ENCYCLOPEDIA

OF

ZIONISM

AND

ISRAEL

1

A-J

THEODOR HERZL, 1860–1904

ENCYCLOPEDIA

OF

ZIONISM

AND

ISRAEL

EDITED BY

RAPHAEL PATAI

HERZL PRESS / McGRAW-HILL
NEW YORK, 1971

ENCYCLOPEDIA OF ZIONISM AND ISRAEL

Library of Congress Catalog Card Number: 68-55271 ISBN: 07-079635-1

ENCYCLOPEDIA OF ZIONISM AND ISRAEL

Editor: Raphael Patai

Associate Editor: S. Z. Abramov

Consulting Editors: Oskar K. Rabinowicz; Joseph B. Schechtman

Assistant Editors: Gertrude Hirschler; Tovia Preschel

McGRAW-HILL STAFF

Editor in Chief: David I. Eggenberger
Director of Design and Production: Gerard G. Mayer
Sponsoring Editor: Robert A. Rosenbaum
Managing Editor: Tobia L. Worth
Copy Editor: Beatrice E. Eckes
Administrative Assistants: Rosemary DeMaria; Linda M. Lovisolo
Picture Research: Bernice Epstein
Art and Design: Richard A. Roth

FOREWORD

The birth of the State of Israel in 1948 and its early days produced a mounting stream of books in many languages. In the years which have since passed, replete with dramatic events, the stream has not subsided but has risen at times to near flood proportions. Every aspect of the new State and every turn in its fortunes were recorded, described, and analyzed, often in great detail.

One aspect of this Zionist Revolution has not as yet received the full measure of attention it merits: it is the genesis of the Zionist movement itself—the linear progenitor of the Jewish State. The latter cannot be fully understood without the former. Zionism is in itself a remarkable epic. It is the story of a people so long exiled from its ancestral home, scattered and dismembered and buffeted by unrelenting storms, yet zealously guarding its personality and its claim to nationhood and at long last gathering up its strength in a desperate effort to establish a new polity on ancient soil. It is a tale without parallel in human history.

This is perhaps the most noteworthy aspect of the whole process: the fact that in rebuilding its National Home the Jewish people, still dispersed, has been rebuilding itself—no longer a conglomeration of individuals, of separate groups and communities, but one people united in its diversity and firm in its collective determination to reshape its destiny.

In the perspective of history both phenomena, Zionism and Israel, are but two aspects of the same process inextricably woven together. The changes wrought by Zionism in the Jewish Diaspora are second in importance only to the transcendent events in the land of Israel.

It was felt that the time was ripe to produce an inclusive work of reference which thoughtful men could consult for authentic knowledge of the whole subject. This *Encyclopedia* is the first of its kind in any language; as a pioneering work it required considerable effort to overcome the difficulties inherent in the nature of the subject matter. Certainly the many men and women, scholars and writers, who have produced it have given it of their best.

The members of the Editorial Advisory Committee express their appreciation to all who have participated in the preparation of the *Encyclopedia* including, of course, its editor, Dr. Raphael Patai, and his associates.

Unfortunately, in the several years which have elapsed since the work was begun four members of the Committee have passed away. They are Zvi Lurie, Samuel K. Mirsky, Oskar K. Rabinowicz, and Joseph B. Schechtman. They were all men of erudition and great devotion. They are most gratefully remembered.

EMANUEL NEUMANN

PREFACE

The *Encyclopedia of Zionism and Israel* was conceived by Dr. Emanuel Neumann, chairman of the Jewish Agency Executive in New York, some 12 years ago as a "Zionist Encyclopedia" which would fill the increasingly felt need for a reliable reference book on Zionism. Dr. Neumann's original plan called for an encyclopedia that would contain the answers to questions interested individuals would be likely to ask in connection with the Zionist movement—questions about its history and ideologies, its party formations, its institutions and organizations, and the men and women who created and led it.

When Dr. Neumann first asked me, as far back as 1964, to undertake the editorship of such an encyclopedia, I began to consider the subject matter to be encompassed in the volume. It soon became evident that virtually every phase and aspect of the World Zionist movement was inextricably linked to events that took place in Palestine and in the life of the Yishuv, Palestine's Jewish community, which owed its development directly to Zionist work. I therefore felt strongly that if an article were to present the complete story of any Zionist subject, it would have to deal not only with its Diaspora phases but also with its ramifications in Palestine and, after 1948, in the State of Israel.

Take such an institution as the Hebrew University of Jerusalem. For many years plans to establish a Hebrew institution of higher learning in Palestine were the subject of discussion at Zionist Congresses and in Zionist circles and committees, and were bound up with a specific trend in Zionist ideology. There could thus be no question but that the planned Zionist encyclopedia would have to contain an article on the Hebrew University. But soon after it actually opened its doors in Jerusalem the Hebrew University developed into an indigenous institution of the Yishuv, and its ties to the World Zionist Organization gradually slackened. By the time Israel achieved independence, the Hebrew University was an integral part of the educational system of the new State. For our encyclopedia article on the Hebrew University to describe the Zionist efforts that went into its establishment and then to stop short of telling about the fruit that these efforts have yielded would clearly, therefore, have been a most unsatisfactory way of handling the subject.

The Editorial Advisory Committee, which had been set up by Dr. Neumann in the meantime, considered this question. It was agreed that since Zionism and Israel were so closely intertwined, the nature of the material to be covered in the encyclopedia required that they be given equal attention. This, in brief, was the genesis of the *Encyclopedia of Zionism and Israel.*

Many questions, of course, still remained to be decided. If Israel were to be included in our encyclopedia, what specific aspects of the country should be covered? Here, the answer was that we would confine ourselves to modern Israel; we would not go back historically beyond the second half of the 19th century, when the first new Jewish settlers, the so-called Bilu pioneers, began to arrive in Palestine (1882). There is only one exception: the acticle giving a general historical survey of Israel covers, albeit very briefly, the total history of the country from the Old Stone Age to the present (*see* ISRAEL, HISTORY OF). This was done to establish a background that would provide a setting for, and add meaning to, the developments that took place in the country within the last century.

As for the Zionist movement itself, it was decided to include its immediate precursor, the Hibbat Zion (Love of Zion) movement, which, from 1882 on, laid the foundations for the political Zionism of Theodor Herzl.

Once the general framework had been established, we were ready to turn to details. It was decided that the *Encyclopedia* would contain three principal types of articles:

Places in Israel. These articles are mostly very brief, two- or three-line items, which should be studied together with the foldout map of Israel. To this category, also, belong a few longer articles dealing with the major cities, towns, natural features, regions, and other places of special importance in Israel.

Biographies. This category includes primarily Zionist leaders and Israeli statesmen and public officials. In the case of persons who were prominently active in Zionism but whose primary claim to fame lay outside their Zionist activities or interests, their general biographical data have been held to the barest minimum, in most instances compressed into the first paragraph of the article. In addition, we included biographies of major literary and cultural precursors of Zionism as well as non-Jewish political figures whose activities bore on the course of the Zionist movement or on the history of Jewish Palestine and Israel. Here, too, general biographical information is brief, with the major portion of the article devoted to the role of the individual in the areas of immediate concern to the *Encyclopedia.*

Topical subjects. This category includes articles on the following areas of interest:

Zionism. The history of the Zionist movement and its constituent organizations in various countries; Zionist institutions in Israel and elsewhere; milestones in the history of Israel and Zionism; Zionist ideologies and concepts; pro-Zionist, anti-Zionist, and general Jewish movements and organizations and their impact on Zionism and Israel.

Israel. Social, cultural, economic, religious, political, and agricultural developments in the Yishuv and Israel; governmental agencies and various institutions that constitute the framework of the nation's life; various aspects of everyday life in the Jewish State (e.g., clothing in Israel, ethnic groups and problems in Israel, family in Israel, food in Israel, manners in Israel, population of Israel). Other articles describe the waves of Jewish immigration that have come to Palestine (later Israel) since 1882 and their role in the history and growth of the Jewish State. A special group of articles describes the position in Israel of immigrants from various countries and their contributions to Israel's development (e.g., BRITISH JEWS IN ISRAEL). A considerable number of articles deal with the Arabs in Palestine and Israel and with the relationships between the Jewish State and its Arab neighbors. Still other articles trace the history of relations between the great powers and Zionism, Palestine, and Israel.

The articles in the *Encyclopedia,* which number nearly 3,000, are the work of some 285 contributing authors, most of whom are either Israeli or American scholars or experts in the fields they discuss. Individual articles were contributed by authors living in as many as 34 different countries. The authors include statesmen (headed by Zalman Shazar, President of the State of Israel), officials and specialists attached to various departments of the Israeli government and the Jewish Agency, staff members (historians, sociologists, etc.) of universities in Israel, the United States, and elsewhere, and Zionist leaders of major Jewish communities. Most of the contributors composed their articles on the basis of scholarly research; some wrote from personal recollection of events in which they themselves had participated.

Every encyclopedia contains some articles that were written several years prior to publication. In this volume, wherever possible such articles were updated. Given the rapid changes that have been taking place in Israel, especially during the last four or five years, however, this was not always feasible. As a result, we had no choice but to publish certain articles which present a picture of their subject matter as of 1966 or 1967.

The editor enjoyed the help of a number of experts specializing in the historical study of one or another aspect of Zionism and Israel. He wishes to avail himself of this opportunity to express his appreciation to them.

S. Z. Abramov, member of the Knesset and distinguished Zionist historian, served as associate editor of the *Encyclopedia.*

Dr. Oskar K. Rabinowicz and Dr. Joseph B. Schechtman, both outstanding scholars in the history of Zionism, and themselves prominent figures on the Zionist scene, served as consulting editors. It is a matter of deep sorrow to the editor that these two men, whose personal friendship he was privileged to enjoy, did not live to see the completion of this work.

Gertrude Hirschler and Prof. Tovia Preschel were assistant editors of this *Encyclopedia.* For five years they shared with the editor the day-to-day problems involved in the editing of this volume, in addition to contributing signed and unsigned articles.

Beyond these colleagues, the Editorial Advisory Committee, chaired by Dr. Emanuel Neumann, rendered valuable service by helping the editorial staff reach decisions on general policy issues.

The staff of the Herzl Press also included Ruth Salinger Hyman, who was the first editorial assistant of the project, and Betty Gross, the editor's secretary of many years.

This *Encyclopedia* could not have been compiled without the ever-ready help and advice so generously supplied by the staff of the Zionist Archives and Library: its director, Sylvia Landress, and her assistants Rachel Schechtman, Esther Togman, and Rebecca Zapinsky.

Invaluable help was given by the editorial staff of the McGraw-Hill Book Company: David I. Eggenberger, editor in chief of the McGraw-Hill Professional and Reference Book Division, Robert A. Rosenbaum, sponsoring editor, Tobia L. Worth, managing editor, and Beatrice E. Eckes, copy editor and proofreader, who brought to our *Encyclopedia* experience and knowledge based on their work with many other encyclopedias; and Bernice Epstein, who did the picture research.

RAPHAEL PATAI

EXPLANATORY NOTES

Alphabetization

The alphabetizing principle used in the *Encyclopedia of Zionism and Israel* is that of letter-by-letter rather than word-by-word. For example, a series of compound place names all beginning with the word "Gan" is interrupted by unrelated titles: Gan, Gan HaDarom, Ganne 'Am, Gannot, Gan Sh'lomo, Gan Sh'muel.

Cross-references

1. *The asterisk.* An asterisk in the text indicates that an article may be found in the *Encyclopedia* under a title which is identical with the word or words following the asterisk (e.g., "We will now consider *clothing in Israel."). It is placed at the first mention only of the name or subject within the article. No asterisks have been placed in front of place names and other geographical names, it being understood that these are covered by articles in the *Encyclopedia*. No asterisk was placed in front of the name Theodor Herzl, the founder of modern Zionism.

2. *The "see" reference.* There are conventional *see* references to present the exact article title in cases where the form varies from singular to plural (e.g., text mention of Zionist Congresses necessitates the cross-reference *see* CONGRESS, ZIONIST) or in cases where the historical mention of a variant name requires the presence of the frozen form chosen by the editors as the article title (e.g., text mention of Y'hoshu'a Eisenstadt carries a parenthetical *see* BARZILAI, Y'HOSHU'A next to it). *See also* references are also employed to make the reader aware of related articles within a specific area.

3. *The main reference.* The main reference, or reference entry, has been used throughout the *Encyclopedia* to indicate variant spellings (BEERSHEBA. *See* B'ER SHEVA'.); pseudonyms (NATZIV, THE. *See* BERLIN, NAPHTALI TZ'VI Y'HUDA.); changes in name (GREEN, DAVID. *See* BEN-GURION, DAVID.); alternate titles of conferences (ROUND TABLE CONFERENCE OF 1939. *See* ST. JAMES CONFERENCE.); and so on. In such cases the variant will appear in the article title itself in parenthetical form. Main references are also used to direct the reader from a general subject to a specific title or titles (SECTS IN ISRAEL. *See* ARABS IN ISRAEL; BAHAI COMMUNITY IN ISRAEL; etc.), from a specific subject to the general title under which it is treated (MACCABI. *See* SPORTS AND PHYSICAL EDUCATION IN ISRAEL.), or from one formulation to another (SECURITIES MARKET IN ISRAEL. *See* FINANCE IN ISRAEL.).

Transliteration

For the purposes of this *Encyclopedia* the editor has devised a simplified and phonetic system of transliteration. It is simplified as compared with scientific transliteration systems in that it uses no diacritical marks. It is phonetic in that it endeavors to approximate the way Hebrew is pronounced in Israel today, rather than attempting to reproduce Hebrew orthography. The accompanying table can be consulted for details.

The *sh'va na'* is transliterated by an apostrophe (e.g., l'umi), except in those few cases where the word in question is in common use in English in a different form (e.g., Knesset instead of K'neset, Rehovot instead of R'hovot).

TRANSLITERATION OF HEBREW			
Hebrew	**English**	**Hebrew**	**English**
א or אַ or אָ	a (as in c<u>a</u>r)	נ	n
בּ	b	או or אֹ	o
ד	d	פּ	p
א or אֶ or אֵ*	e (as in <u>e</u>gg)	ר	r
פ	f	שׂ or ס	s
ג	g (as in g<u>e</u>t)	שׁ	sh
ח or ה	h	ט or תּ or ת	t
אִי or אִ	i (as in h<u>i</u>t)	אוּ or אֻ	u (as in t<u>oo</u>l)
ק or כּ	k	ב or ו	v
כ	kh (as in German a<u>ch</u>)	י	y
ל	l	ז	z
מ	m		

*In the modern Israeli colloquial practically no differentiation remains between these three vowels. In classical Hebrew אֶ and אֵ were pronounced like the "e" in egg, and אַ like the "a" in name.

No attempt was made to reproduce the *dagesh hazak* (reduplication, double stress) in Hebrew consonants, because in the Hebrew spoken in Israel no trace remains of such reduplication. Thus we transliterated Aderet rather than Adderet, HaShomron rather than HaShShomron, and so on. Exceptions, however, were made in cases where the Hebrew name in question has consistently been transliterated with the double consonant and has become familiar to the reader in this form, for example, Abba, 'Akko, Egged, Knesset (the last two words have, in fact, no double consonant in Hebrew).

The *matres lectionis* (reading aids) א at the beginning, middle, or end of the word, ה at the end of the word, and ו and י in the middle or at the end of the word are not transliterated.

The inverted comma (') stands for the ע ('ayin), which was a distinct consonant in classical Hebrew but of which barely a trace is left in modern Israeli Hebrew.

The transliteration of given names presented a special problem. In many cases, an individual first became known by a non-Hebrew form of his given name, but after he settled in Palestine or Israel he took to using the Hebrew form of his name (e.g., Yitzhak for Isaac, Sh'muel for Samuel). In other cases, an individual known by the Hebrew form of his given name became known also by various non-Hebrew forms of his name (e.g., when his writings were published in English or German translations). In the case of such names, we tried to adhere, as far as possible, to using the Hebrew form.

Many individuals Hebraized their last names (e.g., Moshe Shertok became Moshe Sharett; Meir Berlin became Meir Bar-Ilan). In referring to these, we used the non-Hebrew form when the reference was to the period during which the individual himself still used his non-Hebrew name. From the date of the name change, we used the Hebrew form.

In order to distinguish between the article (Heb., Ha-) and the word following it (treated as one word in Hebrew), we capitalized both the article and the noun following it (e.g., HaShomer HaTza'ir, or The Young Watchman). This facilitates the identification of the same noun which appears at times with, and at others without, the article (e.g., Ha'Ahdut, Ahdut 'Avoda, Kibbutz, HaKibbutz).

Bibliography

The last section of Volume 2 of the *Encyclopedia of Zionism and Israel* contains an extensive bibliography organized under relevant subject heads.

CONTRIBUTORS
(with partial list of articles they wrote)

Abrahamson, Aaron. *Assistant to the Director General, Keren HaYesod, Jerusalem.* KEREN HAYESOD.

Abramov, S. Zalman. *Member of the Knesset, Jerusalem.* BEN-GURION, DAVID; BRANDEIS, LOUIS DEMBITZ; "CONQUEST OF LABOR"; G'DUD HA'AVODA V'HAHAGANA 'AL SHEM YOSEF TRUMPELDOR; GENERAL ZIONISM; GOVERNMENT OF ISRAEL; HAGANA; HALUTZIYUT; HASHOMER; PRESIDENCY OF ISRAEL; SECOND 'ALIYA; YISHUV, SELF-GOVERNMENT IN THE; other articles.

Adler, Joseph. *Author of* The Herzl Paradox, *New York.* CHURCHILL, SIR WINSTON LEONARD SPENCER; DREYFUS AFFAIR; EL-'ARISH SCHEME; JEWISH STATE, THE; OLD-NEW LAND; other articles.

Adler, Selig. *Samuel P. Capen Professor of American History, State University of New York, Buffalo.* ROOSEVELT, FRANKLIN DELANO.

Akzin, Benjamin. *Professor of Political Science and Constitutional Law, Hebrew University, Jerusalem.* RETURN, LAW OF.

Alperin, Aaron. *Managing Editor,* Day–Jewish Journal, *New York.* Biographical articles.

Antonier, Avraham. *Deputy General Director, Ministry of Transport, Jerusalem.* SHIPPING IN ISRAEL (with Naftali H. Wydra); TRANSPORTATION IN ISRAEL.

Antonovsky, Aaron. *Senior Research Associate, Israel Institute of Applied Social Research, Jerusalem.* SOCIAL STRUCTURE OF ISRAEL.

Arnon, Ya'akov. *Director General, Ministry of Finance, Jerusalem.* DIAMOND INDUSTRY IN ISRAEL.

Aronowsky, Eliezer S. *President, Cultural Section, Zionist Union, Havana.* CUBA, ZIONISM IN.

Ashkenazy, Hillel. *Deputy Director General, Ministry of Housing, Tel Aviv.* DOMESTIC TRADE IN ISRAEL (with Gad Soen).

Assaf, Michael. *Orientalist; Chairman, Federation of Journalists in Israel, Tel Aviv.* HAQIQAT AL-AMR; WAQF.

Attias, Moshe. *Historian and folklorist; formerly Secretary of the Va'ad L'umi.* ASEFAT HANIVHARIM; COUNCIL OF THE SEPHARDI COMMUNITY OF JERUSALEM; VA'AD L'UMI; WORLD FEDERATION OF SEPHARDI COMMUNITIES.

Avidor, Moshe. *Israeli Ambassador to UNESCO, Paris.* ISRAEL ACADEMY OF SCIENCES AND HUMANITIES.

Bachi, Roberto. *Director, Central Bureau of Statistics, Jerusalem.* IMMIGRATION TO PALESTINE AND ISRAEL (section); POPULATION OF ISRAEL.

Baker, Henry E. *President, District Court, Jerusalem.* HIGH COMMISSIONER FOR PALESTINE (section); JUDICIARY IN ISRAEL; LEGISLATION IN ISRAEL; MANDATE FOR PALESTINE (section); RELIGIOUS COUNCILS IN ISRAEL.

Band, Arnold J. *Professor of Hebrew Literature, University of California, Los Angeles.* LITERATURE, MODERN HEBREW AND ISRAELI (section).

Bar-David, Molly Lyons. *Author, Tel Aviv.* FOOD IN ISRAEL.

Barlas, Hayim. *Formerly Director, Immigration Department, Jewish Agency, Jerusalem.* IMMIGRATION TO PALESTINE AND ISRAEL (section); PALESTINE OFFICES.

Bar-Moshe, Isaac. *Author, Jerusalem.* IRAQI JEWS IN ISRAEL.

Baroway, Aaron. *Vice-president, PEC Israel Economic Corporation, New York.* AMERICAN ECONOMIC COMMITTEE FOR PALESTINE, INC.

Bat-Yehuda, Geula (Mrs. Yitzhak Raphael). *Translator and editor, Rabbi Kook Foundation, Jerusalem.* Biographies of religious Zionists.

Bauer, Yehuda. *Head, Department of Holocaust Studies, Institute of Contemporary Jewry, Hebrew University, Jerusalem.* B'RIHA; "EXODUS 1947"; ILLEGAL IMMIGRATION; PALMAH; "STRUMA."

Bein, Alex. *Director, Central Zionist Archives, Jerusalem.* HERZL, THEODOR.

Benari, I. (Yehuda). *Chairman, Board of Directors, Jabotinsky Institute, Tel Aviv.* B'RIT HAHAYAL; B'RIT NASHIM L'UMIYOT; HERUT; KUPAT HOLIM L'OVDIM L'UMIYIM; LOHAME HERUT ISRAEL; TRUMPELDOR, JOSEPH; other articles.

Bentwich, Norman. *Formerly Professor of International Relations, Hebrew University, Jerusalem.* CITIZENSHIP IN ISRAEL; HOLY PLACES IN ISRAEL; IHUD; RELIGION AND STATE IN ISRAEL.

Ben-Ya'akov, Avraham. *Author and educator, Jerusalem.* KURDISH JEWS IN ISRAEL.

Ben Yehuda, Barukh. *Principal, Herzliya High School, Tel Aviv.* HERZLIYA HIGH SCHOOL.

Berger, Ludwig. *Director, Economic Research Office, Jewish Agency, Jerusalem.* INDUSTRY IN ISRAEL (section).

Bergmann, Ernest D. *Professor of Organic Chemistry, Hebrew University, Jerusalem.* ATOMIC RESEARCH IN ISRAEL.

Bernhard, Carlos. *Honorary Consul of Israel; formerly President, Zionist Organization of El Salvador, San Salvador.* EL SALVADOR, ZIONISM IN.

Bibrowski, Henry. *Brussels.* BELGIUM, ZIONISM IN.

Bloch, M'nahem. *Executive Director, Book Publishers Association of Israel, Tel Aviv.* PUBLISHING AND PUBLISHERS IN ISRAEL.

Boas, Henrietta. *Author and educator, Amsterdam.* Biographies of Dutch Zionists.

Braham, Randolph L. *Associate Professor of Political Science, City College of the City University of New York.* HUNGARY, ZIONISM IN; biographies of Hungarian Zionists.

Brand-Auraban, Aron, M.D. *Chairman, Jerusalem Academy of Medicine, Jerusalem.* JERUSALEM ACADEMY OF MEDICINE.

Braver, Bernhard. *Editor, Die Stimme, Vienna.* AUSTRIA, ZIONISM IN (with Josef Fraenkel).

*Caplan, Sam. *Research consultant, American Committee for the Weizmann Institute of Science, New York.* HOVEVE ZION (section); ZIONIST ORGANIZATION OF AMERICA.

Cherniak, Saadia. *Executive Director, American Friends of the Alliance Israélite Universelle, New York.* ALLIANCE ISRAELITE UNIVERSELLE.

Chertoff, Mordecai S. *Executive Director, Histadrut Cultural Exchange, New York.* AVUKAH.

Chorin, Yehuda. *Chairman, Advisory Board, Bank of Israel, Tel Aviv.* CITRUS INDUSTRY IN ISRAEL.

Chouraqui, André. *Permanent Delegate, Alliance Israélite Universelle, Paris and Jerusalem; member of the Jerusalem Municipal Council.* NORTH AFRICAN JEWS IN ISRAEL.

Cohen, Aharon. *Author, Sha'ar Ha'Amakim.* KALWARISKI-MARGOLIS, HAYIM; LAWRENCE, THOMAS EDWARD.

Cohen, Benno. *Member of the Knesset, Jerusalem.* 'ALIYA HADASHA.

Cohen, Hayim J. *Lecturer in Contemporary Jewry, Hebrew University, Jerusalem.* IRAQ, ZIONISM IN.

Comet, Ted. *Consultant on Overseas Services, Council of Jewish Federations and Welfare Funds, New York.* AMERICAN ZIONIST YOUTH COUNCIL; AMERICAN ZIONIST YOUTH FOUNDATION; NORTH AMERICAN JEWISH YOUTH COUNCIL.

Dickman, Irving R. *Formerly Director, Public Relations, American Jewish Joint Distribution Committee, New York.* AMERICAN JEWISH JOINT DISTRIBUTION COMMITTEE.

Dienstag, Jacob. *Professor of Bibliography and Chief, Judaica Division, Yeshiva University Library, New York.* FRIEDENWALD, HARRY; LAZARUS, EMMA; RIVKIND, ISAAC; SCHOLEM, GERSHOM GERHARD; other biographical articles.

Doron, Alexander. *Formerly Secretary, Bank L'umi L'Yisrael; Joint Secretary, Jewish Colonial Trust Ltd. and Anglo-Palestine Bank Ltd., Tel Aviv.* BANK L'UMI L'YISRAEL.

Duffield, Walter. *General Secretary, Zionist Federation of Australia and New Zealand, Melbourne.* AUSTRALIA, ZIONISM IN (with Max D. Friedman).

Easterman, Alex L. *Formerly Director, Political Department, World Jewish Congress, London.* WORLD JEWISH CONGRESS (with A. Max Melamet).

Eisen, Aaron. *Author, Jerusalem.* PANAMA, ZIONISM IN.

Eisenstein, Ira. *President, Jewish Reconstructionist Foundation, New York.* RECONSTRUCTIONISM AND ZIONISM.

Eliav, Arye. *Member of the Knesset; Secretary-General, Israel Labor party; Deputy Minister for the Absorption of Immigrants, Jerusalem.* DEVELOPMENT TOWNS.

Engelman, Uriah Zvi. *Formerly Director, Department of Research, American Association for Jewish Education, New York.* JEWISH EDUCATION IN THE DIASPORA (with Abraham P. Gannes).

Epstein, Bernice. *Picture researcher, New York.* GOVRIN, 'AKIVA.

Epstein, David. *Executive Director, Histadrut 'Ivrit of America, New York.* HADOAR.

Even, Arye. *National Director, Masada organization, New York.* MASADA.

Farkas, Tibor. *General Secretary, Hitahdut 'Ole Hungaria, Tel Aviv.* HUNGARIAN JEWS IN ISRAEL.

Feilchenfeld, Werner. *Economic consultant, Great Neck, N.Y.* HA'AVARA.

Feinberg, Charles W. *Formerly National Director, American Red Mogen Dovid for Israel, New York.* AMERICAN RED MOGEN DOVID FOR ISRAEL, INC.

Feuer, Leon I. *Rabbi, Collingwood Avenue Temple, Toledo, Ohio; member of the Jewish Agency Executive, New York.* REFORM JUDAISM AND ZIONISM.

Figler, Bernard, Q.C. *Head, Judgment Department, Provincial Court, Montreal.* CANADA, ZIONISM IN; CANADA AND ZIONISM; biographies of Canadian Zionists.

Fishman, Aryei. *Lecturer in Sociology, Bar-Ilan University, Ramat Gan.* HAKIBBUTZ HADATI.

Foerster, Gideon. *Lecturer in Classical Archeology and Jewish Art, Hebrew University; Archeologist, Northern District, Department of Antiquities and Museums, Ministry of Education and Culture, Jerusalem.* ARCHEOLOGY IN ISRAEL; M'TZADA.

Fraenkel, Josef. *Research officer, Information Department, World Jewish Congress; founder of the World Federation of Jewish Journalists, London.* AUSTRIA, ZIONISM IN (with Bernhard Braver); GREAT BRITAIN: RELATIONS WITH ZIONISM AND ISRAEL (section); GREAT BRITAIN, ZIONISM IN (sections); HOVEVE ZION (sections); JEWISH CHRONICLE; JEWISH WORLD; ORDER OF ANCIENT MACCABEANS; other articles.

Frank, Moshe Z. *Journalist; author of* Sound the Great Trumpet, *Teaneck, N.J.* AMERICAN JEWISH LEAGUE FOR ISRAEL; HASHILOAH; HOVEVE S'FAT 'EVER.

Frankel, Ella Siona. *Editor, Jewish Women's Review, London.* SIEFF, REBECCA DORO MARKS.

Friedman, Max D. *Formerly General Secretary, Zionist Federation of Australia and New Zealand, Edgecliff, New South Wales.* AUSTRALIA, ZIONISM IN (with Walter Duffield).

Friedman, Menahem. *Hebrew University, Jerusalem.* AGUDAT ISRAEL; ME'A SH'ARIM; N'TURE KARTA.

Furman, John. *Formerly President, PEC Israel Economic Corporation, New York.* PEC ISRAEL ECONOMIC CORPORATION.

*Deceased.

xvii

Gannes, Abraham P. *Director, Department of Education and Culture, Jewish Agency, New York.* JEWISH EDUCATION IN THE DIASPORA (with Uriah Zvi Engelman).

Gassman, Rosalie. *General Secretary, Federation of Women Zionists of Great Britain and Ireland, London.* WOMEN'S INTERNATIONAL ZIONIST ORGANIZATION (with Raya Jaglom).

*Gelber, Nathan Michael. *Zionist historian, Jerusalem.* AUSTER, DANIEL; BADER, GERSHOM; CONGRESS, ZIONIST (with Oskar K. Rabinowicz); HERLITZ, GEORGE JOSEPH; HERRMANN, LEO; MAHLER, ARTHUR; REICH, LEON; ROTHBLUM, DAVID; ROTTENSTREICH, EFRAYIM FISHEL; SCHMORAK, EMIL; SOFERMANN, RAPHAEL; SOMMERSTEIN, EMIL; TENENBAUM, JOSEPH; THON, OSIAS; THON, YA'AKOV YOHANAN; WERNER, SIEGMUND; other biographical articles.

Gidron, Michael. *Director, Israel Government Tourist Office, Boston.* TOURISM IN ISREAL.

Gilbert, Jennie Z. *Chairman, Zionist Council of Ireland, Dublin.* IRELAND, ZIONISM IN.

Gillon, Philip. *Member of the editorial board,* Jerusalem Post, *Jerusalem.* MANNERS IN ISRAEL.

Gitlin, Marcia. *Formerly in charge of publicity in English, Hebrew University, Jerusalem.* HEBREW UNIVERSITY OF JERUSALEM; SOUTH AFRICAN JEWS IN ISRAEL (with Louis I. Rabinowitz).

Gjebin, Rafael, M.D. *Director General, Ministry of Health, Jerusalem.* MEDICINE IN ISRAEL.

Goldberg, David. *Educational consultant, American Zionist Youth Foundation, New York.* LEARSI, RUFUS; YOUTH MOVEMENTS.

Goldberg, Hannah. *Executive Director, Hadassah, New York.* HADASSAH.

Goldman, Paul L. *Vice-president, United Labor Zionist Organization of America, New York.* AHDUT 'AVODA—PO'ALE ZION OF AMERICA.

Goldschlag, Yitzhak. *General Secretary, Mizrahi—HaPo'el HaMizrahi, Jerusalem.* MIZRAHI.

Gourgey, Percy Sassoon, M.B.E. *Joint Treasurer, World Jewish Congress, British Section, London.* INDIA, ZIONISM IN; INDIAN JEWS IN ISRAEL.

Gradenwitz, Peter E. *Lecturer in Musicology, Tel Aviv University, Tel Aviv.* FOLK MUSIC IN ISRAEL; GERSON-KIWI, EDITH; HUBERMAN, BRONISLAW; IDELSOHN, ABRAHAM ZVI; ISRAEL BROADCASTING SERVICE; ISRAEL PHILHARMONIC ORCHESTRA; MUSIC IN ISRAEL; biographies of Israeli musicians and composers.

Gross, David C. *Formerly Director of Public Relations, American Society for Technion; Editor, Sabra Books, New York.* TECHNION.

Grossmann, Kurt R. *Formerly consultant on German and Austrian affairs, Jewish Agency, New York.* GERMAN-ISRAEL AGREEMENT; GERMANY, ZIONISM IN.

Grunwald, Kurt. *Formerly Manager, Palestine Corporation Ltd.–Union Bank of Israel, Ltd., Jerusalem.* JEWISH COLONIZATION ASSOCIATION.

Gutman, Israel. *Director, Moreshet Memorial Institution and Mordecai Anilewicz Museum, Yad Mord'khai.* ANILEWICZ, MORDECAI; KOVNER, ABBA.

Gutmann, Emanuel. *Senior Lecturer in Political Science, Hebrew University, Jerusalem.* POLITICAL PARTIES IN ISRAEL.

Guvrin, Yehoshu'a (Oskar Gruenbaum). *Advocate and notary, Tel Aviv; formerly Vice-president, General Zionist party.* AUSTRIAN JEWS IN ISRAEL.

HaCohen, Mordecai. *Director, Research and Information Center, Ministry of Religious Affairs, Jerusalem.* RABBINATE OF ISRAEL.

Hadas, Avraham. *Managing Director, Israel Wine Institute, Rehovot.* WINE INDUSTRY IN ISRAEL (with Pinhas Spiegel-Roy).

Halevi, Hayim Shalom, M.D. *Assistant Director General, Ministry of Health, Jerusalem.* PUBLIC HEALTH IN ISRAEL (section).

Halpern, Ben. *Professor of Near Eastern Studies, Brandeis University, Waltham, Mass.* MANDATE FOR PALESTINE (section).

Hamlin, Isadore. *Executive Director, Jewish Agency, New York.* HALPRIN, ROSE; KIRSHBLUM, MORDECAI; SCHECHTMAN, JOSEPH B.

Harris, Lucien. *Director, Hadassah Information Services, Jerusalem.* BRITISH JEWS IN ISRAEL.

Hashimshoni, Aviah. *Associate Professor of Architecture and Town Planning, Technion, Haifa.* ARCHITECTURE AND TOWN PLANNING IN ISRAEL.

Hasson, Yaacov I. *Executive Director, Office of Human Relations, B'nai B'rith, Lima.* FELDMAN, ABRAHAM; PERU, ZIONISM IN.

Hasson, Zvi. *HaNo'ar HaTziyoni, Tel Aviv.* HANO'AR HATZIYONI.

Hausner, Gideon M. *Advocate; Member of the Knesset, Jerusalem.* EICHMANN TRIAL; PROGRESSIVE PARTY IN ISRAEL.

Hellman, Yehuda. *Executive Director, Conference of Presidents of Major American Jewish Organizations, New York.* CONFERENCE OF PRESIDENTS OF MAJOR AMERICAN JEWISH ORGANIZATIONS.

Henkin, Judah H. *Formerly General Secretary, Mizrahi HaTza'ir, New York.* MIZRAHI HATZA'IR.

Hershman, Ruth. *Executive Secretary, American Israel Public Affairs Committee, New York.* AMERICA-ISRAEL SOCIETY; EMERGENCY COMMITTEE FOR ZIONIST AFFAIRS (sections).

Hesky, Moshe George. *Formerly Deputy Director, Philatelic Services, Ministry of Posts, Jerusalem.* STAMPS OF ISRAEL.

Heth, Meir. *Examiner of Banks, Bank of Israel, Jerusalem.* BANKING IN ISRAEL; BANK OF ISRAEL.

Hirschberg, Binyamin W. *Chairman, Executive Council, HaKibbutz HaDati, Lavi.* B'NE 'AKIVA.

Hirschler, Gertrude. *Assistant Editor, Encyclopedia of Zionism and Israel, New York.* BERGSON GROUP; BOARD OF DEPUTIES OF BRITISH JEWS; CHINA, ZIONISM IN; DANZIG, ZIONISM IN; DECLARATION OF INDEPENDENCE; EAST AFRICA SCHEME; EGYPT, ZIONISM IN; JAPAN, ZIONISM IN, AND RELATIONS WITH ISRAEL; JEWISH TERRITORIAL ORGANIZATION; LODGE-FISH RESOLUTION; NORTH AFRICA, ZIONISM IN; PITTSBURGH PROGRAM;

*Deceased.

PRACTICAL ZIONISM; SYKES-PICOT AGREEMENT; WILHELM II; WILSON, (THOMAS) WOODROW; WOLFF-SOHN, DAVID; other articles.

Horovitz, Ruth. *Senior Research Officer, Ministry of Social Welfare, Jerusalem.* SOCIAL WELFARE SERVICES IN ISRAEL.

Hubner, Samuel. *Rabbi and author, New York.* BERGMANN, SAMUEL HUGO; FLEG, EDMOND; KLEE, ALFRED; SOLOVEITCHIK, MAX; WELTSCH, ROBERT; other biographical articles.

Hutner, Jehoshua. *Rabbi, Executive Director, Yad HaRav Herzog, Jerusalem.* YAD HARAV HERZOG; YESHIVOT IN ISRAEL.

Jaffe, Benjamin. *Director, External Relations Department, Jewish Agency, Jerusalem.* JAFFE, LEIB.

Jaglom, Raya. *Chairman, World Executive, Women's International Zionist Organization, Tel Aviv.* WOMEN'S INTERNATIONAL ZIONIST ORGANIZATION (with Rosalie Gassman).

Kadury, Abigail. *Supervisor, Girls' Vocational Schools, Tel Aviv.* CLOTHING IN ISRAEL.

*Kamrat, Mordecai. *Founder and Director, Ulpan 'Etzyon, Jerusalem.* ULPAN.

Kanev, Yitzhak. *Director, Economic and Social Research Institute, Histadrut, Tel Aviv.* KUPAT HOLIM; PUBLIC HEALTH IN ISRAEL (section); SOCIAL INSURANCE IN ISRAEL.

Kaplan, Aline. *Assistant Executive Director, Hadassah, New York.* JUNIOR HADASSAH.

Kaplan, Jerachmiel. *Director, Forestry Department, Land Development Authority, Jewish National Fund, Kiryat Hayim, Haifa.* FORESTRY IN ISRAEL.

Karmon, Yehuda. *Professor of Geography, Hebrew University, Jerusalem.* GALILEE; GAULAN HEIGHTS; GEOGRAPHY OF ISRAEL; JORDAN RIVER; NATIONAL WATER CARRIER; NEGEV; other geographical articles.

Kashani, R'uven. *Author, Jerusalem.* AFGHAN JEWS IN ISRAEL.

Katz, Barney. *General Secretary, Central African Zionist Organization; Chairman, Bulawayo Chovevei Zion Society, Bulawayo.* RHODESIA AND ZAMBIA, ZIONISM IN.

Kenen, Isaiah L. *Executive Vice-chairman, American Israel Public Affairs Committee, Washington; Editor, Near East Report.* AMERICAN JEWISH CONFERENCE.

Kerem, Moshe. *Formerly General Secretary, HaBonim, New York.* HABONIM.

Kitron, Gad. *Legislative adviser to members of the Knesset; Deputy Attorney General, Government of Israel, Jerusalem.* STATE COMPTROLLER OF ISRAEL; TAXATION IN ISRAEL.

Kitron, Moshe. *Director, Education Department, Histadrut Executive, Tel Aviv.* LATIN AMERICAN JEWS IN ISRAEL.

Klausner, Israel. *Deputy Director, Central Zionist Archives, Jerusalem.* BILU; B'NE B'RIT SOCIETY; ESRA; HOVEVE ZION (sections); KATTOWITZ CONFERENCE; LIBRARIES AND ARCHIVES, ZIONIST (section); MINSK CONFERENCE; ODESSA COMMITTEE; SAFA B'RURA SOCIETY; USSISHKIN,

M'NAHEM MENDEL; other biographical articles.

Kling, Simha. *Rabbi and author of* Nahum Sokolow, *Louisville, Ky.* SOKOLOW, NAHUM; TSCHLENOW, YEHIEL.

Klinger, Shalom. *Editor,* Unzer Veg, *Paris.* GINSBOURG, BENJAMIN; LAZARE, BERNARD; ROTHEMBERG, NEHEMIA; ROTHSCHILD, BARON EDMOND-ADOLPHE DE; TOPIOL, MEILICH.

*Kobler, Franz. *Author, San Francisco.* CHURCHILL, CHARLES HENRY.

Kohen-Sidon, Sh'lomo. *President, Jehuda Halevi Lodge, Israel B'nai B'rith; formerly Member of the Knesset, Jerusalem.* EGYPTIAN JEWS IN ISRAEL.

Kol, Moshe. *Minister of Tourism; formerly Head, Youth 'Aliya Department, Jewish Agency Executive, Jerusalem.* YOUTH 'ALIYA.

Kolatt, Israel. *Head, Division on Zionism and the New Yishuv, Institute of Contemporary Jewry, Hebrew University, Jerusalem.* ANTI-ZIONISM; ARABS AND ZIONISM; AUXILIARY FARMS; B'RIT SHALOM; CANAANITES AND SEMITIC ACTION; COMMISSIONS OF INQUIRY, ZIONIST; DEMOCRATIC FACTION; EMANCIPATION; EXECUTIVE, ZIONIST; FRENCH REPORTS; HA'ARETZ V'HA'AVODA; HAKHSHARA; HAPO'EL HATZA'IR; HAYCRAFT COMMISSION OF INQUIRY; HOPE-SIMPSON REPORT; ISRAEL, HISTORY OF (section); JEWISH AND ARAB LABOR; PARTITION OF PALESTINE; PO'ALE ZION; RURAL SETTLEMENT IN PALESTINE AND ISRAEL (Public Sector); TZIYONE ZION; UNITED NATIONS SPECIAL COMMITTEE ON PALESTINE; WOODHEAD COMMISSION; biographical articles.

Kressel, Getzel. *Zionist historian; Editor,* Leksikon HaSifrut Ha'Ivrit, *Holon.* HAMAGGID; HATZ'FIRA; HEBREW PRESS; HISTADRUT; JEWISH NATIONAL FUND; KEREN HAG'ULA; MIN HAY'SOD; SELBST-EMANZIPATION; biographical articles.

*Krinitzi, Abraham. *Mayor of Ramat Gan.* RAMAT GAN.

*Kubovy, Arye Léon. *Chairman, Yad VaShem, the Heroes' and Martyrs' Authority, Jerusalem.* YAD VASHEM.

Labunsky, Margot de. *Caracas.* VENEZUELA, ZIONISM IN.

Lachman, Frederick R. *Executive Editor, American office,* Encyclopedia Judaica, *New York.* AMERICA-ISRAEL CULTURAL FOUNDATION.

Landau, Jacob M. *Associate Professor of Political Science, Hebrew University, Jerusalem.* AL-HUSAYNI, HAJJ AMIN; ARAB HIGHER COMMITTEE; ARAB LEAGUE; ARABS IN ISRAEL; DRUZE COMMUNITY IN ISRAEL; GAZA STRIP (with Yehuda Karmon).

Landress, Sylvia. *Director, Zionist Archives and Library, New York.* LIBRARIES AND ARCHIVES, ZIONIST (section); BIBLIOGRAPHY (Zionism and Israel).

Laufer, Leopold. *International Development Officer, Bureau for Latin America, Agency for International Development, U.S. Department of State, Washington.* FOREIGN AID PROGRAM OF ISRAEL.

Lavi, Theodor. *Project director,* Encyclopedia of Jewish Communities, *Yad VaShem, Jerusalem.* ROMANIA, ZIONISM IN; ROMANIAN JEWS IN ISRAEL.

Leaf, Hayim. *Professor of Hebrew Literature, Yeshiva University, New York.* BEN AVI, ITAMAR; BIALIK, HAYIM

*Deceased.

xix

NAHMAN; BIN-GORION, MIKHA YOSEF; BLUVSTEIN, RACHEL; BRAININ, REUBEN; BRAUDES, REUBEN ASHER; BURLA, YEHUDA; FICHMAN, YA'AKOV; GORDON, Y'HUDA LEIB; HADANI, 'EVER; HAMEIRI, AVIGDOR; HAZAZ, HAYIM; KARNI, YEHUDA; LEVIN, SH'MARYA; PERSKY, DANIEL; RIBALOW, MENAHEM; SHIM'ONI, DAVID; TSCHERNICHOWSKY, SAUL.

Leftwich, Joseph. *Director, Federation of Jewish Organizations, London.* ANGLO-AMERICAN COMMITTEE OF INQUIRY (with Raphael Patai); GUEDALLA, PHILIP; LEAGUE OF BRITISH JEWS; MCMAHON CORRESPONDENCE; PEEL COMMISSION; STAVSKY TRIAL; biographical articles.

Lehman, Emil. *Director, Theodor Herzl Institute, New York.* GOLDSMID, ALBERT EDWARD WILLIAMSON; THEODOR HERZL INSTITUTE.

Levenberg, Schneier. *Head, Jewish Agency, United Kingdom, London.* GREAT BRITAIN: RELATIONS WITH ZIONISM AND ISRAEL (section); GREAT BRITAIN, ZIONISM IN (sections); LATVIA, ZIONISM IN; LITHUANIA, ZIONISM IN; LONDON ZIONIST CONFERENCE OF 1920; STEIN, LEONARD JACQUES.

Levine, Susan M. (Mrs. Moshe Dworkin). *Formerly of Near East Report, Washington.* ARAB BOYCOTT OF ISRAEL.

Lieberman, Judith B. *Public Affairs Chairman, Mizrahi Women's Organization of America, New York.* BERLIN, NAPHTALI TZ'VI Y'HUDA.

Linton, Joseph I. *Formerly Political Secretary, Jewish Agency, London; former member of the Israel Foreign Service with personal rank of Ambassador.* WEIZMANN, CHAIM; WEIZMANN, VERA CHATZMAN.

Livneh, Eliezer R. *Author; formerly Member of the Knesset, Jerusalem.* GERMANY: RELATIONS WITH ZIONISM AND ISRAEL; LEVI-BIANCHINI, ANGELO; MOSHAV.

Loewenstein, Kurt. *Leo Baeck Institute, Tel Aviv.* GERMAN JEWS IN ISRAEL.

Lorch, Netanel. *Director, Latin American Division, Ministry of Foreign Affairs, Jerusalem; formerly Chief, Military History, Israel Defense Forces.* FOREIGN RELATIONS OF ISRAEL; ISRAEL DEFENSE FORCES; SINAI CAMPAIGN; SIX-DAY WAR OF 1967; WAR OF INDEPENDENCE.

Luft, Freddy. *Secretary, Congregación Israelita de Nicaragua, Managua.* NICARAGUA, ZIONISM IN.

Mahler, Raphael. *Professor of Jewish History, Tel Aviv University, Tel Aviv.* BOROCHOVISM.

Malachy, Yona. *Editor, Christian News from Israel, Ministry of Religious Affairs, Jerusalem.* RESTORATION MOVEMENT.

Malamud, Samuel. *President, Federation of Jewish Organizations, Rio de Janeiro.* BRAZIL, ZIONISM IN.

Mann, Daniel. *Coordinator, American Zionist Federation; formerly Executive Director, Po'ale Zion and League for Labor Israel, New York.* PO'ALE ZION IN AMERICA.

Margolinsky, Julius. *Librarian, Jewish Community of Copenhagen.* DENMARK, ZIONISM IN.

*Margulies, Morris. *Executive Director, B'rit Rishonim,* New York. B'RIT RISHONIM OF THE UNITED STATES.

Marton, Jehuda. *News Editor, Israel Broadcasting Authority, Jerusalem.* BRAND, JOEL EUGEN; KASZTNER, REZSO RUDOLF; UJ KELET.

Mashiah, Avidan. *Public relations officer, municipality of Jerusalem.* BULGARIAN JEWS IN ISRAEL; HABANI JEWS IN ISRAEL; SYRIA AND LEBANON, ZIONISM IN.

Maslin, Simeon J. *Formerly Rabbi, United Netherlands Portuguese Congregation, Curaçao.* CURACAO, ZIONISM IN; SURINAM, ZIONISM IN.

Melamet, A. Max. *Executive Director, North American branch, World Jewish Congress, New York.* WORLD JEWISH CONGRESS (with Alex L. Easterman).

Mendelsohn, Ezra. *Lecturer in Contemporary Jewry and Russian Studies, Hebrew University, Jerusalem.* ANTISEMITISM.

Mendelsohn, Oskar. *Educator and author, Oslo.* NORWAY, ZIONISM IN.

Meri, U. *Author; member of the kibbutz Manara.* D'ROR.

Meyuhas, Yoseph B. *Director, Youth Department, Ministry of Education and Culture, Jerusalem.* SCOUTING IN ISRAEL.

Minerbi, Sergio. *Ambassador of Israel to the Ivory Coast, Abidjan.* ITALY: RELATIONS WITH ZIONISM AND ISRAEL; VATICAN: RELATIONS WITH ZIONISM AND ISRAEL (with Gertrude Hirschler).

Mizrahi, Hanina. *Educator, Jerusalem.* IRAN, ZIONISM IN, AND RELATIONS WITH ISRAEL; IRANIAN JEWS IN ISRAEL.

Morris, Ya'akov. *Consul General of Israel, Bombay.* 'ARAVA (with Yehuda Karmon).

Moshe, Itzhak Ben David (Itzhak Nathani). *Vice-president, Zionist Federation of the United Kingdom of Great Britain and Northern Ireland, London.* GREAT BRITAIN, ZIONISM IN (Mapam).

Musaph-Andriesse, Rosetta C. *Formerly Honorary Secretary, Nederlandsche Zionistenbond, Amsterdam.* NETHERLANDS, ZIONISM IN (with Gertrude Hirschler).

Nardi, Shulamit. *Assistant to the President of Israel, Jerusalem.* SHAZAR, SH'NEUR ZALMAN.

Nedava, Joseph. *Formerly Lecturer in Political Science, Bar-Ilan University, Ramat Gan; Visiting Professor of Political Science, Dropsie University, Philadelphia.* AARONSOHN, AARON; AGNON, SH'MUEL YOSEPH; AGUDAT HASOFRIM HA'IVRIM B'YISRAEL; GREENBERG, URI ZVI; KLAUSNER, JOSEPH GEDALIA; NILI; SAMUEL, HORACE BARNETT.

Negbi, Moshe. *Senior Lecturer in Botany, Hebrew University, Jerusalem; editorial coordinator, Israel Journal of Botany.* FLORA AND VEGETATION OF ISRAEL.

Nesson, Sylvia N. *Formerly of American Committee for Bar-Ilan University, New York.* BAR-ILAN UNIVERSITY.

Neumann, Oskar. *Chairman, Hitahdut 'Ole Tshekhoslovakia, Tel Aviv.* CZECHOSLOVAK JEWS IN ISRAEL; EDELSTEIN, JAKOB; FLEISCHMANN, GISI.

Ornstein, Judith (Ben-David). *Choreographer; Director, Studio Ornstein of Modern Dance, Tel Aviv.* DANCE IN ISRAEL (with Peter E. Gradenwitz).

Palgi, Phyllis. *Chief Anthropologist, Ministry of Health,*

*Deceased.

XX

Tel Aviv; Lecturer, Department of Behavioral Science, Medical School, Tel Aviv University. FAMILY IN ISRAEL.

Parzen, Herbert. *Research associate, Theodor Herzl Institute, New York.* CONSERVATIVE JUDAISM AND ZIONISM; EMERGENCY COMMITTEE FOR ZIONIST AFFAIRS (sections); FRIEDLANDER, ISRAEL; KING-CRANE REPORT; UNITED JEWISH APPEAL; UNITED PALESTINE APPEAL; UNITED STATES OF AMERICA, ZIONISM IN; biographical articles.

Patai, Raphael. *Editor, Herzl Press, New York; Professor of Anthropology, Fairleigh Dickinson University, Rutherford, N.J.* ASHKENAZIM; COMMUNITIES IN ISRAEL; ETHNIC GROUPS AND PROBLEMS IN ISRAEL; ORIENTAL JEWS; SEPHARDIM; TRUMAN, HARRY S; ZIONISM, HISTORY OF; other articles.

Patai, Saul. *Professor of Organic Chemistry, Hebrew University, Jerusalem.* NATIONAL COUNCIL FOR RESEARCH AND DEVELOPMENT; SCIENTIFIC RESEARCH IN ISRAEL.

Pechenik, Aharon. *Director, Religious Information, Hekhal Sh'lomo, Jerusalem.* HEKHAL SH'LOMO.

Philipp, Dan. *Probation officer, Welfare Office, Government of Israel, Tel Aviv.* CRIME IN ISRAEL (with Sh'lomo Shoham).

Philipp, Israel. *Archivist, Central Zionist Archives, Jerusalem.* RUPPIN, ARTHUR.

Pinner, Hayim. *Executive Director, B'nai B'rith of Great Britain and Ireland; Chairman, Po'ale Zion of Great Britain, London.* ANGLO-ISRAEL ASSOCIATION; ANGLO-JEWISH ASSOCIATION; BRIDGE IN BRITAIN; ELIOT, GEORGE; GREAT BRITAIN, ZIONISM IN (section); OLIPHANT, LAURENCE; SAMUEL, EDWIN HERBERT.

Porzecanski, Leopold. *Federación Sionista, Montevideo.* URUGUAY, ZIONISM IN.

Prag, Jehuda L. *Head, Patrol and Training Department, Police Headquarters, Tel Aviv.* POLICE IN ISRAEL.

Preschel, Tovia. *Assistant Editor,* Encyclopedia of Zionism and Israel, *New York.* AMERICAN ZIONIST MEDICAL UNIT; BALFOUR DECLARATION; BIROBIDZHAN; EDUCATION IN ISRAEL (section); HAIFA; HEBREW; ISRAEL, HISTORY OF (section); JAFFA; JERUSALEM; LANGUAGE WAR; LEGISLATIVE COUNCIL; MACDONALD LETTER; MORRISON-GRADY PLAN; PASSFIELD WHITE PAPER; TEL AVIV–JAFFA; WESTERN WALL; WHITE PAPER OF 1939; ZIONIST COMMISSION; ZION MULE CORPS; other articles.

*Rabinowicz, Oskar K. *Zionist historian, Scarsdale, N.Y.* BASLE PROGRAM; CONGRESS, ZIONIST (with Nathan Michael Gelber); CZECHOSLOVAKIA, ZIONISM IN; SAN REMO CONFERENCE; WHITE PAPER OF JUNE, 1922.

Rabinowitz, Louis I. *Jerusalem; formerly Chief Rabbi, Union of South Africa.* SOUTH AFRICAN JEWS IN ISRAEL (with Marcia Gitlin).

Rader, Jack. *Assistant Executive Director, American ORT Federation, New York.* ORT.

Rahmani, Hayim Pinhas (Derbaremdiger). *Head, Synagogues Department, Ministry of Religious Affairs, Jerusalem.* SYNAGOGUES IN ISRAEL.

Raicher-Schapire, Rosa Perla. *Diaspora Research Institute,*

Tel Aviv University, Tel Aviv. ARGENTINA, ZIONISM IN (with Moises Senderay).

Raphael, Yitzhak. *Member of the Knesset; President, Rabbi Kook Foundation, Jerusalem.* Biographies of religious Zionists.

Ravikovitch, Shlomo. *Professor of Soil Science Emeritus, Hebrew University of Jerusalem, Rehovot.* SOILS OF ISRAEL.

Raviv, Shabtai. *Manager, Israel Communications Ltd.; formerly public relations officer, Port Authority, Tel Aviv.* PORTS OF ISRAEL.

Reiss, Anzelm-Anshel. *Member of the Actions Committee and of the Executive, World Labor Zionist movement, Tel Aviv.* HOVEVE ZION (section); POLISH JEWS IN ISRAEL.

Remba, Oded. *Professor of Economics, Staten Island Community College of the City University of New York.* ECONOMY OF ISRAEL; STANDARD OF LIVING IN ISRAEL.

Resnikoff, Natalie. *Mizrahi Women's Organization of America, New York.* MIZRAHI WOMEN'S ORGANIZATION OF AMERICA.

Richman, Sarabeth. *Formerly Director, Student Zionist Organization, Chicago.* STUDENT ZIONIST ORGANIZATION.

Ritov, Israel. *Member of the Zionist Executive and of the Central Committee, Israel Labor party, Tel Aviv.* COOPERATIVES IN ISRAEL.

Romano, Giorgio. *Correspondent,* Il Messaggero, *Tel Aviv.* ITALIAN JEWS IN ISRAEL; ITALY, ZIONISM IN; biographies of Italian Zionists.

Ronall, Joachim O. *Economist, Federal Reserve Bank of New York; Adjunct Associate Professor, Fordham University, New York.* EUROPEAN COMMON MARKET AND ISRAEL; FINANCE IN ISRAEL; FOREIGN TRADE OF ISRAEL; GOVERNMENT CORPORATIONS IN ISRAEL; INDUSTRY IN ISRAEL (section).

Ronnen, Meir. *Editor,* Jerusalem Post Weekly, *Jerusalem.* ART IN ISRAEL; MUSEUMS IN ISRAEL.

Rosenak, Michael. *Hebrew University, Jerusalem.* RELIGION AND RELIGIOUS ATTITUDES IN ISRAEL; SABBATH AND HOLIDAYS IN ISRAEL.

Rosenan, Naftali. *Formerly Deputy Director, Meteorological Service of Israel, Bet Dagan.* CLIMATE OF ISRAEL.

Rosetti, Moshe. *Clerk of the Knesset, Jerusalem.* GREAT BRITAIN, ZIONISM IN (section).

Rotem, Zvi I. *President, Association of Yugoslav Jews in Israel, Tel Aviv.* YUGOSLAVIA, ZIONISM IN.

Ruben, Herbert. *President, Zionist Council of New Zealand, Wellington.* NEW ZEALAND, ZIONISM IN.

Rubin, Jacob. *Author of* History of Israel, *New York.* AMERICAN ZION COMMONWEALTH; JEWISH BRIGADE; articles on Israeli newspapers.

Rubinstein, Leon. *Director, National Committee of the Jewish Folk Schools, New York.* TZ'IRE ZION HITAHDUT OF AMERICA.

Samuel, Viscount. *Principal, Israel Institute of Public Administration, Jerusalem and London.* CIVIL SERVICE IN ISRAEL; HIGH COMMISSIONER FOR PALESTINE (section); LOCAL GOVERNMENT IN ISRAEL.

*Deceased.

*Schechtman, Joseph B. *Author; former member of the Jewish Agency Executive, New York.* ARAB REFUGEES; B'RIT TRUMPELDOR; HOVEVE ZION (section); IRGUN TZ'VAI L'UMI; JABOTINSKY, VLADIMIR YEVGENIEVICH; JEWISH LEGION; NEW ZIONIST ORGANIZATION; NORDAU, MAX; OPERATION 'EZRA AND NEHEMIA; OPERATION MAGIC CARPET; REVISIONISTS; RUSSIA: RELATIONS WITH ZIONISM AND ISRAEL; RUSSIA, ZIONISM IN; TERRORIST ORGANIZATIONS, ARAB; TRANSJORDAN; UNITED NATIONS AND PALESTINE-ISRAEL; UNITED STATES OF AMERICA: RELATIONS WITH ZIONISM AND ISRAEL; other articles.

Schenker, Avraham. *Head, Organization and Information Department, World Zionist Organization, Jerusalem.* AMERICANS FOR PROGRESSIVE ISRAEL—HASHOMER HATZA'IR; HASHOMER HATZA'IR; HASHOMER HATZA'IR ZIONIST YOUTH IN NORTH AMERICA; MAPAM.

Schepansky, Israel. *Instructor in Talmud, Yeshiva University, New York.* HASIDIC JEWS IN ISRAEL.

Schönkopf, Bertil. *Author, Stockholm.* SWEDEN, ZIONISM IN.

Senderay, Moises. El Diario Israelita, *Buenos Aires.* ARGENTINA, ZIONISM IN (with Rosa Perla Raicher-Schapire).

Shadmon, Asher. ISRAEL ELECTRIC CORPORATION, LTD.

Shaikovski, Zosa. *Historian; Fellow of the American Academy of Jewish Research, New York.* KOMITEE FUR DEN OSTEN.

Shakow, Zara. *Artistic Director, Acting Training Center, New York.* THEATER IN ISRAEL.

Shamir, Aaron. *Supervisor of Secondary Schools, Ministry of Education and Culture, Tel Aviv.* RUSSIAN JEWS IN ISRAEL.

Sharabi, Israel Y'sha'yahu. *Member of the Knesset; formerly Minister of Posts, Jerusalem.* YEMENITE JEWS IN ISRAEL.

Shavitt, Edna. *Author, Tel Aviv.* ENTERTAINMENT IN ISRAEL.

Shazar, Zalman. *President of Israel, Jerusalem.* BEN ZVI, ITZHAK.

Sherman, C. Bezalel. *Visiting Professor of Sociology, Stern College, Yeshiva University, and Jewish Teachers Seminary, New York.* AMERICAN FEDERATION OF LABOR—CONGRESS OF INDUSTRIAL ORGANIZATIONS; AMERICAN JEWISH COMMITTEE; AMERICAN JEWISH CONGRESS; AMPAL; ASSIMILATION; B'NAI B'RITH; BUND; COLUMBUS PLATFORM; CONGRESS OF INDUSTRIAL ORGANIZATIONS; FARBAND; GALUT NATIONALISM; HISTADRUT CAMPAIGN; IHUD 'OLAMI; JEWISH FRONTIER; LABOR ZIONISM; PIONEER WOMEN; PITTSBURGH PLATFORM; WORKMEN'S CIRCLE; YIDISHER KEMFER; biographical articles.

Shoham, Sh'lomo. *Director, Institute of Criminology and Criminal Law, Tel Aviv University, Tel Aviv.* CRIME IN ISRAEL (with Dan Philipp).

Shulov, Aharon S. *Professor of Zoology, Hebrew University, Jerusalem.* ANIMAL LIFE IN ISRAEL.

Shultz, Lillie. *Director of Public Relations, American Committee for the Weizmann Institute of Science,* New York. WEIZMANN INSTITUTE OF SCIENCE.

Sieff, Israel Moses (Baron Sieff). *Business executive; Chairman, European Executive, World Jewish Congress, London.* ANGLO-ISRAEL CHAMBER OF COMMERCE.

Silberschlag, Eisig. *Dean, Hebrew Teachers College, Brookline, Mass.* LITERATURE, MODERN HEBREW AND ISRAELI (section).

*Simon, Sir Leon, C.B. *Author, London.* AHAD HA'AM; CULTURAL ZIONISM.

Simri, Uriel. *Scientific Director, Wingate Institute for Physical Education and Sport, Tel Aviv–N'tanya road.* SPORTS AND PHYSICAL EDUCATION IN ISRAEL.

Skulsky, Sh'lomo. *Author and teacher, Levinsky Teachers Seminary, Tel Aviv.* BEN 'AMI, MORDECAI; CAHAN, YA'AKOV; SMILANSKY, MOSHE.

Slutsky, Y'huda. *Lecturer in the History of the Labor Zionist Movement in Israel, Tel Aviv University, Tel Aviv.* AHDUT 'AVODA; AHDUT 'AVODA–PO'ALE ZION; COMMUNISTS IN ISRAEL; FIFTH 'ALIYA; FIRST 'ALIYA; FOURTH 'ALIYA; HANO'AR HA'OVED V'HALOMED; HAT'NU'A HAM'UHEDET; HEHALUTZ; HITAHDUT; ISRAEL, HISTORY OF (section); KIBBUTZ MOVEMENT; MAPAI; MERKAZ HAKLAI; MO'ETZET HAPO'ALOT; RURAL SETTLEMENT IN PALESTINE AND ISRAEL (Private Sector); SELF-LABOR; "STOCKADE AND TOWER" SETTLEMENTS; THIRD 'ALIYA; T'NU'AT HAMOSHAVIM; TZ'IRE ZION; other articles.

Soen, Gad. *Director, Internal Trade Division, Ministry of Commerce and Industry, Jerusalem.* DOMESTIC TRADE IN ISRAEL (with Hillel Ashkenazy).

*Spar, Samuel. *Religious Zionists of America, New York.* RELIGIOUS ZIONISTS OF AMERICA.

Spiegel-Roy, Pinhas. *Head, Department of Horticulture, Volcani Institute of Agricultural Research, Bet Dagan.* WINE INDUSTRY IN ISRAEL (with Avraham Hadas).

Spira, Shirley. *Author; contributor,* Israel *magazine, Ashk'lon.* AMERICAN AND CANADIAN JEWS IN ISRAEL.

Stavi, Joseph. *Librarian, Knesset, Jerusalem.* BURG, SH'LOMO YOSEPH; FRANKEL, ABRAHAM HALEVI; GELLMAN, LEON; SHAPIRA, (HAYIM) MOSHE; UNTERMAN, ISSAR Y'HUDA; WAHRHAFTIG, ZERAH.

Steinglass, Meyer. *National Director of Public Relations, State of Israel Bonds Organization, New York.* STATE OF ISRAEL BONDS.

Stendel, Ori. RASSCO, *Jerusalem.* ARAB DELEGATIONS; ARAB RIOTS IN PALESTINE.

Sultanik, Kalman. *Executive Vice-chairman, World Confederation of General Zionists, New York.* WORLD CONFEDERATION OF GENERAL ZIONISTS.

Super, Arthur S. *Chief Minister, United Progressive Jewish Congregation, Johannesburg.* SOUTH AFRICA, ZIONISM IN.

Syrkin, Marie. *Author; Editor,* Jewish Frontier; *formerly member of the Jewish Agency Executive, New York.* MEIR, GOLDA.

Tal, Shim'on. *Director, Fish Culture Division, Ministry of Agriculture, Tel Aviv.* FISHING IN ISRAEL.

Tarshish, Abraham. *Editor, HaKibbutz HaM'uhad Pub-*

*Deceased.

lishing House, Tel Aviv. B'RIT 'OLAMIT AHDUT 'AVODA-
PO'ALE ZION.

Tartakower, Arye. *Chairman, Israeli Executive, World
Jewish Congress, Jerusalem.* AUTONOMY, JEWISH;
B'RIT 'IVRIT 'OLAMIT; POLAND, ZIONISM IN; SILBER-
SCHEIN, ABRAHAM; TARBUT.

Teich, Meyer. *Editor in chief,* Die Stimme, *Ramat Gan.*
BUKOVINIAN JEWS IN ISRAEL.

Telsner, David. *Head, Religious Department, Ministry for
the Absorption of Immigrants, Jerusalem.* GREENBERG,
AHARON YA'AKOV HALEVI; SHRAGAI, SH'LOMO ZALMAN.

Unna, Moshe. *Formerly Member of the Knesset; Deputy
Minister of Education and Culture; Chairman of the
Board for Religious Education, Ministry of Educa-
tion and Culture, Jerusalem.* TORA VA'AVODA.

Vardi, Martha. *Director, Arts and Crafts Center, Israel
Export Institute, Tel Aviv.* CRAFTS IN ISRAEL (with
Gertrude Hirschler).

Voss, Carl Hermann. *Author, Saratoga Springs, N.Y.; for-
merly Chairman, Executive Council, American
Christian Palestine Committee, New York.* AMERICAN
PALESTINE COMMITTEE.

Wainstein, Baruch. *Member of the Executive, World Union
of General Zionists, Tel Aviv.* WORLD UNION OF GEN-
ERAL ZIONISTS.

Wardi, Chaim Y. *Senior Lecturer in Church History, Tel
Aviv University, Tel Aviv.* CHRISTIAN COMMUNITIES
AND CHURCHES IN ISRAEL; CHRISTIAN MISSIONS IN
ISRAEL.

Warkoff, Irving. *Formerly Executive Director, Boys' Town,
Inc., New York.* BOYS' TOWN, JERUSALEM.

Weill, Georges. *Director, Services d'Archives des Hauts-
de-Seine, Chaville, France.* FRANCE: RELATIONS WITH
ZIONISM AND ISRAEL; FRANCE, ZIONISM IN.

Weinfeld, Eduardo. *Editor,* Enciclopedia Judaica Castel-
lana, *Mexico City.* FASTLICHT, ADOLFO; MEXICO, ZION-
ISM IN; MITRANI, VICTOR.

Weinstein, Jacob I. *Formerly Executive Secretary, Jewish
Community, Helsinki.* FINLAND, ZIONISM IN.

Weisberg, Bernard M. *National Director, Hadassah Zionist
Youth Commission, New York.* AMERICAN ZIONIST
YOUTH COMMISSION; YOUNG JUDAEA.

Weiser, Max W. *Consul of Israel, Quito.* ECUADOR, ZIONISM
IN.

Weisgal, Meyer W. *Chancellor, Weizmann Institute of
Science, Rehovot.* SHARETT, MOSHE.

Weitz, Ra'anan. *Member of the Executive and Head,
Agricultural Settlement Department, Jewish Agency,
Jerusalem.* AGRICULTURE IN ISRAEL.

Weitz, Yoseph. *Member, Curatorial Board, Jewish National Fund, Jerusalem.* LAND POLICY IN ISRAEL; LAND
RECLAMATION IN ISRAEL.

Weltsch, Robert M. *Chairman, London branch, and Editor
of the* Year Book, Leo Baeck Institute, London. FEI-
WEL, BERTHOLD.

Werner, Alfred. *Art Editor,* Encyclopedia Judaica, *New
York.* ARDON, MORDECAI; CASTEL, MOSHE; GUTMAN,
NAHUM; JANCO, MARCEL; MOKADY, MOSHE; RUBIN,
REUVEN; SCHATZ, BORIS; STEINHARDT, JACOB; TICHO,
ANNA.

Wiener, Aaron. *President, Tahal Consulting Engineers,
Ltd., Tel Aviv.* WATER AND THE UTILIZATION OF
WATER RESOURCES IN ISRAEL.

Willner, Dorothy. *Associate Professor of Anthropology,
University of Kansas, Lawrence, Kans.* IMMIGRANTS'
VILLAGES.

Winkelman, Yisrael. *Formerly National President, B'rit
Trumpeldor–Betar.* B'RIT TRUMPELDOR, U.S.A.

*Wohlmann, Leon. *President, Schweizerischer Zionisten-
verband, Zurich.* SWITZERLAND, ZIONISM IN.

Wormann, Curt D. *Director, Jewish National and University Library, Jerusalem.* JEWISH NATIONAL AND UNI-
VERSITY LIBRARY, JERUSALEM; LIBRARIES IN ISRAEL.

Wulman, Leon L., M.D. *Physician and author, New York.*
OSE.

Wydra, Naftali H. *Chairman, Israel Port Authority; Chair-
man and General Manager, Israel Shipping Research
Institute, Haifa.* SHIPPING IN ISRAEL (with Avraham
Antonier).

Yahil, Hayim. *Chairman, Israel Broadcasting Authority;
formerly Director General, Ministry of Foreign Affairs,
Jerusalem.* BOHEMIA AND MORAVIA, ZIONISM IN.

Y'hoshu'a, Ya'akov. *Director, Muslim and Druze Division,
Ministry of Religious Affairs, Jerusalem.* KARAITES IN
ISRAEL.

Yoel, Marcel M. *Editor,* Jewish Review, *Athens.* GREECE,
ZIONISM IN.

Yudelevich, Mateo. *Federación Sionista, Santiago.* CHILE,
ZIONISM IN.

Yudin, Yehuda. *Member of the Histadrut Executive;
Chairman, Department of Workers' Participation in
Management, Tel Aviv.* TRADE UNIONS IN ISRAEL.

Yussef, Norma. *Executive Secretary, Organización Sionista de Guatemala, Guatemala City.* GUATEMALA,
ZIONISM IN.

Zakin, Dov. *Mapam Political Secretary; Member of the
Knesset, Jerusalem.* YA'ARI, MEIR.

Zenner, Walter P. *Associate Professor of Anthropology,
State University of New York, Albany.* SYRIAN AND
LEBANESE JEWS IN ISRAEL.

*Zidon, Asher. *Deputy Secretary of the Knesset, Jerusa-
lem; author of* Knesset: The Parliament of Israel.
KNESSET.

Ziv-Av, Yitzhak. *Director General, Farmers' Federation
of Israel, Tel Aviv.* HITAHDUT HAIKKARIM.

Zohn, Harry. *Professor of German and Chairman, Department of Germanic and Slavic Languages, Brandeis
University, Waltham, Mass.* NEW GHETTO, THE.

Zwergbaum, Aaron. *Legal Adviser, World Zionist Organi-
zation, Jerusalem.* CONGRESS TRIBUNAL; ISRAEL AND
THE DIASPORA; JEWISH AGENCY FOR ISRAEL; SEPARATE
UNIONS; SHEKEL; WORLD ZIONIST ORGANIZATION; ZION-
IST TERRITORIAL ORGANIZATIONS.

*Deceased.

xxiii

A

AARONSOHN, AARON. Agronomist and Jewish statesman (b. Bacău, Romania, 1876; d. 1919). At the age of six he was brought by his parents to Palestine. His father was one of the founders of Zikhron Ya'akov. Aaronsohn studied in France and on his return to Palestine was employed as an agronomist by Baron Edmond de *Rothschild at M'tula (1895). He made extensive explorations in Palestine and neighboring countries and in 1906 discovered specimens of wild wheat *(Triticum dicoccoides)* at Rosh Pina, a discovery that made him famous among botanists throughout the world.

At the invitation of the U.S. Department of Agriculture, Aaronsohn visited the United States in 1909–10. With the help of influential Jewish leaders and philanthropists (Louis D. *Brandeis, Louis *Marshall, Julius *Rosenwald, Julian W. *Mack, Nathan *Straus, Jacob *Schiff, Judah L. *Magnes, and Henrietta *Szold, among others), he raised funds for the establishment of an agricultural experiment station at 'Atlit, near Haifa.

In 1915, with Avshalom Feinberg and members of their

Zionist aspirations. Moving to Cairo, he helped British headquarters there in planning the campaign for the invasion of Palestine. In 1916 he visited London and there circulated a memorandum on the future of Palestine, which helped to make the idea of a Jewish National Home in Palestine part of British policy in the Near East. In 1918 Aaronsohn worked in conjunction with the *Zionist Commission in Palestine, and in 1919 he cooperated with the Zionist delegation to the Paris Peace Conference, dealing especially with the problem of the Palestine boundaries (*see* COMITÉ DES DÉLÉGATIONS JUIVES).

Aaronsohn was killed in an airplane crash over the English Channel on May 15, 1919. His researches on Palestine *flora and part of his exploration diaries were published posthumously. The Institute for Agriculture of the *Hebrew University of Jerusalem is named for him.

J. NEDAVA

AARONSOHN, SARAH. Sister of Aaron *Aaronsohn (b. Zikhron Ya'akov, 1890; d. there, 1917). She played a leading role in

Aaron Aaronsohn.
[Zionist Archives]

Sarah Aaronsohn.
[Zionist Archives]

families, Aaronsohn organized *Nili, a secret intelligence group with the aim of assisting the British forces under Gen. Edmund H. H. *Allenby to conquer Palestine, thus helping to realize

*Nili, a secret intelligence group in Palestine, and succeeded in collecting much vital information for the British. In the spring of 1917, while on a secret mission to Egypt, she was asked by her

brother Aaron to remain there rather than endanger her life by further efforts on behalf of this intelligence service. Refusing, she returned to Palestine to head the Nili group. She was arrested by the Turkish military authorities in the fall of the same year. In an effort to obtain information about the group, the Turks tortured her for three days. She endured heroically and disclosed no secrets. To escape further torture, she shot and killed herself.

'ABDUL HAMID II. Thirty-fourth Sultan of the Ottoman Empire (b. Constantinople, 1842; d. Manisa, Turkey, 1918). Hamid's rule (1876–1909) was marked by violence, censorship, espionage, bribery, murder, and terrorism. European encroachments on Ottoman territory continued throughout his reign, resulting in the loss of Cyprus (1878), Tunis (1881), and Crete (1897). The ineffectiveness of the Sultan's policies led to the rise of the Young Turk movement, culminating in 1908 in the Young Turk Revolution. In 1909 the Sultan was deposed and banished.

'Abdul Hamid's attitude toward the Jews of Turkey was liberal. In 1876 the Jews of the Ottoman Empire gained equality before the law. Three Jews were elected to Parliament, two were nominated by the Sultan to the Senate, and the Hakham Bashi (Chief Rabbi) was nominated to the Divan (State Council). Isaac Molho Pasha, a Jew, became an admiral in the Turkish Navy.

In the Palestine area 'Abdul Hamid introduced new administrative methods, thereby improving the situation of the population, and built the Hejaz Railway down to Medina and Mecca. But he was adamantly opposed to Jewish national aspirations in Palestine, primarily because he feared that the influence of the European powers there would be increased by the immigration of their nationals. Because of the influx of Jews from Russia in the wake of the 1881 pogroms, the Sultan prohibited Jewish *immigration into Palestine in 1882. This prohibition was rescinded in 1883, but renewed in 1891. The law, however, was not stringently enforced, and Jews were able to immigrate and found settlements in Palestine.

On June 28, 1896, 'Abdul Hamid awarded Herzl the Commander's Cross of the Mejidiye Order, and five years later, on May 18, 1901, he received Herzl in a long private audience, which, although the Sultan assured Herzl of his sympathy for the Jews, yielded no tangible results for Zionism. On that occasion 'Abdul Hamid bestowed on Herzl the Grand Cordon of the Mejidiye. 'Abdul Hamid resisted Herzl's attempts to obtain from him a political *Charter for an autonomous Jewish settlement in Palestine, rejecting national Jewish concentration there and suggesting instead that individual Jewish families settle in various parts of the Ottoman Empire.   J. ADLER

'ABDULLAH I. *See* TRANSJORDAN.

ABELES, OTTO. Zionist worker and writer (b. Brno, Moravia, Austria, 1879; d. Bergen-Belsen, 1945). After his graduation from the University of Vienna, he served as legal adviser to the Austrian railways. A Zionist since his youth, he contributed to and served as editor of German-language Zionist publications. With Ludwig Bato he edited the Viennese *Jüdischer National-kalender Almanach* (1917–21).

In 1926 he entered the service of the *Keren HaYesod (Palestine Foundation Fund), for which he had previously worked in a voluntary capacity, and from 1931 to 1939 directed its activities in the Netherlands. During World War II the Nazis deported

him to Bergen-Belsen, where he died of exhaustion several days after the liberation of the camp.

Abeles published the following books (all in German): *Jewish Refugees* (1918), *A Visit to the Land of Israel* (1926), *Ten Jewish Women* (1931), and *Meetings with Jews* (1936).

ABERSON, DAVID. Journalist, Zionist propagandist, and *Po'ale Zion organizer (b. Russia, 1873; d. Chicago, 1929). Little is known about his life prior to his immigration to the United States from England in 1903. From 1904 he was one of the most energetic organizers of American Po'ale Zion groups, and he contributed much toward their crystallization into one party in 1905. Aberson was a leader in the party's early struggle against the Socialist-Territorialists, on the one hand, and the assimilationist Jewish Socialists, on the other. An orator of great eloquence and a most effective propagandist of the young Po'ale Zion movement, he carried its message from town to town.

Aberson also enjoyed a considerable reputation as a writer. He contributed to all Po'ale Zion publications and served on the governing bodies of the organization. In 1910 he moved from New York to Chicago and joined the staff of the *Jewish Courier,* a Yiddish daily. In 1916 he established his own weekly, *Undzer Lebn,* which was short-lived. Returning to New York, he became a staff member of the *Zeit,* a daily published by the Po'ale Zion in 1920–22. Broken in health, he moved back to Chicago in the mid-1920s and remained there until his death.

C. B. SHERMAN

ABRAHAMS, ABRAHAM. Writer and Zionist leader (b. London, 1898; d. Johannesburg, 1955). A talented publicist and political analyst, he was editor of the London *Jewish Youth* (1928) and *Jewish Weekly* (1932). In 1933 he became editor of the New York office of the *Jewish Telegraphic Agency, in which capacity he visited Nazi Germany to report to the Jewish press on the situation of the German Jews.

An early adherent of the Revisionist movement, Abrahams served as editor of many of its publications (*see* REVISIONISTS). In 1934 he was political editor of the Jerusalem *HaYarden,* and between 1937 and 1941 he edited in London the Zionist Press Service of the *New Zionist Organization. From 1940 to 1948 he edited the *Jewish Standard.* In this London weekly Abrahams forcefully attacked Britain's anti-Zionist Palestine policy and, during World War II, clamored for the rescue of European Jewry and propagated the idea of a Jewish army. In 1945 he wrote *Background of Unrest: Palestine Journey, 1944.*

Abrahams held prominent positions in the Revisionist movement and later was a member of the Presidium of the New Zionist Organization as head of its Political Committee. At the time of his death, which occurred while he was guest editor of the South African *Jewish Herald,* he was a member of the Executive of the Zionist Revisionist movement and chairman of its organization in Great Britain.

In 1932 Abrahams published a volume of *Poems,* which was awarded the first Israel *Zangwill Memorial Prize.

ABRAMOV, S. ZALMAN. Lawyer and Israeli political leader (b. Minsk, Russia, 1908). After studying at the *Herzliya High School in Tel Aviv (1920–26) and Western Reserve University in Cleveland (1927–34; M.A., J.D.), he practiced law in Tel Aviv. He was chairman of the Israel-America Friendship League (1951–65) and a member of the *Actions Committee (1955–59), the Central Committee of the General Zionist party (1955–60), and the Central Committee of the *Liberal party (1960–   ).

From 1959 on Abramov was a member of the *Knesset, serving on the Constitution, Law, and Justice Committee and the House (Knesset) Committee. He represented Israel as an observer at the Council of Europe in Strasbourg (1963–68) and from 1965 on served on the Executive Committee of the World Liberal Union in London. A frequent contributor to the Israeli and American Jewish press on political and historical subjects, he undertook several lecture tours throughout the United States.

ABSORPTION OF IMMIGRANTS. *See* IMMIGRATION TO PALESTINE AND ISRAEL.

ABU. Arabic word, meaning "father," that forms part of the name of many Arab tribes in Israel and Arab countries, as in Abu Balal (Father of Balal).

ABU 'ABDUN. Nomadic Arab tribe in the B'er Sheva' region of the Negev. Population (1968): 268.

ABU 'AMRE. Nomadic Arab tribe in the B'er Sheva' region of the Negev. Population (1968): 148.

ABU BALAL. Nomadic Arab tribe in the B'er Sheva' region of the Negev. Population (1968): 467.

ABU GHOSH. Arab village west of Jerusalem, on the highway leading to Tel Aviv. The inhabitants of the village were known for their friendly relations with the Jews. During the *War of Independence, they did not participate in the fighting and submitted to the Jewish forces. Population (1968): 1,710.

The Arab village of Abu Ghosh. [Israel Information Services]

Abu Ghosh is the site of interesting prehistoric finds from the Neolithic period (pottery and the remains of a square building) indicating Syrian influences and of a 12th-century Crusaders' church built on the remains of a Roman structure.

ABU J'WEI'AD. Nomadic Arab tribe in the B'er Sheva' region of the Negev. Population (1968): 1,500.

ABU K'RENAT. Nomadic Arab tribe in the B'er Sheva' region of the Negev. Population (1968): 2,060.

ABU MU'AMER. *See* MAS'UDIN AL-'AZAZME.

ABU RABI'A. Nomadic Arab tribe in the B'er Sheva' region of the Negev. Population (1968): 3,150.

ABU RAKIK. Nomadic Arab tribe in the B'er Sheva' region of the Negev. Population (1968): 3,950.

ABU SINAN. Druze village in western Galilee. Population (1968): 2,490.

ABU S'REHAN. Nomadic Arab tribe in the B'er Sheva' region of the Negev. Population (1968): 215.

ACADEMY OF HEBREW LANGUAGE. *See* HEBREW LANGUAGE ACADEMY.

ACADEMY OF MEDICINE. *See* JERUSALEM ACADEMY OF MEDICINE.

ACCO. *See* 'AKKO.

ACHER, MATHIAS. *See* BIRNBAUM, NATHAN.

ACHIMEIR, ABBA. *See* AHIMEIR, ABBA.

ACHOOZA (ACHUSA, ACHUZA) SOCIETIES. *See* AHUZA SOCIETIES.

ACRE. *See* 'AKKO.

ACRE PRISON. *See* 'AKKO PRISON.

ACTIONS COMMITTEE. Greater Actions Committee, *see* ZIONIST GENERAL COUNCIL. Inner Actions Committee, *see* EXECUTIVE, ZIONIST. *See also* WORLD ZIONIST ORGANIZATION.

ADAMIT. Village (kibbutz) in western Upper Galilee. Founded in 1958 and affiliated with the *Kibbutz Artzi Shel HaShomer HaTza'ir.

'ADANIM. Village (moshav) in the southern Sharon Plain. Founded in 1950 and affiliated with *T'nu'at HaMoshavim. Population (1968): 195.

ADEN, JEWS FROM. *See* YEMENITE JEWS IN ISRAEL.

ADERET. Village (moshav) in the Judean Plain. Settled in 1961 and affiliated with *T'nu'at HaMoshavim.

ADIRIM. Village (moshav) in the Jezreel Valley. Founded in 1956 and affiliated with *T'nu'at HaMoshavim. Population (1968): 335.

ADLER, CYRUS. Orientalist, educator, and Jewish communal leader (b. Van Buren, Ark., 1863; d. Philadelphia, 1940). He taught Semitic languages at Johns Hopkins University (1887–93) and was curator of historic archeology and historic religions at the United States National Museum in Washington (1889–1908) and librarian (1892–1905) and assistant secretary (1905–08) of the Smithsonian Institution.

Cyrus Adler.
[Jewish Theological Seminary of America]

Adler helped found the *American Jewish Joint Distribution Committee, of whose Cultural Committee he was chairman until his death. He was also one of the founders of the Jewish Publication Society of America (1888) and the American Jewish Historical Society (1892) and eventually served as president of both bodies. He was president of the Dropsie College for Hebrew and Cognate Learning in Philadelphia (from 1908) and of the Jewish Theological Seminary of America in New York (1924–40). From 1914 to 1918 he was presiding officer of the United Synagogue of America.

A prominent and active member of the *American Jewish Committee, Adler served with Louis *Marshall as its spokesman before the Paris Peace Conference and helped secure minority rights for the Jews of Eastern Europe. On Marshall's death (1929), he succeeded him as president of the American Jewish Committee.

Though not a Zionist, Adler had been associated before World War I with constructive efforts in Palestine. After the issuance of the *Balfour Declaration, he advocated collaboration between non-Zionists and Zionists in the building of the Jewish National Home. He helped found the enlarged *Jewish Agency and after its establishment (1929) became cochairman of the Agency's Council. In 1930 Adler prepared a *Memorandum on the Western Wall*, which, annotated by a committee of scholars in Jerusalem, was submitted by the Jewish Agency to the special Commission of the League of Nations that had been appointed to study and define the claims and rights of Jews and Muslims at the *Western (Wailing) Wall in Jerusalem. He edited numerous books and wrote on a variety of topics. His autobiography, *I Have Considered the Days*, was published posthumously, in 1941.

'ADULAM REGION. Development area in the Jerusalem corridor. Started in 1957, it covers an area of 25,000 acres. By 1969, 5 of a projected 10 moshavim (*see* MOSHAV) had been established. The region was named for the Biblical city 'Adulam, which existed in the area.

AELIA CAPITOLINA. *See* JERUSALEM.

AFEINISH. Bedouin tribe in the B'er Sheva' area. Population (1968): 433.

AFEK. Village (kibbutz) in the Z'vulun Valley. Founded in 1939 and affiliated with the *Kibbutz M'uhad. Population (1968): 417.

AFFORESTATION IN ISRAEL. *See* FORESTRY IN ISRAEL.

AFGHAN JEWS IN ISRAEL. Apart from legends and a few medieval references, the earliest historical information about Afghan Jews is dated 1839, when part of the Jewish community of Meshed, Persia, chose to flee to Herat, Afghanistan, rather than submit to the demand of conversion to Islam. The refugees infused the small Jewish community of Herat with a new vitality. After the Russian Revolution of 1917 the community grew again, as a result of the arrival of Jewish refugees from Bukhara and other cities.

Prior to World War I several Afghan-Jewish families had gone to Palestine, primarily to fulfill the Mitzva (religious commandment) of being buried there. After the war, however, some Jewish pilgrims who had visited Palestine returned to tell of the rebuilding of the Holy Land and inspired groups of Afghan Jews to settle in Jerusalem.

Although the borders of Afghanistan were closed to foreigners and particularly to Zionist organizers, nonetheless, from 1933 to 1937, many Jewish families liquidated their businesses, sold their property at great loss, and sought to migrate to Palestine. A few received *immigration certificates; many more arrived as illegal immigrants (*see* ILLEGAL IMMIGRATION). By 1937 their number was close to 1,000, of whom 700 lived in Jerusalem.

At the beginning of World War II a wave of *anti-Semitism, fomented by Nazi agents, swept through Afghanistan. The Jews were forced to leave the border areas and were confined to certain areas in the interior, and their situation, never favorable, deteriorated also in other respects. Many sought to emigrate to Palestine, but the Afghan government forbade them to leave the country and the British *White Paper of 1939 prevented their entry into Palestine.

Since the creation of the State of Israel, the Jewish community in Afghanistan has virtually disappeared. In 1949 there were some 3,500 Jews in Afghanistan, but their situation had become so difficult that the leaders of the community requested the help of the *Jewish Agency to settle in Israel. Since then almost all the Jews of Afghanistan have moved there. In 1967 fewer than 100 families remained in Herat and Kabul, while the number of Afghan Jews in Israel had reached 7,000, of whom about one-half were immigrants and the other half their descendants born in Israel.

In 1926 the Afghan Jews established in Jerusalem a community council composed of seven leaders; similar councils were subsequently formed in Haifa, Tel Aviv, and Tiberias. In 1936 mutual-aid funds and loan associations were formed to assist the immigrants in finding homes and employment. In 1943 some of the younger generation in Jerusalem formed the Organization of Afghan Youth to sponsor educational and cultural projects.

During World War II many Afghan-Jewish youths joined the British Army and the *Jewish Brigade. Many young men and women were active in the *Hagana, *Palmah, and various underground movements prior to and during the Israel *War of Independence. In the 1960s the Afghan Jews were scattered throughout Israel, but the large majority lived in Tel Aviv and Jerusalem.

R. KASHANI

AFIKIM. Village (kibbutz) in the Jordan Valley. Settled in 1932 and affiliated with the *Ihud HaK'vutzot V'haKibbutzim. Population (1968): 1,300.

AFL-CIO. *See* AMERICAN FEDERATION OF LABOR–CONGRESS OF INDUSTRIAL ORGANIZATIONS.

'AFULA. City in the heart of the Jezreel Valley. Founded in 1925 by the *American Zion Commonwealth on a site formerly occupied by an Arab village, it has developed as the market and communication center of the Jezreel Valley. Its inhabitants are mainly farmers, tradespeople, and artisans. With the rapid growth of the city since the establishment of the State, industrial enterprises have come to 'Afula, including a sugar refinery and textile and flour mills. The city's hospital and educational and vocational institutions serve a wide area. In the 20-year interval from 1948 to 1968 the population of 'Afula grew from 2,000 to 16,400.

'Afula is the site of prehistoric finds from the Upper Chalcolithic period, belonging to the so-called Esdraelon (Jezreel) subculture, characterized by pottery with a burnished gray slip. In addition, remains of buildings from this period were found on the site.

'AGMON, NATHAN. *See* BISTRITSKY, NATHAN.

AGNON (CZACZKES), SH'MUEL YOSEPH. Outstanding Hebrew novelist (b. Buchach, Galicia, Austria, 1888). Agnon began writing Hebrew and Yiddish poetry at the age of nine. A Zionist from his early youth, he settled in Palestine in 1907 and was appointed secretary to the *Hoveve Zion committee in Jaffa. He published his first story in Palestine in Simha *Ben-

Sh'muel Y. Agnon.
[Israel Information Services]

Zion's periodical, *Ha'Omer.* At about that time he adopted the pen name Agnon. His story *W'Haya He'Akov L'Mishor* (And the Crooked Shall Be Made Straight) was published in book form in 1912. In 1913 Agnon left for Berlin; in 1924 he returned to Palestine and settled in Jerusalem.

Agnon's style is original, drawing from old Midrashic, rabbinic, and Hasidic sources. His works depict the epic of the Galician small town before the Nazi holocaust as well as the

'Afula is the Jezreel Valley's market center. [Zionist Archives]

spirit of the *Second 'Aliya and character types of modern Jerusalem. His major works are *Hakhnasat Kalla,* 1931 (*The Bridal Canopy,* 1937); *Sippur Pashut* (A Simple Story, 1935); *Oreah Nata LaLun* (A Wayfarer Tarried the Night, 1937); and the prize-winning *T'mol Shilshom* (Yesterday and the Day Before, 1950). Several of these were translated into other languages, including English, Polish, German, Swedish, Hungarian, Italian, and Croatian. Agnon also compiled an anthology, *Yamim Noraim* (High Holidays, 1938). He was twice awarded the Bialik Prize and the *Israel Prize for literature, and in 1966 he received the Nobel Prize for literature.

J. NEDAVA

AGRANAT, SHIM'ON. Chief Justice of Israel's Supreme Court (b. Louisville, Ky., 1906). Agranat studied law at the University of Chicago. He was attracted to Zionism and served as chairman of the local chapter of *Avukah, the Zionist student federation. Settling in Palestine in 1930, he was in private law practice for many years. From 1940 to 1948 he served as a magistrate and subsequently was chief judge of the Haifa District Court. He was named to the Supreme Court in 1950 and appointed Chief Justice in 1965.

AGRICULTURAL EXPERIMENT STATION. *See* VOLCANI INSTITUTE OF AGRICULTURAL RESEARCH.

AGRICULTURAL SETTLEMENTS. *See* IMMIGRANTS' VILLAGES; KIBBUTZ; MOSHAV; MOSHAVA; RURAL SETTLEMENT IN PALESTINE AND ISRAEL.

AGRICULTURAL UNION. *See* IHUD HAKLAI.

AGRICULTURAL WORKERS' FEDERATION. *See* MERKAZ HAKLAI.

AGRICULTURE IN ISRAEL. Ever since the beginning of Zionist *immigration to Palestine, stress has consistently been laid on the agricultural development and settlement of the country. This trend has continued, even after the rise of the State of Israel, to the present day.

Consequently, a major concern of the *Jewish Agency has been to develop the agricultural sector of the economy of the *Yishuv (Jewish population of Palestine) and primarily the cooperative and communal agricultural settlements. From 1948 on these tasks and responsibilities have been shared by the Agency with the *government of Israel. The agricultural settlements of the private sector are dealt with in a separate article.

Economic and Social Functions of Agriculture. In 1965 only 10 per cent of Israel's national income derived from agriculture, which employed 13 per cent of the country's labor force. However, the role of agriculture was far more important than would appear from these figures.

Of the 875 towns and villages in Israel in 1965, more than 750 were agricultural settlements whose inhabitants were engaged primarily in farming. Agricultural settlement thus constituted a principal factor in the distribution of the population, the adequate dispersal of which was a main objective of government policy.

One of Israel's major problems in the economic field was the

An orchard in Upper Galilee. [Israel Information Services]

Spreading fertilizer in Galilee. [Israel Information Services]

excess of imports over exports. This problem had been temporarily met by capital imports in the form of contributions and German reparations or loans. However, the country's main efforts were directed toward increasing its exports and thereby improving its balance of payments. The necessity of doing so was expected to become all the more pressing as capital imports decreased, a trend which was expected to continue in the future. Here agriculture played a major part. In 1963 agricultural exports accounted for one-third of Israel's total exports, and in 1965, for about one-fourth.

TABLE 1. EXPORTS, 1962–65
(In millions of dollars)

Category	1962	1963	1965
Agricultural produce	68.4	89.2	86.8
Industrial products	117.6	139.6	181.2
Diamonds	83.9	104.0	131.7
Miscellaneous	1.5	3.2	3.7
Total	271.4	336.0	403.4

In actual fact, the share of agriculture in Israel's total exports was greater because of its relatively low import component. Agriculture, moreover, was an activating factor in many other areas of the economy. A considerable section of Israel's industry was based on the processing of agricultural produce (e.g., vegetable and fruit preserves, textiles), while other industries were engaged in supplying agriculture with the required means of production (e.g., fertilizers, tools).

The rapid development of Israel's agriculture thus provided work for other sectors of the economy and gave employment both to those engaged directly in farming and to those contributing indirectly to the process of agricultural production. The growth of the country's agriculture was stimulated also by the need to supply the ever-growing population with fresh food products which could not be imported, such as milk, vegetables, and fruit. Before the establishment of the State, a considerable part of these foods had been either imported from the neighboring Arab countries or produced locally by Arab peasants. When Israel was cut off from these sources of supply, she had to produce these commodities locally on her own.

Apart from these social and economic factors, the development of agriculture in Israel was closely connected with emotional and psychological motives, in that the return of the Jewish people to their Homeland was intimately linked with the ideological emphasis on the "return to the soil." Since the beginning of Zionist immigration late in the 19th century, farming had been regarded as the basis of national revival.

Development of Agriculture. For these reasons, special stress was laid on agricultural development. During the years of mass immigration, many of the newcomers were settled in agricultural villages. Agriculture received priority in public investments, both for the establishment of new villages and for the agricultural development of existing settlements. Special emphasis was placed on the development of water sources, which constituted the very basis of intensive agriculture in the country. As compared with 300 million cubic meters in 1949, over 1,300 million cubic meters were used in 1965, of which 1,000 million were expended in agriculture. This increase was made possible through extensive engineering projects, culminating in the completion of the *National Water Carrier Project for the diversion of large quantities of water from the Jordan River and Lake

TABLE 2. TOTAL INCREASE IN VALUE OF AGRICULTURAL PRODUCTION, 1948/49–1964/65

	1948–49	1954–55	1957–58	1959–60	1961–62	1964–65
Index of production (1948–49 = 100)	100	240	366	439	526	610
Value of production at 1948–49 prices (in millions of IL*)	44.4	106.5	162.5	184.9	233.5	271.1
Value of production at current prices (in millions of IL*)	44.4	337.4	675.8	747.5	968.0	1,345.9

*Israeli pounds.

TABLE 3. GROWTH OF AGRICULTURE, 1949–1964/65

Branch	Unit	Output			
		1949	1953–54	1962–63	1964–65
Wheat and barley	tons	41,200	123,900	131,000	217,000
Green fodder	tons	372,800	672,000	1,756,000	1,593,000
Peanuts	tons	300	15,000	13,000	13,500
Cotton fibers	tons		250	13,400	21,500
Sugar beets	tons		6,750	249,600	294,600
Vegetables and potatoes	tons	106,000	284,000	405,800	415,400
Citrus fruit	tons	272,000	470,000	736,400	878,300
Other fruit	tons	47,400	79,300	207,550	249,400
Milk	kiloliters	85,950	176,800	358,500	383,800
Eggs	thousands	242,500	414,000	1,113,300	1,296,000
Beef	tons	2,010	4,000	31,000	42,700
Poultry	tons	5,040	9,300	67,000	74,000

Kinneret to the southern part of the country. It was thus possible to expand the area under irrigation from 75,000 acres in 1948 to about 385,000 acres in 1966. During this period agricultural production grew almost sixfold.

Changes in Agricultural Production. During the first years of the State's existence efforts were directed mainly toward the production of fresh food for local consumption, such as vegetables, fruit, eggs, milk, and dairy products. Within a few years local demands for these commodities were fully met, and there was even a surplus in some items, including vegetables, eggs, and milk. This, together with the need to improve the national balance of payments, led to changes in the production pattern. Greater stress was placed on export crops and on the replacement of imports, and the development of new branches of agriculture was begun. In 1953 the cultivation of cotton and sugar beets was started, and by 1959 Israel was able not only to produce all its cotton requirements but also to export considerable quantities of raw cotton and finished products. During the same period locally grown sugar beets had been able to satisfy about one-third of the local consumption. Agricultural exports, which had formerly consisted solely of citrus fruit, expanded to include peanuts, cotton, vegetables, and other fruits such as avocados, melons, and bananas.

As Table 3 shows, less intensively cultivated crops having a relatively lower yield per land unit, such as green fodder or some cereals, were increasingly replaced by more intensively cultivated crops, for both local and export markets. This trend toward high-yield crops became still more pronounced in the middle 1960s owing to the lack of basic production factors and to the water shortage. The latter made it necessary to institute a careful selection of crops and branches of cultivation with a view to obtaining maximum returns from the quantities of water available and at the same time satisfying the needs of the population for perishable products.

Patterns and Systems of Settlement. Certain changes also took place in the patterns and systems of settlement adopted, without altering the main underlying principles of settlement on nationally owned land, "self-labor," and a fair distribution of production factors in order to provide an equal income level to all farmers. Model farm types were evolved, and the projected income from all the available production factors was planned on a more or less uniform basis, approximating the average income of trained urban industrial workers. The type of farm was determined by the natural conditions of the locality—its *soils, topography, and *climate—and by the general trends affecting the composition of agricultural output. In the early years of the State, when agricultural production was still mainly concerned with supplying fresh products to the local population, most farms were planned as mixed farms, whose principal products were vegetables, milk, and other fresh produce. For the transition to export and industrial crops new farm types were evolved: field-crop farms cultivating mainly industrial crops; citrus farms concentrating mainly on citrus plantations; and, subsequently, export farms engaging chiefly in the production of export vegetables. These farm types were set up in both moshavim (cooperative villages) and kibbutzim (communal villages).

Concomitantly with the change that took place in the types of farming and in the settlement pattern, some modification was introduced into the settlement system itself. In the past the settlements established were isolated and had no close contact with one another. In 1954, however, the regional settlement system was introduced, based on clusters of agricultural settlements around rural centers to supply services to the surrounding villages instead of leaving each village to cater to its own needs. Regional settlement was intended to serve both economic and social ends. From the point of view of economy the centralization of services for a number of villages led to greater efficiency and lower costs. Socially, it was intended to encourage the

ı the Jezreel Valley. [Israel Information Services]

ts. In the 1960s the pace of agricultural develop-
vn with the decline in new settlement activities.
ainly to the shortage of water and the ample
tural produce. In both respects, however, pros-
y favorable. The water shortage was relieved
the completion of the National Water Carrier
he erection of water desalination plants was
g a radical solution to this problem by 1972.
)duction trends, the cultivation of new areas,
r region in the western Negev, the 'Arava, and
ions, was expected to lead to an ever-increasing
produce, since these areas were naturally suited
n of export crops such as citrus fruit, peanuts,
egetables. At the same time the existing farming
ensify production in order to meet the growing
)cal market.
s agriculture was at the initial phase of renewed
signed to strengthen the national economy and
the development and settlement of new parts of

L SETTLEMENT IN PALESTINE AND ISRAEL.

R. WEITZ

)NSKY), GERSHON. Journalist and mayor of
ena, Ukraine, Russia, 1893; d. Jerusalem, 1959).
Jnited States in 1906, he immediately became
an Zionism. In 1915 he began to contribute to

the *Jewish World* (Philadelphia), and in 1917 he became editor
of *Dos Yidishe Folk* (New York). In 1918 Agron volunteered for
the *Jewish Legion. In 1920–21 he was a member of the press
office of the *Zionist Commission, from 1921 to 1929 editor of
the New York *Jewish Telegraphic Agency, and from 1924 to
1929 director of the press office of the Zionist *Executive in
Jerusalem. He was also Palestine correspondent for American
and British papers. From 1931 to 1932 he edited the *Palestine
Bulletin,* published by the Zionist Executive and the Jewish
Telegraphic Agency.

On Dec. 1, 1932, Agron became editor in chief of the *Palestine
Post,* which after the establishment of the State changed its
name to *Jerusalem Post.* As the only English-language daily
in Palestine, the *Post* exerted considerable influence on British
officials in the Middle East and on its English readers in general.
Its criticism of British policy and its unwavering support of the
plan for a Jewish State were resented by the British administration. After the establishment of the State, Agron was appointed
head of the Information Services of the Israeli government,
which office he held from 1949 to 1951. From 1955 until his
death, he was mayor of Jerusalem.

G. KRESSEL

**AGUDAT HASOFRIM HA'IVRIM B'YISRAEL (Hebrew
Writers' Association in Israel).** Organization founded in Tel Aviv
in April, 1921, by some 70 charter members, to promote Hebrew
literature and protect the interests of Hebrew writers. Hayim

Cotton is an important export crop. [Israel Information Services]

Tending young plants in the Negev. [Israel Information Services]

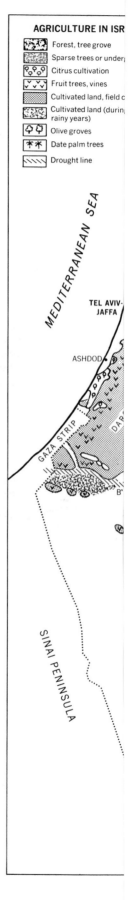

AGRICULTURE IN ISR

- Forest, tree grove
- Sparse trees or under
- Citrus cultivation
- Fruit trees, vines
- Cultivated land, field c
- Cultivated land (durin, rainy years)
- Olive groves
- Date palm trees
- Drought line

MEDITERRANEAN SEA

TEL AVIV-JAFFA

ASHDOD

GAZA STRIP

DAR

SINAI PENINSULA

Varied farmi

Future Pro
ment slowed
This was du
supply of agr
pects were h
considerably
Project, whil
expected to
In regard to
such as the E
several other
output of exp
to the cultiva
and off-seaso
areas were to
demands of t

In 1968 Isr
development
to contribute
the country.

See also RU

AGRON (AG
Jerusalem (b.
Settling in the
active in Ame

process of integration among different ethnic *communities. The rural center served as a meeting place for the inhabitants of the various villages. Each village was peopled by members of a single community in order to make for greater local stability. The center provided an opportunity for intermingling; children from all villages attended the same school and adults met at various social events as well as at communal institutions such as the clinic, the tractor station, and the sorting shed. The system was expected in time to bring the different communities closer together.

The regional structure was also designed to prevent or reduce social gaps between urban and rural populations. In the rural centers services and industries were to be established to absorb the population surplus of the villages. These ensured an adequate standard of services not inferior to that supplied in the city. By absorbing the surplus rural population in the centers, the rural areas avoided the risk of becoming depopulated as was generally the case in most developed countries.

In the middle 1960s the regional settlement system embraced widespread parts of the country and was being expanded to new areas with a view to aiding in their social and economic consolidation and agricultural development.

Nahman *Bialik headed the organization from 1927 until his death (1934) and was succeeded by Saul *Tschernichowsky. The association's headquarters, situated in Tel Aviv, is called Bet HaSofer 'Al Shem Shaul Tschernichowsky. With branches in Jerusalem and Haifa, the organization numbers more than 300 members, affiliated on a nonpolitical basis and representing all literary schools. A conference is held every two years to elect its central bodies.

The central organ of the association, *Moznayim,* a monthly, has appeared almost without interruption since 1931. The association also publishes various periodicals: *M'assef* (mainly for extensive literary works), *Nefesh* (for works of deceased authors), and *Sifriyat Makor* (for original works). At the suggestion of Asher *Barash, the association established G'nazim, a bio-bibliographical institute, for the purpose of collecting unpublished literary works, letters, and photographs of writers, cataloging and indexing the material, and providing for the publication of all works of literary merit. It also organized an annual Hebrew Book Week, regular lectures, and symposia with the participation of Hebrew writers. The association maintained contact with writers' associations abroad, and its members constituted the panels of judges for awarding literary prizes.

J. NEDAVA

AGUDAT ISRAEL. Political and religious movement which views the Tora, as interpreted by traditional commentators throughout the ages, as the only legitimate code of laws binding upon the Jew as an individual and upon the Jewish people as a whole.

HISTORY

The movement, initiated by members of a neo-Orthodox group in Frankfurt on the Main, held its founding convention, attended by 300 delegates, in Kattowitz in 1912. (The group had held a series of meetings three years earlier, in Homburg, Germany.) Agudat Israel had originally sought to combine all Orthodox groups in Eastern and Western Europe into a united front in opposition to the Zionist movement and its demands for changes in the structure and content of Jewish life. When the 10th Zionist *Congress (1911) decided to include cultural projects within the scope of the Zionist movement, however, several Orthodox Zionist delegates from Germany dissociated themselves from the Congress and joined Agudat Israel, thus providing a decisive impetus to its formal organization.

Agudat Israel was comprised of three main groups, differing in religious practice as well as in attitude toward the structure of Jewish communal life: (1) German neo-Orthodox followers of

An Agudat Israel delegation at the United Nations in 1948 (left to right): Michael Tress, Dr. Isaac Lewin, Jacob Rosenheim, Rabbi Yitzhak Meir Levin, and Meier Schenkolewski. [Zionist Archives]

Samson Raphael Hirsch, (2) Hungarian Orthodoxy, and (3) Orthodox Jewry in Poland and Lithuania.

German neo-Orthodoxy meticulously observed all traditional Jewish religious commandments but adapted itself to the Western social patterns of its non-Jewish environment, as expressed in a broad knowledge of general culture, Western dress, and the use of the German language.

Hungarian and Polish Orthodoxy, including both Hasidic groups and the rabbis of the Lithuanian Yeshivot, opposed the acquisition of Western knowledge and culture. On the other hand, Hungarian Orthodoxy agreed with some of the Hirschian neo-Orthodox groups that Orthodox Kehillot (religious congregations) should be completely separate from non-Orthodox Jewry, while Polish and Lithuanian Orthodoxy and other Orthodox leaders in Frankfurt on the Main were opposed to this practice.

Such differences in outlook hindered organizational unification. The question of the introduction of Western culture in particular was viewed as potentially destructive to the traditional Eastern European Jewish community, and it was placed on the agenda of the founding convention in Kattowitz. The differences concerning Kehilla organization, summarized in the "Hungarian demand," were resolved at the Second K'nesiya G'dola (Agudat Israel's assembly; Vienna, 1929), which advocated the preservation of the status quo in each country.

The founding convention in Kattowitz established the representative bodies for Agudat Israel, including a Council of Rabbinic Leaders. This council distinguished Agudat Israel from secular Jewish political organizations and movements and assured, in effect, that Agudat Israel would undertake no political action that would run counter to the Tora. The council consists of individuals possessing Halakhic authority, each an outstanding rabbinic leader in his own right.

The Nazi holocaust and the ensuing political and social upheavals led to changes in the executive bodies of Agudat Israel. At the convention of the Central World Council (Marienbad, 1947) three world centers were created: one in New York, headed by Jacob Rosenheim, world president of Agudat Israel; one in London, headed by Harry Goodman; and one in Jerusalem, headed by Rabbi Yitzhak Meir *Levin.

In the early years of the organization the influence of the neo-Orthodox elements was decisive, owing to their high economic, social, and general cultural level in Central and Western Europe. During World War I the group took a strong pro-German stand, and the Agudat Israel group in Poland received the support of the German occupation forces. The defeat of Germany and the subsequent independence of Poland and the Baltic states gave relatively greater influence to the Agudat Israel of Poland, which, as opposed to the Western groups, was a movement of the masses. The Hasidim of Góra Kalwaria were the single most significant element within this group. Subsequently, the rise of Nazism and the outbreak of World War II led to the almost total disappearance of neo-Orthodox influence in the leadership of Agudat Israel.

AGUDAT ISRAEL AND PALESTINE

Originally, Agudat Israel was ambivalent in its attitude toward the resettlement of Palestine. On the one hand, Jewish law considers it meritorious, if not mandatory, for a Jew to settle in Palestine; nor could Agudat Israel ignore the upheaval within Eastern European Jewry between the two world wars and the fact that Palestine was one of the solutions to this problem.

On the other hand, Agudat Israel was not willing to aid Jewish settlement of Palestine unless it was based on the complete observance of Jewish law. It therefore opposed the concept of a Jewish *National* Home and of a Jewish State not founded on Jewish law and tradition. Moreover, Agudat Israel opposed the Zionist view that Jews had to leave the *Diaspora, settle in Palestine, and build a new society there. The Orthodox groups held that the *Ingathering of the Exiles and the Return to Zion could not be separated from the Messianic redemption, for which the time had not yet come.

Nevertheless, Agudat Israel established a Palestine settlement fund (Keren HaYishuv), a society for the Homeland (HaBayit), a Land and Building Corporation in the United States, a special agricultural school (Hirschhof), near Falkengesäss, Germany, and two colonization societies in Poland (Giv'at Y'huda and Nahlat Lublin). In Palestine, it acquired land, founded the settlement Mahane Yisrael, and established schools in Jerusalem, Tel Aviv, and Safed.

In London, Agudat Israel established a Political Department (headed by Harry Goodman) and initiated direct negotiations with the British government. It denied the *Jewish Agency's right to act as the representative of the Jewish people and demanded recognition, but was turned down (as had had happened earlier when Winston *Churchill refused it recognition in 1922). In 1925 it undertook steps in Palestine to be recognized as a religious community separate from the *Yishuv (the Jewish population), but this effort, too, remained unsuccessful. Its representatives appeared before the Royal Commission (see PEEL COMMISSION; SHAW COMMISSION) and maintained in their testimony, for the first time, that the *Balfour Declaration and the *Mandate for Palestine were in the spirit of the divine promise of redemption.

In Palestine, Agudat Israel at first identified itself with the old Yishuv in Jerusalem in its bitter war against the organization of the Jewish community along the lines of the Zionist ideology, that is, within the *K'nesset Yisrael. In 1922–24 the Agudat Israel carried on, at times in cooperation with Arab leaders, an active anti-Zionist political campaign in British circles and in the world press. The tension between the new Yishuv and the Agudat Israel reached its climax when Jacob de Hahn, the political spokesman of the Aguda, was murdered in Jerusalem.

Not only did the Aguda opt out of the officially recognized Jewish community (K'nesset Yisrael), but it did not recognize the Chief *Rabbinate set up by the British Mandatory administration and established its own rabbinical court in Jerusalem. Consequently, it stayed outside the autonomous framework of the Yishuv.

However, the late 1920s saw the arrival in Palestine of significant numbers of Agudat Israel members from Poland who, desiring to participate in the economic and social development of the new Yishuv, could not accept the concept of complete isolation from the *World Zionist Organization and its agencies. The clash between these two approaches was further complicated by the immigration of German Jews who sought to carry over into Palestine their principle of combining Tora and secular studies, which was diametrically opposed to the practices and basic philosophy of the old Yishuv.

In 1934 a delegation from the Central World Conference, comprised mainly of leaders of the Polish Agudat Israel, came to Palestine and broke the old Yishuv's control over Agudat Israel by giving equal representation in the conference to immigrants from Poland and Germany. Following the reorganization of Agudat Israel leadership in Palestine, some elements of the old Yishuv broke away from the movement and subsequently formed the *N'ture Karta.

The internal conflicts reached a peak at the Third K'nesiya G'dola (Marienbad, 1937). On the agenda was the question of Agudat Israel reaction to the report of the Peel Commission, which advocated the establishment of a Jewish State in part of Palestine. Isaac *Breuer claimed that the goal of Agudat Israel should be to "prepare and bring together the people of God and the land of God, in order to create anew a kingdom of God under the rule of God." Opposing him was a coalition of part of the neo-Orthodox group headed by Jacob Rosenheim, Hungarian Orthodoxy, and some of the Polish rabbis who were unwilling to make a definite decision on the matter.

The genocide of European Jewry tragically proved the validity of the Zionist concept. Agudat Israel thereupon granted de facto recognition to Zionist work in Palestine and began cooperating increasingly with the Zionist agencies, although it maintained its reservations on the establishment of an independent Jewish State in Palestine and its spokesmen used the term "Jewish authorities in Palestine."

Prior to the creation of the State, however, a certain settlement was reached with David *Ben-Gurion, then chairman of the Jewish Agency, in which Agudat Israel agreed to support the State on condition that the status quo in matters of religion be maintained. Agudat Israel then joined the Provisional Council of State and participated in Israel's first coalition government.

In the early 1920s *Po'ale Agudat Israel, the labor offshoot of the movement, had been formed. In line with the philosophy of Isaac Breuer, this organization sought to play an active role in the settlement and rebuilding of an independent Jewish community in Palestine. Its members established moshavim and kibbutzim in cooperation with the settlement agencies of the Zionist movement. Agudat Israel set up its own autonomous school system (referred to as Hinukh 'Atzma'i; see EDUCATION IN ISRAEL), which in the 1960s numbered more than 20,000 pupils and was largely financed by the Israeli government. During the 1960s the split between Agudat Israel and Po'ale Agudat Israel became pronounced. The former remained in opposition to the government, while the latter joined the government coalition. The Aguda objects to a written constitution for the State and opposes the drafting of girls into the *Israel Defense Forces.

Agudat Israel is one of the small political parties in the State of Israel. In the elections to the Second Knesset (1951), Agudat Israel and Po'ale Agudat Israel obtained 3.6 per cent of the votes. In the elections to the Fifth Knesset (1961) the two groups obtained 5.6 per cent of the votes, their strength coming mainly from the urban settlements of the old Yishuv, particularly from the Orthodox sections of Jerusalem and Tel Aviv. In the 1965 elections Agudat Israel obtained 3.30 per cent of the votes (four seats) and Po'ale Agudat Israel 1.83 per cent (two seats), or a total of 5.13 per cent. In the 1969 elections to the Seventh Knesset Agudat Israel and Po'ale Agudat Israel obtained the same number of seats as in 1965.   M. FRIEDMAN

AGUDAT PO'ALIM. First Jewish agricultural workers' organization in Palestine, established in 1887 in Rishon L'Tziyon by workers employed by the settlers of the colony and by the Rothschild administration. It was organized primarily for the purpose of mutual aid, but its program also included assistance to new immigrants by training them in agricultural work. That same year the association participated in the settlers' revolt against Baron Edmond de *Rothschild's administrators of the colony. The subsequent repressive measures taken by the administrators contributed much to the disintegration of the association.

Y'hiel Mikhael *Halpern was one of the association's founders.

'AGUR. Village (moshav) in the Judean Plain. Founded in 1950 and affiliated with *T'nu'at HaMoshavim. Population (1968): 298.

AHAD HA'AM. Pseudonym invariably used by the Hovev Zion (see HOVEVE ZION) and Hebrew essayist Asher Zvi Ginzberg (b. Skvira, near Kiev, Russia, 1856; d. Tel Aviv, 1927). Ahad Ha'Am is a Hebrew phrase meaning "one of the people" or

Ahad Ha'Am.
[Zionist Archives]

"a plain man." The only son of Isaiah Ginzberg, a pious Hasid, Asher received a Heder education until he was 12 years old, when his father took the position of administrator of a large estate near a remote village in the district of Kiev and moved there with his family. Thereafter Asher continued his Hebrew studies under private tutors and soon became a prodigy in rabbinic learning. He also managed unaided to acquire mastery of a number of European languages and read widely in their literatures, especially in his favorite fields of history, sociology, and moral philosophy.

Even as a child Ahad Ha'Am had begun to show a rationalistic and critical bent, which first estranged him from Hasidism and finally, after a period when he espoused the ideals of the *Haskala (Enlightenment), led him to religious agnosticism, without, however, diminishing his fervent attachment to the cultural heritage, and particularly the ethical ideals, of Judaism. During the years of intellectual isolation which ended when, at the age of 30, he settled in Odessa to engage in commerce, he had come to the conviction that of all the remedies being advocated to alleviate the plight of Russian Jewry, the one offering the most hope was the resettlement of Jews in Palestine. Accordingly, he became an active but critical member of the Central Committee of the Hoveve Zion movement.

In his first essay, published in *HaMelitz* in 1889, he argued that there was no hope of success for the movement unless it ceased its attempt to attract settlers to Palestine by illusory appeals to self-interest and devoted its efforts instead to awakening their latent Jewish patriotism and love of Zion, so that they would be willing to face the hardships of life in the ancestral Homeland in order to help lay the foundations for a national rebirth. At the same time he became the spiritual head of the secret order *B'ne Moshe, which for some years had tried, with little success, to show by example how the task of colonizing Palestine should be approached. The impression made by his first essay was reinforced by two critical studies of actual conditions in the "colonies," which he published after visiting Palestine in 1891 and 1893. Though his outspoken strictures shattered formerly unquestioned illusions, he was recognized as a friendly critic of independent mind, rare objectivity, and outstanding literary gifts. During the next few years he elaborated his views in response to criticism, outlining his philosophy of Judaism and Jewish nationalism. In 1895 most of his essays published in Hebrew periodicals were reissued in a volume entitled 'Al Parashat D'rakhim (At the Crossroads). Between that year and 1914 three more volumes of essays appeared under the same title. These four volumes, together with an anthology of his letters (also in four volumes), constitute the whole of his literary output except for some autobiographical reminiscences.

In 1895 business reverses compelled him to turn to writing as a profession, and in 1896 he became editor of *HaShiloah, a new Hebrew monthly. In the six years of his editorship, Ha-Shiloah attained a standard never before reached by a Hebrew periodical, mainly because he insisted that all contributors adhere to those canons of style, taste, and moderation of language that were taken for granted in any reputable European journal but were all too often disregarded by Hebrew writers of those days.

During this period the 1st Zionist *Congress (1897) inaugurated the political Zionist movement, of which Ahad Ha'Am became the most uncompromising nationalist opponent. On practical and ideological grounds, he rejected the Jewish State as an immediate object of national policy. In his view, what was required was not a "refuge" for the persecuted Jewish masses but a truly Jewish State that could be established only after a long process of national self-education, through which the Jewish people would rid itself of the evil effects of centuries of *Diaspora (Galut)—not only the shiftlessness and stagnation associated with the ghetto but also emancipated Jewry's attenuated Jewish consciousness and slavish acceptance of non-Jewish standards and ways of thinking. Such a process, which could be powerfully assisted by a "national spiritual center" in Palestine, would, he felt, enable the Jewish people once more to contribute creatively to human progress in ways determined by its own essential character and ideals. His opposition to the policy of Herzl's movement earned him much misrepresentation and obloquy but did not affect the eminence which he had already attained as a Jewish thinker of unquestioned integrity and high moral stature. He was revered by a large part of the Eastern European Jewish intelligentsia; and translations of his essays into English, French, German, and other languages made his name and ideas familiar to thinking Jews all over the world.

After giving up the editorship of HaShiloah in 1902, he returned to business, and in 1908 he settled in London as manager of the office of the Wissotzky tea firm there (see WISSOTZKY, KALONYMUS-Z'EV). His 14 years in London were chiefly noteworthy for two of his best-known essays and for his participation in the negotiations of the Zionist leaders with the British government which led to the *Balfour Declaration. Otherwise, his activity during this period was severely restricted by ill health, which continued after he settled in Tel Aviv at the beginning of 1922. During the last five years of his life he was unable to engage in public activity or to do any literary work except for the preparation for publication of the four volumes of letters mentioned above.

The influence of Ahad Ha'Am's doctrine on the Zionist movement persisted. The Ahad Ha'Amists continued to emphasize *cultural Zionism rather than the political Zionism and *practical Zionism to which most leaders of the movement devoted their energies.

SIR LEON SIMON

AHARONI (AHARONOWITZ), ISRAEL. Palestinian zoologist (b. Vidzy, Lithuania, 1882; d. Jerusalem, 1946). He received a religious education in Lithuania, attended high school in Prague, and studied zoology and Semitic philology at the University of Prague. While still in high school, he and Egon Erwin Kisch founded a nationalist Jewish youth journal. Later he taught Hebrew in Zionist societies in Prague. In 1901 Aharoni settled in Palestine. At first he was a teacher in Rehovot and Rishon L'Tziyon. He then moved to Jerusalem, where he taught at the *Bezalel School, and devoted himself to the study of the fauna of Palestine and neighboring countries. He undertook numerous scientific expeditions and discovered animal species which had been previously unknown or considered extinct. During World War I he was the zoologist attached to the Fourth Turkish Army. After the war he became agricultural adviser to the *Zionist Commission and zoological adviser to the British Palestine administration. He was the founder of the Zoological Museum of the *World Zionist Organization, which was later taken over by the *Hebrew University of Jerusalem.

Aharoni published numerous zoological studies and wrote on the names of animals in the Bible and Talmud. He was also the author of an autobiography, Zikhronot Zo'olog 'Ivri (Memoirs of a Hebrew Zoologist), an account of his pioneering zoological researches in Palestine.

G. KRESSEL

AHARONOWITZ, JOSEPH. See ARONOWICZ, JOSEPH.

AHARONSON, SH'LOMO HAKOHEN. Chief rabbi of Tel Aviv (b. Kruchi, Mogilev District, Russia, 1863; d. Tel Aviv, 1935). He began his rabbinical career at the age of 24 in Halochov and became rabbi of Kiev in 1906. A Hovev Zion (see HOVEVE ZION) since his youth, he became a supporter of political Zionism. Aharonson was active in Russian-Jewish affairs and protested to the Tsarist government against the pogroms. He served in an advisory capacity in the defense of Menahem Mendel Beilis at the blood libel trial in Kiev (1911–13). In Kiev, in 1917, Aharonson founded Ahdut Israel, which became a national religious organization under his guidance. When the Communists took control, he moved to Germany, serving as rabbi of the Russian-Jewish refugee community in Berlin. In 1923 he was chosen Ashkenazi chief rabbi of Tel Aviv, where he founded the Tel Aviv Yeshiva. In 1924 he participated in the Jewish World Relief Conference in Karlovy Vary, Czechoslovakia.

Y. RAPHAEL

AHAVAT ZION. Palestine colonization society in Vienna, founded in 1881–82 by Reuben *Bierer and Peretz *Smolenskin. Though it succeeded at first in enlisting a considerable number of members, it later disintegrated and was dissolved in 1885. Solomon Benjamin Spitzer, rabbi of Vienna's strictly Orthodox synagogue known as the Schiffschul, was among its early members but left with his followers when Smolenskin refused to give the society an Orthodox character.

AHAVAT ZION (novel). *See* MAPU, ABRAHAM.

AHDUT 'AVODA (United Zionist Labor Party). Zionist Socialist party in Palestine from 1919 to 1929. Its Hebrew name means "Union of Labor." Toward the end of the *Second 'Aliya support emerged among a group of Jewish laborers in Palestine for the establishment of an all-embracing trade union as well as a political organization outside the party framework of the then-existing political parties *Po'ale Zion and *HaPo'el HaTza'ir. Consequently, a "nonparty" workers' group was formed; led by Berl *Katznelson, it devoted itself to the creation of an agricultural workers' federation in Judea and Galilee. During the final year of World War I the Jewish workers of Palestine expected that the complexion of the *Yishuv (Jewish population) would be radically changed by the arrival of large numbers of Halutzim (pioneers; *see* HALUTZIYUT). To absorb these Halutzim and to guide them in the ideals which had crystallized during the Second 'Aliya, full unification of all trends among the workers appeared necessary. Talks for unity were held in the tents of the Jewish battalions which formed part of the British Army, and a large proportion of whom had come from the ranks of the workers. At the end of the war, a Unity Committee was established; it consisted of David *Ben-Gurion, Itzhak *Ben Zvi, Yitzhak *Tabenkin, Sh'muel Yavn'eli, Berl Katznelson, and David *Remez. The committee prepared a merger proposal which was submitted to the conference of the Agricultural Workers' Federation in February, 1919. Most of the Po'ale Zion accepted the proposal and, with the nonparty delegates, assured its acceptance by the conference. HaPo'el HaTza'ir, which was a minority at the conference, seceded and established its own agricultural workers' federation and other institutions.

The founding conference of Ahdut 'Avoda was held in March, 1919. Of the 81 delegates attending, 47 were agricultural workers, 15 came from the cities, and 19 were soldiers of the Jewish battalions. They represented a total of 1,870 members. Since HaPo'el HaTza'ir did not join the union, those who demanded that the new movement stress its Socialist character prevailed. The movement was given the name Hitahdut Tziyonit-Sotzialistit Shel Po'ale Eretz Yisrael–Ahdut 'Avoda (Zionist Socialist Union of the Workers of Palestine–Ahdut 'Avoda). It published a weekly organ, *HaKuntres* (Notebook).

In the beginning Ahdut 'Avoda was an activist party. It advocated the continued existence of the Jewish battalions and spearheaded the organization of *Hagana (Hagana was founded at the Ahdut 'Avoda conference held in Kinneret in July, 1920). The party followed the teaching of Nachman *Syrkin (whom it regarded as one of its mentors) that the ideals of Zionism could be realized only in thoroughgoing socialism. It was considered that private capital, interested as it was in financial gain, would employ cheap Arab labor, which would bar the possibility of large-scale Jewish *immigration. Ahdut 'Avoda advocated large K'vutzot and developed the *G'dud Ha'Avoda V'haHagana 'Al Shem Yosef Trumpeldor and workers' enterprises such as HaMisrad La'Avodot Tziburiyot–Bureau for Public Works (later called Solel Bone; *see* HISTADRUT).

Although Ahdut 'Avoda did not, in theory, give up the idea of a complete political union of all the Jewish workers in the country, it was forced to renounce it under the pressure of the new immigrants. At the general conference of the workers held late in 1920 (at which 42 per cent of all the delegates were from Ahdut 'Avoda), it proposed establishing the labor federation Histadrut, with authority also in political and cultural matters. Ahdut 'Avoda devoted its major efforts to Histadrut. It repre-

sented the central force in Histadrut (58 per cent of all voters for the second conference of the Histadrut, 1923; and 53 per cent of all voters for the third conference, 1927). At the second conference of Ahdut 'Avoda, held late in 1922, the necessity for the continued existence of Ahdut 'Avoda as a political party was discussed, and it was decided to continue the party so that it might guide the activities of the Histadrut in the spirit of Socialist Zionism. At this conference Ahdut 'Avoda also formulated its attitude toward the class struggle, which was to include the professional struggle of the workers employed in private enterprise, as well as the establishment of cooperative farms and workers' villages, as a means of creating a Socialist Commonwealth in Palestine.

Within the Histadrut, Ahdut 'Avoda continued to seek a broadening of its field of activities. It was under the influence of Ahdut 'Avoda that *Davar, the daily newspaper of the Histadrut, was established in 1925 under the editorship of Berl Katznelson. The Histadrut HaNo'ar Ha'Oved (Federation of Working Youth) was founded. Ahdut 'Avoda created within its framework the Bahrut Sotzialistit, which organized older and younger youths to educate them in the spirit of the party. Ahdut 'Avoda also devoted great efforts to bring about the unification of Zionist labor groups in the *Diaspora. Under its influence, Po'ale Zion (Right) and the Zionists-Socialists merged in 1925, the first in a series of mergers that were to take place in ensuing years.

While characterizing itself as the standard-bearer of Socialist Zionism, Ahdut 'Avoda did not limit the ideological views of its members. The party had a Marxist-Borochovist wing, but generally it had a Socialist-Constructivist character, regarding as its main task the establishment of workers' enterprises and communities in cities and villages.

The late 1920s saw the beginning of a rapprochement between Ahdut 'Avoda and HaPo'el HaTza'ir. On the one hand, Socialist tendencies, advocated by Hayim *Arlosoroff, prevailed in HaPo'el HaTza'ir. On the other, Ahdut 'Avoda moved toward the moderate wing in the world Socialist camp (it joined the Second International in 1923 and consistently moved closer to the British Labor party). An additional factor in the rapprochement between the two parties was the criticism by right-wing circles in the Zionist movement of the workers' settlements, especially the kibbutzim, which intensified during the Fourth 'Aliya and the years of crisis that followed. It became apparent that the labor movement would have to unite "to capture the Zionist movement" (B. Katznelson). In the spring of 1929 the merger agreement between the two parties was signed and a common program formulated. In a referendum among 2,500 members of the party, more than 80 per cent ratified the union. The *Arab riots of August, 1929, further strengthened the feeling for immediate fusion. Early in January, 1930, both parties held their final separate conferences. On January 5, the merger conference took place. This conference, which represented 5,650 members, announced the establishment of the Mifleget Po'ale Eretz Yisrael (*Mapai, or Palestine Labor party). Y. SLUTSKY

AHDUT 'AVODA–PO'ALE ZION. Zionist Socialist workers' party in existence from 1944 to 1948 and from 1954 to 1968 in Palestine and Israel. In the late 1930s and early 1940s an opposition faction was formed within *Mapai. It was composed of the majority of the active members of *Kibbutz M'uhad, who were critical of the policies of the party's Executive and of its representatives in the national institutions (*Va'ad L'umi, *World

Zionist Organization, and so on), and of a minority of the active members of the trade unions in the cities, who demanded a stronger struggle for workers' rights. It was also a protest against the powerful *Histadrut (General Federation of Labor) bureaucracy. The faction was known by the unofficial name of Si'a Bet (Faction B). The Mapai Conference, held in K'far Witkin in August, 1942, adopted a resolution prohibiting the establishment of factions within the party. In reaction, the members of the faction discontinued their participation in the party's institutions. After the representatives of the faction at an Executive Committee meeting of the Histadrut joined the minority parties and voted against the *Biltmore Program, an open rift developed in February, 1944. In May, 1944, the faction established the T'nu'a L'Ahdut Ha'Avoda (Movement for the Unity of Labor). In the elections to the sixth convention of the Histadrut, the party received 17.7 per cent of the votes.

In the years of the struggle with the British (1945–47) the party pursued an extreme activist policy. Its members occupied key positions in the *Hagana self-defense organization and in the command of the *Palmah (commando units). In April, 1946, the party was joined by the remnants of the Left *Po'ale Zion and changed its name to Ahdut 'Avoda–Po'ale Zion. At the same time the World Confederation of the party (see B'RIT 'OLAMIT AHDUT 'AVODA–PO'ALE ZION) was established; constituent members in the *Diaspora were the Left Po'ale Zion of Western Europe and the United States and the youth organizations affiliated with the Kibbutz M'uhad. Ahdut 'Avoda–Po'ale Zion sought to eliminate the British Mandate and replace it by an international mandate over Palestine.

In February, 1948, Ahdut 'Avoda–Po'ale Zion united with *HaShomer HaTza'ir to form Mifleget HaPo'alim HaM'uhedet (United Workers' party, or *Mapam). The unification was not far reaching, however, and the constituent parties never actually merged. The strong left-wing tendencies which dominated the united party caused a rift in the Kibbutz M'uhad (1951) that shook the entire kibbutz movement. Even the expulsion in August, 1953, of the extreme leftist elements, whose views amounted to a denial of Zionism, did not promote a further rapprochement between the two groups. In August, 1954, the members of Ahdut 'Avoda–Po'ale Zion decided to launch a daily of their own, *LaMerhav, and thus renewed the independent existence of their party. They were represented by 8 to 10 members in the *Knesset and participated in the coalition governments.

Nonetheless, the desire for unity within the party grew even stronger. Instead of an unrealistic call for complete unity of all the workers' parties, a call for prompt union with Mapai was issued. In January, 1963, Yitzhak Ben Aharon published his article "'Oz LiT'mura—B'Terem Pur'anut" (Courage for Change Prior to the Catastrophe), in which he advocated unity of the workers' movement, even if only partial unity, in view of the increased strength of the right-wing parties and the crisis in Mapai at that time. In September, 1965, Ahdut 'Avoda–Po'ale Zion and Mapai signed an agreement for an alignment (Ma'arakh), which expressed itself in a united list of candidates for the Knesset and Histadrut elections and a united representation in the Knesset. The alignment helped maintain the political predominance of the Histadrut despite the withdrawal of David *Ben-Gurion and some of his friends from Mapai to launch a separate party, Rafi (*R'shimat Po'ale Yisrael). The alignment brought about in January, 1968, the complete unification of Ahdut 'Avoda–Po'ale Zion with Mapai and Rafi in the Mifleget Ha'Avoda HaYisr'elit (*Israel Labor party).

During the years of its existence Ahdut 'Avoda–Po'ale Zion was in the main the political spokesman of the Kibbutz M'uhad. Its leading figures, Yitzhak *Tabenkin, Israel *Galili, Yitzhak Ben Aharon, Yigal *Allon, and others, came from the Kibbutz M'uhad. The party evolved neither a separate ideology nor a program of its own but stressed the need for the strengthening of the pioneering and settlement movements, especially the kibbutz movement. It advocated a positive attitude toward the U.S.S.R., while criticizing the Soviet position on Zionism and Israel. Having advocated unity among the workers' parties, it completed its tasks when it merged into the Mifleget Ha'Avoda HaYisr'elit, the Israel Labor party.

Y. SLUTSKY

AHDUT 'AVODA–PO'ALE ZION OF AMERICA. American Labor Zionist movement established under this name in 1947. The antecedents of the movement go back to 1920, when a left-wing group of the original Po'ale Zion Organization of America (see PO'ALE ZION IN AMERICA) split from the parent body and called itself Left Po'ale Zion. In 1947 this group joined the *B'rit 'Olamit Ahdut 'Avoda–Po'ale Zion (World Confederation of Ahdut 'Avoda–Po'ale Zion), which had been founded in 1946, adopted the name Ahdut 'Avoda–Po'ale Zion of America, and from then on functioned as part of the world body. Early in 1968 the World Confederation merged with the *Ihud 'Olami (World Union of Zionists-Socialists) under the new name T'nu'at Ha'Avoda HaTziyonit (Zionist Labor Movement), whose affiliate the Ahdut 'Avoda–Po'ale Zion of America now became.

As a labor wing of the Zionist movement, the Ahdut 'Avoda–Po'ale Zion of America engages in activities relating to Zionist as well as general Jewish life on the American scene. Considering itself also a part of the labor movement in the United States, it is active in matters of concern to the organized American labor movement. It is affiliated with, and gives support to, the pioneering elements in Israel and publishes in the United States a Yiddish monthly, *Undzer Veg* (Our Way). It has participated in the establishment of cultural institutions in several kibbutzim affiliated with the *Kibbutz M'uhad and in its seminary in Ef'al.

Considerable help from the American movement enabled its sister movement in Israel to establish the largest Yiddish publishing house, the I. L. Peretz Publishing Company, and a chain of libraries under that name. The *D'ror young Zionist organization is connected with the Ahdut 'Avoda–Po'ale Zion of America.

P. GOLDMAN

AHDUT ISRAEL (political grouping in Israel). See HERUT.

AHIASAPH. Hebrew publishing house founded in Warsaw in 1893 at the initiative of the *B'ne Moshe society. It published numerous important original Hebrew works as well as translations and for many years issued a literary annual, *Luah Ahiasaph*.

In 1896 *Ahad Ha'Am, who had served Ahiasaph as literary adviser from the outset, was made a director. He then founded the Hebrew periodical *HaShiloah (which Ahiasaph continued to publish until 1921). In 1902 Ahad Ha'Am resigned from the editorship of *HaShiloah* and from Ahiasaph.

In 1901 Ahiasaph published *HaDor*, a Hebrew weekly edited by David *Frischmann. During its more than three decades of publishing activities, Ahiasaph contributed greatly to the progress and spread of modern Hebrew literature.

AHI'EZER. Village (moshav) in the Judean Plain northwest of Lod. Settled in 1950 by *Yemenite Jews and affiliated with HaPo'el HaMizrahi (see MIZRAHI). Population (1968): 850.

AHIHUD. Village (moshav) in western Lower Galilee. Settled in 1950 by immigrants from Yemen and affiliated with *T'nu'at HaMoshavim. Population (1968): 463.

AHIMEIR (ACHIMEIR), ABBA. Journalist and Zionist leader (b. Dolgi, near Bobruisk, Russia, 1896; d. Ramat Gan, 1962). He was educated in Bobruisk and at the *Herzliya High School in Tel Aviv, later returning to Europe to study history and philosophy at the Universities of Kiev, Liège, and Vienna (Ph.D., 1924).

While in Russia, Ahimeir was active in the youth group *Tz'ire Zion and in 1917 participated in the All-Russia Zionist Conference in Petrograd. Settling in Palestine in 1924, he worked for a time as an agricultural laborer and as a teacher. He was associated with the Socialist youth organization *HaPo'el HaTza'ir and contributed to the Hebrew press. In 1928 he joined the Revisionist movement (see REVISIONISTS), within which he founded and headed a radical wing, B'rit HaBiryonim.

In 1930, when Drummond Shiels, the British Under-secretary of State for the Colonies, visited Palestine, Ahimeir was arrested for leading an anti-British demonstration. Elected to the Third *Asefat HaNivharim (Elected Assembly) in 1931, he was arrested again for agitating against the population census. In June, 1933, he was charged with complicity in the assassination of Hayim *Arlosoroff but in the spring of 1934 was acquitted of the charge. He was not released, however, but tried as an organizer of the B'rit HaBiryonim and sentenced to 18 months' imprisonment.

As coeditor of the Revisionist paper *Hazit Ha'Am*, he advocated opposition to British anti-Zionist policies, attacked the official Zionist leadership, and strongly opposed all forms of socialism, his main target being Marxian theories.

After his retirement from organized political activities, Ahimeir devoted himself to journalism. His reminiscences of imprisonment and selections from his articles appeared in book form. He also translated into Hebrew Vladimir *Jabotinsky's *Story of the Jewish Legion*.

I. BENARI

AHISAMAKH. Village (moshav) south-southeast of Lod. Founded in 1950 by immigrants from Tripoli and affiliated with *T'nu'at HaMoshavim. Population (1968): 625.

AHITUV. Village (moshav) in the Sharon Plain. Settled in 1951 by immigrants from Iraq and affiliated with *T'nu'at Ha-Moshavim. Population (1968): 650.

AHUZAM. Village (moshav) in the Darom. Settled in 1950 by immigrants from North Africa and affiliated with Ha'Oved HaTziyoni. Population (1968): 525.

AHUZA (ACHOOZA, ACHUSA, ACHUZA) SOCIETIES. Societies organized in the United States "to purchase land in Palestine and improve same by plantation of fruit trees." The Ahuza movement was launched in St. Louis in 1908 by Simon Goldman, who had lived in Palestine for several years and was a member of the St. Louis Dorshe Zion Society. The local Zionist group endorsed the plan, and shortly thereafter Goldman issued a pamphlet calling on American Zionists to raise $1,000,000 to buy land for eventual settlement in Palestine. The first Ahuza land company was formed in St. Louis with 50 members; it was soon followed by similar groups in other American cities. According to the company's statutes, each member had to make quarterly payments, accumulating over a period of five years the sum of $1,400, for which he was entitled to 50 dunams (12½ acres; see DUNAM) of land planted with almonds. After this crop yielded the first income, the members were to settle on the land, each bringing with him more capital to enable him to build a house and set up a farm on his plot.

At the 12th convention (1909) of the Federation of American Zionists (see ZIONIST ORGANIZATION OF AMERICA), Goldman's draft resolution on the establishment of Palestine land development companies was not approved, whereupon he left for Palestine on his own and purchased land in Poriya, near Tiberias, to accommodate a settlement for the St. Louis society. The planting of olive and almond trees was begun in 1910, and although Goldman died soon thereafter, his idea spread, so that by 1913 there were 20 Ahuza groups in the United States and Russia with some 1,000 members (including 7 groups in the United States—2 in Chicago and 1 each in St. Louis, New York, Los Angeles, Cleveland, and Pittsburgh—with a membership of about 250 and an aggregate capital stock of nearly $500,000). In 1914 the American societies combined into the United Hoachooza of America. In the same year, Arthur *Ruppin, who advised the Ahuza groups, wrote from Palestine to the 17th convention of the Federation of American Zionists to the effect that "the American colony Poriya is a living example of the energy and ability of American Jews. . . ."

Subsequently, the American Ahuza movement stimulated the *American Zion Commonwealth idea. Ahuza Alef (founded in New York in 1912) established the settlements Ra'anana (1921) and Gan Yavne (1931).

A number of factors—lack of credit, absence of working hands, and political developments in Russia—prevented the Ahuza societies from developing.

AHUZAT BAYIT. Name of a group of Jewish merchants and clerks, residents of Jaffa, and of a suburb of Jaffa they founded in 1909, from which Tel Aviv eventually developed.

AHUZAT NAFTALI. Religious educational institution in eastern Lower Galilee. Founded in 1949 by *Po'ale Agudat Israel. In 1967 its staff and student body numbered 76; in 1968, 27.

AIR FORCE OF ISRAEL. See ISRAEL DEFENSE FORCES.

AIRPORTS IN ISRAEL. See AVIATION IN ISRAEL.

AKABA, GULF OF. See ELAT, GULF OF.

AKADEMIYA LALASHON HA'IVRIT. See HEBREW LANGUAGE ACADEMY.

'AKHB'RA. Arab village in eastern Upper Galilee south of Safed. In ancient times 'Akhb'ra was a Jewish village; in the 11th century Jews were still residing there. Population (1968): 352.

AKHZIV. Ancient name of the deserted Arab village ez-Zib, situated on the Mediterranean shore 3 miles north of Nahariya. The village was occupied in 1948 by units of the *Israel Defense Forces. Later a small museum was established on the site to house local antiquities. In 1961 the harbor site of Akhziv was chosen by the Club Méditerranée for its Israeli camp.

Akhziv is an important archeological site. Its Iron Age cemetery contains tombs cut into the rock, in some cases closed with masonry dressed in the characteristic 8th-century B.C.E. Phoenician manner. Rich funerary equipment, consisting of pottery vessels, masks, figurines of pregnant women, musicians, and breadmakers, and models of boats, was also found on the site.

'AKIVA. Youth organization founded in 1924 in western Galicia, Poland, by Jewish students. It instilled in its membership a deep sense of identification with Jewry and Jewish values and educated them toward pioneering and kibbutz life in Palestine. Graduates of the movement established several settlements in Palestine.

'AKKO (Acco, Acre). Coastal city in western Galilee, at the northern tip of Haifa Bay. First mentioned in Egyptian documents from the 19th and 18th centuries B.C.E., 'Akko, at the time of the Israelite conquest of the country, was assigned to the tribe of Asher but not conquered by it. Captured in 701 B.C.E. by the Assyrian king Sanherib (Sennacherib), the city was later ruled by the Persians and by Alexander the Great, after whose death it passed to the Egyptian Ptolemies (who renamed it Ptolemais) and subsequently to the Syrian Seleucids. The Hasmonean rulers tried unsuccessfully to subdue the heathen city, which was hostile to the Jews. During the Roman-Jewish War (C.E. 66–70), 'Akko, by then a Roman colony, served as a base

for the Roman legions fighting to suppress the Jewish revolt in Galilee.

After the destruction of the Second Temple (C.E. 70), a sizable Jewish community developed in the city, and Jews lived there also during the Byzantine, Arab, and Crusader (1104–1291) periods. In the reconquest of the city by the Muslims, 'Akko was destroyed and many of its inhabitants massacred. Only in the second half of the 13th century was it resettled, and a small Jewish community was established there once again.

'Akko rose again to some importance in the 18th century, when Sheikh Dhaher el-'Amr, who revolted against the Turks and controlled Galilee, made 'Akko his headquarters and invited Jews to settle there. For some time a larger Jewish community was in existence, but many of the Jews left because of the internal wars in the area. In 1775 Ahmed Pasha, known as el-Jazzar (the Butcher) because of his cruelty, restored Galilee to the Sultan. He retained 'Akko as the capital of the district, fortified it, and erected new buildings there. In 1799, backed by the British Navy, he successfully defended the city against Napoleon.

'Akko continued to be an important trade center in the first half of the 19th century. In 1821–22 the Turks laid siege to the city in an unsuccessful attempt to subdue Ahmed Pasha's son and successor, who had revolted against the Sultan. Ten years later, Ibrahim Pasha of Egypt conquered it, but 'Akko was restored to the Turks as a result of a three-hour bombardment by a combined British-Austrian-Turkish fleet in November, 1840.

In the second half of the 19th century 'Akko went into a

The old Arab section of 'Akko. [Israel Information Services]

decline as the result of the sanding up of its port and the gradual transfer of its larger maritime traffic to neighboring Haifa. The importance of the city dwindled even more after the conquest of the country by the British, who made Haifa the administrative headquarters of the area.

In the British Mandatory era (1917–48), 'Akko, by then an all-Arab town, was a center of Arab hostility to Jewish aspirations. It was captured by Jewish forces on May 17, 1948, after having been abandoned by most of the inhabitants. It was resettled by Jewish immigrants and subsequently developed by the building of new residential districts and the establishment of numerous industrial plants. With its mosque, Arab market, old wall, and fortifications, 'Akko has become an important tourist center. Archeologically, interest in 'Akko is occasioned by the remains of a Hellenistic temple and of early Roman tombs found near the modern city. From Crusader times there remain the Crypt of St. John and a tower overlooking the bay. The double circuit of walls and the Mosque of Ahmed el-Jazzar date from the 18th century.

The rapid growth of 'Akko after the independence of Israel is illustrated by the following figures. In 1948 the city had 5,000 inhabitants; in 1968, 32,800, of whom 8,450 were non-Jews. In 1949–50 it had a municipal budget of IL 54,000; in 1968–69, one of IL 9,039,700. The number of municipal employees in 1968 was 450. The same year 5,264 students were enrolled in elementary schools, 501 in high schools, and 433 in trade schools.

T. PRESCHEL

'AKKO (ACRE) PRISON. During the period of the British *Mandate for Palestine (1917–48), the medieval fortress of Acre ('Akko) served as the country's central prison for criminals as well as political prisoners. Here Vladimir *Jabotinsky and 19 of his followers were detained in 1920 for their self-defense activities during the *Arab riots in Jerusalem in April of that year. During the 1930s and 1940s hundreds of members of the three Jewish underground organizations languished in the large prison. Here Sh'lomo *Ben Yosef (on June 29, 1938), Dov *Gruner, Y'hiel Dresner, Eliezer Kashani, and Mordecai Alkahi (on Apr. 16, 1947), and Meir Nakar, Avshalom Haviv, and Ya'akov Weiss (on June 16, 1947), all members of the *Irgun Tz'vai L'umi, went to the gallows singing Jewish national songs as a last gesture of defiance. On May 4, 1947, in a daring and brilliantly conceived and executed action, the Irgun stormed the fortress of Acre and freed many of the prisoners. This exploit, one of the heaviest blows dealt by the Jewish underground to the British security forces and British prestige, caused a worldwide sensation.

After the establishment of the State of Israel, the 'Akko fortress was converted into an institution for the mentally ill. Years later part of the citadel, including the death cell and the cell of Jabotinsky, was dedicated as a national shrine.

See also 'AKKO.

AKZIN, BENJAMIN. A leader of the *Revisionists and an expert in government and international law (b. Riga, Latvia, 1904). He completed his studies in law and government in Vienna (1926), in Paris (1929), and at Harvard (1933). From 1920 he was active in the Zionist youth organization in Latvia, and during his student days in Vienna he was among the leaders of the student Zionist organization HeHaver. A member of the Revisionist movement from its inception in 1925, first in Vienna,

The Israeli flag flies over 'Akko Prison. [Histadrut Foto-News]

then in France, he served on the editorial board of the newspaper *Rassviet* in Paris. From 1929 to 1930 he was general secretary of the Revisionist movement in London, thereafter devoting himself to scholarly pursuits. In 1936 he became active once again in the *New Zionist Organization and assisted Vladimir *Jabotinsky in his political work. He tried to bring the Revisionist movement back into the *World Zionist Organization; failing to do so, he dropped out (1940). From 1941 to 1944 he was head of the Legal Department of the Library of Congress in Washington, D.C. From 1945 to 1949 he served the American Zionist Emergency Council (*see* EMERGENCY COMMITTEE FOR ZIONIST AFFAIRS) as an adviser and representative, in Washington and then in New York.

Akzin settled in the new State of Israel in 1949 and became a professor of government and constitutional law at the *Hebrew University of Jerusalem, where he served a number of terms as dean of the Faculty of Law. He published books on law, public administration, and politics (in Hebrew, French, and English), wrote for the Israeli press on current problems, and lectured at universities in the United States, Germany, and elsewhere.

G. KRESSEL

AL-ASSIFA. *See* EL-FATAH.

ALEINIKOV, MICHAEL. Zionist leader in Russia (b. Smolensk, Russia, 1880; d. Chamonix, France, 1938). He studied law in Kharkov, then practiced law, and later engaged in business. Active in the Russian Zionist movement and in Jewish communal affairs, he participated in the *Helsingfors Conference (1906), from 1913 to 1919 was a member of the Central Committee of Russian Zionists, and from 1913 to 1921 a member of the Greater *Actions Committee. He was also a member of the editorial board of *Rassviet*. After the Russian

Revolution he headed the Executive Committee of the Russian Jewish Communities.

In 1919 Aleinikov left Russia. For several years he served as deputy secretary of the *Comité des Délégations Juives in Paris. Then, in 1926, he settled in Palestine. From 1928 to 1933 he was director of the Haifa Bay Land Development Company and for some years was also chairman of the Hadar HaKarmel Council.

AL-FATAH. *See* EL-FATAH.

ALGERIA, ZIONISM IN. *See* NORTH AFRICA, ZIONISM IN.

ALGERIAN JEWS IN ISRAEL. *See* NORTH AFRICAN JEWS IN ISRAEL.

'AL HAMISHMAR (newspaper). Israeli daily newspaper, founded in Tel Aviv on July 30, 1943. Born in the midst of the debate over the *Biltmore Program, *'Al HaMishmar* (On Guard) claimed to represent the extreme Zionist left, which opposed that program and campaigned for a binational Jewish-Arab state in Palestine (*see* IHUD). These political concepts were supplemented by a more radical, Marxist approach to social problems in general and to *Histadrut policies in particular. As the organ of *HaShomer HaTza'ir, a faction within the Histadrut, *'Al HaMishmar* by its very appearance challenged the assertion that *Davar* reflected the entire spectrum of opinions and organizations prevailing in the Histadrut. Seeking to explain this formal parting of ways, Meir *Ya'ari, the ideological mentor of HaShomer HaTza'ir, stated in the first issue of *'Al HaMishmar:* "We are well aware of the feelings the existence of two workers' dailies will evoke in the camp of labor. But we sincerely believe that this duplication is imperative; we believe, too, that it will result in a fruitful and creative tension, and will strengthen freedom of judgment, independence and public control."

'Al HaMishmar had a ready-made readership in the kibbutzim of HaShomer HaTza'ir. Its literary supplement became an important medium of artistic expression for young Israeli writers emerging from the kibbutz elements. Abraham *Shlonsky's editorship of this supplement added to its literary distinction. After the establishment of *Mapam, *'Al HaMishmar* served as its party organ, with Mordecai *Bentov, Eleazar Peri, and Jacob Amit as editors. In 1966 *'Al HaMishmar* reported a circulation of 15,500.   J. RUBIN

'AL HAMISHMAR (Zionist political group). *See* POLAND, ZIONISM IN.

AL-HUSAYNI, HAJJ AMIN. Mufti of Jerusalem (b. Jerusalem, 1893). He was educated first in Jerusalem, then at al-Azhar University in Cairo, but did not complete his studies there. After serving in the Ottoman Army during World War I, he turned to teaching. In 1920 he was sentenced to 10 years' imprisonment by a British military court for inciting Arab mob violence in the Jewish quarter of Jerusalem but managed to flee to Transjordan. Amnestied by Herbert *Samuel in 1921, he returned a year later.

In the hope of making al-Husayni into a "British mufti," Samuel's administration was instrumental in nominating him mufti of Jerusalem, to succeed his half-brother Kamal. Within a short time he was appointed president of the Muslim Supreme Council and of the religious courts. His eminent religious position, his control of the large *Waqf funds, and his violent opposition to Jewish colonization all made him a prominent leader in the Arab nationalist movement in Palestine. His position enabled him to appoint preachers in the mosques and judges in the Muslim courts, all loyal to him and the anti-Jewish course he advanced; his funds, to finance nationalist propaganda and smuggle arms from Syria and Transjordan. His hand was behind the pogroms of May, 1921, and September, 1929 (*see* ARAB RIOTS IN PALESTINE).

During the 1920s and 1930s (up to 1937) his prestige increased in the Arab and Muslim countries and in Palestine. He organized a Pan-Islamic Congress in Jerusalem (1931), traveled widely, and obtained political support and funds. In 1935 he founded the Palestinian Arab party, a political group headed by his relative and associate Jamal al-Husayni. The creation, in 1936, of the 10-member *Arab Higher Committee, which included leaders of all six existing Arab political formations, bolstered his position still further, and he soon became the dominant figure in this coalition. Overriding the objections of more moderate members of the committee, he launched, in April, 1936, the "Arab Revolt" against both the British and the Jews.

Belatedly realizing that the mufti was not only anti-Jewish but also anti-British, the British, in March, 1937, removed him as head of the Muslim Supreme Council and of the Waqf Committee. In October, 1937, he fled to Lebanon; for a while he continued to direct terrorism in Palestine from Beirut and Damascus. In 1938 his bands killed 297 Jews and wounded 427. Some of his Arab opponents, mainly from the Nashashibi clan, were also attacked and murdered. At the beginning of World War II (in October, 1939), the mufti moved to Baghdad, where he induced Iraqi Prime Minister Rashid 'Ali al-Gailani to launch, in May, 1941, an anti-British coup, with promised Axis support. When this armed movement failed, the mufti fled to Teheran and then to Italy and Germany.

In Berlin he became active in speeding up Hitler's scheme to annihilate European Jewry, collaborating eagerly with the Nazi war machine, organizing sabotage in Arab countries under Allied rule, and rallying political and military support for Germany among Muslims in Axis-occupied countries.

After the collapse of Hitler's Third Reich, the mufti fled to Switzerland; there he was handed over to the French, who interned him in a villa near Paris. In May, 1946, he was permitted to "escape" to Cairo. From there, he maintained close relations with the offices of the *Arab League and with the newly reconstituted Arab Higher Committee in Palestine, dominated by his relatives and associates. He played an important role in the attempts to organize militarily the Arabs of Palestine in 1947–48. Following the Arab-Israeli War of 1948 (*see* WAR OF INDEPENDENCE), the Arab Higher Committee moved to the Egypt-held *Gaza Strip, where a "Palestine government" was proclaimed, with the mufti as president of the "National Assembly." Later, in Cairo, he continued his subversive activities; the murder of King 'Abdullah of Jordan in July, 1951, was widely attributed to him, though this has never been proved conclusively. In 1951 the mufti presided over the World Muslim Conference in Karachi, West Pakistan, and in 1955 he played a minor role in the Afro-Asian Conference in Bandung, Indonesia. His Egyptian support flagging, he settled in Beirut in 1959. His advocacy of a "Palestinian army" found support from Iraq's dictator, 'Abdul Karim Qassem. After Qassem's overthrow (February, 1963) the mufti lost Iraq's patronage. Damascus became his headquarters, but in 1966 the new Syrian regime found him expendable; in 1967 he was living in Riyadh, as the guest of King Feisal of Saudi Arabia.   J. M. LANDAU

'ALIYA (Immigration). A basic concept and ideal in Zionist pioneering ideology, 'Aliya meant more than mere *immigration to and settlement in Palestine and, from 1948, Israel. It implied, as the literal meaning of the Hebrew word *'aliya* (ascent) indicates, the fulfillment of an ideal and, at the same time, the elevation of one's personality to a higher ethical level.

In the early days of immigration to Palestine, most of the 'Olim (immigrants) were actually Zionist idealists who went to the Land of Israel because they preferred living there, even under primitive conditions, to living in the *Diaspora (Galut). With the growth of *anti-Semitism following the emergence of Nazi Germany, an increasing number of 'Olim went to Israel to escape persecution, or its threat, or social or economic pressures, in Europe. After Israel achieved independence (1948), large-scale 'Aliya movements started in the Muslim lands and especially in the Arab countries of the Middle East and North Africa. In addition, "idealistic" 'Aliya during this period came largely from the free countries of the Western world and primarily from the United States.

See also FIRST 'ALIYA; SECOND 'ALIYA; THIRD 'ALIYA; FOURTH 'ALIYA; FIFTH 'ALIYA.

R. PATAI

'ALIYA BET. *See* ILLEGAL IMMIGRATION.

'ALIYA HADASHA. Political party founded in October, 1942, at K'far Sh'maryahu, Palestine. It developed from the Hitahdut 'Ole Germania V'Austria (Association of Immigrants from Germany and Austria), after it had become apparent that immigrants to Palestine from Central Europe had their own political views which made it difficult for them to find their place within the existing parties on Palestine's political scene. 'Aliya Hadasha (New Immigration) entered the political arena as a "political, but not party-bound organization," while all work connected with *immigration, social welfare, and cultural integration was left to the nonpolitical Irgun 'Ole Merkaz Europa (Organization of Immigrants from Central Europe), which was open to all parties. It opposed the newly formulated *Biltmore Program, which called for the establishment in Palestine of a Jewish Commonwealth, while upholding the old concept of the establishment of the Jewish National Home as the goal of Zionism. 'Aliya Hadasha stressed the priority of the fight against Hitler on all fronts and demanded the mass immigration of European Jewry into Palestine, the lifting of restrictions on Jewish ownership of land in Palestine, and efforts to create cooperation and goodwill between Jews and Arabs.

For the most part, the Hebrew press greeted the new group with harsh criticism because of its views on external policy. In 1943 the party scored successes in a number of communal elections. A countrywide conference held in Haifa showed that the party had grown considerably and achieved a large measure of internal consolidation. 'Aliya Hadasha developed into a party of internal reform, calling for a strengthening of the *Va'ad L'umi's power and autonomy, increased efficiency and integrity in public life, and a public labor exchange. First and foremost, it insisted that elections to the *Asefat HaNivharim (Elected Assembly), which were long overdue, be held at the earliest possible moment. It elected Felix Rosenblüth (Pinhas *Rosen) chairman.

In 1943 a Hebrew organ, *'Amudim,* with Gustav Krojanker as editor, was founded. There was also a German-language organ, the *Mitteilungs-Blatt* (popularly known as "M.B."), whose editor was Robert *Weltsch.

It was during a meeting of the Irgun 'Ole Merkaz Europa in 1944 that claims against Germany for Jewish lives and property lost to the Nazi regime were first discussed.

Early in 1944 those members of 'Aliya Hadasha who belonged to the *Histadrut (General Federation of Labor) formed an independent group under the name 'Aliya Hadasha 'Ovedet, which participated in the 1944 Histadrut elections. Women's and young people's groups were also formed.

In the elections to the Asefat HaNivharim held on Aug. 1, 1944, 'Aliya Hadasha ran on the following platform: thoroughgoing reforms in the organizational framework of Palestine's Jewish community, a broadening of the *Yishuv's social services, a planned program of immigrant integration, a campaign against corruption, and, above all, the cessation of violence and terrorism. 'Aliya Hadasha won second place with 18 mandates (*Mapai won first place with 63 mandates). The party received four seats in the Va'ad L'umi and one in the Zionist *Executive, which was assigned to Georg Landauer.

After World War II 'Aliya Hadasha sharply attacked the British Labor Government's restrictions on immigration to Palestine and insisted that the gates of the country be opened to the survivors of the Nazi holocaust. At the same time the party was definitely opposed to acts of violence against the British administration and even to the "activism" of the *Hagana in its struggle against the anti-Zionist policy of British Foreign Secretary Ernest *Bevin. Its reaction to further outbreaks of terrorism in 1946 was an appeal to the *Jewish Agency to put before the *Anglo-American Committee of Inquiry every conceivable alternative for the solution of the Palestine problem.

Late in 1946 'Aliya Hadasha participated in the elections to the 22d Zionist *Congress in Basle, receiving about 6.5 per cent of the total votes cast in Palestine. There, together with Chaim *Weizmann, 'Aliya Hadasha voted for Jewish Agency participation in a new British Palestine conference which was to include Arab and Jewish representatives. The majority's decision against such participation led to Weizmann's resignation.

Following the appointment of the *United Nations Special Committee on Palestine (UNSCOP), the Central Committee of 'Aliya Hadasha, contrary to resolutions passed in 1946, decided (June 12, 1947) to accept Felix Rosenblüth's proposal to support the *partition scheme, defeating Georg Landauer's plan for the setting up of an interim regime aimed at the creation of an Arab-Jewish binational state.

When it became clear, late in 1947, that the British intended to give up the mandate and withdraw from Palestine, a temporary governmental organization was formed in which 'Aliya Hadasha was represented by Rosenblüth, who subsequently became a member of Israel's provisional government and Minister of Justice in several coalition Cabinets. In the summer of 1948, after conferences with the labor organization Ha'Oved HaTziyoni and the progressive wing of the General Zionist party, 'Aliya Hadasha combined with these two groups to form the *Progressive party. At the last countrywide conference of 'Aliya Hadasha (Sept. 17–18, 1948), the Progressive party was officially founded and took over the political activities of 'Aliya Hadasha. The Irgun 'Ole Merkaz Europa continued its activities as a welfare and cultural organization.

B. COHEN

ALKALAI, DAVID. Zionist leader in Yugoslavia (b. Belgrade, 1862; d. there, 1933). He studied law in Vienna, where he joined *Kadimah, a student organization. With the advent of Herzl, he became his ardent follower and participated in the 1st

Zionist *Congress (1897) and subsequent ones. After his return to his native country, where he practiced law, Alkalai founded and led the local Zionist Organization. He was a member of the Greater *Actions Committee and participated in the drafting of the constitution of the *Jewish National Fund.

ALKALAI, JUDAH SOLOMON HAI. Precursor of modern Zionism (b. Sarajevo, Bosnia, 1798; d. Jerusalem, 1878). At the age of 28 he became reader and teacher of the Sephardi community of Zemun, near Belgrade. Some years later he was appointed rabbi of the community, serving in this capacity until his emigration to Palestine.

Steeped in the study of the Kabbala, Alkalai believed that the year 5600 (1840) would usher in the Messianic redemption of the Jewish people. In the introduction to *Darkhe No'am,* a book dealing with Hebrew grammar which he published in 1839, he called upon his fellow Jews to prepare for the redemption by prayer and spiritual devotion to Zion and by rendering material assistance to those already residing in the Land of Israel. He further developed his ideas in *Sh'lom Y'rushalayim* (1840), in which he warned his people that misfortune would befall them if they did not prepare for redemption and exhorted them to give concrete expression to their devotion to Zion by dedicating one-tenth of their income ("tithe") to the support of those who dwelled in Jerusalem.

The Damascus affair (1840) had far-reaching effects on Alkalai's views on the redemption of the Jewish people. On the one hand, he saw in the blood accusation a danger signal, warning the Jews to leave the lands of the *Diaspora. On the other, the united Jewish effort led by Jewish notables from Western Europe and the intervention of European powers on behalf of the victims revealed to him that a Return to Zion could be achieved with the help of the nations. In *Minhat Y'huda* (1843) and subsequent brochures and articles, Alkalai advocated the formation of an "Assembly of Jewish Notables" which would serve as the representative body of the Jewish people, appeal to the nations to permit the Jews to return to their ancient Homeland, and organize the gradual settlement of the Jews with the funds of the tithe. Supporting his ideas and arguments with ample quotations from Jewish religious literature, Alkalai asserted that the final and supernatural redemption to be brought about by the Messiah must be preceded by the physical return of the Jews to Zion. To spread his ideas, Alkalai developed a prolific literary activity, and in 1851–52 he toured several foreign countries, including Great Britain, where he published a pamphlet in English and established a short-lived Palestine settlement society.

Alkalai joined the *Colonisations-Verein für Palästina, established by Chaim *Lorje, and was very active in its behalf. In 1871 he visited Palestine, where he established a settlement society, which, however, soon disintegrated. In 1874 Alkalai settled permanently in Palestine.

T. PRESCHEL

ALLENBY, EDMUND HENRY HYNMAN (1st Viscount Allenby). British army officer, conqueror of Palestine (b. Brackenhurst Hall, near Southwell, Nottinghamshire, England, 1861; d. London, 1936). He saw active service in Bechuanaland (1884–85) and Zululand (1888) and was in command of British cavalry operations during the Boer War (1899–1902). In 1905 he became a brigadier general, in 1909 a major general, and from 1910 until 1914 he was inspector general of the British cavalry.

Lord Allenby. [Zionist Archives]

During World War I Allenby was at first appointed commander of the British cavalry in France. In 1917 he led the Third Army at the Battle of Arras. Later that year he was named commander of the British Expeditionary Force in Egypt.

In October, 1917, after intensive secret preparations, he launched an offensive against the Turks in Palestine. Within a few weeks the first phase of the offensive brought the southern part of the country, including Jaffa and Jerusalem, under his control. He entered the Holy City on foot and was greeted by the Jewish population as their liberator.

The transfer of a large part of his troops to France in the spring of 1918 prevented Allenby from continuing his advance. In September, 1918, after his army had been reinforced by troops from India and Iraq and by the *Jewish Legion, he renewed the offensive and in a brilliantly conceived attack won a decisive victory at Megiddo. Pursuing the retreating Turks, he captured Damascus and Aleppo. While still in the midst of his campaign, he was made military governor of the conquered territory.

In recognition of his services he was promoted to the rank of field marshal and elevated to the peerage as Viscount Allenby of Megiddo and Felixstowe. From 1919 to 1925 Allenby was British High Commissioner in Egypt.

While he was military governor of Palestine, Allenby was indifferent to Zionism. Later, his attitude became more favorable to it, and he delivered an enthusiastic address at the opening of the *Hebrew University of Jerusalem in 1925.

ALLIANCE ISRAÉLITE UNIVERSELLE. Jewish charitable, educational, and defense organization, with headquarters in Paris, active in many areas of Europe, Asia, and Africa. Founded in 1860 by French Jews, it was later joined by many thousands of people in various countries with the purpose of providing assistance to needy Jews anywhere in the world, including help in their fight against persecution and discrimination. Its founders included Adolphe Crémieux, a French-Jewish statesman and political leader of note, who fought throughout his life for Jewish rights and, in 1870, in his capacity as Minister of Justice, proclaimed the complete emancipation of the Jews of Algeria. He served for many years as president of the Alliance.

Although denouncing "servile assimilation," the leaders of the Alliance Israélite Universelle as such did not accept the Zionist doctrine of a territorial solution to the Jewish problem. However, the Central Committee of the organization often included adherents of the Zionist movement.

In 1911, when David *Wolffsohn, president of the *World Zionist Organization, charged Alliance representatives with participation in the anti-Zionist movement among the Jewish population of the Ottoman Empire, Jacques Bigart, Alliance secretary from 1892 to 1934, emphatically denied the accusation and declared that all representatives of the Alliance, in Turkey and elsewhere, were under strict orders to eschew ideological controversy. The attitude of the Alliance in this respect was in some measure influenced by the responsibilities it had shouldered with regard to educational work among the Jews in many parts of the empire.

In 1919 Prof. Sylvain Lévy, who in 1920 was to become president of the Alliance, testified before the Supreme Council of the Allied Powers, which was drafting the peace treaties in Paris, submitting what at the time was considered an anti-Zionist statement. In 1947, however, Prof. René Cassin, then president of the Alliance, submitted a memorandum to the *United Nations Special Committee on Palestine urging a solution that would "permit large-scale immigration and colonization and the free development of the Jewish National Home in Palestine."

In 1945, in its first post-World War II statement of policy, the Central Committee of the Alliance Israélite Universelle, which at that time returned to liberated Paris, took a definitely positive attitude toward Jewish aspirations in Palestine.

It was in Palestine that, motivated by the desire to alleviate the misery of the Jewish population, the Alliance had begun its activities in 1867. In 1866 Charles *Netter, a founder of the Alliance who went to Palestine to see how the 13,000 Jews were living there, reported to the Central Committee that, with the exception of a few relatively well-to-do individuals, the Jewish population was faced with the alternatives of starving, leaving the country, or asking aid from the various Christian missions that were seeking Jewish converts.

Since modern education was considered the only way out of this desperate situation, the Alliance opened elementary schools in Jerusalem, Haifa, Jaffa, Safed, and Tiberias during the latter part of the 19th century. These schools provided secular as well as religious instruction and were at the time almost the only modern Jewish schools in the country.

In 1870 the Alliance opened an agricultural school, Mikve Yisrael, near Jaffa, to train Jewish farmers. The desire to make Palestine Jewry more productive also prompted the Alliance to open, a few years later, a vocational school in Jerusalem. This was the first school of its kind not only in Palestine but in the entire Middle East.

French-language instruction was an important feature of the curriculum of the Alliance schools because, as *Ahad Ha'Am explained in his essays, a knowledge of French seemed essential to the development of a productive economy in the Near and Middle East. However, *Hebrew also had an important place in the Alliance program from the very beginning. It was in these schools that the father of modern Hebrew, Eliezer *Ben Yehuda, and the educators David *Yellin and Abraham *Elmaleh were first given an opportunity to apply modern methods to the teaching of Hebrew. In 1932 the Alliance opened in Jerusalem a school for deaf-mute children, the first of its kind in that part of the world.

After World War II the Alliance concentrated its efforts in Palestine, and later in Israel, on secondary education. It opened *lycées* (high school and junior college combined) in Jerusalem, Tel Aviv, and Haifa. The largest of these schools, in Tel Aviv (named for Edmond, Maurice, and Edmond de *Rothschild in memory of the "Father of Palestine Colonization," his son, and grandson), is operated jointly by the Alliance and the municipality.

In 1968 there were about 5,000 pupils in the schools of the Alliance in Israel, distributed among 12 schools in six localities; they were taught by 340 teachers. The language of instruction in all Alliance schools in Israel was Hebrew, and the curriculum conformed to the requirements of Israeli law and educational procedure. French, however, was still an important part of the curriculum; it was the first foreign language taught in these schools, in conformity with the wish expressed by Israel's leaders, eager to strengthen cultural ties with the French-speaking world.

During its century of existence, the Alliance has, through its schools, radically influenced the lives of great numbers of Jews in Israel, as it has done in many other countries of the Near and Middle East and North Africa. It is estimated that about 650,000 Jewish boys and girls received their secular and Jewish education in the schools of the Alliance in various countries of the region. There were in 1968 about 30,000 students in the schools founded by the Alliance.

Tens of thousands of young men and women who graduated from Alliance schools in Palestine-Israel, among them about 6,000 graduates of Mikve Yisrael, have helped, in their turn, to effect radical changes in the economic and social structure of the *Yishuv (Jewish population of the country). The historical importance of the schools of the Alliance lies also in the fact that they served as pioneers in the country and effectively assisted in the work of all who became active in Palestine toward the end of the 19th century and thereafter.

S. CHERNIAK

ALLON, YIGAL. Israeli Army commander and Cabinet member (b. K'far Tavor, 1918). He studied at the *Kadourie

Yigal Allon.
[Israel Information Services]

Agricultural School, and in 1937 he helped found the kibbutz Ginnosar, of which he still was a member in 1969. Joining

*Hagana at an early age, he was one of the founders of *Palmah (commando units). In 1943 he became deputy commander in chief of Palmah, and later, in 1946–48, its commander in chief. During the *War of Independence, Allon was in charge of military operations which liberated various parts of the country from the Arab invaders. He was a leader in *Ahdut 'Avoda and *Kibbutz M'uhad. First elected to the *Knesset in 1955, he was reelected in 1959 but resigned in 1960 to accept a research fellowship at Oxford University. In 1961 he was again elected to the Knesset and that year was appointed Minister of Labor. In 1968 he was appointed Deputy Premier and Minister for the Absorption of Immigrants. In 1969, on the death of Prime Minister Levi *Eshkol, he became Acting Prime Minister. Allon has written on security problems and on the history of the Palmah.

G. KRESSEL

'ALMA. Village (moshav) in eastern Upper Galilee. Founded in 1949 and settled by Tripolitanian immigrants and proselytes from Sannicandro Garganico, Italy. Affiliated with HaPo'el HaMizrahi (*see* MIZRAHI). Population (1968): 585.

ALMAGOR. Village (moshav) in eastern Upper Galilee. Founded in 1961 and affiliated with *T'nu'at HaMoshavim. It was frequently a target of Syrian attacks.

ALMALIAH, AVRAHAM RAPHAEL. *See* ELMALEH, ABRAHAM RAPHAEL.

ALMOGI, JOSEPH. Israeli labor leader and Cabinet member (b. Rubishów, Poland, 1910). Almogi settled in Palestine in 1930. Prominently active in *Hagana, he became a member of its command. During World War II he served as a volunteer with the British Army. Taken prisoner in Greece, he spent four years in a prisoner-of-war camp in Silesia, where he was the spokesman of the Jewish inmates. After his return to Palestine, he was secretary of the Haifa Labor Council, from 1945 to 1959, and

ALONE ABBA. Village (moshav) in western Lower Galilee. Founded in 1948 and named for Abba Berditchev, one of the Palestinian Jewish *parachutists of World War II. Affiliated with Ha'Oved HaTziyoni. Population (1968): 223.

ALONE YITZHAK. Children's youth village in Samaria. Founded in 1949 and named for Itzhak *Grünbaum. Population (1968): 328.

ALONIM. Village (kibbutz) in the Jezreel Valley. Settled in 1938 and affiliated with the *Kibbutz M'uhad. Population (1968): 490.

ALTALENA. Literary pseudonym of Vladimir *Jabotinsky.

ALTERMAN, NATAN. Hebrew poet and translator (b. Warsaw, 1910). Settling in Palestine in 1925, Alterman attended the *Herzliya High School in Tel Aviv and studied at the agricultural institute in Nancy, France. He served on the editorial board of *Ha'Aretz from 1934 to 1943, when he joined the *Histadrut daily *Davar. Beginning in 1931, he wrote lyric poems, which subsequently were published in several volumes, as well as articles on current topics; he was also engaged in translation from world literature (plays by Shakespeare, Molière, and so on). In his satirical *Tur Shevi'i* (Seventh Column) he created a new genre of topical verse, reacting sharply to contemporary social and political events. His poetry fulfilled an important function during the period of struggle with the British. He was also the author of *Kinneret, Kinneret,* a play about the *Second 'Aliya (performed by the Kameri Theater), one of the important songwriters for the Hebrew theater, and the composer of children's songs (*see* THEATER IN ISRAEL).

G. KRESSEL

ALTMAN, ARYE. Zionist Revisionist leader (b. Balta, Russia, 1902). An active Zionist since his youth, he was from 1922 to

Joseph Almogi.
[Israel Information Services]

Arye Altman.
[Zionist Archives]

general secretary of *Mapai, from 1959 to 1962. Elected to the *Knesset for the first time in 1955, he became, in 1961, a member of the Cabinet without portfolio. From 1962 until his resignation in 1965 he was Minister of Development and Housing. He joined Ben-Gurion, helped found *R'shimat Po'ale Yisrael (Rafi), and was elected to the Knesset as a representative of this party in 1965. In 1968 he was appointed Minister of Labor.

1929 chairman of the Odessa chapter of *Tz'ire Zion. He was arrested several times by the Bolsheviks and was sentenced to exile in Siberia. However, he succeeded in having his sentence, as well as that of hundreds of other Zionists, changed into expulsion from the country. In 1924 he settled in Palestine, becoming active in *HaPo'el HaTza'ir, but he later joined the *Revisionists. During studies in the United States (1928–35), he was active in the American branch of this movement and served for several years as its vice-president. In 1936 he became president of the movement in Palestine and held that position until 1949. He was also on the Presidium of the world movement.

Altman was a member of the Executive of the *Va'ad L'umi, of the Presidium of the *Actions Committee, and of the Constituent Assembly of Israel. From 1951 to 1965 he was a *Herut representative in the *Knesset.

ALTNEULAND. *See* OLD-NEW LAND.

ALUMA. Rural center in the Darom. Founded in 1965.

'ALUMIM. Village (kibbutz) in the Negev. Founded in 1966 and affiliated with HaPo'el HaMizrahi (*see* MIZRAHI).

ALUMOT. Village (kibbutz) in eastern Lower Galilee. Founded in 1941 in nearby Poriya and later moved to its present site. Affiliated with *Ihud Ha'Kvutzot V'haKibbutzim. Population (1968): 146.

AL-YOM (al-Yawm). Arabic daily paper, established in 1948 by the Department for Arab Affairs of the *Histadrut. Michael Assaf, the member of the *Davar editorial staff in charge of Arab affairs, was its first editor. He was succeeded by Nissim Rejwan, a Jewish immigrant from Iraq and an authority on Middle Eastern affairs. *Al-Yom* discontinued publication in 1968. In 1970 two Arabic dailies were published in Jerusalem: *al-Anba,* owned partly by the *Jerusalem Post,* and the Arab-owned *al-Quds.*

AMATZYA. Village (moshav) in the Lakhish region. Founded in 1955 and affiliated with *Herut.

AMERICA-ISRAEL CULTURAL FOUNDATION. American Jewish philanthropic organization, founded by Edward Norman and dedicated to the furtherance of cultural life in Israel. It was officially established on Dec. 22, 1939, as the "first agency for joint and unified fund raising on behalf of the cultural institutions" of what today is Israel. In 1968 the Foundation supported projects in some 50 cultural institutions in Israel, helped with the cultural integration of new immigrants, provided talented Israeli youngsters with scholarships for study in all the arts, collected art treasures to be exhibited in Israel's *museums, served Israeli as well as American institutions as a clearinghouse for cultural information, organized two-way cultural exchanges between the United States and Israel, and supported an important building program of cultural institutions in Israel. It created in New York City the America-Israel Culture House as a showcase for the best Israel has to offer in the arts.

The financial help and cultural assistance provided by the Foundation have benefited orchestras, choirs and music academies, museums, art exhibits and art schools, theaters (*see* THEATER IN ISRAEL), and *dance ensembles. The Foundation tried to develop these institutions and to raise their standards of performance. It financed pilot projects designed to serve the cultural needs of the rural settlements in Israel and to be taken over later by the *government or other Israeli authorities. In deciding on these projects and allocations the Foundation worked through its Israel Advisory Board, but the actual decisions were made exclusively by the American Board of Directors.

By the end of 1968 the Foundation had awarded scholarships

America-Israel Culture House, New York.

to 2,500 talented Israeli youngsters for the continuation and completion of their studies in Israel and, in some exceptional cases, other countries. A considerable number of former scholarship students have become internationally known, for example, the violinists Sh'muel Ashkenazi and Itzhak Perlman, the conductors Daliah Atlas and Moshe Atzman, the pianist Daniel Barenboim, the painter Sh'muel Boneh, the soprano Netania Davrath, and the sculptor Hava Mechutan.

In the field of cultural exchange, the Foundation has brought to the United States the *Israel Philharmonic Orchestra, the Israel National Youth Symphony–Gadna', the Rinat Choir, HaBimah Theater, Inbal Dance Theater, and so on. An outstanding Israeli art exhibit was circulated for two years through museums in the United States and Canada. On the other hand, the Foundation has sent to Israel teachers of music and art, conductors, and soloists, some of whom have taken a prominent part in Israel's festivals of music and drama, such as the Pablo Casals Violoncello Competition and the International Harp Contests. In 1966, as an addition to its exchange program, the Foundation took over the organization of study tours to Israel by American Christian clergymen and other prominent persons.

Within the framework of its building program the Foundation has provided Israel with cultural centers in agricultural areas and with museums, theaters, and music academies in the cities. Among them are the Fredric R. Mann Auditorium in Tel Aviv, the HaBimah and Kameri Theaters, and the Rubin Academies of Music. The Foundation played a major role in the construction of the Israel Museum in Jerusalem and in bringing to Israel valuable collections (e.g., the Billy Rose Art Garden exhibited at the Israel Museum).

The Foundation's America-Israel Culture House, opened in New York on Feb. 8, 1966, contains the permanent Gallery of Israeli Art and the Israeli Arts and Crafts Center. In its music recital and meeting rooms regular programs, concerts, film showings, and lectures are offered to the Foundation's members and guests. In the mid-1960s the house was rapidly becoming a center where outstanding men and women of America's and Israel's cultural spheres could meet and where visitors could get vivid impressions and first-hand information on Israel's cultural achievements. In 1968 the violinist Isaac Stern was president of the Foundation.

F. R. LACHMAN

Memorial to war dead at Gesher HaZiv, one of the villages founded by American pioneers. [Israel Information Services]

AMERICA-ISRAEL SOCIETY. Organization founded in 1954 in Washington, D.C., to advance mutual understanding and strengthen the bonds of friendship between Israel and the United States and to interpret the spiritual and democratic heritage that binds the two nations together. Its projects included educational and student exchange programs, seminars for educators and clergymen, an information program, and a speakers' bureau. An annual Summer Study Tour to Israel for 50 college instructors and clergymen was a featured part of its program.

Theodore R. McKeldin, a former Governor of Maryland, was president of the organization from 1954 to 1966. In March, 1964, the Society transferred its headquarters from Washington to New York, and in 1966 it became part of the *America-Israel Cultural Foundation. The Baltimore chapter, however, continued to function under the Society's own name, under the chairmanship of William Rogers.

R. HERSHMAN

AMERICAN AND CANADIAN JEWS IN ISRAEL. The interest and participation of North American Jewry in the Return to Zion dates back to the 1820s, when an American Jew, Maj. Mordecai Manuel *Noah, envisioned the establishment of "Ararat, a City of Refuge for the Jews" on Grand Island, in the Niagara River, in upstate New York. Noah hoped that his "city of refuge" would become a useful proving ground for the eventual establishment of the Jewish nation in Palestine. In his *Discourse on the Restoration of the Jews,* written in 1844, Noah urged the return of the people of Israel to Palestine.

Early Years. In 1844 Warder Cresson was the United States Consul in Jerusalem. He embraced Judaism and changed his name to Michael Boaz Israel. In 1852 he announced his intention of establishing a farm near Jerusalem for the purpose of promoting agricultural pursuits among the Jews. His enterprise was to serve as a beginning of Israel's return to its ancestral soil. Though he had the support of Jewish individuals in various countries as well as of a group in Jerusalem, his plan did not materialize.

One of the men who supported Cresson was the American Jewish philanthropist Judah Touro. When Touro died (1854),

he left a large legacy for the benefit of the Jewish poor in Palestine, which was used by Sir Moses *Montefiore for the building of houses in Jerusalem.

In 1870 Simon Berman, a Galician Jew who had lived in the United States for many years, arrived in Palestine. Advocating the establishment of Jewish agricultural settlements, he organized the Holy Land Settlement Society in Tiberias, which had a membership of 150, but the society's plan to found a settlement was not realized.

In 1904 *HeHalutz, whose aim was to train members for *'Aliya (immigration) to Palestine, was founded in the United States, preceding the Eastern European HeHalutz by many years. Five of its members emigrated to Palestine and worked on the Kinneret Farm. One of them, Eliezer Lipa *Joffe, became a leading figure in the Palestine labor movement and was instrumental in defining the organization and structure of the Moshav 'Ovdim (*see* MOSHAV), which soon became a widespread form of settlement.

In 1913 *Hadassah, which had been founded a year earlier by Henrietta *Szold, sent two American Jewish nurses, Rose Kaplan and Eva Levin, to Palestine. They established themselves in Jerusalem, treating thousands of children for trachoma and giving maternal-care instruction.

During World War I Hadassah organized the *American Zionist Medical Unit. In June, 1918, 44 men and women of the Unit, including physicians, nurses, social workers, and administrators, arrived in Palestine. They were later joined by additional Americans and local personnel. Many of the Unit's members remained in Palestine, where they continued to be active in the medical institutions and health services established by the Unit and played a prominent role in the country's public health activities.

Also in 1918, 2,000 American and Canadian volunteers for the *Jewish Legion arrived in Palestine. After the disbandment of the Jewish battalions, about 500 of the American volunteers remained in the country, assisting in its rebuilding in various capacities.

Under the British Mandate. Between the end of World War I and 1927, some 4,300 settlers went to Palestine from North America, most of them setting up private enterprises in the growing towns and villages. The first members of the American *Po'ale Zion, *Gordonia, and other Labor Zionist groups began to arrive in Palestine during the *Fourth 'Aliya (1923–28). Many joined established villages in ones and twos. Some, however, came in larger groups; for example, 12 members of the Detroit K'vutza settled at Ramat Yohanan.

In 1931 *HaShomer HaTza'ir, the pioneer youth movement, sent its first group to Palestine and eventually founded 'En HaShofet (named for Justice [shofet] Louis D. *Brandeis), the first kibbutz set up by Americans. Similar pioneer Zionist youth organizations were subsequently formed in the United States and Canada, and they systematically began to train young people for life in the kibbutz.

Between the beginning of the *Fifth 'Aliya (1933) and the establishment of the State of Israel in 1948, some 5,350 Americans and Canadians, including about 850 who had originally gone there as tourists, settled in Palestine, many of them after doing volunteer work in the European underground and manning ships carrying "illegal" immigrants to Palestine (see ILLEGAL IMMIGRATION).

All in all, during the 30-year period between 1918 and the founding of the State of Israel, a total of 11,000 Americans and Canadians settled in Palestine. Of these, 6,600 were registered immigrants from the United States and 285 registered immigrants from Canada. The rest entered under a variety of categories, both official and "illegal." Of the 11,000, some 3,500 eventually returned to their country of origin. By 1948 American and Canadian pioneers had established, in partnership with youth groups from other countries, the villages of Avihayil (founded by former members of the Jewish Legion), 'En HaShofet, K'far M'nahem, K'far Blum, Bet Herut, Hatzor, Gesher HaZiv, Ma'ayan Barukh, and 'En Dor.

This period saw significant contributions by many Americans. Among them were Dr. Judah L. *Magnes, one of the founders and the first president of the *Hebrew University of Jerusalem; Henrietta Szold, the most outstanding leader in social work; Alexander *Dushkin, a leading educator; Judge Shim'on *Agranat; Gershon Agronsky (later *Agron), mayor of Jerusalem and founder and editor of the English-language daily Palestine Post (later *Jerusalem Post); Jessie *Sampter, the poet; and Dr. Israel Jacob Kligler and Louis Cantor, who were instrumental in introducing and developing public health services. Other Americans who contributed to the development of the Yishuv were Simon Goldman of St. Louis, founder of the *Ahuza societies; Israel *Goldstein, head of the *Keren HaYesod (Palestine Foundation Fund); Robert Kesselman, an executive of the Federation of American Zionists and chief auditor of the *Zionist Commission; Elias Passman, representative of the *American Zion Commonwealth and later of the *American Jewish Joint Distribution Committee; and Mendes Sachs, a citrus expert and manager of the M'hadrim society.

Immigration since 1948. During the *War of Independence, 1,770 Americans and Canadians enlisted in *Mahal, the organization of volunteers from overseas who joined the fighting forces in Israel. Of these, approximately 500 eventually settled in Israel, mostly in urban areas, engaging in white-collar jobs, professions, and academic life, and a few in kibbutzim and cooperative settlements.

Between 1948 and 1967 about 12,000 Jews from the United States and Canada settled in Israel. Among the villages they founded or helped to start were Sasa, Barkai, HaSol'lim, Yiftah, Kissufim, Urim, Orot, Gal'on, Nahshon, and K'far

Darom as well as the agricultural suburb of Bet Hatzor. During the same period some 1,500 Americans who were originally tourists settled in the country; about a quarter of this number eventually returned to their country of origin. Of the immigrants, close to 1,100 were young professional men and women who came to Israel under the auspices of the *Professional and Technical Workers' 'Aliya (PATWA); 500 were retired men and women with independent means who transferred their social security and other pension benefits to Israel. Some 200 Americans and Canadians went after making investments in the country under special conditions facilitating the transfer of capital at favorable rates of exchange. Two communities of *Hasidic Jews also moved in their entirety from America to Israel, but their numbers were small.

A fairly complete statistical survey of American and Canadian immigration was compiled from the close of 1961 through 1966 by the Association of Americans and Canadians in Israel. During those years 6,300 adults from the United States and Canada settled in Israel. Of the immigrants, 34 per cent were 30 years of age and below, 17 per cent were from 31 to 45, 10.5 per cent were from 46 to 60, and 22.5 per cent were over 60. The ages of 16 per cent, mostly wives of the heads of families, were not listed.

Geographic and Professional Distribution in Israel. A survey as of March, 1963, showed 789 Americans and Canadians in a total of 94 kibbutzim and 239 in a total of 34 moshavim. It is estimated that another 200 to 250 had joined kibbutzim and moshavim by the end of 1966; an additional 400 were in private agricultural settlements. By 1968 it was estimated that of 23,000 settlers of all types from the North American continent, some 10 per cent were pioneers, somewhat less than the national average. On the other hand, their proportional participation in kibbutzim soared well above it.

More than 17,000 were settled in towns and cities, engaged in trade, in the professions, in academic life, in technical and service work, and in academic studies. Close to half of the 6,300 who arrived after 1961 were in professions requiring a university education. Of these, 10 per cent were teachers, primarily concentrated in large urban areas. Another 25 per cent were members of the professions, including doctors, engineers, psychologists, social workers, economists, scientists, architects, computer programmers, occupational therapists, rabbis, and cantors. The nonprofessional group included skilled workers, businessmen, salesmen, secretaries, typists, and so on. Also, a number of American artists, dancers, and musicians settled in Israel. Slightly less than 1 per cent of the total immigration after 1961 became members of kibbutzim.

In the 1960s, many immigrants from the United States and Canada held key positions in Israel. Heading the list of officials were Golda *Meir, Prime Minister, and Dov *Joseph, Minister of Justice, an American and a Canadian respectively. At the Hebrew University, the Haifa *Technion, the Negev Institute for Arid Zone Research, and the *Weizmann Institute of Science, heads of departments and prominent research scientists and instructors were of American and Canadian origin. A mining engineer in the Timna Copper Mines had trained for his work in his native Canada; the head of the *Institute of Applied Social Research was an American; a Canadian had regular broadcasting time on Kol Yisrael's light radio program (see ISRAEL BROADCASTING SERVICE). A citrus-grove manager in Ra'anana, an old-time farmer in Avihayil, the personnel manager of a large factory near Haifa, the public relations director of an important child-care institution, an outstanding specialist in a large government hospital—these are only a few of the hundreds of Americans and Canadians who are making important contributions to the development of the State of Israel.

Special Problems of Acclimatization and Absorption. The educated, physically healthy, and technologically oriented manpower emigrating from the United States and Canada was highly essential to Israel's developing agriculture, industry, science, and art and left its mark on numerous aspects of the new State's life and culture. Efforts were made to understand and solve some of the problems specific to members of this immigrant group, who, unlike immigrants from numerous other lands, had not been forced to leave their original countries but had come to Israel of their own free will. Every effort was made to reduce the numbers of those who, unable to overcome the obstacles to adjustment in Israel, returned to America.

In the 1960s the largest number of immigrants arriving from the Western Hemisphere were young professionals, and it was expected this trend would continue in the near future. These individuals required conditions that would enable them to follow their professions and to maintain a standard of living for their families not too far below that to which they had been accustomed in their former homes. Relatively lower salaries and higher expenses for housing inferior to their housing abroad created difficulties. Certain amenities considered normal in America, such as a car or a refrigerator, were heavily taxed as luxury items in Israel. What appeared to be an adequate salary in foreign currency was frequently not sufficient to support a family in Israel. The profusion of rules, laws, and customs inherited from the Turks and the British, added to attempts at reorganization and modernization on the part of Israeli legislative bodies, made the initial formalities of immigration confused and inefficient. Highly specialized experts would find that their field had no counterpart in Israeli science and industry. Such professional people sometimes had to forgo the work for which they had trained and change to a related, less specialized field. Members of the legal profession had a particularly difficult problem to face, as they could not practice in Israel without a thorough knowledge of the Hebrew language and Israeli law.

In the mid-1960s two organizations in the United States and Canada were attempting to facilitate the immigration and absorption in Israel of Americans with established occupations or professions. The Commission on Manpower Opportunities in Israel was working to secure advance placement in jobs and housing of candidates of 'Aliya. The candidates had to obligate themselves to go wherever they would be sent and to remain in the country for at least three years. PATWA was also making efforts to fit people with special skills into the scheme of Israeli life prior to their arrival in the country. There was an elaborate program of training institutes, youth leaders' seminars, and kibbutz training centers, most of them connected with youth movements abroad or with the *Jewish Agency for Israel, to prepare young people for the pioneering aspects of life in Israel.

In an attempt to find new approaches and create conditions which would facilitate the successful absorption of immigrants from the United States and Canada, an Israeli 'Aliya Committee was formed, comprising all governmental and Jewish Agency bodies, together with the Association of Americans and Canadians in Israel. Special housing projects were constructed, the problem of customs rates and availability of loans for newcomers was tackled, and efforts were made to simplify the many overlapping official details involved in the initial period of settlement. In 1967, 1,777 Americans immigrated to Israel.

Early in 1968 a new 'Aliya group, the Association of Americans and Canadians for Aliyah (AACA), was established with Norman Schanin as chairman (replaced in May by Pesach Schindler), in affiliation with the American Zionist Council and the Association of Americans and Canadians in Israel. Its purpose was to facilitate the settling of Americans and Canadians in Israel, and by May, 1968, it reported a membership of more than 600. A considerable portion of the members prepared for 'Aliya to Israel in the summer of the same year. The total number of immigrants to Israel from the United States and Canada in 1968 was about 4,000. It was expected that in 1969 the number would be 5,500.

S. SPIRA

AMERICAN CHRISTIAN PALESTINE COMMITTEE. *See* AMERICAN PALESTINE COMMITTEE.

AMERICAN COMMITTEE FOR BAR-ILAN UNIVERSITY. *See* BAR-ILAN UNIVERSITY.

AMERICAN COMMITTEE FOR THE WEIZMANN INSTITUTE OF SCIENCE. *See* WEIZMANN INSTITUTE OF SCIENCE.

AMERICAN ECONOMIC COMMITTEE FOR PALESTINE, INC. Nonprofit association whose primary objective was to help increase the economic absorptive capacity of Palestine. Established in 1932 by Israel B. Brodie and Robert *Szold in response to the *Passfield White Paper, the Committee was in operation until 1954. The project was supported by Justice Louis D. *Brandeis and Judge Julian W. *Mack.

From 1932 to 1942—through the height of *immigration from Germany and Central Europe into Palestine—the Committee devoted itself primarily to encouraging and guiding private enterprise in Jewish Palestine. Through offices in New York and Tel Aviv it furnished to immigrants in Palestine and to prospective immigrants (numbering about 9,000 individuals originating from more than 50 countries) factual surveys of specific economic aspects of Palestine. These reports were used by the recipients in making their decisions whether to establish factories, workshops, farms, or service businesses in Palestine and resulted in the creation of settlement and labor opportunities for thousands of Jews and in the investment of millions of dollars of new capital. The establishment of most new factories in Palestine in the 1930s was determined on the basis of data prepared by the Committee. Its information services prevented waste of capital by newcomers in unfamiliar operating conditions and directed persons with capital and valuable experience to potentially viable projects.

The Committee's Tel Aviv office was regarded as the central source of economic information on Palestine by leading Jewish institutions, including the *Jewish Agency, the Palestine Manufacturers Association, the Farmers' Federation, the *Histadrut (General Federation of Labor), the municipality of Tel Aviv, the Tel Aviv–Jaffa Chamber of Commerce, and the German and Polish immigrants' associations. Its reports on specific areas and subareas of Palestine industry and agriculture were used by the *Palestine Offices of the Jewish Agency in Germany, Austria, Hungary, Czechoslovakia, Poland, and Romania.

The Tel Aviv office was discontinued late in 1939, after the outbreak of World War II and the cessation of immigration.

The New York office was closed in 1942, but it resumed activity in 1943 with emphasis on furnishing highly specialized technical information designed to assist Palestine manufacturers and farmers in producing and marketing better products. The organization regularly forwarded to Palestine—and later to Israel—technical descriptions of advances in manufacturing processes as well as information relating to machinery and equipment, new products, and the improvement of manufactured products. The Committee operated the New York office independently until 1951, when this office became affiliated with the Jewish Agency for Israel within the latter's Economic Department in New York. The affiliation terminated on June 30, 1954, when the Committee ceased operations.

The Committee's services were rendered free of charge. Its membership was composed of individuals whose knowledge and experience could be utilized in the development of Palestine's—and Israel's—industry and agriculture.

A. BAROWAY

AMERICAN EMERGENCY COMMITTEE FOR ZIONIST AFFAIRS. *See* EMERGENCY COMMITTEE FOR ZIONIST AFFAIRS.

AMERICAN FEDERATION OF LABOR–CONGRESS OF INDUSTRIAL ORGANIZATIONS (AFL-CIO). National labor organization in the United States. In 1955 the American Federation of Labor (AFL), organized in 1886, merged with the Congress of Industrial Organizations (CIO), founded in 1935, under the name American Federation of Labor–Congress of Industrial Organizations (AFL-CIO). This central body of American trade unions has had a consistent record of supporting the Zionist program, the Jewish effort in Palestine, the development of the State of Israel, and the work of the *Histadrut (General Federation of Labor). The record goes back to a convention held by the AFL in Buffalo, N.Y., in November, 1917, a few days after the issuance of the *Balfour Declaration. The AFL was the first national trade-union organization to endorse that document and to commit itself to its implementation. This commitment was subsequently reaffirmed by successive conventions of the organization and translated into action. AFL and CIO hailed Jewish accomplishments in Palestine and protested against breaches of the promises contained in the Balfour Declaration. AFL demanded the repeal of the *Passfield White Paper in 1930 and condemned the MacDonald *White Paper of 1939. At its 64th convention (New Orleans, 1944) AFL called for "the reconstitution of Palestine as a free and democratic Jewish Commonwealth." When the State of Israel was proclaimed, AFL greeted it with a resolution adopted at its 67th convention, reading in part: "Mankind has at last arrived at the historic moment when this great people have won a homeland which they can call their own." AFL called for military, political, and economic support of Israel throughout the years, warning that attacks on the Jewish State endangered the peace of the world and the progress of the Middle East. A resolution passed by the Unity Convention, which effected the merger of AFL and CIO (New York, December, 1955), urged "the United States, Britain and France to reaffirm their tripartite Declaration of 1950 and to implement it by enabling the Republic of Israel to obtain arms and other means necessary for the maintenance of its territorial integrity and national independence."

Nor was the interest of this labor organization manifested only at national conventions or in public statements. It reached down to local and state federations and to the national and international unions affiliated with AFL-CIO, taking the form of tangible assistance to Palestine and later Israel through the *Histadrut Campaign, which was officially endorsed at an AFL convention in 1928, and through the American Histadrut Trade Union Council. Organized in 1945, this council included the most important figures in American organized labor, among them William Green and Philip Murray, presidents of AFL and CIO respectively, who were its first honorary chairmen. Their successors, George Meany and Walter P. Reuther, also held this office. Numerous delegations from American trade unions visited Israel, strengthening the ties between the two countries; and affiliates of AFL-CIO offered substantial financial aid. AFL-CIO also participated in projects not directly related to Histadrut. Thus it endorsed the *State of Israel bonds, a fact which induced many unions to make sizable purchases of these bonds and to give other evidence of their concern for the welfare of Israel.

C. B. SHERMAN

AMERICAN FRIENDS OF A JEWISH PALESTINE. *See* BERGSON GROUP.

AMERICAN FRIENDS OF THE HEBREW UNIVERSITY. *See* HEBREW UNIVERSITY OF JERUSALEM.

AMERICAN HISTADRUT TRADE UNION COUNCIL. *See* AMERICAN FEDERATION OF LABOR–CONGRESS OF INDUSTRIAL ORGANIZATIONS.

AMERICAN ISRAEL PUBLIC AFFAIRS COMMITTEE (originally American Zionist Committee for Public Affairs). American Jewish organization established in 1954 to work for stronger United States policies in the Near East looking toward an Arab-Israel peace settlement. Organized by American Zionist bodies, the committee was subsequently broadened to include representative non-Zionist leadership. It has advocated direct Arab-Israel peace negotiations, resistance to the *Arab boycott, and economic and military aid to Israel. It has also worked to combat Arab propaganda.

The committee has a unique day-to-day function in Washington. Since it advocates legislation, it registers with Congress under domestic lobbying laws. Accordingly, the committee may not be financed by tax-exempt organizations but must depend on contributions from individuals for its budget. Legislation supported includes United States foreign aid, grants and loans to Israel for refugee resettlement and economic development, grants to UNRWA for Arab refugee resettlement, and declarations against aid to countries that persist in boycotting, economic warfare, aggression, and interference with freedom of navigation in international waterways, such as the Suez Canal and the Strait of Tiran.

The committee holds annual policy conferences and carries its program to the executive and legislative branches of the United States government and to the national political conventions. It has maintained a nonpartisan position, appealing for the support of both national parties.

The committee was headed by Louis *Lipsky in 1954, by Rabbi Philip S. Bernstein of Rochester, N.Y., from 1955 to 1968, and Irving Kane of Cleveland, Ohio, from 1968 on. I. L. Kenen has served as its executive director from the committee's inception and edits the *Near East Report,* a biweekly newsletter circulated to public officials, contributors, and subscribers.

AMERICAN JEWISH COMMITTEE. Jewish organization in the United States, organized in 1906. Its aims in the 1960s were to prevent the infraction of the civil and religious rights of Jews in any part of the world, to promote Jewish integration on the basis of full participation in American life and retention of Jewish identity, and to combat prejudice by scientific techniques aimed at strengthening the forces of democracy and instilling understanding and cooperation among all racial and religious groups. Originally formed as a limited body with three classes of individual members, formally representing Jewish communities and national organizations but largely chosen by the committee itself, it began in 1945 to broaden its organizational base by establishing chapters. By the end of 1964 it had units in 60 cities with a total membership of about 28,000. However, the authority to make decisions regarding national policy and action remained, as before, exclusively in the hands of the Executive Committee.

The American Jewish Committee rendered significant aid to Jewish communities the world over. In the United States, in addition to being on guard against infringement of the rights of Jews as full-fledged citizens, it supported Jewish educational and cultural efforts and played a leading role in the rise and development of Jewish philanthropic and social services. It was especially active in the fight for free immigration to the United States. Its most notable achievements included the abrogation, in 1911, of the American trade treaty with Tsarist Russia because of the discrimination practiced by the latter against Jewish citizens of the United States; the founding of the American Jewish Relief Committee, forerunner of the *American Jewish Joint Distribution Committee; countermeasures against the anti-Semitic propaganda of Henry Ford in the 1920s which resulted in an apology and retraction by Ford; and the publication of scholarly works of Jewish interest. Beginning with the 1930s the committee played a leading role in Jewish community relations and interfaith work.

It was the policy of the organization not to join central Jewish bodies, preferring to "go it alone" and carry on its work in its own way. In the few instances when it reluctantly entered such bodies, it left them at the first opportunity. During World War I it joined the first *American Jewish Congress only after making sure that the congress would deal solely with peace problems as they affected European Jews and with Palestine and would disband on the conclusion of this task. During World War II it withdrew from the *American Jewish Conference on finding itself alone in opposition to the resolution endorsing a Jewish Commonwealth in Palestine. In 1952 it withdrew from the National Community Relations Advisory Council (NCRAC). Until 1967 the committee was the only major Jewish organization not participating in the *Conference of Presidents of Major American Jewish Organizations. Since the crisis of May–June, 1967, preceding the *Six-day War, it has participated in the affairs of the conference on a "cooperating" basis.

Although the committee has never fully accepted the concept of Jewish peoplehood, it has extended its activities among Jewish communities outside the United States in recent years. In 1964 it had offices in Tel Aviv, Paris, and Buenos Aires and lay committees in a number of other foreign cities.

Although not Zionist in its philosophy, the committee adopted at its annual meeting in 1918 a resolution receiving the *Balfour Declaration "with profound appreciation." It went on record that it was "not unmindful that there are Jews everywhere who, moved by traditional sentiment, yearn for a home in the Holy Land for the Jewish people," declaring its "whole-hearted sympathy with this hope." The committee joined with other Jewish organizations in urging Pres. Woodrow *Wilson to secure the endorsement of the Balfour Declaration by the Paris Peace Conference.

During the period of the British *Mandate for Palestine the committee supported the efforts of the *Yishuv (Jewish population of Palestine) without subscribing to the principle of a Jewish State. In response to Chaim *Weizmann's invitation, the committee helped to bring into being the extended *Jewish Agency in order to induce Zionists and non-Zionists to cooperate in upbuilding the Jewish National Home. It effectively supported Zionist resistance to the restrictions imposed on Jewish *immigration by the White Papers of 1930 and 1939 (see PASSFIELD WHITE PAPER; WHITE PAPER OF 1939). In January, 1943, the committee adopted a resolution calling for the abrogation of the White Paper of 1939 and urging continued immigration to and settlement in Palestine under an international trusteeship that was to be replaced "within a reasonable period of years by a self-governing commonwealth." In April, 1946, it urged the admission to Palestine of 100,000 refugees as recommended by the *Anglo-American Committee of Inquiry. The committee exerted its influence on the government of the United States and in the United Nations on behalf of acceptance of the Palestine *partition proposal. Ever since the establishment of the State it has rendered constant and valuable assistance to Israel.

Among those instrumental in founding the American Jewish Committee were Cyrus *Adler, Adolf Lewisohn, Julian W. *Mack, Judah L. *Magnes, Louis *Marshall, Julius Rosenwald, Jacob H. *Schiff, Oscar S. *Straus, Cyrus L. *Sulzberger, and Mayer Sulzberger. The following men have served as presidents of the committee: Mayer Sulzberger (1906–12), Louis Marshall (1912–29), Cyrus Adler (1929–40), Sol. M. Stroock (1941), Maurice Wertheim (1941–43), Joseph M. Proskauer (1943–49), Jacob *Blaustein (1949–54), Irving M. Engel (1954–59), Herbert B. Ehrmann (1959–61), Frederick F. Greenman (1961), Louis Caplan (1961–62). A. M. Sonnabend (1962–64), Morris B. Abram (1964–68), Arthur J. Goldberg (1968–69), and Philip E. Hoffman (1969–   ).

The American Jewish Committee publishes (in conjunction with the Jewish Publication Society of America) the *American Jewish Year Book* and *Commentary*, a monthly magazine.

C. B. SHERMAN

AMERICAN JEWISH CONFERENCE. Representative body organized at the height of World War II by American Jewish citizens of every shade of opinion and affiliation for the purpose of formulating and carrying out an action program to meet the problem that would confront the Jewish people in the postwar period in Europe and Palestine.

Responding to the invitation of Henry *Monsky, national president of *B'nai B'rith, representatives of 32 national organizations, with an aggregate membership of 1,000,000, held a preparatory meeting in Pittsburgh, Pa., on Jan. 23–24, 1943. They convened the conference on Aug. 29, 1943, at the Waldorf-Astoria Hotel in New York. The 502 delegates included 123 who represented 64 national membership organizations and 379 delegates who were elected by secret ballot, in a system of proportional representation, at special electoral conferences in 77 cities and 59 regions. The conference spoke for 2,250,000 American Jews.

On the eve of the conference, black headlines reported the holocaust of Europe's Jews and the organization broadened its agenda to include an urgent appeal to democratic nations to rescue those who might still be saved.

The question of the future status of Palestine and of the Jewish National Home became the focus of the attention at the conference and the major controversial issue. The Zionists were committed to the *Biltmore Program calling for the establishment of a Jewish Commonwealth in Palestine. The delegates of the *American Jewish Committee, the National Council of Jewish Women, and the Jewish Labor Committee sought to avoid the adoption of the Biltmore Program and urged that, for the sake of unity, a resolution calling for free *immigration and settlement in Palestine be adopted. A number of Zionist leaders appeared to favor such a compromise. It was at this juncture that Abba Hillel *Silver made an impassioned plea on behalf of a Jewish Commonwealth, which changed the climate of the conference and led to the adoption of a pro-Commonwealth resolution, carried by all, with only 4 negative votes and with 19 delegates representing the National Council of Jewish Women and the Jewish Labor Committee abstaining. The American Jewish Committee withdrew from the conference. Subsequently, in 1944, the Jewish Labor Committee withdrew for organizational reasons.

The conference elected an Interim Committee, headed by three cochairmen, Monsky, Israel *Goldstein, and Stephen S. *Wise, to implement its resolutions. Louis *Lipsky was chairman of the Executive Committee. The Interim Committee created three working commissions: one on rescue, headed by Rabbi Irving *Miller and Herman Shulman; one on postwar problems, headed by Rabbi Maurice Eisendrath; and one on Palestine, headed by Abba Hillel Silver. The commissions were serviced by conference staff personnel (I. L. Kenen, executive director; Meir *Grossman, director of overseas relations; and Dr. Alexander Kohanski, director of research).

Between 1943 and 1947 the American Jewish Conference sought to win the support of the United States government and public opinion for its program. It maintained offices in New York and Washington. It sponsored mass meetings and demonstrations, adopted policy statements, issued publications, and submitted testimony to Congress. It sent delegations to all international conferences.

In 1945 the U.S. Department of State selected the American Jewish Conference and the American Jewish Committee to serve among the 42 national organizations designated as consultants to the United States delegation to the UN Conference on International Organization at San Francisco. The American Jewish Conference proposed and obtained the inclusion of Article 80 of the United Nations Charter, which was designed to safeguard Jewish rights in Palestine if the United Nations adopted a trusteeship there. It also offered testimony to the *Anglo-American Committee of Inquiry in 1946 and to the *United Nations Special Committee on Palestine (UNSCOP) in 1947.

The conference always tried to unify American Jewry and to establish a united front with Jewish organizations in other countries. It cooperated with the *World Jewish Congress and the *Board of Deputies of British Jews in submitting proposals for an international bill of rights and for the restoration of rights and status for the Jews of Europe. The conference played a leading role in uniting 11 international and national Jewish organizations in the submission of proposals for the peace treaties at the Paris Peace Conference in 1946.

In 1947 the conference joined with the Board of Deputies of British Jews and the South African Jewish Board of Deputies to create the Coordinating Board of Jewish Organizations, which served as a consultant to the Economic and Social Council of the United Nations.

The role of the American Jewish Conference as a unifying instrument raised expectations that it might become a permanent organization, speaking for American Jewry and dealing with domestic as well as overseas problems. This issue divided the conference in stormy debates at its national conventions in Pittsburgh in 1944 and Cleveland in 1946, and at its final session in Chicago, which opened on Nov. 29, 1947, on the very day the UN General Assembly recommended the *partition of Palestine and the establishment of a Jewish State. The conference had won its objective, but this success removed its major reason for existence. Early in 1949, after major constituents had registered their opposition to plans for a permanent body, the conference voted to dissolve.

I. L. KENEN

AMERICAN JEWISH CONGRESS. American Jewish organization, founded in 1922. According to the formulation of its program in the 1960s, it "seeks to eliminate all forms of racial and religious bigotry; to advance civil liberties, and defend religious freedom and separation of church and state; to pro-

American Jewish Congress House, New York.

mote the creative survival of the Jewish people; to help Israel develop in peace, freedom and security."

Shortly after the beginning of World War I a movement developed for a democratically elected Jewish Congress to express the will of the Jewish community on Jewish aspirations for Palestine and on demands for according internationally guaranteed minority rights to the Jewish people in Eastern Europe. After two years of preparatory work a preliminary conference was held in Philadelphia in March, 1916. It adopted a program for convening a congress that would labor "for the attainment of full rights for Jews in all lands, for national rights wherever such are recognized, and for the furtherance of Jewish interests in Palestine." Louis D. *Brandeis was chosen as chairman of the organizing committee.

The congress, which met in Philadelphia on Dec. 15, 1918, was the most significant gathering in the history of Jews in the United States. Of the 400 delegates, 100 were named by the leading national organizations; the rest were chosen in popular elections in which 335,000 votes were cast. The congress elected Julian W. *Mack president; Louis *Marshall, Henrietta *Szold, Adolf Kraus, and Harry *Friedenwald vice-presidents; and Jacob H. *Schiff treasurer. Three important decisions were taken: (1) to send a delegation to Europe to cooperate with the representatives of Jews of other lands for the recognition of Jewish rights by the Paris Peace Conference; (2) to cooperate specifically with the *World Zionist Organization "to the end that the Peace Conference might recognize the aspirations and historic claims of the Jewish people in regard to Palestine" as set forth in the *Balfour Declaration; and (3) to secure national rights for the Jews in Eastern Europe. A delegation of 10, elected to represent the congress at the peace conference and composed of both Zionists and non-Zionists, was instrumental in securing recognition for Jewish rights in Palestine as well as for Jewish minority rights in the "new or enlarged states" of Eastern Europe (see COMITÉ DES DÉLÉGATIONS JUIVES). On its return from Paris the delegation presented a report to a second session of the congress, held on May 31, 1920. Thereafter the congress adjourned sine die.

In June, 1922, the Zionist groups and their allies, the initiators of the Jewish Congress, assembled to organize the American Jewish Congress as a permanent body. The new organization did not limit its sphere of activity to the safeguarding of the rights of Jews in other countries but included action on the American Jewish scene, resolving "to deal with all matters relating to and affecting specific Jewish interests."

During the 1930s and 1940s, the American Jewish Congress was the leading force in the protest movement against Nazi atrocities in Europe and in combating rising *anti-Semitism in the United States. Since its leaders were also leaders in the Zionist movement, it took an unequivocally Zionist position on the Palestine problem. Much of its attention was devoted to efforts to bring about democratic community organization and unity. It played a major part in organizing the *American Jewish Conference, and the delegates of its bloc voted solidly for the resolution in favor of a Jewish Commonwealth. In the field of community relations, it pioneered social action and legislation as the means for extending civil rights and civil liberties.

For nearly two decades the American Jewish Congress functioned as a central body, with affiliated Jewish organizations constituting its units. In 1938 it revised its structure to include individual members, who soon became the dominating factor within the organization, making the position of the affiliated

organizations untenable. In time these organizations withdrew from the congress and formed an American section of the *World Jewish Congress, of which the American Jewish Congress was also a constituent member. The American Jewish Congress concentrated more and more on the fight for civil rights, and although its pro-Israel sentiments remained strong, its commitment to Israel faded perceptibly.

In the 1960s the congress published the *Congress Weekly* and *Judaism,* a quarterly devoted primarily to Jewish theological issues.

C. B. SHERMAN

AMERICAN JEWISH JOINT DISTRIBUTION COMMITTEE. American Jewish overseas relief organization. The organization had its beginnings in the fall of 1914, when Henry *Morgenthau, then United States Ambassador to Turkey, cabled to Louis *Marshall and Jacob H. *Schiff for $50,000 to save 60,000 Jews in Palestine (then under Turkish rule) from starvation.

On Nov. 27, 1914, two relief organizations—the American Jewish Relief Committee and the (Orthodox) Central Relief Committee—combined under the chairmanship of Felix M. *Warburg to form the Joint Distribution Committee of American Funds for Jewish War Sufferers (JDC). Early in 1915 the People's Relief Committee, representing labor groups, also entered JDC. All during World War I, even after the United States had entered the conflict on the side of the Allies, JDC found channels to send funds raised in America to local relief committees formed in Berlin, Vienna, Moscow, and St. Petersburg.

As the major Jewish agency aiding the uprooted populations of Eastern Europe, JDC found itself faced with tremendous new crises at the end of World War I. Following the war, the Russian Revolution, and the liquidation of the Austro-Hungarian Monarchy, hundreds of thousands of Jews were trying to return to their old homes or to find new ones. In Poland, the Baltic countries, Russia, Czechoslovakia, Romania, and Hungary, Jews were suffering from famine, disease, pogroms, and attacks by roving bandits. Their homes had been destroyed, their economic and social institutions wrecked.

As an interim measure, while a field staff was being organized, JDC distributed funds through public and private agencies already on the scene, such as the American Relief Administration,

Hebrew is taught in a JDC-sponsored village for the aged in Israel. [Israel Information Services]

the YMCA, the Red Cross, and the Near East Relief Commission. Next, between 1919 and 1923, American experts and field workers—doctors, nurses, social workers, child-care experts, administrators, and accountants—were sent abroad. They wore American uniforms for their protection but worked at the risk of their lives. Two of them, Prof. Israel *Friedlaender and Rabbi Bernard Cantor, were murdered and robbed of JDC relief funds while traveling in the Ukraine.

As time went on, JDC became firmly convinced that local committees should take over relief activities and raise the necessary funds. As early as 1924 most of the American workers went home and JDC was making plans for the liquidation of its direct operations.

When it became clear that in large areas of Russia the majority of Jews, who had been traders or artisans, were being deprived of their citizen rights as "nonproductive" elements, JDC empowered its representative, Dr. Joseph A. Rosen, to start an agricultural-settlement experiment with an initial grant of $400,000. Farmers thus settled recovered their citizen rights for themselves and their children. In 1924 the American Jewish Joint Agricultural Corporation (Agro-Joint) was founded; it established new settlements on a large scale, with the full cooperation of Soviet authorities. In order to enlarge the scale of settlement, the American Society for Jewish Farm Settlement in Russia was set up in 1928; it provided funds to Agro-Joint that were obtained from private subscribers and was legally independent of the public fund-raising efforts of JDC. Up until 1934, when the industrialization of the Soviet Union and the granting of equal rights to formerly deprived classes of citizens ended the settlement efforts, Agro-Joint settled some 60,000 to 70,000 persons on the land, mainly in the Crimea and the Ukraine. Other organizations followed suit, and together with the old prerevolutionary settlements, the number of Jews settled on the land was brought to about 250,000. The total investment in the Agro-Joint colonies amounted to $40,000,000, of which $16,000,000 came from America and the rest from Soviet funds. After the onset of the Stalin dictatorship, Agro-Joint had to leave the Soviet Union (1938); many colonists left the settlements because better opportunities beckoned in the cities, and in 1941–42 the Nazis overran the Crimea and most of the Jewish settlers were murdered. After the war an attempt was made by the Soviets to resettle some of the colonies, and in 1966 a few of them were reported to be still partly Jewish.

When the Nazis took over the government of Germany, JDC immediately made funds available to local Jewish organizations and committees for relief purposes. Later, money was supplied by a clearance method which prevented any dollars from entering Germany. The concerted efforts of JDC and the European organizations with which it worked enabled some 85,000 persons to leave Germany between 1933 and 1938, while many more were prepared for emigration by programs of vocational retraining. In European countries, JDC helped to maintain many of the 150,000 refugees who had left Germany, and later Austria and Czechoslovakia, and, wherever possible, helped them to emigrate. In the year following the pogroms of November, 1938, JDC intensified its fund-raising activities. In 1939, after false starts in 1930, 1934, and 1935, JDC and the *United Palestine Appeal joined to form the *United Jewish Appeal, which became the chief fund-raising instrument for both organizations in the United States.

In 1939 JDC obtained permits for the Jewish refugees who sailed from Germany on the S.S. "St. Louis" to enter the Netherlands, Belgium, France, and England. In 1940 it helped establish a Jewish colony in Sosúa, in the Dominican Republic, on a large estate made available by General Trujillo.

JDC also helped support a refugee settlement in Bolivia, which was a haven for several thousand Jews who fled from Germany. In Shanghai, JDC organized a relief program for some 20,000 refugees from Central and Eastern Europe.

Until the United States entered the war, in December, 1941, JDC in Poland, especially in Warsaw, continued to give relief to Jews in ghettos. Although contact with New York was indirect, monies were mostly borrowed locally against a promise of repayment after the war. Even after Hitler had launched his "final solution" to the "Jewish problem," JDC continued this welfare work—until the final stages of extermination.

Working through its European headquarters in Lisbon, JDC helped many thousands to escape from Europe between 1939 and 1944. Thousands of others were maintained in hiding throughout the war. In France, aid was smuggled to Jewish prisoners in the labor battalions. In Yugoslavia, JDC supplies that could not be sent any other way were dropped by parachute. More than $50,000,000 was spent on its various programs during the war.

JDC went into the liberated areas late in 1944 on the heels of the Allied armies. After a slow start, large quantities of supplies were brought to the displaced-persons camps in Central Europe.

After 1945 JDC's aid assumed gigantic proportions, supported by a massive effort of the American Jewish community. Thousands of tons of goods were shipped into Europe, and an army of doctors, nurses, social workers, educators, and administrators—composed of Americans and of the survivors themselves—was mobilized to work in the camps and the communities. After 1947 more than 600,000 men, women, and children were helped to emigrate. Of these, JDC helped over 500,000 go to Israel.

From May 15, 1948, the date of the establishment of the State of Israel, to Dec. 31, 1950, JDC had primary responsibility for aiding Israel-bound migrants. One of the most dramatic of its rescue operations was *Operation Magic Carpet, the airlift which flew 46,000 *Yemenite Jews from Aden to Israel.

In Eastern European countries, JDC worked until it was asked to leave by the Communist governments—in Romania until March, 1949; in Bulgaria until May, 1949; in Czechoslovakia until January, 1950; and in Hungary until early in 1953. Asked to withdraw from Poland in December, 1949, it was invited back in 1957 to help some 20,000 Jews who were repatriated from the Soviet Union, most of whom subsequently went on to Israel.

In 1949 JDC inaugurated its Malben welfare program in Israel to relieve the government and the *Jewish Agency of the burden of caring for the aged, chronically ill, and handicapped among the newcomers pouring into the country. To this end, JDC-Malben established a network of homes for the aged, hospitals, clinics, sheltered workshops, and other installations. Following these emergency measures, in cooperation with the Israeli government and other voluntary agencies in Israel, public facilities were developed together with extramural services such as housekeeping assistance and special housing programs for the aged to enable them to continue to live independently in the community. In 1966 an estimated 85,500 persons benefited from JDC's and Malben's direct or indirect services in Israel: 37,500 from Malben, more than 23,000 from aid to *Yeshivot and cultural and religious programs, and 25,000 from *ORT vocational training programs.

In 1965, from a total Jewish population of some 176,000 in Algeria, Morocco, Tunisia, and Iran, approximately one out of every three persons benefited from JDC services, provided wherever possible through local Jewish organizations such as ORT, *OSE, *Alliance Israélite Universelle, Otzar HaTora, and the Lubavitch schools. JDC stood ready to meet emergencies as they arose, such as the influx of more than 100,000 Algerian Jews into France. In addition, its program included the supplying of food, clothing, shelter, medical aid, child care, cultural assistance, vocational training, economic rehabilitation, and other aid to distressed Jews all over the world.

JDC celebrated its 50th anniversary on Nov. 27, 1964. This "Jewish Red Cross," as it has been called, was a pioneer in the whole modern movement of international voluntary agencies to relieve misery and suffering among the unfortunate. The $810,000,000 it has channeled to the help of the needy and distressed is an impressive sum, not only in terms of the money raised (mostly from American Jewry) but as a measure of JDC's achievements in saving and restoring human lives.

I. R. DICKMAN

AMERICAN JEWISH LEAGUE FOR ISRAEL. American Zionist organization founded in 1957 by a group of prominent members of the opposition in the *Zionist Organization of America (ZOA), including two former presidents of that body. The main reason for the disaffection of these dissidents with the ZOA was the latter's link with the General Zionist party in Israel (see GENERAL ZIONISM). The league advocated a policy of non-affiliation and noninterference in Israel's internal affairs. The organization deliberately omitted the word "Zionist" from its name, but immediately after its inception it joined the *World Zionist Organization and later joined the *World Confederation of General Zionists.

Its first president was Ezra Shapiro of Cleveland, who several years later was succeeded by Samuel Daroff of Philadelphia. During the first year of its existence, the organization's membership reached 1,100.

During the first 18 months of its existence, the American Jewish League for Israel published a monthly magazine, *American Israel Review,* edited by Moshe Z. Frank, and continued to issue bulletins of its activities after Frank's resignation. In the first two years of its existence, it sponsored activities such as a Youth Pilgrimage to Israel, seminars, and mass meetings. The pilgrimage was conducted under the auspices of the *Jewish Agency.

M. Z. FRANK

AMERICAN LEAGUE FOR A FREE PALESTINE. *See* BERGSON GROUP.

AMERICAN PALESTINE CAMPAIGN. *See* UNITED PALESTINE APPEAL.

AMERICAN PALESTINE COMMITTEE. Organization of prominent Americans, predominantly non-Jewish in its composition, that aimed to provide moral and political support for the Jewish National Home in Palestine. It was first projected by Emanuel *Neumann, American member of the World Zionist *Executive, late in 1931, after the publication (1930) of the *Passfield White Paper by the British government had marked

a line of retreat from the commitments of the *Balfour Declaration and the *Mandate for Palestine.

The American Palestine Committee was launched publicly at a dinner in Washington on Jan. 17, 1932, that was attended by members of both houses of Congress and other government dignitaries, including Vice President Charles Curtis. The principal speeches were delivered by Felix *Frankfurter, Emanuel Neumann, and Elwood Mead. A letter from Pres. Herbert Hoover, expressing sympathy and approval, was read.

The event was widely noted, but despite this auspicious beginning the committee drifted into an inactive and dormant state when Neumann left for Palestine to assume his duties there. It was reconstituted only about a decade later, when the British *White Paper of 1939 and the impact of World War II on British policy in the Middle East threatened to put an end to Zionist aspirations.

The second and more sustained effort undertaken on Neumann's return to the United States in 1940 was notably successful. Among those who agreed to sponsor and head the revived Palestine Committee were Senators William H. King of Utah, Charles McNary of Oregon, Robert F. Wagner of New York, and Robert A. Taft of Ohio. By the time the reconstituted committee held its initial dinner meeting in 1941, the first of a series of such annual events, its roster included more than two-thirds of the U.S. Senate and hundreds of members of the House of Representatives, as well as many other leaders in public life.

The committee was soon expanded to include such men as Paul Kellogg of *Survey,* William F. Albright of Johns Hopkins University, commentator Raymond Gram Swing, 'soil expert Walter Clay *Lowdermilk, columnist Edgar Ansel Mowrer, essayist and critic Lewis Mumford, and many other molders of public opinion. The membership of the committee grew eventually to 15,000, including governors, members of state legislatures, mayors of cities, and men and women in all walks of life, many of whom lent their services as speakers in a campaign of public education and in other ways.

In Great Britain officials of the Foreign and Colonial Offices were disturbed by these activities and by the resulting impression in Arab circles that the United States was preparing to exert its influence in the anticipated postwar settlement in a pro-Jewish and pro-Zionist direction. On certain occasions the British Embassy in Washington made representations to the Department of State in the hope of restraining such public manifestations of pro-Zionist sentiment. These attempted interventions were unsuccessful.

Christian Council on Palestine. Whereas the American Palestine Committee was largely political in its makeup, additional significant support was forthcoming with the founding of the Christian Council on Palestine as an allied though independent cooperating group. The initial impetus was given late in 1942 by prominent Protestants such as Reinhold Niebuhr, S. Ralph Harlow, Henry A. Atkinson, Daniel A. Poling, and Paul Tillich. Working with them as liaison with the *Emergency Committee for Zionist Affairs were Milton Steinberg and Philip Bernstein, who enjoyed the full cooperation of Stephen S. *Wise and Emanuel Neumann. This group was animated by the conviction that "the destiny of the Jews is a matter of immediate concern to the Christian conscience, the amelioration of their lot a duty that rests upon all who profess Christian principles." The Christian Council emphasized the need to destroy racial and religious discrimination and to demand justice for the Jewish people everywhere, but it considered Zionist

Founders of the American Palestine Committee in January, 1932, included (left to right): Dr. Emanuel Neumann, Justice Harlan F. Stone, U.S. Vice President Charles Curtis, Sen. William H. King, Prof. Felix Frankfurter, Rep. John Q. Tilson, and Rep. Henry T. Rainey. [Zionist Archives]

objectives in Palestine the paramount goal and the basic solution to Jewish national homelessness. The council strove to gain the sympathy of churchmen and clergy by organizing conferences, arranging seminars, and publishing literature. The influence it exerted was out of proportion to its relatively limited membership.

In 1944 the American Palestine Committee sponsored a National Conference on Palestine. The conference, which was held in Washington and attended by leaders from all parts of the country, adopted resolutions with regard to the Jews of Europe and the future of Palestine, demanding maximum Jewish *immigration to Palestine and the reconstitution of the country as a Jewish Commonwealth. The same year members of the American Palestine Committee in both houses of Congress lent their support to the efforts of Abba Hillel *Silver and the American Zionist Emergency Council, which he headed, to have Congress adopt a resolution favoring Zionist aims in Palestine. The resolution was finally adopted late in 1945.

Council leaders were prominently associated with the International Christian Conference for Palestine, held in Washington in November, 1945, and attended by representatives of 30 nations. The conference passed resolutions for free Jewish immigration to Palestine, repeal of the anti-Jewish land purchase laws in the country, and immediate transportation and settlement there of 100,000 Jews from Europe. It also urged the establishment of Palestine as a Jewish State at the earliest possible moment. At this assembly a *World Committee for Palestine was established, with Sir Ellsworth Flavelle of Canada as chairman.

American Christian Palestine Committee. In 1946 the American Palestine Committee and the Christian Council on Palestine were merged under the name American Christian Palestine Committee (ACPC), with Dean Howard LeSourd, of Boston University, and Dr. Carl Hermann Voss as codirectors. Before the establishment of the State of Israel the ACPC concentrated on combating the British White Paper policy, demanding the admission to Palestine of Jewish displaced persons from Europe, and mobilizing Christian public opinion behind its aim to encourage the establishment of the Jewish State.

Once the State of Israel came into being, the organization, concerned with the necessity of spreading democracy throughout the Middle East, adopted as one of its primary aims the presentation and interpretation of Israel's achievements as a democratic force in this underdeveloped area. ACPC study tours to Israel, Jordan, Syria, Lebanon, Egypt, Turkey, and Greece were organized to enable Americans to view at first hand the situation in these countries and the problems confronting the various peoples in the area.

Throughout the years of its existence, the ACPC and its predecessors carried their message to large numbers of people throughout the United States by means of radio, press, lectures, and sermons. From 1950 to 1961 the ACPC published *Land Reborn,* both a house organ and a journal of opinion. The ACPC terminated its program in 1961.

C. H. VOSS

AMERICAN PALESTINE CORPORATION. *See* AMPAL.

AMERICAN PALESTINE JEWISH LEGION. *See* JEWISH LEGION.

AMERICAN RED MOGEN DOVID FOR ISRAEL, INC. American support and supply wing of *Magen David Adom, the Israel national ambulance and first-aid service. Founded in 1941, it is a nationwide agency with chapters and supporting groups in a number of American cities, including Los Angeles, Chicago, Syracuse, Hartford, and Washington. In Greater New York the activities of the agency are carried on by national headquarters supported by the Women's Division. The principal activity is the establishment of first-aid centers for Magen David Adom, equipping them with ambulances, bloodmobiles, and other vitally needed emergency aid supplies, and affording any other support needed to enable Magen David Adom to fulfill its function as Israel's national first-aid and civilian defense agency.

C. W. FEINBERG

AMERICANS FOR PROGRESSIVE ISRAEL-HASHOMER HATZA'IR. Adult arm of *HaShomer HaTza'ir world movement in the United States, constituent organization of the American Zionist Council (*see* EMERGENCY COMMITTEE FOR ZIONIST AFFAIRS). Its Socialist Zionist ideology is reflected in its commitment to the *Kibbutz Artzi Shel HaShomer HaTza'ir (the federation of 75 HaShomer HaTza'ir kibbutzim in Israel) and in its association with the World Union of *Mapam.

A relative latecomer to the American Zionist scene, the Americans for Progressive Israel–HaShomer HaTza'ir (API) was not organized until the post-World War II period. In 1946–47 a group of former members of HaShomer HaTza'ir youth movement, who had served in the Allied armies during World War II, joined with a number of progressive-minded individuals seeking a synthesis between their Socialist world outlook and their Jewish national consciousness to form the Progressive Zionist League–HaShomer HaTza'ir, which quickly established branches in New York, Philadelphia, Baltimore, Detroit, and Los Angeles.

Almost simultaneously, an organization appeared under the name Progressive Palestine Association, whose purpose was to support the agricultural labor settlements in Palestine, to identify with the left-wing forces in the *Histadrut (General Federation of Labor), and to form a liberal wing in American Zionism. This group did not last long. In 1948, however, shortly after the establishment of the State of Israel, some of its leaders—notably Mrs. Irma Lindheim, national president of *Hadassah, and Leon Mohill, a Pittsfield, Mass., businessman active in liberal movements—helped establish Progressive Israel Projects to obtain financial and material support for HaShomer HaTza'ir kibbutzim, particularly for educational and industrial facilities.

In the late 1940s the Progressive Zionist League took an active interest in the development of the American Labor party in New York State and in the presidential bid of Henry A. Wallace on the Progressive party ticket in 1948. Through these activities, the league attracted leading figures in American left-wing and liberal circles whom the establishment of the Jewish State had led to seek identification with some pro-Israel organization.

In 1950 the Progressive Zionist League merged with friends and parents of HaShomer HaTza'ir youth and members of Progressive Israel Projects to form Americans for Progressive Israel. In 1955 the latter was amalgamated with HaShomer HaTza'ir to constitute the present Americans for Progressive Israel–HaShomer HaTza'ir.

In the late 1960s the API was primarily concerned with Jewish-Arab friendship and the expression of Jewish identity through secular means. In September, 1966, the organization was instrumental in the establishment of secular Pioneer Hebrew Schools in various communities in the United States.

In Israel, API supported (1968) the activities of Kibbutz Artzi Shel HaShomer HaTza'ir; Giv'at Haviva, the Kibbutz Institute for Advanced Studies; the Jewish-Arab Friendship Fund, for activities furthering Arab-Jewish rapprochement; the Kibbutz Scholarship Fund, which enables the children of new and needy immigrants to attend kibbutz high schools; and the Kibbutz Education Fund, which provides equipment and supplies for kibbutz high schools, and helps set up libraries in immigrant centers. It also maintains and assists three cultural centers, in Haifa, Ashdod, and Kiryat Sh'mona.

In the United States, API offers a program of educational, social, and cultural activities, sponsors the youth movement HaShomer HaTza'ir, the *HeHalutz training farm Shomria, and the HeHalutz Israel Institute at Hightstown, N.J. In addition, it participates in Zionist and pro-Israel endeavors and in general American Jewish community affairs, including the struggle against neo-Nazism and the other forms of *anti-Semitism. It is an affiliate of the American section of the *World Jewish Congress.

Its publications in 1968 were *Israel Horizons,* a monthly issued in New York (since 1951); *New Outlook,* a Middle East monthly, issued in Israel (since 1957) by Jews and Arabs; and *Yisroel Shtimme,* a Yiddish-language weekly published in Israel. Officers of the organization were Avraham *Schenker, chairman, replaced in 1968 by Moshe Kagan; and Mrs. Valia Hirsch, executive director.

A. SCHENKER

AMERICANS IN ISRAEL. *See* AMERICAN AND CANADIAN JEWS IN ISRAEL.

AMERICAN SOCIETY FOR TECHNION–ISRAEL INSTITUTE OF TECHNOLOGY, INC. *See* TECHNION.

AMERICAN ZION COMMONWEALTH. American Jewish organization for the purchase and development of land in Palestine, founded in 1914 by Bernard *Rosenblatt, then honorary secretary of the Federation of American Zionists (*see* ZIONIST ORGANIZATION OF AMERICA). Incorporated in Palestine in 1924, it provided for individual holdings of about $2\frac{1}{2}$ acres, which was considered sufficient for a single homestead. Each holding represented a single share certificate. Members who intended to engage in farming in Palestine were expected to purchase a minimum of 10 certificates. In an effort to achieve a compromise between private and communal land ownership, it was stipulated that 10 per cent of the land purchased by the American Zion Commonwealth was to be kept as inalienable communal property which might be leased but never sold. Rents and profits accruing from this land went to members. Because membership in the American Zion Commonwealth, unlike membership in the *Ahuza societies, was not restricted to those desiring to settle in Palestine but was open also to those willing to invest in Palestine landholdings, opponents of this concession to private initiative labeled the whole plan "real estate colonization." Close to 10,000 purchases were made by the American Zion Commonwealth.

Bernard Rosenblatt was the first president of the organization; he was succeeded by Solomon J. Weinstein and, later, David Freiberger.

In 1919 the Commonwealth entered into a contract of affiliation with the Zionist Organization of America (ZOA), under which the ZOA became the agent for the sale of American Zion Commonwealth land certificates. Eventually, land bought by the Commonwealth totaled 36,000 acres.

Among the settlements founded on American Zion Commonwealth land were 'Afula, Balfouriya (founded in 1919), and Herzliya (for which land was purchased in 1923 on the recommendation of Arthur *Ruppin). After acquiring the Meshek Company, which represented Jewish investors from Poland, the American Zion Commonwealth bought sufficient shares to gain a controlling interest in the Haifa Bay Land Development Company, a purchase which had been urged on Rosenblatt by Chaim *Weizmann in 1924.

When the Zion Commonwealth ran into financial difficulties owing to British Mandatory policies and the inability of Polish Jewish investors to keep up their payments, the *Keren HaYesod (Palestine Foundation Fund) came to its aid and a greater part of Commonwealth assets passed into national ownership. The Commonwealth held its last annual convention in November, 1931, and soon thereafter liquidated its assets and disbanded.

J. RUBIN

AMERICAN ZIONIST, THE. Monthly published by the *Zionist Organization of America (ZOA). Founded in 1921 under the name the *New Palestine* (which had succeeded the *Maccabean*) as a small weekly bulletin featuring news about Palestine and Zionist activities, it soon broadened its scope to include essays and longer articles on Zionist problems and on various aspects of Jewish life and creativity. In 1941 it became a biweekly. In 1944, while continuing to publish twice a month, it began to appear alternately in two different formats—a monthly *News Reporter Issue* presenting news and designed for the broad membership of the ZOA, and a monthly magazine devoted to articles and features of political, literary, and educational interest; in 1947 the two formats merged. In 1949 the *New Palestine* became a monthly, changing its name in 1951 to the *American Zionist*.

During the many decades of its existence the publication has contributed greatly to the spread of Zionist activities in the United States. Contributors have included noted authors and journalists and world leaders of the Zionist movement.

Editors of the *American Zionist* were Ernest E. Barbarash (1951–52; 1954–61), Marvin Lowenthal (1952–54), and David E. Hirsch (1961–   ).

AMERICAN ZIONIST COMMITTEE FOR PUBLIC AFFAIRS. *See* AMERICAN ISRAEL PUBLIC AFFAIRS COMMITTEE.

AMERICAN ZIONIST COUNCIL. *See* EMERGENCY COMMITTEE FOR ZIONIST AFFAIRS.

AMERICAN ZIONIST EMERGENCY COUNCIL. *See* EMERGENCY COMMITTEE FOR ZIONIST AFFAIRS.

AMERICAN ZIONIST FEDERATION. *See* ZIONIST ORGANIZATION OF AMERICA.

AMERICAN ZIONIST MEDICAL UNIT. During World War I health conditions in Palestine deteriorated alarmingly, with epidemics of typhus and cholera aggravated by a serious shortage of physicians, drugs, and hospital facilities. The *World Zionist Organization sought to relieve the situation by raising medical recruits in European countries, but because of the war such personnel were not available. In the summer of 1916 the World Zionist Organization turned to the Provisional Executive Committee for General Zionist Affairs in the United States, which asked *Hadassah to organize a medical corps. As a result of American diplomatic intervention, Great Britain and France agreed to grant a safe-conduct to the Unit. Germany agreed to extend to it the same recognition secured for the Red Cross by the Geneva Convention. Turkey, however, refused to admit the Unit, and it was only after southern Palestine had been occupied by the British that the necessary permits were obtained and all obstacles removed. Sailing from New York on June 11, 1918, equipped with vehicles, ambulances, and large supplies of drugs, instruments, blankets, linen, and clothes, the Unit arrived in Jaffa on August 17. Its personnel of 44 men and women included physicians, nurses, social workers, and administrators. The Unit was subsequently augmented by local personnel and more Americans.

From August to November, 1918, the Unit grappled primarily with emergency situations. Later it was able to devote itself to the establishment of regular health services. It opened hospitals and dispensaries in Jerusalem, Jaffa, Tiberias, Safed, and Haifa, sent medical aid to different parts of the country, conducted antimalaria campaigns, and engaged in other preventive activities. It also established a school for nurses in Jerusalem.

The budget of the Unit, which reached a considerable sum, was provided by Hadassah, the *Zionist Organization of America, the *American Jewish Joint Distribution Committee, and the Palestine Restoration Fund. E. W. Lewin-Epstein served as chairman, and Miss Alice L. *Seligsberg as vice-chairman, of the Executive Committee in charge of the affairs of the Unit.

T. PRESCHEL

AMERICAN ZIONIST YOUTH COMMISSION. Agency formed in 1940 by *Hadassah and the *Zionist Organization of America (ZOA) to further the growth of their individual youth programs under a single sponsorship. Youth groups sponsored by the commission were *Avukah, *Junior Hadassah, *Masada, and *Young Judaea. The commission also maintained a Program Department, which published material on Israel and Zionism for the general Jewish community, and in particular for camp programs and the training of camp counselors. In 1967 the partnership between Hadassah and the ZOA was dissolved, and the commission ceased to exist.

B. WEISBERG

AMERICAN ZIONIST YOUTH COUNCIL. National representative body of the 10 Zionist youth movements in the United States, with a total membership of 25,000 in 1966. The con-

Medical Unit staff in Jerusalem, 1919. [Zionist Archives]

stituent groups were *B'rit Trumpeldor (Betar), *B'ne 'Akiva, D'ror HeHalutz HaTza'ir (*see* D'ROR), *HaBonim, *HaShomer HaTza'ir, *Junior Hadassah, *Mizrahi HaTza'ir, *Student Zionist Organization, *Masada of the *Zionist Organization of America, and *Young Judaea.

The council, sponsored by the *American Zionist Youth Foundation, represented Zionist youth before the American Zionist Council and the *World Zionist Organization as well as before peer groups. It published a magazine (the *Maccabean*), distributed informational materials, printed program guides, and undertook national projects such as sponsorship of the *Jewish National Fund's Gilboa Youth Forest in Israel.

A major council objective was the servicing of local Zionist youth councils in leading cities around the country. These local councils planned intermovement activities and considered methods of involving the general Jewish community. Israel folk dance festivals, Israel Independence Day celebrations, leadership training institutes, meetings with outstanding Zionists, and sports and social events represented the combined efforts of the youth movements to bring worthwhile programs to the public.

In 1968, as a result of reorganization, 8 Zionist youth movements were represented in the American Zionist Youth Council. Junior Hadassah was absorbed in Young Judaea, and the Student Zionist Organization was replaced by a network of independent Zionist students' groups operating on some 120 campuses and served by the Campus Service Department of the American Zionist Youth Foundation.   T. COMET

AMERICAN ZIONIST YOUTH FOUNDATION. Instrument of the Zionist movement in the United States and Canada for

developing educational programs in Israel and America to give American youth a better understanding of Jewish life, values, and history and to foster a deeper commitment to the creative survival of the Jewish people. Established in 1963, the Foundation carried out the work previously handled by the Youth Departments of the American Zionist Council (*see* EMERGENCY COMMITTEE FOR ZIONIST AFFAIRS) and the *Jewish Agency for Israel–American Section, Inc.

The programs of the Foundation in Israel offered work, study, travel, and leadership-training opportunities for teen-agers, young adults, and students through the Summer Institute in Israel (started in 1948), Summer-in-Kibbutz, Year Workshops, and Sherut La'Am. There were special seminars for professional group workers.

The Foundation strengthened and consolidated the work of the 10 Zionist youth movements on the American scene: *B'rit Trumpeldor (Betar), *B'ne 'Akiva, D'ror HeHalutz HaTza'ir (*see* D'ROR), *HaBonim, *HaShomer HaTza'ir, *Junior Hadassah, *Mizrahi HaTza'ir, *Student Zionist Organization, *Masada of the *Zionist Organization of America, and *Young Judaea. Zionist youth councils on the national and local levels provided a platform for the opinions of Zionist youth and enabled the planning of a variety of intermovement activities. Youth directors and Sh'lihim (emissaries from Israel; *see* SHALIAH) were brought together periodically to deal with programs and problems of mutual concern. In 1968 the Student Zionist Organization, exclusively sponsored by the Foundation, was restructured and Junior Hadassah was absorbed in Young Judaea, leaving a total of 8 Zionist youth organizations affiliated with the Foundation.

The 26 Zionist summer camps in operation in the United States and Canada in 1968 were one of the most vital and successful of all Zionist youth activities. Each year they offered to 6,000 young people Jewish camping that combined Israel-centered cultural programs with sports and social activities. Several camps were conducted completely in *Hebrew, and all included some Hebrew studies. The Foundation serviced these camps through meetings of camp directors and by providing educational and Hebrew study materials, establishing counselor training seminars, advising on camping problems, and organizing intercamp cultural and sports events.

The Foundation also serviced general Jewish youth organizations and institutions through its Israel programs, by supplying information material and speakers, organizing worldwide and regional Jewish youth conferences, and arranging visits of educators and youth workers from Israel. It worked closely with all major Jewish youth organizations, including 'Atid, the B'nai B'rith Youth Organization, the Hillel Foundations, Jewish community centers, the Jewish Welfare Board, the National Federation of Temple Youth, the National Conference of Synagogue Youth, the United Synagogue Youth, Yavneh, and the Young Israel Intercollegiate Council.

The culmination of these efforts was the formation in September, 1966, of the *North American Jewish Youth Council, comprising all 24 national Jewish youth organizations in the United States and Canada. The council, whose activities dealt with the American Jewish community and Israeli and Soviet Jewry, was administered by the Foundation, as was the Association of National Jewish Youth Directors.

The American Zionist Youth Foundation also reached large numbers of youth through such community projects as Salute to Israel parades, Maccabias, Israel folk dance festivals, and training institutes.

T. COMET

AMERICAN ZIONIST YOUTH MOVEMENTS. *See* AMERICAN ZIONIST YOUTH COUNCIL.

'AMI'AD. Village (kibbutz) in eastern Upper Galilee. Founded in 1946 and affiliated with *Ihud HaK'vutzot V'haKibbutzim. Population (1968): 275.

'AMIDAR. *See* SHOSHANAT HA'AMAKIM.

'AMIEL, MOSHE AVIGDOR. *Mizrahi leader and chief rabbi of Tel Aviv (b. Porozovo, Russian Poland, 1882; d. Tel Aviv, 1945). Educated in Yeshivot, he was ordained by leading rabbinical authorities. After serving as rabbi of Švenčionys, Lithuania, and Grajewo, Poland, he became chief rabbi of Antwerp, Belgium, in 1920, and was chief rabbi of Tel Aviv from 1936 to his death. He was an eminent Talmudist and a leading exponent of a new system of Talmudic study (Havana), which opposed the casuistry of pilpulism and sought instead a basic analysis of sources and logic. An early adherent of the Mizrahi movement, he soon became one of its leading personalities and chief ideologists, representing the organization at Zionist Congresses (*see* CONGRESS, ZIONIST).

'Amiel was an eloquent orator and a prolific writer. His literary output ranged from weighty volumes of Halakhic novellas to homiletics, essays on religious philosophy, and dissertations on religious Zionism. Extremely active in the field of Jewish education, he founded the well-known Tahkemoni School and other educational institutions in Antwerp and Yeshivat HaYishuv HeHadash in Tel Aviv.

'AMIKAM. Village (moshav) in Samaria. Founded in 1950 and affiliated with *Herut. Population (1968): 140.

'AMINADAV. Village (moshav) in the Jerusalem Mountains. Founded in 1950 and affiliated with *T'nu'at HaMoshavim. Population (1968): 257.

'AMI 'OZ. Village (moshav) in the northern Negev. Founded in 1957 and affiliated with *T'nu'at HaMoshavim.

'AMIR. Village (kibbutz) in the Hula Valley. Founded in 1939 and affiliated with the *Kibbutz Artzi Shel HaShomer HaTza'ir. Population (1968): 400.

AMIRIM. Village (moshav) of naturalists in eastern Upper Galilee. Founded in 1950 and affiliated with *T'nu'at HaMoshavim. Population (1968): 130.

'AMKA. Village (moshav) in western Galilee. Founded in 1949 by *Yemenite Jews and affiliated with *T'nu'at HaMoshavim. Population (1968): 130.

'AM 'OLAM (Eternal People). Jewish emigration movement from Russia to the United States. Like the *Bilu movement, it arose as a reaction to the Russian pogroms of the early 1880s, which made large segments of Russian Jewry realize that there was no future for them in their native country.

Founded in Odessa in 1881 by Monye Bokal and Moishe Herder, it soon spread to other cities. The name of the movement was derived from Peretz *Smolenskin's essay "'Am 'Olam." Its emblem featured the two tablets of the Law with the Ten Commandments and a plow and carried the legend: "Eternal People, arise from the dust, cast off the scorn of the nations, for it is high time."

The programs of the various groups varied with the background of their members. Their common aim was the rehabilitation of the Jews on the basis of productive work, primarily farming, and the establishment of Jewish colonies in the United States. Some even toyed with the idea of founding a Jewish canton there. People from all walks of life—merchants, tradesmen, workers, students, and Russianized Jewish intellectuals—rallied to the movement. The Russianized Jewish intellectuals, some of whom had been active in the revolutionary movements, stressed collectivism and Socialistic ideals, while the other groups were imbued with strong Jewish national feelings.

In 1881–82 the first 'Am 'Olam groups left Russia for the United States. On their way through Europe they received aid from local Jewish groups and individuals. After their arrival in the United States some groups dissolved while others established "communes" in the New York area. There were short-lived attempts to establish collective agricultural settlements. Bethlehem Judea in South Dakota, founded in 1882, was dissolved in 1885; another colony, New Odessa, in Oregon, founded the same year, existed until 1887.

T. PRESCHEL

AMPAL (American Palestine Corporation). Business corporation organized for the purpose of promoting constructive ties between the United States and Israel through investment, shipping, and export and import transactions, incorporated in the state of New York in February, 1942. The idea of Ampal originated with Abraham Dickenstein, representative in the United States of the Bank HaPo'alim (Workers' Bank) of Tel Aviv, who with a group of American friends had conceived and developed a detailed plan for the establishment of an American corporation to attract and mobilize large-scale investment capital for the development of the basic economy of Palestine.

In October, 1941, Dickenstein presented the idea to the directors of Hevrat Ha'Ovdim, Ltd., and Bank HaPo'alim at a meeting in Tel Aviv and was commissioned to return to the United States to execute the plan without delay. He encountered considerable difficulty in convincing wealthy and influential Jewish businessmen to invest money in a country that was then in real danger of being overrun by the Nazi Afrika Korps.

In February, 1942, Ampal was incorporated with a share capital of $99,000 by a board of directors consisting of Albert K. Epstein and Benjamin R. Harris, of Chicago; Mayer S. Hiken, of Milwaukee; Edmund I. *Kaufmann, of Washington; Charles Brown, of Los Angeles; Dr. Herman Seidel, of Baltimore; and Abraham Dickenstein, Isaac *Hamlin, and Louis *Segal, of New York. Ampal's first loan, in the amount of $110,500 made through the *Jewish National Fund, was used to finance a water pipeline to serve the first four new settlements in the heart of the Negev. Since no Palestinian institution could then sell Palestine currency securities in the United States because of wartime regulations, Ampal undertook to extend its financing against promissory notes of American fund-raising agencies such as the Jewish National Fund and the *Histadrut Campaign negotiating in United States currency. Through its financing activities Ampal acted as resident buyer in the United States and Canada for the large *Histadrut cooperative institutions in Palestine.

Later in World War II, when the threat of a Nazi invasion of Palestine had receded and Palestine was able to begin a limited transition from its wartime economy, Ampal issued new loans for land purchase, agricultural settlement, and housing and loans to agricultural, industrial, and transport cooperatives for the expansion of their economic activities.

During the period of large-scale *'Aliya (immigration) after the war and the subsequent establishment of the State of Israel, Ampal arranged for additional long-time financing of settlement and irrigation and for new industrial, transportation, and agricultural equipment. Loans were increased to supply housing through Shikun, Inc., for mortgage loans on other housing developments, for the irrigation work of the *Mekorot Water Company, for citrus- and vegetable-processing cooperatives, and for the expansion of maritime activities.

In 1968 the Ampal group consisted of the following units: Ampal–American-Israel Corporation (established in 1942), Israel Development Corporation (established in 1954), Israel-American Industrial Development Bank, Ltd. (established in 1956), Israel Securities Corporation (established in 1939), Israel Purchasing Service (established in 1946), Canpal–Canadian-Israel Trading Company, Ltd. (established in 1949), and Ampal–Israel Development Corporation, Ltd. (established in 1965). At the end of 1967 the combined resources of these organizations exceeded $96,000,000.

Ampal granted credits to industry, trade, and development institutions in Israel—including large loans to the Israel *government, Histadrut, the *Jewish Agency, and other public bodies—totaling over $500,000,000. In the 1960s it placed increased emphasis on investment and financing industrial projects. The enterprises it initiated or helped found include the Zim–Israel Shipping Company, Ltd.; Koor Industries; the Lapidoth Israel Petroleum Company, Ltd., the Naphtha Petroleum Corporation, Ltd., and the Delek Company (three companies engaged in prospecting, refining, and marketing oil and gas products); the Israel Sugar Works; the Tri-Continental Pipe Lines; and numerous other undertakings—all of decisive importance in Israel's expanding *economy. Outstanding loans and investments of the Ampal group at the end of 1967 totaled approximately $55,000,000. The group had paid annual dividends and interest to stockholders and debenture holders throughout its existence. Between 1942 and end of 1967, it paid a total of $13,862,672 in dividends. The amount of dividends paid in 1966 was $1,443,425; in 1967 the amount was over $1,500,000. In 1968 Abraham Dickenstein was president and Ralph Wechsler chairman of the board.

C. B. SHERMAN

'AMRIYE. Nomadic Arab tribe in the Haifa area. Population (1968): 98.

ANGLO-AMERICAN COMMITTEE OF INQUIRY. Committee of British and American representatives appointed in 1945 to study the question of Jewish *immigration into Palestine and the future of that country. In the fall of that year special envoy Earl Harrison, an American businessman who had made a personal investigation in Europe, reported to United States Pres. Harry S *Truman that the only solution to the problem of the European Jews surviving the Hitler destruction was emigration to Palestine. Truman thereupon suggested to British Prime Minister Clement Attlee that 100,000 Jews be admitted to Palestine immediately. This suggestion was followed by a proposal from Ernest *Bevin, British Foreign Secretary, that a joint Anglo-American Committee of Inquiry be appointed to look into the whole question. President Truman gave his consent, and the agreement on the establishment of such a committee of inquiry was announced simultaneously in London and Washington on Nov. 13, 1945. Bevin promised that he would implement the Committee's recommendations.

The American Zionist Emergency Council (*see* EMERGENCY COMMITTEE FOR ZIONIST AFFAIRS), cochaired by Abba Hillel *Silver and Stephen S. *Wise, condemned the proposed inquiry, calling it a device whereby the British government might procrastinate and avoid the fulfillment of its pledges. It felt that the United States government, by agreeing to the proposal, had fallen into a carefully prepared trap. The Zionist Inner *Actions Committee, which met in Jerusalem, emphasized its opposition to the British policy but did not adopt any decision on the question of whether to cooperate with the Committee, leaving the matter to the *Jewish Agency Executive. Subsequently, Zionist leaders testified before the Committee. Abba Hillel Silver refused to do so.

The Committee began its hearings in Washington in January, 1946. There were two chairmen, Justice John E. Singleton, representing Great Britain, and Judge Joseph C. Hutcheson, representing the United States. Its American members were James G. *McDonald, who had been League of Nations High Commissioner for Refugees; Bartley C. Crum, a San Francisco lawyer; Frank W. Buxton, editor of the *Boston Herald*; Dr. Frank Aydelotte, director of the Institute for Advanced Study at Princeton; and William Phillips, a career diplomat. The

The Anglo-American Committee of Inquiry on its arrival in Jerusalem. [Zionist Archives]

British members included Richard H. S. *Crossman, M.P., and Maj. Reginald E. Manningham-Buller, M.P., both of whom later became Ministers, in Labor and Conservative Governments respectively.

The full Committee or subgroups of it also held meetings and heard witnesses in London and in various parts of Europe (including the displaced-persons camps in the British, American, and French zones of Germany, where it talked with the DPs). They were not allowed to enter the Russian zone, but they went to Poland, met leading Jews there, and visited the site of the Warsaw ghetto. After leaving Europe, they visited and took testimony in Cairo, Palestine, Damascus, Beirut, Baghdad, Riyadh, and Amman.

In Washington, London, and Jerusalem the Committee heard evidence from Chaim *Weizmann, David *Ben-Gurion, Selig *Brodetsky, Emanuel *Neumann, Stephen S. Wise, Henry *Monsky (for the *American Jewish Conference), Joseph M. Proskauer (for the *American Jewish Committee), Walter C. *Lowdermilk, Albert *Einstein, Martin *Buber, Judah L. *Magnes, Viscount *Samuel (the first British *High Commissioner for Palestine), Chief Rabbis Isaac Halevi *Herzog and Ben-Zion M. H. *'Uziel of Palestine, Rabbi Issar Y. *Unterman of the British *Mizrahi (who later became Chief Rabbi of Israel), Itzhak *Ben Zvi (later President of the State of Israel), and Moshe *Sharett (later Israeli Foreign Minister and Prime Minister), among others, as well as from several representatives

of the Arab states, headed by Emir Feisal, then Crown Prince and Viceroy of Saudi Arabia. The *Jewish Agency submitted to the Committee in Jerusalem a memorandum printed under the title *Zionism and the Arab World.*

The Jewish position, as presented by the great majority of the Jewish witnesses, consisted in the main of demands for the establishment of a Jewish Commonwealth in Palestine (*see* BILTMORE PROGRAM) and the immediate admission of 100,000 Jewish refugees into the country. They included also the transfer of control over immigration from the British Mandatory authorities into the hands of the Jewish Agency and repeal of the restrictions on the sale of land (*see* WHITE PAPER OF 1939).

The Arab demands, expressed by delegates from the Arab states to the United Nations and by representatives of the *Arab League, the *Arab Higher Committee, and other Arab organizations, were for the immediate independence of Palestine, complete cessation of Jewish immigration, and the prohibition of all land sales by Arabs to Jews.

The report of the Committee, which was completed on Apr. 20, 1946, contained the following recommendations: (1) The British and United States governments should make every effort to find new homes for displaced persons. (2) Immigration certificates to Palestine for 100,000 Jewish victims of Nazi and Fascist persecution should be issued immediately. (3) Palestine shall become neither a Jewish nor an Arab State; the form of government ultimately established shall, under international guarantees, fully protect and preserve the interests of Christianity, Islam, and Judaism in the Holy Land; and "Palestine must ultimately become a state which guards the rights and interests of members of the three faiths and accords to the inhabitants, as a whole, the fullest measure of self-government." (4) The government of Palestine shall continue under the mandate pending the execution of a trusteeship agreement under the United Nations. (5) Measures should be taken to bridge the gap between Arab and Jewish standards of living. (6) "Pending the early reference to the United Nations and the execution of a trusteeship agreement, the Mandatory should administer Palestine according to the Mandate." (7) The *Land Transfer Regulations of 1940 should be rescinded and replaced by regulations based on a policy of freedom in the sale, lease, or use of land. (8) Plans for the large-scale agricultural and industrial development of Palestine should be examined, discussed, and carried out with the cooperation of the Jewish Agency and Arab states. (9) The Arab and Jewish educational systems should be reformed and compulsory education introduced. (10) Violence from any side should be resolutely suppressed.

The Jewish Agency, refraining from taking any stand on the report as a whole, welcomed the recommendation to admit immediately 100,000 Jews to Palestine and expressed the hope that this recommendation would be implemented without delay. The Arabs declared the report unacceptable. President Truman expressed gratification with many of its features, especially the recommendation of the immediate admission of 100,000 Jews to Palestine. The subsequent report was not accepted by the British government, which instead referred the entire Palestine problem to the United Nations, and a new committee, the *United Nations Special Committee on Palestine (UNSCOP), was appointed.

J. LEFTWICH AND R. PATAI

ANGLO-ISRAEL ASSOCIATION. Organization, with headquarters in London, established in 1949 to foster understanding between Britain and Israel and to provide opportunities for Jews and non-Jews to acquire a wider knowledge of the Middle East and of the place of Israel there. The Association arranged for an exchange of students through scholarships, organized lectures, discussions, and exhibitions, and issued literature. Primarily an educational and cultural body, it was independent of governmental and political organizations. Its counterpart in Israel was the Israel and British Commonwealth Association.

H. PINNER

ANGLO-ISRAEL CHAMBER OF COMMERCE. First binational chamber of commerce connected with the new State of Israel. It was founded in 1950.

The aims and objects of the Chamber, as outlined by the Memorandum and Articles of Association, were (1) to promote and develop trade, commerce, and shipping between the United Kingdom and Israel; (2) to study the problems entailed in the promotion of trade relations; (3) to deal with all obstacles which might affect or retard the development of trade between the two countries; (4) to act as a committee of arbitration to settle disputes arising out of commercial transactions between persons engaging in trade and commerce between the United Kingdom and Israel; and (5) to study ways and means of increasing and expanding trade between the two countries. In its day-to-day work the Anglo-Israel Chamber of Commerce also served as an information center for firms interested in trade between the two

countries by providing statistical and other economic information on Israel, and it was instrumental in the appointment of agents in Israel for British firms wishing to be represented there and of agents in the United Kingdom for Israeli firms.

From its foundation the Chamber published a monthly, *Trade Journal;* up to 5,000 copies of it were distributed to its members and to other chambers of commerce, the press, trade associations, and so on, many of which looked to the Chamber for factual information concerning Israel.

BARON SIEFF

ANGLO-JEWISH ASSOCIATION. Organization founded by British Jews in 1871 for the purpose of promoting the social, moral, and intellectual advancement of the Jewish people. Throughout its existence, the Anglo-Jewish Association (AJA) has intervened in behalf of persecuted Jewish communities and individuals and has maintained or helped maintain Jewish educational institutions in various countries.

In 1878 the AJA and the *Board of Deputies of British Jews set up a joint political action committee (Conjoint Foreign Committee); it was disbanded in 1946, mainly because of disagreements between the two bodies on Palestine policies. In the 1890s AJA became prominently associated with the projects sponsored by the *Jewish Colonization Association (ICA), after receiving a sizable block of ICA shares as a gift from Baron Maurice de *Hirsch.

For many years AJA opposed the concept of Jewish nationalism. In May, 1917, it published, through the Conjoint Foreign Committee, a letter in the London *Times* protesting against Zionism. Subsequently, however, it supported the British *Mandate for Palestine and even declared its readiness to support the augmented *Jewish Agency. It maintained its opposition to Jewish statehood until 1948; but later a declaration of AJA principles, while reiterating the aim of maintaining "independence of thought and discussion of Jewish matters in the belief that Anglo-Jewry must not be subordinate to any one political movement or international body," went on to speak of the need to give support "to the upbuilding of Israel and to the welfare of our fellow-Jews who have found a home there."

At one time AJA maintained branches not only throughout the British Empire but also in Japan, China, and Iraq. However, since World War II its international scope and activities have been greatly reduced.

The membership of AJA has been small and not truly representative of the Anglo-Jewish community. Among the presidents of the organization were Jacob Waley, Baron de Worms (Lord Pirbright), Sir Julian Goldsmid, Claude G. Montefiore, Osmond G. d'Avigdor-Goldsmid, Leonard Goldsmid Montefiore, Leonard J. *Stein, Ewen Montagu, and Maurice Edelman (Labor member of Parliament and avowed Zionist, elected in 1965).

H. PINNER

ANGLO-PALESTINE BANK LTD. *See* BANK L'UMI L'YISRAEL.

ANGLO-PALESTINE COMPANY. *See* BANK L'UMI L'YISRAEL.

ANILEWICZ, MORDECAI. Commander of the Jewish Fighting Organization of the Warsaw ghetto and leader of the ghetto revolt (b. Warsaw, ca. 1919; d. there, 1943). He studied at the Warsaw Hebrew High School and was a member of *HaShomer HaTza'ir. During World War II he helped organize illegal

Statue of Mordecai Anilewicz at the kibbutz Yad Mord'khai. [Israel Information Services]

Zionist activities in Russian-occupied Poland. Attempting to make his way to Palestine, he was arrested by Soviet guards on the Romanian border. After his release he volunteered to return to German-occupied Poland to help in the illegal activities of HaShomer HaTza'ir. He became the head of HaShomer Ha-Tza'ir in the Warsaw ghetto, organized widespread activities, and left the ghetto illegally to establish contact with Jews in other cities.

Anilewicz was among the organizers of the Jewish Fighting Organization of the Warsaw ghetto (1942), of which he eventually became commander. He led his men in the first brief fights in January, 1943. In the following weeks he organized the remnants of the ghetto for the final battle. On April 19, well-armed German forces moved into the ghetto, where they were met by Jewish resistance. Anilewicz commanded his men from fighting positions and from the organization's headquarters. In his last message, sent to his deputy, Yitzhak Zuckerman, who was then staying outside the Warsaw ghetto, he wrote: "The dream of my life has been fulfilled. I have lived to see Jewish defense in all its greatness and glory." Anilewicz was killed with other leading fighters at the organization's headquarters at Mila 18. Kibbutz Yad Mord'khai was named for him.

I. GUTMAN

ANIMAL LIFE IN ISRAEL. Changes in animal life in Israel brought about by climatic conditions have been demonstrated by excavations carried out in different parts of the country,

such as those in the Carmel caves and in several places along the Jordan Valley. The excavations revealed large mammals, such as elephants and rhinoceroses, long extinct in this part of the world. It appears that even as late as the period of the conquest of Canaan (ca. 1200 B.C.E.), the fauna of the country was comparatively rich. In later periods, however, many species became extinct, and of the numerous wild animals mentioned in the Bible, only a few have survived into the 20th century.

Mammals. Leopards have appeared from time to time in the vicinity of the Syrian and Lebanese borders and along the Jordan Valley and the 'Arava. The same is true of the cheetah (hunting leopard), apparently rarer than the leopard. It is possible that the two last-mentioned big cats, together with caracals and jungle cats, have even increased in numbers since the establishment of the State of Israel, when effective protection of wildlife was begun. The wild Libyan cat, ancestor of all breeds of domestic cats, was also still numerous in the 1960s.

Wolves are still present in the country and are not only encountered occasionally in sparsely populated areas but also attack flocks of sheep and goats almost every winter, sometimes even invading sheds on the outskirts of agricultural settlements. There are several species of foxes, of which the Egyptian fox, which lives in the hills and along the coastal plain, seems the most abundant. Jackals have been more abundant than prior to the establishment of the State, as they are able to find more food in the garbage heaps on the outskirts of the populated areas, and their wailing is often heard even near the large cities.

Of the smaller carnivorous animals, the badger, mongoose, and Oriental polecat seem to be quite abundant, as are the striped hyenas, which, like the jackals, find their food in garbage heaps.

Only a few hoofed wild animals have been saved from extinction. Two species of gazelles still survive, a Mediterranean variety which increased to such an extent in the 1960s that it caused damage to plant nurseries, and a desert variety, which is very rare. The Nubian ibex, which was on the verge of extinction before the establishment of the State of Israel, has increased in numbers and is rather well established in the hills around 'En Gedi.

Hoofed domestic animals include horses, mainly of the Arabian breed, dromedaries (one-humped camels), local breeds of donkeys, mules, and various breeds of cattle, either imported long ago or introduced recently.

The largest rodent in the Near East, the porcupine, is very common in the Mediterranean area, causing damage to vegetable gardens. Israel has harbored up to 80 species of various murines, some of which are still flourishing. The most important one from the human point of view is the golden hamster, domesticated in 1926 at the *Hebrew University of Jerusalem and representing an important contribution of Israel to modern biological and medical research. Of agricultural importance is the vole, and to a lesser degree the jird, which periodically increases in numbers, causing considerable damage to farm crops in valleys and foothills.

There are at least three species of rats, of which one, the sewer rat, is concentrated near the harbors and along the coastal plain. The Alexandrian gray rat occurs more often in hilly regions; the black rat, in the north. In the 1960s squirrels were no longer present. Dormice are very scarce, found primarily in the north in the remnants of primeval forests. Spalax, the blind mole rat, occupies the territory of the European mole, and its

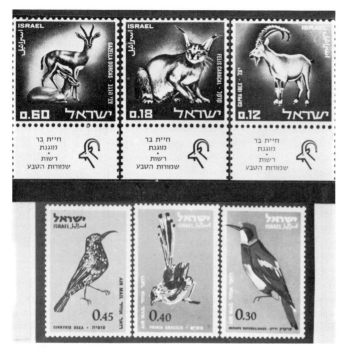

Gazelle, caracal, ibex (top); sunbird, warbler, bee-eater (bottom). [Israel Philatelic Agency in America]

mounds of excavated earth are quite conspicuous, especially in winter. Two species of hedgehogs, the European and the long-eared, are very common and are found even in the center of towns.

Birds. About 350 species of birds are known in Israel, of which approximately 100 are permanent. The others pass through the country during their seasonal migration.

Several species of birds, especially those eating grain, cause some damage to crops and plant nurseries, and attempts are being made to control them, with as yet incomplete results. The house sparrow appears in two species and exists in large numbers all over the country. The chukar partridge in the hills and various larks are conspicuous. Of the birds of prey, the griffon vulture and the black vulture are found sporadically; Egyptian vultures and kites are particularly abundant near garbage heaps. Many kinds of ravens, such as the big black raven, the hooded crow, and the fan-tailed raven, are found in the forests, especially in the hilly regions. Brightly colored Oriental jays are fairly common, frequenting small woods. There are many species of doves: the rock dove (the ancestor of all the domestic doves), the collared dove, and the laughing dove are permanent residents; the turtledove is a regular visitor. Among the owls is the screech owl, whose hoot is often heard near settlements in sparsely populated regions. The barn owl, which seems to be useful in hunting voles and other murines, is quite common in the Mediterranean section of the country. The eagle owl still nests in the crevices of higher hills, hunting mainly small birds as well as hares. White storks are frequently seen in passage to the north. Quails, while less common, are also met in migration. Other small birds frequently seen in Israel are the black-and-white wagtail, shrikes, plovers, and swifts.

Reptiles. Among the venomous snakes, the most common are the Palestine viper found in the Mediterranean region, the *Efa* in the desert, and three species of sand vipers. The black cobra, the most poisonous of the Israeli snakes, is found in the southern

Negev. The most common of the nonpoisonous varieties are the black Syrian snake, reaching a length of almost 10 feet, the plump Montpellier snake, and the vividly colored coin-marked snake.

The most common lizard is the grayish agama. Also very common are geckos and several species belonging to the genus *Lacerta*. The big desert monitor, which reaches a length of 3 feet including the tail, is still common in sandy regions, as is the large spiny-tailed lizard *Uromastix*, found to the south of the Dead Sea.

Chameleons are quite common in the hilly areas. The Mauretanian tortoise is frequently seen in the Mediterranean part of the country, especially on the light soils of the coastal plain. The water terrapin is common in inland waters and fish-ponds, and toads and frogs are quite common during the winter.

Fish. Lake Kinneret abounds in fish, the most common species being the Galilean comb. By the 1960s, however, most fresh-water fish was coming from man-made fish nurseries, where carps were bred. The coastal waters of Israel are poor in fish in comparison with other parts of the Mediterranean. However, the fishing industry is being developed intensively on the Red Sea, where the port of Elat serves as the home base for the fishing fleet.

Insects and Arachnids. Of the invertebrates, the insects and arachnids are most worth mentioning. In the 1960s the known number of insect species in Israel was in excess of 7,000. Desert locusts frequent the country in large swarms, arriving from their breeding grounds in the Sudan and the Arabian Peninsula. The migratory locusts of the species that cause damage in Eastern Europe are also present in Israel but do not appear in flocks.

The scale insects have caused damage to Israel's agriculture, especially to the orange plantations. Research conducted in Israel has resulted in the breeding of several species of insects, mainly wasps, which prey on the scale insects, thus reducing the damage and the need to use toxic substances, which may be harmful to human beings and to the livestock.

There are many species of butterflies, some extremely beautiful, such as the swallowtails and the various Danainae, which are very common in the fields in winter and spring. Moths of various families are abundant, some, such as the *Prodenia* and *Agrotis,* causing much damage to crops. The tiger moth bores into olive and other fruit trees.

The peculiar ecological conditions resulting from a hot, dry climate explain the presence of a wide group of black beetles. Among the vast number of other beetles, *Capnodis* causes severe destruction to plants and especially to fruit trees, and the newly introduced tropical batocera damages fig trees.

Israel's climatic conditions provide food for many wasps and bees, both solitary and social. Of the social form, the large Oriental wasp is very common and in the 1960s presented the main obstacle to the development of beekeeping in semidesert regions. There are many species of ants, of which *Messor barbarus,* the harvesting ant, is the most common. The honey bee in Israel is of the imported Italian race, which is more productive and more easily kept than the native Syrian type. To the smaller parasitic wasps belong those imported beneficial insects which are used for biological control.

By the 1960s flies, long a serious problem in the Middle East, seemed to be under control owing to scientifically designed methods of control and of garbage disposal. In rural areas, however, people working in fields were still suffering from bloodsucking chironomid mosquitoes known by their Arabic name, *barkhash.*

The malaria parasite carried by mosquitoes seems to have been completely eradicated in Israel owing to extensive scientific research that led to the elimination of swamps and breeding places of mosquitoes, along with effective medical treatment in malaria-infested areas. Of the arachnids, there were some 13 species of scorpions. The sting of the common yellow one may be fatal, especially to children. There seemed to be at least 500 species of spiders, of which 3, related to the American black widow, were of major importance.

A. S. SHULOV

ANNUAL CONFERENCE. *See* JAHRESKONFERENZ.

ANTI-SEMITISM. The term "anti-Semitism," like so many other "isms," first appeared in the European vocabulary in the 19th century. Although of recent vintage, it describes a phenomenon as old as the Jewish *Diaspora. In the Hellenistic-Roman world Jews were often regarded as an alien group, guilty of political disloyalty and distasteful exclusiveness. Their religion and customs were held up to ridicule and their economic activities resented. To these familiar anti-Semitic accusations Christianity added some new elements. The church, emerging from the synagogue, laid claim to the sacred writings of Judaism, at the same time charging the Jewish people with the crime of deicide. The anti-Jewish attitudes of the Church Fathers found expression in secular legislation which sought to segregate and humiliate the Jew. These same attitudes became deeply embedded in the consciousness of the medieval Christian, leading ultimately to blood libel accusations and mass attacks on Jews.

Medieval anti-Semitism cannot be ascribed entirely to religious factors. The economic function of the Jew, who was barred from owning land and becoming a member of artisan guilds, made him vulnerable to attacks from both kings and peasants. Jewish loyalties continued to be suspect, especially during times of war and invasion. In Eastern Europe, where the Jews had fled from persecution in the West, a combination of religious, social, and national conflicts created an explosive situation, resulting eventually in the Chmielnicki massacres of the 17th century. Nevertheless, religion was the determining factor in the Christian's attitude toward the Jew. In the words of one expert, "A medieval Christian, if he were asked what was the substance of his hostility to the Jews, would undoubtedly place first the Crucifixion" (James Parkes, *The Conflict of the Church and the Synagogue: A Study in the Origins of Anti-Semitism,* Meridian Books, Cleveland and New York, 1961, p. 69).

The tenets of the European Enlightenment, together with the rise of the secular national state, gradually undermined the medieval attitude toward the Jews. The widespread acceptance of the principle of religious toleration, added to the need of the modern state to destroy the remnants of feudalism, combined to break down the ghetto status of the Jews and allow them to attain full citizenship. Beginning with the French Revolution and continuing throughout the 19th century, Jews were granted political and legal *emancipation in Western and Central Europe. In return, they were expected to renounce their separateness and assimilate into the dominant culture. A new type of Jew appeared, imbued with the spirit of the *Haskala, or Jewish Enlightenment, and convinced that the attainment of emancipation would ensure both political equality and the right to participate freely in the economic and cultural life of Europe. It was also believed that this emancipation, which freed the Jews from their medieval ghettos, would put an end to the centuries-old hatred between Jew and Gentile.

However, 19th-century Europe witnessed the rise of a new anti-Semitic movement, which, while drawing on the medieval heritage, added some new and ominous elements of its own. Among these was the doctrine of racism, which found its classic expression in the writings of Comte Joseph-Arthur de Gobineau and Houston Stewart Chamberlain and was vulgarized for popular consumption in scores of books and pamphlets. Respected scholars "discovered" that the Jews were an inferior race; from this assumption it was easy to advance one step further and to accuse the Jews of gradually poisoning European civilization. Indeed, Semitic "plots" to conquer and subjugate the world were "revealed" in such scurrilous documents as the *Protocols of the Elders of Zion.* Wilhelm Marr, in one of the classic works of the new anti-Semitism entitled *Der Sieg des Judentums über das Germanentum* (The Victory of Judaism over Germanhood, 1879), warned Germany of the "social and political domination" of the Jewish race, while Édouard-Adolphe Drumont described in *La France juive* (Jewish France, 2 vols., 1886) the Jewish "conquest" of France. Racism, in the writings of many, supplemented religion as the basic ingredient of anti-Semitism. This racial element lent to anti-Semitism a degree of finality which its medieval predecessor had lacked. It had always been possible to escape persecution by conversion, but it was clearly impossible to convert from one race to another.

In an age of growing nationalism, Jews were declared to be an alien, hostile people, incapable of assimilation. Their economic activities were especially attacked by anti-Semites, who tended to regard all Jews as potential Rothschilds. Capitalists and conservatives charged Jews with radicalism, while Socialists often denounced them as exploiters. Politicians found in anti-Semitic propaganda a convenient method of marshaling discontent. There arose specifically anti-Semitic parties, such as Karl Lueger's Christian Socialist party in Vienna, whose successes so impressed the young Adolf Hitler.

The impact of the new anti-Semitism on the emancipated Jew was enormous. To those Jews who believed in the rationalism of the Enlightenment, the anti-Semitic agitation appeared to be a terrible throwback to the Dark Ages. Jews were accused of every possible crime, and the sober mustering of evidence to disprove these accusations made no impression. Incredibly, the blood libel and pogrom, symbols of medieval fanaticism, made their reappearance in civilized Europe. As a result, many Jews were forced to admit that their sanguine hopes had been unrealistic and that new solutions would have to be sought. To be sure, Jewish reactions to 19th-century anti-Semitism were varied. Some clung even more strongly to assimilation; others went so far as to convert. Some looked to socialism to end anti-Semitism forever; still others, shaken by their confrontation with anti-Semitism, turned to political Zionism as their own solution to the Jewish question.

The case of Moses *Hess, an assimilated German Jew who had dedicated his life to the amelioration of human society, was typical. Profoundly shocked by the Damascus blood libel accusation of 1840, Hess wrote in his pre-Zionist classic *Rome and Jerusalem:* "As far back as twenty years ago, although I was then far from Judaism, I already had the desire to express my Jewish patriotic feelings in a cry of pain. It was at the time of the Damascus Affair resulting from an absurd charge against the

Jews. . . . It was at that time, while I was in the midst of my socialist endeavors, that the realization came to me anew that I belonged to a slandered people, forsaken by all the world, spread in all lands, but not dead" (English translation by Maurice J. Bloom, New York, 1958, p. 31). The same Damascus affair had a similar effect on another important forerunner of political Zionism, Rabbi Judah S. H. *Alkalai.

In Russia, where Jews were still encumbered by legal restrictions, the pogroms of 1881–82 had a profound impact on them. A generation of educated Russian Jews, previously concerned with the struggle for emancipation, was forced to consider new solutions. Thus Leo *Pinsker, an assimilated Jew active in the Society for the Promotion of Enlightenment among Russian Jews, came to the conclusion that anti-Semitism was "based upon an inherited aberration of the human mind . . ." (Auto-Emancipation, New York, 1935, p. 9). The only remedy for anti-Semitism, in his view, lay in the "creation of a Jewish nationality, of a people living upon its own soil, the auto-emancipation of the Jews" (Ibid., p. 32). The events of 1881–82 had a similar effect on two other prophets of the Jewish national idea, Moshe Leib *Lilienblum and Peretz *Smolenskin. Moreover, it was in 1882, immediately after the pogroms and in their shadow, that the *Bilu group set out from Russia to settle on the land in Palestine.

The most famous confrontation between the assimilated Jew and the new anti-Semitism occurred in Paris, where Herzl, as a correspondent for the Neue Freie Presse, witnessed the Dreyfus trial (see DREYFUS AFFAIR). Herzl had previously been disturbed by anti-Semitism, and the works of the German anti-Semite Karl Eugen Dühring had made an impression on him. He later wrote in his diary: "When did I actually begin to concern myself with the Jewish question? Probably ever since it arose; certainly from the time that I read Dühring's book" (Complete Diaries, New York, 1960, vol. I, p. 4). The Dreyfus affair presented Herzl with final evidence of "the emptiness and futility of all efforts to 'combat anti-Semitism'" and provided the final impetus for his conversion to Zionism (Ibid., p. 6). Similarly, Bernard *Lazare, a French Socialist, was moved by the Dreyfus affair to affiliate himself with Zionism. "I am a Jew," he wrote, "and I know nothing about the Jews. . . . I must learn who I am and why I am hated, and that which I can be" (Job's Dungheap, New York, 1948, p. 44).

Herzl never denied the direct impact of anti-Semitism on his own development: "I was indifferent to my Jewishness; let us say that it was beneath the level of my awareness. But just as anti-Semitism forces the half-hearted, cowardly, and self-seeking Jews into the arms of Christianity, it powerfully forced my Jewishness to the surface" (Complete Diaries, vol. I, p. 109). In the same vein, Max *Nordau declared at the 4th Zionist *Congress: "We have become Zionists because the distress of the Jewish race has appealed to our hearts, because we see with sorrow a steadily increasing misery which will lead to sudden and calamitous catastrophes, and because our earnest and painful investigations show us but one way out of the labyrinth of affliction, and that is the acquisition of a legally assured and guaranteed home for the persecuted Jewish millions" (Max Nordau to His People, New York, 1941, p. 117).

Anti-Semitism not only influenced many Jews to become Zionists but also had an effect on the development of Zionist ideology. Such aspects of the Zionist philosophy as the "negation of the Exile" (Sh'lilat haGola), the contempt for the ghetto Jew, the dislike of the Yiddish language, and the attacks on Jewish economic activities in the Diaspora owed something to anti-Semitic propaganda. Consciously or unconsciously, some Zionists tended to accept certain features of the Jewish stereotype as presented in anti-Semitic literature.

It would be a grave mistake, however, to consider the emergence and evolution of political Zionism as a simple reaction to 19th-century anti-Semitism. For one thing, Zionism drew on the general spirit of the times and, especially, on the modern doctrines of nationalism. More important, Zionist aspirations were firmly rooted in the Jewish past, and in those areas of Europe where Jewish national forms had not been eroded by assimilation Zionism was never far from the surface. Speaking of pre-Herzlian Zionism in White Russia, Chaim *Weizmann noted that "our Jewishness and our Zionism were interchangeable; you could not destroy the second without destroying the first" (Trial and Error, London, 1949, p. 27). The Zionism advocated by *Ahad Ha'Am was concerned not so much with the problem of the Jews as with the problem of the spiritual condition of Judaism. In the last analysis, 19th-century anti-Semitism provided only the stimulus for the emergence of political Zionism. The movement itself, aiming at the physical and spiritual regeneration of the Jewish people on its own soil, quickly assumed a permanent value of its own, irrespective of the existence or nonexistence of anti-Semitism.

During the years following the 1st Zionist Congress (1897), anti-Semitism continued to act as a spur to 'Aliya (*immigration to Palestine) and as a stimulus for embracing Zionism. An example of this continued impact was the *Kishinev pogrom of 1903, during which hundreds of Jews were killed and wounded while the Tsarist police stood by. The pogrom heightened the feeling within the Zionist movement that something must be done immediately and contributed to Herzl's championing of the *East Africa scheme. It played a role in making a Zionist of Vladimir *Jabotinsky, who in 1903 helped organize a self-defense group against the possibility of a pogrom in Odessa. The Kishinev pogrom, along with other Russian pogroms of 1905–06, stimulated a new wave of immigration to Palestine. The influence of anti-Semitic agitation on leading Christian statesmen was also marked, and it played a definite role in the drafting of the *Balfour Declaration. Balfour himself stated in 1905 that the treatment of the Jews "has been a disgrace to Christendom" (L. Stein, The Balfour Declaration, New York, 1961, p. 149). Balfour as well as other statesmen clearly viewed Zionism as an opportunity for Christians to redeem themselves for past behavior.

During the British Mandate period, anti-Semitic excesses continued to spur emigration to Palestine. The *Third 'Aliya was, in part, a reaction to the Ukrainian pogroms of 1919, while the large influx of Polish Jews into Palestine in the 1920s was the result of anti-Jewish economic measures taken in Poland. Similarly, Hitler's anti-Semitic legislation provided the impetus for the first major 'Aliya of German Jews. Within Palestine itself, the mandate period witnessed the growth of Arab hostility to Jewish settlement, a hostility which manifested itself in economic boycotts (see ARAB BOYCOTT OF ISRAEL) and in extended anti-Jewish rioting. These events were not inspired by anti-Semitism in the European sense of the word; rather, they resulted from the Arabs' negative reaction to Jewish inroads in Palestine. Nonetheless, the impact of these anti-Jewish actions was similar to that engendered by European anti-Semitism;

they served to strengthen the resolve of the Jewish community in Palestine, at the same time tightening the bonds between that community and the Diaspora.

The anti-Semitism of Nazi Germany, which culminated in the genocidal holocaust of 6 million Jews in Europe, was a completely new phenomenon in the 2,000-year-old history of anti-Jewish excesses. Here, for the first time, persecution and, finally, the systematic extermination of the entire Jewish people was made an official part of the ideology and program of a state. The Jews were singled out for mass destruction for the simple reason that they were Jews. In Nazi eyes, the mere fact of their Jewishness stamped them with an indelible stigma which could not be removed by conversion to Christianity or by inter-marriage with gentiles and which, according to the Nürnberg laws, attached even to the children and grandchildren of mixed marriages.

The Nazi holocaust had a profound effect on the fortunes of Jewish Palestine and the Zionist movement. Refugees from Nazi terror fled to Palestine during and after World War II, exacerbating relations with the British and contributing to growing Arab opposition. The war experience strengthened Jewish demands for the establishment of a Jewish State, while world opinion, horrified by Nazi extermination policies, tended to favor the founding of such a State. Thus, immediately after the war, the Congress of the United States passed a unanimous resolution demanding that "Palestine shall be opened for free entry for Jews" and calling for "the upbuilding of Palestine as the Jewish national home..." (cited by O. Janowsky, *Foundations of Israel*, Princeton, N.J., 1959, p. 164). The *Anglo-American Committee of Inquiry, charged with investigating the Palestine situation, stressed in its report the persecution of Jews by Nazis and Fascists and urged the immediate admission of these Jews to Palestine. Those members of the United Nations who voted in 1947 for the *partition of Palestine (*see* UNITED NATIONS AND PALESTINE-ISRAEL) were undoubtedly influenced by wartime events. Finally, the Israeli *Declaration of Independence recognized the impact of Nazi persecution when it stated: "The recent holocaust . . . proved anew the need to solve the problem of the homelessness and lack of independence of the Jewish people by means of the re-establishment of the Jewish State."

Events from 1948 to 1968 continued to indicate the close relationship between Zionism and anti-Semitism. The immigration to Israel of *Oriental Jews was partly the result of rising anti-Jewish sentiment in Arab lands. With the rise of anti-Semitism in South America, 'Aliya from that continent increased. Meanwhile, the Soviet Union's refusal to allow emigration kept Russian Jewry from making its contribution to Israel. Just as anti-Semitism, or the lack of it, affected immigration to Israel, so it played a role in internal Israeli politics. The *Eichmann trial and the issue of political and cultural relations with Germany are but two examples.

In a sense, anti-Semitism constituted one aspect of the foreign relations of the Jewish people. As such, it seems safe to conclude that as long as Jews continue to exist, anti-Semitism will never entirely disappear. It will undoubtedly continue to play a role in Jewish history in general and in the history of Israel and the Zionist movement in particular.

E. MENDELSOHN

ANTI-ZIONISM. On the whole, the basic aim of Zionism, the reestablishment of a Jewish State in Palestine, met with favorable response in Jewish and non-Jewish circles alike, as shown by the increasing support received by the Zionist movement, which culminated in the State of Israel in 1948. In the course of its relatively brief history, however, Zionism also encountered opposition from various quarters. This article is concerned with the manifestations of this negative attitude.

Anti-Zionism is both an inner Jewish phenomenon and a non-Jewish trend directed against the Zionist idea in its various manifestations or against Zionism as a political movement, or both. In general it can be stated that anti-Zionism in the Jewish camp was directed primarily against the Zionist idea, whereas non-Jewish anti-Zionism was aimed mainly at the political movement and its achievements.

The anti-Zionism of Orthodox and Reform Jews rejected any definition of Jewry in nonreligious terms. The Orthodox anti-Zionists criticized Zionism for adopting secular policies in order to establish a Jewish Homeland in Palestine instead of relying on Divine Providence. The Reform movement considered Zionism an obstacle to the universal mission of Judaism.

Other anti-Zionist trends within Judaism were opposed either to the concept of a Jewish nation, which would separate the Jews from the social and cultural milieus in which they live and unite them all over the world, or to political aspirations that would free Jews from their minority status and establish a Jewish State.

The emancipatory movement, which feared that Zionism might prejudice the civil rights recently acquired by the Jews, opposed it as did the universalists, who denounced all forms of so-called religious, national, or racial segregation. Many anti-Zionists considered Zionism a mere Jewish counterpart of *anti-Semitism that was bound to wither away as mankind continued its progress. Some Jewish anti-Zionist trends accepted nationalism but rejected the idea of Jewish territorial concentration, while others objected to the idea of concentration in Palestine.

The revival of *Hebrew as a secular language connected with Zionism was considered blasphemy by some Orthodox Jews, a betrayal of Yiddish, the living language of the Jewish masses, by the Yiddishists, and a regression to an obsolete language by modernists.

Common to many versions of anti-Zionism (the religious Orthodox excluded) was the rejection of the Zionist interpretation of Jewish history as a national history centered in Palestine, either in actuality or at least in the dreams and aspirations of the Jewish people.

The social gamut of opposition to Zionism was as wide as the intellectual one. In the beginning, all major Jewish organizations either opposed it or, at best, took a non-Zionist position. The Jewish communities and the Jewish press sympathized with Zionism only to a very limited extent. Individual Jews in high positions in politics and finance were reserved and often hostile toward Zionism. Jewish labor was influenced by general socialism and communism. Intellectuals and the youth were attracted by universal culture and only rarely found universal values in Zionism. The Jewish middle class was often repelled by the allegedly impractical and visionary aspects of Zionism or by the dull economic prospects and need for vocational readjustments in Palestine.

Thus anti-Zionism, while not a coherent movement either ideologically or from the social or organizational point of view, was embraced by individuals and groups following different and often contradictory trends in Jewish life.

Non-Jewish anti-Zionism rested mainly on political or economic considerations and interests and on sympathy for Arab rights and claims in Palestine. A special case was Soviet anti-Zionism, which combined a rigid ideological opposition to Zionism with a somewhat more flexible political attitude.

JEWISH ANTI-ZIONISM

The early stages of Zionism (up to 1897) aroused controversy within the Jewish camp only to a limited extent. The bold affirmation of the Jewish national entity by such men as Peretz *Smolenskin and Eliezer *Ben Yehuda, or the rejection of *assimilation and the pessimistic view of *emancipation of Moshe Leib *Lilienblum and Leo *Pinsker, did not create a great stir in Jewish life, although they occasioned ideological discussions in the Jewish press, for example, the debate between Rabbi Adolf Jellinek of Vienna and Pinsker. There was also a controversy on the direction Jewish emigration should take and on the progressive or reactionary character of a Jewish national concentration from the point of view of enlightenment and social structure. The *Hoveve Zion movement, which grew up in the 1880s, sought to avoid intra-Jewish controversy, to conciliate Orthodox as well as Western Jews, and to achieve a Jewish consensus on the colonization of Palestine.

The ideological affirmation was blurred for the sake of practical work; the definition of the "Jewish problem," the rejection of the "exile status," and the demand of national self-identification were not considered points for immediate controversy. The poignancy of *Ahad Ha'Am's protest against the neglect of national education for the sake of practical work and of his harsh criticism of Western Jewry was attenuated by the lack of political content in his brand of Zionism.

Outspoken and vehement anti-Zionism was evoked by Herzl's call for the 1st Zionist *Congress and the establishment of the *World Zionist Organization. The declaration of the political nature of Jewish nationalism resulted in a sharp reaction. Among the foes of Zionism were a number of modern-minded rabbis. Moritz *Güdemann, chief rabbi of Vienna, at first showed sympathy for, but later denounced, Zionism. While opposing the elimination of "Zion" and "Jerusalem" from the prayer book, he insisted on regarding these references as religious symbols only. Defining Judaism as a religious covenant, he rejected the concept of a Jewish nation, in which he saw an anti-Semitic label that reduced everything to race and nationalism.

The anti-Zionism of the Reform movement in Judaism preceded the emergence of political Zionism by half a century. Since 1840 the Reform doctrines had opposed Jewish nationalism and all national interpretations of Messianic hopes.

On the eve of the 1st Zionist Congress (1897), the Executive Committee of the Association of Rabbis in Germany (comprising different religious trends), later labeled "protest rabbis" by Herzl, made public its anti-Zionist position. Rejecting Zionism on the ground that the aspiration for a Jewish national state in Palestine contradicted the Messianic promises of Judaism, the association proclaimed that Judaism was a faith requiring its adherents to serve with complete devotion the fatherlands in which they lived.

However, the rejection of the idea of a Jewish State did not preclude support of colonization in Palestine. A statement to this effect was released at a time when Herzl still planned to hold the 1st Zionist Congress in Munich. When the Jewish community of Munich objected to having the Congress take place in Munich, Basle was selected instead. Subsequently Ludwig Geiger wrote, in *Die Stimme Der Wahrheit* (1905), that Zionism was as dangerous to the German spirit as social democracy and ultramontanism and that the German Jew who was German in all his national traits had no national ties with Jews outside Germany.

After Herzl's death, opposition to Zionism emerged among some of its former adherents as well. Both *Galut nationalism and *Territorialism attracted affiliated Zionists, and, while taking over some of the Zionist tenets, rejected the Zionist insistence on both geographical concentration and Palestine. When, at the *Helsingfors Conference, Zionism lent its support to the program of Jewish autonomy in the *Diaspora, a certain rapprochement developed between autonomism (*see* AUTONOMY, JEWISH) and Zionism. As for Territorialism, it petered out in its original form after the *Balfour Declaration, only to be revived in 1933.

The *Bund (founded in 1897) bitterly opposed Zionism on both general and specific Jewish grounds (the affirmation of the Diaspora). In this it shared common cause with Folkism, an aspect of Galut nationalism. In 1912 *Agudat Israel was established, and it assumed anti-Zionism as one of its basic principles in 1919.

Other centers of anti-Zionism in the pre-World War I years were the *Kultusgemeinden* (religious communities) of the Jews in Germany, which enjoyed official recognition and controlled Jewish education. In France, the *Alliance Israélite Universelle was initially opposed to Zionism. It withheld cooperation with Zionism in 1903 and rejected it as incompatible with "Ottomanism" in 1910.

Anti-Zionism reached new heights on the eve of World War I. In 1913 a resolution against Zionism was adopted by the Centralverein Deutscher Staatsbürger Jüdischen Glaubens (Central Union of German Citizens of the Jewish Faith), with the stated reason that Zionism ran counter to German national feelings. The same year, 300 prominent leaders of Jewish organizations in Germany blamed Zionism for creating controversy and dissension within the Jewish community itself.

In England, the two principal Jewish organizations, the *Board of Deputies of British Jews and the *Anglo-Jewish Association, were hostile to early Zionism. In May, 1907, the former resolved against cooperation with the Zionist Organization. Both the Orthodox and the Liberals denied the concept of Jewish nationalism inherent in Zionism.

Also among the opponents of Zionism was Dr. Herman Adler, Chief Rabbi of Great Britain. And, on ideological grounds, Zionism was rejected by the prominent Jewish philosopher Hermann Cohen, who flatly denied the existence of such a thing as a Jewish nation.

Many Jewish scholars, intellectuals, and writers denounced Zionism in a variety of terms. Lucien Wolf (1857–1933) found it contrary to the concept of a "holy nation" and "kingdom of priests" and considered it a threat to the safety of Jews everywhere, because it would expose them to the allegation of foreign loyalties. Laurie Magnus (1872–1933) found Zionism a threat to safety and called it "material Messianism." Claude Montefiore (1858–1938) preached the "denationalization of Judaism."

During World War I, when Zionist efforts in Britain were aimed at a pro-Zionist declaration by the British government, anti-Zionism played an active role. Political activities of British Jewry were mainly in the hands of the Conjoint Foreign Committee (of the Board of Deputies and the Anglo-Jewish Association), whose main interest lay in attaining personal security and equal rights for the Jews in Russia and in intervention against anti-Jewish discrimination in other countries. While accepting this obligation of Jewish solidarity, the committee positively rejected the "national postulates of Zionism," the implied "perpetual alienage of the Jews everywhere outside Palestine," and the "unassimilability of the Jews." Negotiation between the Zionists and the Conjoint Foreign Committee on a common moderate formula failed in 1915; the anti-Zionists regarded any demand for "special rights" for the Jews in Palestine as endangering the rights enjoyed by the Jews in any other country.

When, in the summer of 1917, the Conjoint Foreign Committee did not agree that Palestine should become the Jewish National Home, the Board of Deputies, changing its former position, withdrew from the committee. Nevertheless, as a result of the influence of Edwin Montagu, the Jewish anti-Zionist Secretary of State for India, a passage on the Jewish rights in countries other than Palestine was included in the Balfour Declaration. After the issuance of the declaration, opposition to, and even reservations about, pro-Zionist policy diminished in many parts of world Jewry.

The establishment of the enlarged *Jewish Agency in 1929 marked the readiness of certain non-Zionist and anti-Zionist groups, particularly in the United States, to cooperate with the Zionist movement in its practical work without subscribing to its nationalist ideology. Thus the *American Jewish Committee, originally anti-Zionist, subsequently adopted a non-Zionist, and eventually a pro-Zionist, position. In 1918–19 it welcomed the Balfour Declaration but added that the United States is a "home" for American Jewry and Palestine a "haven" for refugees.

Following the creation of the State of Israel, all the Jewish bodies, except *N'ture Karta and the American Council for Judaism, adopted a positive attitude toward the Jewish State. This represented a marked diminution of anti-Zionism in the Jewish camp.

JEWISH ANTI-ZIONISM IN THE UNITED STATES

The exclusion by the Reform movement of the national element from the Jewish religion foreshadowed a future rejection of Zionism. The *Pittsburgh Platform, adopted in 1885, proclaimed the pure, universal nature of the Jewish religion and declared the Exile a blessing. Isaac M. Wise and Kaufmann Kohler, mentors of classic Reform Judaism, repeatedly asserted their views on the universalism of the Jewish religion. They denounced Zionism as abandoning hope for the moral progress of humanity by emphasizing the abiding nature of anti-Semitism. Kohler even went so far as to describe Zionism as a "degeneracy" and "demoralization" of the Jewish people.

As early as 1890 the Reform movement's Central Conference of American Rabbis (CCAR) adopted a resolution opposing the idea of the "Return to Zion." In 1897, the year of the 1st Zionist Congress, the CCAR restated its earlier position by resolving that "we totally disapprove of any attempt for the establishment of a Jewish State. Such attempts show a misunderstanding of Israel's mission which, from the narrow political and national field, has been expanded to the promotion among the whole human race of the broad universalistic religion first proclaimed by the Jewish prophets. We affirm that the object of Judaism is not political nor national but spiritual. . . ." *See also* REFORM JUDAISM AND ZIONISM.

In spite of dissenting voices in their midst, anti-Zionist resolutions were adopted by the CCAR in 1898, 1899, 1906, 1911, 1917, 1918, and 1920. In 1907 pro-Zionist professors were purged from the Hebrew Union College in Cincinnati. At the same time, however, some of the most outstanding Zionist leaders were Reform rabbis, for example, Stephen S. *Wise and Abba Hillel *Silver. In reaction to the Balfour Declaration the CCAR expressed its gratitude to Great Britain for helping to rebuild Palestine for "some Jews" but added that "Israel is not a nation and this is not Geulah [i.e., Redemption]." Following the Balfour Declaration, a petition signed by 299 American Jews who disavowed the declaration on the ground of "dual loyalty" was submitted to the United States government.

In the late 1920s Reform anti-Zionism changed to non-Zionism, and cooperation with the Zionist Organization for the sake of rebuilding Palestine was accepted. This made possible the foundation of the expanded Jewish Agency (1929). After 1933 the settlement of Jewish refugees in Palestine was favored; in 1935 former anti-Zionist resolutions were modified: Zionism became a matter of personal choice, and cooperation in the upbuilding of Palestine from the economic, cultural, and spiritual aspects was affirmed.

In 1937 the *Columbus Platform was substituted for the Pittsburgh Platform. It accepted the concept of "the Jewish people" and considered Palestine no longer merely a haven but a center of Jewish cultural and spiritual life.

However, a far-reaching resolution in favor of a Jewish army, adopted in 1942, caused a rift in the Reform movement and gave birth to the American Council for Judaism, the first and only explicitly anti-Zionist Jewish organization in the United States. Those who seceded from the increasingly pro-Zionist Reform camp were interested in curbing the Zionist wave which swept American Jewry. In April, 1943, Lessing J. Rosenwald, a Reform Jew of Philadelphia, placed his talents and considerable financial resources at the disposal of the council and was elected its president.

The ideology of the American Council for Judaism was founded on a continuation of the universalistic interpretation of Jewish religion characteristic of early classic Reform Judaism. It rejected any notion of "peoplehood" insofar as the Jews are concerned. It insisted on a separation between the "Jewish problem" as it existed in Europe and the Zionist solution of a Jewish State in Palestine. It further assumed that the American "melting pot" implied abandonment of all specific group traits except religious ones and that American democracy demanded total and undivided loyalty. Hence the council's attitude toward the Zionist analysis of the "exile" status of the Jews, and particularly toward the Zionist call for immigration to Israel, was rigidly negative. It denied the existence of any special relationship between Israel and American Jewry and regarded the assumption of any such relationship as an infringement of American citizenship.

The council, whose main activity consisted of anti-Zionist and anti-Israel propaganda, frequently supported the Arab cause vis-à-vis Israel. Estimates of its numerical strength varied from 2,000 to 15,000 members (1964), most of whom belonged to Reform Judaism and to the richer echelons of American Jewish society.

NON-JEWISH ANTI-ZIONISM

This section is confined to a discussion of the opposition to Zionism in various countries of the world, in which, along with pro-Zionist trends, in many cases very strong, there appeared also anti-Zionist manifestations. For a proper perspective, these outcroppings of anti-Zionism should have been placed against the background of the simultaneous pro-Zionist manifestations in the same places and, often, in the same circles. Such a treatment, however, would have resulted in an overlong essay on the larger subject of the varied reactions Zionism evoked in the non-Jewish world. Instead, the present section on non-Jewish anti-Zionism should be read in conjunction with such articles as those dealing with Great Britain and Zionism, the United States and Zionism, and so on, and the general article on the history of Zionism.

British Anti-Zionism. The strong trend in Great Britain favoring the restoration of the Jews to Palestine prepared the ground for a generally positive attitude on the part of British statesmen toward the goals of Zionism. Nevertheless, beginning with the end of World War I, there emerged a number of factors making for anti-Zionism in British circles. Among these were British pledges to the Arabs, the assumption that the Arab population of Palestine had certain preexisting rights, and certain views as to what was essential to British interests in the Middle East. Some felt frustrated by the "dual obligations" Britain had assumed during the war, which were considered mutually incompatible. There were British anti-Zionists who gave frank expression to anti-Zionist convictions; others tried to undermine the policy of the British *Mandate for Palestine by demonstrating its impracticability.

In discussing British anti-Zionism, a distinction must be made between the policy of the British government in London, the conduct of the "men on the spot," and British public opinion. In Great Britain itself there was some opposition to Zionism before 1914; it was alleged that Zionism was a pro-German movement whose settlement work and political activity served to strengthen the German position in the Middle East. The opposition to the issuance of a pro-Zionist declaration during the first stage of the negotiations stressed the impracticability of Zionism and rejected any expansion of British obligations.

Nevertheless, despite some unfriendly utterances by Thomas Edward *Lawrence (Lawrence of Arabia) on the Jewish villages in Palestine, there was no active opposition to the Balfour Declaration on the part of the Arab Bureau of the British government. The first stubborn opposition to Zionism came from Gen. Gilbert Falkingham Clayton, the political officer of Gen. Edmund H. H. *Allenby, on the eve of the Palestine Campaign. There was fear that a pro-Zionist policy would add to Arab discontent and alienate Palestine's population. This feeling grew after the British administration was established in Palestine.

One of the decisive developments in British anti-Zionism took place during the term of the OETA (Occupied Enemy Territory Administration), which ruled Palestine until July, 1920. The officers and officials of the OETA considered Zionism a nuisance both administratively and from the viewpoint of relations with the Arabs. As for the *Zionist Commission, they regarded it as a shadow government encroaching on the sphere of competence reserved for the British authorities.

As a result of these attitudes, the instructions sent by the British government to the Palestine administration to implement the Balfour Declaration were not published in Palestine until 1920, no facilities were given to Jewish *immigration and land settlement, and Jewish influence in the administration was frowned upon. While the Zionists wished to begin practical work for the realization of the National Home, the authorities

clung to the status quo of a military regime in accordance with international law. According to some authorities, British officers even instigated anti-Jewish disturbances to demonstrate Arab opposition. In July, 1920, a civil administration was set up, but some officials in the new government of Palestine persisted in the anti-Zionism of the OETA.

Another manifestation of British anti-Zionism occurred in the Conservative party and in the press during the 1920s. Growing discontent in Palestine, which necessitated an increase in British troops, was considered expensive to the British taxpayer, and in June, 1922, a motion was introduced in the House of Lords rejecting the pro-Zionist form of the mandate on the grounds that it violated the pledges to the Arabs and opposed the wishes of the majority of the people of Palestine. The motion, introduced by Lord Islington and supported by Lord Sydenham, an alleged anti-Semite, was carried; the Government was defeated by a large majority.

Anti-Zionism in Britain gained momentum after the enforced resignation of David *Lloyd George and the Conservative victory in the general elections of 1922. Lord Northcliffe joined the camp of anti-Zionism after his visit to Palestine in February, 1922. The London *Times* and *Daily Mail* began to publish anti-Zionist propaganda, J. M. N. Jeffries, who served as a correspondent in the Middle East, presented the anti-Zionist cause.

Both the *Shaw Commission and the *Hope-Simpson Report were to a considerable extent hostile to Zionism. The *Passfield White Paper was an expression of policy as well as of an attitude toward Zionism. Although the British Labor party was generally sympathetic to Zionism and felt an affinity with the Jewish labor movement, Passfield, whom Christopher Sykes called "the most anti-Zionist Secretary of State with whom Zionists had to deal at that time," somehow came to identify Zionism with capitalism and viewed it as a violation of the rights of the Arab population.

Anti-Zionism as a policy, molded between 1937 and 1939, was influenced by the *Arab riots and the preparations for war. The policy of the *White Paper of 1939 was in line with the intentions of the anti-Zionist elements in the British administration in Palestine.

Ernest *Bevin's anti-Zionism from 1945 to 1948 can be attributed to his rigid stand on what seemed to him British interests in the Middle East and to a touch of anti-Semitism. He believed that a pro-Zionist solution would alienate the Arabs and turn them to Moscow and that British strategic and economic interests required military bases in the Middle East and a united Palestine. *Partition, he thought, would create two nonviable states. Zionist resistance, which he feared would endanger the vital Anglo-American alliance, aggravated Bevin's opposition to Zionism.

British public opinion, however, remained quite favorable to Zionism even after the change in government policy. Only the acts of terrorist Jewish groups during the 1940s alienated it. *See also* GREAT BRITAIN: RELATIONS WITH ZIONISM AND ISRAEL.

American Anti-Zionism. Like other variants of anti-Zionism, American anti-Zionism was a combination of various factors. It was rooted largely in American educational activities in the Arab world, particularly in Syria and Lebanon, and in the resulting feeling of sympathy toward Arab aspirations. It was also nourished by the application to the Arabs in Palestine of the idea of self-determination, proclaimed by Pres. Woodrow *Wilson. At times it was motivated by a negative attitude to the Zionist idea itself. In the main, however, it was based on a certain view of American interests in the Middle East and of the political role Zionism appeared to play in that context, and, to some extent, on anti-Jewish bias in certain State Department circles.

American interest in political Zionism did not arise until World War I, although the Protestant Mission and the circle around the American University in Beirut had not favored an expansion of Jewish influence in Palestine. Immediately prior to World War I, when Standard Oil received a concession from the Ottoman government (1913), American oil interests started to play their role. After the outbreak of the war, when the Jewish settlement was in danger of extinction, humanitarian relief work was generously engaged in, and the anti-Zionism apparent in American prewar policy disappeared. There was, however, a strong anti-Zionist wing among the aides of President Wilson. Nevertheless, the President approved the draft of the Balfour Declaration.

American opposition to Zionism grew during the Paris Peace Conference. Reports sent by William Yale, an American agent in the Middle East, to the U.S. Department of State foresaw a Jewish-Arab conflict in Palestine. Yale reported on the bitterness of the Arabs over Jewish settlement work and on their resentment over what they considered unfulfilled promises made to them. He predicted that the Arabs would appeal to the United States as a disinterested party. The role of Zionism seemed to him that of a pawn in the British Empire, and he regarded Palestine as a buffer state between the French dependencies and Suez.

During the Paris Peace Conference, Secretary of State Robert Lansing and staff members of the American delegation worked to mitigate the pro-Zionist attitude of President Wilson. Zionism was presented as a British tool to dominate Palestine against the will of the Arabs and was described as contrary to the principle of self-determination. American support of Zionism was considered harmful to the American interest of impartiality. Dispatches from the U.S. Consulate in Jerusalem warned of Arab outbursts; opposition to the dismemberment of the Ottoman Empire (the United States not being at war with Turkey) added to the flavor of anti-Zionism.

President Wilson issued a declaration in favor of a Jewish Commonwealth; however, a commission which was supposed to be sent by the peace conference to investigate the wishes of the population in Syria, and which became finally a purely American group, delivered an anti-Zionist report (*see* KING-CRANE REPORT).

After Wilson's administration, American policy, generally isolationist, concentrated on securing American economic rights in Palestine, particularly the protection of oil interests in the Middle East. The United States insisted on an open-door policy in the mandated territories and on being consulted on any change in the political status of Palestine, but it refrained from taking any share of responsibility in the mandate and its pro-Zionist provisions. Anti-Zionism prevailed in the State Department, which insisted on a disentanglement from all obligations toward Zionism. Zionist leaders asking for American support were given no hearing. A joint resolution adopted by both houses of Congress in 1922 in favor of Zionism was treated with anger and contempt by American policy makers (*see* LODGE-FISH RESOLUTION). Congress was accused of arousing the hostility of the Muslim majority in the Middle East and the Catholic Church and of committing the United States to the defense of the Jewish National Home.

During the 1930s the view persisted in the United States administration that the Jewish National Home was not consonant with American interests. Only in 1937, when a change in the political status of Palestine was envisaged, did the United States consider intervention. Two years later, the British White Paper was not objected to by Pres. Franklin D. *Roosevelt.

Anti-Zionism in the United States government manifested itself in a refusal to render any assistance to Zionist endeavors, such as the abolition of the 1939 White Paper, the question of immigration, the organization of Jewish army units, and so on, The wish not to disturb Great Britain during the early stages of World War II, and later the fear of alienating the Arabs, impeded any pro-Zionist move. The State Department recoiled from any declaration in favor of Zionist aims. The oil interests contributed their share in opposing any pro-Zionist policy. A resolution in favor of Zionism introduced in both houses of Congress was opposed by the Departments of War and State in 1944.

During the decisive phase of Zionist action in the United States, between 1945 and 1948, anti-Zionism, too, gained momentum. Oil became a major strategic commodity. Growing tension between the United States and the Soviet Union made the Middle East and its resources a pawn in the cold war. The military establishment considered Palestine a valuable strategic base and preferred that it remain under British control. The military potential of Palestinian Jewry was considered vastly inferior to that of the Arabs, and any clash between the two seemed to make American military intervention inevitable. The suggested partition of Palestine was regarded as a move which would facilitate Soviet penetration of the Middle East. In addition to political considerations, emotional attitudes, too, prevented the development of an American policy not concurred in by Britain. American missionaries persisted in their pro-Arab sympathies, and some circles resented the emergence of Jewish intellectual and spiritual influence in the Middle East. In 1946 the Foreign Mission Conference of North America testified before the *Anglo-American Committee of Inquiry against Zionist aims. Such was the alignment of anti-Zionist forces in the United States on the eve of the establishment of the State of Israel. *See also* UNITED STATES OF AMERICA: RELATIONS WITH ZIONISM AND ISRAEL.

French and Italian Anti-Zionism. During World War I and following it there was considerable anti-Zionist sentiment in French and Italian imperialist circles, which regarded Zionism as a tool of British imperialism and thus opposed to their own interests. Also, the Catholic character of both states created in them an interest in the *holy places (particularly in Jerusalem) and their protection. Nevertheless, France actually approved both the Balfour Declaration and the Mandate for Palestine. *See also* FRANCE: RELATIONS WITH ZIONISM AND ISRAEL; ITALY: RELATIONS WITH ZIONISM AND ISRAEL.

Ottoman Anti-Zionism. In spite of the traditionally friendly attitude of the Ottoman government toward Jewish immigrants, it was hostile to the new Jewish settlement movement from its inception in 1882. The Ottoman authorities feared that mass immigration from Russia and Romania would create a new national problem in their empire. In 1882 the entry of Russian and Romanian Jews into Palestine was forbidden; after a relaxation in the implementation of this prohibition in the late 1880s, the ban was renewed in the summer of 1891.

In 1891 the sale of state-owned lands was forbidden to all Jews, including Ottoman subjects not residing in Palestine. In

1900 the rules were consolidated, and Jewish visitors to Palestine were allowed to stay no more than three months in the country. In 1914 there was a certain legal attenuation of these regulations due to a Turkish attempt to negotiate with the World Zionist Organization.

Anti-Zionism in the Socialist Camp. Zionism met with violent opposition from certain elements within the Socialist movement, which counted many Jews among its leaders. These Socialists criticized Zionism for seeking to preserve the Jewish entity, which was considered in Western Europe a combination of religion and bourgeois ideals. Zionism was sharply attacked by prominent Socialists such as Viktor Adler and Otto Bauer in Austria and Karl Kautsky (a non-Jew) in Germany and by Yuliy Osipovich Martov and other Jewish Mensheviks in Russia.

In Eastern Europe, where, because of the existence of a sizable Jewish working class, it was not possible to identify the Jews with the bourgeoisie, Zionism was charged with seeking to divert the attention of the Jewish workers from their real needs. It was also alleged that Zionism sought to quench the workers' revolutionary zeal and deluded them with romantic visions of a utopian future in backward Palestine.

Following World War I, Zionism gained adherents in Western Socialist circles, which were attracted by the Socialistic and idealistic features of Jewish settlement in Palestine. But even then Socialists such as Kautsky entertained doubts as to the historic claim of the Jews to Palestine, the Zionist alliance with Great Britain, and the ability of a Jewish Palestine to become integrated in the Middle East.

Soviet Anti-Zionism. Soviet opposition to Zionism is based on ideological struggles in Russian political life prior to the Communist Revolution and on political considerations of the Communist world.

Lenin opposed all shades of Jewish nationalism and adopted Georgi Plekhanov's definition of the Bundists as "Zionists afraid of seasickness." To the Communists, Jewish nationalism appeared the expression of parochial segregationalism on a "mystic" and "petit bourgeois" basis and of a cultural particularism as contrasted with proletarian internationalism. When Stalin's ideological work *Marxism and the National Question* (1913) legitimized the existence of nations, the Jews were still considered an exception because they lacked the attributes required by the definition of nationality, namely, a territory, a language, and an economic identity.

After the revolution, communism assumed an outright hostile attitude toward Zionism, which seemed to compete with communism for the allegiance of the Jewish masses by calling for Jewish affiliations beyond barriers of class and country. All this negated Communist ideology. Moreover, Zionist cooperation with Great Britain was regarded as making common cause with imperialism.

Until the middle of 1919 Zionist activity continued in the Soviet Union, with the Zionist Organization adopting a neutral attitude toward Soviet domestic affairs. At that time both the Soviet authorities and the Jewish Communist sections were preoccupied with the liquidation of Jewish communal, welfare, and religious organizations. Zionism was at first shunned because its main interest lay outside the Soviet lands. Particularly active against Zionism was the Yevsektzia (the network of Jewish sections in the Communist party), which at its second conference (June, 1919) adopted a resolution demanding the suppression of all Zionist activities.

The year 1920 marked a definite hardening in the Soviet attitude to Zionism. The Second Congress of the Comintern, which convened that year, resolved that Zionism was a tool of imperialism. In 1921 there followed a certain retreat. The Soviet authorities took pains to explain that their policy was not directed against Zionism as such but against the "bourgeois" elements embracing it. As a proof, the Left *Po'ale Zion was permitted to continue its activities. There was no uniformity in the treatment of *HeHalutz and the Hebrew language; some branches were allowed to go on with their work while others were persecuted. Nevertheless, the general trend was clear. Even when policy vacillated, arrests and persecutions were carried on by local authorities, many of which took orders from the Yevsektzia. However, the attempt to create in 1927 and 1934 an autonomous Jewish area of colonization and Jewish culture in *Birobidzhan carried the implication of a certain concession to Zionism.

In 1928 an end was put to all shades of Zionist activity in the Soviet Union. Even in 1948–49, when the Soviet Union supported the establishment of the State of Israel, Ilya Ehrenburg gave expression to the basic Soviet view by affirming that the Jewish problem can be solved only by general progress. Zionism was declared nationalistic and mystic. *See also* RUSSIA: RELATIONS WITH ZIONISM AND ISRAEL.

AFTER THE ESTABLISHMENT OF THE STATE OF ISRAEL

The establishment of the State of Israel in 1948 forced the anti-Zionists to recast their ideology. The acceptance and support of the new State by most Jews, except extremists on the political left and in the ultra-Orthodox and classic Reform camps, tended to blur the distinction between anti-Zionism and anti-Semitism.

While in some instances maintaining their reservations on issues such as the Israeli border and Arab refugee problems, political opponents of Zionism eventually reconciled themselves to the existence of the State. In the 1960s even such opposing elements as the American Friends of the Middle East confined their criticism of the State to the fact that "Israel [is] supported by tremendous contributions of money and other means from International Zionism" instead of being "nonexpansionist and integrated into Near East Society." (This last charge referred to Israel's acceptance of large-scale immigration.)

The *War of Independence and the emergence of Israel as an independent state gave rise to negative attitudes toward Zionism in certain intellectual circles whose main spokesman, the historian Arnold J. Toynbee, would prefer to have the Jewish people, which he defines as a "fossil" of Syrian civilization, remain a strictly religious community in a pluralistic society.

In the 1960s the most irreconcilable hostility to Zionism and the State of Israel came from the Arab world, which continued to seek the annihilation, or at least mutilation, of the Jewish State. *See also* ARABS AND ZIONISM.

I. KOLATT

'AQABA, GULF OF. *See* ELAT, GULF OF.

'ARA. Arab village in Samaria. Population (1968): 2,050.

'ARABA. Arab townlet in eastern Lower Galilee. Site of an ancient Jewish village called 'Arav, mentioned in the Talmud. Population (1968): 4,970.

ARAB BOYCOTT OF ISRAEL. In contravention of the 1949 *armistice agreements between Israel and the Arab states, the latter have, since that date, maintained an economic boycott of Israel. These measures were part of the general effort of the Arab states to destroy Israel, along with guerrilla raiding, political warfare, attempted interference with Israel's utilization of its water resources, and other hostile acts. Until April, 1950, the boycott barred only Arab businessmen from dealings with Israel. After that date, however, all foreign shippers carrying goods or immigrants to Israel were informed that they would be blacklisted in Arab countries and denied the facilities of Arab ports. By 1955 not only shippers but also firms represented in Israel became subject to boycott by all 13 *Arab League members and 4 Persian Gulf sheikhdoms.

As of the late 1960s, there were 12 reasons for which a firm might be subject to boycott by the Arab states:

1. Maintaining main or branch factories in Israel.
2. Maintaining assembly facilities in Israel.
3. Maintaining general or main offices for Middle East operations in Israel.
4. Permitting Israeli companies the use of the firm name or trademark.
5. Holding shares in Israeli companies.
6. Having "know-how" agreements in Israel.
7. Refusing to answer questionnaires distributed by Arab boycott authorities.
8. Acting as the representative of an Israeli company.
9. Promoting or selling products made in Israel.
10. Belonging to Israeli chambers of commerce in overseas countries.
11. Appointing an Israeli a corporate officer.
12. Selling shares to Israeli citizens.

The mere fact of selling to Israel was not an "offense" under boycott regulations, as long as no sales apparatus was established within the country. Likewise, buying from Israel was tolerated, as long as no attempt was made to reexport Israeli goods or goods containing Israeli materials to the Arab world. The Central Boycott Office in Damascus, Syria, and local boycott offices maintained a blacklist of firms which were boycotted and whose products were forbidden in Arab countries.

Questionnaires requesting information about dealings with Israel were sent to businessmen throughout the world. In addition to requesting information which most businessmen would consider confidential, these questionnaires stipulated that the firm not initiate business with Israel or that, if a relationship already existed, it be discontinued. Such a commitment was a precondition for dealing with Arab countries.

A firm doing business in the Arab world for the first time was required to have a corporate officer sign a notarized affidavit to the effect that it did not and would not violate boycott regulations. Firms shipping to Arab countries for the first time were required to submit a negative certificate of origin attesting that no Israeli materials had been used in the goods to be shipped. In the United States and Western Europe these certificates were usually provided by chambers of commerce as a service to businessmen.

Despite the fact that the boycott regulations and apparatus loomed powerful and intimidating, hundreds of firms throughout the world defied them. Occasionally the boycott regulations were waived by Arab officials when they proved detrimental to the economic self-interest of Arab countries; foreign businessmen could often secure cooperation from the Arabs in circum-venting Arab boycott obstacles. As Israel became increasingly viable economically, the Arab boycott became more and more of a propaganda device, intended to frighten the unknowing businessman but not designed to stand up against the will of more sophisticated business organizations.

Peripheral effects of the boycott and its propaganda were felt in shipping, commercial air transport, the entertainment industry (entertainers with known Zionist sympathies were boycotted in Arab countries), censorship of books and films, and regular tourism (non-Israeli Jews had to conceal their religious affiliation to gain entrance into some Arab countries).

In general, governments of the Western countries gave little protection to businessmen threatened by the Arab boycott, permitting them to make their own choice between dealing with Israel or with the Arabs. Recognizing that the boycott did not hinder economic growth, the Israeli government took no countermeasures against it until 1965, when Israeli import authorities revoked the import licenses of eight foreign firms which had refused to sell to Israel directly because of Arab boycott pressure. Several of these firms reestablished a direct trading relationship almost immediately rather than lose the Israeli market.

Some governments, notably that of Italy, made sure that its chambers of commerce did not issue negative certificates of origin. This action of the Italian chambers of commerce in August, 1963, initially met with resistance in the Arab world but was subsequently acquiesced in.

By far the most significant governmental action was that taken by the United States. On June 30, 1965, Pres. Lyndon B. Johnson approved Public Law 89-63, by which the Export Control Act of 1949 was amended to include antiboycott provisions. According to the law, "it is the policy of the United States to oppose restrictive trade practices or boycotts fostered or imposed by foreign countries against other countries friendly to the United States." American exporters were called on "to refuse to take any action, including the furnishing of information or the signing of agreements, which supports such restrictive practices or boycotts."

Pursuant to the law, the U.S. Department of Commerce issued regulations, effective Oct. 7, 1965, stipulating that firms receiving requests for information, affidavits, or negative certificates of origin must report that fact and their reply to the Department of Commerce within 15 business days from the date of receipt. This meant that the United States government, in addition to requesting American concerns to ignore the boycott, wanted to acquire an idea of the scope and effectiveness of that boycott. Also, the United States Congress in its 1965 session reenacted an amendment to the Foreign Assistance Appropriation Act which called on the administration to withhold aid from countries which discriminate against Americans on the ground of race or religion.

The strong stand taken by the United States had immediate effect in France, Switzerland, the Netherlands, and Denmark, where forceful action was taken against the boycott. In the Arab world active reaction to these measures was minimal.

S. M. LEVINE

ARAB DELEGATIONS. Pressure groups used by the Arabs of Palestine and of neighboring Arab countries from 1919 to 1948 in their struggle against Zionism and the *Yishuv (Jewish population of Palestine). Arab delegations were usually most active at crucial meetings of the various commissions of inquiry.

As a rule their stand was extreme, and their claims remained unchanged. They demanded the establishment of an Arab State encompassing the entire territory of mandated Palestine and the total cessation of all Zionist activities in the country.

The following Arab delegations were active along these lines:

1. *The Syrian Delegation to the Paris Peace Conference (January, 1919).* This delegation differed from the others in its approach. It was headed by Emir *Feisal I, whose attitude toward the Zionist aspirations was positive, in keeping with his agreement with Chaim *Weizmann.

2. *The Syro-Palestinian Arab Delegation to the Paris Peace Conference (February, 1919).* This second delegation to the peace conference, headed by Shukri Ghanem, appeared on Feb. 13, 1919, and made statements that were even more friendly to the Zionist movement than those of Feisal. Ghanem not only welcomed the Jews back to "the southern portion of our country" but suggested an autonomous Palestine, to be joined to Syria in a federation. He said, "If the Jews form a majority there [i.e., in Palestine], they will be the rulers. If they are in the minority, they will be represented in the government in proportion to their numbers."

3. *The Syro-Palestinian Delegation to the League of Nations (1920–21).* It urged the gradual unification of "Greater Syria" and displayed extreme anti-Zionism. The delegation was led by the Syrian leaders Emir Shakib Arslan and Ihsan Jabri.

4. *The Delegation of the Arab Executive to Europe (1921).* This was the first purely Palestinian Arab delegation. Led by Musa Kazim al-Husayni, the chairman of the Arab Executive, it visited various European capitals and participated in the Syro-Palestinian Conference at Geneva; its main task, however, was to present its views to the Colonial Office in London. It had a twofold program: the repudiation of the *Balfour Declaration and the achievement of independence for an Arab Palestine. It rejected the British proposal to set up a *Legislative Council in Palestine. An attempt by the heads of the Zionist movement in London to get in touch with this delegation was of no avail. In spite of the failure to achieve its major aims, the influence of the delegation was considerable: European press and political circles were exposed to its propaganda and the allegations concerning the Yishuv.

5. *The Arab Executive.* After the *Arab riots of 1929, Arab political activity was controlled by the Arab Executive, which appointed delegates to present its stand before the *Shaw Commission. The Commission's conclusions encouraged the Arab leadership to increase its pressure. In March, 1930, prior to the appearance of another British commission, headed by Sir John Hope-Simpson, the Executive sent a six-member delegation to London to conduct direct negotiations with His Majesty's Government. This delegation, in which leaders of the two rival factions—the Husaynis and the Nashashibis—participated, claimed to represent the entire Arab population of Palestine and demanded the cessation of Jewish *immigration and the prohibition of Jewish land purchases. These negotiations laid the foundations for the conclusions of the *Hope-Simpson Report, which were considered the delegation's first concrete achievements. It opened a permanent office in London for propaganda purposes, directed by three delegates who remained there after the departure of the rest: Emir 'Adel Arslan, a Lebanese Druze who later showed Nazi leanings; Jamal al-Husayni, a nephew and political right arm of Hajj Amin *al-Husayni, the mufti of Jerusalem; and 'Izzat Tannous, a Christian Arab doctor, of the Greek Catholic community in Palestine.

6. *The *Arab Higher Committee.* The next phase in the struggle over Palestine was the outbreak of the "revolt" of 1936, which resulted in the appointment of the *Peel Commission in November of that year. The Palestine Arab Higher Committee decided to boycott the Commission and to block the dispatching of any delegation to it, even preventing institutions and private persons from appearing before the Commission. However, in the final week of the Commission's stay in the country, rulers of neighboring Arab countries succeeded in persuading the heads of the Arab Higher Committee to change their attitude and to appear before the Peel Commission. In order to strengthen their claim, a delegation was sent to London, headed by Jamal al-Husayni and 'Izzat Tannous. An additional delegation, composed of Greek Orthodox leaders and headed by Emil Gouri, was sent to the Balkan states to stir up public opinion there and gain support for the Arab claims.

7. *Arab Delegations to the *St. James Conference in London (February–March, 1939).* These delegations took advantage of the international situation on the eve of World War II, and their very composition indicated the conciliatory attitude of the British government toward the Arabs: for the first time, representatives of five Arab states (Egypt, Iraq, Saudi Arabia, Transjordan, and Yemen) were invited to discussions on Palestine. Moreover, the British government allowed members of the Arab Higher Committee, which had been exiled to the Seychelles, to participate in the Palestinian delegation and to confer with Hajj Amin al-Husayni, by then a political refugee in Beirut. The Palestinian delegation was composed solely of Husaynis and their followers, under the leadership of Jamal al-Husayni; the opposition sent a separate delegation under Ragheb Bey Nashashibi. The conference opened on July 2, 1939. During the entire proceedings there was never a joint meeting of all the delegations, because the Palestinian Arabs refused to sit with the *Jewish Agency delegation.

Nevertheless, several meetings did take place between Jewish delegates and delegates from other Arab states, although without concrete results. The *White Paper of 1939, subsequently issued by the British government, met many of the Arab demands by stifling the development of the Yishuv.

8. *Arab Delegations before the *Anglo-American Committee of Inquiry (1945–46).* In the course of its travels, the Anglo-American Committee of Inquiry heard the testimony of 42 Arab representatives. On Jan. 11, 1946, the first Arab delegation testified before the Committee in Washington; its three members, representing the Institute for Arab-American Affairs, attacked the Balfour Declaration and emphasized the right of the Arab people to an independent state in Palestine. A delegation of Arab representatives from Syria, Lebanon, Iraq, and Saudi Arabia appeared before the Committee in London. In Cairo, the Committee heard 'Abd er-Rahman 'Azzam, Secretary-General of the Arab League, Fadel Jamali, Director General of the Iraqi Foreign Office, Habib Bourguiba, a representative from Arab North Africa, and representatives of youth and religious organizations. The Committee also visited Syria, Iraq, Lebanon, Saudi Arabia, and Transjordan. Everywhere, the Arab representatives reiterated their absolute opposition to Zionism, referring to it as a foreign factor in the region. No new arguments were introduced, but two points emerged: (1) The Syrian Orthodox community in the Middle East and the Maronite community had expressed support for the establishment of a Jewish State; they communicated their views through memoranda submitted to the Committee at Beirut on

Mar. 19, 1946, after their delegates had been prevented by the Arab governments from appearing before the Committee. (2) In contradistinction, the governments of Syria and Iraq deemed it necessary to include in their respective delegations two representatives of the Jewish communities of their countries. On Mar. 17, 1946, David Tutah testified in Damascus in the name of the Jewish community of the city, expressing the loyalty of his people to Syria and emphasizing its dissociation from the Zionist movement. In Baghdad, Rabbi Sasson Kaddouri appeared before the Committee, whose members, however, were fully aware that his testimony was far from spontaneous. He evaded direct questions as to his own feelings in regard to Zionism, pleading that he was merely a religious functionary, though he mildly criticized the Arab attitude toward the Jews in Iraq. After Rabbi Kaddouri had finished, Sir John Singleton, the Committee's chairman at Baghdad, felt prompted to point out that his testimony was forced. The Committee also held two sessions in Jerusalem, hearing representatives of the Arab Higher Committee, heads of the Christian communities, and Muslim notables. Spokesmen for the Arab Higher Committee went to great lengths to emphasize the strength of the Arabs in Palestine and to negate the right of the Committee to decide the fate of Palestine.

Arab demands may be summarized under four headings: (1) recognition of complete independence of their country, (2) cessation of all attempts to build a Jewish Homeland in Palestine, (3) termination of the mandate and the setting up of a sovereign Arab State, and (4) immediate cessation of all Jewish immigration and Jewish land purchases.

These were the constant claims of the Arab delegations, with no change, with no attempt to reach a practical solution, and with no prospect of compromise. No new elements of any importance were introduced by the various delegates. The only difference was in tone: the representatives of the Arab Higher Committee were the most extreme in presenting their demands.

9. *At the *United Nations Special Committee on Palestine.* The Arab Higher Committee boycotted the UN Special Committee on Palestine. Thus, only representatives of Arab states were heard, repeating their fierce opposition to a Jewish State.

O. STENDEL

ARAB EDUCATION IN ISRAEL. *See* EDUCATION IN ISRAEL.

ARAB EXECUTIVE. *See* ARABS AND ZIONISM.

ARAB HIGHER COMMITTEE.
Organization founded on Apr. 25, 1936, to coordinate nationalist activities of various factions among Palestine's Arabs. The founding members, all Palestinian Arabs, claimed to constitute the Arab leadership in Palestine. Some of them actually had represented political groups, and the committee supplanted the activity of these groups. The paramount influence in the committee was, from the start, in the hands of the extremist Husayni clan; the chairman was Hajj Amin *al-Husayni, mufti of Jerusalem. The program of the committee resembled, almost to the point of being identical with it, the platform of the political group led by the Husayni clan: Arab rule in Palestine, the end of Jewish *immigration to Palestine, and the prevention of the sale of Arab land to Jews.

The main activities of the committee were propaganda, the organization of demonstrations, and strikes and terrorist acts against Jews and British and Arab moderates. Terrorism against

Arabs was carried out by pressure, threats, and violence intended to press recruits into armed bands, which were meant to execute the policies of the committee. Between waves of terrorism, the committee organized propaganda campaigns, fund raising, and gunrunning in Palestine and abroad, and in 1946 it functioned as the self-appointed representative of Palestine's Arabs before British commissions of inquiry.

In July, 1937, the intensification of Arab terrorism in Palestine caused some of the moderates, chiefly the Nashashibi clan and its allies, to leave the committee, which thus came even more fully under the domination of the Husaynis, and its extremism became even more pronounced. When the British district officer of Nazareth was murdered, the British authorities took drastic steps. On Oct. 1, 1937, the committee was disbanded and outlawed; Amin al-Husayni, its chairman, was removed from the presidency of the Muslim Supreme Council, which was also abolished. Some members of the committee were arrested and others exiled to the Seychelles, but most succeeded in escaping to neighboring countries and later to Europe. Amin al-Husayni himself escaped to Lebanon, then to Iraq and Iran, and later to Germany, where he assisted the Nazis in their propaganda efforts.

Throughout World War II the leaders of the Arab Higher Committee continued their political activities abroad. Late in 1945 and early in 1946 some were allowed to return to Palestine, and the committee was reconstituted in November, 1945. Since Amin al-Husayni was not allowed to return, another leader of the clan, Jamal al-Husayni, became the key personality of the committee. Meanwhile, however, new bodies and organizations had sprung up among Palestine's Arabs, some of which favored fighting the Jews on the economic level. The committee was no longer as powerful as it had been before World War II. Even the backing of the *Arab League, in June, 1946, did not make the committee the unchallenged leader of Palestine's Arabs, who were thus weakened and divided prior to the Arab-Israeli War of 1948, the *War of Independence, after which the committee ceased to exist in all but name.

J. M. LANDAU

ARAB-ISRAELI WAR OF 1948. *See* WAR OF INDEPENDENCE.

ARAB-ISRAELI WAR OF 1967. *See* SIX-DAY WAR OF 1967.

ARAB LEAGUE.
Official organization founded by the heads of government of the Arab states in March, 1945, to promote a union between all independent Arab states. The British, aware of the desire of some Arab leaders and intellectuals for union, encouraged these sentiments. Anthony Eden, then British Foreign Secretary, was particularly active behind the scenes in preparing the ground for the creation of the League. The seven founding members were Egypt, Yemen, Saudi Arabia, Transjordan (later Jordan), Syria, Lebanon, and Iraq. The covenant between these states was a compromise between Pan-Arabism and the particularist tendencies of each individual state. Members agreed to cooperate in certain matters, mainly political, but reserved the right to independent action in any issue. Article 7 of the League's covenant stipulated that every member state was bound only by its own vote.

Soon after its foundation, it became evident that the importance of the Arab League lay in its functioning as a body for the exchange of views, the smoothing over of differences, and concerted action in matters of common interest. As the

Arab League lacked the power to impose sanctions, many decisions were actually the outcome of hard behind-the-scenes bargaining among the member states. On the whole, the more powerful members, chiefly Egypt, wanted wider powers for the League, thus hoping, probably, to increase their influence in the Arab countries via the League; the smaller states, however, strove to obtain safeguards for their sovereignty and freedom of action within the framework of the League. This seemed to hold true even after the number of states had grown to include, in addition to the founders, Morocco, Mauretania, Algeria, Tunisia, Libya, Sudan, and Kuwait. Furthermore, this growth in membership increased the possibilities for a divergence of views; the Maghreb states (Northwest Africa) were less immediately concerned about the Arab-Israeli issue and thus lukewarm in their attitudes.

Through its press releases the Council, the supreme body of the League, succeeded in glossing over differences of opinion between the members on inter-Arab and international issues (or differences of tactics vis-à-vis Israel). One such case was the plan for the internationalization of Jerusalem, supported by some League members but bitterly and consistently opposed by Jordan. A series of agreements attempted to draw the Arab states closer to one another in the military field, but these agreements were not put to use, as in the *Sinai Campaign of 1956. Nor did the Joint Arab Command, founded by the League in January, 1964, to prevent Israel from diverting the Jordan River, move when Israel diverted water. A Palestine Liberation Front, under the orders of the Joint Arab Command, was created early in 1965, but soon thereafter it split and was discouraged by the Jordanian authorities. Its role in the *Six-day War of 1967 was also insignificant. The economic efforts were partly successful in the *Arab boycott of Israel but less so in inter-Arab cooperation. Thus, even concerted Arab action for the diversion of the Jordan River tributaries in Syria, Lebanon, and Jordan made but little progress, owing to differences of opinion and lack of funds from Arab League sources. The Arab League was more successful in the cultural field, assigning personnel and funds for the study of Arab civilization and education as well as for the treatment of technical problems; it convened

Arab League meeting in Cairo, 1947. [Zionist Archives]

inter-Arab conferences and encouraged exchanges of scholars.

The main interests of the Arab League, however, remained in the political arena, where it achieved success in a number of instances. Although the United Nations had not recognized the Arab League as an official regional organization, it approved (in November, 1950) the invitation of a representative of the Arab League as an observer to all meetings of the General Assembly (*see* UNITED NATIONS AND PALESTINE-ISRAEL). The Arab League often coordinated Arab political activity and propaganda at the United Nations and in a number of European and American states. In so doing, it increasingly became the mouthpiece of Egyptian inter-Arab and international policies, both because its headquarters was in Egypt and because its Secretary-General was an Egyptian. This, in turn, resulted in the defection of Tunisia from the League and in the boycotting of many of its sessions by Jordan—so that the League's work was often virtually paralyzed. In addition, its activities were somewhat overshadowed, in the 1960s, by the Arab summit meetings.

J. M. LANDAU

ARAB REFUGEES. Former Arab inhabitants (and their descendants) of those areas of Mandatory Palestine which now constitute the territory of Israel. They fled the country in 1948–49, when, in the wake of the Proclamation of the State of Israel (May 14, 1948), armies of five Arab states invaded Israel's territory. Since then they have lived in Jordan, Syria, Lebanon, and the Gaza Strip. Arab spokesmen contend that the mass flight of Palestinian Arabs was caused by "Zionist terror." In fact, Israel's authorities were eager to prevent the exodus; they ascribe it to the inducement and horror propaganda of the Arab leadership. Within a few years after the Arab refugees left their homes (1949–52), Israel received from the Arab countries a comparable number of Jewish refugees who had fled to escape political, economic, and often physical insecurity (*see* IRAQI JEWS IN ISRAEL; NORTH AFRICAN JEWS IN ISRAEL; YEMENITE JEWS IN ISRAEL). Thus what happened following the Proclamation of Israel's independence was in effect a spontaneous and unplanned population exchange.

The Arabs claim that the original number of refugees was in excess of 800,000. Yet, according to British official figures for the end of 1944, not more than 640,000 Arabs were living in the present area of Israel; the natural increase during the following 40 months (until 1948), estimated at 56,000, would bring the total to 696,000. Not all these Arabs fled; some 142,000 remained, and 35,000 were subsequently permitted to return to Israel to be reunited with their kin. This leaves a maximum of 519,000 refugees. Although United Nations relief organizations reported in July, 1949, that close to 1,000,000 Arab refugees were registered for relief, the accuracy of this figure was challenged two months later by the UN Relief for Palestine Refugees (UNRPR, which preceded UNRWA), whose report stressed that "in many cases, individuals who could not qualify as being *bona fide* refugees are in fact on the relief rolls" (*Assistance to Palestine Refugees,* UNRPR Report for December, 1948–September, 1949). This early, unwarranted padding of the relief rolls resulted in the years that followed in a continued inflation of the figures of alleged refugees, with their children being automatically added to the total, and thus in perpetuating a magnified, distorted picture of the true size of the refugee population. In fact, no actual census of the refugees was ever taken by UNRWA (UN Relief and Works Agency for Palestine

Refugees in the Near East, established in 1949), which has submitted annually the rising figures of Arab refugees it was caring for; the latest figure, for 1965–66, was 1,317,749. The Agency has repeatedly admitted that the refugees under its care, while always registering births, usually conceal deaths. Between 1950 and 1966 a total of 570,785 births and only 112,275 deaths were registered—a unique and utterly unbelievable ratio. As early as 1959, UNRWA's director averred that ration rolls in Jordan alone included 150,000 ineligibles and many persons who had died.

On Dec. 11, 1948, the UN General Assembly passed a 15-paragraph resolution setting up a Palestine Conciliation Commission. Paragraph 12 of the resolution stated that "the refugees wishing to return to their homes and live in peace with their neighbors should be permitted to do so at the earliest practicable date" and instructed the Commission to "facilitate the repatriation, resettlement and economic and social rehabilitation of refugees and payment of compensation." The Arab governments, which had voted against the resolution, have since made the wholesale and unconditional repatriation of the refugees their *sine qua non* prerequisite for any peace negotiations with Israel. This stand has frustrated all the efforts of the Conciliation Commission to achieve a political settlement. In 1949 an attempt was made to solve the problem of Arab refugees by an economic approach, mainly through their integration into the economies of their actual countries of residence. An authoritative Economic Survey Mission advocated substitution of constructive works for philanthropic relief and suggested several limited pilot projects. In 1952 the Assembly allocated a $200,000,000 fund for this purpose. The allocation remained unused because of the Arab governments' refusal to cooperate. The UNRWA Report for 1959–60 admitted that its rehabilitation function, intended to render a substantial number of refugees self-supporting, had failed. Since then the Agency has concentrated on direct relief only. The refugees have gradually found themselves better off with regard to health, education, and nutrition than they had been at home or than were the people in the neighboring Arab countries. For example, as against 1.51 hospital beds per 1,000 refugees, in Egypt there were in the 1960s only 1.25 hospital beds per 1,000 population; among the refugees 78 per cent of the school-age population received education, as against 65 per cent in Egypt.

In the 1960s, UNRWA's inflated relief rolls continued to swell. Promises of rectification remained unfulfilled, since the Arab governments refused to permit any verification among the refugees in their respective territories. It was nevertheless established that, in spite of the official obstacles put in the way of the integration effort, a large-scale de facto integration of refugees was taking place. This is evident even from some Arab sources. A Lebanese daily, *al-Hayat,* writing on this subject on June 25, 1959, said: "Of the 120,000 refugees who entered [Lebanon], not more than 15,000 are still in camps. Taking into account a natural increase of 15,000, we may conclude that 120,000 refugees have been absorbed in Lebanon and her economy." The official government broadcasting service of Jordan stated on Jan. 18, 1961: "We can see, as the years go by, that this [integration] is materializing automatically, because it is unnatural that after 13 years of exile the refugees should continue to live without roots; neither is it natural that they should continue to remain beyond the pale of human society."

The UNRWA Report for 1962 reveals that more than three-fifths of them (61.1 per cent) were living outside camps. The

report for 1959–60 admitted that "hundreds of thousands of refugees have established themselves in the expanding economies of the Arab countries." In July, 1966, U.S. Secretary of State Dean Rusk told the Senate Subcommittee on Refugees and Escapees that "almost half a million refugees have jobs ... living reasonably normal lives" outside the camps and should be removed from UNRWA's relief rolls. Time and economic realities have thus shown themselves powerful factors in the gradual, de facto solution of the Arab refugee problem.

As a result of the *Six-day War of 1967, Israel found itself in possession of some 32,000 square miles of territory formerly controlled by Jordan (the West Bank area), the United Arab Republic (the Gaza Strip and the Sinai area), and Syria (the Gaulan Heights), with an Arab population of more than 1 million which, according to UNRWA statistics, included 628,182 refugees from the 1948 war. A census conducted in August, 1967, by the Israeli Central Bureau of Statistics established that the UNRWA figures were highly inflated. A total of 220,000 Arab refugees were found in the Gaza Strip, as against 317,000 on UNRWA's most recent (May 31, 1967) relief rolls; in the West Bank area, UNRWA's count registered 311,182 refugees, while the Israeli census found 120,000. The total number of refugees in these two areas (there were no refugees in Sinai and the Gaulan Heights) was thus 280,000 smaller than the one appearing on UNRWA's rolls. Almost simultaneously with the Israeli count, UNRWA itself, for the first time in 20 years, completed a ration-card–checking operation, which resulted in the cancellation of some 43,000 cards that had proved to be forged, duplicated, or belonging to persons who had long since died or left the area in search of employment abroad.

A new category of Arab refugees emerged in the wake of the Six-day War. According to the latest (July, 1968) Jordan data, 354,000 Arabs from the Israeli-held West Bank and Gaza Strip had crossed into Transjordan. Israeli sources contested this figure; they estimated the total to be about 200,000, including 120,000 "old" refugees from the 1948 war.

On July 2, 1967, the Israeli government announced that the West Bank residents who had left for Transjordan on or shortly after June 7 would be permitted to return to their homes until August 10, under the supervision of the International Committee of the Red Cross; the deadline was subsequently extended to August 31. By mid-July, the first application forms were handed over to Red Cross representatives for distribution to prospective returnees. Meanwhile, thousands were reported returning without authorization by wading across shallow fords in the Jordan River. On July 18, the first group of 50 was admitted under the official repatriation program. Yet, at a very early stage, Jordanian authorities started putting obstacles in the way of organized return. They objected to the distribution of application forms bearing the heading "State of Israel," even though the forms were counterstamped by the International Red Cross. It was not until August 6 that an agreement was reached to the effect that new forms would be printed carrying the names of Israel, Jordan, and the Red Cross. The Jordanian government then launched an all-out propaganda campaign urging the refugees to go back, in order, as Finance Minister 'Abdul Wahhab Magali put it, to be "a thorn in the flesh of the [Israeli] aggressor"; those declining to return were warned that they would be refused further governmental aid.

By the end of August, 32,000 applications from prospective returnees, representing 100,000 persons, had been received by

Israeli authorities, but only 14,056 persons had actually re-crossed the Jordan River. Jordanian officials asserted that many of those granted permits could not be found. On September 12, Israel announced that some 7,000 refugees who had missed the August 31 deadline would be permitted to return without any time limit. The great majority of the returnees were settled farmers and farm workers with their families rather than 1948 refugees.

In July, 1967, the Israeli authorities permitted the exchange of produce between the west and east banks of the Jordan. In the fall of that year, residents of Israel-held areas were granted permits to visit in the Arab countries.

Simultaneously with the return movement, the exodus of West Bank Arabs to Transjordan continued. As late as December, 1967, UNRWA reported that "several thousand a month" were still leaving for the East Bank. They were not prevented from leaving by the Israeli authorities and were received without difficulties by the Transjordan officials. In 1968 also, many Gaza Strip refugees from the 1948 war started moving in the direction of Transjordan. The UNRWA director in the area stated at the end of May, 1968, that "there has been a fairly healthy movement out of the Gaza Strip," amounting to some 40,000 of the original 300,000 refugees. After the end of July, 1968, however, Gaza residents were being turned back on the Jordanian side of the Allenby Bridge. The Jordanian representative at the United Nations charged that Israel was coercing the refugees in Gaza to emigrate. The Israel Ministry of Defense categorically denied the charge.

In July, 1968, Prime Minister Levi *Eshkol reiterated in the *Knesset Israel's readiness to participate in the settlement of the Arab refugees within the framework of a regional arrangement with international assistance; Israel, he insisted, could not undertake such a task alone.

J. SCHECHTMAN

ARAB RIOTS IN PALESTINE. From its inception, in 1882, the modern Jewish settlement in Palestine repeatedly encountered opposition from the Arab population. From 1904 on, with the rise of Arab nationalism, attacks became more highly organized. Jewish reaction led to the founding of *HaShomer (Jewish watchmen's organization), which remained limited in

Arab rioters looted this house in Jerusalem during the 1929 terrorism. [Zionist Archives]

The library of Prof. Joseph Klausner was sacked in the 1929 riots. [Zionist Archives]

scope until the British conquest. From 1920 on the Arab leadership resorted to terrorist tactics in its attempts to hamper Zionist activity in Palestine and to prevent the formation of a Jewish National Home there. Riots were also an expression of the internal power struggles within the Arab leadership and especially between the more radical Husayni faction, led by Hajj Amin *al-Husayni, mufti of Jerusalem, and the more moderate Nashashibi faction, headed by Ragheb Bey Nashashibi, mayor of Jerusalem.

The riots followed a typical pattern: they usually began with anti-Jewish incitement in the Arab press and in mosques, mostly on the theme of alleged murders of innocent Arabs and desecration of Muslim shrines by Jews. Then came street attacks on individuals, often coinciding with popular festivals when emotions were easily aroused. Inflammatory speeches sent mobs out to loot and slaughter; commercial activity was brought to a standstill; Arab gangs repeatedly blocked highways and raided isolated settlements. British reaction was generally slow and feeble, further encouraging violence. In contrast, after 1929 the *Hagana acted with increasing efficiency and in time became a definite deterring factor.

Among the political effects of the disturbances were restrictions on Jewish *immigration and, in general, a British tendency to appease the Arab leadership. Four major disturbances took place under the British Mandate.

1920–21. In order to exert pressure on the *San Remo Conference, attacks were made on Jewish settlements, culminating in riots in Jerusalem in the spring of 1920. British activity hindered Jewish self-defense. In May, 1921, further riots broke out in several parts of the country, with 47 Jews killed and many injured. Following these outbreaks, the *White Paper of June, 1922, was issued and Jewish immigration restricted to what was deemed the "economic absorptive capacity" of Palestine. At the same time, the disturbances led to the consolidation of Hagana.

1929. In direct reaction to the setting up of the extended *Jewish Agency and as a result of Husayni defections in local elections in 1927, Arab demonstrations—developing into violence—broke out in Jerusalem, Hebron, and Safed, in which 133 Jews were killed and 400 injured. Again, British police action remained ineffective, but the outbreaks were checked by Hagana and the arrival of British troops. The political results were manifold: the Husaynis gained power, the *Shaw Commission further appeased the Arab leadership, and the White Paper of 1931 limited Jewish immigration, Jewish land purchases, and the powers of the Jewish Agency. These events led to factionalism in the *Yishuv (the Jewish population of Palestine) and the Zionist movement: the militant *Revisionists and the *B'rit Shalom, which sought a Jewish-Arab understanding, emerged at the two opposite extremes, and the group which formed *Mapai in 1930, in the center. Hagana was reorganized under a unified national command, enabling it to take widespread concerted action.

1933. The Istiqlal, a new Arab political party, instigated riots, which, however, were quickly put down by the British.

1936-39. These disturbances, climaxing many years of tension, were unique in extent and duration. The Arabs referred to them as "the Arab Revolt," a name well justified by their organized nature. Zionism was not alone in bearing the brunt; this time the British also came under attack. Several factors account for this: the rise of fascism and Nazism in Europe, nationalist developments in Egypt and Syria, the progress of Zionist work in Palestine, and the British refusal to grant even limited self-rule in Palestine, which would have meant Arab (majority) rule.

The first of two major phases of the revolt consisted of an Arab general strike lasting from April through October, 1936. The rival Arab factions united in their efforts, and an Arab High Command, under the leadership of the mufti, was set up. A boycott of the Yishuv was instigated, Arab villagers lent their hands to terrorist activities, and considerable aid was also received from neighboring countries. Iraqi reinforcements arrived under Fawzi al-Kawukji, who took over command of all the terrorist bands, molding them into a cohesive military organization. Nevertheless, internal factionalism (more Arabs were killed by Arabs than by Jews), the strength of the Yishuv, and, above all, the British Army brought about the revolt's collapse.

The second phase, which lasted from the summer of 1937 to 1939, began after the murder of a British district commissioner, arousing the British Army to action. The Arab High Command was outlawed, the mufti fled, and other leaders were exiled. Disturbances continued, however, until they were finally quelled by the British, largely by means of Capt. Orde C. *Wingate's *Special Night Squads.

In the three years from 1936 to 1939, 91 Jews were killed, 369 were injured, and much property was damaged. Arab losses were much higher. During these years the number of Jewish constables in the British police forces grew considerably, and the Yishuv learned to consolidate its defense and supply potential. The Arab strike, which closed the port of Jaffa, also brought about the opening of an embryonic Jewish port at Tel Aviv.

These disturbances were the last Arab attempts to dislodge the Yishuv. During World War II the situation in Palestine was quiet. Hostile Arab acts against Jews were renewed only in 1947, in reaction to the *partition decision of the United Nations.

O. STENDEL

ARABS AND ZIONISM. The Arab attitude to Zionism is a compound phenomenon in which basic premises of Arab nationalism are intermixed with reactions to historical incidents and with clashes of political interests and destinies.

Under Ottoman Rule. Prior to World War I, Jewish-Arab relations had two aspects: the relations between the Jewish settlers and their Arab neighbors, and those between the Jewish and Arab national movements. As to the first, there was Arab discontent with certain economic effects of the Jewish settlement, such as the rise in land prices; the eviction, in certain cases, of peasants by landlords who sold the land to Jews; and commercial rivalry. On the other hand, the growing Jewish economy offered many jobs to Arabs. As to the Arab national movement, Zionism impelled it to view its problems in a wider perspective. Naguib Azouri, one of the harbingers of Arab nationalism, took an early adamant stand against Zionism and foresaw an irreconcilable rivalry between the two movements. After the revolution of the Young Turks (1908), when a struggle developed between the centralist and decentralist tendencies in the Ottoman Empire, the Arabs aligned themselves with the latter. Against this background, some approaches were made by the Arab leaders toward Zionism with a view to rallying Jewish political influence and economic power to the Arab side. In general, however, there was mounting Arab opposition to Zionism and propaganda against it.

The Arab press started agitation against Jewish expansion in Palestine. Petitions were sent to the central government and complaints were raised in the Parliament in Constantinople against the sale of land to Jews, Zionist symbols, and Jewish institutions of self-government and education; these were considered alien and separatist factors.

In 1909 and again in 1914 the public order was threatened in different parts of the country, particularly in Galilee, by Arab nationalist agitation against the Jews, which led to repeated assaults on Jews. In 1911 an anti-Jewish association was founded in Jaffa with the stated aim of stopping Jewish progress in Palestine.

On the other hand, there was also a certain inclination on the part of the Arabs to endorse the Zionist efforts in Palestine provided the Jews, in return, would use their means and influence in support of the Arab cause. During the Arab Congress that took place in Paris in 1913, some Arab-Jewish contacts were initiated along these lines. Subsequently, however, the Arabs retreated and returned to their anti-Zionist position. In the second half of 1914, disillusioned with the Turkish government, the Arabs renewed their approaches to the Jews. The Zionist leadership, however, reacted with hesitation, because it doubted the genuineness of these feelers and because it did not wish to antagonize the Ottoman government.

During World War I, Arab nationalists and Zionists were both persecuted by the Turkish authorities. While the political negotiations which led to the *Balfour Declaration were in progress, severe Arab opposition was not foreseen. In fact, some of its initiators considered the Balfour Declaration a prelude to a Zionist-Arab-Armenian alignment on which British influence in the Middle East was to rest.

Only after the issuance of the declaration did Arab opposition loom large. Arab nationalism had changed its character during the war years; its political ambition had increased, and while it allied itself with the Hashemite dynasty, other groups became more influential. Chaim *Weizmann, who went to Palestine in 1918 with the *Zionist Commission, tried to calm Arab fears and initiated negotiations with Emir *Feisal in that year and again in early 1919 in Paris. These resulted in the Feisal-Weizmann Agreement, which was based on the hope for a United Arab Kingdom with Syria as its center and on Feisal's expectations of Jewish political help. However, if there was an understanding between Weizmann and Feisal, this did not greatly affect the Syrian and Palestinian Arab opposition to Zionism, which was encouraged by certain British officials.

During the British Mandate. Soon after the British conquest of southern Palestine late in 1917 and after the armistice agreement late in 1918, Arab rallies, petitions, and demonstrations gave expression to strong opposition to all Zionist aspirations. The arrival of the Zionist Commission in 1918 served as an impetus to greater Arab animosity. The Arab leaders of Palestine, who considered Palestine an integral part of Syria, referring to it as "southern Syria," opposed the Balfour Declaration, not only because of their fear of Jewish domination or their insistence on Arab civil and political rights, but primarily because they wished to be included in the envisaged Syrian Arab state. The desire to achieve this goal was strong enough to overcome, for the moment at least, the age-old antagonism between Muslim and Christian Arabs; thus, in February, 1919, Christian-Muslim associations were formed, characterized by opposition to Zionism and the Balfour Declaration.

The first anti-Zionist demonstration was held by the Arabs in Jerusalem on Feb. 27, 1920 (*see* ARAB RIOTS IN PALESTINE). A few days later (March 8) a second demonstration took place. April, 1920, saw the eruption of Arab mob violence during the Nebi Musa festivities in Jerusalem, and in the following year (May, 1921) terrorist outbreaks occurred in Jaffa.

At the same time Arab quasipolitical anti-Zionist organizations took shape in Palestine. In December, 1921, the Muslim Supreme Council was created, and it was given authority by the British Palestine administration to control the *Waqf, the religious-charitable foundations. In 1921 Hajj Amin *al-Husayni, who was to become the foremost Palestinian Arab champion of anti-Zionism, was elected mufti of Jerusalem with the help of the British *High Commissioner, Sir Herbert *Samuel. In 1922 he was elected head of the Muslim Supreme Council.

When the hopes for an Arab state under Feisal were shattered by the French, the center of the Arab movement shifted to Palestine. The Third All-Syrian Congress, which was held in Haifa in December, 1920, elected an Arab Executive and adopted a resolution against recognition of the Zionist Commission by the government, Jewish *immigration, and recognition of the Hebrew language. It demanded home rule and the formation of a house of representatives elected by the Arabic-speaking population which lived in the country before World War I. The collection of all the anti-Zionist resolutions adopted since 1919 was called the National Covenant.

While the British *Mandate for Palestine was being formulated, Arab opposition mounted and was given expression in the dispatching to London and Geneva of the first of several *Arab delegations in February, 1922. The official Arab position condemned the constitutional framework of the mandate and until the end of 1928 refused to cooperate in any scheme of political representation.

In the late 1920s, after the final ratification of the mandate, there was a certain relaxation in Arab enmity toward Zionism, although All-Syrian Congresses continued to be convened in Palestine (four more took place between 1921 and 1928), and there was an Arab general strike in March, 1925, in protest against Lord *Balfour's visit to inaugurate the *Hebrew University of Jerusalem. (Other strikes were directed against the French Mandate in Syria.) Among the factors which contributed to the mitigation after 1922 of Arab anti-Zionism were the lessening of the fear of Zionist domination in Palestine and the emergence of strong intra-Arab rivalries and feuds.

In the late 1920s the Muslim religious factor became prominent in Arab anti-Zionist propaganda, led by the mufti of Jerusalem. In it, the danger to the *holy places was stressed (especially the problem of the *Western, or Wailing, Wall). This agitation resulted in the Arab riots of 1929.

The exacerbation of Arab anti-Zionism in the 1930s can be attributed to the fear of rapid Jewish progress following the establishment of the expanded *Jewish Agency, to the growing Arab interest in self-rule in face of the advancing independence in the region as a whole, to the general development of Arab society, and to the claim that not only the national aspirations but also the specific rights of the Arab population (and particularly its rural sector) were being violated by the Jewish settlement. Eviction of peasants, Jewish national lands, and the slogan "Jewish Labor" were the main complaints.

In 1934 the Arab Executive fell into decay; in 1936 the *Arab Higher Committee was formed and began to spearhead Arab anti-Zionist activities. Arab anxiety in view of the sizable Jewish immigration, the delay in considering their demands for a *Legislative Council, the deterioration of international stability due to the Italo-Ethiopian War, and Fascist and Nazi incitement resulted, from 1935 on, in rapidly increasing tension which, in 1936, culminated in the Arab rebellion. The rebellion manifested itself in terrorist acts, a general strike, and an attempt at civil disobedience.

During the investigation by British commissions of inquiry, Arab representatives rejected all solutions other than complete domination of Palestine by the Arab majority, on whose will the fate of the Jews would depend.

The Arab line emerged clearly from the testimony given by the mufti of Jerusalem before the *Peel Commission: he went so far as to deny the right even of the existing Jewish population to live in Palestine and proposed to leave the issue to a future Arab state. Nevertheless, when the possibility of the creation of a Jewish State emerged, some attempts were made to establish Jewish-Arab contacts. These failed, however, mainly because of the problem of free immigration. The intransigence of the Husayni party, led by the mufti, was so extreme that it rejected at first even the anti-Zionist *White Paper of 1939, although subsequently influential factions among the Arabs were ready to accept its provisions.

In September, 1937, a Pan-Arab Conference, called under the auspices of the Syrian Committee for the Defense of Palestine, in which the Arab states were not officially represented, met in Bludan, near Damascus. It was attended by 400 delegates from all the Arab countries except Yemen, and resolved unanimously that Palestine was an integral part of the Arab homeland, no part of which can be alienated without Arab consent. The conference demanded the annulment of the Balfour Declaration and the abrogation of the British Mandate. The only concession the conference made to the existing non-Arab population of Palestine was an expressed willingness to include guarantees for the safeguarding of the rights of minorities in the British-Palestine treaty it envisaged.

During World War II, the Arabs in Palestine were without effective leadership. The only nationalistic activity in evidence was the resuscitation of financial instruments such as the Nation's Fund (first created in the 1930s), for the prevention of the transfer of Arab lands to Jewish hands.

Toward the end of the war and following it, a split developed in the Arab camp which had bearings also on Arab-Jewish relations: the Istiqlal (Arab Independence party) was ready to accept the 1939 White Paper, while the more extreme Husayni Palestinian Arab party insisted on the "dissolution of Jewish nationalism."

After 1945, two Arab paramilitary terrorist societies, al-Futuwwah (Heroism), under Husayni influence, and al-Najadah (Valor), sponsored by the Muslim Brotherhood, arose in Palestine. They merged in September, 1946. Arab anti-Zionist propaganda bureaus were opened in Western centers. The main proponent of the Arab cause became the *Arab League (established in March, 1945), which continued to intervene in Palestinian affairs in the name of the entire Arab nation. It conducted the Arab political campaign in 1945–48, trying to avoid the most extremist overtones. In 1947–48 the League was in charge of the preparations for the Arab attack on Israel (see WAR OF INDEPENDENCE).

The Arab anti-Zionist position was summarized by George Antonius, an eloquent exponent of the Arab cause, to the effect that the Arabs had the right to Palestine through both historical connections and the acquisition of political rights. He claimed that the conquest, the Arabization of the existing Palestinian population by intermarriage and assimilation, and the attachment to the soil made for the historical right; the political rights were based on commitments made to the Arabs during and after World War I. According to Antonius, Arab opposition to Zionism stemmed from these rights as well as from grievances of the existing Arab population, whose economic situation was deteriorating because of Zionist colonization. He viewed Zionism as an outcome of European atrocities toward Jews, for which the Arabs could not be made responsible.

In sum, it appears that Arab nationalism from the very beginning resented all foreign domination (including that of the Turks), to which it attributed the Arab decline. Zionism was unable to convince the Arabs that it was neither foreign to the Middle East nor a movement seeking domination. Arab nationalism is based on the memory of the grandeur of the Arab Empire and on the concept of the divine right of conquest. The Jewish hold on Palestine seems to impair this concept, even apart from the particular rights of the Arab inhabitants of the country. Owing either to European policies after World War I or to intra-Arab disunity, a united Arab state failed to materialize. In Zionism Arab nationalism found a target on which to focus; the common opposition to it could serve as a sorely needed uniting factor.

After 1948. Following the War of Independence, the Arab attitude to Zionism became interwoven with Arab hostility to the new State of Israel. Contributing factors to the intensification of Arab opposition to both Zionism and Israel were the *Arab refugees and the loss of Palestine, claimed to be part of the undivided Arab homeland.

Soon after the signing of the *armistice agreements it became evident that the Arab countries were not prepared to recognize Israel or to sign a peace treaty with her. This clearly implied that another round in the war was, if not imminent, at least a very real possibility. An arms race soon began and an anti-Israel campaign consisting of an *Arab boycott of Israel, infiltration, sabotage, and hit-and-run attacks was launched against the young State. Also, efforts were made to impede the development and utilization of Israel's natural resources, such as the Hula Lake and the *National Water Carrier. Although all this was directed against Israel, nevertheless, in Arab propaganda, whenever a distinction was made between Israel and Zionism, it was the latter that was given the connotation of an aggressive expansionist all-Jewish movement bent on dominating Palestine and neighboring Arab lands.

A whole fabric of ideology was elaborated in order to provide a foundation and justification for the conflict between the Arab world and Zionism. Apart from the rights of the Palestinian Arabs, the soil of Israel was considered an inalienable part of the common Arab homeland. Israel itself was represented as an alien factor, the main arguments being that it disrupted the continuity between the Arab lands of Asia and Africa, that it was a potential dominating factor in the Middle East, or again, that it was culturally alien and constituted a danger to the spiritual entity "Arabism."

Israel was also presented as a state based on race and religion which denied equal rights to its non-Jewish citizens, and as an artificial and immoral state which accordingly should be expelled from the international community. A quantity of literature describing Jewish history and the Jewish character in damaging terms and making use of anti-Semitic stereotypes endeavored to refute Jewish claims on Palestine as a homeland. The drift of some Arab states toward leftism and the trend of "revolutionary unity" in the Arab camp brought about a further intensification of Arab anti-Zionism. Israel was presented as an agent of imperialism in the Middle East. The struggle against Israel became a central issue of the new regimes in Egypt (United Arab Republic) and Syria, as well as one of the most important causes that preoccupied the Arab League.

The *Sinai Campaign of 1956 was seized upon as an illustration of Israeli aggression and imperialism.

In April, 1963, when a federal union between Egypt, Syria, and Iraq was envisaged, its proposed constitution included the duty to liberate the Arab nation from the "peril of Zionism."

In 1964–65 a Joint Arab Command and a Palestine Liberation Front were established. The slogan "popular revolutionary war" was adopted, particularly by the Syrians and by *el-Fatah (the Conquest), a terrorist organization which represented the accumulation of frustration and hate among the Palestinian refugees. The longing for the lost homeland and the yearning for revenge were fanned by an incessant stream of inflammatory speeches broadcast especially from Syria and Egypt.

To sum up, the Arab position on Zionism and Israel envisaged the practical liquidation of Israel in a number of stages. It began with the demand that Israel retreat to the borders specified in the United Nations partition resolution of 1947 and absorb the Arab refugees. It went on to require that Israel be "de-Zionized" by cutting its ties with world Jewry and stopping immigration. It further insisted that the State of Israel itself be abolished and a Palestinian Arab state be established in its place, in which the Jewish population was to be given a certain autonomy. As an alternative, preferred by the more extreme Arab leaders, Jewish emigration from Palestine was to be energetically encouraged, under the threat of the annihilation of Israel's Jewish population in the country itself; this was to be attained by terrorism and open warfare. These were the demands and aims that culminated in the Egyptian preparations of May, 1967, to attack Israel, which, in turn, led to the *Six-day War of 1967. See also ARABS IN ISRAEL.   I. KOLATT

ARABS IN ISRAEL. Ever since the beginnings of the *Hoveve Zion movement and the establishment of the first modern Jewish agricultural settlements in Palestine (in 1882; *see* MOSHAVA), the relationship of the Arab population of Palestine to the Jewish efforts to settle in the country and develop a Jewish National Home in it was of crucial importance. In general, the numerical increase of the *Yishuv (Jewish population of Palestine) was paralleled by an increase in the numbers of the Palestinian Arabs, a rise in their standard of living, and a development of an anti-Zionist political consciousness.

PALESTINE (1918–47)

In 1918 there were some 600,000 Arabs in Palestine; by 1947 their number had doubled. This increase was due partly to natural factors and partly to the influx of Arabs from the surrounding countries, who were attracted by Palestine's higher standard of living and economic development, brought about by the Jewish settlement work. The Zionist attempt to find a common language with them bore little fruit; one of the tragedies of Jewish-Arab relations in Palestine stemmed from the fact that a nationalist revival occurred at the same period in the history of both peoples. Despite general improvement in material conditions and public health, owing in large measure to Jewish capital and assistance, Arab suspicions of Jewish *immigration and land buying remained unabated, and it was on these two themes that the extremist elements, led by the Husayni clan, organized anti-Jewish (and, periodically, anti-British) riots in the years 1920–21, 1929, and then again, most violently, in 1936–39 (*see* ARAB RIOTS IN PALESTINE).

Rapid numerical increase did not essentially change the socioeconomic structure of Palestine's Arab population. Two-thirds of the Palestinian Arabs remained agricultural villagers who owed allegiance, through the chieftains of their clans, to certain influential families in the cities. Because of this allegiance the Husayni political party was able to keep its followers together and spur them on to acts of violence. Other Arab parties, also urban-centered and rural-supported, were less inclined to extremism. Internal feuds, Jewish armed resistance, and the British crackdown in 1937 on the extremist Arab leaders, and their exile, brought about a demoralization of the Palestinian Arabs on the eve of the creation of the State of Israel.

A Negev Bedouin operates farm machinery provided by the State.
[Israel Information Services]

Arab women sort wool at Umm al-Fahm, a town in Samaria.
[Israel Information Services]

ISRAEL (1948–   )

The 1948 Arab-Israeli War (*see* WAR OF INDEPENDENCE) left within Israel's boundaries about 120,000 Arabs; the others had fled or remained in the territories that were brought under Jordanian or Egyptian control. By the end of 1966 the Arab population in Israel had grown to about 300,000, owing to the high rate of natural increase and the partial return of *Arab refugees, sponsored by the Israel government under the Unification of Families Plan. This numerical rise notwithstanding, the Arabs' feeling of shock at having been suddenly reduced to minority status persisted. The division into religious groups added to this feeling: 69.1 per cent were Muslims (Moslems); 20.5, Christians (*see* CHRISTIAN COMMUNITIES AND CHURCHES IN ISRAEL); 9.8, Druzes (*see* DRUZE COMMUNITY IN ISRAEL); and 0.6 belonged to other communities. The Christians, two-thirds of whom were urban residents, were in turn divided into many denominations, the largest being the Greek Catholic (40 per cent) and the Greek Orthodox (37 per cent). All communities enjoyed a large degree of autonomy in matters of religion, personal status, and education. The State contributed to the salaries of their officials and to the upkeep of denominational schools (tuition in the State schools, attended by most Arab children, was free).

Localities. Up to the *Six-day War of 1967 Israeli Arabs lived in six "mixed cities" with a Jewish majority (Jerusalem, Tel Aviv–Jaffa, Ramle, Lod, Haifa, and 'Akko); two all-Arab towns (Nazareth and Sh'far'am); 104 villages, numbering between 200 and 5,000 persons; and Bedouin encampments in the Negev and Galilee, numbering some 27,000. About 60 per cent of the Arabs lived in Galilee; another 20 per cent, approximately, in the "Little Triangle" near the middle portion of the Jordanian border.

The Arab concentrations on Israel's frontiers presented difficult problems to the State. The Arab minority was expected to be loyal to the State, but its ethnic, religious, and cultural ties (even its kinship) often were with the Arabs beyond the frontiers, with whom no peace had yet been concluded. Hence the military administration in the Arab border areas, imposed during the Arab-Israeli War, had to continue, although its control was considerably eased. Arabs not living near the borders enjoyed equality with the Jews in every respect; those who lived near the borders had to obtain travel permits from the military administration to leave the restricted zones (after 1963 this applied to only a very limited area at the borders, and at the end of 1966 the military administration was abolished).

Political Attitudes. One of the remarkable new developments in the life of the Arab population was its growing participation in public affairs, both locally and nationally. Under Ottoman rule and even under the British *Mandate for Palestine, only a few of the Arab townspeople and hardly any of the villagers had shown an interest in public affairs. In Israel, more than half of the Arab population was organized in two townships and more than 30 local councils, constituted under the same statutes which applied to their Jewish counterparts, and many Arabs became intensely active in their local affairs. Particular interest was shown by the younger generation, which asserted itself as never before.

Even more significant was a change from the previous apathy in questions of national politics. Under Ottoman rule, politics had always been considered the prerogative of certain influential families, mainly in the cities. Subsequently, the British had offered opportunities for a few more Arabs to enter politics, but it was only in Israel that the poorer and younger Arabs increasingly entered political life. Arabs began to vote in all local and national elections alongside their Jewish fellow citizens; and, for the first time in the history of the Arabs in Palestine, suffrage was extended to women as well.

Although no Arab political parties of national significance emerged until 1965, some were being planned. Nevertheless, Israel's Arabs eagerly exercised their right to vote in all elections and to hold office; indeed their proportionate participation in all parliamentary elections—with the exception of the first one (1949)—was higher than that of the Jews, amounting to more than 80 per cent of the Arab electorate. A sizable number of their ballots went to Opposition lists, thus showing the absence of both pressure and fear of authority. Of the 120 members of the *Knesset, there were 3 Arabs in 1949, 8 in 1951 and 1955, and 7 in 1959, 1961, and 1965. In the 1961 parliamentary elections Israeli Arabs gave the Communist party about 21,000 votes, or half of its total ballots, representing a protest vote of over one-fifth of the total valid Arab ballots; the results of the Arab vote remained almost the same in the 1965 elections (despite the split of the Communist party into two groups).

Social and Economic Change. The impact of Jewish settlement left its mark on the Palestinian Arabs even during the period of the British Mandate. Following the establishment of the State of Israel, an increasing number of Arab women joined the labor force in many capacities, including office work and teaching. Previously, most Arab women had worked at home or in agriculture. A rising number of youngsters left their villages and found remunerative work in "mixed" or Jewish towns. Many of them were sons of large families who were no longer able to make a satisfactory living in agriculture and sought employment in *industry and handicrafts such as the manufacture of paper, metalwork, weaving, the fashioning of mother-of-pearl jewelry, and souvenir making. Still others, high school or university graduates, had little interest in the routine life of their villages and looked for suitable employment in the cities. Since 1960 the *Histadrut (General Federation of Labor) has admitted Arab members; at the end of 1964 there were in the Histadrut 34,959 Arabs, numbering together with their dependents 82,054,

or 28.7 per cent of the total Arab population in Israel at the time. By 1968 more than half of all the Arab workers belonged to the Histadrut, which organized and trained them and safeguarded their interests, including equal pay for equal work.

Nazareth. Socioeconomic change was strongest in Nazareth, the largest Arab town in Israel, with a population of some 30,000 Arabs (alongside a steadily growing "new" Nazareth nearby, peopled with Jewish immigrants). Arab Nazareth still kept much of its picturesque character, but it was being modernized by new schools, hospitals, and municipal and governmental institutions. The number of Arabs commuting to jobs in Haifa or 'Afula equaled that of those working in Nazareth itself. The considerable growth in income and the resultant rise in the standard of living, as well as Jewish influence and example at work and leisure, had a far-reaching impact on the way of life of Nazareth's Arabs. Arab men (the Arab women less so) dressed like their Jewish neighbors and sought the same amusements (*see* ENTERTAINMENT IN ISRAEL). Their new houses and apartments closely resembled Jewish buildings, both in exterior and interior, with living-room furniture imitating Jewish taste and kitchens displaying an increasing number of modern electrical appliances.

Arab Villages. The Arab villages in Israel were not free from differences between old and young. These, however, were less sharp than in the towns, since the households of the peasants, or fellahin (*see* FELLAH), often still consisted of large extended families whose members also worked together. Here too, however, the traditional patriarchal structure of the family was gradually disintegrating. Not only were sons and daughters less dependent on the elders' authority, but a new set of values was evolving, altering former patterns of sociopolitical leadership. The heads of clans and families were no longer the only ones to have relations with officialdom. The younger generation in the villages, many of whom had learned Hebrew in Israeli schools, had personal contacts with the civil or military authorities of the State, local party representatives, the Histadrut, or other organizations. Close contacts with the Jews increased the knowledge of these young Arabs of how to attain political or economic power in their villages. For example, since land was

Arabic is the language of instruction in this Arab high school at Tira. [Israel Information Services]

gradually ceasing to be the only status symbol in the Arab village, Arab contractors were using their outside contacts and ready cash to produce new sources of employment away from the village, thus acquiring a growing socioeconomic role and importance as job providers.

The Bedouins, too, felt the impact of modernization. Of the 27,000 Israeli Bedouins, only some 7,000 (or about one-fourth) still could be described as "desert nomads." The rest had settled and cultivated the land. What still set them apart from the fellahin was mainly their traditions and customs. The Bedouins of the northern Negev still preserved most of their ancient customs, moving around with their sheep and cattle in search of water and pastureland, living in tents, and adhering to tribal structure. However, even they had been affected by the creation of the State of Israel: they could no longer roam, as previously, across the political frontiers, which were now closely guarded by military forces. Therefore, the Negev Bedouins also turned increasingly to agriculture, a step which led to sedentarization. Many lived in collapsible huts or houses instead of tents; men and women often wore Western-style shoes and clothes when going to work in the cities. Neighboring kibbutzim and the State authorities assisted Bedouins as well as fellahin in their attempts to adapt to the modern conditions prevailing in Israel.

Problems of Education. Although in principle the educational laws of Israel apply equally to Jews and Arabs, in practice a greater effort was needed in the Arab than in the Jewish sector, owing to the high Arab illiteracy rate, the lack of suitable teachers and textbooks, and the continuing opposition of some Muslim parents to the schooling of their daughters, not only out of religious inhibitions but also because the girls were often needed for agricultural work. By 1968 more than 74,000 Arab children, of a total Arab school-age population (aged 6–17) of 104,000, were attending school. Many attended high schools, and an increasing number studied at Israeli institutions of higher learning. Success was also evident in that, in the general drive to increase the number of Arab schoolteachers, another important achievement was scored: almost one-third of these teachers were women. *See also* EDUCATION IN ISRAEL.

Thanks to full-time courses for new teachers and refresher courses for experienced personnel, the quality of Arab teaching is improving. Learning by rote has been replaced by modern pedagogical and didactic approaches, and much-needed textbooks have been published in Arabic, since the basic educational philosophy required that Israeli Arabs learn their own language, history, and literature first of all. Beyond that, they study Hebrew and then English. A problem still unsolved is how to reconcile the study of Arab cultural values with the training for loyalty to the State of Israel.

Literature and the Press. Prior to 1948 the literary production of the Palestinian Arabs was mediocre compared with that in Egypt or Lebanon; it was primarily of a political character. After the founding of the State of Israel, the Arab minority was culturally cut off from the mainstream of Arabic literary creativity. This isolation was eased only by the radio, which broadcast literary works in Arabic (*see* ISRAEL BROADCASTING SERVICE). Up to 1958 not one Arabic full-length novel was printed in Israel; only about 15 slim volumes of poetry appeared, mostly published by the authors themselves. In the early 1950s an impetus to Arabic literature in Israel was given by Jewish immigrants from Arab countries. Many of these newcomers had been active in journalism and literature, chiefly in Iraq. Now they joined those writing in Arabic and also provided a

greater number of readers for Arabic literature. After these Jewish immigrants had learned Hebrew and been integrated in Israel, they ceased to write in Arabic; but the impetus they provided was sufficient. A spate of novels, pamphlets, and newspapers of all kinds (many of the latter subsidized by the political parties) appeared in print.

Significantly, although in the early years of the State Arabic literature consisted mostly of love stories and poems, increasing political and social writing in Arabic was to be noted after 1955. Contributing factors were the widening circle of potential readers of Arabic, made up of Arab school graduates and students, the example of the intense Jewish interest in political and social affairs, and the sustained efforts of the Arab states to stir up the feelings of Israeli Arabs. The complete freedom of expression, which all Israelis enjoyed, offered some of the more articulate Israeli Arabs an opportunity to attack the new State in their writings, on either nationalist or Communist grounds. Others defended the State, pointing to the economic advantages and educational opportunities it offered. Either way, the politicizing of Arabic literature, so prevalent under the British Mandate, seems to have taken a new turn in the same old direction in the State of Israel.

Arabs in Occupied Territories. After the Six-day War of 1967, about 1 million Arabs were added to the territories under Israeli control. Of these, about two-thirds were inhabitants of the so-called West Bank, that part of the kingdom of Jordan which lay west of the Jordan River, and one-third of the *Gaza Strip. In the Gaulan Heights, in the southwestern corner of Syria, only a few thousand Druzes actually remained. While these Druzes welcomed Israeli rule and fully cooperated with Israel, the attitudes of the Arabs in the conquered territories varied from animosity and suspicion to wholehearted cooperation with the Israeli authorities. Practically all Arabs in those territories were quick to take advantage of the economic benefits offered by Israeli rule, and cases of sabotage or other forms of active or passive resistance (such as strikes) were rare. On the whole, the Arab population of these areas suffered relatively little disturbance in its economic, social, and cultural life. The farmers were enabled by the Israeli authorities to continue the sale of their produce to consumers on the east bank of the Jordan River, and the Arab economic, educational, religious, and other institutions, including the municipal organizations, were able to resume their normal activities soon after the cessation of the June hostilities.

J. M. LANDAU

'ARAD. Townlet in the eastern Negev, in the area between B'er Sheva' and the Dead Sea. Founded in 1961, when a project to populate the whole area was begun. The name was derived from the Bible. Population (1968): 2,000.

Remains of a large town of the early Bronze period and of a sanctuary dating from the early Hebrew monarchy were discovered and excavated at 'Arad.

ARANNE (ARONOWICZ), ZALMAN. Israeli Minister of Education and Culture (b. Russia, 1899). He studied at Yeshivot and academic institutions in Russia. Early active in the Zionist movement, he was in 1924–25 a member of the Central Committee of the illegal Zionists-Socialists in Russia. In 1926 he settled in Palestine, where he came to occupy high offices in *Mapai and in the *Histadrut. He was also a member of the Presidium of the Zionist *Actions Committee. From 1948 to 1951 he was general secretary of Mapai.

Newly built 'Arad is 25 miles east of B'er Sheva'. [Zelda Haber]

A member of the *Knesset from its inception in 1949, he was in 1954–55 a member of the Cabinet without portfolio. Sub-

Zalman Aranne.
[Israel Information Services]

sequently, in 1955–60, he was Minister of Education and Culture. He was again appointed to this post in 1963, and still held it in 1968.

'AR'ARA. Arab townlet in the 'Iron Valley, which leads from the Sharon Plain to the Jezreel Valley. Population (1968): 2,560.

'ARAVA. Long, narrow plain (100 miles long by 10 miles wide) stretching from north to south, from the Dead Sea to the Gulf of Elat. The frontier between Israel and Jordan runs through the middle of the 'Arava, from north to south. Arid throughout

its length, the plain forms part of the Negev. Starting at the southern end of the Dead Sea in an area of salt swamps, at a depth of 1,286 feet below sea level, it ascends gradually to a watershed 62 miles farther south, at an elevation of 650 feet above sea level. In this part it is drained by the Nahal 'Arava, which forms here the boundary between Israel and Jordan. From there to the Red Sea there is no drainage line, only some salt flats, and the boundary is not clearly marked. The 'Arava is covered mainly by gravel, with some sand and loess, and large sandy alluvial fans in the east. Along its western edge runs the new Elat-S'dom highway. There is no road along its eastern edge. A few springs provide water for three agricultural pioneer settlements and for the town of Elat.

The 'Arava is a narrow corridor between the mountains of Edom (in Jordan) and the Negev, in which air is compressed in summer. At night the air becomes sharp and cold. Under the midday sun, when cooled by slight breezes from the sea, the temperature reaches 115°F. When there is no breeze, it reaches 125°. At night dewfall totals one-fifth of an inch. Evaporation exceeds precipitation throughout the year. Light rain often evaporates before it reaches the ground. The combination of high-salt and low-water content is the cause of sterility in the plain. The 'Arava, nevertheless, was inhabited at various times, and through it ran an important caravan route linking the Red Sea and the Mediterranean. Habitation was made possible by the flood discharge from the surrounding hills, which, on occasion, can exceed 600 cubic meters per second.

In 1938 the kibbutz Bet 'Arava was founded not far from the Dead Sea. It became famous for its successful experiments in leaching salt from the soil and growing vegetables and fruit. It was destroyed in 1947 by the Transjordan Arab Legion. By then it had 30 acres under cultivation and obtained 36 tons of tomatoes per acre.

Evidence of settlement in the 'Arava seven centuries before the first Judean kingdom has been found throughout the region. Iron Age sites dating back to the 13th century B.C.E. reveal a once-large population.

Settlement in the 'Arava in the 1960s consisted of the Gadna' training settlement of B'er Ora and the villages of Yotvata, 'En Yahav, and G'rofit. Agriculture is based on cultivation of silt soil islets, deposited by short, sharp winter floods from the hills. Besides vegetables, 'Arava farmers grow gladioluses for export and cultivate date palms. Additional settlement plans were based on the assessment of soil experts that some 14,000 acres of land are cultivable and that sufficient water resources exist for irrigation. At Yotvata the wells of 'En Radian (a caravan station in Roman times) were discovered. This is the main water source for Elat, the 'Arava Red Sea port. Large phosphate deposits and copper are the 'Arava's main minerals and the basis for 'Arava industrial development. The copper deposits were once worked by the miners of King Solomon.

Y. KARMON AND Y. MORRIS

ARBEL. Village (moshav) in eastern Lower Galilee. Founded in 1949 and affiliated with *T'nu'at HaMoshavim. It derives its name from the ancient city of Arbel, which was located nearby and whose ruins can still be seen. Population (1968): 157.

ARCHEOLOGY IN ISRAEL. Living in a country with a documented history of more than three millenniums, the people of Israel are keenly aware of Palestine's archeological past. In fact, interest in archeology and amateur archeological exploration have become something of a national pastime. Among the amateur archeologists are political leaders, high army officers, students, workers, and members of kibbutzim. Discoveries of important archeological sites, monuments, and documents such as the ruins of Masada, the Dead Sea Scrolls, the Bar Kokhba letters, ancient Canaanite sanctuaries, and Biblical towns are treated by press and public alike as major, if not sensational, events in the nation's life. The Israeli public at large feels that each such discovery strengthens the ties of the *Yishuv (the Jewish population of Israel) to the land of its forefathers as well as the connection with its past, in addition to contributing to an understanding of the Bible, which is the most influential book in the life of modern Israel. The archeological exhibits in the Israel Museum and (since the *Six-day War of 1967) the Rockefeller Museum, in Jerusalem, and in the Ha'Aretz Museum, in Tel Aviv (*see* MUSEUMS IN ISRAEL), have aroused a lively interest in all segments of the Yishuv and continue to draw large numbers of visitors.

Professional archeology in Israel is served by a number of local and foreign institutions of higher learning and by scholarly societies. Yet beyond the professional and scholarly interest, archeological work in the country is of considerable importance

Archeologists of the Hebrew University explore a Dead Sea cave. [Israel Information Services]

to the non-Jewish world as well and especially to Christendom, which understandably wishes to learn more about the life and history of the early Christians of Palestine, their contemporary Jewish environment, and their roots in ancient Israel.

HISTORY

The ancient Land of Israel was a geographical bridge between the great political and cultural centers of Mesopotamia in the northeast and Egypt in the southwest. With the settlement of the Israelites and the establishment of their kingdom, it achieved an importance of its own. In the 10th century B.C.E., the kingdom split into two countries, Judah and Israel, both of which were destroyed by superior forces from the north, Israel late in the 8th century B.C.E. and Judah early in the 6th.

Holy to the major monotheistic religions, the country, throughout the centuries, attracted pilgrims, scholars, and students who went there to trace the history of their religions. However, serious study of the country did not begin until the 15th century. The first major work in this field, *Palestina ex monumentis veteribus,* by the Dutchman Adrian Reland, was published in 1709. The author, who had never visited Palestine, assembled all that was known in his day about the antiquities of the country. A further advance was marked by the important topographical studies of Edward Robinson, an American theologian, who in 1838 spent several months in Palestine. The first "modern" archeologist to work in the country was the Frenchman Félicien de Saulcy. Although the results of his excavations in 1850 were not accurate, they were of pioneering value. Later, excavations and surveys were conducted, mostly by British scholars, on behalf of the Palestine Exploration Fund. These concentrated chiefly on Jerusalem. Palestinian archeology was advanced also by Charles Clermont-Ganneau, a young Frenchman. With the exception of epigraphic material of clearly defined age, these scholars had no means to help them in the dating of their findings, nor were they aware of the importance of stratigraphy, without which modern archeology is unthinkable.

The first scholar to introduce more scientific methods was Sir Flinders Petrie. From 1880 on, he applied the principle of relative chronology on the basis of successive layers of deposits and the potsherds found in them. Aided by the results of his excavations in Egypt, he was also able to establish some definite dates for the potsherds and the objects found with them.

In the first decade of the 20th century, when Palestine was still under Turkish rule, British, American, and German archeologists began excavations on the important mounds of the country. Diggings at Ta'anakh, Gezer, Megiddo (M'giddo), Jericho, Samaria, Jerusalem, and other places yielded a large number of finds ranging from the prehistoric era to the Canaanite, Israelite, and Roman periods. They included remnants of buildings as well as potsherds, epigraphic material, and other objects indicative of the state of civilization.

The main deficiency of these widespread diggings, despite the relative advances they represented, was the lack of order in cataloging the findings, at both the excavation site and the place of their examination. The absence of trained personnel, due to the paucity of funds, was the cause of numerous inaccuracies in the cataloging of the objects found, which, in turn, reduced their value as a means of dating. From the point of view of modern archeology, the result of most of these excavations was a collection of objects useful for purposes of comparison only. The greater part of the conclusions drawn from these ex-

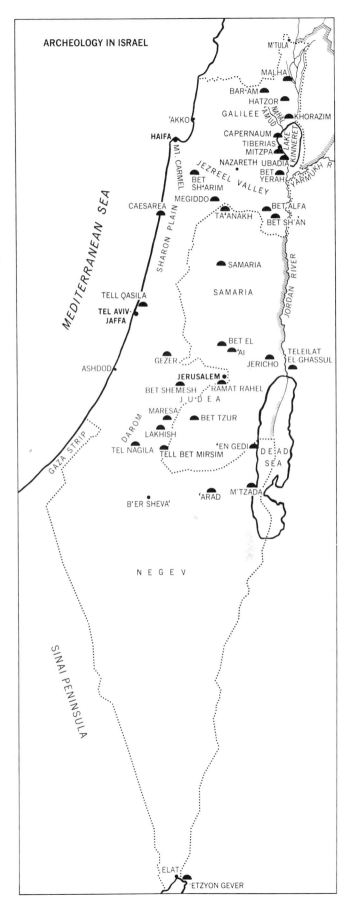

An underground Chalcolithic dwelling of the 3d millennium B.C.E. [Israel Information Services]

A Dead Sea Scroll exhibited in the Shrine of the Book, Jerusalem. [Israel Information Services]

peditions proved incorrect. Most of the mounds on which excavations were carried out in the beginning of the 20th century were redug in later years with a view to establishing their stratigraphy and chronology.

After the occupation of Palestine by the British, a new phase of archeological activity was initiated with the establishment of the Department of Antiquities, headed by John Garstang. From 1920 to 1948 great forward strides were made in both methods and scope of excavations. Schools for archeology and for the study of the Near East and various scientific institutions in Jerusalem contributed much to this progress. These included the American School of Oriental Research in Jerusalem (founded in 1903), whose work reached its peak under the leadership of William F. Albright, the greatest of Palestine archeologists; the British and French schools of archeology; and institutes affiliated with the various religious orders, which had developed a widespread archeological activity. The establishment, in 1913, of the Jewish Society for the Exploration of Palestine and Its Antiquities marked the entry of the Jews of Palestine into archeological study of their country.

This period witnessed the development of the study of the prehistoric era through discoveries of great importance from the Paleolithic period in caves at the Nahal (brook) 'Amud and on Mount Carmel. Garstang resumed his excavations at Jericho in a quest to find traces of Joshua's conquest. Various American expeditions made diggings at the important mounds of Bet Sh'an and Megiddo, the results of which have been modified by later archeological study in Israel and elsewhere. Other American expeditions uncovered important Judean cities, including Mitzpa and Bet Shemesh. The excavation of the Biblical D'vir, begun in 1926 by the American School of Oriental Research under Albright's direction, served as a model of accuracy in methods of work and deduction of historical inferences. Though the digging yielded no spectacular results, the methods employed in the expedition and the impeccable publication of its findings served as guides for all subsequent archeological work. Important results were yielded by the excavations at Lakhish, carried out by the British under the leadership of John L. Starkey. An expedition organized jointly by the Americans, the British, and the *Hebrew University of Jerusalem continued excavations at Samaria between 1931 and 1937 which brought to light significant material from the Israelite and Roman epochs.

In addition to these larger excavations, which were devoted mostly to the Canaanite and Israelite epochs, other, no less important digs into remains from these periods were carried out in 'Etzyon Gever near Elat, in Teleilat el-Ghassul near the Dead Sea, and at 'Ai. Findings at 'Ai did not support its identification with the Biblical 'Ai. In the 1930s an American expedition in the arid Negev explored remnants of Byzantine cities, which the desert sand had protected from the devastation of man and weather.

In addition to its participation in the Samaria expedition, the Hebrew University also engaged in diggings in other parts of the country. Professors Eleazar L. *Sukenik and Leo A. Mayer studied the topography of Jerusalem during the era of the Second Temple. Prof. Benjamin *Mazar, followed by Prof. Nathan Avigad, conducted excavations in Bet Sh'arim, the large necropolis of Mishnaic and Talmudic times. Extremely important excavations of the early Canaanite period were made in Bet Yerah under the direction of Professors Michael Avi-Yona and Moshe Stekelis. Jewish scholars, particularly Sukenik, devoted themselves to the study of the remains of ancient synagogues in the country.

The establishment of the State of Israel opened a new period for the archeological study of the country. All archeological endeavors came under the supervision of three institutions: the Department of Antiquities of the Ministry of Education and Culture (replacing the department of the same name of the mandatory period), headed (1966) by Dr. Avraham Biran; the Society for the Exploration of the Land of Israel and Its Antiquities, headed by Mazar and Yigael *Yadin; and the department of archeology of the Hebrew University, with which Professors Avigad, Avi-Yona, Yadin, Mazar, Stekelis, and Aharoni were prominently affiliated. Besides these official bodies, persons in all sections of the population displayed an intense interest in archeology and volunteered for archeological activities.

Many teams from other countries, including expeditions from the United States, Japan, Italy, and France, carried out excavations in Israel. There were also joint diggings by foreign teams and Israeli institutions.

RESULTS

The main results of archeological activities up to 1968 are outlined below according to periods.

Archeologists work on the west side of the fortress M'tzada (Masada). [Israel Information Services]

Carvings in black basalt once decorated a synagogue in Khorazim. [Israel Information Services]

Paleolithic and Mesolithic Periods (600,000–10,000 B.C.E.). Important archeological remains were discovered in Ubadia, south of Lake Kinneret near the Jordan River, where Stekelis found remains of men and animals, such as elephants and hippopotamuses, together with stone vessels dating back about 600,000 years, which correlate with findings made in East Africa. The Jordan Valley may have been one of the centers of early man. At the brook 'Amud, near Lake Kinneret, an expedition from Tokyo University discovered a cave containing a human skeleton from a much later period (80,000 B.C.E.). At the same place were found remains of a human whom scholars call Galilee man. Interesting methods of burial and remains of temporary settlements from the Mesolithic period (10,000 B.C.E.) were discovered, mainly in Malha, in the north. These remains indicate the importance of Palestine as one of the cradles of mankind.

Neolithic Period (10,000–5000 B.C.E.). In this period man began to live in well-ordered settlements and knew how to make clay vessels. Remains from this period were unearthed mainly in Jericho, Jordan, where a strongly fortified settlement was discovered. In Israel, they were found chiefly in the Jordan Valley.

Chalcolithic Period (5000–3000 B.C.E.). The chief remains of this flourishing civilization were discovered in the southern part of the country. The first excavation, at Teleilat el-Ghassul, opposite Jericho, yielded a well-developed settlement whose inhabitants knew how to work copper and lived in houses with ornamented walls. Excavations in the B'er Sheva' area, led by the French archeologist Georges Perrot, brought to light Chalcolithic settlements, some with underground dwellings. Stone sculptures and copper and salt vessels were also found. Interesting finds included clay sarcophagi shaped like houses with gabled roofs and other architectural features, from which was learned the building style of the period. However, the most important finds were the unearthing in 1961 of a sanctuary in 'En Gedi and the discovery in the same year, by Pesah Bar-Adon, of a trove of about 400 excellently preserved copper vessels in a cave in the Judean Desert. It may be assumed that these vessels were used for cultic purposes and that the priests of 'En Gedi, forced to flee from their homes, had hidden them, hoping to recover and restore them to use at some future time.

Early Bronze Period (3000–2000 B.C.E.). From this period dates the first historical information about Palestine. The early

Bronze period marks the beginning of urbanization in the country. Archeological remains were unearthed in various places; only the main sites are mentioned here. Palaces, sanctuaries, and city fortifications were discovered in 'Ai, Megiddo, and Bet Yerah. In 1962 Dr. Aharoni and Ruth 'Amiran of the Hebrew University began excavating the fortifications, houses, and streets of 'Arad, in the northern Negev, which was a large town in that period. In addition to architectural remains, a rich assortment of household articles and other objects were discovered. Indications are that the town was abandoned suddenly.

Middle Bronze Period (2000–1550 B.C.E.). This period is referred to in the Bible, for the 18th century B.C.E. was the era of the Hebrew patriarchs. Rich archeological remains, relating to the Egyptian rule in the country as well as to its later domination by the Hyksos, who also occupied Egypt, were discovered. The towns were fortified by strong walls. In the lower parts of the walls remains of beautiful palaces and sanctuaries were found.

Important remains were unearthed near Tel Aviv by Sukenik prior to the establishment of the State of Israel. Finds were also made at Megiddo. Teams from Israeli archeological institutions, headed by Yadin, made extensive excavations at Hatzor. Findings showed that Hatzor was a large city in that period. Other important excavations, carried on at Tel Nagila in the south of the country by an American expedition and local institutions, brought to light the remains of a large city.

Late Bronze Period (1550–1200 B.C.E.). This was the period of the Exodus and the conquest of the country by Joshua. Disturbances in Palestine, which was then governed by Egypt, weakened Egyptian rule and provided an easy setting for its conquest by the tribes of Israel. Many mounds, such as Bet El, D'vir, Lakhish, and Hatzor, are survivals from destruction by fire toward the end of the 13th century, a date which coincides with the Hebrew conquest of Canaan.

Remains of the materially rich civilization of the Canaanites were found in Bet Sh'an, Megiddo, Hatzor, and Lakhish. The temples testify to Egyptian as well as Syrian-Anatolian influences. Their fortifications were strong and the palaces stately. For the first time, documents written in Akkadian cuneiform writing, the official language of the period, appeared. The art objects, too, reveal a mixture of Syrian and Egyptian styles as well as Aegean influences.

First Iron Period (1200–930 B.C.E.). Also called the first Israelite period, it embraces the eras of the Judges and of the kingdoms of David and Solomon. From the various excavations, archeologists have gained knowledge about the difficulties experienced by the tribes of Israel in the process of settling the country. Only at a later stage, after the first generation, did the Israelites begin to fortify their settlements.

To this period belong also the many remains of Philistine civilization discovered at Bet Sh'an, at excavations on Tell Qasila conducted by Mazar, and more recently at Ashdod, dug up by a joint Israeli-American expedition directed by Dr. Moshe Dothan, of the Israeli Department of Antiquities.

King Solomon employed Phoenician craftsmen and architecture in his monumental construction projects. Their influence is visible in the remains of his buildings, fortifications, and palaces, chiefly at Megiddo and Hatzor, and in the copper mines, discovered by Nelson Glueck in Tel el-Khuleife ('Etzyon Gever), which probably date from the same time.

Second Iron Period (930–586 B.C.E.). This period was crucial in the history of the Jewish people. It encompasses the eras of

An ark carved in solid rock in the catacombs of Bet Sh'arim.
[Israel Information Services]

the kings of Judah and Israel and the destruction of both kingdoms. At many sites in the country remains of this period were discovered, such as the Samaria of King Ahab's days with its fortifications and beautiful palaces. Ahab's stables were found at Megiddo. In Hatzor fortifications, the town's fortress, and dwellings of characteristically Israelite design have been uncovered. In Samaria, capital of the kingdom of Israel, dozens of documents written in ink on clay were also unearthed. These are important not only because of their contents but also for the study of early Hebrew epigraphy. Strata with ruins of its ancient cities attest to the destruction of the kingdom of Israel toward the end of the 8th century B.C.E.

In the territory of the kingdom of Judah, many sites of that period have also been discovered, the most important of them being Lakhish. The double fortifications of Lakhish as well as the dozens of letters found in the guardrooms tell of the difficult position of the kingdom in the days of Sennacherib. In D'vir and Mitzpa substantial remains of fortifications and buildings have been unearthed. In Ramat Rahel (Biblical Bet HaKerem?) Dr. Israel Aharoni of the Hebrew University dug up remains of a fortified palace from the time of King Jehoiakim, which had been utterly destroyed. He also unearthed a fortress in 'Arad, in the Negev, where many cultural documents of the period were found, including letters written in ink on clay and the remains of a sanctuary erected no later than the reign of Solomon. Nebuchadnezzar's destruction of Judah is recalled by the thick burned layers on sites of its ancient cities.

From the Return to Zion to the Arab Conquest (536 B.C.E.– C.E. 636). This long period—more than a millennium—

witnessed the domination of Palestine by the empires of Persia, Greece, Rome, and Byzantium.

The Return to Zion from the Babylonian Exile took place during the period of Persian rule in the country. Phoenician and Greek influences are seen in the few important settlements of the period, which were unearthed chiefly by Israeli archeological institutions, situated at 'En Gedi (on the western shore of the Dead Sea), Lakhish, Ramat Rahel, Mikhmash (near Tel Aviv), and Hatzor (in Galilee). The conquest of the country by Alexander the Great late in the 4th century B.C.E. initiated the Hellenistic period, during which the Syrian Seleucids and the Egyptian Ptolemies ruled intermittently. From about 150 to 50 B.C.E. Palestine was ruled by the independent Jewish dynasty of the Hasmoneans. Only a few remains from that period have been unearthed. As early as 1902 the remains of Maresa, a Hellenistic town in Judea, were excavated. Remains from the Hasmonean period were discovered in Jerusalem; fortresses were dug up in Bet Tzur and Gezer. With the conquest of Judea by Pompey in 63 B.C.E., the rule of the Hasmoneans, for all practical purposes, came to an end. Years later Herod, an Idumean who was made king by the Romans, executed large building projects, of which remains of fortifications, of a sanctuary, and of other buildings in Samaria were excavated. Parts of the port of Caesarea, which Herod had planned and built, were uncovered by an Israeli-Italian expedition. Part of the port, sanctuaries, an amphitheater, aqueducts, and fortifications were laid bare.

Another large archeological undertaking was the unearthing of M'tzada (Masada), Herod's fortified palace, built atop a high and steep rock in the Judean Desert and captured by the Jews on the eve of their great rebellion against Rome. Among its ruins were discovered objects which had belonged to the families of the Zealots who heroically defended the fortress for three years after the destruction of Jerusalem and the Temple by the Romans (C.E. 70). During the excavations, conducted by Yigael Yadin, fragments of parchment scrolls were found, proving the authenticity of the dating of the Dead Sea Scrolls.

Expeditions of Israeli archeological institutions searched the caves of the Judean Desert in 1960 and 1961. In one of the caves Yadin found family archives of Bar Kokhba's soldiers. After the suppression of the Bar Kokhba uprising, the majority of the Jews in the country was concentrated in Galilee. One of the important Galilean cities of the period was Bet Sh'arim, the large necropolis which served not only Palestine Jewry but also Jews from abroad. The excavations of ancient Bet Sh'arim brought to light dozens of catacombs abounding in examples of Jewish art and inscriptions in Hebrew, Greek, and other languages.

To this period belong also the remains of numerous beautifully decorated synagogues, discovered in Galilee. Their art is clearly Jewish but also shows pagan motifs. Foremost among them are those of Capernaum (K'far Nahum), Khorazim near Lake Kinneret, and Bar'am in northern Galilee.

A different type of synagogue was developed between the 4th and 6th centuries of the Common Era, with richly decorated mosaic floors picturing the Ark, the 12 signs of the zodiac, and so on. The synagogue of Hammat-Tiberias and that of Bet Alfa belong to this type. The mosaic art found in the Christian churches of the period resembles that of the synagogues in general design and motif.

Since the Six-day War of 1967 archeological surveys have been carried out by Israeli archeologists in the newly occupied territories, and excavations have been begun in the area of the Temple Mount in Jerusalem, especially near the *Western Wall (Wailing Wall).

For individual prehistoric and archeological sites in Israel, *see* ABU GHOSH; 'AFULA; AKHZIV; 'AKKO; ASHK'LON; 'ATLIT; 'AVDAT; AZEKA; AZOR; B'ER SHEVA'; BET ALFA; BET GUVRIN; BET SH'AN; BET SH'ARIM; BET SHEMESH; BET YERAH; CAESAREA; CAPERNAUM; DOR; 'EVRON; GEZER; HADERA; HAIFA; HALUTZA; HATZOR; JAFFA; JERUSALEM; KEDESH; K'FAR BIRIM; KHIRBET MINYE; KHORAZIM; LAKHISH; LOD; MALHA; MANAHAT; MARESA; MESER; M'GIDDO; MONTFORT; M'TZADA; NAHARIYA; NAZARETH; NIRIM; NITZANA; RAMAT RAHEL; RAMLE; ROSH HA'AYIN; SAFED; SHA'ALVIM; SHA'AR HAGOLAN; SHARUHEN; SHAVE TZIYON; SHIVTA; TABGHA; TELL ABU HAWAM; TELL BET MIRSIM; TELL EL-HESI; TELL EL-JUDEIDAH; TELL ES-SAFI; TELL JEMME; TELL QASILA; TIBERIAS; TZIPPORI; WADI HEVER.

See also ISRAEL, HISTORY OF.

G. FOERSTER

ARCHITECTURE AND TOWN PLANNING IN ISRAEL. The challenge to architects and town planners in Israel has been to create an authentic style of architecture and urban design that would not only be appropriate to Israel's landscape and climate but would also meet the requirements of the new social, economic, political, and demographic structure evolving in the young Jewish State. Having no "native" tradition on which to rely, modern Palestinian, and later Israeli, architects have had to borrow their guiding principles and techniques from

Mass-produced housing in Elat. [Israel Information Services]

New residential section in Ashdod. [Israel Information Services]

various Occidental schools of contemporary architecture. Frequently, particularly in the early years of modern Jewish settlement in Palestine, the principles of architecture and urban planning imported from Europe have not been suited to giving appropriate physical expression to the new social realities of the *Yishuv (Jewish population of Palestine)—the *kibbutz, the *moshav, and mass housing for immigrants—and have conflicted with climate and budgetary limitations.

A dominant factor in much of Israeli architecture has been the element of urgency, the need for large-scale planning done with great dispatch to accommodate the masses of immigrants who have come to Israel, especially in the period immediately following the establishment of the State, and to keep pace with urban and industrial expansion. Given the pressure under which the work has had to be completed, many of Israel's buildings bear the characteristics of improvisation and of stereotyped formulas not calculated to create an impression of beauty or congeniality with their environment. In a country where the first priority has had to be assigned to the needs of mass shelter and to survival in the face of constant threats from unfriendly neighbor nations, esthetic considerations frequently have been subordinated.

HISTORY

The history of modern Palestinian and Israeli architecture may be divided into five distinct phases: mid-19th century to the early days of the British Mandate (1880s to mid–1920s); mid–1920s to early 1930s; war and struggle for statehood (mid–1930s to 1948); early statehood (1948–55); and the present (1955–   ).

Mid-19th Century to Early Days of the British Mandate (1880s to Mid–1920s). This era, which saw the first organized attempt by Jews to establish rural and urban settlements in Palestine, preceded the emergence of a specifically Israeli architecture. The following architectural and town-planning developments date from this period:

1. Jerusalem neighborhoods such as Y'min Moshe and Me'a Sh'arim and others, where immigrants settled by land of origin. These neighborhoods show the influence of housing development ideas current in England at the time.

2. Villages built under the sponsorship of Baron Edmond de *Rothschild, which show a distinct French influence.

3. Villages such as Petah Tikva and Hadera, planned by German engineers of the Templar colonies (*see* TEMPLARS).

4. Early residential areas of the new Jewish town of Tel Aviv and of Haifa at the foot of Mount Carmel. Their architecture followed Mediterranean patterns.

5. Early public buildings such as the *Herzliya High School in Tel Aviv (1905) and the Reali High School in Haifa (1911), built in an "Oriental" style incorporating Middle Eastern, Arab, Persian, and ancient forms in the framework of otherwise modern design.

Mid-1920s to Early 1930s. This period, which was marked by the heavy post-World War I *immigration, the establishment of Jewish quasigovernmental institutions under the British Mandate, the early *Arab riots, an economic slump (1928–32), and a proliferation of kibbutzim and moshavim, gave rise to eclectic construction in the newly developed residential sections of Jerusalem, Haifa, and Tel Aviv and to the beginnings of contemporary functional styles. Characterized by straightforwardness and mass composition reflecting the physical and psychological functions of the building and unhampered by preconceived notions, this new architectural trend produced a style in keeping with the Zionist goal of creating an entirely new environment as the basis for the future Jewish State.

The chief ideologist of this trend was Alex Baerwald, who made his influence felt as the designer of various buildings and also as the first lecturer in architecture at the Haifa *Technion. Born in Germany, Baerwald had come to Palestine before World War I to design the Reali High School and Technical College compound. For this purpose he drew on Muslim and Mediterranean architectural styles, consulting Arab builders who had had experience in working for English, French, and German clients. In the last years of his life (he died in 1931), however, he abandoned the eclectic approach and became a leading exponent of the search for a new style.

Another architect who first attained prominence in this period was Richard *Kaufmann, who designed many of the villages and garden suburbs established between 1919 and 1929 and planned the settlement of Nahalal in the form of a circle. Born in Germany, he brought with him new ideas of town planning influenced by the British view of the garden city as the city of the future. This approach was in keeping with the Zionist ideal, which not only advocated a return to farming and nature but also sought to put the achievements of science to work in the creation of the Jewish State. Free from eclecticism, Kaufmann

brought to his work new concepts of planning and the extensive use of reinforced concrete. The buildings he designed in the warmer regions of the country show the manner in which he utilized climatic elements in relation to contemporary tropical building. He was able to combine rational planning with monumental design. Meanwhile, British architects pursued a style of their own, typified by the police stations erected in various parts of the country with a mixture of details from Arab and Cycladic architecture. Their designer, Austen St.-B. Harrison, also planned the Palestine Archaeological Museum (Rockefeller Museum) and the High Commissioner's Palace near Jerusalem.

Two buildings of interest dating from that period are the old premises of the Technion in Haifa (1925) and the National Institutions compound in Jerusalem (1930). The Technion building still reflected the eclectic approach, with a fusion of Persian and European elements. The National Institutions compound, which housed the *Jewish Agency and *Jewish National Fund headquarters and the offices of the *Va'ad L'umi (National Council), typified the analytical and functional style. It was designed by Yohanan (Eugene) Ratner, who had been born in Russia and educated in Germany and had come to Palestine in the 1920s. The framework and interior walls of the National Institutions buildings were of reinforced concrete. Their outside walls were made of the Jerusalem stone quarried from the Jerusalem Mountains. Under an ordinance adopted by the British authorities at that time, all buildings in the new city of Jerusalem had to be constructed or faced with this local sandstone, which lent the city a charm and beauty all its own.

Most of the public buildings of the period were commissioned

Dizengoff Circle, Tel Aviv. [Israel Government Tourist Office]

King David Boulevard, Tel Aviv. [Israel Information Services]

Hilton Hotel, Tel Aviv. [El Al Israel Airlines]

on the basis of competitions, which did much to encourage architectural talent. Prominent among the judges in these contests were Ratner and Prof. Alexander Klein, the chief architect for the Jewish National Fund.

War and Struggle for Statehood (Mid-1930s to 1948). This period saw large-scale immigration from Germany, increased Arab agitation, World War II, and the victorious struggle against the British authorities for an independent Jewish State. The architecture showed a strong Central European influence imported by prominent Palestinians who had gone to Europe to study and, particularly, by architects of professional standing who had come to Palestine as refugees from Nazi persecution. Many of the apartment buildings, theaters, and schools built during these years were constructed in the formalized Western European Bauhaus style, which failed to take into account the climate of the country and soon looked dreary against the strong light and brilliant colors of the country. In contrast, the middle 1930s also brought a new style of rather small apartment houses of reinforced concrete which were better adapted to the climate, taking advantage of the breezes that brought relief from the heat.

One of the architects who devoted much effort to adaptation of the formal values of functional architecture to local conditions of climate and light was Leopold Krakauer of Jerusalem. His designs incorporated such aids to comfort as ventilators.

Considerable influence was exerted by the world-renowned German-Jewish architect Eric Mendelsohn, who was active in Palestine during this period. His school brought a measure of uniformity to Palestinian architecture, drawing together the efforts of many architects and setting them on a common path. Among the public, commercial, and private residential buildings designed by Mendelsohn were the Anglo-Palestine Bank (*see*

BANK L‘UMI L’YISRAEL), the Mount Scopus *Hebrew University–Hadassah Medical Center (Jerusalem, 1937), and the home of Chaim *Weizmann in Rehovot.

Other architects who first came into prominence in the late 1930s were Dov Carmi and Z’ev Rechter, in Tel Aviv, and Joseph Neufeld, Heinz Rau, and Arye Sharon. Sharon, who was born in Israel, had gone to Germany in the 1920s to study at the Bauhaus school and eventually became Israel’s first Director of Planning.

Early Statehood (1948–55). The first precarious years of the Jewish State saw an unprecedented wave of immigration, which necessitated a massive building program after a period of comparative inactivity during World War II. The rickety Ma‘abarot (transit villages; *see* MA‘ABARA) composed of huts, tents, and packing crates, in which the immigrants were given makeshift shelter on their arrival, had to be replaced as quickly as possible by more adequate and permanent dwellings. Frequently such apartment buildings would rise adjacent to the Ma‘abara they were intended to replace. This was not a period of new architectural styles; the overriding concern was the provision of decent homes for the greatest possible number of families at minimum cost. Some 70 per cent of Israel’s dwellings were built after 1949. In 1948 town-planning activities along comprehensive lines were initiated with the establishment of an official Planning Department that anticipated the requirements of a total population of 2.5 million by planning new towns (*see* DEVELOPMENT TOWNS), industrial zones, and educational and recreational areas.

To conserve space, the trend in housing design began to shift from relatively small units with adjacent private gardens to multidwelling residential units. Regional development policy sought the dispersal of the population throughout the country,

El 'Al building, Tel Aviv. [El Al Israel Airlines]

in preference to concentration around Tel Aviv, Haifa, and Jerusalem, and the creation of rural regions with easily accessible urban facilities. The latter aspect of regional planning endeavored, among other purposes, to facilitate the integration of immigrants from divergent backgrounds. It enabled them to live together in their own nationality groups, while bringing them into contact with 'Olim from other parts of the world through the urban facilities which they all shared.

The Present (1955–). As conditions in the young State attained stability and the post-1948 austerity was eased to some extent, architects were again free to pay greater attention to esthetic and artistic considerations. The Israeli architect of the 1960s was particularly concerned with the following objectives: (1) the breakup of the repetitive character of living space units and the reorganization of apartments in a manner conducive to active social relationships (entertainment of guests at home plays a paramount role in Israeli social life); (2) the siting of apartments near areas of greenery in the form of small court-yards or large squares; and (3) the improvement of the exterior appearance of buildings.

Architects gained inspiration from southern architectural concepts originating in the French Midi and Latin America, from Scandinavian trends, and from ancient Hebrew decorative motifs found on artifacts unearthed by archeologists. High-rise buildings made their first appearance in the early 1960s, and air conditioning became increasingly prevalent.

Even the kibbutz was beginning to make concessions to beauty and comfort. With improved economic conditions, the older and wealthier kibbutzim built modern dining halls, cultural centers, schools, and living quarters catering to the growing

desire for individual privacy. Foreign industrial enterprises and tourist hotels built in Israel by international hotel chains (e.g., the Hilton and the Sheraton in Tel Aviv) represented the most recent advances being made in modern Western architecture.

A group of architects including Benjamin Idelson, Alfred Mansfeld, Arye Sharon, and M. Weinrob set up large studios in which they gave employment to young colleagues. These men attached particular importance to the use of new building materials. Yohanan Ratner and Heinz Rau continued to be active, each developing a distinctive mode of design. Ratner designed his buildings as continua of functional and spatial relationships. His approach to the overall design of buildings and his somewhat cursory attitude to the finish of details aroused considerable debate in Israeli architectural circles. Rau, who was born in Germany, emphasized light and shade and the establishment of a sophisticated relationship between a building and its surroundings. He strove for a clear approach and precise handling of relations between detail and mass. His buildings included the Synagogue on the Hebrew University campus (1957) and the Hebrew Union College building in Jerusalem (1962). He became known for highly polished exteriors and exterior decorations.

Among other Israeli architects prominent in the 1960s were Robert Bannet, who built a shopping center (1960) and housing projects (1962) in Ramat Aviv and the dining hall of the kibbutz Giv'at Brenner (1962); D. A. Brutzkus, who designed the Applied Physics Laboratory of the Hebrew University (1958); Ram Carmi, son of the late Dov Carmi (Carmi's Tel Aviv firm, Carmi & Associates, participated in the construction of various buildings on the new Hebrew University campus in Jerusalem and helped build the *Histadrut headquarters, 1955, the Mann Auditorium, 1959, and the El 'Al building, 1963, all in Tel Aviv; Aviah Hashimshoni, dean of the Faculty of Architecture and Town Planning of the Haifa Technion, who designed public buildings and sports and housing projects all over the country; Yosef Klarwein, designer of the new *Knesset building; Sh'muel Mestiechkin, who designed the Nautical School at Caesarea (1947), the chicken house in the kibbutz HaZore'a

Administration Building of the Hebrew University of Jerusalem. [Israel Information Services]

(1955), and the Mona Bronfman Scheckman Amphitheater on the new Hebrew University campus (1958); and Z'ev Rechter, who worked with the Carmi firm.

A. HASHIMSHONI

PROFESSIONAL TRAINING AND ORGANIZATION

In the first four decades of its existence, the Haifa Technion Faculty of Architecture, inaugurated by Alex Baerwald in 1925 and headed for many years by Yohanan Ratner, produced more than 500 graduates, or 90 per cent of all architects at work in Israel. The standard course takes five years, town planning being offered as an elective subject during the senior year. In 1953 the Technion set up a Building Research Station where students could learn about materials and scale models of projected important buildings could be tested. The station is a branch of the Israel Bureau of Standards. The Association of Engineers and Architects of Israel had (1965) 600 architects in a total membership of 3,500 and published its own magazine.

POINTS OF ARCHITECTURAL INTEREST

Numerous points of architectural interest are found in Haifa, Jerusalem, Tel Aviv and its environs, and the Negev.

Haifa. Among the outstanding recent architectural additions to this city are the ultramodern Haifa Technion campus on Mount Carmel, including the Winston S. *Churchill Auditorium (designed by Arye Sharon and Benjamin Idelson) and the new Medical Center (by Rechter and Zarhy). Plans have been made to replace deteriorated sections in the middle sector of Mount Carmel and to build luxury houses overlooking Haifa Bay. A Haifa landmark is the Dagon grain silo, which represents modern architecture at its most functional and bears decorations symbolic of the Promised Land of the Bible.

Jerusalem. Modern Jerusalem is famous for its public buildings. It boasts the two Hebrew University–Hadassah Medical Centers, the older one on Mount Scopus and the new one in 'En Karem (1961), with the synagogue featuring the famous Marc *Chagall windows. The 'En Karem center was designed by the American architect Joseph Neufeld. In addition to the new Hebrew University campus there is the new building of the Israel Academy of Sciences and Humanities (by Resnik and Powsner), with the closed stone forms, interior courtyards, and low scale typical of Jerusalem architecture. The Israel Museum (by Alfred Mansfeld and Mrs. D. Gad) with its Shrine of the Book (by Frederick Kiesler and Armand Bartos) attracts large numbers of visitors each year (*see* MUSEUMS IN ISRAEL). The Knesset building has mosaics and tapestries by Marc Chagall.

Most impressive are two memorials, one to the 6 million Jewish victims of Nazism and the other to the late Pres. John F. Kennedy. The holocaust memorial, *Yad VaShem (by Arye Sharon, Benjamin Idelson, and Arye Elhanani), is a simple low structure with walls looking as if they had been built from random fallen boulders. The Kennedy Memorial, Yad Kennedy, which was dedicated in 1966, is on top of a mountain 20 minutes from Jerusalem. It is designed in the shape of a cut-down tree trunk. The interior contains only an eternal light and a bust of the late President.

Much new housing has gone up around the new city to accommodate the constantly increasing population. The reunification of the eastern and western sectors of Jerusalem after the *Six-day War of 1967 offered new problems and challenges to architects and town planners, particularly the renovation of blighted sections in the Old City and the beautification of the area around the *Western Wall (Wailing Wall).

Tel Aviv and Environs. In addition to the buildings previously mentioned, Tel Aviv has a few "skyscrapers": an eight-story apartment block designed by Nahum Zolotov, the Shalom Tower, and the El 'Al building. Designed by Yitzhak Perlstein and Gidon Ziv, the Shalom Tower, with 36 floors, is the tallest (1968) building in Israel and the largest office building (1 million square feet) in the Middle East. It straddles Herzl Street, one of the city's busiest thoroughfares. The El 'Al building, with shops and parking area below, was built by Carmi & Associates. It features a curved façade and an exterior spiral staircase.

Tel Aviv was in a constant process of construction in the late 1960s. Work was under way on a project to redevelop the waterfront between Tel Aviv and Jaffa. Giv'atayim, a suburb of Tel Aviv, acquired a futuristic hexagonal apartment building designed by Neumann, Hecker, and Sharon. The same group of architects designed the City Hall of Bat Yam, south of Tel Aviv. This strange-looking structure was built in the form of an inverted ziggurat.

Negev. New plans for B'er Sheva' called for a large project (by Carmi & Associates) including high-rise buildings, offices, a motion-picture theater, and a supermarket and a shaded environment reminiscent of the traditional bazaar. Elat, seaport and tourist attraction, might become a "Venice of the Red Sea." Plans envisioned a network of canals built as inlets to allow water to enter the desert city. A marina along the canal banks would eventually be lined with hotels and cafés.

OUTLOOK FOR THE FUTURE

As of the late 1960s, Israeli architects had yet to develop a typical Israeli style. The proportionate role of European, Oriental, and "early Palestinian" tradition in the evolution of Israeli architecture remained to be seen. In the ultimate analysis, much of the future character of Israel's architecture would be shaped by economic and political factors. Only economic stability and freedom from the constant burden of national defense against unfriendly neighbors could provide a practical and psychological climate that would impel the people of Israel to demand more than mere shelter for survival and free Israeli architects to commit their creative talents to the beautification of their land.

G. HIRSCHLER

ARCHIVES, ZIONIST. *See* LIBRARIES AND ARCHIVES, ZIONIST.

Mordecai Ardon.
[Zionist Archives]

ARDON (BRONSTEIN), MORDECAI. Israeli painter (b. Tuchów, Galicia, Austria, 1896). He studied at the Bauhaus under Kandinsky, Feininger, and Klee. In 1933 he left Germany for Palestine, settling in Jerusalem. From 1935 until 1952 he taught at the New Bezalel School of Arts and Crafts (*see* BEZALEL SCHOOL), becoming director of the school in 1940. In 1952 he was appointed artistic adviser to the Israeli Ministry of Education and Culture. Ardon's symbol-fraught, usually very large canvases found recognition all over the world. He had several one-man shows and received a number of awards, including the *Israel Prize of 1963.

A. WERNER

ARGENTINA, ZIONISM IN. The first Jews to settle in Argentina were Marranos, who came in the 16th century during the early period of Spanish colonization and were eventually absorbed in the Christian population. There were small groups of Jews in the country in the second half of the 19th century, and in 1868 the first Jewish congregation was established. Mass immigration of Jews started in 1891 with the founding by Baron Maurice de *Hirsch of the *Jewish Colonization Association (ICA), which established Jewish agricultural settlements in the country. Many Jews came from Eastern Europe, but there was also a large influx of *Sephardim from Mediterranean countries. After the rise of Nazism in Europe, thousands of German Jews found refuge in Argentina. In 1968 there were 450,000 Jews in the country, 350,000 of whom lived in the capital city, Buenos Aires.

Early Years (1889–1905). Zionism in Argentina dates to 1889, when a group of Russian Jews arrived in the country to engage in agriculture. Among them were members of *Hoveve Zion. Immediately after landing on Argentine soil, they made a collection of funds for the colonization of Palestine. Organized Zionism in Argentina began in 1897, when J. Becker, Jacobo Simon Liachovitzki (b. Grodno, Russia, 1875; d. Argentina, 1937), an active and much-discussed figure in the movement, and Enrique Ana San founded in Buenos Aires a group called Hoveve Zion. It soon split, and a second group, Zion, came into being. Jacob Joselevich, a prominent figure whose active participation was of importance to the Zionist movement, was the secretary of the Hoveve Zion group and also served as treasurer of the Zion group. In the provinces, too, notably in the Jewish agricultural settlements of Entre Rios, Zionist societies were founded. Groups in widely separated places, though unable at first to act jointly, showed their identification with the Zionist movement. From the outset, the groups in Buenos Aires and the provinces kept in close touch with the central bodies of the Zionist movement and its leaders.

Several publications began to appear simultaneously in 1898. The first Argentinian-Jewish periodical, the lithographed *Widerkol*, with Michael Hacohen Sinai as editor, revealed both Zionist and Socialist tendencies. *Di Folkshtime*, which appeared from time to time between 1898 and 1914, was published and edited by Abraham Vermont, a former partner in the *Widerkol*. It provided an outlet for the complaints of settlers against the ICA and for criticism of various Zionist groups, thereby arousing the opposition of other publications such as *Der Phonograph*, *Di Blum*, and *Der Poik*.

In 1897, when there were only 50 organized Zionist members in the country, Becker, Liachovitzki, and San sent the 1st Zionist *Congress a cable expressing solidarity. A year later, the Argentinian Zionists decided to send a delegate to the 2d Congress. Discussions on this point led to a further split in the Hoveve Zion groups. The religious members founded a group of their own, called Hoveve Zion–Zikhron Sh'muel, after Rabbi Sh'muel *Mohilever. San appointed himself a delegate and went

to the Congress without the consent of his fellow workers. His purpose was to draw the attention of the Congress to the serious situation of the settlers in the ICA agricultural settlements and to suggest their transfer to Palestine. San's appearance at the Congress proved a failure. Speaking half in Russian and half in French, he could not make himself understood. His name was not included in the official Congress minutes, and he was not recognized as a representative of the Hoveve Zion in Argentina. He died without returning to that country.

By that time the Hoveve Zion of Argentina counted 300 affiliated members. Outstanding among them was Sh'lomo Liebeshutz (b. Russia, 1857; d. Argentina, 1932).

In 1899 Liachovitzki founded the Theodor Herzl League in opposition to the existing organizations. The new society soon gained importance. Joined by groups in Buenos Aires and the provinces, it was recognized by the Central Zionist Office as representing Argentine Zionism. The league had 200 nominal members and two branches in the provinces, in Basavilbaso and Córdoba. In 1900 it launched a Yiddish periodical, *Der Zionist*, which later also printed a Spanish edition (1904); and it opened a library and developed a youth group, Pirhe Zion, which attracted about 100 children between the ages of 7 and 15. It also sold 500 shares of the *Jewish Colonial Trust, organized a shareholders' club named for Max *Nordau (1901) with approximately 50 members, and established a Zionist synagogue, whose initiators were Rabbi Reuben Hacohen Sinai and Simha Fleischhecker. There were two other Zionist houses of worship in Buenos Aires: Hevra Tehillim, founded in 1895, and a private synagogue established in 1900 in the home of the Krehavitchev family.

In the early 1900s, while Zionism in the ICA settlements became weaker owing to the opposition of officials, the movement made headway in the Jewish community as a whole. As early as 1901 Zionist societies were formed in the small Jewish communities of Santa Fé and Córdoba. On Apr. 16–18, 1904, the first countrywide Zionist conference, chaired by Enrique Rubinsky, was held in Buenos Aires. It was attended by 35 delegates representing 16 societies, including both Sephardi and Ashkenazi organizations and a women's organization. The Zionist Association of Entre Rios, at the time an important center of Jewish life, refused to participate because it disagreed with the Theodor Herzl League on Zionist matters as well as on local Jewish issues. The conference, which was dominated by the league, established the Federation of Zionist Groups. Among its founding members was Adolfo Krenovich, who at the 6th Zionist Congress was elected to the Greater *Actions Committee as member for the Americas. The Zionist organization in the provinces, called the Central Zionist Federation of Argentina, had its center at the Clara settlement in Entre Rios. The newly formed Federation of Zionist Groups founded the Zionist Argentine People's Bank in July, 1904, as a branch of the Jewish Colonial Trust, introduced collections for the *Jewish National Fund at Jewish functions and affairs, and established Theodor Herzl Leagues in Coronel Suárez (province of Buenos Aires) and Rosario.

In 1905 a second Zionist conference, held in the province of Entre Rios, was attended by 34 delegates from 21 groups. Buenos Aires was represented by Zeev Zeitlin, J. S. Liachovitzki, and Dr. E. de Benedetti. The conference did not accomplish unification between the federation and the Entre Rios groups, although both were aware of the need to create a territorial organization that would embrace the entire Zionist movement in Argentina.

Second Period (1905–14). The large wave of Jewish immigration that followed the failure of the Russian Revolution of 1905 brought new Zionist elements to the country. The ideology and background of these immigrants were the same as those of the pioneers of the *Second 'Aliya, which began at that time. The Jews who settled in Argentina and took root there were mainly workers and skilled artisans, nourished by the Jewish culture and traditions of Eastern European communities and by contemporary Jewish ideologies. In this spirit they established their own organization, Tiferet Zion, which soon attracted the support of the Entre Rios Zionist groups led by Dr. Noah Iarcho (d. 1912), an outstanding physician in the settlements.

New immigrants from Russia also established the Territorialist organization Herut, which, a year later (1906), changed its name to Zionists-Socialists (see PO'ALE ZION). This group published the Yiddish bulletin *Nachrichten,* which was edited by Meir Pollack.

In 1906 a group of followers of Ber *Borochov was organized. Its periodical was *Broit und Ehre* (Bread and Honor). The leaders of this Zionist Socialist group included Zalman Soskin and Dr. León Hazanovitch. Both men were subsequently deported from the country by the Argentinian authorities for Socialist activity.

The years 1906 to 1908 saw the struggle between Tiferet Zion and the federation for leadership in Argentinian Zionism. In 1906 the federation still seemed to be quite strong. In the *Shekel (membership fee) report of that year, Liachovitzki, head of the federation, submitted a list of 1,247 Shekel holders as against the 120 submitted by Tiferet Zion. However, at the third Zionist conference, held in 1907, again without the participation of the Entre Rios group, it developed that only seven groups were actively affiliated with the federation. This conference decided to establish a youth movement, called Pirhe Herzl.

Tiferet Zion appealed to the Actions Committee to recognize it as the official representative of the *World Zionist Organization in the country. The request was granted after two members of Tiferet Zion, who were preparing to settle in Palestine, had stopped on their way in Europe to attend the 8th Zionist Congress (1907) and reported to the Actions Committee the situation in Argentina. In an effort to retain its status, the federation offered to coopt to its committee three members of Tiferet Zion, but the offer was not accepted. In 1908 Tiferet Zion launched its periodical, *Dos Yidishe Lebn,* and, with Dorshe Zion (founded by middle-class elements that had seceded from Tiferet Zion) and other groups, established a new representative body, the Central Committee of the Zionist party in Argentina, which by 1910–11 had 2,000 members. The committee embarked on widespread propaganda activity and began to publish a paper of its own, *Di Yidishe Hofnung.* This periodical, which existed until 1917, was edited by Jacob Joselevich.

In 1910 Nathan Gezang went to Argentina to take charge of Zionist activities. Having been sent by the Actions Committee of the Zionist Organization at the request of the local representative body, Gezang soon became a leader of Argentinian Zionism. He was assisted in his work by Joselevich, Sh'lomo Liebeshutz, and José Reich. Reich founded the periodical *Di Yidishe Velt,* which eventually became the organ of the federation and was edited by I. Gorelik, D. Lomonosuf, and M. Maidenik.

In 1913 a countrywide Zionist conference was convened. The conference, which established the Zionist Federation of Argentina, deliberated not only on Zionist affairs but also on general problems of Argentinian Jewry and expressed the need for community organizations and a board of communities. Joselevich was elected president of the new federation; Akiva Moses, secretary; José Jacubov, treasurer; and Nathan Gezang, technical director.

World War I Period. With the outbreak of World War I, Zionists became leaders of the local Jewish Aid Committee. In 1917 the Zionist Federation convened a conference of Jewish organizations to discuss aid to war victims and general Jewish problems. The main speakers at the conference, whose resolutions included a call on the future peace conference to secure full equality for Jews everywhere and to establish a Jewish National Home in Palestine, were the Zionists Joselevich, Sh'lomo Liebeshutz, Nathan Gezang, José B. Fleischer, Noah Katzovitch (of Mosesville, the first of the ICA settlements), and Rabbi Dr. Sh'muel Halfón (Jalfón).

In 1917 Dr. Boris Epstein, an emissary of the Actions Committee, toured Argentina. His addresses contributed much to the strengthening of Zionism. The issuance of the *Balfour Declaration toward the end of the year created great enthusiasm among Argentine Jewry. A Redemption Fund was established, and a volunteer movement was started for the *Jewish Legion by Vladimir German, a former Jewish officer in the Russian Army. Negotiations with the British Embassy were protracted because of British indifference and the cool attitude of the pacifist-minded Zionist Federation toward the project. However, German was able to overcome all the difficulties, and shortly before the end of the war a group of 35 volunteers sailed from Argentina. A second group of volunteers was in the process of formation when the armistice was declared. The Argentinian legionnaires participated in Jewish self-defense activities during the postwar riots in Palestine. Most of them remained in the country, with only a few returning to Argentina.

In 1920, a short time prior to the *London Zionist Conference, the Zionist Federation organized a great public demonstration in Buenos Aires. As a result of the enthusiasm generated, a collection for the *Keren HaYesod (Palestine Foundation Fund), which at that time had not yet been officially established by the Zionist Organization, realized £50,000. In 1921, when the decisions of the *San Remo Conference were adopted, enthusiastic public rallies took place in Buenos Aires.

In 1921 Dr. Alexander *Goldstein toured Argentina as first emissary of the Keren HaYesod. He was followed in 1922 by Leib *Jaffe. Another great public demonstration was organized in connection with the opening of the *Asefat HaNivharim (Elected Assembly) in Palestine. Thousands of Jews, led by Rabbi Shabetai Hesekia, former rabbi of Damascus, Leib Jaffe, and the leaders of the Zionist Federation, marched through the main thoroughfares of the capital past the Parliament and government buildings. A delegation was received by Pres. Hipólito Irigoyen and the Cabinet.

Between the Two World Wars. Like Zionism everywhere, Argentinian Zionism, especially after World War I, was divided into parties, factions, and splinter groups of different ideologies.

In 1918 Tiferet Zion left the Zionist Federation and established itself as an independent party, *Tz'ire Zion–*Hitahdut. The same year the Zionists-Socialists, who had never been part of the federation and had not been active for some time, were reactivated by the arrival of Marcos Regalski, an emissary of their party, and launched *Di Naye Zeit,* an organ that was still in existence in 1968.

The years that followed saw splits in the Tz'ire Zion as well as in Po'ale Zion into moderate, right-wing, and left-wing factions. The Left Po'ale Zion, which called itself *Ahdut 'Avoda, was very active in education and developed a school system of its own. Its activities influenced other parties to engage in educational work. In 1932 the Po'ale Zion emissary, J. Razilai, succeeded in uniting the Right Po'ale Zion and the Left Tz'ire Zion into Po'ale Zion–Hitahdut, which the Right Tz'ire Zion later joined.

In 1930 the Zionist Federation, which after the secession of the Tiferet Zion represented only the General Zionists, split into A and B sections; these subsequently reunited, only to split up a number of times thereafter.

With the birth of the Zionist Revisionist world movement, a branch was also established in Argentina (see REVISIONISTS). A *Mizrahi organization was established in 1940, when Rabbi Z'ev *Gold toured the country on behalf of religious Zionism.

The first Zionist women's organization in Argentina was the *Women's International Zionist Organization (WIZO). It came into being in 1920, in connection with a jewelry drive on behalf of Keren HaYesod conducted by a group of women. This group formed the nucleus of what later grew into a strong organization. Active for many years in WIZO and holding leading positions in it (1968) were Esther Shapira and Beruria Elnecave. A *Pioneer Women organization, established in 1948, was headed in 1968 by Mania Butler and Elena Kuziner.

In addition to those already mentioned, Zionist emissaries who visited Argentina after World War I included a number of other prominent figures. Ben-Zion *Mossinsohn toured the country on behalf of Keren HaYesod in 1925. That year Albert *Einstein was the guest of the University of Buenos Aires, and his presence helped strengthen Zionist influence. Abraham Mibashan arrived in Argentina in 1930 and served as the representative of the *Jewish Agency there until his death in 1960. Rabbi Yudah Leib Zlotnik came in 1935 as an emissary of the Jewish National Fund and initiated a drive for the raising of 500,000 pesos to buy land for the establishment of a settlement of Argentinian Jews. The drive encountered some difficulties but was completed in 1944 with the visit of Nathan *Bistritsky. Ten years later the projected settlement was established in the central sector of Israel and named Nir Tz'vi in memory of Baron Maurice de Hirsch (Hirsch, the German word for "hart," is "Tz'vi" in Hebrew). Because many of its settlers came from Argentina, the village was at first known as K'far Argentina.

In 1937 Lord *Melchett visited Argentina and initiated the establishment of a branch of the extended Jewish Agency there. Ezra Teubel was elected president, and Nathan Gezang, Simon Mirelman, and Marcos Regalski served as vice-presidents. In 1941 an office of the Jewish Agency was organized. Headed by Mibashan, the local Agency representative, it existed until the establishment of the State of Israel.

In 1940 the various Zionist groups in Argentina established the Zionist Central Committee to coordinate their activities. Represented in this body were the Zionist Federation, Po'ale Zion–Hitahdut, *HaShomer HaTza'ir, and the Revisionists. Its first president and secretary were Marcos Regalski and Moshe Kostrynski, respectively. In the years that followed, Isaac Halperin, Moisés Slinin, Mateo Goldstein, Isaac Harcabi, Isaac Goldenberg, and Nachman Radzichovski were presidents, and Mordechai Kaufman, M. Zion, S. Rotberg, Moshe Starkman, and Jacobo Breiter, secretaries. In 1946 the committee, which in 1943 had been renamed the Zionist Central Council of

Argentina, initiated (in cooperation with the Jewish Agency) the first Latin American conference, held in Montevideo, Uruguay, with Mibashan as a leading participant.

Establishment of the State of Israel. After the United Nations *partition resolution of November, 1947, Argentinian Jewry rallied to the support of the besieged and fighting *Yishuv (Jewish population of Palestine). A special *Hagana appeal, proclaimed by Ruth Klieger from Palestine and spearheaded by a committee presided over by Dr. Moyses Goldman, evoked an unprecedented response. The establishment of the State of Israel was celebrated by street demonstrations in Buenos Aires and other cities.

From the very beginning of the Zionist movement, the Jewish community of Argentina was clearly Zionist-minded. Especially following the establishment of the State of Israel, Zionists dominated Jewish life in the country. All major communal institutions, such as DAIA (Delegación de Asociaciones Israelitas Argentinas, founded to help the victims of Nazism), the community organization (Kehilla), and the Central Education Committee, were Zionist-directed and Zionist-oriented.

In 1956 the Zionist Territorial Organization of Argentina, a new central body formed to coordinate the activities of all Zionist parties, was initiated. In 1958 the Zionist parties, together with other Jewish groups, participated in the elections to the Jewish Community of Buenos Aires. Although the *Bund and the Communists, too, competed in these elections, the leadership of the community remained in the hands of the Zionists, who refused to cooperate with either group.

The Zionist Territorial Organization of Argentina was formally established in 1961, with Elimelech Gutkin as president and Abraham Mittelberg and Antonio Klein as secretaries. They represented Po'ale Zion–Hitahdut, Ahdut 'Avoda, and the Zionist Federation (General Zionists), which had become the largest Zionist groupings in the country. In all the larger cities Zionist councils coordinated the activities of the local groups and societies. The Zionist parties had their youth movements, which played an important role in education and *'Aliya (immigration), participated in Zionist work, and trained Halutzim (pioneers; see HALUTZ). These youth movements became influential, especially after World War II. They included Ihud *HaBonim, HaShomer HaTza'ir, *D'ror, *HaNo'ar HaTziyoni, *B'rit Trumpeldor (Betar), and *B'ne 'Akiva. LaMerhav was a nonparty training farm in Mosesville.

Argentinian Jews have given substantial material aid to Israel, principally through the United Campaign, which was inaugurated in 1948. Several hundred volunteers went to Israel to participate in the *War of Independence, and after the establishment of the State many Jews from Argentina made their permanent home in Israel. By the end of 1969 more than 4,000 Argentinian Jews had settled there.

M. SENDERAY AND R. P. RAICHER-SCHAPIRE

ARLOSOROFF, HAYIM VICTOR. Zionist leader (b. Romny, Ukraine, Russia, 1899; d. Tel Aviv, 1933). He received his education in Germany, where he was brought by his family when he was six years old. After World War I, while a student at Berlin University (where he received his doctorate in economics), he helped found *HaPo'el HaTza'ir in Germany and became editor of its periodical, *Die Arbeit*. He was instrumental in the founding of *Hitahdut (1920), the union of HaPo'el HaTza'ir and *Tz'ire Zion, and became one of its leaders. In 1923 he was elected to the *Actions Committee of the *World Zionist Organization. Settling in Palestine in 1924, he soon played a leading role in the *Yishuv (Jewish population). In 1926 he was elected a member of the *Va'ad L'umi and was in the Yishuv's delegation to the League of Nations in Geneva.

Hayim Arlosoroff.
[Zionist Archives]

He went to the United States in November, 1926, as a member of the delegation accompanying Chaim *Weizmann. The Tz'ire Zion utilized his stay in the United States and Canada to get in touch with various other Jewish student groups, particularly *Avukah. At the invitation of the Tz'ire Zion leadership Arlosoroff went to the United States again in the fall of 1927 for a longer stay, to participate in the educational and organizational work of the movement.

Arlosoroff supported the idea of an enlarged *Jewish Agency and with its establishment (in 1929) was named a member of its Administrative Committee. Two years later he was elected a member of the Agency's Executive, directing its Political Department in Jerusalem. After the rise of Nazism he visited Germany and set to work organizing the settlement of German Jews in Palestine. He helped prepare the agreement which enabled German Jews to transfer part of their assets from Germany to Palestine (*see* HA'AVARA).

One of the theoreticians of the Zionist labor movement, Arlosoroff was a prolific writer, in Hebrew and German, on political and economic problems. He was assassinated by unknown assailants in June, 1933, on the seashore of Tel Aviv (*see* STAVSKY TRIAL). In 1934–35 a collection of his Hebrew writings was published in seven volumes. In 1950 his *Yoman Y'rushalayim* (Jerusalem Diary) appeared; it contains Arlosoroff's private notes from the period during which he was director of the Jewish Agency's Political Department.

ARMISTICE AGREEMENTS. Treaties concluded between Israel and the Arab states following the *War of Independence (1947–48). Responding to a call by the UN Security Council on Nov. 16, 1948, to the parties involved in the Palestine conflict to seek agreement with a view to an immediate armistice and thereby to facilitate the transition from truce to permanent peace in the country, Israel and the Arab states entered into negotiations under United Nations chairmanship (*see* UNITED NATIONS AND PALESTINE-ISRAEL). Egypt was the first Arab state to sign an armistice agreement with Israel, at Rhodes (Feb. 24, 1949). Later, agreements were signed with Lebanon, at Rosh HaNikra on the Israeli-Lebanese border (Mar. 23, 1949); with Jordan, at Rhodes (Apr. 3, 1949); and with Syria, at Mahanayim, on the Israeli-Syrian border (July 20, 1949). The negotiations were guided by Ralph J. *Bunche, Acting UN Mediator for Palestine. *See also* BOUNDARIES OF THE STATE OF ISRAEL.

The agreements, which were similar in structure, delineated permanent armistice demarcation lines, limited the use of armed forces in areas adjoining these lines, and provided for the exchange of prisoners of war and the setting up of Mixed Armistice Commissions to enforce the agreements. The agreement between Israel and Jordan contained, in addition, a provision for the establishment of a special committee to formulate plans and make arrangements designed to enlarge the scope of the armistice agreement, including free access to the *holy places, the resumption of normal activities on the Mount Scopus campus of the *Hebrew University of Jerusalem and at the *Hadassah-University Hospital, and the use of the Jewish cemetery on the Mount of Olives. This last paragraph, however, was never honored by the Jordanian authorities. The armistice agreements were to remain in force until a peaceful settlement between the parties had been achieved.

The armistice agreements contained the statement that, having been "negotiated and concluded in pursuance of the resolution of the Security Council of 16 November 1948 calling for the establishment of an armistice in order to eliminate the threat to the peace in Palestine and to facilitate the transition from the present truce to permanent peace in Palestine, they shall remain in force until a peaceful settlement between the Parties is achieved."

During the same period, the Palestine Conciliation Commission was set up under a United Nations resolution of Dec. 11, 1948. Composed of French, Turkish, and United States members, it was to assist the governments and authorities concerned in carrying out the task of seeking agreement by negotiations with a view to the final settlement of all questions outstanding between them.

For more than a year following the signing of the armistice agreements, the Mixed Armistice Commissions set up in accordance with them supervised the armistices so effectively that the chief of staff of the UN Truce Supervision Organization felt that the number of truce observers could be reduced from 500 to 30. During this period there were no more than three or four violations by military action; consequently, the chief of staff suggested that all future incidents of this nature could be effectively handled by the Mixed Armistice Commissions, whose bases should be "broadened by means of conversations or conferences between the parties themselves."

However, the attitude of the Arab states on the question of negotiations with Israel hardened to the point where they adamantly refused to entertain even the suggestion that they should enter into peace negotiations with the Jewish State. When France, the United Kingdom, and the United States issued a Tripartite Declaration (May 25, 1950) to the effect that they would control the arms balance in the Middle East and prevent any violation of frontiers and armistice lines, the members of the *Arab League Council responded by stating that they "take note of the assurances that they have received to the effect that the three powers did not intend by their declaration... to exert pressure on the Arab states to enter into negotiations with Israel. . . ."

In the absence of any actual pressure toward negotiating a peace, the situation on Israel's frontiers deteriorated to the point where border incidents became very frequent along all the Arab-Israeli frontiers with the exception of the Lebanese. In 1954 conditions on the Israel-Jordan armistice line became so intolerable that Israel invoked the article in the armistice agreement which provided that, after one year, either party could request the Secretary-General of the United Nations to call a conference to review the agreements, with attendance mandatory. The Jordanians refused to attend, however, and the Secretary-General gave up the attempt to call a conference.

Meanwhile, the frontier incursions continued. Irregular Arab contingents repeatedly and frequently crossed into Israel, perpetrating sabotage, espionage, and terrorist missions. Israeli retaliation followed at longer intervals but with the deployment of greater force. Throughout, the Mixed Armistice Commissions proved powerless not only to prevent these incidents but, in many cases, even to fix the blame for them. The Egyptian-Israel armistice became totally inoperative. The Syrian-Israeli Mixed Armistice Commission ceased functioning altogether because the Syrians insisted on placing the question of sovereignty over the demilitarized zones on the Commission's agenda as its first item, whereupon Israel felt constrained to boycott the Commission.

In November, 1955, after a clash between Israeli and Egyptian troops in the El-'Auja demilitarized zone, which resulted in the ejection of the Egyptians, UN Secretary-General Dag Hammarskjöld negotiated a new armistice agreement in which the parties committed themselves to the United Nations (not to each other, as formerly) to open fire only if the other side violated the cease-fire provisions. Other breaches of the armistice agreement were not to be considered sufficient ground for opening fire. This modification of the armistice agreement led directly to the launching of *fedayeen raids by Egypt. It was this development, together with the closing of the Suez Canal by Egypt to Israeli shipping (July, 1956), that led to Israel's *Sinai Campaign late in 1956.

Several months later, Israel withdrew from Sinai on the basis of a new set of "understandings" that superseded the old Egyptian-Israeli armistice agreement. A United Nations presence was established along the Egyptian side of the Egyptian-Israeli border; as a result, that frontier became almost as peaceful as the frontier between Israel and Lebanon in the north. The removal of the United Nations units from the border at Egypt's demand in May, 1967, was the first step leading to the *Six-day War of 1967.

The Syrian-Israeli armistice agreement contained a provision which established demilitarized zones on the Israeli side of the border. In these Israel was barred from using her military forces and from effecting changes that would give her military advantages while she was allowed to proceed with the civilian development of the zones. Syria's interpretation of these provisions was that they gave her the right to contest irrigation and electrification works in the zones and to deny Israel's sovereignty in them. When Syria insisted on discussing the question of sovereignty over the zones in the Syrian-Israeli Mixed Armistice Commission, Israel boycotted the Commission, which thus ceased functioning. Meanwhile, the Syrians continued the intermittent shelling of the Israeli villages and fields lying in the valley below their own elevated fortified positions. When, as late as October, 1966, Israel tried once again to obtain redress through the Security Council, a widely approved compromise formula was blocked by a Soviet veto. In January, 1967, UN Secretary-General U Thant attempted to reactivate the Syrian-Israeli Mixed Armistice Commission. Although an advance agreement was reached to the effect that only matters pertaining to cultivation in the demilitarized zones would be discussed, the Syrians ignored this agreement when the body met. Thereupon, the meetings of the Commission were suspended by its United Nations chairman. During all this time, Syrian shelling and sabotage continued. On Apr. 7, 1967, when Israel employed planes to silence Syrian tanks and gun positions, the Syrians sent out their own Russian-built planes to meet the Israeli fliers, who, however, managed to destroy part of the Syrian Air Force.

The Jordanian-Israeli armistice suffered from the fact that Jordan had the longest and least clearly demarcated border with Israel and that Jordan was used as the staging area from which other Arab states launched their sabotage attacks against Israel. After one such raid, organized by Syria from the Jordanian village of Es-Samu, Israel retaliated by a severe attack on the village on Nov. 13, 1966.

The 1948 armistice agreements were effectively terminated by the Six-day War of 1967, which resulted in a complete obliteration of the 1948 cease-fire and armistice lines. During the 19 years that those lines existed, they represented a tenuous de facto and temporary border between the areas controlled by Israel and those controlled by her Arab neighbors. While the armistice agreements themselves did not prevent the Arab states from manifesting their hostility and belligerence on a small scale, they helped at least to prevent the recurrence of a large-scale Arab incursion into Israel such as took place in the very hour of her birth in 1948.   R. PATAI

ARMY OF ISRAEL. *See* ISRAEL DEFENSE FORCES.

ARON, ROBERTO. Lawyer and Zionist leader in Chile (b. Mendoza, Argentina, 1915). At an early age Aron founded the Ahad Ha'Am Youth Center in Argentina. In 1937 he moved to Chile. After obtaining a law degree from the University of Chile, he became president of the Zionist Federation of Chile and of the General Zionist party (*see* GENERAL ZIONISM). He was a founder of the Latin American Confederation of General Zionists.

In 1958 he settled in Israel, and from 1960 to 1964 he was a member of the Zionist *Actions Committee. He was also a member of the Board of Directors of the Otzar Hityashvut HaY'hudim (Jewish Settlement Fund), a founder and vice-president of Kiron (a new development near Tel Aviv), a founder of the Israel American Medical Center, and chairman of the Council of the *World Confederation of General Zionists.

ARONOWICZ (AHARONOWITZ), JOSEPH. Writer and Palestine labor leader (b. Kirivka, near Bershad, Ukraine, Russia, 1877; d. Tel Aviv, 1937). To avoid military service in Tsarist Russia, he moved to Brody, Galicia, Austria, where he became active as an educator among Zionist youth. In 1906 he settled in Palestine. At first a laborer in various Jewish settlements, he was invited to edit *HaPo'el HaTza'ir,* the first labor periodical in Palestine, published by the *HaPo'el HaTza'ir party. During World War I he was expelled from Palestine and went to Egypt. After his return at the end of the war, he resumed his work with *HaPo'el HaTza'ir* until 1922. Subsequently, he served as director of Bank HaPo'alim (Workers' Bank). He was prominently active in the labor movement and represented first HaPo'el HaTza'ir, then *Mapai, in the institutions of the Zionist movement, the Palestine Jewish community, and the *Histadrut. His thinking made a great impact on the Palestinian Jewish labor movement, of which he and Berl *Katznelson were regarded as the two most prominent intellectual leaders and spokesmen. A selection of Aronowicz's articles was published in two volumes in 1941.   G. KRESSEL

A gallery of Israeli paintings in the Israel Museum in Jerusalem. [America-Israel Cultural Foundation]

ARONOWICZ, ZALMAN. *See* ARANNE, ZALMAN.

ART IN ISRAEL. The general impression one gets in viewing the artistic production of the *Yishuv (Jewish population of Palestine and later of Israel) is one of a mosaic picture in the making, in which the many colorful stones have not yet been set in place so as to make an organized whole. It is not yet possible to speak of typical Israeli art, not even of Israeli schools of art. Foreign influences abound, and in the work of many artists, even of the youngest native-born generation, one feels the traces of this or that European or American artistic trend.

Painting. Prior to the 1930s, only a few Palestinian painters were known beyond the confines of the Yishuv, most of whom had acquired fame prior to settling in Palestine. The Yishuv, in the era of *"stockade and tower" settlements, had little time for any recreation other than *music and only a limited interest in architecture (*see* ARCHITECTURE AND TOWN PLANNING IN ISRAEL).

A few veteran painters, such as Hermann *Struck in Haifa and Nahum *Gutman and Reuven *Rubin in Tel Aviv, had been active for many years. Pinhas Litvinovsky, Ludwig Blum, and Abel Pann had been working in Jerusalem since World War I. Blum and Pann were chiefly landscape painters, though Pann's Biblical scenes were peopled with Oriental nymphets. Gutman

and Rubin were the romantics of the multiracial Levant, the exotic genre of their time. Blum was a classical impressionist realist.

In the early 1930s refugee painters poured into Palestine, representing almost every artistic trend then current in Europe. Joseph *Budko took over the *Bezalel School and was joined by the woodcut master Jacob *Steinhardt. Mordecai *Ardon came fresh from the Bauhaus to teach the art as well as the craft of painting. Z'ev Ben Zvi had come earlier from Poland, having persuaded Boris *Schatz, the founder and director of the Bezalel School, to take him on as a teacher of sculpture. David Gumbel and Ludwig Wolpert took over the classes in metalwork. Other refugee artists found a place in the kibbutzim, where they taught and also continued to paint. *Youth 'Aliya rescued a younger generation of talent that later came to the forefront in Israeli painting.

This burst of activity, involving hundreds of painters, from Marcel Janco to Jankel Adler, from Joseph Zaritzky to Anna *Ticho, was stopped short by World War II and then by Israel's struggle for independence. It was not until the 1950s that Israeli artists began to renew their ties with the outside art world. As late as 1960 there was still a great deal of resistance to abstraction, and it was not until the 1960s that master abstract painters such as Joseph Zaritzky, Zvi Meirowitch, Avigdor

Stematsky, and Lea Nikel were firmly established. Abstract expressionism too made its appearance only in the 1960s, at a time when it was beginning to be submerged by assemblage and pop art elsewhere. A colony of nearly 100 Israelis lived in Paris, working in assemblage and other avant-garde media, but some of them seemed unaware that the focus of invention had shifted from Paris to New York and London. The vast majority of the nearly 4,000 artists in Israel were still working routinely in formalized realism. Fewer than 100 of them were really outstanding by any international standards, although some 2,000 were registered exhibiting members of the Israeli Painters and Sculptors Association. Of all these, only a dozen or so seemed to be consciously evaluating art developments elsewhere in relation to their own work. A few artists, such as Arie Aroch, made an effort to integrate some of the "discoveries" of America's Rauschenberg and Johns into their works. Fortunately, Aroch has gone on to more personal triumphs with his collage oils and "crayon on print" (oil pastels worked over glossy reproductions).

If the great majority of the painters survived on the heritage of the culture they had brought with them, it was largely because their public had come to Israel with them and still subscribed to the same esthetic ideas. Even the pioneers of the 1910s were still in demand and continued to be active. The landscape had been a dominating influence in Israeli art, even in abstract painting.

On the other hand, there was a group of young painters who concentrated on Jewish themes, organizing them in semi-abstract, semiformalized compositions, and who consciously aimed at creating an Israeli-Jewish school. The most articulate members of this group were Naftali Bezem, Sh'muel Boneh, and Moshe Tamir, all of whom began painting under Mordecai Ardon. Their themes were taken from the Bible or the festivals, or were based on ritual symbols. Bezem also concentrated on the theme of *'Aliya, which he saw as the great regenerative force of modern Jewish history. One of his 'Aliya murals became the keynote of the Israeli Pavilion at Montreal's Expo 67. This rather intellectual approach is a far cry from the emotional expressionism of Germany, the erstwhile home of so many Israeli painters or their parents. Figurative expressionism has disappeared almost entirely in Israel.

Other painters were drawing on their particular ethnic origins as a source of expression. Most outstanding among these was Yosef Halevy, whose parents had come from Yemen. He painted lyrical abstractions of his people, with one of the richest yet subtlest palettes in the country.

Veteran painters, such as Zaritzky and Aroch, who had succeeded in moving with the times had a great influence on the younger painters. Aroch was one of the trio who represented Israel at the 1964 Venice Biennale, together with Lea Nikel and Yigael Tumarkin, the latter a highly skilled maker of Crucifixion and Hiroshima images in the assemblage technique, using machine parts and various "rejected materials" on a polyester-and-wood panel base. Tumarkin also exhibited some tortured images in bronze and, in 1966, a number of antiwar memorials welded together from casts of machine guns and pistols. He is also an expert maker of sculptured jewelry.

Sculpture. While thousands painted, few worked in the demanding field of sculpture, in which one of the pioneers was Hannah Orloff. The outstanding sculptors have developed in surroundings where tools, time, and materials were available, namely, the kibbutz garage. Prominent among the kibbutz

sculptors were Yehiel Shemi and Ezra Orion, who worked with old iron sheets and rails. Less abstract but no less formal was the work of Yitzhak Danziger, who also exercised much influence as a teacher. The work of this trio was rather typically monumental, but a far cry from the realistic heroic worker-soldier statuary so beloved of most kibbutzim in the past. Lea Vogel has produced some highly original bronze figures in the last few years, in 1966 winning an ACIF scholarship; and Dodo Shenhav has executed equally strong animal abstractions carved from old Turkish railroad ties. In 1966 the polychrome polyester language of London pop reached Israel, fostered chiefly by Buki Schwartz, Aaron Witkin, and Menashe Kadishman. Abstract expressionism found its champion in the fecund forms of Pinhas Eshet's beaten volumes.

In 1968 there was still no sign of an Israeli school in a country characterized by diversity. Israelis are great individualists, and the better younger painters, such as Yosel Bergner, prefer to develop within their own stylistic framework, putting the accent on their highly personal view of things rather than following any particular "ism," though Bergner has become increasingly surrealist. Thanks to rising prices and a growing market both in Israel and abroad, the better painters could afford to go their own way. Many of them obtained commissions to decorate public buildings or new ships. Even Ya'akov Agam's tricky constructions of multiplaned compositions, which change color and form as the observer walks past them, were no longer regarded as avant garde; and in 1964 he executed two murals, one for the S.S. "Shalom" and the other for Jerusalem's Concert Hall.

Public Involvement. As public interest widened, more and more attention was given to art education and painting classes

Hannah Orloff's monument to the defenders of the kibbutz 'En Gev. [Israel Information Services]

in schools, where many painters were employed. Painter Moshe Tamir was appointed chief supervisor of art instruction in the schools. In 1964 the New Bezalel School of Arts and Crafts had 260 students and turned others away for lack of accommodations. Private art schools did well. There were classes and summer courses at the artists' village of 'En Hod, in the Carmel foothills. There was another art colony in Safed. All the larger towns, from Tiberias to Elat, boasted their own municipal art museums and many private galleries. A new art show would open somewhere approximately every day of the week. In addition there was a massive exchange of exhibitions with European museums. Private collections, varying from Amlash (Iran) figures to Chinese porcelain, Japanese prints and painting, French tapestries, and Greek ceramics, also went on show in 1964. Marc *Chagall, whose windows of the Twelve Tribes of Israel had been installed at the *Hebrew University-Hadassah Medical Center, visited Israel in 1964 to prepare studies for three tapestries in the new *Knesset building and again in 1966 to supervise the completion of his mosaics there. The first comprehensive show of Israeli art in the United States took place in 1964, and an Israeli group exhibited in the Galerie Charpentier in Paris. The Tate Gallery in London acquired its first Israeli work, Ardon's triptych "Missa Dura," after his critically successful show in London (followed in 1967 by a show in New York).

A sales boom continued through 1965 and most of 1966, enabling more Israelis to devote themselves to their art full time. The Ten-Plus group of 10 young artists, joined by a few others in group shows, reflected some of the latest trends in British painting, making a further break with abstract expressionism–impressionism, though the latter was bolstered by exhibitions by Fima-Roytenberg and Avigdor Arikha, both of whom came on visits from Paris. But Ten-Plus included such diverse approaches as the delightful Klee-like water colors of Louise Schatz and the intricate, intellectual, formalized abstractions of Reuven Berman. The British trend was reflected in the work of Ten-Plus advocate Aaron Witkin, an op-cum-pop former South African, who, in addition to his iron sculpture, was working in luminous paint on diamond backgrounds; such a work won him the Israel Museum's Young Artists' award for 1967. Other former South Africans to have outstanding shows were architect-painter-industrial designer Arthur Goldreich and expressionist Harold Rubin. More and more painters turned to the execution of design commissions, such as Dani Karavan's abstract sculptured wall for the Knesset and his screen for the new Tel Aviv Law Courts; Bezalel Schatz did decorative iron walls and screens for the *Jewish Agency headquarters and a building at the *Weizmann Institute of Science. Notable examples of the wedding of industry and art were the many commissions decorating the Hecht Dagon silo at Haifa port, in ceramic, enamel, and stained glass. A dozen new galleries, some for crafts as well as painting, opened in Tel Aviv in 1966 alone. A further boost to public interest came from the spate of international shows at the Israel and Tel Aviv Museums, notably those of Paul Klee and Henry Moore and the surrealists, with the young Israelis being given space alongside them; while veterans such as Reuven Rubin and expressionist romantics Menahem Shemi and Isidor Aschheim were given retrospective shows at the Israel Museum. A return to subject matter was also typical of the 1966–67 trend; the international surrealist show was followed by an exhibition of Israeli surrealists. Israeli Sh'muel Bak, formerly an abstract painter, brought a brilliantly

painted surrealist show from Rome and sold every canvas at a time when a general economic recession had brought an end to the sales boom. By 1968 both Israeli painters and the public were clearly in search of content and meaning.

M. RONNEN

'ARUGOT. Village (moshav) in the Judean Plain. Founded in 1949 by immigrants from Romania and Poland and affiliated with *T'nu'at HaMoshavim. Population (1968): 306.

ARZA. See MOTZA 'ILIT.

ASAD. Bedouin tribe in the B'er Sheva' region of the Negev. Population (1968): 410.

A'SAM. Bedouin tribe in the B'er Sheva' region. Population (1968): 1,350.

ASEFAT HANIVHARIM (Elected Assembly). Representative body of Palestine Jewry during the period of the British *Mandate for Palestine (1917–48), elected by members of the *K'nesset Yisrael (Community of Israel), the organization embracing politically the entire Jewish population of Palestine. With the occupation of the southern part of the country by the British Army late in 1917, the leaders of the local Jewish population took steps to form a united representative body to negotiate with the new authorities, who were expected to further the establishment of a Jewish National Home in the country. On Jan. 2, 1918, representatives of political parties and of economic and educational institutions met in Jaffa for a Preparatory Assembly to discuss current problems, particularly the formation of an elected representative body. The conference chose a Va'ad Z'mani (Provisional Council) to serve as interim representatives in internal as well as external matters, to deal with current problems, and to supervise the election of a delegates' assembly. On June 17, 1918, the Second Preparatory Assembly took place. About half a year later a third such assembly was held, with representatives participating from all over the country, which by that time had been occupied in its entirety by the British forces. The Va'ad Z'mani did much to consolidate the Jewish population, divided as it was into different parties and communities, and to prepare it for the assumption of quasigovernmental functions. It had to struggle with Orthodox Jewry, which opposed, on religious grounds, the extension of suffrage to women. On Apr. 19, 1920, the Va'ad conducted elections for the Asefat HaNivharim. The entire Jewish population, without distinctions of sex or class, participated in the elections. Of the 28,765 persons entitled to vote, 77 per cent made use of their prerogative, electing 314 delegates.

During the same period the Jews of Jaffa, Tel Aviv, Jerusalem, and Haifa organized community councils. These, as well as the councils of the rural villages, regarded themselves as cells of a countrywide community organization. At the initiative of the government, a unified Chief *Rabbinate for *Ashkenazim and *Sephardim was chosen.

The Asefat HaNivharim met in Jerusalem on Oct. 7, 1920, and proclaimed itself the "autonomous national leadership of the Jews of Palestine" and their sole representative in internal and external affairs. It elected the *Va'ad L'umi (National Council), which was given the task of drafting the constitution of the autonomous Jewish community and of securing its approval by the British. The *High Commissioner accorded official recognition to the Asefat HaNivharim and the Va'ad L'umi. The constitution drafted by the Va'ad L'umi was debated by the second session of the Asefat HaNivharim, held on Mar. 6, 1922. It was based on the principle that every Jew living in Palestine was obligated to belong to the overall community organization, which had the right to impose taxes for the maintenance of communal and national services. The third session set elections for the Second Asefat HaNivharim. Again the right of women to vote became a subject of heated controversy. The demands of the Orthodox were rejected, and elections were held on Dec. 6, 1925. Of the 64,764 persons entitled to vote, 57 per cent participated, electing 221 delegates.

The first session, held on Jan. 21, 1926, was advised of the Palestine government's refusal to approve a constitution for a national community organization in which membership was to be obligatory and of the government's insistence on the adoption of statutes for a religious community based on voluntary affiliation. After long deliberations the Va'ad L'umi agreed to these demands in order to prevent the breakdown of the community organization which had been built with so much effort. In February, 1926, the government published the Religious Communities Ordinances; within their framework the High Commissioner instituted the Jewish Community Regulations, published on Jan. 1, 1928, which served as the official and legal basis of the Jewish community organization until the establishment of the State of Israel. Under these regulations, Jews were entitled to opt out of K'nesset Yisrael. The *Agudat Israel accordingly withdrew from the K'nesset Yisrael and recognized neither the Va'ad L'umi nor the Chief Rabbinate.

The Asefat HaNivharim was the most authoritative body of all institutions of the K'nesset Yisrael. It served as the representative of the organized Jewish community and approved the budget of the Va'ad L'umi, which included also the budget of the Rabbinical Council. The K'nesset Yisrael took over from the Zionist *Executive the responsibility for the Jewish school system and later the Jewish health institutions. Its yearly sessions issued orders to levy the rates or fees which it asked or authorized the Jewish community councils to impose and collect and assessed taxes to cover the budgets of the Va'ad L'umi and the communities. It debated political issues and problems of security and economy involving the Jewish community. Its decisions were accepted as the official policy of the organized community. The Regulations Defining the Constitution and the System of Election of the Asefat HaNivharim were officially recognized on Mar. 3, 1930. They provided for universal suffrage, a secret ballot, and proportional representation. Every registered member of the Jewish community 20 years of age and over could be a candidate for election, provided he could speak, read, and write Hebrew.

Elections to the Third Asefat HaNivharim were held on Jan. 5, 1931. About 90,000 persons had the right to vote. Some 56 per cent of them voted, electing 71 representatives. Owing to the *Arab riots of 1936–39 and World War II, new elections were postponed and the Palestine government extended the authority of the Third Asefat HaNivharim, which held a total of 18 sessions from its election until the new elections of Aug. 1, 1944. In the elections to the Fourth Asefat HaNivharim, 67 per cent of the 300,000 persons entitled to vote participated, electing 171 representatives. The Asefat HaNivharim functioned until the end of the British Mandate and the establishment of the State of Israel.

Apart from its function as the quasi-governmental body of the Yishuv, the Asefat HaNivharim fulfilled a significant role in training the Jews of Palestine for the exercise of democratic parliamentary self-government. It was formally abolished on Feb. 13, 1949.

M. ATTIAS

'ASERET. Rural center in the Judean Plain. Established in 1954 and named for the 10 (Heb., *'asara*) founders of nearby G'dera, it serves the neighboring settlements of Meshar, Zekher Dov, K'far Mord'khai, K'far Aviv, Sh'dema, and Gan HaDarom. Population (1968): 382.

ASHDOD. Town on the southern coastal plain, named for an ancient town that was located nearby. Modern Ashdod was founded in 1955. A deepwater port, opened in 1966, established

Dockside at Ashdod. [Israel Information Services]

it as the southernmost port of the country. By 1968 Ashdod had a population of 28,600, a school population of 8,500, a municipal budget of IL9,570,940, and 480 municipal employees.

ASHDOT YA'AKOV. Village (kibbutz) in the Jordan Valley. Founded in 1933 and named for James (Ya'akov) de Rothschild, president of the *Palestine Jewish Colonization Association (PICA), on whose land the settlement was built. The settlement split in 1953, and the secessionists established a kibbutz nearby with the same name. Ashdot Ya'akov A and B were affiliated with *Ihud HaK'vutzot V'haKibbutzim and the *Kibbutz M'uhad, respectively. Population (1968): Ashdot Ya'akov A, 520; B, 530.

ASHKELON. *See* ASHK'LON.

ASHKENAZIM. Term derived from Ashk'naz (the traditional medieval Hebrew name for Germany), denoting those Jews whose ancestors lived in German lands. During and after the Middle Ages, the Ashkenazi Jews spread all over Europe (except the Mediterranean countries) and thence migrated overseas, to South Africa, the Americas, and Australia. Until the onset of the period of *Haskala (the Jewish Enlightenment) they retained Yiddish, a medieval German dialect with an admixture of Hebrew words, as their mother tongue, in which they produced a rich religious and secular literature. It was not until the late 19th or early 20th century that Yiddish was gradually replaced by the languages of the countries in which the Ashkenazi Jews lived.

Another result of Enlightenment and *emancipation was the rapid *assimilation, demographically as well as culturally, of many Ashkenazi Jews to the Christian majority populations in Central and Western Europe. This trend brought about a marked Germanization, Hungarianization, Anglicization, and and so on, of the Jews, even though they retained their religious affiliation with Jewish congregations and their Jewish consciousness.

In 1968 the total number of Ashkenazi Jews was estimated at 12 million, or about 88 per cent of the world Jewish population.

The percentage of Ashkenazi Jews in the *Yishuv (Jewish population of Palestine) and the *population of Israel underwent considerable fluctuation as a result of changes in the ethnic composition of Jewish *immigration. Of a total of about 24,000 Jews in Palestine in 1882, most were *Sephardim and *Oriental Jews. The *First 'Aliya (1882–1903) brought to Palestine 25,000 Jewish immigrants, almost all Ashkenazim. The same was true of the approximately 40,000 immigrants of the *Second 'Aliya (1904–13), the 35,000 immigrants of the *Third 'Aliya (1919–23), the 82,000 of the *Fourth 'Aliya (1924–31), and the 248,000 of the *Fifth 'Aliya (1932–39). As a result 345,000, or 77.5 per cent, of the 445,000 Jews living in Palestine in 1939 were Ashkenazim. From 1940 on the percentage of Ashkenazim among the Jewish immigrants steadily declined, and consequently so did their percentage in the Yishuv. In 1948 it was estimated at 76.3, in 1950 at 65.5, in 1952 at 60.3, in 1955 at 55, in 1960 at 53, and in 1965 at 50. It must be noted that the higher natural increase of the Sephardim and Oriental Jews was also an appreciable factor in this decline of the Ashkenazi percentage in the Yishuv.

It can be foreseen that while Ashkenazim will constitute an ever-increasing percentage of the world Jewish population, the reverse may be the case in Israel, where their numbers will probably continue to decrease relatively until about 1980, by which time the Sephardi and Oriental Jewish birthrate may, in all likelihood, have fallen to the level of the Ashkenazi birthrate.

R. PATAI

ASHK'LON (Ashkelon). City on the southern coastal plain. It was formed in 1955 by the amalgamation of Migdal Gad and Afridar. Migdal Gad, formerly the Arab townlet Majdal, was resettled by Jewish immigrants soon after its abandonment by the Arabs during the *War of Independence. Afridar, a modern suburb not far from the site of ancient Ashk'lon, was founded in 1951 by South African promoters. In 1968 the city consisted of five suburbs: Migdal, Afridar, Barne'a, Shimshon, and Shikune HaDarom.

The oldest settlement on the site dates back at least to the Bronze Age, and there is a heavy accumulation of later remains. In the late Bronze level sub-Mycenaean pottery was found. Other finds include a 3d-century B.C.E. bouleuterion with relief sculptures of Nike, Atlas, and Isis, an adjacent portico, a Roman tomb, and a Byzantine-Crusader wall.

Ashk'lon's economy is based on agriculture, which includes large citrus groves (see CITRUS INDUSTRY IN ISRAEL), cotton plantations, and *industry. Its beaches, historic sites, and relative proximity to the large urban centers of the country have made it a favorite resort. An area of the ancient city that is rich in antiquities has been developed into a national park.

The growth of Ashk'lon in the two decades following the

Communal and shopping center at Ashk'lon. [Zionist Archives]

independence of Israel is illustrated by the following figures. In 1948 the city had 2,000 inhabitants; in 1968, 37,400. In 1968 the municipal budget amounted to IL 12,000,000, and municipal employees numbered 550. The same year 13,000 pupils were enrolled in Ashk'lon's kindergartens and elementary, high, and trade schools.

ASHMURA (formerly Dardara). Village in the Hula Valley. Founded in 1949 by members of Nahal, a unit of the *Israel Defense Forces that is also trained in agriculture.

ASSAF, SIMHA. Scholar, Israel Supreme Court justice, and rector of the *Hebrew University of Jerusalem (b. Russia, 1889; d. Jerusalem, 1953). A product of the Yeshivot of Slutsk and Telšiai, he was well read in history, Judaica, and Hebrew journalism. In 1913 he became an instructor of Talmud in the Yeshiva of Odessa, and served as its principal during World War I. After the war his first scholarly papers on Jewish literature, history, sociology, and jurisprudence appeared. Leaving Russia in 1920, he studied in France and Germany, then settled in Palestine, where he became a lecturer in Talmud and the history of Jewish education at the Mizrahi Teachers Seminary in Jerusalem. In 1922 he lectured on Jewish law at the Jerusalem Law School, set up by the British Mandatory government, and in 1925 joined the faculty of the Hebrew University. Becoming a professor in 1937, he served as a member of the university's Executive Council, chairman of the department of Jewish studies, dean of the School of Humanities, and rector (1948–50). In addition to his lectures at the university he delivered weekly radio broadcasts and gave private lessons to outstanding students. His appointment to Israel's Supreme Court in 1948 required special approval by the *Knesset, as he did not have a law degree. He was a member of the World and Israel Executives of *Mizrahi and the first chairman of the Israel government's Council of Religious Education. He published many articles and books on Jewish history, education, and law and was active in various scholarly organizations.

Y. RAPHAEL

ASSIMILATION. In Jewish history assimilation is the term denoting the process whereby a Jewish community or its members become socially and culturally similar to the majority in whose midst they dwell. As individuals people always assimilate to one another in some form, and nations influence one another politically and culturally. Assimilation endangers group survival when the group tries to take on the nature of other groups at the expense of its own individuality. An early example of assimilation of this type was the submission of the Jews to Hellenizing influences during the Second Jewish Commonwealth. Similar instances may be found throughout the history of the Jews as a minority group amid non-Jewish majorities as well as among other minority groups.

Assimilation became an acute problem early in the 19th century, when *emancipation transformed the legal status of the Jew from that of a ghetto dweller to that of an equal citizen. Entering the mainstream of political and cultural life of the state that granted him the rights of citizenship, he felt that he had to reconcile his loyalty to the Jewish heritage with his loyalty to his country. While these two loyalties were not in any way incompatible, many found the attempt of bringing them into a harmonious relationship too taxing and gave up at the start. Striving to take on the image of the dominant groups among whom they lived, they jettisoned their Jewishness, thus giving the term "assimilation" the connotation it has had since: a process of accommodation to surrounding attitudes, living patterns, and scales of values which leads to a loss of identification with the group into which one was born.

Another type of assimilation is that imposed by external force. This happened in the Soviet Union, where, in keeping with the Bolshevik thesis that the solution of the Jewish problem lay in total assimilation, the Jews were denied the right to function as a community and were deprived of all organizational and cultural opportunity to lend meaning to their Jewish identity, to live in accordance with Jewish values, or to give expression to Jewish national needs and aspirations.

(To be sure, the Communist leaders have not always been able to practice what they preached. Despite their theoretical denial of the existence of a Jewish people, they were forced, after seizing power, to deal with the Russian Jews as a group in order to integrate them into the social order ushered in by the October Revolution. The Soviet government was thus impelled to undertake special economic measures—agricultural and industrial—to make the declassed Jews a productive element in the framework of the Soviet system. This also necessitated the establishment of cultural institutions in the Yiddish language, which made great progress until the 1930s, when a slow process of liquidating them was set in motion by the Stalin regime. This process, interrupted during the war against Nazi Germany, came to a head in 1948 with the closing of all Jewish cultural institutions and the arrest and execution of leading Jewish writers and artists. In the 1960s, although a Yiddish monthly was appearing in Moscow and a few Yiddish books were being published in the Soviet Union, the policy of imposed assimilation was nevertheless in full effect. Paradoxically, the Jews were legally regarded as a nationality in the Soviet Union. In the late 1920s the government even decided to consolidate this nationality by autonomous territorial concentration in *Birobidzhan.)

In the Western world, assimilation was more the result of free choice than of legal coercion. In modern times assimilation has manifested itself as both an objective process and a subjective urge. In each case it has been, on the one hand, the result of economic factors and of the spiritual attrition to which the Jew is subjected, and, on the other, the result of a deepening acculturation which has been changing his relations with the non-Jewish society.

Subjective assimilation is never the basis for mass action. Rarely has a movement arisen among Jews with the avowed purpose of bringing about the dissolution of the Jews as a group. In the few instances when such a movement did appear, it was in connection with either some universal religion, as in the case of the early Christians, or an international ideal, as in the case of many Jewish Socialists and practically all Jewish Communists. Subjective assimilation is fundamentally an individual impulse; one who loses interest in Jewish survival does not take the trouble to form organizations to further Jewish self-liquidation, for even such an organization would constitute an objective brake on assimilation. Nor should subjective assimilation be confused with conversion. The latter requires a formal act and an official change of faith; conversely, full subjective assimilation, resulting in a complete severance of relations with the Jewish community, may be effected without any public declaration or announcement, particularly in countries such as the United States, Great Britain, and Canada, where Jewish "belonging" has been largely a matter of free choice.

The pressure toward objective assimilation has been inherent in the very freedom that the Jew enjoys in the democracies. Here the pressure is strong because the inner resistance to it grows progressively weaker. As the Jew weaves himself organically into the social fabric of his native land, the factors making for Jewish group distinctiveness fade. The greater his access to the means of economic, political, and social advancement and the more frequent and intimate his mingling with non-Jewish fellow citizens, the greater becomes his urge to cut the distance between himself and them by adopting their outlook and patterns of living. Also, the higher his general educational attainment, the larger looms the deficit in the Jewish, as against the gentile, component in his cultural makeup. Shifting of occupational structure, residential mobility, growing engagement in the professions and public services, new skills removed from traditionally Jewish crafts, increasing participation in civic affairs and social action, adaptation to prevailing forms of entertainment and recreation—all this, combined with a rising laxity in Jewish religious observance, a declining appreciation of Jewish values, and an ever-increasing pull from the general community, have made the Jew more susceptible to conformity and rendered his "otherness" less relevant. This has brought in its wake an increasing rate of intermarriage, a growing indifference to things Jewish, and a nagging uncertainty as to the value of Jewish survival. The Jew's vulnerability to assimilatory tensions has increased correspondingly.

This vulnerability has been further enhanced by certain philosophies and ideologies which underlie the programs of some Jewish groups and which, whatever the subjective intentions of their proponents, objectively breed assimilation. Such was the philosophy of classical Reform Judaism, taken over in the 1940s by the American Council for Judaism (see ANTI-ZIONISM), which rejected the concept of Jewish peoplehood and reduced the concept of a worldwide Jewish people to the status of a loosely knit religious sect. Anti-Zionism has had the same long-range effect.

That assimilation has not made even greater inroads into Jewish life in the past was due to the ability of Jews in some cases to forge antiassimilationist instrumentalities out of assimilationist pressures. Owing to their long experience in adjusting to new conditions and to alien and hostile environments, Jews have acquired a capacity to achieve, by accommodation and adaptation, a degree of integration in the life of their native lands which other ethnic minorities managed to achieve only by group dissolution. For the latter, therefore, assimilation has been the road to disappearance; in Jewish life, assimilation has thus far not assumed such debilitiating proportions. *Anti-Semitism and anti-Jewish discrimination have tended to foster Jewish group cohesion and strengthen Jewish resistance to assimilation. The emergence of Zionism played a central role in combating both assimilationist tendencies and ideologies. Jewish communities have functioned vigorously in the larger democracies; in the smaller countries they have somehow managed to hold their own. They have all been profoundly affected by assimilation, but their power of resistance has not been totally lost. This resistance is reinforced by anti-Semitism and other forms of anti-Jewish bias to which Jews are exposed in larger or smaller measure even in the most liberal countries. Whether they will continue to be able to counter the effects of the disintegrating objective factors by mobilizing sufficient subjective forces rooted in the Jewish will to survive, only time will tell.

Already it appears that the existence of the State of Israel will be a decisive factor in the interplay of positive and negative forces marking Jewish life in the *Diaspora. In Israel, too, Jews are influenced materially and spiritually by the outside world. However, while the Jews of the Diaspora have sought to shape their distinctive values so as to fit them into the value system of the majorities among whom they live, the Jews of

Israel have endeavored to incorporate general values into their own value system. Assimilation there is not the one-way passage that it has been in the communities of the Diaspora.

C. B. SHERMAN

'ATAWNA. Nomadic tribe in the B'er Sheva' region of the Negev. Population (1968): 625.

'ATLIT. Community on the Mediterranean coast south of Haifa. Founded in 1903 by the *Jewish Colonization Association (ICA). An agricultural and fishing village, it is also the site of a plant for extracting table salt by evaporation of seawater. Population (1968): 2,110.

Archeologically, 'Atlit goes back at least to the Iron Age, when Phoenician settlers cremated their dead here. The finds in the deep pit tombs include Attic pottery, Greek seals and weapons, and Egyptian jewelry and amulets. The large Templar castle dates from the Crusader period.

It was in 'Atlit that Aaron *Aaronsohn established his agricultural experiment station in 1912, the first in the Middle East. During World War I the station served as a base for the *Nili intelligence ring led by Aaronsohn. It was abandoned late in 1917 after some members of the group had been apprehended by the Turks.

During the last years of their regime, the British erected a large detention camp in 'Atlit for illegal immigrants (*see* ILLEGAL

A Crusaders' castle near 'Atlit. [Israel Information Services]

IMMIGRATION). In 1945 *Hagana raided the camp and freed many of its inmates. After the establishment of the State, the camp became an important reception center for immigrants.

ATOMIC RESEARCH IN ISRAEL. One of the very first tasks with which the scientists of the young State of Israel were charged by Prime Minister David *Ben-Gurion, in 1948, was the formation of a plan for the development of atomic energy as a source of power in a country devoid of the conventional sources of fuel and as a tool for the furtherance of basic and applied research. This plan entailed, to begin with, the training of a reasonable number of scientists and engineers, the search for uraniferous ores, and the study of processes for the production of heavy water. The whole nuclear program of Israel was—and remained—based on the combination of natural uranium and heavy water as the most convenient source of energy.

After the successful execution of this initial program, it was decided in 1956 to establish a research reactor at Nahal Sorek, near the old town of Yavne. This reactor, which is of the "swimming pool" type and has a level of 1 to 5 megawatts, went critical on June 16, 1960, and became a major facility for research and teaching, utilized by all the scientific institutions of the country. While this research reactor was still in the planning stage, the decision was taken to build in the Negev a second experimental reactor, based on natural uranium and heavy water and destined to be the pilot plant for subsequent large-scale (and no longer experimental) reactors. This second reactor, located near Dimona, became operative late in 1964. It was surrounded by well-equipped laboratories which, it was hoped, were to become the center of modern scientific research and the point of crystallization for the planned University of the Desert in southern Israel.

In the laboratories of the Nahal Sorek establishment, a variety of research projects were carried out in both pure and applied science. It is, of course, impossible to list here even the most important results achieved; one might perhaps mention the theoretical work on the Omega minus and the theory of elementary particles in general, experimental studies on the Mössbauer effect, the structure of ferroelectric compounds and the chemistry of concentrated solutions and molten salts, the development of new analytical methods based on various aspects of what is called activation analysis, and the most accurate proof achieved thus far of Einstein's theory that the velocity of light is independent of the velocity of the light source (*see* EINSTEIN, ALBERT).

In the applied field, the production of radioactive isotopes, especially those of short life for medical use, should be mentioned first; a successful attempt was also made to introduce the use of such isotopes into agriculture and industry, into the hydrological projects of the country, and even into police work. The two major projects in progress in 1965 were the preservation of food by irradiation and the eradication of insect pests by sterilization with the help of such irradiation—both techniques of particular importance to tropical and subtropical countries.

The Nahal Sorek reactor establishment, in cooperation with the *Weizmann Institute of Science, maintained a Radioisotope Training Center. In addition to the courses given at the center for Israeli scientists, technicians, and teachers, a number of international courses and seminars were organized there, such as two international courses in radiobiology, attended by scientists from more than 20 countries, and a course for secondary school teachers from the developing countries.

A new atomic reactor at Nebi Rubin, near Rishon L'Tziyon. [Israel Information Services]

In general, the Israel Atomic Energy Commission, mindful of the fact that international collaboration is essential for satisfactory progress in this field, endeavored to cooperate with corresponding establishments in other countries. Good relations were maintained with France, the United States, the United Kingdom, Norway, Italy, and Japan. An attempt was also made to establish cooperative projects with other developing countries such as Turkey, Greece, Iran, Thailand, and the Philippines.

Although up to 1968 electric power stations based on atomic reactors were not economically feasible in Israel, because the planned annual increase in the installed capacity was too small to warrant the operation of nuclear reactors, there seemed to be no doubt that a dual-purpose reactor producing sweet water and *at the same time* electricity from the ocean was an economically sound possibility, provided the reactor was sufficiently large. Apart from defense, the adequate supply of sweet water was Israel's major problem. Without the solution of this problem, the reclamation of the Negev would remain a dream; a solution by means of a nuclear desalting plant would amply justify all the effort, thought, and devotion invested in the development of atomic energy in Israel.

E. D. BERGMANN

AUSTER, DANIEL. Zionist leader and mayor of Jerusalem (b. Stanislav, Galicia, Austria, 1893; d. Jerusalem, 1963). He was active in student Zionist circles in his birthplace and Vienna. After completing his law studies, he settled in Palestine in 1914 and became a teacher. During World War I he was drafted into the Austro-Hungarian Army and served as an officer in Damascus. Returning to Palestine after the war, he became secretary of the Legal Department of the *Zionist Commission and in this capacity founded and directed the Jewish arbitration courts. He practiced law in Jerusalem and was a cofounder of the Rehavia quarter of that city. From 1935 to 1944 he was deputy mayor of Jerusalem, then briefly served as acting mayor. After the establishment of the State of Israel, he became mayor of Jerusalem, serving in that capacity until 1951.

In 1947 he was named to the directorate of the *Jewish National Fund. Ideologically and politically he was affiliated with the General Zionist Organization (*see* GENERAL ZIONISM).

N. M. GELBER

AUSTRALIA, ZIONISM IN. Jews began to settle in Australia in the early 1800s, and congregations were formed in the second quarter of the 19th century. In 1900 there were about 15,000

Jews on the continent. By 1933 their number had grown to 24,000; by the end of World War II, to 32,000. In 1968 the Jewish population was 72,000. The largest Jewish communities were Melbourne (35,000) and Sydney (30,000).

Early Origins. The first Zionist society was formed on Feb. 15, 1900, in Perth, Western Australia. Its founder and first president was Rev. David Isaac Freedman, the rabbi of the community. The society existed until 1913, when it was reorganized into the West Australian Zionist Society. On Jan. 13, 1901, the N.S.W. (New South Wales) Zionist League came into being in Sydney. One of its founders was Alfred Harris, owner and publisher of the *Hebrew Standard,* which from its inception in 1895 had published favorable items about Palestine and later about political Zionism.

In 1902 organized Zionism came to Victoria. On March 2 of that year, a meeting held at the home of Abraham Goldman in Cardigan Street, Carlton, resolved to form the Victorian Zionist League with Goldman as the first president. An enthusiastic meeting with more than 100 persons present, held on March 23 at the East Melbourne Synagogue in Albert Street, acclaimed the new society. At the first annual meeting, held on Mar. 1, 1903, the Rev. Solomon Mark Solomon of the Bourke Street Synagogue, who later became honorary secretary of the league, put in a strong plea for Zionism. S. Kozminsky was elected president to replace Goldman, whose health was failing.

In Brisbane, Queensland, Joseph Blumberg acted unofficially on behalf of the Zionist movement for several years, until, in June, 1910, he was appointed by the N.S.W. Zionist League to represent it in Queensland. The first organized Zionist Society there was formed in 1913.

In South Australia there was no Zionist or pro-Palestine activity until July, 1920, when Israel *Cohen, general secretary of the *World Zionist Organization, came from England on behalf of the Palestine Restoration Fund, the forerunner of the *Keren HaYesod. The interest stimulated by his visit resulted in sporadic efforts during the 1920s. In May, 1928, a Young Men's Club was formed with the idea of developing it into a Zionist body. In March, 1929, this club, together with certain other groups, formed the Zionist Council of South Australia, with Israel Golovsky as its first president.

The Zionist groups continued in existence throughout World War I, maintaining their connection with the movement through the Provisional Executive Committee for General Zionist Affairs in the United States and also through the *Copenhagen Bureau of the World Zionist Organization. With the appointment of Great Britain as the mandatory power and the inclusion of the *Balfour Declaration in the *Mandate for Palestine, Zionism in Australia entered upon a new phase.

The Zionist Federation. In 1927 representatives of the five state Zionist organizations met in conference in Melbourne to form the first federated body, the Australian Zionist Federation, under the honorary presidency of Sir John Monash. Rabbi Israel Brodie of Melbourne, who later became Chief Rabbi of the United Hebrew Congregations of the British Empire, was elected first federal president. At the second annual conference of the federation, held in Sydney in May, 1929, a constitution was adopted which linked Australian Zionism with the Zionist *Congress. Some 10 years later, the name "The Zionist Federation of Australia and New Zealand" was adopted, although in fact New Zealand has always been an independent territorial Zionist entity.

Zionist activities continued unabated throughout World War

II. In 1947 federation officers provided much of the material and briefing required by Dr. Herbert Vere Evatt, then Australia's Deputy Prime Minister and Minister for External Affairs, who was chairman of the General Assembly of the United Nations, which voted for the establishment of a Jewish State in part of Palestine.

The federation embraces all Zionist political parties as well as youth movements. The federation's Executive and its Keren HaYesod Department also act as the federal Keren HaYesod of Australia, and the Keren HaYesod committees referred to below are campaign committees formed each year on the initiative of the state Zionist councils. The other major fund-raising organizations for Israel, such as the *Jewish National Fund (Keren Kayemet L'Yisrael), *Women's International Zionist Organization (WIZO), and the Australian Friends of the *Hebrew University of Jerusalem, are also affiliated with the federation and its state Zionist councils. The supreme authority of the federation is the biennial Conference, composed of a fixed number of delegates nominated by each of the states. The state Zionist councils not only include all Zionist party and fund-raising organizations but also have provisions for affiliation of nonparty Zionist organizations and individuals and for associated organizations. Such organizations include congregations, *Landsmannschaften,* and any other communal organizations that work for Israel.

The Executive of the federation maintains a close liaison with the Israel Embassy and Executive Council of Australian Jewry, the organized lay body of the entire Jewish community of the Commonwealth. The president of the federation Executive (1968) was Nathan Jacobson. Past presidents were Rabbi Dr. Israel Brodie, Dr. Leon Yona, Alec Masel, Rabbi Max Schenk, Samuel Wynn, Horace B. Newman, Max Freilich, and Joseph Solvey.

Keren HaYesod–United Israel Appeal. The first Keren Ha-Yesod campaign committees were established in the early 1940s, when Dr. Michael Traub came to Australia for an extended visit. The Zionist Conference held in Sydney in 1943 resolved to have yearly fund-raising drives alternating between Keren HaYesod and the Jewish National Fund. In 1951 the name of the campaign was changed to Keren HaYesod–United Israel Appeal (UIA). Since then the Keren HaYesod–UIA has been the only Zionist appeal conducted in the Australian Jewish communities (other Zionist fund-raising organizations raise funds through membership, social functions, projects, and other means but make no direct appeal to the communities). Outstanding personalities from abroad visit Australia annually to lead the fund-raising drives.

Jewish National Fund. The first practical Zionist work in Australia was done through the Jewish National Fund. Records tell of contributions in 1907. By 1908 the Golden Book was known. The first page of the first volume contains an inscription of an early Australian Zionist, A. Vecht. Collection boxes and JNF stamps were sent from the head office in Cologne, Germany, with which regular contact was maintained until World War I. There was, however, no organized JNF in Australia until 1939, when Dr. Sh'lomo Lowy of the head office in Jerusalem arrived on an extended mission and established JNF offices in five state capitals of the Commonwealth. In 1944 the Jewish National Fund of Australia and New Zealand, a federal coordinating roof organization, was created.

Noteworthy Israel projects of the Australian JNF included Nahlat Anzac, the Evatt Forest, Nahlat Sydney, Nahlat N.S.W., the Sir Eric and Lady Woodward Nahla in 'Adulam, Nahlat Victoria in N'ot HaKikar, "Forest Pools" (jointly with WIZO), N've Tzipora and Australia Park (jointly with the National Council of Jewish Women of Australia), and the Menzies Forest near Bat Sh'lomo in honor of Sir Robert G. Menzies, Prime Minister of Australia, and Lady Menzies, and the Anzac Memorial and Forest near Gaza.

Women's International Zionist Organization. The Australian Federation of WIZO, an affiliate of the Zionist Federation, was the roof organization of the WIZO state councils, which existed in all Australian states. The history of WIZO in Australia goes back to the early 1930s, when Rieke Cohen established Ivria, the first WIZO group in Sydney, and a group of Zionist women in Melbourne simultaneously formed themselves into a women's Zionist group that, under the guidance of Rabbi Brodie, was introduced to and adopted the principles of WIZO. The firm establishment of the organization in the Commonwealth was accomplished by Ida Wynn–Ben Zion, who came to Australia in 1937 as an emissary of World WIZO.

In the late 1960s Australia had 54 WIZO groups with a membership of approximately 6,500. These formed one of the strongest Zionist membership organizations in Australia and united women in fund-raising and educational tasks on behalf of Israel on a nonparty basis. In addition to participating in the activities of World WIZO, Australian WIZO supported its own project, the Australian WIZO Children's Home.

National Council of Jewish Women (NCJW). Also an affiliate of the Zionist Federation, NCJW was the first women's Zionist organization in Australia. Founded in 1923, it had two outstanding projects, the settlement N've Tzipora (named for Dr. Fanny Reading, founder and life national president of the council) in Gan Yavne and the NCJW Australia Park in Jerusalem.

M. D. FRIEDMAN AND W. DUFFIELD

AUSTRIA, ZIONISM IN. By the time Herzl came upon the scene, there were in Vienna many enthusiastic young people ready to work with him. Zionism in Austria proper and particularly in Vienna, then the hub of the far-flung Austro-Hungarian Monarchy, was greatly strengthened by an influx of Jews from the provinces of Galicia, Bukovina, and Moravia. Many of them had come from circles much more receptive to the Zionist idea than their brethren in the West.

Following the publication in the London *Jewish Chronicle* of an article by Herzl that was an abridgement of his *Jewish State,* a Jewish students' deputation called on Herzl (Feb. 7, 1896), and on the following day he attended and addressed their meeting in the Jüdische Akademische Lese- und Redehalle. His words were received with great enthusiasm, which greeted him also when he participated, on February 20, in a gathering of *Kadimah. In those weeks numerous Viennese Jewish writers and thinkers, among them Saul Raphael *Landau, Nathan *Birnbaum, Heinrich *York-Steiner, and Richard *Beer-Hofmann, called on Herzl, and on March 7 the local Zionists suggested to him that a propaganda drive be launched in Vienna. On April 5, a delegation of the Zion society brought him its support, and the propaganda drive began. By June, 1896, a Zionist Association of Vienna was in existence with Moritz *Schnirer as president. On September 15, an important Zionist debate took place in the Viennese Café Louvre, and on October 21, Herzl was enthusiastically received at a gala gathering of Kadimah. Among the early opponents in Vienna of Herzl and

Zionism were Chief Rabbi Moritz *Güdemann and Josef Samuel *Bloch, the editor of the influential weekly *Österreichische Wochenschrift.*

On March 6 and 7, 1897, a Zionist conference took place in Vienna, called by Osias *Thon, Willy *Bambus, and Nathan Birnbaum. Herzl's Viennese friends Johann *Kremenetzky, Oser *Kokesch, Heinrich York-Steiner, and Leon *Kellner participated, as well as Marcus *Ehrenpreis of Diakovar (Djakovo), Moses Moses of Kattowitz (Katowice), Abraham *Salz of Tarnów, and Isaac *Turoff of Breslau. At this meeting Herzl's suggestion to convene a Zionist *Congress was adopted.

The first public meeting of Zionists in Vienna took place on Mar. 16, 1897; it was chaired by Leon Kellner and attended by almost 1,000 persons. Within two months the Zionist Organization in Vienna took shape. It was greatly enhanced by the election of an Executive during a meeting (May 20, 1897) which, of course, recognized Herzl as head of the movement. About a week before this meeting Herzl decided to launch a weekly in the service of the movement. On May 11, Die *Welt, the central organ of the World Zionist movement, was founded, and on June 2 its first issue was published.

From the First Congress to the Death of Herzl. At the 1st Zionist Congress (Basle, 1897), the Zionists of Austria were represented by a delegation of 18, including Michael *Berkowicz (Herzl's Hebrew secretary), Nathan Birnbaum (then secretary-general of the Zionist Organization), Isidor *Schalit (Herzl's secretary), and Albert Donreich (secretary of the 1st Zionist Congress). During Herzl's lifetime the head office of the *World Zionist Organization, under his presidency, remained in Vienna. All members of the Inner *Actions Committee were Viennese. They were elected by the various Zionist Congresses between 1897 and 1903. (Oser Kokesch was elected by all six Congresses; Moritz Schnirer, by the first four; Johann Kremenetzky, by the 1st, 5th, and 6th; Alexander Mintz and Oskar *Marmorek, by the 1st; and Leopold *Kahn, by the 2d through the 6th.) The first Zionist head office was in Vienna (Türkenstrasse 9), together with the editorial offices of *Die Welt,* which continued to appear in Vienna until 1904.

With the approval of the Inner Actions Committee, Leon Kellner founded in Vienna (1901) a Jewish Toynbee Hall (see JEWISH TOYNBEE HALLS) where a number of Zionist leaders, including Martin *Buber, Wilhelm Jerusalem, Leopold Kahn, Ernst Müller, Siegmund *Werner, and Heinrich York-Steiner, lectured on Jewish history and literature and on Palestine. Another frequent speaker at Zionist gatherings in Vienna was the Rev. William H. *Hechler, the British Protestant minister who had become Herzl's trusted adviser.

*Labor Zionism in Austria began in Vienna with an organization named Ahva (Brotherhood), which was founded in 1898 by Saul Raphael Landau. Meetings of Ahva, which were attended by Zionist workingmen and white-collar employees, were frequently disrupted by the Social Democrats, a party then bitterly opposed to Zionism. On Aug. 1, 1898, Landau brought out the first issue of Der Jüdische Arbeiter, a periodical aimed at attracting Jewish working people to Zionism and at effecting a synthesis between Zionism and Social Democratic ideology. It attacked the leaders of the Social Democratic party of Vienna, who, it was asserted, were opposed not only to Zionism but to all things Jewish. Other pro-Zionist Jewish papers appearing in Vienna in this period included Der Jüdische Arbeiter (Socialist Zionist, 1897–1914), Jüdische Volkszeitung (1899–1915), Neue Nationalzeitung (1899–1914), and Jüdische Zeitung (1907–21).

After the formal approval of the *Jewish National Fund by the 5th Congress (1901), Johann Kremenetzky established the Fund's headquarters in Vienna, where it remained under his chairmanship until 1907.

From Herzl's Death to the End of World War I. After Herzl's death (1904), Vienna ceased to be the center of World Zionism, and the interests of Herzl's former colleagues in the world leadership and of Zionism turned to the internal reorganization of the movement. In the years prior to 1918, Austria proper, like the other provincial units of the monarchy, constituted an autonomous Zionist district with its own leadership and headquarters. Among the well-known heads of the Austrian Zionist district were Max Bernhard, Isidor *Margolis, J. H. Körner, Ludwig Bato, and Max Marcus. In 1908 the Zionist groups of Austria, Bohemia, Moravia, and Silesia, while retaining their district organizations, formed a larger organizational unit, the West Austrian Zionist Organization, with headquarters in Vienna. For many years Adolf *Böhm acted as its chairman. Its primary purpose was to synchronize Zionist activities, policies, and cultural pursuits.

The work of Austrian Zionists during those years centered on two aspects: the upbuilding of the organization and the enlargement of the Zionist program beyond concentration on Palestine to pursue positive political and cultural work in the *Diaspora (these programs were called *Gegenwartsarbeit* and/or *Landespolitik*).

A strong organization could be built up only by dislodging the assimilationists (*see* ASSIMILATION) from the leading positions they held in Austria's Jewish community. Herzl had advised Zionists as far back as 1898 to work for the "capture of the Jewish religious communities." The Zionists of Vienna were among the first to heed his call and to make efforts to penetrate the official Jewish Religious Community of Vienna (Wiener Israelitische Kultusgemeinde). In the forefront of this struggle were Jakob Ehrlich, Leopold Plaschkes, Karl Pollak, Robert *Stricker, Egon Michael Zweig, and many others. The first success came in 1912, when Ehrlich and Stricker were elected to the board of the Community. Twenty more years had to elapse before a Zionist majority was able to transform the Community into a stronghold of Zionism.

The attainment of a voice in general political affairs as an independent Jewish nationality group was a much more formidable task. For political reasons it was regarded expedient not to pursue this work in the name of the Zionist Organization but to form a separate political party of national minorities under Zionist leadership. At a conference in Cracow (July 1, 1906) it was decided to establish such a party with headquarters in Vienna; it was headed by Isidor Schalit, whose first attempt, however, to gain a seat in the Vienna Parliament (1907) was unsuccessful. Among other leading Zionists taking an active part in Austrian political life were Herman Kadisch, Adolf Böhm, and Oskar Karbach.

Between the Two World Wars. Concrete Zionist achievements in Austrian politics materialized only after the establishment of the republic in Austria, when Stricker was elected to Parliament (1919) and Jakob Ehrlich, Leopold Plaschkes, and Bruno Pollak-Ponnan were elected to the Municipal Council of Vienna.

Outside Vienna, among the Zionist groups in the provincial areas of Austria proper, those in Graz, Innsbruck, Krems, Linz, Mödling, Sankt Pölten, Salzburg, and Wiener-Neustadt were particularly active in the period between the two world wars.

Even while the Religious Community of Vienna was still ruled by an assimilationist majority, Zvi Peretz *Chajes, an ardent and leading Zionist, became chief rabbi of the city. David Feuchtwang, who succeeded Chajes in the chief rabbinate in 1933, had a record of many years of service to the Zionist cause.

Vienna was the scene of two Zionist Congresses, the 11th (1913) and the 14th (1925). Zionist conferences also took place in the Austrian capital, particularly after 1918. The Zionists-*Revisionists held their world conferences there in 1932 and 1935.

At the 12th Zionist Congress in Karlovy Vary (Carlsbad, 1921), Chief Rabbi Chajes was elected president, and Robert Stricker vice-president, of the Actions Committee, with the result that the seat of the committee was moved to Vienna—for the first time since Herzl's death.

A Palestine Office (*see* PALESTINE OFFICES) was set up in Vienna in 1918 to assist prospective immigrants to Palestine. In the 1920s, hundreds of Halutzim (pioneers; *see* HALUTZIYUT) on their way to Palestine from Poland and elsewhere found themselves stranded in Vienna when they were refused *immigration certificates into Palestine by the British administration. A Keren 'Aliya (Immigration Fund) was set up to support them while they waited. The initiator and first director of the Vienna Palestine Office (1918) was Egon Michael Zweig. He was succeeded by Martin *Rosenblüth (1921), Nahum Blauer (1923), Leo Goldhammer (1926), Hayim Tartakower (1930), Simon Horowitz (1932), and Alois Rothenberg (1934).

Zionist influence was also strong in Jewish sports in Austria. The first Jewish sports club was established in 1903, under the impact of Max *Nordau's speech at the 5th Zionist Congress (1901) calling for the physical regeneration of Jewry. But it was only in 1921 that, during the 12th Congress in Karlovy Vary, the Maccabi World Federation was formed, in which Austria played an important part. On the occasion of the 14th Congress (1925) Maccabi put on a great sports show which gave impetus to the organization of additional Jewish sports clubs. International renown was gained by HaKoah, a popular Zionist sports organization, which participated in national and international meets and won many championships.

Zionist influence made itself felt in every aspect of Jewish life in Austria. Each group in Vienna and in the provinces organized its own public discussion meetings, invited well-known lecturers, and arranged other functions which were well attended by audiences of all ages and of all walks of life. Many of these groups had reading rooms where the local and world Jewish newspapers could be read; usually there would also be a library. Courses in history and Hebrew were held there regularly. In the 1920s and 1930s Vienna had a number of Hebrew kindergartens, a Zionist-oriented high school (Chajes Gymnasium), and a school for the training of teachers of modern Hebrew language and literature.

Austria, particularly Vienna, was frequently visited by Zionist personalities of international stature and renown, such as Hayim Nahman *Bialik, Kurt *Blumenfeld, Nahum *Goldmann, Itzhak *Grünbaum, Vladimir *Jabotinsky, Sh'marya *Levin, Leo *Motzkin, Max Nordau, Moshe *Sharett (Shertok), Nahum *Sokolow, M'nahem M. *Ussishkin, and Chaim *Weizmann.

This period was marked by a spate of periodicals. From 1919 to 1927 there appeared the *Wiener Morgenzeitung*, a Zionist daily published by Robert Stricker, who subsequently edited *Die Neue Welt* (1929–38). *Die Stimme* (1928–38), the organ of the Austrian General Zionists, and *Der Jüdische Weg* (1932–35) were edited by Leopold Plaschkes. There also appeared *Der Judenstaat* (1931–32), a Revisionist weekly, and *Palästina* (1926–38), a scholarly monthly on Palestine problems edited by Adolf Böhm.

Zionist activity in Austria reached its climax at the time of the 14th Zionist Congress (Vienna, 1925). In addition to the 15 provincial groups and 14 Viennese district sections, the following Zionist groupings were active: the Zionist Organization of Academicians (2,500 registered members), the Association of Sephardi Zionists (400 members), the Austrian district of the Maccabi World Federation (4,500 members), the *Women's International Zionist Organization (WIZO, 400 members), and *Hitahdut (at that time part of the Austrian Zionist Organization, 400 members).

The growing influence of the Austrian movement became manifest in the results of the elections to the Jewish Religious Community held on Dec. 4, 1932. For the first time the Zionists attained an absolute majority. Desider Friedmann, a prominent Zionist, was elected president. The victorious Zionist majority immediately embarked on a program to reshape the purely religious community organization along more national lines. Among the prominent members of the community board were Jakob Ehrlich, Rudolf Glanz, Siegfried Graubart, Oskar Grünbaum, Josef Grünhut, Josef Löwenherz, Max Schwarz, Mendel Singer, Robert Stricker, and Saul Weinreb.

Zionist Parties and Organizations. The parties within the World Zionist Organization were well represented in Austria. In 1937, the year before Austria's occupation by the Nazis, the General Zionist party had 18 groups in Vienna and 12 in the provinces; 8 of their Zionist youth organizations had a total of 2,077 members. Among the leaders of the General Zionists were Paul Berger, Desider Friedmann, Leo Goldhammer, Oskar Grünbaum, Alfred Löwy, Sofie Löwenherz, Eduard Pachtmann, Sabine Passweg, and Leo Schmerler. *See also* GENERAL ZIONISM.

The Revisionists also had organized groups in every section of Vienna and in the provinces. When, in 1935, they participated in the founding of the *New Zionist Organization, they attained over 22,000 votes. Those active in the movement included David Bukspan, Paul Diamant, Josef *Fraenkel, Siegfried Graubart, Norbert Hoffmann, Arthur *Koestler, Willy Perl, Hans Perutz, Robert Stricker, and Z'ev (Wolfgang) *von Weisl.

When the *Jewish State party emerged after the split in the Revisionist ranks, Vienna became one of its important centers. The Vienna office was headed by Robert Stricker, Josef Fraenkel, Theodor Grubner, and Fritz Richter.

*Mizrahi did not command a strong organization in Austria. Its membership there was headed by Rabbi Israel Friedmann (a member of the famed rabbinic dynasty in Sadagura), Viktor Bauminger, and Dr. Rosner.

The Zionist Socialist *Po'ale Zion, arising out of the Ahva society, commenced its activities at an early date. By 1918 Vienna had become part of the headquarters of its world movement, with Sh'lomo *Kaplansky heading the Central Secretariat (the secretariat for practical work had been set up in Palestine), and J. Wachmann had joined the Vienna office as second in command. Po'ale Zion in Austria opposed national Diaspora politics as expounded by the Zionist Organization and did not participate in the elections of "national" Jews to Parliament and other legislative bodies. It stood under the influence of Ber *Borochov, who had visited Vienna in 1912 to outline his concept of Socialist Zionism. After the split in the Po'ale Zion

and as a result of the unification conference in Prague (1920), the membership joined other Zionists-Socialists to form the Po'ale Zion–Hitahdut, which from then on represented the Socialist wing of Zionism in Austria. Its most prominent leaders were Mendel Singer, editor of Borochov's works in German, Hayim Tartakower, Paul Sokal, and Saul Weinreb.

Beginning in 1923 the *Radical Zionists rallied around Robert Stricker and counted among their other leaders Josef Fraenkel, Leopold Plaschkes, and Israel Waldmann. They continued activities on a considerably reduced scale when Stricker joined the Revisionist party (1930).

WIZO had 10 groups in Vienna and 3 branches in the provinces. In 1937 it counted a membership of 832. Among the leaders were Martha Hoffmann, Sofie Löwenherz, Anita *Müller-Cohen, Sabine Passweg, and Erna Patak.

In addition to these parties and groupings there existed at various periods different Zionist groups or associations of groups, or both. Most important among them were the Zionist students' organizations in Vienna. Even in the early years there was an Association of Zionist Academic Fraternities (Zionistische Akademische Korporationen), which included Bar Giora, Bar Kokhba, Emunah, Eretz Yisrael, Leo Pinsker, Theologia, and the Association of Jewish College Students. The Organization of Jewish Academic Associations (Verband der Jüdischen Akademischen Verbindungen) comprised Ivria (founded in 1892), Kadimah, Makkabea, and Libanonia (1895). At various periods these student organizations, both as individual societies and as unified associations, played an important part in the growth of the Zionist movement in Austria, and often beyond its borders.

There were also in Austria a *Binyan Ha'Aretz group (1933–37, 925 members) and an Adolf *Stand Club (1931–37, 236 members).

Austria, like many other countries, also had a large representative Pro-Palestine Committee, which counted among its members prominent scholars, statesmen, and men of affairs, both Jewish and non-Jewish. It became a very important instrument for the enlightenment of the general public on the Palestine problems which crystallized after the issuance of the *Balfour Declaration.

Austria had a great number of Halutz organizations, which functioned up to World War II: General *HeHalutz (the Austrian Federation of Halutzim) and its affiliates 'Akiba (Mizrahi), B'rit Bilu, B'rit Herzl, *Gordonia, *HaShomer HaTza'ir, He'Atid, Makkabi HaTza'ir, Miriam (WIZO), *T'khelet-Lavan, HeHalutz HaK'lal-Tziyoni, HeHalutz HaL'umi, HeHalutz HaMizrahi, Halutz Group of the Radical Zionists, and Halutz Youth of the Jewish State party. In addition, there was the Austrian *B'rit Trumpeldor (Betar), which was not affiliated with the General HeHalutz but was part of the Revisionist (later New Zionist) organization, which prepared its members for pioneer work in Palestine.

The last report covering the period to March, 1938, when Austria was occupied by the Nazis, showed that the Zionist Federation of Austria comprised 8,634 members in 18 district societies in Vienna and 12 societies in the provinces. The constituents of the federation included WIZO and the youth organizations B'rit Zion, HeHalutz, Maccabi HaTza'ir, B'rit Tz'irenu, Jewish Youth Club, Miriam, 'Akiba, and the Palestine Club.

Under Nazi Occupation. The Nazi occupation of Austria (Mar. 12, 1938) brought about a strong movement of Jewish emigration. Some Zionist leaders were immediately arrested, among them Desider Friedmann, who was taken to the Buchenwald concentration camp but subsequently released, only to be rearrested later. Others were able to continue their activities, and, in fact, the cooperation among the existing Zionist groups became even closer. By February, 1939, the following additional groups had joined the Zionist Federation: Jewish National Fund, Keren HaYesod, Mizrahi, and Maccabi—giving the federation a total membership of 12,245. The federation continued its activities, opening Hebrew classes and establishing urban and rural training centers where members were prepared for immigration to Palestine. The sole organ that the federation was permitted to publish was the weekly *Zionistische Rundschau,* but in November, 1938, this paper, too, was forced to suspend publication.

In March, 1939, the federation was reorganized as the Zionist Territorial Federation, Vienna (Zionistischer Landesverband, Wien). In its report of June, 1939, it gave its registered membership as 21,600, comprising all affiliated groups. By that time the Jewish population in Vienna had dropped from 180,000 (March, 1938) to 100,000 (May, 1939). The last president of the federation before the outbreak of World War II was Karl Gutwald, who was assisted by an Executive Board consisting of Siegfried Knopfmacher, Josef Grünberger, Ezechiel Nussbaum, and Alfred Weisshut. The veteran leaders who had made Vienna important as a Zionist center had been deported. The federation had no organ of its own; there was, however, a Vienna edition of the *Jüdisches Nachrichtenblatt,* which began publication in February, 1939, under the auspices of the Jüdischer Kulturbund of Germany and its Vienna branch.

The principal activity of all Zionist groups throughout 1938 and as long as possible in 1939 was the organization of "illegal" transports of emigrants to Palestine. The groups collaborated closely with their counterparts in Czechoslovakia, particularly with the Revisionist organization, which began to organize these transports at an early date. Subsequently, the Palestine Office in Vienna, jointly with Palestine Offices in other European countries, was able to organize additional illegal transports and thus save hundreds of Jews from certain death (*see* ILLEGAL IMMIGRATION).

After World War II. At the end of World War II only a few thousand of Austria's prewar Jewish population of 190,000 were alive—mostly persons married to non-Jews. Later, this number was augmented by an influx of displaced persons and returnees from abroad. In 1968 the total estimated Jewish population of Austria was 11,500, residing mostly in Vienna.

In February, 1946, a Palestine Office was opened in Vienna, and between 1945 and 1948 a total of 170,000 Jews from various concentration camps and from Poland, Romania, and Hungary passed through Vienna on their way to Palestine.

Within months after Austria's liberation the Zionists formed a club which paved the way for the foundation of the Zionistischer Landesverband (Zionist Territorial Federation) in Austria by Bernhard Braver, veteran Zionist and former executive director of the Jewish Religious Community of Vienna. This group, which had much support from Asher Ben-Natan (later Israel's Ambassador to Bonn), sponsored lectures and *'Oneg Shabbat meetings and published a newspaper, *Die Stimme.* The Landesverband was soon followed by the establishment in Austria of the Jewish National Fund, Keren HaYesod, *Ha-No'ar HaTziyoni, and WIZO.

Owing to fragmentation and factionalism, the Landesverband,

which was originally meant to be a roof organization for all Zionist activity in Austria, evolved into a General Zionist party, of which Anton Winter was secretary-general in 1968. Winter was also president of Keren HaYesod and vice-president of the Jewish National Fund in Austria.

After the war a *Mapai organization emerged. One of its prominent members, David Schapira, an attorney, was elected president of Vienna's Jewish Religious Community in 1948, the first Zionist to hold that office after World War II. The Zionist Revisionist Union of Austria published soon after 1946 a weekly, *Die Neue Welt,* edited by Denes Szilagyi, and later another paper, *Heruth,* edited (1968) by Alfred Reischer. Mizrahi–HaPo'el HaMizrahi was presided over (1968) by Lazar Kahan.

*Mapam, at first strongly influenced by Vienna's Jewish Communists, was reorganized in the early 1960s by Ya'akov Schoenfeld, an emissary from Israel, and since then has veered away from politics to concentrate on the Zionist education of the young. In the 1960s Mapam's youth movement was the leading Zionist youth organization in Austria.

In 1968 all Austrian Zionist groups were concentrated in Vienna, with individuals residing elsewhere in the country belonging to the Viennese organizations. These groups were constituent bodies of the Zionist Federation of Austria (Zionistische Föderation in Österreich, ZFÖ), which sponsored discussions on local Jewish and Zionist problems, lectures on Jewish culture and Yiddish literature, reports by visitors from Israel, Hebrew courses, and summer seminars. Each of the Zionist organizations had a youth group with its own cultural programs, holiday celebrations, and summer camps.

B. BRAVER AND J. FRAENKEL

AUSTRIAN JEWS IN ISRAEL. Neither Herzl's *Jewish State,* which was published in Austria in 1896, nor the activity of the early Zionist groups in Vienna and the provinces succeeded in producing an *immigration from Austria proper to Palestine prior to World War I.

In November, 1918, a Palestine Office (*see* PALESTINE OFFICES) was set up in Vienna under the leadership of Egon Michael Zweig to receive Halutzim (*see* HALUTZ) from Eastern Europe (Bukovina and Galicia) passing through Austria on their way to Palestine and to arrange for the next lap of their journey. Because of Vienna's relative proximity to the Mediterranean seaport of Trieste, where the Palestine-bound emigrants would embark for Jaffa, World Zionist leaders took a particular interest in the work of this Palestine Office.

The period immediately preceding Germany's annexation of Austria saw the rise of Halutz youth movements in the Austrian branches of *Po'ale Zion, the General Zionist party, and *B'rit Trumpeldor (Betar). From its foundation in 1934 until Oct. 1, 1939, *Youth 'Aliya brought to Palestine a total of 997 Austrian Jewish teen-agers and children.

From 1938, the year of the Nazi take-over in Austria, to 1941, when the shortage of "legal" immigration certificates became acute, Dr. Alois Rothenberg, director of Vienna's Palestine Office, and Dr. Josef Löwenherz, then the president of Vienna's Jewish Religious Community, set up an agency known as Overseas Transports which organized "illegal" transports to Palestine (*see* ILLEGAL IMMIGRATION).

According to *'Aliya Notes—Thirty Years of 'Aliya to Israel, 1919–49,* a statistical survey published by the *Jewish Agency in 1949, a total of 12,189 Austrian Jews reached Palestine during the three decades from 1919 to 1949. Hundreds, perhaps thousands, of Austrian Jews who attempted to get to Palestine after the Nazi annexation of their country were caught and murdered by the Gestapo on the way. Others were killed when their ships were torpedoed, or died of disease or exposure aboard unseaworthy vessels.

The children and teen-agers who succeeded in reaching Palestine during World War II were received by the Hitahdut 'Ole Austria (Association of Immigrants from Austria), led by David Weiser and Anita *Müller-Cohen, the Austrian-born philanthropist and social worker. They were offered courses in Hebrew and English and placed in jobs. Many went to kibbutzim or moshavim, where a large number of them were still residing in 1968.

Unlike many of their brethren from Germany who had been able to transfer part of their assets to Palestine, most of the Austrian Jews who managed to get there in the months immediately preceding World War II arrived penniless. To add to their plight, Palestine was just then undergoing a severe economic crisis, and former merchants, physicians, and lawyers were happy to find "unofficial" employment as errand boys and in menial jobs. In numerous instances, wives went to work as cleaning women. The situation did not improve until after the outbreak of World War II, when many of the younger newcomers joined the British Army or the Palestinian Supernumerary Police, and when skilled and white-collar workers, physicians, and other professional personnel were so badly needed by the army and the hospitals that even "illegal" immigrants were accepted for employment there.

After the war, in 1945, *B'riha in Austria, under the leadership of Asher Ben-Natan, brought large numbers of "illegal" immigrants to Palestine.

In the 1960s, Jews from Austria were found in practically every walk of life in Israel. Many who had arrived there entirely without funds had risen to prominence in politics, the professions, public service, and business.

Theodore (Teddy) *Kollek was elected mayor of Jerusalem in 1965. Prof. Naphtali H. *Tur-Sinai (Torczyner) was president of the *Hebrew Language Academy. Immigrants from Austria sitting in Israel's *Knesset in 1966 included Dr. Hans Klinghofer, professor of law at the *Hebrew University of Jerusalem; Dr. Elimelekh *Rimalt of Ramat Gan, who had been a rabbi in Innsbruck; and Sh'lomo Perlstein of Tel Aviv, a member of the Executive of the World Hotel Union.

In 1966 Ehud *Avriel and Asher Ben-Natan, who had come to Palestine from Austria as Halutzim, were Israel's ambassadors to Rome and Bonn, respectively.

Senior officers in the Israeli armed forces included Col. Yosef Geva (Glasberg), military attaché in Washington, D.C., and Col. Etan Avissar (formerly Capt. Edler von Friedmann), who presided over Israel's highest military court. Dr. Josef Michael Lamm had senior rank among Israel's Austrian-born judges.

Other immigrants from Austria playing a prominent part in Israel's public life were the physicians Nahman Frey and Isidor Klaber, both formerly of Vienna, who were known for their charity work; and the late Nathan Michael *Gelber, noted historian and writer.

Among Israel's outstanding musicians were Zvi Haftel, music director of the *Israel Philharmonic Orchestra, and the cellist Joachim Stutchewski.

Benjamin *Akzin and Max Frankl were professors of political science and organic chemistry, respectively, at the Hebrew University. The university's Medical School had a number of professors who were born or trained in Austria, including Emil Adler, Ernst Amoz Braun, Arye *Feigenbaum, and Walter Kornblüth.

Ephraim Heinrich Frei was professor of electronics at the *Weizmann Institute of Science. Also on the staff of the institute was Dr. Hugo Boyko, ecologist, president of the World Academy of Arts and Sciences, and winner of the Weizmann Award in 1957. His wife, Dr. Elizabeth Boyko, was a prominent horticulturist. Dr. Victor Kellner, former principal of Vienna's Chajes Gymnasium, and Moshe Rath, head of the University Extension Courses, were engaged in the advancement of the Hebrew language.

The veteran Zionist Isidor *Schalit spent the last years of his life in Palestine, as did Martin *Buber, who was born in Vienna.

Hans Perutz, Rudolf Weitz, and Julius Klein were active in the manufacture and export of textiles.

Aided by the Austrian government and the Jewish Religious Community of Austria, and by funds from heirless Austrian-Jewish assets, the Hitahdut 'Ole Austria founded a home for the aged in Ramat Hen which is named for Anita Müller-Cohen.

Y. GUVRIN

AUTOEMANCIPATION (pamphlet). *See* PINSKER, LEO.

AUTONOMY, JEWISH (Jewish Self-government). The idea of Jewish self-government is as old as the Jewish *Diaspora. Self-government as an existing reality, based on certain political or cultural assumptions, has been well known in Jewish life for 2,000 years. It reached its highest expression first in Babylonia in the Talmudic period. It accompanied the Jews on their wanderings and settlement in the various countries of Europe, reaching its climax in Poland, where it was officially recognized by the government almost up to the end of Polish independence in the second half of the 18th century. Its organs were the Jewish communities and unions of communities whose scope of activities embraced virtually all affairs of social life: this was, as Heinrich Heine put it, "the portable Jewish State." Despite its important role in Jewish life, this autonomy was far from being considered a permanent institution; rather it was regarded as a temporary expedient until such time as the Jewish people, by the grace of God, would return to their Homeland, the Land of Israel.

From the *Emancipation to the End of the 19th Century. The emancipation, beginning with the French Revolution, or actually with the *Haskala, the period of enlightenment which had set in one or two generations earlier, brought far-reaching changes in this respect, especially in the Western countries. In Eastern and Central Europe, communal self-government continued to exist, even being strengthened by official recognition (laws in Germany, 1847 and 1876; in Austria, 1890; in Russia, 1835, abolished a few years later). However, this recognition confined the activities of the communities to religious and charitable affairs. In the West, with the progress of *assimilation, the Jewish communities lost much of their former influence. They were not backed by the authority of the state, whose avowed principle of separation of church and state prevented it from either supporting or interfering in the affairs of religious communities. No longer was membership in the Jewish community self-evident, as it had been in former generations; on the contrary, many Jews, especially the immigrants from Eastern Europe, failed to join the existing communities, establishing organizations of their own. In the United States, whose entire Jewish population consisted of immigrants, the very concept of an inclusive Jewish community was unknown. The immigrants limited themselves to establishing societies to fulfill special needs (for the most part, the maintenance of synagogues) or for such purposes as uniting people who had come from a particular city or area in Europe (the so-called *Landsmannschaften*).

Rise of Jewish "Autonomism." Just at the time when Jewish communal self-government lost much of its former significance, the idea of making it the basis for Jewish survival in the Diaspora arose. Jewish autonomism in its modern form was born at the beginning of the 20th century, although a few signs of it (such as the propaganda of the French-Jewish writer Bernard *Lazare) had appeared several years earlier. It originated in the ranks of various Jewish Socialist and nationalist groups, frequently in combination with one another, and was strongly influenced by the general political ideology in the two multinational states, Russia and Austria-Hungary: in both, ways and means were sought to enable the various nationality elements to coexist in peace, at the same time satisfying their nationalist aims. Of special significance from this point of view was the work of enlightenment done by the Socialist movement of Austria, in whose ranks the idea of national autonomy was launched, according to which each national minority group was to enjoy autonomy regardless of the place of residence of its individual members. This idea was adopted enthusiastically by the Jewish Socialist parties, especially the *Bund and the various Zionist Socialist groups, as the best possible solution to the problem of Jewish survival.

The real founder of the idea of Jewish autonomism was the historian Simon *Dubnow, who developed it from 1897 to 1906 in a series of articles in the St. Petersburg Russian-Jewish periodical *Voskhod* (republished as *Letters on Ancient and Modern Judaism* in St. Petersburg in 1907). Dubnow's basic assumption was that the Diaspora was not to be considered an anomaly but rather an important step forward in the development of the idea of nationalism, since it proved that a nation could exist without a territorial base, just as it could without bonds of blood; the decisive factor was the will of the nation to exist without being artificially separated from other nations, as had happened in former generations, but also without the danger of assimilation. National (as distinct from religious) autonomy was the best possible path to this goal. The Jewish people, Dubnow asserted, should enjoy self-government based on Jewish national communities and should develop their own language and culture; this, and not a Jewish National Home, would solve the Jewish problem.

Dubnow's ideas caused strong repercussions, especially in Eastern Europe, where they led to the establishment of the movement of Folkism, or *Galut nationalism. Also, many other Jewish, and even Zionist, groups adopted the idea of autonomism as a way of safeguarding Jewish national survival in the Diaspora which did not necessarily clash with the idea of a Jewish National Home in Palestine. Practically, however, not much could be done in the years before World War I to make autonomism a reality, since the Tsarist regime in Russia suppressed every effort of this kind and in the Hapsburg monarchy the Jews were not recognized as a national minority.

Between the Two World Wars. Only after the war, when those two empires broke up into independent states, was the way clear for the realization of Jewish self-government in its modern form. The first attempt was made in the Ukraine, which, after the out-break of the Russian Revolution, declared itself an independent state and late in 1917 granted autonomy to the three national minority groups in its territory, the Jews, the Poles, and the Russians. A Ministry of Jewish Affairs and a Jewish National Council composed of representatives of the communities were established. However, the incessant civil strife in the new state and its occupation by the Red Army early in 1919, with the ensuing incorporation of the Ukraine into the Soviet Union, prevented any practical achievements along these lines. Jewish national autonomy in Lithuania, granted in 1919 and based on a Union of Jewish Communities with a Jewish National Council and a Ministry for Jewish Affairs as its organs, did not fare much better. It existed for a few years, only to be abolished by the new nationalist regime established in 1922. Of the original program, only state support of the Jewish schools continued until the end of Lithuania's independence (1940). Similar to a certain degree was Jewish cultural autonomy in the two other Baltic states, Latvia and Estonia; it, too, was limited to the support of Jewish schools and came to an end with the incorporation of the two states in the Soviet Union in 1940.

Much more significant was Jewish autonomy in the Soviet Union. With the establishment of the new regime, it was granted to Jews in the same way as to other nationalities in the Soviet Union. In order to enable the Jews to enjoy this autonomy despite their dispersion throughout the country, the government proclaimed the few districts in the Ukraine and the Crimea having a Jewish majority population (mostly districts of Jewish agricultural colonization) Jewish autonomous districts, adding to them a considerable number (over 200 in the 1930s) of urban and rural communities in which Jews were in the majority. In all these places Yiddish was recognized as an official language. Not content to stop there, the Soviet government decided to have one of the provinces of the country turned into an autonomous Jewish territory by way of large-scale colonization. The Far Eastern province of *Birobidzhan was chosen for this particular purpose, and it was proclaimed a Jewish national territory in 1934. The work of colonization progressed slowly, however, and the Jews remained a minority within the general population.

In the West, the governments were not willing to grant the Jews national autonomy, nor was the Jewish population interested in autonomy or in national minority rights. Although Jewish communities and unions of communities existed in many Western countries, their character was for the most part exclusively religious and the scope of their activities rather limited. In the United States, the process of establishing both congregations for religious purposes and other Jewish bodies continued. Among these, the bodies organized for fund-raising purposes (welfare funds) and the Jewish community councils frequently approximated, to a degree, the character of the European communities, without, however, achieving the significance and scope of the latter. An effort to establish a Kehilla (religious community) in New York early in the 20th century remained isolated and short-lived. The efforts to unite American Jewry, especially during World War I, were also not very successful. The *American Jewish Congress, established to protect the interests of European Jewry in the postwar period, lost its original representative character after a few years and became one of the many public bodies of American Jewry. Only in Latin America, and especially in Argentina, did the Jewish population succeed in reviving the tradition of the European Kehillot, based solely on voluntary membership. The community of Buenos Aires became the first body of this kind and was followed by similar ones elsewhere in Argentina and in Latin America in general.

World War II and the Postwar Period. The great network of institutions of Jewish self-government in Europe broke down in the years of Nazi domination under the impact of cruel persecution. After World War II it was restored in those countries where it had existed with the exception of the Soviet Union, where virtually nothing remained of the national autonomy of the previous period apart from the disintegrating autonomous Jewish territory of Birobidzhan and a few local congregations for the maintenance of synagogues. In other countries of the Soviet bloc, unions of Jewish communities were reestablished, but they mostly limited their activities to religious and, to some extent, educational work. In general, the same is true of the Western European Jewish communities and of those in the Middle East and in the British Commonwealth. No progress could be seen in the United States in this particular field, aside from efforts to unite the forces of American Jewry, whether on a permanent basis, such as the *American Jewish Conference or, more recently, the *Conference of Presidents of Major American Jewish Organizations, or for specific purposes, such as assistance to Soviet Jewry. In the countries of Latin America, the work of organizing the Jewish communities and establishing their national representative bodies was carried on successfully.

Attempts at World Organization. Efforts to unite the Jewish communal organizations on a worldwide scale partially succeeded with the establishment of the *World Jewish Congress in 1936. There were also a few other bodies of international character, such as *Agudat Israel, *B'nai B'rith, the *World Federation of Sephardi Communities, and the Conference of Jewish Organizations (COJO). All these were trying to continue the tradition of concerted action of previous Jewish generations, and, by adapting it to modern needs, paving the road to Jewish survival in the Diaspora.

A. TARTAKOWER

AUXILIARY FARMS. Small farms, adjacent to moshavot (*see* MOSHAVA), for the settlement of hired workers employed in the moshavot.

Beginning with the 1890s the ability of Jewish agricultural workers to attain a satisfactory income became a matter of growing concern to the settlement authorities cooperating with the *Hoveve Zion movement. One of the suggested ways of meeting the problem was to create smallholdings of about 10 to 15 dunams ($2\frac{1}{2}$ to $3\frac{3}{4}$ acres; *see* DUNAM) for the settlement of the workers.

The acquisition of land and the erection of buildings were to be financed from public funds. The lots were planned so as to provide employment for the workers' families and to supply them with food. In this manner it was hoped that the income level might be raised without corresponding increases in wages and that the Jewish workers would be enabled to compete with Arab labor, which was cheaper.

During the period of the *Second 'Aliya several auxiliary farms, such as 'En Ganim and B'er Ya'akov, were established by the *Odessa Committee. Subsequently it was found that precautions had to be taken to prevent the sale of land by the settlers. Other settlers devoted themselves completely to their own plots of land and gave up working for wages in the moshavot. Some of the lessons learned from this experience were applied in the creation of the Moshav 'Ovdim (*see* MOSHAV).

The expansion of citriculture in the late 1920s and early 1930s created a renewed need for auxiliary farms for the workers in the citrus groves. However, this time the auxiliary farms were meant mainly to develop into independent farms in the future, and the time during which a man worked as a hired laborer was considered a transitional training period.

Objections were raised to this scheme because it was considered unjustified for the *Jewish National Fund to purchase for this purpose costly land in the plantation area already predominantly in Jewish hands.

I. KOLATT

'AVDAT. Site of an ancient city in the central Negev hills, on the way from B'er Sheva' southward to the port of Elat. Archeological remains indicate that the site was occupied by Nabateans from the 3d century B.C.E. to C.E. 106, when their kingdom was annexed by Rome. Among the finds are a temple and a pottery kiln. The city was resettled in the 3d century, and in the Byzantine period two churches and a fortress were erected on top of the town hill.

'AVDON. Village (moshav) in western Upper Galilee. Founded in 1952 and affiliated with *T'nu'at HaMoshavim. Population (1968): 346.

AVI'AD-WOLFSBERG, Y'SHA'YAHU. Physician, writer, and Israeli statesman (b. Hamburg, 1893; d. Bern, 1957). He studied philosophy, medicine, and Judaica at Heidelberg, Würzburg, and Berlin and became a successful pediatrician. Interested in Zionism from an early age, he edited the *Jüdische Presse,* became president of *Mizrahi, and served on the Zionist *Actions Committee and on the executive boards of various Jewish institutions. In 1934 he settled in Jerusalem, dividing his time between medicine and public service and writing and lecturing on problems of religion, Zionism, and politics. He was Israel's first envoy to the Scandinavian countries.

Y. RAPHAEL

AVIATION IN ISRAEL. The proclamation of Israel's independence (May 14, 1948) found the young State with almost no civil aviation. Lod Airport, the country's only large modern facility, was surrendered by the departing British to the Arabs, and international airlines which had maintained regular flights to Palestine ceased their operations.

During the first and most crucial weeks of its existence, the State of Israel was forced to operate an improvised air service based on smaller airfields. In July, 1948, Lod Airport was captured by the *Israel Defense Forces, and a short time later it was reopened for regular flights. The first foreign company to use Lod for scheduled flights was the Czechoslovak airline. Gradually, other foreign companies, defying threats by the Arab states to deny them the use of their airports, resumed scheduling flights to and from Israel.

In the fall of 1948 the Israeli *government, in conjunction with several corporate groups, founded *El 'Al, Israel's national airline, which began operations in July, 1949. Owing to the hostility of the Arab states and the closing of all its land borders, air and sea traffic formed the only link between Israel and the outside world. This factor, as well as the rapid expansion of civil aviation in general during the years following World War II, contributed to the development of civil aviation in Israel.

In 1968, 16 international airlines maintained regularly

Byzantine fortress at 'Avdat. [Israel Government Tourist Office]

scheduled flights to and from Israel. El 'Al had direct flights between Lod and numerous cities in Europe, North America, Africa, and Asia, handling about half of the total air passenger traffic to and from Israel. Lod Airport, which has been enlarged and modernized, developed into an important air-traffic connection for numerous intercontinental flights.

In 1964 (the last year for which data were available at the time of writing), 4,411 planes brought to Israel a total of 208,822 passengers and 3,553,000 kilograms of freight from abroad. By 1967–68 El 'Al alone carried 364,360 passengers, in 3,872 flights.

In 1968 several local Israeli airlines served the internal needs of the country. Arkia, a subsidiary of El 'Al founded in 1950, operated flights from Tel Aviv to B'er Sheva', Elat, M'tzada, Haifa, and Rosh Pina. It had in 1968 five 50-passenger prop-jet planes which were also used for air tours to the Sinai Peninsula, the Gaulan Heights, and other areas. Avitor operated flights between Haifa and Elat and also served agricultural purposes (e.g., air spraying), as did Chimavir and Marom. Monavir operated an air-taxi service.

Israel Aircraft Industries, established in 1953, is located near Lod Airport, where it operates an internationally approved repair station. It carries out modifications and complete overhauls and manufactures jet trainers and spare parts.

The Israel Aero Club is a member of the Fédération Aéronautique Internationale and participates in international glider competitions.

T. PRESCHEL

AVIDOM (MAHLER-KALKSTEIN), M'NAHEM. Israeli composer (b. Stanislav, Galicia, Austria, 1908). Settling in Tel Aviv in 1937, he served for several years as secretary of the *Israel Philharmonic Orchestra and later with the Binyane HaUma organization. He then became director-general of Acum Limited, the Society of Israeli Authors and Composers, and chairman of the Israeli Composers' League.

Most of Avidom's music, which is characterized by a light and lucid symphonic style, reflects his French musical education. His later works were influenced by dodecaphonic methods. His compositions include seven symphonies, including *The Song of Elat* (Symphony No. 5, with contralto voice), *Psalm Cantata*, chamber music, piano works, and music for small instrumental ensembles.

P. GRADENWITZ

AVIEL. Village (moshav) in Samaria. Founded in 1949 by members of the *Herut movement. It was named for Israel Epstein (Aviel), an emissary of the *Irgun Tz'vai L'umi, who was killed in Rome. Population (1968): 226.

AVI'EZER. Village (moshav) between the Judean Mountains and the Judean Plain. Founded in 1958 and named for Sigmund Gestetner, president of the *Jewish National Fund of Great Britain (*see* GREAT BRITAIN, ZIONISM IN). Affiliated with HaPo'el HaMizrahi (*see* MIZRAHI).

AVIGDOR. Village (moshav) in the Darom. Founded in 1950 by veterans of a transport unit of the *Jewish Brigade, it was named for Sir Osmond Elim d'Avigdor-Goldsmid, British Jewish leader and chairman of the *Jewish Colonization Association (ICA), whose son commanded the unit. Population (1968): 330.

AVIHAYIL. Village (Moshav 'Ovdim) in the Sharon Plain. Established in 1932 by veterans of the *Jewish Legion and affiliated with *T'nu'at HaMoshavim. Its economy is based on citriculture, dairy products, and poultry. Population (1968): 600.

AVITAL. Village (moshav) in the Jezreel Valley. Founded in 1953 and affiliated with *T'nu'at HaMoshavim. Population (1968): 321.

AVIVIM. Village (moshav) in eastern Upper Galilee. Founded in 1960 and affiliated with *T'nu'at HaMoshavim.

AVNIEL, BENJAMIN. Member of the *Knesset (b. Jerusalem, 1906). Avniel studied at Brussels University and served for many years as director of the Labor Department of the Palestine Manufacturers Association. From 1947 to 1949 he was chairman of the draft board that organized recruitment during the *War of Independence. In 1951 he was elected to the Knesset on the *Herut slate and still served there in 1968. Avniel's publications include books on political and labor problems.

'AVODA 'IVRIT (Jewish Labor). *See* "CONQUEST OF LABOR."

AVRIEL, EHUD. Israeli diplomat (b. Vienna, 1917). In his youth he was active in the Viennese Zionist youth organization Blau-Weiss (Blue-White; *see* T'KHELET-LAVAN), and in 1939 he settled in Palestine. In 1943–44 he engaged in rescue work in behalf of the *Jewish Agency in Istanbul and after the end of World War II was prominently associated with organizing *illegal immigration to Palestine.

After the establishment of the State, Avriel became Israel's first Minister to Prague and Budapest and in 1950 was envoy to Romania. Subsequently he served as Director General of the Prime Minister's Office and of the Ministry of Finance. Elected to the *Knesset on the *Mapai slate in 1955, he later resigned to become Israel's Ambassador to Ghana and Liberia (1957–60). Thereafter he served as Ambassador to the Congo. In 1961 he became Deputy Director General of the Ministry of Foreign Affairs, serving until 1966, when he was appointed Ambassador to Italy and Malta.

At the 27th World Zionist *Congress (Jerusalem, 1968), Avriel was named chairman of the Presidium of the Zionist *Actions Committee (General Council).

AVUKAH. American Zionist students' organization, initiated in 1925 by members of the Intercollegiate Zionist Association in cooperation with a *Histadrut (General Federation of Labor) delegation then in the United States. Prime movers in the United States were Samuel Blumenfield, Max Rhoade, and Joseph S. Shubow. Starting out with fewer than 100 members, it had several thousand, in 65 chapters, at the outbreak of World War II. Avukah was affiliated with the *Zionist Organization of America, which subsidized its activities.

In its early years Avukah was a loose federation of independently working chapters conducting cultural activities; the Zionist platform was not stressed. In 1928 a new group took over the Avukah leadership, and in the following three years the increase in publications, the founding of the Avukah Summer School, and the issuance of the *Brandeis Avukah Annual* (in 1932 and again in 1936), an elaborate Zionist anthology, marked an era of growth in the life of the organization. Palestine travel fellowships, a system of regional organization, and the *Avukah Bulletin* were established in 1934. Great strides in educational and propaganda work were made in 1935. Among the publications Avukah issued were *A Short History of Zionism* by S. H. Sankowsky, *Analysis of Zionism* by Meir *Ya'ari, *Call to the Educated Jew* by Louis D. *Brandeis, *Study Programs for Avukah Chapters*, and the *Avukah Zionist Analysis*, dealing with the theoretical basis of Zionism.

In 1936 an experiment in cooperative management, which had proved effective, became the pattern for the Avukah Summer School camps. By 1940 there were three camps, one each in the New York, New England, and Middle Western areas, organized around an intensive program of lectures and discussions.

At Avukah's 13th annual convention (1937) discussion of the problems of Zionism and its relation to American Jewry resulted in a three-front Program for American Jews. Developing the interrelationship between Jewish needs in the United States and other countries, it presented Zionism in its world political perspective and indicated the necessity for Jewish action against fascism and for the mobilization of the Jewish community for maximum support of Zionism.

Late in 1937 Avukah issued *My Impressions of Palestine*, by John McGovern, M.P., and *Diagram of Zionism*, a statement of the theory of Zionism, and established a national pamphlet service. *Avukah Student Action*, a journal of news and comment, appeared in 1938. At the same time a sociological survey of Jewish college youth was undertaken.

In 1939–40 Avukah published *Associations of American Jews*, a study of the American Jewish community by Adrian Schwartz, and the New Discussion Series. Its newly developed Activity Plan called for units suggesting concrete activity by chapters on themes such as "Zionism Now," "War and Antifascism," "Modern Palestine," and "The American Jewish Community." A number of pamphlets outlining the ideological background of these topics were issued.

Besides its activities along political and cultural lines, Avukah, throughout the United States and Canada, established a comprehensive social program. It attracted some talented and energetic young Zionist intellectuals who later became leaders in their communities and in the Zionist movement, including Ambassador Arthur Goldberg, who was president of the Chicago chapter, Philip Klutznick, president of *B'nai B'rith, and Shim'on *Agranat, Chief Justice of Israel.

After the outbreak of World War II, army service claimed more and more of the Avukah membership, and in 1943 Avukah's New York headquarters was closed down permanently.

M. S. CHERTOFF

'AYANOT. Agricultural training farm south-southwest of Rishon L'Tziyon. Founded in 1930 and affiliated with *T'nu'at HaMoshavim. Population (1968): 484.

AYELET HASHAHAR. Village (kibbutz) in eastern Upper Galilee. Settled in 1918 and affiliated with the *Ihud HaK'vutzot V'haKibbutzim. During the Israel *War of Independence the village was damaged by heavy bombardments, but after the war it recovered and developed at an increased rate. Population (1968): 720.

'AZARYA. Village (moshav) southeast of Ramle. Founded in 1949 and affiliated with *T'nu'at HaMoshavim. Population (1968): 485.

AZEKA (Tell Zakhariya). Archeological site in the foothills of Judea. It was developed in the middle and late Bronze Age. The Israelites fortified Azeka with a citadel. In the upper part of the tell (mound) a Hellenistic level was found.

AZOR (Yazur). Township southeast of Tel Aviv. Founded in 1948 by immigrants living in the Arab village of Yazur, which was abandoned by its inhabitants during the *War of Independence. Population (1968): 5,100.

In this general region were found several Chalcolithic sites, including tomb caves that yielded a great quantity of house-shaped ossuaries (containers of bones), as well as some in the form of human faces.

'AZRIEL. Village (moshav) in the Sharon Plain. Founded in 1951 and named for Rabbi Azriel *Hildesheimer. Affiliated with HaPo'el HaMizrahi (*see* MIZRAHI). Population (1968): 465.

'AZRIKAM. Village (moshav) in the Darom. Founded in 1950 and affiliated with *T'nu'at HaMoshavim. Population (1968): 575.

B

BACHAD. *See* B'RIT HALUTZIM DATIYIM.

BADER, GERSHOM. Zionist writer and journalist (b. Cracow, Poland, 1868; d. New York, 1953). One of the early Zionist publicists and a pioneer of the Yiddish press in Galicia, he contributed regularly to *HaMaggid* and *'Ivri Anokhi* and in 1889 became editor of *HaShemesh,* a weekly, in Kolomyya. In 1894 he settled in Lvov (Lemberg), where he became active in local Zionist and literary life. He contributed to numerous Hebrew, Yiddish, Polish-Jewish, and German-Jewish periodicals and edited a variety of Hebrew and Yiddish publications, including the Yiddish daily *Togblat* (1904–06), the first Yiddish daily in Galicia, and *Dos Naye Lemberger Togblat.* In 1912 he settled in New York, where he became a prominent contributor to the American Yiddish press.

Bader also wrote plays, feuilletons, historical monographs, literary essays, and a Hebrew biographical lexicon of Galician writers and scholars.

N. M. GELBER

BADER, YOHANAN. Journalist and member of the *Knesset (b. Cracow, Poland, 1901). He was educated at the Universities of Cracow and Warsaw. In his early youth he joined the Jewish Socialist organization *Bund and, later, *HaShomer HaTza'ir. Dissatisfied with the latter's political orientation, he joined the Revisionist movement (*see* REVISIONISTS), served as chairman of its Central Committee in western Galicia, and edited its weekly, *Tribuna Narodova.* In 1936 he was elected to the Central Committee of the *New Zionist Organization in Poland.

After the collapse of Poland in 1939, Bader was arrested by the Soviet authorities in Lvov for his Zionist activities and deported to Arkhangelsk. Under the Soviet-Polish agreement of 1941, he was released from detention and enlisted in the Polish Army. In 1943 he settled in Palestine and joined the *Irgun Tz'vai L'umi. He was interned in 1945 by the British authorities in the concentration camp in Latrun.

Bader served on the Executive of *Herut from its inception. Beginning in 1949 he represented the Herut party in the Knesset, where he was a member of the Finance Committee. He regularly contributed to the party paper, *Herut,* on legal, political, economic, financial, and social problems.

I. BENARI

BAHAI COMMUNITY IN ISRAEL. Sect purporting to be an all-embracing world religion. It originated as a movement of dissenters from Shi'ite Islam in Persia. The founder of Bahaism, Husayn 'Ali, known as Baha'ullah ("Glory of God"), was exiled

Bahai Shrine, Haifa. [Israel Government Tourist Office]

from Persia in 1853 and subsequently imprisoned by the Ottoman government in the jail-fortress of 'Akko (Acre). After his death in 'Akko in 1892, the leadership of the movement passed to his son 'Abdul-Baha. The shrines and administrative buildings of the Bahais are located in 'Akko and Haifa, the world centers of the Bahai faith. The best-known Bahai shrine is the beautiful temple with the golden dome on the slopes of Mount Carmel, standing in the middle of an exquisite flower garden. In 1961 the total number of Bahais in Israel was 156.

BAHAN. Village (kibbutz) in the Sharon Plain. Founded in 1953 and affiliated with the *Ihud HaK'vutzot V'haKibbutzim.

BAHAN. Village (moshav) in the Hefer Valley. It was founded in 1953 by Nahal (see ISRAEL DEFENSE FORCES) and settled in 1954 by immigrants from South America, most of whom were sons of Jewish colonists in Argentina.

BAKSTANSKY, LAVY. British Zionist leader (b. Slonim, Russia, 1904). He was educated at the *Herzliya High School in Tel Aviv and graduated from the London School of Economics. In 1930 he was appointed secretary-general of the Zionist Federation of Great Britain and Ireland. He influenced and led Zionist activities in Great Britain and helped establish Jewish day schools. Bakstansky played an important role in the *World Confederation of General Zionists, served as director of the Joint Palestine Appeal, and was a member of the European Executive of the *World Jewish Congress.

BALABAN, MEYER SAMUEL. Historian (b. Lvov, Galicia, Austria, 1877; d. Warsaw ghetto, 1942–43?). Balaban studied at Lvov University and began to teach while still a student. During World War I he was a military chaplain and officer for Jewish affairs in Lublin, then occupied by the Austro-Hungarian Army. After the war he directed a Jewish high school in Częstochowa. Subsequently he became one of the directors of the Tahkemoni Rabbinical Seminary in Warsaw. He also taught Jewish history at Warsaw University and at the Warsaw Institute for Jewish Studies, of which he was rector at two different periods.

An early Zionist, Balaban was in his student days extremely active in the academic Zionist circles of his native Galicia, especially in culture and education. He contributed to the Zionist periodicals *Przyszlosc* and *Voskhod,* disseminating Zionism in the localities where he taught and fighting assimilationist tendencies in education.

Balaban was the author of numerous books, monographs, and essays on the history of the Jews of Poland. His prolific output included histories of the Jews of Lvov, Cracow, and Lublin, studies on the Karaite sect in Poland and on the 18th-century heretical Jewish Frankist movement, a book on Jewish antiquities in Poland, and a variety of essays dealing with personalities and events in Polish-Jewish history.

BALFOUR, ARTHUR JAMES (1st Earl of Balfour and Viscount Traprain). British statesman, philosopher, and author (b. Whittingehame, East Lothian, Scotland, 1848; d. Fisher's Hill, near Woking, England, 1930). Trained early by his mother in the teachings of the Old Testament, Balfour was not only a profound thinker but also a deeply religious man. He was the author of several books on religious philosophy: *A Defense of Philosophic Doubt* (ca. 1879); *Foundations of Belief, Being Notes Introductory to the Study of Theology* (1893); and *Theism and Thought: A Study of Familiar Beliefs* (1923).

Balfour was Prime Minister from 1902 to 1905. It was during this period (July 10, 1905) that he made a statement in Parliament cautioning against the continued admission of Jewish immigrants to England, since their refusal to mingle with the majority population would pose a threat to the country. This statement was attacked by Parliament, the press, and the 7th Zionist *Congress (Basle, 1905). However, Balfour was, in fact, deeply interested in the Jews and once declared that Christianity

owed to the People of the Book "an immeasurable debt shamefully ill repaid." It was during his premiership that Britain offered Herzl land in British East Africa (see EAST AFRICA

Lord Balfour.
[Zionist Archives]

SCHEME). Impressed by the refusal of the Zionists to consider this proposal, Balfour became interested in Zionism. It was through a Mr. Dreyfus, a Manchester Jew, that, in 1905, he first met Chaim *Weizmann, with whom he again discussed Zionist objectives in 1915.

As Great Britain's Foreign Secretary (1916–19) under David *Lloyd George, Balfour played a crucial role in the prolonged negotiations with Zionist leaders which resulted in the historic British policy statement that was to bear his name. In April, 1917, Balfour visited the United States, on which occasion he met and conferred with Louis D. *Brandeis, leader of the American Zionists. The *Balfour Declaration was released on Nov. 2, 1917, in the form of a letter to Lord Rothschild (Lionel Walter Rothschild), a leading English Jew (see ROTHSCHILDS: BRITISH BRANCH).

Balfour's part in the issuance of the pro-Palestine declaration won for him the acclaim and affection of a large segment of Jewry. He continued to be active in favor of Zionism after World War I. In December, 1920, as chief British representative, he submitted the draft of the Palestine Mandate (see MANDATE FOR PALESTINE) to the League of Nations. In June, 1922, as Lord President of the Council, he spoke against a motion proposed in the House of Lords calling on Britain not to accept the Palestine Mandate, and that same year he participated in the London meeting of the League of Nations at which the mandate was ratified.

In 1925 Balfour visited Palestine, where he spoke at the inauguration ceremonies of the *Hebrew University of Jerusalem. After the *Arab riots of 1929, Balfour, with Jan Christiaan *Smuts and David Lloyd George, signed a letter to the London *Times* urging the British government to appoint a special commission to investigate the disorders in Palestine.

In 1922 he was made a knight of the Garter and raised to the peerage. The village (moshav) Balfouriya, founded in 1922 in the Jezreel Valley by settlers from the United States, is named for him.

G. HIRSCHLER

BALFOUR DECLARATION. Official statement issued on Nov. 2, 1917, by British Foreign Secretary Arthur James *Balfour to Lionel Walter Rothschild (2d Baron Rothschild),

Foreign Office,
November 2nd, 1917.

Dear Lord Rothschild,

I have much pleasure in conveying to you, on
behalf of His Majesty's Government, the following
declaration of sympathy with Jewish Zionist aspirations
which has been submitted to, and approved by, the Cabinet.

"His Majesty's Government view with favour the
establishment in Palestine of a national home for the
Jewish people, and will use their best endeavours to
facilitate the achievement of this object, it being
clearly understood that nothing shall be done which
may prejudice the civil and religious rights of
existing non-Jewish communities in Palestine, or the
rights and political status enjoyed by Jews in any
other country"

I should be grateful if you would bring this
declaration to the knowledge of the Zionist Federation.

Balfour Declaration. [Zionist Archives]

declaring that the British government favored "the establishment in Palestine of a national home for the Jewish people." *See* ROTHSCHILDS: BRITISH BRANCH.

Background. The entry of Turkey into World War I in November, 1914, on the side of the Central Powers brought to the fore the question of the future status of Palestine. An Allied victory was expected to result in major territorial changes in the Ottoman Empire, of which Palestine was a part.

At the first meeting of the General Council of the *World Zionist Organization (WZO) held after the outbreak of the war (Copenhagen, Dec. 3–6, 1914), it was decided that the Zionist Organization would maintain its neutrality toward the belligerents and that the head office of the WZO would remain in Berlin so that it might be in a strong position to invoke the friendly interest of the German government in behalf of Palestine Jewry, which was then under the rule of Germany's ally, Turkey. It was considered that Zionist efforts should be directed toward securing Jewish rights in Palestine following the termination of hostilities and that, with this aim in view, Zionist diplomacy should cultivate public opinion as well as the governments in the belligerent camps and in neutral countries. To pursue Zionist diplomacy in the Allied countries, two members of the Zionist *Executive, Nahum *Sokolow and Yehiel *Tschlenow, were sent to England, where they arrived at the end of 1914. Of the neutral countries, the United States had the largest Jewish population, of which the majority were refugees from Tsarist persecution in Russia and thus sympathetic toward the Central Powers.

It was in England that the question of Palestine first aroused public and official interest. In March, 1915, Herbert *Samuel,

then a member of the British Cabinet and not a Zionist, circulated a memorandum among his colleagues pointing out that "the establishment of a great European Power so close to the Suez Canal would be a continual and formidable menace to the essential lines of communication of the British Empire.... We cannot proceed on the supposition that our present happy relations with France will continue always." Samuel therefore advocated an autonomous Jewish settlement in Palestine under British suzerainty. This memorandum followed previous oral conversations Samuel had had with his colleagues in the British Cabinet. Sir Edward Grey, then Foreign Secretary, and David *Lloyd George, who was Chancellor of the Exchequer, evinced interest in the proposal, while Prime Minister Herbert Henry Asquith opposed it; the matter was not pursued.

Chaim *Weizmann was the only member of the Zionist *Actions Committee residing in England. On Turkey's entry into the war, he commenced a political campaign on behalf of Zionism. He was soon joined by Sokolow, who as a member of the Zionist Executive had the authority to negotiate in behalf of the Zionist movement. It was Sokolow who initiated discussions with Lucien Wolf of the Conjoint Foreign Committee (*see* BOARD OF DEPUTIES OF BRITISH JEWS) with a view to establishing a common Jewish front on the issue of the future of Palestine. Lengthy negotiations ensued but were without result, since the Zionist and non-Zionist positions could not be reconciled. Meanwhile, Weizmann had won Charles P. *Scott, editor of the *Manchester Guardian,* to his ideas, and the latter introduced him to Samuel. Samuel in turn introduced Weizmann to Lloyd George.

Soon thereafter Weizmann developed a new method of producing acetone (a basic material in the manufacture of explosives), and this greatly contributed to the esteem in which he was held by Lloyd George, who in 1915 became Minister of Munitions. During this period Weizmann met with Balfour, whom he had already met many years earlier. In September, 1915, Weizmann became technical adviser on acetone supplies to the Admiralty, of which Balfour was then First Lord. Weizmann sought to win prominent personalities in British and Anglo-Jewish society to his ideas.

Toward the end of 1915 British governmental circles found it expedient to undertake steps to gain the support of Jewish public opinion in the United States and elsewhere which had not been favorable to the Allies because of their alliance with the Jew-baiting Tsarist Russian government. Lucien Wolf, himself an anti-Zionist, suggested to the British government that in view of the fact that Zionism had lately captured Jewish public opinion, an Allied declaration of sympathy with Zionist aspirations, support of Jewish colonization, and some sort of Jewish autonomy in Palestine would create a pro-Allied attitude in American Jewry as a whole. He submitted a draft of a declaration to Edward Grey, and the latter circulated it to the Allied governments. This draft, however, was dropped as unacceptable to the Zionists and as unlikely to gain the support of Jews in neutral countries.

Early in 1916 Sir Mark *Sykes, representing the British, and François-Georges Picot, on behalf of the French, had come to a secret agreement on the division of the Middle East. The agreement was designed to reconcile the British and French interests in the area with the national aspiration of the Arabs, who were encouraged to revolt against the Turks. It took into account the international religious interest in the Holy Land and provided for the internationalization of Palestine (the area extending from Hebron to Nazareth) and for the establishment of British and French zones of influence in part of which an Arab state or Arab states were to be established (see SYKES-PICOT AGREEMENT).

In February, 1916, soon after the agreement had been made, Sykes was introduced by Samuel to Zionism, which attracted him personally and appealed to him politically. Like other English statesmen at the time, Sykes assumed that British support of Zionism would win Jewish public opinion in the United States for Britain, and he also envisaged an Arab-Armenian-Jewish alliance in the Middle East, which would be of great economic and political importance to the Allies.

Encouraged by Samuel, Moses *Gaster approached Sykes and maintained contact with him. Sykes was further strengthened in his Zionist policy by meetings with Aaron *Aaronsohn, who had arrived in London in the fall of 1916 to offer the War Office his services and those of his comrades in Palestine to aid the British Army in its operations against the Turks (see NILI).

In the second half of 1916 the Zionist leaders, who until then had contented themselves with cultivating personal contacts with influential persons, began efforts to bring the aims of Zionism to the attention of a wider British public. To that end they published a collection of essays, "Zionism and the Jewish Future." Toward the end of the year the British Palestine Committee was established to "reset the ancient glory of the Jewish nation in the freedom of a new British Dominion in Palestine." The moving spirits of the committee were Weizmann's Manchester friends, Harry *Sacher, Simon *Marks, and Israel M. *Sieff, and Herbert *Sidebotham, the military commentator of the *Manchester Guardian,* who had argued all along that a friendly Palestine was necessary to the British Empire for the defense of Egypt and the Suez Canal.

During this period several developments that greatly advanced the cause of Zionism took place. After a Cabinet crisis in December, 1916, David Lloyd George became Prime Minister and Arthur James Balfour, Foreign Minister. Both these men and some of their immediate subordinates were outspoken supporters of Zionist aspirations. Next, in January, 1917, the British occupied Rafa, on the coast of southern Palestine. Though the advance of the British was halted before Gaza, Britain remained committed to the total expulsion of the Turks from Palestine. As a consequence, Zionism once again attracted attention on the political scene.

Effects of War Developments. New elements entered the situation with the March Revolution in Russia and the entry of the United States into the war in April, 1917. The upheaval in Russia encouraged the emergence of pacifist tendencies there. Overestimating the political influence of Russian Jewry, the British government hoped that if the Russian Jews were given reason to link an Allied victory with the fulfillment of Zionist aspirations, they might keep Russia from making a separate peace with the Central Powers. The British also felt that if they would support Zionist aims, American Jewry might bring its influence to bear in support of a British protectorate over Palestine.

Meanwhile, Sir Mark Sykes was assiduously at work on his own plans. In January, 1916, he had succeeded in getting France to agree to the internationalization of Palestine. However, Sykes did not consider the internationalization plan, or even an Anglo-French condominium, a satisfactory solution. In addition to the other motives that led him to support Zionism, he also came to regard support of Jewish national aspirations in Palestine as a

Field Marshal Allenby, Lord Balfour, and Sir Herbert Samuel (left to right) in Jerusalem in 1925. [Zionist Archives]

way of sidestepping the agreement with Picot and of denying French rights in Palestine. After making contact with Moses Gaster (who did not hold an official post in the British or World Zionist Organizations), Sykes sought contacts with persons holding positions of official leadership in the Zionist movement. On Jan. 28, 1917, a meeting took place between Sykes and Weizmann. On this occasion Weizmann was accompanied by Leopold J. *Greenberg, editor of the *Jewish Chronicle,* and Sykes by James A. *Malcolm, the London representative of the Armenian national delegation.

On Feb. 7, 1917, Sykes held a conference with several Zionist leaders at Gaster's home. All those present, including Lord Rothschild, Harry Sacher, Herbert Samuel, and Nahum Sokolow, agreed that Zionist aspirations would be greatly benefited if Britain were to come into control of Palestine. Sykes said that the Palestine problem had become acute. He urged the Zionists to do what they could to induce the French to give way in Palestine. The task of negotiating with the French was assigned to Sokolow, a member of the Zionist Executive.

In March, 1917, Weizmann met with Lloyd George and Balfour. The Zionists had not yet received any definite commitment from the British government, but they had become increasingly confident of British support. They had also been given to understand that the British government would look favorably on Zionist propaganda designed to impress on world Jewry the idea that British control of the Holy Land would be the best guarantee for the fulfillment of Jewish aspirations in Palestine. Satisfied that the Zionists would support a British protectorate over Palestine, Sykes urged Sokolow in April, 1917, to negotiate with the other Allied Powers to secure their support for Zionist aims. It was Sykes who prepared the ground for Sokolow's diplomatic efforts in Paris, at the Vatican, and in Rome. Late in April and again in May, Sokolow negotiated with Stéphen Pichon, the French Foreign Minister, and although he intimated that the Zionists would prefer British rule, under which he considered the Jews would be in a better position to develop their national culture, Sokolow managed to obtain a French written statement of sympathy with Zionist aspirations. While this statement did not imply a renunciation of French claims to Palestine, Sykes was content with the result, since he felt that it aided British ambitions for a British protectorate over Palestine. Sokolow also secured the moral support of Pope Benedict XV and the friendly attitude of the Italian government.

At the same time Weizmann and his colleagues were urging American and Russian Zionist leaders to declare their support for a Jewish National Home in Palestine under Great Britain as the protecting power. Louis D. *Brandeis pledged such support on behalf of the Zionist movement in the United States. He also discussed the matter with Pres. Woodrow *Wilson and had satisfactory meetings with Balfour when the British Foreign Minister visited the United States in April and May, 1917. The Russian Zionist leaders, on the other hand, clinging to the principle that the Zionist movement had to remain neutral in the world conflict, remained cool to the proposal.

Anti-Zionist Opposition. In May and June, 1917, a violent conflict erupted between the British Zionists and the anti-Zionists, who were represented by the Conjoint Foreign Committee. The anti-Zionists, fearing that British support for Jewish nationalism might have an adverse effect on their own status as Englishmen, sought in vain to deflect British policy from giving support to Jewish national aspirations in Palestine. Finally, the committee issued a statement (published in the *Times* on May 24, 1917) that they objected to the Zionist theory that regarded the Jews of the world as homeless and in need of a political center and an always available homeland in Palestine. They also declared that they opposed the granting of special colonization rights to the Zionists in Palestine. The statement aroused a furor in Anglo-Jewry. Many Jewish personalities condemned it, as did the *Times*. On June 17, 1917, the Board of Deputies of British Jews, one of the two parent bodies of the Conjoint Foreign Committee, condemned the committee's action, and the committee was dissolved. The dissolution of this prestigious committee, representing an influential Anglo-Jewish group, emboldened the Zionists in their activities. A few days after the vote of the Board of Deputies Lord Rothschild and Weizmann were received by Balfour. They conveyed to the Foreign Minister their feeling that the time had come for Britain to identify herself openly with the Zionist cause. Balfour asked them to draft a declaration that would be satisfactory to the government and which he would then submit to the War Cabinet.

Preliminary Draft. Numerous drafts were prepared by the Zionists and discussed with British representatives, but none were accepted. On July 18, 1917, Lord Rothschild submitted a draft declaration to Balfour, who circulated it early in August among the members of the War Cabinet. The draft read as follows:

1) His Majesty's Government accepts the principle that Palestine should be reconstituted as the National Home of the Jewish People.
2) His Majesty's Government will use its best endeavours to secure the achievement of this object and will discuss the necessary methods and means with the Zionist Organization.

This proposal was, in fact, prepared by the British, and, at their instance, it was submitted by Lord Rothschild. On Sept. 3, 1917, the War Cabinet, in the absence of Prime Minister Lloyd George and Foreign Secretary Balfour, discussed this draft. Edwin Montagu, Secretary of State for India, though not a member of the War Cabinet, was invited to state his views. Montagu, an assimilated Jew, vehemently opposed the declaration, and his protest prevented a favorable decision. The meeting was inconclusive, and it was decided to seek the views of President Wilson on the advisability of a British declaration of sympathy with Zionist aspirations.

On Sept. 11, 1917, the Foreign Office was informed by Washington of Wilson's view that the time was not opportune for a definite declaration, except, perhaps, a statement of sympathy without any real commitment.

The outlook was bleak. It seemed that the declaration had been shelved for the moment. Taken aback by the chilling communication from President Wilson, Weizmann cabled Brandeis the text of the draft declaration submitted by Rothschild and asked him to support it and also to intercede with Wilson. A few days later Brandeis cabled that Wilson was in complete sympathy with the declaration. Owing to the efforts of Charles P. Scott, Lloyd George met with Weizmann on Sept. 28, 1917. Lloyd George placed the discussion of the declaration on the agenda for the next Cabinet meeting. On October 3, the eve of the Cabinet meeting, Weizmann and Rothschild, in order to forestall another setback through intervention from Montagu, sent a memorandum to the War Cabinet stating that the Jews and the Zionists had entrusted their fate to the British government in the hope that Zionist aims would be considered in the light of the British Empire's best interests and of the principles for which the Allies were fighting. The Zionists stated their reluctance to believe that the War Cabinet would allow the divergence of views on Zionism existing in Jewry to be presented to them in a strikingly one-sided manner.

When the War Cabinet met, both Lloyd George and Balfour were present. The hand of the pro-Zionists was strengthened by reports to the effect that if the British government continued to delay issuing a pro-Zionist declaration it might be forestalled by the Germans. Once again Edwin Montagu argued vehemently against the declaration, repeating that the recognition of a Jewish nationality with a homeland in Palestine would reflect adversely on the status of Jews in the *Diaspora. Refuting Montagu's arguments, Balfour declared that the French supported Zionism and that President Wilson was in favor of the movement. He also informed the War Cabinet that the German government was making every effort to capture the sympathies of the Zionist movement.

Final Draft. At a meeting on Oct. 4, 1917, the War Cabinet decided to consult President Wilson once again. It was explained to Wilson that the debate had been reopened because of the apparent imminence of an official pro-Zionist move on the part of the German government.

In view of Montagu's stubborn opposition, it was decided to invite the views of both Zionist leaders and anti-Zionist representatives. This decision was acutely resented by the Zionists, who felt any further concession to the anti-Zionists to be unwarranted.

When the War Cabinet was discussing the declaration on October 4, it had before it a draft prepared by Leopold S. Amery (a member of the War Cabinet Secretariat) at the request of Lord Milner, who had asked him to prepare a statement "which would go a reasonable distance to meeting the objections, both Jewish and pro-Arab, without impairing the substance of the proposed declaration."

In August, 1917, Milner himself had prepared a draft more cautious than the formula submitted by Rothschild to Balfour. Amery followed Milner's draft. It was his version, with certain amendments, that was finally approved by the War Cabinet on Oct. 31, 1917, and became the Balfour Declaration. The text of Amery's draft was cabled to Wilson in Washington on October 6. On October 13 Wilson approved the formula. In accordance with the resolution of the War Cabinet, the draft was submitted for comment to Zionist and British personalities: Chief Rabbi Dr. Joseph H. *Hertz, Rothschild, Sokolow, Weizmann, Leonard (later Sir Leonard) Cohen (president of the Jewish Board of Guardians), Sir Philip Magnus, M.P., Claude G. Montefiore (president of the *Anglo-Jewish Association), and Sir Stuart Samuel, M.P. (president of the Board of Deputies of British Jews).

Although they proposed some changes in the formula, Weizmann, Sokolow, and Rothschild welcomed the declaration. Chief Rabbi Hertz hailed it as marking an epoch in Jewish history. Montefiore, Cohen, and Magnus stated the anti-Zionist case. Sir Stuart Samuel, without stating his own opinion, expressed the view that the majority of Jews resident in Britain were in favor of the establishment of a Jewish National Home in Palestine. Herbert Samuel, who was also consulted, reiterated the view he had held throughout the war with regard to the establishment of a large Jewish population in Palestine under a British protectorate and called the declaration a wise step.

Issuance of the Declaration. On Oct. 31, 1917, addressing the War Cabinet, Balfour explained the meaning of the concept "national home": "It did not necessarily involve the early establishment of an independent Jewish State, which was a matter of gradual development in accordance with the ordinary laws of political evolution."

At that meeting the declaration was adopted. Two days later, on November 2, Lord Balfour wrote a letter to Lionel Walter Rothschild, enclosing a copy of the declaration and requesting him to communicate it to the Zionist Federation. Only on November 9 was the declaration published in the press.

The British War Cabinet and the British statesmen and officials who had worked for the promulgation of the Balfour Declaration were personally motivated by a variety of considerations. In the first place, there was the general British interest in gaining the sympathies of the Jews at a critical juncture in the war and in safeguarding British interests in the Middle East. The British were further mindful that Zionist support would enable them to control a territory adjacent to the Suez Canal, thus protecting imperial lines of communication. There was also a genuine interest in the fate of the Jewish people and a desire to assist their resettlement in their ancient homeland.

The declaration was endorsed by France in February, 1918, by Italy in May, and subsequently by other Allied governments (China, Japan, Greece, and Siam). President Wilson had given his assent, although the American government could not formally endorse the declaration since the United States was not at war with the Ottoman Empire. The declaration was formally discussed by the Allied Powers at the Paris Peace Conference (1919). The Allied Supreme Council, which met in San Remo in April, 1920, and awarded the *Mandate for Palestine to Great Britain, decided to incorporate the declaration into the peace treaties with Turkey. The text of the declaration was incorporated in the preamble to the Palestine Mandate granted by the League of Nations to Great Britain.

Effects. The declaration was received with great enthusiasm by Jews the world over. It created a profound impression not only in the Jewish communities of the Allied countries but also among the Jews of Germany and Austria-Hungary. It was the first time since the loss of Jewish independence in the 1st century of the Common Era that a great power had recognized the Jews as a nation entitled to a homeland and committed its help to facilitate the attainment of this goal. Although at first

a British pronouncement, the declaration became an internationally recognized instrument by virtue of its incorporation in the mandate of the League of Nations. By paving the way for a Jewish National Home in Palestine, the Balfour Declaration helped lay the foundations for the future State of Israel.

See also PEEL COMMISSION; SHAW COMMISSION; WHITE PAPER OF JUNE, 1922; WHITE PAPER OF 1939.

T. PRESCHEL

BALFOURIYA. Village (moshav) in the Jezreel Valley. Founded in 1922 and affiliated with *T'nu'at HaMoshavim. Population (1968): 243.

BAMBUS, WILLY. German-Jewish communal worker (b. Berlin, 1862; d. there, 1904). He was active in *Esra, the Berlin *Hoveve Zion group, and was coeditor of the periodical *Serubabel* (1886–88), which fought *assimilation and advocated the colonization of Palestine. Active in *Jung Israel, the Berlin pre-Herzlian Zionist society, Bambus joined Herzl soon after the appearance of the latter's *Jewish State* but later turned against him and against political Zionism, stressing that practical settlement work in Palestine must take precedence over diplomatic activity. He visited Palestine several times and established firms in Germany for the sale of Palestine produce and goods.

In addition to engaging in widespread activities for the colonization of Palestine, Bambus was extremely active in other Jewish communal endeavors. He played a leading role in the formation of societies for Jewish history and literature in Germany and combated *anti-Semitism. He also participated in the founding of the *Hilfsverein der Deutschen Juden and served as its general secretary.

His publications include *Palästina: Land und Leute* (Palestine: Land and People), *Die Kriminalität der Juden* (Criminality among the Jews), and *Die Juden als Soldaten* (The Jews as Soldiers).

BANKING IN ISRAEL. Israel has two different types of financial institutions designated as banks:

1. Commercial banks and cooperative credit societies, legally permitted to engage in the banking business, which is defined as "receiving from the public on current account money which is to be repayable on demand by check, and making advances to customers" (Banking Ordinance, 1941).

2. Mortgage banks and other specialized lending institutions, which raise long-term funds and finance housing as well as industrial and agricultural development.

COMMERCIAL BANKING

The inception of modern banking in Israel dates back to 1903, when the Anglo-Palestine Company (known after the establishment of the State as *Bank L'umi L'Yisrael) was founded at the initiative of the Zionist movement. But the real development of the banking system began only under the British *Mandate for Palestine, after World War I. Liberal banking legislation, coupled with the influx of Jewish immigrants and capital, led to a rapid growth in the number of banks and credit cooperatives (80 and 50, respectively, by 1935). More restrictive legislation, introduced in 1936–37, together with events preceding and during World War II, brought about a consolidation of the banking system. By 1944 the number of banks had declined to 25. Prominent among them were the Jewish Anglo-

Palestine Bank, the British Barclays Bank D.C.O., and the Ottoman Bank, as well as 2 Arab banks that served the Arab population. Most of the other banks were Jewish, as were all the credit cooperatives (66 in 1944).

Structure of the System. After the establishment of the State, the number of commercial banks in Israel remained virtually constant (23 in 1948, 27 in 1967) because of the restrictive licensing policy followed by the monetary authorities. In all other respects, however, the development of the banking system was rapid and variegated.

The number of bank offices was determined by two simultaneous processes: (1) the opening of new branch offices by banks and several credit cooperatives and (2) the absorption of credit cooperatives by banks. The cooperatives, many of which were small-town institutions, could not withstand the competition of bank branches and were adversely affected by the restrictive monetary policy of the *Bank of Israel.

TABLE 1. NUMBER OF BANKS AND CREDIT COOPERATIVES AND THEIR BRANCH OFFICES

	1950	1954	1958	1963	1967
Banks:					
Head offices	23	23	25	26	27
Branches	72	135	291	543	621
Cooperatives:					
Head offices	85	95	52	25	17
Branches	24	62	48	76	83

Major Institutions. In 1967 three banks accounted for more than two-thirds of all banking business in Israel. The largest was Bank L'umi L'Yisrael. With its four affiliated banks (one of them the Union Bank of Israel Ltd., which ranked fourth in the State), it was about equal in size to its two nearest competitors combined: the Israel Discount Bank, a privately owned institution; and Bank HaPo'alim (Workers' Bank), which was owned by the *Histadrut (General Federation of Labor). Other major banks, although considerably smaller, were the Foreign Trade

Bank (an affiliate of the Swiss-Israel Trade Bank of Switzerland), several privately owned banks (Israel-British Bank, Jacob Japhet & Co.), and Bank HaMizrahi, controlled by the religious organization whose name it bore (*see* MIZRAHI). In 1967 the Israeli branch of the Barclays Bank D.C.O. apparently was a medium-size institution. The biggest credit cooperative in 1967 was Halvaa VeHisakhon Tel Aviv–Jaffa (Tel Aviv–Jaffa Loan and Saving Association).

Banking Operations. In 1967 demand deposits were the single most important source of funds for Israeli banking institutions, but their share had gradually declined from more than 50 per cent of total resources in the early 1950s to less than one-fourth in 1967. Owing to persistent inflationary pressures, ordinary time and saving deposits never exceeded 10 to 15 per cent of total resources. A very substantial portion of the banks' resources was in the form of deposits from the government and other institutions earmarked for the granting of credit. In recent years, banks had accumulated large amounts of foreign currency deposits, most of which belonged to recipients of German restitution payments (these funds were redeposited in their entirety with the Bank of Israel).

Equity capital, which amounted to about 3 per cent of total resources during the 1950s, increased to 5 or 6 per cent between 1962 and 1964 as a result of public shares issued by some of the banks, but it declined once more in 1967.

The uses to which the banks put their funds were dictated by the liquidity and credit control regulations issued by the Bank of Israel. Reserve requirements were gradually raised from 58 per cent of deposits in 1958 to 69 per cent, in Israeli currency, in 1965 and cut back to 65 per cent during 1966. (The banks were allowed, however, to reduce their liquid assets by the amount of credit granted, subject to Bank of Israel directives. Their effective liquidity ratio had never exceeded 50 per cent.) Foreign currency was deposited in full with the Bank of Israel unless express approval for its use had been issued by the authorities. These reserve requirements made the banks highly liquid. In addition, a considerable proportion of the credit granted by them was subject to the directions of the depositors or to the approval of the Bank of Israel or the Israeli Treasury. The combination of

TABLE 2. CONDENSED BALANCE SHEET OF COMMERCIAL BANKS AND CREDIT COOPERATIVE SOCIETIES, 1955, 1961, AND 1967
(In millions of IL*)

Assets	1955	1961	1967	Liabilities	1955	1961	1967
Liquid assets†	*165*	*494*	*2,377*	Capital and reserves	*32*	*70*	*323*
Credit	*403*	*992*	*3,227*	Debentures	. . .	. . . . .	*117*
Regular	240	573	1,820	Demand deposits	267	624	*1,567*
From earmarked deposits‡	143	411	1,275	Time deposits	91	374	*2,344*
To the government	20	8	132	Regular	88	171	926
Foreign currency assets	. . .	*166*	*660*	Of restitution recipients	3	203	1,418
Securities	*34*	*128*	*591*	Deposits earmarked for loans	156	447	*1,300*
Government	23	54	214	Government	156	258	548
Other securities	11	74	377	Other	. . .	189	752
Fixed assets	*8*	*32*	*90*	Foreign liabilities¶	. . .	137	875
				Other liabilities	*64*	*160*	*419*
Total	*609*	*1,812*	*6,945*	Total	*609*	*1,812*	*6,945*
Contingent accounts§	*158*	*434*	*1,457*	Contingent accounts	*158*	*434*	*1,457*

*Exchange rate in 1955, IL = $0.56; in 1961, IL = $0.56; in 1967, IL = $0.33.

†Mostly balances with the Bank of Israel.

‡Of the government and institutions (mainly pension funds).

§Major item, guarantees.

¶Borrowings and deposits of nonresidents.

high liquidity ratios and a legal interest rate ceiling, under circumstances of persistent credit demand and inflationary pressures, led to the creation of a sizable "free" credit market in the early 1960s. The banks acted in this market as both brokers and guarantors of their customers' notes. This activity explained the size of the item "contingent accounts" in their balance sheets.

Investments of Israeli banks in securities were relatively small, but several banks invested extensively through investment affiliates. Other subsidiaries of commercial banks were prominent among mortgage banks and trust companies.

In addition to their deposit and credit business, Israeli commercial banks engaged in foreign exchange transactions and were active in the securities market both as brokers and as underwriters. Commercial banks were, as a whole, the most important financial institutions in Israel.

Besides an exceptional rate of growth, the Israeli banking system showed until 1967 a remarkable degree of stability. This pattern was upset in early 1967 by the failure of two medium-size institutions, which caused the collapse of a third. The failures, brought about by the economic slowdown in 1966–67 and deficiencies in management, were likely to bring about further consolidation of the banking system.

MORTGAGE AND DEVELOPMENT BANKS

Commercial banks were usually limited by the character of their resources to short-term credit transactions. To grant long-term loans for housing and for agricultural and industrial development, the Anglo-Palestine Bank Ltd. set up several subsidiary companies prior to the establishment of the State. These subsidiaries, together with a few other publicly sponsored finance companies, provided to the developing economy vital though modest amounts of long-term capital.

After 1948 the need for development capital increased enormously, but lending institutions were unable to raise the necessary amounts in the local capital market. This opened the way for public, mainly government, initiative. The government deposited with mortgage banks, chiefly the General Mortgage Bank Ltd. and the Housing Mortgage Bank (subsidiaries of Bank L'umi and Bank HaPo'alim, respectively), large sums that were lent out to purchasers of apartments. In 1961 the government established its own mortgage bank, T'fahot, which soon became the largest of its kind in the country.

TABLE 3. CONDENSED BALANCE SHEET OF MORTGAGE AND DEVELOPMENT BANKS, 1963 AND 1967
(In millions of IL)

Assets	1963	1967	Liabilities	1963	1967
Cash	22	48	Capital and reserves	385	680
Long-term loans	1,614	3,144	Debentures	406	931
Regular		711	1,254	Deposits	1,002	1,939
From institutional deposits	100	635	Public	33	121
From government deposits	803	1,255	Institutions†	147	548
Loans to the government*	203	579	Government	822	1,270
Securities	32	92	Loans received	13	102
Other assets	5	18	Other liabilities	70	229
Total	1,876	3,881	Total	1,876	3,881
Contingent accounts	56	140	Contingent accounts	56	140

*Includes deposits with the Treasury.

†Includes pension funds and participation of financial institutions in loans.

In 1951 the Israel Bank of Agriculture was established to provide long-term financing for agriculture, and in 1957 a similar government-sponsored institution, the Industrial Development Bank of Israel, was founded for the financing of industrial development. The establishment of the Maritime Bank followed in 1962.

Mortgage and development banks expanded at an extremely rapid pace. Despite the fact that beginning in 1953–54 both their debentures and their long-term loans were value-linked either to the rate of exchange or to the consumer price index, they could raise only a small portion of their resources on ordinary commercial terms and relied to a great extent on Development Budget funds, although regular commercial financing was gradually growing in importance. After the 1962 devaluation the government gradually relieved most borrowers from linkage commitments. The banks continued, however, to raise value-linked money, the most important purchasers of their debentures being pension funds. They depended, therefore, on the government's undertaking to cover differentials that might arise between their interest income and the interest cum linkage increments payable on their debentures.

M. HETH

BANK L'UMI L'YISRAEL (Bank Leumi le-Israel B.M.). Israel's oldest and largest bank. Its head office is in Tel Aviv. In 1968 it had 175 branches in Israel and banking subsidiaries in London (Anglo-Israel Bank Ltd.) and Switzerland (Cifico Bank Ltd., Zurich and Geneva), as well as representative offices in Paris, Frankfurt on the Main, Buenos Aires, Panama City, Caracas, and Mexico City. A branch which was opened in New York in 1961 was replaced in 1968 by the First Israel Bank and Trust Company, a subsidiary of the Bank L'umi.

Bank L'umi L'Yisrael headquarters, Tel Aviv. [Zionist Archives]

Assets. On Dec. 31, 1967, the bank's capital and open reserves were IL69,127,739; a capital note of $5,000,000 was issued to the Ford Foundation in 1967. Total deposits at that date were IL2,305,000,000 (about $659,000,000), and the balance sheet total was IL2,981,000,000 (about $852,000,000).

The bank has a number of significant subsidiaries in Israel, including the Union Bank of Israel Ltd., which is Israel's fourth largest commercial bank (total assets, IL370,000,000, or

$106,000,000), the General Mortgage Bank Ltd. (total assets, IL462,000,000, or $132,000,000), the Bank Leumi Investment Co. Ltd. (total assets, IL230,000,000, or $66,000,000), Ya'ad Agricultural Development Bank (total assets, IL152,000,000, or $43,000,000), and Otzar LaTa'asiya (long-term industrial credit; total assets, IL105,000,000, or $30,000,000). The total of consolidated assets of the bank and its subsidiaries as of Dec. 31, 1967, was IL4,489,000,000, or $1,283,000,000. The bank ranked 222d among the 500 largest banks in the free world in the annual listing of the *American Banker* (Sept. 1, 1967). If the consolidated deposits of other banks owned as to 50 per cent or more were included, the bank ranked 158th (*American Banker,* Sept. 27, 1967).

Early History. The bank was incorporated in London in 1902 under the name Anglo-Palestine Company Ltd. (later changed to Anglo-Palestine Bank Ltd.) as a subsidiary of the *Jewish Colonial Trust, which was set up by Herzl as the financial instrumentality of the *World Zionist Organization. Its object was to serve as a banking and financial instrument to further Zionist reconstruction activities. Its first branch was opened in Jaffa in 1903. Since most would-be borrowers were then not individually creditworthy, the bank organized cooperative societies in towns and villages, to which it granted modest credits. In 1909 it assisted a project to set up a new residential suburb near Jaffa and, after obtaining the necessary long-term loan money for the purpose, granted 18-year loans for the construction of the first 60 houses of what has since become Israel's largest city, Tel Aviv.

When Turkey entered World War I, the bank, as an English company, was closed and later ordered into liquidation but managed to continue certain of its activities clandestinely, especially relief activities on behalf of the *American Jewish Joint Distribution Committee. The bank emerged from the war rather stronger than it started.

Development in the 1930s. A great impetus was given to the country and to the bank by the immigration from Germany in the 1930s, which the bank fostered by participating in the establishment of certain capital transfer arrangements. In 1934 the bank was able to help the *Keren HaYesod (Palestine Foundation Fund) obtain from Lloyds Bank Ltd., London, the first foreign loan for Zionist reconstruction activities. This loan was large by the standards then prevailing—£500,000 sterling. During the 1930s the bank was able to foster the country's industrialization by granting medium- and long-term loans to the growing industrial enterprises, which later served the Allied war effort in World War II with the help of credits obtained from the bank.

Under the State of Israel. After the establishment of the State of Israel the bank was, by agreement with the provisional government, authorized in August, 1948, to issue its own bank notes as the legal tender of the new State and appointed government banker and financial agent. These functions were carried on in a separate issue department until December, 1954, when a central bank, the *Bank of Israel, commenced operations and in the course of time printed its own notes. In May, 1951, a new Israeli company, Bank Leumi le-Israel B.M., took over the undertaking, assets, and liabilities of the old English company.

Control and Direction. Control of the bank is in the hands of Otzar Hityashvut HaY'hudim B.M. (an Israeli successor company to the Jewish Colonial Trust), which holds a majority of the bank's voting stock. The first chairman of the bank's board of directors was David *Wolffsohn; another prominent chair-

man was Eliezer Siegfried *Hoofien. Dr. Yeshayahu *Foerder has been chairman since 1957. The first general managers were, successively, Zalman David *Levontin, Hoofien, and Aron *Barth. As of 1967, there were three general managers, Dr. Ernst Lehmann, Dr. Heinz Gruenbaum, and Mr. Ernst I. Japhet.

A. DORON

BANK OF ISRAEL. Central bank of the State of Israel, established in accordance with the Bank of Israel Law in 5714 (1954). It started operations in December, 1954.

The functions of the bank were defined in section 3 of the law as follows: "... to administer, regulate and direct the currency system, and to regulate and direct the credit and banking system in Israel, in accordance with the economic policy of the *government and the provisions of this Law, with a view to promoting by monetary measures (1) the stabilization of the value of the currency in Israel and outside Israel; (2) a high level of production, employment, national income and capital investments in Israel."

Accordingly, the major activities of the bank are as follows:

1. As a bank of issue it issues currency, both notes and coins. The amount to be issued is determined by the governor of the bank, with the approval of the Israeli government. The bank must hold assets to cover the currency issued but is not limited as to the types of assets to be held.

2. As sole banker and fiscal agent of the Israel government, the bank holds the government's deposits, makes provisional advances to the government, and administers the State loans.

3. As banker to the banks and regulator of Israel's banking and credit system, the bank accepts deposits from banking institutions and prescribes the amount and composition of liquid assets to be held by them. The law authorizes the bank to grant credit to banking institutions, to rediscount bills, to conduct open-market operations, and to prescribe rates of interest for deposits and loans.

4. The Examiner of Banks, who is an official of the bank, exercises general control and supervision over the conduct of banking business.

CONDENSED BALANCE SHEET AS OF DEC. 31. 1955, 1963, AND 1967
(In millions of IL*)

Assets	1955	1963	1967	Liabilities	1955	1963	1967
Gold and foreign exchange	100	1,565	2,501	Capital and reserves	11	20	20
Advances to the government	51	180	728	Currency in circulation	184	550	998
Government securities	146	222	184	Government banks		87	1,180	2,316
Rediscounts	16	86	409	Government deposits	16	336	561
Loans to foreign governments	...	46	34	Payment agreements	11	8	.....
Other accounts	48	389	48	Other accounts	52	394	9
Total	361	2,488	3,904	Total	361	2,488	3,904
Contingent accounts	32	335	466	Contingent accounts	20	335	466

* Exchange rate in 1955, IL = $0.56; in 1963, IL = $0.33; in 1967, IL = $0.33.

5. The bank holds the foreign exchange reserves of the State.

The bank is managed by a governor (David *Horowitz since its establishment), who consults with an Advisory Committee of seven members. The Research Department of the bank publishes a periodical *Bulletin* and an *Annual Report*.

M. HETH

BANNER OF JERUSALEM. *See* DEGEL Y'RUSHALAYIM.

BAQA AL-GHARBIYA. Large Arab village at the foot of the Samaria Mountains. Population (1968): 6,400.

BARAK. Village (moshav) in the Jezreel Valley. Founded in 1956 and named for the Biblical judge Barak, who defeated the Canaanites in this area. Affiliated with *T'nu'at HaMoshavim. Population (1968): 262.

BAR'AM. Village (kibbutz) in eastern Upper Galilee. Founded in 1949 and affiliated with the *Kibbutz Artzi Shel HaShomer HaTza'ir.

BARASH, ASHER. Hebrew author (b. Lopatin, near Brody, Galicia, Austria, 1889; d. Tel Aviv, 1952). A teacher in Galicia, he settled in Palestine in 1914 and taught Hebrew and Hebrew literature in Tel Aviv high schools. He began writing at an early age and was the author of tales of Jewish life in Galicia and of the life of *Second 'Aliya immigrants in Palestine, historical stories, and poetry. In cooperation with Ya'akov Rabinovitz, he established *Hedim* (1922–30), which served as a literary mouthpiece and proving ground for beginning writers.

Barash was for many years president of the Palestine Hebrew Writers' Association and of the biobibliographical institute G'nazim, which was renamed in his honor after his death. His collected writings were published in three volumes. He cooperated in the translation into Hebrew of the writings of Herzl and the memoirs of Chaim *Weizmann.   G. KRESSEL

BARATZ, YOSEF. Israeli labor leader (b. Kosnica, Russia, 1890; d. D'ganya, 1968). Active in *Tz'ire Zion in Kishinev, he settled in Palestine in 1906 and worked as an agricultural laborer at Hadera and Kinneret. He helped found D'ganya, the

Yosef Baratz.
[Zionist Archives]

first communal settlement, and lived in it thereafter. Baratz was active in *HaPo'el HaTza'ir and later in *Mapai, representing these organizations in Zionist and communal institutions. From

World War II until 1963 he was head of the Committee for Soldiers' Welfare. In 1921 he was a member of the first delegation of the *Histadrut (General Federation of Labor) to the United States and for a number of years traveled widely on a variety of missions. He wrote on contemporary events but especially on the communal settlements. His story of D'ganya, *A Village by the Jordan,* appeared in Hebrew and in an English translation.

G. KRESSEL

BARBASH, SAMUEL. Russian-Jewish banker (b. Podolia, Russia, ca. 1850; d. 1922). Settling in Odessa in the early 1880s, he founded a large banking house there and became a leader in the *Hoveve Zion movement, serving as treasurer of its *Odessa Committee. He purchased land in Talpiyot, near Jerusalem, and in Merhavya; attended Zionist Congresses (*see* CONGRESS, ZIONIST); and with the establishment of the *Jewish Colonial Trust became one of its directors and its representative in southern Russia. After the Russian Revolution his fortune was confiscated, and he died alone and in poverty.

BAREKET. Village (moshav) in the Petah Tikva area. Founded in 1952 and affiliated with HaPo'el HaMizrahi (*see* MIZRAHI). Population (1968): 690.

BAR GIYORA. Village (moshav) in the Judean Mountains. Founded in 1950 by *Yemenite Jews and named for Shimon Bar Giyora, leader of the rebellion against Rome (C.E. 66–70). Affiliated with *Herut. Population (1968): 200.

BAR-ILAN (BERLIN), MEIR. Religious Zionist leader (b. Volozhin, Russia, 1880; d. Jerusalem 1949). The youngest son of Rabbi Naphtali Tz'vi Y'huda *Berlin, he was trained at Yeshivot in Russia. An early adherent of religious Zionism, he soon became one of its most prominent leaders and over a period of more than 40 years helped build and expand the *Mizrahi movement as well as shape its ideology and program. In 1905 he served for the first time as a delegate to the Zionist *Congress. In 1910 he settled in Berlin, where he founded and edited the Hebrew weekly *Ha'Ivri.* In 1911 he became a member of the Executive, and in 1912 was named general secretary, of the Mizrahi World Movement, which then opened its central office in the German capital.

Meir Bar-Ilan.
[Zionist Archives]

In 1913 Bar-Ilan visited the United States for the purpose of organizing and strengthening the young Mizrahi movement there. He returned during World War I for a prolonged stay,

The campus of Bar-Ilan University, in Ramat Gan. [Zionist Archives]

during which he developed local Mizrahi groups into a national organization, resumed the publication of *Ha'Ivri,* and played a leading role in American Zionism and Jewish communal life. He was president of the Mizrahi Organization from 1916 to 1926, when he became honorary president. He served as president of the Rabbi Isaac Elchanan Theological Seminary (nucleus of Yeshiva University) in New York and was active in the *American Jewish Joint Distribution Committee and other organizations that rendered assistance to the war-ravaged Jewish communities of Eastern Europe.

In 1926 Bar-Ilan settled permanently in Jerusalem. He headed the Mizrahi World Movement with only a brief interruption from then until his death.

Elected to the Zionist *Actions Committee in 1921, he filled leading posts in the *World Zionist Organization in the years that followed. He served on the Presidium of Zionist Congresses beginning with the 12th (Carlsbad, 1921), was a member of the Executive Committee of the *Jewish National Fund (from 1925) and of its Presidium (from 1941), served on the Zionist *Executive, and was a member of the *Va'ad L'umi (National Council).

Bar-Ilan was a proponent of strong Zionist policies. In 1937 he was one of the leaders of the opposition in the Zionist movement to the British plan for the *partition of Palestine. In 1939 he participated in the *St. James Conference in London but left in protest when British anti-Zionist designs became ap-

parent. After the publication of the *White Paper of 1939, he advocated a Jewish policy of noncooperation vis-à-vis the British administration in Palestine.

Throughout the *War of Independence he remained in besieged Jerusalem. After the siege had been broken, he hastened to Tel Aviv and addressed a plea to the Provisional Council of State for unity and aid to embattled Jerusalem.

An eloquent orator, Bar-Ilan frequently toured Jewish centers all over the world on behalf of his party and the Zionist movement. He wrote numerous journalistic articles and ideological essays, some of which have been collected in book form. His books include *Fun Volozhin bis Yerushalayim* (From Volozhin to Jerusalem), a two-volume autobiography (Yiddish, 1933; Hebrew, 1939–40), and *Rabban Shel Yisrael* (Teacher in Israel, 1943), a biography of his father in Hebrew. He was also the founder and first editor of *HaTzofe,* Mizrahi's Hebrew daily newspaper, initiated the Mif'al HaTora (for the financial support of Yeshivot in the Land of Israel), and planned and helped edit the *Talmudic Encyclopedia* (1946 ff.). ·

T. PRESCHEL

BAR-ILAN UNIVERSITY. University located in Ramat Gan, a suburb of Tel Aviv, on a 45-acre campus off the highway to Tel HaShomer. An independent coeducational institution of higher learning, it was founded in 1955 by Dr. Pinhas Michael *Churgin, who served as its first president until his death in

1957, when Rabbi Joseph H. Lookstein of New York became acting president. Prof. Moshe (Max) Jammer was president from 1966 to 1968.

Named for Rabbi Meir *Bar-Ilan and founded under the auspices of the *Religious Zionists of America, the university was created to answer the need for a traditional Jewish institution of higher learning in Israel and to train men and women to integrate religious learning with secular knowledge. In 1963 a provisional charter was granted the university by the Board of Regents of the Department of Education of the State of New York, thus making it the only American-chartered institution of higher learning in the State of Israel and placing it on a par with other American colleges in the Middle East. The university receives substantial support from the American Committee for Bar-Ilan University, which has its headquarters in New York.

The officers of the university in 1970 were Rabbi Joseph H. Lookstein, chancellor; Moshe Hayim *Shapira, chairman of the Executive Council; Matityahu Adler, director general; and Prof. Harold Fisch, rector. The university is governed by a Board of Trustees (Phillip Stollman, of Detroit, chairman) and an Academic Senate, headed by the rector.

Academic Structure. In 1968 there were 4,000 students. They included Israelis, Europeans, North and South Americans, and South Africans. Courses were grouped in five divisions:

1. Jewish studies: Bible, Talmud, Jewish history, and Jewish philosophy.

2. Languages and literatures: Hebrew, Arabic, English, French, German, Latin, Greek, ancient Semitic languages, Hebrew literature, and world literature.

3. Social sciences: history, philosophy, psychology, sociology, economics, political science, and education.

4. Mathematics and natural sciences: general biology, botany, zoology, microbiology, biochemistry, chemistry, physics, and mathematics.

5. School of Social Work.

Degrees. Completion of a full course of study (150 credits) leads to the degree of B.A. or B.S., which entitles graduates to a New York State Board of Regents diploma. The university also grants a Ph.D. in Jewish studies.

Faculty. In 1968 the faculty numbered 400.

S. N. NESSON

BARKAI. Village (kibbutz) in the Sharon Plain. Founded in 1949 and affiliated with the *Kibbutz Artzi Shel HaShomer HaTza'ir.

BAR KOKHBA (Bar Kochba). Zionist organization of Jewish students in Prague, named for the leader of the Jewish revolt in Palestine against the Romans in the 2d century of the Common Era. Established in 1893 as Maccabia, it was one of many national Jewish students' organizations formed in response to the situation and problems of Jewish students at German universities. The students' encounter with the world of secular learning, their wish to retain Jewish identity, their exclusion from Christian fraternities, and their feeling of responsibility toward the Jewish people were all factors which gave impetus to the establishment of Bar Kokhba.

In 1899, following a period during which the organization was non-Zionist and was called the Verein der Jüdischen Hochschüler in Prag (Association of Jewish College Students in Prague), it changed its name a second time to Bar Kokhba and

joined the *World Zionist Organization. Within the organization, Bar Kokhba emphasized educational and cultural work, looking not only for political achievements but for some kind of Jewish renaissance and seeing in Zionism not only a solution to the problems of the Jewish masses but also a means of lending Jewish content to the life of the individual Jew. Bar Kokhba, was, in a sense, close to the *Democratic Faction but was more favorably inclined than the latter toward Jewish religious tradition, if not religious institutions. Bar Kokhba gained general recognition and importance during the lull in political activity in the Zionist movement in the years 1909–14.

It was at Bar Kokhba gatherings that Martin *Buber held his famous "Three Lectures on Judaism," which greatly influenced Jewish youth in Central Europe. In these lectures, Buber sought to trace the development of the Zionist idea to the situation of the Jewish individual in the West, where he was not persecuted but was torn between the impressions of his environment on the one hand and his Jewish heritage on the other.

Bar Kokhba published *Vom Judentum* (1914), a collection of essays edited by Hans Kohn, in which its ideas were expressed: the search for a living content of Judaism, the longing for Jewish identity, and the quest for living values in the East (i.e., Asia) as against Western utilitarianism and materialism. The participants rejected the identification of Judaism with realism and materialism, which was common at that time in anti-Semitic circles. They were influenced by the ideas of philosophers such as Immanuel Kant, Johann Gottlieb Fichte, Wilhelm Dilthey, and Henri Bergson.

Among the members of Bar Kokhba were Samuel Hugo *Bergmann and Robert and Felix *Weltsch. The organization disintegrated during World War I.

I. KOLATT

BAR-LEV, HAYIM. Israeli soldier and chief of staff (b. Austria, 1924). Bar-Lev emigrated to Palestine in 1939 from Zagreb, Yugoslavia, where he had spent most of his childhood. In 1942, after completing his studies at the Mikve Yisrael Agricultural School, he enlisted in *Palmah (commando units), receiving his first command in 1944. During the *War of Independence, he was placed in command of a battalion of the Negev Brigade, which repulsed the Egyptian attack from the Sinai Peninsula, occupied S'dom, and led the first Israeli thrust into the north of the Sinai Desert.

After the war Bar-Lev served as instructor of a battalion commanders' course. In 1952 he became head of the Northern Command, and in 1954–55 he commanded the Giv'ati Brigade. During the years that followed, he was several times sent abroad for military studies and also attended university courses, eventually obtaining a degree from the *Hebrew University of Jerusalem and a master's degree in economics and business administration from Columbia University. In 1956 he was a colonel in command of the Armored Corps in the *Sinai Campaign. Bar-Lev's forces were among the first Israeli units to reach the Suez Canal.

Bar-Lev remained commanding officer of the Armored Corps until 1961, when he was sent to study in the United States for two and one-half years. On his return to Israel in 1964, he was appointed chief of operations of the *Israel Defense Forces. In May, 1966, he went to Paris for advanced military courses but was recalled in May, 1967, to become deputy chief of staff of the Israel Defense Forces. In this capacity he shared the responsibility for the conduct of the *Six-day War with Chief of Staff Itzhak *Rabin and Brig. Gen. 'Ezer *Weizmann. He succeeded Rabin as chief of staff of the Israel Defense Forces in January, 1968.

BARONDESS, JOSEPH. Labor and Zionist leader in the United States (b. Kamenets Podolsk, Russia, 1867; d. New York, 1928). Settling in New York in 1888, Barondess worked as a tailor while attending New York University Law School at night. He became a labor organizer and was instrumental in the organization of the Cloakmakers Union, the Ladies Garment Workers Union, the Hebrew Actors Union, and the Hebrew American Typographical Union. The *Kishinev pogrom (1903) made him turn to Zionism, and from then on, though continuing to play a prominent role in the Jewish labor movement, he devoted more and more of his time to the Zionist cause. Barondess was one of the founders of the *American Jewish Congress, a member of the American Jewish delegation to the Paris Peace Conference, and Nasi (president) of the fraternal order *B'nai Zion. At the time of his death he was an honorary vice-president of the *Zionist Organization of America.

BAROU, NOAH. Economist, Labor Zionist pioneer, and *World Jewish Congress leader (b. Poltava, Russia, 1889; d. London, 1955). Barou joined the *Po'ale Zion movement at an early age and became a leading figure in it. Arrested for anti-Tsarist activities while a student at the University of Kiev, he left Russia upon his release to continue his studies in Germany. In 1914 he returned to Russia to become secretary-general of the underground Po'ale Zion party. In 1922 he left Russia permanently and, after a brief stay in Berlin, settled in London, where he gained renown as an economist and authority on the cooperative movement. He continued his Jewish activities, serving as chairman of the British section of the World Jewish Congress. The author of many books and articles in Russian and English, Barou was also active in the Fabian Society and in the British Labor party. He initiated with the West German government the negotiations that culminated in the agreement by the latter to pay out a large sum of money in reparations to the surviving victims of Nazi atrocities (see GERMAN-ISRAEL AGREEMENT).

C. B. SHERMAN

BARTA'A. Arab village in northern Samaria. Population (1968): 650.

Aron Barth.
[Zionist Archives]

BARTH, ARON. *Mizrahi leader and financial expert (b. Berlin, 1890; d. Tel Aviv, 1957), He was educated by his father, Prof. Jacob Barth, at the Berlin Rabbinical Seminary, which had been founded by his grandfather, Rabbi Azriel *Hildesheimer, and at the Universities of Berlin and Heidelberg (Dr.Jur., 1911). Barth practiced law in Berlin and served as legal adviser to various industrial concerns and banks. He was a leader of Adat Yisrael, the Orthodox community in Berlin, president of Mizrahi in Germany, and a member of the *Keren HaYesod (Palestine Foundation Fund) Executive. He was also active as attorney of the Zionist *Congress in the framework of the *Congress Tribunal. In 1933 he settled in Palestine, later becoming general manager of the Anglo-Palestine Bank (see BANK L'UMI L'YISRAEL) and its affiliates. Barth helped establish Israel's monetary policy and supervised various public bond issues. He was a founder and chairman of the board of the religious youth village near K'far Hasidim and the author of a philosophical work on Judaism.

G. BAT-YEHUDA

BARTH, ELIEZER. Editor and writer (b. Berlin, 1880; d. Tel Aviv, 1949). A brother of Aron *Barth, he was educated at the Berlin Hildesheimer Rabbinical Seminary. Later he turned to business and Zionist activities. Barth served on the national Executive of the Zionist Organization of Germany and headed its Berlin branch. During World War I he served in the German Army and headed the Office for Jewish Affairs in Warsaw. Barth edited *Mizrahi's *Jüdische Presse* and its monthly, *Zion*, writing articles signed "Eldad and Medad." He headed the Zionist *Executive's Department of Propaganda in London for two years. In 1933 he settled in Palestine.

Y. RAPHAEL

BARUCH, JOSEPH MARCOU. Adventurer and early Zionist (b. Constantinople, 1872; d. Florence, 1899). Baruch studied at the *Alliance Israélite Universelle school and the University of Constantinople. Following brief sojourns in Austria, France, and Algeria, he settled in Plovdiv (Philippopolis), Bulgaria, in 1895, joined the Zionist youth movement HaShahar there, and founded and edited its magazine, *Carmel* (in French with a Ladino supplement). In 1897 Baruch became the principal of the Ashkenazi school in Cairo. Shortly thereafter he joined the Greek anti-Turkish armed forces, rising to the rank of sergeant. His war diaries, published in Italian translation in a Jewish paper in 1897–98, express a fierce desire to die a hero's death for the liberation of Palestine.

There followed a second period of wanderings through Egypt, Algeria, Tunisia, Asia Minor, and the Balkans. When he learned about Herzl and political Zionism, Baruch engaged in vigorous Zionist propaganda, often walking from one country to another. One of his projects was that the Jews should purchase a small Mediterranean island, declare it an independent Jewish state, and organize from it a military expedition for the armed conquest of Palestine. Baruch's strange behavior caused apprehension in people who met him, as can be gathered from Herzl's statements about him in his *Diaries*. Following an unhappy love affair, he committed suicide in Florence.

BAR-YEHUDA, ISRAEL. Israeli labor leader (b. Ukraine, Russia, 1895; d. Jerusalem, 1965). He was active in the Zionist movement in Russia until he was exiled to Siberia by the Communists in 1922. Freed in 1923, he settled in 1926 in Palestine, where he became a road worker and later joined the Yagur kibbutz. He soon rose to leadership in the *Histadrut (General Federation of Labor), was prominently associated with *Hagana work, and at various times held high positions in the *Mapai, *Ahdut 'Avoda, and *Mapam parties.

Bar-Yehuda was a member of the *Knesset from its inception in 1949. From 1956 to 1959 he was Minister of the Interior, and from 1962 until his death, Minister of Transport.

BARZILAI (EISENSTADT), Y'HOSHU'A. Leader of the *Hoveve Zion movement (b. Kletsk, Minsk District, Russia, 1855; d. Geneva, 1918). He went to Palestine in 1887 and became active in communal affairs. A year later he returned to Russia, where he became one of the founders of the secret order *B'ne Moshe, and at the first general meeting of the *Odessa Committee was chosen a deputy member of the committee. In 1890 he went to Palestine once again and became a member of the Jaffa Executive of the Odessa Committee. He initiated the founding of the workers' society *Agudat Po'alim and of a fund for land purchase and support of the institutions of the Jewish community, and he aided many other important enterprises. He wrote articles on the situation in the country in Hebrew periodicals and edited the bulletin *Mikhtavim MeEretz Israel* (1893–95).

With the advent of Herzl, Eisenstadt joined the political Zionist movement. He participated in the *Minsk Conference of Russian Zionists in 1902 and during the Uganda debate (*see* EAST AFRICA SCHEME) was one of the leaders of the *Tziyone Zion in Palestine. In 1904 he began to work for the Anglo-Palestine Bank (*see* BANK L'UMI L'YISRAEL). He was also one of the founders of the Jerusalem Hebrew High School and of the Bet 'Am, the Jewish communal and cultural center.   I. KLAUSNER

BARZILAI, YISRAEL. Member of the Cabinet of Israel (b. Nieszawa, Russian Poland, 1913). Settling in Palestine in 1934, Barzilai joined a kibbutz and later helped found the kibbutz Negba, where he made his home. Active in *HaShomer Ha-

Yisrael Barzilai.
[Israel Information Services]

Tza'ir from his youth on, he held leading positions in the *Kibbutz Artzi Shel HaShomer HaTza'ir, the *Histadrut (General Federation of Labor), and other Labor Zionist bodies. In 1946 he participated in the formation of the World Union of HaShomer HaTza'ir and served as its first secretary. After the merger of HaShomer HaTza'ir with *Ahdut 'Avoda to form *Mapam (1948), he became a member of Mapam's Central Committee and its Political Commission. From 1948 to 1951 he served as Israel's Minister to Poland, and from 1955 to 1961 he was a member of the *Knesset. From 1955 to 1961 and again from 1966 on, he served as Minister of Health.

BASCH, VICTOR-GUILLAUME. Scholar, author, and Zionist leader (b. Budapest, 1863; d. Lyon, France, 1942). The son of the Hungarian-Jewish publicist Rafael Basch, he began his academic career in Nancy and Rennes, France, at the time of the *Dreyfus affair. He became professor of literature at the Sorbonne in Paris and wrote numerous books on the classics of German philosophy, art, and literature. Joining the Zionist movement at its inception, he became a lifelong associate of Max *Nordau in his Zionist work.

During World War I, in 1915–16, Basch was sent by the French government to the United States, ostensibly as an official representative of the French Ministry of Public Instruction but in reality for the purpose of attempting to influence American Jewry to support the Allied cause. Basch considered his mission a failure.

Basch was president of the French League of Human Rights for many years. He was murdered in Lyon by the Nazis.

BASLE PROGRAM. Program of the *World Zionist Organization as formulated and adopted at the 1st Zionist *Congress, held in Basle in 1897. It reads as follows (translated from the German original):

> Zionism strives to create for the Jewish people a home in Palestine secured by public law. For the attainment of this aim the Congress envisages the following means:
> 1. The promotion, on suitable lines, of the settlement of Palestine by Jewish agriculturists, artisans, and tradesmen.
> 2. The organization and unification of the whole of Jewry by means of appropriate local and general institutions in accordance with the laws of each country.
> 3. The strengthening of Jewish national sentiment and national consciousness.
> 4. Preparatory steps toward securing the consent of governments, which is necessary to attain the aim of Zionism.

A controversy arose as regards the term *öffentlich-rechtlich* (secured by public law). Originally it was proposed to insert only "legally" and, subsequently, *völkerrechtlich* (by international law), which actually came nearest to Herzl's views. The problem could not be settled in the plenum of the Congress and was handed over to a special commission in which all shades of opinion were represented. Max *Nordau, Alexander Mintz, Hermann *Schapira, Max *Bodenheimer, Nathan *Birnbaum, Saul Raphael *Landau, and Adam *Rosenberg (the last named was from the United States) were members.

The first draft prepared by this commission was rejected by the Congress, and the commission sat again and inserted the term *öffentlich-rechtlich* as Nordau had suggested. The significance of this revision in terminology lay in the following considerations: The use of *völkerrechtlich* would have been regarded by Turkey (then the sovereign over Palestine) as an attack on its sovereignty; thus the phrase *öffentlich-rechtlich* was used to obviate the implication that any infringement of Turkish sovereignty over Palestine was intended. At the same time, this term was left so vague that it was open to the interpretation of being merely the opposite of "private" right.

The four points which the Congress adopted were not regarded as an integral part of the Basle Program but only as guiding principles for carrying it out. Twenty years later, the formulation of the Basle Program ("home for the Jewish people in Palestine") was incorporated in the *Balfour Declaration.

The Basle Program became the authentic and authoritative pronouncement on the aims of Zionism and remained unaltered

The beach at Bat Yam. [Israel Information Services]

for more than 50 years. The 23d Zionist Congress (1951), the first to be held in the State of Israel, adopted a new statement concerning the objectives and tasks of the Zionist movement. This came to be known as the Jerusalem Program (for text, *see* CONGRESS, ZIONIST: 27th Congress).

O. K. RABINOWICZ

BAT SH'LOMO. Village (moshav) in the Zikhron Ya'akov area. Founded in 1889 and named for the father-in-law of Baron Edmond de *Rothschild. Affiliated with *Hitahdut HaIkkarim. Population (1968): 186.

BAT YAM. Coastal city south of Tel Aviv. Founded in 1926 by a group of pioneers, it was originally called Bayit VeGan. In 1948 its population was only about 1,500, but after the establishment of the State it grew considerably through the absorption of thousands of newcomers and developed into a thriving industrial center and popular seaside resort. Population (1968): 62,000.

BEDOUINS IN ISRAEL. *See* ARABS IN ISRAEL.

BEER, SAMUEL FRIEDRICH. Sculptor (b. Brno, Moravia, Austria, 1846; d. Florence, 1912). After studying at the Vienna Academy of Fine Arts, he worked in Rome and Vienna. In 1875 he moved to Paris, where his statues and busts gained him world fame. A friend of Herzl and of Max *Nordau, he was an early adherent of Zionism and participated in the 1st Zionist *Congress, designing the medal struck to commemorate this event. "Shema Yisrael," a statue he executed in Florence, where he had settled in 1902, symbolized the tragedy of the Jewish people. Beer also executed a bust of Herzl, which is now in the Herzl Museum on Mount Herzl in Jerusalem.

BEER-HOFMANN, RICHARD. Playwright, poet, and novelist (b. Vienna, 1866; d. New York, 1945). Beer-Hofmann studied law at the University of Vienna but never engaged in the legal profession. He made his literary debut in 1893 with the publication of a volume of short stories.

His "Schlaflied für Mirjam" (Lullaby for Miriam, 1898) has been regarded as one of the most beautiful poems in the German language. His drama *Jaakobs Traum* (Jacob's Dream, 1918), which was to serve as preface to a dramatic trilogy on the life of King David, describes the turning point in Jacob's life at Bet El and his choice to accept the mission of God and the suffering and persecution it would entail. The drama was translated into Hebrew and English and presented on the German stage and by HaBimah (*see* THEATER IN ISRAEL). *Der junge David,* the first part of the trilogy, appeared in 1933.

Beer-Hofmann, who settled in the United States in 1939 as a refugee from Nazi-occupied Austria, was one of the first to write to Herzl approvingly of his *Jewish State,* and although he never officially joined the Zionist movement, he was a supporter of Zionism throughout his life. He visited Palestine in 1936.

BEERSHEBA. *See* B'ER SHEVA'.

BEGIN, M'NAHEM. Chairman of the *Herut movement, member of the *Knesset, and journalist (b. Brest Litovsk, Russia, 1913). Educated at Warsaw University Law School, he joined *B'rit Trumpeldor (Betar), the Revisionist youth movement (*see* REVISIONISTS), in 1929 and was cofounder of the Jewish Student Defense Unit. In 1932 he joined the Betar command in Poland, was in charge of its Organizational Department, and contributed to *HaM'dina, HaMadrikh,* and *HaM'tzada,* the

M'nahem Begin.
[Israel Information Services]

official organs of the movement. In 1936 he was appointed commander of Betar in Czechoslovakia. On returning to Poland in 1939, he joined the radical wing of the Revisionist movement, which was ideologically linked with the B'rit HaBiryonim group in Palestine, and assumed a responsible position in the executive organs of Betar and the Revisionist Union, taking an active part in the organization of *illegal immigration to Palestine. The same year, while leading a protest demonstration against the British policy in Palestine, Begin was arrested by the Polish security forces in Warsaw.

In 1938 Begin represented the Polish Betar at the World Congress of the organization in Warsaw, where, under his influence, the Betar oath of allegiance was amended to include a vow to conquer the Jewish Homeland by force of arms. Early in 1939 Begin was appointed commander of Betar in Poland. After the collapse of Poland at the outbreak of World War II, he resumed work in Vilna, which had come under Soviet rule. Late in 1940 he was arrested for his Revisionist activities and sentenced to eight years' forced labor. He served his sentence in a Vilna prison until the end of 1941, when he was transferred to a con-

centration camp in Pechora. Released under the Soviet-Polish agreement of that year, Begin joined the Polish Army and in 1942 went to Palestine. While still serving in the Polish armed forces, he assumed command of the Palestinian Betar and, on his discharge from the army, became commander of the *Irgun Tz'vai L'umi. Beginning in 1944, he led Irgun's armed uprising against British rule in Palestine. The British authorities offered a reward of £10,000 for his arrest.

After the proclamation of the State, Begin, together with other Irgun leaders, founded the Herut movement, and he was elected its chairman. Beginning in 1949 he served on the Knesset's Foreign Affairs and Defense Committee and, later, on the Constitution, Law, and Justice Committee. In June, 1967, he was appointed minister without portfolio in the Government of National Unity formed on the eve of the *Six-day War.

Begin was a regular contributor to the paper *Herut on political, social, legal, and other issues and the author of *The Revolt* and *The White Nights.*

I. BENARI

BEHAM, ARYE. Physician and pioneer in Palestine (b. Lithuania, 1877; d. Tel Aviv, 1941). Beham studied medicine at the University of Kharkov, where he organized Zionist societies. He was a delegate to the 4th Zionist *Congress in 1900 and to the *Minsk Conference of Russian Zionists in 1902. In 1903 he was sent by Kharkov Jewry to Kishinev to organize aid for the pogrom victims (*see* KISHINEV POGROM). Two years later he was drafted into the Russian Army as a physician and served in the Far East during the Russo-Japanese War. On his way home in 1906, he passed through Palestine and decided to devote himself to the improvement of the poor health conditions he found there. After working for some time at the Pasteur Institute in Kiev and at the Hamburg Institute for Tropical Diseases, he returned to Palestine and established a Pasteur Institute in Jerusalem. Later he opened branches of the institute in Petah Tikva (1925) and Haifa (1926).

During World War I, Beham served as a physician in the Turkish Army. After the war he was active in Palestinian Jewish public life, especially in Jewish physicians' organizations and in public health institutions.

BEILINSON, MOSHE. Journalist and publicist (b. northern Russia, 1890; d. Petah Tikva, 1936). He received his early schooling in Russia and later studied at the Universities of Moscow, Freiburg, and Basle. For some time he practiced medicine but left the profession to devote himself to Zionist work and journalism. From 1917 to 1924 he lived in Italy and was active in the Zionist movement and the Zionist press there. After settling in Palestine in 1924, he worked as an agricultural laborer until, with the establishment of the Histadrut daily *Davar (1925), he was invited to join its editorial board. At first, he wrote his articles in Italian, German, and Russian, from which languages they were translated into Hebrew, but from 1926 on he wrote in Hebrew. As one of *Davar*'s chief publicists, he published numerous articles, his prolific output reaching its height during the time of the Arab terror in the last year of his life. His books on the Arab problem and the Italian Renaissance were published during his lifetime. After his death, a selection from his articles appeared in two volumes. Beilinson was a member of the *Va'ad L'umi (National Council), the *Histadrut Executive Committee, and the Central Committee of *Mapai. He was also prominently active in the institutions of *Kupat

Holim, the Sick Fund of the Histadrut, serving as chairman of its National Supervisory Committee.

G. KRESSEL

BEIN, ALEX. Zionist historian (b. Steinach, Germany, 1903). He studied at Berlin University and from 1927 to 1933 was a researcher at the German State Archives in Potsdam. In 1933 he settled in Palestine. There he served as deputy director of the Central Zionist Archives (*see* LIBRARIES AND ARCHIVES, ZIONIST)

Alex Bein.
[Zionist Archives]

in Jerusalem from 1936 to 1954, becoming director in 1955. A year later he was also appointed State Archivist of Israel. Bein's writings include a biography of Herzl (translated into several languages) and books on other Zionist leaders and on Jewish settlement in Palestine, including *Return to the Soil* (1952).

BEISAN VALLEY. *See* BET SH'AN VALLEY.

BELGIUM, ZIONISM IN. There were Jewish communities in what is now Belgium even during the Middle Ages, but because of severe persecution, settlement was not continuous. Jews did not settle in Belgium in large numbers until the 19th century. In 1939 there were about 80,000 Jews in Belgium, more than half of whom were subsequently murdered by the Nazis during World War II. In the 1960s, Belgium's Jewish population was 40,000, most of whom were concentrated in Brussels (24,000) and Antwerp (13,000).

Early Years. Most of the Jews in Antwerp prior to World War II were active in the diamond trade, which they helped to develop, making Antwerp the world's largest diamond center. German Jews who had come to Brussels early in the 19th century were concentrated mainly in the leather industry.

The advent of political Zionism found a warm response in Belgium, particularly among the newcomers from Central and Eastern Europe. The native Belgian Jews, descendants of immigrants from the Netherlands, Alsace, and Turkey, at first remained aloof. At the 1st Zionist *Congress (1897) Belgian Zionists were represented by one delegate, Boris Barbasch, a medical student in Brussels.

In the early 1900s, a Zionist Federation came into existence, with headquarters in Antwerp. It was headed by Jean *Fischer (who was the leader of Belgian Zionism until his death in 1926), his brother Oscar Fischer, Joseph Grunzweig, Ruben Kohn, and Samuel *Tolkowsky.

The Zionist Federation included the following groups: Agudat Zion, *Tz'ire Zion, B'ne Zion, Zionist students, and Zionist women.

The federation engaged in cultural and propaganda activities. In 1905 it began to publish *HaTikva*, a German-language monthly which also featured French articles from time to time and which appeared until World War I. It also established, in Antwerp, a group called S'fat Zion to further the study of *Hebrew and a Friends of the *Bezalal School of Jerusalem. Samuel Tolkowsky established a branch of the Rehovot Settlement Society. Annual conferences were held at which reports of federation activities were presented. In 1906 a session of the Zionist *Actions Committee was held in Brussels, with delegates from 80 countries attending.

The same year Oscar Fischer was appointed director of the *Jewish National Fund (JNF) of Belgium. In Antwerp the Zionists succeeded in winning two seats on the Jewish Community Council. Jean Fischer represented the Zionists of Belgium at Zionist Congresses, on the Actions Committee, and on the Executive Committee of the JNF, and he served on all other major financial bodies of the Zionist Organization.

In 1907 the Ahavat Zion group was established in Brussels. From time to time it held joint meetings with the Antwerp Zionists. Zionist students' groups, under the name Kadima, with Jewish students from Russia as the driving force, were founded in Brussels, Liège, Ghent, and later in Antwerp.

In 1912, 1,300 Sh'kalim (membership fees; *see* SHEKEL) were sold in Belgium. At the time, the city with the largest number of Zionists was Antwerp, where the local Agudat Zion had its headquarters. The JNF engaged in widespread fund-raising activities.

The *Mizrahi movement of Belgium cooperated closely with its counterpart in the Netherlands. Zionist activity in Belgium came almost to a standstill when the country was occupied by the Germans in World War I.

World War I and After. Still, the Zionist Federation of Belgium and a Belgian *Po'ale Zion group participated in a Zionist Conference held in The Hague on Dec. 24–25, 1916, and the federation held a conference in Scheveningen, Netherlands, on Apr. 29, 1917. It was during that period, too, that Arye Kubowitzki (later *Kubovy, chairman of *Yad VaShem), Pesah Helman, and Maurice Weisbart founded Tz'ire Zion (a nonpolitical group) and Na'are Zion (a youth group).

In 1918 a Mizrahi branch, led by Abraham Zvi Kubowitzki, was organized in Brussels. At the time the General Zionists of Antwerp (*see* GENERAL ZIONISM) were led by Jean Fischer and Numa *Torczyner; the Brussels organization was headed by Itzhak Kubowitzki and Max Podliaschuk.

In 1921 Po'ale Zion founded a branch in Brussels, and a Left Po'ale Zion was organized. Three years later *HaShomer HaTza'ir was founded, and in 1926 a Borochov Youth group (of the Left Po'ale Zion) was established. In 1929 a branch of the *Gordonia youth movement was set up, as was a branch of the Revisionist movement (*see* REVISIONISTS) and of the *B'rit Trumpeldor (Betar) youth organization. This movement published a Yiddish-language monthly, *Unzer Front.*

At the time of the creation of the expanded *Jewish Agency that same year, a Comité Belgique-Palestine was organized under the chairmanship of Prof. Herbert Speyer of the University of Brussels.

In 1932 Po'ale Zion and Tz'ire Zion merged, and the federation began to publish *HaTikva,* a French-language journal, edited first by Arye Kubowitzki and later by Joseph Szulsinger.

In 1933 the *D'ror youth movement of Po'ale Zion, the only youth movement to maintain branches in all the major cities of Belgium, was organized, Gordonia set up a *Hakhshara farm in Villiers-la-Ville, and a branch of *HaNo'ar HaTziyoni was founded. A number of very active students' organizations representing all shades of Zionism came into being. The Zionist Federation developed an extensive program to help refugees arriving from Germany, where Hitler had come to power in 1933.

During the period preceding World War II, the Jewish National Fund was not only a fund-raising instrument but also a social force in the Jewish community. The annual JNF Ball (later the JNF Bazaar) was the main social event on the Jewish communal calendar.

Until World War II, Belgium was represented at Zionist Congresses by Numa Torczyner (General Zionist movement) and Arye Kubowitzki (Labor Palestine). Except for two years during which Jef Prouzanski, leader of Po'ale Zion, held the position, Torczyner was chairman of the Zionist Federation from 1926 until 1940.

World War II and After. Zionist groups in Belgium continued their activity even during World War II. Regular *'Oneg Shabbat gatherings were held. The Zionist leaders Itzhak Kubowitzki and Joseph Rotkel were active also on the Jewish Community Council. Two Hebrew schools sponsored by the council were organized. A library was also founded and remained in existence until the liberation. The Left Po'ale Zion published a Yiddish-language underground newspaper, *Unzer Vort.* An underground Palestine Office (see PALESTINE OFFICES), headed by Abraham Szatan, was organized, providing those in hiding with prisoner exchange papers from Palestine.

After the liberation, the *Jewish Brigade units stationed in Belgium gave much help to the Zionist effort. The Zionist parties were reconstituted. The Zionist Federation had its seat in Brussels, which then had the largest Jewish community in the country. Itzhak Kubowitzki was elected chairman and held this post until 1948. The federation initiated the publication of a French-language bimonthly journal, *La Tribune Sioniste,* which has continued to appear without interruption.

In the 1960s all Zionist parties had branches in Belgium, united in the federation. The *Women's International Zionist Organization (WIZO) was quite active, as were JNF and the United Campaign. Zionists were active in the community councils and had established several day schools: the Tahkemoni School, a model school with 800 students in Antwerp; and one Orthodox and one Traditional school, in Brussels.

Non-Jews also took an interest in the Zionist movement of Belgium and in the upbuilding of Palestine, and leaders of various political parties supported Zionism. Camille Huysmans, the secretary of the Second International, mayor of Antwerp, and (after World War II) President of the Belgian Parliament, was one of the earlier supporters of the Zionist cause. Émile Vandervelde, one of the outstanding personalities of the immediate postwar period, visited Palestine, and the lectures he gave on his return created a tremendous amount of interest. King Albert and Queen Elizabeth had visited Palestine, where they were the guests of Chaim *Weizmann, later President of Israel, and Queen Mother Elizabeth maintained a lifelong interest in the growth of the *Yishuv (Jewish population of Palestine) and Israel.

H. BIBROWSKI

BELKIND, ISRAEL. Early Zionist pioneer and educator (b. Lahoisk, Russia, 1861; d. Berlin, 1929). One of the founders of the *Bilu immigration movement, Belkind settled in Palestine in 1882. He worked first as a laborer in Mikve Yisrael and later in Rishon L'Tziyon, where he led the settlers' revolt against Baron Edmond de *Rothschild's administration. In 1889 he founded a school in Jaffa in which Hebrew was the language of instruction. Later he served as a teacher in various localities. After the *Kishinev pogrom of 1903 he brought orphans to the country and provided for them in the Kiryat Sefer Agricultural School in Sh'feya, which he founded. The institution closed in 1906. Years later he sought to revive the school, and for this purpose he brought to Palestine, after World War I, children orphaned by the Ukrainian pogroms, but his efforts were not successful.

Belkind was the author of Hebrew textbooks and wrote also on Jewish history and the modern Jewish settlement in Palestine.

BELKOVSKY, ZVI. Zionist leader in Russia (b. Odessa, 1865; d. Tel Aviv, 1948). He studied law in Odessa. Offered a professorship in Russia if he would agree to be converted to Christianity, he refused and, from 1893 to 1897, taught at Sofia University in Bulgaria. In 1898 he returned to Russia, settling in St. Petersburg, where he contributed to scholarly publications and practiced law.

Zvi Belkovsky.
[Zionist Archives]

While still a student, Belkovsky was active in pre-Herzlian Zionist associations. He developed widespread Zionist activities in Bulgaria, and in 1893, with Nathan *Birnbaum and others, planned a world Zionist convention. With the advent of Herzl he became one of his earliest followers, participated in the 1st and other early Zionist Congresses (see CONGRESS, ZIONIST), and helped draft the statutes of the *Jewish Colonial Trust and the *Jewish National Fund. For years he was a member of of the Greater *Actions Committee and head of the St. Petersburg district of the Russian Zionist Organization. Because of his Zionist activities he was arrested by the Tsarist authorities.

After the Russian Revolution, in 1918–19, he served as chairman of the Executive Committee of the Russian Jewish Communities. From 1922 to 1924 he was head of the illegal Russian Zionist Central Committee. Arrested in 1924, he was sentenced to deportation to Siberia, but the sentence was commuted to exile from the country, and he settled in Palestine.

In Palestine Belkovsky was active in the General Zionist movement (see GENERAL ZIONISM), practiced law, and was a member of the Jewish Arbitration Court in Tel Aviv. His publications included a Zionist bibliography with 4,000 entries, the first work of its kind.

BEN. Hebrew word, meaning "son," that forms part of many place names in Israel, as in Ben Shemen (Son of Oil).

BEN 'AMI (RABINOVITZ), MORDECAI. Author and publicist (b. Podolia, Russia, 1854; d. Tel Aviv, 1932). He received a Jewish and a secular education and studied at the Universities of Kiev and Odessa. In 1881 he began his career as a publicist with an article on the teaching of Russian at Jewish schools. During the pogroms of that period he called for and helped organize Jewish self-defense in Odessa. Later he went to Paris to secure aid from the *Alliance Israélite Universelle for the pogrom victims who had fled to Brody, Galicia. Subsequently he resided in Geneva, where he wrote his first stories of Jewish life. On his return to Odessa in 1887, he became active in the *Hoveve Zion movement and was a member of the *Odessa Committee of the organization from its inception. Ben 'Ami became an ardent follower of Herzl and served as a delegate to the 1st and subsequent Zionist Congresses (*see* CONGRESS, ZIONIST). After the Russian Revolution of 1905 he settled in Geneva, emigrating to Palestine in 1923.

In his articles, Ben 'Ami championed Jewish *nationalism and fought *assimilation. His stories, which express love for Jewish tradition, were immensely popular and were translated into Hebrew and other languages from the original Russian.

S. SKULSKY

BEN 'AMI, 'OVED. Israeli civic leader (b. Petah Tikva, 1905). He was active in youth organizations and served as secretary of the Jewish settlers' organization *B'ne Binyamin from 1924 to 1928 and as chairman from 1929 on. He was a member of the *Asefat HaNivharim (Elected Assembly) and of the *Va'ad L'umi (National Council).

Ben 'Ami helped found several settlements in addition to N'tanya, which, owing to his efforts and under his guidance, developed into one of the largest cities of Israel. He served as mayor of N'tanya from its founding in 1929 to 1965. He was also instrumental in building the port city of Ashdod and in the establishment of the *diamond industry in Israel and was prominently associated with other business enterprises.

BEN 'AMI. Village (moshav) in western Galilee. Founded in 1949 and affiliated with *T'nu'at HaMoshavim. The village was named for Ben-'Ammi Pechter, *Hagana commander, and 46 of his soldiers, who fell in the area during the *War of Independence. Population (1968): 341.

BEN AVI, ITAMAR. Hebrew writer (b. Jerusalem, 1885; d. East Orange, N.J., 1943). The son of the Hebrew lexicographer Eliezer *Ben Yehuda, Ben Avi was the first child in modern times whose mother tongue was Hebrew. He studied at the Teachers Seminary of the *Alliance Israélite Universelle in Paris and at the University of Berlin. Ben Avi helped his father in the publication of his newspapers and wrote articles as well as belles lettres. During World War I he was in the United States, where he conducted Jewish nationalist propaganda. In 1919 he helped found the Palestine Hebrew daily *Do'ar HaYom, serving as its editor for many years. He also edited other publications, including the *Palestine Weekly,* and served as correspondent for foreign newspapers. A founder of the settler

organization *B'ne Binyamin, he went on missions abroad on behalf of the *Jewish National Fund and the *Keren HaYesod (Palestine Foundation Fund). He urged a renaissance of Jewish seafaring. Like his father, he coined many new Hebrew words. He advocated the romanization of the Hebrew script and experimented with Hebrew publications printed in roman characters. His autobiography, 'Im Shahar 'Atzma'utenu (At the Dawn of Our Independence), was published posthumously, in 1961.

H. LEAF

BEN DOR. *See* NESHER.

BENE B'RAK. *See* B'NE B'RAK.

BEN ELIEZER, ARYE. Leader in *Irgun Tz'vai L'umi and Deputy Speaker of the *Knesset (b. Vilna, Russia, 1913; d. Ramat Gan, 1970). Brought to Palestine in 1920, he joined in 1926 the Revisionist youth movement *B'rit Trumpeldor (Betar) and during the 1929 and 1936 *Arab riots in Palestine took part in the defense of Jerusalem and Tel Aviv. In 1931 he was arrested for agitation against the population census, which the *Revisionists opposed as a first step toward a *Legislative Council in Palestine. Two years later he was again arrested, on suspicion of belonging to the radical Revisionist group B'rit HaBiryonim. Between 1937 and 1939 he visited Poland, Romania, and other Balkan states, where he organized Irgun Tz'vai L'umi cells. In 1939 he was sent by the Irgun High Command to the United States, where he helped form the Committee for a Jewish Army, the Emergency Committee to Rescue the Jewish People of Europe, and the Hebrew Committee of National Liberation (*see* BERGSON GROUP).

Ben Eliezer returned to Palestine in October, 1943, on behalf of the Emergency Committee to work for the rescue of European Jewry and joined the Irgun High Command. In 1944 he was interned in Latrun and later was transferred to Cairo, the Sudan, and Asmara, Eritrea. In January, 1947, he escaped to Ethiopia and from there to Djibouti, French Somaliland. After 4 months' imprisonment for illegal entry into the country, he spent 15 months in Djibouti, evaded extradition to British authorities, and reached Paris (1948), where he joined the *Diaspora command of the Irgun. After returning to Israel in June, 1948, he was instrumental in the formation of the *Herut movement, which he represented in the Knesset from 1949 on. In 1956 be became Deputy Speaker of the Knesset.

I. BENARI

BEN-GURION, DAVID (David Green). Zionist labor leader, Jewish statesman, architect of the Jewish State, and the first Prime Minister of Israel (b. Płońsk, Russian Poland, 1886). He obtained his early education in a modern Heder founded by his father, Avigdor Green, an early Hovev Zion (*see* HOVEVE ZION). As a boy, he founded a Zionist youth society. In 1904 he went to Warsaw, joined the *Po'ale Zion, and became active in the controversy over the *East Africa scheme, opposing any territorial solution of the Jewish problem outside Palestine.

Ben-Gurion immigrated to Palestine in 1906. Until 1910 he worked as a farmhand, first in the settlements of Judea and later in Galilee. In 1906 he attended a conference of Po'ale Zion in Ramle, at which the party platform was drawn up. It was at this conference that Ben-Gurion first voiced objection to the *Diaspora-based Po'ale Zion program and sought to infuse the party's program with a Palestinian quality and make it relevant

Ben-Gurion in the uniform of the Jewish Legion, during World War I. [Zionist Archives]

to the realities of the new country. He further advocated the supremacy of the *Hebrew language over Yiddish. At subsequent conferences of Po'ale Zion in Palestine and other countries he stressed the central importance of the Palestine branch of the Po'ale Zion within the Po'ale Zion World Movement.

In 1910 Ben-Gurion moved to Jerusalem, joining Itzhak *Ben Zvi in editing *Ha'Ahdut,* the Po'ale Zion periodical. The Young Turk Revolution (1908–09) and the prospect of a modern multinational structure within the framework of the Ottoman Empire prompted him to take up the study of law so as to be better equipped to participate in the political life that seemed to open itself to the *Yishuv (the Jewish population of Palestine). In 1911 he proceeded to Salonika, where he studied Turkish and established contacts with Jewish labor groups. In the summer of 1912 he enrolled as a law student at the University of Constantinople, at the same time continuing his party activities. In 1913 he attended the 11th Zionist *Congress in Vienna and was elected to the Central Committee of Po'ale Zion.

Ben-Gurion's studies in Constantinople were interrupted by World War I. To forestall the deportation from Palestine of large numbers of Jews who were Russian nationals and hence enemy aliens, Ben-Gurion, with other Palestinian leaders, urged Palestinian Jews to adopt Ottoman nationality. He himself

became an Ottoman national, which, however, did not prevent Ahmed *Jamal Pasha, commander of the Turkish forces in Syria and Palestine, from expelling him (spring, 1915) on the ground that the program of Po'ale Zion was inimical to the interests of the Ottoman Empire. Reaching Alexandria, he met Joseph *Trumpeldor and Vladimir *Jabotinsky, who were engaged in recruiting volunteers for a Jewish battalion among the Jewish refugees from Turkish-held Palestine. Since the battalion was intended to fight on the side of the Allies, Ben-Gurion disapproved of the initiative, because he felt that it would expose the Yishuv to the wrath of the Turkish authorities.

Arriving in New York in May, 1915, Ben-Gurion and Ben Zvi set out to organize *HeHalutz, an organization of young Jews who would do pioneering work in Palestine. Ben-Gurion also joined the proponents of the creation of a democratically elected *American Jewish Congress. Early in 1918, when part of Palestine was no longer under Turkish control, Ben Gurion supported the recruiting in the United States of a *Jewish Legion that was to be a part of the British Army and fight on the Palestine front against the Turks. He himself enlisted in this battalion, which reached Palestine in the summer of 1918. While still a soldier, Ben-Gurion was active in campaigning for the formation of a united Labor party; this initiative led to a conference in Petah Tikva (1919) at which Po'ale Zion and nonaffiliated laborites joined in forming a new party, *Ahdut 'Avoda.

Ben-Gurion was one of the founders of the *Histadrut (General Federation of Labor) and as its secretary-general (1921–35) was its effective leader as well as the undisputed head of Ahdut 'Avoda. With the merger of Ahdut 'Avoda and *HaPo'el HaTza'ir in 1930, he became the leader of the Palestine Labor party (*Mapai). At Zionist Congresses, in the *Va'ad L'umi (National Council), and from the platforms of his own party, he fought leftist tendencies within the labor movement on the one hand and the rightist orientation of the Zionists-*Revisionists on the other, always stressing the overriding importance of Jewish settlement work in Palestine as the way to the attainment of the Zionist goal. Until 1937, when the *Peel Commission recommended the *partition of Palestine into an Arab and a Jewish State, Ben-Gurion opposed the demand of the Revisionists to make the principle of a Jewish State the basis of Zionist policy vis-à-vis the British government. At the same time, he strenuously objected to the policy of the *B'rit Shalom group, which advocated renunciation of the demand for a Jewish majority in Palestine as a means of reconciling the Arabs to a limited measure of Jewish progress there. In an attempt to reduce the tension between the Histadrut and the Revisionists that developed in the early 1930s as a result of labor disputes, Ben-Gurion signed (October, 1934) an agreement with Jabotinsky, leader of the Revisionists, providing for a settlement of such disputes and the avoidance of clashes between them. This agreement, however, was rejected in 1935 in a referendum of Histadrut members.

From 1935 until the establishment of the State of Israel in 1948, Ben-Gurion served as chairman of the Executive of the *Jewish Agency in Palestine and assumed an increasingly important role in shaping the policies of the Yishuv and of the Zionist movement. He favored the partition plan of the Peel Commission on the ground that a Jewish State, even in a greatly reduced area, would afford a refuge to European Jewry, whose very existence was then menaced by Nazi Germany. In the spring of 1939 he was a member of the Jewish delegation to the London Round Table Conference, where an unsuccessful attempt was made to reconcile Zionist aspirations with British policy. When the British policy of appeasing the Arabs culminated in the anti-Zionist *White Paper of 1939, which aimed at reducing the Yishuv to the status of a permanent minority within an Arab-dominated Palestinian state, Ben-Gurion led an uncompromising opposition to this policy. At the outbreak of World War II, however, he advocated an all-out mobilization of the Yishuv for the Allied war effort and the formation of Jewish units in the British Army. His policy was "to combat the anti-Zionist White Paper as though there was no war, and to fight the Germans on the side of England as though there was no White Paper." Recognizing that Britain would not implement the *Balfour Declaration as provided in the *Mandate for Palestine, Ben-Gurion saw the establishment of a Jewish State after the war as the objective of Zionist policy. In 1940–41 he toured the Jewish communities of the free world, explaining his views on the postwar solution of the Palestine problem. He was one of the proponents of the *Biltmore Program (1942), which committed the Zionist movement to the principle of a Jewish Commonwealth as its postwar political objective.

When it became apparent after the war that the British Labor Government, which assumed office in 1945, was bent on enforcing the White Paper, Ben-Gurion initiated a resistance policy that in its first stage assumed the form of promoting Jewish *immigration to Palestine contrary to the White Paper's regulations. When the British reacted vehemently against *illegal immigration and employed force to prevent it, Ben-Gurion authorized armed resistance to the British forces. At first, Ben-Gurion was opposed to the armed attacks launched on British military installations by the two dissident underground military organizations, *Irgun Tz'vai L'umi and *Lohame Herut Israel (Lehi), as endangering the safety of the Yishuv. In 1946, however, he authorized the *Hagana to mount, in cooperation with the two dissident groups, country-wide attacks on British installations. The British retaliated by arresting members of the Jewish Agency Executive and Hagana leaders. The subsequent British proposals for the solution of the Palestine problem, all of which aimed at perpetuating the Yishuv as a minority in Palestine, were opposed by Ben-Gurion, who, in his appearances before the *Anglo-American Committee of Inquiry (1946) and the *United Nations Special Committee on Palestine (UNSCOP, 1947), reiterated the demand for a Jewish Commonwealth. At the 22d Zionist Congress (Basle, 1946), Ben-Gurion, Abba Hillel *Silver, and their supporters defeated a proposal for a further round table conference in London offered by the British government and supported by Chaim *Weizmann. As a result Weizmann failed to be reelected president of the *World Zionist Organization.

On his return to Palestine, Ben-Gurion, realizing that an armed clash with the Arabs was unavoidable, took charge of Hagana, secured funds for the setting up of a clandestine arms industry, made arrangements for the purchase of weapons, and placed the Yishuv on a war footing. In the weeks prior to the *Declaration of Independence, he firmly resisted pressures from within and without to postpone the Proclamation of the State. On May 14, 1948, he chaired the session of the People's Council, read the Proclamation of Independence, and assumed the office of Prime Minister and Minister of Defense in the provisional government of Israel.

In 1949, following the elections to the First *Knesset, Ben-Gurion headed a coalition government, holding the offices of Prime Minister and Minister of Defense until his first retirement in December, 1953. The reason he gave for his unexpected decision to retire was the need to rest. In February, 1955, he was asked to rejoin the government as Minister of Defense under the premiership of Moshe *Sharett. Following the results of the elections to the Third Knesset in 1955, Ben-Gurion again assumed the premiership and the post of Minister of Defense, holding both offices until his final retirement in June, 1963.

Ben-Gurion was in all respects the builder of the Army of Israel (see ISRAEL DEFENSE FORCES). While the invasion of Palestine by the Arab armies (May–June, 1948) was in progress, he set out to mold the volunteer militia that defended the infant State into a modern and effective fighting force. With firmness and in the teeth of opposition from both left and right, he eliminated the dissident armed units of Irgun Tz'vai L'umi and Lohame Herut Israel, abolished the special status enjoyed by *Palmah (commando units), then under leftist influence, and merged them all in one national army. He followed the policy of entrusting army leadership to young commanders and assuring the steady flow of new blood into the High Command by retiring chiefs of staff every three or four years. Also, it was his policy to draw scientific talent and academically trained people into the service of the army.

In his capacity as Prime Minister and Defense Minister, Ben-Gurion decisively shaped the foreign policy of Israel. His overriding principle that, in the absence of peace with the neighboring Arab countries, foreign policy must be subordinated to defense considerations, often led to differences with his Foreign Ministers, Moshe Sharett and Golda *Meir. Early in 1956 he succeeded, through his associates in the Defense Ministry, in initiating friendly relations with the French government, assuring Israel of a steady flow of arms at a time when other Western powers were unwilling to aid Israel with military hardware. Ben-Gurion planned and decided on the *Sinai Campaign of 1956, thereby further strengthening Franco-Israeli cooperation. In June, 1960, he met French President Charles de

Ben-Gurion in retirement. [Israel Information Services]

Gaulle and assured the continuation of French friendship. The same year he conferred with German Chancellor Konrad Adenauer in New York and laid the groundwork for close cooperation with the Federal Republic of Germany in economic and other fields. Without weakening his pro-American orientation in any way, Ben-Gurion strove to forge a close link with the principal powers in continental Western Europe, France and Germany, regarding the support of both countries as essential for Israel's defense potential and for its association with the *European Common Market.

In matters of internal policy, Ben-Gurion increasingly stressed the preeminence of the national interest over the particularist tendencies which were dominant in the pre-State period and had been carried over, with other pre-State institutions, into the political, economic, and social structure of the sovereign State. He fought successfully for the elimination of the party "trends" from the school system and, in the face of opposition from many leaders in his own Mapai party and from the more leftist Ahdut 'Avoda and *Mapam parties, succeeded in having the Knesset enact a law abolishing these trends and establishing a single State-supported and -controlled educational network. He failed, though, in his advocacy of a public medical service administered by the State, because he was unable to carry along his own party, which preferred to keep as many State functions as possible in the hands of the Histadrut. He succeeded in inducing his party to approve a program of electoral reform providing for the introduction of a constituency system as practiced in Great Britain and the United States rather than a proportional system of representation. In doing so, he sought to abolish the proliferation of parties, reduce their number, and bring the Israeli party structure closer to the British and American models. Because of opposition from other parties, however, this reform failed to materialize.

After the establishment of the State Ben-Gurion, recognizing the importance of the Negev and of the Gulf of Elat as Israel's outlet to the Indian Ocean and the African continent, bent his energies to the development of this large and desolate area. It was due to his insistence that considerable investments were made in the building of the city of Elat and its port. To symbolize the vital importance of this region, Ben-Gurion, when he first retired from the government in 1953, settled in S'de Boker, a kibbutz south of B'er Sheva', where he later founded a secondary school and a teachers training college.

Ben-Gurion's achievements were in no small measure made possible by his undisputed leadership and control of Mapai, the dominant party in Israeli politics. His pursuit of national policies, at times in disregard of, or even in opposition to, the particularist doctrines of his party, lifted him to the level of a national figure.

His unchallenged authority within his party was shaken as a result of the Lavon affair. Being unable to impose his will on the government, he brought about the dissolution of the Knesset in March, 1961. During his last two years in office (1961–63), when he served as both Prime Minister and Minister of Defense, he drew considerable criticism for his pro-German policy. On June 17, 1963, he announced his resignation, suggesting the appointment of Levi *Eshkol as his successor, and retired to S'de Boker. This event signified the end of an era in the history of Israel; the foundations of the State were firmly established, and its structure bore the imprint of Ben-Gurion's personality.

A year later Ben-Gurion reentered the public arena by reviving the Lavon affair and later by opposing Premier Eshkol's plan to form an alignment between Mapai and the left-wing Ahdut 'Avoda. When, in January, 1965, the Mapai Convention approved the alignment plan by a majority of 60 per cent, Ben-Gurion organized his adherents with a view to appearing with a separate list in the forthcoming Knesset elections. For this, the Mapai party tribunal expelled him from the party he had founded and led for 25 years. At the head of a new party, the *R'shimat Po'ale Yisrael (Rafi), which he formed with his close associates Moshe *Dayan, Minister of Agriculture, and Shim'on *Peres, Deputy Minister of Defense, Ben-Gurion was elected in 1965 to the Sixth Knesset. When, following the *Six-day War of 1967, Rafi disbanded and rejoined Mapai, Ben-Gurion remained a lone member in the Knesset, unaffiliated with any party.

Despite a crowded life, Ben-Gurion devoted much of his time to historical studies, stressing the importance of the Bible rather than of post-Biblical literature as the principal source of inspiration and guidance for the nascent Jewish culture in Israel. He added the study of the classical Greek language and literature as well as Indian philosophy to his intellectual pursuits. A prolific writer and publicist, he published a number of studies on the Jewish labor movement and the revival of Israel.

S. Z. ABRAMOV

BEN-HAIM (FRANKENBURGER), PAUL. Israeli composer (b. Munich, 1897). Settling in Tel Aviv in 1933, he became one of the best-known representatives of Eastern-Mediterranean music in a lyrical, pastoral-romantic vein. In 1957 he received the *Israel Prize for his symphonic work *The Sweet Singer of Israel,* which has been recorded by the New York Philharmonic under Leonard Bernstein. Ben-Haim's compositions also include two symphonies, a concerto and a capriccio for piano and orchestra, concertos for violin and for violoncello, piano and chamber music, the cantatas *Vision of a Prophet* and *Hymn from the Desert,* and a liturgical cantata, the motet *Lift Up Your Heads,* three psalms for soloists, chorus, and orchestra, and choral works *a cappella.*

R. GRADENWITZ

BENI 'UQBA. See 'UQBI.

BEN JACOB, JACOB. Bibliographer and early member of the *Hoveve Zion movement (b. Vilna, Russia, 1858; d. Zoppot, Danzig, 1926). A son of the bibliographer Isaac Ben Jacob, he posthumously published his father's magnum opus, a bibliographical list of approximately 17,000 Hebrew books published prior to 1863. He earned his livelihood as a merchant but devoted his major efforts to bibliography. Ben Jacob was one of the founders of the Hoveve Zion group in Vilna and in 1890 attended the first general meeting of the *Odessa Committee. With the advent of Herzl, he became his ardent follower and participated in early Zionist Congresses (*see* CONGRESS, ZIONIST). When Herzl visited Vilna in 1903, he stayed at the home of Ben Jacob.

BEN SHEMEN. Village (moshav) in the Judean Plain, neighboring the youth village of the same name. Founded in 1952 and affiliated with *T'nu'at HaMoshavim. Population (1968): 200.

Not far from the present settlement, Boris *Schatz established in 1911 a settlement for Yemenite silver-filigree workers (*see*

YEMENITE JEWS IN ISRAEL), which was abandoned at the outbreak of World War I. In 1922 a moshav named Ben Shemen was established on the site. During the *War of Independence, this moshav, which was in the area of fighting, had to be abandoned.

BEN SHEMEN. Youth village and agricultural school in the Judean Plain, east of Lod. Established in 1921, it became famous for specific advanced educational methods. During World War II and in the period thereafter it was an important absorption center for children saved from the Nazi holocaust, who were brought to the country by *Youth 'Aliya. During the *War of Independence it withstood a long siege by the Arabs. Population (1968): 740.

BENTOV, MORDECAI. *Mapam party leader (b. Grodzisk, near Warsaw, 1900). He studied at Warsaw University and the Warsaw Institute of Technology and was active in *HaShomer HaTza'ir in Poland. In 1920 he went to Palestine, where he worked as a laborer and settled in the kibbutz Mishmar Ha-'Emek, which he helped establish. After graduating from law school in Jerusalem, he came to hold leading positions in HaShomer HaTza'ir, the kibbutz movement, and the *Histadrut (General Federation of Labor). In 1935 he was elected a member

Mordecai Bentov.
[Israel Information Services]

of the *Actions Committee. He was a member of the Zionist delegation to the *St. James Conference in London (1939) and of the *Jewish Agency delegation to the United Nations (1947). After the establishment of the State of Israel, he served as Minister of Labor and Reconstruction from 1948 to 1949 and Minister of Development from 1955 to 1961. He was a member of the *Knesset from its inception (1949) until 1965, representing Mapam, of which he was a prominent leader. Bentov founded the Mapam daily *'Al HaMishmar and served for some time as its editor.

BENTWICH, HERBERT. Lawyer and British Zionist leader (b. London, 1856; d. Jerusalem, 1932). Bentwich studied law at University College, London, edited the *Law Journal,* practiced law, and was an expert on copyright. He was a cofounder of the *Order of Ancient Maccabeans (1891) and joined the *Hoveve Zion movement (1892), eventually becoming its vice-president. Inspired by Herzl's second address before the Maccabeans (July 6, 1896), Bentwich organized a "pilgrimage" from England to Palestine, which lasted from Apr. 6 to May 14, 1897. Among the 21 pilgrims was Israel *Zangwill. Bentwich was cofounder of the Zionist Federation of Great Britain and Ireland and a

member of the Presidium of the 2d Zionist *Congress (1898). He helped draft the statutes of the *Jewish Colonial Trust and opposed the *East Africa scheme. He became grand commander of the Maccabeans and president of the London Zionist League, and propagated the establishment of a Maccabean colony.

Bentwich was a member of a political committee formed to assist Chaim *Weizmann and Nahum *Sokolow in their work that resulted in the *Balfour Declaration. In 1919 he was a member of the Jewish delegation to the Paris Peace Conference. He settled in Jerusalem in 1929.

J. FRAENKEL

BENTWICH, NORMAN. Lawyer and Zionist leader (b. London, 1883). He was a son of Herbert *Bentwich and, following in his father's footsteps, devoted his life largely to Zionism. In World War I he volunteered for the Palestine Campaign, and when the British Mandatory government (*see* MANDATE FOR PALESTINE) was established, he was appointed its Attorney General. Although he was an ardent advocate of Jewish-Arab cooperation, he encountered much Arab hostility and once was shot and wounded by an Arab. After the *Arab riots of 1929, the fact that he was a Jew precluded him from representing the government at the Commission of Inquiry and eventually brought about his retirement in 1931. He then threw himself into work at the *Hebrew University of Jerusalem, where he was professor of international relations. After Hitler's accession to power in 1933, Bentwich was named Deputy of the League of Nations High Commissioner for Refugees from Germany and subsequently became active in British Jewish rescue work for European Jewry. In 1953 he became vice-chairman of the Hebrew University's Board of Governors. He wrote many books, including *Fulfilment in the Promised Land* (1938), *Judea Lives Again* (1944), *Israel and Her Neighbours* (1955), *Israel Resurgent* (1960), *The New-Old Land of Israel* (1960), and an autobiography, *My 77 Years* (1961). With his sister Margery, Bentwich wrote a biography of their father, under the title *Pilgrim Father* (1940).

J. FRAENKEL

BEN-YA'AKOV, TZ'VI. *See* PARACHUTISTS, PALESTINIAN JEWISH.

BEN YEHUDA, ELIEZER. Pioneer of the restoration of *Hebrew as a living language (b. Lushky, Lithuania, 1857; d. Jerusalem, 1922). He received a traditional and a secular education in his native country and, in 1878, went to Paris to study medicine. Impressed by the struggles of the Balkan peoples for freedom from the Turks (1877–78), Ben Yehuda became interested in the restoration of the Jews to their ancient Homeland and in the revival of Hebrew as a living language. In 1879 he published in the Hebrew periodical *HaShahar* an article in which he demanded that the Jews colonize Palestine and use Hebrew as their daily language and that Hebrew literature be dedicated to a renaissance of the Hebraic spirit. In subsequent articles he reiterated his views and asked that Hebrew replace other languages as the language of instruction in the Jewish schools in Palestine.

Forced to interrupt his medical studies because of tuberculosis, Ben Yehuda spent the winter of 1880–81 in the warm climate of Algeria, and in the autumn of 1881 he settled in Palestine with his wife. In Jerusalem he helped edit the periodical

Havatzelet and taught at the *Alliance Israélite Universelle school, having been given permission to teach Jewish subjects in Hebrew. In 1884 he established *HaTz'vi*, his own weekly, which eventually developed into a daily. He also edited other periodicals. In his papers Ben Yehuda fought against the *Halukka, the religious charity organization on whose funds a considerable part of the old *Yishuv (Jewish population of Palestine) subsisted. He advocated work in agriculture and propagated the use of Hebrew in daily life.

In 1889 Ben Yehuda, with several collaborators, established the Va'ad HaLashon Ha'Ivrit, or Hebrew Language Council (*see* HEBREW LANGUAGE ACADEMY), among whose tasks was the coining of new Hebrew words. Ben Yehuda, who himself enriched the Hebrew language with many new words, served as chairman of the council until his death.

In addition to his varied activities as publicist and author, Ben Yehuda, throughout his years of residence in Palestine, worked on the compilation of a comprehensive dictionary of the Hebrew language containing Hebrew words ranging from those found in the Bible to those in modern Hebrew literature. He traveled to Europe several times to consult rare Hebrew books and manuscripts and to raise funds for his projects. After the outbreak of World War I, fearing persecution by the Turkish authorities of Palestine, he went to the United States, where he continued work on his dictionary. Several volumes of this great thesaurus were printed in his lifetime. By 1959 the complete edition of 17 volumes had appeared.   T. PRESCHEL

BEN YOSEF, SH'LOMO (Shulim Tabacnik). Palestinian Jewish martyr (b. Lutsk, Russia, 1913; d. 'Akko, 1938). He received a traditional education. Joining the Revisionist youth organization *B'rit Trumpeldor (Betar) at an early age, he immigrated illegally to Palestine in 1937 and worked with a Betar labor group in Rosh Pina. On Apr. 21, 1938, Ben Yosef and two of his comrades, outraged by Arab terror, made a retaliatory attack on an Arab bus. They were arrested and tried. Though no one was hurt in the attack, two of the accused, Ben Yosef and Abraham Shein, were sentenced to death. Shein's sentence was commuted to life imprisonment, but Ben Yosef was executed despite worldwide protests and appeals.

BEN ZAKKAI. Village (moshav) in the Judean Plain. Founded in 1950 and named for the Talmudic sage Yohanan Ben Zakkai. Affiliated with HaPo'el HaMizrahi (*see* MIZRAHI). Population (1968): 605.

BEN-ZION, SIMHA (Simha Alter Gutmann). Hebrew writer (b. Teleneshty, Bessarabia, Russia, 1870; d. Tel Aviv, 1932). He lived for some time in Odessa, where he taught at a modern Heder (Jewish elementary school) and was one of the founders of *Moriah, the Hebrew publishing house. Settling in Palestine in 1905, he edited literary miscellanies as well as periodicals. In addition to writing short stories, novels, and poetry, Ben-Zion compiled textbooks and translated German classics into Hebrew. He wrote monographs on the *Bilu immigration movement and on the settlements of Rishon L'Tziyon and G'dera. One of the first settlers of Tel Aviv, Ben-Zion was active in the communal life of the city. He was prominently affiliated with *General Zionism.

BEN ZVI, ITZHAK (Yitzhak Shimshelevitz). Second President of the State of Israel (b. Poltava, Ukraine, Russia, 1884; d.

Jerusalem, 1963). His father, Z'vi Shimshelevitz, an ardent Hovev Zion and a member of the secret order *B'ne Moshe, went to Palestine in 1891 as representative of the Agudat HaElef of Minsk, which planned the settlement of 1,000 families in Palestine.

Because of the restrictive Jewish quotas at secondary schools, young Ben Zvi was not admitted to the Gymnasium (high school) until 1901, when he was 17. He continued his Hebrew studies and belonged to a Hebrew-speaking circle organized by one of his teachers, A. M. Borochov, whose son Ber was his close friend (*see* BOROCHOV, BER).

In the summer of 1904, Ben Zvi realized his dream of visiting Palestine. On his way he made the acquaintance, for the first time, of *Sephardim in Constantinople, Smyrna, Salonika, and Beirut. During his two months in Palestine he explored Jewish villages and met the workers and teachers of the *Second 'Aliya, some of them his own townsmen. He returned to Poltava, determined to settle in Palestine. Immediately after completing his high school studies, he went to nearby towns to organize self-defense groups and *Po'ale Zion.

In June, 1906, the Russian police searched the house of Ben Zvi's parents and discovered, hidden in the yard, the arms cache of the Poltava Jewish self-defense movement which Ben Zvi headed. His father was sentenced to life exile in Siberia (he was able, however, to get to Palestine in 1922) and the rest of the household to terms of imprisonment. Ben Zvi himself managed to escape to Vilna, where he continued his clandestine work for Po'ale Zion. He participated in the movement's secret regional conference in Minsk (*see* MINSK CONFERENCE) in June, 1906, and then traveled to Germany, Austria, and Switzerland in an attempt to attract Jewish students to the Po'ale Zion movement. Late in 1906 he returned to Vilna, where he served for a while as editor of *Der Proletarisher Gedank*, the organ of the movement, and was imprisoned twice. In the spring of 1907, he left Vilna for Palestine.

As a delegate of Po'ale Zion in Palestine, Ben Zvi took part in the 8th Zionist *Congress, held in 1907 in The Hague. At the First World Conference of Po'ale Zion, also held in The Hague that year, Ben Zvi was selected the Po'ale Zion World Movement's representative in Palestine. In 1908 Rahel *Yanait arrived in Palestine and worked with him in the leadership of Po'ale Zion and in *HaShomer (Jewish watchmen's organization). Ben Zvi and Rahel Yanait also helped establish the Hebrew High School in Jerusalem in 1909 and were among its first teachers.

With the Young Turk Revolution of July, 1908, the Po'ale Zion movement took a new turn. In the fall of 1909, Ben Zvi went to Turkey to establish contact with the Turkish-Jewish workers and intelligentsia and with Bulgarian and Armenian leaders.

In 1910, with Rahel Yanait, David *Ben-Gurion, Z'ev Ashur, and others, Ben Zvi founded the first Palestinian Hebrew-language Socialist journal, *Ahdut* (Jerusalem, 1910–15). To be better equipped for the political work of Po'ale Zion, he and Ben-Gurion went to the University of Constantinople to study law. With the outbreak of World War I he returned to Jerusalem, where Ahmed *Jamal Pasha's anti-Zionist policy soon led to the imprisonment of both Ben Zvi and Ben-Gurion and, in the spring of 1915, to their exile. They went to Egypt, from where, with great difficulty, they managed to reach New York. In the United States they founded the Zionist pioneer youth organization *HeHalutz. With Pinhas *Rutenberg, Nachman *Syrkin,

Chaim *Zhitlowsky, and Ber Borochov, they founded the Jewish Congress movement and formulated its proposals to the Paris Peace Conference (*see* AMERICAN JEWISH CONGRESS). With the entry of British forces into Palestine, Ben Zvi and Ben-Gurion devoted their efforts to a recruiting campaign for the *Jewish Legion and were among the thousands of volunteers who reached Egypt in the summer of 1918 and the Palestine front in the fall. That same fall Ben-Zvi and Rahel Yanait were married.

In October, 1920, Sir Herbert *Samuel, the first British *High Commissioner for Palestine, appointed Ben Zvi to membership in the Government Advisory Council. After the *Arab riots of May, 1921, in Jaffa and the subsequent stoppage of Jewish *immigration, Ben Zvi resigned from the Council in protest. He was active in the ranks of the *Hagana and represented the Jewish Community in its negotiations with the mandatory government (*see* MANDATE FOR PALESTINE).

Itzhak Ben Zvi, second President of Israel. [Israel Information Services]

Ben Zvi played a central part in the development of the Jewish labor movement. With the foundation of the *Histadrut he was elected a member of its Secretariat.

In 1929 he edited the *Va'ad L'umi's *Memorandum on Jewish Rights at the Wailing Wall* (*see* WESTERN WALL). In 1931 he was elected chairman, and later president, of the Va'ad L'umi (National Council). In this capacity he represented the *Yishuv (Jewish population of Palestine) at the coronation of King George VI in 1937 and the London *St. James Conference in 1939 and testified before the *Anglo-American Committee of Inquiry in 1946. In the *War of Independence, Ben Zvi lost his 24-year-old son Eli, who fell defending the kibbutz Bet Keshet in Galilee.

After the death of Chaim *Weizmann on Dec. 8, 1952, Ben Zvi was elected President of Israel by the *Knesset. On Oct. 28, 1957, he was elected for a second term of five years, and in 1962 for a third term.

President and Mrs. Ben Zvi were hosts to Queen Mother Elizabeth of Belgium and to the Presidents of Dahomey, Upper Volta, the Malagasy Republic, Costa Rica, Gabon, Liberia, and the Ivory Coast. President Ben Zvi's own state visits took him to the Netherlands, Belgium, Burma, the Congo (Brazzaville), and Liberia. He paid an unofficial visit to the Congo (Léopoldville).

To the official and constitutional aspects of the Presidency, Ben Zvi added new perspectives and new roles in the nation's life. His personal modesty and his genuine concern for all the "tribes" and communities that constitute Israel brought the Presidency close to the people and made the President himself a popular and beloved figure. He kept in constant touch with the citizenry by frequent visits to various parts of the country and by making the President's House in Jerusalem the scene of important cultural and public activities (the President's Office had been moved from Tel Aviv to Jerusalem after Ben Zvi's first election).

Throughout his administration, Ben Zvi continued his literary and scholarly work, most of it being devoted to the various Jewish sects and communities and to the Land of Israel, its geography, ancient settlements, antiquities, and population. In 1948 Ben Zvi's special interest in Oriental Jewry led him, with the support of the *Jewish Agency, the Ministry of Education and Culture, and the Histadrut, to establish an institute devoted to the study of the Oriental communities and their history. In 1953 this institute was given the name Ben Zvi Institute, and it thereupon became affiliated with the *Hebrew University of Jerusalem.

Z. SHAZAR

BERDITCHEV, ABBA. *See* PARACHUTISTS, PALESTINIAN JEWISH.

BERDYCZEWSKY, MIKHA YOSEF. *See* BIN-GORION, MIKHA YOSEF.

BEREGI, ÁRMIN (Benjamin). Engineer and Zionist leader (b. Budapest, 1879; d. Tel Aviv, 1953). He received his engineering degree from the Budapest Technical University in 1901. A founder (1903) of Makkabea, the Hungarian Zionist students' organization, he served as president of the Hungarian Zionist Organization from 1911 to 1918. Beregi was instrumental in the establishment of two Jewish military defense units which played an important role in the preservation of law and order in Budapest between November, 1918, and March, 1919. A delegate to many Zionist Congresses (*see* CONGRESS, ZIONIST), Beregi visited Palestine in 1921. On his return he gave his impressions in lectures and articles in many Jewish periodicals, including *Zsidó Szemle* (Jewish Spectator) and *Mult és Jövő* (Past and Future). In 1933 he published a novel about life in Palestine. As director of the Palestine Office in Budapest (*see* PALESTINE OFFICES) from 1920 to 1925, he helped organize the first group of Hungarian-Jewish technicians and engineers to emigrate to Palestine, a group that played an important role in the economic development of the *Yishuv, the Jewish population of Palestine (*see* HUNGARIAN JEWS IN ISRAEL). In 1935 he settled in Palestine, where he continued his activities in support of Zionist causes until his death. The municipality of Tel Aviv named a street in Yad Eliyahu after him.

R. L. BRAHAM

BERENSTEIN, SAMUEL FRANZIE. Early Zionist leader in the Netherlands (b. The Hague, 1877; d. there, 1918). A member of a well-known Orthodox family in The Hague, Berenstein was active as a speaker and writer for the Zionist movement. Elected to the *Actions Committee at the 8th Zionist *Congress (The Hague, 1907), he was chairman of the Dutch Zionist Federation from 1908 to 1912.

BERGER, JULIUS. Early Zionist leader (b. Niederbreisig, Germany, 1884; d. Israel, 1948). Berger began his work in the Central Office of the *World Zionist Organization in Cologne, Germany, under the presidency of David *Wolffsohn, and was head of the office of the central Zionist weekly *Die *Welt* for many years. He became one of the first leaders of the *Keren HaYesod (Palestine Foundation Fund) in 1921. Settling in Palestine in 1923, Berger joined the *Jewish National Fund headquarters as an executive. He initiated many Zionist activities in fund raising and land purchasing.

BERGER, YEHUDA LEIB. Zionist propagandist (b. Minsk, Russia, 1867; d. Beirut, Lebanon, 1917). He studied at the Yeshiva of Volozhin, where he helped found the *Hoveve Zion group Nes Tziyona. Later he settled in Pinsk, where he established a modern Heder (Jewish elementary school) and became the leader of the local Hoveve Zion. Berger exerted a great influence on Jewish youth, including Chaim *Weizmann. He participated in the founding conference of the *Odessa Committee in 1890 and was a member of the secret order *B'ne Moshe. With the advent of Herzl he became a political Zionist, attending the 1st Zionist *Congress (1897) and subsequent Congresses as a leader of Russian Zionists. He traveled through Russia, Poland, and Lithuania disseminating Zionism and directing the work of the *Jewish National Fund. In 1912 he settled in Palestine.

BERGMANN, DAVID ERNST. Israeli scientist (b. Karlsruhe, Germany, 1903). Bergmann studied at the University of Berlin (Ph.D., 1924) and was a lecturer there from 1928 to 1933. In 1934, the year he settled in Palestine, he became scientific director of the Sieff Research Institute, and in 1949 of the *Weizmann Institute of Science, retaining this post until 1952.

During World War II Bergmann was engaged at various times in scientific work in France and England. He was also a member of *Hagana, serving on its Technical Committee. In 1948 he was appointed Director of the Scientific Research Department of the Israel Ministry of Defense and, in 1952, after the discovery of uranium in the Negev, Chairman of the Israel Atomic Energy Commission, holding both positions until 1966. From 1953 on he was professor of organic chemistry at the *Hebrew University of Jerusalem. He was visiting professor at the Haifa *Technion (1953–55), Yale University (1952), and Columbia University (1959). In 1953 he was named an honorary life member of the New York Academy of Sciences. In 1968 he was a member of Israel's *National Council for Research and Development and the *Israel Academy of Sciences and Humanities.

BERGMANN, SAMUEL HUGO. Professor of philosophy (b. Prague, 1883). He studied at the Universities of Prague and Berlin. Except for the years of World War I, when he was in the Austro-Hungarian Army, Bergmann was an assistant at the library of the University of Prague from 1907 to 1919. He subsequently served as secretary of the Cultural Department of the Zionist *Executive in London. Settling in Palestine in 1920, he became director of the *Jewish National and University Library and lecturer in philosophy at the *Hebrew University of Jerusalem. In 1935 he was appointed professor at the university, holding that post until his retirement in 1955. From 1935 to 1938 he was also rector of the university.

Samuel Hugo Bergmann. [Zionist Archives]

Bergmann began his Zionist activity in *Bar Kokhba, the Zionist students' organization in Prague. He was one of the builders of the Zionist labor movement in Western Europe and an organizer of the founding conference of *Hitahdut in Prague (1920). In Palestine he was first a member of the Socialist Zionist youth organization *HaPo'el HaTza'ir. He then joined the *B'rit Shalom (Covenant of Peace) and was editor of its organ *Sh'ifotenu* (Our Aims), while remaining active also in the labor organization *Histadrut.

In 1919 Bergmann represented Czechoslovak Jewry in the Jewish delegation to the Paris Peace Conference. In 1943 he headed the delegation of the Jewish Community of Palestine to the Pan-Asia Conference in New Delhi. Bergmann contributed to a variety of publications and was the author of numerous books on philosophical topics.

S. HUBNER

BERGSON, PETER (Hillel Cook or Kook). Organizer and leader of the Hebrew Committee of National Liberation (b. Lithuania, 1915). Bergson was taken by his parents to Palestine at the age of 10. A member of *Hagana, he joined the *Irgun Tz'vai L'umi at its foundation in 1937. Sent abroad that year, he was active on behalf of the Irgun in Warsaw and London. In 1940 he arrived in the United States, where he soon emerged as a powerful propagandist for Jewish national causes. He was a cofounder and leader of the Committee for a Jewish Army of stateless and Palestinian Jews, the Emergency Committee to Rescue the Jewish People of Europe, the American League for a Free Palestine, and the Hebrew Committee of National Liberation. The two last-named organizations publicized and gave propaganda support to the struggle of the Palestine underground movements, especially the Irgun, against the British.

After the establishment of the State, Bergson was a member of the First *Knesset (1949–51), representing *Herut.

BERGSON GROUP. Name commonly applied to a group of young men, Palestinian and non-Palestinian, who were active in the United States between 1939 and 1948 in connection with a variety of Zionist and Jewish causes. The name refers to the leader of the group, Peter *Bergson.

The group created a chain of fund-raising committees, each operating under a different name: American Friends of a Jewish Palestine, Committee for a Jewish Army, Emergency Committee to Rescue the Jewish People of Europe, Hebrew Committee of National Liberation, American League for a Free Palestine, Repatriation Supervisory Board, and Palestine Resistance Fund. The activities of these groups were in conflict with those of the official Zionist organizations.

American Friends of a Jewish Palestine (1939–41). The program of this body included support for *illegal immigration to Palestine and dissemination of propaganda for the idea of a Jewish army. Initially it was led mainly by members and supporters of the *New Zionist Organizations.

Committee for a Jewish Army (1941–43). According to one of its founders, Samuel Merlin, this group sought to avoid entanglement in political issues in order not to embarrass the British and American governments in their war effort. It advocated the formation of a Jewish army consisting only of Palestinian Jews and stateless Jews of the world to the exclusion of all other Jewish communities. Its president for a time was Pierre van Paassen, the Protestant pro-Zionist author and clergyman.

Emergency Committee to Rescue the Jewish People of Europe (1943–45). This group grew out of a conference (July 20–25, 1943) called in response to the first reports of mass extermination of Jews in Europe by the Nazis. Emphasizing the humanitarian rather than the political aspects of the Jewish problem, the Emergency Committee sponsored a resolution in the Congress of the United States, recommending that the President create a commission of experts to formulate a plan for the rescue of the surviving Jews of Europe. Such a commission actually materialized in January, 1944, as the War Refugee Board. In August, 1944, the Emergency Committee urged the War Refugee Board to adopt the "free port" plan providing for the setting up by all non-Axis countries of areas where refugees could be "held" until the end of the war and the opening of Palestine to Jewish *immigration. In June, 1944, the committee asked the British government to set up emergency shelters for Jewish refugees in Palestine.

Hebrew Committee of National Liberation and American League for a Free Palestine (1944–45). The call for the formation of the Hebrew Committee of National Liberation was issued in 1944 in Washington, D.C., by Peter Bergson, Arye *Ben Eliezer, Theodore Bennahum, Pinhas Delougar, Capt. Yirmiyahu *Halpern, Eri Jabotinsky, and Samuel Merlin. In a departure from the classic Zionist concept of a worldwide Jewish people, the committee constituted itself "trustees" of a "Hebrew nation," taken to include only the Jews of Palestine and the stateless Jews of Nazi-held Europe. The committee set up an "embassy" in Washington to seek Allied recognition for the Hebrew nation as a cobelligerent in the struggle against Nazism. It also sought representation on the UN War Crimes Commission and on the boards of other United Nations organizations such as the UN Relief and Rehabilitation Administration (UNRRA).

The American League for a Free Palestine, a nonsectarian group which had among its leaders the author Ben Hecht, was founded to support the Hebrew Committee of National Liberation.

Repatriation Supervisory Board (1947). This much-publicized body was created by the American League for a Free Palestine to raise funds for the league's illegal immigration projects.

Palestine Resistance Fund (1947). This was another project of the American League for a Free Palestine, created to raise funds for the support of the resistance activities of the *Irgun Tz'vai L'umi in Palestine.

The leadership of most of the above-named organizations consisted of practically the same persons. They all were agreed on the necessity for vigorous propaganda among Jews and non-Jews to attain their common goal: the rescue of the remnants of European Jewry and their free immigration to Palestine.

G. HIRSCHLER

B'ERI. Village (kibbutz) in the western Negev. Founded in 1946 and named for Berl *Katznelson. Affiliated with the *Kibbutz M'uhad. During the *War of Independence its property was destroyed by the Egyptians, and the settlers lived in bunkers for many months. The settlement was rebuilt at the end of the war.

BERKOWICZ, MICHAEL. Writer and teacher (b. Borislav, Galicia, Austria, 1865; d. Szezryk, Poland, 1935). After being educated in Lvov and Brody, he went in 1893 to Vienna, where he studied at the rabbinical seminary and the university. While still in Galicia, he began to contribute to Jewish periodicals and became active in pre-Herzlian Zionist circles. In 1890 he helped found the first Zionist society in Brody. In Vienna he was secretary of the Zion organization of settlement societies. With the advent of Herzl, Berkowicz became his follower. He translated Herzl's *Jewish State* into Hebrew soon after its appearance and served as Herzl's secretary for Hebrew and Yiddish from 1896 to 1898.

Later Berkowicz lived for some years in Cracow, Poland, where he was one of the editors of the Zionist Yiddish weekly *Der Yud.* On his return to Vienna, he helped edit the Yiddish edition of Die *Welt. In addition to widespread activity as a publicist, he engaged also in scholarly research, collaborating on the *Monumenta Judaica.* In 1910 the Vienna Academy published his *Der Strophenbau in den Psalmen.* The following year he became an instructor in religion at a secondary school in Bielsko, a position he held until his retirement.

During his long journalistic career Berkowicz contributed to numerous Jewish periodicals in Hebrew, Yiddish, and German and was active also as a translator. Between 1921 and 1924 he published a Hebrew translation of Herzl's Zionist writings. In the last years of his life he devoted himself to editing the writings of the Jewish Socialist Aaron Samuel Liebermann (1844–80) and documents relating to his activities.

BERLIGNE, ELIAHU. Israeli public official (b. Mogilev, Russia, 1866; d. Jerusalem, 1959). He studied law at Moscow University and became a prosperous businessman. Active in the *Hoveve Zion movement and in political Zionism, he attended several Zionist Congresses (*see* CONGRESS, ZIONIST). At the 5th Congress (1901) he associated himself with the *Democratic Faction. Settling in Palestine in 1907, he participated prominently in the economic and social life of the country. As a resident of Jaffa, he helped found the committee that built the suburb of Ahuzat Bayit, which was the beginning of Tel Aviv.

Under the British Mandatory regime (*see* MANDATE FOR PALESTINE) he helped found the *K'nesset Yisrael and was a member of the *Asefat HaNivharim (Elected Assembly) and of the *Va'ad L'umi (Jewish National Council), serving for many years as the treasurer of the latter.

Berligne was a signatory of Israel's *Declaration of Independence and a member of the Provisional Council of State and of the *Actions Committee of the *World Zionist Organization.

BERLIN, SIR ISAIAH. Political scientist in England (b. Riga, Latvia, 1909). During World War II he was attached to the British Information Service in New York and served as First Secretary of the British Embassy in Washington from 1942 to 1946. He was knighted in 1957.

Berlin had a distinguished academic career at Oxford University, serving from 1966 as president of Wolfson College. His second Herbert Samuel Lecture on Chaim *Weizmann and his Lucien Wolf Memorial Lecture, "The Life and Opinions of Moses Hess," both given in London in 1957, were published in booklet form (*see* HESS, MOSES; SAMUEL, SIR HERBERT LOUIS). Sir Isaiah was the author of a number of books, including *Karl Marx: His Life and Environment* (1939).

J. FRAENKEL

BERLIN, MEIR. *See* BAR-ILAN, MEIR.

BERLIN, NAPHTALI TZ'VI Y'HUDA (known as "the Natziv," from his initials). Rabbi and author (b. Mir, Russia, 1816; d. Warsaw, 1893). His first publication, which made him famous, was a commentary on the 8th-century rabbinic work *Sh'eltot* of Rav Ahai. This was followed by *Ha'ameq Davar,* a commentary on the Pentateuch. Other works included *responsa* and *novellae* on the Talmud. He served for almost 40 years as head of the Volozhin Yeshiva, the foremost institution of its kind in Russia, and was thus the mentor of most of the spiritual leaders of Russian Jewry.

An early adherent of the *Hoveve Zion movement, Berlin saw in the upbuilding of the Land of Israel a beginning of the final redemption and did not shrink from collaboration with nonobservant Jewish elements. "Did not Jews of all kinds participate in the Return to Zion at the time of Ezra?" he would demand. At the *Druskenik Conference of the Hoveve Zion (1887) he was elected, and at the Vilna Conference (1889) reelected, one of the three rabbinical advisers to the leadership of the movement. The important role he played in the Hoveve Zion contributed much to the spread of the movement among the religious masses. It also could not fail to influence his numerous disciples. Many of his former students, among them Hayim Nahman *Bialik and Alter *Druyanow, became standard bearers of the Jewish national renaissance, while his youngest son, Meir *Bar-Ilan (Berlin), was to become a world leader of *Mizrahi.

After the closing of the Yeshiva of Volozhin by the Russian authorities in 1892, Berlin went to Warsaw. He hoped to settle in Palestine but died before he could do so.

J. LIEBERMAN

BERMAN, JACOB. Rabbi and educator (b. Salantai, Lithuania, 1878). Educated at the Telšiai Yeshiva, he was active in religious Zionist groups and in 1903 participated in the conference of the *Mizrahi Organization in Lida. He studied law at the University of St. Petersburg (1906), then served as lecturer at the Odessa School of Jewish Studies (1908). From 1910 to 1921 he was rabbi in Berdichev, where he was active also in the rescue of thousands of refugees who fled from Galicia and Lithuania during and after World War I. In 1919 he was arrested by the Yevsektzia, the office of the Communist party dealing with Jewish affairs, but was soon released. Two years later he settled in Palestine, where he served as headmaster and chief inspector at the Mizrahi schools and vice-chairman (1925–44) of the Education Department of the *Va'ad L'umi (National Council).

From 1944 to 1948 he was head of the Mizrahi Organization in Palestine. He also served for many years as a member of the Zionist *Actions Committee.

BERMUDA CONFERENCE. Anglo-American conference held in Bermuda on Apr. 19–30, 1943, to study what was officially described as "the refugee problem in all its aspects, including the position of potential refugees who are still in the grip of Axis powers without any immediate prospect of escape." Though its terms of reference made no specific statement to that effect, the conference was called primarily to study the situation of the Jews in Europe. The proceedings were kept secret. No representatives of Jewish groups were permitted to attend, but Jewish organizations submitted memorandums in which they pleaded for negotiations with the German government for the release of the Jews, for the establishment of places of refuge in Allied and neutral countries, and for the opening of the gates of Palestine. As is already clear from the statement issued at its conclusion, the conference did not produce practical results.

From documents published in Arthur D. Morse's book *While Six Million Died* (1968), it became clear that the instructions given to the American delegation by the U.S. Department of State were calculated to make the conference totally ineffective in advance. Myron C. Taylor, the vice-chairman of the Intergovernmental Committee on Refugees, declared following the conference that, in his view, "the Bermuda Conference was wholly ineffective, and we knew it would be." In 1965 Lord Coleraine (Richard Kidston Law), who had headed the British delegation at the conference, stated: "It was . . . a façade for inaction."

BERNADOTTE, COUNT FOLKE. Swedish diplomat (b. Stockholm, 1895; d. Jerusalem, 1948). A nephew of King Gustav V of Sweden, he held a variety of official positions. During World War II he served as vice-chairman (1943) of the Swedish Red Cross, arranging for the exchange of disabled British and German prisoners of war. Early in 1945 he was sent by the Swedish government to Germany for the rescue of concentration camp prisoners whom SS chief Heinrich Himmler had agreed to free, and he subsequently organized the transfer to Sweden of more than 20,000 displaced persons of various nationalities, including many thousands of Jews. Soon after the war Bernadotte continued the transfer of concentration camp survivors to Sweden.

After the outbreak of the *War of Independence in May, 1948, Bernadotte was appointed UN Mediator for Palestine. Following a resolution by the UN Security Council, a 30-day truce went into effect on June 11, 1948. During that period Bernadotte submitted to the Jews and the Arabs a peace proposal that envisaged Palestine, including Transjordan, as a political and economic union of two states, one Jewish and one Arab. The proposal suggested the following changes in the territorial arrangements of the United Nations *partition plan: the city of Jerusalem and all or part of the Negev were to be Arab territory, while all or part of western Galilee was to be Jewish; Haifa was to have a free port (the free area was to include the oil refineries and terminals) and Lod (Lydda) a free airport; and the status of Jaffa was to be determined at a later date. The proposals were rejected by both Israel and the Arabs.

On July 9, 1948, the fighting was resumed. The Security Council ordered a cease-fire, and Bernadotte fixed July 18 as the cease-fire date. In September, he sent a report to the United Nations, urging it to take decisive action to establish peace. In his recommendations he said that the State of Israel was a fact and that the Arabs should resign themselves to its existence. On the other hand, the Jews, in the interest of promoting friendly relations with their Arab neighbors, would do well to define their *immigration policy and to consider measures and policies to allay the fears of the Arabs. The right of *Arab refugees to return to their homes, if they so desired, was to be safeguarded. In his report to the United Nations, Bernadotte discarded the idea of political and economic union and modified some of his earlier territorial suggestions. Jerusalem was to be put under United Nations control; the Negev was to be Arab territory and western Galilee Jewish; and Ramle and Lod, which had been captured by the Israelis in the fighting between the two truces, were to be Arab.

On Sept. 17, 1948, while on an inspection tour, Bernadotte was assassinated in the Jewish part of Jerusalem, along with a member of his staff, Col. André P. Gerot of France. A group calling itself Hazit HaMoledet claimed responsibility for the assassination. The assailants were never caught but were believed to be members of the Stern group (see LOHAME HERUT ISRAEL). The *government of Israel arrested hundreds of members of the group and tried and sentenced two of its leaders for illegal activities.

Bernadotte's report reached the UN General Assembly session in Paris shortly after his death. Its recommendations were supported by the United States and Great Britain but were rejected by the Arabs. Israel stated it was willing to explore all proposals which would be "put forward as a basis for a final lasting peace," but it rejected the suggestion that the Negev be excluded from its territory. Arab and Soviet opposition to the immediate discussion of the Bernadotte Plan by the UN Assembly prevailed, and subsequently, in the wake of political developments, the matter was dropped altogether.

T. PRESCHEL

BERNFELD, SIMON. Historian and Hebrew essayist (b. Stanislav, Galicia, Austria, 1860; d. Berlin, 1940). He studied at the university and at the Hochschule für die Wissenschaft des Judentums in Berlin. From 1886 to 1894 he served as chief rabbi of the Sephardi Jewish community of Belgrade.

Bernfeld, a many-sided and prolific Hebrew writer, embarked early on a literary career. He contributed articles, essays, and studies to all the important Hebrew periodicals of his time, writing also in Yiddish and German. His many books included *Sefer HaD'ma'ot* (Book of Tears, 3 vols., 1924–26), an anthology of Jewish martyrology; *Da'at Elohim* (Knowledge of God, 2 vols., 1897–99), a history of Jewish philosophy; books on the age of Moses Mendelssohn and on the birth of modern Jewish scholarship; a history of the movement for

religious reform in Judaism; and monographs on Jewish scholars and writers through the ages. He also wrote a voluminous book on the Bible.

Bernfeld was among the early workers of the *Hoveve Zion but did not participate in the political Zionist movement. His many studies, written in a style of great clarity, were widely read and contributed much to the strengthening of the attachment to Jewish national ideals, to the Hebrew language, and to the ancestral Homeland.

T. PRESCHEL

BERNSTEIN, PERETZ. Zionist leader (b. Meiningen, Germany, 1890). He acquired a classical education and a broad knowledge of literature and modern languages. From 1915 to 1935 he engaged in business in Rotterdam. From 1924 to 1930 he was a member of the Executive of the Dutch Zionist Federation and from 1930 to 1934 served as its president. He was also editor of the Dutch Zionist weekly.

Peretz Bernstein.
[Zionist Archives]

Settling in Palestine in 1936, Bernstein was active in the General Zionist party, of which he eventually became president (see GENERAL ZIONISM). From 1937 to 1946 he was editor of *HaBoker,* and from 1946 to 1948 a member of the Executive of the *Jewish Agency, heading its Department of Trade and Industry in Jerusalem. After the establishment of the State, he became a member of the Provisional Council of State and served as Minister of Commerce and Industry from 1948 to 1949 and again from 1953 to 1955.

Bernstein was a member of the *Knesset from its inception (1949) until 1965, representing the General Zionist party (which in 1961 constituted itself as the *Liberal party). A regular contributor to newspapers and other periodicals, he was also the author of several books, including one on *anti-Semitism (*Der Antisemitismus als Gruppenerscheinung,* 1925; published in English, 1951).

BERNSTEIN, SIMON GERSON. Hebrew and Yiddish writer and scholar (b. Jēkabpils, Latvia, 1884; d. New York, 1962). He studied at the Universities of Berlin, Strasbourg, and Bern. Active in the Zionist movement and in the Hebrew press from his youth, Bernstein became in 1912 secretary of the World Zionist *Executive, which then had its headquarters in Berlin. During World War I he worked in the *Copenhagen Bureau of the Zionist Organization and subsequently joined the staff of the Central Zionist Office in London. In 1922 he became editor of

Dos Yidishe Folk, the Yiddish weekly of the *Zionist Organization of America, and served in that capacity until 1953. From 1922 to 1949 he was also director of the Palestine Office in New York (*see* PALESTINE OFFICES), which handled primarily matters relating to *immigration to Palestine.

A student of Jewish history and literature, Bernstein wrote historical essays and edited poetry of medieval and later Hebrew poets.

BERNSTEIN-COHEN, JACOB. *See* KOHAN-BERNSTEIN, JACOB.

B'EROTAYIM. Village (moshav) in the Sharon Plain. Founded in 1949 by immigrants from Czechoslovakia and affiliated with *T'nu'at HaMoshavim. Population (1968): 282.

B'EROT YITZHAK. Village (kibbutz) north of Lod. Named for Yitzhak *Nissenbaum and affiliated with HaPo'el HaMizrahi (*see* MIZRAHI). Population (1968): 295.

Founded initially (1943) in the Negev, the village was heavily attacked by Egyptian invaders during the *War of Independence. The Egyptians succeeded in occupying the peripheral buildings but not the kibbutz as a whole. After the war, the settlers abandoned the destroyed settlement and relocated at the present site.

B'ER SHEVA' (Beersheba). Principal city of the Negev. Its name is of Biblical derivation, meaning either "Well of Seven" or "Well of Oath." Population (1968): 69,500.

The earliest settlement in the area dates to the Chalcolithic age. First the inhabitants lived in caves, but toward the end of the period they built houses. Silos found in excavations testify to their practice of agriculture, while bones show that they engaged in animal husbandry. Finds include numerous pottery and finely polished stone vessels as well as highly artistic small ivory statuettes of men, women, and animals. The Negev Museum in B'er Sheva' contains exhibits from regional excavations.

Ancient B'er Sheva', near which the modern city was built, played an important role in the history of the Biblical patriarchs. Abraham, Isaac, and Jacob encamped there. After the conquest of Canaan by the Twelve Tribes, B'er Sheva' was the southernmost settlement in the land; hence the Biblical expression "from Dan to B'er Sheva' to denote the extent of the settled area from the north to the south of Palestine. An important center during the times of the Second Commonwealth and Roman rule, ancient B'er Sheva' was destroyed and abandoned in the Middle Ages, and thereafter, for centuries, served merely as a camping area for the nomadic tribes of the Negev.

Modern B'er Sheva' had its beginnings toward the end of the 19th century, when it was established by the Turks as an administrative center for the Bedouin tribes of the Negev. The new town developed around the government buildings and the police station. By the 1940s its population was about 4,000. At the beginning of the *War of Independence, the then all-Arab town was occupied by the invading Egyptian Army. The *Israel Defense Forces took B'er Sheva' in the autumn of 1948 during their great offensive in the Negev. In April, 1949, the city, which had been evacuated prior to the entry of the Israeli forces, was opened to Jewish settlers. Since then, B'er Sheva' has grown rapidly.

B'er Sheva'. [Israel Information Services]

Mosaic floor of the 6th-century synagogue at Bet Alfa. [Israel Government Tourist Office]

BERTINI, GARY. Israeli conductor and composer (b. Bessarabia, Romania, 1927). He studied in Tel Aviv and Paris. A founder and conductor of the Rinat Choir, with which he toured Europe and the United States, he was a guest conductor of the *Israel Philharmonic and Kol Yisrael symphony orchestras. He composed film and stage music, songs, chamber music, and concertos for the French horn.

P. GRADENWITZ

B'ER TOVYA. Village (moshav) in the Darom. Founded in 1930 and affiliated with *T'nu'at HaMoshavim. Population (1968): 645.

As early as 1887 a Jewish settlement was established on the site. However, many of the settlers left because of a shortage of water and isolation from other Jewish settlements. In 1896 the *Hoveve Zion renewed the settlement, which was destroyed in 1929 during the *Arab riots. The present moshav was established near the ruins of old B'er Tovya.

B'ER YA'AKOV. Township in Judea. Founded in 1907 by religious Jews from Dagestan in the Caucasus, with the help of *Hoveve Zion. The settlers were led by Rabbi Ya'akov Yitzhaki, for whom the settlement was named. Population (1968): 3,950.

BET. Hebrew word, meaning "house of" (the *status constructus* of *bayit*, "house"), that forms the first part of many place names in Israel, as in Bet Ha'Emek (House of the Valley).

BET ALFA. Village (kibbutz) in the eastern Jezreel Valley. Established in 1922 as the first communal settlement of *HaShomer HaTza'ir and affiliated with the *Kibbutz Artzi Shel HaShomer HaTza'ir. Population (1968): 670.

An early 6th-century synagogue was excavated at Bet Alfa, indicating a vital Jewish settlement on the site. The surviving mosaic pavement depicts a Biblical scene of the Sacrifice of Abraham and several symbolic motifs, including the signs of the zodiac and the seven-branched *Menora.

BETAR (Revisionist Zionist youth organization). *See* B'RIT TRUMPELDOR.

BET 'ARIF. Village (moshav) in the Judean Plain. Founded in 1951 and affiliated with *T'nu'at HaMoshavim. Population (1968): 535.

BET-ARYE, DAVID. HaPo'el HaMizrahi leader (b. Kaunas, Lithuania, 1903). He studied agronomy at Bonn University and in 1929 settled in Palestine, where he helped found the Yavne kibbutz. Bet-Arye was a cofounder of *B'rit Halutzim Datiyim (Bachad) in Germany (1928) and was prominently associated with various institutions of the HaPo'el HaMizrahi (*see* MIZRAHI). In 1946 he became a member of the Zionist *Actions Committee, and in 1951 a member of the Executive of the *Jewish Agency. After serving for several years in New York as a member of the American section of the Executive, he was in 1956 made head of the Agency's Jerusalem Department of Religious Education and Culture in the Diaspora.

BET BERL. Educational institution of the *Israel Labor party, located near K'far Saba. Founded in 1949 and named for Berl *Katznelson. Population (1968): 377.

BET DAGAN. Township southeast of Tel Aviv. Founded in 1948. Population (1968): 2,680.

BET EL'AZARI. Village (moshav) in the Judean Plain. Founded in 1948 and named for Yitzhak *Elazari-Volcani. Affiliated with T'nu'at HaMoshavim. Population (1968): 500.

BET ESHEL. Settlement in the Negev, east-southeast of B'er Sheva'. Founded in 1943, it was heavily attacked by the Egyptians during the *War of Independence. The settlers heroically resisted the attacks, but the settlement was completely destroyed in the fighting. In 1949 its members founded a new settlement, HaYogev, in the Jezreel Valley.

BET 'EZRA. Village (moshav) in the Darom. Founded in 1950 and named for Ezra, the Biblical scribe. Affiliated with *T'nu'at HaMoshavim. Population (1968): 545.

BET GAMLIEL. Village (moshav) in the Judean Plain. Founded in 1949 and affiliated with HaPo'el HaMizrahi (*see* MIZRAHI). The village was named for Rabban Gamliel, head of the Sanhedrin (ancient Jewish High Court), which had its seat in nearby Yavne after C.E. 70. Population (1968): 425.

BET GAN. *See* YAVN'EL.

BET GUVRIN. Village (kibbutz) in the Darom. Founded in 1949 and affiliated with the *Kibbutz M'uhad. It is named for the ancient city of Bet Guvrin.

Following the destruction of the Israelite city of Maresa in 40 B.C.E., a new town called Bet Guvrin rose on an adjacent site and took its place. This new town later was called Eleutheropolis; excavations yielded a series of fine Byzantine mosaics.

BET HA'EMEK. Village (kibbutz) in western Galilee. Founded in 1941 and affiliated with the *Ihud HaK'vutzot V'haKibbutzim. Population (1968): 300.

BET HAGADI. Village (moshav) in the northern Negev. Founded in 1949 and affiliated with HaPo'el HaMizrahi (*see* MIZRAHI). Population (1968): 632.

BET HAKEREM. Residential suburb within the municipal area of Jerusalem.

BET HALEVI. Village (moshav) in the Sharon Plain. Settled in 1945 by *Sephardim from the Balkan countries and named for Yehuda Halevi, the medieval Hebrew poet. Affiliated with *T'nu'at HaMoshavim. Population (1968): 219.

BET HANA'ARA. *See* 'EN VERED.

BET HANAN. Village (moshav) in the Judean Plain. Founded in 1930 and affiliated with *T'nu'at HaMoshavim. Population (1968): 383.

BET HANANYA. Village (moshav) north of Hadera. Founded in 1950 on *Palestine Jewish Colonization Association (PICA) land and named for Hananya Gottlieb, the PICA director in Israel. Affiliated with *T'nu'at HaMoshavim. Population (1968): 284.

BET HASHITTA. Village (kibbutz) in the eastern Jezreel Valley. Founded in 1935 and affiliated with the *Kibbutz M'uhad. Population (1968): 885.

BET HERUT. Village (moshav) in the Sharon Plain. Founded in 1933 and affiliated with *T'nu'at HaMoshavim. Population (1968): 280.

BET HILKIYA. Village (moshav) in the Judean Plain. Founded in 1953 and affiliated with *Po'ale Agudat Israel. Population (1968): 280.

BET HILLEL. Village (moshav) in eastern Upper Galilee. Settled in 1940 and named for Hillel *Joffe. Affiliated with *T'nu'at HaMoshavim. Population (1968): 173.

BETHLEHEM (Bet Lehem). City on the West Bank of the Jordan, south of Jerusalem. Population (1968): 22,000, the majority of whom were Christian Arabs.

An ancient town, Bethlehem is often mentioned in the Bible. Rachel died on the way to Bethlehem (Genesis 35:19; *see* RACHEL, TOMB OF). After the Israelites' conquest of Canaan, the town was allotted to the tribe of Judah. It was there that the prophet Samuel anointed David king. A Jewish settlement existed there also in the time of the Second Commonwealth and thereafter until the Hadrianic persecutions of the 2d century of the Common Era.

Bethlehem was the reputed birthplace of Jesus, and Constantine, the first Christian Emperor (4th cent.), built the Church of the Nativity there. For centuries the town has been a Christian center and a major Christian pilgrimage site and has, in recent decades, attracted many tourists. Annexed by the kingdom of Jordan in 1948, Bethlehem was occupied by Israel during the *Six-day War of 1967.

BET JAN. Druze village in western Upper Galilee. Population (1968): 4,110.

BET JIMAL. Christian monastery and agricultural school for Arab children in the Judean Plain. Population (1968): 47.

BET KAMA. Village (kibbutz) in the northern Negev. Founded in 1949 and affiliated with the *Kibbutz Artzi Shel HaShomer HaTza'ir. Population (1968): 245.

BET KESHET. Village (kibbutz) in eastern Lower Galilee. Founded in 1944 and affiliated with the *Kibbutz M'uhad. Population (1968): 338.

BET LEHEM. *See* BETHLEHEM.

BET LEHEM HAG'LILIT. Village (moshav) on the border of Lower Galilee and the Jezreel Valley. Founded in 1948 and affiliated with *T'nu'at HaMoshavim. Population (1968): 270.

BET LID. *See* SH'VUT 'AM.

Bethlehem. [Israel Information Services]

BET MEIR. Village (moshav) in the Jerusalem Mountains. Founded in 1950 and named for Meir *Bar-Ilan (Berlin). Affiliated with HaPo'el HaMizrahi (*see* MIZRAHI). Population (1968): 270.

BET N'HEMYA. Village (moshav) near Lod. Founded in 1950 by immigrants from Iran and named for Nehemiah, the Biblical Jewish leader. Affiliated with Ha'Oved HaTziyoni. Population (1968): 205.

BET NIR. Village (kibbutz) in the Darom. Founded in 1955 and affiliated with the *Kibbutz Artzi Shel HaShomer HaTza'ir. Population (1968): 121.

BET N'KOFA. Village (moshav) in the Jerusalem Mountains. Founded in 1949 and affiliated with *T'nu'at HaMoshavim. Population (1968): 202.

BET OREN. Village (kibbutz) on Mount Carmel. Founded in 1939 and affiliated with the *Kibbutz M'uhad. Population (1968): 225.

BET 'OVED. Village (moshav) in the Darom. Founded in 1933 and affiliated with *T'nu'at HaMoshavim. Population (1968): 202.

BET RABBAN. Teachers seminary of the religious State schools, in the Rehovot area. Founded in 1946. Population (1968): 355.

BET SH'AN. Israeli town in the Bet Sh'an Valley south of Lake Kinneret. Formerly an Arab townlet, it was abandoned by its inhabitants and captured by Jewish forces in May, 1948. It was resettled by Jews in 1949. Population (1968): 12,500.

Archeological finds at Bet Sh'an include four Canaanite temples of the late Bronze Age showing the influence of Egyptian style and decoration (the city was occupied by Egyptian troops for three centuries, beginning under Thutmosis III, ca. 1469–1436 B.C.E.). In addition, a fortress, a governor's residence, and a monumental silo were found. In Hellenistic times, when the city was called Scythopolis, it spread into the plain surrounding the tell (mound). The finds from this period include a Hellenistic-Roman temple, a bust of Alexander, decorated sarcophagi, and a large Roman theater. From the Byzantine period date a round Byzantine church and a 6th-century monastery containing mosaics. Many of the finds are deposited in the local archeological museum.

Captured by the Israelites in the days of King David, Bet Sh'an was an important town in antiquity. In Hellenistic times it was settled by Greeks. John Hyrcanus (2d cent. B.C.E.) conquered it, and it remained in Jewish hands for several decades until it was taken by the Romans. During the great rebellion against Rome (C.E. 66–70), a large number of Jews were massacred in the city. Later a Jewish community was reestablished there. Bet Sh'an was of importance and Jews resided there during the Middle Ages. Estori Farhi (fl. 14th cent.), the earliest Jewish topographer of Palestine, lived in Bet Sh'an. Excavations begun in 1927 unearthed remnants of the ancient settlement, including a Roman hippodrome.

BET SH'AN (BEISAN) VALLEY. Eastern section of the great transverse valley of Israel which connects Haifa Bay with the Jordan Valley and separates Galilee from Samaria. The Bet Sh'an Valley is the lowest part of this trough, sloping from 330 feet below sea level in the west, where it adjoins the Harod Valley,

to 985 feet below sea level in the east, where it is bounded by the Jordan River. It extends 10 miles from north to south and from east to west. The climate, ranging from semiarid in the northwest to arid in the southeast, is very hot in summer because of the low elevation, but in winter frost occasionally occurs at night. Therefore subtropical fruit, such as bananas and citrus, can be grown only in specially sheltered areas. Much of the soil is poor, being too rich in lime and often saline.

The great asset of the valley is an abundance of springs and rivers. From the foot of Mount Gilboa, which bounds the valley to the south and southwest, rise numerous rich springs that form short rivers crossing the valley to join the Jordan. Many of these springs are saline, and during the last few centuries all of them formed swamps, which turned the valley into a malarial area that was visited only by Bedouins. Jewish settlement started in 1936, but full drainage and utilization were not accomplished until the creation of the State of Israel. The outstanding feature of the valley now is its elaborate system of irrigation which carries water in concrete channels, separated according to salinity, and mixes these waters in central places to meet the needs of different crops. The principal crops are dates, other fruits, and cotton. The cotton is processed in Bet Sh'an, the

Roman theater at Bet Sh'an. [Israel Information Services]

Entrance to the catacombs at Bet Sh'arim. [El Al Israel Airlines]

central town of the valley. The most saline waters are used for fishponds.

Y. KARMON

BET SH'ARIM. Village (moshav) in the Jezreel Valley. Founded in 1936 and affiliated with *T'nu'at HaMoshavim. Population (1968): 317.

The village was named for the neighboring ancient town of Bet Sh'arim, where Rabbi Judah HaNasi (2d cent.), compiler of the Mishna, resided for some time. One of the most important archeological sites in Israel is the series of 26 catacombs in which HaNasi and, following him, many Jews from places as far as Palmyra were buried up to the middle of the 4th century. About four-fifths of the inscriptions are in Greek; many of the sarcophagi are decorated with reliefs. Near the catacombs is a site at which excavations brought to light a synagogue and a basilica.

BET SHEMESH. Town in the Judean Mountains. Founded in 1950 and named for the Biblical Bet Shemesh, which was situated in the area. Population (1968): 9,850.

Excavations at the site of ancient Bet Shemesh unearthed fortifications from the early Bronze Age, which were destroyed in the middle Bronze Age. In the Hyksos period the city was refortified, and a necropolis was laid out. During the Egyptian New Kingdom the city reached its zenith under the 19th dynasty. Israelites and Philistines contested for the city's domination into the first Iron period. In Byzantine times a large monastery was established on the ruins of the city.

BET SHIKMA. Village (moshav) in the Darom. Founded in 1950 and affiliated with *T'nu'at HaMoshavim. Population (1968): 510.

BETTELHEIM, SAMU. Journalist (b. Bratislava, Slovakia, Hungary, 1872; d. Budapest, 1942). Bettelheim studied at the Bratislava (Pressburg) Yeshiva. He organized the first Hungarian Zionist group in 1897 and convened the 1st Hungarian Zionist Conference, which was held in Bratislava. After the establishment of the Hungarian Zionist Organization, he served as its president for three years (1904–07). He was also one of the organizers of the First World Conference of the *Mizrahi (Bratislava, 1904). In 1908 Bettelheim founded the Zionist *Pressburger Jüdische Zeitung* (later transferred to Budapest and named the *Ungarländische Jüdische Zeitung*), which he edited until 1915.

During World War I Bettelheim was sent to the United States by the Austro-Hungarian government to enlist support for the Central Powers. After the war he was editor in Bratislava of *Die Jüdische Presse,* which served the *Agudat Israel. From 1934 to 1937 he edited *Judaica*, a literary and scholarly periodical.

R. L. BRAHAM

Bet Yosef. [Zionist Archives]

BET TZ'VI (also called K'far Sitrin). Combined Yeshiva and vocational training school on the seashore south of Haifa. Founded in 1953 by *Mizrahi. Population (1968): 300.

BET 'UZIEL. Village (moshav) in the Judean Plain. Founded in 1956 and named for Chief Rabbi Ben-Zion Meir Hay *'Uziel. Affiliated with HaPo'el HaMizrahi (*see* MIZRAHI). Population (1968): 405.

BET YANNAI. Village (moshav) in the Sharon Plain. Founded in 1933 and named for the Hasmonean king Alexander Janneus. Population (1968): 229.

BET YERAH (Khirbet Kerak). Notable archeological site near Lake Kinneret. The early Bronze Age buildings, which include a large stone communal granary with places for nine silos, were surrounded by a thick mud-brick wall. From later periods date Hellenistic-Roman houses, a rectangular Roman fortress into which a basilical synagogue was subsequently built, a church (529), and baths that remained in use up to the Arab period.

BET Y'HOSHU'A. Village (moshav) in the Sharon Plain. Founded in 1938 and named for Osias (Y'hoshu'a) *Thon. Affiliated with Ha'Oved HaTziyoni. Population (1968): 260.

BET YITZHAK. Village (moshav) in the Sharon Plain. Founded in 1940, it was named for Isaak *Feuerring, the veteran German Zionist with whose legacy the land for the settlement was purchased. Population (1968): 825.

BET YOSEF. Village (moshav) in the Jordan Valley. Founded in 1937 and named for Joseph *Aronowicz. Affiliated with *T'nu'at HaMoshavim.

BET ZAYIT. Village (moshav) in the Jerusalem Mountains. Founded in 1949 and affiliated with *T'nu'at HaMoshavim. Population (1968): 436.

BET ZERA' (K'far Natan). Village (kibbutz) in the Jordan Valley. Established in 1927 by *HaShomer HaTza'ir. Population (1968): 660.

BETZET. Village (moshav) in western Upper Galilee. Founded in 1949 and affiliated with *T'nu'at HaMoshavim. Population (1968): 244.

BEVIN, ERNEST. British trade union leader and Foreign Secretary (b. Winsford, Somerset, England, 1881; d. London, 1951). Bevin served as Minister of Labor and National Service in Winston *Churchill's wartime Cabinet (1940–45). He subsequently became Foreign Secretary in Clement Attlee's Labor Government, serving in that capacity until shortly before his death.

Bevin was largely responsible for Britain's anti-Zionist policy during the period immediately preceding the establishment of the State of Israel. Soon after the election of the Labor Government (in the summer of 1945), it became apparent that the Government would not honor the party's preelection pledges to facilitate Zionist aspirations. On Nov. 13, 1945, in cooperation with U.S. Pres. Harry S *Truman, Bevin announced the appointment of an *Anglo-American Committee of Inquiry to investigate the Palestine issue and the plight of the remnants of European Jewry and to recommend solutions. In the interim, the *White Paper of 1939 was to remain in force. Bevin's announcement left no doubt that he felt in no way bound by the promises made by his party. He spoke of the resettlement of the Jews in Europe and asserted that Palestine could make only a small contribution to the Jewish refugee problem. By making the United States a partner in the Committee of Inquiry, Bevin sought to alleviate United States pressure on his Government to admit to Palestine immediately a large number of European survivors and to get the United States to acquiesce in his policy. When the Committee proposed the immediate admission of 100,000 Jewish survivors (against the expectation of Bevin, who had promised to carry out its recommendations if they were adopted unanimously), the Government refused to adopt the proposal.

In the meantime, Jewish resistance in Palestine mounted. Measures taken at Bevin's instance to suppress the underground groups and to prevent the landing of "illegal" immigrants in Palestine (*see* ILLEGAL IMMIGRATION) met with little success. In June, 1946, the government of Palestine arrested members of the *Jewish Agency and thousands of persons suspected of being members of the *Hagana. Several weeks later, the British government began to intern "illegal" immigrants in Cyprus (*see* CYPRUS, DETENTION CAMPS IN), and a year later the ship *"Exodus 1947" was turned back to Germany and the immigrants forced to land there. In January–February, 1947, Bevin held talks with Jewish Agency leaders, which, however, were fruitless.

On Feb. 15, 1947, after the *Morrison-Grady Plan had been rejected by both the Arabs and the Jews, Bevin told the British Parliament that he would submit the Palestine problem to the United Nations (*see* UNITED NATIONS AND PALESTINE-ISRAEL). When the *partition proposal was debated at the United Nations, British statements implied a rejection of the proposal. At the vote (Nov. 29, 1947), Britain abstained, and subsequently the British government and the Palestine administration not only refused to help in the implementation of the United Nations plan, particularly in the formation of a Jewish State, but actually attempted to sabotage the plan. Even after the establishment of the State, Bevin continued to pursue an anti-Zionist policy, and it was not until Jan. 29, 1949, that the British government extended de facto recognition to the Jewish State. In his last two years in office Bevin adopted a more sympathetic attitude to the State of Israel.

BEZALEL NATIONAL ART MUSEUM. *See* MUSEUMS IN ISRAEL.

BEZALEL SCHOOL. School of arts and crafts in Jerusalem, named for Bezalel (Exodus 35:30), the builder of the Biblical Sanctuary. The original school was founded in 1906 by Boris *Schatz, who conceived it as an institution not only for the spreading of arts and handicrafts among the Jews of Palestine

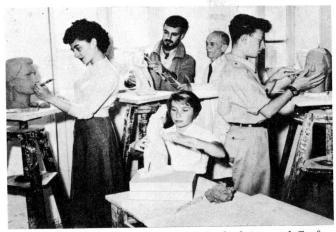

Sculpture class at the New Bezalel School of Arts and Crafts.
[Zionist Archives]

but also for the development of a new national Jewish style of art which would emphasize the historical characteristics of Jewish craftsmanship and at the same time express the spirit of the Jewish national renaissance. The school was supported by the Bezalel Association, which had its headquarters in Berlin and was directed by Otto *Warburg. It developed rapidly, and 457 persons were working at the school and in its studios by 1911. Also in 1911, a Bezalel colony of Yemenite engravers was established in Ben Shemen (*see* YEMENITE JEWS IN ISRAEL). The school's activities included carpet weaving, tapestry, filigree work, wood turning, ivory carving, and embroidery. Bezalel work, notably religious objects and souvenirs, was much in demand among Jews all over the world.

During World War I the Bezalel School closed, but after the war Schatz was able to reopen the institution with the financial help of the *World Zionist Organization. However, it did not regain its former size and importance and was closed again in 1929. Throughout the school's existence, Schatz was its sole director, with the exception of a period prior to World War I when he shared this responsibility with Richard Goldberg.

In 1935 Bezalel was reorganized under the name New Bezalel School of Arts and Crafts by Joseph *Budko, who directed it until his death in 1940. His successors were Mordecai *Ardon (Bronstein), Jacob *Steinhardt, and J. Schechter. The school became Israel's leading art academy, in which drawing, painting, sculpture, applied graphics, metalwork, hand weaving, art theory, and history were taught.

T. PRESCHEL

BIALIK, HAYIM NAHMAN. Most influential Hebrew poet of modern times (b. Radi, Volyn District, Russia, 1873; d. Vienna, 1934). Son of a pious learned family, Bialik received a traditional education in his native Ukraine but in secret read modern Hebrew literature. Subsequently, he studied in the Yeshiva of Volozhin, where he helped found a *Hoveve Zion group, Netzah Yisrael. In 1891 he went to Odessa, then a center of Hebrew literary activity. At first he remained there for only a short period, but he returned in 1900 after having lived in the Ukraine and having served for three years as a teacher in Sosnowiec, Russian Poland.

He resided in Odessa, with one short interruption, until 1921, when he left Russia. The period from his stay at the Yeshiva of Volozhin, where, under the influence of the works of the Russian-Jewish poet Simon Frug, he began to write poetry, until World War I was the most fruitful in his career.

In many of his poems Bialik stressed the vital role of the Bet HaMidrash (house of study) and extolled the tradition of learning in Jewish life (*'Al Saf Bet HaMidrash*, 1894; *HaMatmid*, 1894–95; *Im Yesh Et Nefshkha Lada'at*, 1898), but his main preoccupation was with the rebirth of the Jewish people and its Return to Zion. He spoke out, like a prophet of old, calling on his people to awaken from its slumber and take its rightful place among the nations (*Akhen Hatzir Ha'Am*, 1897).

After the *Kishinev pogrom (1903), Bialik published his poem *In the City of Slaughter,* wherein he depicted the horrors of the pogrom but also expressed shame that the Jews had not resisted their attackers: "For great is the anguish, great the shame on the brow, but which of these is greater, son of man, say thou. . . ." The powerful poem had a tremendous influence on Russian-Jewish youth and inspired it to form self-defense groups.

Because of his intense identification with the Jewish people's past and present, Bialik soon became the most beloved figure in the world of modern Hebrew letters. In addition to poetry, Bialik wrote stories and essays. He also wrote in Yiddish and translated Yiddish, Russian, and German literature into Hebrew. His translations include Friedrich Schiller's *Wilhelm Tell.*

In Odessa he founded (1905) with several partners the *Moriah publishing house, which exerted a great influence on modern Hebrew education. Moriah's publications included textbooks and the *Sefer HaAggada* (compiled by Bialik and Y'hoshu'a Hana *Rawnitzky), which endeavored to acquaint the modern Jew with the world of the Midrash. For some years Bialik was editor of the belletristic section of *HaShiloah* and in this capacity resided in Warsaw for a time.

Hayim Nahman Bialik.
[Zionist Archives]

After he left Russia, he lived for several years in Germany, where he established the D'vir publishing house. In 1924 he settled in Palestine and continued his publishing activities there. He propagated the idea of the ingathering of all the literary treasures created by the Jewish people through the centuries, and he hoped to serve this idea through D'vir. He himself, in cooperation with Rawnitzky, edited the poems of Solomon Ibn Gabirol and Moses Ibn Ezra.

In Palestine, Bialik was active in numerous cultural institutions and was also a president of the Va'ad HaLashon Ha'Ivrit, or Hebrew Language Council (see HEBREW LANGUAGE ACADEMY). It was Bialik who originated the Sabbath afternoon assemblies known as 'On'ge Shabbat (see 'ONEG SHABBAT). In 1926 he toured the United States on behalf of the *Keren HaYesod (Palestine Foundation Fund) and D'vir. He died in Vienna, where he had gone to seek medical treatment.

H. LEAF

BIALIK FOUNDATION (Mosad Bialik). Publishing house in Jerusalem named for Hayim Nahman *Bialik. Its aim is to "encourage Hebrew writing, both literary and scientific, and to built a bridge between modern Hebrew literature and the literature of earlier generations, as well as between the literature of the Jewish people and world literature in general, and to encourage research in and advancement of the Hebrew language."

By 1965 the foundation had published about 600 books, including critical editions of Hebrew classics, source books and studies in the religion, history, and literature of the Jews, Palestinography, belles lettres, and science, as well as translations of important works written by Jewish writers in foreign languages and Hebrew renderings of world literature. Larger projects of the foundation include the *Hebrew Biblical Encyclopedia*, five of whose planned seven volumes were published between 1955 and 1970.

BIBAS, YEHUDA. Rabbi and precursor of Zionism (b. Gibraltar, ca. 1790; d. Hebron, 1854). For a time he lived in London and Italy. In 1831 he was chosen rabbi of the Jewish community of Corfu, where, with the exception of a few years (1839–44), he served until his departure for Palestine early in 1852.

Bibas traveled through the continent of Europe in 1839–40. He also visited England, where he is reported to have gone to see what could be done for his oppressed brethren and to have propagated the instruction of Jews in the sciences as well as in the use of arms—the latter so that they might be able to liberate Palestine from the Turks. Rabbi Judah Solomon Hai *Alkalai quoted him as having said that repentance of the Jews must consist first of all in their return to the Land of Israel: God would redeem the Jews only if they would make an effort on their own to return to the land of their fathers.

BIBLIOGRAPHY OF ZIONISM. See last section of Vol. 2.

BIENENSTOCK, MAX. Educator, public figure, and Labor Zionist leader in Poland (b. Tarnów, Galicia, Austria; d. Lwów, Poland, 1923). He studied at the University of Cracow and then taught in high schools, subsequently becoming principal of a private Jewish high school in Lvov (later Lwów). Joining the Zionist movement during his student days, he helped found the *Po'ale Zion movement in Galicia and Austria. After World War I he was briefly interned by the Poles, who falsely suspected him of pro-Ukrainian activities. In 1922 he was elected to the Polish Senate, where he served until his death.

A journalist and writer, Bienenstock wrote on Zionism, socialism, and Jewish literature, and on the theater. He was the author of a number of books in Polish and German on Polish literature and on literature in general.

BIENSTOCK, YEHUDA LEIB. Rabbi and writer (b. Volhynia, Russia, 1836; d. Jaffa, 1894). He studied at the rabbinical seminary in Zhitomir and served as official government rabbi of that city from 1859 to 1862. Later he worked with a Russian newspaper and served as official adviser on Jewish affairs to the Governor of Kiev. Bienstock contributed to Russian and Russian-Jewish journals and in 1890 made a study of Jewish settlements in the district of Yekaterinoslav.

In 1892 he was appointed Jaffa representative of the *Odessa Committee of the *Hoveve Zion movement. He acted on instructions of the committee, helped the settlements develop their farms, and aided in the establishment of the first Hebrew school in Jaffa.

I. KLAUSNER

BIERER, REUBEN. Physician and early Zionist (b. Lvov, Galicia, Austria, 1835; d. there, 1930). After practicing medicine in his birthplace, he went to Vienna in 1878 to complete his medical studies. He subsequently returned to Lvov, where with the exception of a period during the 1880s and 1890s when he practiced medicine in the Balkans, he remained for the rest of his life.

An early Jewish nationalist, Bierer founded a Zionist group in Lvov. In Vienna, with Peretz *Smolenskin, he established the Palestine settlement society *Ahavat Zion, and he participated in the founding of *Kadimah, the Jewish national students' fraternity. Bierer maintained contact with the *Hoveve Zion movement in Russia and corresponded with Leo *Pinsker. He also created the first nationalist Jewish organizations in Sofia.

Bierer hailed Herzl as the leader chosen by Providence, became his faithful follower, and contributed much to the dissemination of political Zionism in Galicia.

BIERER, YOSEF SH'MUEL. Physician (b. Lvov, Galicia, Austria, 1870; d. Vienna, 1937). A son of Reuben *Bierer, he studied medicine in Vienna and settled in Czernowitz (now Chernovtsy), Bukovina. He founded the Zionist student society Hashmonia in Czernowitz and the Histadrut 'Ivrit (Hebrew Society) of Bukovina.

BILTMORE PROGRAM. Eight-point declaration adopted by the Extraordinary Conference of American Zionists held at the Biltmore Hotel in New York, on May 9–11, 1942. It was the first official American Zionist pronouncement using the phrase "Jewish Commonwealth," that is, explicitly advocating the establishment of an independent Jewish State in Palestine.

Background. In the years prior to the outbreak of World War II, Zionists in the United States had tended to concentrate on the practical tasks of rebuilding Jewish Palestine and on gaining the support of non-Zionists for this work rather than on formulating political programs. America's entry into the war, the news of Nazi atrocities, and plans for a new world order following a hoped-for Allied victory shifted the focus of attention to the ultimate political status of Palestine.

The Biltmore Conference was called by the *Emergency Committee for Zionist Affairs for the purpose of discussing the future of Palestine, possibilities of cooperation with non-Zionist groups, and methods for obtaining a united representation of Jewry at the eventual peace conference. It was the first joint meeting of all American Zionist parties since World War I, with the four major organizations—the *Zionist Organization of America, *Hadassah, *Mizrahi, and *Po'ale Zion—participating.

Among the nearly 600 delegates in attendance, there were Zionist leaders from 17 foreign countries. The presence of these, and of World Zionist figures such as Chaim *Weizmann, David *Ben-Gurion, and Nahum *Goldmann, gave the conference some aspects of a World Zionist *Congress.

The Presidium of the conference consisted of Leon *Gellman, Louis E. *Levinthal, Louis *Lipsky, Tamar de Sola *Pool, Robert *Szold, David Wertheim, and Stephen S. *Wise. In addition to the above, speakers included Gedalia *Bublick, Z'ev *Gold, Israel *Goldstein, Hayim *Greenberg, Meir *Grossman, Jacob *Hoffman, Emanuel *Neumann, and Abba Hillel *Silver.

The Program. The Biltmore Program, which was to guide the future efforts of Zionism in the United States, was drafted on the urging of Ben-Gurion, to reaffirm the original intention of the *Balfour Declaration and the *Mandate for Palestine, and of Abba Hillel Silver, who warned against making distinctions between "political Zionism" and "philanthropic humanitarianism."

The declaration submitted by Judge Levinthal on behalf of the Presidium reaffirmed the devotion of American Zionism to the cause of freedom, sent a message of hope and encouragement to the Jews in Nazi-held Europe, commended the *Jewish Agency and the *Yishuv (Jewish community of Palestine), and expressed the readiness and desire of the Jewish people to cooperate fully with Palestine's Arab neighbors. Praising the contribution of the Yishuv to the war effort, the declaration asserted the right of the Jews of Palestine to play their full part in the war "through a Jewish military force fighting under their own flag and under the high command of the United Nations."

The most important part of the declaration was contained in points 6 and 8. Point 6 reaffirmed the rejection of the *White Paper of 1939 and called for the fulfillment of the original purpose of the Balfour Declaration and the mandate, which, "recognizing the historical connection of the Jewish people with Palestine, was to afford them the opportunity, as stated by President *Wilson, to form there a Jewish Commonwealth." Point 8 declared that the new world order which would follow an Allied victory could not be established on foundations of peace, justice, and equality unless the problem of Jewish homelessness would be permanently solved. It demanded that "the gates of Palestine be opened; that the Jewish Agency be vested with control of *immigration into Palestine and with the necessary authority for upbuilding the country, including the development of its unoccupied and uncultivated lands; and that Palestine be established as a Jewish Commonwealth integrated in the structure of the new democratic world."

World Reaction. Non-Zionist groups such as the *American Jewish Committee regarded the Biltmore Program as a victory for the "extreme" Zionist position, since it called for an independent Jewish Palestine rather than the mere lifting of barriers to future Jewish immigration.

On Nov. 10, 1942, the Biltmore Program was endorsed by the Inner *Actions Committee in Jerusalem by a vote of 21 to 4. The opposing votes were cast by *HaShomer HaTza'ir, which offered a substitute resolution calling for a binational (Arab-Jewish) rather than a Jewish state.

The Biltmore Program was overwhelmingly accepted by the *American Jewish Conference held the following year, by Zionist organizations throughout the democratic world, and finally at the World Zionist Conference held in London in August, 1945, so that it became the official policy of the *World Zionist Organization.

G. HIRSCHLER

BILU. Movement of Palestine pioneers who spearheaded the *First 'Aliya. It derived its name from the initials of "Bet Ya'akov L'khu V'Nelkha" ("O House of Jacob, come ye and let us go," Isaiah 2:5), which served as its slogan. Founded in Kharkov in 1882 by students who reacted against the Russian pogroms of the time, it had members also in other localities, and membership was not restricted to students. Bilu's aim was the national renaissance of the Jewish people, the development of its productiveness, and its return to agriculture. The organization called on its members to settle in Palestine, and its central office sent representatives to Constantinople to seek out the British author and forerunner of Zionism Laurence *Oliphant and request his help. However, Oliphant was not able to render it much assistance. Of the Bilu members who reached Constantinople, a group of 14 went on to settle in Palestine in July, 1882. Those who remained in Constantinople and additional members who had come there directly from Russia later went to Palestine, where they worked as farmhands at first in Mikve Yisrael. Some of the Biluim (i.e., Bilu immigrants) settled in Rishon L'Tziyon, while others remained working as agricultural laborers in Mikve Yisrael. Still others learned a trade and worked as artisans in Jerusalem.

Bilu pioneers. [Zionist Archives]

The Biluim planned to establish a model colony on cooperative lines, but their plans did not materialize because of lack of funds. Baron Edmond de *Rothschild was unwilling to establish a settlement for them, although he subsequently did extend aid to the existing Bilu settlements. Some of the Biluim left the country, and for those who had not settled in Rishon L'Tziyon, Yehiel Mikhel *Pines purchased a tract of land on which they founded the settlement of G'dera in 1884. The leadership of the Russian *Hoveve Zion movement supported the settlement and assisted its consolidation.

Although the Biluim were few in number and their concrete achievements in establishing settlements were limited, the moral and historical effect of the movement was substantial because of the ideals which it represented and which continued to inspire successive generations.

I. KLAUSNER

BI'NA. Arab village in western Galilee. Population (1968): 1,960.

BIN-GORION (BERDYCZEWSKY), MIKHA YOSEF. Hebrew essayist and novelist (b. Medzhibozh, Russia, 1865; d. Berlin, 1921). The son of a rabbi, he received a traditional Jewish education and studied at the famous Yeshiva of Volozhin. Later he studied at the Universities of Breslau, Bern, and Berlin.

In his early novels, Bin-Gorion poignantly presented the dilemma of the young Jew who, though fettered by ancient tradition, craved the beauty and freedom of modern European culture. In his later essays, he championed the rights of the individual against what he described as the stifling and oppressive dogmas of historical Judaism. He espoused the cause of the deviationists in Jewish history, such as false prophets, heretics, and rebels against tradition. Lashing out against *Ahad Ha'Am's stress on spiritual values, he emphasized the need for Jewish participation in the realities of the present. A leader of the group known as Tz'irim (the Young), he introduced Nietzschean ideas into Hebrew literature, interpreting them in the light of the Jewish struggle for individual freedom.

Set against the background of the Jewish *shtetl* (small town) in the *Diaspora, his novels and short stories encompass a wide range of themes and modes of life. In his stories the natural instincts and impulses of the characters are given free play. In some, the mood is gently reminiscent as he describes the longing of the traditional Jew for Zion. Bin-Gorion also edited collections of Jewish legends and Hasidic lore, lending them his individual style and interpretation. Although he did not align himself with Zionism, his positive identification with man's natural impulses greatly influenced the individualistic drives of Jewish youth for national self-expression. His best-known novels include *Me'Ever HaNahar* (From Across the River), *B'Seter Ra'am* (Hidden Thunder), and *Miriam.*

H. LEAF

BINYAMINA. Township in the northern Sharon Plain. Founded in 1922 by the *Palestine Jewish Colonization Association (PICA), it was named for Baron Edmond (Binyamin) de *Rothschild. Its prime source of income has been citrus growing. Population (1968): 2,570.

BINYAN HA'ARETZ. Hebrew name of several Zionist groups, meaning "Upbuilding of the Land." One group was active in Germany in the early 1920s. Based on ideas espoused by Dr. Ignatz *Zollschan in *Revision des jüdischen Nationalismus* (1919), it was founded in 1920 by Alfred *Klee, Karl Lewin, Max Kollenscher, and Gotthold Weil. The group rejected all Zionist activities other than those concerned directly with the upbuilding of Palestine; it thus strongly opposed political activities in the *Diaspora (the so-called *Landespolitik*). It called for the unification of all Jews, Zionists and non-Zionists alike, for the rebuilding of Palestine. To this end, Binyan Ha'Aretz stressed the important role of private initiative in Palestinian economic and industrial projects, in opposition to the Socialist trend that had been making considerable headway in Germany after World War I and was based on party and selective principles. The group felt that overemphasis of Jewish nationalism would cost the Zionist movement the cooperation of broad segments of non-Zionist Jewry. Binyan Ha'Aretz met with sharp opposition from leaders of the Zionist Organization of Germany including Kurt *Blumenfeld, Arthur *Hantke, Fritz Löwenstein, and

Egon Rosenberg, who established a National Unity Bloc to counteract its activities. The success of the bloc at a Zionist convention in Hannover (May, 1921), which was simultaneous with the defeat of the Brandeisists, who had expressed similar ideas, at Cleveland that year, dealt a severe blow to Binyan Ha'Aretz, which to all practical purposes ceased to function by 1922. *See also* GERMANY, ZIONISM IN.

A Zionist group of the same name existed in 1921 in Czechoslovakia. A similar group, numbering 925 members, was active in Austria from 1933 to 1937.

BIR AL-MAKSUR. Arab village in western Lower Galilee. Population (1968): 1,780.

BIRAM, ARTHUR YITZHAK. Educator (b. Bischofswerda, near Dresden, Germany, 1878; d. Haifa, 1967). He studied at the university and the Hochschule für die Wissenschaft des Judentums in Berlin and at the University of Leipzig. Later he taught classical languages and literature at high schools in Prussia. While still a student, he joined the Zionist movement. Beginning in 1899, he published polemical articles in the Berlin Zionist journal *Jüdische Rundschau* against the rabbis who opposed Zionism. Subsequently, he contributed to many Zionist periodicals and publications in Germany.

In 1914 he settled in Palestine and became principal of Bet Sefer Reali, the Hebrew high school in Haifa. Biram directed the institution until his retirement and during his long period of service developed it into a model school. His educational principles were modesty, integrity, and discipline. He made intensive physical education a part of the curriculum and in 1953 initiated the establishment of a school for premilitary training attached to the Reali High School. Some of the most prominent officers of the *Israel Defense Forces, including chiefs of staff, were products of this school, which emphasized not only physical fitness but also patriotism and devotion to duty.

Biram also carried out Biblical researches and was the author of several studies in this field, as well as of a book on the history of the Jews in Biblical times. In 1954 he was awarded the *Israel Prize for outstanding achievement in the field of education.

G. KRESSEL

BIRANIT. Rural settlement in western Upper Galilee. Founded in 1964.

BIR AS-SIKA. Arab village in the Sharon Plain. Population (1968): 357.

BIRNBAUM, NATHAN (pseudonym, Mathias Acher). Author, publicist, and originator of the term "Zionism" (b. Vienna, 1864; d. Scheveningen, Netherlands, 1937). While a student at the University of Vienna, he independently formulated ideas similar to those of Leo *Pinsker. In 1882 he published his first pamphlet opposing *assimilation, and in 1883 helped found *Kadimah, the first Jewish nationalist-oriented student fraternity in Vienna. In 1885 he began to edit *Selbst-Emanzipation, a Jewish-national periodical promulgating the ideas of the *Hoveve Zion movement. It was during this period that Birnbaum coined the term "Zionism." In 1893 he published a brochure entitled *Die nationale Wiedergeburt des jüdischen Volkes in seinem Lande als Mittel zur Lösung der Judenfrage* (The National Rebirth of the Jewish People in Its Homeland as a Means of Solving the Jewish Problem), in which he expounded ideas similar to those that Herzl was subsequently to promote.

An early adherent of Herzl, Birnbaum played a prominent part at the 1st Zionist *Congress (1897) and took a leading role at the Vienna headquarters of the Zionist Organization. Gradually, however, differences developed between him and Herzl. Birnbaum began to question the political aims of Zionism and to attach increasing importance to the national-cultural content of Judaism. In 1898 he left the Zionist movement and became a leading spokesman of *Galut nationalism. He came to stress the Yiddish language as the basis of Jewish culture and was one of the chief promoters of the Conference on Yiddish held in Czernowitz (now Chernovtsy), Bukovina, in 1908, which was attended by many Yiddish writers and which proclaimed Yiddish as the national language of the Jewish people. Birnbaum propagated his ideas in writing and lectures in many Jewish communities. In the years preceding World War I he gradually abandoned his materialistic and secular outlook and turned to religious problems, eventually embracing extreme Orthodoxy. He expounded his new beliefs in articles and brochures, including *Divre Ha'Olim* (Words of the Ascendants, 1917) and *Gottes Volk* (The People of God, 1917). Dissatisfied with the spiritual complacency of the religious masses, he called for constant spiritual preparedness for the advent of the Messiah. He also advocated the return of the Jews to agricultural work and the formation of select "orders" or communities whose saintly mode of life would serve as an example to the rest of the Jewish people. During the latter part of his life he again gave the Holy Land a place of prime importance in Jewish living. In his book *Im Dienste der Verheissung* (In the Service of the Promise, 1927), he called on the Jewish people to work in and for Palestine out of love for the land, but without political aspirations.

Several years after World War I, Birnbaum, who resided in Germany for a time, became secretary-general of the World *Agudat Israel movement. After the rise of Nazism, he left Germany for the Netherlands, where he edited *Der Ruf* (the Call), a platform for his ideals, and where he died.

BIROBIDZHAN.

Autonomous region in eastern Siberia, U.S.S.R. In 1928 the Soviet government set aside an area of some 10 million acres for a Jewish settlement in Birobidzhan, which was intended eventually to evolve into an autonomous Jewish territory. The decision was prompted by a variety of motives, including the plan to develop Soviet Far Eastern territories as a barrier against Japanese encroachment, as well as efforts being made to rehabilitate the Jewish masses that had been economically uprooted by Soviet economic policy. In line with these considerations it seemed expedient to some Soviet leaders to grant the Jews a national territory where, like all other nationality groups in the U.S.S.R., they would be able to develop their own Yiddish culture, national in form and Socialist in content. The plan to establish a Jewish settlement was also used by Soviet policy makers to enlist the goodwill of Jewish communities abroad and to discourage Zionism in the ranks of Soviet Jewry. Jewish committees to help in the realization of the project were established in some countries.

Soon after the announcement of the project, Soviet authorities embarked on a vigorous program of propaganda and pressure to generate Jewish mass migration to Birobidzhan. The Jewish masses, however, were not tempted to become pioneers in a territory with which they had no historical link, nor could the prospects of a Jewish settlement whose Jewishness was to consist solely in the cultivation of the Yiddish language have a wide appeal.

By 1934 about 20,000 Jews, including small groups from outside Russia, had gone to Birobidzhan, but half of them left again, having found conditions much worse than they had expected. That year Birobidzhan, which had been declared a Jewish National District in 1928, was officially promoted to the status of Jewish Autonomous Region. The years immediately following saw further Jewish immigration. In 1936 there were approximately 18,000 Jews in Birobidzhan, or about one-third of the total population of the area.

During the Soviet purges in the latter 1930s, the entire leadership of the Jewish Autonomous Region project, in European Russia as well as in Birobidzhan, was liquidated. Numerous leading officials in Birobidzhan were arrested on charges of treason, sabotage, or Jewish nationalistic and Zionist counterrevolutionary activities. These developments resulted in a setback for the program of Jewish colonization. While the general population of the region increased, Jewish migration to Birobidzhan decreased materially.

In the period immediately following World War II there was an increase in the Jewish influx to Birobidzhan. Those who came were mostly survivors of the war years who, on returning from evacuation, the army, partisan groups, and slave labor camps, had found their families slaughtered, their houses occupied, and the local population of their former places of residence in many cases hostile and had therefore decided to start life anew in Birobidzhan. The Soviet authorities encouraged their immigration and called on the Jews in Western countries for new efforts to develop the Jewish Autonomous Region. An estimated 15,000 Jews seem thus to have moved to Birobidzhan, increasing the Jewish population of the territory to a total of 35,000. At that time preparations were made to revive some of the Yiddish institutions which had been closed. These developments were cut short in 1948, when the Stalin regime embarked on an anti-Jewish drive; Jews in Birobidzhan were charged with conspiring to make the region secede from the Soviet Union and to turn it over to the Japanese.

In the post-Stalin era, beginning in 1953, there was no renewal of efforts to promote Jewish immigration to Birobidzhan. Though the Soviet authorities never changed Birobidzhan's official designation as a Jewish Autonomous Region, it was obvious that they had definitely abandoned their scheme. In 1958 Premier Nikita Khrushchev, in an interview with a French editor, admitted that the Jewish colonization project in Birobidzhan had failed.

It was estimated that in 1968, out of a total population of over 160,000, there were about 25,000 Jews in Birobidzhan. There were no Yiddish schools. The *Birobidjaner Stern,* the only Yiddish newspaper in the Soviet Union, appeared three times weekly. But there was hardly any Jewish cultural life in the territory which once had been intended to become a Jewish Autonomous Region.

T. PRESCHEL

BIRYA.

Agricultural settlement in eastern Upper Galilee. Founded in 1949. Population (1968): 312.

Birya was a Jewish village in the Talmudic period, and the locality had a Jewish population also in later times. Joseph Karo, the 16th-century codifier, lived there for some time. Before the establishment of the present settlement, a kibbutz of HaPo'el HaMizrahi (see MIZRAHI), founded in 1945, existed on the site. Early in 1946 the British arrested all the settlers on the pretext that they had fired at an Arab Legion camp in the neighborhood

Fire tower at Birya. [Jewish National Fund]

and "occupied" the settlement. A short time later, 3,000 young people from all parts of the country came to Birya and erected new temporary settlement facilities. These were destroyed by the British, but the young pioneers rebuilt them. Finally the British permitted 20 youths to remain in the settlement. The British left Birya in the summer of 1946.

BISMET TAB'UN. Arab village in the Haifa area. Population (1968): 710.

BISSELICHES, MÓZES. Engineer and Zionist leader (b. Brody, Galicia, Austria, 1878). He studied at the rabbinical seminary and the technical university in Budapest. After earning his degree in mechanical engineering, he became a manufacturer of metal goods. Bisseliches was drawn to Zionism early in his youth and was one of the founders and pioneers of the Zionist movement in Hungary. He served as president of Makkabea, the Hungarian Zionist students' organization, and of the Hungarian Zionist Organization. For a while he edited the organization's official organ, *Zsidó Szemle* (Jewish Spectator), and served as the first president of *Keren HaYesod (Palestine Foundation Fund) in Hungary. After World War I, he became active in the work of the *American Jewish Joint Distribution Committee. A frequent contributor to the Hungarian Zionist press, he played a leading role in the Hungarian section of the *World Jewish Congress, which he represented at the Montreux Congress of 1948.

R. L. BRAHAM

BISTRITSKY ('AGMON), NATHAN. Author, translator, and official of the *Jewish National Fund (b. Zvenigorodka, Ukraine, Russia, 1896). Bistritsky settled in Palestine in 1920, and from 1922 to 1952 he headed the Information and Public Relations Department of the Jewish National Fund. Traveling throughout the world and publicizing the Zionist movement, he exerted a particularly strong influence on youth groups. He edited a series of books explaining the work of the Fund and the personalities associated with it. Bistritsky also published several stories and plays and a novel, *Yamim V'Lelot* (Days and Nights, 1924), which describes the *HaShomer HaTza'ir colonization of Bet Alfa. He translated a number of literary works, such as

Don Quixote and the poems of the Chilean poet Pablo Neruda, into Hebrew.

G. KRESSEL

BITAN AHARON. Village (moshav) in the Sharon Plain. Founded in 1936 and named for Archibald Jacob (Aaron) *Freiman, the Canadian Zionist leader. Affiliated with *Ihud Haklai. Population (1968): 130.

BIT'HA. Village (moshav) in the Negev. Founded in 1950 and affiliated with *T'nu'at HaMoshavim. Population (1968): 665.

BITIR. Arab village in the Judean Mountains. It is the site of ancient Betar, the last Jewish fortress in the rebellion led by Bar Kokhba against the Romans in the 2d century of our era.

BITZARON. Village (moshav) in the Darom. Founded in 1935 and affiliated with *T'nu'at HaMoshavim. The founders were Halutzim (pioneers; see HALUTZIYUT) from Russia who had been imprisoned by the Soviet authorities, and the name alludes to a reference in Zechariah 9:12: "Return to the stronghold [Bitzaron], ye prisoners of hope." Population (1968): 420.

BIYADA. Arab village in the Hadera district of Samaria. Population (1968): 224.

B'KO'A. Village (moshav) in the Judean Plain. Founded by *Yemenite Jews in 1951 and affiliated with *T'nu'at HaMoshavim. Population (1968): 470.

BLANKENSTEIN, SOLOMON. *See* SCHILLER, SOLOMON.

BLAUSTEIN, JACOB. Industrialist and Jewish communal leader in the United States (b. Baltimore, 1892). In 1910 he and his father, Louis Blaustein, founded the American Oil Company. A director of a number of business corporations, including the Standard Oil Company of Indiana, Blaustein was active in Jewish communal life and American public affairs. From 1949 to 1953 he served as president of the *American Jewish Committee, of which he subsequently became honorary president.

A consultant to the American delegation at the United Nations Conference on International Organization in San Francisco in 1945, Blaustein was chairman of the delegation sent by the American Jewish Committee to the Paris Peace Conference in 1946 and chairman of the American delegation to the Conference of Jewish Organizations which met in London that same year.

He was a senior vice-president and Presidium member of the *Conference on Jewish Material Claims against Germany and a member of the Executive Committee on Jewish Claims against Austria. He also served as vice-president of the Jewish Restitution Successor Organization and, in 1967, as senior vice-president of the cultural foundation supported by Claims Conference funds. At the invitation of Prime Minister David *Ben-Gurion in 1949, 1950, 1958, 1960, and 1961 and at the invitation of Premier Levi *Eshkol in 1963, he went on missions to Israel. He conducted discussions with Ben-Gurion that were intended to clarify the relationship between the State of Israel and American Jews. Subsequently Ben-Gurion issued a statement outlining the limitations of Israel's authority in relation to the Jewish communities of the *Diaspora.

BLOCH, JOSEF SAMUEL. Rabbi, editor, and parliamentarian (b. Dukla, Russia, 1850; d. Vienna, 1923). Bloch studied at Yeshivot and attended the Universities of Zurich and Munich. He served as preacher and rabbi in various communities in Germany, in Brüx (now Most), Bohemia, and finally in Floridsdorf, an outlying district of Vienna.

Bloch first became widely known in 1882, when he sharply attacked and ridiculed the anti-Semitic professor August Rohling, of the University of Prague, who had defamed the Talmud. In 1883 he was elected to the Austrian Parliament, where he represented electoral districts in Galicia. Reelected twice, he served until 1895. Soon after he had entered Parliament, he founded the *Österreichische Wochenschrift,* a weekly of which he was editor for 37 years. In Parliament as well as in his weekly, Bloch valiantly defended Jewish rights and courageously fought *anti-Semitism.

A prolific writer, he published scholarly books on the Bible, the Talmud, Jewish history, and apologetics and an autobiography. A member of the *Hoveve Zion movement, he became a friend of Herzl. As early as February, 1896, Bloch reprinted in his weekly a Zionist article by Herzl which had previously been published in the London *Jewish Chronicle,* but he later became an antagonist of Herzl and political Zionism. In his last years, however, he assumed a more positive attitude toward Zionism and in 1922 spent a few months in Palestine.

BLUESTONE, EPHRAIM MICHAEL. American physician and hospital administrator (b. New York, 1891). The son of Joseph Isaac *Bluestone, he graduated from the Columbia University Medical School in 1916 and served as first lieutenant in the U.S. Army Medical Corps in 1918–19. In 1920, after a year in private practice, he entered the field of hospital administration as assistant director of Mount Sinai Hospital in New York. In 1926 he went to Palestine to serve as director of the *Hadassah medical organization and chairman of the Nathan and Lina Straus Health Center. On his return to the United States two years later, he became director of Montefiore Hospital in New York, a position he held until 1951, after which he was a consultant at the hospital. From 1939 to 1950 he was chairman of the Medical Reference Board of the Hadassah-University Hospital. From 1945 on he was assistant professor of hospital administration at Columbia University.

BLUESTONE, JOSEPH ISAAC. Physician and Zionist leader (b. Kalvarija, Lithuania, 1860; d. New York, 1934). Bluestone studied at Yeshivot and began to write Hebrew poetry at an early age. In 1878 he went to the United States and studied medicine, which he practiced all his life. In 1883 he founded the first *Hoveve Zion society in the United States and in 1889 became editor of *Shulamith,* the movement's first organ in the country. Bluestone was a founder and grand master of the fraternal order *B'nai Zion, and he served as a delegate to the Zionist Congresses of 1903 and 1907 (*see* CONGRESS, ZIONIST). An early adherent of the Mizrahi movement in the United States (*see* RELIGIOUS ZIONISTS OF AMERICA), he served as its first secretary-general in 1912. An able promoter of Mizrahi ideals throughout the United States, he was the author of "Mizraha," the anthem of the American Mizrahi. Bluestone visited Palestine and there published *Shirim UM'Shalim* (1931), which also includes a number of Zionist songs.

Y. RAPHAEL

BLUM, LÉON. Author, literary critic, social philosopher, French Socialist leader and statesman, and supporter of the Jewish National Home in Palestine (b. Paris, 1872; d. there, 1950). After a brilliant literary career in his youth, Blum met Jean Jaurès, the French Socialist leader at the time of the *Dreyfus affair, in 1896, and was greatly influenced by him. Joining the Socialist movement in 1899, he became prominent in party affairs through his writings in party publications and was elected to the French Parliament after World War I. Although never actively identified with a Zionist organization, in 1919 Blum was a firm supporter of Zionist aims in Palestine, asserting his Zionist views in French political circles and at the congresses of the international Socialist movement. In 1927 he joined the France-Palestine Committee. In 1929 he accepted the invitation of Chaim *Weizmann to participate in the Zurich Conference called for the purpose of founding the enlarged *Jewish Agency. Blum was the first Jew and the first Socialist to become Prime Minister of France, a position he held from 1936 to 1938. After the French defeat in 1940 he was arrested and tried in Riom as "one responsible for the war," but his heroic self-defense resulted in an interruption of the proceedings against him. Subsequently he was deported to a German concentration camp. He survived World War II and served briefly as Prime Minister of France in 1945–46. Blum was an active supporter of the establishment of the State of Israel and played a prominent role in securing French recognition for the newly created Jewish State.

BLUMENFELD, KURT (Yehuda). Zionist leader and theoretician (b. Marggrabowa, East Prussia, Germany, 1884; d. Jerusalem, 1963). His Zionist activities date from his student days in Berlin, in 1904. In 1909 he became secretary of the Zionist Organization of Germany, and two years later he was named general secretary and chief of publications of the Executive of the *World Zionist Organization, which then established itself in Berlin. In 1913–14 he was editor of *Die *Welt.* In 1920

Kurt Blumenfeld.
[Zionist Archives]

he became a member of the Greater *Actions Committee. After the establishment of the *Keren HaYesod (Palestine Foundation Fund) in 1920, he launched the fund in Germany. In 1924 he became president of the Zionist Organization of Germany, a position he held for many years.

A leading Zionist theoretician and a brilliant orator, Blumenfeld toured Germany and other countries preaching Zionism to well-established Jewries as a movement of personal self-realization and self-redemption from the spiritual complexities and contradictions of *assimilation. He was instrumental in gaining many adherents to Zionism. Leaders whom he attracted to the movement and enlisted in its cause included Albert *Einstein.

In 1933, after the rise of Nazism, Blumenfeld settled in Palestine, where he joined the Board of Directors of the Keren HaYesod. From 1939 until 1944 he was in the United States on behalf of the fund. In Palestine he was also chairman of the Hitahdut 'Ole Germania (Association of Immigrants from Germany). Shortly before his death his memoirs, *Erlebte Judenfrage* (1962; Hebrew edition, 1963), were published.

BLUVSTEIN, RACHEL. Hebrew lyric poet (b. Vyatka, Russia, 1890; d. Tel Aviv, 1931). Rachel, as she was generally known, endeared herself to Hebrew readers by her warm and melodic poems of the Palestinian countryside. Arriving in Palestine at the age of 19, she mastered the Hebrew language while living there.

Rachel worked as a laborer first in Rehovot and later at the agricultural training farm of Kinneret in the Jordan Valley. In 1913 she went to France to study agriculture and from there to Russia, where she spent the years of World War I teaching refugee children. While in Russia she contracted tuberculosis. After the war she returned to Palestine. She lived for some time at D'ganya, but ill health forced her to leave the kibbutz. Her illness lent a sad and nostalgic mood to her poetry. Love of country and love of fellowman are the dominant themes of her poems, many of which have been set to music. She was buried at Kinneret.

H. LEAF

B'NAI (B'NE) B'RITH. Oldest Jewish service organization in the world, organized in the United States in 1843. With about 400,000 members (including men, women, and youth), it was the world's largest Jewish organization of its kind. The great majority of its members lived in the United States and Canada. Founded in New York by 12 German Jews with "the mission of uniting Israelites in the work of promoting their highest interests and those of humanity," it has engaged throughout its existence in the defense of Jewish rights, in educational and philanthropic activities, in community relations and mutual-aid services, in citizenship and civic affairs, and in social fellowship. In the 1960s it was the only American Jewish organization to have branches in other countries.

In 1909 B'nai B'rith Women was organized; and in 1913 the Anti-Defamation League was formed as the agency of B'nai B'rith in combating *anti-Semitism and other manifestations of racial and religious discrimination and bigotry and in promoting civil liberties and civil rights. The B'nai B'rith Hillel Foundations came into being in 1923; at the end of 1964 they were providing religious, cultural, social, and counseling services to Jewish college and university students on 247 campuses in the United States, Canada, Israel, and other countries. Since 1924 the B'nai B'rith Youth Organization has been active among Jewish teen-agers, and since 1938 its vocational service has conducted occupational research and provided direct guidance to Jewish youth seeking careers.

Aid to Jewish communities in need of economic, moral, and political assistance from the United States has always occupied a prominent place on the agenda of B'nai B'rith. Palestine has engaged its attention since 1865, when it made its first financial contribution to aid victims of a cholera epidemic. In 1888 the first B'nai B'rith lodge was founded in Palestine. About that time, the order supported a vocational school and an orphan asylum in Jerusalem. In later decades it rendered aid to the *Jewish National and University Library, Jerusalem, and to the Haifa *Technion. In the 1920s B'nai B'rith built homes for new immigrants in Jerusalem and provided a research scholarship at the newly opened *Hebrew University of Jerusalem.

in 1936 the order decided to provide $100,000 for the *Jewish National Fund to enable it to purchase land for a settlement in honor of B'nai B'rith's president, Alfred M. Cohen. The settlement, called B'ne B'rit–Moledet, was founded in Lower Galilee in 1937. B'nai B'rith also planted through the Jewish National Fund a forest in memory of its secretaries Boris Bogen and Isaac Rubinow and provided funds for *Youth 'Aliya.

In 1941 the order again decided to provide $100,000 for the Jewish National Fund, this time for the establishment of a settlement in the name of its president, Henry *Monsky; in 1942 this settlement, Ramat Tz'vi, was founded near B'ne B'rit–Moledet.

Never committed to the ultimate aims of Zionism, B'nai B'rith has slowly veered toward the practical Zionist program since the *Balfour Declaration, particularly since the 1930s. It participated in the National Conference for Palestine called by the *Zionist Organization of America in Washington in 1935. In 1943 Henry Monsky, then president of B'nai B'rith, initiated the *American Jewish Conference; all 65 delegates forming the B'nai B'rith bloc at the conference voted for a resolution calling for a Jewish Commonwealth in Palestine.

In 1947 B'nai B'rith urged Pres. Harry S *Truman to support the recommendation of the *United Nations Special Committee on Palestine (UNSCOP) to partition Palestine into Jewish and Arab states. During the first year of the existence of Israel, B'nai B'rith sent clothing, medical supplies, trucks, and other equipment valued at $4,000,000 to the State. In subsequent years it sponsored the establishment of a rehabilitation center for disabled war veterans in Tel Aviv, a children's home in Jerusalem, and the Hillel Foundation at the Hebrew University. In 1951, when Israel began to issue its bonds, B'nai B'rith became a major organization in promoting their sale (*see* STATE OF ISRAEL BONDS).

In 1954 the order played a prominent role in the formation of the *Conference of Presidents of Major American Jewish Organizations, which initially limited its scope to matters concerning Israel and ways in which it might help the State. Later, the conference broadened the scope of its activities. Subsequently, B'nai B'rith was among the initiators of the World Conference of Jewish Organizations (COJO).

In 1959 B'nai B'rith held its general convention in Israel. At the time of the convention it dedicated the B'nai B'rith Martyrs' Forest, planted in memory of European members of B'nai B'rith who had perished in the Nazi era. In 1965 the order again held its general convention in Israel.

In 1962 B'nai B'rith decided to help build a library at S'de Boker, to serve as the nucleus of the Negev College which David *Ben-Gurion planned to establish there. In 1966 B'nai B'rith launched its Israel Technical Corps for the recruitment of American and Canadian Jewish technicians and skilled workers for Israel.

Presidents of B'nai B'rith have included Julius Bien (1868–1900), Leo N. Levi (1900–04), Simon Wolf (1904–05), Adolph

Kraus (1905–25), Alfred M. Cohen (1925–38), Henry Monsky (1938–47), Frank Goldman (1947–53), Philip M. Klutznick (1953–59), Label A. Katz (1959–65), and Dr. William A. Wexler (1965–   ).

B'nai B'rith in Israel. The first B'nai B'rith lodge in Palestine was established in Jerusalem in 1888. From the beginning it insisted on Hebrew as the language of the lodge, and the order's constitution and ritual were translated into that tongue by Eliezer *Ben Yehuda, who was the lodge's first secretary. Soon after its creation the lodge opened an evening school for adults in the city. Members of the Jerusalem lodge in 1894 established the settlement of Motza in the vicinity of Jerusalem.

Gradually lodges were established all over the country. They developed widespread charitable activities and participated in the efforts of the *Yishuv (Jewish population of Palestine). Some of the leading citizens of the country were members of B'nai B'rith. In the 1960s the order erected a spacious B'nai B'rith building in Tel Aviv to serve the local lodges. Gad Frumkin was for many years president of B'nai B'rith in Israel.

C. B. SHERMAN

B'NAI (B'NE) ZION. American fraternal Zionist organization, founded in 1908 under the name Order Sons of Zion. The organization was dedicated to three principles: Americanism, Zionism, and fraternalism. The organizational convention was held on Apr. 25, 1908, at Clinton Hall, in New York, under the chairmanship of Judah L. *Magnes. Among its founders were Stephen S. *Wise, Joseph I. *Bluestone, Zvi Hirsch *Masliansky, Nathan Chasan, and Joshua Sprayragen. At this convention David Blaustein was elected president.

In the 60 years of its existence, the order has contributed to the spread of Zionist activities in the United States and to reconstruction work in Palestine. During World War I it participated in the establishment of the Provisional Executive Committee for General Zionist Affairs in the United States. It also helped to organize the *American Jewish Congress. It affiliated with the *Zionist Organization of America (ZOA) and in 1921 helped launch the *Keren HaYesod (Palestine Foundation Fund) in the United States. It organized the Judea Industrial Corporation and the Judea Insurance Company Ltd., the first Jewish insurance company in Palestine. In addition, it made massive contributions to the *Jewish National Fund and supported individual institutions such as the *Bezalel School in Jerusalem.

In 1943 B'nai Zion participated in the formation of the *American Jewish Conference. The year 1947 saw the dedication in Palestine of B'ne Zion, an agricultural settlement (moshav) in the Sharon Plain named for the order and built partly with funds provided by it.

Since the establishment of Israel, members of the order as individuals and the organization as a whole have intensified their activities on behalf of the State. The order established several health clinics and Maccabi youth centers in the country. On the American scene it encouraged the study of *Hebrew through the award of scholarships to students and financial aid to Hebrew educational institutions.

By 1968 the order had 25,000 members organized in 112 chapters in 16 states. Its annual dinners were addressed by important persons in American, Israeli, or general Jewish life. Presidents of B'nai Zion since its inception were David Blaustein, Joseph I. Bluestone, Leon *Zolotkoff, Joseph *Barondess, Jacob S. Strahl, Abraham Shomer, Nathan Chasan, Sol Fried-

land, Max Perlman, Isaac Allen, Joseph Kraemer, Harris J. Levine, Harry Grazer, Harry A. Pine, Louis *Lipsky, Abraham A. *Redelheim, Jacob I. Steinberg, Louis K. Bleeker, Arthur Markewich, Nathaniel S. Rothenberg, Hyman J. Fliegel, Norman G. Levine, Edward Sharf, and Raymond M. Patt. Secretaries of the order included Jacob Ish-Kishor (1910–27) and Herman Z. Quittman (1938–   ). The order's organ was the *B'nai Zion Voice*.

G. HIRSCHLER

B'NAYA. Village (moshav) in the Judean Plain. Founded in 1949 and affiliated with *T'nu'at HaMoshavim. Population (1968): 278.

B'NE. Hebrew word, meaning "sons of," that forms part of a number of place names in Israel, as in B'ne Darom (Sons of [the] South), and of the names of Jewish organizations, as in B'ne B'rit (Sons of [the] Covenant).

B'NE 'AKIVA. Youth branch of the *Mizrahi–HaPo'el Ha-Mizrahi World Movement, founded in Palestine in 1922. Its original purpose was to train religious young people in agriculture and crafts and to obtain for them suitable places of employment that would enable them to earn their living while pursuing a traditionally religious way of life. In time, it became an ideological movement with the specific aim of training its members for a life of *Tora va'Avoda (Tora and Labor) expressed in a concrete way by religious *Halutziyut (pioneering) as exemplified by the kibbutzim of *HaKibbutz HaDati. Accordingly, B'ne 'Akiva established an educational framework to direct its members toward life in the religious kibbutz.

Soon B'ne 'Akiva was ready to establish its own kibbutzim. In 1946 the kibbutz 'En Tzurim was founded in the Hebron Hills. After the occupation of that region by the armed forces of Jordan during the Israel *War of Independence and after a period of 10 months in Jordanian prisons, the members of 'En Tzurim reestablished their settlement in the Darom. In 1947 the kibbutz Sa'ad was founded in the Negev. A third kibbutz was established in 1946 at Birya, Upper Galilee, in the face of strong opposition from the British Mandatory government (*see* MANDATE FOR PALESTINE) and despite efforts of British troops to dismantle it.

From 1949 on, settlement units of B'ne 'Akiva joined and augmented many kibbutzim of HaKibbutz HaDati; by 1965 they were to be found in all the older kibbutzim. Units of B'ne 'Akiva served in the Nahal unit of the *Israel Defense Forces. In 1962 a B'ne 'Akiva Nahal unit founded an army outpost on Mount Gilboa, near the Jordanian border, which slowly grew into a thriving kibbutz, at the same time maintaining its purpose of defending Israel's borders.

In addition to developing a pioneering force, B'ne 'Akiva founded Yeshivat B'ne 'Akiva, a unique educational institution with part of its daily program devoted to the regular high school curriculum of the Ministry of Education and Culture and the rest to the Bible, the Talmud, and related subjects. On completion of the four-year program, students may take a university entrance examination. In 1965 B'ne 'Akiva had 15 Yeshivot for boys and two Ulpanim (*see* ULPAN) for girls, with additional institutions in the planning stage.

Similar religious Zionist youth movements developed in other countries. In the early years they had little or no contact with each other, and there was no central body to coordinate their activities and development. They existed, in fact, under different names, such as HeHalutz HaMizrahi, HaShomer HaDati (Shomer Dati), Bachad (*B'rit Halutzim Datiyim), and HaNo'ar HaDati. After a few ineffectual attempts to bind these organizations together, a successful effort was made in September, 1954, when the founding conference of the World B'ne 'Akiva was held at K'far HaRo'e, the site of the first Yeshivat B'ne 'Akiva. Movements from 22 countries were represented at the conference, which elected a World Secretariat to be responsible for standardization of the names, aims, programs, and structure of the constituent organizations.

In 1966 B'ne 'Akiva branches existed in 23 countries. They had a total of 32,000 members, of whom 21,000 were in Israel. On the national level, B'ne 'Akiva's affairs were directed by locally elected executives, who were assisted in educational work by Sh'lihim (emissaries from Israel; see SHALIAH) sent by the World Secretariat, which worked very closely with the Religious Section of the Youth and HeHalutz Department of the *Jewish Agency.

In Israel B'ne 'Akiva maintained three training centers for graduates of the youth movements in the *Diaspora to train and prepare them for youth leadership abroad and for eventual settlement in Israel. Such centers were set up at the kibbutz Yavne for North Americans, the kibbutz 'En Tzurim for South Americans, and the kibbutz Lavi for Europeans. In addition, B'ne 'Akiva members from all countries participated in annual leadership courses organized by the Youth and HeHalutz Department of the Jewish Agency.

B. HIRSCHBERG

B'NE 'ATAROT. Village (moshav) in the Petah Tikva area. Founded in 1948 and affiliated with *T'nu'at HaMoshavim. Population (1968): 295.

B'NE 'AYISH. Rural settlement in the Judean Plain. Founded in 1958 and named for Akiba Joseph *Schlesinger (known by his initials, 'Ayish). Population (1968): 840.

B'NE BINYAMIN. Organization of the sons of the farmers who came with the *First 'Aliya to Palestine and founded the first Jewish agricultural settlements in the country. Founded in 1921, it was named for Baron Edmond (Binyamin) de *Rothschild, who had supported those settlements. The organization established settlements for its members and engaged in agricultural contracting. N'tanya, Even Y'huda, K'far Aharon (which was subsequently incorporated into Nes Tziyona), and part of Herzliya were founded by B'ne Binyamin. The organization was disbanded during World War II.

B'NE B'RAK (Bene B'rak). City northeast of Tel Aviv. Population (1968): 64,700.

Established in 1924 as an agricultural settlement by a group of Hasidim from Poland, B'ne B'rak has developed into an industrial center. The city, the great majority of whose population are observant Jews, is also the seat of numerous *Yeshivot and other higher religious educational institutions, including the Ponevezh Yeshiva. Yitzhak Gerstenkorn, one of the founders of B'ne B'rak, served as its mayor from 1924 to 1954.

B'NE B'RIT (village). See MOLEDET.

B'NE B'RITH. See B'NAI B'RITH.

B'NE B'RIT SOCIETY. Organization founded in Kattowitz, Germany (now Katowice, Poland), in 1882 to support the settlement in Palestine of Jews from Russia, Romania, and Morocco. Its founders were Selig Freuthal, a teacher, and Moses Moses, a businessman. According to its statutes, which were ratified by the authorities on May 8, 1882, the aim of the society was to render through the establishment of colonies moral and material support to Jews who were persecuted because of their faith. The society formed branches in many localities in Silesia and also had members in Berlin, Cracow, and Warsaw. Beginning in September, 1882, it published a monthly report of its activities. Early in 1883 the report became a weekly paper entitled *Der Colonist,* the first periodical in Germany to be dedicated wholly to the colonization of Palestine.

The society gave financial support to the colonies of Rosh Pina and Zamarin (see ZIKHRON YA'AKOV). It maintained contact with *Hoveve Zion groups abroad, including those of Galaţi, Warsaw, Vienna, and Lvov, and with Rabbi Sh'muel *Mohilever of Białystok and others, and invited them to participate in a conference to be held in Kattowitz in October, 1883. The conference was attended by the B'ne B'rit members of Kattowitz and by representatives of the society's branches in Silesia. The only delegates to come from abroad were Dr. Karpel *Lippe, who represented the Romanian Central Committee of the Hoveve Zion, and two delegates from Warsaw. A year later, in November, 1884, Kattowitz was the scene of a larger conference that laid the foundations for a centralized Hoveve Zion movement. This conference, known as the *Kattowitz Conference of the Hoveve Zion, was initiated by the Warsaw Hoveve Zion group, and thereafter the leadership of the movement passed to the Hoveve Zion in Russia. From the Kattowitz B'ne B'rit only Moses Moses was elected to the Central Committee. Freuthal, disappointed, ceased publication of *Der Colonist.*

About the same time, the B'nai B'rith, a branch of the service organization *B'nai B'rith founded in the United States in 1843, was formed in Germany. Freuthal assisted in the foundation of the branch and of its lodges in Silesia, in the hope that these would support the national aspirations of the Hoveve Zion. The B'ne B'rit settlement society of Kattowitz merged with the local Concordia Lodge of B'nai B'rith on condition that work for the colonization of Palestine would be continued. The agreement was kept for only a short time, however, because the Berlin center of B'nai B'rith directed its affiliated lodges not to support settlement work in Palestine.

I. KLAUSNER

B'NE DAROM. Village (moshav) southwest of Rehovot. Established in 1949 by settlers of K'far Darom in the Negev, which had been abandoned during the *War of Independence after prolonged and heroic resistance against the Egyptian invaders. Affiliated with HaPo'el HaMizrahi (see MIZRAHI). Population (1968): 144.

B'NE D'ROR. Village (moshav) in the Sharon Plain. Founded in 1946 by veterans of the British armed services in World War II. Affiliated with *T'nu'at HaMoshavim. Population (1968): 231.

B'NE ISRAEL. See INDIA, ZIONISM IN; INDIAN JEWS IN ISRAEL.

B'NE MOSHE (Sons of Moses). Secret order of the *Hoveve Zion movement, founded in Odessa in 1889 and dissolved in 1897. The aim of the order was to bring into being an elite body of dedicated "lovers of Zion," who would serve their people with complete unselfishness and devotion and prepare it for national rebirth in the ancestral Homeland. The ideal to which the members aspired was the personality of Moses, his moral character and humility. Membership was not open to all but was limited to men of high moral caliber. New entrants were inducted in a solemn ceremony and sworn to observe the order's rules and to keep its existence secret. The B'ne Moshe was divided into chapters, each of which elected its own leaders and "advisers."

The order's statement of policy was written by *Ahad Ha'Am, who was its spiritual guide and for some time served as leader of its main chapter in Odessa. Control later passed to the chapter in Warsaw and subsequently to that in Jaffa, the only chapter outside Russia.

Though B'ne Moshe never had more than about 100 members, its influence on the Hoveve Zion was notable, for some of the outstanding leaders of the movement were affiliated with it. Its main achievements were in education. B'ne Moshe established in Jaffa the first elementary school in which Hebrew was the medium of instruction, while in Russia it opened Hebrew libraries and prepared the ground for the establishment of modern Heders. The Warsaw chapter of the order assisted in the founding of the agricultural settlement of Rehovot and of two Hebrew publishing houses, *Ahiasaph and Tushiya.

Internal differences concerning the aims of the order and the lack of a clearly defined practical program, as well as the opposition of Hoveve Zion leaders who regarded colonization work as the main task of the movement and of Orthodox Jews in Palestine who suspected the order of tendencies toward religious reform, brought about the disintegration of B'ne Moshe. The rise of political Zionism sealed the fate of the order, which during its last years had abandoned its secret character.

B'NE R'EM. Village (moshav) in the Judean Plain. Founded in 1949 and named for the rabbi of Góra Kalwaria, Abraham Mord'khai Alter (1864–1948), whose Hebrew initials form the word R'em. Affiliated with *Po'ale Agudat Israel. Population (1968): 316.

B'NE ZION. Village (moshav) in the Sharon Plain. Founded in 1947 and affiliated with the *Ihud Haklai. It was named for *B'nai Zion, the American Zionist fraternal organization which participated in the acquisition of the land. The name has reference also to Joel 2:23 ("Be glad then, ye children of Zion . . ."). Population (1968): 380.

B'NE ZION (fraternal order). *See* B'NAI ZION.

BOARD OF DEPUTIES OF BRITISH JEWS. Body of British Jewry recognized as the authorized spokesman on behalf of the Anglo-Jewish community before the British government. It had its beginnings in 1760 when a delegation of the Sephardi Jewish community of London (*see* SEPHARDIM) was formed under the name the London Committee of Deputies of British Jews to present a loyal address to King George III on his accession to the throne. The committee was inactive for several decades. Eventually the Ashkenazi community (*see* ASHKENAZIM) joined, and, in the 1820s, the body began to hold periodic meetings as the Board of Deputies of British Jews. In 1835 it adopted a formal constitution.

In the late 1960s the board admitted to membership all properly constituted synagogues in England and the British Commonwealth as well as secular institutions such as the provincial representative councils, the interuniversity Jewish federations, and veteran groups. Its aims were to watch over the interests of British Jews, to maintain the good name and religious rights of the community, and to use its influence in favor of Jewish communities and individuals abroad.

Until the middle of the 19th century, the Board of Deputies concerned itself primarily with securing the political and civic *emancipation of Jews. From 1835 on, under the presidency of Sir Moses *Montefiore, it scrutinized legislation affecting Jews and began to act as the recognized representative of the Jewish community in dealing with the British authorities on questions such as marriage laws, grants for schools, burials, registration, and the rating of synagogues. The Marriage Registration Acts, passed by Parliament in 1836, empowered the board to appoint the marriage secretaries of synagogues.

In 1840 the board, still under Montefiore's administration, called a conference on the Damascus and Rhodes blood libels, which was attended by the French statesman Adolphe Crémieux.

After British Jewry had won full emancipation in 1858, the board took an increasing interest in the situation of Jews in other lands. In 1878 it joined with the *Anglo-Jewish Association to form the Conjoint Foreign Committee, which acted much like a Foreign Office for Jewish Affairs. As the range of the board's activities grew, it gained worldwide prestige, particularly owing to the efforts of Montefiore, whose championship of Jewish rights the world over enjoyed the support of Queen Victoria.

The Board of Deputies first took an active interest in Palestine in 1865, when it established a Holy Land Relief Fund. The board refused, however, to take a leading role in the settlement of Palestine, despite Montefiore's endeavors in this respect. When Montefiore retired from office in 1874, the board set up a Testimonial Fund designed to improve the situation of Palestinian Jewry through the founding of industrial enterprises and the erection of model dwellings.

At first the board was opposed to political Zionism; however, the pro-Zionist influence of provincial Jewish leaders soon made itself felt. When the Conjoint Foreign Committee published a letter in the *Times* (May 24, 1917) opposing the political aims of Zionism as a threat to the civic rights of Jews the world over, David Lindo Alexander, the president of the board, who had co-signed the letter with Claude G. Montefiore, president of the Anglo-Jewish Association, was forced to resign. He was succeeded by Sir Stuart Montagu Samuel, a leader in the *Mizrahi movement, whose attitude toward the *Balfour Declaration was positive. This incident caused the dissolution of the Conjoint Foreign Committee in the summer of 1917. It was reconstituted in February, 1918, as the Joint Foreign Committee, which was in operation until 1943.

The elections of 1919 brought to the board a pro-Zionist majority. Thereafter the board formally expressed support of the British *Mandate for Palestine, and in 1925 it incorporated into its constitution a clause which enabled it to cooperate with the *Jewish Agency.

Through the 1930s the board's principal activity was aid to refugees from Nazi-held countries and defense work against *anti-Semitism. Meanwhile, Zionism in England had grown to such an extent that the board elections of 1943 were fought on

Zionist versus non-Zionist lines, and a large majority of first-generation British Jews of pro-Zionist orientation was brought in. That same year pressure from the *World Jewish Congress put an end to the cooperation between the board and the non-Zionist Anglo-Jewish Association in the Joint Foreign Committee.

The president of the Board of Deputies during World War II and the years of struggle for Jewish statehood was Selig *Brodetsky, who energetically fought against the White Paper policy of the British Mandatory authorities (see WHITE PAPER OF 1939). On Nov. 5, 1944, the Board of Deputies, in a statement of policy on Palestine, passed a resolution calling for a Jewish State or Commonwealth in Palestine in the terms of the Balfour Declaration, expressing the hope that this state might become part of the British Commonwealth of Nations. The resolution also requested support from the United Nations for the transfer and resettlement of European refugees in Palestine. In a memorandum to the *Anglo-American Committee of Inquiry (Jan. 23, 1946), the board reaffirmed its 1944 statement, condemned the White Paper with its plan for a permanent Jewish minority in Palestine, and urged the immediate opening of Palestine to displaced persons.

Recent presidents of the Board of Deputies include Abraham Cohen (1949–55), Sir Barnett *Janner (1955–64), Abraham Moss (1964), Solomon Teff (1964–67), and Alderman Michael M. Fidler, J.P. (1968–   ).

G. HIRSCHLER

BODENHEIMER, MAX ISIDOR. Lawyer and Zionist leader (b. Stuttgart, Germany, 1865; d. Jerusalem, 1940). He studied law at German universities and practiced in Cologne. In 1891 Bodenheimer published a pamphlet, *Wohin mit den russischen Juden?*, advocating the establishment of settlements in Syria and Palestine for Russia's persecuted Jews. Two years later,

Max Isidor Bodenheimer.
[Zionist Archives]

with David *Wolffsohn, he founded a Zionist society (Die Nationaljüdische Vereinigung) in Cologne. After the appearance of *The *Jewish State* he became an ardent follower and close collaborator of Herzl. He was a member of the Presidium of the 1st Zionist *Congress (1897), at which he participated in the formulation of the Zionist aims (see BASLE PROGRAM), and served as deputy chairman at later Zionist Congresses. He drafted the statutes of the *World Zionist Organization. In 1898 he was a member of the delegation that accompanied Herzl to Con-

stantinople and Palestine for his meetings with Emperor *Wilhelm II of Germany.

Bodenheimer was one of the organizers and the president (1897–1910) of the Zionistische Vereinigung für Deutschland (Zionist Organization of Germany) and a member of the Greater *Actions Committee from its inception in 1897 until 1921. He was also president (1907–14) of the *Jewish National Fund, whose statutes he had drafted. During World War I he helped found in Berlin the Committee for the Liberation of Russian Jewry (later renamed *Komitee für den Osten), which sought to ease the lot of Polish and Russian Jews under the German occupation and to ensure the granting of equal rights as well as political autonomy to Jews in Eastern European territories occupied by Germany.

From 1929 to 1934 he was affiliated with the *Revisionists. In 1935 he settled in Jerusalem. A contributor to Die *Welt and other Zionist periodicals, Bodenheimer wrote Zionist pamphlets as well as a monograph on Max *Nordau. His memoirs were published posthumously (in Hebrew, *Darki L'Tziyon*, 1953; in German, *So Wurde Israel*, 1958; in English, *Prelude to Israel*, 1963).

BOGRASHOV (BOGER), HAYIM. Zionist leader and educator (b. Berdianik, Ukraine, Russia, 1876; d. Tel Aviv, 1963). After receiving a traditional Jewish education, he continued his studies in Switzerland, obtaining a Ph.D. degree at the University of Basle. He first attended a Zionist *Congress in 1903. The next year he was sent to Palestine to investigate the possibility of establishing a high school with Hebrew as the sole language of instruction, and he subsequently carried on a campaign in Russia for the project. Returning to Palestine in 1906, he was one of the founders of the *Herzliya High School in Tel Aviv, where he was to serve as a teacher of geography and geology, and later as principal, for more than 40 years. Bograshov assembled a mineralogical collection and published researches in the geology of Palestine. Expelled from Palestine by the Turkish authorities after the outbreak of World War I, he spent the war years in Spain, where he was engaged in cataloging medieval Jewish manuscripts in the Escorial. In 1919 he returned to Palestine. In addition to teaching, he was active in the public life of the *Yishuv (Jewish population of Palestine). He was one of the founders of Tel Aviv, and in 1921 he established the Nordia quarter on the outskirts of the city to accommodate refugees who fled from Jaffa after the *Arab riots in May of that year. In 1932 he founded the middle-class settlement Tel Tzur. A leader of the General Zionist party (see GENERAL ZIONISM), he was a member of the *Knesset from 1951 to 1955.

BOHEMIA AND MORAVIA, ZIONISM IN. This article deals with the history of the Zionist movement in Bohemia and Moravia until late 1918, that is, the period in which these two provinces formed the western part of Austria. For the subsequent history of Zionism in Bohemia and Moravia, see CZECHOSLOVAKIA, ZIONISM IN.

The first development of interest in the history of Zionism in Bohemia and Moravia-Silesia was the rise of a Jewish nationalist student society in Prague in 1836. Founded by Moritz Steinschneider (1816–1907), the bibliographer and Orientalist, a native of Prostějov (Prossnitz), Moravia, and Abraham Benisch (1811–78), the scholar and journalist, a native of Drossau (Drosau), near Klatovy (Klattau), Bohemia, this organization declared its aim to be the "reestablishment of Jewish independence in Palestine."

The violent struggle between Czech and German nationalist trends in the late 19th century made the Jews of Bohemia and Moravia-Silesia aware not only of modern nationalism but also of the fact that they, the Jews, were still regarded as foreign elements by the nations among which they lived. The first Bohemian Jews to join the Jewish nationalist movement were from the area where Czech rather than German culture predominated. These Jews had turned to Jewish nationalism in reaction to the cool reception the Czechs had given their expressions of sympathy with the struggle of the Czech people for intellectual, cultural, and political independence.

Even before the advent of Herzl a number of nationalist Jewish organizations calling themselves Zionist had sprung up in various Bohemian and Moravian cities. The first such group was founded in 1893 in the Bohemian town of Horaždovice (Horaschdowitz). It was soon followed by other groups in several small and middle-size Bohemian communities. In Moravia, too, Zionist societies and students' *Ferialverbindungen* (vacation societies) were formed by young people who had gone to study in Vienna because there were no universities in Moravia at the time. These groups were in touch with the pre-Herzlian Zionist movement under the guidance of Nathan *Birnbaum.

Moravia. The advent of Herzl and the 1st Zionist *Congress (Basle, 1897) had a strong impact on the Jews of Moravia and Silesia, who sent to Basle nine delegates, including Berthold *Feiwel, a native of Pohořelice (Pohrlitz) and the founder of the Veritas students' society in Brno (Brünn). Many other communities of the province sent greetings to the Congress. The Jewish nationalist movement in Moravia received added impetus from the anti-Semitic demonstrations that broke out in several Moravian cities, notably in Holešov (Holleschau), after the notorious Polna case (1899), in which a Jew, Leopold Hilsner, was accused of ritual murder (*see* ANTI-SEMITISM).

The first conference of Austrian Zionists was held in Olomouc (Olmütz), Moravia, in March, 1901. It was at this conference that Berthold Feiwel delivered the speech in which he set forth the aims of the Zionist movement and that the structure of the West Austrian Zionist Organization was formulated, with the provinces of Bohemia and Moravia-Silesia each forming one of the country's six Zionist districts.

Initially the seat of the Moravian Zionist Executive was Brno, the capital of the province. The first chairman of the committee was Max Hickl, who in 1900 founded the Zionist weekly *Jüdisches Volksblatt.* In 1910 Zionist headquarters was moved to Opava (Troppau), where Gustav Finzi succeeded Hickl as chairman. In 1917 the seat of the Executive was moved once more, this time to Bielsko (Bielitz), a town on the border between Silesia and Galicia (then Austrian Poland). This choice was an unfortunate one, for when the Austro-Hungarian Monarchy collapsed the following year, Bielitz was incorporated into Poland.

From the outset the Zionist movement in Moravia not only received much popular support but also proved highly effective in practical work, with the result that it soon gained considerable influence in most Moravian Jewish communities. After the founding of the Czechoslovak Republic the headquarters of the Zionist movement in the country remained in Prague, the national capital, only until 1921, when it was moved to Moravská Ostrava (Mährisch-Ostrau).

In addition to Feiwel, Finzi, and Hickl, prominent Zionists in Moravia included Rabbi Leopold Goldschmied, Friedrich Löwe, Adolf Pollak, Egon Michael Zweig, who led the work of the *Jewish National Fund, and, particularly, the physician Siegmund Werner of Jihlava (Iglau), who was Herzl's secretary and one of the editors of Die *Welt. Moravian-born Zionist leaders who later assumed important positions in the Zionist movement in Vienna included the poet Otto *Abeles, Rabbi David Feuchtwang of Mikulov (Nikolsburg), who later became chief rabbi of Vienna, Desider Friedmann, Oskar Grünbaum (later known as Joshua Guvrin and chairman of the Zionist Federation of Austria), Leopold Plaschkes (a member of the Vienna Municipal Council), and Robert *Stricker of Brno.

Bohemia. In Bohemia the progress of organized Zionism was a little slower than in Moravia. At the 1st Zionist Congress, Bohemian Jewry was represented by only one delegate, Rabbi David Neumark, who had come from Galicia that very year to assume the pulpit of a small congregation in Bohemia. Before long, however, many Bohemian Jews were drawn to Zionism by reports from the Congresses and also by the rude awakening dealt them by the rising tide of anti-Semitism, particularly in the German (Sudetenland) sector. The plight of the Bohemian Jews, caught between the conflicting Czech and German nationalist trends, was described by Herzl himself in an article, "Die Jagd in Böhmen" (The Hunt in Bohemia), in Die Welt (Nov. 5, 1897), signed with the pseudonym Benjamin Seff. Zionist organizations were formed in Prague and in smaller towns in Czech- as well as German-speaking areas. The 4th Zionist Congress (London, 1900) was attended by a sizable delegation from Bohemia.

Among the leading Zionists of Prague were Filip Lebenhart, Friedrich Mautner, and Karl Resek. Lebenhart, a popular orator and labor organizer, set up a Jewish People's Bank and in 1900 founded *Jung Juda,* a biweekly for Jewish youth. Resek was the first chairman of the provincial Zionist Executive of Bohemia, a position he held for a number of years, and a member of the World Zionist *Executive. These leaders remained loyal to Herzl even during the controversy set off by the *East Africa scheme, which threatened to tear the Zionist movement apart.

An important place in the history of Zionism in Bohemia is held by the *Bar Kokhba students' society of Prague, which was founded in 1899 and reached the peak of its activity during the decade preceding World War I. The central figure in this circle was Samuel Hugo *Bergmann. Among other Bar Kokhba leaders who later held important positions in the World Zionist movement were Oskar Epstein, Viktor Freud, Ernst Gütig, Leo and Hugo *Herrmann, Julian Herrnheiser, Sigmund Katznelson, Victor Kellner, Hans Kohn, Alfred Löwy, Friedrich Thieberger, and Felix and Robert *Weltsch. Some of these men were natives of Prague; others had been born in the Sudeten area. At a later date, they were joined by Max *Brod and gained the support of intellectuals such as Franz Kafka.

The Bar Kokhba circle was not content with purely political Zionist work. Known for its high intellectual level, it sought to effect a Jewish cultural and intellectual renaissance by rediscovery of the past literary creations of the Jewish people and by contact with Jewish cultural and communal life in Eastern Europe. Its views were close to those expressed by the *Democratic Faction and *cultural Zionism and, at a later date, to the ideas that characterized the *Halutz (pioneer) movement in Palestine, especially the teachings of Aharon

David *Gordon. It was under the auspices of Bar Kokhba that Martin *Buber delivered his "Three Lectures on Judaism" (1909–10). The influence of Buber, Feiwel, and Adolf *Böhm was readily discernible in the development of Bar Kokhba. Bar Kokhba took the initiative in the founding of the biweekly *Selbstwehr* (1907) and in the publication of an anthology, *Vom Judentum* (1913). During the conflict over the East Africa scheme, Bar Kokhba members were among the opponents of the plan; after Herzl's death they opposed the administration of David *Wolffsohn and supported practical work in Palestine (*see* PRACTICAL ZIONISM) and *Gegenwartsarbeit* and cultural activities in the *Diaspora. As Zionism spread to Czech-speaking student circles, the Theodor Herzl Student Society was founded (1909) as a counterpart to Bar Kokhba.

An entirely different type of student society was Barissia, which was founded in Prague in 1903 and whose organizational structure and trappings were patterned on the German *Couleur* student societies. Barissia stood for militant Zionism, supported the political Zionism of Wolffsohn and Max *Nordau, and raised a generation of devoted Zionist leaders. Among its founders was Walter Kohner, who later was to serve for many years as chairman of the Council of the Czechoslovak Zionist Territorial Federation.

The last few years before World War I saw the founding of the Blau-Weiss (*T'khelet-Lavan) youth movement in Bohemia and Moravia. Strongly influenced by German-Jewish youth movements, Blau-Weiss after the war developed into the Halutz movement.

World War I. Among other outstanding Zionists in Bohemia prior to World War I were Rabbi Heinrich (Hayim) *Brody, a noted scholar; Alfred Engel, an educator; Prof. Arthur *Mahler, an archeologist who was elected to the Austrian Parliament in 1907 after the introduction of universal suffrage; Emil *Margulies, an articulate advocate of political Zionism and Jewish nationality rights in the Diaspora; Ludwig *Singer, a native of Kolin and spokesman of the young Czech-speaking generation of Zionists, who in 1911 was elected chairman of the Executive of the Zionist Organization of Bohemia; and Hugo Zuckermann, a poet who was killed in action in 1914.

Despite the induction of many Zionist leaders into the armed forces and the precarious political situation, World War I did not stop Zionist activity in Bohemia and Moravia. The Zionists were in the forefront of the individuals and organizations aiding the Jewish refugees from Galicia, who poured into Bohemia and Moravia by the tens of thousands. At the same time, they continued their political and practical work, laying the foundations for many educational and social institutions. Aware of the impending political changes and their significance for the Jews of the region, the Zionist leadership in Prague under Ludwig Singer got in touch with the leaders of the Czech nationalist movement.

Early in October, 1918, national Jewish committees were set up in Prague and Brno. Immediately before the establishment of the Czechoslovak Republic at the end of October a Jewish National Council was set up under Singer's chairmanship. One of the vice-chairmen was Max Brod. This body succeeded in obtaining from the Czechoslovak government recognition of the Jews as a distinct nationality group in the new republic, with full civil and national minority rights. It also carried out a democratization of the official Jewish religious congregations and set up a central national body that included all the local religious congregations in the country.

In these and other endeavors the Zionist movement, led by Singer, assumed the leadership of Czechoslovak Jewry as a whole.

H. YAHIL

BÖHM, ADOLF. Zionist leader, publicist, and historian (b. Teplice-Šanov, Bohemia, Austria, 1873; d. Vienna, 1941). Böhm grew up in assimilationist surroundings, joining the Zionist movement only after the death of Herzl. He became one of the leading personalities and theoreticians of Zionism in the pre-World I period. From 1907 to 1911 he was, with Chaim *Weizmann and M'nahem M. *Ussishkin, one of the chief advocates of practical work in Palestine. Böhm was a member of the Greater *Actions Committee and of the Executive Committee of the *Jewish National Fund. An expert on Palestine, he served from 1910 to 1912 as editor of the monthly *Palästina*, which was devoted chiefly to the economic development of the country. He revived the publication in 1927 and edited it until its demise in 1938. Böhm was also the author of *Die zionistische Bewegung* (1920–21; second enlarged edition in two volumes, 1935–37), a standard work on the history of Zionism until 1925. He was working on a continuation of this study but was unable to complete it. Other publications were booklets on the Jewish National Fund (translated into several languages) and the *Keren HaYesod (Palestine Foundation Fund).

BOKHARAN JEWS IN ISRAEL. *See* BUKHARAN JEWS IN ISRAEL.

BONAVENTURA, ENZO. Psychologist and Zionist leader (b. Pisa, Italy, 1891; d. Jerusalem, 1948). A professor of philosophy, he was vice-president of the Italian Zionist Federation in the early 1920s and had a profound influence on the moral thinking of Jewish youth in Italy. Settling in Palestine in 1939, he served as professor of psychology at the *Hebrew University of Jerusalem from 1939 until he was killed in an Arab ambush of the convoy in which he was traveling to Mount Scopus, on Apr. 13, 1948.

G. ROMANO

BONDS OF ISRAEL. *See* STATE OF ISRAEL BONDS.

BONFIGLIOLI, RENZO. Italian-Jewish musicologist, bibliophile, art collector, philanthropist, and Zionist leader (b. Ferrara, Italy, 1904; d. there, 1963). Bonfiglioli held degrees in law and in political science. An active Zionist, he was interned during World War II in a concentration camp for anti-Fascists and was subsequently very active in the resistance movement. He served as president of the Jewish Community of Ferrara (1945–53), president of the Union of Italian-Jewish Communities (1952–53), and president of the Italian Zionist Federation (1962–63). During the last years of his life he was particularly active in the reorganization of the federation and in the revival of Zionist groups throughout Italy. He was a delegate to the Zionist Congresses (*see* CONGRESS, ZIONIST) held in Jerusalem in 1956 and 1960.

G. ROMANO

BOROCHOV, BER. Theoretician of the *Po'ale Zion movement (b. Zolotonosha, Ukraine, Russia, 1881; d. Kiev, Russia, 1917). Borochov received a secular education and independently studied literature, languages, philosophy, and sociology. He was a member of the Russian Social Democratic party (1900–01), but the party's attitude toward the Jewish problem led him to establish Po'ale Zion, one of the first groups to synthesize socialism and Zionism. Thereafter, he developed his "proletarian Socialist Zionist" ideology and published its fundamentals in Russian Zionist periodicals (*see* BOROCHOVISM). In 1906 Borochov published "Our Platform," which elucidated the Po'ale Zion party's aims and ideology.

Ber Borochov.
[Zionist Archives]

In 1907, after having been arrested and then released, Borochov left Russia and went to The Hague, where he helped found the World Union of Po'ale Zion and became its secretary. He traveled widely in Europe, spreading the ideas of proletarian Zionism and studying the Jewish workers' movement. His researches were eventually published in his statistical book *The Jewish Labor Movement in Figures* (1918). Following the outbreak of World War I, he went to the United States, where he was active not only in his party but on behalf of the *American Jewish Congress as well. He also helped the movement for the *Jewish Legion and wrote on the economic development of the Jewish people.

With the outbreak of the Russian Revolution, he returned to his native country, where he died in 1917 at the age of 36. In 1963 his remains were transferred to Israel. In addition to his political work and sociological studies, Borochov engaged in research in the Yiddish language, laying the groundwork for its scientific investigation. His collected works were published in Yiddish. Selections from his writings appeared in several languages, and Hebrew translations of his collected works were published from 1955 on.

G. KRESSEL

BOROCHOVISM. Theory of Jewish socialism, particularly Zionist socialism, formulated by Ber *Borochov. In 1905, in his polemics against Territorialism, Borochov characterized Zionism as realistic and at the same time idealistic, declaring that the predominant causal factor in the national Jewish movement was the acute suffering of the Jewish masses, and that the ideal toward which the movement was striving derived its impetus from the Jewish ethos. In Borochov's opinion, Zionism stood for the redemption of the Jewish people, the renaissance of Jewish culture, and the return to the ancestral Homeland.

In the same year Borochov set forth his ideas on a synthesis of Zionism and socialism. Basing his thesis on Karl Marx's theory, he defined a nation as a sociological entity deriving from conditions of production shared in common and united by the awareness of a common historic past. Each class within the nation had its own interest in the conditions of production, especially the factor of territory, which was the reservoir of all conditions of production. The proletariat had a vital interest in the territory as the locale of its activities and as the strategic basis for its class struggle. Since the proletariat was the most progressive class in the nation, its nationalism, in contradistinction to other nationalisms, was a realistic nationalism, aiming at the practical liberation of the nation, the normalization of working conditions, and the creation of circumstances conducive to true freedom in the search for national self-determination.

In 1906 Borochov published "Our Platform," the theoretical program of *Po'ale Zion, of which he was the leader in Russia. In subsequent articles he set forth the interest of the Jewish proletariat in Zionism and its task in the realization of the Zionist ideal. The conditions under which the Jewish people lived and worked were "extraterritorial." Such a nation, without an independent economic base, must of necessity become isolated, for the majority population in whose midst it lives will debar it from those areas of economy that are considered the preserve of the host nation. As a consequence, the Jews were consistently forced into the weakest and least important branches of production.

The field of activity and the basis for the strategic battle of the Jewish proletariat being therefore anomalous, the solution of the Jewish problem, according to Borochov, lay in the attainment of a geographical territory for the Jewish people. The Jewish bourgeoisie and the Jewish proletariat were both interested in this aim. The Jewish emigrant masses would inevitably concentrate in a certain territory. This territory, Borochov said, was the Land of Israel, because it was half agrarian and because the local population—he was speaking in the early part of the 20th century—had not yet crystallized into a socioeconomic organism able to compete with the capital and labor force of the Jews. Just as the will of the proletariat, operating through the class struggle, had a share in the developments inevitably leading to the fulfillment of the aims of socialism, so too the will of the class-conscious Jewish working masses played a role in the developments inevitably leading to the attainment of a geographical territory for the Jewish people.

The class struggle was also the only means through which the Jewish proletariat would be able to improve its own position and that of the entire Jewish people in the *Diaspora, by the democratization of communal life and the achievement of a maximum of national rights, that is, national political autonomy. The attainment of this autonomy was, of course, dependent on the democratization of the capitalist societies in the lands where the Jews resided.

The task of the Jewish proletariat was thus twofold. The Jewish proletarian masses who went to Palestine, together with Jewish capital, would there conduct the political and economic class struggle that would be directed also against the Turkish government, thus accelerating the attainment of national independence by the Jewish people in the land. Meanwhile, in the Diaspora, too, the Jewish proletariat would fight for the improvement of the condition of the Jewish people in their host countries. Both struggles were interdependent because any achievement on one front inevitably benefited the other.

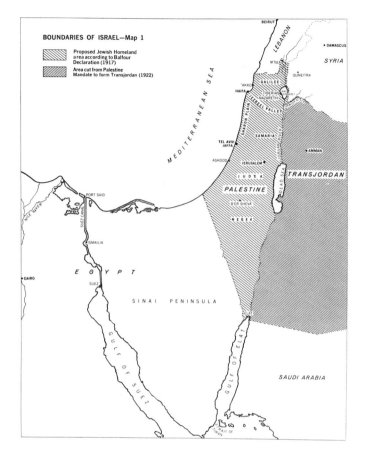

BOUNDARIES OF ISRAEL—Map 1

Proposed Jewish Homeland area according to Balfour Declaration (1917)

Area cut from Palestine Mandate to form Transjordan (1922)

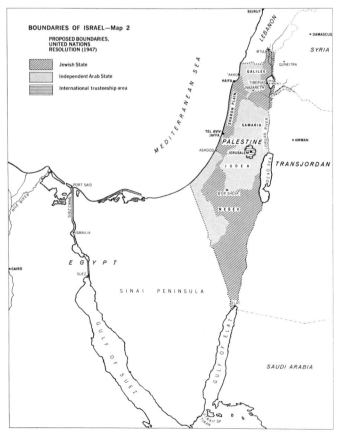

BOUNDARIES OF ISRAEL—Map 2

PROPOSED BOUNDARIES, UNITED NATIONS RESOLUTION (1947)

Jewish State

Independent Arab State

International trusteeship area

In the final year of his life Borochov made far-reaching changes in his philosophy. In his speech at the Russian Po'ale Zion conference held in September, 1917, in Kiev, a short time before his death, he stressed the necessity of elaborating on his ideology. In addition to striving for the concentration of the Jewish masses in the Land of Israel and for the achievement of Jewish territorial and political autonomy there, Zionism also aimed at the fulfillment of the people's desire to return to its Homeland. Borochov explained why, in the first decade of its existence, his party's ideology had not been concerned with this emotional element: the party had then still been young and it had conceived of life in strictly practical terms; but with the expansion and consolidation of the party, esthetic-cultural needs began to demand their due. The main reason for the absence of "romanticism" in its earlier programs, however, was the confrontation of the party with other Jewish parties. As against the General Zionists (*see* GENERAL· ZIONISM), who believed in volunteerism, the Po'ale Zion party stressed the inevitability of the historical process. In opposing the *Bund, the party had to purge its program of all "romanticism" so as not to be confused with the General Zionists. From then on Borochov regarded Palestine not only as the strategic basis for the struggle of the Jewish working class but also as the "basis for its constructive activities."

The workers' party that most closely followed classical Borochovism was the Left Po'ale Zion, which was formed in 1920.

R. MAHLER

BOSCOVICH, ALEXANDER URIA. Israeli composer and educator (b. Kolozsvár, Hungary, 1907; d. Tel Aviv, 1964). A native of what is now Cluj, Romania, he was on the staff of the Conservatory of Music in Tel Aviv and of the Israel Academy of Music, and he also served as music critic for *Ha'Aretz,* the liberal democratic daily. Boscovich was a proponent of the Eastern-Mediterranean school of music. His work exemplified a new florid musical style in Near Eastern melodic and rhythmical patterns and an instrumentation evoking the sound of Near Eastern ensembles.

P. GRADENWITZ

BOTZRA. Village (moshav) in the Sharon Plain. Founded in 1946 by veterans of the British armed services in World War II and affiliated with the *Ihud Haklai. Population (1968): 430.

BOUNDARIES OF THE STATE OF ISRAEL. In the five decades between the British conquest of Palestine (1917–18) and the *Six-day War of 1967, the boundaries of the Jewish Homeland underwent four major changes, as illustrated by Maps 1 to 4: the separation of *Transjordan from the rest of the *Mandate for Palestine (1922); the *partition resolution adopted by the United Nations (1947); the *armistice agreements (1949); and the cease-fire lines resulting from the Six-day War in June, 1967. Map 1 shows the area within which the Jewish Homeland was to be created according to the *Balfour Declaration (1917), and Transjordan, which was cut off from Palestine in 1922 by the British in an effort to conciliate the Arabs. Map 2 shows the Jewish State as proposed by the United Nations resolution of 1947 (heavily shaded area). The lightly shaded area shows the Palestine Arab State envisioned in the resolution. Map 3 shows the additional territory, primarily in Galilee and the Negev, held by Israel as delineated in the armistice agreements (1949) signed with Egypt, Jordan, and Syria. Map 4 shows the Israeli-held territory after June 10, 1967, including East Jerusalem, the Gaulan Heights, the West Bank, the Sinai Peninsula, and the Gaza Strip, in accordance with the United Nations cease-fire resolution accepted by Israel, the United Arab Republic, Jordan, and Syria.

BOYCOTT, ARAB. *See* ARAB BOYCOTT OF ISRAEL.

BOYS' TOWN, JERUSALEM. Secondary-level educational institution in the Bayit VeGan section of Jerusalem, founded in 1953. It provides a comprehensive program of academic, vocational, and spiritual training for teen-age youths. The idea of Boys' Town originated with Rabbi Alexander S. Linchner, formerly of New York, who in 1966 was dean and vice-president of the institution. Rabbi Jacob Leshinsky served as director. One-half of the 700 students enrolled in Boys' Town in 1967 were of Middle Eastern background. Almost half of the total were scholarship students. The extensive dormitory facilities were used by students from 68 Israeli communities.

The Israel Ministry of Defense adopted a proposal to establish special army industrial units of Boys' Town graduates, combining military training with industrial work and helping to bring skilled workers to development areas. The institution also set up a special Technical Teachers Training School at government request. In 1964 Boys' Town received the Ministry of Education and Culture Award for excellence and achievement. From the beginning the institution has been maintained and supported primarily by an American committee under the presidency of Ira Guilden.

I. WARKOFF

BRAININ, REUBEN. Hebrew literary critic, essayist, editor, publicist, and major figure in the renaissance of the *Hebrew language and literature (b. Lyady, Russia, 1862; d. New York, 1939). He gained fame with his first story, "G'sisat HaSofer" (The Writer's Agony, 1888), which seems to have been based on the last days of Peretz *Smolenskin.

Brainin was a harbinger of new trends in Hebrew literature. He widened the horizons of the Hebrew reader, introducing him to the creative forces, ideas, and beauty of modern Hebrew letters. He was among the first to write analytical, socioscientific studies on Hebrew works, in which the esthetic, impressionistic approach was dominant.

In Vienna, Brainin founded the magazine *MiMizrah Umi-Ma'arav* (From East and West, 1894–99), which served as a vehicle for his advanced literary concepts. He then moved to Berlin, where he was the leading spirit in the Welt Organisation für die Verbreitung der Hebräischen Sprache und Kultur (World Organization for the Dissemination of Hebrew Language and Culture). Among his many published biographies are those of Abraham *Mapu, Smolenskin, and the young Herzl. A close friend of Herzl, Brainin attended the 1st Zionist *Congress (1897). In 1909 he went to the United States, where he edited the Hebrew literary weekly *HaD'ror* (The Swallow).

From 1912 to 1915, Brainin edited a Yiddish daily, the *Canadian Eagle,* in Montreal, where he was one of the founders of the Canadian Jewish Congress and also founded the Jewish Public Library. Subsequently, he resumed his literary activities in the United States, where he edited *HaToren* (The Mast) and was a contributing editor to the Yiddish daily *Der Tog.*

After a visit to Palestine and the Soviet Union in 1926,

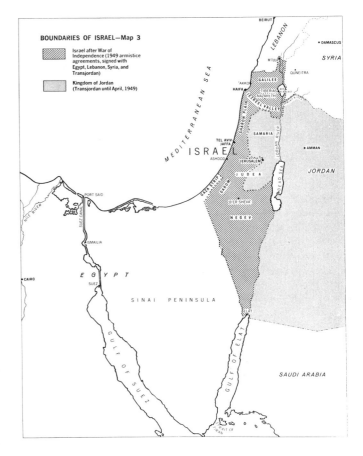

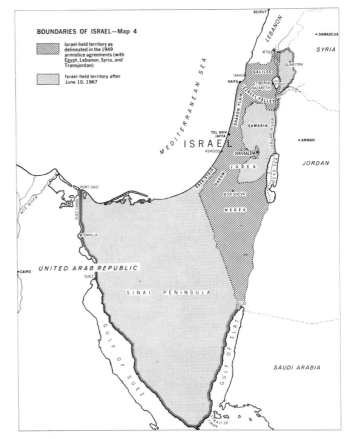

he approved and advocated Jewish colonization in the Soviet Union. This attitude made him a controversial figure and alienated him from some of his former colleagues. However, he remained a fervent Zionist and Hebraist until his death.

There are 102 volumes of his diaries in manuscript form in the *Jewish National and University Library, Jerusalem. The Brainin Archives, which contain his correspondence and other documents, are in a special room of the Jewish Public Library in Montreal.

H. LEAF

BRAND, JOEL EUGEN. Liaison worker in Jewish refugee activities (b. Naszód, Transylvania, Hungary, 1906; d. Bad Kissingen, Germany, 1964). Educated in Germany, Brand left home at the age of 18, worked his way around the world, and then returned to work as a clerk. He was jailed by the German authorities in 1933. Freed the following year, he immediately fled the country. He joined the Zionist Workers' movement in Budapest, becoming active in leftist political organizations. His activities on behalf of Jewish refugees from Poland brought him into contact with the German counterespionage, and from 1943 on he worked with Rezső *Kasztner in the rescue of Jewish refugees.

On May 19, 1944, at the instigation of Adolf Eichmann, Brand left German-occupied Hungary to convey to the *Jewish Agency representatives in neutral Turkey a German offer to spare Hungarian Jewry in exchange for military supplies. After meeting the Agency representatives on June 16, 1944, he continued en route to Palestine. The following day, however, he was arrested by the British in Aleppo, Syria; he was allowed to meet Moshe *Sharett but was transferred to detention in Cairo. His mission failed because the British refused to consider the German offer, and by the time Brand was freed in Jerusalem on Oct. 7, 1944, the Jews of the Hungarian provinces had already been sent to Auschwitz, where most of them were to perish.

Brand remained in Palestine. In the summer of 1964, he went to testify at the Frankfurt trial of the Nazis Hermann Krumey and Otto Hunsche. He died of a heart attack while in Germany and was buried in Tel Aviv.

J. MARTON

BRANDEIS, LOUIS DEMBITZ. Statesman, jurist, and World Zionist leader in the United States (b. Louisville, Ky., 1856; d. Washington, 1941). The son of immigrants from Prague, Brandeis graduated with high honors from Harvard Law School and soon became known as an outstanding lawyer. While working as a corporation lawyer, he embarked on an active policy of defense of the consumer and the workingman and earned a reputation as "the people's advocate." His broadly framed social philosophy and uncompromising adherence to principle brought him close to the progressive forces of American society and to Pres. Woodrow *Wilson. Writing to the Senate Committee on the Judiciary in 1916, Wilson said of Brandeis: "In every matter in which I have made test of his [Brandeis's] judgment and point of view, I receive from him counsel singularly enlightening, singularly clear-sighted and judicial, and above all, full of moral stimulation." On June 5, 1916, Wilson appointed him associate justice of the Supreme Court, the first Jew to hold that office. With Justice Oliver Wendell Holmes, Brandeis was the author of many dissenting opinions that differed radically from the majority of the Court in matters of social and economic policy.

Louis Dembitz Brandeis. [Zionist Archives]

Prior to and during the Wilson administration, Brandeis was in close touch with Wilson, who asked his advice on a variety of subjects. Brandeis retired from the Supreme Court in 1939. In the proceedings before the bar of the Supreme Court in his memory (Dec. 21, 1942), the resolution of the bar included this statement: "Mr. Justice Brandeis stands with a one half dozen giants of our law, wise, strong and good."

During the greater part of his life, Brandeis had no Jewish affiliation, religious or otherwise. His first contact with the Jewish masses occurred in 1910, when he was called on to arbitrate the garment workers' strike in New York, and he was impressed by the moral fiber of the Jewish working class and with its sense of solidarity. He was not drawn to Zionism until late in life, although he is reported to have said to his wife on reading a report of the 1st Zionist *Congress in 1897: "Here is a cause to which I could dedicate my life." It was not until his meeting with Jacob *de Haas, Herzl's former secretary, in Boston in 1912 that he evinced interest in Zionism. His association with the Zionist movement was first demonstrated by his acceptance of the chairmanship of a reception held in Boston in honor of Nahum *Sokolow in March, 1913.

In response to an appeal by De Haas in August, 1914, Brandeis, by accepting the chairmanship of the Provisional Executive Committee for General Zionist Affairs in the United States, assumed in fact the leadership of the Zionist movement in the country. Within a short time he transformed Zionism from the concern of a small group in the Jewish community into a dynamic and dominant factor on the American scene. From a membership of about 12,000 in 1914, the movement grew to 176,000 in 1919, and its budget from $15,000 to $3,000,000. Taking charge of the movement, giving his personal attention to political and organizational problems, drawing into Zionist ranks some of the finest Jewish talents of the day, Brandeis before long became the unchallenged leader of American Zionism. He was the moving spirit behind the movement for the creation of a democratically elected *American Jewish Congress that would represent American Jewry on questions concerning the future status of the Jews of Eastern Europe and Palestine in the settlement after World War I.

Brandeis dealt at length with the accusations of dual loyalty leveled against Zionism and rejected the melting-pot theory of Americanism, which envisioned the obliteration of ethnic differences and would bring forth a homogeneous nation claiming the undivided loyalty of its members. He advocated what has come to be known as cultural pluralism or cultural democracy. The term he applied to what he regarded as the essential feature of true Americanism was "inclusive brotherhood." In his famous Fourth of July address at Symphony Hall, Boston, in 1915, he declared: "America has believed that in differentiation, not in uniformity, lies the path of progress." In his address "The Jewish Problem—How to Solve It" (originally delivered at the Eastern Council of the Central Conference of American Rabbis in New York in 1915 and widely distributed in pamphlet form), Brandeis concluded that Zionism, far from being inconsistent with American patriotism, was actually the inevitable consequence of true Americanism:

> Multiple loyalties are objectionable only if they are inconsistent. A man is a better citizen of the United States for being also a loyal citizen of his state, and of his city; for being loyal to his family, and to his profession or trade; for being loyal to his college or his lodge.... Every American Jew who aids in advancing the Jewish settlement in Palestine, though he feels that neither he nor his descendants will ever live there, will be a better man and a better American for doing so.

The first task of the Provisional Executive Committee was to organize relief for the Jews of Palestine, whose economic position had been undermined as a result of the war. With the help of the U.S. Navy, supplies were rushed to Palestine. At Brandeis's initiative, the American Ambassador in Constantinople kept a constant watch over Jewish interests in Palestine when the *Yishuv (Jewish population) was threatened by the unfriendly Turkish military authorities. Until the entry of the United States into the war in April, 1917, the Provisional Executive Committee was the financial as well as political mainstay of the Yishuv, then suffering from war privations and oppression at the hands of the Turkish authorities.

In accordance with the declared policy of the *World Zionist Organization (WZO), the Provisional Executive Committee and, later, the reorganized *Zionist Organization of America (ZOA) maintained an attitude of neutrality toward the belligerent camps as long as the United States was neutral. Numerous attempts by pro-German elements to infiltrate the ZOA were facilitated by the pro-German sentiments of American Jewry. Brandeis managed to keep these elements at arm's length. Banking on an Allied victory, Brandeis early in 1915 made unofficial contact with the British and French Ambassadors in Washington, putting before them the Zionist views on the future of Palestine. This contact was preceded by a discussion with President Wilson, who expressed his sympathy for Zionist aspirations. In May, 1917, contacts with Wilson became more frequent. It was Wilson who arranged for Foreign Secretary Arthur James *Balfour, who then headed the British mission to Washington, to confer with Brandeis on the Palestine question. Brandeis was also requested by Wilson to cooperate in collating the material that was to serve as the basis for the peace negotiations. From May to November, 1917, Brandeis was in constant touch with Chaim *Weizmann, who was then negotiating with the British for a pro-Zionist declaration, and, at Weizmann's request, made representations in Washington to secure American approval of the declaration. During this period Brandeis lent his support to the formation of a *Jewish Legion that would fight for Palestine as part of the British Army.

After the issuance of the *Balfour Declaration, Brandeis turned his attention to the elaboration of the principles that were to guide the upbuilding of the Jewish National Home in Palestine. True to his social philosophy, he drafted what later became the official program of the ZOA, the *Pittsburgh Program of 1918. It called for national ownership of land to prevent speculation and urged public ownership of natural resources and utilities and encouragement of cooperative measures in the development of agriculture and industry.

Brandeis remained in close touch with the Zionist delegation at the Paris Peace Conference in 1919 (see COMITÉ DES DÉLÉGATIONS JUIVES). In the summer of that year he visited Palestine. On his way back he stopped in Paris and London to confer with Zionist leaders. He again met Balfour and made strong representations to him regarding the anti-Zionist activities of some of the British administrators in Palestine. As a result of this intervention, some of the administrators were replaced by friendlier officers. In 1920, on the eve of the *San Remo Conference, which allotted the *Mandate for Palestine to Great Britain, Brandeis successfully intervened with Wilson for adjustment of Palestine's northern frontier.

At the head of a large delegation of American Zionists, Brandeis attended the *London Zionist Conference of 1920 and was elected its chairman. He was offered the presidency of the WZO; although he declined the offer, he did accept the honorary presidency. It was at this conference that a rift first appeared between Brandeis and the European Zionists led by Weizmann. Now that Britain had been entrusted with the implementation of the Balfour Declaration, Brandeis felt that the period of Zionist political action had virtually come to an end, the political interests of Zionism should be handled largely by the representatives of the Jewish community in Palestine, and the Zionist movement ought to concern itself primarily with the practical problem of rebuilding the Jewish Homeland. He considered it important to obtain the support also of those Jews who would not join the Zionist Organization. Most European Zionists, on the other hand, considered the era of political work and propaganda far from over and were also opposed to Brandeis's plan to draw into the Zionist *Executive prominent men of affairs, including non-Zionists, who would assume responsibility for the economic development of the National Home.

The establishment by the London Conference of the *Keren HaYesod (Palestine Foundation Fund) as the principal fund-raising agency of the WZO exacerbated relations between the American and European Zionists. In a memorandum drawn up by Brandeis on his return from London (the so-called Zeeland Memorandum), he reiterated the social principles embodied in the Pittsburgh Program but objected to the use of part of the philanthropic funds to be raised by Keren HaYesod for investment purposes. Investments, in his view, were to be promoted and carried out according to business principles and left to private initiative. Keren HaYesod funds were to be applied solely for purposes which, by the nature of things, were not remunerative, such as *land reclamation and development, public health, education, and initial expenses in land settlement. Brandeis repeatedly stressed that economic policy must be directed primarily toward making the new settlers self-reliant and, at the earliest possible time, self-supporting. In 1921, when Weizmann arrived in the United States to inaugurate the Keren HaYesod campaign, attempts to effect a reconciliation between him and Brandeis failed. Among American Zionists, the majority of whom were of recent European origin, opposition to Brandeis developed. Matters came to a head at the Cleveland Convention of the ZOA (June, 1921), in which Weizmann and other European Zionist leaders participated. The majority of the delegates sided with Weizmann. As a result, Brandeis and his associates withdrew from the leadership of American Zionism.

Thereafter, Brandeis confined his continuing interest in Palestine primarily to economic activity. He devoted his attention to the Palestine Cooperative Company, established under his guidance in 1920, which later absorbed the groups known as Palestine Development Leagues and the Palestine Development Council formed by his followers after 1921. The Palestine Cooperative Company became in 1925 the Palestine Economic Corporation (see PEC ISRAEL ECONOMIC CORPORATION), which played an important role in the economic life of the Yishuv. Brandeis encouraged plans for land settlement in the Negev and for securing a foothold in 'Aqaba (Elat), the extreme southern tip of the Negev. During the Anglo-Zionist crisis resulting from the promulgation of the *Passfield White Paper in 1930, Brandeis intervened with Pres. Herbert Hoover. Following Hitler's rise to power in 1933, Brandeis maintained close contact with Pres. Franklin D. *Roosevelt on Palestine developments. During the controversy over the *Peel Commission scheme of 1937 for the *partition of Palestine into two independent states, Brandeis insisted on the whole of Palestine as the legitimate area of a Jewish National Home.

Brandeis was an outstanding figure in the history of American Zionism. In addition to unflagging efforts for the Zionist cause, he set a personal example by making substantial contributions to Zionist funds and Palestine causes. In his will, after making provision for his wife and daughters, he bequeathed half of the residue of his considerable estate to the Palestine Endowment Funds, Inc., and *Hadassah, "to be used by each of them for the upbuilding of Palestine as a national home for the Jewish people." Although his essentially American approach to Zionism was criticized by many European Zionists, his Zionist philosophy and the principles he expounded for the economic development of the Jewish Homeland eventually gained a greater measure of appreciation and respect.

S. Z. ABRAMOV

BRANDEISISTS. *See* UNITED STATES OF AMERICA, ZIONISM IN.

BRAUDE, MARKUS (Mord'khai Z'ev). Rabbi and Zionist leader (b. Brest Litovsk, Russia, 1869; d. Haifa, 1949). Braude received a traditional and a general education in Galicia and later studied at the Universities of Berlin and Freiburg and at the Berlin Rabbinical Seminary. From 1900 to 1906 he was rabbi and preacher of the modern synagogue of Stanislav, Galicia (then in Austria; later Stanisławów, Poland). In 1908

he received a similar position in Łódź and served there until after the outbreak of World War II, when he escaped from German-occupied Poland. He arrived in Palestine in 1940.

Active in Zionist circles in Galicia from his youth, Braude helped found the *Jung Israel organization (1891) during his student days in Berlin. He was one of the builders and leaders of the Zionist Organization of Galicia and participated in the 1st (1897) and subsequent Zionist Congresses (*see* CONGRESS, ZIONIST). An advocate of Zionist participation in local national politics, he worked for the election of Zionist candidates to the Austrian Reichsrat (Parliament). In 1907 he was himself a candidate in Stanislav, and although he received a majority of the votes, the local Polish authorities, voiding a large number of votes cast in his favor, declared the Polish candidate elected.

In Łódź, Braude developed widespread Zionist and Jewish-national cultural activities. In 1912 he founded a new type of Zionist bilingual (Hebrew and Polish) high school. The school served as a model for similar institutions which came into being in many cities of independent Poland and were organized in a network headed by Braude. He also helped found (1928) the Institute for Jewish Studies in Warsaw. Braude was a member of the Polish-Jewish delegation to the Paris Peace Conference (1919) and from 1922 to 1927 was a deputy in the Polish Sejm (Parliament).

His memoirs, *Zikhronot* (1960), were published posthumously in Hebrew.

A. ALPERIN

BRAUDES (BROYDES), ABRAHAM. Hebrew poet and pioneer of Jewish labor organization in Palestine (b. Vilna, Russia, 1907). Braudes began his literary career while a student at a Hebrew high school in Vilna. In 1923 he went to Palestine as a *Halutz (pioneer) and spent his first years there working as a laborer in the building trades during the day and studying at night. He became a protégé of Hayim Nahman *Bialik, with whose support he was appointed in 1928 secretary-general of the *Agudat HaSofrim Ha'Ivrim B'Yisrael (Hebrew Writers' Association in Israel), a position he held until 1964. He published many volumes of poetry, for which he received several literary awards.

BRAUDES, REUBEN ASHER. Hebrew novelist (b. Vilna, Russia, 1851; d. Vienna, 1902). Braudes received a traditional education but in his early youth came under the influence of the *Haskala (the Jewish Enlightenment). He began his literary career with scholarly articles. Later he turned to belles lettres and journalism. In his articles he opposed excessive religious restrictions and pleaded for a more tolerant approach to secular culture. From 1876 to 1879 he lived in Lvov, Galicia, where he helped edit the periodical *HaBoker Or*. He moved with the periodical to Warsaw and later lived in Vilna. After the Russian pogroms of 1881 he went to Romania, where he joined the *Hoveve Zion movement and published a Yiddish periodical, *Yehudit*, devoted to the dissemination of its ideas. From 1884 to 1896 he lived again in Galicia, editing periodicals in Hebrew and Yiddish and spreading the ideas of Hoveve Zion. In 1896 he settled in Vienna. He was an early and ardent follower of Herzl, under whose direction he took charge of the Yiddish edition of *Die *Welt*.

A prolific writer, Braudes was the author of numerous articles and works of fiction, including two great novels, *HaDat V'haHayim* (Religion and Life, 1877) and *Sh'te HaK'tzavot*

(The Two Extremes, 1888). *HaDat V'haHayim* ranks high among the literary works of the Haskala period. In it Braudes presents a realistic though tendentious contest between the old and the new generations. *Sh'te HaK'tzavot* portrays the changing attitudes of emancipated Jews toward Jewish life and tradition and their attempts to synthesize traditional and modern ways of life.

H. LEAF

BRAZIL, ZIONISM IN. Jews first went to Brazil in the 16th century as Marrano refugees from the Portuguese Inquisition. Most of the first Jewish immigrants were of Sephardi origin (*see* SEPHARDIM) and settled in the northern states, especially Pernambuco, Amazonas, and Pará. In the 17th century, Jewish immigrants came primarily from Amsterdam. They settled in Recife, in the north of the country, where their situation was good under Dutch rule. When the Portuguese defeated the Dutch, most of the Jewish population was forced to flee. However, some Jewish groups remained in the country, mainly in Belém.

Only in the latter half of the 19th century did *Ashkenazim come to Brazil. They came from England, Germany, France, Austria, and Eastern European countries, some as emigrants and some as representatives of European business concerns. Most of them settled in Rio de Janeiro and in the states of São Paulo and Minas Gerais. Many families in these communities became assimilated.

The present Brazilian Jewish community is of recent origin. Large numbers of Jewish immigrants from Eastern European countries reached Brazil after World War I, and since the 1920s Sephardi Jews have come from Turkey and Syria. Late in the 19th and early in the 20th century, the *Jewish Colonization Association (ICA), as part of its Argentine colonization plan, purchased a large tract of land near the Argentinian border in the far south of Brazil, in the state of Rio Grande do Sul. Its colonies failed to prosper, however, and most of the colonists left to settle in Pôrto Alegre, the state capital, which in 1968 had the third largest Jewish community in Brazil (12,000 inhabitants). Rio de Janeiro and São Paulo were the cities with the largest Jewish communities (50,000 and 70,000 inhabitants, respectively). Whereas in 1914 there were only 7,000 Jews in Brazil, by 1968 their numbers had increased to 140,000.

Early Years. At the beginning of the 20th century there was a nucleus of a Zionist group in the city of Belém. Its members exchanged correspondence with leaders of the Zionist movement, among them Max *Nordau. In March, 1913, a meeting held in the home of Jacob Schneider in Rio de Janeiro marked the foundation of what was for all practical purposes the first organized Zionist group in the country.

The year 1915 saw the appearance, in Pôrto Alegre, of Brazil's first Yiddish weekly, *Die Menshheit*. In 1916 a Portuguese-language weekly, *A Coluna* (The Pillar), appeared in Rio de Janeiro. It was edited by Dr. David José Pérez, a young intellectual of Sephardi descent, and was openly Zionist-oriented.

The group of Rio de Janeiro, which adopted the name Tiferet Zion, began its work with a campaign in behalf of the *Jewish National Fund. In 1916 a committee to raise funds for the relief of war victims was created by the *American Jewish Joint Distribution Committee (JDC) in Rio de Janeiro. Following instructions from the *World Zionist Organization, with which it had been in touch from the outset, Tiferet Zion requested and, after lengthy debates with anti-Zionists on the war relief com-

mittee, received an allocation from the funds raised in the JDC campaign.

By 1916 Rio de Janeiro had a Jewish school under the principalship of Saadiyahu Lozinsky, a member of the *Mizrahi movement. When the *Balfour Declaration was issued in 1917, Tiferet Zion sent a message of appreciation to the British government through the British Embassy in Rio de Janeiro.

Between the Two World Wars. In 1921 the first *Keren HaYesod (Palestine Foundation Fund) campaign was launched in Brazil. When D. I. Wilensky, the emissary sent to Brazil for this purpose, landed in Recife, he was met by Jacob Schneider and taken to Maceió and Salvador. He then went to Rio de Janeiro, São Paulo, and other cities, where Zionist groups had been founded despite their small Jewish populations.

In 1922 the first conference of delegates representing all the Zionist organizations in the country met under the chairmanship of Mauricio Klabin. At this conference, the Zionist Federation of Brazil was founded with Jacob Schneider as president and Eduardo Horowitz, who had been the secretary of Tiferet Zion since 1917, as secretary. The federation began holding biennial conventions. Growing steadily because of immigration from Eastern Europe, it soon assumed a leading role in Brazilian Jewish life. The various Zionist groups all over the country became active in many fields, including the organization of a system of Jewish education. In those early days, the General Zionists (*see* GENERAL ZIONISM) were the predominant element in the federation.

In 1926 Nathan Becker, Naphtali Jaffe, Moses Costa, and others organized Brazil's first *Po'ale Zion group. They paid special attention to educational problems, establishing Jewish schools in which Hebrew was taught as well as courses for adults. The arrival in Brazil (1927) of Aaron Bergman, noted Polish journalist and Po'ale Zion leader, gave added impetus to the growth of Po'ale Zion in the country, the younger generation being attracted in large numbers. Subsequently, other Zionist parties also arose, each acting independently and working with the others only for fund-raising purposes. The steady growth of the Jewish community in Brazil led to the formation of a number of new institutions but also to ideological differentiation, since the immigrants tended to transplant to the new country the ideas and attitudes that had prevailed in their countries of origin. Most of the arrivals during this period were from Eastern European countries.

In 1924 Kadima, the first Zionist youth organization in Brazil, was founded in Rio de Janeiro. This group engaged in cultural activities, raising funds for various Zionist endeavors and for the first campaign to be conducted in Brazil on behalf of the *Hebrew University of Jerusalem. The organization was disbanded in 1928.

In 1928 the HaT'hiya Library was established in Rio de Janeiro to take the place of the Sholom Aleichem Library, which had come under the control of Progressive elements. HaT'hiya soon became the first nucleus of *Halutziyut (pioneering) in Brazil, under the influence of the Po'ale Zion. The first members of this group emigrated to Palestine in 1934. Among the leading members of HaT'hiya at that time were Sh'lomo Steinberg, Sh'muel Griver, Dr. Zvi Lerner (who died in Israel in 1965), and Dov Zaigarnikas, who belonged to the first group of Halutzim (pioneers).

In 1929, at the conclusion of a mass demonstration in Rio de Janeiro, a memorandum was handed to the British Embassy for forwarding to the British Mandatory authorities (*see* MAN-

DATE FOR PALESTINE). It protested the refusal of the authorities to take positive action to stop Arab attacks on Jews in Palestine (see ARAB RIOTS IN PALESTINE). Under the dictatorship of Getúlio Vargas, from 1937 to 1945, all foreign political activity was banned. This meant the end also of the political work of Brazil's Zionist movement, which thereafter confined its activities to the maintenance of its schools and to collections for the Jewish National Fund.

World War II and after. When, during World War II, a war relief committee was organized in Brazil on the initiative of the *World Jewish Congress, the Zionist leaders requested that 50 per cent of the proceeds of the war relief campaign be turned over to the Keren HaYesod. After some debate, this request was granted.

In July, 1945, the ban on Zionist activity in Brazil was lifted. The General Zionists and Po'ale Zion established contact with each other for the purpose of founding a united Zionist organization based on individual membership. That November the Histadrut HaAhida (United Federation) of Brazil was founded. All Zionist parties and adherents participated in the federation, and branches were formed throughout the country. Jacob Schneider was chosen chairman and Samuel Malamud secretary-general.

The new Zionist organization developed an intensive program. In 1946, under the leadership of its secretary-general, it set up a Political Committee. The task of this committee, which included Eduardo Horowitz, Naphtali Jaffe, Aaron Bergman, and Jacob Schneider, was to mobilize public opinion in favor of Zionism. Later that year mass meetings were held throughout Brazil, with Brazilian political and intellectual leaders participating, to protest the arrest of the leaders of the *Jewish Agency in Palestine by the British Mandatory authorities. Soon thereafter, the Political Committee helped organize a Pro-Palestine Committee. This committee, of which Prof. Ignacio Azevedo Amaral, then chancellor of the University of Brazil, was chairman, distributed propaganda and educational material edited by the committee's secretary, Leão Padilha. Sen. Hamilton Nogieira, vice-president (later president) of the committee, made a speech on the floor of Parliament urging Brazilian support of Pres. Harry S *Truman's proposal to admit 100,000 Jewish refugees into Palestine immediately.

At the time of the United Nations debate (see UNITED NATIONS AND PALESTINE-ISRAEL) on the *partition of Palestine, the Zionist organization of Brazil made every effort to secure the support of the Brazilian government for the plan. Led by Horacio Lafer, a Jewish member of the House of Deputies, a parliamentary delegation representing all political parties obtained an interview with the Foreign Minister. Telephone conversations were held with Brazilian Ambassador Oswaldo Aranha, who was then President of the UN General Assembly and who had received a telegram from his own mother urging him to support the partition plan.

With the renewal of Zionist work in Brazil in 1945, several youth organizations, among them *HaShomer HaTza'ir, *B'rit Trumpeldor (Betar), and Ihud HaNo'ar HaHalutzi (*D'ror-*Gordonia), were founded. After the rise of the Jewish State, hundreds of young people took training in Hakhsharot agricultural training centers (see HAKHSHARA) and then settled in Israel, where they established kibbutzim such as B'ror Hayil and Ga'ash. A number of young men and women from Brazil saw service in the *War of Independence. From 1948 to 1968, 3,400 Jews from Brazil emigrated to Israel.

Under the auspices of the Zionist organization, children's groups went to Israel each year for a month's visit and young men and women were sent to attend seminars of a year or longer. In Brazil itself, the Zionist organization built a number of new schools in the 1960s, sponsored Hebrew courses in many of the larger Jewish communities, and published the periodical *Aunde Vamos.* The organization also called periodic conferences to plan its various activities and to elect its Executive Board and Council. In the mid-1960s it continued to be the most important institution of Jewish life in Brazil, working through its various departments for the State of Israel as well as for Jewish cultural and traditional life in Brazil itself.

In 1968, apart from the Zionist organization, there were in Brazil two Zionist women's organizations, the *Women's International Zionist Organization (WIZO) and the *Pioneer Women. WIZO, the older of the two, had been founded after World War II. Both organizations had a large membership and were quite active, particularly in the mobilization of young women for Zionist work in Brazil.

S. MALAMUD

B'REKHYA. Village (moshav) in the Darom. Founded in 1950 by Tunisian immigrants and affiliated with *T'nu'at Ha-Moshavim. Population (1968): 720.

BRENNER, YOSEPH HAYIM. Hebrew writer and pioneer in the Palestinian labor movement (b. Novy Mlini, Ukraine, Russia, 1881; d. Jaffa, 1921). After receiving a traditional Jewish education and studying at a Yeshiva, Brenner went to Gomel, where he was drawn into the Jewish labor movement and became secretary to Mord'khai ben Hillel *Hacohen. At that time he

Yoseph Hayim Brenner.
[Zionist Archives]

came under the influence of Fyodor Dostoyevsky and Leo Tolstoy and began to write. At the turn of the 20th century he lived in Białystok and Warsaw, where he eked out his subsistence by teaching Hebrew. In 1901 his first book, a collection of short stories, was published in Warsaw. Late that year he was drafted into the Russian Army, but on the outbreak of the Russo-Japanese War in 1904 he was smuggled out of the country.

Settling in London, Brenner found employment in a print shop, became active in the *Po'ale Zion movement, and from 1906 to 1907 published *HaM'orer,* a Hebrew monthly, which exerted considerable influence on the young generation of the *Second 'Aliya. When lack of funds forced him to cease publication, he went to Lvov, where he worked as a typesetter on a Yiddish daily and published (1908–09) *R'vivim,* a periodical that later appeared briefly in Jerusalem and Jaffa. In 1909 he emigrated to Palestine, where he became a regular contributor to various newspapers and the publicist of the Second 'Aliya generation.

During World War I Brenner taught at the *Herzliya High School in Tel Aviv. When the British occupied Palestine, he went to Jaffa, where he took part in the publication of *HaKuntres,* the weekly of the *Ahdut 'Avoda movement, and later edited the literary monthly *Ha'Adama.* Late in 1920 he moved to Galilee, where he worked on road construction projects and taught Hebrew at *Halutz (pioneer) camps. In 1921 he participated in the founding conference of the Jewish labor federation *Histadrut. In May, 1921, he was killed in the *Arab riots in Jaffa. The kibbutz Giv'at Brenner, in the Judean Plain, is named for him.

Brenner wrote short stories, the play *Beyond the Frontiers,* and several novels, including *MiSaviv LiN'kuda* (Around the Point, 1904) and *Sh'khol V'Khishalon* (Bereavement and Failure, 1920), and translated many Russian and German works into Hebrew. His penetrating observations and pessimistic, at times cruel, descriptions truthfully mirrored the difficulties faced by his generation in Russia and Palestine. His works depict the wretched life of a people lacking an independent material and spiritual basis—a life of anomalies and purposeless, unending agony. Brenner encouraged young writers and felt a special kinship with young workers who wrote of their lives and problems. His collected works were published in eight volumes in Tel Aviv (1924–30).

G. KRESSEL

BRESSLER, MAX. Jewish communal and Zionist leader in the United States (b. Ukraine, Russia, 1901; d. Miami, Fla., 1966). Active in Zionism in Russia during the Russian Revolution, he continued his Zionist work after his arrival in the United States in 1920 and was active in the *Zionist Organization of America, of which he was president from 1960 to 1962.

Bressler was national president of the *Jewish National Fund, a member of the National Cabinet of the *United Jewish Appeal, and chairman of the Guardians of the *State of Israel Bonds Organization. He was also prominently associated with Jewish educational institutions in the United States and Israel. In 1966 he was a board member of the *Weizmann Institute of Science, *Bar-Ilan University, and the American Friends of the *Hebrew University of Jerusalem and was also a member of the Zionist *Actions Committee.

BREUER, ISAAC. Attorney and leader of *Agudat Israel (b. Pápa, Hungary, 1883; d. Jerusalem, 1946). He grew up in Frankfurt on the Main, where he studied at the Yeshiva directed by his father, Solomon Breuer, who was rabbi of the Secessionist Orthodox Jewish community of the city. Breuer also studied at a number of German universities. While practicing law, he engaged in widespread communal and literary activities. He was a founder of the ultrareligious movement Agudat Israel, representing its pro-Palestine wing. While rejecting secular Jewish nationalism, he advocated reconstruction activities in Palestine, stating that his aim was to make "our people turn to the Land, and the Land turn to our people, and both turn to the God of the people and of the Land." He was the director of the Keren HaYishuv (Palestine Fund) of Agudat Israel. In 1936 he settled

in Palestine, where he continued to serve in the leadership of Agudat Israel and was also president of *Po'ale Agudat Israel.

Breuer represented Agudat Israel before governmental bodies and commissions. In his final appearance on its behalf, he testified before the *Anglo-American Committee of Inquiry, strongly defending the Jewish rights to Palestine. A prolific writer, he was the author of a number of religious philosophical works and of essays on Agudist ideology. He also wrote several novels with religious themes.

BRIDGE IN BRITAIN. Independent British nondenominational, nonpolitical organization that cooperates with its Israeli counterpart, Bridge in Israel, in arranging "bridging" schemes. By encouraging and enabling actual and potential leaders in communal and social work to study and serve in exchange projects between Britain and Israel, these programs seek to promote good citizenship in Britain and Israel and goodwill between the two countries.

In 1965 Bridge in Britain operated a four-point program: (1) scholarship awards to young men and women between the ages of 18 and 30 from Britain and Commonwealth countries, to enable them to work in Israel without pay during the summer, (2) six-week summer work tours of Israel for groups of schoolboys accompanied by their teachers, (3) a six-month social or agricultural service period in Israel for young people from Britain and Commonwealth countries who had completed their secondary education and were waiting to enter a university or a technical college, and (4) three- and four-week visits to Britain by Israeli youngsters in organized groups accompanied by their leaders. During the period from 1961 to 1964 some 200 British youngsters visited Israel and an equal number of young Israelis visited England as part of the Bridge program. In 1965 Jews as well as non-Jews served as officers of the organization, of which the Duke of Edinburgh, husband of Queen Elizabeth II, was an honorary member.

H. PINNER

B'RIHA. Mass migration of Jews from Eastern Europe to Western and Southern Europe between 1944 and 1948; also, the name of the organization, B'riha (Heb., "Flight"), that facilitated the movement. During World War II, Jews in German-occupied territories attempted to cross Europe's frontiers to save their lives. Some groups were organized by Zionist youth movements with the aim of getting Jews to Palestine. With the end of the war, many of the survivors were unwilling to rebuild their lives in the countries in which their brothers had been murdered and in the midst of populations that had assisted in the massacres. Thus a Palestine-oriented mass exodus began. Late in 1944 Jewish partisans in the Vilna and Rovno areas, led by Abba *Kovner and Eliezer Lidovsky respectively, and consisting mostly of members of Zionist youth movements (*HaShomer HaTza'ir, *D'ror, *HaNo'ar HaTziyoni, *B'rit Trumpeldor), combined to take Jews from the Soviet Union to Romania. After a failure at Cernăuți (Chernovtsy), a coordinating committee in which returnees from the Soviet Union and ghetto fighters from Warsaw participated was set up in Lublin, Poland, in January, 1945. After Kovner's departure for Romania in February, the B'riha command passed to Mordecai Rosman (until May, 1945) and then to Moshe Meiri (until December, 1945), subject to the authority of the B'riha committee representing all Zionist groups. Between February and May, 1945, some 1,500 persons crossed illegally into Romania, where they were received by Palestinian emissaries. Disappointed in their hopes for an early departure for Palestine, they reached Italy after passing through Hungary and Yugoslavia and the Graz area of Austria, where they set up B'riha points. After May, 1945, the Polish B'riha sent people directly via Bratislava and Vienna or Budapest. Some 15,000 persons, aided by *Jewish Brigade units, entered Italy. Another 12,000 remained in the Graz area and gradually infiltrated Italy in late 1945. B'riha points in Aš and Prague transferred others to Germany and Austria. Beginning in February, 1946, the return of 175,000 refugees from the Soviet Union to Poland created a large new reservoir for the Polish B'riha.

Late in June, 1945, the Palestinian soldiers of the Jewish Brigade established contact with Jewish displaced persons in Central Europe, and small-scale transfer to Italy soon gave way to large-scale organization, dovetailing with the earlier Polish B'riha. A committee (Merkaz LaGola) put Mordecai Surkiss in charge of operations. Beginning in September, 1945, the Mosad L'Aliya Bet ("illegal" immigration center, under Shaul Avigur) in Palestine sent emissaries who took over command in Vienna (Asher Ben Natan), Germany (Ephraim Frank), and Poland (Itzhak *Ben Zvi), though in Poland actual control remained in the hands of local youth movements until the spring of 1946. Jewish chaplains in the United States Army helped whenever they could.

After October, 1945, B'riha directed the flow of refugees to Germany, Italy having been "flooded" with 23,000 displaced persons. The main transit center was at the Rothschild Hospital in Vienna. Some groups, mainly members of youth movements, went to Italy, where they filled the reservoir for "illegal" immigration.

After the July, 1946, pogrom in Kielce, a frantic exodus from Poland began. Through the mediation of the *American Jewish Joint Distribution Committee, the Czechoslovak government agreed to provide transit facilities to Bratislava. An agreement with Poland allowed unofficial but legal exit via Kudowa and Náchod. Between July 1 and Sept. 30, 1946, a total of 73,000 Jews left Poland with B'riha. During the winter months the movement slackened, but it was resumed in the spring of 1947 with the unorganized flight of some 17,000 Jews from Romania. Money usually came through indirect channels from the Joint Distribution Committee. B'riha was aided by important Jews in Europe and unofficially by most of the European governments. An approximate total of 250,000 Jews left Eastern Europe with B'riha or in its wake. Of these, 170,000 came from Poland (63,000 in 1945, 100,000 in 1946, 6,000 in 1947). Some 35,000 came from Romania and the rest mainly from Czechoslovakia and Hungary. European commanders of B'riha were Ephraim Dekel (1946–48) and Meir Sapir. Tapering off after the establishment of the State of Israel, B'riha was dissolved early in 1950, after another 17,000 Jews had reached Austria from Eastern European countries. The quarter of a million refugees constituted the largest migratory movement organized by Jews in modern times. They formed the large reservoir in Central Europe's displaced-persons camps whose pressure was instrumental in the establishment of the State of Israel.

Y. BAUER

BRILL, YEHIEL. Hebrew journalist (b. Podolia, Russia, 1836; d. London, 1886). While still young, he went to Constantinople and from there made his way to Palestine. Together with Yoel Moshe *Salomon and Michael Hacohen, he established a print-

ing press in Jerusalem and, in 1863, published *HaL'vanon,* the first Hebrew periodical in the country, which was closed a year later because it lacked a government permit. Brill then proceeded to Paris, where in 1865 he resumed publication of *HaL'vanon,* which appeared as a weekly starting in 1868. It ceased publication in 1870 but reappeared a year later in Mainz, Germany, in the form of a Hebrew supplement to the local Orthodox periodical *Der Israelit* of Dr. Marcus Lehmann. From 1873 on, Brill also published in Mainz *HaYisraeli,* a weekly in Yiddish.

Brill was an early adherent of the *Hoveve Zion movement, collaborating with Rabbi Sh'muel *Mohilever in his efforts to establish a colony for Russian Jews in Palestine. After Mohilever had secured the support of Baron Edmond de *Rothschild, Brill accompanied him to Russia. Toward the end of 1882, Brill went to Palestine at the head of a group of settlers from the village of Novo-Pavlovka, near Ruzhany in Grodno District, and helped them find suitable land for settlement. He returned to Europe six months later and described the venture of these immigrants, who later founded Kiryat 'Ekron, in a book, *Yesud HaMa'ala* (1883). Brill later settled in London, where he established a Yiddish periodical, *HaShulamit.* In 1886, a few months before his death, he resumed publication of *HaL'vanon,* of which 11 issues subsequently appeared.

I. KLAUSNER

B'RIT HAHAYAL. Association of Jewish reservists in the Polish Army, formed in December, 1932, in Radom, Poland. In February, 1933, the Radom group set up the first branch of the association in Warsaw, with the aim of "taking part in the struggle of the Jewish people for the reconstruction of the Jewish State on both sides of the Jordan." The association recognized Vladimir *Jabotinsky as its political and spiritual leader.

Thirty-one Polish branches participated in the first meeting, which took place in Warsaw in August, 1933. A provisional High Command was elected. The first conference of the association, which was convened in Warsaw in October, 1933, with Jabotinsky and 1,500 delegates present and 170 branches represented, accepted as its program the basic principles of Revisionism (*see* REVISIONISTS), including the priority of national interests over individual concerns. Freedom of conscience, based on respect for the values of Jewish tradition, was also accepted as one of the basic principles of the association. Growing militant *anti-Semitism impelled B'rit HaHayal to include in its otherwise Palestine-centered program the task of organizing units for the defense of Jewish life, dignity, and property in Poland.

By the end of 1934, branches of the association had been set up in eight European countries. The first world conference of B'rit HaHayal was convened in Cracow in January, 1935. The conference endorsed the program formulated by the Polish group and decided to establish regional military and political training schools for members of the association.

The organization was modeled on the army unit and based on strict discipline with a well-defined chain of command. At the outbreak of World War II, B'rit HaHayal claimed a total of 25,000 members in Argentina, Belgium, Danzig, Estonia, France, Greece, Latvia, Lithuania, Poland, Romania, and Palestine.

I. BENARI

B'RIT HAKANA'IM. *See* JEWISH STATE PARTY.

B'RIT HALUTZIM DATIYIM (Bachad). Religious pioneering Zionist youth movement. *See* MIZRAHI.

BRITISH JEWS IN ISRAEL. It was estimated that in 1966 some 8,000 to 10,000 British Jews were living in Israel, with each year bringing an average of 700 new arrivals from the British Isles. Jews from Britain were to be found chiefly in the liberal professions, public administration, and agriculture and less prominently in commerce and industry. In the days of Turkish rule, British immigrants were rare in Palestine, but there are records of one Elijah Goodall (1841–1932), who came to Jerusalem in 1868 and initiated long-term mortgage facilities to encourage the creation of new suburbs outside the walls of the Old City, and of Zerah Barnett, a London tailor who was one of the founders of Petah Tikva.

In the early 1900s the *Order of Ancient Maccabeans, a British Zionist organization, acquired land at Gezer, but this was not followed up by any settlement of British Jews there. On the other hand, four pioneers from Glasgow were among the original settlers of the moshav Merhavya in 1911. Some of the intellectual leaders of British Zionism, including Herbert *Bentwich and Israel *Zangwill, visited Palestine in those days, and one of Bentwich's daughters, Mrs. Nita Lange, settled there in 1912. Miss Annie Landau came from London in the early 1900s to serve as principal of the Evelina de Rothschild School, an institution supported by the *Anglo-Jewish Association, and set a tradition in which devotion to Orthodox Judaism was synthesized with a high sense of civic duty.

The arrival of the *Jewish Legion in 1917 produced the first group of British Jews to settle in Palestine. Six Jewish officers of the legion stayed on in the country. They included Capt. Thomas Coussin, of Glasgow, who was paymaster in the British Mandatory Police Force and later head of the Pay Department of the Israel Police Force; Julius Jacobs and Victor Levy, both of whom were among the most senior Jewish civil servants in the British Mandatory government (*see* MANDATE FOR PALESTINE) and were to meet a tragic death in the King David Hotel explosion in 1947; and Lieut. Leon *Roth, who later became professor of philosophy at the *Hebrew University of Jerusalem.

Among the Anglo-Jewish officials who served with the mandatory government under Sir Herbert *Samuel, *High Commissioner for Palestine, were Edwin *Samuel, son of Sir Herbert, who founded the Institute of Public Administration in the country; Norman *Bentwich, who was Attorney General for a time; and Mordekhai *Nurock, who later became Israel's Minister to Australia. No less than seven sons and daughters of Herbert Bentwich made their home in Palestine during this period, which also saw the first attempt at Anglo-Jewish group settlement on the land. The first London Ahuza (*see* AHUZA SOCIETIES), headed by David Harris, founded the village of Karkur in 1911, braving malaria as well as the attacks of Arab marauders.

Anglo-Jewish settlers in Palestine soon after World War I included Cecil Hyman, later Israel's Minister to South Africa; Elias *Epstein, a senior *Jewish National Fund official and later director of the ZOA House in Tel Aviv; and Prof. Saul Adler, F.R.S., a world-famous parasitologist. In the 1930s these were followed by David Goitein, a London jurist who, at the time of his death, was a justice of Israel's Supreme Court, and Henry E. Baker, an Oxford-trained lawyer who subsequently became presiding judge of the Jerusalem District Court.

Because of severe mandatory government regulations restrict-ing Jewish *immigration, the limited quotas of *Halutz (pioneer) certificates made available to the *World Zionist Organization were distributed to those Eastern European Jews who lived under unstable regimes. Prior to the founding of the British *HeHalutz in 1932, there was no substantial *'Aliya (immigration) movement in British Zionism.

The first graduates of Britain's HeHalutz arrived in Palestine in the midst of the *Arab riots of 1936, and later moved up to what were then malarial swamps in the Hula area, founding the *HaBonim village of K'far Blum in 1943. In subsequent years, British pioneers set up K'far HaNasi (HaBonim) on the Syrian border; the kibbutz Labi (*B'rit Halutzim Datiyim, or Bachad); the kibbutzim Yas'ur and Zikim (*HaShomer HaTza'ir); the kibbutzim 'Ami'ad and Bet Ha'Emek (both HaBonim); HaBonim and Bet Hever (Moshavim Shitufiyim; *see* MOSHAV SHITUFI); K'far Mord'khai (middle-class moshav), near G'dera; and Massu'ot Yitzhak (Moshav Shitufi of HaPo'el HaMizrahi; *see* MIZRAHI).

In 1944 a movement was founded in London to attract the professional and technical workers in British Zionist ranks who had no place in the conventional "Halutz" or "capitalist" categories. This movement, known as PATWA (*see* PROFESSIONAL AND TECHNICAL WORKERS 'ALIYA), organized its members in professional groupings (physicians, nurses, engineers, administrators, scientists, etc.) and encouraged them to study Hebrew. PATWA's first chairman was Dr. Eli David (subsequently professor of internal medicine at the Hebrew University–*Hadassah Medical School), and Walter *Eytan (subsequently Israel's Ambassador to France) was its first honorary secretary. PATWA's charter members were drawn from the ranks of professional men and women who had been active during the preceding 10 to 15 years in the University Zionist Federation, HaBonim, and the Association of Young Zionist Societies.

In 1948 hundreds of young idealists from the British Isles went to help Israel in the *War of Independence in the ranks of *Mahal, and in 1949 the small group of PATWA members already settled in the land helped establish the British Mahal Resettlement Office in Tel Aviv. PATWA principles—the casework approach and careful vocational guidance—were put to work, mortgage funds were set up with the aid of the Joint Palestine Appeal (JPA), and hundreds of British Mahal men and women were helped to settle in kibbutzim and moshavim and placed in urban occupations.

Early in 1949 the Israel Office of the Zionist Federation of Great Britain and Ireland was opened in Tel Aviv. At its disposal were special JPA funds earmarked for consolidation loans to the "British" kibbutzim and moshavim, as well as a loan fund whose trustees were authorized to issue loans on easy terms to individual newcomers. The kindness, speed, and lack of red tape with which these loan applications were handled earned the office a well-merited reputation among British settlers.

Among the British Zionist leaders who settled in Israel soon after the Declaration of Independence were Prof. Selig *Brodetsky (who became president of the Hebrew University after the death of Judah Leon *Magnes), Sir Leon *Simon (who laid the plan for the establishment of Israel's Post Office Savings Bank), and Mrs. Rebecca *Sieff, leader of the *Women's International Zionist Organization (WIZO).

In 1950 the Hitahdut 'Ole Britannia (HOB) was set up with the following aims:

1. To assist, promote, and facilitate the settlement of its members in the State of Israel.

2. To encourage members to make their maximum individual and collective contribution to the development of the country.

3. To secure the maximum possible immigration to Israel from Great Britain and Ireland.

HOB branches all over Israel have helped thousands of new immigrants from Britain to become integrated into life in Israel, to find a home and suitable employment and friends of similar background who can best interpret to them the ways and customs of their new home.

In 1952, HOB joined with the Association of Americans and Canadians in Israel and other similar groups from the Western world to form the Council for Western 'Aliya. This body is in regular contact with the *government of Israel and the *Jewish Agency, with a view to streamlining facilities for the absorption of Western 'Aliya. Amendments to customs regulations were secured, previous army service was recognized as exempting a newcomer from all but three months' service in the Army of Israel, *Ulpan (Hebrew-language seminar) and *Sh'nat Sherut ("Year of Service" in Israel) schemes were improved, hostel accommodations for unmarried immigrants and for families were provided in the principal cities, and better mortgage facilities were arranged.

The invitation extended by President and Mrs. Itzhak *Ben Zvi to a representative group of British 'Aliya to call on them at their residence in Jerusalem in 1956 made it clear that British 'Olim (immigrants) were honorably represented in public administration, the *judiciary and the *Rabbinate, the medical, legal, engineering, nursing, and teaching professions, the institutions of higher learning, journalism, broadcasting, and public relations, and a network of villages throughout Israel. Abba *Eban, formerly Israel's Ambassador to the United States and to the United Nations, became Deputy Prime Minister and Minister of Foreign Affairs; Moshe Rosetti, Clerk of the *Knesset, was elected president of the International Association of Parliamentary Clerks; and Dr. Henry Tabor, head of the National Physical Laboratory of Israel, achieved international renown for his researches into the use of solar energy.

—See also GREAT BRITAIN: RELATIONS WITH ZIONISM AND ISRAEL; GREAT BRITAIN, ZIONISM IN.

L. HARRIS

BRITISH MANDATE FOR PALESTINE. See MANDATE FOR PALESTINE.

BRITISH MANDATORY. See MANDATE FOR PALESTINE.

B'RIT 'IVRIT 'OLAMIT (World Hebrew Federation). Central representative body of organizations and groups in many countries that are active in the field of *Hebrew language and culture. B'rit 'Ivrit 'Olamit (BIO) was established in its present form at a conference held in Berlin in June, 1931. Efforts to unite Hebrew-language movements throughout the world, such as the 1903 conference on the occasion of the 6th Zionist *Congress in Basle or a conference held in Berlin in 1909, had been made earlier, but they had failed to yield the desired results. As against this, the new body managed to survive, although its organizational structure underwent many changes.

The program of BIO, as formulated at the Berlin Conference of 1931, included furthering the knowledge of Hebrew language and culture among all segments of the Jewish people, fostering Hebrew education in all its forms, securing the position of Hebrew as the language of Jewish national bodies and institu-

tions, and propagating the idea of a Hebrew renaissance. The membership consisted mainly of Hebrew-language organizations in Eastern Europe, although there were affiliated bodies also in many Western European countries.

The end of World War II and especially the establishment of the State of Israel marked the beginning of a new era in the history of BIO. In 1950 the First World Hebrew Congress was convened in Jerusalem and proclaimed BIO's close cooperation with the *World Zionist Organization and the State of Israel. This was followed by a second congress in 1955 and a third in 1962. In 1959 the government of Israel recognized BIO as a representative body charged with furthering Hebrew language and culture among the Jews in the *Diaspora. A similar statement on behalf of the World Zionist Organization was issued by the 25th Zionist Congress in Jerusalem in 1960. BIO itself decided to enlist the cooperation of other Jewish bodies. In answer to this call, several national and international Jewish organizations, among them the *World Jewish Congress, the world movement of *B'nai B'rith, the *Board of Deputies of British Jews, and the *Alliance Israélite Universelle, sent representatives to the Third World Hebrew Congress and pledged their support. They were joined by representatives of the leading Jewish women's and youth organizations.

In the mid-1960s, 21 countries were represented in BIO. The most important BIO groups were those in the United States (*Histadrut 'Ivrit of America), Argentina, Canada, France, and South Africa.

The ideology of BIO, as reformulated at the Third World Hebrew Congress, aimed at the Hebraization of the Diaspora by strengthening the Hebrew-language movement, by education, and by propaganda. The seat of the Executive Committee and of the Central Office of BIO is in Jerusalem, where its organ, the quarterly 'Am VaSefer, is published.

A. TARTAKOWER

B'RIT NASHIM L'UMIYOT. World union of nationally oriented women, affiliated with the *New Zionist Organization and founded by the World Union of Revisionist Women (WURW; see REVISIONISTS). WURW had been formed in 1930 by Naomi von Weisl and Edith Lachman with the aim of enlisting Jewish women in the active struggle for the implementation of the Revisionist program and of assisting Revisionist youth organizations, such as *B'rit Trumpeldor (Betar), the *Masada organization, and student organizations, in Palestine and the *Diaspora. Conceived originally as a purely political organization, it subsequently extended its activities and assumed responsibilities for the Revisionist welfare institutions in Palestine and in the Diaspora, creating kindergartens, dispensaries, child care institutions, and the like.

During the Constituent Congress of the New Zionist Organization in Vienna in September, 1935, WURW convened a conference and formed B'rit Nashim L'umiyot to enlist Jewish women in the struggle for the reconstruction of the Jewish State with its historical boundaries, foster national education, and combat *assimilation. The activities of the organization extended over Austria, Belgium, Latvia, Romania, Palestine, Poland, South Africa, and Czechoslovakia.

After the foundation of the *Herut movement in Israel in 1948, the Israeli organization became affiliated with it under the name B'rit Nashim Herut. It set up a chain of kindergartens in urban and development areas and organized welfare and adult educational institutions in Herut agricultural settlements on the

Israeli borders. The organization became active also in the Committee for Soldiers' Welfare. In the Diaspora, the organization, apart from participating in the activities of the Revisionist movement, actively engaged in fund raising in behalf of the *Tel Hai Fund, maintained social and welfare institutions in Israel, especially the *Youth 'Aliya farm in B'ne Ya'akov, and assisted the *Kupat Holim L'Ovdim L'umiyim (National Workers' Sick Fund) kindergartens and youth clubs directed by B'rit Nashim Herut in Israel.

B'rit Nashim L'umiyot was represented on the governing bodies of the Revisionist movement in the Diaspora and in Israel.

I. BENARI

B'RIT 'OLAMIT AHDUT 'AVODA–PO'ALE ZION (World Confederation of *Ahdut 'Avoda–Po'ale Zion).
Organization founded in April, 1946, as the result of the unification of two Palestinian Zionist Socialist parties, T'nu'a L'Ahdut Ha'Avoda and Mifleget Po'ale Zion (Left). At the elections to the 22d Zionist *Congress (1946), the two parties appeared with a united ticket. With the *Diaspora delegates of the Left Po'ale Zion, their faction had 30 delegates. In December, 1946, soon after the Congress, the first world conference of the new World Confederation was held. Participants included ghetto fighters, members of *HeHalutz who were associated with Ahdut 'Avoda, members of the Left Po'ale Zion, and delegates from North and South America and Western Europe.

In the beginning the unification was not complete, and for some time the parties outside Palestine continued to work independently. The Confederation had no time to solidify its structure, for in 1948 the United Workers' party, uniting Ahdut 'Avoda–Po'ale Zion with *HaShomer HaTza'ir, came into being (see MAPAM). In that year a world federation, including also members of HaShomer HaTza'ir, was established, but unity was not complete and was expressed solely in a unified appearance at Zionist Congresses and international gatherings. After Ahdut 'Avoda–Po'ale Zion had split away from Mapam in 1954, the organizational framework of the World Confederation of Ahdut 'Avoda–Po'ale Zion was gradually strengthened. The Confederation convened almost yearly conferences in Israel and maintained a central office there. Early in 1968, after the establishment of the *Israel Labor party, uniting Mapai, Ahdut 'Avoda–Po'ale Zion, and *R'shimat Po'ale Yisrael (Rafi), the corresponding world movements, *Ihud 'Olami and B'rit 'Olamit Ahdut 'Avoda–Po'ale Zion, merged into the T'nu'at Ha'Avoda HaTziyonit (Zionist Labor Movement).

A. TARSHISH

B'RIT RISHONIM OF THE UNITED STATES.
Society of American Jews who joined the Zionist movement prior to 1930. At the founding conference in 1961, the following Governing Board and officers were chosen: Louis *Lipsky, president; Dr. Simon Federbush and Dr. Samuel *Margoshes, vice-presidents; Meyer Brown, treasurer; Morris Margulies, honorary secretary; and Paul L. Goldman, Rose *Halprin, Rabbi Mordecai (Max) *Kirshblum, Dr. Joseph *Schechtman, Louis *Segal, and Robert *Szold.

The program of B'rit Rishonim includes meetings at which addresses are delivered on the lives and work of deceased founders of the American Zionist movement. These memorial addresses are published in pamphlet form.

M. MARGULIES

B'RIT SHALOM.
Jewish organization in Palestine, with connections in other countries, devoted to the promotion of a peaceful modus vivendi between Zionism and Arab nationalism. Consisting mainly of intellectuals and other eminent personalities in the *Yishuv (Jewish population of Palestine), B'rit Shalom reached the peak of its activities during the late 1920s and early 1930s.

The beginnings of B'rit Shalom go back to 1925, when the *Hebrew University of Jerusalem was opened. At that time, several prominent persons formed a circle which stressed the need for shifting the emphasis of Zionist activities from relations with the British Mandatory government (see MANDATE FOR PALESTINE) to work for friendly relations with the Arab nationalists. At no time did B'rit Shalom reach a clear definition of its structure. Some of its members felt that the organization should be a study group whose purpose would be to draw the attention of the Zionist movement to the urgency of the Arab problem. Others advocated wide public activity. B'rit Shalom never became a party with a large following. Its ideas served more to stimulate public debate than to shape policies.

The main political aim of B'rit Shalom was to promote the cause of a binational state in Palestine with political and civil equality for Jews and Arabs irrespective of the numerical proportions of the two groups. In this manner, Jewish rights were to be assured as long as the Jews were in the minority, while the rights of the Arabs were to be safeguarded if and when the Jews became a majority in Palestine. This concept implied the renunciation of plans for a Jewish State. A few of the members went so far as to express readiness to forgo even the right of free Jewish *immigration to Palestine for the sake of keeping peace with the Arabs.

The plan had certain ideological undertones, rooted in a particular view of Jewish history. To B'rit Shalom Zionism seemed more a cultural promise than a political fulfillment. B'rit Shalom did not seek a solution for the problems of the Jewish masses, nor did it believe that they would all settle in Palestine. Some members denounced the Zionist-British nexus in the mandate as alienating the Arab nationalists. They believed that the close racial and cultural affinity between Jews and Arabs, based on their common Semitic origins and their joint cultural achievements in the Middle Ages, could and should serve as a basis for an understanding in Palestine.

The actual policies recommended by B'rit Shalom included the development of self-governing institutions, Jewish-Arab cooperation in municipal administration and in economic life, the advancement of Arab agriculture and education with Jewish help, and mutual assistance. B'rit Shalom issued a journal in Hebrew as well as publications in English and Arabic. In these the policies of the *Histadrut (General Federation of Labor) toward Arab workers were criticized.

The Arabs rejected the B'rit Shalom program as a camouflaged Zionist front, and despite the participation of personalities such as Samuel Hugo *Bergmann, Rabbi Binyamin (see RADLER-FELDMAN, Y'HOSHU'A), Arthur *Ruppin, Hayim *Kalwariski-Margolis, and Gershom *Scholem, and its connections with Judah L. *Magnes and Martin *Buber, its influence on the Yishuv was minimal. The activities of B'rit Shalom ceased in the early 1930s. Groups with a similar outlook were the Pan-Semitic Kedma Mizraha, which was founded in 1936; the League of Jewish-Arab Rapprochement, which came into existence in 1939; and *Ihud, which was organized in 1942.

I. KOLATT

B'RIT TRUMPELDOR (Betar).

Revisionist youth movement named after Joseph *Trumpeldor (*see* REVISIONISTS). Founded in 1923 in Riga, Betar counted nearly 100,000 members in 26 countries on the eve of World War II. Adhering to the general ideological tenets of Revisionism, Betar, though independent in its organizational structure and internal educational work, was subordinated in matters of a general political nature to the decisions of the central and local organs of the Revisionist Union. The head of the organization was Vladimir *Jabotinsky.

The seven major tenets of Betar's ideology were (1) Jewish statehood; (2) Zionist monism, or the centrality and unqualified primacy of the integral Zionist idea, without the admixture of any other ideology; (3) cultivation of the *Hebrew language; (4) military preparedness for self-defense and readiness to join the *Jewish Legion; (5) mobilization, obliging every Betar member to devote the first two years after his arrival in Palestine to national service, in whatever capacity and locality directed by the Betar bodies; (6) strict discipline; and (7) Hadar (dignity), an exacting code of personal behavior in the spirit of chivalry, courtesy, good manners, and awareness of the inherent worth of the Jewish nation. Alongside intensive training for defense duty in Palestine, Betar branches in several countries have, in various degrees, engaged in establishing *Hakhshara farms which prepared the members for *Halutz (pioneer) duty in Palestine and enabled them to qualify for the much-coveted certificates of *immigration to Palestine. Strongly opposed to *Histadrut's Socialist ideology and methods of class struggle (such as strikes) during the process of national upbuilding, Betar formed the first nucleus of the National Workers Federation (1934; *see* HISTADRUT HA'OVDIM HAL'UMIT), which advocated obligatory national arbitration of conflicts between workers and employers instead of strikes and lockouts. They also constituted the main cadres of the *Irgun Tz'vai L'umi (1936) and the *Lohame Herut Israel (1940). The first Jewish naval training center, in Civitavecchia, Italy, was established and manned by Betar (1934), as were the first Jewish training centers for aviation in Paris (1934), Lod (Lydda, 1938), Johannesburg (1939), and New York (1941).

During the years of the holocaust, the bulk of the Betar movement in Europe perished in Nazi-occupied Poland. Those who fled to the Soviet Union and those in Soviet-annexed eastern Poland, Bessarabia, Bukovina, and the Baltic states were considered counterrevolutionaries and British agents, as were all other Zionists, and were deported to forced-labor camps in the north of Russia, where many died.

The remnants of Betar in Nazi-held Poland played an active part in the Jewish resistance movement. They formed the backbone of the Jewish Military Organization (Zydowski Zwiasek Wojskowy), one of the two fighting underground bodies in the Warsaw ghetto uprising of 1943. The survivors of the uprising joined the various partisan groups. Many Betar members were active in the partisan movement in Lithuania.

After World War II, Betar activities were resumed in the free countries of Europe. In the 1960s Betar organizations were also functioning in most of the Latin American countries and in the United States, Canada, South Africa, Australia, and Israel. Shilton, the supreme body of the World Betar movement, is based in Israel.

J. SCHECHTMAN

B'RIT TRUMPELDOR, U.S.A.

B'rit HaNo'ar Ha'Ivri 'Al Shem Yosef Trumpeldor, popularly known as Betar, was officially organized in the United States in 1929, although for two years previously members had been meeting informally. During the 1930s the American Betar protested British policy in Palestine and that of Nazi Germany. In 1939 it began to work for a Jewish army to fight alongside the Allies, and in 1941 it established the Jabotinsky Aviation School in Rockaway, N.Y. After the war Betar began to transfer arms and supplies to the underground struggle waged by the *Irgun Tz'vai L'umi and *Lohame Herut Israel (Lehi). Several American Betar members were aboard the "Ben Hecht," an illegal immigrant ship. The munitions ship "Altalena" was partially outfitted and staffed by United States Betar members, and many others participated in the Israeli *War of Independence.

In Israel, members of B'rit Trumpeldor, U.S.A., founded M'vo Betar and joined other agricultural settlements. Many others have participated in numerous aspects of the Israeli economy and society. Just before the *Six-day War of 1967, 10 American Betar members formed one of the first volunteer groups from anywhere in the world to go to Israel's aid.

Betar maintains a camp at Liberty, N.Y., where a leadership training course is held. The program of the Betar units covers a wide range of activities, including the study of Jewish and Zionist history, Betar thought, Israeli songs and folk dancing, and sports. In addition, Betar actively participates in the Jewish causes of the day.

National headquarters is in New York City. Regional chapters function in Manhattan, the Bronx, Brooklyn, Queens, Great Neck, Paterson–Fair Lawn, Chicago, Detroit, Philadelphia, and Los Angeles. Montreal and Toronto are affiliated with an all-inclusive North American Executive.

Y. WINKELMAN

BROD, MAX.

Author and Zionist leader (b. Prague, 1884; d. Tel Aviv, 1968). He studied law, philosophy, and music at the German University of Prague. After working in the civil service for some time, he joined the staff of the *Prager Tageblatt*. The author of numerous works of fiction, including some of an auto-biographical character, as well as of biographies and philosophical works, Brod is regarded as one of the most significant modern German writers. Many of his books deal with Jewish life and personalities or are otherwise related to Judaism. His *Reubeni, Fürst der Juden,* 1925 (Reubeni, Prince of the Jews, 1928), describes the life of the 16th-century adventurer; *Unambo,* 1949 (published in English, 1952), is a novel of Israel's *War of Independence. In his philosophical *Heidentum, Christentum und Judentum* (Paganism, Christianity, and Judaism, 1916), Brod compares Judaism with paganism and Christianity with respect to reality and human needs. Brod became the biographer and editor of the works of his friend Franz Kafka, and it is due mainly to his efforts that Kafka was discovered by modern literature. He was the author also of poetry, plays, and several translations, and he composed music.

An ardent Zionist, Brod wrote much on Zionism and was active in Zionist affairs in his native Czechoslovakia. After World War I he helped found in Prague the Jewish National Council, which aimed to represent the Jews of the country as a separate nationality group. He served as vice-president of the body, and in his negotiations with the authorities in that capacity strove to gain their support for Jewish nationalism and Zionism. After settling in Palestine, Brod served as literary adviser to the HaBimah (*see* THEATER IN ISRAEL).

BRODETSKY, SELIG.

Mathematician and Zionist leader (b. Olviopol, Ukraine, Russia, 1888; d. London, 1954). In 1893 he moved to England with his family, settling in London's

Whitechapel section, where his father, Akiva Brodetsky, a religious functionary, became active in the British Zionist movement. Despite financial difficulties, Brodetsky early began a distinguished academic career. In 1906 he won a scholarship to Cambridge University, where he studied until 1911 and attained high academic honors. He was a founder and honorary secretary

Selig Brodetsky.
[Zionist Archives]

of the Zionist Society at Cambridge and soon became well known in British Zionist circles. In 1912 he entered the University of Leipzig, where he obtained his doctorate in 1913. While at Leipzig, he was chairman of the local Zionist Students' Society.

Returning to England in 1914, Brodetsky was appointed lecturer in applied mathematics at the University of Bristol. He continued his Zionist work, was elected to the Executive Council of the Zionist Federation of Great Britain and Ireland, and became actively interested in plans for a *Hebrew University in Jerusalem. In 1920 he joined the faculty of the University of Leeds as lecturer in applied mathematics, becoming a professor in 1924 and remaining on the university staff until his retirement in 1948.

Along with his academic duties Brodetsky carried on a full schedule of Zionist activity. Soon after his arrival in Leeds he became president of the local Zionist Council, and in 1920 he attended the *London Zionist Conference. He attended all Zionist Congresses (*see* CONGRESS, ZIONIST) from the 12th (Karlovy Vary, 1921) to the 22d (Basle, 1946) and was appointed to the Zionist *Executive in 1928, serving until 1951. In 1925 he made his first visit to Palestine to attend the opening of the Hebrew University, and the next year he visited the United States on behalf of the university and *Keren HaYesod (Palestine Foundation Fund).

For many years Brodetsky was president of the Zionist Federation of Great Britain and Ireland and served as its honorary president at the time of his death. In 1935 he was elected grand commander of the *Order of Ancient Maccabeans, an office he held until 1949, and honorary president of the Maccabi World Federation.

In 1939 Brodetsky joined the *Board of Deputies of British Jews and two months later was elected its president, serving until 1949. In this capacity he spoke out as the leader of British Jewry against the policy of the British Mandatory authorities (*see* MANDATE FOR PALESTINE). While emphasizing British Jewry's loyalty to the Crown, he was outspoken in his attacks on British government policies. However, he was consistently opposed to acts of terrorism in the *Yishuv (Jewish population in Palestine).

In January, 1946, he testified in London before the *Anglo-American Committee of Inquiry. In 1949 Brodetsky moved to Israel to take over the presidency of the Hebrew University, but he resigned in 1951 because of illness and disagreements with the university's Board of Governors.

Brodetsky was the author of a number of works on mathematics and aeronautics. His autobiography, *Memoirs: From Ghetto to Israel,* was published by his widow, Mania Brodetsky, in 1960.

G. HIRSCHLER

BRODSKY, BENCIÓN. Zionist worker in Peru (b. Bessarabia, Russia, 1903). In 1927 he settled in Peru, where he became prominent in Jewish communal life and Zionism. He was head of the first *Jewish National Fund and *Keren HaYesod (Palestine Foundation Fund) committees and served as secretary and president of the Zionist Organization of Peru. From 1947 to 1948, Brodsky was president of the Unión Israelita del Peru, the community organization of Eastern European Jews in Peru.

J. HASSON

BRODY, HEINRICH (Hayim). Rabbi, scholar, and communal leader (b. Ungvár, Hungary, 1868; d. Jerusalem, 1942). He studied at Yeshivot and at the Hildesheimer Rabbinical Seminary in Berlin. In 1912 he became chief rabbi of Prague, serving in that capacity until 1930, when he became head of the Schocken Institute for Research in Hebrew Poetry in Berlin (*see* SCHOCKEN INSTITUTE FOR JEWISH RESEARCH). He continued to head the institute after it moved to Jerusalem.

Brody was prominent in the Zionist movement, and in speeches and writing propagated the idea of the Return to Zion. He had joined *Mizrahi at its foundation in 1902, and during his period of service as chief rabbi of Prague was president of the Mizrahi Organization of Czechoslovakia.

A great authority on medieval Hebrew poetry, Brody edited the writings of various medieval Hebrew poets and published numerous studies in this field.

G. BAT-YEHUDA

BRONSTEIN, MORDECAI. *See* ARDON, MORDECAI.

B'ROR HAYIL. Village (kibbutz) in the Darom. Founded in 1948 and affiliated with *Ihud HaK'vutzot V'haKibbutzim. Population (1968): 520.

B'ROSH. Village (moshav) in the northern Negev. Founded in 1953 and affiliated with *T'nu'at HaMoshavim. Population (1968): 365.

BROT, SAMUEL. Rabbi and *Mizrahi leader (b. Łódź, Russian Poland, 1885; d. Tel Aviv, 1963). After serving as rabbi in various communities in Poland, he became a rabbi in Antwerp, Belgium, in 1935. During World War II he escaped to the United States, where he served as a rabbi in New York until he settled in Israel after the establishment of the State. In Israel he was a member of the Rabbinical Court of Appeals and of the Council of the Chief *Rabbinate.

One of Poland's leading rabbis, Brot was a Zionist from his youth onward. An early adherent of Mizrahi, he played a leading role in the movement and eventually became president of the Mizrahi Organization of Poland. He was also a member of the Polish Sejm (Parliament) and a member of the Zionist *Actions Committee.

BROWDY, BENJAMIN G. Manufacturer and Zionist leader in the United States (b. Slabode, Lithuania, 1895). Browdy studied at the Slobodka (Slabode) Yeshiva and at Columbia University. He was active in the *Zionist Organization of America, serving as its president from 1950 to 1952, and was a member of the Presidium of the American Zionist Council and of the Executive of the *Jewish Agency. Browdy also served as national president of the *Keren HaYesod (Palestine Foundation Fund) from 1950 to 1955 and was a member of the boards of the *United Jewish Appeal, the United Israel Appeal, and the *State of Israel Bonds Organization.

BROYDES, ABRAHAM. *See* BRAUDES, ABRAHAM.

BRUCK, ZVI. Physician, Zionist, and communal leader (b. Chernigov, Russia, 1869; d. Berlin, 1922). He studied at the University of Kiev and subsequently practiced medicine in various localities.

Bruck joined the *Hoveve Zion movement while still a youth and after the 1st Zionist *Congress (1897) became an ardent political Zionist. He was soon one of the most prominent figures in Russian Zionism and at the 3d Zionist Congress (1899) was elected a member of the Greater *Actions Committee. Following Herzl's call to win over the Jewish communities to Zionism, he successfully ran for the position of government rabbi of Vitebsk in 1901. In 1905 he was elected to the First Russian Duma (Parliament) as representative of the Jews of Vitebsk. After the dispersal of the Duma by the government, he was among the signatories of the antigovernment Viborg Manifesto. Like the others, he was sentenced to prison and was dismissed from his position as government rabbi.

He was opposed to the Helsingfors Program (1905; *see* HELSINGFORS CONFERENCE), which advocated local political activity by the Zionists, and withdrew from the Zionist leadership. However, he returned to Zionist activity after the Russian Revolution. Escaping the Communist regime, he settled in Palestine in 1920. In 1921 he participated as a delegate at the 12th Zionist Congress in Karlovy Vary. He died in Berlin while seeking medical treatment there.

A. ALPERIN

BRUSSELS CONFERENCE. Zionist-initiated conference of Jewish organizations, opened in Brussels on Jan. 29, 1906. The conference had been called by David *Wolffsohn, president of the *World Zionist Organization (WZO), to consider ways of aiding pogrom-stricken Russian Jewry. Eight delegates from various countries (none from the United States), representing the WZO, the *Hilfsverein der Deutschen Juden, the *Anglo-Jewish Association, the *Odessa Committee, and the *Jewish Territorial Organization, attended. The *Alliance Israélite Universelle and the *Jewish Colonization Association (ICA) had declined Wolffsohn's invitation. The conference heard reports from Max Emanuel *Mandelstamm of Kiev and Jacob *Kohan-Bernstein of Kishinev. Mandelstamm declared that the Jews of Russia had no reason to hope for an improvement in their status by revolution or by governmental reforms and that the only solution to their problem would be the foundation of a Jewish Homeland. Kohan-Bernstein stated that eventually all the Jews would have to leave Russia and proposed Egypt or Asia Minor as suitable sites for a Jewish settlement. He opposed Jewish emigration to Great Britain and the United States in view of the laws against aliens which were in force in those countries.

The conference passed resolutions calling for cooperation among all Jewish organizations to aid Russian Jewry and, on Wolffsohn's initiative, for the formation of a committee to explore in the various countries, especially in Eastern Europe, the possibilities of Jewish emigration and settlement. Although the resolutions did not yield concrete results, the conference brought the Zionist movement into the forefront as the initiator in seeking ways of dealing with a situation of immediate concern to all Jews.

BRUTZKUS, JULIUS. Physician, historian, and writer (b. Polangen, Lithuania, 1870; d. Tel Aviv, 1951). Brutzkus studied medicine in Moscow and subsequently settled in St. Petersburg. He was prominently active in Jewish communal life in Russia, participating in the work of the Society for the Promotion of Enlightenment among Russian Jews and in the activities of the *Jewish Colonization Association (ICA). He was on the editorial board of *Voskhod* but resigned in 1902, when that Russian-Jewish periodical became strongly anti-Zionist. In 1905 he was one of the leaders in the struggle for equal rights for the Jews of Russia. After the Revolution of 1917, he was elected to the Russian Constituent Assembly on a Jewish slate. In 1921 he was appointed Minister for Jewish Affairs in Lithuania and in 1922 became a member of the Lithuanian Sejm (Parliament). He later lived in Berlin and Paris, where he worked on behalf of *OSE and HIAS (Hebrew Immigrant Aid Society). During World War II he escaped to the United States and ultimately settled in Israel.

Brutzkus was the author of a variety of studies on the history of Eastern European Jewry. A Zionist as early as his student days, he was one of the leaders of Russian Zionism. An ardent advocate of practical work in Palestine, he wrote much on Zionism. In 1909 he was elected to the Greater *Actions Committee of the *World Zionist Organization. After the Russian Revolution, the Central Committee of Russian Zionists entrusted him with the task of organizing cooperative groups for emigration to Palestine. In the 1920s Brutzkus helped form the Zionist Revisionist party (*see* REVISIONISTS).

B'SOR REGION. Development area southwest of B'er Sheva'. It covers an area of 175,000 acres, more than half of which is suitable for vegetable farming and citriculture (*see* CITRUS INDUSTRY IN ISRAEL).

BUBER, MARTIN. Religious philosopher (b. Vienna, 1878; d. Jerusalem, 1965). While he was still a student, Buber became involved in the Zionist movement. He was cofounder of the Zionist Society and the Zionist Students' Society in Leipzig in 1898, and in 1901 he was invited to be editor of Die *Welt. In the same year he was one of the founders of the Jüdischer Verlag. As early as 1902 Buber advocated the establishment of a Jewish institution of higher learning in Palestine. In 1916 he founded the magazine Der *Jude, which under his editorship (1916–24) became the leading intellectual forum for German-speaking Jews. From 1924 to 1933 he taught comparative religion and Jewish studies at the University of Frankfurt, and he served as director of the Jüdisches Lehrhaus (Jewish Academy) there from 1933 to 1938. In 1938 he settled in Jerusalem and became professor of social philosophy at the *Hebrew University of Jerusalem, from which post he retired in 1951. After settling in Jerusalem, he joined Dr. Judah L. *Magnes and the *Ihud movement in advocating Arab-Jewish rapprochement and an Arab-Jewish binational state in Palestine.

Israeli philosopher Martin Buber. [Israel Information Services]

Buber was the author of a large number of books on the Bible, Jewish and general philosophy, Hasidism, theology, and Zionist theory. His fame, which was greater in the non-Jewish world than in Israel itself, was based primarily on his philosophy of a dialogue between God and man, as expressed in his books *Between Man and Man* (1947) and *I and Thou* (1958).

BUBLICK, GEDALIA. Journalist, Yiddish writer, and religious Zionist leader (b. Grodno, Russia, 1875; d. New York, 1948). Educated at the Yeshivot of Łomża and Mir, he also studied Jewish literature, general philosophy, and sociology. In 1900 he headed a *Jewish Colonization Association (ICA) group of 50 families from Białystok that settled in Mosesville, Argentina, where he taught school for three years.

Moving to New York City, he worked on the daily *Yidisher Tagblat,* becoming its editor in 1915. When the *Tagblat* went out of existence in 1928, he wrote for the *Morgen Journal.* He was a founder and vice-president of the *American Jewish Congress, a founder and president (1928–32) of the Mizrahi Organization of America (*see* RELIGIOUS ZIONISTS OF AMERICA), and a member of the Zionist *Actions Committee.

In his writings he fought Jewish secularism, socialism, and Reform Judaism. Arguing that Judaism must be accepted as a complete religious-national entity, he regarded religious education as the only deterrent to Jewish assimilation in the United States.

G. BAT-YEHUDA

BUCHMIL, JOSHUA HESHEL. Zionist propagandist (b. Ostrog, Russia, 1869; d. Jerusalem, 1938). Buchmil received traditional training as well as a general education. At first he studied agriculture but later became a law student at the University of Montpellier. He was one of the leaders of a student Zionist society, 'Atid Yisrael, and was among the earliest supporters of Herzl. Subsequently he spread Herzl's ideas in Russia and was instrumental in securing the participation of Russian *Hoveve Zion delegates at the 1st Zionist *Congress (1897). In 1901 he was a founder of the *Democratic Faction after the 4th Zionist Congress and one of the leaders of the opposition to the Uganda project (*see* EAST AFRICA SCHEME). In

1906 Buchmil went to Palestine on behalf of the *Odessa Committee to study the legal and economic prerequisites for Jewish settlement in the country.

After the Russian Revolution of 1917, Buchmil was elected a member of the Central Committee of Russian Zionists. In 1921 he escaped from the Soviet Union, settling in Jerusalem in 1923. From there he frequently went on missions abroad on behalf of the *Keren HaYesod (Palestine Foundation Fund).

Buchmil contributed to the Zionist press and wrote (in French) *Jewish Renaissance* (1926) and *Problems of the Jewish Renaissance* (1936). His wife, Shoshana, was also active in the Zionist movement. At the 2d Zionist Congress (1898) she helped lay the foundation for an organization of Zionist women.

G. HIRSCHLER

BUDKO, JOSEPH. Painter and engraver (b. Płońsk, Russian Poland, 1888; d. Jerusalem, 1940). He attended Yeshivot and later studied in Vilna and in Berlin, where he was a student of Hermann *Struck. In 1933 he settled in Palestine and two years later reopened the *Bezalel School in Jerusalem, serving as its principal until his death.

Budko created a highly original artistic style, blending traditional Jewish art with modern modes of expression. His engravings, woodcuts, and paintings mostly depict the Bible, Jewish history, and contemporary Jewish life. He illustrated books of the Bible, the Aggada, and works of modern Hebrew and Yiddish authors. His woodcut "Men Like Myself Do Not Run Away" symbolized Jewish courage in Palestine during the period of Arab terror.

BU'ENA. Arab village in eastern Lower Galilee. Population (1968): 1,090.

BUKHARAN (BOKHARAN) JEWS IN ISRAEL. Bukhara, a region in central Asia which came under Russian control in 1868 and became part of the Soviet Union in 1920, has an ancient Jewish community, the first historical evidence of Jews there dating to the 13th century. In contrast to the Jewish communities in European Russia, the Bukharan Jews have been able, under Soviet rule, to maintain to some degree their traditional way of

Bukharan men. [Israel Information Services]

life and religious institutions. There are no reliable estimates as to the number of Jews in Bukhara in 1967; however, according to the 1959 census, there were 94,344 Jews in the Uzbek S.S.R., of which Bukhara Oblast forms part.

Early Years. The first Bukharan Jew to settle in Palestine arrived in 1868. In the following years several more arrived, and in 1882 larger numbers began to immigrate. This trend was due partly to an increase in road security and to an improvement in the economic position of Bukharan Jewry, effected by the consolidation of Russian rule in the country.

In 1889 Bukharan Jews in Jerusalem established a society for the purpose of building communal institutions of their own: a synagogue, schools, and a guesthouse. Sometime later the committee began the building of a residential quarter. The quarter, which was called Rehovot, was distinguished for its comparative modernity and wide streets.

The establishment of the quarter attracted more immigrants, and by the outbreak of World War I (1914) the Jerusalem community numbered about 1,500 souls. Most of the immigrants brought with them some capital, which they invested in the building of houses for rent. Some returned to Russia to carry on their businesses, leaving their children in Jerusalem and coming there for holidays.

The Jerusalem community boasted several learned men, who engaged in supplying literature for their brethren abroad. Numerous books in Hebrew and in the Judeo-Persian vernacular (in Hebrew characters) were printed by the community in Jerusalem. Most of them were of a religious character, and the Jerusalem community thus formed a spiritual center for Bukharan Jewry. The community had its own rabbinate and lay leadership but otherwise was affiliated with the Sephardi community (*see* SEPHARDIM).

Bukharan woman.
[Israel Information Services]

World War I and the Interwar Period. Jerusalem's Bukharan Jews suffered greatly during World War I. They lost most of their property, and the remainder was confiscated by the Turkish authorities, who requisitioned their houses for army quarters and stables. Almost all the men left the country with the outbreak of war. Only the aged, children, and women remained behind. Their numbers were decimated by poverty and disease. About 700 Bukharan Jews perished during the war in Jerusalem. After the war, Bukhara's Jews could not aid the rehabilitation of the Jerusalem community, for they had been impoverished by the Russian Revolution.

As long as the doors of Russia were not tightly shut, Bukharan Jews emigrated to Palestine, and in the 1930s the number of Bukharan Jews in Palestine was about 3,000. While some of the post-World War I immigrants settled in Jerusalem, as the earlier settlers had done, others settled in Tel Aviv and Haifa or joined agricultural settlements.

Development since the Establishment of the State. By the time the State of Israel was established, the Bukharan quarter was considered one of the poorest sections of Jerusalem. Its large mansions had been converted into schools, its streets were unpaved, and although a few traces of past prosperity still remained (notably the Old Bukharan Synagogue), the general impression was one of decay.

In the 1960s members of the younger generation of Bukharans were displaying a revived interest in, and attachment to, many of the community's religious and social customs, and they manifested a renewed appreciation of the traditional Bukharan jewelry and folk costumes, which rival in beauty and richness those of the *Yemenite Jews. The popularity of Bukharan singers, choirs, and dance groups contributed to this trend. On the other hand, only a few of the younger generation still spoke Tajiki, the traditional Judeo-Persian vernacular of the Bukharan Jews, and most of the articles in *T'vuna*, the magazine of the Bukharan community in Israel which was published at irregular intervals in Tel Aviv, were in Hebrew.

BUKOVINA, ZIONISM IN. *See* ROMANIA, ZIONISM IN.

BUKOVINIAN JEWS IN ISRAEL. The incorporation of Bukovina (formerly a part of the Austro-Hungarian Monarchy) in Romania after World War I put an end to the freedom and prosperity enjoyed by the Jews of that province during the Hapsburg regime. Many were deprived of their citizenship, and the economic situation of the Jews in Bukovina deteriorated steadily, resulting in large-scale emigration to Palestine in the period between World Wars I and II.

The Goga-Cuza government openly persecuted the Jews of Bukovina and the rest of Romania in 1938. After Romania's pro-Nazi government, led by Ion Antonescu, declared war on the U.S.S.R. in 1941, there were pogroms and mass deportations, ending in the annihilation of most of Bukovina's prewar Jewish population of 150,000.

Those of Bukovina's Zionists who succeeded in reaching Palestine formed the Hitahdut 'Ole Bukovina (Union of Immigrants from Bukovina), popularly known as HOB, with headquarters in Tel Aviv and branches throughout Israel. In addition, immigrants from nearly every town in Bukovina formed *Landsmannschaften* of their own in Israel, with clubhouses, institutions, and mutual-assistance funds. These organizations did much to aid later immigrants in their integration into life in Israel, and after World War II they successfully pushed restitution claims of their countrymen against Germany.

The leaders of the Bukovinian immigrants in Israel included Meir *Ebner, a former president of the Zionist Organization of Bukovina, former editor of the *Ostjüdische Zeitung* in Czernowitz (Cernăuţi; now Chernovtsy), and a regular contributor of articles to Israel's Hebrew and German-language press. Some of the immigrants attained prominent places in Israeli politics, particularly Berl *Locker, who served on the Executive of the *Jewish Agency from 1931 to 1956, acting as its Jerusalem chairman from 1947 to 1956; and Yehuda Sha'ari, who represented the *Progressive party in the *Knesset. A number of businessmen from Bukovina established large concerns in Israel, such as Argaman, a textile corporation, with Abraham Klier as president, and Ivanier Brothers, a wholesale firm with branches throughout the country.

M. TEICH

BULGARIA, ZIONISM IN. The modern state of Bulgaria was established by the Congress of Berlin (1878) on territory taken from the Ottoman Empire. Jews had been living in that region ever since Roman times, and following the expulsion of the Jews from Spain (1492) several Sephardi communities (*see* SEPHARDIM) were formed, particularly in Sofia, Nikopol, and Pleven. At the time Bulgaria was established, it had a Jewish population of some 27,000 in a total of more than 2 million inhabitants.

Although the Jews of Bulgaria were accorded full civil rights under the law, they suffered from poverty and considerable anti-Jewish prejudice among the general population, circumstances that aided the rapid growth of Zionism in the country. Even before the 1st Zionist *Congress (1897) there had been a Zionist society in Sofia, the 'Ezrat Ahim Society. In 1895 this group purchased land in Hartuv, Palestine, on which 10 Bulgarian-Jewish families settled in 1896. When Herzl passed through Sofia on his way to Constantinople in June, 1896, he was given an enthusiastic reception by masses of Jews as his train stopped in the city. "I, myself, was quite touched," he reported in his *Diaries*. By 1898 there were 15 and, a few years later, 42 Zionist societies in the country. The Zionists met with some opposition from the assimilationists and from the *Alliance Israélite Universelle, which was engaged in educational work in Bulgaria. Although at first the Zionists constituted a minority in the representative organizations of Bulgarian Jewry, they made their influence felt as early as 1899, when they defeated the nomination of an anti-Zionist chief rabbi and replaced him with a Zionist candidate. Zionists helped close a centuries-old gap in Bulgaria between the Sephardim and the *Ashkenazim, who joined to work together for Palestine. By the eve of World War I, the Zionists had obtained majorities on the boards of almost all the official Jewish communities, and there was a Zionist Federation, which published a weekly, *HaShofar*.

Between the two world wars the Zionist Federation grew apace, with more than 2,400 members in the 1920s, and a number of new Zionist papers, in Bulgarian and Ladino, appeared. The *Women's International Zionist Organization (WIZO) had chapters in 14 localities, Maccabi had branches in 22 towns with a total membership of 2,700, and *HaShomer HaTza'ir had 800 members in 6 towns. There were also branches of *Po'ale Zion, the Revisionist party (*see* REVISIONISTS), and *B'rit Trumpeldor (Betar). In the summer of 1930 a branch of the pioneering organization *HeHalutz was founded with 120 members; they set up the He'Atid *Hakhshara (agricultural training) farm near Pazardzhik. A Palestine Office (*see* PALESTINE OFFICES) had been opened in Rustchuk (Ruse) soon after World War I. Most young people were eager to emigrate to Palestine; in the early 1920s, 599 persons from Bulgaria, some of them skilled artisans, went on *'Aliya. In the 1930s settlements of Bulgarian Jews were established in K'far Hittim and Bet Hanan. The *Jewish National Fund and *Keren HaYesod (Palestine Foundation Fund) were both active.

During the period of Nazi domination in World War II all Zionist activity in Bulgaria was discontinued. However, Bulgaria was the only Nazi-ruled country in Europe not to carry out mass deportations of Jews, and its prewar Jewish community of some 48,000 persons survived the war almost intact. Soon after Bulgaria's liberation, the Zionists of Bulgaria reconstituted themselves at a conference (Oct. 8, 1944) and began to publish a Zionist paper, *Bama Tziyonit (Zionista Tribuna)*. On Jan. 10, 1946, the United Zionist Organization of Bulgaria held its first

postwar conference, with 126 delegates in attendance. As a result of the Communist take-over, however, all Zionist activity in Bulgaria had ceased by the summer of 1949 and nearly all the Jews of the country had emigrated to Israel.

G. HIRSCHLER

BULGARIAN JEWS IN ISRAEL. Prior to the establishment of the State of Israel there were about 7,000 Bulgarian Jews in Palestine, concentrated mainly in Tel Aviv, with small groups in Haifa and Jerusalem. In 1896 Bulgarian Jews settled the colony of Hartuv. Between 1947 and 1949 about 38,000 Jews arrived in Israel from Bulgaria, and by 1966 there were 60,000 Bulgarian Jews in the country. About 80 per cent were living in Tel Aviv–Jaffa, 7,000 in Haifa, and the rest in Jerusalem, Ramle, Lod, 'Akko, Safed, Kinneret, and the settlements of Tel Hanan, K'far Hittim, and Tzur Moshe.

Bulgarian Jews, who comprise a strong academic element in the Sephardi group (*see* SEPHARDIM), have adjusted with ease to the economic, social, and cultural life of Israel. Several professors and scholars from this group serve on the faculties of the *Hebrew University of Jerusalem, the *Weizmann Institute of Science in Rehovot, and the *Technion in Haifa. The younger generation is eager for higher education, and a large number of young Bulgarian Jews have entered medicine, engineering, architecture, economics, and other professions. The Bulgarian

Bulgarian immigrants processed at Haifa. [Zionist Archives]

community has also produced writers, poets, actors, opera singers, journalists, upper-echelon officers in the *Israel Defense Forces, and senior officials in the *government, the *Histadrut (General Federation of Labor), and public and private institutions. The older generation is engaged mainly in trades, business, and various service industries.

The Bulgarian community does not play an active role in Israel's religious life. While Bulgarian Jews maintain synagogues in all the larger towns in Israel, they are, in general, secularists. Despite their lack of religious commitment they have a strong sense of Jewish identity; there was almost no intermarriage among the Jews of Bulgaria. They have a well-developed community organization which encompasses many aspects of their cultural and social life.

The Association of Immigrants from Bulgaria in Israel supports a home for the aged of the community and handles matters involving German reparations and Jewish property left in Bulgaria. Benjamin Arditi, a member of the Third, Fourth, and Fifth Knessets (*Herut party), wrote a history of the Jews of Bulgaria and later undertook the compilation of a bibliography of writings by Bulgarian Jews. The Ahva Bank was founded by Bulgarian Jews, and Kupat 'Aliya, a cooperative bank, has a board of directors composed of Bulgarian Jews. Although the community has few welfare cases, it supports several charitable institutions in the three large cities.

Within the community the Bulgarian language is retained, although the younger generation (those under 20 years of age), whether *Sabra or Bulgarian-born, speaks Hebrew. A Bulgarian-language paper, *Far Tribuna,* had a daily circulation of 7,000 and a Friday (weekend) circulation of 10,000 in 1966. The various political parties also print Bulgarian-language weeklies. An attempt to form a Bulgarian theater was unsuccessful, but the Tzadikov Chorus (composed of children and adults), established by the Bulgarian community, is considered the finest in Israel.

By 1968 there were still about 5,000 Jews left in Bulgaria, and emigration to Israel had slowed down to an insignificant number.

A. MASHIAH

Ralph J. Bunche.
[Zionist Archives]

BUNCHE, RALPH JOHNSON. United Nations official (b. Detroit, 1904). Grandson of a Negro slave and orphaned as a child, Bunche studied in Los Angeles while working to support himself. In 1941, after a distinguished academic career during which he did postgraduate work in Europe, Africa, and Southeast Asia, he joined the Office of Strategic Services (OSS), in which he filled major posts. From 1944 to 1946 he was with the U.S. Department of State. He served as Director of the UN Trusteeship Division from 1946 to 1955, when he was appointed UN Under-secretary for Special Political Affairs.

In 1947 Bunche served as secretary of the *United Nations Special Committee on Palestine (UNSCOP). During the Arab-Israeli War (*see* WAR OF INDEPENDENCE) he served as special United Nations representative in Palestine, and after the assassination of Count Folke *Bernadotte, in September, 1948, he was appointed Acting UN Mediator for Palestine. In this capacity he succeeded in obtaining *armistice agreements between Israel and the neighboring Arab states. For his role in ending this war, Bunche was awarded the Nobel Peace Prize in 1950.

BUND. One of the first Jewish Socialist mass organizations and modern Jewish political parties in the world. It was founded at a secret conference in Vilna (Sept. 25–27, 1897) as the Algemeiner Yidisher Arbeterbund fun Russland un Poilen (General Jewish Labor Federation of Russia and Poland) and later added Lita (Lithuania) to its name. During its early years it stressed economic activities designed to improve the lot of the Jewish worker. Later it developed a wide and dynamic program of political action which led to its persecution and suppression by the Tsarist regime. Hundreds of Bundists were imprisoned, deported to Siberia, or executed. Despite police persecution, its following grew and its activities were intensified. However, the victory of communism in November, 1917, marked the beginning of its end. Following a number of futile attempts to become adjusted to the new situation, a majority of delegates at a conference held in March, 1921, resolved to disband the organization. The remaining minority group was speedily suppressed by the Soviet authorities.

Brutally liquidated in Russia, the Bund emerged as an important force in independent Poland following World War I. Its influence was felt in the country at large and in all walks of Jewish life, particularly in areas of cultural and political interest. Despite its secularist philosophy and ideology, it became a significant factor in the Kehillot (Jewish communities) which had received government recognition as Jewish religious bodies. On the eve of Hitler's invasion, the Bund was probably the largest Jewish party in Poland. Smaller Bundist parties functioned in Romania, Lithuania, and Estonia. The Nazi holocaust put an end to all of them.

It took the Bund a long time to evolve its specifically Jewish program, and its views remained nebulous to the very end in many areas of Jewish concern. One aspect it never relinquished was its rabid *anti-Zionism. Starting out with a position of neutrality on the question of Jewish peoplehood, it recognized the Jews of Russia as a nationality group in 1901, and at its sixth convention, held in October, 1905, it decided to demand cultural autonomy for the Jews, in addition to civic rights and political equality. Yiddish, at first employed as an expedient means of reaching the Jewish working masses, was later acknowledged (rather than Hebrew) as the national language of the Jewish people.

Although the Bund had a great record of Jewish creative accomplishments, its activities were always of a localized nature. It was only after World War II, when it practically ceased to exist as a serious factor, that the scattered tiny Bundist groups set up a world committee to coordinate their activities. The Bund never took hold in countries where the status of Jews was secure. The small groups it had in the free world were made up of émigrés and refugees. Groups of this kind still functioned in the 1960s in a number of countries, including Israel.

C. B. SHERMAN

BUND ZIONISTISCHER VERBINDUNGEN (BZV). Association of Zionist academicians and Zionist student societies in Germany. Founded in 1920 by a group seceding from the *Kartell Jüdischer Verbindungen (KJV), it was active in several German cities between World Wars I and II. The association strove to educate students for Zionism and Zionist activity. Though not very strong in numbers, it was a very well-organized body, known for the strong ties of comradeship that united its members. See also GERMANY, ZIONISM IN.

BUQEI'A. See P'KI'IN.

BURG, SH'LOMO YOSEPH. Leader in Hapo'el HaMizrahi (b. Dresden, Germany, 1909). Burg studied at the Universities of Leipzig and Berlin and at the Hildesheimer Rabbinical Seminary. A leader of *Mizrahi in Germany, he participated prominently in the organization of *Youth 'Aliya (youth immigration) and in the promotion of Jewish adult education. After settling in Palestine, he taught Talmud and history at the *Herzliya High School in Tel Aviv from 1941 to 1946. Later, he was active in rescue work in Europe.

Sh'lomo Burg.
[Israel Information Services]

Burg was a member of the *Knesset from 1949 on and served as Deputy Speaker. Subsequently he was Minister of Health from 1951 to 1952 and Minister of Posts from 1953 to 1958. In the following year he became Minister of Social Welfare, a position he still held in 1966. From 1939 to 1950, Burg was a member of the Greater *Actions Committee of the *World Zionist Organization. He was a leader of the progressive wing of HaPo'el HaMizrahi.

J. STAVI

BURG'TA. Village (moshav) in the Sharon Plain. Founded in 1949 by immigrants from Turkey and affiliated with *T'nu'at HaMoshavim. Population (1968): 330.

BURLA, YEHUDA. Hebrew novelist (b. Jerusalem, 1886; d. 1969). Scion of a Sephardi family of rabbis (see SEPHARDIM), Burla studied at Yeshivot and at the Jerusalem Teachers Seminary. He taught school, first in Jerusalem and later in Damascus, where he was principal of the Hebrew school of the Zionist Organization from 1919 to 1922, and in Zikhron Ya'akov, Haifa, and Tel Aviv. He was also a director of the Department for Arab Affairs of the labor organization *Histadrut. In 1947 he visited South America in behalf of the *Keren HaYesod (Palestine Foundation Fund). After the establishment of the State of Israel he served as a director of the Department for Culture, Press, and Information in the Ministry of Minorities.

Burla, who began writing at an early age, was a raconteur of the life of the Sephardi and *Oriental Jews in Palestine and neighboring countries. He depicts their seemingly simple yet conflict-ridden world, portraying their customs and time-honored traditions, their outlook on life, and their fanciful mode of speech. Burla received the Bialik and Ussishkin Prizes for literature (1942 and 1949, respectively).

H. LEAF

BUSSEL, JOSEPH. Founder of D'ganya (b. Lyakhovichi, Russia, 1891; d. Palestine, 1919). As a youngster Bussel prepared himself for pioneering life in Palestine by undergoing agricultural training on Jewish farms in Russia. In 1908 he settled in Palestine. While working in the fields of Kinneret, he advocated among his fellow workers the idea of the K'vutza (see KIBBUTZ) and organized them in a commune. The group worked subsequently in Hadera and in 1910 moved to D'ganya, settling there permanently a year later. The guiding spirit of the group, Bussel was instrumental in formulating the theoretical and practical principles governing K'vutza life. During World War I he helped to draw the agricultural settlements of Lower Galilee into cooperative action and aided Jaffa and Tel Aviv Jews who had been expelled from their homes by the Turkish authorities.

Bussel was active in *HaPo'el HaTza'ir and contributed to its magazine. He drowned in Lake Kinneret when his boat capsized in a storm. Busslia youth groups that remained in existence in Eastern Europe until World War II were named in his honor.

G. KRESSEL

BUSTAN HAGALIL. Village (moshav) in western Galilee. Founded in 1948 by new immigrants, mostly from Romania, and affiliated with the *Ihud Haklai. Population (1968): 340.

BYCHOWSKI, SHNEUR ZALMAN. Physician and Zionist publicist (b. Korets, Volhynia, Russia, 1865; d. Warsaw, 1934). After obtaining his medical degree at Warsaw University, he settled in Warsaw, where he became a noted physician. A veteran member of the *Hoveve Zion movement, he was an early follower of Herzl and participated in the 1st Zionist *Congress (1897). A forceful writer, Bychowski disseminated the ideas of Zionism in the Polish press. He also wrote in German, Russian, and Yiddish, and published medical and psychiatric studies in Hebrew in *Ha Tz'fira* and *Ha T'kufa.*

BZV. See BUND ZIONISTISCHER VERBINDUNGEN.

C

CABINET OF ISRAEL. *See* GOVERNMENT OF ISRAEL.

CAESAREA. Ancient city on the Mediterranean coast, 22 miles south of Haifa. The earliest settlement on the site was an anchorage called Strato's Tower. The city itself was founded by King Herod the Great toward the end of the 1st century B.C.E. and named in honor of the Roman emperor Augustus; it served as the capital of Palestine for 600 years. Herod erected a Roman temple and other magnificent buildings and constructed a port. Caesarea developed rapidly and became the largest city in the country, rivaling Jerusalem. It was the seat of the Roman Governor and the base of the Roman garrison. Frequent clashes occurred between the Jews of the city and the Roman and Greek settlers, who despised them. The Roman authorities, supporting the pagan population, deprived the Jews of their civil rights. In one of the clashes many Jews were killed, and the rest fled the city. Subsequent developments helped unleash the great Jewish revolt against Rome (C.E. 66–70).

After the destruction of the Temple, a Jewish community reestablished itself in the city, which continued to be a major Roman center. Many Talmudic sages lived in Caesarea, which also had a large number of Christians and Samaritans. The Muslims took the city from the Byzantines in 690. In 1107 it was captured by the Crusaders, under whose reign the Jewish and Samaritan communities diminished considerably. Then, in 1291, Caesarea was destroyed by the Egyptian Mamelukes. In subsequent centuries the site was generally abandoned.

Since the establishment of Israel, large-scale excavations have been carried out on the site of the ancient city, in the course of which many remnants of the Roman period, including the amphitheater, hippodrome, two aqueducts, and a synagogue, as well as an open-air enclosure decorated by the Byzantines with Roman statues and an extramural church with a mosaic pavement, have been unearthed. A small museum in the nearby kibbutz, S'dot Yam, contains finds from Caesarea.

In 1958, the government of Israel, in partnership with the Rothschild interests, formed the Caesarea Development Corporation with the aim of developing modern Caesarea. Since then an area has been designated a tourist resort, in which beaches with bathing facilities, a golf course, a riding school and racetrack, and modern hotels have been opened.

CAHAN, YA'AKOV (Jacob Cohen). Hebrew poet (b. Slutsk, Minsk District, Russia, 1881; d. Petah Tikva, 1960). Raised in Poland, he studied at the Universities of Bern, Munich, and Paris. In 1907, while a student in Bern, he helped set up the world office of 'Ivriya, an organization for the promotion of the renaissance of the Hebrew language. When 'Ivriya developed into Histadrut LaSafa V'laTarbut Ha'Ivrit (Society for Hebrew Language and Culture), Cahan was its secretary (1910–13) and later served as director of its Berlin headquarters (1913–14).

After World War I he worked for the Stiebel publishing house in Warsaw, was supervisor of Hebrew education in Jewish high schools (1924–27), and lectured at the Institute for Jewish Studies (1927–33). After serving on the Revisionist party's Central Committee in Poland (*see* REVISIONISTS), he joined the minority which seceded from the movement and became active in the *Jewish State party. In 1934 he settled in Palestine, where he became prominently affiliated with the *Bialik Foundation and the *Hebrew Language Academy. He was a president of the Hebrew PEN Club in Poland and later in Israel.

Cahan's writings include ballads, epic poems, plays, and folktales. In many of his poems he gave militant expression to the striving of the Jews for national redemption. He also edited periodicals and translated works of world literature into Hebrew. His collected writings were published in 10 volumes. Literary awards conferred upon him included the *Israel Prize for 1953 and 1958.

S. SKULSKY

CANAAN. *See* PALESTINE.

CANAANITES AND SEMITIC ACTION. Splinter groups in the *Yishuv (Jewish population of Palestine) and in Israel which hold the view that the new nation created in the Land of Canaan has no links with world Jewry but is rooted in the ancient traditions of the land and its soil. The movement began in the

Roman theater at Caesarea. [Israel Information Services]

early 1940s, when it gained influence in circles of young intellectuals active in the press, literature, and the arts.

Rejecting the spiritual traditions of Judaism, the Canaanites denied that the Jewish community in the *Diaspora had any national attributes and claimed that Jewish influence from abroad only 'hindered the development of a new nation in the Land of Canaan. They held that the only connection between the Jews in Israel and those in the Diaspora was the tenuous one of common origin, and they looked toward the ancient East as a source of inspiration from which to draw their themes and symbols. They propounded the idea of a wide Middle Eastern area-space (Heb., *merhav*), which preceded both the ancient Hebrew and the Arab conquests, as an all-embracing cultural unit. Some even advocated the utilization of Astarte, ancient Canaanite goddess of fertility, as an inspiring symbol.

In the 1950s the Canaanites as an organized intellectual force declined, to be replaced by the more politically oriented Semitic Action, a movement less extremist in its intellectual position and much more explicit on political issues. It, too, claimed that the Hebrew nation in Israel was a new national entity, and it rejected any influence of Diaspora Jewry in its affairs. While admitting that there were some "spiritual, sentimental, and personal" ties between Jews in Israel and those in the Diaspora, it maintained that once Israel ceased to be an instrument of Diaspora Jewry, the country would be on the path to integration with the rest of the Middle East. This aspiration, to be integrated into the new political world of the Middle East, was the basic motivation of Semitic Action, which was also opposed to the party system as it existed in Israel and to fund raising for Israel

in the United States. As to internal affairs, it claimed to represent a "humanistic" approach to social issues and accused the existing regime of "statism." It opposed the cultural isolation of the Israeli Jew and called for contact with "Semitic civilization" as well as with foreign culture in general.

The Canaanites published a number of periodicals in which they gave expression to their ideas. In 1946 they issued *Eretz Yisrael HaTz'ira* (Young Eretz Israel) and *BaMa'avak* (In the Struggle), and later they drafted the platform of the *Young Hebrews* and *Aleph*.

In 1950 Uri Avneri assumed the editorship of the magazine *Ha'Olam HaZe* (This World) and soon became one of the main political proponents of the Canaanites and of Semitic Action. Although the latter group had a journal of its own, *Etgar* (Challenge), Avneri later founded a separate political movement embodying the attitudes and program of Semitic Action. This new body was also called Ha'Olam HaZe and Koah Hadash (New Force). In the mid-1960s the Canaanite movement, at least on the organizational level, disintegrated, and after the *Six-day War of 1967 its influence waned.

I. KOLATT

CANADA, ZIONISM IN. Jews first began to settle in Canada in appreciable numbers in the middle of the 19th century. By the end of 1966, Canada had a Jewish population of 275,000, in a total population of 20 million.

Being largely of Eastern European origin (with a small group of *Sephardim, residing mainly in Montreal), Canadian Jewry provided fertile soil for Zionism from the beginning. Adherents of the classic Reform ideology, represented in the United States by mid-19th-century Jewish immigrants from Germany, were not present in sufficient numbers to put up opposition, tacit or organized, to the Zionist movement.

From the outset, too, the Zionist movement in Canada benefited from the proximity of the large and influential Zionist community in the United States. Developments within American Zionism had a strong bearing on Jewish life in Canada. For the most part, the various Zionist party groupings were "imported" from the United States and retained close links with their counterparts in that country, and important visitors from Palestine (and later, Israel) and from the World Zionist movement stopped in Canada on their way to or from the United States.

Early Beginnings. The first Zionist society in Canada was organized in 1887 by Alexander Harkavy (1863–1939), the lexicographer, but its life-span was brief. In 1889, when *Ahad Ha'Am formed his secret Zionist order, *B'ne Moshe, it counted only one member in all North America, Lazarus Cohen of Montreal.

In 1892 another Zionist society, Shave Zion (locally spelled Shavey Zion) No. 2, a branch of the American Shave Zion, was formed in Montreal. A considerable sum of money was raised for the purchase of land in Palestine, and two families were sent to settle there. When, owing to restrictions imposed by the Turkish regime, the two families were obliged to return to Canada, the members of the society became discouraged, their contributions were refunded, and the society ceased to exist.

In 1898 a permanent basis was laid for organized Zionism in Canada with the formation in Montreal of Agudat Zion, a men's Zionist society. On receipt of an invitation from Herzl, the society named Jacob *de Haas its delegate to the 2d Zionist *Congress, which was held that year.

By the following year Zionist societies had sprung up in several cities. Their representatives met at a conference in Montreal in November, 1899, formed the Federation of Zionist Societies of Canada, and elected as president Clarence I. *de Sola, who held the office until 1919. The name of the federation was changed in 1923 to Zionist Organization of Canada (ZOC). The first convention of the federation was held in 1900; subsequent meetings were held annually until the outbreak of World War I and less frequently in the years immediately following.

The first women's Zionist group, the Young Ladies' Liberal Progressive Zionist Society, was formed in Montreal in 1901. In 1903 the *Jewish National Fund (JNF) began its activities in Canada with collections undertaken by the Federation of Zionist Societies of Canada.

In 1905 the Canadian delegates to the 7th Zionist Congress registered their vote against the *East Africa scheme. That same year, the *Po'ale Zion party was introduced into Canada. The ideological parent of the Labor Zionist movement in the country, this party was to be instrumental in the founding of Jewish schools in a number of Canadian cities and of the Canadian Jewish Congress in 1919. In 1909 it helped set up the first Canadian branch of the *Farband (Labor Zionist fraternal order) in Montreal.

Zionist youth in Canada came into its own at an early date. By 1910 a *Young Judaea Club was active in Montreal; six years later, there was a Young Judaean League in that city, and in 1917 the Federation of Zionist Societies approved the formation of the Young Judaean National League, its first

president being Bernard (Barney) Joseph, who was to become better known as Dov *Joseph of Jerusalem.

In 1911 a group of religious Zionists organized a *Mizrahi chapter in Toronto. Three years later, on the occasion of a visit by Rabbi Meir Berlin (*Bar-Ilan), Mizrahi became a national body and an affiliate of Mizrahi in the United States.

In 1911 *World Zionist Organization (WZO) headquarters reported that receipts from Canada for the preceding 12 months had totaled $14,475, an unusually high amount at the time. Since there was then no Zionist administrative setup, the entire amount was remitted to the WZO without any deductions for local expenses. In addition, $10,000 had been raised in Canada by the JNF for the purchase of land in Palestine between 1910 and 1912.

The outbreak of World War I brought a lull in Zionist fundraising activity since the forwarding of funds to Palestine, then ruled by Turkey, an enemy country, was forbidden. Organizational work, however, continued. In 1915 the first Po'ale Zion youth group was formed. A year later Anna Selick (later Anna *Raginsky) founded the first Canadian chapter of Hadassah in Toronto. By the end of the war, there were Hadassah chapters in four other Ontario cities, which had formed a provincial body. Canadian Hadassah had no connection with the *Hadassah of the United States, but it subsequently affiliated with the *Women's International Zionist Organization (WIZO).

When recruiting for the *Jewish Legion began in the United States, Canadian Zionists also enlisted. Eventually, the number of recruits from Canada reached 300; of these, 150 were from Toronto; the rest came from Montreal, Hamilton, Winnipeg, and points west. Together with the volunteers from the United States, they received their basic training in Windsor, Ont., in York Redoubt, off Halifax, and elsewhere in Nova Scotia. Among the legionnaires from Canada who after the war remained in Palestine, or eventually returned to settle there, were A. Aisenstadt, Leon Cheifetz, M. Epstein, A. Feldman, A. H. Friedgut, Saul Glazer, Bernard (Dov) Joseph, Philip Joseph, and S. C. Kernerman.

Between the Two World Wars. The two decades from 1919 to 1939 were a period of intensive Zionist growth and propaganda. The 1921 (Jan. 30–Feb. 1) convention of the Zionist Federation adopted a resolution to raise $1,000,000 for the *Keren HaYesod (Palestine Foundation Fund). The total Jewish population of Canada being no more than 125,000 at the time, however, this amount had to be raised in installments as follows: 1922—$262,500; 1923—$151,500; 1925—$160,000; 1927—$218,000; and 1929—$208,000. On May 2, 1921, Chaim *Weizmann made his first visit to Canada, appealing for maximum support for Keren HaYesod. In addition to Weizmann, Canadian Jewry played host to such spokesmen of World Zionism as Itamar *Ben Avi, Brig. Gen. Sir Wyndham *Deedes, Sh'marya *Levin, Leo *Motzkin, Maurice *Samuel, and Nahum *Sokolow.

Increased Jewish immigration also brought to Canada educators and men of letters, whose influence made for a growing interest in things Jewish. The Anglo-Jewish press grew, Yiddish dailies made their appearance, the Yiddish theater flourished, and Yeshivot and Talmud Toras (Hebrew schools) were developed and modernized. The Yiddishist schools—Yiddish was still the common language of Canadian Jewry—became increasingly Zionist-oriented.

This period of intensified Jewish life, in which Zionism and Zionists played a seminal role, saw the continued development of Zionist ideological groupings. Several Labor Zionist organizations were established. The Canadian *Ahdut 'Avoda was founded in Toronto in 1921; by 1922 it had branches in Montreal, Windsor, Hamilton, Winnipeg, and Calgary. In 1924 the Labor Zionist movement introduced the *Histadrut Campaign into Canada, and the year 1926 saw the beginnings of a women's division which later became the Pioneer Women's Organization of Canada (see PIONEER WOMEN). The *HaBonim Labor Zionist Youth movement did not come to Canada until 1938.

That year the activities of Po'ale Zion, Farband, Pioneer Women, HaBonim Labor Zionist Youth, and the Canadian Histadrut Campaign were united into the Labor Zionist Movement of Canada, a national roof organization. The initiator of this development was the Labor Zionist leader Moshe Dickstein, who was national president of the Labor Zionist Movement from 1938 to 1956.

Religious Zionist youth organized the *Tora va'Avoda youth movement in the early 1930s. Several years later the Canadian Mizrahi became an autonomous part of the Mizrahi World Movement.

Under the leadership of Mrs. Archibald J. (Lillian) *Freiman, O.B.E., of Ottawa, who in 1919 had been elected chairman of the Hadassah Society of Canada by the ZOC, many new Hadassah chapters were organized across the country. When the Women's International Zionist Organization was formed in 1920, Canadian Hadassah became one of its constituent federations. The first Canadian national convention of Hadassah met in 1921 and elected Mrs. Freiman to the national presidency, an office she held until her death in 1940.

Mrs. Freiman's husband, Archibald J. *Freiman, was elected president of the Federation of Zionist Societies in 1919 (after 1923, the Zionist Organization of Canada), remaining in office until 1944. His long tenure was typical of the stability of Zionist leadership in Canada during the early decades of the century. Under his administration the 21st annual convention of the ZOC (1927) undertook to purchase the Hefer Valley, a region bordering on the Mediterranean, and raised $1,000,000 for this purpose within five years.

The ZOC approved the founding, in 1923, of the Zionist order HaBonim by Rabbi Judah L. *Zlotnick and supplied the major part of its budget. The members of this organization, of which Rabbi Julius Berger was the first president, earned the reputation of being Zionist shock troops. They organized lodges in a number of cities and held national conventions. One of the major achievements of the order was its part in the founding of Kissufim, a kibbutz in the Negev, by a group of young Canadians. Between 1931 and 1932, and again in 1946, the order published a periodical, *HaBoneh*. In 1950 the name of the order was changed to Zionist Men's Association of Canada (Bone Zion). In 1963 it ceased to be an autonomous body, becoming part of the Membership and Organization Department of the ZOC.

Until the formation of the United Zionist Council of Canada (see below) in 1941, the ZOC conducted all Zionist public relations work in the country. Outstanding events in this sphere in the years preceding World War II were addresses by Richard B. Bennett, Prime Minister of Canada, on a nationwide radio hookup on Apr. 15, 1934, and Governor-General Lord Tweedsmuir (John Buchan) on Apr. 20, 1936, in each case to launch the *United Palestine Appeal in Canada.

The *Shekel (membership fee) was the highly regarded symbol of World Zionist affiliation, and elections of delegates to World Zionist Congresses were at times hotly contested affairs. When asked, after the formation of the extended *Jewish Agency in 1929, whether non-Zionists would be coopted on the councils of the ZOC, Freiman asserted that there were no "non-Zionists" in Canada.

With the growing emphasis on the need for *'Aliya, *Hakhshara (agricultural training) farms were founded in the provinces of Quebec and Ontario, the first being established at Chambly Basin, Que., in 1933.

World War II. Zionist conventions during the war years adopted a number of resolutions appealing to the Canadian government and to world opinion to support the effort on behalf of a Jewish National Home, and a resolution in 1941 urging the formation of a Jewish army and the admission of Palestine as a member of the British Commonwealth.

In 1941 the ZOC, Po'ale Zion–*Tz'ire Zion, and Mizrahi formed the United Zionist Council of Canada (UZC) for the purpose of planning concerted political action and establishing pro-Palestine committees. The council also planned cooperative fund-raising campaigns, regulated collections for Palestine by agencies not sponsored by any of the above-named Zionist parties, conducted Shekel registration, and carried on propaganda and educational campaigns to attract the young and the unaffiliated.

That same year, the JNF was set up as a separate department of the ZOC, with Rev. Jacob K. *Goldbloom, who had come to Canada from England, serving as its first executive director.

In 1942 the Mizrahi Women's Organization of Canada began to function as a national body, and Young Judaea set up its first summer camp.

Zionist cultural activities continued throughout the war years. The Keren HaTarbut (Canadian Hebrew Culture Organization), organized in Montreal in 1942 on the initiative of the Zionist order HaBonim, became a national body in 1944, holding its first convention in Toronto. In 1944, too, the Canadian Friends of the *Hebrew University of Jerusalem, which had first been formed in 1937 in Montreal, set up a national organization with Allan Bronfman as national president. He still held that office in 1967.

Since the Establishment of the State of Israel. After 1948 Canadian Zionists continued to provide economic and cultural support for the State of Israel and to aid 'Aliya. Beginning in 1949 the United Israel Appeal collected between $3,000,000 and $3,500,000 annually.

Several new organizations were formed to give economic assistance to the young State. In 1948 Canpal–Canadian-Palestine Trading Company, Ltd., was incorporated and soon thereafter was renamed Canpal–Canadian-Israel Trading Company, Ltd. (see AMPAL). Its objective was to introduce Israeli products to the Canadian market. By 1966 Canpal's total volume of business and trade with Israel reached $21,000,000. The Canada-Israel Corporation was founded in 1951 jointly by the ZOC and the Canadian Jewish Congress to provide Israel with a revolving credit of several million dollars for the purchase of wheat and other commodities in Canada.

In 1953 Canada-Israel Securities, Ltd., was organized to sponsor the sale of Israel bonds (see STATE OF ISRAEL BONDS). By the end of 1966 total bond purchases in Canada reached $59,600,000.

In 1955 JNF began to plant 2 million trees in a Canada Forest at 'En HaKerem. Thousands of dunams (see DUNAM) of land were purchased in the western Negev, in the B'er Sheva' area, and many "family forests" were planted. In 1963 the Fund adopted as its project the development of the D'vir region, in the northern Negev, bordering on Jordan. The Canadian Foundation, established in 1955, was instrumental in obtaining substantial subscriptions for various JNF projects. In 1962 the JNF of Canada, which until then had been administered by a committee of the United Zionist Council of Canada, was incorporated as an autonomous body.

Canadian Jewry took an active interest in Israel's institutions of culture and higher learning. In 1962 the Canadian Friends of the Hebrew University launched a Family Endowment Plan, adopted and extended by the Board of Governors of the university into a World Endowment Plan, with a goal of $100,000,000. By 1966 the Friends of the University had 56 chapters in Canada. The organization developed a steady network of scholarships and had dental and pharmacy divisions to help the respective schools in Israel. Through its efforts, several buildings were erected on the new campus of the university and at Rehovot.

In 1951 the Canadian Technion Society was founded to aid the Haifa *Technion (Israel Institute of Technology). By the end of 1966 this organization had branches in Montreal, Ottawa, and Toronto, with a membership of 2,500. A large number of scholarships were established by the Men's and Women's Divisions. In 1966 the construction of the Canada Building, which houses the Technion's department of natural resources, was completed at a cost of $2,000,000. The *Technion Review* was published four times yearly. In 1966 D. Lou Harris of Toronto was national president, and Mrs. Lillian Mendelssohn of Montreal, national president of the Women's Division.

The Canadian Friends of *Bar-Ilan University, formed in 1954 as an autonomous body, contributed funds toward the erection of several buildings on the Ramat Gan campus and established many scholarships.

In October, 1957, Louis M. Bloomfield, Q.C., and Mendel Ladsky founded the Israel Maritime League of Canada, to raise funds for scholarships for the Nautical College at 'Akko (Acre) and for the Fisheries and Seamanship School at M'vo'ot Yam. The league also supports the Haifa Maritime Museum and the training of naval cadets in Israel. Since 1958 the group has published an annual, *Ha Yam* (The Sea). In 1966 the league had a membership of 1,500, with branches in all Canadian ports.

To foster 'Aliya, the Jewish Agency established in Canada a Youth and HeHalutz Department in 1954 and, in 1959, an Economic Department and an 'Aliya Office. The latter functioned as a department of the United Zionist Council of Canada. During the period from 1948 to the end of 1963, 1,466 persons from Canada settled in Israel. By the end of 1963 there were some 2,100 former Canadians in the country. As of 1967 Canadian Jewry was represented in Israel by two settlements in the Hefer Valley: Bitan Aharon and Havatzelet HaSharon, named for Archibald J. Freiman and Lillian Freiman, respectively.

Election of delegates to Zionist Congresses on the basis of Shekels sold was obviated by an agreement allotting representation to the various Zionist parties. Thus, the number of delegates to the 1960–61 World Zionist Congress was as follows: ZOC and Hadassah, 6; Labor Zionists, 4; Mizrahi–HaPo'el HaMizrahi, 3; *Herut, 1; and Ahdut 'Avoda, 1.

Although it was influenced by Zionist cultural and spiritual activity in the United States, Zionism in Canada developed a life and character of its own, colored in no small part by interchanges with British Jews, significant numbers of whom settled in Canada, particularly after World War II.

Zionist Organizations. In the mid-1960s the following Zionist organizations were active in Canada:

Zionist Organization of Canada (ZOC). The largest and most influential Zionist body in Canada in the 1960s, the ZOC was the parent body of Canadian Hadassah, of Canadian Young Judaea, and of the Zionist order HaBonim (which in 1950 changed its name to Zionist Men's Association and was dissolved in 1963) and sponsor of the *Student Zionist Organization. Until their merger in more recent years with local community appeals, all Keren HaYesod, United Palestine Appeal, and United Israel Appeal campaigns were conducted by the ZOC. Its official organ is the *Canadian Zionist* (first issued in 1934), which is published 10 months in the year.

The following men succeeded Archibald J. Freiman as president of the ZOC: a Presidium of Three—Michael *Garber, Samuel E. Schwisberg, and Samuel *Zacks (1944–46); Samuel Zacks (1946–50); Edward E. *Gelber and Samuel E. Schwisberg (copresidents, 1950–52); Edward E. Gelber (1952–56); Michael Garber (1956–58); Lawrence *Freiman (1958–62); Joseph N. Frank (1962–64); Lawrence Freiman (1964–67); and Julius Hayman (1967–   ). In 1968 the organization had about 40,000 members (membership comprises contributors of $15 or more to the United Israel Appeal).

Ahdut 'Avoda–Po'ale Zion (United Labor Zionist party). At the end of 1966 the party in Canada, which was affiliated with the Ahdut 'Avoda party of Israel, had 800 members and sponsored a fraternal organization, the Independent Workers Circle. It maintained schools and three kindergartens in Toronto; a youth group, *D'ror, numbering 110 boys and girls; and a summer camp in Ontario. A Yiddish-language monthly, *Unzer Veg,* was published in Toronto. By the mid-1960s, nearly 40 Canadian families and individuals belonging to the party had settled in various kibbutzim in Israel.

Farband (Labor Zionist fraternal order). At the end of 1966 this organization, which was affiliated with the order in the United States, had 25 branch groups in Montreal, Toronto, Winnipeg, Windsor, and Hamilton, with a membership of 3,500.

*Friends of Pioneering Israel–*Mapam.* Founded in 1956 as successor to the Progressive Zionist League (which had been formed in 1948), this organization supported joint Arab-Jewish centers in Israel and the Dr. William Cantor House in Haifa (a social center for youth), a joint project of the United States and Canadian membership. In 1964 it had about 500 members, a national headquarters in Montreal, and branch offices in Halifax, Ottawa, and Toronto.

HaBonim Labor Zionist Youth. Affiliated with the HaBonim of North America, the HaBonim Labor Zionist Youth was sponsored by the Labor Zionist Movement of Canada, which furnished its entire Canadian budget. The total membership of Canadian HaBonim in 1966 was 500. There were three HaBonim summer camps. A large number of HaBonim graduates went to Israel, settling in Urim, K'far Blum, and other kibbutzim.

Hadassah–WIZO Organization of Canada. In 1958 the name of the Hadassah organization was changed to Hadassah–WIZO Organization of Canada. Although it remained an affiliate of the ZOC, it set up its own treasury in 1950 and became autonomous in 1963 by virtue of a charter from the Dominion government.

Canadian Hadassah was the sole representative of *Youth 'Aliya and *Magen David Adom in Canada, raising funds for the many projects of the latter in Israel. Since 1948 the annual budget has been at least $1,000,000. Its past achievements include the planting of the Canadian Hadassah Forest and the building and equipping of the Chaim Weizmann Memorial Biology Science Building, Canada Hall, and Massey Hall at the Hebrew University; the Hanna *Maisel-Shohat Agricultural School at Nahalal; the children's and youth village Hadasim for agricultural training; and the temporary hospital at Elat.

The organization published a monthly magazine, Ora, and had a supplement in the Canadian Zionist. In 1966 there were 325 chapters in 70 cities, with a membership of 16,000 and an additional 10,000 contributors.

The following women served as national presidents after Mrs. Freiman: Anna Raginsky (1941–47); Mrs. H. (Rosa) Singer (1947–51); Mrs. D. P. (Sarah) Gotlieb (1951–55); Mrs. William (Lottie) Riven (1955–60); Mrs. Harry (Nina) Cohen (1960–64); Mrs. Charles (Anne) Eisenstat (1964–68); and Mrs. Hyman Wisenthal (1968–   ).

*HaShomer HaTza'ir Zionist Youth movement. Part of the HaShomer organization of North America, whose central office is in New York, HaShomer HaTza'ir had no Canadian national office or officers in the 1960s. Its members were among the founders of the kibbutz 'En HaShofet in 1937. A summer camp, Shomria, was maintained at Otto Lake, Perth, Ont. Hakhshara farms were maintained for a time at Prescott and Smithville, Ont., and a Bet HeHalutz in Montreal. In 1966 the membership in Canada comprised 300 boys and girls, aged 10 to 20, mainly in Montreal and Toronto.

Histadrut Campaign. The Histadrut Campaign was conducted by the Canadian Association for Labor Palestine (later called Labor Israel). Affiliated with the *Histadrut in Israel, the association was responsible for many specific Israeli projects in the fields of medical care, vocational training, and economic rehabilitation. Affiliated with the association were Histadrut Leagues and Canada-Israel Fellowship Clubs in several Canadian cities. The income in 1963 was $569,000. The cumulative total income from 1924 to the end of 1966 was more than $9,000,000.

Keren HaTarbut (Canadian Hebrew Culture Organization). An affiliate of ZOC since 1963, this organization maintained Hebrew-speaking camps, organized a women's group, HeN, and published Hebrew literature for children.

Labor Zionist Movement of Canada. This central body coordinated the activities of the Po'ale Zion, Farband, Pioneer Women, HaBonim Labor Zionist Youth, the Canadian Histadrut Campaign, Canpal–Canadian-Israel Trading Company, Ltd., and five summer camps.

The Labor Zionist Movement was the only Zionist organization in Canada to maintain a Jewish school system. It was active in instituting the sale of Israel bonds in Canada and was affiliated with the *Ihud 'Olami, the world federation of the Labor Zionist movement. Its official organ was the English-Yiddish bimonthly The Voice–Dos Vort. The following men served as national president after Moshe Dickstein: Isidore M. Bobrove, Q.C. (1956–60); Dr. Samuel B. Hurwich (1960–63); and Leon Kronitz (1963–   ).

Mizrahi–HaPo'el HaMizrahi Organization of Canada. A part of the worldwide religious Zionist movement, this organization has regional offices in Toronto and Winnipeg.

HaPo'el HaMizrahi, formerly known as the Tora va'Avoda youth movement, merged with Mizrahi in 1956. The Canadian Mizrahi made possible the establishment of Youth 'Aliya hostels and trade schools. It published the Mizrahi Voice, in Yiddish and English, five times yearly. It sponsored and provided the budget for the *B'ne 'Akiva youth movement, which in

1966 had a membership of 1,800 and owned a summer camp in Ontario. In 1966 Joel Sternthal of Montreal was national president, and Rabbi Seymour M. Zambrowsky, national chairman.

Mizrahi–HaPo'el HaMizrahi Women's Organization of Canada. In 1966 this women's organization had a membership of 4,000, organized in 52 chapters in 10 communities. Canadian projects in Israel included several nursery schools, dormitories, and vocational schools. The organization also contributed to projects of the World Mizrahi Women's Organization in Israel. In 1966 Mrs. I. I. (Miriam) Lieff was national president.

Pioneer Women's Organization of Canada. The women's division of the Labor Zionist Movement of Canada raised funds for all projects of the *Mo'etzet HaPo'alot (Working Women's Council of Israel), with which it is affiliated, and also supported all the activities of the Labor Zionist Movement of Canada. Several former national officers have settled in Israel. In 1966 the organization consisted of 100 clubs in 12 cities, with a membership of 3,500.

Po'ale Zion party. In 1966 the party existed in larger cities in the form of local clubs that were represented directly on local and national bodies of the Labor Zionist Movement of Canada. The Po'ale Zion was instrumental in founding several Jewish schools in a number of Canadian cities.

Student Zionist Organization (SZO). The SZO began its activities in Canada in 1954 as a continuation of the former IZFA (Intercollegiate Zionist Federation of America) and as a subsidiary of the International Student Zionist Organization. The ZOC provided the major part of its Canadian budget. In 1966 the SZO of Canada had a membership of 400 students at eight universities, in seven cities.

United Zionist Council of Canada (UZC). Originally the council consisted of 18 members representing constituent organizations as follows: ZOC, 12; Labor Zionists, 4; and Mizrahi, 2. This representation was later changed to 12, 6, and 4, respectively. In 1960 the council was reconstituted to include all Zionist groups in Canada recognized by the World Zionist Organization. The major parties were to have equal representation, and the ZOC was to have the right of veto with respect to financial and budgetary matters. The United Zionist Revisionist party (see REVISIONISTS), Friends of Pioneering Israel–Mapam, and Ahdut 'Avoda were admitted to the council, and in 1962 'Aliya was added to its program.

In the mid-1960s all public statements regarding Zionism and all representations to the Canadian government were made jointly by the UZC and the Canadian Jewish Congress.

Young Judaea. Renamed Federation of Young Judaea of Canada in 1922 and Canadian Young Judaea in 1931, this organization had its full budget provided by the ZOC. Between 1948 and 1963, 40 Young Judaeans went on 'Aliya, 83 took one-year courses in Israel, and 75 took summer courses there. In 1951 Canadian Young Judaea became affiliated with *Ha-No'ar HaTziyoni, the worldwide liberal Zionist youth movement.

By 1966 Young Judaea had five summer camps. It published an official monthly, the Judaean, which had first appeared in 1917. In 1966 the organization had 2,000 members, distributed over 40 communities. Membership consisted of boys and girls aged 8 to 25, divided into five age groups.

Zionist Revisionist Organization of Canada. Affiliated with the Herut party of Israel, it had members in Montreal, Toronto, Hamilton, and Winnipeg, including women's chapters. It published a weekly in Toronto, the *Daily Hebrew Journal,* in Yiddish and English, and for a number of years published a *Year Book.* The president in 1966 was Nathan Silver.

The organization sponsored the *B'rit Trumpeldor (Betar) youth movement in Montreal and Toronto. Members attended the Betar summer camp in the United States, and a number of them went to work and study in Israel for various periods of time.

Federated Zionist Organization. From Mar. 31 to Apr. 4, 1967, the founding convention of the Federated Zionist Organization, which embraced all Canadian Zionist groups and parties, took place in Toronto. Sam Chait, Q.C., was elected president and John R. Devor and Leon Kronitz, deputy presidents. Early in 1968 six regional executive boards were set up and began wide-ranging programming and other activities.

B. FIGLER

CANADA AND ZIONISM. Christian sentiment in Canada was always favorable to the Zionist ideal. One outstanding Canadian Christian Zionist was Henry Wentworth Monk, of Ottawa, who gave up a promising career and marriage to dedicate his life to the ideal of Israel's Return to Zion. He made pilgrimages to the Holy Land in 1854 and 1863, decades before the first Canadian Jew, Lazarus Cohen of Montreal, visited Palestine in 1893. As early as 1882 Monk proposed the establishment of a Bank of Israel, and in 1891 he petitioned Queen Victoria "to issue a Royal Proclamation on behalf of the Jews, promising to restore them to Palestine." He died in 1896, one year before the birth of the Zionist movement.

Prime ministers, Cabinet members, mayors, and other prominent Canadians were guests at every Canadian Zionist convention and spoke out in favor of the Zionist movement. Although the Canadian government was thus well aware of the deep interest of Canadian Jews in Zionism, the Zionist aims were also brought to its attention by the British government, which in 1917 consulted it on the text of the proposed *Balfour Declaration. When Lord *Balfour came expressly to Ottawa for that purpose, the president of the Federation of Zionist Societies of Canada, Clarence I. *de Sola, was summoned to Ottawa to meet with him. In 1920 the Canadian government intervened officially with the British government to advocate a British trusteeship for the establishment of a Jewish National Home in Palestine.

In general, however, the Canadian government as such had little occasion to express itself officially regarding Zionism, nor did it adopt any policy on the subject until the establishment of the State of Israel. For one thing, it was only toward the end of this period that a Department for External Affairs evolved. Until then the Prime Minister would express the stand of the government in personal statements, and members of the government would state their personal views on Zionism or on a particular situation in response to appeals by Jewish or Zionist leaders. Moreover, since Britain had the *Mandate for Palestine, all that the Canadian government could do was transmit such Zionist petitions as it received from Canadian Zionist organizations to the British government for consideration. Only from the early 1940s on did the Canadian government have its own diplomatic service and could it receive and act on Zionist submissions.

Beginning as early as 1897, every Canadian Prime Minister expressed his sympathy with the Zionist cause. Shortly after the issuance of the Balfour Declaration, Prime Minister Arthur Meighen addressed a Zionist gathering and expressed his government's support and approval of the declaration.

In 1943, during World War II, a Canadian Palestine Committee modeled after the *American Palestine Committee was formed by prominent Christians in various walks of life, to lend their voice and influence in molding public opinion on behalf of Zionist aims. In 1946 the committee submitted a brief to the External Affairs Committee of the House of Commons, recommending a policy of Canada in support of a Jewish State in Palestine (reported in Minutes of Proceedings and Evidence of External Affairs Committee Nos. 14 and 15, Session 1946, House of Commons).

Sir Ellsworth Flavelle was elected chairman of the Canadian Palestine Committee in 1943. In 1945 a *World Committee for Palestine was formed in Washington, D.C., by similar committees representing 30 nations. Sir Ellsworth was chosen president of this world body, which was active from 1945 to 1949 and made representations to the United Nations on behalf of a Jewish State in Palestine. Its work was praised by the government of the new Jewish State. In 1948 the name of the Canadian committee was changed to Canada-Israel Association; the organization was still active in 1967. Sir Ellsworth was the national chairman, and Herbert A. Mowat was the national director.

In 1947 Mr. Justice Ivan C. Rand of the Supreme Court of Canada represented Canada on the *United Nations Special Committee on Palestine (UNSCOP), which recommended the establishment of a Jewish State. Lester B. Pearson, later Prime Minister of Canada, who represented Canada at the United Nations, strongly supported the plan to partition Palestine and played a leading role in the acceptance of the proposal by the United Nations in November, 1947. Prominent as a mediator in international disputes, Pearson proposed the UN Emergency Force in the Suez crisis of 1956, and in February, 1957, he proposed that the *Gaza Strip be internationalized. In the same year, he became the first Canadian to win the Nobel Peace Prize. In connection with the *Six-day War of 1967, Canada again demonstrated her traditional friendship to Israel.

The Canadian government extended de facto recognition to Israel on Dec. 24, 1948, and de jure recognition on May 11, 1949. The following persons served as Canadian ambassadors to Israel: Terrence W. L. MacDermot (1954), E. D'Arcy McGreer (1957), Margaret Meager (1958), A. J. Andrew (1962), and R. L. Rogers (1962). The first Israeli Consul General, Avraham *Harman, arrived in Canada in 1949. Michael S. *Comay, Israel's first Minister to Canada, arrived in Canada in 1953 and was raised to the rank of ambassador in 1954.

B. FIGLER

CANADIAN JEWS IN ISRAEL. *See* AMERICAN AND CANADIAN JEWS IN ISRAEL.

CANPAL–CANADIAN-ISRAEL TRADING COMPANY, LTD. *See* AMPAL.

CANTONI, RAFFAELE. Zionist leader and banking consultant in Italy (b. Venice, 1896). Persecuted under the Fascist regime, Cantoni was very active in helping refugees from Germany prior to World War II. Interned by the Italians at the outbreak of the war, he was then arrested by the Germans but escaped from a deportation train. After the war, in 1945, he was Financial Commissioner of northern Italy. He organized the Jewish Community of Milan, served as president of the Union of Italian-Jewish Communities, and headed fund-raising campaigns from 1948 to 1950. A member of the Council of the Italian Zionist Federation and Italian member of the Executive of the *World Jewish Congress, Cantoni was also the founder of the Fondazione Italiana per la Gioventù Ebraica (Italian Foundation for Jewish Youth) and supported it for many years. He was president of the *OSE and headed many other Jewish and Zionist activities in Italy after World War II.

G. ROMANO

CANTONIZATION PLAN. *See* MORRISON-GRADY PLAN.

CAPERNAUM (K'far Nahum). Archeological site on the north shore of Lake Tiberias. A late-2d-century synagogue, representing the purest version of the early type, has been unearthed here. It is decorated with a notable relief frieze showing a mixture of religious and fertility symbols.

CAPITAL FOR ISRAEL, INC. American corporation founded in 1966, at the request of the Israel *government, by leaders of the *State of Israel Bonds Organization to offer Israeli securities in the United States. The first offering of Capital for Israel, Inc., was stock in the Industrial Development Bank of Israel, and in 1968 the corporation was in the process of selling $20,000,000 in shares (preferred stock) in the bank. In 1968 Capital for Israel had headquarters in New York; Sydney Lubarr was national director, and Samuel Rothberg, of Peoria, Ill., and Joseph J. *Schwartz were president and vice-president, respectively.

CARLEBACH, AZRIEL. Writer and journalist (b. Leipzig, Germany, 1908; d. Tel Aviv, 1956). Scion of a German rabbinic family, he received his education in Yeshivot in Eastern Europe, in Jerusalem, and at German universities. In his youth he wrote mainly belles lettres, but later he devoted himself to journalism, serving numerous major Jewish newspapers and other periodicals. From 1929 to 1933 he was editor of the *Jüdisches Familienblatt* (Hamburg). After the rise of Nazism in Germany, he lived for some time in Poland, where he served on the editorial board of the daily *Hajnt,* and in London, where he edited the *Yidishe Post.*

Settling in Palestine in 1936, he founded in 1939 the afternoon paper *Y'di'ot Aharonot* and was its editor until 1948. That year he founded the afternoon paper *Ma'ariv,* which he developed into the country's most widely read newspaper. Carlebach was not only one of Israel's ablest and most influential publicists but also the author of several books and studies, including travel impressions.

CARMEL, MOSHE. Israeli labor leader and Cabinet member (b. Mińsk Mazowiecki, Russian Poland, 1911). Settling in Palestine in 1924, he was active in *HaNo'ar Ha'Oved V'ha-Lomed and joined kibbutz Na'an. Working in the *Hagana, he was arrested by the British and spent more than a year and a half in *'Akko Prison. Subsequently he held major positions in the Hagana, including that of commander of the Haifa District. During the *War of Independence he was commander of the Northern District. Carmel played a leading role in Israel's labor movement, serving in the *Knesset for a number of years as the representative of *Ahdut 'Avoda. From 1955 to 1959 and again from 1966, he was Minister of Transport. He wrote *Within the*

Walls, letters from 'Akko Prison, and *The Battles of the North,* on the War of Independence, both in Hebrew.

Moshe Carmel.
[Israel Information Services]

CARMEL, MOUNT. The only mountainous area in Israel that approaches the Mediterranean Sea and forms a distinct cape. Geologically it is a tilted block that rises abruptly in the east above the valleys of Z'vulun and Jezreel to an average height of 1,200 feet, with the peak in Rom Carmel (1,791 feet). From there it slopes gradually to the west with a final steep descent to the Carmel coast, which is approximately 2 miles wide. The proximity to the sea causes very steep dissection by rivers and divides the mountain into isolated spurs, which are connected only by a road along the watershed. It also makes for greater rainfall (up to 30 inches) than in the neighboring parts of the country. The greater moisture and the strong dissection have preserved here large tracts of natural forest, which today form the main attraction of Mount Carmel.

The mountain is mainly limestone, which formed numerous caves; in some of them remains of one of the oldest human species (Carmel man) have been discovered. Others have been connected with legends, especially of the prophet Elijah. Settlement is sparse; prior to Jewish settlement it comprised only two Druze villages (*see* DRUZE COMMUNITY IN ISRAEL). In recent years a number of kibbutzim have settled on its spurs. Its main utilization, however, is for purposes of recreation and urban development. The city of Haifa, which is built on a spur, occupies large tracts of its slopes and spreads along its crest toward the south. Its northern flanks are utilized as limestone quarries and supply raw material to the largest cement factory of Israel.

Y. KARMON

CARPI, LEONE. Lawyer and Zionist leader (b. Rome, 1887; d. Tel Aviv, 1964). Carpi was a member of the Italian Committee of *Keren HaYesod (Palestine Foundation Fund) from 1924, of the Zionist Organization of Milan, and of the World Union of Zionists-Revisionists (*see* REVISIONISTS), serving as the Italian representative from 1928. He headed the Revisionist youth organization *B'rit Trumpeldor (Betar) in Italy to 1936. Editor of the magazine *L'Idea Sionnista* from 1930 to 1938, Carpi published a selection of the writings and speeches of Vladimir *Jabotinsky in 1960. He was active in the organization of *illegal immigration into Palestine. World War II interrupted his activities, but after the war he was active again in the *New Zionist Organization, and from 1947, when the Revisionists reentered the *World Zionist Organization, he was their representative. Carpi was a member of the Council of the Italian Zionist Federation from 1948 to 1956 (vice-president from 1949 to 1951) and a delegate to the 23d, 24th, and 25th Zionist Congresses (see CONGRESS, ZIONIST).

G. ROMANO

CASTEL, MOSHE. Israeli painter (b. Jerusalem, 1909). Descended from an old Sephardi family (see SEPHARDIM), he is one of the few older artists born in Palestine. From 1927 to 1940 Castel lived and studied in Paris. His style of painting changed repeatedly, and his later works were very close to pure abstraction. Castel founded the Ofakim Hadashim (New Horizons) group, gathering around him the young and progressive artists of Israel. He participated in the 24th Venice Biennale, and in 1959 received the Grand Prize at the 5th Bienal of São Paulo, Brazil.

A. WERNER

CAZALET, EDWARD. British industrialist and advocate of Jewish settlement in Palestine (b. Brighton, England, 1827; d. Constantinople, 1883). In factories he owned in Russia, Cazalet came into contact with the Jewish masses and was shocked by their lack of civil rights, their poverty, and the persecution they suffered. He recognized the attraction of Palestine for the Jews and the interests of the British in the area. From 1878 on he propagated in speeches and in writing the mass settlement of Jews in Palestine under a British protectorate. He also advocated the establishment of a Jewish university there. Later, after his project had failed to make headway, he sought a concession from the Turkish government for the settlement of Jews in some part of Asiatic Turkey, promising that he and his friends would provide financial means for the development of the region, but his efforts did not meet with success.

J. FRAENKEL

CAZALET, VICTOR ALEXANDER. British soldier and member of Parliament, grandson of Edward *Cazalet (b. London, 1896; d. 1943). From 1924 until his death in an air crash over Gibraltar while returning from the Middle East, Cazalet was a Conservative member of the British Parliament. A constant defender of Zionism in the House of Commons, he pleaded in speeches and articles for the restoration of the Jewish State. He and Josiah *Wedgwood (later Baron Wedgwood) were joint chairmen of the Parliamentary Palestine Committee. Cazalet was also chairman of the Parliamentary Committee on Refugees, the National Committee for Rescue from Nazi Terror, and the Committee for a Jewish Fighting Force.

CENTRAL ZIONIST ARCHIVES. See LIBRARIES AND ARCHIVES, ZIONIST.

CERTIFICATE. See IMMIGRATION TO PALESTINE AND ISRAEL.

CHAGALL, MARC (Moshe). Surrealist artist (b. Vitebsk, Russia, 1889). His works include paintings, engravings, murals, costume and décor designs for ballet and theater, and ceramics, and are distinguished for their lively fantasy and striking use of color. His work has been exhibited in museums throughout the world, including those in Jerusalem and Tel Aviv.

Chagall drew his inspiration largely from the life of the Hasidim and village Jews in Eastern Europe. His better-known works of specifically Jewish interest include "I and My Village," the "Rabbi of Vitebsk," and illustrations for the Bible (1956).

He first visited Palestine in 1931 and later returned to Israel several times. In June, 1959, he was commissioned by *Hadassah to design stained-glass windows for the synagogue of the new Hebrew University–Hadassah Medical Center in the 'En Ha-Kerem quarter of Jerusalem. The 12 windows, installed in 1962, interpret the story of the Twelve Tribes of Israel. Chagall also designed a tapestry and mosaic floors and murals for the new *Knesset building which was opened in 1966.

CHAJES, ZVI PERETZ. Rabbi, scholar, and Zionist leader (b. Brody, Galicia, Austria, 1876; d. Vienna, 1927). He studied at the Yeshiva of Brody, Vienna Rabbinical Seminary, and the University of Vienna. In 1902 he became a professor at the Collegio Rabbinico Italiano in Florence, and two years later professor of Hebrew at the university there as well. In 1912 he was elected chief rabbi of Trieste and in 1918 chief rabbi of Vienna, a position he held until his death.

Chajes was the author of numerous studies on the Bible and the Talmud as well as in Jewish history and literature; he wrote commentaries on the Psalms and the Book of Amos and published from manuscript an 11th-century commentary on the Talmudic tractate Mo'ed Katan. Prominently associated with Jewish relief and educational activities, he established a variety of educational institutions in Vienna, including a teachers seminary and a Hebrew high school.

One of the outstanding personalities in the Zionist movement, Chajes actively promoted the idea of Jewish national rebirth. A brilliant orator, he visited various countries, including the United States, on behalf of Zionist fund-raising campaigns. From 1921 to 1925 he was chairman of the Zionist *Actions Committee. He also headed the Austrian committee for the *Hebrew University of Jerusalem, whose opening in 1925 he attended.

CHAMBERLAIN, JOSEPH. British statesman (b. London, 1836; d. Birmingham, 1914). Chamberlain was President of the Board of Trade from 1880 to 1885 and Secretary of State for the Colonies from 1895 to 1902 in the Cabinet of Lord Salisbury and in 1902–03 in Arthur James *Balfour's Cabinet.

Chamberlain first met Herzl on Oct. 22, 1902. During the one-hour interview, the Zionist leader suggested the establishment of an autonomous Jewish settlement in Sinai (El-'Arish area and the Pelusiac Plain; see EL-'ARISH SCHEME). According to Herzl's Diaries, Chamberlain agreed, provided that Lord *Cromer recommended it, and next day, at a short meeting, he arranged for Herzl to open negotiations with the Foreign Secretary, Lord Lansdowne, and the Foreign Office. At the end of 1902 Chamberlain visited South Africa, returning to London in March, 1903. On April 23 of that year, he again received Herzl and suggested a self-governing Jewish settlement in Uganda, which Herzl was unwilling to consider. Four weeks later, on May 20, Chamberlain offered to Leopold J. *Greenberg another, as yet not clearly defined, territory in the East Africa Protectorate. In the meantime the Sinai scheme had to be given up owing to the negative position taken by the Egyptian government. Herzl regarded it politically wise to maintain close contact with Britain and therefore advised the 6th Zionist *Congress not to reject outright Britain's offer but to send a commission to the area to investigate it.

Chamberlain, who resigned his post on Sept. 18, 1903, supported in subsequent years the *Jewish Territorial Organization in public statements but only insofar as the ITO contemplated the establishment of a Jewish settlement within the British Empire. In the course of years he also expressed on several occasions great admiration for Herzl and his policy.

Chamberlain was a significant figure in Zionist history because he was the first British statesman to understand the importance of the Zionist movement and to induce the British government to recognize and deal officially with the *World Zionist Organization. Herzl and the Zionist leadership endeavored to preserve this relationship in the conviction that Britain would continue to propose various areas for Jewish settlement until this would ultimately lead to British assistance in enabling the national colonization in Palestine. This is precisely what happened. Thus Chamberlain had an important share in laying the foundations for the later negotiations that led to the *Balfour Declaration.

J. FRAENKEL

CHAMBER THEATER. *See* THEATER IN ISRAEL.

CHANCELLOR, SIR JOHN ROBERT. British soldier and civil servant (b. Edinburgh, 1870; d. Lanark, Scotland, 1952). After a distinguished career in the British Army, Chancellor served as Governor and commander in chief of several British possessions (Mauritius, 1911–16; Trinidad and Tobago, 1916–21; Southern Rhodesia, 1923–28). From 1928 to 1931 he was British *High Commissioner for Palestine.

Chancellor arrived in Palestine after the Seventh Arab Congress (1928), which, in addition to passing the usual resolution repudiating the *Balfour Declaration, had demanded parliamentary institutions run along democratic lines. These, the delegates hoped, would be instrumental in bringing about the curtailment of Jewish *immigration to Palestine. Evaluating the situation from the point of view of British strategic interests and trained in the British colonial tradition, Chancellor was not in favor of Zionist aspirations and doubted the loyalty of the *Yishuv (Jewish population of Palestine) to the British Empire. The *Arab riots of 1929 broke out while he was on leave in London discussing the plan to set up a *Legislative Council. On his return to Palestine a week later, he issued a proclamation branding Arab onslaughts as savage crimes and promising measures to punish the guilty and to restore order. However, a subsequent proclamation was less outspoken in its condemnation of the Arabs, and Chancellor was said to have had a part in the framing of the anti-Zionist *Passfield White Paper. At a farewell reception tendered him by the mayor of Jerusalem when he left his post in Palestine, Chancellor said: "I came hoping to increase the country's prosperity and happiness. I am leaving with my ambition unfulfilled. The conditions have gone against me."

In August, 1945, Chancellor wrote a letter to the London *Times* supporting the *partition of Palestine in which he stated: "There is little moral value in maintaining political unity in Palestine at the cost of perpetual strife and bloodshed." He felt that "with the air forces of the great powers available within a few hours' range for the defense of Palestine, there will be little temptation for either state to attack its neighbor." Regarding possible financial difficulties, Chancellor believed that "the Jewish State can be supported by large subsidies from wealthy American Jews and will, undoubtedly, be self-supporting. The Arab State, on the other hand, will,

at least in its early days, require financial assistance from without."

I. KOLATT

CHARTER. Term derived from the Latin *charta* (paper or letter), denoting a letter of license or franchise of specified rights made by a government or a ruler to a person or corporation. When Herzl adopted this term, he seems to have had in mind the charter obtained on Oct. 20, 1889, by the British South African Company, in which the British government granted the company full autonomy in the Zambezi area with regard to administration of the territory and political activity in relation to the native population, under the supervision of the British government. In a similar manner, Herzl felt that the Zionist movement must endeavor to obtain a Charter for Palestine from the Turkish Sultan, under whose suzerainty the country was at the time. At the 3d Zionist *Congress (1899), Herzl accordingly stated: "Only when we will be in possession of this Charter, which must contain the necessary safeguards secured by public law, can we commence large-scale practical colonization."

The Charter concept was also advanced when the settlement schemes of El-'Arish and East Africa were negotiated with the British government (*see* EAST AFRICA SCHEME; EL-'ARISH SCHEME). Herzl himself had drafted a few Charter proposals.

Within the *World Zionist Organization bitter controversies had arisen with regard to the Charter, particularly after Herzl's death, when the "Charterites" continued to make practical settlement work dependent on the prior attainment of a Charter. But the movement rejected this concept. The *Balfour Declaration and the *Mandate for Palestine are often described in Zionist literature as the fulfillments of the Charter idea.

CHASAN, JACOB. *See* HAZAN, YA'AKOV.

CHASANOVICH, JOSEPH. Physician, founder of the Jewish National Library (subsequently renamed *Jewish National and University Library) in Jerusalem (b. Grodno, Russia, 1844; d. Yekaterinoslav, Russia, 1919). He studied medicine in Germany and practiced in Białystok, Russian Poland. An early follower of the *Hoveve Zion movement, he attended the *Kattowitz Conference and was a member of the secret order *B'ne Moshe. With the advent of Herzl, Chasanovich joined the Zionist movement and participated in Zionist Congresses (*see* CONGRESS, ZIONIST). In 1890, while on a visit to Jerusalem, he conceived the idea of establishing a Jewish National Library there. On his return to Russia, he began to collect books for the projected library and in 1895 sent 8,800 volumes to Jerusalem, continuing to gather books for the library until his death. He would accept books from his patients in lieu of cash fees and went into considerable debt to acquire books. During World War I he fled into the interior of Russia, where he died in poverty.

CHASANOWITSCH, LEON (Kasriel Schub). Pioneer and leader of *Labor Zionism, author, and editor (b. Širvintos, Lithuania, 1882; d. Vlachovze, Czechoslovakia, 1925). He organized the first *Po'ale Zion movement in Russian Poland and was subsequently arrested for his activities by the Tsarist authorities. After his release, he went to Galicia, where, in 1908, he became editor of *Der Yidisher Arbeter,* the Po'ale Zion periodical in Cracow and later in Lemberg (now Lvov). In 1909 Chasanowitsch toured the agricultural colonies of the *Jewish

Colonization Association (ICA) in Argentina, voicing severe criticism of their management and system of operation. As a result, he was deported from Argentina as an alleged anarchist. In 1910 he published *Der Krizis fun der Yidisher Kolonizacie in*

Leon Chasanowitsch.
[Zionist Archives]

Argentina (The Crisis of Jewish Colonization in Argentina), in which he outlined his critical observations. He later headed, with Ber *Borochov, the Central Office of Po'ale Zion in Vienna.

After the outbreak of World War I, Chasanowitsch went to The Hague, where he founded the periodical *Di Yidishe Arbeter Korrespondenz* to hold various factions of the Po'ale Zion party together during the war. In 1917 he went to the United States, where he participated in the campaign for the founding of the *American Jewish Congress and the People's Relief Committee, and until 1922 he served as editor of *Die Zeit,* the Po'ale Zion Yiddish daily in New York. He died while on a mission for *ORT in Czechoslovakia.

A. ALPERIN

CHIEF RABBINATE OF ISRAEL. *See* RABBINATE OF ISRAEL.

CHILE, ZIONISM IN. Marranos settled in Chile during the earliest period of Spanish rule and suffered greatly when the Inquisition was introduced there in 1570. Only after the country had gained independence (1810) and after the proclamation of religious liberty did the era of recent Jewish immigration begin.

In 1914 there were about 3,000 Jews in the country. Between 1934 and 1946, 15,000 Jews arrived; groups of 200 to 300 arrived in the 1950s, and a small group of Jewish refugees from Hungary immigrated in 1957. In 1968 there were in Chile about 35,000 Jews (90 per cent *Ashkenazim), of whom 33,000 lived in Santiago, the capital, and 1,200 in Valparaiso.

Zionist activity in Chile originated in 1910, when the first campaign on behalf of the *Jewish National Fund was begun. The first Zionist group came into being in 1911. In 1917, in the wake of the *Balfour Declaration, which aroused great enthusiasm, a National Jewish Committee was formed with the aim of unifying the entire Jewish community under the Zionist banner.

In 1919 the first Congress of Chilean Jewry, with the participation of representatives of 13 societies, was held. At the final session of this congress, the Zionist Federation of Chile was established. The main points of the federation's statutes and program, as laid down by the 1st Chilean Zionist Conference (1920), were as follows: (1) The Zionist Federation of Chile was

to include all Jewish and Zionist societies of the capital and the provinces. (2) The functions of the federation were *(a)* to represent the Jewish community before the authorities and before the public, *(b)* to spread the Zionist ideal, *(c)* to develop Jewish education, *(d)* to contribute to the rebuilding of the Jewish National Home in Palestine, *(e)* to guide the Zionist movement in Chile, and *(f)* to maintain contact with the headquarters of the *World Zionist Organization in London and Jerusalem.

Within the framework of the federation, Zionist groups of various ideologies cooperated harmoniously in work toward the common ideal, and for two decades the federation was the representative body of Chilean Jewry. In 1940 the Comité Representativo was set up at the initiative of several Chilean Zionist leaders to serve as the central communal authority, and it assumed the federation's function of representing the community in local matters.

During World War II and throughout the period leading to the *War of Independence and the establishment of the State of Israel, Zionist sentiment struck firm roots among the Jews of Chile. It persisted thereafter and was manifested on numerous occasions in the great response to the Solidarity Campaigns and the mass demonstrations held in honor of distinguished Israeli visitors. Among the Israeli statesmen who visited Chile were Zalman *Shazar, Moshe *Sharett, Golda *Meir, M'nahem *Begin, Sh'lomo Yoseph *Burg, Eliyahu *Dobkin, Berl *Locker, and Yoseph *Serlin.

There was practically no aspect of communal Jewish life in Chile that was not in some form linked with Israel and Zionism. The great majority of the Jewish population was, in some way, connected with the Zionist movement. The Cultural Department of the Zionist Federation played a very important role in communal life, and there were active Zionist workers in the Board of Education, which was responsible for Jewish schools, which had a total enrollment of 1,300 in 1968.

Almost all political tendencies and ideologies in the Zionist movement found adherents among the Jews of Chile, and with the passing of time parties and groups identifying themselves with the various Zionist ideologies were established in the country. In the 1960s the following Zionist groups were affiliated with the Zionist Federation: *Po'ale Zion (*Mapai), founded in 1933 as the successor to the League for Labor Palestine, was one of the two major Zionist parties in Chile; the General Zionist party (*see* GENERAL ZIONISM), founded in 1947, grew to become the other major party; the *Revisionists (*Herut),

Zionist conference in Santiago, Chile, in 1923. [Zionist Archives]

founded in 1932, became a potent force only at the end of World War II; the Independent Zionist party, established in 1955, did not identify itself with any political party in Israel but was affiliated with the General Zionist faction headed by Israel *Goldstein and Rose *Halprin; and *Mapam was established by former members of *HaShomer HaTza'ir and sympathizers. At one time, Mapam was quite influential, but later, owing largely to the emigration of its outstanding members to Israel, it lost some of its importance.

Two women's organizations were affiliated with the federation: the *Women's International Zionist Organization (WIZO) and *Pioneer Women. WIZO, established in 1926, had a fine record of Zionist activities; it helped maintain WIZO institutions in Israel and took a prominent part in Jewish National Fund drives. Pioneer Women, founded in 1948, became an important factor in local Zionist life and in activities on behalf of Israel.

Representation of the various parties in the federation was proportionate to their strength as established by elections. The president of the federation in 1968 was Enrique Alcalay; vice-presidents were Felipe Fliman, Miguel W. Maldavsky, Isaac Icekson, and León Tchimino.

A large segment of Jewish youth in Chile identified itself with Zionism. There were *Halutz (pioneer) youth organizations as well as groups of a social and sporting character. The former were HaShomer HaTza'ir, *HaNo'ar HaTziyoni, *B'rit Trumpeldor (Betar), Ihud HaBonim (see HABONIM), and LaMerhav. From their ranks came large numbers of pioneers who made their home in kibbutzim or elsewhere in Israel. Non-Halutz youth organizations were the Maccabi HaTza'ir, a social and athletic group, the Centro Universitario Judío (CUJ), and Barkai. They developed widespread activities, among which Zionism held a prominent place.

The efforts of the Zionist Federation on behalf of *'Aliya and capital investments in Israel were eminently successful. Hundreds of Chilean Jews settled in Israel. The Jewish community of Chile planted a forest dedicated to Gabriela Mistral, the great Chilean poet.

M. YUDELEVICH

CHINA, ZIONISM IN. This article deals with the development of Zionism in Shanghai, Tientsin, and Harbin, Manchuria, the three main centers of Jewish life in China, from the middle of the 19th century until the nearly total emigration of Jews following the Communist take-over in the late 1940s.

Historical Background. Jews had been living in China as early as C.E. 1000, but by the end of the 18th century their principal community, in Kaifeng, had virtually disappeared through assimilation. China's modern Jewish community can be said to have originated in the 1840s, when Sephardi Jews, mainly merchants from Baghdad, settled in China, primarily in Shanghai. They were followed by Russian Jews, mainly middle-class business people, who came in large numbers after the Russo-Japanese War (1904–05) and the Russian Revolution (1917). At first the Russian Jews were concentrated mainly in Harbin, where Russian influence was strong in the early 20th century, but in the 1930s many of them moved to Tientsin and Shanghai. They kept themselves apart from the Sephardim and largely retained the customs and way of life they had brought with them from Russia. Third and last to reach China were the refugees from Nazi Europe, who poured into Shanghai by the thousands between 1938 and 1941.

Before the Sino-Japanese War, 1903–37. In 1903 a Zionist group was founded in Shanghai (which by that time had a

Jewish population of 600) under the leadership of Nissim Ezra Benjamin Ezra (1880–1936), a merchant who had come to the city from India. Ezra was the honorary secretary of the Shanghai Zionist Association for many years, but he was best known as the editor of the newspaper *Israel's Messenger.* Except for an eight-year interruption (1910–18), *Israel's Messenger,* which identified itself as the "fearless exponent of Traditional Judaism and Jewish Nationalism" and the "official organ of the Shanghai Zionist Association and of the *Jewish National Fund Commission for China," was issued every other month (for a time, every month) from 1904 to 1941. After Ezra's death, his widow became editor. Through this newspaper Ezra secured pro-Zionist statements from the governments of China (which had endorsed the *Balfour Declaration in the form of a letter, dated Dec. 14, 1918, from Tcheng Loh, Vice-Minister in charge of Foreign Affairs, to Eliezer Silas Kadoorie, president of the Shanghai Zionist Association), Siam, and Japan. The most prominent of these statements was the following letter, addressed to Ezra on Apr. 24, 1920, by Sun Yat-sen, the founder of the Chinese Republic:

> Dr. Mr. Ezra:
>
> I have read your letter and the copy of *Israel's Messenger* with much interest, and wish to assure you of my sympathy for the movement—which is one of the greatest movements of the present time. All lovers of Democracy cannot help but support the movement to restore your wonderful and historic nation, which has contributed so much to the civilization of the world and which rightfully deserves an honourable place in the family of nations.
>
> I am,
> Yours very truly,
>
> SUN YAT-SEN

When Sun's remains were reentombed in the memorial built for him in Nanking (1929), Ezra and Mrs. R. E. Toeg, president of the Shanghai Zionist Association, were invited by the Chinese government to attend the ceremonies.

In October, 1929, Ezra published an open letter to Mohandas K. Gandhi to protest a statement purportedly made by Gandhi and other Hindu leaders to the Viceroy of India, to the effect that they would be willing to send 20,000 Hindus to Palestine to protect the Muslim holy places against supposed Jewish aggression. In reply, Gandhi sent a denial, which was published in *Israel's Messenger.*

Another prominent Zionist leader in Shanghai in the first three decades of the 20th century was Sir Elly (Eliezer Silas) Kadoorie, a member of a prominent mercantile family, who contributed generously to Zionist causes from 1900 on. He was president of the Shanghai Zionist Association from 1915 to 1928. In 1921 the Zionists of Shanghai paid tribute to his late wife, Laura Kadoorie, by founding a settlement named for her in Palestine. This settlement merged with the "China Jewish colony" that had been established the year before. Most of the funds for the settlement had come from Sir Elly; an additional £10,000 had been raised for this purpose by the Jews of Shanghai during World War I.

In 1923 Albert *Einstein visited Shanghai, where he addressed a pro-Palestine meeting. Another visitor that year was Mrs. Caroline Greenfield, a representative of *Hadassah. In 1925 Dr. Uriel Bension, representing *Keren HaYesod (Palestine Foundation Fund), visited Shanghai and helped found a pro-

Zionist society with non-Jewish members—Chinese, Japanese, Parsees, Hindus, and Muslims.

In 1928 Mrs. R. E. Toeg became president of the Shanghai Zionist Association. In November, 1929, she headed a Zionist delegation that called on Malcolm MacDonald, son of British Prime Minister (James) Ramsay *MacDonald, who was then visiting Shanghai. The delegation read him a statement for transmission to his father, protesting the atrocities perpetrated by the Arabs earlier that year (see ARAB RIOTS IN PALESTINE). The younger MacDonald assured Mrs. Toeg and her colleagues that the British government would never repudiate the Balfour Declaration and would always support the movement to rebuild the Jewish Homeland. On Nov. 2, 1930, Mrs. Toeg presided over a meeting held in Shanghai to protest the *Passfield White Paper. In the spring of 1934 she visited England, where she was honored at a luncheon by the London Zionist *Executive.

The Russian Jews of Shanghai had their own society, called Kadimah. Despite the refusal of the Chinese authorities to give legal recognition to the Zionist movement in Harbin, the Jewish community of that city was strongly Zionist. Harbin's democratically elected Jewish Council of 40 members had on its board (1920) 13 General Zionists (see GENERAL ZIONISM) and 3 representatives each of *Po'ale Zion, *Tz'ire Zion, and *Mizrahi. There were also two youth organizations, Maccabi and *B'rit Trumpeldor (Betar); and two Zionist newspapers, *Yevreiskaya Zhizn* (Jewish Life), a Russian-language publication of the General Zionists, and *HaDegel,* published by the *Revisionists.

The Zionist Society of Tientsin was formed as a result of a visit from Israel *Cohen, who traveled through China during the winter of 1920–21. The president of the Tientsin group for some years was Leo Gershevitch, a fur dealer and native of Irkutsk, Siberia, who attended the meeting of the Zionist *Actions Committee held in London in July, 1926.

War and Communism, 1937–50. At the outbreak of the Sino-Japanese War in 1937, the Jewish population of China (including Manchuria but not Hong Kong) was about 20,000 in a total population of nearly 458 million: 8,000 Jews lived in Harbin, 3,500 in Tientsin, and 5,500 in Shanghai. From 1938 to 1941 thousands of Jewish refugees from Germany, Austria, and Poland went to Shanghai, a free port that accepted them without visas. By July, 1939, there were 10,000 refugees in the city; during World War II the number rose to nearly 20,000. At war's end, there were 14,874 refugees, some 8,000 having died, many from hunger and lack of health facilities. Most of the Shanghai refugees lived in Hongkew, the Japanese-occupied sector of the city. The Japanese did not perpetrate Nazi-style atrocities on the Jews in the Chinese territory they had occupied but treated them as foreigners, subject to certain restrictions.

The Shanghai refugee community remained in existence until 1950. After the liberation in 1945 there were three General Zionist organizations, one for the Central European refugees, Kadimah for the "old-timers" from Russia, and the *Women's International Zionist Organization (WIZO). Next in numbers were the United Zionists-Revisionists, Po'ale Zion, and Mizrahi. Youth groups were *B'rit Halutzim Datiyim (Bachad), Betar, and *HaBonim. Most of the emigration from Shanghai in 1946–47 was directed not to Palestine but to the United States. Only after the establishment of the State of Israel was there a large-scale *'Aliya from Shanghai, Harbin (Jewish population, 1,800 in 1948), and Tientsin (Jewish population, 800 in 1948).

Before the coming of civil war and Communist rule to China, the Jews of the country were quite active in Zionist political work. There were two biweekly Russian-English magazines, *Our Life* (General Zionist) and *Tagar* (Revisionist). In May, 1947, at a mass meeting held in the Hongkew section of Shanghai, more than 8,000 Jews protested the hanging of Dov *Gruner by the British in Palestine. That summer the Zionists obtained a pro-Zionist statement from Sun Fo, son of Sun Yat-sen and Vice President of the Chinese Republic. In a letter to Miss Judith Hasser, a Revisionist leader in Shanghai and a delegate to the 22d Zionist *Congress (Basle, 1946), Sun Fo reconfirmed his father's sympathetic regard for Zionism.

The final victory of the Communist forces in China put an end to Zionist activity and to China's Jewish communities. Some members of the Sephardi community moved to Hong Kong; others, Iraqi citizens with relatives in Baghdad, had to disavow Zionism. By the mid-1960s it was estimated that no more than 100 Jews were left in all China.

G. HIRSCHLER AND T. PRESCHEL

CHISSIN (HISSIN), HAYIM ISSER. Physician, early member of the *Bilu movement, founder of Tel Aviv, and leader of the *Yishuv (b. Ukraine, Russia, 1865; d. Tel Aviv, 1932). Arriving in Palestine in 1882 with a Bilu group, Chissin settled first in Mikve Yisrael and then in Rishon L'Tziyon, where he worked as a farmhand. In 1887 he went to Switzerland to study medicine and practiced in Russia for a time. In 1905 he returned to Palestine, where he practiced medicine, headed the *Hoveve Zion office in Jaffa, led all the activities of the organization in Palestine, and played an active role in community affairs. Chissin was among the founders and outstanding personalities of Tel Aviv. His memoirs of the early days of Bilu have appeared in Russian and Hebrew.

G. KRESSEL

CHRISTIAN COMMUNITIES AND CHURCHES IN ISRAEL. A Christian community in the Middle East is a more complex organism than a church in the West (see COMMUNITIES IN ISRAEL). It is not only a religious but also an ethnic entity, a small nation, as it were, constituted as a church and molded by it. Its supreme leader is usually a Patriarch, who acts as its religious and secular head. The following communities, formerly recognized by the Turkish government and subsequently by the British Mandatory administration (see MANDATE FOR PALESTINE), have enjoyed official status in Israel since 1948: the Greek Orthodox, the Roman Catholic, the Gregorian Armenian, the Armenian Catholic, the Syrian Catholic, the Chaldean, the Melkite (or Greek Catholic), the Maronite, and the Syrian Orthodox. This list, which is included in a schedule added in 1939 to the Palestine Order-in-Council of 1922, contains no provision for the Church of England or for any other Protestant denomination. In recent years, however, the Church of England and the Evangelical Lutheran Church have been granted official status by the government of Jordan, and a group of Protestant churches has applied for such recognition to the government of Israel.

Results of the *Six-day War of 1967. The normal functioning of the churches in the Holy Land, as it had developed and become stabilized during the 30 years of British Mandatory rule, suffered considerable disturbance in 1948 as a result of the *partition of Palestine and the annexation of the Old City of Jerusalem by the then kingdom of *Transjordan. The Christian

Nativity Square, Bethlehem. [Israel Government Tourist Office]

communities of Israel, whose heads and central administration had been located for centuries in Jerusalem, were separated from their leadership and placed under vicars, exarchs, and other representatives. Although Patriarchs and other dignitaries from abroad were free to visit their Israeli communities, they did this, in fact, rather rarely and were, moreover, considered foreign, exposed as they were in their own countries to influences and pressures which were not always of a religious character. This anomaly disappeared following the reunification of Jerusalem and its reintegration in the State of Israel after the Six-day War of 1967. Today the Christian communities of the Holy Land once again form more or less organic units, grouped around their hierarchs and sacred shrines. True, now as in mandatory times, the diocesan boundaries do not coincide with the political frontiers, but Israel's consistent policy is to ensure uninterrupted contacts between Jerusalem and the Christians of Jordan.

The Christian population of Israel in 1968 numbered a little more than 100,000. Most of the Christians, especially the Catholics and Protestants, lived in urban centers, but there were also many village communities. The most important concentrations of Christians were to be found in the districts of Jerusalem, Nazareth, Haifa, Tel Aviv, and Jaffa. In the West Bank area,

most Christians were concentrated in the Ramallah and Bethlehem districts. The level of education was comparatively high. All children received primary education, increasing numbers attended high schools, and not a few pursued higher studies in universities. In addition to the government, religious orders and missionary agencies greatly contributed to the furthering of Christian education.

Jerusalem is at present (1968) the seat of three Patriarchs, three Archbishops, two Bishops, and five patriarchal Vicars. They "represent" there almost all principal branches of the Christian Church. The territorial boundaries of their jurisdictions include not only Jerusalem and Israel but also Jordan. Only one of them, the Greek Orthodox Patriarch, is the head of an autocephalous church; all others are more or less dependent on foreign hierarchs, such as the Pope, the Catholicos of All Armenians, the Oriental Patriarchs of Antioch and Alexandria, and the Archbishop of Canterbury. This by no means implies that their churches are "foreign"; in fact, their communities are predominantly indigenous.

Most of the churches established in Jerusalem in ancient or medieval times (but also some of the more recent ones) are intensely attached to the *holy places, especially to those recalling the birth, Passion, and Resurrection of their Lord. Not all churches, however, enjoy equal rights in those major sanctuaries. The three Patriarchs take pride of place, the Syrian and Coptic Archbishops have fewer privileges, and others have no privileges at all. All churches, however, possess either sanctuaries or places of worship of their own.

Orthodox Church. Any survey of churches in Israel must begin with the Church of Jerusalem, for 15 centuries embodied in the Greek Orthodox Patriarchate of Jerusalem. If not exactly the direct continuation of the primitive Judeo-Christian community of St. James, it is surely its closest successor and has a record of more than 1,800 years. Of minor significance in the 2d and 3d centuries, this gentile Greek-speaking church gained importance in the days of the emperor Constantine and came to the fore in C.E. 451, when its bishop, Juvenal, obtained the rank of Patriarch. The present (1968) Patriarch, His Beatitude Kyr Benedictos, is Juvenal's 95th successor.

The Church of Jerusalem flourished in Byzantine times, decayed under the Arabs, nearly disappeared during the Crusades, recovered some of its strength in the later Middle Ages, fought for the possession of the holy places under the Turks, and reached the beginning of the 20th century with flying colors. Not as numbers go, however, for at that time the entire Christian population of Palestine numbered a mere few thousands. In 1968 there were more than 37,000 Orthodox in Israel territories and about 33,000 in Jordan.

As in most Eastern churches, the ecclesiastical framework of the Church of Jerusalem exhibits a fundamentally monastic character. At its core is an order, known as the Brotherhood of the Holy Sepulchre, made up of 100 monks, almost all of them of Hellenic origin. Greek historians trace the order's beginnings to the 4th century; their Western opponents, to the 16th. The head of the brotherhood is the Patriarch, who is also the head of his church and community. In the government of the church he is assisted by a Synod of 14 to 18 members. Most of the members reside in the patriarchate. There is, however, a residential Metropolitan Bishop in Nazareth and another in Amman, Jordan. All members of the Synod as well as other dignitaries and office bearers of the patriarchate are chosen from among the members of the brotherhood and, except for one Arab Bishop, are all Greek-speaking. Only the local (secular) clergy, mostly married and often poor, are Arabs; but most of the members of the church are Arabs.

The Patriarch, as an ethnarch, exercises jurisdiction over the whole community and administers its religious and cultural institutions. These include many historic churches, lauras, and monasteries, some of them dating to early Byzantine times. The patriarchate also maintains schools and charitable institutions. It possesses a fine collection of ancient manuscripts and incunabula, most of them deriving from the famous Monasteries of St. Saba and the Holy Cross. Its primary function, however, is the guardianship of the holy places and the ministering to the pilgrims who convene there from all corners of the world.

In accordance with a set of rules, evolved in the course of

The Garden of Gethsemane. [Israel Government Tourist Office]

'En HaKerem, a suburb of Jerusalem, is the traditional birthplace of John the Baptist. [Israel Government Tourist Office]

centuries and made binding by sultanial rescripts of 1852 and 1853 (enforcing the so-called status quo), the patriarchate exercises rights of possession and worship in the Church of the Resurrection in Jerusalem, in the Church of the Nativity in Bethlehem, and in the Tomb of the Virgin in the Kidron Valley. In the first, it enjoys sole possession of the catholicon (the main body of the church), the Seven Arches and the chapels beneath them, and half of Mount Golgotha. The rest of the basilica and, especially, the Aedicula of the Holy Sepulchre are held in common with the Latins and Armenians. The basilica in Bethlehem, except for a corner controlled by the Armenians, is in the sole possession of the Greek Patriarchate, while the Grotto of the Nativity is shared with the Latins and Armenians. Finally, the Tomb of the Virgin is held in common with the Armenians only.

In the shadow of the Greek Orthodox Patriarch, three foreign Orthodox missions operate in Israel. Two of them are Russian, and the third is Romanian. One of the Russian missions represents the Moscow Patriarchate; the other, the Russian Church in Exile (with headquarters in the United States). Each of them claims to be the legitimate heir and successor of the Russian Ecclesiastical Mission of Tsarist memory. Established in the middle of the 19th century for the purpose of strengthening Orthodoxy in the Holy Land and of defending it "against Roman and Protestant encroachments," this institution had exercised considerable influence on the life of the Orthodox communities of the Middle East until it was discontinued in 1914. In 1948, upon the recognition of Israel by the Soviet Union, the Patriarchate of Moscow sent a mission to Israel, which took over the *sobor* in the capital and a few churches and properties in Jaffa, Haifa, Nazareth, and the vicinity of Tiberias. This mission never gained ground in the Old City of Jerusalem, where

a representation of the Russian Church in Exile remained in charge of eight churches and monasteries, including the characteristic Church of St. Mary Magdalene in the Garden of Gethsemane. Since the unification of Jerusalem both missions have been in Israel. The Mission of the Russian Church in Exile, being out of communion with the Patriarch of Moscow, is not recognized by the Greek Orthodox Patriarch of Jerusalem, but it is recognized by the Israel Ministry of Religious Affairs.

Catholics. The Catholic world is represented in the Holy Land by what might aptly be termed a "commonwealth" of communities. In fact, the Latins as well as the Melkites, the Maronites, the Chaldeans, and the Armenian, Syrian, and Coptic Catholics, though belonging to separate and independent jurisdictions, are all severally connected with the Sacred Congregation of Oriental Churches in Rome.

The Latins are by far the most important Catholic community in the Holy Land. Made up of Arabs, Europeans, and others, the community is one of the largest, probably the wealthiest, and surely the best organized and educated. In 1968 it numbered more than 22,000 in Israel territory and some 33,000, mostly Arabs, in Jordan and Cyprus. The prevalently autochthonous character of the Latin diocese is also manifest in the composition of the patriarchal clergy, now in majority Arabic-speaking.

The Latin community is headed by a Patriarch (since 1947 Msgr. Alberto Geri), who is assisted by a Coadjutor, two Auxiliary Bishops, and a chapter of canons. Diocesan clergy to the number of 70 are in charge of 47 parishes. A Patriarchal Seminary, founded in 1853, trains new recruits.

The patriarchate is assisted in the exercise of all its pastoral, missionary, educational, and charitable functions by contingents of men and women from more than 40 religious orders and congregations. Only a few of these can be mentioned: the Salesians with their trade schools and theological institute; the Brethren with their flourishing colleges; the Fathers of Bet Harram and the White Fathers with their seminaries for the training of clergy; the Trappists with their Abbey of Latrun; the Benedictines with their Abbey of the Dormition; the Dominicans with their École Biblique, famous for its archeological and exegetical work, *Revue Biblique,* and, especially its translation and commentary of the Bible, the *Bible de Jérusalem*; the Carmelites with their sanctuaries on Mount Carmel; the Assumptionists with their organization for large pilgrimages; the Jesuits with their Biblical Institute; and, finally, the Franciscans. Among the religious communities of women, some 25 in number with more than 12,000 recruits and several hundred houses, special mention must be made of the Sisters of the Rosary, both for their merits and for their autochthonous character. This order is probably the only indigenous congregation for whose foundation and development a woman of this country, Sister Alphonsine Danil, was largely responsible. Mention should also be made of the Sisters of St. Joseph, the Filles de la Charité, the Carmelite Sisters, and the Poor Clares.

Most members of these orders came to the Holy Land during the last 120 years, admitted or called in by the Latin Patriarchs. (The Latin Patriarchate of Jerusalem was founded by the Crusaders in 1099. It ceased to exist, except in idea, in 1291. It was reestablished in 1847–48.) But centuries before the first of them came to the country, the Franciscans had been there. For more than 500 years, their Custody of the Holy Land took care of Catholic interests in Palestine and the Middle East, endeavoring to regain rights of worship and possession in the major sanctuaries, rehabilitating abandoned shrines, attending to numberless pilgrims, and ministering to the tiny "Latin" communities that sprang up around their convents. In 1848 they surrendered to the restored patriarchate some of their functions and prerogatives, but neither all nor the most important. With a personnel of more than 400, drawn from 28 nations, they still are the guardians of the most important sanctuaries. While sharing, under the status quo, the Church of the Holy Sepulchre and the Grotto of the Nativity with the Orthodox and the Armenians, they hold in exclusive possession numerous sacred sites in Nazareth, Cana, K'far Nahum (Capernaum), Tabor, Gethsemane, Bethany, Bethphage, and Mount Nebo (Pisgah). Aided by worldwide Catholic generosity, they have erected on them churches and chapels and, *inter alia*, finished in 1967 a monumental basilica in Nazareth.

It should be borne in mind that the Franciscan Custody, though having its headquarters in the Old City of Jerusalem, is a "province" spread over 50 localities in Egypt, Israel, Jordan, Lebanon, Syria, and Cyprus. In most of these places the Franciscans are in charge of the Latin parishes; in Israel, of 14 only, among them those of Jerusalem, Bethlehem, Jaffa, and Nazareth. In all these places they also attend to the poor, maintain orphanages and workshops, run schools and colleges (with about 14,400 students), and engage in other social and cultural activities.

Mention must also be made of the scientific endeavors of the Franciscans, especially of their Studium Biblicum (now a section of the Theological Faculty of the Pontifical University of St. Anthony in Rome), renowned for its archeological and exegetical work and for its numerous publications.

Supervising the activities of the Latin Church is the Apostolic Delegate, representing the Holy See in Jordan, Israel, and Cyprus.

Uniates. Jerusalem is also the seat of several patriarchal Vicars representing the Patriarchs of the Oriental churches in communion with Rome. The Patriarchs themselves reside in the neighboring Arab countries; their jurisdiction, however, is recognized both in Israel and in Jordan.

The largest Uniate church in the country is the Greek Catholic, or Melkite, numbering about 26,500 faithful (23,000 in Galilee and 3,500 in Jerusalem and the West Bank). Its origins go back to the 17th century, when a number of Greek Orthodox Syrians, although retaining their Byzantine forms of worship and the use of Greek and Arabic in their ceremonies, seceded from their church and united with that of Rome. The present Melkite Patriarch of Antioch, Jerusalem, and Alexandria, Maximus V (who until 1967 had been Archbishop of Haifa and Galilee), resides in Damascus. Owing to their close association with the Roman Catholic Church, the Melkites of Israel are a well-organized and well-disciplined community. Under the able leadership of their former Archbishop, George Hakim, they made great strides after the establishment of the State, erecting churches, founding schools and seminaries, and taking part in the social and economic life of the country.

Also in close touch with Rome are the Maronites, some 3,000 strong and concentrated mainly in several villages not far from the Lebanese border. They follow an ancient Syrian ritual, using Syriac and Arabic in their liturgy. Their Patriarch resides in Lebanon, where the Maronites form the largest single religious community.

The other Uniate churches (Chaldean, Syrian, and Armenian) are much smaller, with a mere few hundred faithful all together. None of the Uniate churches has rights of independent worship in the principal holy places. The Armenian Catholics, however, are in possession of the Chapel of Our Lady of the Spasm near the fourth station on the Way of the Cross.

Non-Chalcedonians. The Non-Chalcedonian, or, as they are rather improperly called, Monophysitic, churches are represented in Jerusalem by an Armenian Patriarchate, a Syrian Orthodox Archbishopric, a Coptic Archbishopric, and an Ethiopian monastic community headed by a Bishop.

The Armenians seem to have been there since ancient times. In the 7th century they had no less than 70 monasteries in the Holy Land. Their numbers increased considerably in the times of the Crusades. In 1311 their Bishop was raised to the rank of Patriarch. Today, though no longer as numerous as in mandatory times, the Armenian community still numbers about 7,000 persons (2,650 in Israel and the occupied territories). Its ecclesiastical framework, the Armenian Patriarchate of Jerusalem, is of great significance to the entire Armenian nation because of the holy sites and the religious and cultural institutions of which it is in charge. In fact, the Armenian Patriarch enjoys, under the status quo, rights and privileges similar to those of the other two Patriarchs of Jerusalem, with whom he shares the Church of the Holy Sepulchre, the Basilica of the Nativity, and the site of the Ascension. He also holds in common with the Greeks the Tomb of the Virgin.

Apart from these principal holy places, the Armenian Patriarchate enjoys sole ownership of the Church of St. James (its cathedral), which is believed to stand on the site of the house of St. James the Less, the first Bishop of Jerusalem. The cathedral is the center of the Armenian monastery and quarter, which occupy almost one-sixth of the Old City within the walls. There a number of historic sites and institutions are located, among them the House of Caiaphas, the Chapel of St. Theodore, the residence of the Patriarchs, the Gulbenkian Library, and the Library of Manuscripts. The patriarchate also has monasteries in Bethlehem, Jaffa, and Ramle.

The patriarchate is organized as a monastic community, known as the Brotherhood of St. James, and composed of 9 Bishops, 32 archimandrites, and 70 monks. Thirty-six members of this brotherhood attend to work in Jerusalem and the holy places; the others serve as bishops and priests in the Armenian diaspora or study in Echmiadzin, U.S.S.R. The head of the brotherhood is the Patriarch, the leader of the church, the president of all its assemblies, and the governor of the church property. He also represents his community before the State. In the discharge of his spiritual and administrative duties, he is assisted by a Holy Synod, which derives its authority from a General Assembly of all members of the brotherhood.

The Armenian Patriarch of Jerusalem is in communion with and to some extent dependent upon the Catholicos of All Armenians, who resides in Echmiadzin, the original religious capital of Armenia.

Syrian Orthodox, Copts, and Ethiopians. These are also ancient communities in Jerusalem, enjoying status and rights of worship in certain holy places. The Syrians have had a Bishop there since 1140; the Copts, since 1236. Though small in numbers, they enjoy some sort of recognition, have sanctuaries, and minister to pilgrims coming from their respective countries.

The Syrian Orthodox, or Jacobite, community, numbering about 2,000 in Jordan (with only a handful in Jerusalem and the West Bank), is headed by an Archbishop residing in the ancient Monastery of St. Mark. According to one tradition, this monastery was built in the 5th or 6th century on the site of the house of Mary the mother of John, who was surnamed Mark (Acts 12:12). The Syrian Orthodox Patriarch of Antioch, now Mar Ignatius Jacob III Severios (who also has a large following in India), since 1924 has resided in Homs, Syria. In Jerusalem, the Jacobites have a chapel of their own in the Rotunda of the Holy Sepulchre.

The Copts are even less numerous—a mere few hundred. Their Archbishop resides in a convent behind the Church of the Holy Sepulchre. Inside the basilica the Copts are in possession of a tiny chapel behind the Aedicula of the Holy Sepulchre. They also have a large monastery for pilgrims in Jaffa and a newly built church in Nazareth. The Coptic Patriarch of Alexandria resides in Cairo.

The Ethiopians, a monastic community headed by a Bishop, represent in Jerusalem a church and nation which have greatly grown and developed in recent times. The Church of Ethiopia became independent of the Coptic Church in the 1950s. The Ethiopians, who in the Middle Ages owned a large number of chapels and altars in the Church of the Holy Sepulchre and elsewhere, are today confined to the roof of St. Helen's Chapel, on which they have a monastery called Deir es-Sultan. They also have a church near the Jordan River and a monastery and monumental church in the new city of Jerusalem.

Protestant Churches. Reformed Christianity came to the Holy Land in the 1820s. In 1837 the liturgy of the Church of England was translated and published in Hebrew. In 1841, as a result of an accord between Queen Victoria and King Frederick William IV of Prussia, a joint bishopric was established in Jerusalem. Its first incumbent was Michael Solomon Alexander, a convert from Judaism. The original Anglican-Lutheran accord broke down in 1881, and when the bishopric was reconstituted in 1887, it was as a solely Anglican enterprise. The Lutherans were to carry on independently. Under Bishop Blyth, in 1898, the Collegiate Church of St. George the Martyr was consecrated in Jerusalem.

Anglicanism prospered especially in mandatory times; after 1948 its importance in the country slightly decreased. On the other hand, it became more thoroughly grounded in its environment; the overwhelming majority of the Evangelical Episcopal community (as it is called) is now Arabic-speaking. Moreover, in 1957 the bishopric was raised to archiepiscopal rank. The Archbishop presides over a Synod composed of the Bishops of Egypt and Libya, Sudan, Iran, and Jordan, and he exercises direct diocesan jurisdiction over the Anglican congregations in Israel and Cyprus. The (Arab) Bishop of Jordan is in charge of the Anglicans in Syria and Lebanon.

The Anglican Archbishop has no rights in the Church of the Holy Sepulchre; he enjoys, however, the privilege of occasionally celebrating Holy Communion in the adjacent Chapel of St. Abraham, owing to the hospitality accorded by the Greek Orthodox Patriarch.

The Lutherans established in the Holy Land schools, hospitals, and other institutions. Despite the setbacks suffered as a result of the two world wars, they are present and active. Led by a Propst residing in the building of the characteristic Church of the Redeemer (near the Basilica of the Holy Sepulchre), they now number about 1,500, mostly Arabic-speaking. Their best-known institutions are the Augusta Victoria Hospital on Mount Scopus, the Hospice of the Order of St. John, and the Talitha Kumi School at Bet Jala. Mention should also be made of the German Evangelical Institute for Archaeological Research in the Holy Land, which was directed by Gustaf Dalman from 1902 to 1914 and of which Martin Noth has been in charge since 1963. Of the non-German Lutheran institutions, mention should be made of the Swedish Theological Institute in Jerusalem, the Swedish School and Hospital in Bethlehem, and the Finnish Missionary School and the Scandinavian Seamen's Church in Haifa.

The Church of Scotland continues to maintain its Memorial Church and Hospice of St. Andrew and its schools in Jaffa and other cities. The once-renowned hospital in Tiberias is now a hospice and cultural center run by Dutch Calvinists.

Reformed Christianity is also represented by a number of minor Protestant groups and agencies, which, being mostly of foreign and recent origin, do not enjoy the status of official communities. This fact, however, does not prevent Israeli Presbyterians, Baptists, Pentecostalians, Friends, Adventists, Brethren, and others from practicing their religion freely and carrying on their activities.

Status. The Christian communities of Israel enjoy considerable internal autonomy. They own property and administer it freely. Their religious leaders and other officials are elected or appointed without government interference. Matters of personal status, such as marriage, divorce, inheritance, and alimony, are within the competence of their clergies and ecclesiastic courts (*see* JUDICIARY IN ISRAEL). The Patriarchs and their representatives are free to leave and enter Israel at will and to exercise their pastoral and other duties. The rulings of the patriarchal courts, especially in matters of personal status, even if given abroad, are recognized by Israeli law and therefore are binding on the members of the communities living in Israel.

In many cases the communities maintain and manage their own schools; if not, they avail themselves of government or foreign schools. In government schools, religious education is provided free of charge according to the preferences of the parents (*see* EDUCATION IN ISRAEL).

Apart from the holy places held in common by several communities, such as the Basilicas of the Nativity and the Holy Sepulchre, each community has its own shrines and churches. Access to them is free for all. Their integrity and inviolability are safeguarded by laws and regulations.

C. WARDI

CHRISTIAN COUNCIL ON PALESTINE. *See* AMERICAN PALESTINE COMMITTEE.

CHRISTIAN MISSIONS IN ISRAEL. Although the Christian churches and missions in Israel enjoy complete legal freedom to carry on missionary activities, there has been some opposition to them, primarily on the part of Orthodox Jews. In addition to Orthodox opposition, which stems from religious motives, other sectors of the Jewish majority have opposed missionary work because they are against introducing further dissension into a society which is badly in need of coalescence and consolidation.

Catholic missionary activity in Israel, discreet, tactful, and subtle, was carried on by religious, educational, and charitable institutions. In 1965 the total number of Catholic institutions in Israel, most of which operated in non-Jewish areas, was 95, including 35 schools and 8 hospitals and clinics, with some 800 clergy attending to their work. Protestant activity was more direct but less coordinated and disciplined. Many free-lance missionaries were engaged in distributing religious tracts and trying to influence individuals. In the 1960s there were in all some 25 Protestant missionary agencies with about 240 workers active in Jewish areas. The most common method of carrying out religious propaganda was by means of schools. There were Anglican, Scottish, Lutheran, Baptist, and even Hebrew-Christian educational institutions.

The success of missionary endeavor in Israel has not been spectacular. According to a statement by Prime Minister Levi *Eshkol at a Cabinet meeting in 1964, only 900 Jewish children were attending a total of 11 Christian schools, of which only 3 openly proselytized (2 using Hebrew as the language of instruction). According to Zerah *Wahrhaftig, Minister of Religious Affairs, the total enrollment of Jewish pupils in Christian schools was 1,380, and the schools, including kindergartens, numbered 29.

From 1950 to 1964 only 11 Jewish children attending the above schools were converted to Christianity. The total number of Jews who embraced Christianity or Islam during the same period was 200. To these must be added several hundred converts who had embraced Christianity before coming to Israel. The total number of Christians, Muslims, Druzes, and Circassians who adopted Judaism in the same period was 407.

The Eastern churches were not engaged in missionary activity to any appreciable extent (see CHRISTIAN COMMUNITIES AND CHURCHES IN ISRAEL).

C. WARDI

CHRISTIAN ZIONISTS. *See* RESTORATION MOVEMENT.

CHURCH AND STATE IN ISRAEL. *See* RELIGION AND STATE IN ISRAEL.

CHURCHILL, CHARLES HENRY. British army officer, diplomat, and author (b. Madras Province, India, 1808; d. Bihwarah, Lebanon, 1869). The son of Charles Henry Churchill, an official of the East India Company, he was a descendant of Gen. Charles Churchill, brother of the 1st Duke of Marlborough, and thus, contrary to popular assumption, is not identical with Charles Henry Spencer Churchill (1815–77), a grandson of the 5th Duke of Marlborough. He participated in the campaign against Mohammed 'Ali, Viceroy of Egypt (1840–41), as a staff officer. In an address he delivered at the home of Raphael Farhi in Damascus on Mar. 1, 1841, after the liberation of Palestine and Syria, Churchill advocated the restoration of Israel's political existence. In pursuance of the same goal, Churchill, in his capacity as Resident Officer of Damascus, addressed a letter to Sir Moses *Montefiore, dated June 14, 1841, in which he declared the resumption of the political existence of the Jewish people a perfectly attainable object "if the Jews will take the matter up universally and unanimously." He urged the beginning of an "agitation" by which the Jews would "conjure a new element in Eastern diplomacy," and ultimately obtain "the sovereignty at least of Palestine."

Unperturbed by Montefiore's failure to reply, Churchill undertook another attempt to stir up a movement which, had it materialized, would have anticipated political Zionism. On Aug. 15, 1842, he again wrote to Montefiore, enclosing the draft of an appeal to the Jews of Europe for an application, to be made jointly with the Jews of England, to the British government for the creation of a special British office to watch over the interests of Jews residing in Syria and Palestine. Montefiore referred Churchill's letters to the *Board of Deputies of British Jews,

which, late in 1842, informed Churchill that it "was precluded from originating any measures for carrying out [his] benevolent views." This refusal terminated Churchill's pro-Zionist activity. He settled on Mount Lebanon and espoused the cause of the Lebanese people, particularly of the Druzes (see DRUZE COMMUNITY IN ISRAEL).

F. KOBLER

CHURCHILL, SIR WINSTON LEONARD SPENCER. British statesman and writer (b. Blenheim Palace, Oxfordshire, England, 1874; d. London, 1965). Churchill began his political career in the so-called khaki elections of 1900 and served as a member of Parliament intermittently for more than six decades (1900–64). His ministerial posts included those of Undersecretary of State for the Colonies (1906–08), President of the Board of Trade (1908–10), Home Secretary (1910–11), First Lord of the Admiralty (1911–15), Chancellor of Duchy of Lancaster (1915), Minister of Munitions (1917), Secretary of State for War and Air (1919–21), Secretary of State for the Colonies (1921–22), Chancellor of the Exchequer (1924–29), First Lord of the Admiralty (1939–40), Prime Minister, First Lord of the Treasury, and Minister of Defense (1940–45), leader of the Opposition (1945–51), and Prime Minister and First Lord of the Treasury (1951–55).

Sir Winston's views on Judaism, *anti-Semitism, and Zionism evolved slowly and paralleled his emergence as a public figure. A confirmed Bible reader, he greatly admired the spiritual and ethical side of Judaism. He intervened, for the first time in his political career, in a matter affecting Jews when as a Liberal M.P. he strenuously opposed the Aliens Bill of 1904. His early stand against restrictive immigration legislation and his later support of Saturday Closing and Sunday Opening Bills and specified Jewish educational rights won for him the admiration of the English Jewish community.

Sir Winston Churchill.
[Zionist Archives]

As Home Secretary (1910–11), Churchill played a prominent role in suppressing the anti-Jewish riots of 1911 in south Wales. As Secretary of State for War and Air in 1919, however, he was criticized for his failure to curb the anti-Semitic excesses of the White Russian armies of Gen. Anton Denikin, which Churchill vigorously supported in their struggle against the Bolsheviks. In defense of his position, Churchill published the telegrams he had sent to Denikin demanding a halt to anti-Jewish excesses. But these were obviously disregarded.

As early as 1906 Churchill expressed interest in the efforts of

Israel *Zangwill's *Jewish Territorial Organization to find a haven for the Jews somewhere in the British Empire. However, by 1908 he had definitely moved toward Zionism and its goal of Palestine. "I am in full sympathy with the historical aspirations of the Jews," he wrote to a Zionist meeting in Manchester on Feb. 2, 1908. "The restoration to them of a center of racial and political integrity would be a tremendous event in the history of the world."

As Colonial Secretary (1921–22), Churchill laid down the principles of Great Britain's policy and responsibilities under the *Mandate for Palestine. To be able to do so he called in Cairo a conference of all British diplomatic representatives in the area (March, 1921). Britain was confronted with a new situation owing to the French occupation of Damascus (1920) and the expulsion of King *Feisal from Syria; thus the pledge of independence given by Britain to the Arabs could not be fulfilled. The Cairo Conference therefore decided to set up Feisal as King of Iraq and his brother 'Abdullah as Emir of *Transjordan. This made it necessary to detach Transjordan from the Palestine area, a step that was submitted by the British government to the League of Nations and approved by it on Sept. 16, 1922.

On June 22, 1922, the Churchill White Paper (see WHITE PAPER OF JUNE, 1922) was issued. It reassured the Arabs that Great Britain did not intend to create a wholly Jewish Palestine and that Jewish nationality would not be imposed on the inhabitants of Palestine as a whole, and it advised them that it would be best for them to cooperate with the *High Commissioner in setting up rudimentary self-governing institutions. Jewish *immigration, in addition, was to be limited and was not to exceed the economic capacity of the country to absorb new arrivals. Regarded by most Zionists as a serious whittling down of the *Balfour Declaration, the White Paper did, however, reaffirm that the declaration "was not susceptible of change," that the Jewish community should freely develop its capacities in Palestine, and that "it is essential that it should know that it is in Palestine as of right and not on sufferance. That is the reason why it is necessary that the existence of the Jewish National Home in Palestine should be internationally guaranteed, and that it should be formally recognized to rest upon ancient historic connection."

Churchill firmly believed that his White Paper would remain the basis of future Anglo-Jewish cooperation. His subsequent condemnation of the *Passfield White Paper (1930), the *partition scheme of 1937, and the *White Paper of 1939 was based on the premise that they constituted a breach of agreed upon policies expressed in his 1922 statement.

Under Churchill's premiership during World War II, no practical rescue efforts were made by the British government to save the remnants of European Jewry. Indeed, the Prime Minister remained silent in the face of both appeals and attacks to abrogate the White Paper of 1939. "I do not advise any decision at the present time on the Palestine policy," he wrote on June 29, 1944, to Anthony Eden, the Foreign Secretary. "I am determined not to break the pledges of the British Government to the Zionists expressed in the Balfour Declaration, as modified in my subsequent statement at the Colonial Office in 1921 [should read 1922]. No change can be made in policy without full discussion in Cabinet. We have so little to do now, it should be easy to find an opportunity to do this."

When approached by Chaim *Weizmann in 1940, Churchill expressed sympathy for the creation of a *Jewish Brigade to fight alongside the Allies against the Nazis. Nevertheless, he did not take energetic steps to bring this plan to a speedy realization, particularly against the objections of the military and some Foreign Office officials. It was only in July, 1944, that he took decisive action. "I certainly understood and hold very strongly the view that a brigade group should be made," he wrote on July 10, 1944, to Sir Edward Bridges. By September the brigade was officially established.

While, on the whole, Churchill did not concern himself during the war with the future boundaries and independence of countries, including Palestine, it is a fact that prior to the assassination of Lord *Moyne in Cairo in 1944 he had set up a commission to investigate the possibility of a sensible partition of Palestine after the war. He also had another plan and revealed it to Weizmann before the latter's departure to the United States in 1942. "I would like to see Ibn Saud [King 'Abdul 'Aziz Ibn Sa'ud of Saudi Arabia] made the lord of the Middle East—the boss of bosses—provided he settles with you [that is, the Zionists]. It will be up to you to get the best possible conditions. Of course we shall help you. Keep this confidential, but you might talk it over with [Pres. Franklin D.] *Roosevelt when you get to America. There's nothing he and I cannot do if we set our minds on it." (It is known that St. John Philby, Ibn Saud's representative, had approached Weizmann and brought him an "offer" which coincided with Churchill's "plan," but subsequently Halford L. Hoskins of the U.S. Department of State informed Weizmann that on a visit to Ibn Saud the latter had informed him of his complete rejection of any such plan.)

Immediately after the collapse of Germany, Weizmann endeavored to induce Churchill to commence serious consideration of Palestine's future. Churchill, however, evaded the issue by insisting that Palestine could not be considered until "the victorious Allies were . . . seated at the peace table." A short time later he was out of office, winding up his historic ministry with the White Paper of 1939 unabrogated and his vaunted personal commitment to Zionism unfulfilled. Shorn of power, his voice was now again heard from the Opposition benches castigating the new Government for not giving Zionism its due.

Churchill was one of the first to insist on the recognition of Israel, an act which the Labor Government bestowed de jure in 1950. Sir Winston's second premiership (1951–55) witnessed no radical change in Middle East strategy. A policy of conciliation toward the Arabs was adopted. The sale of arms to Israel's neighbors increased, and negotiations for a British evacuation of the Suez area were concluded without any provisions for the security of Israel.

J. ADLER

CHURCHILL WHITE PAPER. *See* WHITE PAPER OF JUNE, 1922.

CHURGIN, PINHAS MICHAEL. *Mizrahi leader, educator, and founder and first president of *Bar-Ilan University (b. Pogost, Minsk District, Russia, 1894; d. New York, 1957). In his youth Churgin's family settled in Palestine, where he was educated by his father and grandfather, both rabbis, and at Yeshiva Torat Hayim in Jerusalem. He later studied at the Yeshiva of Volozhin.

In 1915 he went to the United States and attended Clark College and Yale University, where he received his Ph.D. degree in 1922. He taught Jewish history at Yeshiva College (later Yeshiva University) in New York City, and in 1923 he became principal of the Teachers Seminary founded by Mizrahi, which subsequently became associated with Yeshiva College. Churgin helped formulate programs of religious-Zionist–oriented education in the United States and trained hundreds of Hebrew teachers. He was on the Board of Directors of the *Histadrut

Pinhas Churgin.
[Zionist Archives]

'Ivrit of America and many Jewish pedagogical associations. Active in Zionist affairs, he represented Mizrahi at Zionist Congresses (*see* CONGRESS, ZIONIST). He was president of the Mizrahi Organization of America from 1949 to 1952 and was one of the foremost advocates of the merger between Mizrahi and HaPo'el HaMizrahi. In 1953 he helped found and formulate the policy of Bar-Ilan University in Ramat Gan. As its first president, he assumed responsibility for its support until his death. He was the author of scholarly studies and edited (1933–54) the literary-historical quarterly *Horev* as well as other Mizrahi publications. His articles on education, current Jewish problems, and Zionism appeared in many Hebrew and Yiddish journals in the United States.

G. BAT-YEHUDA

CIO. *See* CONGRESS OF INDUSTRIAL ORGANIZATIONS.

CITIZENSHIP IN ISRAEL. During the period of the British *Mandate for Palestine, the British government defined Palestinian citizenship in an order-in-council enacted in 1925. Immigrants to Palestine could obtain naturalization after two years' residence and after acquiring knowledge of one of the three official languages: English, Hebrew, and Arabic. The Israel Citizenship Law was enacted in 1952, four years after the establishment of the State. Under that law, which was designed to confer Israeli citizenship on the greatest possible number of Jews residing in the country, citizenship was obtained by virtue of "return" under the 1950 Law of *Return, by residence in Israel, by birth, or by naturalization. Every Jew who had come to Israel as an immigrant or had been born there either before or after the enactment of the Law of Return was a citizen of Israel unless, being over 18 years of age and a citizen of a foreign country, he expressly declared that he did not wish to be a citizen of Israel. The provisions for the acquisition of Israeli citizenship by non-Jews were more complicated.

Citizenship was conferred at birth in accordance with either the *jus soli* (by birth in Israel territory) or the *jus sanguinis* (by birth anywhere in the world, with an Israeli parent). A child born of an Israeli mother and a foreign father, whether in Israel or abroad, had dual citizenship at birth. The law did not contain any provision for loss of citizenship by desuetude, except for naturalized citizens. Conditions for naturalization were liberal. Jewish immigrants who came to Israel to stay obtained citizenship automatically; non-Jews could be naturalized five years after immigration (provided they spent three of those five years in Israel) and on acquiring some knowledge of Hebrew. Generally, a person declaring himself a Jew was accepted as such. However, if he converted to another faith prior to settling in Israel—as happened in the case of the Polish Roman Catholic monk Brother Daniel—he was not accepted as a Jew, even though religious law (Halakha) still considered him as such.

Israeli citizenship could be lost by renunciation or by revocation of naturalization. Only persons not resident in Israel could renounce their Israeli citizenship. A naturalized Israeli could be deprived of his citizenship only if he had acquired it under false pretenses, if he had been abroad for seven consecutive years and had no substantial connection with the country, or if he had committed an act regarded as a breach of loyalty to the State of Israel. The Minister of the Interior could exempt an applicant for naturalization from any or all of the legal requirements if in his opinion there was good reason for doing so.

A woman did not automatically acquire Israeli citizenship by marrying an Israeli citizen. However, in cases where either the husband or the wife was an Israeli citizen or had applied for naturalization, the other spouse could receive Israeli citizenship even if he or she did not comply with the conditions for naturalization. Special provisions were made for the naturalization of children under 18 years of age whose parents were not living in Israel, had died, or were unknown. The effect of the Citizenship Law was that the vast majority of persons resident in Israel, both Jews and Arabs, became Israeli citizens. Many persons in Israel held dual citizenship, except in cases where the law of the other country involved stipulated that they would lose their citizenship there once they had acquired citizenship in any other country.

N. BENTWICH

CITRUS INDUSTRY IN ISRAEL. In the period preceding World War II citriculture in what was then Palestine developed rapidly, covering an area of 300,000 dunams (75,000 acres; *see* DUNAM). About one-half of this area belonged to Jewish growers;

Loading grapefruit at Haifa. [Trans World Airlines]

the other half was owned by Arabs. Owing to the interruption of exports, lack of income, and neglect during World War II, the acreage was reduced to 230,000 dunams (57,500 acres). The resultant poor condition of the land led to a steady decline in area and yield even in the immediate postwar period.

After the *War of Independence and the consequent difficulties in continuing cultivation even on a minimum scale, the acreage was reduced to 125,000 to 130,000 dunams (31,250 to 32,500 acres), and even this acreage was in bad condition. The entire crop for 1948–49 was 6.5 million boxes, of which 4 million were exported, as compared with 15 million boxes exported in 1938–39 (over 60 per cent from Jewish orchards and less than 40 per cent from Arab groves).

After 1948. After the establishment of the State of Israel the authorities, recognizing the importance of the citrus industry as a source of employment and foreign currency earnings, decided to adopt extensive measures for the restoration of existing plantations and the development of new ones. In the early years, steps were taken mainly to rehabilitate neglected plantations. This involved the restoration of about 130,000 dunams of neglected fruit-bearing groves, left over from the 1938–39 area of 300,000 dunams.

Comprehensive and planned rehabilitation work led to improvements in the methods of cultivation and to considerable economy in the resulting outlay. With increased yields and improved cultivation, favorable results were achieved within a relatively short time. Citrus growing recovered from the severe crisis it had undergone during and after World War II and began to regain the favored position it had formerly enjoyed.

Furthermore, great advances were made in packing methods by the abolition of "domestic" packing and the transition to modern centralized packinghouses. Forty up-to-date packinghouses were set up by the various citrus growers' organizations.

New Plantings. In the 1950s a constant and rapid expansion of citrus planting took place throughout the world, particularly in the Mediterranean area. The growing demand for the fruit in the postwar period and the improvement in standards of living and nutrition induced the producers to expand their groves.

In Israel, there was at first considerable doubt regarding the desirability and possibility of expanding the industry, for public confidence in the stability of the markets had been shaken during the period of crisis through which the industry had passed. In the course of time, however, it was found that even if citrus

Packing citrus fruit at Hadera. [El Al Israel Airlines]

fruit was subject to price fluctuations, it was, from the long-term point of view, a fundamentally sound and worthwhile investment for State and growers alike.

New planting commenced in 1952–53. The center of new planting shifted from private initiative to communal settlement. There was a steady expansion in the plantations sponsored by the *Jewish Agency. Between 1952 and 1967 about 280,000 additional dunams (70,000 acres) were planted, bringing the total to 410,000 dunams (102,500 acres).

The final plan for plantation decided on by the Agricultural Planning Authority aimed at a total area of 450,000 dunams (112,500 acres). New planting was being carried out in new regions and on soils which had not formerly been used for citrus growing. Another characteristic of the new planting was the relative decline of the Shamouti orange and the increase in other citrus varieties, such as grapefruit, Jaffa Lates, and lemons. While in the older groves the Shamouti was grown to the extent of 80 per cent, the production of the new groves was as follows: Shamouti, about 55 per cent; grapefruit, 15 per cent; Jaffa Lates (Valencia types), 15 per cent; lemons, 5 per cent; navel oranges, clementines, and so on, 10 per cent. This diversification of species made it possible to prolong the shipping season and permitted a ready adaptation to the needs of foreign markets.

Marketing Possibilities. The 1966–67 yield was estimated at 25 million cases, of which 17.5 million were for export (as against 15 million in 1938–39 and 5 million in 1949–50). The expected export in the 1967–68 season was 19 million cases, and the forecast for 1970–71 was 30 million cases (22 million for export).

In assessing marketing possibilities throughout Europe, it was necessary to consider not only the production of Israel but also that of the entire Mediterranean area supplying citrus fruits during the winter season to the markets in question. If one takes into account the total citrus consumption in Europe and the volume of production in the Mediterranean area, the annual increase of 1 million to 1.5 million cases that Israel envisaged exporting for 1967–72 seemed insignificant compared with the increasing natural demand.

Israeli exports of citrus fruit in 1966–67, in thousands of tons, are shown in the accompanying table. In that year, exports of oranges by the other principal Mediterranean producers were as follows, in thousands of tons: Spain, 1,050; franc area (Morocco, Algeria, Tunisia), 570; Italy, 140.

A market survey showed that during the 1966–67 season the Western European countries, with full employment, high standards of living, and a total population of 300 million, consumed fewer than 100 million cases of fruit as compared with the nearly 200 million cases consumed annually in the United States with its population of 200 million. Some of the Central European countries, for various reasons, imported only a small part of their actual demand, while the markets of Eastern Europe still seemed entirely unaware of the nutritional value and economic importance of citrus fruit imports.

In 1966 the State of Israel officially applied for membership in the European Economic Community, or Common Market. The three-year agreement signed with the Market in 1964 was due to end in the middle of 1967. Because this agreement failed by far to satisfy Israel, every effort was made to agree on an approach to the economic network of the European Market countries, the principal customers for Israeli products.

In 1968 there was a substantial deficit in the commercial balance of Israel with these countries. Israeli citrus growers were particularly concerned about the marketing chances for

CITRUS EXPORTS FROM ISRAEL, 1966–67
(In thousands of tons)

Market	Oranges	Grapefruit	Lemons	Total
Western Europe:				
United Kingdom	149.8	31.2	2.5	183.5
West Germany	121.6	33.4	0.1	155.1
Scandinavian countries	89.2	11.3	2.7	103.2
Benelux	64.1	14.7	1.3	80.1
France	27.0	25.7	4.9	57.6
Switzerland	19.4	6.8	0.2	26.4
Austria	20.1	1.6	0.1	21.8
Italy	.....	....	3.3	3.3
Total	491.2	124.7	51.1	631.0
Eastern Europe (except U.S.S.R.)	22.0	0.5	6.0	28.5
Canada	6.6	.....	....	6.6
Other countries	11.5	0.2	0.6	12.3
Grand total	531.3	125.4	21.7	678.4

that season, owing to the influence of the preference prices established by the Market committee aiming to protect the Italian citrus industry.

Industrial Utilization. In 1966 there were in Israel about 30 factories with a capacity to process 350,000 tons of citrus fruit in season. About 80 per cent of the industry's output was directed to export. Israel's citrus products, including concentrates, frozen and other types of juices, grapefruit segments, and pectin, were well established in the European markets owing to their quality and competitiveness and were an important earner of foreign currency.

The export of citrus fruit from Israel in 1966–67 (fresh fruit and by-products) represented about 25 per cent of total Israeli exports and about 30 per cent of the total in added value.

Total citrus fruit and by-products exports reached about $110,000,500 in 1967, and it was expected that with the increase of crops, foreign currency earnings would increase also, thus strengthening the economy of the country.

Y. CHORIN

CIVIDALLI, GUALTIERO BENIAMIN. Engineer and Zionist leader (b. Florence, 1899). A member of the 'Avoda group in Rome and "blue box" commissioner of the *Jewish National Fund from 1926 to 1938, Cividalli was one of the most influential members of the small group of Italian Zionist leaders between the two world wars. A resident of Palestine from 1938 on, he was senior officer of *RASSCO in 1966.

G. RÓMANO

CIVIL AVIATION IN ISRAEL. *See* AVIATION IN ISRAEL.

CIVIL SERVICE IN ISRAEL. In 1966 the civil service in Israel, as presented by its own official statistics, consisted of all employees of the State of Israel paid from government funds, including those in the railways and ports, the police, the Land Development Authority, the *Knesset, the President's Office, and the Office of the *State Comptroller but excluding judges, schoolteachers, and *Israel Defense Forces and their civilian employees, as well as arsenal workers, local employees of Israel diplomatic missions and consular offices abroad, the staffs of local authorities and of government corporations (except those of the Ministry of Tourism), and seasonal laborers employed by the Ministries of Agriculture and Labor (in the latter, mostly in the Department of Public Works).

On this basis, the total number of civil servants employed in April, 1966, was 57,850. Together with 22,900 teachers this made 3.1 per cent of the population, a proportion that had remained constant each year since the founding of the State in 1948. These 57,850 civil servants were distributed in 1966 among the larger ministries as in the accompanying table.

DISTRIBUTION OF CIVIL SERVANTS, 1966

Ministry	Number of civil servants	Percentage of civil servants
Posts	11,040	19.1
Police	9,230	16.0
Health	8,470	14.6
Finance	6,890	11.9
Labor	3,560	6.2
Transport	3,470	6.6
Agriculture	2,680	4.6
Social Welfare	1,620	2.8
Education and Culture (excluding teachers)	1,680	2.9
Defense (excluding military personnel, etc.)	1,520	2.6
Justice	1,270	2.3

These larger ministries employed 89.6 per cent of all civil servants. The remaining 10.4 per cent, or 6,340 persons, were distributed among 12 other units, each of which employed fewer than 1,000 persons.

In 1966 the civil service included 39,000 administrative personnel, 9,000 professional personnel, and 9,000 police officers, policemen, and prison wardens. Of the 39,000 administrative staff, 30,000 were permanent and pensionable; the rest were on special contract, were paid by the hour, or were casual laborers.

The total salary bill for the civil service in 1965–66 amounted to $282,500,000. There were 20 grades, the top being that of directors general, the permanent heads of ministries. The difference in take-home pay between one grade and the next was remarkably small. The top salary in 1948 was only three times the bottom salary. With inflation, payment of cost-of-living and family allowances, and the imposition of a steeply graduated income tax, the take-home pay of a director general at one time was only 30 per cent higher than that of his own typist. This anomaly was remedied, often by automatic promotion on reaching the maximum of the grade, which destroyed the normal pyramidal structure of the civil service.

Recruitment. During the period of the British Mandate (see MANDATE FOR PALESTINE), nearly all the top posts in the Palestine administration were held by British civil servants, who were withdrawn when the British left the country. Of the middle and lower positions, two-thirds were held by Arabs, nearly all of whom left the country when Israel became independent. Of the one-third who were Jews, some were not reappointed by the Israel government and some did not wish to continue.

The severe shortage of trained civil servants at the beginning of the new State was offset, in part, by the transfer to the State of many employees of the former *Va'ad L'umi, the National Council of the Jews of Palestine, particularly from its Department of Health, Education, and Social Welfare. A certain number of men and women who had risked their lives in under-

ground defense movements or in organizing clandestine immigration came to the surface with the establishment of the State and entered the civil service in the Ministry of Defense and elsewhere. Some of them found the work routine and left after a while. On the other hand, economists and statisticians were loaned from banks and other enterprises; so were temporary volunteers from law offices and private medical practice, often at considerable financial loss. Many key posts were filled by political nominees of the minister in charge. The lower ranks of postal and railway employees were filled from another source of personnel, new immigrants who had acquired Israeli citizenship on entry and were willing to take on such work, which had no high educational requirements, until something better turned up. Those immigrants who had had public service experience abroad were first put to learning Hebrew intensively at residential Hebrew-language seminars, Ulpanim (see ULPAN), at the expense of the *Jewish Agency. Lastly, there were young Israelis leaving primary school who entered the lowest ranks of the civil service as a career and worked their way up, often by means of additional training at night school. Others, who had had a secondary education, entered the middle ranks, while those with a university education came directly into the upper levels. By the 1960s the young Israeli was, naturally, the mainstay of the civil service. Everything possible was done to reduce the intake from political party patronage.

In the early years, the turnover was very high, but in 1965–66 it amounted to only 4,800 (excluding police and some other types of employees), or 8.2 per cent. Vacancies in the lower ranks of the civil service were filled directly from the labor exchanges. Those in the middle and upper ranks (new appointments as well as promotions) were selected on the recommendation of ad hoc selection boards. In 1965–66 some 1,200 such boards were appointed, and 20,500 individuals who appeared before them sat for written civil service and other examinations.

Conditions of Service. The minimum age of appointment was 14, while the normal age of retirement on pension was 65 for both men and women. Israeli citizenship was a prerequisite for permanent civil service appointment. All candidates for permanent employment were required to pass a medical board examination, but disabled persons, mostly war veterans, received special, lenient treatment.

The hours of work in government offices were based on a 45-hour week, differing somewhat in summer and winter. Offices normally opened at 7:30 A.M. six days a week and closed at 4 P.M. on two days a week with only a half-hour break for lunch. On three of the remaining days, there was one long shift to 3 P.M., which was not a healthy practice but one which the civil service unions insisted on maintaining.

Civil servants were normally eligible for 13 to 26 days of annual leave, depending on age, seniority, and length of service. There were, in addition, several days off for public and religious holidays.

Training. Apart from general education at school and, in some cases, on the university level, there was little preentry training. Nearly all civil servants had undergone 30 months (24 in the case of women) of compulsory military service. Those immigrants who had not completed their primary education abroad were required to do so at public expense while in military service.

Brief ministerial orientation courses were provided for all new entrants. In 1966 there was still no cadet system in operation for prolonged full-time in-service training. Postentry part-time training was the responsibility of each ministry, and all the larger ministries had full-time training officers to organize it. The Civil Service Commission provided joint courses for regular clerical services such as typing, stenography, and accountancy. Full-time residential training was provided for senior staff at the Public Service College in Jerusalem. Evening courses for civil servants and others were also provided by a number of outside bodies for a fee, of which half was normally refunded by the government on successful completion. A small number of civil servants were sent abroad on fellowships each year for further specialized training. Training in the civil service was supervised by a Supreme Training Council.

Discipline. Standing instructions for the civil service were issued from time to time in loose-leaf form by the Civil Service Commission and were kept in a volume known as the *Takhshir*. Discipline was primarily the responsibility of each ministry. Serious infractions were brought before a standing disciplinary court, which could recommend a graduated series of punishments, the most severe being dismissal with loss of separation pay. If a breach of the penal law was found to be involved, the case was handed to the police for prosecution. Reports of the more important cases (without the names of the accused) were circulated throughout the civil service as object lessons.

In general, it was very difficult to secure the dismissal of an inefficient civil servant in Israel once he had completed his short probationary period, except through the disciplinary court process. When no actual breach of discipline was disclosed, this procedure could not be applied.

Civil Service Commission. Originally established as part of the Prime Minister's Office, the Commission was responsible to the Minister of Finance, who, in any case, was involved in all changes in salary scales. Its seat was in Jerusalem, and it had branch offices in Tel Aviv and Haifa. In April, 1966, its staff totaled 151; its budget for 1966–67 amounted to $700,000. The staff were grouped in the following units: Division of Regulations, Division of Employment (including the Central Index and examinations, and the Establishment and Planning Divisions, which covered job classification), Training Service, Public Service College, Pensions, Organization and Methods Service, Publications, Statistics, and Disciplinary Proceedings.

The Civil Service Commission was aided by the Va'adat HaSherut (Service Committee) and by an Advisory Council composed of the assistant directors general of the several ministries. The work of the Commission was impeded by continuous salary negotiations with the trade unions. Strikes and threats of strikes were formerly frequent, largely on questions of status and salary, but after 1964 strikes were few and far between.

Efficiency. The efficiency of the Israeli civil service varied from ministry to ministry and from unit to unit within a given ministry. One of the main causes of inefficiency was the cramped space provided, often in leased premises, owing to the rapid expansion of the civil service and of the population in general. Other causes were the undertaking of ambitious schemes without adequate personnel or enough trained personnel, failure to agree on priorities, a disinclination to delegate authority to subordinates, a reliance on numerous interoffice committees stemming from interministerial and interdepartmental rivalry and suspicion, and the difficulty in dispensing with the services of inefficient personnel.

In the 1960s the civil service was still highly politicized in spite of attempts to set limits to the political activities of civil servants, especially in the upper ranks. The obtaining of preferential or priority treatment through the intervention of someone in the department concerned was widely sought by the public in order to cut through red tape. Corruption and embezzlement were rare, and the indignation expressed in the press and in the Knesset whenever such criminal cases were revealed was a healthy sign that the public did not consider these weaknesses inevitable. The occurrence of these evils was largely due to inadequate inspection.

VISCOUNT SAMUEL

CLIMATE OF ISRAEL. Situated in the southeastern corner of the Mediterranean Sea, Israel extends south to the northern tip of the northeastern extension of the Red Sea, the Gulf of Elat, and covers an area influenced by both the Mediterranean Sea and the planetary desert belt south of it. Its climate, therefore, varies from a pure Mediterranean to a desert climate. The former is characterized by dry summers and rainy winters and by a moderate range of temperature between day and night and between summer and winter. A desert climate shows not only lack of rainfall throughout the year but also considerable annual and even daily variations of temperature.

The most important climatic element in Israel is rainfall, which varies from 44 inches annually in the hills of Upper Galilee to 1 inch at Elat. Rainfall decreases from north to south and from the sea inland; it increases with elevation. Thus the rainfall map is well in conformity with the geography and the relief of the country. The length of the rainy season is almost uniform throughout Israel. Rain of measurable quantities starts falling in October, reaches its maximum during December, January, and February, and practically comes to an end by April. The months of June to August are rainless. Two-thirds of the total annual rainfall is distributed over the three winter months. The number of rain days is almost proportional to the rainfall and varies from 70 in Upper Galilee to 5 at Elat. A typical winter month has 10 to 15 rain days and collects 4 to 8 inches of rainfall in the northern half of the country. Typical figures for the annual average are as follows: Haifa, 24 inches of rainfall on 55 days; Tel Aviv, 22 inches on 50 days; Jerusalem, 20 inches on 45 days. Rain occurs mainly in showers, so that continuous rain for several hours is relatively rare. Snow may fall once a year on hilltops and remain on the ground once every three years.

Temperatures vary from moderately warm to hot. The annual mean temperature is 61°F on the hilltops of Upper Galilee, Judea, and the Negev; 68°F in the plains along the Mediterranean and inland; and 77°F at the Dead Sea and Elat. The annual run of temperature is characterized by an increase in the annual range from the Mediterranean eastward: from a difference of 22°F between the mean temperatures of the hottest and the coldest months, to 27°F along the axis of the hill ridge, and to 32°F in the southern Jordan Rift down to Elat. Thus we find similar winter temperatures at places of the same elevation, whereas the differences are considerable in the summer. Mean temperatures for January in the lowlands range from 54 to 59°F, whereas in August, the hottest month at most places, readings are 79°F near the Mediterranean, 82°F in the inland plains, and 91°F at Elat. Hill locations are, of course, cooler: Jerusalem's mean temperatures vary from 48°F in January to 75°F in August, as against 61°F and 93°F, respectively, at the Dead Sea. The daily range of temperature is influenced by the proximity of bodies of water and by relief, being narrow near

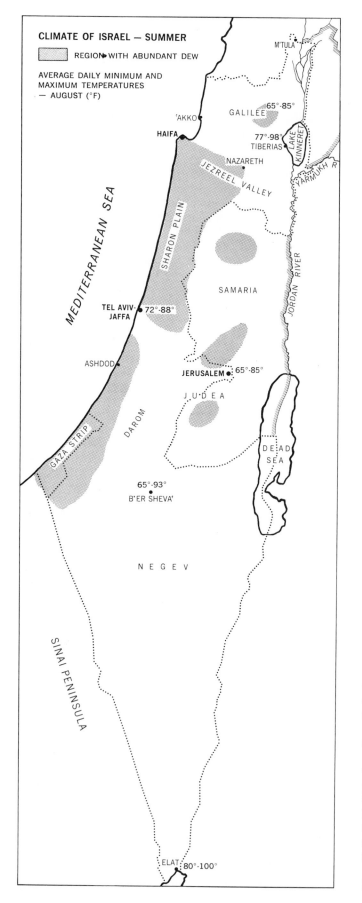

CLIMATE OF ISRAEL — SUMMER

REGION WITH ABUNDANT DEW

AVERAGE DAILY MINIMUM AND
MAXIMUM TEMPERATURES
— AUGUST (°F)

M'TULA

GALILEE   65°-85°

'AKKO

HAIFA

TIBERIAS   77°-98°

LAKE KINNERET

NAZARETH

JEZREEL VALLEY

YARMUKH R.

MEDITERRANEAN SEA

SHARON PLAIN

SAMARIA

JORDAN RIVER

TEL AVIV-
JAFFA   72°-88°

ASHDOD

JERUSALEM   65°-85°

JUDEA

DAROM

DEAD SEA

GAZA STRIP

65°-93°
B'ER SHEVA'

NEGEV

SINAI PENINSULA

ELAT   80°-100°

the sea and wider in valleys than on hilltops. The smallest difference between daily maximum and minimum temperatures is found on Mount Carmel, near the sea, whereas the greatest is found in inland valleys (e.g., 25°F at B'er Sheva'). The mean daily maximum temperatures in August are 80°F at N'tanya on the Mediterranean coast and at Jerusalem, as against 104°F at the Dead Sea and Elat. Whereas, on the average, August is the hottest month and January the coolest, the highest actual temperatures are almost never experienced in the hottest months. These are caused by *sharav* (khamsin) situations, occurring most frequently in the transitional seasons (April–May, September–October), when interruptions of the usual circulation pattern with its influx of cool air from the Mediterranean cause the air to stagnate over the country or to be advected from the desert areas surrounding Israel. Temperatures may rise to 95°F and above in the coastal plain and the hills and to 104°F and above in the Jordan Rift and its southern extension. On the other hand, frost may occur occasionally during the winter in the hill region and the inland valleys in connection with the influx of polar air.

The third element characterizing Israel's climate is the humidity of the air. Here again the main source is the Mediterranean Sea, and therefore absolute measures of humidity decrease from the sea inland. Relative humidity (a fraction of the vapor-holding capacity of the air), which again rises with temperature, varies according to the temperature regime. Thus conditions are very stable along the Mediterranean shore, with almost unvarying mean monthly relative humidities of 70 per cent all year round. On the hills variability is relatively large: over 70 per cent in winter and 50 per cent or less in summer. In the Jordan Rift relative humidities decrease from north to south down to Elat, where the climate is extremely dry, with humidity varying between 50 per cent in the winter and 30 per cent or less in the summer. Daily variations of relative humidity vary inversely with those of temperature, being small on the Mediterranean coast and large inland: a normal summer midday relative humidity of 70 per cent at Tel Aviv contrasts with one of 20 per cent at Elat.

The wind regime of Israel is characterized by a season of regular daily alternation of land and sea breezes in summer and one of winds subject to the influence of passing weather systems during the rest of the year. In general, winds are moderate, and the regular sea breeze from the Mediterranean reaches very far inland during the daytime in summer with a moderating effect on the inclemency of temperature and humidity conditions.

N. ROSENAN

CLOTHING IN ISRAEL. The urban population of Israel dresses in the modern Western style, following seasonal changes and the latest fashions. The styles are derived mainly from France, Italy, and the United States. Until the mid-1960s, local designers exerted only a limited influence on Israeli fashions.

Israeli dress had changed markedly since the early 1900s, when Palestine was under Turkish rule. At that time the Jewish population of the country was relatively small, and there were no textile and clothing industries. The early Jewish pioneers in Palestine stressed simplicity in dress, a trend still reflected in the clothing seen in villages and collectives in the 1960s. The men abandoned ties and jackets, the women went without sheer stockings and girdles, and wardrobes were relatively limited.

Because of the intense sun, hats had to be worn in the summer. In the city, women wore wide-brimmed straw or cloth hats;

men chose straw for the summer and felt for the winter. In the rural areas, the narrow-brimmed blue or khaki linen *tembel* hat was the usual headgear. It was also worn by children throughout Israel and by many tourists and had become a form of national costume.

Typical Israeli work clothes consisted of a sports shirt worn with pants or a four-gored skirt. Winter weather called for a sweater or a wool jacket and high-laced shoes. Simple leather-thonged sandals (known as Biblical sandals) were worn in the summer. Formerly summer clothing in the kibbutzim was completely white. By the 1960s, however, summer clothing throughout Israel was made of lightweight colored materials, mainly of Israeli manufacture.

Clothing Industry. Israeli textiles in the 1960s were made of cotton, linen, wool, and synthetic fibers. The cotton was mainly of local origin. Small quantities of flax were grown locally; the rest was imported from Belgium and processed, dyed, or printed in Israel. Wool was imported from Australia, New Zealand, South Africa, and Argentina. Synthetic fibers, which were used in combination with cotton, linen, wool, and rayon, were imported from Japan, the Netherlands, England, Germany, and the United States.

Israel manufactured smooth and stretch nylon, Acrylan, Saran, and other synthetics for use in bathing suits, girdles, stockings, blouses, knitwear, braided and woven goods, purses, and accessories. The wide variety of patterned and textured textiles manufactured in Israel was comparable in quality to similar materials manufactured elsewhere, but as they were produced in limited quantities, they were expensive. Nonetheless, Israel's modern, well-equipped factories were increasingly able to compete in the world market.

Israel's textile industry included knitting, weaving, finishing, dyeing, and printing of materials for men's, women's, and children's wear, upholstery and curtain fabrics, table linens, and bedding. Some factories housed under one roof an entire series of operations, from the spinning of raw fibers into thread to the production of finished items of clothing. A considerable part of the textiles manufactured in Israel was exported; Israeli knitwear—dresses, suits, blouses, and bathing suits—was particularly well received abroad.

In the 1960s Israel had an important leather-goods industry. Leather was imported from Cyprus, Turkey, and Iran and made into shoes, suits, jackets, coats, gloves, handbags, and luggage. These goods also found a market abroad. No import taxes were levied on raw materials imported by the leather and textile industries for the purpose of manufacture and export.

In 1965, 42,000 workers, or one-sixth of all the industrial workers of Israel, were employed in Israel's clothing (textile and leather) industry. A large number were new immigrants who had learned their trade in Israel. The factory owners were mainly of European origin with European experience and know-how. It was anticipated that the textile and leather industries would double their production by 1970.

The Fashion Center of the Israeli Export Board encouraged Israeli textile and clothing designers by sponsoring awards and granting preferential tax rates for outstanding local designs. Through its efforts, Israeli designs were exported in increasing quantities in the 1960s.

Israel participated in international trade fairs, where it displayed its textiles, leather goods, and clothing. During the annual Fashion Week in Israel, the latest clothing and textile designs were on display and buyers came from large stores throughout

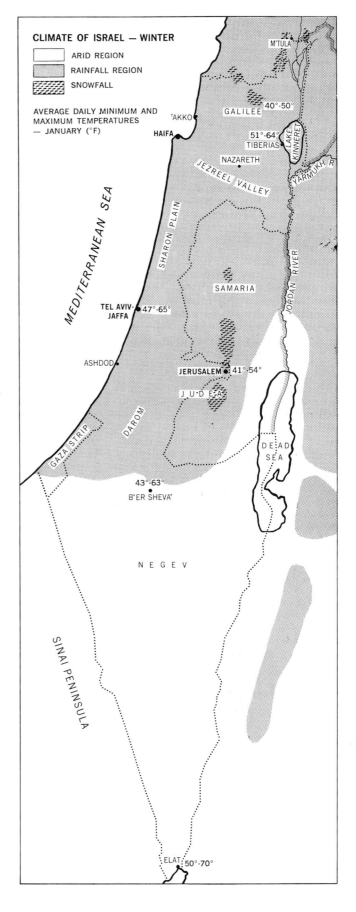

CLIMATE OF ISRAEL — WINTER

ARID REGION

RAINFALL REGION

SNOWFALL

AVERAGE DAILY MINIMUM AND MAXIMUM TEMPERATURES — JANUARY (°F)

the world. The Levant Fair, held biannually in Tel Aviv, also served as a showplace for Israeli fashions, textiles, and leather goods.

A Contemporary "National Costume." In the 1960s the necessity of providing a unique and easily distinguishable costume for the *dance troupes and student exchange groups going abroad led to attempts to create a "national costume" for Israel. Some suggestions were drawn from the clothing brought to Israel by the *Yemenite Jews. The *Women's International Zionist Organization (WIZO) pioneered in the development of Yemenite-inspired clothing through the employment of Yemenite women to embroider garments sold in the WIZO shops. This had the dual result of providing home employment for women and of helping to preserve the beautiful traditional embroidery patterns, which were, however, adapted to contemporary taste.

Maskit, a government-supported firm, attempted to bolster home industry by employing immigrant women from many *ethnic groups in various handicrafts. Although these immigrants brought with them a variety of lovely national costumes, they rapidly abandoned them for modern dress.

Israeli designers drew inspiration for new fashions from the interesting collections of jewelry and clothing of the various ethnic groups within Jewry, which were displayed in Israel's folklore *museums on life-size dummies depicting the physical traits of each of the ethnic groups. Some of these new designs were executed in cotton batik and fishnet; the Yemenite influence could be seen in loose garments worn with long, tight pants edged with embroidery.

A. KADURY

COCHIN JEWS IN ISRAEL. *See* INDIAN JEWS IN ISRAEL.

COHEN, DAVID. Scholar, communal worker, and Zionist leader in the Netherlands (b. Deventer, Netherlands, 1882; d. Amsterdam, 1967). A brother of Isaac *Cohen and Rudolf *Cohen, he founded Maccabi, the first Zionist youth group in the Netherlands. Cohen was honorary secretary of the Dutch Zionist Executive (1908–10) and editor in chief of the Zionist weekly *De Joodse Wachter* (1910–12). In 1918 he became the first chairman of the Dutch Zionist Youth Federation. An adherent of the practical school of Zionism, which stressed settlement and reconstruction work in Palestine as distinct from political action in behalf of a Jewish State, Cohen represented a minority view against leading Dutch Zionist thinkers such as Samuel Franzie *Berenstein and Nehemia *de Lieme.

In 1926 Cohen was appointed professor of ancient history at the University of Amsterdam. From 1933 to 1940 he served as honorary secretary of the Committee to Aid Jewish Refugees from Germany. In 1941 he was appointed cochairman of the Joodse Raad (Jewish Council) by the Nazi occupation authorities. He was later interned at Westerbork and in Theresienstadt. After his return to Netherlands in 1945, Cohen was no longer active in Zionist and Jewish communal affairs.

COHEN, ELIYAHU BEN SAUL (Eli). Israeli secret agent (b. Alexandria, 1924; d. Damascus, 1965). A graduate of the School of Engineering at Farouk University in Cairo, he joined the Zionist movement in 1941 and was a member of the pioneering youth movement HeHalutz HaTza'ir from 1941 to 1946 (*see* HEHALUTZ). Settling in Israel after the *Sinai Campaign

of 1956, he later reached Syria via Argentina and, under the assumed Arab name Camile Amin Thabbet, established himself in Damascus. There he became friendly with Syrian leaders, including Cabinet ministers and high-ranking army officers, from whom he obtained information which he regularly radioed to Israel, where he visited his wife and children each year.

Cohen was considered one of the boldest and most successfull agents in the history of espionage. Arrested in February, 1965, he was given a staged trial presided over by two Syrian officers, a Colonel Daali and Maj. Salim Hatum, who had been among his friends. Convicted on May 8, 1965, on charges of entering a military area in disguise and passing classified information to Israel, he was hanged in a public square in Damascus on May 18, 1965, despite appeals for clemency from world leaders, including Pres. Charles de Gaulle, Queen Mother Elizabeth of Belgium, and a representative of Pope Paul VI, and despite Israel's offer to exchange any or all of the Syrian prisoners it was holding in return for a commutation of Cohen's death sentence. He was buried in the Jewish cemetery in Damascus. Syria refused Israel's requests, made through the UN Mixed Armistice Commission and the Red Cross, for Cohen's body.

COHEN, GUSTAV GABRIEL. Merchant and early Zionist (b. Hamburg, Germany, 1830; d. there, 1906). He was the owner of a large business in Port Elizabeth, South Africa, and later in Manchester, England. A pre-Herzlian Zionist, he became a close friend and collaborator of Herzl. Cohen was the author of *Die Juden-Frage und die Zukunft* (The Jewish Question and the Future, 1891, 1896). His daughter became the wife of Otto *Warburg.

COHEN, ISAAC. Zionist leader and Chief Rabbi of Ireland (b. Llanelly, Wales, 1914). In 1965 Rabbi Cohen was a member of the Standing Committee of European Rabbis; honorary president of the Mizrahi Federation of Ireland (*see* MIZRAHI), the Joint Palestine Appeal of Ireland, the Association of Jewish Clergy and Teachers of Ireland, the Dublin Jewish Friendship Club, and the Dublin Hebrew Speakers' Circle; and honorary superintendent of the Dublin Talmud Tora. In 1964 he served as a delegate to the 26th Zionist *Congress.

COHEN, ISAAC (Chi). Attorney and Zionist leader in the Netherlands (b. Deventer, Netherlands, 1884; d. Bergen-Belsen, 1944). A brother of David *Cohen and Rudolf *Cohen, he was honorary editor of the Zionist weekly *De Joodse Wachter* (1920–26) and served for a time as vice-chairman of the Dutch Zionist Executive. He was head of the Palestine Office in the Netherlands (*see* PALESTINE OFFICES) from 1920 to 1924 and again from 1934 to 1940.

COHEN, ISRAEL. Author and Zionist leader (b. Manchester, England, 1879; d. London, 1961). Cohen studied at Jews' College and London University. He attended several Zionist Congresses (*see* CONGRESS, ZIONIST) and in 1910 became the English secretary of Zionist headquarters in Cologne, and in 1911, in Berlin. At the beginning of World War I he was interned in the Ruhleben prison camp, in Germany, and was not released until June, 1916. After the war he toured Poland and Hungary and reported on the manifestations of *anti-Semitism he found there. From 1918 to 1922 Cohen served as director of publicity, and from 1922 to 1939 as general secretary, of the *World Zionist Organization in London. He also edited the reports of the Zionist *Executive to several Zionist Congresses.

Cohen was one of the early outstanding Zionist journalists and writers in Great Britain, and his articles appeared in Jewish Zionist and English journals. He also published 15 books, among them *Jewish Life in Modern Times* (1914); *The Zionist Movement* (1945); *A Short History of Zionism* (1951); *A Jewish Pilgrimage: The Autobiography of Israel Cohen* (1956); and *Theodor Herzl: Founder of Political Zionism* (1959). In addition, he published pamphlets on Jewish affairs, Zionism, and anti-Semitism and edited *The Rebirth of Israel: A Memorial Tribute to Paul Goodman* (1952).   J. FRAENKEL

COHEN, JACOB. *See* CAHAN, YA'AKOV.

COHEN, RUDOLF (Ru). Zionist leader in the Netherlands (b. Deventer, Netherlands, 1888; d. Bergen-Belsen, 1945). A younger brother of David *Cohen and Isaac *Cohen, he was a founder and honorary secretary of Maccabi, the first Zionist youth group in the Netherlands. From 1918 until his deportation by the Nazis he was active in the training of Halutzim (pioneers; *see* HALUTZIYUT) and for this purpose founded the Deventer Vereniging. In 1947 an agricultural training center in Bet HaShitta, Israel, was named for him and his wife, Eva.

COHN, ARTHUR (Asher Michael). Rabbi and early Zionist sympathizer (b. Flatow, West Prussia, Germany, 1862; d. Basle, Switzerland, 1926). As rabbi of the Jewish community of Basle from 1885 until his death, Cohn was an outspoken opponent of Reform Judaism. Opposed to political Zionism for religious reasons, he nevertheless attended the 1st Zionist *Congress (Basle, 1897) as an observer. Deeply impressed by the Congress and by Herzl, he visited a number of the early Congresses, but at the time of the 10th Congress (Basle, 1911) he was one of the group that called on Orthodox Jews to leave the Zionist movement, a step which resulted in the formation of *Agudat Israel. His addresses were published after his death in an anthology entitled *Von Israels Lehre und Leben* (Israel's Law and Life, 1927).

COHN, EMIL BERNARD. Rabbi, author, and Zionist leader (b. Berlin, 1881; d. Los Angeles, 1948). Cohn served as a preacher in Berlin and later as rabbi in the German cities of Kiel, Essen, and Bonn, where he edited (1919–23) *Der Jüdische Bote vom Rhein*. Beginning in 1926 he served in Berlin again. After the rise of Nazism, he emigrated to the Netherlands and from there to the United States, where he was killed in an automobile accident.

An ardent Zionist, Cohn played a prominent role in Zionism in pre-Hitler Germany. Because of his Zionist views, he was forced to leave his first Berlin pulpit in 1907. He was the author of several plays and books, the latter including *Ein Aufruf an die Zeit* (1923), an appeal on behalf of traditional Judaism; and *David *Wolffsohn, Herzl's Successor*, a biography of the second president of the *World Zionist Organization, which appeared in both German (1939) and English (1944).   S. HUBNER

COHN, HAYIM HERMANN. Israeli jurist and Supreme Court justice (b. Lübeck, Germany, 1911). Cohn received his high school education in his native city, where he also studied at the rabbinical school founded by his grandfather, Rabbi Solomon

Carlebach. He briefly attended the Universities of Munich and Hamburg before settling in Palestine in 1930. Between 1930 and 1932 he studied at the *Hebrew University and at the Merkaz HaRav Yeshiva in Jerusalem. In 1932 he left Palestine for a year to study at the University of Frankfurt, where he earned his law degree in 1933.

After his admission to the Palestine bar in 1937, Cohn engaged in private legal practice until 1947, when he became secretary of the Legal Council of the Emergency Commission of the *Jewish Agency. He was subsequently State Attorney of Israel (1948–49) and Director General of the Ministry of Justice (1949–50). In 1950 he was appointed Attorney General, an office he held until 1960 except for a brief period (June–December, 1952) when he served as Minister of Justice. In 1960 he was named justice of Israel's Supreme Court, an office he still held in 1968.

Cohn represented Israel at the United Nations on the Committee on International Criminal Jurisdiction (Geneva, August, 1951) and on the UN Commission on Human Rights (1957–59, 1965–67). From 1961 on he was a member of the Permanent Court of Arbitration at The Hague. In 1959 he became Chairman of the Israel national section of the International Council of Jurists, and in 1964 Chairman of the Israel section of the Association Internationale de Droit Pénal.

Cohn wrote *The Foreign Laws of Marriage and Divorce* (1937) and numerous articles in Israeli and foreign legal journals.

COHN, MARKUS MORDEKHAI. Attorney and *Mizrahi leader in Switzerland (b. Basle, 1890; d. Switzerland, 1953). The son of Arthur *Cohn, he attended the Universities of Leipzig, Berlin, Heidelberg, and Basle (J.D., 1914). In 1919 he opened a private legal practice in Basle. Cohn was a Presidium member of the Mizrahi Organization of Switzerland and president (1931–36) of the Swiss Zionist Federation. A delegate to the 16th (Zurich, 1929), 17th (Basle, 1931), and 19th (Lucerne, 1935) Zionist Congresses (*see* CONGRESS, ZIONIST), he served on the *Congress Tribunal from 1935 to 1953. In 1933 he founded the Swiss branch of the Palestine Office (*see* PALESTINE OFFICES). He was a delegate to the Montreux session of the *World Jewish Congress in June, 1948. In 1950 he went to Israel to become adviser on Jewish law to the Ministry of Justice. In 1953 he returned to Switzerland for medical treatment and died there. Cohn was the author of numerous works on Jewish civil law.

COLLECTIVE SETTLEMENTS. *See* KIBBUTZ.

COLONISATIONS-VEREIN FÜR PALÄSTINA (Settlement Society for Palestine). Society founded in 1860 in Frankfurt on the Oder by Chaim *Lorje for the purpose of establishing a large Jewish agricultural settlement in Palestine and of encouraging and assisting individual Jewish agriculturists there. Lorje developed a widespread publicity campaign and succeeded in enlisting the aid of a number of prominent Jews.

Members of the society included such precursors of Zionism as Rabbis Judah Solomon Hai *Alkalai, Elijah *Gutmacher, and Moses *Hess. Most active on its behalf was Rabbi Zvi Hirsch *Kalischer, whose treatise *D'rishat Zion*, printed by the society in 1862, advocated the establishment of a Jewish agricultural community in Palestine and subsequently became the ideological basis of the Hibbat Zion movement (*see* HOVEVE ZION).

The Colonisations-Verein ceased to exist in 1864. Though it

made no concrete achievements during its short existence, it contributed much to the rise of the Hibbat Zion movement.

COLONIZATION. *See* RURAL SETTLEMENT IN PALESTINE AND ISRAEL.

COLUMBUS PLATFORM. Revised platform of American Reform Judaism, announced in Columbus, Ohio, in 1937. It modified the original anti-Zionist stand of American Reform Judaism (*see* ANTI-ZIONISM). While an increasing number of rabbinical and lay leaders of the Reform movement had been manifesting Zionist sympathies since World War I and particularly after the issuance of the *Balfour Declaration, the Central Conference of American Rabbis (CCAR) and the Union of American Hebrew Congregations (UAHC) as bodies stood on the *Pittsburgh Platform as the source of their official anti-Zionism for half a century. A formal change took place in 1935, when CCAR adopted the following resolution: "We are persuaded that acceptance or rejection of the Zionist program should be left to the determination of the individual members of the Conference themselves . . . the Central Conference of American Rabbis takes no official stand on the subject of Zionism." The same resolution pledged CCAR to "continue to cooperate in the upbuilding of Palestine, and in the economic, cultural, and particular spiritual tasks confronting the growing and evolving Jewish community there."

At a convention held in Columbus, Ohio, in 1937, CCAR went a step further and, in what has become known as the Columbus Platform, adopted the concept of Jewish peoplehood and stated that it was "the obligation of all Jewry to aid in [the] upbuilding [of Palestine] as a Jewish homeland by endeavoring to make it not only a haven of refuge for the oppressed but also a center of Jewish cultural and spiritual life." In the same year, the UAHC declared in a resolution: "The time has now come for all Jews, irrespective of ideological differences, to unite in the activities leading to the establishment of a Jewish homeland in Palestine, and we urge our constituency to give their financial and moral support to the work of rebuilding Palestine." With few exceptions, the union's constituent congregations and groups responded to this call in the affirmative.

See also REFORM JUDAISM AND ZIONISM.

C. B. SHERMAN

COMAY, MICHAEL SAUL. Israeli diplomat (b. Cape Town, South Africa, 1908). A graduate of Cape Town University, he early became active in the Zionist movement. He served in the South African Army from 1940 to 1945 and was mentioned twice in military dispatches. Settling in Palestine in 1946, he was special representative of the South African Zionist Federation attached to the Political Department of the *Jewish Agency in Jerusalem from 1946 to 1948.

Comay served as Director of the British Commonwealth Division of the Israeli Ministry of Foreign Affairs from 1948 to 1953 and as Assistant Director General of the Ministry from 1951 to 1953 and again from 1957 to 1960. He was Israel's Minister and then Ambassador to Canada from 1953 to 1957, a member of the Israeli delegation to numerous sessions of the UN General Assembly, and chairman of the delegation at the 15th, 16th, and 17th sessions. In 1960 he became Permanent Representative of Israel to the United Nations, serving until 1967, when he was named Political Adviser to the Ministry of Foreign Affairs.

COMITÉ DES DÉLÉGATIONS JUIVES. Body of Jewish organizations formed in Paris on Mar. 25, 1919, for the purpose of presenting the peace conference with demands for Jewish national rights in certain countries, particularly in the newly established "succession states" in Central and Eastern Europe. Its official title was Comité des Délégations Juives auprès de la Conférence de la Paix (Committee of Jewish Delegations to the Peace Conference). As distinct from delegations sent to Paris by other organizations, such as the Joint Foreign Committee of the *Anglo-Jewish Association and the *Alliance Israélite Universelle, which merely sought the attainment of equal civic rights for all Jews, the Comité represented the Zionist, or nationalist, approach to Jewish issues.

The delegations comprising the Comité represented the Jews of the United States, Canada, Palestine, and a number of European countries including the Ukraine, Russia, Austria-Hungary, Poland, Romania, Turkey, Italy, and Greece. They began to assemble in Paris soon after the armistice (November, 1918). Some of them had been chosen by popular election through Jewish congresses or national assemblies; others came as representatives of Jewish national councils or official Jewish communities.

Julian W. *Mack, president of the *American Jewish Congress and chairman of its delegation to the Paris Peace Conference, was elected chairman of the Comité. Before the conclusion of the work of the Comité in Paris, Mack was succeeded by Louis *Marshall, who in turn was followed by Nahum *Sokolow. In addition to the officers, prominent members of the Comité included Joseph *Barondess, Leopold Benedict, Bernard G. Richards, Nachman *Syrkin, and Stephen S. *Wise of the United States; Aaron Eisenberg, Isaac Wilkansky (*see* ELAZARI-VOLCANI, YITZHAK AVIGDOR), and David *Yellin of Palestine; Wilhelm Filderman, Jacob *Niemirower, and Philippe Rosenstein of Romania; M'nahem M. *Ussishkin of the Ukraine; Émile Reich, Michael *Ringel, and Joseph *Tenenbaum of eastern Galicia; and Markus *Braude, Leon *Levite, and Osias *Thon of Poland. Chaim *Weizmann was one of the representatives of the *World Zionist Organization.

The Comité submitted two memorandums to the conference, one on the civil and cultural rights of Jews in various countries, and the other on the historic claim of the Jewish people to Palestine. Members of the Comité were officially received by members, experts, and advisers of the peace conference. The international treaties guaranteeing the rights of all minority groups, Jewish and non-Jewish, were considered one of the major achievements of the Comité and, more specifically, of the American Jewish delegation to the Paris Peace Conference.

The Comité, with headquarters in Paris, remained in existence for the protection of Jewish rights until the early 1930s. Leo *Motzkin, who succeeded Sokolow as chairman, remained at the head of the Comité until his death in 1933. The Comité subsequently merged with the *World Jewish Congress.

G. HIRSCHLER

COMMERCE OF ISRAEL. *See* DOMESTIC TRADE IN ISRAEL; FOREIGN TRADE OF ISRAEL.

COMMISSIONS OF INQUIRY, ZIONIST. Commissions of inquiry within the Zionist movement were appointed mainly to investigate sources of disagreement between the central authorities in the movement and the men on the spot in Palestine. In April and May, 1914, a delegation including Nahum *Sokolow, Leo *Motzkin, Julius *Simon, and Boris *Goldberg, which had been appointed that January, was in Palestine to investigate the work of Zionist institutions there, such as the Palestine Office (see PALESTINE OFFICES) and the Anglo-Palestine Bank (see BANK L'UMI L'YISRAEL). This delegation devoted special attention to the problem of Jewish labor and the operations of the bank. However, its report was prepared too late to influence Zionist work in Palestine before the outbreak of World War I.

In September, 1920, the Zionist *Executive set up a Reorganization Commission. Created in the face of a severe shortage of funds (revenue had fallen far behind the expectations held prior to the *London Zionist Conference), the Commission was charged with the introduction of changes necessary to ensure the effective continuation of the settlement work and with drawing up plans for future development. It was strongly supported by the Brandeis group, which intended to gain control of the economic management of the *Zionist Commission.

The Reorganization Commission consisted of Julius Simon, director of the Palestine Office in London, Nehemia *de Lieme, managing director of the *Jewish National Fund (JNF), and Robert *Szold, a former member of the Zionist Commission. They arrived in Palestine on Nov. 4, 1920, and stayed about six weeks. The solutions they offered were in line with their general economic concept, namely, that a retrenchment in unproductive expenses should be effected wherever possible and that the approved development budget should not be exceeded in any item.

For economic reasons the Commission curtailed attempts at settlement of the Jerusalem Mountains. This aroused resentment in the *Yishuv (Jewish population of Palestine). A major point of contention was the acquisition by the JNF of the Jezreel Valley, to which the Commission objected, arguing that the price was too high. De Lieme was of the opinion that land should be acquired in Jerusalem and the Negev instead.

The report of the Commission was published by the Brandeis group during its conflict with Chaim *Weizmann and was thus given a factional tinge. The main points of criticism pertained to economically unproductive expenditures. The report recommended that a clear distinction be made between basic investments without returns and economically sound investments. It suggested that the budget of the *World Zionist Organization (WZO) be relieved of the burden of education and that the funds thus saved be directed toward immigration and settlement. Political activity also seemed to the Commission to lie outside the sphere of the WZO, since it considered that political work had been completed for the most part with the ratification of the *Mandate for Palestine.

Among the institutions for economic development recommended by the Commission were a mortgage bank, a cooperative agricultural bank for granting short-term loans, an agricultural bank for providing settlers with essentials, a loan fund for craftsmen and small manufacturers, a workers' bank, an equipment fund for public-works employees, a large purchasers' cooperative designed to lower the prices of essential commodities, a central land-buying agency to prevent competition among private purchasers and between them and the JNF, and a research institute. All these institutions were to be independent of one another and headed by experts whose decisions were to be governed by purely economic considerations within the framework of the general policy of the WZO. In this manner it was hoped that a separation would be effected between economic action and public needs, on the one hand, and political influence, on the other.

The funds thus freed were to be spent on land purchases. The Reorganization Commission objected to the method of providing new settlers with their entire equipment and suggested that the settlers themselves bear part of the expenses of settlement out of future savings.

The 12th Zionist *Congress, which met in Karlovy Vary, Czechoslovakia, in 1921, rejected the Commission's criticism and approved the work done in Palestine. Simon and De Lieme thereupon resigned from the Zionist Executive.

After a series of consultations between Zionist and non-Zionist leaders, a Common Inquiry Commission was set up in June, 1927. Its task was to examine Palestine economic resources and conditions in order to plan future work there. The members of the Commission were Sir Alfred Mond (see MELCHETT OF LANDFORD, 1ST BARON), Felix M. *Warburg, Oskar *Wassermann, and Lee K. *Frankel. The Common Inquiry Commission was assisted by subsidiary commissions composed of experts in different fields. Among them was a Commission of Agricultural Experts under the chairmanship of Dr. Elwood Mead, Commissioner of Reclamation of the United States. The main conclusions of this Commission favored Jewish agricultural settlement work, particularly that in the coastal plain, the Jezreel Valley, and the Jordan Valley, where water for irrigation had been made available. The progress which had been made seemed to the Commission to give assurance that, with the right methods, success was possible. Exception was taken only to the cultivation of the mountainous areas.

On the other hand, the Commission was critical of certain social aspects, particularly of interference by the labor organizations in immigration and settlement, to which it attributed the premature establishment of settlements prior to the consolidation of existing villages. The Commission also disapproved of the methods of settlement pursued by the WZO, preferring the methods employed by private settlers. It recommended that national ownership of land be limited, that hired labor be used, and that private investment capital be attracted. It felt that a social system which did not reward individual initiative and ability was not conducive to development and considered the collective settlements mere "social experiments."

The report aroused strong objections in the WZO, particularly in the labor parties, which accused the Commission of disregarding the "human factor" and of lacking appreciation for social progress.

I. KOLATT

COMMITTEE FOR A JEWISH ARMY. See BERGSON GROUP.

COMMITTEE FOR THE EAST. See KOMITEE FÜR DEN OSTEN.

COMMITTEE OF JEWISH DELEGATIONS TO THE PEACE CONFERENCE. See COMITÉ DES DÉLÉGATIONS JUIVES.

COMMON MARKET AND ISRAEL. See EUROPEAN COMMON MARKET AND ISRAEL.

COMMONWEALTH IDEA IN PALESTINE. See REVISIONISTS.

COMMUNE. See KIBBUTZ.

COMMUNISTS IN ISRAEL. The first Communist organization in Palestine was the Mifleget Po'alim Sotzialistim (Socialist Workers party), founded in 1919 by a group of members of the *Po'ale Zion movement who did not join the *Ahdut 'Avoda (United Zionist Labor party). In an effort to gain recognition by the Comintern, the group departed from Zionism, opposing Jewish *immigration and settlement in Palestine and the revival of the *Hebrew language and changing its name to the Yiddish Palestinishe Kommunistishe Partei (PKP). The Communists recruited their members from among Halutzim (pioneers; *see* HALUTZIYUT) who despaired of the realization of Zionism, leftist elements that had come to Palestine by chance, and young people who were attracted by underground activities (communism was illegal in Palestine until 1941, and the British authorities persecuted Communists, many of whom were expelled from the country). In February, 1924, the Comintern recognized the PKP as its branch in Palestine. In that year the PKP sided with the Arab nationalists in the quarrel over land in 'Afula. In April, 1924, the *Histadrut (General Federation of Labor) expelled all its Communist members because of their activities against the Jewish people and the working class in Palestine. The Communists urged their adherents to leave Palestine. Emigrants included a group of leftists who were with the *G'dud Ha'Avoda V'haHagana 'Al Shem Yosef Trumpeldor (1927) and one that departed for *Birobidzhan (1932). During the 1929 *Arab riots in Palestine the Communists helped defend the Jewish population against the Arab attackers, but immediately thereafter, in accordance with instructions from Moscow, they adopted an anti-Jewish line, referring to the pogroms as a "revolt of the fellahin" (*see* FELLAH). The party was ordered to undergo "Arabization." Young Arabs were sent to Moscow for indoctrination. One of these, Ridwan El-Hilu ("Mussa"), was appointed secretary of the party in 1934. Between 1936 and 1939 Arab Communists participated in the terrorist activities of the Arab bands. During the Spanish Civil War about 400 Communists went to Spain to join the International Brigade. When World War II broke out, the Communists had reservations about what they called the "imperialist war." When Nazi Germany attacked Russia in June, 1941, however, they immediately joined the Allied war effort and assumed the status of a legal party.

With the growth of Palestine's Jewish population, the Jewish Communists there began to react to the realities of life in the country. In May, 1943, after prolonged inner dissension, the party split into an Arab faction, which continued as the Arab League of National Liberation and adopted an Arab nationalist line, and a Jewish splinter group. A third splinter group, the Communist Educational Association, leaned more toward Zionist views and established contact with Jewish activist circles, the Ahdut 'Avoda and *Lohame Herut Israel. In 1944 the Communists again became active members of the Histadrut.

With the establishment of the State of Israel the various Communist splinter groups were reunited into the Israel Communist party (Miflaga Komunistit Yisraelit, or Maki), which accepted the new State, recognized its *flag and anthem, but denied the bond between the Jewish people in Israel and the *Diaspora, supported the "right of the Arab refugees to return and to receive compensation," and advocated the establishment of an Arab Palestinian state in the territory allotted to it by the United Nations *partition resolution of 1947. The support of the Soviet Union for Israel in the initial period of the State gained the Communists a measure of popularity in certain left-wing Zionist quarters. In 1955, after *Mapam split, activists led by Moshe *S'ne joined the Communist party. At about that time the Communist kibbutz Yad Hanna Szenes was founded. However, the party's main sphere of influence was among the Arabs, many of whom supported it as an anti-Zionist party. In spite of this, the Communists did not disappear from the lower echelons of Jewish public life. In the *Knesset the number of their representatives moved between 3 and 6 (in a total of 120 representatives). Soviet policy toward the Jewish citizens and toward Israel caused unrest among the Communists. In the early 1960s the internal differences in the party increased. The Arab Communists began to show nationalist tendencies, some going as far as to sympathize with Arab *terrorist organizations. A significant number of Jewish Communists, however, did not agree with the pro-Arab manifestations in the policy of the Soviet Union and other Communist parties. Thus, in the summer of 1965, the party split again. The Mikunis-S'ne faction, which included the majority of the Israeli Jewish Communists, leaned toward Zionist views, such as the recognition of the bond between the Jewish people in Israel and the Diaspora, the demand that the Arab states, as a preliminary condition for peace negotiations with the Arabs, recognize the right of the State of Israel to exist, and so on. In the mid-1960s the paper *Kol Ha'Am served as this faction's mouthpiece. The Wilner-Toubi faction, which included the Arab Communists and a group of Jewish Communists, adhered to the old views of the party. Their organs were Zu HaDerekh and Al Ittihad. Both factions held conferences simultaneously in August, 1965, and both were recognized by Moscow.

The *Six-day War of 1967 deepened the disagreement between the two sections of the Communist party. The Mikunis-S'ne faction took the position that the policy of Israel was, generally, justified both before and after the war. The Wilner-Toubi faction, on the other hand, unreservedly followed the official Soviet line, which accused Israel of aggression. These attitudes, in turn, determined the relationship of the Soviet Union to the two factions, which was expressed in the fact that only the anti-Israel faction was invited to the festivities commemorating the 50th anniversary of the October Revolution of 1917.

Y. SLUTSKY

COMMUNITIES IN ISRAEL. In Israeli parlance the term "communities" (Heb., 'edot; singular, 'eda) refers to (1) Jewish *ethnic groups and (2) non-Jewish religious groups.

Each immigrant group (as well as its Israeli-born descendants) coming from one place of origin is referred to by the term "'Eda." The place of origin can be a country, in which sense all the Moroccan Jews, for instance, are termed a "community" (*see* NORTH AFRICAN JEWS IN ISRAEL). Or it can refer to a territory (e.g., the 'Eda of the *Kurdish Jews derived from Kurdistan, an ethnic area divided politically among several countries) or even to a town (e.g., the 'Eda of the Aleppo Jews). More rarely, the term is used to refer to an Ashkenazi Jewish ethnic group, in a sense paralleling that of the Yiddish Landsmannschaften. In most but not all cases, an 'Eda has an immigrants' organization or is centered on a synagogue with its Kehilla (religious congregation).

The non-Jewish religious communities, also called 'Edot, derive their present status in Israel from the Ottoman millet system, under which recognized religious groups were given a degree of internal autonomy and representation vis-à-vis the central and local governments. In the case of the non-Jewish

'Edot the differentiating criterion is always and exclusively a religious one. Therefore, the term is not applied to the *Arabs in Israel, among whom there are Muslims (referred to as "the Muslim 'Eda") and Christians, who form a part of the Christian community of Israel, which is composed of such groups as the Greek Orthodox community and the Greek Catholic community (*see* CHRISTIAN COMMUNITIES AND CHURCHES IN ISRAEL). The Druzes and Bahais are considered separate communities because they constitute religious sects (*see* BAHAI COMMUNITY IN ISRAEL; DRUZE COMMUNITY IN ISRAEL). The *Karaites and *Samaritans, inasmuch as historically they formed religious groups separate from the main body of (Rabbanite) Judaism, are still referred to as 'Edot.

In addition to the communities mentioned above, *see also* N'TURE KARTA; SEPHARDIM; and separate articles on the Afghan, American and Canadian, Austrian, British, Bukharan, Bukovinian, Bulgarian, Czechoslovak, Egyptian, German, Habani, Hasidic, Hungarian, Indian, Iranian, Iraqi, Italian, Latin American, Polish, Romanian, Russian, South African, Syrian and Lebanese, and Yemenite Jews in Israel.

R. PATAI

COMPTROLLER'S OFFICE. *See* STATE COMPTROLLER OF ISRAEL.

CONFEDERATION OF GENERAL ZIONISTS. *See* WORLD CONFEDERATION OF GENERAL ZIONISTS.

CONFERENCE OF PRESIDENTS OF MAJOR AMERICAN JEWISH ORGANIZATIONS. Organization of American Jewish leaders, informally established in March, 1955, for the purpose of considering issues relating to Israel and of common interest and concern to the Jewish community of the United States. Periodic meetings continued under the chairmanship of Dr. Nahum *Goldmann until December, 1960. The presidents of the following major Jewish organizations participated: American Histadrut Trade Union Council (*see* AMERICAN FEDERATION OF LABOR–CONGRESS OF INDUSTRIAL ORGANIZATIONS); *American Israel Public Affairs Committee; *American Jewish Congress; American Zionist Council; *B'nai B'rith; *Hadassah; *Jewish Agency for Israel—American Section; Jewish Labor Committee; Jewish War Veterans of the U.S.A.; Labor Zionist Organization of America–Po'ale Zion (*see* PO'ALE ZION); Mizrahi–HaPo'el HaMizrahi (*see* RELIGIOUS ZIONISTS OF AMERICA); National Community Relations Advisory Council; National Council of Jewish Women; Union of American Hebrew Congregations; Union of Orthodox Jewish Congregations of America; United Synagogue of America; and *Zionist Organization of America.

In December, 1960, the conference decided to change its ad hoc character, organize itself on a permanent basis, and formalize its procedures. A professional staff was employed and a regular budget adopted. At the same time it was decided that the chairman or president of any of the 17 member organizations would be eligible to serve as chairman of the conference for a one-year term, with provision for reelection for one additional year. Late in 1961 the president of the National Council of Young Israel joined the conference. In September, 1963, the conference broadened its scope to include problems of Jews in other countries.

In 1965 the presidents of the three American rabbinical organizations—namely, the Central Conference of American Rabbis, the Rabbinical Assembly, and the Rabbinical Council of America (Reform, Conservative, and Orthodox respectively)—joined the conference, increasing the number of its members to 21. In March, 1966, it was unanimously resolved that the conference should become the central body of the major American Jewish organizations and that the president of the conference should exchange memorandums and information with international multiorganizational Jewish organizations.

The activities of the conference have centered on disseminating the view that a strong and secure Israel is in the best interests of American policy and world peace, helping American business firms challenge the *Arab boycott of Israel, calling attention to the dangers of neo-Nazi movements and international *anti-Semitism, demanding the release and resettlement of Jews victimized in Arab lands as a result of the *Six-day War of 1967, and denouncing Soviet incitement against Israel and the Jewish people. These activities have included the publication of documents and special conferences and meetings with leaders in world politics and Jewish communities in other lands. The conference played a vital role in the education of public opinion and the enlistment of the American Jewish community in support of Israel before and during the Six-day War. It sponsored the Solidarity with Israel rally held in New York on May 27, 1967, and the National Emergency Leadership Conference for Israel which took place in Washington on June 7–8 of that year.

Past chairmen of the conference, in order of succession, were Nahum Goldmann, Philip M. Klutznick, Label A. Katz, Rabbi Irving *Miller, Lewis H. Weinstein, Rabbi Joachim Prinz, and Rabbi Herschel Schacter. In 1970 Dr. William A. Wexler was chairman and Yehuda Hellman, executive director.

Y. HELLMAN

CONFERENCE ON JEWISH MATERIAL CLAIMS AGAINST GERMANY. *See* GERMAN-ISRAEL AGREEMENT.

CONGRESS, ZIONIST. Parliament of the Zionist movement, created by Herzl. At first it symbolized rather than represented the self-determination sought by the Jewish people and their sense of national unity. It was an expression of their desire for statehood.

In contrast to earlier Jewish conclaves, which were primarily of a philanthropic character, the Zionist Congress was the first representative Jewish political assembly. The Congress, Herzl wrote in his *Diaries,* was to become the national assembly of the Jewish people and was to arouse in every Jew the feeling that "today he was still in exile, but next year he might be in his ancient homeland." Herzl sought to make the Congress a forum also for the "poor victims of our philanthropists and their officials." He sought to convert it into a permanent platform providing the Jewish people with their first means of national expression.

Originally, the Congress met every year (1897–1901), then every second year (1903–13, 1921–39). Following World War II it met at irregular intervals (1946, 1951, 1956, 1960–61, 1964–65, 1968). Elections to the Congress also varied. The 1st Congress was an assembly of self-appointed volunteer participants; for the 2d Congress, the *Shekel (membership fee) was introduced, and with it the election of delegates by Shekel holders. The exact way of determining the number of delegates on the basis of Shekels sold was changed repeatedly. In 1921 Shekel holders of the *World Zionist Organization (WZO) who lived in

Palestine were given the advantage over the *Diaspora membership of enabling them to elect twice as many delegates in relation to their numbers. In general, the number of delegates was determined by the total number of Shekels sold in the two-year period preceding each Congress. Since 1959 Zionists residing in Israel have been allotted 38 per cent of all the Congress seats. Israel's Zionist parties are represented in proportion to the number of votes obtained in elections to the *Knesset. The share of the United States in Congress seats has been fixed at 29 per cent and that of all other Diaspora countries together at 33 per cent.

The function of the Congress, as it crystallized in the course of the years, was to make decisions which were binding on the Zionist Organization until they were changed by a subsequent Congress. Between Congresses, the *Actions Committee was the supreme authority of the Organization. The Inner, or Smaller, Actions Committee (or Zionist *Executive) carried on the work of the Organization.

1st Congress. Basle, Aug. 29–31, 1897. President, Herzl; vice-presidents, Max *Nordau, Abraham *Salz, and Samuel *Pineles. Participants, 204, from 17 countries. Karpel *Lippe, the dean of the delegates, delivered the opening speech, in which he reviewed the development of the Zionist idea. Herzl then addressed the gathering. He set forth the aim of the Congress in one sentence: "We are here to lay the foundation stone of the house which is to shelter the Jewish nation." Then he went on to outline the broad program of Zionism, which, he said, sought to awaken the Jewish people everywhere to self-help. The Jewish problem could not be solved through a continuation of the slow colonization methods without a basis of legal recognition. Legal rights were the indispensable condition of large-scale settlement, and these could be achieved only by open political negotiations. Nordau's review of the general condition of world Jewry, which was to become a regular feature of the early Congresses, was one of the high points. The ideological substance and the historical and economic justification of Zionism were dealt with in the speeches of David *Farbstein and Nathan *Birnbaum. A large part of the discussion was devoted to the situation of the settlements in Palestine. All three speakers on this subject, Jacob *Kohan-Bernstein (Kishinev), Moses Moses (Kattowitz), and Adam *Rosenberg (New York), demanded immediate large-scale settlement work on a national basis. Prof. Hermann *Schapira (Heidelberg) urged the setting up of a land fund, from which the *Jewish National Fund was later to develop. Marcus *Ehrenpreis demanded intensified *Hebrew studies, and Schapira suggested the establishment of an institution of higher learning in Palestine (*see* HEBREW UNIVERSITY OF JERUSALEM).

The agenda of the Congress was devoted mainly to the formulation of the Zionist program and the organization of the Zionist movement. The Congress established the World Zionist Organization and drafted (on the basis of Max Nordau's suggestion) the Zionist platform which became known as the *Basle Program.

The first organization statutes, submitted by Heinrich *York-Steiner, were adopted. Herzl was elected president of the Zionist Organization, and an Inner Actions Committee and a Greater Actions Committee were elected to conduct the current affairs of the movement. The Executive (Inner Actions Committee) elected at the 1st Congress consisted of Herzl, president, and Oser *Kokesch, Johann *Kremenetzky, Alexander Minz, and Moritz *Schnirer.

Summarizing the results of the Congress, Herzl wrote in his *Diaries*: "In Basle I founded the Jewish State. If I were to say this aloud I would meet with general laughter; but in another five years, and certainly in another fifty years, everyone will be convinced of this. The state is created mainly upon the people's will for a state."

2d Congress. Basle, Aug. 28–31, 1898. President, Herzl; vice-presidents, Max Nordau, Moses *Gaster, and Max E. *Mandelstamm. Delegates, 349. In the face of the opposition to Zionism on the part of the leaders of the local Jewish community councils, Herzl proclaimed the need to "capture the Jewish communities" for Zionism. This became the political slogan of the Congress and led to various projects to strengthen Zionist loyalty within Jewish life. Nordau, for the first time, introduced the *Dreyfus affair into the discussion. Schnirer reported on the growth of the movement since the 1st Congress: the number of Zionist groups had increased from 117 to 913. Leo *Motzkin, who had been sent to Palestine by Herzl, reported on conditions there and submitted a program of further settlement activities. At this Congress the General Hebrew Language Society, the predecessor of *Tarbut, was founded.

On the basis of a report by David *Wolffsohn, the Congress decided to establish the *Jewish Colonial Trust, a financial agency designed to aid in the development of Palestine. The Executive elected consisted of Herzl, president, and Leopold *Kahn, Oser Kokesch, Oskar *Marmorek, and Moritz Schnirer.

3d Congress. Basle, Aug. 15–18, 1899. President, Herzl; vice-presidents, Max Nordau, Moses Gaster, and Max E. Mandelstamm. Delegates, 153. Herzl reported on his reception by Kaiser *Wilhelm II in Constantinople and in Palestine and followed his report with a discussion of wider political issues and the *Charter. The political methods of Zionism and the policy of the Jewish Colonial Trust aroused heated debate. It was decided not to allow the use of Trust funds for Zionist or other activities outside Palestine and Syria. Other items on the agenda dealt with cultural, settlement, and organizational questions. The Executive elected consisted of Herzl, president, and Leopold Kahn, Oser Kokesch, Oskar Marmorek, and Moritz Schnirer.

4th Congress. London, Aug. 13–16, 1900. President, Herzl; vice-presidents, Max Nordau, Moses Gaster, and Max E. Mandelstamm. Delegates, 498. The British capital was chosen as the place of the Congress to acquaint the British public with the aims of Zionism and to enlist its support for the Zionist cause.

Propaganda was one of the main topics on the agenda. The Congress also dealt with the persecution of Jews in Romania and the subsequent increase in emigration from that country. It was decided to establish a migration fund and to promote the establishment of Jewish economic institutions in the Diaspora in order to improve the economic situation of the Jewish population.

In the discussion on cultural problems, the Orthodox delegates, led by Rabbi Yitzhak Ya'akov *Reines, demanded that the Zionist Organization abstain from dealing with cultural matters and concentrate solely on political work. The Congress also took up, for the first time, the economic problems of Jewish workers in Palestine.

Professor Mandelstamm reported on Jewish athletic activities. This speech, together with that of Nordau on *Muskeljudentum* (muscle Jewry) at the 5th Congress, led to the formation of what later developed into the national Jewish sports movement and the Maccabi organization (*see* SPORTS AND PHYS-

ICAL EDUCATION IN ISRAEL). The Congress resolved to establish a national fund (details were to be presented at the subsequent Congress). Nordau, for the first time, expanded the program of Zionism to include also Diaspora activities, which later led to *Landespolitik*, that is, political work in the Diaspora countries. The Executive was reelected.

5th Congress. Basle, Dec. 26–30, 1901. President, Herzl; vice-presidents, Max Nordau, Yehiel *Tschlenow, and Moses Gaster. Delegates, 358. Herzl reported on his meeting with Sultan *'Abdul Hamid II of Turkey and on the beginning of the work of the Jewish Colonial Trust with a capital of £250,000. The Congress approved the formation of the Jewish National Fund.

At this Congress the *Democratic Faction, led by Leo Motzkin, Martin *Buber, and Chaim *Weizmann, made its first appearance. It urged the adoption of Hebrew cultural activity as a function of the WZO and a larger measure of democracy in the leadership of the movement.

Nordau called for an improvement of the physical, economic, and spiritual condition of the Jewish people. The question of whether the Zionist Organization should engage in cultural activities was once again the subject of heated debate. The Orthodox delegates strenuously objected to cultural projects championed by the Democratic Faction. This led to the emergence of political parties within the previously unified Zionist Organization (see MIZRAHI; PO'ALE ZION).

This was the first Congress at which a group of delegates walked out of a session. On the last day of the Congress, the Democratic Faction insisted that culture, art, and related matters be debated, whereas Herzl insisted that the Congress proceed to the elections lest it have to adjourn without a duly elected leadership. The faction then walked out in protest, and elections were held in its absence. After the return of the faction, Herzl lent his support to its proposals, which in consequence were adopted. The Congress also decided to open a branch of the Jewish Colonial Trust in Jaffa. The Executive, except for Schnirer, was reelected.

6th Congress. Basle, Aug. 23–28, 1903. President, Herzl; vice-presidents, Max Nordau, Max E. Mandelstamm, Sir Francis Abraham *Montefiore, and Max *Bodenheimer. Delegates, 592. In his opening speech Herzl reported on his negotiations with the British statesmen Joseph *Chamberlain and Lord Lansdowne regarding a Jewish settlement in *Sinai and explained the circumstances which had led to the abandonment of this project. He then outlined the proposal made to the Organization by the British government for an autonomous Jewish settlement in East Africa (see EAST AFRICA SCHEME). He did not suggest that the offer be accepted by the Congress, stressing the fact that no country on earth could supersede Palestine as the Jewish Homeland. But he advised the Congress not to reject the offer, which, made by the British government to the Zionist Organization, deserved to be treated with proper consideration. Herzl therefore moved that the Congress dispatch a commission to investigate the suitability of East Africa as an area of settlement and report back to the next Congress.

A heated debate ensued. Herzl was supported by Nordau, who termed the proposed territory a *Nachtasyl* (refuge for the night), and opposed by Yehiel Tschlenow, M'nahem M. *Ussishkin, and other Russian Zionists. A roll-call vote gave Herzl's motion a 295-to-178 majority, whereupon the opposing delegates walked out. They returned only after Herzl pleaded with them to maintain the unity of the movement. At the concluding session Herzl recited the verse from Psalm 137 which

became a Zionist credo: "If I forget thee, O Jerusalem, let my right hand forget her cunning."

Among other items on the agenda of the Congress was a report by Franz *Oppenheimer on cooperative agricultural settlement in Palestine (see COOPERATIVES IN ISRAEL), which contained a proposal leading to the establishment of Merhavya. At the suggestion of Selig E. *Soskin a Palestine Commission, paralleling the East Africa Commission, was formed.

At this last Congress attended by Herzl, the report showed that the number of Zionist groups all over the world had increased to 1,572. The former Executive was reelected.

7th Congress. Basle, July 27–Aug. 2, 1905. President, Max Nordau; vice-presidents, Jacob Kohan-Bernstein, Alexander *Marmorek, Sir Francis Abraham Montefiore, Zinovi *Tiomkin, and David Wolffsohn. Delegates, 497. The first meeting was devoted to a eulogy of Herzl by Nordau.

The central topic of the debate was again the controversial issue of the establishment of a Jewish settlement outside Palestine, particularly in the proposed area of East Africa (Guas Ngishu Plateau). The Congress dealt with the issue in a special session. Although the report of the investigation committee considered the territory unsuited for large-scale Jewish settlement, Israel *Zangwill advocated acceptance of the British proposal without, however, loosening the movement's ties to Palestine. The "Territorialists," as Zangwill's followers were called, argued that the essence of Zionism was not organically connected with Palestine and that Zionist effort could be directed to any country suitable for mass settlement and national autonomy. The *Tziyone Zion firmly opposed this concept. The Congress voted overwhelmingly to reject all settlement programs other than those in Palestine and immediately adjacent countries. When the regular sessions were resumed, the Territorialists met separately and formed the *Jewish Territorial Organization (ITO).

Prof. Otto *Warburg (Berlin) outlined the plan for practical work in Palestine as part of his report on the Palestine Commission. For the first time the attention of the Congress was focused on "*practical Zionism." Along with political work, it was decided to embark on practical settlement activities in Palestine, through greater support of industry, agriculture, and the like.

No president was elected to fill the place of Herzl. Leopold J. *Greenberg, Jacobus H. *Kann, Jacob Kohan-Bernstein, Alexander Marmorek, M'nahem M. Ussishkin, Otto Warburg, and David Wolffsohn were elected to the Executive. Wolffsohn was elected by the Executive as its chairman and thus became president of the World Zionist Organization as well. Since he resided in Cologne, the seat of the Executive was moved from Vienna to Cologne.

8th Congress. The Hague, Aug. 14–21, 1907. Presidents, David Wolffsohn and Max Nordau; vice-presidents, Moses Gaster, Jacobus H. Kann, Alexander Marmorek, Isidor *Schalit, Yehiel Tschlenow, M'nahem M. Ussishkin, and Otto Warburg. Delegates, 324. Discussion was concentrated mainly on programs for practical work in Palestine, that is, rural settlement, or, as it was called at the time, colonization. Those who favored political activities, that is, obtaining a Charter for a political framework for colonization, did not easily agree to practical projects. There was a lengthy ideological debate between the "practical" and the "political" Zionists. To designate the combination of both trends, Rabbi Jacob *Niemirower coined the name "*Synthetic Zionism." Weizmann was the most eloquent spokesman of the concept that the sought-for Charter could be obtained only as a result of simultaneous practical and political accomplishments in Palestine.

The Congress decided to establish a Palestine Office (*see* PALESTINE OFFICES) in Jaffa, which was opened in 1908 with Arthur *Ruppin as director, and to form a Palestine Land Development Company with a capital of £50,000. A three-member Inner Actions Committee—David Wolffsohn as chairman, Otto Warburg, and Jacobus H. Kann—was elected.

9th Congress. Hamburg, Dec. 26–30, 1909. President, Max Nordau; vice-presidents, Max Bodenheimer, Adolf *Stand, Yehiel Tschlenow, and M'nahem M. Ussishkin. Delegates, 364. The Congress discussed the political consequences of the Young Turk Revolution for Jewish colonization in Palestine. Strong opposition developed to Wolffsohn, who was an exponent of political Zionism. The practical Zionists demanded an expansion of practical projects in Palestine. The Congress decided to create a cooperative settlement society *(Siedlungsgenossenschaft)*, as suggested by Franz Oppenheimer; subsequently Merhavya, the prototype of the later K'vutza (*see* KIBBUTZ) and Moshav 'Ovdim (*see* MOSHAV), was founded. Since the Congress could not agree on a new leadership, the old Executive remained, with Cologne as its seat.

10th Congress. Basle, Aug. 9–15, 1911. President, Max Nordau; vice-presidents, Max Bodenheimer, Alexander Marmorek, Adolf Stand, Yehiel Tschlenow, and M'nahem M. Ussishkin. Delegates, 388. The 10th Congress marked the complete victory of "Synthetic Zionism." Detailed discussions were held on practical projects in Palestine, and the Congress decided that such projects were urgent. Hebrew cultural activities were discussed, and for the first time a session, chaired by Ussishkin, was held in Hebrew.

The Congress declared that the Jewish problem could be solved only by Jewish emigration to Palestine. In the face of the growing need for migration, however, the Zionist Organization was to support all efforts aimed at organizing migrants and at democratizing assistance to them. The Executive elected consisted of Otto Warburg, chairman, and Arthur *Hantke, Sh'marya *Levin, and Nahum *Sokolow. The seat of the Executive was moved to Berlin.

11th Congress. Vienna, Sept. 2–9, 1913. President, David Wolffsohn; vice-presidents, Adolf Stand, Moses Gaster, Julius *Simon, Max Bodenheimer, and Jakob Ehrlich. Delegates, 539. The work of the Congress was entirely dominated by the impact of practical Zionism and by Palestine projects, on which Ruppin gave a detailed report. Weizmann and Ussishkin proposed the establishment of a university in Jerusalem, a project which was enthusiastically approved. Sokolow announced that Louis D. *Brandeis had joined the Zionist Organization. The Congress welcomed the Ahuza movement (for purchasing and developing land in Palestine) that had been initiated in the United States and subsequently received support in other countries (*see* AHUZA SOCIETIES). It passed the first resolution defining *'Aliya (immigration) as a Zionist obligation: "In view of the overwhelming importance of the Palestine principle in the Zionist movement, the Congress declares that it is a duty of each Zionist—in the first place of those who are economically able to do so—to get personally acquainted with Palestine on the basis of first-hand observation, to create there personal economic interests, and to adopt the plan of settling in Palestine as part of his life's program." The Executive was reelected in its entirety with the addition of Yehiel Tschlenow.

12th Congress. Karlovy Vary (Carlsbad), Sept. 1–14, 1921. President, Nahum Sokolow; first vice-president, Leo Motzkin. Beginning with this Congress, the first to be held after World War I, the other vice-presidents were nominated by territorial federations and factions. They were Meir Berlin (*Bar-Ilan) and Y'hoshu'a Heshel *Farbstein for the Mizrahi, Sh'lomo *Kaplansky and Yosef *Sprinzak for Po'ale Zion–*Hitahdut, and Meir *Klumel and Louis *Lipsky for all territorial federations. Delegates, 512, of whom 376 represented territorial federations, 95 the Mizrahi, and 41 the Labor parties (*Tz'ire Zion, Hitahdut, *HaPo'el HaTza'ir, and Po'ale Zion).

The Congress welcomed the *Balfour Declaration and the decision of the principal Allied Powers at the *San Remo Conference (April, 1920) to assign the *Mandate for Palestine to Great Britain and called for the ratification of the Palestine Mandate by the League of Nations. It passed resolutions on all aspects of Zionist work in Palestine, whose ramifications had grown significantly in the years preceding the war. The activities of the *Keren HaYesod (Palestine Foundation Fund), its organizations, and its expansion were discussed, as was the duty of each Zionist to pay a Ma'aser (tithe). Echoes of the Brandeis-Weizmann controversy reached the Congress in some of the speeches of delegates criticizing the Executive. The Congress also declared that the Zionists endeavored "to live in relations of harmony and mutual respect with the Arab people," and called on the Executive to achieve a "sincere understanding with the Arab people on the basis of this declaration."

Weizmann was elected president of the Zionist Organization, Sokolow president of the Executive, and the following members of the Executive: Joseph *Cowen, Montague David *Eder, Berthold *Feiwel, George *Halpern, Vladimir *Jabotinsky, Richard *Lichtheim, Leo Motzkin, Isaac *Naiditsch, Hermann *Pick, Bernard *Rosenblatt, Arthur Ruppin, Max *Soloveitchik, Yosef Sprinzak, and M'nahem M. Ussishkin. One part of the Executive was to have its headquarters in London; the other, in Jerusalem.

13th Congress. Karlovy Vary, Aug. 6–18, 1923. President, Nahum Sokolow; vice-presidents, Itzhak *Ben Zvi, Meir Berlin, Y'hoshu'a Heshel Farbstein, Eliezer *Kaplan, Sh'marya Levin, Louis Lipsky, and Leo Motzkin. Delegates, 331 (territorial federations, 165; Mizrahi, 76; left-wing groups, 69; *Radical Zionists, 21). The Congress welcomed the award of the Palestine Mandate to Great Britain by the League of Nations and debated the proposal to establish an expanded *Jewish Agency which, in accordance with article 4 of the Palestine Mandate, was to "secure cooperation of all Jews who are willing to assist in the establishment of the Jewish National Home."

Weizmann was elected president of the Zionist Organization, and Sokolow president of the Executive; the members of the Executive were Joseph Cowen, Berthold Feiwel, George Halpern, Col. Frederick Herman *Kisch, Louis Lipsky, Isaac Naiditsch, Hermann Pick, Arthur Ruppin, Max Soloveitchik, Yosef Sprinzak, and Siegfried *Van Vriesland. The seat of the Executive remained in London and Jerusalem.

14th Congress. Vienna, Aug. 18–31, 1925. President, Nahum Sokolow; vice-presidents, Meir Berlin, Y'hoshu'a Heshel Farbstein, Arthur Hantke, Eliezer Kaplan, Meir Klumel, Leon *Levite, Leo Motzkin, David *Remez, Henrietta *Szold, M'nahem M. Ussishkin, and Stephen S. *Wise. Delegates, 311 (territorial federations, 166; Mizrahi, 55; Po'ale Zion, 11; Radicals, 15; *Revisionists, 5; Hitahdut, 37; Tz'ire Zion, 11). The Congress was attended by a Revisionist delegation headed by

Jabotinsky, who demanded a more active Zionist policy and opposed the inclusion of non-Zionists in the Jewish Agency.

The Congress discussed the first five years of the British Mandate and took note of the termination of Sir Herbert *Samuel's high commissionership. In the wake of the achievements of the *Fourth 'Aliya and its problems, one of the central and most controversial topics of the Congress debates was the respective advantages of public and private colonization. Dissatisfied with the Executive, the Congress voted on August 26 to discharge it without the usual vote of appreciation. The Executive resigned on the following day. The crisis was resolved on August 29, when the Congress adopted a resolution to the effect that its resolution of August 26 was no reason for the Executive to resign, since it had confidence in the Executive's political leadership. Weizmann was reelected president of the Zionist Organization and Sokolow president of the Executive. It was left to them to choose the members of the Executive, and they later appointed Joseph Cowen, Berthold Feiwel, George Halpern, Col. Frederick Herman Kisch, Louis Lipsky, Isaac Naiditsch, Hermann Pick, Arthur Ruppin, Yosef Sprinzak, and Siegfried Van Vriesland.

15th Congress. Basle, Aug. 30–Sept. 11, 1927. President, Nahum Sokolow; vice-presidents, Meir Berlin, Y'hoshu'a Heshel Farbstein, Hayim *Fineman, Max Heller, Eliezer Kaplan, Leo Motzkin, Abraham Podliszewski, Leon *Reich, Isidor Schalit, Henrietta Szold, and M'nahem M. Ussishkin. Delegates, 281 (territorial federations, 151; Mizrahi, 46; Po'ale Zion, 30; Hitahdut, 33; Radicals, 11; Revisionists, 10). The Congress was greatly concerned with the unemployment and difficult economic situation prevailing in the *Yishuv (Jewish population of Palestine), and several suggestions for remedying the situation were discussed. A large part of the discussion was also devoted to the expansion of the Jewish Agency. The disagreements were so pronounced that, for the first time since 1921, neither the Mizrahi nor the left was represented in the Executive elected by the Congress before it adjourned. Weizmann and Sokolow were reelected to the positions they had held, and the following were elected members of the Executive: Montague David Eder, Col. Frederick Herman Kisch, Louis Lipsky, Pinhas Rosenblüth (*Rosen), Harry *Sacher, and Henrietta Szold, all of whom called themselves representatives of "Constructive Zionism."

16th Congress. Zurich, July 29–Aug. 10, 1929. President, Nahum Sokolow; vice-presidents, Leo Motzkin (chairman of the Presidium), David *Ben-Gurion, Meir Berlin, Adolf Bernhardt, Y'hoshu'a Heshel Farbstein, Archibald J. *Freiman, Abraham Podliszewski, Leon Reich, Abba Hillel *Silver, Selig E. Soskin, and Yosef Sprinzak. Delegates, 315 (General Zionists—see GENERAL ZIONISM—formerly territorial federations, 145; Mizrahi, 51; Hitahdut, 42; Po'ale Zion, 39; Revisionists, 21; Radicals, 12). All parties except the Revisionists decided to support the expanded Jewish Agency that was to be formally constituted immediately after the Congress. The Congress prepared and adopted a constitution for the Jewish Agency. Chaim Weizmann was elected president of the WZO, Nahum Sokolow president of the Executive, and Lazarus Barth, Meir Berlin, Selig *Brodetsky, Sh'lomo Kaplansky, Col. Frederick Herman Kisch, Louis Lipsky, Pinhas Rosenblüth, Arthur Ruppin, Harry Sacher, Yosef Sprinzak, and Henrietta Szold members of the Executive.

Following the Congress, the founding conference of the expanded Jewish Agency was held, also in Zurich.

17th Congress. Basle, June 30–July 15, 1931. President, Leo Motzkin; vice-presidents, Meir Berlin, Montague David Eder, Y'hoshu'a Heshel Farbstein, Eliezer Kaplan, Julian *Mack, Emil *Margulies, Anshel *Reiss, Emil *Schmorak, Abraham *Silberschein, Selig E. Soskin, Zinovi Tiomkin, and M'nahem M. Ussishkin. Delegates, 254 (General Zionists A, 25; General Zionists B, 59; Labor parties, 75; Mizrahi, 35; Revisionists, 52; Radicals, 8). The Congress protested the *Passfield White Paper, which, following the 1929 *Arab riots in Palestine, recommended the drastic limitation of Jewish immigration and Jewish land purchases and advocated policies detrimental to Zionist activities (see also SHAW COMMISSION).

The Revisionists proposed a resolution spelling out the establishment of a Jewish State as the ultimate goal of Zionism. The Congress, however, refused to put this resolution to a vote, whereupon Vladimir Jabotinsky and his followers left the Congress hall in protest.

Weizmann was severely criticized because of a statement he had given the *Jewish Telegraphic Agency, to the effect that he did not regard the attainment of a Jewish majority in Palestine essential to the realization of the aims of Zionism. The Congress considered his subsequent explanation unsatisfactory and did not reelect him to the presidency of the WZO. On the other hand, the Congress declared the *MacDonald letter of Feb. 13, 1931, acceptable as a basis for continued negotiations with Great Britain. Nahum Sokolow was elected president of the WZO, and Hayim *Arlosoroff, Selig Brodetsky, Y'hoshu'a Heshel Farbstein, Berl *Locker, and Emanuel *Neumann were elected members of the Executive.

18th Congress. Prague, Aug. 21–Sept. 4, 1933. President, Leo Motzkin; vice-presidents, Itzhak *Grünbaum, Eliezer Kaplan, Sh'lomo Kaplansky, Joseph *Rufeisen, and M'nahem M. Ussishkin. Delegates, 318 (General Zionists A and B, 74; Labor, 138; Mizrahi, 39; Revisionists, 45; Radicals, 15; *Jewish State party, 8). The Congress met under the shadow of the persecution of German Jewry which had begun with Hitler's rise to power. Arthur Ruppin presented a broad program for the settlement of German Jews in Palestine. The delegates were also agitated by the murder of Hayim Arlosoroff. Tension between the Labor party, which in 1930 had formed a united front, and the Revisionists, now split into Revisionists and the Jewish State party, was particularly apparent in the general debate and interfered with the work of the Congress. Nahum Sokolow was elected president of the WZO and David Ben-Gurion, Selig Brodetsky, Itzhak Grünbaum, Victor *Jacobson, Eliezer Kaplan, Louis Lipsky, Berl Locker, Arthur Ruppin, and Moshe Shertok (*Sharett) members of the Executive.

19th Congress. Lucerne, Aug. 20–Sept. 4, 1935. President, Chaim Weizmann; vice-presidents, Nahum *Goldmann, Sh'lomo Kaplansky, John M. *Machover, Ben-Zion *Mossinsohn, Anshel Reiss, and Yosef Sprinzak. Delegates, 463 (General Zionists A, 99; General Zionists B, 50; Mizrahi, 74; Po'ale Zion–Hitahdut, 226; Jewish State party, 13; unaffiliated, 1). The Revisionists, who had seceded from the WZO in 1935 and established the *New Zionist Organization, did not participate.

Deliberation revolved mainly around the problem of the German Jews and the ways of rescuing them. Nahum Sokolow was elected honorary president of the WZO; Chaim Weizmann, president; and David Ben-Gurion, Selig Brodetsky, Y'huda L. Fishman (*Maimon), Itzhak Grünbaum, Eliezer Kaplan, Efrayim Fishel *Rottenstreich, and Moshe Shertok members of the Executive. M'nahem M. Ussishkin was elected chairman of the Greater Actions Committee.

20th Congress. Zurich, Aug. 3–16, 1937. President, M'nahem M. Ussishkin; vice-presidents, Meir Berlin, Nahum Goldmann, Sh'lomo Kaplansky, John M. Machover, Anshel Reiss, Emil Schmorak, Yosef Sprinzak, and Stephen S. Wise. Delegates, 484 (Labor, 224; General Zionists A, 128; General Zionists B, 43; Mizrahi, 80; Jewish State party, 9). The Congress considered the *Peel Commission's report (July, 1937), which proposed the establishment of a Jewish State in a partitioned Palestine. Opinions were divided. The advantages of an independent State were weighed against the smallness of the territory offered and the loss of the major part of Biblical Palestine.

Weizmann, though deeply dissatisfied with the scheme, was in favor of negotiation with the British government with a view to obtaining a plan that would enable the Jews of Palestine to have independence and at the same time alleviate the situation of Jews in other countries. Ussishkin, who led the uncompromising opposition, rejected partition altogether, since, he held, the Jewish people could not renounce their right to any part of their Homeland. He was in favor of a Jewish State in the whole of Palestine. After long debate, the Congress by a large majority adopted a resolution declaring the partition scheme unacceptable, but it empowered the Executive to negotiate with the British government to clarify the specific terms of the British proposal to establish a Jewish State in Palestine.

The Congress marked the 40th anniversary of the 1st Zionist Congress with a special celebration in which delegates to the 1st Congress participated. Weizmann was reelected president of the WZO; David Ben-Gurion, Selig Brodetsky, Y'huda L. Fishman, Itzhak Grünbaum, Eliezer Kaplan, Efrayim Fishel Rottenstreich, and Moshe Shertok were elected members of the Executive. M'nahem M. Ussishkin was reelected chairman of the Greater Actions Committee.

21st Congress. Geneva, Aug. 16–25, 1939. President, M'nahem M. Ussishkin; vice-presidents, Solomon *Goldman, Nahum Goldmann, Sh'lomo Kaplansky, John M. Machover, Yosef Sprinzak, Meir *Ya'ari, and Ya'akov *Zerubavel. Delegates, 527 (Labor, 234; General Zionists A, 159; General Zionists B, 33; Mizrahi, 75; Jewish State party, 10; Left Po'ale Zion, 13; unaffiliated, 3). The Congress rejected the British *White Paper of 1939, which threatened Zionist projects and endeavors.

The shadow of World War II hovered over the Congress, and in view of the international situation the Standing Committee suggested that the Executive as constituted by the previous Congress be empowered to continue in office. Chaim Weizmann was elected president of the WZO; David Ben-Gurion, Selig Brodetsky, Y'huda L. Fishman, Itzhak Grünbaum, Eliezer Kaplan, Emil Schmorak, and Moshe Shertok, members of the Executive; and Nahum Goldmann, Louis Lipsky, Arthur Ruppin, and M'nahem M. Ussishkin members of the Executive with restricted rights.

22d Congress. Basle, Dec. 9–24, 1946. President, Chaim Weizmann; vice-presidents, Rabbi Sh'muel HaLevi Brod, Judith G. *Epstein, Leo Garfinkel, Rev. Jacob Koppel *Goldbloom, Hayim *Greenberg, Moshe Kleinbaum (*S'ne), Tzivya *Lubetkin-Zuckerman, Elimelech Neufeld, Mordekhai *Nurock, Levi-Yitzhak Rabinowitz, David Remez, Joseph *Schechtman, Abba Hillel Silver, Yosef Sprinzak, and Meir Ya'ari. Delegates, 385 (General Zionist bloc, 123; World Union of Po'ale Zion–Hitahdut, 101; Mizrahi, 58; Revisionists, who

after the war had returned to the WZO and joined with the Jewish State party to form the United Zionists-Revisionists, 41; *HaShomer HaTza'ir, 26; *Ahdut 'Avoda–Po'ale Zion, 26; *'Aliya Hadasha, 5; unaffiliated, 5).

This first Congress to meet after World War II marked the nadir of British-Jewish relations. The conviction that Great Britain was not prepared to search honestly for a constructive solution to the problem of Palestine in accordance with the Palestine Mandate had become nearly universal in the Zionist movement. Describing in retrospect the mood prevailing at the Congress, the report by the Political Department of the Jewish Agency, submitted five years later to the 23d Congress in Jerusalem, stated:

> Grief and bitterness filled the hearts of the delegates. . . . Resentment against the Mandatory power, which was keeping the gates of the Jewish National Home closed to the survivors of the Holocaust, was universal. Faith in its readiness to live up to its international obligations had been shattered beyond repair. The conviction was general that the end of a chapter had come, that the Mandate was dead, and that only the establishment of a Jewish commonwealth in Palestine could ensure the implementation of Zionist aspirations and the rescue of the survivors in Europe.

Political activism was the dominant trend among the Congress delegates. Their resolutions reflected the new outlook of the Zionist movement. The Congress recorded its firm opposition to the latest British scheme of a five-year trusteeship over Palestine, "by which the establishment of the Jewish State would be prevented or postponed." It also resolved that "in the existing circumstances, the Zionist Movement cannot take part" in one more British-Arab-Jewish conference on Palestine called by the mandatory power. Chaim Weizmann, who, notwithstanding his deep disappointment with the anti-Zionist British policy in Palestine, pleaded for Zionist participation in the London discussions as a last attempt to reach a settlement with Great Britain, was not reelected to the presidency of the World Zionist Organization. The office of president remained vacant. David Ben-Gurion, Peretz *Bernstein, Selig Brodetsky, Eliyahu *Dobkin, Y'huda L. Fishman, Z'ev *Gold, Nahum Goldmann, Hayim Greenberg, Itzhak Grünbaum, Rose *Halprin, Eliezer Kaplan, Moshe Kleinbaum, Berl Locker, Golda Meyerson (*Meir), Emanuel Neumann, Moshe *Shapira, Moshe Shertok, Sh'lomo Zalman *Shragai, and Abba Hillel Silver were elected members of the Executive.

23d Congress. Jerusalem, Aug. 14–30, 1951. President, Nahum Goldmann; vice-presidents, Benjamin G. *Browdy, Judith G. Epstein, Rev. Jacob Koppel Goldbloom, Mordecai Goldstein, Itzhak *Harkavi, Marc *Jarblum, Joseph *Klarman, Golda Meir, Elimelech Neufeld, Mordekhai Nurock, Louis *Segal, Yosef Sprinzak, Meir Ya'ari, and Ya'akov Zerubavel. Delegates, 446 (Union of Po'ale Zion–Hitahdut, 161; General Zionists, 118; Mizrahi and HaPo'el HaMizrahi, 69; United Workers, 60; Revisionists, 33; unaffiliated, 5).

This, the first Congress to be held in the State of Israel, was solemnly opened on Mount Herzl. It was faced with momentous changes in Zionist concepts and organizational structure resulting from the establishment of Israel. Its deliberations largely centered on the question of the relationship of the Zionist Organization to the State and its government. Berl Locker, chairman of the Jewish Agency Executive, reviewed the development of Zionism from Basle to Jerusalem. Prime Minister David

Ben-Gurion spoke on behalf of the Israel government, and Nahum Goldmann stressed the paramount importance of the partnership between the Jewish people and the State of Israel.

The Congress outlined the new tasks of the Zionist movement following the establishment of the State of Israel, which represented the realization of the Basle Program. It resolved: "The task of Zionism is to strengthen the State of Israel, to gather the exiles in the Land of Israel, and to guarantee the unity of the Jewish people."

The Congress also set forth the following program for the WZO: encouragement of 'Aliya, strengthening of *Halutziyut (pioneering) and *Hakhshara (agricultural training), supreme efforts to enlist funds for the realization of the Zionist aims, promotion of private capital investment in Israel, deepening of Jewish consciousness, mobilization of world public opinion for Israel and Zionism, participation in the organization of Jewish communal life on a democratic basis, and the safeguarding of Jewish rights. Resolutions delineated the new tasks of Zionism and proposed that Israel enact appropriate legislation recognizing the WZO as the representative body of the Jewish people in all matters that involved the organized participation of Diaspora Jewry in the development of Israel.

No president of the WZO was elected. Nahum Goldmann was elected chairman of the Executive in New York and Berl Locker chairman of the Executive in Jerusalem. Yehuda Braginsky, Eliyahu Dobkin, Levi *Eshkol, Z'ev Gold, Zvi Herman, Giora *Josephthal, Moshe *Kol, Emanuel Neumann, Yitzhak *Raphael, and Zalman *Shazar were elected members of the Jerusalem Executive; David *Bet-Arye, Benjamin G. Browdy, Israel *Goldstein, Hayim Greenberg, Rose Halprin, Zvi *Lurie, and Baruch *Zuckerman, members of the New York Executive.

24th Congress. Jerusalem, Apr. 24–May 7, 1956. President, Yosef Sprinzak; 17 vice-presidents. Delegates, 496 (*World Confederation of General Zionists, 158; World Union of Po'ale Zion–Hitahdut, 151; Mizrahi–HaPo'el HaMizrahi, 69; *Herut-Revisionists, 52; *Mapam, or United Workers, 34; Ahdut 'Avoda–Po'ale Zion, 29; unaffiliated, 3). In a political declaration, the Congress voiced its "profound awareness of the dangers threatening the State of Israel" because of openly voiced "aggressive intentions" of the Arab states, which received "constant and growing consignments of arms from East and West." Proclaiming "the indissoluble historical bond between the Jewish people and the Land of Israel," the Congress called on "the Jews throughout the world to fulfill their responsibility towards the State of Israel by rallying to its support and by mobilizing the fullest measure of devotion and strength for its well-being, prosperity and security." Stressing the urgency of large-scale immigration to Israel, the Congress called for the "creation of a regime of absorption in the State of Israel which will encourage the immigration of Jewish masses."

The Congress gave close attention to the organizational structure of Zionism. It rejected the proposal that a single united Zionist organization function in every country, adopting instead a more flexible motion "to maintain in every country a territorial framework that shall include all the Zionist parties and organizations." Further proposals for organizational reform were referred to the Zionist General Council "for consideration and decision." See also ZIONIST TERRITORIAL ORGANIZATIONS.

Nahum Goldmann was elected president of the WZO and chairman of the Jewish Agency Executive. David **Bet-Arye**,

Yehuda Braginsky, Eliyahu Dobkin, Arye Leon *Dultzin, Levi Eshkol, Israel Goldstein, Meir *Grossman, Rose Halprin, Avraham *Harman, Giora Josephthal, Mordecai *Kirshblum, Moshe Kol, Zvi Lurie, Emanuel Neumann, Louis Segal, Zalman Shazar, and Sh'lomo Zalman Shragai were elected members of the Executive.

25th Congress. Jerusalem, Dec. 27, 1960–Jan. 11, 1961. Presidents, Nahum Goldmann and Moshe Sharett; 25 vice-presidents. Delegates, 521 (World Union of Po'ale Zion–Hitahdut, 166; World Confederation of General Zionists, Goldstein-Halprin, 80; World Confederation of General Zionists, Neumann, 75; Mizrahi–HaPo'el HaMizrahi, 63; Mapam, or United Workers, 51; Herut-Revisionists, 35; World Union of Ahdut 'Avoda–Po'ale Zion, 29; *Progressive party in Israel, 13; *Women's International Zionist Organization—WIZO, 6; unaffiliated, 3). For the first time in Zionist history, representatives of non-Zionist bodies and of Jewish communities in 14 countries participated in the Congress as associate members and fraternal delegates, without voting rights.

The Congress heard addresses by Nahum Goldmann, Itzhak Ben Zvi, and David Ben-Gurion. Deliberations centered on immigration, particularly from the free Western countries, and *Jewish education in the Diaspora. Addressing the Congress on "The People and the State," David Ben-Gurion, Israel's Prime Minister, said: "The existence of the State of Israel and the existence of Jewry in the Diaspora are mutually dependent and conditioned. . . . They depend on two factors—increasing 'Aliya, both pioneering and constructive, and the Jewish education of the younger generation in the Diaspora—in order to intensify its personal attachment to both Judaism and Israel."

Nahum Goldmann was elected president of the WZO. David Bet-Arye, Eliyahu Dobkin, Arye Leon Dultzin, Levi Eshkol, Israel Goldstein, Rose Halprin, Dov *Joseph, Mordecai Kirshblum, Moshe Kol, Hayim Levanon, Zvi Lurie, Emanuel Neumann, Louis Segal, Moshe Sharett, Zalman Shazar, Sh'lomo Zalman Shragai, and Aharon Zisling were elected members of the Executive; and Avraham *Schenker, deputy member.

26th Congress. Jerusalem, Dec. 30, 1964–Jan. 11, 1965. Nahum Goldmann and Moshe Sharett (the latter was prevented from attending by ill health) were elected presidents of the Congress. Delegates, 529 (Po'ale Zion–Hitahdut, 154; *World Union of General Zionists, 95; World Confederation of General Zionists, 91; Mizrahi–HaPo'el HaMizrahi, 69; Herut-Revisionists, 53; Mapam, 35; Ahdut 'Avoda–Po'ale Zion, 27; WIZO and others, 15). In his opening speech, Nahum Goldmann defined as a major task of the Congress the inauguration of a new era of cooperation between *Israel and the Diaspora. It was Israel's responsibility, he said, to help Diaspora Jewry in the struggle against spiritual disintegration and assimilation. Zionists must take an increasing part in communal affairs and spread the knowledge of Hebrew and of national and traditional values.

Speakers in the general debate dealt with various dangers confronting Diaspora Jewry, problems of immigration from Western countries, and various aspects of Zionist work. Resolutions of the Congress included a call to governments to stop arms deliveries to nations in the Middle East which threatened their neighbors, an appeal to the U.S.S.R. to alleviate the situation of Russian Jewry and to permit those who wished to settle in Israel to do so, and a call for intensified Jewish and Zionist cultural work and for 'Aliya to Israel. The Congress reelected Nahum Goldmann president of the Zionist Organization and Moshe Sharett chairman of the Executive. The election of the Executive was referred to the Zionist General Council, which subsequently (Jan. 18, 1966) elected Arye *Pincus chairman of the Executive and the following new Executive: in Jerusalem, Itzhak Artzi, David Bet-Arye, Eliyahu Dobkin, Arye Leon Dultzin, Israel Goldstein, Itzhak Harkavi, Joseph Klarman, Hayim Levanon, Tzivya Lubetkin-Zuckerman, Zvi Lurie, Woolf Perry, Sh'lomo Zalman Shragai, Ra'anan Weitz, and Avraham Ziegel (Cygel); and in New York, Rose Halprin, Mordecai Kirshblum, Emanuel Neumann, Joseph Schechtman, Marie *Syrkin, and Avraham Schenker (deputy member). The General Council also appointed the following as members of the Executive on a nonparty basis: Simon *Greenberg, Astorre *Mayer, J.-G.-A. *Narboni (Sephardim), Emanuel *Rackman, Joseph J. *Schwartz, Lord Sieff (Israel Moses *Sieff), Dewey *Stone, and Raya Jaglom (in an advisory capacity). On Sept. 20, 1966, the Executive appointed Leon Feuer a member of the New York Executive. Rose Halprin and Emanuel Neumann alternated as chairman of the New York Executive.

27th Congress. Jerusalem, June 9–19, 1968. The Presidium was composed of 16 members, headed by Nahum Goldmann. Delegates, 529 (Labor Zionist movement, 181; World Union of General Zionists, 95; World Confederation of General Zionists, 81; Mizrahi–HaPo'el HaMizrahi, 69; B'rit Herut-HaTzohar, 53; Mapam, 35; unaffiliated, 3; WIZO, 12). Of the delegates, 190 were Israelis and 145 came from the United States. The participants at the Congress, including some 300 invited to serve in an advisory capacity, represented 40 countries.

This Congress marked the 20th anniversary of Israel and was the first to be held in united Jerusalem. Dignitaries present included Pres. Zalman Shazar, the entire Israeli Cabinet, and 25 heads of foreign diplomatic missions.

In his keynote address, Goldmann set forth the major tasks facing the Jewish State and Diaspora Jewry. Israel must "find the way . . . for becoming an integrated part of the Middle East." The Zionist movement "will stand or fall by what happens to the question of 'Aliya." It is essential that both Zionism and Israel submit to thoroughgoing changes. The challenges and ideals of yesterday no longer appeal to the young generation, and before young people from the Western world will want to settle in Israel, they will have to learn to identify with Jewish values.

The principal themes of the Congress were the *Six-day War of 1967 and resultant problems, and the promotion of unprecedented 'Aliya from the Western world. Resolutions of the Congress condemned attempts to make a distinction between Zionism and the Jewish people; called on Soviet Russia to change her attitude toward Israel and Russian Jewry; urged the Zionist Executive to strengthen its public relations work, with special emphasis on Jewish students; appealed to the Arab peoples and their leaders to help bring peace to the Middle East; called on "peace-loving nations to supply Israel with defensive weapons" in the absence of an international arrangement to limit the arms race in the Middle East; and expressed concern about the situation of the Jews in Arab lands. The Jerusalem Program, adopted originally by the 23d Congress in 1951, was reformulated to read:

> The aims of Zionism are: The Unity of the Jewish People and the centrality of Israel in its life; the ingathering of the Jewish People in its historical homeland, Eretz Yisrael, through aliya from all lands; the strengthening of the State of Israel,

founded on the Prophetic ideals of justice and peace; the preservation of the identity of the Jewish People through the fostering of Jewish and Hebrew education and of Jewish spiritual and cultural values; the protection of Jewish rights everywhere.

The election of a successor to Nahum Goldmann as president of the World Zionist Organization was referred to the Actions Committee, of which Ehud *Avriel was elected chairman. Arye Pincus was reelected chairman of the Executive. The Jerusalem Executive was reduced from 25 to 12 full-fledged members. The following new members were elected to the Executive: Col. Mord'khai Bar-On, Chaim Finkielsztein of Buenos Aires, Charlotte Stone *Jacobson of New York, and Avraham Schenker. The following members were reelected: Arye Dultzin, Israel Goldstein, Raya Jaglom, Joseph Klarman, J.-G.-A. Narboni, Emanuel Neumann, and Ra'anan Weitz. Two seats, left open for representatives of Mizrahi–HaPo'el HaMizrahi, were subsequently filled by Mordecai Kirshblum and Moshe Krona. Five additional prominent Jewish leaders were to be coopted to the Executive on a nonparty basis.

N. M. GELBER AND O. K. RABINOWICZ

CONGRESS COURT. *See* CONGRESS TRIBUNAL.

CONGRESS OF INDUSTRIAL ORGANIZATIONS (CIO). Central body of American industrial trade unions, founded in 1938. It first took a clear-cut stand on Palestine at its 7th convention (Chicago, 1944), at which it passed a resolution calling for "removal of the *White Paper [of 1939] policy, and the full implementation of the *Balfour Declaration towards the ultimate establishment of a Palestinian Jewish commonwealth in accordance with the principles of democratic action." From that time until its merger with the American Federation of Labor in 1955 (*see* AMERICAN FEDERATION OF LABOR–CONGRESS OF INDUSTRIAL ORGANIZATIONS), it wholeheartedly supported Zionist demands in relation to Palestine and rendered great financial and political service to the *Histadrut (General Federation of Labor). An official delegation of the organization, composed of Jacob S. Potofsky, president of the Amalgamated Clothing Workers of America, and Joseph Curran, president of the National Maritime Union, visited Israel in 1949. After receiving their report, which characterized Israel as "indeed a bastion of democracy in the Middle East," the 11th convention (Cleveland, 1949) passed a resolution recommending the appointment "of a C.I.O. Israel-American Committee to provide adequate channels for handling our fraternal relations with the Histadrut." The 14th convention (Atlantic City, N.J., 1952) endorsed the *State of Israel bonds issue.

The CIO cooperated with the AFL in matters of concern to Israel and the Histadrut even before the two organizations merged. The two bodies made joint representations to the United States government in behalf of Israel and cooperated in forming the American Histadrut Trade Union Council, of which Philip Murray, president of the CIO, acted as honorary co-chairman, a post subsequently taken over by his successor, Walter P. Reuther. Affiliates of the CIO made substantial financial contributions to Histadrut enterprises and continued to do so after they had become part of the united AFL-CIO.

C. B. SHERMAN

CONGRESS TRIBUNAL. High court of the *World Zionist Organization (WZO). It dates back to the *Organisationsstatut* enacted by the 5th Zionist *Congress in 1901, which provided for a *Kongressgericht*. According to the new constitution of the World Zionist Organization adopted in 1960, the Congress Tribunal combined the functions of the two courts which had existed under the constitution of 1921, the Congress Court and the Court of Honor.

In 1966 the Congress Tribunal consisted of a maximum of 25 members, including the chairman and as many as 5 deputy chairmen, all of whom were elected for the duration of the inter-Congress period by the Zionist Congress or, on express authorization, by the Zionist General Council (*see* ACTIONS COMMITTEE).

Under article 49 of the constitution, the Congress Tribunal was authorized (1) to interpret the constitution; (2) to examine the legality of decisions of central Zionist bodies; (3) to hear and arbitrate certain disputes between Zionist bodies or between a central Zionist body and an individual (except for disputes involving money matters); (4) to deal with objections to decisions to postpone a Zionist Congress or a session of the Zionist General Council; (5) to confirm, annul, or alter the results of Congress elections; (6) to decide complaints lodged by the attorney of the WZO that a certain act constituted an infringement of the constitution or was detrimental to the interests or prestige of the WZO; and (7) to deal with appeals from judgments of judicial bodies of territorial Zionist organizations and against decisions of the Committee for Determining the Number of Congress Delegates.

The number of judges forming a bench of the Congress Tribunal varied from 3 to 7, depending on the nature of the case. The judgments of any bench were final and not subject to further appeal. The cases were conducted under the special Rules of Procedure of the Congress Tribunal, which also provided for sanctions to be imposed on Zionist bodies and individuals, ranging from a warning to suspension or cancellation of membership.

The Congress Tribunal is busiest before the opening of a Zionist Congress because most cases brought before it pertain to election matters. Though not formally bound by its previous judgments and decisions, it usually decides cases in conformity with the precedents handed down in the course of seven decades. Owing to its impartiality, the high standards of its proceedings, and the eminence of the personalities who have served as chairmen of the tribunal (Dr. Max *Bodenheimer, Sammy *Gronemann, Dr. Aron *Barth, Judge Shneur Zalman Cheshin, and Chief Justice Shim'on *Agranat), the Congress Tribunal is held in high esteem.

The Congress Tribunal in its 1970 composition was elected by the 27th Zionist Congress (Jerusalem, 1968); its chairman was Justice Moshe *Landau, of Israel's Supreme Court. Of the 23 judges, including 5 deputy chairmen, 15 were Israelis, 5 resided in the United States, and 1 each resided in Great Britain, Canada, and South Africa.

A. ZWERGBAUM

"CONQUEST OF LABOR" (Kibbush 'Avoda). Doctrine developed by the *Second 'Aliya (1904–14) and, in particular, by *HaPo'el HaTza'ir, stressing the importance of Jewish labor as the basis for a Jewish society in Palestine. By the beginning of the 20th century, the development and consolidation of the Jewish agricultural settlements, especially those in Judea and Samaria, had reached a stage at which they were in need of hired labor. Most of the laborers employed were Arabs (*see* ARABS IN ISRAEL); some worked on a permanent basis, but by far the larger number were seasonal laborers drawn from neighboring Arab villages. Joseph *Aronowicz, leader of the HaPo'el HaTza'ir party and editor of its weekly, preached the replacement of Arab labor by Jewish labor, not only because of the need to provide employment for Second 'Aliya immigrants but because without Jewish hired labor a Jewish majority in Palestine would be unattainable. Palestine would not be made Jewish by the mere possession of title to properties or merely by Jewish management but only by the performance by Jews of their own manual labor, whether on the farm or in the factory; in other words, only the "Conquest of Labor" by Jews and not the mere "conquest" of land by purchase would assure the realization of Zionism and the attainment of a Jewish majority. Aronowicz's appeal was directed both to the old settlers and to the new arrivals; to the settlers he pointed out the dangers inherent in Arab labor, and to the young workers he stressed the importance of becoming hired laborers themselves.

Kibbush 'Avoda gave rise to considerable tension between the settlers and the Second 'Aliya, who were, on the whole, radical-minded and permeated with the ideas of the Russian intelligentsia of the Revolution of 1904–05. The settlers were not always ready to pay the inexperienced new immigrants a higher wage than the one paid to the Arabs. In the course of time, however, wages were increased considerably, and the conflicts that arose were not due primarily to wage disputes. There was a feeling of estrangement between the settlers and the new immigrants. The latter, often better educated and politically minded, felt superior to the rather conservative settlers, who resented the assertion of superiority and the radical slogans of the 'Olim. In places such as Petah Tikva acute conflicts developed because young workers, who generally were not observant, offended the sensibilities of the Orthodox elements particularly by failing to observe the Sabbath. Since most of the new arrivals were unmarried, there was no compelling need for them to become attached to their places of employment, and their easy mobility from settlement to settlement and from Judea to Galilee earned them the reproof of Aronowicz. HaPo'el HaTza'ir impressed the importance of Kibbush 'Avoda both on the *Hoveve Zion movement of Russia and on the Palestine Office of the *World Zionist Organization headed by Arthur *Ruppin. With their assistance the smallholders' settlement of 'En Ganim was founded near Petah Tikva in 1908, the intention being that the workers hold small tracts of land and cultivate them in their spare time, thus supplementing the income derived from their work in the orange groves of Petah Tikva. 'En Ganim was followed by Nahlat Y'huda, near Rishon L'Tziyon, and it was hoped that these developments would attach the new arrivals both to the land and to the status of hired laborers in the nearby settlement (*see* MOSHAV).

The total number of Jews employed in the settlements did not exceed 10 to 12 per cent of the labor force, and by 1914 it was estimated at 1,500. The doctrine of the "Conquest of Labor" was challenged by Joseph *Witkin, who in 1908 appealed for the settlement of new arrivals on the land as self-employed farmers. Knowing the middle-class origins and the mentality of the Second 'Aliya, Witkin realized that the status of hired farmhands would not appeal to them and that only the prospect of becoming independent farmers would attach them to the land. In this respect Witkin was the precursor of the various K'vutzot (communal settlements; *see* KIBBUTZ) and smallholders' settlements which were established prior to World War I. Aronowicz, on the other hand, rejected Witkin's policy:

since the new 'Olim had no means, they would be dependent on a settlement agency and dominated by it. Aronowicz preferred to have persons of means developing the economy of Palestine and employing Jews, thus avoiding the dangers of the *Halukka (religious charity), from which not only the old *Yishuv (Jewish population of Palestine) but also the new Yishuv was suffering. New settlements, he argued, would draw labor from the existing Jewish villages; their success, on the other hand, would create a demand for new labor, which would inevitably be Arab. Thus the establishment of Jewish workers as independent farmers would merely increase the demand for Arab labor and remove the prospect of a Jewish majority in Palestine.

The controversy over Kibbush 'Avoda agitated the Yishuv and the Zionist movement in the decade preceding World War I. *Ahad Ha'Am, who devoted considerable attention to the problem, did not believe that it would be possible to create a Jewish working class to replace the Arabs employed in the colonies.

With the advent of the *Third 'Aliya (1920–24), Kibbush 'Avoda in agriculture was replaced by the principle of 'Avoda 'Ivrit (Jewish Labor) in all sectors of the rapidly developing economy of Palestine. During the period of the British *Mandate for Palestine (1917–48), the application of this principle gave rise to a number of conflicts, nearly all in the citrus plantations of the old colonies. In Jewish-owned trades and industries, including the building trades, the principle was generally accepted. *See also* JEWISH AND ARAB LABOR.

S. Z. ABRAMOV

"CONQUEST OF THE SOIL" (Kibbush Ha'Adama). Concept in the ideology of the Palestinian pioneers of the *Second 'Aliya, complementing their more comprehensive aim of the *"Conquest of Labor." The "conquest" of the soil meant specifically the acquisition and utilization of the soil of Palestine by settling it with Jewish farmers who engaged personally in all branches of agricultural work.

In 1908 Joseph *Witkin suggested at the conference of *HaPo'el HaTza'ir that the "Conquest of Labor" should take the form of the "Conquest of the Soil" through the establishment of workers' settlements. However, the principal contributor to the development of this ideology was Aharon D. *Gordon, who taught that devotion to agricultural work would cleanse the Jewish soul of "parasitism," which had infected it as a result of the economic restrictions forced on the Jews by life in the *Diaspora. In the Diaspora the Jews were barred from primary economic activities and cut off from direct contact with the soil, and this, above all, stunted their normal psychological development. The tilling of the soil of their old-new National Homeland was considered by Gordon and his followers the basis not only of a viable and balanced national economy but also of the psychological regeneration of the people.

R. PATAI

CONSERVATIVE JUDAISM AND ZIONISM. Conservative Judaism takes a historic view of Judaism, regarding it as an evolving religious civilization. Zionism, too, is based on one of the chief historical elements in Jewish tradition, the Messianic faith in the Ingathering of the Jewish people to its Homeland. Therefore, despite the tensions stemming from the indifferent attitude of a substantial part of the Zionist leadership toward the religious aspects of Judaism, these two movements have stood side by side during the years of struggle, growth, and achievement. Conservative Judaism is sufficiently broad to include Zionism with its nationalist implications. Large numbers of the Conservative rabbinate and laymen in the United States have remained within the framework of *General Zionism and the *Zionist Organization of America (ZOA); smaller segments have affiliated themselves with *Labor Zionism. Understandably, therefore, the Conservative organizational setup in the United States—the Jewish Theological Seminary of America, the Rabbinical Assembly, the United Synagogue of America, and their ancillary bodies—has been effective in winning American Jewry to Zionism.

In Europe, Conservative Judaism did not develop into an organized movement, nor did it advance the Zionist cause as much as it did in the New World. Among the more important causes of this lack of vitality were the monolithic national structure of the European states, the staid and custom-ridden posture of the official Jewish communities, the psychological block against Zionism erected by the fear that newly won *emancipation might be undermined, and the paucity of adherents to the Conservative interpretation of Judaism.

In the United States students of the Jewish Theological Seminary were drawn to modern Zionism as early as 1896, when they organized the first intercollegiate Zionist association, the Young American Zionists, which was modeled after the *Kadimah of Vienna. In 1898 this group became the first Zionist fraternity in the country under the name ZBT. The letters stood for the Hebrew initials of Zion B'Mishpat Tipade (Zion shall be redeemed through justice). It is a historical curiosity that several years later this body became an exclusive social Greek-letter fraternity, Zeta Beta Tau, a hotbed of *anti-Zionism and *assimilation.

In all its history, the faculty of the seminary has had only one member ideologically opposed to Zionism. A number of professors have been active in the affairs of the ZOA and have held important posts in its administrations. The most outstanding among them was Solomon *Schechter, who headed the seminary and was an intellectual force in the life of the Federation of American Zionists, although he frequently disagreed with the secular trend of its leaders. Dr. Israel *Friedlaender was the interpreter of Zionism in the Jewish community and its spokesman to non-Jews. Both men created the bonds which bound Conservative Judaism and Zionism.

The Conservative rabbis have been the backbone of the local Zionist districts, the teachers of Zionism, the fosterers of modern Hebrew literature in their communities, and the key men in local *Keren HaYesod (Palestine Foundation Fund) and *United Palestine Appeal drives. Many of these rabbis have been among the leading figures in the Zionist movement in the United States. In brief, the members of the Rabbinical Assembly have unquestionably been an important factor in educating American Jewry to understand and support Zionism.

The congregations affiliated with the United Synagogue of America, the congregational arm of the Conservative movement, have definitely reflected the Zionist viewpoint of their spiritual leaders, provided a significant percentage of the membership of the ZOA, supplied a substantial number of Zionist leaders on various levels, and supported the upbuilding of Palestine during the days of strife and stress.

Until the end of World War II, the lay Board of Overseers of the seminary, which included a number of prominent Reform

Jews, consisted in the main of non-Zionists. Some of the members were even anti-Zionist. Nevertheless, the board did not even attempt to influence the ideology of the Conservative constituency.

Cyrus *Adler, president of the seminary from 1916 to 1940, who was closely allied with the history of the Conservative movement for two generations, was not a Zionist in the organizational sense but a "pro-Palestinian." He fought the ZOA leadership on crucial issues such as the *American Jewish Congress. But he was aware that his attitude did not reflect the views of the bodies representing Conservative Judaism in the United States. In the last decade of his life he became non-Zionist cochairman of the *Jewish Agency.

From its beginnings in the mid-1930s, the Reconstructionist movement, originated by Prof. Mordecai M. *Kaplan of the Jewish Theological Seminary, had as part of its official platform the reestablishment in Israel of a Homeland not only for the Jews but for the historic Jewish civilization, even while it called for the formation of organic Jewish communities in the *Diaspora. See also RECONSTRUCTIONISM AND ZIONISM.

Since the establishment of the State of Israel, the future of the *World Zionist Organization in the Diaspora, misunderstandings between the Jewries of Israel and the United States, and the need to introduce tolerance in the religious community of Israel have been issues of concern to American Conservative Judaism. In 1964 the Rabbinical Assembly organized an Israel Commission to study the relevant problems and prepare a plan of action. The result was the publication of the Blue Paper, which proposed the reorganization of the Zionist movement to create a proper rapprochement between Israel and the Diaspora. Although it was bitterly criticized by various Zionist leaders, the paper was seriously discussed at the 1965 convention of the Rabbinical Assembly and recommitted for continued consideration at the next convention.

The 1966 convention resolved to issue a series of studied statements dealing with the religious and social "significance of the State of Israel for Jewish communities throughout the world." The first of these statements set forth the following basic premises:

1. The Conservative movement has been committed from the beginning to Zionism as a Mitzva (commandment) obligatory on all Jews.

2. Every Jew has an equal spiritual and religious share in the ongoing life of the State of Israel.

3. Without seeking political power or social coercion, the Conservative movement is prepared to present its case to the Jews of Israel in the form of diverse religious viewpoints so that Israeli society may be made aware of alternative interpretations of authentic Jewish tradition.

Steps have been taken to implement a program of action in Israel, including the encouragement of *'Aliya (immigration) and the sending of rabbis to Israel to minister in various capacities, the establishment of two camps and a high school there, and the broadening of the summer programs of the Conservative youth movement. In 1962 the Jewish Theological Seminary of America opened the American Student Center in Jerusalem, to serve students of the seminary's rabbinical school who spend a year of study in Israel. The students' program is supervised by a resident faculty. The building of the center also serves as headquarters for American youth groups touring Israel under the auspices of the United Synagogue of America. Thus the Conservative movement has begun to grapple ideologically and pragmatically with the task of building a series of associations to bridge the gap between the Jews of Israel and the Conservative Jews of the United States.

H. PARZEN

CONSTITUTION OF ISRAEL. See LEGISLATION IN ISRAEL.

COOK, HILLEL. See BERGSON, PETER.

COOPERATIVE SETTLEMENTS. See COOPERATIVES IN ISRAEL; IMMIGRANTS' VILLAGES; MOSHAV; MOSHAV SHITUFI.

COOPERATIVES IN ISRAEL. Pardes, the first modern cooperative in Palestine, was registered under Ottoman law in 1900. It was formed for the purpose of cultivating and marketing citrus fruit raised by the Jewish farmers, and its nine founders—Arye Leib Weiss, Asher Levin, Dr. Aaron M. *Mazia, Moshe Maklev, Haim Solomon, Johann *Kremenetzky, Peretz Pascal, Shimon *Rokah, and Joshua *Stampfer—included the heads of the *Yishuv (Jewish population of Palestine) at that time. In 1967 Pardes had 1,300 members, 37,000 dunams (9,250 acres; see DUNAM) of orchards, and a yearly income of IL35,000,000 ($10,000,000).

The cooperative movement started in 1904, at the beginning of the *Second 'Aliya. The pioneers, mainly young unmarried men and women, received minimal wages. Being without means, they resorted to the principle of mutual aid and began to establish all kinds of cooperative organizations in order to alleviate their lot. Thus, cooperative workers' kitchens, laundries, grocery stores, credit associations, health clinics, and other such groups were formed.

Agricultural Cooperatives. During the Second 'Aliya, the settlement of Sejera (Ilanya) served as the center for the workers of Galilee; later it was a center of both ideology and action for all the workers of Palestine. Here the "collective," or agricultural cooperative, was born. Late in 1907 a collective group assumed complete responsibility for agricultural production at the farm of the *Jewish Colonization Association (ICA). The valuable experience thus gained helped lay the groundwork for the formation in 1910 of D'ganya, the first K'vutza (see KIBBUTZ). This was the seed from which the cooperative agricultural settlement has grown, with the help of the *Jewish National Fund and, later, the *Histadrut (General Federation of Labor), all factions of the pioneering population, the *Keren HaYesod (Palestine Foundation Fund) of the *World Zionist Organization, and, since the establishment of Israel, the government, through the Ministry of Agriculture and other departments.

In 1912 an attempt was made in the *moshava (village) of Merhavya to found an agricultural cooperative based on the ideas of the German-Jewish Zionist economist and sociologist Prof. Franz *Oppenheimer. This cooperative, which tried to combine the advantages of a private village with those of a communal settlement, had to disband after seven years of struggle, but many of its ideas and experiences were later incorporated in various forms of cooperative rural settlements.

In 1921 Nahalal, the first Moshav 'Ovdim (smallholders' settlement; see MOSHAV), was founded. It was (and still is) a cooperative settlement of smallholders, with land leased individually to each settler by the Jewish National Fund, work done by the individual families on their own farms, mutual aid practiced, and cooperative organizations functioning primarily in the field of joint marketing. The moshav differed from the kibbutz in that land ownership (leasehold) in it was private and each settler was responsible for working his own farm. The *Moshav Shitufi, which was developed subsequently, is a form of rural settlement in which a group of families cooperates in everything pertaining to production. They work together, are jointly responsible for the work of the settlement, and jointly own the income from their work. However, each family is free to spend its monthly budget allowance as it sees fit and independently of the community.

In 1967 the number of agricultural cooperatives including kibbutzim and moshavim registered with the government totaled 938. They were grouped as shown in Table 1.

TABLE 1. AGRICULTURAL COOPERATIVES, 1967

Group	Cooperatives	Persons
Kibbutzim: Group I		
*Ihud HaK'vutzot V'haKibbutzim	82	29,000
*Kibbutz M'uhad	58	24,500
*Kibbutz Artzi Shel HaShomer HaTza'ir	73	30,500
*HaKibbutz HaDati	10	4,000
Kibbutze Ha'Oved HaTziyoni	5	1,200
Kibbutze *Po'ale Agudat Israel	2	550
Unaffiliated kibbutzim	3	900
Total	233	90,650
Cooperative rural settlements:		
Mosh've 'Ovdim	301	
Moshavim Shitufiyim	20	
Total	554	
Marketing and processing cooperatives	30	
Water supply associations	53	
Agricultural insurance cooperatives	6	
General agricultural cooperatives	130	
Miscellaneous	165	
Grand total	938	

In addition, there were 62 Arab water supply associations and 9 Arab general agricultural cooperatives. An additional 20 cooperatives had not yet been officially registered.

Production and Service Cooperatives. In 1908 the first non-agricultural cooperatives (transportation, tailoring, shoe repairing, carpentry, etc.) were formed, but of these only the Ahdut Press (founded in 1910) was still in existence in 1967.

The main types of production cooperative organizations were as follows: metal and electrical work, woodworking, building materials, printing and paper manufacture, leatherwork, clothing, bakeries and pastry shops, food preparation, pharmaceuticals and soap, plastics, diamond polishing, manufacture of glass and glass products, dentures, cigarettes, ceramics, and rubber.

Following the establishment of the State of Israel the number of production (or industrial) cooperatives decreased considerably. Some of the successful cooperatives of this type became to all intents and purposes private enterprises. On the other hand, many attempts to set up such cooperatives failed in spite of the encouragement they received from the government.

Service cooperatives were active in the distribution of meat,

kerosine, ice, milk, and so on; agricultural labor (plowing, leveling land, excavation, drilling, etc.); quarrying of sand and gravel for construction; laundering; barbershops; dyeing; luncheonettes; engineering and architecture; garages; gardening; schools; hotels; restaurants; health projects; motion-picture theaters; sailing; fishing; cleaning and painting of boats; cleaning of offices, shops, and homes; and garbage collection and processing.

The largest groups were the cooperatives for passenger and freight transport. The public bus system was controlled by two cooperatives, Egged and Dan, which had been formed by a lengthy process of merger of more than 60 cooperatives of varying sizes. This concentration of public transport within one cooperative framework was unique in the world. Cooperatives carried about 40 per cent of the freight tonnage of Israel. There was also a cooperative which handled sea freight and had four ships.

In 1967 production and service cooperatives as shown in Table 2 were registered with the government. One of the most

TABLE 2. PRODUCTION AND SERVICE COOPERATIVES

Type of cooperative	Number*	Number of workers	Yearly income IL1,000	Wages IL 1,000
Production	129	3,200	90,000	30,000
Service	85	2,300	40,000	12,000
Passenger transport (buses and taxis)	3	9,000	240,000	128,000
Freight transport	34	1,550	50,000	19,000
Total	251	16,050	420,000	189,000

*Plus 13 Arab cooperatives (7 production, 1 service, 2 passenger transport, and 3 freight transport) established prior to the *Six-day War of 1967.

complex problems involved in cooperative organization concerned hired labor. In some cooperatives, especially the industrial cooperatives, the number of hired employees exceeded that of the members of the cooperatives. Membership in the production and service cooperatives was generally drawn from the ranks of young people, new immigrants, veterans, and similar groups lacking capital. As a result, the cooperatives suffered from a shortage of investment and circulating capital.

Consumer Cooperatives. In 1916 the workers of Galilee, in an effort to combat the inflation and hunger prevalent during World War I, formed HaMashbir, a cooperative organization to supply goods to, and purchase produce from, Jewish workers in Palestine. With the formation of T'nuva in 1927 as a cooperative for the sale of produce grown on Jewish farms, HaMashbir became HaMashbir HaMerkazi, the central whole-sale supplier of kibbutzim and consumer groups in settlements, villages, and cities. In the course of this development, the consumer cooperatives served by HaMashbir split into three groups: consumer associations in cities and moshavot, area purchasing organizations for kibbutzim, and area purchasing organizations for Mosh've 'Ovdim.

Consumer cooperatives played an important role not only within the many-branched cooperative undertaking but also within the broad agricultural perspective of Israel. They covered the country with a network of wholesale and retail operations, serving over half a million people in urban and rural areas.

In 1967 the income of the consumer groups associated with the Alliance of Consumer Cooperatives reached IL191,000,000; that of HaMashbir HaMerkazi, IL320,000,000. To this must be added the income of the area purchasing groups.

Marketing Cooperatives. Marketing cooperatives existed mainly in the agricultural sector of the economy. The most important was T'nuva, which handled the marketing and export of manufactures as well as agricultural produce. Its income in 1966–67 was IL631,000,000. The income from produce grown on its own farms was IL190,000,000. T'nuva marketed 70 per cent of Israel's agricultural produce. Its members included 546 cooperative agricultural settlements as well as hundreds of individual farms.

T'nuva Export (registered in 1936) marketed the citrus fruit grown on 300 shareholder cooperatives. It handled transport, packing, delivery to the port, loading, and marketing abroad. In 1961–62 T'nuva Export marketed 2,000,000 crates of fruit; in 1963–64, 3,580,000 (32 per cent of the citrus production of Israel). Its income was IL35,000,000 for 1961–62, IL57,000,000 for 1963–64, and IL91,000,000 for 1966–67.

Credit Cooperatives. The credit cooperative movement, which had grown steadily since its inception in the early 1900s, dwindled in the 1960s and faced a serious crisis. Some of the causes of the decline were changes in the legal and financial status of the credit cooperatives vis-à-vis the commercial banks, discrimination against them by banks dealing in foreign currency and increasing their capital by issuing shares to the public, and the general policy of the Histadrut to bring the credit cooperatives under the control of the Bank HaPo'alim (Workers' Bank). The workers' savings and loan associations closed and merged with the Bank HaPo'alim. The credit groups belonging to the central Merkaz organization numbered only 18 in 1967, as against 62 in 1955. The number of members, which had always fluctuated, was 233,000 in 1955 and 180,000 in 1967.

Housing Cooperatives. The 4th Conference of the Histadrut in 1935 established the basis for workers' housing cooperatives. It held that cooperatives provided a social climate in housing projects and guaranteed that the apartments would belong to the members and to their children without danger of speculative practices. With the establishment of the State of Israel, the mass influx of immigrants, and the assumption of responsibility by the government and the *Jewish Agency for immigrants' and workers' housing, cooperatives flourished and came to number hundreds of groups comprising hundreds of thousands of families. In 1967 there were nearly 200 groups in Histadrut projects (300,000 occupants) and 150 in private projects. But these figures actually reflected a decrease in cooperative housing. For various reasons, including the growth of a middle class in Israel and the desire to become free of burdensome restrictions, many persons had left the cooperative framework. Since 1956 the formation of new housing cooperatives had remained static, and some of the existing cooperatives had divested themselves of their cooperative character.

Benefit Associations. In 1967, 240 benefit associations were registered as cooperative organizations. Of these, 195 were regular benefit associations in which members' savings equivalent to a fixed percentage of their earnings accumulated with specific parallel payments by their employers, and 45 were pension funds based on the cumulative-pension principle. The capital of these organizations in 1967 totaled IL1,912,000,000.

Merkaz HaKooperatziya (Cooperative Center). The central body of the Histadrut, which initiates, subsidizes, and supervises Histadrut-affiliated cooperatives. The Merkaz is headed by a governing board elected once every four years by the Conference of Cooperatives. It comprises the following departments and institutions: Organization, Education and Culture, Comptroller, Guidance and Supervision (the so-called B'rit Pikuah), Finance (Kupat HaKooperativim), Equipment and Supply, Insurance, and Legal. Three professional or trade divisions are active within the Merkaz: Production, Transportation (passenger and freight), and Public Services.

Department of Cooperative Associations. The government agency responsible for cooperative affairs is the Department of Cooperative Associations of the Ministry of Labor. It is headed by the Registrar of Cooperative Associations, and it operates within the framework laid down by the Cooperative Societies Ordinance. Its functions include registration of cooperative societies, approval of their bylaws, supervision of the activities of cooperative societies, especially from the legal aspect, and liquidation of cooperative societies that cannot continue to maintain themselves. The Department also concerns itself with cooperative legislation. An Advisory Council attached to the Department advises the government on all questions concerning the cooperative movement in Israel. Headed by the Minister of Labor, it includes representatives of all the main central societies.

I. RITOV

COOPERATIVE VILLAGE. See K'FAR SHITUFI.

COPENHAGEN BUREAU, 1915–18. Clearinghouse for Zionist affairs during World War I. The outbreak of World War I in July, 1914, confronted the *World Zionist Organization (WZO) with a threat to its unity. Neutrality toward the belligerents was the only possible attitude to adopt for any international Jewish organization. The head office of the WZO was in Berlin, and it was proposed to transfer it either to New York or to The Hague. With the entrance of the Ottoman Empire into the war in November, 1914, on the side of the Central Powers and with the anxiety felt for the fate of the *Yishuv (Jewish population of Palestine) under the Turks, it was decided, on further consideration, that the head office should remain in Berlin. The Zionist *Executive would thus be left in as strong a position as possible for invoking the friendly interest and the good offices of the German government on behalf of Palestine Jewry.

The first meeting of the General Council of the WZO after the outbreak of the war was held in neutral Copenhagen on Dec. 3–6, 1914. It was decided to leave the head office in Berlin in charge of two members of the Executive, Otto *Warburg and Arthur *Hantke. Victor *Jacobson was sent to take charge of the Zionist Office in Constantinople, and it was decided to open an office in Copenhagen to be directed by Dr. Leo *Motzkin. The Copenhagen Bureau was to act as a clearinghouse for Zionist affairs and as a link between the head office in Berlin and Zionist federations in neutral and belligerent countries. The bureau was under the control of the head office in Berlin.

At the end of 1916, Dr. Jacobson took charge of the Copenhagen Bureau and established close contact with the German Legation there. His immediate purpose was to invoke the help of the German Foreign Office in averting the danger to which the Jews and the Jewish institutions in Palestine were exposed from the moment the Turks entered the war.

In July, 1917, Itzhak L. *Goldberg and Yehiel *Tschlenow, leaders of the Russian Zionists, had a meeting in Copenhagen with Jacobson and with the two members of the Berlin Executive, Warburg and Hantke. At this meeting, Goldberg passed on information about the progress of the negotiations which were then being carried on by Chaim *Weizmann and Nahum *Sokolow with the British government. Neither the German members of the Executive nor Tschlenow favored a pro-British orientation but advocated adherence to the principles of neutrality. On returning from Copenhagen, Warburg and Hantke established a German pro-Zionist committee, on the model of the British Palestine Committee, and urged the Foreign Office in Berlin to exercise its influence in Constantinople in favor of Jewish settlement in Palestine. The Copenhagen Bureau remained the link connecting the Zionists of Berlin, Petrograd, London, and, later, the United States and enabled the Berlin office, on the basis of the information received from Copenhagen, to exert pressure on the German government.

With the outbreak of the Bolshevik Revolution in November, 1917, and the elimination of Russian Jewry from the world Jewish scene, the bureau's importance as a center of Zionist diplomacy declined, until it closed down shortly after the end of the war.

The Copenhagen Bureau published a bimonthly *Bulletin* and, on Oct. 28, 1918, issued the *Copenhagen Manifesto. It also published two books by Siegfried Bernstein, one pamphlet by Yehiel Tschlenow, and one by Henri Nathansen, a Danish-Jewish author.   S. Z. ABRAMOV

COPENHAGEN MANIFESTO. Appeal issued by the *Copenhagen Bureau of the *World Zionist Organization on Oct. 28, 1918, in which it set forth the demands of the Jewish people addressed to the forthcoming Paris Peace Conference. It stressed the fact that lasting peace would be achieved only when the just demands of all nations, great or small, were fulfilled and when every nation was given the opportunity to develop its potentialities in the service of mankind. The demands of the Jewish people, as enumerated in the manifesto, were:

1. The confirmation of Palestine in its historical boundaries, which were identical with those set by political and economic necessity, as the National Home of the Jewish people and the creation of the conditions necessary for its unhindered development.

2. The granting of full equality to Jews in all countries.

3. The granting of national autonomy—cultural, social, and political—to the Jewish population in countries of Jewish mass settlement and in all other countries where the Jewish population might demand it.

The appeal called on Zionist organizations in all countries to present these demands to their governments and to the public and to press for their realization through the peace treaty, thereby rendering effective aid to the political endeavors of the World Zionist Organization. It concluded with the statement that on the day of the signing of the peace, through which mankind wished to approach the attainment of the Jewish ideal of eternal peace, the 2,000-year suffering of the Jewish people must be atoned for and compensated and "the Jewish people must become an equal member of the covenant of free nations."

CORALNIK, ABRAHAM. Journalist, essayist, and early promoter of Zionism (b. Uman, Ukraine, Russia, 1883; d. New York, 1937). Coralnik began his literary career in 1903,

when, after his graduation from the University of Vienna, he devoted his first writings to Zionism as a contributor to *Die *Welt,* of which he later became editor. During his long and versatile career he wrote extensively in German, Russian, Hebrew, and Yiddish. After World War I he settled in the United States, where he became one of the chief contributors and editorial writers of the leading Yiddish daily newspaper *Der Tog,* on whose staff he remained until his death. His essays and articles were published in Yiddish in five volumes (Warsaw, 1928) and posthumously in three volumes (New York, 1938).

COUNCIL OF CONTINENTAL ZIONISTS. Body of Zionist organizations of the European continent based in England. Created during World War I by the Jacob Ehrlich Society, the Nahum Sokolow Society, the Czech Zionist Society, Igul, *Bar Kokhba, and the Dutch Zionist Federation, the Council called on the members of its affiliated organizations to join the Zionist district societies and thus to participate in decisions on Zionist policy within the British Zionist movement. The basis of the Council's policy was the demand for Palestine as a Jewish State. The Council was dissolved after the establishment of the State of Israel.

COUNCIL OF THE SEPHARDI COMMUNITY OF JERUSALEM. According to a tradition current among the *Sephardim of Jerusalem, their community was founded by Rabbi Moses ben Nahman (Nachmanides), who went from Spain to Palestine in 1267. The community managed to maintain itself despite many hardships and persecutions, and in 1841 the Turkish government issued a firman (imperial decree), officially appointing for the first time a rabbi (Rabbi Hayim Abraham Gaguin) to serve as Hakham Bashi (chief rabbi) of the Jerusalem community. By a decree issued on May 5, 1865, the Hakham Bashi of Constantinople was recognized as the religious representative of the Jewish millet (nation) in the Ottoman Empire. The ordinances confirmed the religious and secular institutions of the community and their authority and prescribed the manner of elections. The larger communities, including that of Jerusalem, were organized on the pattern of that of Constantinople. At the recommendation of the Hakham Bashi of Constantinople, these communities were recognized by the authorities, and the title of Hakham Bashi was bestowed on their rabbis. The ordinance prescribed that the Hakham Bashi must be a Turkish subject and the son of a Turkish subject. As a result, only Sephardi rabbis were able to occupy this position. The Hakham Bashi of Jerusalem also bore the title *Rishon L'Tziyon, which has been preserved to this day.

Following the British occupation of the country, at the initiative of the leaders of the Jerusalem Sephardi community, the World Federation of Sephardi Jews and later the *World Federation of Sephardi Communities were organized. Under by-laws confirmed by the British Mandatory government (*see* MANDATE FOR PALESTINE), the community was headed by an elected Council consisting of 30 members, which continued to function after the establishment of the State of Israel. A Sephardi list participated in the elections for the First *Knesset, and several of its candidates were elected. As a result of the mass *immigration from Muslim countries and of the contact between the immigrants and the Israeli *political parties, the latter attracted more and more Sephardim and members of the other Middle Eastern Jewish communities. Despite the decrease in the stature and role of the Council, however, its leaders have continued their efforts to guard the interests of the community in governmental and public institutions. The Council has established an institute for the training of rabbis for Sephardi communities in Israel and other countries, it maintains a scholarship fund for the benefit of Sephardi students in high schools and higher educational institutions, and it publishes a monthly, *BaMa'arakha,* devoted to the discussion of political and communal problems and to championing the rights of the community. The main efforts of the Council in the late 1960s were directed to widening educational opportunities for the youth of the Oriental communities (*see* ORIENTAL JEWS) and to the constant endeavor to improve their social, cultural, and economic situation.

M. ATTIAS

COUNCIL OF WOMEN'S ORGANIZATIONS IN ISRAEL.
See MO'ETZET IRGUNE NASHIM.

COWEN, JOSEPH. Merchant and early Zionist leader in England (b. Plymouth, England, 1868; d. London, 1932). A London businessman, Cowen was one of the first British Jews to join Herzl and his Zionist movement. He attended the 1st Zionist *Congress (Basle, 1897) and became one of Herzl's most efficient co-workers in Great Britain. In 1902 he accompanied Herzl on his visit to Constantinople. He was a founder of the *Jewish Colonial Trust, of which he became chairman in 1919. After Herzl's death, Cowen collaborated closely with his successor, David *Wolffsohn, and became the guardian of Herzl's son Hans.

Early in 1907, with a number of other Zionist leaders, Cowen acquired a controlling interest in the *Jewish Chronicle,* which from then on had a clearly pro-Zionist orientation. A founder of the Zionist Federation of Great Britain and Ireland (*see* GREAT BRITAIN, ZIONISM IN), Cowen served for a number of years as its president. During World War I he supported Chaim *Weizmann in his efforts to interest British Jews and non-Jews in the aims of Zionism. In 1916 he became chairman of the first political committee established to conduct organized propaganda in England on behalf of Zionist aspirations, an effort that culminated in the *Balfour Declaration. He also supported Vladimir *Jabotinsky in his campaign for a *Jewish Legion.

Cowen was a member of the *Zionist Commission that was sent to Palestine in 1918 and of the Zionist *Executive (1921–25). He was the prototype for the figure of Joe Levy in Herzl's utopian novel *Old-New Land.*

J. FRAENKEL

CRAFTS IN ISRAEL. The first attempt to develop a new Israeli style in arts and crafts was made in 1906 by Boris *Schatz, who founded the *Bezalel School in Jerusalem, where hundreds of craftsmen representing many different countries and cultural backgrounds worked side by side. However, the objects produced by the Bezalel School in the early days were not so much examples of original Palestinian art as reflections of the multitude of cultures and traditions that were joining to form the new *Yishuv (Jewish population of Palestine). Still, it can be said that the confluence of various traditional Middle Eastern forms and patterns and modern Western techniques and styles proved fruitful to some degree, in that it gave rise to what soon came to be recognized the world over as the Bezalel style.

An important new development took place in the 1930s with

Yemenite jeweler. [Israel Information Services]

the arrival of a number of skilled artisans from Central Europe. While some of these craftsmen, in order to win popular acceptance, made it a point to follow styles associated with countries such as the Scandinavian lands and Italy, they gained new inspiration from the landscape, history, and archeology of the Jewish Homeland and initiated the evolution of an original Israeli style.

Mosaics and Pottery. In the 1950s specialists from France and Italy arrived in Israel to teach the repair and restoration of mosaics unearthed on the sites of ancient synagogues, Roman bathhouses, and Byzantine churches. Impressed by the possibilities of this ancient medium, many Israelis who took the specialists' courses began to create their own designs, some being based on ancient motifs and others on more modern themes. The basic material used for mosaics in Israel is stone, including the blue-green Elat stone, sometimes mixed with seashells, whole or crushed, and with bits of colored glass or potsherds to obtain the desired colors, textures, and contrasts.

The most popular local handicraft in Israel, both among artisans and on the market, is pottery. It also has the longest history. In recent years, pottery several millenniums old has come to light and, with the simple Arab village pottery that carried on the age-old tradition, has afforded inspiration to many modern potters. Using glazes and color schemes of their own invention that are reminiscent of the Negev cliffs, the desert hills, and the vivid hues and patterns of Negev stones, Israeli potters emulate the simple, uncluttered lines of the bowls, vases, ewers, pots, and jars uncovered by archeologists. The production of ceramics is probably the most highly organized

Yemenite basket maker. [Israel Information Services]

of all Israeli handicrafts. It ranges from the many small home industries found in the settlements to the widely known pottery-producing concerns working for export as well as for the domestic market. In B'er Sheva' alone, half a dozen potters are at work, using local Negev clay and baking it in their own kilns.

Glass, Woodwork, and Basketry. Glassblowing, like woodworking and basketry, has not yet reached the industrial stage. The use of glass for ornamental purposes is restricted by the very small number of skilled craftsmen in this field. Ornamental glass produced in Israel includes the blue Hebron glass, with air bubbles blown in or with dark metal flecks, and patina-finished glass, inspired by the vases of the Greco-Roman era, which, buried in the debris of ancient cities, acquired a characteristic iridescent sheen. Outstanding modern work reminiscent of ancient glass has been done by Bar Tal, an artist from Italy who settled in Israel in the early 1960s.

The search for production techniques suited to work with olive wood has continued concomitantly with the development of new designs that best bring out the particular beauty of this material.

Very popular abroad are the gaily colored items of Israeli basketry, which are characterized by unpretentious charm. Basketwork is widely taught in immigrant settlements and *development towns.

Textiles. The influx of immigrants from Yemen and other Middle Eastern countries, coupled with the growing enthusiasm of a number of young Israeli artists and designers, has given rise to a revival of handweaving. Products in this field include a wide range of bedspreads, tablecloths, wall hangings, and rugs made of wool, cotton, linen, or combinations of these materials with synthetic fibers. Some of the handwoven materials have a rough yet airy texture similar to that of Bedouin cloth and come in shades reminiscent of desert sand dunes. The rugs, which are widely used on cool tile floors, are appearing in new forms, including the loomed Porat rug, with its intricate design of lozenges alternating with stripes, made by former cave dwellers from Libya, and the practical and decorative knotted rugs woven by immigrants from Iran and Yemen.

An interesting new line in textiles has evolved from the use of batik, a process originating in Indonesia in which materials are colored through wax. Batik prints are widely used in mural panels and lampshades.

Jewelry and Metalwork. The presence in the country of women of widely differing cultural backgrounds may account for the rich variety of jewelry available in Israel, from the highly ornamental, heavily ornate work for which Yemenites and Iranians are justly famous to the modern classic look much favored in Israel—simple, solid jewelry, much of it in silver, with semiprecious stones (many of them mined in the country) in heavy and unusual settings. The Yemenites, whose lives reflect the ancient tradition they brought with them to Israel, produce a profusion of colorful articles, exquisitely worked, with special appeal to folk art enthusiasts. Their famous filigree patterns appear in various designs on shawls, blouses, handbags, and belts, embroidered or interwoven with fine strands of silver or gold, dramatically offset against backgrounds of black, sand beige, or brick red. These patterns are taken from silver jewelry—handsome collar necklaces, wide bracelets, and long, dangling eardrops set with semiprecious stones.

Though most homes still have their old-fashioned candlesticks and heavily embossed Sabbath tray, the trend in Israel today, in religious art as well as in jewelry, is toward uncluttered silver with a smooth, almost sculptured finish.

A good deal of development has taken place in the fashioning of metalwork. From the simple beginnings in the suq (the Arab market), where copper jars, jugs, plates, bowls, and cups could be picked up for pennies, this traditional art has spread to encompass not only copper but also iron and brass.

For many people in the *Diaspora the entry of the new State of Israel into the world of handicrafts was heralded by the appearance of a multitude of highly colored knickknacks, such as ashtrays and inkstands, made of the heavy green-patina metal which was very popular in the country at one time. To these have been added many attractive articles of copper, in the form of finjans (for serving coffee), jars, and platters, and the ubiquitous candlestick or candleholder in somber black iron, of simple design.

Dolls. Israel-made character dolls represent an entire industry in their own right. The presence in the country of people from more than 80 different places of origin acts as a constant source of inspiration for dollmakers. In addition, many local groups lend themselves readily to portrayal in puppet form. No collection of Israeli dolls is complete without the mystical Bible scholar, the sturdy kibbutznik in shorts and the Israeli national headgear known as the *kova' tembel,* and, of course, Little Israel, the fun figure of so many local cartoons. Apart from appearing in everyday garb, dolls make their debut on the local scene fashioned of wood and ceramics.

Encouragement of Crafts. Israeli craftsmanship is still too highly individual to be called indigenous. It is the lack of overall organization which has so far been the greatest blessing for the renascent arts and crafts industry in Israel in that it affords the artist greater creative freedom. There are, however, several enterprises that encourage local talent, provide training, and serve as outlets for the products of Israeli artisans, particularly newcomers.

The Home Industries Department of the *Women's International Zionist Organization (WIZO), originally known as Shani, set up a project to encourage traditional arts and crafts among Yemenite and other Oriental Jewish immigrants in Israel. WIZO advisers visited these newcomers in their villages and urban residential neighborhoods, providing the craftsmen with the expensive raw materials they needed and informing them of the type of work most likely to have a ready market in Israel and abroad. The finished work was then paid for and either put up for sale at the WIZO Home Industries Shops in Jerusalem, Tel Aviv, and Haifa or exported. In 1966 the WIZO gift shops marketed the products of more than 600 workers, representing 20 countries of origin. Merchandise sold included linen tablecloths, bags and shoes made of Negev flax, and a wide variety of religious objects, embroidered shawls, scarves, aprons, blouses, decorative items, and character dolls.

Maskit, a government-sponsored enterprise founded in 1954 through the initiative of Ruth Dayan, wife of Moshe *Dayan, began by selling the products of 60 workers from 2 villages. By the end of 1965 it had two shops in Tel Aviv and one each in Jerusalem, Nahariya, N'tanya, and Petah Tikva, which processed the products of 600 artisans working in more than 20 villages under the guidance of 20 professional designers and experts. At an exhibit held at a California savings bank in the early 1960s, Maskit sold $50,000 worth of arts and crafts. Maskit wares include handwoven fabrics, wool and cotton rugs, fashion items, jewelry, ornaments, embroidered and handwoven tablecloths and napkins, bedspreads, basketwork, dolls, and toys. They are made of local material—willows from the Hula Valley, wool from Negev flocks, flax from fields in the Lakhish area, and wood from olive trees in the Jerusalem Mountains.

In contrast to the practice of Maskit, the Bathsheva Shop and Bathsheva Crafts, Ltd., in Tel Aviv, founded in 1958 by Bethsabée de Rothschild, concentrates on modern arts and crafts.

The 1960s have brought a fresh upsurge in the development of Israeli arts and crafts. More Israeli artists have been traveling abroad, local buyers have become more affluent and hence more discriminating, and new groups of settlers as well as native inhabitants (Bedouins, Druzes, and Arab villagers) have a larger market than they had in the early days of austerity.

The terse, uncluttered *Hebrew language, the landscape of bright, clean colors, and the *climate characterized by extremes of sunlight and rainfall have all had a profound effect on the work of Israel's artists. It may be expected that the Israeli design of these craftsmen will evolve and be characterized by simplicity to the point of starkness.

M. VARDI AND G. HIRSCHLER

CREECH-JONES, ARTHUR. British labor leader and Cabinet member (b. Bristol, England, 1891; d. London, 1964). A trade union official, Creech-Jones became active in Britain's Labor party, which he represented in Parliament from 1935 until shortly before his death. Considered one of the party's leading experts on colonial affairs, he had expressed pro-Zionist views in Parliament and within the party earlier in his career. When the Labor party came to power in 1945, he was appointed Parliamentary Under-secretary of State to the Colonial Office; in October, 1946, he became Secretary of State for the Colonies, an office he held until the spring of 1950.

It was during his term of office that Anglo-Zionist relations reached their lowest point and that the *Yishuv (Jewish population of Palestine) was in armed revolt against the British administration. Creech-Jones, however, did not deal with the Palestine problem, which because of its gravity was removed from the Colonial Office and transferred to the Foreign Office, then headed by Ernest *Bevin.

A member of the United Kingdom delegation to the UN General Assembly in 1946 and again in 1947–48, Creech-Jones presented the British case regarding Palestine before the Assembly (September, 1947), before the Security Council (February, 1948), and again at the special Palestine session of the Assembly in April, 1948.

CRIME IN ISRAEL. When one attempts to present a picture of criminality in Israel, the data available for Palestine under the British Mandate become significant for purposes of comparison. In Table 1, the data for Jews and non-Jews are presented from 1940 to 1945 (during the mandatory period) and from 1951 to 1960 (after the establishment of the State of Israel).

TABLE 1. CONVICTIONS FOR MAIN OFFENSES BY POPULATION GROUPS, 1940–60, PER 1,000 OF POPULATION

Year	Non-Jews		Jews	
	Aged 9 and above	All ages	Aged 9 and above	All ages
1940	....	13.8	8.7	7.1
1941	....	17.0	7.3	6.0
1942	....	16.5	6.7	5.5
1943	....	17.0	6.1	5.0
1944	....	19.8	6.5	5.3
1945	....	21.3	6.7	5.5
1951	15.2	10.5	8.3	6.6
1952	23.3	16.1	10.9	8.5
1953	24.7	17.1	12.6	9.7
1954	24.3	17.0	11.1	8.5
1955	22.4	15.8	10.0	7.7
1956	23.1	16.3	9.8	7.5
1957	17.8	12.5	10.4	8.0
1958	24.5	17.0	9.9	7.7
1959	20.7	14.2	8.8	6.9
1960	27.4	18.8	9.9	7.8

The table shows that the rate of convictions of Jews increased by about 50 per cent between the end of the mandate and the period following mass *immigration. These figures indicate that the incidence of crime among the Jews in Palestine during the mandatory period was lower than that in Israel of the 1950s. This is not surprising, considering the composition of the Jewish population in the mandatory period, particularly the select, pioneering character of a large part of the immigrants at that time. In view of the rapid growth and increased diversity of the Jewish population following independence, the mass arrivals from underdeveloped countries or from the horrors of the Nazi holocaust, and the hardships of absorption for many of the new immigrants, it is significant that the crime rate did not increase more than it actually did. By the middle 1950s it had settled at a constant level which was maintained for about 10 years. (Data taken from statistical police and court reports indicate a rise, though a relatively slight one, in the general extent of crime in 1962–63.) Together with this stability in the relative crime rate in general, there has been a persistent increase in the percentage of recidivists among the convicted offenders. In 1960 every second offender had had at least one previous conviction.

The rate of conviction for non-Jews at the end of the mandatory period was at about the same, rather high level as it was from 1952 on, after the establishment of the State. The offenses of non-Jews comprised a limited number of types: disturbance of the peace, assaults, thefts, and destruction of property. Quarrels between clans in Arab localities gave rise to violence, sometimes in the form of wholesale brawls, and to a chain of acts of vengeance against property and persons.

Population Growth. In examining the annual figures of criminal statistics, one must take into consideration the rapid growth of the population of the State, adopting 1951 as the base year. This was the first year in which the criminal statistics were

prepared in essentially the same way as in later years, and the average population for 1951 already included persons who had arrived during the mass immigration of the first years of independence.

The data presented in Table 3, which include convicted adult offenders (males aged 17 and above; females aged 19 and above), show that from 1952 to 1960 there was a distinct rise in juvenile delinquency. This was due chiefly to the following factors:

1. An increase in the absolute number of juveniles among the Jews from about 190,000 in 1951 to about 426,000 in 1963 and among the non-Jews from about 36,000 in 1951 to about 54,000 in 1963.

2. An increase in the percentage of juveniles among the Jews from 18 in 1951 to 24 in 1960 and to 25 in 1963.

3. An increase in the percentage of juvenile offenders who were apprehended as a result of the work of special youth branches in the police, which were organized beginning in January, 1959.

Recidivism. For the purposes of the annual statistics, a "recidivist" is defined as a person who has been found guilty

TABLE 2. POPULATION OF ISRAEL AGED 9 AND ABOVE, 1948–62

	Absolute numbers, in thousands				Indices (1951 = 100)			
	1948	1951	1960	1962	1948	1951	1960	1962
Total	654	1,162	1,658	1,793	56	100	143	154
Jews	544	1,045	1,498	1,622	52	100	143	155
Non-Jews	110	117	160	171	94	100	137	146

TABLE 3. OFFENDERS FOUND GUILTY, 1951–60*

Year	Absolute numbers	Indices	Rates	First offenders	Recidivists	Percentage of recidivists	Jews	Non-Jews
All offenders:								
1951	9,392	100.0	8.1	. . . .	. . . .	. . . .	7,080	2,312
1952	15,591	166.0	12.7	. . . .	. . . .	. . . .	11,156	4,435
1953	15,994	170.3	12.7	. . . .	. . . .	. . . .	10,833	5,161
1958	16,999	181.0	11.1	. . . .	. . . .	. . . .	11,915	5,084
1959	16,132	171.7	10.2	. . . .	. . . .	. . . .	11,411	4,721
1960	18,090	192.6	11.1	9,485	8,605	47.6	11,841	6,249
Adults:								
1951	8,320	100.0	8.9	6,360	1,960	23.6	6,222	2,098
1952	13,414	161.2	13.3	10,338	3,076	22.9	9,600	3,814
1953	14,227	171.0	13.9	9,722	4,505	31.7	9,553	4,674
1954	12,836	154.3	12.4	8,071	4,765	37.1	8,623	4,213
1955	12,443	149.6	11.6	7,571	4,872	39.1	7,918	4,525
1956	12,628	151.8	11.4	7,354	5,274	41.8	8,474	4,154
1957	13,736	155.1	11.9	7,782	5,954	43.3	9,674	4,062
1958	14,094	169.4	11.8	7,820	6,274	44.5	9,846	4,248
1959	13,082	157.2	10.7	6,966	6,116	46.7	9,187	3,895
1960	14,102	169.5	11.2	6,825	7,277	51.6	8,969	5,133
Juveniles (boys aged 9–16; girls aged 9–18):								
1951	1,072	100.0	4.8	. . . .	. . . .	. . . .	858	214
1952	2,177	203.1	9.1	. . . .	. . . .	. . . .	1,556	621
1953	1,767	164.8	7.2	. . . .	. . . .	. . . .	1,290	487
1958	2,905	271.0	8.6	. . . .	. . . .	. . . .	2,069	836
1959	3,050	284.7	8.5	. . . .	. . . .	. . . .	2,224	826
1960	3,988	372.0	10.3	2,660	1,328	33.3	2,872	1,116

*As recorded in the charge register of the police. Figures include offenses against Defense (Emergency) Regulations of 1945 but exclude brawls and minor assaults by adults.

TABLE 4. OFFENSES BY POPULATION AND TYPE OF OFFENSE, 1951–60, IN PERCENTAGES

Year	Total	Offenses against public order	Crimes of violence	Sex offenses	Offenses against property	Fraud and forgery	Other offenses
Total population:							
1951	100.0	6.4	19.1	1.8	45.2	1.7	35.8
1952	100.0	5.5	18.0	1.2	43.3	1.3	30.7
1953	100.0	5.7	17.5	1.6	36.1	1.5	37.6
1958	100.0	17.0	21.0	1.9	33.7	1.5	24.9
1959	100.0	17.9	22.6	1.9	34.2	1.7	21.7
1960	100.0	15.5	22.3	2.2	34.5	1.6	23.9
Non-Jewish population:							
1951	100.0	5.0	15.0	0.8	29.7	1.5	48.0
1952	100.0	5.3	15.0	0.5	27.9	0.6	50.7
1953	100.0	2.8	13.2	0.7	19.0	0.4	63.9
1958	100.0	12.9	16.9	0.8	23.5	0.5	45.4
1959	100.0	17.7	17.9	0.9	26.0	0.8	36.7
1960	100.0	11.0	16.9	1.0	22.5	0.5	48.1

in Israel of at least two offenses within one year. During the decade 1951–60 the incidence of recidivism among Jewish adult offenders increased from 1.4 to 3.5 per 1,000; among non-Jews the corresponding figures were 6.6 and 13.9 respectively.

Types of Offense. The available information on the types of offense is summarized in Table 4. We see that offenses against property are always the commonest, offenses against public order and crimes of violence are usually of medium frequency, and sex offenses and fraud and forgery are less common. The 1950s saw a tendency toward a decrease in the proportion of offenses against property and, on the other hand, an increase in the proportion of offenses against public order, crimes of violence, and sex offenses.

TABLE 5. JEWISH OFFENDERS BY PLACE OF BIRTH, 1951–60, IN PERCENTAGES

Year	Israel-born	Asian-born	African-born	European- and American-born
1951	16.8	25.5	13.9	43.8
1952	15.2	32.1	16.4	36.3
1953	14.5	{50.4}		35.1
1958	16.8	28.6	30.7	24.6
1959	16.5	28.7	30.9	23.9
1960	18.5	27.9	32.6	21.0

Ethnic and Social Differentials. Crime rates for Jews, by place of birth, rank as follows in descending order: African-born, Asian-born, Israel-born, European-born. This order has remained stable over the years. Since the mid-1950s the crime rates of the African-born have been about four to five times higher than those of the European-born and almost twice as high as those of the Asian-born. The rates of the Israel-born, consistent with the composite origin of this group, have been between those of the Asian- and African-born, on the one hand, and those of the European-born, on the other (see Table 5).

The tendency shown in Table 5 does not correlate with the changes in the ethnic composition of the Jewish population, as shown in Table 6.

The 1960–61 rates for adult offenders born in specified countries per 1,000 persons of all ages born in those countries and resident in Israel are shown in Table 7. Thus the ranking

TABLE 6. ETHNIC COMPOSITION, IN PERCENTAGES

Year	Israel-born	Asian-born	African-born	European- and American-born
Jews aged 17 and above:				
1951	9.0	18.1	6.4	66.5
1953	9.6	20.7	7.3	62.4
1955	10.9	21.0	9.0	59.1
1958	11.9	20.6	12.9	54.6
1960	13.8	20.4	13.1	52.7
Jews aged 9–16:				
1951	43.9	24.9	9.7	21.5
1953	45.1	27.6	11.1	16.2
1958	43.5	20.9	16.9	18.7
1960	53.0	15.8	14.3	16.9

order of criminal behavior of foreign-born adults, in broad groups and in descending order, is as follows: Moroccan-born; Algerian-, Tunisian-, and Libyan-born; members of Oriental communities from Asia; Asian- and Egyptian-born *Sephardim; Sephardim born in Balkan countries; European- and American-born (except for Balkan countries).

Significant differences can be observed between older and more recent immigrants within each ethnic group, as shown in Table 8. This table presents in concentrated form the great differences in criminality according to population group, place of birth, and period of immigration. The adult crime rates in

TABLE 7. ADULT OFFENDERS PER 1,000 OF SPECIFIED POPULATION, 1960–61

Country of birth	Percentage
All foreign-born	9.6
Morocco	33.4
Algeria, Tunisia, and Libya	18.5
Asia (except for Turkey, Syria, and Lebanon)	15.0
Turkey, Syria, Lebanon, and Egypt	10.6
Greece and Bulgaria	5.7
Hungary and Romania	5.3
Other European countries and America	3.9

TABLE 8. OFFENDERS BY POPULATION GROUP, PLACE OF BIRTH, AND PERIOD OF IMMIGRATION PER 1,000 OF SPECIFIED POPULATION, 1961

	Total	Adults	Juveniles
All offenders	10.9	11.6	8.8
Jews, total	9.5	10.0	8.0
Israel-born, total	8.4	11.6	5.8
Origin, Asia and Africa	16.6–19.5	22.7–29.1	2.1–13.4
Origin, Europe and America	3.4– 3.7	5.2– 5.8	9.1– 2.0
Asia and Africa, total	16.5	17.3	13.5
To 1947	10.3	10.1	} 14.6
1948–54	17.4	18.2	
From 1955 on	17.1	19.3	11.6
Asia, total	13.4	13.9	11.6
To 1947	9.0	8.9	} 12.2
1948–54	14.5	15.1	
From 1955 on	12.5	15.2	5.7
Africa, total	20.8	22.5	15.6
To 1947	20.4	19.0	} 19.2
1948–54	23.4	24.7	
From 1955 on	18.0	20.3	12.7
Europe and America, total	4.7	4.6	5.6
To 1947	3.4	3.4	} 6.3
1948–54	5.3	5.1	
From 1955 on	6.0	6.5	4.3
Non-Jews, total	24.2	28.6	14.0
Muslims	....	34.8	....
Christians	....	18.1	....
Druzes	....	13.8	....

1961 for the groups shown in the table varied from 35 per 1,000 for Muslims to 5 per 1,000 for the European-born. Among the Jews there were marked differences between the high crime rates of the African-born and the Israel-born of Asian and African origin, on the one hand, and the low crime rates of the European-born and the Israel-born of European origin, on the other. Asian-born ethnic groups occupied an intermediate position.

Occupations. The large majority of offenders are described in the police records simply as unskilled laborers. The members of liberal professions, clerks, and sales personnel, on the one hand, and dependents, on the other, constitute rather small groups among the offenders, the first being particularly small among non-Jewish offenders (see Table 9).

Summary. Israel, having brought together populations from widely differing cultural backgrounds, is unique from the demographic point of view. For example, most of the African-

TABLE 9. ADULT OFFENDERS, BY POPULATION GROUP AND OCCUPATION, 1951–60, IN PERCENTAGES

Occupation	1951	1955	1958	1960
Jews:				
Liberal professions, clerks, sales personnel	13.1	14.2	14.9	17.4
Agriculture, industry, construction, transportation, services	73.9	75.2	76.2	76.7
Dependents	13.0	10.6	8.9	5.9
Non-Jews:				
Liberal professions, clerks, sales personnel	4.3	3.3	3.5	7.3
Agriculture, industry, construction, transportation, services	85.1	84.6	87.4	86.9
Dependents	10.6	12.1	9.1	5.8

born immigrants have come from North Africa and belong to the Maghribi community, which, in general, has been characterized by an ethos quite distinct not only from that of the European and American immigrants but also from that of the rest of the Oriental Jews. The clue to the differential crime rates may quite possibly be found in such differences in cultural levels and orientations. It may be that the clash between the cultural codes, norms, and values of these immigrants and those of the receiving community causes a relative increase in the crime rates of such immigrants. The process of integration may also injure the social and economic status of the head of the family, for when he comes to Israel, the different social setup may prevent him from fully exercising his former authority and leave him in a state of confusion in which he cannot retain proper control over his family, so that the children may realize that their father is not the omnipotent patriarch he was supposed to be.

However, these primary findings call for further research into criminality in Israel in relation to the two basic factors of ethnic background and length of sojourn in Israel.

S. SHOHAM AND D. PHILIPP

CROMER, 1ST EARL OF (Evelyn Baring). British Agent and Consul General (1883–1907) in Egypt (b. Cromer, England, 1841; d. London, 1917). In the spring of 1903 he rejected Herzl's plan to establish an autonomous Jewish settlement at El-'Arish in Sinai (see EL-'ARISH SCHEME) because (1) the Egyptian government did not favor the diversion of water from the Nile River for this project, (2) irrigation experts believed the plan impractical, and (3) Cromer felt that the administration of Egypt was complex enough without taking on additional problems.

J. ADLER

CROSSMAN, RICHARD HOWARD STAFFORD. British politician and journalist (b. 1907). Educated at Winchester and at New College, Oxford (where he was a fellow and tutor from 1930 to 1937), Crossman joined the staff of the *New Statesman and Nation,* serving as its assistant editor from 1943 to 1955. During World War II he served briefly with the British Ministry of Information (1939), directed the German section of the Political Intelligence Department of the Foreign Office (1940–43), and served as Deputy Director of Psychological Warfare at Allied headquarters in Algiers (1943–44) and as Assistant Chief of the Psychological Warfare Division at Allied Supreme Headquarters (SHAEF).

Active in Labor politics from the mid-1930s on, Crossman was elected to the British Parliament in 1945 and was still a member in 1968. He was Minister of Housing and Local Government from 1964 to 1966, when he was appointed Lord President of the Council.

In 1946 Crossman was appointed to the *Anglo-American Committee of Inquiry on Palestine by Foreign Secretary Ernest *Bevin. He came to the assignment with little knowledge of Zionism and with an undecided attitude toward it. However, his firsthand observation of the plight of German Jewry under the Nazis (he had spent considerable time in Germany and Austria in the 1930s and had boarded with a Jewish family in Frankfurt on the Main) had aroused his sympathy for the Jews, and his visit to the Nazi concentration camps soon disposed him in favor of the Zionist cause. He led the Labor bloc in Parliament that revolted against Bevin's anti-Zionist policy. Together with Michael Foot, a colleague in Parliament, he published a pamphlet, *A Palestine Munich* (1946), which aroused wide interest in England.

Crossman was the author of *Palestine Mission: A Personal Record* (1947), in which he described his work on the Committee of Inquiry; and *A Nation Reborn,* in which he portrayed the roles of David *Ben-Gurion, Ernest Bevin, and Chaim *Weizmann in the story of the State of Israel. He also wrote numerous articles for the Anglo-Jewish and general press.

CUBA, ZIONISM IN. As early as the 16th century, Cuba had a Jewish community consisting of Marranos from Spain, but this community was destroyed by the Inquisition. After Cuba achieved its independence from Spain in 1898, a new Jewish community was formed by immigrants from the United States, Turkey, and Morocco. During World War I a wave of Jewish immigrants came from Eastern Europe, and the 1930s brought refugees from Nazi persecution. Before the advent of Fidel Castro's regime in 1959, the Jewish community of Cuba numbered 12,000 persons, of whom 5,000 were *Ashkenazim and the rest *Sephardim. Since then the Jewish community in Cuba has been reduced to about 2,100. In the mid-1960s there were four Jewish schools with a combined enrollment of 600.

There were beginnings of Zionist activity in Cuba even before the arrival of the wave of immigrants from Eastern Europe after World War I. Most prominent among Cuba's early Zionists was David Bliss, veteran pioneer and founder of the Zionist Organization and the Jewish Center, of which he was president for a long time. It was Bliss who, in November, 1918, presented a petition to Ricardo Dolz, the President of the Cuban Senate, requesting the Cuban government to give official approval to the *Balfour Declaration. Also present at the interview were Cosmo de la Terriente, chairman of the Senate Committee on Foreign Affairs, and Jorge Fernando de Castro, a member of the editorial staff of the newspaper *El Día,* a friend of Bliss and a supporter of Zionism. As a result of this meeting, the Cuban Congress accorded official recognition to the Balfour Declaration.

In the 1920s, with the coming of immigrants from Europe in large numbers, an active Jewish life began in Cuba. The year 1924 saw the founding of the Centro Hebreo, an institution intended to serve the cultural needs of Jewish youth. That October, a Zionist Organization was founded; it set up a library and reading room and soon sponsored regular meetings and cultural programs, such as lectures, discussions, and choral and dramatic groups. Later, a daily Yiddish-language Zionist radio program was started.

The first *Jewish National Fund campaign, held in 1927, yielded $5,000 within a few days. The first such campaign with active participation of immigrants from Eastern Europe was sponsored by trade unions. Soon thereafter, a League for Labor Palestine was founded. In 1945 the Zionist Organization moved into a new building of its own, the Bet 'Am.

In the 1960s the Zionist movement in Cuba, in addition to the men's organization, included a *Women's International Zionist Organization (WIZO) federation consisting of the Aleph, Bet, Sephardic, Young Women's Chapter, and Hanna *Szenes groups, with a total membership of 1,500, and the following youth groups: *HaShomer HaTza'ir, *HaBonim, and the Youth Club. Nearly all the founders of HaShomer HaTza'ir settled in Palestine, a number of them in kibbutzim.

Prior to the Castro revolution, Cuba's Jewish community actively participated in the campaigns organized by the Jewish National Fund, the *Keren HaYesod (Palestine Foundation Fund), and the *State of Israel Bonds Organization. Following the advent of the Castro regime and the nationalization of industry, 80 per cent of Cuba's Jewish community, which had consisted largely of businessmen and industrialists, left the country. The majority went to the United States; several hundred settled in Israel. While it was no longer possible to raise funds for Israel in Cuba, educational and cultural activity showed no signs of abating. Special attention was given to the teaching of the *Hebrew language, and attendance at some of the Zionist gatherings held in Havana was as large as 700 to 800 persons.

In the 1960s the officers of the Zionist Organization of Cuba were Moshe Baldas, president and official *Jewish Agency representative; Azriel Weitz, secretary; Hayim Terner, treasurer; Joseph Blumenkrantz, administrator; and Eliezer Aronowsky, cultural director. The Zionist Organization continued to be active despite the reduced numbers of the Jewish population and the emigration of many Zionist leaders.

E. ARONOWSKY

CULTURAL ZIONISM (Spiritual Zionism). Term commonly used to designate a philosophy of Jewish *nationalism which, while believing that a measure of reconcentration in its historic Homeland is necessary for the Jewish people, does not accept the postulate of political Zionism that the main reason for that belief is to be found in the persistence of *anti-Semitism and the political and economic disabilities of the Jewish masses. Instead, it sees the greatest threat to Jewish survival under modern conditions in the internal weaknesses of Jewry, in the loss of its sense of unity, and in the weakening of the hold of traditional values, ideals, and hopes. Pre-Herzlian nationalists such as Moses *Hess and Peretz *Smolenskin had emphasized the importance of the cultural factor in Jewish nationalism, and it had its place in the Hibbat Zion movement (*see* HOVEVE ZION); but it was *Ahad Ha'Am who most fully and logically developed the implications of the spiritual or cultural approach, with its insistence on loyalty to the *Hebrew language and the values historically associated with Judaism. When Herzl put forward his Jewish State proposal, Ahad Ha'Am became his foremost critic. He rejected the notion that the primary purpose of the Jewish State should be to provide a "home of refuge" for the victims of anti-Semitism and that the State could be established in a comparatively short time by means of diplomatic and financial activity alone, without any prior attempt to create the necessary psychological and spiritual conditions within Jewry itself. For him the "plight of the Jews," however serious, did not present so urgent a problem as the "plight of Judaism"; and he held that the first aim of the national movement should not be the attainment of political sovereignty, for which in his opinion the Jewish people could wait as long as might be necessary, but the establishment of conditions under which it could regain *spiritual* independence and the possibility of full and free development along the lines dictated by its own spirit and character. He wanted Palestine to be the home of a Jewish settlement which could become the "national spiritual center" of the scattered people and as such would contribute powerfully to that "revival of the spirit" which, in his view, was an indispensable precondition of a successful effort to establish a *Jewish* State when external circumstances became favorable. Spiritual Zionism as preached by Ahad Ha'Am was too uncompromising to have any chance of becoming the basis of a popular movement. However, when the political hopes of Herzl's *World

Zionist Organization in its early years were thwarted and Herzl himself was removed by an untimely death, control passed into the hands of the "practical" wing of the Organization, many of whose leaders were among Ahad Ha'Am's friends or admirers and had been adherents of the Hoveve Zion movement before Herzl came on the scene. Thenceforward the ideas for which Ahad Ha'Am stood were to some extent reflected in Zionist policy.

SIR LEON SIMON

CUNNINGHAM, SIR ALAN GORDON. British soldier and last British *High Commissioner for Palestine (b. Dublin, 1887). Educated at the Royal Military Academy, he had a distinguished

Sir Alan Cunningham.
[Zionist Archives]

military career, rising to the rank of general in 1945. In the fall of that year he was appointed to succeed Viscount *Gort as High Commissioner for Palestine. Cunningham was not inimical to the Jews and Zionism, but the major decisions concerning Palestine policies were not in his sphere of competence; they were handled by the British Foreign Office. Cunningham's task was to keep order during the sessions of the *Anglo-American Committee of Inquiry and the *United Nations Special Committee on Palestine (UNSCOP) in the face of growing Jewish opposition to British policy, *illegal immigration, acts of sabotage by the *Hagana, and attacks by the *Irgun Tz'vai L'umi and the Stern group (see LOHAME HERUT ISRAEL).

After the quota of 75,000 allowed under the *White Paper of 1939 had been exhausted, legal *immigration into Palestine was limited to 1,500 persons per month. All the other Jews who reached the shores of Palestine were sent to Cyprus (see CYPRUS, DETENTION CAMPS IN). An abortive effort was made to split the Jewish community into extremists and moderates and to oust the *Jewish Agency from control. This culminated in the arrests of numerous leaders of the *Yishuv (Jewish population of Palestine) on June 29, 1946. Jewish resistance was to be suppressed by curfews, arms searches, arrests, and executions. However, the British failed in this attempt.

In January, 1947, Cunningham was authorized to use his discretion in enforcing statutory martial law in any area of the country. After the United Nations resolution of Nov. 29, 1947, for the *partition of Palestine, the British Mandatory government (see MANDATE FOR PALESTINE) failed to keep order and to prevent infiltration from the Arab countries. Law enforcement and personal security were limited to British enclaves and to the main highways vital to British evacuation. Although the

government still maintained a certain role of arbitration between the fighting sides in order to prevent excesses, the administration as a whole collapsed.

On May 8, 1948, a truce was reached between the Jews and the Arabs in Jerusalem, so that the High Commissioner was able to leave a semblance of peace in the capital city. On May 14, the day the State of Israel was proclaimed, he left the country from Haifa.

I. KOLATT

CURAÇAO, ZIONISM IN. Curaçao, the largest island and capital of the group known as the Netherlands Antilles, is the site of the oldest Jewish settlement in the Western Hemisphere. The community of *Sephardim dates back to 1651, and its famous synagogue was dedicated in 1732. In 1968 the Jewish population of Curaçao was estimated at 700.

Zionist activity in Curaçao grew out of an organization founded in 1941 and called the Joodsch Hulp Comité (Jewish Aid Committee). In 1945 Rev. Isaac Jessurun Cardozo, with the help of Henri Perlman, called a meeting to found a Zionist organization. In 1946 these same people organized the Curaçao *Jewish National Fund under the chairmanship of José Abady, and in 1949 their wives and several other women organized the Curaçao branch of the *Women's International Zionist Organization (WIZO). The organization was chartered by the government in 1949.

During World War II and immediately thereafter, American, European, and Palestinian representatives of *Keren HaYesod (Palestine Foundation Fund) came to Curaçao periodically for campaigns. They were usually helped by the Reverend Cardozo and by individuals from the Club Union, the Ashkenazi social and religious organization (see ASHKENAZIM). Generally, the Sephardim, whose families had been in Curaçao for two or three centuries, had little connection with Jewish affairs overseas.

In 1949, after returning from a trip to Israel, William Cohen, a local merchant, with the help of Cardozo and the leaders of the Club Union, organized the United Jewish Aid Committee (UJAC). Whereas the Joodsch Hulp Comité was designed to aid refugees and other distressed Jews in Curaçao, the UJAC was formed to conduct an annual campaign for Keren HaYesod and for other smaller Jewish organizations and Yeshivot outside Curaçao. Cohen also set up weekly television broadcasts about Israel on all major channels and stations in the Netherlands Antilles. In recognition of his work, he was appointed honorary Consul of Israel in Curaçao in 1956.

S. J. MASLIN

CURRENCY OF ISRAEL. See FINANCE IN ISRAEL.

CYPRUS, DETENTION CAMPS IN. Detention camps maintained by the British in Karaolos and Xylotymbou, Cyprus, for Jews who arrived in, or were en route to, Palestine on illegal transports between 1946 and 1948. With the increasing arrivals of shiploads of illegal immigrants (see ILLEGAL IMMIGRATION) organized by *Hagana and *B'riha in the post-World War II period, the British abandoned the policy of detaining "illegals" in Palestine and decided to deport them, instead, to the Mediterranean island of Cyprus for internment. The first transports to meet this fate were those arriving on the S.S. "Yagur" and S.S. "Henrietta Szold," which landed at Haifa in August, 1946. The 1,300 immigrants aboard were forcibly transferred by British soldiers to British ships and taken to Cyprus. While the immigrants were being transferred from their ships, Haifa Jews, in violation of curfew regulations, struggled with the British in an attempt to break into the sealed-off port area and to come to the aid of the illegals.

The British hoped that the deportation of immigrants to Cyprus would deter further illegal Jewish immigration. However, shiploads of illegals continued to arrive. Though half of the 1,500 "legal" immigration certificates provided monthly by the British government were allocated to detainees in Cyprus, the camp population kept growing and became a burden to the British. By June, 1947, about 15,000 illegals were being detained in Cyprus.

Upon the arrival of the S.S. *"Exodus 1947" at the shores of Palestine in July, 1947, with more than 4,500 people aboard, the British decided to ship immigrants back to Europe. The subsequent odyssey of these immigrants and the worldwide reaction to their suffering forced the British to revert to their policy of deporting illegals to Cyprus. They continued this policy until the end of the British *Mandate for Palestine, by which time more than 30,000 immigrants were being detained in camps on the island.

The camps were under the joint control of the British Foreign Office, the Colonial Office, the Palestine administration, and the British Army. The internal administration, however, was completely in the hands of the detainees. The camp committees were composed of representatives of the Zionist parties with which the detainees were affiliated. Undercover emissaries of Hagana were active in the camps, recruiting and training people and organizing escapes.

The *American Jewish Joint Distribution Committee (JDC) played a major role in the support and organization of life in the camps. It supplemented the food rations of the detainees and provided special diets for the ailing, for pregnant women, and for children. It brought from Palestine teachers, nurses, and social workers and organized extensive social and educational programs, including a school system from kindergarten to university level, vocational training, Hebrew courses for all, the publication of newspapers, and the formation of artistic ensembles and theatrical troupes. It also catered to the religious needs of the detainees. The JDC issued its own camp scrip, or money, valid only in the camps.

The British promised to release all internees at the end of the mandate, but the promise was broken in the case of immigrants who were considered to be of military age. The continued detention of a large number of immigrants even after the establishment of the State of Israel resulted in the filing of writs of habeas corpus against the British authorities. While the case dragged on, the British government announced the release of all remaining internees in January, 1949. Within a few weeks the last 10,280 illegals were brought to Israel.

Detainees on a muddy street in Camp Xylotymbou, Cyprus. [Zionist Archives]

All in all, 51,000 Jewish immigrants passed through the Cyprus detention camps during the $2\frac{1}{2}$ years of the camps' existence. Of these, 1,800 internees reached Palestine after escaping from the camps; 110 immigrants, including 49 children, died in Cyprus and were buried in the Jewish cemetery in Margo. Two thousand children were born in the camps.

The attitude of the island's population was throughout the period one of friendship and assistance. Many Cypriots helped in the escapes, giving shelter to the escapees and aiding them in reaching Palestine. As a token of gratitude to the Cypriots for their assistance to the detainees, the Israeli government in 1949 financed the building of a playground on the island.

T. PRESCHEL

CYPRUS PROJECT. Plan to establish a Jewish settlement on the Mediterranean island of Cyprus. Soon after Cyprus passed from Turkish to British rule in 1878, voices were heard in the Jewish world for the establishment of a Jewish settlement on the island. In 1883 an attempt at agricultural settlement was made by a group of Russian Jews. This was followed by similar unsuccessful attempts by Romanian Jews in 1885 and 1891. A small settlement of Russian Jews was founded in 1897 at Margo Chiflik under the auspices of the *Jewish Colonization Association and the Ahavat Zion settlement society of London. It existed for some years and then disbanded.

In 1898 Davis *Trietsch, an early adherent of the Zionist movement, advocated the Jewish colonization of Cyprus, which was to form part of a "Greater Palestine." He had conceived the idea several years earlier and had corresponded about it with Herzl. Though he received some unofficial encouragement from Herzl and other Zionist leaders, the Zionist *Congress did not allow Trietsch to present his idea and the Jewish Colonization Association remained cool to it. In 1899 Trietsch founded a committee of Jewish leaders in Berlin to carry out his scheme. He entered into negotiations with the Cyprus authorities and went to the island to make arrangements for the prospective Jewish colonists. On his way to Cyprus he visited Galicia and Romania, where he found much enthusiasm for his plan. In the spring of 1899 the first group of immigrants, consisting of 13 Jewish workers from Borislav, Galicia, organized by the Berlin committee, arrived in Cyprus. At that time, too, a group of Jews came from Romania. The latter had arrived against the advice of Trietsch, who had warned them against emigration without previous arrangement with his committee. The Borislav workers found conditions unsatisfactory and subsequently returned to Galicia.

Despite this failure, Trietsch did not give up his idea. He tried to win over the 5th Zionist Congress (1901) to his concept of a Greater Palestine, and since Palestine proper was not yet open for colonization, he called for the colonization of "Egyptian Palestine," El-'Arish (see EL-'ARISH SCHEME).

During his first meeting with British Colonial Secretary Joseph *Chamberlain, on Oct. 22, 1902, Herzl suggested that permission be given for the establishment of Jewish settlements in Cyprus, the Sinai Peninsula, and El-'Arish. Chamberlain's reaction to the Cyprus plan (the only one of the three over which, as Colonial Secretary, he had jurisdiction) was negative. He pointed out that Jewish immigration into Cyprus would encounter great difficulties but expressed sympathy with the El-'Arish project. Thereafter, Herzl confined his negotiations with the British government to El-'Arish.

After the 6th Zionist Congress (1903), at which Herzl reported

that the El-'Arish–Sinai plan could not be carried out and presented the offer by the British government of a possible Jewish settlement in British East Africa (see EAST AFRICA SCHEME), Trietsch, unaware of the British government's negative attitude toward Jewish immigration to Cyprus, demanded efforts at Jewish colonization on the island. He continued to approach the British authorities on behalf of his Cyprus scheme until the end of 1903, when he was told that they could grant no special privileges to Jewish immigration beyond the ordinary regulations pertaining to the purchase of land and to the aid of destitute immigrants.

CZACZKES, SH'MUEL YOSEPH. See AGNON, SH'MUEL YOSEPH.

CZECHOSLOVAKIA, ZIONISM IN. With the establishment of Czechoslovakia in 1918, after World War I, the formation of a completely new Zionist organizational structure became inevitable. The territorial composition of the new republic made it necessary that the Zionist movement, too, transcend the political boundaries within which it had developed in the prewar years. Prior to 1918 Bohemia and Moravia-Silesia constituted separate, and in many respects autonomous, districts within the West Austrian Zionist Organization, while Slovakia and Subcarpathian Ruthenia were integral parts of the Hungarian Zionist Organization with no autonomous local or regional organizational activity (see AUSTRIA, ZIONISM IN; BOHEMIA AND MORAVIA, ZIONISM IN; HUNGARY, ZIONISM IN). More significant than these external differences were the ideological contrasts. In Bohemia and Moravia-Silesia the Zionist movement long before 1918 had ranked among the important Zionist groups and had left its mark on the ideological development of the World Zionist movement. In Slovakia and Subcarpathian Ruthenia, on the other hand, although various Zionist groups had been in existence since the beginning of the movement, no organization of any significance had emerged, with the probable exception of the religious Zionists, organized in *Mizrahi.

Temporary Central Committee. Actual Zionist work commenced with the first meeting, held in Prague, of Zionist leaders from Bohemia and Moravia-Silesia (Jan. 5, 1919), at which a temporary Zionist Central Committee was set up pending a territorial conference. The committee consisted of the Executive Committee in Prague (Dr. Ludwig *Singer, president, and Norbert Adler, Josef Frey, Paul Grönberg, Viktor Kohn, and Rudolf Wodička, members) and of a larger council of representatives of various local Moravian Zionist groups. This committee laid the foundation for what was to emerge as the Czechoslovak Zionist Territorial Federation. As one of its first acts, the committee drew up new organization statutes whereby each city and town was to have a single Zionist group, comprising all existing local Zionist societies. All the local groups in each area constituted a district. Thus there were Zionist districts in Bohemia (with headquarters in Prague) and Moravia-Silesia (with headquarters in Moravská Ostrava). The provisional committee in Prague immediately initiated contact with Slovakia, and in August, 1919, that territory was proclaimed a newly created district (with headquarters in Bratislava). A temporary joint Zionist-Mizrahi district was formed at the same time in Subcarpathian Ruthenia (with headquarters in Sevluš), but it was definitely proclaimed only in October, 1920 (with headquarters in Mukačevo).

Apart from these first organizational steps, the Prague office laid the foundations for subsequent Zionist activity. It registered the *Jewish National Fund with the authorities, and it established a Palestine Commission that took charge of both *'Aliya (immigration) and *Hakhshara (agricultural training) for Halutzim (pioneers; see HALUTZIYUT). It maintained close contact with the head office of the *World Zionist Organization (WZO), at first in Copenhagen and later in London.

Territorial Conferences. The functions of the provisional Central Committee were handed over to the leadership elected at the 1st Zionist Territorial Conference (Prague, July, 1919). This conference, which was attended by 97 delegates from Bohemia, Moravia, and Slovakia, elected a new executive body, with headquarters in Prague, consisting of Norbert Adler, Alex Feig, Ernst Lebenhart, Hugo Slonitz, and Emil Thein (chairman), and of a larger Council with three representatives from the Bohemian province, eight from Moravia-Silesia, seven from Slovakia, and one from Subcarpathian Ruthenia.

By the time the 2d Zionist Territorial Conference assembled in Brno (March, 1921), the organization had grown to include 66 local groups in Bohemia, 60 in Moravia-Silesia, 55 in Slovakia, and 11 in Subcarpathian Ruthenia, with a total of 7,632 *Shekel-paying members. The deeper penetration of Zionism in the eastern sector of the republic made it necessary to transfer the organization's headquarters nearer to these areas of larger Jewish concentration. The conference therefore decided to transfer the seat of the Executive Committee from Prague to Moravská Ostrava, where it remained until 1939. Dr. Joseph *Rufeisen was elected president of the Territorial Federation, holding office until 1938, when he resigned and was succeeded by Pavel März (later Meretz). Franz Kahn was secretary to the Executive Committee throughout this period. The other committee members, elected at every Territorial Conference, were in charge of the following departments: Athletic, *Diaspora Political Activities, Finance, *HeHalutz, Jewish National Fund, Jewish Religious Congregations, *Keren HaYesod, Organization, Palestine Commission, Press, Propaganda, Schools and Culture (*Tarbut) Commission, Women's, and Youth. The names of these departments indicate the varied areas of Zionist endeavor in which Czechoslovak Zionists engaged in their 20 years of activity.

The supreme body of the federation was the Territorial Conference, consisting of delegates elected on the basis of votes cast by Shekel payers. The Territorial Conference made decisions on all major issues pertaining to Zionist activities and elected the Executive Committee and the Council. The Council consisted of representatives from the four districts and the various groupings within the Territorial Federation and of delegates-at-large ("virilists," or those chosen on the basis of personal merit in Zionist work). The Council was the highest authority between Territorial Conferences and made decisions on all questions pertaining to Zionist activities as they arose. It was headed by a chairman and two vice-chairmen. Altogether, 12 Territorial Conferences were held between 1919 and 1938. The final one met in March, 1938, in Moravská Ostrava.

When Czechoslovak Zionists first began to organize in 1918, the Zionist Territorial Federation, which then emerged, comprised the masses of Zionists who had been members of their respective local Zionist societies prior to 1918 and "automatically" remained within the federation. They were brought together not by any particular ideology or specific aspect of policy, or of problems pertaining to specific conditions in Palestine, but by the simple desire to be Zionists and to make

their contribution to the movement. Such a general view could not long remain the basis of a viable Zionist organization. Rapid developments directly affecting Zionism and its work necessitated a diversification that grew as political, cultural, and economic problems multiplied. These problems affected the World Zionist movement, and Czechoslovakia became a fertile ground for new trends and developments.

*Hitahdut. The first change occurred under the impact of the Prague World Conference of *HaPo'el HaTza'ir–*Tz'ire Zion (1920), which subsequently merged and assumed the name Hitahdut (1922). Several prominent members of *Bar Kokhba of Prague, in association with other Zionists and particularly with a Zionist group in Brno, formed the first branches of HaPo'el HaTza'ir in Prague and Brno. Their leaders were Samuel Hugo *Bergmann (who emigrated to Palestine soon thereafter), Max *Brod, Oskar Epstein, Adolf Grünfeld, Siegfried Spitz, and Karl Teller. Epstein was in charge of the headquarters in Prague. For almost a year this organization remained outside the Territorial Federation, adhering to the opposition policy followed by its world movement. When Hitahdut joined the World Zionist *Executive in 1921, however, the Czechoslovak branch joined the Territorial Federation as an independent group. It differed with the majority in the federation primarily on the question of political activities in the Diaspora, maintaining that such activities were an integral part of Zionist work, whereas the federation's 2d Territorial Conference (1921) had decided to support the establishment of a new organization for Diaspora activities, which became the Jewish party. At first, HaPo'el HaTza'ir (Hitahdut) registered some striking successes, but by 1924, owing to almost complete identity in Zionist political pursuits with the majority in the federation, Hitahdut was no longer noticeably active in Czechoslovakia.

*Radical Zionists. The first split in the ranks of the Territorial Federation was followed in 1923 by the formation of the Radical Zionist (or Democratic Zionist) faction, which arose within the Territorial Federation and remained within it until 1934, when its members seceded and formed an independent Association of Political Zionists. The faction was initiated and led by Emil *Margulies, who was assisted in organizational and propaganda work by such Radical Zionist leaders as Alfred Engel, Pavel März, Miriam Scheuer, and Fritz Tauber. The Radical Zionist faction was an opposition group whose main interest centered in the policies and affairs of the World Zionist movement. It therefore did not deal with strictly Czechoslovak Zionist problems except for the question of support of Chaim *Weizmann's policies, to which the majority of the Territorial Federation adhered. The Radical Zionists never established a proper organization in the republic, nor did they form a youth organization, as most other Zionist groupings did. The faction therefore remained a loose association of like-minded Zionists, and therein lay both its weakness and its strength.

Zionist Realists. In 1925 another group within the federation created its own organization—the Zionist Realists. Its leaders came from the ranks of the Hitahdut, which had ceased activities in Czechoslovakia by 1924. The Zionist Realists, taking their name from the Realist party led by Tomáš G. Masaryk at the beginning of the century, were the only Czechoslovak Zionist grouping that was not a branch of a worldwide movement. The group demanded a realistic approach to Zionist activity and, in fact, returned to the opposition program which the Hitahdut world movement had pursued before joining the

World Zionist Executive (1921–28). In addition to advocating the political program formulated at the Prague Conference of the Hitahdut (1920), the Zionist Realists fought for fundamental changes in Zionist propaganda, based on practical conditions and developments in Palestine and within world Jewry. They further suggested reforms in the WZO and set themselves up as an alternative to the existing Zionist leadership of Czechoslovakia. These activities, which were centered in Brno (Moravia), were led by Oskar Epstein and a number of his colleagues at the Brno Jewish High School, among them Eduard Drachmann, Ernst Lemberger, Leopold Schnitzler, and Alois Zaitschek. Their delegates attended the 7th Zionist Territorial Conference (Brno, July, 1926), but none of their suggestions was adopted. They continued to be active for several years, engaging primarily in distributing circulars and publicizing their ideas in the press. They did not achieve success as an organization. Their importance at that critical juncture in Zionism and in Palestine lay in their ability to help avoid complete stagnation by stimulating debates on Zionist issues all over the republic.

Working Association of Socialist Zionists. Other members of the former Hitahdut in Czechoslovakia, who did not join the Zionist Realist ranks, met during the 7th Zionist Territorial Conference and decided to form a group that later emerged as a new organization under the name Working Association of Socialist Zionists. The initiative for the new group came from Adolf Grünfeld and Karl Teller, both of Brno. Their first success occurred when they reached agreement with the leaders of the Territorial Federation to submit to the 15th Zionist *Congress (Basle, 1927) a joint list of candidates under the heading "left center." The principal ideologist in Czechoslovakia of this concept, which had been imported from Germany, was Hugo *Herrmann, who soon thereafter became a leader in the General Zionist party (see GENERAL ZIONISM). The program of the group was based on a synthesis of the Socialists ("left") and the middle group ("center") of the Territorial Federation; it gave its support to Chaim Weizmann's policies and to labor in Palestine. However, this united group did not survive the Congress, at which a dispute broke out between Weizmann and the labor groups. The two Socialist Zionist delegates from Czechoslovakia voted with labor, and the four other delegates supported Weizmann.

During this critical period the association decided to concentrate on a new organizational drive, which after a few years brought it striking successes. The members were joined by a group of young men who soon emerged as the new leaders of the association in Czechoslovakia. Prominent among these were Dov Biegun, Jakob *Edelstein, Oskar Karpe, Hayim *Kugel, Hans Lichtwitz, Oskar *Neumann, Samuel Rosenkranz, and Viktor Zaitschek. The association's main working basis was the newly created Liga für das Arbeitende Erez Israel (League for Labor Palestine; see PO'ALE ZION), which had been formed in many countries as a nonpolitical group for supporters of Labor Palestine. Actually, however, it was led and headed by Socialist Zionists. Simultaneously, the association began organizational work all over the republic, and within five years it became the strongest grouping in the federation. The association was able to count on the support of *T'khelet-Lavan youth groups and of *HaShomer HaTza'ir, which had become a strong youth organization, particularly in the areas of large Jewish concentration in the eastern section of the republic.

The association adopted the policy pursued by the leaders

of Hitahdut on the international scene. After the reentry of world leaders into the Zionist Executive under Weizmann's presidency, the association supported all the policies of the Executive and the demands of the labor movement in Palestine. As for strictly Czechoslovak problems, the association remained in the Zionist Territorial Federation, within which it concentrated on matters relating to Hakhshara and the 'Aliya Palestine Office (see PALESTINE OFFICES), since it considered this work its link with labor in Palestine.

Between 1927 and 1935 the association held five territorial conferences, at which it assessed its growth and adopted policies. The last conference was held in Moravská Ostrava (January, 1935), where it elected its last group of leaders (Dov Biegun, Fini Brada, Jakob Edelstein, Kurt Grünberger, Oskar Karpe, Hans Lichtwitz, Ernst Polak, and Felix Resek), whose sole task was to establish a united organization of all existing Socialist Zionist groups in Czechoslovakia.

Zionists-*Revisionists. The first leaders and members of the Zionists-Revisionists, who were organized in Brno in 1924, also came from the ranks of the Zionist Territorial Federation. The founding committee consisted of Hans Löw, Leo Pollak, and Oskar K. *Rabinowicz. The official Union of Zionists-Revisionists in Czechoslovakia was established at its first territorial conference (Brno, 1925) with Vladimir *Jabotinsky in attendance. The newly elected leadership consisted of Oskar K. Rabinowicz, chairman, Hans Löw, secretary, and Karl Baum, Leo Baumgarten, Leo Hickl, and Leo Pollak. Baumgarten represented Czechoslovakia on the World Council of the Revisionist movement. The organization was helped in spreading its ideas by the weekly Die Jüdische Volksstimme (edited by Hugo Gold), which permitted the Revisionists to use its pages as their forum. Thus, the Revisionists formed the only group in the Territorial Federation that was able to disseminate its ideas freely through a weekly newspaper. The conference decided that the Revisionists should join the Zionist Territorial Federation as a group, and they did so in 1926, remaining until 1932, when they seceded from the federation.

At the second territorial conference (Brno, November, 1927), which was attended by representatives from all over the republic, Julius Grosz announced the formation of a youth organization, *B'rit Trumpeldor (Betar), which was to become the heart and soul of Revisionist activities in Czechoslovakia. The Revisionist organization grew rapidly, and by 1929 it became necessary to move its headquarters to Bratislava, in Slovakia, which was closer to the area of large Jewish concentration and from which it was headed by Rabinowicz. Meanwhile, a number of prominent Zionists joined the Revisionist movement, became leaders in their respective areas, and were elected to its Council at various conferences. They included Oskar Better, Leopold L. Gottesmann, Martin Lichtner, Viktor Kohn, Josef Löwy, Moshe Rubinstein, Alexander Spiegel, Arno Stampf, Béla Szerényi, and Emanuel Weinberger. In 1929 Szerényi put his Hungarian-language weekly Zsidó Néplap (which appeared in Užhorod, Subcarpathian Ruthenia) at the disposal of the movement, thus giving the Revisionists two forums.

The Czechoslovak Zionists-Revisionists operated as an integral part of the world movement and did not concern themselves with strictly Czechoslovak issues. They were concerned primarily with implementing the policies that the world movement adopted at its various conferences as the Revisionist program. The group began as an opposition party, aiming to take over the leadership of Czechoslovak Zionism, just as the Revisionist world movement sought control of the World Zionist Executive. In the course of its development, however, it became clear that it would have to abandon this aim and focus its concern on building its organizational structure, which eventually was to emerge as an independent body outside the World Zionist movement.

The Revisionist program encompassed all aspects of Zionist endeavor in Palestine and the Diaspora. Its firm opposition to World Zionist leadership embroiled the Revisionists in heated debates with all the other Zionist parties. These differences did not involve strictly Czechoslovak issues but changes in the general political, economic, and financial structure of the World Zionist movement. Such changes could be effected only by attaining a majority in Zionist ranks in each country. But the debates in Czechoslovakia itself absorbed much of the energies of the organization and deflected it from positive pursuits. Accordingly, the Czechoslovak Revisionists, in order to free themselves from these complications, seceded from the Territorial Federation in 1932 and formed a branch of the *New Zionist Organization in 1935.

The Czechoslovak Revisionist organization, which was based on local activities, was headed by a chairman (for most of the period this office was occupied by Oskar Rabinowicz; Hans Löw also served as chairman for a time) and an Executive Committee. Altogether, five territorial conferences were held between 1926 and 1935. From 1934 on the organization had its own organ, Der Judenstaat, which, beginning in 1935, was owned by Rabinowicz, who also served as its editor. The final act of the Revisionist organization (May, 1935) was the holding of a plebiscite in which the membership was asked to decide whether or not it wanted to remain in the WZO. In Czechoslovakia 5,826 duly registered members voted for secession; 140 were opposed. Long before that decision, the Revisionists in Czechoslovakia had paved the way for the formation of an independent group by building up their organization and its subdivisions. They formed a *B'rit HaHayal body, a group of veterans within the movement, headed by Julius Grosz and Berci Baeck; B'rit Yeshurun, a religious faction, headed by Franz Hochhäuser; the woman's organization *B'rit Nashim L'umiyot, headed by Mrs. Emilie Kohn; and a financial instrument, Keren Tel Hai, headed by Alexander Rabbinowitz.

*Jewish State Party. The vote on secession from the WZO was preceded by a controversy within the movement, on whether the Revisionist organization was to be declared an independent body whose members would be free to join or not to join the WZO as they chose. In 1933 this controversy resulted in a schism in the world movement that was reflected in the ranks of Czechoslovak Zionism. Some 350 Revisionists there decided to follow the world leadership of the new Jewish State party, of which they established a Czechoslovak branch at their first territorial conference (August, 1933). The party was headed by Yitzhak Greidinger of Užhorod, Marcell Färber, Jakob Fränkel, Fritz Horowitz, Fritz Steckelmacher, and Ernst Vogel. When the Revisionists left the WZO in 1935, some prominent Revisionists did not follow suit but joined the Jewish State party. The most prominent of them was Martin Lichtner, formerly chairman of the Czechoslovak Revisionist Central Committee.

When it appeared that the Jewish State party could identify itself politically, ideologically, and in many other respects with Emil Margulies and his group, the two parties joined forces

for elections to the 19th Zionist Congress (Lucerne, 1935) but received only 1,208 votes and no mandate. At its second territorial conference (Prostějov, May, 1937), with the participation of Robert *Stricker, the party transferred its headquarters from Prostějov to Prague and Jakob Fränkel became the new chairman. Despite all efforts, however, the party was unable to get more than 352 votes for the 20th Congress (Zurich, 1937). Thereafter it became inactive.

General Zionists. By 1927–28 it had become alarmingly obvious to the center bloc of the Zionist Territorial Federation that the proliferation of various new and preexisting groupings and parties was making inroads in the membership of the center bloc. With other federations of the WZO it attempted to reverse the trend, but it was only thanks to the initiative of Isaac Ignacy *Schwarzbart, head of the Zionist Territorial Federation of Western Galicia, that a conference of the leaders of the various center blocs was held in Zurich during the 16th Zionist Congress (1929) and there decided to form a General Zionist Organization. Joseph Rufeisen joined the world leadership of the new movement. But the next Zionist Congress (Basle, 1931) showed that there was fragmentation within General Zionism itself. At that Congress, Chaim Weizmann was not reelected to the presidency of the WZO and was succeeded by Nahum *Sokolow. Of the 85 General Zionist delegates at the Congress, 58 voted against Weizmann. The minority that remained faithful to him and his policies included the delegates from Czechoslovakia. The General Zionists then split into two parts, General Zionists A (the Weizmann adherents) and General Zionists B (his opponents). The General Zionist Organization of Czechoslovakia remained in group A until the collapse of the republic.

Several years were to pass before the General Zionist Organization was formally established in Czechoslovakia at an initial territorial conference (Brno, June, 1934). The delay was due to the fact that the leaders of the Territorial Federation were then identical with those of the General Zionists. These leaders still hoped that, because of their pro-Weizmann and prolabor policy, the General Zionists in Czechoslovakia could find a basis for closer coordination with the left-wing groups, which pursued the same policies. But these hopes failed when it became clear, in 1934, that all Socialist Zionists in the republic would amalgamate. The Brno Conference of the General Zionist Organization elected its leadership, which consisted of Joseph Rufeisen, chairman, Heinrich B. Zador, secretary-general, and Leo Eisner, Franz Kahn, Leon Kornblüth, Ernst Löwenstamm, Siegfried Schmitz, and Leo Zelmanovits, members. A larger council of representatives from all parts of the republic was also elected; it included all prominent members of the center bloc of the Zionist Territorial Federation. The organization was represented in the world group of General Zionists A by Angelo *Goldstein, Hugo Herrmann, and Joseph Rufeisen.

The decision to establish a proper General Zionist Organization with local branches all over Czechoslovakia was never implemented. The organization continued as a loose association of Zionists from all walks of life with no particular political or ideological program. In fact, the General Zionists refused to formulate a detailed ideological program, for they regarded themselves as the unifying factor in the face of a rapidly growing fragmentation of the Zionist movement. Even in this they failed owing to their own split into pro- and anti-Weizmannists. They had two newspapers, Die Selbstwehr (Prague), a German-language paper edited by Felix *Weltsch, through which they largely influenced the Zionist middle class that carried on the day-to-day practical and fund-raising work of the organization; and *Židovské Zprávy*, a Czech-language weekly.

The General Zionists also tried to establish a General Zionist HeHalutz youth organization, but after some initial success an accommodation with existing Socialist Hakhshara and ʿAliya youth organizations prevented further growth. General Zionism in Czechoslovakia was also supported by the bulk of the membership of the Makkabi athletic association.

*Women's International Zionist Organization (WIZO). The Women's International Zionist Organization was founded in 1920. As a group it was not part of the Zionist Organization. Its individual members supported General Zionism, and some of its leaders were prominent in other Zionist parties. The activities of WIZO in Czechoslovakia were concentrated on the education of women, child care, and welfare work in general. It supported institutions such as hostels and orphanages in Palestine. In addition to its founders in Czechoslovakia, Miriam Mechner and Wally Waldstein, its leaders included Minna Arje, Fini Brada, Gisella Feldman, Gisi *Fleischmann, Lene Hoffmann, Irma Polak, Miriam Scheuer, Marie Schmolka, Bertha Schnabel, Hanna Steiner, and Tony Winkelsberg. WIZO had special supplements in *Selbstwehr* and *Židovské Zprávy*.

Mizrahi. The groups discussed thus far were either parts or outgrowths of the Czechoslovak Zionist Territorial Federation. In addition, there were two Zionist organizations in Czechoslovakia that remained outside the federation from the beginning: Mizrahi and Poʿale Zion. The Mizrahi in Czechslovakia constituted a branch of the Mizrahi World Organization, which had been recognized by the Zionist Congress as a separate union. According to the statutes of the WZO, territorial branches of a union had the right to decide for themselves whether or not to join a territorial federation. Mizrahi in Czechoslovakia remained independent throughout its existence. Its main difference with the other groups was its emphasis on Jewish religion and tradition as the basis and principal guide of Zionism, a position which the other organizations did not accept. In almost all other aspects of Zionism there was little difference between Mizrahi and the other groups.

Mizrahi had in fact been founded in what later became Czechoslovakia, its founding conference having taken place in Bratislava in 1904. Thus the Mizrahi Organization of Czechoslovakia was the oldest Zionist organization in the country when the Czechoslovak Republic was founded in 1918; it was also the only preexisting Zionist group centered in Slovakia. The initiative for the reorganization and adaptation of Mizrahi to the new conditions was taken by Moshe Y. Miller, the Bratislava secretary of the movement. The first committee for Czechoslovakia was soon established; it consisted of Siegfried Steiner, chairman, Moshe Y. Miller, secretary, and Rabbi Moshe Asher Eckstein, Simon Fisch, Wilhelm Fischer, Josef Grünberg, Salomon Hornig, Menachem Katzberg, Franz Lipkovits, Rabbi Chaim Rosenzweig, Baruch Tomaschoff, B. Turk, Rabbi Holle Unsdorfer, and Rabbi Samuel Weinreb.

This committee not only laid the foundations for future organizational and political work but also developed a program of close cooperation with the Zionist Territorial Federation in areas where there were no differences between the two organizations, as in fund-raising campaigns for the Jewish National Fund, Keren HaYesod, the Palestine Office, and other agencies. Mizrahi supported Diaspora political activities in Czechoslovakia and therefore cooperated with the Jewish party. Subcarpathian Ruthenia had become a joint Mizrahi-Zionist district soon after the establishment of Czechoslovakia. Rabbi Heinrich (Hayim) *Brody, chief rabbi of Prague, served for a time as president of the Czechoslovak Mizrahi, representing the organization in the world leadership of the movement. At the 12th Zionist Congress (Karlovy Vary, 1921) the Mizrahi of Czechoslovakia had the largest delegation from the republic, with 3 delegates out of 9. At the time it was the strongest Zionist party in the country. However, it was unable to maintain its lead for long, since other Zionist groupings became increasingly active. Although Mizrahi's membership also grew, the increase in the other groupings outpaced it by far. At the 20th Zionist Congress (Zurich, 1937), the last Congress to include elected delegates from Czechoslovakia, Mizrahi had 3 delegates out of 12.

The change in Mizrahi's relative position was also due to its ideological limitations. Zionism had to cope with many political, economic, and organizational problems that had no bearing on religion. Although Mizrahi generally supported the policies of the Zionist Executive under Chaim Weizmann, it did not do so consistently. This led many religious Zionists who actively fought for political principles to choose a political rather than an ideological alignment in their Zionist affiliation. It was therefore very difficult for Mizrahi to make significant headway in the western sector of Czechoslovakia. Nonetheless, some Mizrahi groups in Moravia and Bohemia were able to accomplish effective organizational work.

The leadership of Mizrahi, which was based in Bratislava, was elected at the territorial conferences of the movement. Mizrahi held eight regular territorial conferences between 1919 and 1937; the final one met in Prešov in December, 1936. In addition to those mentioned above, Mizrahi leaders in Czechoslovakia included Max Amber, Béla Beer, Juda Deutsch, Yehuda A. Eliash, Rabbi Reuben Färber, Rabbi Moses Glaser, Elieser Grünwald, Albert Günsberger, Moshe Arye Kastner, Pinkas Keller, Rabbi Hugo Stransky, and Sh'muel HaKohen Weingarten. Mizrahi had a strong youth movement, HaPoʿel HaMizrahi, which was active primarily in Hakhshara and ʿAliya.

Poʿale Zion. The second organization outside the Czechoslovak Zionist Territorial Federation was Poʿale Zion. This Social Democratic Zionist organization had several branches in Czechoslovak territory even before 1918, but the local societies broke up during the war, so that after the establishment of the Czechoslovak Republic Poʿale Zion had to start all over again. Before long two strong local groups emerged, one in Prague and the other in Brno. The Prague group was headed by Rudolph Kohn; the Brno group, by Siegfried Kessler, who in 1907 had been one of the founders of Poʿale Zion in Moravia.

Poʿale Zion differed from the Territorial Federation primarily on the issue of political activities in the Diaspora. This was an important issue in Czechoslovakia, where Jews had been officially recognized as a national minority group with definite rights set down in the postwar peace treaties and the Czechoslovak Constitution. Poʿale Zion opposed Jews' entering Czechoslovak politics as a group in their own right. Thus Poʿale Zion supported other Social Democratic parties in parliamentary and municipal elections whenever it did not present its own candidates. It was primarily for this reason that Poʿale Zion chose to exercise its right, as a branch of a separate union within the WZO, not to join the Territorial Federation, which strongly supported such Jewish political activity.

The first evidence of Po'ale Zion's strength came in the Prague municipal elections of June, 1919, in which the Jewish national parties received 1,286 votes and one mandate and Po'ale Zion obtained 1,126 votes and one mandate. There were similar results in the municipal elections of Brno, for which Po'ale Zion also presented an independent list. Po'ale Zion seemed about to become a new strong party in Czechoslovakia. When it called its first territorial conference in Prague (July, 1919), it was not aware that a split was about to occur in the movement, which would bring all its activities to a standstill for years to come. This rift, which came at the Vienna Conference (July, 1920) of the Po'ale Zion World Movement, resulted from a debate as to whether the organization should join the Second (Communist) International. In Czechoslovakia most of the leaders of Po'ale Zion (Felix Brunner, Rudolph Kohn, Felix Loria, Joseph Polak) and the majority of the members formed the Communist wing of Po'ale Zion. The pro-Zionist faction was too weak to continue its work and remained dormant until 1928.

In January, 1928, a conference called by three local Moravian groups (Brno, Olomouc, and Prostějov) established an office headed by Julius Huth in Olomouc. At the first territorial conference, which took place in Olomouc in April, 1928, Siegfried Kessler was elected chairman of the new organization and Karl Baum and Hermann Grün became members of the Executive Committee, whose seat was in Brno. Other members were Arthur Heller, Oskar Huber, Rudolf Jokl, and Jakob Reiss. At the second territorial conference (May, 1929), 10 local groups and 4 Socialist Zionist youth groups were represented. The conference decided to publish its own organ, *Der Jüdische Sozialist,* of which Karl Baum became editor. The interest of Po'ale Zion was focused on the League for Labor Palestine. From this time on the movement grew in all parts of Czechoslovakia. It was able to win many new supporters, including young people such as A. Bauer, Menachem Freilich, Hayim Hoffmann (*Yahil), Eldad Lindenbaum, and Ignatz Rokach, who later became leaders in the parent group.

The revived organization remained outside the Zionist Territorial Federation until 1937, when it amalgamated with the Working Association of Socialist Zionists and the unified bloc joined the federation. Before that time it had participated in the various commissions of a "general" Zionist nature (Jewish National Fund, Keren HaYesod, Palestine Office, Tarbut) by special arrangement with the federation, as Mizrahi, too, had done. In 1931 Po'ale Zion moved its headquarters from Brno to Prague, under the direction of Jakob Reiss.

The policies of Po'ale Zion were adopted at its territorial conferences. Between 1928 and 1936 six regular territorial conferences were held. The last one, in Moravská Ostrava (July, 1935), was devoted entirely to the question of unity among Socialist Zionists in the republic. At that time the organization had 27 local groups.

Ihud. Although the Working Association of Socialist Zionists and Po'ale Zion had each passed numerous resolutions suggesting such a step, their merger came about only after many years of effort. The only obstacles to the merger were personal antagonisms within the leadership and the traditional positions taken by the two Socialist groups in Czechoslovakia. The groups were finally brought together by political considerations, namely, elections to Zionist Congresses, to which they submitted joint lists. When such a list was submitted for the 18th Congress (Prague, 1933), the united Socialist Zionist list received 5,476 of 16,246 votes and three of nine mandates. The joint list made the two bodies the strongest Zionist group in Czechoslovakia. Although they did not merge, they submitted joint lists for the next two Congresses (1935, 1937), with increasingly satisfactory results. Finally, in November, 1937, a merger conference was held in Prostějov, where a new bloc called Ihud was established. A joint leadership was elected, and headquarters was established in Prague. The office was headed by Jakob Edelstein, Kurt Grünberger, Wolf Guttmann, Arthur Heller, Ben Josef, Oskar Karpe, Ludwig Kaufmann, Sokolovič, and Jaromir Winternitz. In addition, a 28-man Council was elected. Ihud then joined the Zionist Territorial Federation. But the union was to be short-lived, for Czechoslovakia was already under the threat of war and invasion.

New Zionist Organization. When the Revisionists voted by a large majority for the establishment of an independent organization, they were aware that this step would entail secession from the WZO, but they hoped that it would simultaneously mean the end of internal struggle and an opportunity to do constructive work. In accordance with the decision of the Revisionist World Executive, a plebiscite was held for the formation of an independent organization. Thanks to the work of all members and to help from leaders in other countries, the Revisionist party in Czechoslovakia was able to obtain 36,423 votes in 106 towns and cities. This vote, the largest to be registered by any Zionist group, enabled Czechoslovakia to be represented by 36 delegates at the Constituent Congress of the New Zionist Organization (NZO) in Vienna (1935). Leopold L. Gottesmann reported to the Congress on the Iggeret, a temporary passport of citizens of the future Jewish State, of symbolic value. Oskar Rabinowicz presented the constitution of the new organization, which was adopted. He was then elected to the World Executive of the NZO, which had its headquarters in London. The founding conference of NZO in Czechoslovakia, which took place in Košice in October, 1935, was attended by 116 delegates from all over the country. The temporary leadership, with headquarters in Prague, consisted of J. Goldstein, Pavel Kauders, Viktor Kohn, Moshe Rubinstein, Karl Reiner (chairman), and Arno Stampf. The transition of the NZO from the status of opposition group to an independent organization took longer than had been anticipated. By late 1937 the organization was able to report a considerable increase in membership and agreed to be host to the next world convention of the NZO, which took place in Prague in January, 1938. On that occasion Vladimir Jabotinsky and Oskar Rabinowicz were received by Pres. Eduard Beneš, who welcomed their proposal of direct free elections to a world Jewish Parliament and agreed to help the international committee that was planning an international conference on the Jewish problem.

Last Years. By that time, however, the spread of the Nazi threat forced all Zionists, regardless of affiliation, to shift their attention from the establishment of new organizations to the task of saving Jewish lives. The leaders of NZO, and particularly of Betar, concentrated their energies on *illegal immigration to Palestine and helped thousands of Jews escape there. Other Zionist groups, too, concentrated on this effort. The Zionist Territorial Federation, headed by Pavel März, negotiated with the Czech authorities on the transfer of Jewish property abroad (*see* HA'AVARA). Much of the credit for the success of these difficult negotiations was due Leo *Herrmann, a former leader of Bar Kokhba (Prague) who had come to Czechoslovakia from London to assist in the negotiations. Thus the last days of the Zionist movement in the pre-1939 republic of Czechoslovakia were devoted to the rescue of as many Jews as possible before the outbreak of war closed the gates of Europe.

See also CZECHOSLOVAK JEWS IN ISRAEL.

O. K. RABINOWICZ

CZECHOSLOVAK JEWS IN ISRAEL. During the 20 years of the Czechoslovak Republic (1918–38), about 4,000 'Olim (immigrants) came from Czechoslovakia to Palestine. As early as 1920, members of the Prague *Bar Kokhba academic association established the settlement Heftzi-Bah in the Jezreel Valley. They represented the beginning of a steady *'Aliya, for the most part of Halutzim (pioneers; *see* HALUTZ), graduates of the youth movements of all Zionist parties (*see* CZECHOSLOVAKIA, ZIONISM IN).

Historical Background. Halutzim from Czechoslovakia, either independently or in cooperation with Halutzim from other countries, founded numerous kibbutzim, among them Heftzi-Bah, Sarid, Giv'at Hayim, Gan Sh'muel, B'erot Yitzhak, Ma'agan, N'ot Mord'khai, Sha'ar HaGolan, S'de Nahum, Tel Yosef, Nir 'Etzyon, K'far Makkabi, HaHotrim, Shomrat, Lahavot Haviva, Dorot, Ma'anit, and 'Ogen. A nationwide drive in honor of the 85th birthday of Pres. Tomáš G. Masaryk in 1935 yielded funds that were used for the establishment of the kibbutz K'far Masaryk in 1939.

Following the German annexation of Austria in the spring of 1938, the German occupation of the Sudeten lands later that year, and the capitulation of Czechoslovakia in March, 1939, masses of Czechoslovak Jews applied for permission to go to Palestine, but the Palestine Office in Prague (*see* PALESTINE OFFICES) had only 920 "capitalist" *immigration certificates (issued to immigrants owning personal assets of at least £1,000) and few Halutz certificates at its disposal. The separate Palestine Office that was organized in Bratislava after the German occupation of Bohemia and Moravia had only 20 certificates.

The 920 certificates were covered by the sum of £500,000, which the British government, within the framework of its £8,000,000 loan to the Czechoslovak government as compensation for the Munich Agreement, had put at the latter's disposal for the financing of Jewish emigration. On the basis of this agreement, the *Jewish Agency was able to transfer to Palestine some private as well as institutional Jewish assets. The certificates were allocated to veteran Zionists in Bohemia and Moravia, who comprised the majority of the leading Zionists in the country. In 1939, 1,350 Czechoslovak Jews emigrated to Palestine.

Apart from this official 'Aliya, there was also an unofficial mass emigration to Palestine. From 1939 to 1945, 4,561 illegal Jewish immigrants from Czechoslovakia were able to sail to Palestine, many of them reaching their destination only after great difficulties and contrary to the immigration laws of the mandatory government (*see* ILLEGAL IMMIGRATION). The last groups of illegal immigrants from Czechoslovakia were part of the transports linked with the S.S. *"Patria" disaster and the *Mauritius camps.

At the end of World War II, many concentration camp survivors and other victims of Nazi oppression wanted to go to Palestine to be reunited with members of their families who had settled there. Again, however, the newly established Palestine Office in Prague had only a small number of immigration certificates at its disposal. At that time the Palestine Office was instrumental in arranging the immigration to Palestine of about 1,000 Czechoslovak Jews who had served with the Czechoslovak Legion during the war.

The establishment of the State of Israel marked the start of a new phase. About 2,000 young Jews from Czechoslovakia responded to the call of the *Yishuv (Jewish population of Palestine) and volunteered to serve in the defense of the young State. The Czechoslovak government of that time displayed unusual understanding, giving assistance to the State of Israel as well as to Jewish volunteers and emigrants. In the first two years of the State, about 19,000 Czechoslovak Jews, representing about half of all the Jewish survivors in Czechoslovakia, settled in Israel. Then, suddenly, emigration to Israel was halted by the Czech authorities, to be permitted again only in 1965, after which time it was resumed.

Contributions to Israel. Czechoslovak immigrants have taken an active part in the building of the State of Israel. In 1938, when mass immigration from Czechoslovakia began, the Hitahdut 'Ole Tshekhoslovakia (Association of Immigrants from Czechoslovakia) was organized for the purpose of aiding the immigrants. The immigrants of 1938–39 were able to take part of their property with them, and not only struck roots quickly in the country but also contributed to the development of *agriculture and *industry there. Jews from Czechoslovakia played a leading part in the development of the textile and fashion industries (*see* CLOTHING IN ISRAEL) and in the manufacture of shoes and plastic articles. There was no branch in the economic, intellectual, and artistic life of the country to which Czechoslovak immigrants did not make a significant contribution. They held important positions in the *civil service, the army, and the diplomatic service.

Individual Czechoslovak Jews in Israel whose fame transcends the borders of the country include the late writer Max *Brod and the philosopher Samuel Hugo *Bergmann. Among those active in the arts are the painters Stefan Alexander, Ludwig Blum, Blanka Tauber, and Shraga Weill. The pianist and harpsichordist Frank Pelleg (Pollak) and the conductor Georg Singer are internationally known. The music critic Yehuda Cohen is a lecturer and broadcaster. Irma Singer (now residing in the kibbutz D'ganya Aleph) is the author of Jewish tales for children. Theatrical personalities include Paul Loewy, puppeteer and creator of stage settings, and Joseph Milo, actor, producer, and cofounder of the Tel Aviv Kameri (Chamber) Theater (*see* THEATER IN ISRAEL).

The author Hugo Gold, founder and director of the 'Olamenu publishing firm in Tel Aviv; Dr. Moshe Tavor (Tauber), staff member of the Hebrew daily *Davar; and Moshe Zippor (Vogel), editor of the *Mapam daily *'Al HaMishmar are active in the publishing field. Among those practicing medicine are Otto Kurz, of Beilinson Hospital, and Richard Stein, ophthalmologists; Gustav Aschermann, of Tel Aviv; Jakob Huppert, head of K'far Saba Hospital; Franz Izsak, chief surgeon of Donolo Hospital, Jaffa; and Erich Liban, Bezalel Naor (Lichtwitz), and Tz'vi Kenaan, of the Kaplan Hospital, Rehovot. Erich and Hans Moller founded the Ata textile plants in K'far Ata and Nahariya.

Among Czechoslovak Jews in the Israeli Ministry of Foreign Affairs and Foreign Service are Raffi Ben-Shalom (Friedl); Avigdor Dagan (Viktor Fischl), who was Israel's Ambassador in Poland and Minister to Yugoslavia; Moshe Dak (Daks); Yehuda Gera; Moshe Leshem (Limberski); Uri Naor (Hans Lichtwitz); Ambassador Z'ev Schek; and Hayim *Yahil. The late Dr. Hayim *Kugel was the first mayor of Holon. The veteran Zionist and communal leaders of Czechoslovakia who settled in Israel and became prominent in all fields of private and public endeavor are too numerous to list. Among them are Hugo *Herrmann, Angelo *Goldstein, Joseph *Rufeisen, and Felix *Weltsch.

Throughout the many years of its existence the Hitahdut 'Ole Tshekhoslovakia, in addition to aiding individuals, has rendered valuable services to the State and to the *World Zionist Organization. It has also established a memorial for the 260,000 Czechoslovak Jews murdered by the Germans. The association planted the Memorial Forest of Czechoslovak Jewry in the large Memorial Forest complex of the *Jewish National Fund in the Jerusalem Mountains, where a memorial service is held each year. Marble slabs bearing the names of all the former Jewish communities in Czechoslovakia were erected on the Memorial Plaza.

Another memorial, the Hekhal Y'hude Pressburg (Hall of Pressburg Jewry), was built in Giv'at Shaul, Jerusalem, by Orthodox Jews from Slovakia, particularly from Pressburg (Bratislava), in memory of their community. The memorial includes study facilities and a synagogue, where memorial prayers are recited annually on the anniversary of the start of the deportation of Slovakian Jews by the Nazis. Aharon Grünhut, a former member of the Central Office of the Ortho-dox Community of Pressburg, was instrumental in the erection of this memorial.

Close by, and sharing some of the Hekhal facilities, is the Yeshiva of Pressburg, successor to the famous rabbinical school founded in Pressburg in 1806 by Rabbi Moses Schreiber (known as Hatam Sofer). Reestablished in Jerusalem in 1940 by Rabbi 'Akiba Schreiber, a direct descendant of the founder, the institution had in 1968 an enrollment of almost 100 students between the ages of 15 and 22 and was led by Rabbi 'Akiba Schreiber's grandson, Rabbi Simha Bunim Schreiber, and Rabbi Zalman Weber. There are Hatam Sofer circles (groups of alumni and friends of the original Pressburg Yeshiva) in Jerusalem, Tel Aviv, B'ne B'rak, Petah Tikva, and elsewhere in the country.

A valuable source of information for Israeli students of Czechoslovak-Jewish history is the Oskar Aschermann Library, a collection of 2,000 Czech, German, Hebrew, French, and English books, including some rare volumes in Czech-Jewish and Czech-Palestinian relations. The books were the property of the late Oskar Aschermann, a Prague engineer and veteran Zionist who settled in Palestine in 1939. After Aschermann's death in 1958, his heirs presented the collection to the kibbutz N'ot Mord'khai, in whose library building it is now housed.

The number of Czechoslovak Jews in Israel in 1968 was about 40,000.

O. NEUMANN

CZERNOVICZ, HAYIM (Rav Tza'ir). *See* TCHERNOVITZ, HAYIM.

D

DABBURIYE. Arab village at the foot of Mount Tabor. Population (1968): 2,590.

DAFNA. Village (kibbutz) in eastern Upper Galilee. Founded in 1939 and affiliated with the *Kibbutz M'uhad. Population (1968): 540.

DAHI. Arab village in the Jezreel Valley. Population (1968): 195.

DALIYA. Village (kibbutz) in the Hills of Manasseh. Founded in 1939 and affiliated with the *Kibbutz Artzi Shel HaShomer HaTza'ir. Though predominantly agricultural, it has some industrial enterprises. Population (1968): 610.

Daliya is noted for its colorful folk dance festival, which is held periodically in a natural amphitheater set amid the mountains. The festival, in which hundreds of dancers from all parts of the country participate, was first held in 1924.

DALIYAT AL-CARMEL. Druze village on Mount Carmel (*see* DRUZE COMMUNITY IN ISRAEL). Population (1968): 5,200.

DALTON. Village (moshav) in eastern Upper Galilee. Founded in 1950 and affiliated with HaPo'el HaMizrahi (*see* MIZRAHI). Population (1968): 610.

DAN. Village (kibbutz) in eastern Upper Galilee. Founded in 1939 and affiliated with the *Kibbutz Artzi Shel HaShomer HaTza'ir. During the *War of Independence, Dan suffered from prolonged attacks by the Syrians.

DANCE IN ISRAEL. The dance played an important part in ancient Jewish life and ritual, and many of the famous dancing masters of medieval Europe and Renaissance Italy were Jews; but there was no unbroken tradition on which the dancers and dance instructors of modern Israel could base their work. In Biblical times, rituals, meals, wine festivals, processions, and funerals were accompanied by dancing and appropriate dance music; the dancers were mostly women and children. This probably was the reason why Michal reproached King David for dancing in an unseemly manner before the Ark (II Samuel 6:20), for as a rule only solemn processional dances were executed by men.

Modern Beginnings. In the life of the *Yishuv (Jewish population of Palestine), the dance first began to play a significant role in the early 1920s. The first settlers had brought with them the traditional folk dances of Eastern Europe (*see* HORA), but the dance as an art was not known or accepted by them. Only with immigration from the Central and Western European countries did the dance gain a place in Palestine's education and art. Moreover, while the *theater, *literature, and *music had a heritage on which to build, the dancers had to start from scratch. The Jewish folk dances, particularly the Hasidic dance, influenced the creation of new Hebrew dances, but for the artistic dance they could offer only motifs, gestures, movements, and themes. On the other hand, the dances of the peoples of the Near East, which were completely different in style and expression, represented a source of ever-growing importance.

A scene in the kibbutz Dan. [Israel Information Services]

Folk dancing marks national holidays in Israel. [Zionist Archives]

Although the soil for artistic dancing developed only very slowly, quite a number of dancers, choreographers, and teachers settled in the country. The first studio for dancing in Palestine was founded in Tel Aviv in 1922 by Margalith Ornstein. Subsequently Mrs. Ornstein's two daughters, Shoshana and Judith, who had been trained by their mother, became noted for their varied repertory. Gertrud Kraus, an exponent of the modern dance, came to Palestine from Vienna; her individualistic art exerted great influence, especially in the 1930s. Rina Nikova, a Russian ballerina, came to Palestine in 1925 and founded the first studio for Biblical ballet and a dance group of Yemenite girls. Among later comers were Tile Roessler, who had been trained in the Gert Palacca School; Mia Arbatova, a ballerina from Riga, whose intensive pedagogical and artistic activities greatly benefited the development of young dancers; Deborah Bertonoff, daughter of the noted HaBimah actor Y'hoshu'a Bertonoff, who developed her dance pantomimes with their deeply significant traits of humor and tragedy into a unique art form; Yardena Cohen, a native of Haifa, who was among the first to use the accompaniment of ancient Near Eastern musical instruments and to seek a personal expressive style with which to re-create the characters and episodes of the Bible; Viennese-born Elisheva Mona, who cultivated a Central European style of ballet with outstanding artistry; Archipova, with her classical ballet style; Else Dublon, known for her poetic character studies; and Katia Michaeli (Michaelovsky), Paula Padani, and Flora Weil-Ratner from the Wigman School, each of whom in her own way helped the Wigman style become known and practiced in the country.

With the intensification of cultural interests in the country, many noted dancers and choreographers, among them Udai Shankar of India with his troupe, Marcel Marceau, Yvonne Georgi, and Pola Nirenska, paid influential visits. During the period of isolation in World War II, young and new talents developed. Among them were Naomi Aleskovsky and Hilde Kesten, of the Gertrud Kraus Studio; Chassia Levin, of the Ornstein Studio and a pupil of Else Dublon; Mia Pick; Rahel Nadav, of the Nikova School; and the Ornstein sisters, who in the meantime had taken over branches of the Tel Aviv studio in Haifa and Jerusalem. The war years saw the emergence of Sarah Levy-Tannai, born in Jerusalem of Yemenite parents, who formed a group of young dancers from Yemen and thus prepared the ground for her internationally famed Inbal Dance Theater, founded in 1949.

Development in the State of Israel. After the *War of Independence, dancing joined the other arts of Israel in a flourishing development. The Spanish dancer Juan came to Israel as a volunteer soldier and remained as an active dancer and teacher. Irene Gretry came via a Cyprus refugee camp (*see* CYPRUS, DETENTION CAMPS IN) and appeared in solo recitals. Israeli dancers and teachers could again learn of the progress of their art in other countries, and new talents and teachers came from Europe and the United States. The erstwhile Central European orientation gave way to other influences through the visits of such a variety of artists as Thali Beatty, Martha Graham, Jerome Robbins, Anthony Tudor, Roland Petit, Maurice Bejart, Jean Babile, Harald Kreutzberg, Étienne Decroux, Antonio Y. Rosaria, Anton Dolin, and Alicia Markova, and of folkloristic troupes from India, Africa, the Philippines, and Eastern Europe. Jerome Robbins stayed in Israel for some time and taught part of his *Interplay* to a hand-picked group of students and professionals. Thali Beatty choreographed *Fire in the Mountains*; and Étienne Decroux, Anton Dolin, and Anna Sokolow stayed to teach.

The younger generation of dancers, as well as open-minded professionals, enthusiastically took up the study of the new ways of dancing and dance instruction offered by these authorities, and the technical proficiency of Israel's dancers attained a high standard. The Rubin Academy of Music in Jerusalem opened a studio for dance instructors. The Israel National Opera occasionally presented ballet programs with good choreographers; among these were Mia Arbatova and Adam Darius, who served as temporary directors. Darius, who had come from the United States, left the opera and established a studio and dance group in Haifa. Also from the United States came Dina and Nachum Shachar, Rina Shacham, Rina Glueck, and Ruth Harris. Anna Sokolow founded the Lyric Theater, a dance theater whose membership changed frequently. The Bethsabée de Rothschild Foundation established a professional dance theater in 1964, with Martha Graham assisting in the preparation of the first programs.

While the dancers and dance instructors reared in the Central European tradition saw in the dance an educational and creative medium, there was a growing tendency to perfect the professional, virtuoso, and technical sides of the art. Although dancing and dance instruction in Israel lost something of their erstwhile individual expression as their standards rose, they were in a process of steady, continuous development.

Folk dancing also made great strides; it was strongly influenced by the rites and dances of Asian and African peoples. Folk dance festivals, such as the Daliya Festival, were being held at regular intervals, with Gurit Kadman (Gert Kaufmann) and Jonathan Karmon as the main initiators and organizers. Many Israeli composers wrote musical scores for ballet and dance scenes, and many derived inspiration from traditional Near Eastern dances.

J. ORNSTEIN AND P. GRADENWITZ

DANIEL DERONDA. *See* ELIOT, GEORGE.

DANZIG, ZIONISM IN. Formerly part of Poland and later the capital of West Prussia, Danzig became a free city in 1919 under the protection of the League of Nations. The area included not only the city of Danzig and its seaport but also

New arrivals at K'far 'Etzyon dance the Hora. [Zionist Archives]

nearby communities, which together constituted the free state of Danzig. Annexed by Germany in 1939, the area was assigned to Poland by the Allies after World War II, and since then the city has been known by its Polish name, Gdańsk. In the late 1920s the free state of Danzig had 5,837 Jews in a total population of 235,000.

When Danzig came under League of Nations jurisdiction, the Zionists in the area decided to form an independent federation rather than remain in the Zionist Organization of Germany or join the Polish Zionist Organization. The Zionist Federation of Danzig, which included the Zionists of Danzig, Sopot (Zoppot), and Oliva, had a membership of more than 300; *Mizrahi and the Working Palestine League at first were separate unions but later joined the federation. In 1926 two Zionist youth organizations, Blau-Weiss (Blue-White) and *HaShomer HaTza'ir, were amalgamated to form B'rit HaBonim, with a total membership of 100. In the 1930s Zionist youth was grouped into two organizations, the Socialist B'rit Ha'Olim and the Revisionist *B'rit Trumpeldor (Betar; see REVISIONISTS). Betar held its first world conference in Danzig in April, 1931, with 200 delegates in attendance and Vladimir *Jabotinsky in the chair. Pro-Zionist groups included Bar Kokhba, a sports association, and Kadima, an organization of Jewish students at the technical high school in Danzig-Langfuhr. Later, there was a Jewish gymnastic and athletic society that belonged to the Maccabi World Federation and provided physical training for 400 boys.

In the late 1920s the Zionist Federation began to publish a monthly, Das Jüdische Volk, which served to spread Jewish nationalist ideas and combat *assimilation. There was a Palestine Office (see PALESTINE OFFICES) that processed Halutzim (pioneers; see HALUTZIYUT) from the Ukraine, Lithuania, and Poland who were stranded in Danzig on their way to Palestine. Since most of the pioneers had no means of support while waiting for their passport and visa formalities to be settled, and since, as aliens, they were not permitted to accept employment in Danzig, the Zionist Federation had to give them financial assistance.

The *Jewish National Fund and *Keren HaYesod (Palestine Foundation Fund) were both active, and the *Women's International Zionist Organization (WIZO) also conducted fund-raising campaigns. In 1922 a Jewish Public Bank was founded with the participation of the *Jewish Colonial Trust. *Tarbut conducted a kindergarten and held Hebrew discussions. In 1936 a *Hakhshara (agricultural training) farm for prospective pioneers in Palestine was founded in the village of Schöneberg. By that time Zionism had become a major factor in the Jewish community of Danzig, and one-third of the seats on the Jewish Community Council were held by Zionists.

As the local Nazi party became an increasingly powerful factor in Danzig politics in the 1930s, many Jews emigrated from Danzig. Finally, early in 1939, the Danzig Senate enacted decrees to expel them. By the time the Germans annexed the area most of the Jews had left, largely for Palestine.

G. HIRSCHLER

DARDARA. See ASHMURA.

DAROM. Hebrew geographical term (literally, "the South") denoting the area bounded by the Sh'fela and the Judean hill country on the north, the Negev on the south, the Gaza Strip on the west, and Jordan on the east. Following the establishment of the State of Israel, when a considerable number of new towns and villages were built in the region, the name Darom was chosen for an area comprising parts of the Lakhish, Ashk'lon, G'rar, and B'sor regions, which were established for statistical purposes.

DASHEVSKI, PINHAS. Founder of a Zionist Socialist student association in Kiev (b. Korostyshev, Ukraine, Russia, 1879; d. Siberia, 1934). After the *Kishinev pogrom, the Jewish self-defense organization of Kiev decided to take revenge on the anti-Semitic newspaper editor Pavolachi Krushevan, who had instigated the massacre. Dashevski volunteered for the task and, on June 4, 1903, stabbed and wounded Krushevan in a St. Petersburg street. Dashevski's deed and his proud bearing during the trial, at which he was sentenced to five years at hard labor, did much to strengthen Jewish *nationalism among Russian-Jewish youth.

A chemical engineer by profession, Dashevski worked in the Caucasus and in Siberia. He continued as an active Zionist even after the Communists came to power. He was arrested and died in prison.

DAVAR. Israeli daily newspaper published in Tel Aviv. Established in 1925 by the labor organization *Histadrut, Davar (the Word) was the third Hebrew daily to appear in Palestine under the British *Mandate for Palestine. A declaration of the Histadrut Executive Committee outlined the basic policy of the paper as follows: "The General Federation of Labor is hereby accorded a daily platform from which to address the worker, and which the worker will be able to use as his own medium of expression. It is through this medium that the truth about the life of the worker in the country as mirrored by the workers themselves, about the situation in Palestine, in the *Yishuv and in the labor movement, will reach the rank and file of our membership and our brethren in the *Diaspora."

With the ascendance of the labor movement to leadership in the *World Zionist Organization and the *Jewish Agency in 1933, Davar assumed, for all practical purposes, the role of unofficial organ of the Jewish Agency's Executive. With the establishment of the State of Israel, Davar continued to be considered the unofficial organ of the Israeli *government.

In the 1960s, in addition to news reporting on local and international developments, Davar regularly published articles dealing with Israel's development, problems of the collective sector in the Israeli economy, and Socialist theory and its adaptability to actual conditions in Israel, as well as a weekly literary supplement featuring leading Israeli writers and an illustrated weekly.

Berl *Katznelson, the founder and first editor of Davar, was succeeded by Moshe *Beilinson and later by Zalman *Shazar. Hayim Shurer was editor until 1965, when he was succeeded by Y'huda Gothelf. The circulation of the paper in the late 1960s was close to 40,000.

J. RUBIN

DAVID, SHIELD OF. See MAGEN DAVID.

D'AVIGDOR, ELIM HENRY. *Hoveve Zion leader (b. Provence, France, 1841; d. London, 1895). A civil engineer by profession, D'Avigdor supervised the construction of railways in Syria and Transylvania and of the waterworks in Vienna. A leader of Hoveve Zion in Great Britain, he was active in consolidating the movement there. In 1894 he attended a conference of Western European Hoveve Zion groups held in Paris, and was elected president of the Paris Central Committee set up at that meeting.

D'Avigdor's daughter Sylvie translated Herzl's *Jewish State* into English (1896). The translation was revised by Jacob *de Haas in 1917 and by Israel *Cohen in 1934.

DAVIS, MOSHE. Rabbi and Jewish historian (b. New York, 1916). A graduate of Columbia University (B.S., 1936), Davis was ordained in 1942 at the Jewish Theological Seminary of America and four years later received his doctorate from the *Hebrew University of Jerusalem. Joining the faculty of the seminary in 1942, he became assistant professor of American Jewish history in 1953, also serving as codirector of the seminary's American Jewish History Center from 1953 on and as provost of the seminary from 1951 to 1959. In 1959 Davis obtained a leave of absence from the seminary to join the faculty of the Hebrew University as a visiting professor; beginning in 1963 he was Stephen S. Wise associate professor of American Jewish history and institutions. As of 1968 he was also head of the university's Institute of Contemporary Jewry. Davis wrote a number of books on Jewish history and Jewish religious life.

DAYAN, MOSHE. Israeli soldier and statesman (b. D'ganya, 1915). A son of Sh'muel Dayan, veteran pioneer and later member of the *Knesset, Moshe Dayan was brought at an early age to Nahalal, the first Jewish cooperative village (moshav), and later studied at the agricultural school there. He joined the *Hagana, the Jewish underground defense force, when still in his early teens. During the *Arab riots of 1936 he served with Orde *Wingate's *Special Night Squads. He was arrested by the British in 1939 for possessing illegal arms and sentenced to 10 years' imprisonment in *'Akko Prison, but was released in 1941 to work against the Vichy French forces in Syria and Lebanon. He led a Jewish advance unit in the British-Australian invasion of Syria. During a battle at Lebanon's Litani River, he lost his left eye when a bullet drove his telescope into his eye socket. He served as a liaison officer with the British in Jerusalem until 1944, when he returned to farming.

During the *War of Independence, Dayan held the rank of lieutenant colonel, holding commands on various fronts and leading the forces that captured Lod and Ramle. In 1949 he was senior military representative in the Israeli delegation to the armistice negotiations in Rhodes (*see* ARMISTICE AGREEMENTS) and in this capacity negotiated the armistice with the kingdom of Jordan. Subsequently he served as chief liaison officer to the Mixed Armistice Commissions. In 1952–53 he headed the Southern and then the Northern Command with the rank of brigadier general. While in New York in November, 1953, on a mission connected with United Nations deliberations on the Israel-Jordan border situation, he was recalled to Israel to serve as chief of staff of the *Israel Defense Forces with the rank of major general, a position he held until 1957. He led the Israeli Army in the *Sinai Campaign, a military operation he described in *Yoman Ma'arekhet Sinai* (1965), which was published in English in 1966 as *Diary of the Sinai Campaign*. The book aroused considerable controversy in Israel because in it Dayan revealed costly errors made by his own army.

In 1957 Dayan left the army to enter politics and became

active in the *Mapai party. In the years that followed he returned to school part time, receiving a B.S. degree from the School of Law and Economics in Tel Aviv and taking courses in political science at the *Hebrew University of Jerusalem. He was a close associate of Prime Minister David *Ben-Gurion, who appointed him Minister of Agriculture in 1959, a position Dayan held until 1964, when he resigned as a result of differences with Ben-Gurion's successor, Levi *Eshkol. In 1965 he left Mapai and joined Ben-Gurion's newly formed *R'shimat Po'ale Yisrael (Rafi) party, which elected him to the Knesset that year.

Moshe Dayan.
[Israel Information Services]

Several days before the outbreak of the *Six-day War of 1967, Eshkol, bowing to nationwide pressures, invited Dayan to join the newly formed all-party Government of National Unity as Minister of Defense. In this capacity he had a prominent role in the conduct of the war. As Minister of Defense he was responsible for the military administration of the occupied areas. His firmness and humanity in dealing with the inhabitants of these territories earned him the respect of the Arab population.

DAYAN, YAËL. Israeli journalist and author (b. Nahalal, 1939). The daughter of Moshe *Dayan, she studied at the *Hebrew University of Jerusalem, then joined the Israeli Army in 1956, serving for two years and rising to the rank of lieutenant. It was during her term in the army that she wrote her first novel, *New Face in the Mirror* (1959), the story of an Israeli girl soldier. Her next two novels, *Envy the Frightened* (1960) and *Dust* (1963), deal with pioneering life in modern Israel. The theme of *Death Had Two Sons* (1967) is a father-son relationship shaped by the Nazi holocaust. All these novels were written in English. *Israel Journal, June 1967* (1967; British edition, *A Soldier's Diary, Sinai 1967*) is Miss Dayan's personal account of the *Six-day War, which she covered in Sinai as a war correspondent. She also wrote a travel book and numerous articles for the Hebrew and foreign press.

DEAD SEA. Body of salt water that fills the lowest part of the Jordan Rift Valley. Its shores are the lowest spot on the surface of the earth (1,296 feet below sea level). Its length varies between 47 and 49 miles with fluctuations of the water level; its greatest width is 11 miles; and its average surface is 405 square miles, of which only the southwestern part lies within Israeli borders. The Lisan Peninsula, composed of a special kind of marl (Lisan marl), juts from the eastern shore and divides the sea into two unequal parts. The northern part is bounded by sheer

Salt-coated rocks and wood along the southern edge of the Dead Sea. [Israel Government Tourist Office]

cliffs, which rise perpendicularly, in places to 2,000 feet above the sea, and do not permit even a footpath along the shores. The steepness of the shores is continued under the water, which quickly reaches great depths, with a maximum of 1,309 feet in the eastern section. The smaller southern part of the sea is very shallow, with a maximum depth not exceeding 30 feet; on the shores are narrow level stretches formed by deltas of river gravel. Therefore, only the southern shores are lined by roads, which end abruptly at the edge of the steep cliffs (on the western shore, at 'En Gedi).

Owing to its low elevation, the Dead Sea lies within an arid zone with very high temperatures in summer and warm winters. The mean daily maximum temperatures in July and August exceed 104°F, while in winter even the daily average minimum temperature does not fall below 50°F and the average noon temperature in January may reach 68°F. The high temperatures and low humidity cause a strong evaporation, which balances the water input, 80 per cent of which comes from the Jordan River (about 1,200 million cubic meters per year). The delicate water balance causes strong fluctuations in the sea level, which reflect differences in rainfall and have reached a range as great as 40 feet within the past century.

Another result of the high evaporation rate is the high salt content of the water, which surpasses the saturation point by 33 per cent. Although 52 per cent of the brine is magnesium chloride and 30 per cent sodium chloride, the rest of the soluble matter contains valuable minerals which have made the Dead Sea Israel's largest source of minerals. The Dead Sea Works at the southern end of the sea (*see* DEAD SEA WORKS COMPANY, LTD.) produces mainly potassium chloride and bromides with the aid of huge evaporation pans. In 1966 their area was enlarged with the aid of dams from the 1964 total of 8,000 acres to about 25,000 acres.   Y. KARMON

DEAD SEA WORKS COMPANY, LTD. Corporation created by the Israeli *government to exploit the chemical resources of the Dead Sea. It is the successor to Palestine Potash, Ltd., which had been set up in 1929 by Moshe *Novomeysky (1873–1961), a Russian chemical engineer who first became interested in the Dead Sea in 1906 through the report of a German geologist. Novomeysky noted that the analysis of the salts of the

Dead Sea closely resembled that of the salts found in the Siberian lakes, from which he had been extracting various industrial chemicals. In 1911 he briefly visited Palestine, taking samples of Dead Sea water back with him to Siberia.

In 1920 Novomeysky returned to Tel Aviv with a memorandum on the potentialities of the Dead Sea which he sent to Sir Herbert *Samuel, *High Commissioner for Palestine, with a request for a franchise to operate a potash plant in the area. For the next several years he endeavored to obtain the approval of the British Colonial Office and to raise the funds needed for the project. By May, 1929, he had accumulated £400,000 from various sources and, with Maj. T. G. Tulloch, an Englishman, obtained a 75-year franchise for an enterprise, to be named Palestine Potash, Ltd., with headquarters in London and Novomeysky as managing director. The original board of directors consisted of the 2d Earl of Lytton, as chairman; the 2d Baron Glenconner; Glenconner's cousin Ernest Tennant; a group of Americans, among them Israel Brodie, Bernard *Flexner, Robert *Szold, and Felix M. *Warburg; and G. A. Stolar, as secretary. Despite the lack of experts in Palestine for the type of enterprise Novomeysky was planning and the difficulty of persuading even unskilled workers to face the trying physical and climatic conditions of what is the lowest point on earth, he was able to start production in October, 1929.

Palestine Potash, Ltd., had two plants, one at the north end of the Dead Sea and the other at the south end (now S'dom). By the late 1930s, the enterprise had about 2,000 employees. During its first years, it operated at a loss, having to compete for markets with the powerful Franco-German potash cartel. By 1932, however, it was able to record a profit of £23,000. In 1938–39 Palestine Potash produced 100,000 of the 1.2 million tons of potassium chloride then exported by the world's potash-producing countries. In 1944 the corporation showed a profit of £413,117, and by the end of World War II, 110,000 tons of potash and 1,000 tons of bromine were being extracted annually by the two plants. Extraction was effected by solar power, aided by the strong desert winds, the waters being pumped into huge evaporation pans for exposure. The residue salts were then transported to the plants for separation and processing. After the war agrarian reforms and scientific farming programs in emerging Asian and African states created a sharply increased demand for potash and phosphates, the main ingredients of chemical fertilizer.

Research station, Dead Sea Works. [Israel Information Services]

Work at the Dead Sea plants came to an abrupt halt in 1948 because of the *War of Independence. The northern plant was destroyed by the Arab forces, and the southern plant was cut off from the rest of the country. Before the war, the products of the southern plant had been transported by barge to the northern end of the sea and from there by highway. Under the *armistice agreements, these lines of communication were no longer accessible to Israel. Only 102 of the 405 square miles of the Dead Sea had come under Israeli control, and there was no highway between S'dom and B'er Sheva'. As a result, the S'dom plant lay idle, and its machinery began to deteriorate.

In July, 1952, the Israel government formed the Dead Sea Works Company, Ltd., with a registered and paid-up capital of IL3,600,000, to take over the assets of Palestine Potash and to revive the plant. Fifty-one per cent of the shares were held by the government, and the rest by private concerns, including Solel Bone (see HISTADRUT). In February, 1955, rebuilding operations were begun, and production was resumed that June. By March, 1955, a new highway linking S'dom with B'er Sheva' had been laid. That year, too, Gen. Mordecai Makleff, former chief of staff of the *Israel Defense Forces, was named managing director of the Dead Sea Works, a position he still held in 1968. In February, 1956, the new S'dom plant was completed. In 1962 an expansion project of the Dead Sea Works was begun with an investment of more than IL 200,000,000 in a period of four years.

By 1961 Israel was exporting potash to 15 countries and bromine to 30. In 1966–67 potash production totaled 514,055 tons; that of bromine, 6,607 tons; and that of table and industrial salts, 37,945 tons. That year exports of potash, bromine, and bromides amounted to $17,800,000. Plans were under way to expand annual potash production by an additional 400,000 tons, bringing the total to 1 million tons by 1969.

G. HIRSCHLER

DECLARATION OF INDEPENDENCE. Proclamation issued in Tel Aviv on May 14, 1948 (Iyar 5, 5708), declaring the existence of a sovereign Jewish State in Palestine. Signed by 37 representatives of Palestine Jewry and of the Zionist movement, it sets forth the claim of the Jewish people to the Homeland in Palestine, gives the name of the new State as "the State of Israel," and vests the People's Council (Mo'etzet Ha'Am) and its executive, the People's Administration (Minhelet Ha'Am), with authority to act as the Provisional Council of State and provisional Cabinet (see LEGISLATION IN ISRAEL) until the election of a Constituent Assembly.

Historical Background. The Declaration of Independence set the official seal on the withdrawal of the mandatory authority and opened the road to the conversion of the new de facto state of affairs in Jewish Palestine into a de jure situation. During the months intervening between the adoption of the United Nations *partition resolution (Nov. 29, 1947) and the date set for the termination of the British *Mandate for Palestine (May 15, 1948), the authorities of the *Yishuv (Jewish population of Palestine)—the *Jewish Agency and the *Va'ad L'umi (National Council)—gradually took over control of such vital services as defense, security, information, and food distribution in the area assigned for the Jewish State in Palestine.

On Apr. 6, 1948, the *Zionist General Council, convened in Tel Aviv by the Jewish Agency, judged the time appropriate to set up a provisional Cabinet of 13 and a Council of 37. By

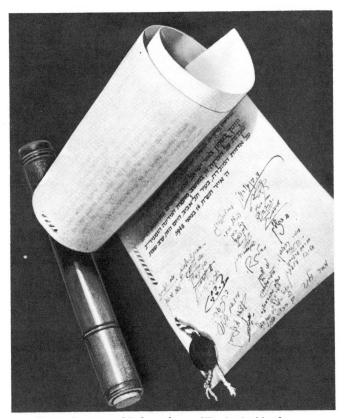

Israel's Declaration of Independence. [Zionist Archives]

early May, many of the functions of the British Mandatory government having been taken over by the Yishuv authorities, the only question that remained to be decided was whether the de facto autonomous government in Jewish Palestine should be declared sovereign or whether it should be made subject to a United Nations trusteeship, as had been proposed by the United States at the UN General Assembly that spring.

On May 12, 1948, three days before the termination of the British Mandate, 10 of the 13 leaders who were to comprise the provisional Cabinet of the new State met to decide which of the two alternatives to follow. The question actually before the group was whether or not to yield to pressure from the U.S. Department of State and accept a truce under which neither the Arabs nor the Jews would proclaim a sovereign state in Palestine and the Arab and Jewish authorities would enforce the truce in the areas under their control. At the meeting, Moshe *Sharett reported on his discussions with U.S. State Department officials who had warned that if the Arabs were to make war on the Jews of Palestine, a world conflict might result, and had made it plain that if the Jews were to proclaim an independent State in Palestine, they could not expect American help in case of an Arab invasion. In fact, it was hinted that if the Jews were to act contrary to American advice and become involved in a war with the Arabs, the United States might place an embargo on dollar remittances to the Yishuv.

In a conference with Secretary of State George C. Marshall and Under-secretary Robert A. Lovett, Sharett found Marshall sympathetic but pessimistic about the chances for survival of the Jewish State in the event of an Arab invasion. Golda *Meir reported on her fruitless efforts to dissuade King 'Abdullah of Transjordan from making war on the Jewish State. Later in the day Israel *Galili, chief of the *Hagana command, and Yigael *Yadin, Hagana's chief of operations, reported on the security situation. They stated that they had 25,000 to 30,000 men and women mobilized but armed only with light weapons. That very day, the 'Etzyon Block settlements between Bethlehem and Hebron were waging a losing battle against the Arab Legion of Transjordan.

All these grim facts notwithstanding, public opinion in Palestine placed paramount importance on the Proclamation of a sovereign Jewish State and held that any delay in issuing a Declaration to that effect might forfeit the efforts made over many decades in behalf of the Zionist cause. In the end, the group decided in favor of a Declaration by a vote of 6 to 4; 3 members of the group were absent (1 in the United States and 2 in Jerusalem), but at least 1 of these 3 was known to have favored the Proclamation.

The draft Declaration had been fashioned over a period of weeks by political leaders and jurists. The final version included revisions made by David *Ben-Gurion.

In framing the text, the drafters of the Declaration were faced with a number of problems including religious considerations, with the religious insisting that the preamble to the Declaration should refer to the fact that Palestine had been promised to the Jewish people in the Bible. An agnostic sought to eliminate the phrase "with trust in the Almighty" from the final paragraph. In the end, the Hebrew term agreed upon was "Tzur Yisrael" (literally, the Rock of Israel).

The decision as to what name to give the new State had been deferred until the very last minute, and the final typewritten version of the Declaration was prepared only an hour or so before it was read. One transcript was taken at once to the vault of the *Bank L'umi L'Yisrael.

Because May 15, the day the British Mandate was to end, fell on a Sabbath, it was decided that independence should be proclaimed the day before, Friday, May 14. At four o'clock that afternoon, a special session of the Provisional Council of State was held at the Tel Aviv Museum. Ben-Gurion read the Declaration and proceeded to announce the establishment of the Provisional Council of State and of the provisional government and to repeal all British legislation restricting Jewish *immigration and development work in Palestine. The Declaration of Independence was then signed by the members of the Provisional Council of State.

Legal Aspects. The Provisional Council of State immediately proceeded to give the Declaration and Proclamation a more solid legal footing by passing the Law and Administration Ordinance of 1948, which, with the Transition Law of 1949, contains the basic constitutional provisions of the State of Israel. ·

According to Shabtai Rosenne, Legal Adviser to the Israel Ministry of Foreign Affairs (*The Constitutional and Legal System of Israel*, Israel Office of Information, New York, 1957), the status of the Declaration of Independence "within the hierarchy of legal norms . . . is not conclusive." He writes: "The implication that the Declaration and the accompanying Proclamation generally lack normative qualities is confirmed by several judicial decisions. In two of its earliest cases the Supreme Court stated that the purpose of the Declaration of Independence was to determine the existence of the State for

international purposes, it giving expression to the national ideal and the beliefs of the people but not being a constitutional law in the light of which the validity of other laws could be determined. Shortly afterward the Court slightly retracted by explaining that it had not meant to imply that the Declaration was merely a political document: it was the equivalent of law for the purpose of determining the fact of the legal establishment of the State, although it was not the criterion for testing the constitutionality of the legislation."

Nevertheless, the Declaration of Independence does possess "a certain invigorating effect of its own" on the intellectual sources of Israel law by "allowing the judiciary of the independent State to have direct recourse to external elements—in the specific instance the general principles of international law—and without being bound by the Common Law of England to the extent that it may have incorporated these same principles." However, the Declaration of Independence did originally envisage an elected Constituent Assembly which would meet and adopt a constitution by Oct. 1, 1948. It was later decided to follow the British system of enacting basic laws instead of adopting a written constitution.

G. HIRSCHLER

TEXT OF THE DECLARATION
(TRANSLATED FROM THE HEBREW ORIGINAL)

Eretz-Israel [*see* ERETZ YISRAEL] was the birthplace of the Jewish people. Here their spiritual, religious and political identity was shaped. Here they first attained to statehood, created cultural values of national and universal significance and gave to the world the eternal Book of Books.

After being forcibly exiled from their land, the people kept faith with it throughout their Dispersion and never ceased to pray and hope for their return to it and for the restoration in it of their political freedom.

Impelled by this historic and traditional attachment, Jews strove in every successive generation to re-establish themselves in their ancient homeland. In recent decades they returned in their masses. Pioneers, *ma'apilim* and defenders, they made deserts bloom, revived the Hebrew language, built villages and towns, and created a thriving community, controlling its own economy and culture, loving peace but knowing how to defend itself, bringing the blessings of progress to all the country's inhabitants, and aspiring towards independent nationhood.

In the year 5657 (1897), at the summons of the spiritual father of the Jewish State, Theodor Herzl, the First Zionist *Congress convened and proclaimed the right of the Jewish people to national rebirth in its own country.

This right was recognized in the *Balfour Declaration of the 2nd November, 1917, and re-affirmed in the Mandate of the League of Nations which, in particular, gave international sanction to the historic connection between the Jewish people and Eretz-Israel and to the right of the Jewish people to rebuild its National Home.

The catastrophe which recently befell the Jewish people— the massacre of millions of Jews in Europe—was another clear demonstration of the urgency of solving the problem of its homelessness by re-establishing in Eretz-Israel the Jewish State, which would open the gates of the homeland wide to every Jew and confer upon the Jewish people the status of a fully-privileged member of the comity of nations.

Survivors of the Nazi holocaust in Europe, as well as Jews from other parts of the world, continued to migrate to Eretz-Israel, undaunted by difficulties, restrictions and dangers, and never ceased to assert their right to a life of dignity, freedom and honest toil in their national homeland.

In the Second World War, the Jewish community of this country contributed its full share to the struggle of the freedom- and peace-loving nations against the force of Nazi wickedness and, by the blood of its soldiers and its war effort, gained the right to be reckoned among the peoples who founded the United Nations.

On the 29th November, 1947, the United Nations General Assembly passed a resolution calling for the establishment of a Jewish State in Eretz-Israel; the General Assembly required the inhabitants of Eretz-Israel to take such steps as were necessary on their part for the implementation of that resolution. This recognition by the United Nations of the right of the Jewish people to establish their State is irrevocable.

This right is the natural right of the Jewish people to be masters of their own fate, like all other nations, in their own sovereign State.

Accordingly we, members of the People's Council, represent- atives of the Jewish community of Eretz-Israel and of the Zionist movement, are here assembled on the day of the termina- tion of the British Mandate over Eretz-Israel and, by virtue of our natural and historic right and on the strength of the resolution of the United Nations General Assembly, hereby declare the establishment of a Jewish State in Eretz-Israel, to be known as the State of Israel.

We declare that, with effect from the moment of the termina- tion of the Mandate, being tonight, the eve of Sabbath, the 6th Iyar, 5708 (15th May, 1948), until the establishment of the elected, regular authorities of the State in accordance with the Constitution which shall be adopted by the Elected Constituent Assembly not later than the 1st October, 1948, the People's Council shall act as a Provisional Council of State, and its executive organ, the People's Administration, shall be the Provisional Government of the Jewish State, to be called "Israel."

The State of Israel will be open for Jewish immigration and for the *Ingathering of the Exiles; it will foster the development of the country for the benefit of all inhabitants; it will be based on freedom, justice and peace as envisaged by the prophets of Israel; it will ensure complete equality of social and political rights to all its inhabitants irrespective of religion, race or sex; it will guarantee freedom of religion, conscience, language, education and culture; it will safeguard the *Holy Places of all religions; and it will be faithful to the principles of the Charter of the United Nations.

The State of Israel is prepared to cooperate with the agencies and representatives of the United Nations in implementing the resolution of the General Assembly of the 29th November, 1947, and will take steps to bring about the economic union of the whole of Eretz-Israel.

We appeal to the United Nations to assist the Jewish people in the building-up of its State and to receive the State of Israel into the comity of nations.

We appeal—in the very midst of the onslaught launched against us now for months—to the Arab inhabitants of the State of Israel to preserve peace and participate in the up- building of the State on the basis of full and equal citizenship and due representation in all its provisional and permanent institutions.

We extend our hand to all neighbouring states and their peoples in an offer of peace and good neighbourliness, and appeal to them to establish bonds of cooperation and mutual help with the sovereign Jewish people settled in its own land. The State of Israel is prepared to do its share in common effort for the advancement of the entire Middle East.

We appeal to the Jewish people throughout the *Diaspora to rally round the Jews of Eretz-Israel in the tasks of immigration and upbuilding and to stand by them in the great struggle for the realization of the age-old dream—the redemption of Israel.

Placing our trust in the Rock of Israel, we affix our signatures to this proclamation at this session of the Provisional Council of State, on the soil of the Homeland, in the city of Tel-Aviv, on this Sabbath eve, the 5th day of Iyar, 5708 (14th May, 1948).

Daniel Auster	Moshe Kolodny [Kol]
Mordecai Bentov	David Ben-Gurion
Itzhak Ben Zvi	Eliyahu Dobkin
Eliahu Berligne	Meir Wilner-Kovner
Fritz [Peretz] Bernstein	Zerah Wahrhaftig
Rabbi Z'ev [Wolf] Gold	Herzl Vardi
Meir Grabovsky	Rachel Cohen
Itzhak Grünbaum	Rabbi Kalman Kahana
Dr. Abraham Granowsky	Saadia Kobashi
[Granott]	Rabbi Yitzhak Meir
Meir David Loevenstein	Levin
Zvi Lurie	Eliezer Kaplan
Golda Meyerson [Meir]	Avraham Katznelson
Nahum Y. Nir [Nahum	Felix Rosenblüth [Pinhas Rosen]
Ya'akov Nir-Rafalkes]	David Remez
Zvi Segal	Berl Repetur
Rabbi Yehuda Leib Hacohen-	Mordekhai Shattner
Fishman [Y'huda Leb	Ben Zion Sternberg
HaKohen Maimon]	B'khor Shitrit
David Zvi Pinkas	(Hayim) Moshe Shapira
Aharon Zisling	Moshe Shertok [Sharett]

DEEDES, SIR WYNDHAM. British soldier, public servant, and ardent Zionist sympathizer (b. East Kent, England, 1883; d. London, 1956). In 1915 Brigadier General Deedes was attached to the intelligence staff of British Near Eastern general headquarters in Cairo, where he worked closely with the bureau formed to win Arab support for the Allies against the Turks. He entered Jerusalem with Gen. Sir Edmund H. H. *Allenby in December, 1917. A deeply religious man, Deedes felt that the only way in which Christian society could atone for its past treatment of the Jews was to help them establish their National Home in Palestine. His sympathy for Zionism was reinforced by his contacts with Chaim *Weizmann, whom he met in Palestine in 1918 and who became his lifelong friend. Placed in an administrative position in the "Occupied Territory of Southern Palestine," he helped the *Zionist Commission in its dealings with the British military authorities. In 1920 Sir Herbert *Samuel, *High Commissioner for Palestine, made him Chief Secretary of the Palestine administration.

A self-effacing and dedicated public servant, Deedes gained universal respect, and Sir Herbert later ascribed the period of comparative calm between 1921 and 1929 in large measure to the procedures he initiated for dealing with Arab-Jewish relations. During the *Arab riots of 1921 Deedes took strong measures to stop Arab attacks on Rehovot and authorized Col. Eleazar *Margolin to enlist Jewish volunteers to defend Jaffa and Tel Aviv and to procure needed arms from government stores. He resigned his post in 1923 to devote the rest of his active life to social work in the London slums. Deedes con- tinued his contacts with Zionist leaders and wrote and spoke on behalf of Zionism in England and elsewhere. When Hitler came to power, Deedes became an active supporter of *Youth 'Aliya. In 1943 he founded the British Association for the Jewish National Home to win public opinion to the Zionist cause.

DEFENSE IN ISRAEL. *See* ISRAEL DEFENSE FORCES.

DEGANIA. *See* D'GANYA.

DEGEL Y'RUSHALAYIM (Banner of Jerusalem). Religious organization founded by Rabbi Abraham Isaac *Kook in London in 1918 for the purpose of imbuing the Jewish national rebirth in Palestine with the religious ideals and traditions of the Jewish people. Its aims included the unification of rabbinical authority in Palestine, the furtherance of religious educational institutions in the settlements, and the establishment of a central Yeshiva in Jerusalem. The organization, which had branches in Switzerland, the Netherlands, and other countries, existed for several years.

DE HAAS, JACOB. Zionist leader and writer (b. London, 1872; d. New York, 1937). At the age of 19 he became the editor of the London *Jewish World* and also contributed to the general British press. In the wake of the publication of Herzl's *Jewish State*, De Haas initiated a correspondence with Herzl. Following Herzl's address at a dinner of the *Order of Ancient Maccabeans in London (1896), he joined the Zionist movement, with the understanding that its aim be establishing the Jewish State in Palestine, and thereafter devoted himself to Zionist work. He served as Herzl's honorary English secretary and as English secretary for the 1st Zionist *Congress (1897). From 1897 to 1905 he was a member of the Zionist *Actions Committee. In 1902, at Herzl's request, he settled in the United States. Introduced by a letter from Herzl to Richard *Gottheil, De Haas became secretary of the Federation of American Zionists, serving from 1902 to 1905. He also edited the *Maccabean* during this period. In 1906 he became superintendent of the Boston Young Men's Hebrew Association, and from 1908 to 1918 he edited the *Boston Jewish Advocate*. Among his notable achievements in the political field was winning to the Zionist cause Justice Louis D. *Brandeis, who subsequently threw himself into Zionist study and activity with De Haas as his right-hand man.

Jacob de Haas.
[Zionist Archives]

From 1916 to 1921 De Haas served as secretary first of the Provisional Executive Committee for General Zionist Affairs and then of the *Zionist Organization of America. In these capacities he was one of the guiding spirits of important American Zionist activities during World War I and the immediate postwar years. During a visit to Palestine in 1919 Brandeis was accompanied by De Haas, who sided with Brandeis in the latter's conflict with Chaim *Weizmann in 1920–21 and later years. Like Brandeis, De Haas was a firm believer in the rebuilding of Palestine by economic corporations established by American and other Western Jewish groups rather than by philanthropic funds. From 1921 to 1924 he served as secretary of the Palestine Development League and the Palestine Development Fund.

A stanch Herzlian political Zionist, De Haas opposed the policies of the American Zionist leadership and the extension of the *Jewish Agency by the inclusion of non-Zionist notables. In 1927, supported by noted spokesmen for the group led by Brandeis and Julian *Mack (Felix *Frankfurter, Samuel Rosenson, Robert *Szold, Harry *Friedenwald, Abraham Tulin), De Haas launched a "back to Herzl" movement; however, the conference of the Zionist opposition, held in Washington in April, 1928, failed to create a strong and effective opposition movement. In 1930 De Haas became a member of the National Administrative Council of the Zionist Organization of America. In the ensuing years he leaned increasingly toward the Revisionist concept (*see* REVISIONISTS) of Vladimir *Jabotinsky, whom he introduced as "the second Theodor Herzl" at a meeting held at the Mecca Temple in New York in January, 1935. Later that year he officially joined Jabotinsky's *New Zionist Organization and presided over its Constituent Congress in Vienna in September.

A prolific writer, De Haas possessed an extraordinary capacity for work and was an indefatigable searcher for facts. His major works are *Zionism: Jewish Needs and Jewish Ideals* (1901); *Zionism: Why and Wherefore* (1903); *Herzl's Jewish State* (1904); *Theodore Herzl* (2 vols., 1927); *Louis D. Brandeis* (1929); *The Great Betrayal* (in collaboration with Stephen S. *Wise, 1930); *History of Palestine* (1934); and *The Encyclopedia of Jewish Knowledge* (1934).

J. SCHECHTMAN

DEINARD, EPHRAIM. Hebrew author, bookdealer, and bibliographer (b. Latvia, 1846; d. New York, 1930). Deinard traveled widely, observing the life of Jewish communities and searching for Hebrew books and manuscripts. He published his travel impressions in the Hebrew press. In 1880 he visited Palestine to study the possibilities for the establishment of a Jewish agricultural settlement there. After returning to Russia, he helped organize Jewish emigration to Palestine from Odessa and was extremely active in the *Hoveve Zion movement. In 1888 he went to the United States, where he founded and edited the short-lived Hebrew weekly *HaL'umi*, which propagated the ideas of Hoveve Zion and urged Jews to engage in agriculture. In 1897 he established a Jewish agricultural colony in Nevada. In 1913 he settled in Palestine, making his home in Ramle and encouraging other Jews to settle in that Arab city, but in 1916 he was expelled by the Turks and returned to the United States.

Deinard was the author of more than 50 books and pamphlets. His writings include travel impressions, scholarly and historical essays, polemics, bibliographies, anti-Hasidic diatribes, and Zionist journalism. As a collector and seller of books, he contributed greatly to the establishment and enrichment of Jewish libraries in the United States.

DEIR AL-ASAD. Arab village in western Upper Galilee. Population (1968): 2,570.

DEIR HANNA. Arab village in eastern Lower Galilee. Population (1968): 2,360.

DE LIEME, NEHEMIA. Economist and Zionist leader in the Netherlands (b. The Hague, 1882; d. there, 1940). Son of a religious functionary, he early acquired an extensive Jewish education. After leaving school at the age of 14, he learned the banking business and, in 1904, with a group of idealistic friends, founded in The Hague the Centrale Arbeiders Verzekeringsbank, a workmen's insurance bank which under his leadership developed into the largest enterprise of its kind in the Netherlands. A sympathizer though never a member of the Socialist movement, he founded the International Institute for Research on Socialism in Amsterdam and managed to acquire, among other historical material, the archives of the *Bund, the Jewish Socialist movement in Russia.

Joining the Zionist movement in 1907, De Lieme became honorary secretary of the Dutch Zionist Federation in 1909. In 1912 he was elected chairman, an office he held for many years. His major contribution to the Zionist movement was his work with the *Jewish National Fund (JNF). Joining the JNF Executive Committee during World War I, he became executive director of JNF headquarters when it was moved to The Hague in 1919. Between 1917 and 1920 he issued a magazine, *Eretz Yisrael*, devoted to Palestine land problems.

At the *London Zionist Conference of 1920, De Lieme was chosen a member of the Executive. In the same year the Zionist *Executive in London decided to send a Reorganization Commission to Palestine to examine the work of the Zionist Commission and recommend changes and reforms. Julius *Simon, Robert *Szold, and De Lieme were members of the Reorganization Commission, which advocated the purchase of urban real estate in addition to rural land in order to prevent speculation, and opposed the acquisition of the Jezreel Valley because it considered the prices asked for the land exorbitant and felt that priority should be given to cheaper tracts with a healthier climate. It urged that the funds of the JNF and the

Nehemia de Lieme.
[Zionist Archives]

*Keren HaYesod (Palestine Foundation Fund) be used exclusively for land purchase and settlement, leaving communal and cultural activities to the *Yishuv (Jewish population of Palestine). It further insisted on the elimination of nonessential personnel on the staff of the Zionist Commission, on budgetary savings, and on greater administrative efficiency.

The recommendations, which were in line with the policy advocated by Justice Louis D. *Brandeis, were resented by the Zionist Commission in Jerusalem and criticized by Chaim *Weizmann and his followers. The entire work of this Commission was related to the Brandeis-Weizmann controversy which arose in 1920. Since the recommendations of the Reorganization Commission were not adopted, De Lieme resigned his seat on the Executive of the *World Zionist Organization. He remained in the movement until 1938, when he relinquished his membership after the decision of the 20th Zionist *Congress (Zurich, 1937) to accept the *partition of Palestine in principle, an action he considered a betrayal of the Zionist ideal.

H. BOAS

DEMOCRATIC FACTION. Faction, composed mainly of intellectuals, within the *World Zionist Organization in the years 1901–03. Its adherents alleged that Herzl concentrated control of the Zionist movement in his hands, opposed his preoccupation with purely political action, and called for a wider basis of membership and leadership and for social and cultural action in both Palestine and the *Diaspora.

The faction originated in circles of Jewish students from Eastern Europe, mainly in Germany and Switzerland. Since the early 1890s these students had been organized in Jewish nationalist study groups, and they were on the point of calling a general congress when Herzl appeared. They accepted political Zionism and joined the Zionist Organization but kept their own ideological flavor, which was influenced by *Ahad Ha'Am on the one hand and by contemporaneous "democratic" movements on the other (at the time the term "democracy" had a radical connotation in Russia and Central Europe). More conscious than the official Zionist leadership of the challenge which the revolutionary movements represented to Jewish youth, they wished the Organization to respond to it in their way.

The faction was initiated after the 4th Zionist *Congress (1900), in which the question of cultural activities resulted in a clash between the religious and the secularly oriented Zionists, the former being strenuously opposed to cultural activities by the Organization. After a preparatory conference in Munich in April, 1901, a general conference was convened in December, 1901, on the eve of the 5th Zionist Congress in Basle. At this conference, in which Chaim *Weizmann and Leo *Motzkin participated, Zvi Aberson in a speech laid the foundation of "democratic Zionism" and of the Democratic Faction. The initiators of this first separate ideological group criticized Herzl's aristocratic manner, the concentration of power in his inner circle, and his appeal to the wealthy and ruling classes both within and outside Jewry. But the main point of criticism was Herzl's neglect of practical and educational work for Jewish settlement in Palestine and for Jewish national consciousness in the Diaspora.

Herzl preferred to keep clear of these fields because he did not believe in action devoid of state authority and wanted to concentrate on the political goal. He was also anxious to avoid friction in the Zionist movement, and any educational or cultural action ran the danger of alienating the Orthodox Jews, who rejected secular nationalism. The Democratic Faction, on the other hand, regarded this attitude as superficial. It claimed that there was an organic relationship between the inner growth of the movement and its external achievements and decried the movement's indifference to the economic situation of the Jewish masses. Its slogan was "Materialization of Zionism for the sake of its idealization." The faction denounced the failure of the Zionist Organization to oblige individual Zionists to realize this ideal by active work. It also called for a change in the principle of organization within the World Zionist Organization, preferring a Zionist Organization composed of factions organized along ideological political lines to national units including all the Zionists from a given country. On this they differed with leaders such as M'nahem M. *Ussishkin.

At the 5th Zionist Congress in 1901, the faction raised a number of educational and cultural problems. When Herzl refused to have the program of the faction debated before the election of the new Executive, members of the faction walked out. When, subsequently, the debate did take place, Herzl voted for the faction's program, which then was adopted by the Congress. The program, which was published in the summer of 1902, called for a scientific study of natural conditions in Palestine, active work, and personal devotion. Although the faction remained a small group of students and did not succeed in forming a popular party or a strong opposition movement to Herzl, its activity stimulated the Orthodox wing of the movement to organize the *Mizrahi in 1902.

After the *Minsk Conference of the Russian Zionists in 1902 had acknowledged two trends of education, a secular and an Orthodox, with equal rights, the faction lost much of its driving force. However, the faction numbered among its members many who were to become great figures in Zionism, including Chaim Weizmann, Leo Motzkin, Berthold *Feiwel, and Martin *Buber. When the East Africa controversy broke out (see EAST AFRICA SCHEME), the faction was engulfed within the wider movement of "naysayers."

Some of the faction's plans, such as the idea of a Jewish or Hebrew university (see HEBREW UNIVERSITY OF JERUSALEM), were to be realized in the coming years. The faction established a publication society (Jüdischer Verlag) and engaged in Jewish statistical research.

I. KOLATT

DEMOGRAPHY OF ISRAEL. *See* POPULATION OF ISRAEL.

DENEKAMP, PAUL. Zionist leader in the Netherlands (b. The Hague, 1907; d. Netherlands, 1940). Member of an assimilated family, Denekamp turned to Zionism in his student days, becoming a leader of the Dutch Zionist Students' Organization and serving as chairman of the Joodse Jeugd Federatie (Dutch Zionist Youth Federation) in 1933–34. He was also an honorary editor of the Zionist weekly *De Joodse Wachter* and a member of the Dutch Zionist Council. A reserve officer in the Dutch Army, Denekamp was killed in the Nazi invasion of the Netherlands.

DENMARK, ZIONISM IN. At the end of the 19th century, the Jewish population of Denmark numbered 3,500 persons, most of whom were natives of the country, their forefathers having arrived from Germany beginning in the late 17th century. From 1814 on, they enjoyed equal civic rights, regarded themselves as Danes, spoke Danish, and showed a tendency toward *assimilation, as is indicated by the high rate of mixed marriages (45 per cent). Jewish cultural life centered in the synagogue and a few religious and charitable organizations. There was no real background or understanding for the emerging Jewish national movement.

Early Years. In May, 1897, Chief Rabbi David Simonsen, jointly with the president of the Copenhagen Jewish Community and nine other prominent Jews, sent an invitation to the Jews of Denmark to enroll in the newly established Copenhagen branch of *Hoveve Zion, which was called the Jewish Society for the Colonization of Palestine. The appeal stressed the possibility that the Jewish agricultural settlements in Palestine might play an important part as places of refuge for the persecuted Jews of Russia and Romania and cited the generosity of Baron Edmond de *Rothschild of Paris to these colonies.

In 1902, five years after the 1st Zionist *Congress, the Danish Zionist Association was founded in Copenhagen by the Danish-born physician Dr. Louis Frankel and Josef Nachemsohn. Their initiative was supported by Rabbi Hirsch Herman Goitein and Joseph Michaelsen.

The preamble to the bylaws of the association, adopted on Jan. 12, 1903, read: "The Danish Zionist Association aspires to spread the Zionist idea according to the *Basle Program. This shall be construed as implying the exclusion of any tendency that might hurt the religious sensitivities of others." The second sentence hints at the opposition facing the Danish Zionists, and it is significant that not until three years later was the new association included in the official almanac of the Copenhagen Jewish Community. For several years the Zionists in Denmark gained little sympathy. They encountered much skepticism, animosity, or ridicule, even by Jewish youth. Nevertheless, two Danish delegates, Dr. Louis Frankel and Josef Nachemsohn, attended the 6th Zionist Congress in August, 1903, representing the Zionists of Copenhagen and of the two Swedish cities Malmö and Lund. Dr. Frankel translated into Danish a pamphlet on Zionism by Max *Nordau and in 1907 started the first Danish-Jewish weekly, *Jødisk Tidsskrift* (Jewish Review).

By 1904 a new epoch in the history of Danish Jewry had begun, signaled by the arrival of Jewish immigrants from Russia following the *Kishinev pogrom. The majority of the new immigrants were connected with the *Bund (Jewish Socialist Workers party). As early as 1908 a small group of Yiddish-speaking Zionists from Eastern Europe organized a Zionist reading club, whose members soon thereafter joined the Danish-speaking Zionist Association, whereupon the latter elected a new board with representatives from both groups. The Yiddish-speaking members became the dominant element in the association, but Dr. Frankel continued as chairman until 1917, when he was succeeded by Josef Nachemsohn.

World War I. At the outbreak of World War I, a new stream of Eastern European Jews, including many Zionists from Russia, arrived in Denmark. In February, 1915, the headquarters of the *World Zionist Organization, then in Berlin, set up an office in neutral Denmark (see COPENHAGEN BUREAU) to raise the necessary funds to carry on Zionist settlement work in Palestine, establish relief committees in the Scandinavian countries (in Denmark, under the leadership of Chief Rabbi Simonsen), make correspondence possible between Jews in the belligerent countries, and effect the transfer of funds from the United States.

The presence of many prominent Zionists from other countries brought about a resurgence of Jewish life in Copenhagen during the war. Scandinavian Zionist conferences were held, a branch of *Mizrahi was founded in 1915 under the chairmanship of Dr. Frankel, and a Yiddish daily, *Yidishe Folkstzaytung*, was edited by Meir *Grossman, who, with Vladimir *Jabotinsky, also published the magazine *Di Tribune*. At the same time, the Zionist movement in Denmark was advanced by the work of Benjamin Slor (b. Petah Tikva, 1892), who for half a century was the undisputed leader in all Zionist activities in the country. During his 23 years as a member of the Executive of the Jewish Community, Slor was able to win over many Danish-born assimilated Jews who earlier had shown themselves indifferent or even hostile to Zionism.

Interwar Period and World War II. Between World War I and the rise of Nazism in Germany, the activities of Danish Zionism were confined to routine work: propaganda, campaigns for the *Jewish National Fund and *Keren HaYesod (Palestine Foundation Fund), and protests against actions adverse to Jewish interests. In 1931 Slor organized an agricultural training farm (*see* HAKHSHARA) in Denmark, and from 1933 until the outbreak of World War II a total of 1,400 pioneers (*see* HALUTZ) from Germany, Austria, and Czechoslovakia received their training from Danish farmers, gardeners, and fishermen. After completing their training, most of the Halutzim joined kibbutzim in Palestine. However, when World War II broke out and Denmark was occupied by the German Army, on Apr. 9, 1940, 350 Halutzim were still living in Denmark. They were able to continue their Hakhshara undisturbed until October, 1943, when, like most other Danish Jews, they were smuggled into neutral Sweden, where they remained until the liberation of Denmark in May, 1945. They subsequently went to Palestine. Slor's fellow workers in this wide-ranging Hakhshara project were Magna Hartvig and Julius Margolinsky. Half of the 300 young people of the *Youth 'Aliya who had arrived in Denmark in 1939 went to Palestine during the first 18 months of the war; the others went after 1945. Melanie Oppenhejm was in charge of this project.

In 1935 all Zionist associations in Denmark, Sweden, Norway, and Finland were united in the Scandinavian Zionist Council. In 1937, following Zionist initiative, Prime Minister Thorvald Stauning published a declaration condemning the persecution of Jews in Germany and expressing his sympathy for the efforts to rebuild the Jewish National Home in Palestine.

Postwar Years. While living in Sweden as refugees, the Danish Zionists joined the Swedish brother organization. After their return to Denmark in May, 1945, they resumed their activities at home. The seven Zionist societies—the Danish Zionist Association (*see* GENERAL ZIONISM), 'Avoda (*Po'ale Zion), Mizrahi, *Tz'ire Mizrahi, *HeHalutz, Bachad (*B'rit Halutzim Datiyim), and the *Women's International Zionist Organization (WIZO)—were united in the Danish Zionist Council, of which Slor was chairman until 1955. A Palestine Office of the *Jewish Agency (*see* PALESTINE OFFICES) was set up in the headquarters of the Jewish Community in Copenhagen. A stenciled information sheet, *Palestine Telegram Service (PTS)*, was circulated for a short time and was succeeded by the printed magazine *Israel*, which still appeared in 1965 as a quarterly, in collaboration with the Danish Israel Club (founded in 1957).

At the time of the United Nations deliberations on the fate of Palestine, in 1947 (*see* UNITED NATIONS AND PALESTINE-ISRAEL), the Danish Zionist Council initiated political intervention in favor of the establishment of a Jewish State, which was supported by the Danish State Church, the Danish Red Cross, and the Danish branch of the Save the Children Organization. Forty young people from Denmark joined the *Hagana and volunteered to serve in the Israel *War of Independence. A committee was set up in Copenhagen with Prof. Erik Warburg

as chairman for the purpose of providing arms for the Hagana.

Since the establishment of the State of Israel, the Danish Keren HaYesod Committee has organized an Israel Appeal every year. In 1950 Jews and gentiles together collected $75,000 and the Danish State added an equal amount for the building and equipping of a tuberculosis hospital in Etanim, near Jerusalem. The institution, named for King Christian X, was opened on Apr. 28, 1952. It was an expression of gratitude to King Christian and to the Danish people in general, who during the German occupation had opposed every Nazi attempt to harm the Jews and had saved them by helping them escape to Sweden. In the 1960s the Israel Appeal realized about $60,000 annually. From 1932 on, Erik Hertz served as chairman of the Jewish National Fund, whose annual income was approximately $10,000. Considerable funds were also collected by Jews and gentiles alike for WIZO and Youth 'Aliya.

In the 1960s the Danish Zionist Council distributed informative material, made available Israeli films for lectures in Danish clubs, and organized Hebrew education and tours to Israel. The religious Zionist youth movement, *B'ne 'Akiva, published its own magazine and arranged seminars and summer camps.

Apart from Halutzim, Youth 'Aliya children, and some temporary residents, immigration to Israel from Denmark was rather sparse until 1965. Before World War II hardly more than a score went to Palestine; about 125 went between 1945 and 1965. In the mid-1960s, however, a tendency to increasing 'Aliya could be observed as a result of the *Sh'nat Sherut ("Year of Service" in Israel) movement and the influence of numerous visitors from Israel.

In 1968 the Jewish population in Denmark numbered 6,000, of whom more than 1,000 were affiliated with the Danish Zionist Council (WIZO, 700 members; Danish Zionist Association, 160; B'ne 'Akiva, 90; Mizrahi, 50; 'Avoda, 50; Zionists at large, about 35).

J. MARGOLINSKY

DE SOLA, CLARENCE I. Shipbuilder and Zionist leader in Canada (b. Montreal, 1858; d. there, 1920). In 1899 he was elected president of the newly formed Federation of Zionist Societies of Canada (*see* CANADA, ZIONISM IN), holding this office until 1919. In 1900 he attended the 4th Zionist *Congress. In 1917 he was consulted by British Foreign Secretary Arthur J. *Balfour, who was then on a visit to Canada, concerning the proposed text of what was to become the *Balfour Declaration. De Sola served as a board member of several shipbuilding companies. In 1904 he became Belgian Consul for Canada and in 1919 was decorated by King Albert of Belgium with the Order of Leopold. He was an officer of many philanthropic and cultural institutions and served as parnas of the Spanish and Portuguese Congregation Shearith Israel of Montreal from 1906 until his death.

B. FIGLER

DESSAU, BERNARDO. Physicist and Zionist leader (b. Offenbach, Germany, 1863; d. Perugia, Italy, 1949). Dessau was professor of physics at Bologna University. A delegate to various Zionist Congresses after the 3d Congress (*see* CONGRESS, ZIONIST) in 1899, he was elected a member of the commission to prepare an expedition to East Africa (*see* EAST AFRICA SCHEME), established in 1903. Active in Italian Zionist work at the beginning of the century, he later also participated in efforts to assist Jewish refugees from Nazi Germany.

G. ROMANO

DEVELOPMENT REGIONS. Areas of planned settlement carried out in accordance with a regional settlement system, which provides for the grouping of four to six settlements around a rural center, the latter containing an elementary school, a cultural center, a dispensary, and farm services. The rural centers, in turn, are grouped around a town with central administrative services and industries based on the farming produce of the region.

The first development region, that of Lakhish, was inaugurated in 1955. Thereafter, the Ta'anakh, 'Adulam, Korazim, and B'sor regions were started.

DEVELOPMENT TOWNS. Towns built in Israel since the attainment of independence, mainly in regions remote from the older population centers in the coastal plain. The three main objectives in the early 1950s, when the planning and building of the development towns began, were the dispersal of population, the distribution of industry, and the creation of administrative and economic centers for the rural areas. In the early years of the State of Israel, hundreds of agricultural villages, mostly cooperative smallholders' settlements of the *moshav type, were established in the country. It soon became evident that to ensure an adequate distribution of the population it was necessary to create new urban centers, since the opportunities for setting up additional farming villages had become extremely limited. The policy adopted by the Israeli government for both security and economic reasons was to distribute new industries throughout the country. In pursuance of this policy

the economy of the new towns was based from the outset on industry as the principal source of livelihood. Many of the new towns were deliberately located within concentrations of new villages, so as to serve as rural centers for storing, packing, and marketing the farm produce and to provide administrative, financial, cultural, and other services for the villages.

History. The history of the development towns can be divided into three main periods: 1949–53, 1953–58, and 1958– . Between 1949 and 1953 security considerations and the need to absorb the great waves of immigrants dictated a policy of re-populating the mixed towns where Jews and Arabs had lived together until the establishment of the State, when the Arabs moved out. At this early stage, the towns of Lod, Ramle, Migdal-Ashk'lon, B'er Sheva', 'Akko, Bet Sh'an, Safed, and Tiberias were repopulated without preconceived plans under the pressure of circumstances. In all these towns, there already was a larger or smaller nucleus of older residents, and the new immigrant population began to fill up the remaining vacant dwellings. Later on, new residential quarters were planned and built, and industrial undertakings were directed to these towns.

From 1953 to 1958 new towns were built throughout the country in locations where no previous urban settlements had existed. Again, the incentive in building the towns was security, the dispersal of population, and the absorption of newcomers. No special stress was then put on industry as the economic mainstay of the new urban areas. Some of the towns built during this period were Kiryat Sh'mona, Hatzor, Sh'lomi, Ma'alot, Migdal Ha'Emek, Or 'Akiva, Bet Shemesh, Kiryat Gat, Kiryat

Kiryat Gat, a development town. [Israel Information Services]

Mal'akhi, Sh'derot, N'tivot, Ofakim, Dimona, Y'roham, and Mitzpe Ramon. After 1958 the authorities made a concerted effort to direct new industrial enterprises to dozens of development towns which had begun to suffer much hardship through unemployment and lack of production outlets. A start was also made on several new towns planned from the outset as industrial towns, such as Notz'rat 'Ilit, 'Arad, and Karmiel.

On the whole, the efforts to direct industry to development towns were successful; life and economy in these towns were revolutionized to such an extent that by the mid-1960s they were suffering from a shortage of manpower.

Planning, Construction, and Administration. The planning and building of each new town called for cooperation among various government departments and public institutions. The initial stages of siting and planning the new towns were supervised by the Planning Department of the Ministry of the Interior and the Ministry of Housing, in cooperation with other bodies such as the Department of Public Works and the army (*see* ISRAEL DEFENSE FORCES).

The initial construction work was in the hands of the Ministry of Housing, whereas the settlers were brought in mainly by the Absorption Department of the *Jewish Agency, which took the new arrivals directly from the ship or airplane to dwellings prepared for them in the new towns. Industrial planning and ways of attracting investors, offering them special facilities and privileges, were the task of the Ministry of Commerce and Industry.

Other ministries, notably the Ministry of Education and Culture, the Ministry of Health, and the Ministry of Social Welfare, also took an active interest in the preparation and implementation of the development town schemes, each in its own sphere of responsibility. These provided the new population with their respective essential services. A prominent factor in the life of the new towns was the *Histadrut (General Federation of Labor), which established local labor councils, dealt with employment problems, developed cultural and sports activities, set up its Sick Fund clinics (*see* KUPAT HOLIM), and participated in new industrial ventures.

In their early stage, the development towns were administered by councils of government-appointed representatives from the various ministries. Two or three years later authority would be handed over to local councils elected by the inhabitants. In the course of time some of the towns that had grown and expanded were promoted to municipal status, which entitled them to government by an elected mayor and town council.

On the whole, economic conditions in most development towns were satisfactory, but there were many social problems. The fact that the population was made up mainly of new immigrants was a formidable obstacle to social integration. The need for adaptation to new ways of life, learning a new language, acquiring new skills, or changing from one profession to another presented difficulties. If one adds the hardships of living in a place still being built, amid the noise and commotion of construction sites and at great distances from the older, more glamorous towns, one can appreciate the psychological resistance among some of the new settlers to integration in their new environment. The authorities attempted to overcome these difficulties by providing good services and directing Israeli-born young people to these towns, since nuclei of native Israelis proved to have a stabilizing and consolidating effect on the rest of the population.

DEVELOPMENT TOWNS IN ISRAEL, 1968

Town	Population	Industries
Northern region:		
Kiryat Sh'mona	15,200	Textiles, farm produce processing, work on neighboring farms.
Hatzor–Rosh Pina	5,250	Canned fruit, work on neighboring farms.
Safed	13,000	Instant coffee, clothing, tourist industry and resort, art center.
Tiberias	23,500	Woodworking, fishing, tourist industry and resort.
Ma'alot	4,750	Afforestation, work on neighboring farms.
Sh'lomi	2,000	Afforestation, work on neighboring farms.
Karmiel	1,250	In initial construction stage; first residents settled in 1965.
Notz'rat 'Ilit (administrative center of Northern District)	11,400	Textiles, candy, tires, workshops, tourist industry.
Bet Sh'an	12,500	Textiles, farm produce processing, work on neighboring farms.
'Afula–'Ir Yezr'el	16,400	Sugar refining, textiles, clothing, plastics, work on neighboring farms.
Migdal Ha'Emek	8,000	Brewing, cosmetics, leather products, building materials, clothing, workshops, work on neighboring farms.
Yokn'am 'Ilit	3,700	Metalwork, work on neighboring farms.
Central and Jerusalem region:		
Tirat HaKarmel	13,100	Automobiles, metalwork.
Or 'Akiva	6,000	Plastics, textiles, tourist industry and resort.
Ramle	28,500	Cement works, metalwork, woodworking, building construction.
Lod	26,100	Aircraft, motors, metalwork.
Bet Shemesh	9,850	Cement works, metalwork, farm produce processing.
Southern and Negev region:		
Kiryat Gat	16,300	Textiles, sugar refining, farm produce processing, plastics.
Kiryat Mal'akhi	7,400	Farm produce processing, meat packing, work on neighboring farms.
Ashdod	28,600	Harbor construction, plastics, textiles, automobiles, metalwork.
Ashk'lon	37,400	Cement products, woodworking, automobile parts, tourist industry and resort, farm produce processing, work on neighboring farms.
Sh'derot	6,700	Building construction, farm produce processing, work on neighboring farms.
N'tivot	4,620	Farm produce processing, work on neighboring farms.
Ofakim	8,550	Textiles, work on neighboring farms.

DEVELOPMENT TOWNS IN ISRAEL, 1968 (continued)

Town	Population	Industries
B'er Sheva' (capital of the Negev and administrative center)	69,500	Chemicals, metalwork, ceramics, transport.
'Arad	2,000	Chemicals, tourist industry and resort.
Dimona	19,000	Textiles, chemicals, atomic reactor, mining, minerals.
Y'roham	4,750	Chemicals, mining, minerals.
Mitzpe Ramon	1,500	Chemicals, mining, minerals.
Elat	11,000	Red Sea port, mining, copper ore processing, tourist industry and resort.

A. ELIAV

D'GANIM. Rural center in the Darom. Founded in 1948. Population (1968): 350.

D'GANYA (Degania). Village, the first *kibbutz in Palestine. In 1909 a controversy broke out between the director of the Kinneret Farm, the agronomist M. Berman, and the workers. Dr. Arthur *Ruppin, director of the Palestine Office (*see* PALESTINE OFFICES) of the *World Zionist Organization, decided to hand over part of the land of the farm to an independent workers' group. In December, 1909, about 3,000 dunams (*see* DUNAM) at Umm Juni, on the east bank of the Jordan south of Lake Kinneret, was put at the disposal of a group of seven workers. The group ended its first year with a profit but disbanded. The land was then given to the Romny group, so called because its first members came from Romny, a town in the Ukraine.

The Romny group, which had lived together as a commune in Hadera, took over the land at Umm Juni on Oct. 28, 1910. After two years it decided to remain on the site permanently, and the first permanent buildings were erected near the exit of the Jordan from Lake Kinneret. The new settlement was named D'ganya. During the first year of its existence, D'ganya was a laboratory of sorts for the form of collective living that came to be known as the K'vutza. At the end of 1911 the Palestine Office suggested that D'ganya be run along the cooperative lines proposed by Franz *Oppenheimer. The group rejected the suggestion, mainly because its members objected to the principle of unequal pay for skilled and unskilled laborers. For years the D'ganya pioneers struggled with the problem of raising their children until the principle of collective child care was finally adopted. It was not until 1926 that the practice of keeping separate accounts for each member was abolished.

In 1919 several members left the group and joined the founders of the Moshav 'Ovdim (*see* MOSHAV). In that year the group sustained a great loss in the untimely death of Joseph *Bussel, one of its founders and ideologists. Aharon David *Gordon was affiliated with D'ganya and spent the last years of his life there.

In the early years the economy of the settlement was based on the growing of *falha* (extensive field crops). This practice caused a number of problems, including a lack of suitable employment for women workers and the necessity of employing outside paid workers at harvesting and threshing time. As a result, the group decided to engage in mixed farming, which gave employment to women members and also made it possible

A view of the kibbutz D'ganya. [Histadrut Foto-News]

to have a balanced work program. The group also decided to maintain the intimate familylike character of the K'vutza (in contrast to the larger K'vutzot and the *G'dud Ha'Avoda V'haHagana 'Al Shem Yosef Trumpeldor) and to limit the membership of D'ganya to 25. Accordingly, it was decided to give up part of the land to another group of settlers (D'ganya Bet, 1919), after which the original D'ganya became known as D'ganya Aleph.

D'ganya was a prototype for all subsequently established communal settlements. In 1925 it participated in the founding of the *Hever HaK'vutzot (League of K'vutzot), which later gave rise to other kibbutz associations (*Kibbutz M'uhad, *Kibbutz Artzi Shel HaShomer HaTza'ir). D'ganya served as a model also for the other kibbutzim that were established in the Jezreel Valley and turned the valley into the first compact area of communal settlements in the world. Members of D'ganya participated in the common organizational, economic, and educational institutions of the kibbutzim of the whole area in order to foster the communal way of life.

In time membership grew and a second and third generation arose, but the K'vutza did not lose its intimate character. During the years of its existence many hundreds of workers and youths, among them *Youth 'Aliya children (from 1934), passed through D'ganya. In 1941 the District Museum for Nature and Agriculture, named for Aharon David Gordon (Bet Gordon), was founded in D'ganya.

On May 18, 1948, D'ganya, with other kibbutzim in the Kinneret Valley, was attacked by the Syrian invaders. Its members fought heroically in nearby Tzemah and, after the fall of Tzemah, stopped the enemy tanks at the gates of D'ganya itself on May 20.

In the history of modern Jewish settlement in the country D'ganya occupies a place of honor as the Mother of the K'vutzot, an expression of the pioneering spirit, and a symbol of Jewish heroism. In 1968 D'ganya Aleph had 440 inhabitants and D'ganya Bet 520. Both were affiliated with the *Ihud HaK'vutzot V'haKibbutzim.

Y. SLUTSKY

DIAMOND INDUSTRY IN ISRAEL. The diamond industry in Israel dates back to 1939. Its pioneers were industrialists who had come to Palestine from the Netherlands and Belgium before World War II and enterprising members of the old *Yishuv (Jewish population of Palestine). Although its beginnings were small, the industry received a tremendous impetus during its second year of existence when the war separated the traditional centers of manufacture—Belgium, the Netherlands, and, to a lesser degree, Germany—from their sources of supply as well as from their customary markets. With the help of a limited number of skilled workers from the Low Countries the industry expanded, and by the end of the war its labor force numbered about 4,000, most of whom were engaged in the cutting of very small stones (eight facets and small brilliants).

After the war, the size of the industry was substantially reduced in Palestine, as it was also in countries such as Brazil and Cuba, where the diamond industry had taken root during the war. In contrast to those countries, however, the nucleus of a skilled labor force remained in Israel, although there were serious difficulties in obtaining sufficient raw materials and the reactivated older European centers offered considerable competition. Beginning in 1950, there was a steady improvement, which was apparent in a marked upward trend after 1957, as illustrated in Table 1.

TABLE 1. EMPLOYMENT IN ISRAEL'S DIAMOND INDUSTRY, 1940–65

Year	Number of workers	Year	Number of workers
1940	200	1953	1,200
1941	1,200	1954	1,900
1942	2,500	1955	2,300
1943	3,750	1956	2,600
1944	3,750	1957	3,000
1945	4,000	1958	3,600
1946	4,000	1959	4,300
1947	2,000	1960	5,000
1948	800	1961	6,000
1949	800	1962	7,100
1950	1,000	1963	8,200
1951	1,200	1964	9,000
1952	1,200	1965	8,000

TABLE 2. IMPORTS OF ROUGH DIAMONDS, 1949–65
(In thousands of Israeli pounds)

Year	Total imports	Imports from syndicate
1949	1,509	1,132
1950	3,224	2,453
1951	3,489	2,801
1952	3,506	2,709
1953	4,212	2,390
1954	4,926	3,060
1955	5,802	2,476
1956	7,710	1,915
1957	10,290	2,107
1958	8,988	2,325
1959	14,817	2,499
1960	17,557	3,725
1961	19,069	7,162
1962	24,277	12,414
1963	33,217	20,176
1964	36,516	22,077
1965	34,502	20,115

In the late 1950s, while the industry maintained its specific system of work, its output, which previously had consisted

mainly of small brilliants (averaging 50 to 130 stones per carat), was composed more generally of melees (averaging 4 to 25 stones per carat). The main obstacle to the industry's growth remained an insufficient supply of rough diamonds, which were allocated by the London Syndicate on a quota basis in accordance with past trade. In the early 1960s, negotiations between the syndicate and Israel's industry led to a change in the syndicate's attitude toward deliveries to Israel, with the result that thereafter Israel received 80 to 90 per cent of all rough melees sold by the syndicate (see Table 2).

In 1968 the diamond industry in Israel comprised some 300 enterprises, including polishing factories, sawing works, and disc-turning workshops. Israel ranked second to Belgium as the world's largest manufacturer of polished diamonds and accounted for about 30 per cent of the world output. Table 3 shows the development of Israel's diamond export trade.

Y. ARNON

TABLE 3. DIAMOND EXPORTS, BY WEIGHT AND VALUE, 1949–65

Year	Weight (in 1,000 carats)	Value (in $1,000)
1949	75	5,118
1950	119	8,810
1951	132	11,652
1952	134	11,462
1953	146	12,712
1954	183	15,698
1955	230	20,616
1956	262	25,982
1957	341	35,221
1958	330	32,959
1959	455	45,195
1960	574	56,318
1961	669	65,284
1962	838	82,339
1963	1,047	104,017
1964	1,084	118,206
1965	1,163	131,761

DIASPORA (Galut). Term of Greek origin denoting the dispersion of the Jews ever since the Babylonian Exile of 586 B.C.E. It is also used to designate the Jewish *communities so dispersed. Originally, the Jews deported from Palestine to Mesopotamia considered themselves people in "exile" (*gola* or *galut* in Hebrew). When a return to Palestine became possible, however, only a few thousand Babylonian Jews availed themselves of the opportunity (Ezra 2:64). The majority either remained behind or even sought new and more remote places of settlement. By the time of the destruction of the Second Jewish Commonwealth by the Romans (C.E. 70), there were considerable Jewish Diasporas in Babylonia and areas immediately adjacent to the north and east, Syria, Egypt, Cyrene, Asia Minor, Greece, and Rome. With the Roman conquests in Europe, Jews settled in the newly opened lands, and the spread of Byzantine influence into Eastern Europe, too, was followed by some Jewish settlement in that part of the world. From Babylonia and Persia, Jews moved on to India, central Asia, and even lands as far east as China. Persecutions in one place gave rise to new Jewish Diasporas in others, and with the movement of European settlers overseas (the Americas, South Africa,

Textile plant at Dimona. [Israel Information Services]

and Australia), the Jewish Diaspora extended to the New World.

In Jewish consciousness as well as in Jewish historiography, *Israel and the Diaspora became the two component parts of the Jewish people. The longing for Israel, symbolized by Zion, never ceased in the Diaspora, but economic ties, political difficulties, and considerations of security only rarely allowed the realization of the dream of return. Nevertheless, the awareness of living in the Diaspora, with its connotation of transience and of strong religious and historical bonds with the Holy Land of the fathers, was an essential prerequisite of the emergence of the *Hoveve Zion movement in the second half of the 19th century and of the great positive response subsequently elicited by Herzl's political Zionism. R. PATAI

DIASPORA NATIONALISM. *See* GALUT NATIONALISM.

DIMONA. Town in the central Negev. Founded in 1955 and named for a city mentioned in Joshua 15:22. Initially planned to house the families of the laborers of the *Dead Sea Works Company, Ltd., at S'dom, it has developed into an industrial center, based on large textile factories and other enterprises. Population (1968): 19,000.

DINUR (DINABURG), BEN-ZION. Historian and educator (b. Khorol, Ukraine, Russia, 1884). After completing Yeshiva training and receiving rabbinical ordination in 1901, Dinur was active in the Zionist movement and later in the revolutionary

movement in Russia. Beginning in 1904, he taught at various Jewish educational institutions in Russia. From 1911 to 1914 he studied at the Universities of Berlin and Bern and subsequently at the University of Petrograd (1917). In 1921 he

Ben-Zion Dinur.
[Israel Information Services]

settled in Palestine, where he taught Hebrew and Jewish history at the Bet HaKerem Teachers Training School in Jerusalem, becoming its principal in 1943. From 1936 to 1952 Dinur was a member of the history department of the *Hebrew

University of Jerusalem, and from 1951 to 1955 he served as Minister of Education and Culture in the Israeli *government. He initiated the distribution of the Israel Prizes on *Independence Day (*see* ISRAEL PRIZE), introduced the government's Education Bill in the *Knesset, and conceived *Yad VaShem (a memorial to the victims of the Nazi holocaust), which he headed from 1956 to 1959.

Both in Russia and in Israel, Dinur wrote prolifically on themes of Jewish history. His magnum opus, *The History of Israel*, based on original source material, consists of two parts, *Israel in the Diaspora* and *Israel in Its Land* (each comprising several volumes not yet completed in 1968). He conceived the series of books known as *Sefer HaTziyonut* and wrote *Precursors of Zionism* (1939) as part of the series. Dinur was the author also of two autobiographical volumes and the editor of various historical journals. A jubilee volume was published in his honor in 1949.   G. KRESSEL

DISHON. Village (moshav) in eastern Upper Galilee. Founded in 1953 and affiliated with Ha'Oved HaTziyoni. Population (1968): 266.

DISRAELI, BENJAMIN (1st Earl of Beaconsfield). British statesman and author (b. London, 1804; d. there, 1881). Disraeli was the eldest son of Isaac D'Israeli, a member of the London Spanish and Portuguese Congregation. When he was 13, his father had him baptized and admitted to the Church of England. After a series of unsuccessful business ventures, Disraeli turned to literature, attracting wide attention with his novel *Vivian Grey* (1826). He traveled in the Middle East and was fascinated by the Holy Land. Disraeli entered politics and, after several defeats, was elected to Parliament by the Conservative party in 1837, becoming a leader of the Young England faction. He was leader of the House of Commons and Chancellor of the Exchequer in 1852, 1858–59, and 1866–68. In 1868, and again from 1874 to 1880, he was Prime Minister. Representing Great Britain at the Berlin Congress of 1878, he was an exponent of British imperialism and acquired Cyprus and an interest in the Suez Canal Company for Britain. Disraeli is regarded as one of the founders of modern British parliamentary democracy, the molder of the British Empire, and the initiator of far-reaching political and social reforms. He was elevated to the peerage in 1877.

Throughout his public career Disraeli never failed to stress his Jewish origin. He saw no conflict between his Christian affiliation and Jewish ancestry, since he considered Christianity only a further stage in the development of Judaism. He regarded the Semites as a superior race by virtue of the fact that they had been privileged to receive the divine revelation on Mount Sinai. His pride in his descent was his reaction to the anti-Semitic gibes directed at him by the British aristocracy. Actually, his conception of Judaism was rather confused, as is apparent, for example, in his indiscriminate use of the terms "Jew" and "Semite." His writings contain various allusions to the restoration of Israel. His novel *The Wondrous Tale of Alroy* (1833) is a debate of sorts between a Zionist and an assimilationist approach. In his novel *Tancred* (1847) the prospect of a Jewish restoration to Zion is conceived as a return to a Jewish Christ. In his biography of Lord Bentinck (1851) he develops a synthesis between Judaism and Christianity, while in his later novel *Lothair* (1870) he reverts to the theme of Jewish revival in Palestine.

As a statesman, Disraeli championed the cause of Jewish *emancipation in Parliament. At times he was accused of being motivated by Jewish sentiment, especially in his anti-Russian policy during the Russo-Turkish War of 1877 and at the Berlin Congress.   S. Z. ABRAMOV

DISTURBANCES, ARAB. *See* ARAB RIOTS IN PALESTINE.

DIZENGOFF, MEIR. Mayor of Tel Aviv (b. Akimowzi, Bessarabia, Russia, 1861; d. Tel Aviv, 1936). While serving a term of imprisonment for activity in the Russian revolutionary movement, young Dizengoff decided that on his release he would devote himself to the betterment of his people. In 1886 he helped found a *Hoveve Zion group in Kishinev, and in the following year he participated in the *Druskenik Conference.

While studying chemical engineering in France, Dizengoff was commissioned by Baron Edmond de *Rothschild to establish a bottle factory at Tantura, Palestine, and went there in 1892. After the enterprise failed, he returned to Russia, where he became one of the members of the *Odessa Committee of Hoveve Zion. He attended Zionist Congresses (*see* CONGRESS, ZIONIST) and was an ardent follower of Herzl. At the 6th Zionist Congress (1903) he opposed the *East Africa scheme. In 1904 he founded the *G'ula land purchase society. Returning to Palestine in 1905, he established the *Ahuzat Bayit society in 1909 as the basis of a modern all-Jewish suburb of Jaffa. In 1911 he was elected chairman of the governing body of the suburb, which later became Tel Aviv. It was his aim to make Tel Aviv the largest city and the cultural center of the *Yishuv (Jewish population of Palestine).

During World War I Dizengoff was active in aiding the Jewish population, which was being harassed by the Turkish authorities. He was among the Jews exiled by the Turks from Tel Aviv in 1917, went into exile in Haifa and Damascus, and organized help for the deportees. Returning to Tel Aviv in 1918, he continued as chairman of the town council, making every effort to obtain independent municipal status for the city. In 1921, when Tel Aviv was granted municipal status, he was chosen its first mayor. He served in that capacity, with an interruption of three years (1925–28), until his death.

Meir Dizengoff.
[Zionist Archives]

Dizengoff contributed significantly to the development of Tel Aviv. He was instrumental in the founding of numerous business enterprises and cultural and social institutions, and he made many trips abroad in the interest of the city. He obtained a loan for Tel Aviv in the United States. It was largely due to his efforts that the first Levant Fair and the first Maccabia sports rally were held. He established friendly relations with Arab leaders and assisted the *Jewish National Fund in acquiring land. He also obtained from the *High Commissioner for Palestine the concession for building a port in Tel Aviv. The new port freed the Yishuv from dependence on Arab dockers in Jaffa, who frequently refused to handle Jewish goods.

Dizengoff was the founder (1919) of HaEzrah, a middle-class organization, and a member of the First *Va'ad L'umi (National Council). He served at one time as deputy mayor of Jaffa and and was a member of the Zionist *Executive from 1927 to 1929, as director of its Department of Urban Colonization. In 1936 he was made honorary commander of the Order of the British Empire for his services in behalf of Palestine. Dizengoff bequeathed his home and estate to the Tel Aviv Museum, which he had founded in 1931 in memory of his wife, Zina (see MUSEUMS IN ISRAEL). It was in this building that the *Declaration of Independence was proclaimed.

DJEMAL PASHA, AHMED. *See* JAMAL PASHA, AHMED.

DO'AR HAYOM. Hebrew daily founded in 1918 in Jerusalem by Itamar *Ben Avi, eldest son of Eliezer *Ben Yehuda. Conceived as the organ of the "old-timers" of the Palestine Jewish community, *Do'ar HaYom* (Daily Mail) opposed the groups that stood behind the other Hebrew daily, *Ha'Aretz*.

Until the end of Ben Avi's editorship in 1928, *Do'ar HaYom* was identified with his "cantonization" proposal, which called for the division of Palestine into autonomous Jewish and Arab cantons and gained the support of certain circles in the *Yishuv (Jewish population of Palestine) and of some officials of the British Mandatory administration in Palestine.

In 1928 the paper was taken over by the *Revisionists and began to advocate the immediate establishment of an independent Jewish State. In 1930 it reverted to Itamar Ben Avi. The paper carried a weekly literary supplement. It ceased publication in 1937.   J. RUBIN

DOBKIN, ELIYAHU. Zionist labor leader (b. Bobruisk, Russia, 1898). Dobkin studied at the University of Kharkov and then moved to Poland, where he was secretary of the pioneer

Eliyahu Dobkin.
[Zionist Archives]

youth organization *HeHalutz of Byelorussia and Poland from 1918 to 1923. From 1923 to 1932 he was chairman of the Executive Committee of the World Federation of HeHalutz,

becoming a member of the Zionist *Actions Committee in 1926. Settling in Palestine in 1932, he served as director of the Immigration Department of the *Histadrut (General Federation of Labor) from then until 1934. In 1937 he became a deputy member of the Executive of the *Jewish Agency (a full member in 1945), and was director of the Agency's Youth and HeHalutz Department. During World War II, as director of the Agency's Immigration Department, he traveled widely in Europe, North and South America, and South Africa on Agency missions, and he attended many Zionist Congresses (*see* CONGRESS, ZIONIST). From 1956 to 1961 he was chairman of the Board of Directors of *Keren HaYesod (Palestine Foundation Fund). He wrote *'Aliya V'Hatzala BIme HaSho'a* ('Aliya and Rescue during the Holocaust, 1946).

DOLITZKI, M'NAHEM MENDEL. Hebrew writer and poet (b. Białystok, Russian Poland, 1856; d. Los Angeles, 1931). One of the first *Hoveve Zion, he published (1881–82) an article in *HaMelitz*, calling for Jewish emigration to Palestine rather than to the United States. His sentimental poems about Zion made him widely known and esteemed as a nationalist poet. He won the prize offered in 1886 by the B'ne Zion Society of Moscow for a poem in a contest for a Jewish national anthem. Dolitzki also wrote stories describing the situation of Russian Jewry after the pogroms of 1881. He was a teacher and, from 1882 to 1892, literary secretary to Kalonymus-Z'ev *Wissotzky. After the expulsion of the Jews from Moscow in 1892, Dolitzki went to the United States, where he worked for the Yiddish press and wrote novels in Yiddish. In 1895 his collected poems, *Kol Shire M'nahem* (2 vols.), were published in New York.

                                               I. KLAUSNER

DÖMÉNY, LAJOS. Jurist and Zionist leader in Hungary (b. Ádánd, Somogy County, Hungary, 1880; d. Russian front, 1914). Dömény became acquainted with Zionist ideas while studying law at the University of Budapest and subsequently emerged as one of the most active leaders of the Zionist movement in Hungary. He helped establish the Hungarian branch of the *Jewish National Fund and organized the *Kadimah scout movement (1913). With Ármin Bokor, he was instrumental in launching *Zsidó Néplap*, the first Zionist organ in Hungary, which he edited for some time. He cooperated in the establishment of Zionist organizations in Budapest and provincial cities of Hungary and published a series of articles on Zionist subjects in Hungarian and foreign papers. Dömény died on the Russian front soon after the outbreak of World War I and was posthumously decorated for bravery.   R. L. BRAHAM

DOMESTIC TRADE IN ISRAEL. The bulk of Israel's population consists of immigrants who have arrived since the formation of the State. Thus, the character of Israel's domestic trade is a natural outgrowth of the country's general development and specific features.

General Character. In 1968 domestic trade was based mainly on the marketing of domestic products; imports had ceased to play the outstanding part they had played in earlier years. The *government of Israel no longer exercised control over marketing and prices, since all goods were available in abundance and in more or less satisfactory quality. Early in 1961 official governmental controls had been introduced for cartels and monopolies where these proved detrimental to the public interest.

Israeli law required the display of price tags in all branches of the retail trade as well as quality and quantity labeling of foodstuffs and many other goods. The government retained indirect influence over the production and marketing of goods, marketing methods, and the level and stability of prices.

The most important food products, such as wheat, seeds, sugar, meat, and milk powder, were imported by the government. One of the unique aspects of the market situation was the problem of the Jewish religious dietary laws with respect to certain meat and dairy products.

Trade was concentrated in the three largest cities, Tel Aviv, Haifa, and Jerusalem, which accounted for more than 50 per cent of sales, although their population was only 31.6 per cent of the country's total. Tel Aviv and Haifa in particular played prominent roles as national centers of commerce.

Following the establishment of the State of Israel, shops expanded considerably in size, equipment, appearance, variety of merchandise in stock, and service. The main stimuli for this development were the steady rise of the general *standard of living and the arrival of experienced businessmen as immigrants to the new State (see Tables 1 and 2). As shown in Table 3,

TABLE 1. LEVEL OF CONSUMPTION PER CAPITA AT 1967 PRICES

	1959	1961	1963	1965	1967
All consumption (in millions of Israeli pounds)	3,815	4,526	5,497	6,584	6,895
Consumption per capita (in Israeli pounds)	1,850	2,067	2,310	2,569	2,540

the increase in expenditures for private consumption in the 1960s was due mainly to a rise in purchases of durable goods.

Wholesale Trade. In 1967 there were in Israel 3,700 wholesale businesses, which supplied a livelihood for 21,600 persons. Of these, 17,800, or 82 per cent, were employees. Wholesale trade was concentrated largely in Tel Aviv (65 per cent) and Haifa (20 per cent); only 4 per cent was located in Jerusalem. The

TABLE 2. EXPENDITURES BY MAJOR ITEMS FOR AVERAGE WAGE-EARNING JEWISH FAMILY OF FOUR PERSONS, 1964

Item	Per cent
Food, including fruit and vegetables	35.7
Furniture and household goods	10.8
Clothing and footwear	11.4
Household maintenance	8.4
Miscellaneous	33.7
All expenses except shelter	100.0

greater part of the wholesale trading houses in the country had been founded after the establishment of the State.

In view of the fact that in Israel distances are relatively small and the major markets are highly concentrated, the scope of wholesale trade is more limited than in larger countries. Moreover, its functions, particularly those of financing and production scheduling, had not been thoroughly developed by the 1960s. In 1967 there were 27 purchasing organizations of collectives and cooperative rural settlements. Rural marketing was done through centralized channels such as T'nuva (see HISTADRUT), which held more than 80 per cent of the agricultural marketing system in its hands, and such smaller organizations as Tene and 'Amir.

Retail Trade. Retail trade in Israel, other than the traditional Oriental bazaars, began with small, primitive retail outlets in the towns and equally primitive cooperative stores in the agricultural settlements. The rising standard of living, accompanied by the refinement of consumer items, brought an ever-increasing demand for better service and for more expensive, higher-quality products. Competition acted as a spur in all fields of consumer sales to improve services and facilities.

In 1967 the bulk of consumer goods sales was in the hands of about 30,000 retail outlets of the private enterprise sector, while the collective sector owned about 400 retail outlets (see Table 4). Large-scale retailers marketed 18 per cent of total retail sales in 1966, as against 21.4 per cent in Western Europe. In 1967, 84.5 per cent of the retail stores (all branches) employed one or two persons, while 2.4 per cent employed more than five persons. The employment status of the persons occupied in the retail trade (all branches) was as follows: store owners, 53.7

TABLE: 3. PERCENTAGE OF ISRAELI FAMILIES POSSESSING DURABLE GOODS

	1961	1962	1963	1964	1965	1966	1967
Radio	79.6	86.8	88.4	89.3	89.9	90.9	76.8*
Gas range or gas cooking stove	62.3	73.0	79.4	84.5	85.5	83.1	84.3
Refrigerator	50.2	58.8	64.3	68.8	77.6	80.1	82.9
Washing machine	18.3	19.2	23.4	27.0	28.5	29.5	31.8
Second radio	....	15.4	18.7	24.2	30.5	31.8	2.2*
Mixer	....	9.2	12.8	14.4	17.7	19.7	21.8
Vacuum cleaner	....	....	8.7	10.3	13.8	14.1	18.1
Private car	....	4.1	5.2	6.9	7.7	10.5	13.3
Tape recorder	....	....	3.2	3.9	6.7	6.1	9.2
Transistor radio	....	....	....	....	....	....	50.6*

*Until 1966 transistor radios were included in the items "Radio" and "Second radio."

TABLE 4. ESTIMATED NUMBER OF RETAIL BUSINESSES AND PERSONS OCCUPIED IN THE RETAIL TRADE, 1967

	Number of businesses	Number of persons occupied		Number of inhabitants	
		Total	Average per business	Average per business	Average per employed persons
Foods	13,400	25,900	1.9	202	104
Textiles and clothing	7,600	15,700	2.1	357	172
Household goods and furniture	4,400	8,000	1.8	609	338
Building materials, agricultural equipment, work utensils, and vehicles	1,300	3,700	2.9	2,114	733
Department stores and other retail establishments	3,800	6,600	1.7	721	412
Total	30,500*	59,900*	2.0	89	45

*Peddlers excluded.

per cent; family members, 23.4 per cent; salaried employees, 22.9 per cent. Most of the stores were owned and operated by families. In 1967 females accounted for 31.1 per cent of the persons occupied in retail trade. In all, 56 per cent of the persons engaged in retail trade were 45 years of age or older. This meant that not enough young blood was going into trade.

In most of the retail trade branches the short-circuit (producer-retailer) system prevailed. Wholesalers were active mainly in such lines as food, household goods, light apparel, furniture, and a number of electrical-appliance lines.

The average size of stores was small by Western standards (frequently there was no more than 220 to 330 square feet of floor space). It seems that Israeli stores did not have sufficient floor space to ensure proper service. Stock turnover generally exceeded that of other countries. This may be attributed to the relatively low stock levels in most Israeli stores. The average profit margin, especially in foodstuffs, was lower than in the countries of Western Europe (20 per cent in Israel, as against 33 per cent in Western Europe).

Changes in Domestic Trade. In the mid-1960s the commercial life of Israel was in a state of rapid change and development. Israel being essentially a pioneering country, the people previously had concentrated on problems of settlement, immigrant absorption, construction, production, and defense, and it was only in the 1960s that they became more conscious of the importance of proper marketing and selling. This consciousness generated an increased desire to study and learn marketing and sales promotion and to develop commercial patterns accordingly.

Through legislation and incentives, the Israeli government endeavored to guide trade toward more progressive ways of doing business and toward higher standards of service. Fair-trade bureaus, consumer organizations, and the trade associations cooperated in achieving these goals.

H. ASHKENAZY AND G. SOEN

DOMINICAN REPUBLIC, ZIONISM IN. The present small Jewish community in the Dominican Republic was started in the 19th century by Jewish immigrants from the neighboring island of Curaçao, in the Netherlands Antilles. A second wave of immigration, consisting of refugees from Tsarist Russia, came in the 1880s. During the era of Nazi persecution and World War II, about 1,000 Jewish refugees were settled in a colony set up for their accommodation in Sosúa. In 1968 the Jewish community in the country numbered almost 400, in a

total population of 3,889,000. There were 200 Jews in Santo Domingo and about 120 in Sosúa.

Following the establishment of the State of Israel the Unión Sionista de la República Dominicana (Zionist Organization of the Dominican Republic) became largely inactive. In December, 1963, a treaty of friendship was signed by the Dominican government and the State of Israel. The following year, the Israeli Legation was raised to the rank of embassy. The *Jewish National Fund maintains an office in Santo Domingo.

DOR (El-Burj). Village (moshav) in the Sharon Plain. Founded in 1949 and affiliated with *T'nu'at HaMoshavim. Population (1968): 186.

A Bronze and Iron Age city was located at Dor. In addition, the remains of a Hellenistic temple and jetty and of a Roman theater and Byzantine church were found.

DORI, YA'AKOV. Israeli military commander (b. Odessa, Russia, 1899). Brought to Palestine as a child, he joined the *Jewish Legion after the British occupation of the country. While still in uniform, he participated in the defense of the Jewish population of Tel Aviv and Jaffa during the *Arab riots of May, 1921. He subsequently studied engineering in Ghent, Belgium. After his return to Palestine, he worked in the Technical Department of the Zionist *Executive and was active in the *Hagana. Dori served as deputy commander and later as commander of the Hagana in Haifa, where he was in charge of personnel training. In 1938 he became chief of staff of the Hagana. From 1948 to 1950 he was chief of staff of the *Israel

Ya'akov Dori.
[Zionist Archives]

Defense Forces and in this capacity commanded the Israeli Army during the *War of Independence. Subsequently he headed the Scientific Research and Development Department

Dreyfus facing the military court at Rennes. [Zionist Archives]

of the Israel government, and from 1951 to 1965 he was president of the *Technion, the Israel Institute of Technology.

DOROT. Village (kibbutz) on the northern border of the Negev. Founded in 1941 and affiliated with the *Ihud Ha-K'vutzot V'haKibbutzim. In 1946 part of the settlement was destroyed during searches by the British Army. In the *War of Independence Dorot suffered heavily from Egyptian air attacks. Population (1968): 370.

DOVEV. Village (moshav) in eastern Upper Galilee. Founded in 1963 and affiliated with *T'nu'at HaMoshavim.

DOVRAT. Village (kibbutz) in the Jezreel Valley. Founded in 1946 and affiliated with the *Ihud HaK'vutzot V'haKibbutzim. Population (1968): 290.

DREYFUS AFFAIR. Trials of Capt. Alfred Dreyfus (1859–1935), a Jew and a General Staff officer in the French Army, on charges of high treason and espionage. The Dreyfus affair provided the setting for a crisis in French democracy that divided the nation into warring camps of republicans and monarchists, freethinkers and clericalists, pacifists and militarists, liberals and anti-Semites.

In December, 1894, a military court, sitting *in camera*, convicted Captain Dreyfus of high treason and espionage on behalf of Germany. He was publicly degraded and sentenced to life imprisonment on Devil's Island, a penal colony off the coast of French Guiana. In 1896 Col. Georges Picquart, chief of France's army intelligence, discovered evidence proving that Dreyfus was innocent and that the real culprit was one Maj. Ferdinand-Walsin Esterhazy. Picquart promptly submitted his findings to his superiors but was commanded to remain silent. When he refused to be silenced, Picquart was ordered to Tunisia. The increasing clamor of the Dreyfusards for justice finally resulted in the arrest of Esterhazy in 1897. However, despite overwhelming evidence of his guilt, Esterhazy was quickly acquitted.

Outraged by these events, Émile Zola wrote his famous article "J'accuse" (1898). As a result, he was charged with libel and forced to flee to England to avoid punishment. Anti-Dreyfusard sentiment now reached a new high level. Colonel Picquart was court-martialed and imprisoned. Anti-Semitic riots erupted throughout France and Algeria. A new and unexpected turn was given the affair by the confession and suicide of Col. Hubert-Joseph Henry, a French officer and one of the original accusers of Dreyfus, who, under rigorous interrogation, had admitted having forged evidence against Dreyfus. Esterhazy, learning of this development, fled to England. Finally, in the summer of 1899, the Court of Cassation ordered a review of the Dreyfus case. Dreyfus was brought back to France and tried by a military court at Rennes. Once again, largely through the machinations of Gen. Auguste Mercier, he was found guilty and given a 10-year sentence. However, soon afterward, Dreyfus received a pardon from Pres. Émile Loubet, which he accepted against the advice of his strongest supporters. In

1906 the Court of Cassation set aside the verdict of Rennes and completely exonerated Dreyfus. He was reinstated in the army, promoted to the rank of major, and awarded the Legion of Honor. He retired with the rank of lieutenant colonel.

Herzl, as Paris correspondent of the *Wiener Neue Freie Presse*, covered the story of the first Dreyfus court-martial and witnessed the public degradation of the condemned officer. The realization that this incident could have occurred in republican France confirmed Herzl's conviction that *assimilation could not be a solution to the Jewish problem. It is in this sense that Herzl could declare in 1899 that the Dreyfus affair had made him a Zionist.

J. ADLER

D'ROR. Youth movement of the *Kibbutz M'uhad within the framework of the *Histadrut (General Federation of Labor). In the 1960s it had branches (S'nifim) in Israel and throughout the *Diaspora and was variously known as HeHalutz HaTza'ir and Mahanot Ha'Olim. D'ror (Heb., "Freedom") educated its members toward the self-realization of their social and national ideals through *Halutziyut (pioneering) and *'Aliya (immigration) to kibbutzim in Israel.

D'ror in North America is an autonomous organization sponsored by the *American Zionist Youth Foundation. Its activities include discussions and seminars on Zionism, social values, Jewish history, and contemporary Israeli and Jewish problems, as well as Israeli songs and folk dancing and celebrations of Jewish holidays in the kibbutz spirit. D'ror maintains three summer camps and three winter camps in North America and holds yearly seminars for youth leaders and counselors. Three weeklies for the members and various educational materials are published by the main office in New York.

The D'ror Workshop Program takes participants for a year's work and study on a kibbutz in Israel, where they can learn Hebrew and other subjects, tour the country, and participate in seminars. Several members of D'ror have moved to Israel and made their homes in settlements throughout the country. The kibbutz Kissufim in the Negev was established by members of D'ror in North America.

U. MERI

DRUSKENIK CONFERENCE. Second conference of the *Hoveve Zion societies in Russia, held in 1887 with 30 delegates participating. The conference decided to continue efforts to obtain official Russian approval for the establishment of a Palestine settlement society to intensify propaganda among the Jews; to support the settlements of G'dera, Y'sud HaMa'ala, and Petah Tikva; and to establish an office in Palestine that would advise prospective Jewish land buyers. At the conference Leo *Pinsker was reelected chairman of Hoveve Zion, and Rabbis Sh'muel *Mohilever, Naphtali Tz'vi Y'huda *Berlin, and Mordecai *Eliasberg, the writer Samuel Joseph *Fünn, Israel *Jasinovsky, and Meir Freidenberg were chosen as his principal aides and advisers.

DRUYANOW, ALTER. Hebrew writer and publicist (b. Druya, Vilna District, Russia, 1870; d. Tel Aviv, 1938). Druyanow received a traditional education and studied at the Yeshiva of Volozhin. From 1899 to 1905 he was secretary of the *Odessa Committee of the *Hoveve Zion, and during the years preceding World War I he served as secretary and member of the Central Committee of Russian Zionists. A noted Hebrew stylist, he

began his literary career in 1890 with a feuilleton in *HaMelitz*. He subsequently wrote for Hebrew and Yiddish periodicals and, from 1910 to 1914, was editor of *Ha'Olam. In 1921 he settled in Palestine, where he had lived previously from 1906 to 1909. While devoting himself to research and literature, Druyanow continued to play a prominent role in Jewish public life and contributed to the daily press. In 1932 he visited Poland and Lithuania on behalf of the *Jewish National Fund.

Druyanow's major literary work is the *Sefer HaB'diha V'haHidud* (1922; 2d enl. ed., 3 vols., 1932–38), a collection of Jewish wit and humor. Among his other publications are *K'tavim L'Toldot Hibbat Zion* (documents relating to the history of the Hibbat Zion movement, 3 vols., 1919–32), *Tziyonut B'Polania* (Zionism in Poland, 1932; with impressions of his visit there), and a monograph on Leo *Pinsker (first published chapter by chapter in periodicals in the 1920s and 1930s). He also served as an editor of the *Encyclopedia Judaica*, the Hebrew *Eshkol Entziklopedia Yisr'elit* (2 vols.); the first four volumes (1918–26) of *R'shumot*, a collection devoted to Jewish folklore; *Mi Yamim Rishonim* (1934–35), a monthly which published material on the history of the Jewish national renaissance as well as on Jewish folklore; and *Sefer Tel Aviv* (1936).

DRUZE COMMUNITY IN ISRAEL. The Druzes are the followers of a religious sect which split off from Islam in the 11th century. Most of its adherents live in Syria and Lebanon. Druzes first came to Palestine from their centers in southern Syria soon after the foundation of the sect. By the 13th century, they had settled in a number of Galilean villages. In the 1960s practically all of Israel's Druzes (about 14,500 in 1949; 24,282 according to the 1961 census) lived in Galilee, between Mount Carmel and the Israel-Lebanon frontier. Most of them lived in 18 villages. Their greatest concentration was near 'Akko; their largest village was Yarka, and their religious center was in nearby Julis. Some villages were almost exclusively Druze; in others, Druzes lived side by side with other groups, mainly

Druze chieftains. [Zionist Archives]

Christian Arabs. The tomb of Nebi Shu'ayb (the prophet Jethro), near Tiberias, is a revered pilgrimage center for the Druzes every spring. The Druzes in Israel are industrious agriculturists, raising olives, grapes, and tobacco (although their religion forbids drinking alcohol and smoking).

Under Ottoman and British rule, the Druzes were never recognized as a separate community. They were therefore refused juridical autonomy and subjected to Muslim court procedure. In the State of Israel, the Druzes have obtained the special status they desire: they are recognized as an independent religious community (see COMMUNITIES IN ISRAEL). The spiritual leadership of their community is acknowledged as an official Religious Council, and under the Druze Religious Courts Law they are subject to the authority of their own courts in all matters of personal status within the competence of religious courts in Israel.

Politically, the Druzes in Israel have been interested in the activities of the larger Druze centers in Syria and Lebanon. However, because of past differences with the Arabs, most of them have cast their lot with the State of Israel and even serve in the *Israel Defense Forces. Socially, they have been affected by Israel's dynamism, and the younger Druzes compete with their elders for leadership in the community.   J. M. LANDAU

DUBNOW, SIMON. Historian, theorist of Jewish autonomism, and founder of the Folkspartei (b. Mstislavl, Mogilev District, Russia, 1860; d. Riga, Latvia, 1941). Dubnow received a thorough Jewish education and at an early age had mastered the Hebrew and Russian languages in addition to Yiddish, his mother tongue. His name appeared in print for the first time in 1881, with a Russian essay on the history of Jewish thought. From then on he contributed regularly to Hebrew and Russo-Jewish publications, first writing on current events and literary topics and later increasingly on Jewish history. He lived in Odessa from 1890 to 1903, in Vilna from 1903 to 1907, and then in St. Petersburg until his departure for Berlin in 1922. After Hitler came to power in Germany, he moved to Riga, where he was shot in 1941 by the invading Nazis.

Dubnow's work, which includes countless articles on various subjects, a history of Hasidism, and a history of Russian Jewry, was crowned by a 10-volume world history of the Jewish people. His was primarily a sociological approach to Jewish history, which he presented as a struggle between positive and negative forces waged around the different centers which had arisen at various periods of Jewish national life. What sustained the Jewish people in the *Diaspora, he contended, was its ability to create new Jewish centers to replace the old ones whenever they were destroyed.

Applying his conceptions of history to contemporary Jewish life, Dubnow published (1897) a series of letters which laid the theoretical foundations of *Galut nationalism. He postulated three types of group structure in human society: the tribal group, the political nation, and the spiritual people. The last form represented the highest stage of national development, which only the Jewish people had attained. Far from being an unmitigated tragedy, Jewish extraterritoriality presented a challenge to the Jewish people to measure up to its full potential as a spiritual nation. But even a spiritual nation needed a structural framework to hold it together, and he therefore propounded the idea of a network of autonomous communities spanning the Jewish world and united in a general Jewish council, to "encompass all aspects of self-government" in

matters relating to internal Jewish affairs. The idea was the core of the platform of the numerically small Folkspartei Dubnow founded in 1906, whose influence was felt widely outside its own ranks. Dubnow was neither a Zionist nor an anti-Zionist (see

Simon Dubnow.
[YIVO Institute for Jewish Research]

ANTI-ZIONISM). In the mid-1930s he referred to the progress the *Yishuv (Jewish population of Palestine) had made since the *Balfour Declaration as the greatest miracle in contemporary Jewish history. In his later years, he moved closer to full acceptance—with overtones of *Ahad Ha'Am—of the Zionist program.   C. B. SHERMAN

DUGDALE, BLANCHE ELIZABETH CAMPBELL BALFOUR. British supporter of Zionism (b. London, 1880; d. Kilkerran, Scotland, 1948). A niece of Arthur James *Balfour, she married Edgar Trevelyan Stratford Dugdale. She was employed in the British Naval Intelligence Department and in 1932 became a member of the League of Nations Union and of the British government's delegation to the League of Nations Assembly.

A firm believer in Zionism and in the justice of the Zionist struggle, and a trusted adviser of Chaim *Weizmann, she was part of the inner circle which helped shape the policies of the Zionist *Executive. She frequently interceded with Cabinet ministers and the *High Commissioner for Palestine, addressed public meetings and Zionist conferences, visited Palestine, and was a guest at Zionist Congresses (see CONGRESS, ZIONIST). During World War II she served on various committees formed to aid Jewish refugees. She published articles regularly in the *Zionist Review*, participated in the protest march to Trafalgar Square on July 8, 1946 (see GREAT BRITAIN, ZIONISM IN), and was a member of the delegation which went to Downing Street to hand over the resolution of the conference of the Zionist Federation of Great Britain and Ireland.

Mrs. Dugdale was the author of a two-volume biography, *Arthur James Balfour* (1936), and of a pamphlet, *The Balfour Declaration: Origins and Background* (1940). When she was told two days before she died in Scotland that the State of Israel had been proclaimed, she exclaimed, "This is the happiest day of my life." On the 10th anniversary of her death, a memorial to her was unveiled in the Balfour Forest in Galilee.

J. FRAENKEL

DULTZIN, ARYE LEON. Zionist leader and member of the Zionist *Executive (b. Minsk, Russia, 1913). In 1928 Dultzin emigrated from Russia to Mexico, where he attended the

National University of Mexico and became active in Zionist circles, serving as secretary (1931–37) and president (1938–44) of the Zionist Federation of Mexico. From 1951 to 1956 he was a member of the Zionist *Actions Committee and of the Executive of the Latin American Confederation of General Zionists (*see* GENERAL ZIONISM). He was a delegate to the 23d (1951) and 24th (1956) Zionist Congresses (*see* CONGRESS, ZIONIST).

In 1956 Dultzin settled in Israel and became a member of the Executive of the *Jewish Agency for Israel and head of the Agency's Economic Department and Companies and Investment Department. Vice-president of the *World Confederation of General Zionists, he was also a member of the Board of Directors of *Keren HaYesod (Palestine Foundation Fund) and of the Executive Committee of Israel's *Liberal party. At the 27th Zionist Congress (Jerusalem, 1968), Dultzin was reelected to the Jewish Agency Executive and placed in charge of its Treasury. In 1969 he became Minister without Portfolio in the government of Israel.

DUNAM. Metric surface measure equal to 1,000 square meters, or roughly one-fourth of an acre. It is used in Israel to the exclusion of all other units of surface measurement. The term is derived from the Turkish *dönüm*.

DUSHKIN, ALEXANDER MORDECAI. Jewish educator (b. Suwałki, Russian Poland, 1890). Dushkin studied at the City College of New York (B.A., 1911), Columbia University (M.A., 1913; Ph.D., 1917), and the Jewish Theological Seminary of America (teacher's certificate, 1916). In 1916 he went to Europe with Judah L. *Magnes as secretary of the European Commission of the American Jewish Relief Committee, and in 1918 he became field secretary for the Education Department of the *Zionist Organization of America (ZOA). A year later he went to Palestine as secretary of the Department of Education of the *Zionist Commission in Jerusalem. He was also inspector of Jewish schools for the Palestine government (1921–22), organization secretary of the *Keren HaYesod (Palestine Foundation Fund), and instructor at the Hebrew Teachers Seminary in Jerusalem.

Returning to the United States in 1922, Dushkin worked in the field of Jewish education. From 1934 to 1939 he was again in Palestine, as lecturer in pedagogy at the *Hebrew University of Jerusalem and principal of the Bet HaKerem Secondary School. In 1939 he returned to the United States, serving for the next 10 years as director of the Jewish Education Committee of New York.

Settling permanently in Israel in 1949, Dushkin served as professor of education at the Hebrew University. Retiring in in 1958, he became director of the Section for Jewish Education at the university's Institute of Contemporary Jewry. He edited several professional journals and wrote scholarly studies on Jewish education.

D'VIR. *See* TELL BET MIRSIM.

D'VIRA. Village (kibbutz) in the Darom on the border of the Negev. Founded in 1951 and affiliated with the *Kibbutz Artzi Shel HaShomer HaTza'ir.

D'VORA. Village (moshav) in the Jezreel Valley. Founded in 1956 and named for the prophetess Deborah, who defeated the Canaanites in this area (Judges 4:4–24; 5). Affiliated with *T'nu'at HaMoshavim. Population (1968): 315.

E

EAST AFRICA SCHEME (popularly and incorrectly known as Uganda Scheme). Proposal for the settlement of Jews in British East Africa, made in 1903. On April 23 of that year Joseph *Chamberlain, Colonial Secretary of Great Britain, mentioned to Herzl that Uganda in East Africa seemed an ideal location for a Jewish settlement. At first Herzl ignored the suggestion, fearing that it might endanger his negotiations for an autonomous Jewish settlement in Sinai (*see* EL-'ARISH SCHEME). When it became clear that the Sinai project was doomed, Chamberlain repeated his proposal to Herzl's representative, Leopold J. *Greenberg. This time, Herzl instructed Greenberg to pursue the matter.

In August, 1903, while in Russia negotiating with Foreign Minister Vyacheslav K. von Plehve for the Tsarist government to discontinue the suppression of Zionist activity there, Herzl received the copy of a letter Sir Clement Hill, Superintendent of African Protectorates, had written to Greenberg, indicating Great Britain's readiness to consider a Jewish settlement in the East Africa Protectorate. The exact area was not then defined. Subject to the approval of the officials concerned, Hill wrote, this settlement could be politically independent with a Jewish governor and a Jewish administration.

Herzl was unable to accept or reject this proposal on his own authority. After meetings with the Greater *Actions Committee and an unofficial conference (Saturday, Aug. 22, 1903) in Basle in the hotel room of Joseph *Cowen with a number of Zionist leaders, he informed the 6th Zionist *Congress (Aug. 23–28, 1903) of the offer.

In his opening address, Herzl reported on his discussions with Chamberlain and Lord Lansdowne regarding Jewish settlement in Sinai and outlined the reasons why the project had to be abandoned. He then presented the East Africa proposal. He did not suggest that the Congress accept it and stressed that no country could supersede Palestine as the Jewish Homeland. On the other hand, he did not urge the Congress to reject it, for he felt that an offer by the British Empire to the *World Zionist Organization deserved diplomatic and objective treatment, especially in view of the significance it might have for victims of persecution, which was then the subject of worldwide attention and protest. He considered contact with England most important and the East Africa offer a significant first step that was to lead the Jews to Palestine. He suggested, therefore, that the Congress send out an expedition to investigate the territory and to report back to the next Congress.

In the course of the debate, Max *Nordau delivered an oration in support of Herzl's argument. Although basically opposed to the plan because he felt that the East Africa project, like the colonies in Argentina (*see* JEWISH COLONIZATION ASSOCIATION), was bound to fail because it lacked the emotional appeal of Palestine, Nordau was impressed by Herzl's plea for an objective attitude to the British offer and was reluctant to abandon him at this point. In his speech, Nordau characterized the projected East Africa settlement as a *Nachtasyl* (shelter for the night) on the road to Palestine.

At the end of his detailed report on the negotiations with England, Leopold J. Greenberg made the following statement:

> I am a strong Palestinian, and am anxious to see our people gathered together again in their own beloved ancient land. But remember one thing—the way to Palestine need not necessarily be only the geographical way. The political road we must never lose sight of.

Nordau was seconded by a number of prominent leaders. The principal leader of the opposition was Yehiel *Tschlenow, who felt that serious consideration of colonization in a country other than Palestine would undermine the *Basle Program.

In the actual vote on the proposal, the Congress decided by a majority of 295 to 17 to send experts to British East Africa to investigate possibilities of Jewish settlement there. The Congress commission chosen to appoint the members of the planned expedition was composed of Joseph Cowen, Leopold J. Greenberg, Leopold *Kessler, and Chaim *Weizmann.

A serious crisis developed at the Congress. The Russian members of the Actions Committee handed Herzl a declaration stating their opposition to the plan and then left the Congress hall, followed by the entire body of the "anti-Ugandist" camp, mostly delegates from Russia. After a final vote, which yielded a majority of 295 to 178 in favor of the proposal (98 delegates, including Herbert *Bentwich, Yitzhak Ya'akov *Reines, and Nahum *Sokolow, abstained), the session was adjourned. Later that evening, Herzl decided to go to the opposition, the *Tziyone Zion (Zionists of Zion), as they called themselves, who had gathered in a smaller meeting room for consultation. He explained his motive in considering the British offer and assured them that he had not abandoned Palestine as the goal of the Zionist movement. It was only then that the group reluctantly returned to the Congress.

While Herzl continued his efforts to heal the rift, the opponents of the plan were joined by the English colonists in East Africa. On August 28 the London *Times* published a telegram of protest from Nairobi, signed by Lord Delamare, claiming that the offer of such excellent land on the Uganda road, built with British funds, to foreigners was unfair to the British taxpayers and would antagonize the natives as well. The *Times* also received a letter from Lucien Wolf, of the *Anglo-Jewish Association, reiterating the arguments of the assimilationist Jews against Herzl and the East Africa proposal. These protests, together with the dim view taken of the project by prominent British non-Jews, caused a perceptible cooling of the attitude of the British government.

On Dec. 19, 1903, an attempt on the life of Nordau was made in Paris by Chaim Zelig Louban, an overzealous young "anti-Ugandist," who cried out "Death to Nordau, the East African" as he took aim at Nordau with a gun. The attempted assassination caused great indignation in the Zionist world.

On Apr. 11, 1904, Herzl called a meeting of the Greater Actions Committee in Vienna, at which reconciliation was effected with the Russian "anti-Ugandists." Herzl died on July 3, 1904. On July 27, 1905, the 7th Zionist Congress met in Basle, with Nordau presiding. The most important item on the agenda of this Congress—the first without Herzl—was a discussion of the East Africa proposal. The Congress now had before it the report of the investigating commission, which had found the territory unsuitable for Jewish settlement. The unfavorable report notwithstanding, Israel *Zangwill advocated acceptance of the British proposal without, however, loosening the ties of the Zionist movement to Palestine. In the general debate that followed, Zangwill and his followers claimed that the essence of Zionism was not necessarily dependent on Palestine and that the Zionists could make use of any country suitable for mass colonization. Led by the Tziyone Zion, the Congress voted by overwhelming majority to reject all colonization programs other than those in Palestine and adjacent countries. It was then that 40 dissident delegates, led by Zangwill, founded the *Jewish Territorial Organization.

G. HIRSCHLER

EBAN, ABBA (AUBREY) SOLOMON. Israeli statesman (b. Cape Town, 1915). After completing his early education in private schools, Eban entered Cambridge University, where he specialized in Oriental studies and first made a name for himself as a debater in the Zionist youth movement and the League of Nations Union. Proficient in seven languages including Arabic, Hebrew, Persian, and Yiddish, he served as a lecturer in Arabic and Oriental studies at Cambridge (1938–40). Joining the British infantry as a private shortly after the outbreak of World War II, he asked for assignment to the Middle East and soon rose to the rank of major. He was stationed in Cairo for a time as military censor for Hebrew and Arabic material. Beginning in 1942, Eban was in Jerusalem as liaison officer between Allied military

headquarters and the *Jewish Agency, charged with the task of stimulating the Jewish war effort, organizing Jewish guerrilla troops against the threatened Axis invasion of Palestine from Africa, and securing volunteers for special and dangerous mis-

Abba Eban.
[Israel Information Services]

sions in Europe and the Middle East. In 1943–44 he was chief instructor at the Middle Eastern Center of Arabic Studies in Jerusalem, which had been established to train administrators and diplomats for duty in the area. During this period he traveled widely in the Middle East, lecturing in Hebrew to Jewish, and in Arabic to Arab, audiences.

In 1946, at the urging of Chaim *Weizmann, Eban joined the Political Department of the Jewish Agency, where he dealt primarily with matters affecting Jewish-Arab relations. In 1947 he became the Agency's liaison officer with the *United Nations Special Committee on Palestine (UNSCOP) and presented the Jewish case at the Palestine debates before the UN General Assembly as a member of the Jewish delegation to that body. In 1948 the provisional government of Israel appointed him its representative to the United Nations. In this capacity he represented Israel before the Security Council in efforts to secure international intervention to stop Arab attacks and obtain a truce and later argued for Israel's admission to the United Nations.

When Israel was admitted to the United Nations, in May, 1949, Eban was appointed its chief delegate, a position which he held until 1959 and in which he earned a name as an eloquent speaker and effective advocate of his country's interests. In July, 1951, Eban induced the Security Council to declare Egypt's blockade of the Suez Canal unjustified. Although the Council's declaration was ignored by Egypt, it became the legal basis for the later doctrine of "free and innocent passage" in the Gulf of 'Aqaba (see ELAT, GULF OF). Earlier in 1951 he had helped draft the principles announced by the United Nations as a possible basis for settling the Korean War. From 1950 to 1959 Eban also served as Israel's Ambassador to the United States.

In 1959 Eban was elected to the *Knesset on the *Mapai slate and became a minister without portfolio. He was named Minister of Education and Culture in 1960, Deputy Prime Minister in 1963, and Foreign Minister in 1966. During the period of the *Six-day War of 1967 and the months that followed, Eban argued Israel's case before the UN Security Council and General Assembly against the Arab countries and their Communist supporters. His speeches, which were heard on radio and television by audiences throughout the world, earned him the reputation of being one of the finest orators in the world assembly.

In 1958 Eban was appointed president of the *Weizmann Institute of Science, serving until 1966. From 1960 he was a member of the American Academy of Arts and Sciences and a fellow of the World Academy of Arts and Sciences. His works include *Zionism and the Arab World* (1947), *Britain's Middle East Strategy* (1947), *Voice of Israel* (1947), *Tide of Nationalism* (1959), and *My People* (1968). He was coauthor of *Chaim Weizmann: A Biography by Several Hands* (1962).

EBNER, MEIR (Mayer). Zionist leader (b. Czernowitz, Bukovina, Austria, 1872; d. Tel Aviv, 1955). Ebner studied law at the University of Czernowitz (now Chernovtsy, U.S.S.R.) and subsequently practiced law there. While a student, he helped found Hasmonea, a Jewish national student association. He was also active in pre-Herzlian Zionist circles and with the advent of Herzl became one of his early followers. He participated in the 1st Zionist *Congress (1897) and subsequent Congresses and was a member of the Greater *Actions Committee from its inception.

During World War I Ebner was taken by the Russians as a hostage and sent to Siberia. After his release he headed, in 1918, the newly established National Council of Bukovinian Jews, and a year later he founded the Zionist *Ostjüdische Zeitung*, which he edited until 1938. Ebner served for several years in the Romanian Parliament and Senate, where he was a stanch spokesman for Jewish rights.

ECONOMY OF ISRAEL. The main features of Israel's economy in the first 20 years of its development were rapid growth and rising living standards, large-scale inflow of capital from private and public sources abroad, and significant participation by the government in economic development and social welfare.

Economic Growth. Israel's economic growth rate was one of the world's highest. According to Israel's Economic Planning Authority, in the period 1950–67 real gross national product (GNP), or the total value of goods and services produced at constant prices, rose at an annual average of 9.3 per cent. Only a very few countries, notably Japan, exceeded this growth rate during the entire period.

Since few other countries had seen their populations increase by $2\frac{1}{2}$ times in the 1950–67 period, it is more meaningful to compare the growth rate on a per capita basis than in terms of total GNP. Israel's performance by the per capita measure (that is, after allowing for population growth) came to 3.4 per cent, which was slightly above the average rate of developed nations and still higher than that of developing countries. Both the rapid population increase of the early 1950s and the severe recession of 1966 and 1967 (when per capita GNP actually declined by 1.6 and 1.0 per cent respectively) lowered Israel's average. In the period from 1955 to 1964, per capita GNP rose by 5.5 per cent annually, a figure exceeded by relatively few countries, mainly those that combined a high rate of economic growth and a fairly stable population. Other estimates, covering similar periods but using a different base year for prices, indicate even higher total and per capita GNP growth rates for Israel than those computed by the Planning Authority. But even if the more conservative estimates are used, the almost steady rise in the output of goods and services per person made it possible for the average *standard of living of Israel's population nearly to double during the period under review.

This record of economic progress can be attributed to four factors: (1) a growing labor force, (2) full employment, (3) a high rate of investment in capital goods (i.e., factories, machinery, and power plants), and (4) the rising productivity of both labor and capital. The civilian labor force grew from 450,000 in 1950 to 927,000 in 1967. Even though a large part of the labor force consisted of new immigrants, many of them initially untrained for the job requirements of a modern industrial economy, there was relatively little unemployment, particularly during the years 1955–65. From May 15, 1948, to the end of 1951, 685,000 immigrants arrived in Israel, well over half of the total number (1,253,000) that had come as of the end of 1967. Unemployment reached a high of 11.3 per cent in 1953 but then declined almost steadily until 1964. The annual average rate of unemployment fell from 8.0 per cent in 1954–56 to 6.3 per cent in 1957–59 and to 4.0 per cent in 1960–64; it reached a low of 3.3 per cent in 1964, when only 29,000 persons were jobless. The unemployed were concentrated largely in small pockets of certain development areas in the north and south of the country. At the same time, the country experienced a shortage of skilled workers, estimated officially at more than 25,000. The slowdown in economic activity raised the unemployment level sharply during the years 1965–67, but the country was back on the road toward full employment in 1968.

The increase in the input of labor was accompanied by proportionately far greater increases in the input of capital goods. Productive capital stock per gainfully employed worker increased fourfold between 1950 and 1967. During this period gross investments totaled IL32,300,000,000 (at 1966 prices); about one-third of the total was invested in housing. Excluding housing, investments were distributed as follows: agriculture, 14 per cent; water and irrigation, 7 per cent; industry and mining, 26 per cent; power, 6 per cent; transportation and communication, 22 per cent; business and personal services, 5 per cent; and public services, 20 per cent. The share of investment in the GNP was higher than in most countries, amounting to 27 per cent in 1955–64, as compared with 17.5 per cent in developing countries in 1960–65. But the share of investment in the total resources at the disposal of the economy (23 per cent in 1955–64) was one commonly found in rapidly growing economies, both developed and developing. Total resources include GNP and the import surplus (i.e., imports of goods and services less exports of goods and services). But most countries did not have as substantial an import surplus as Israel, and they had to finance investment largely from GNP. The allocation of nearly one-fourth of total resources to investment and the simultaneous steady expansion of private and public consumption were made possible by an extensive capital inflow that financed the import surplus.

Table 1 shows the total resources available to the economy from domestic production and the import surplus and their distribution between consumption and investment. The basic relationships portrayed in this table will be used in the analysis of other important aspects of the economy.

About two-thirds of the growth in output resulted from the expansion in the inputs of labor and capital, and one-third from the steady improvement in their productivity. The greater efficiency was the result of better management, higher skills, larger units of production, improved technology, and a higher rate of utilization of plant capacity as well as of improvements in outside services to enterprises such as transportation and communications, power supply, finance, and marketing. Pro-

TABLE 1. RESOURCES AND THEIR USES AT 1966 PRICES
(In millions of Israeli pounds)

	1950	1964	1967
Gross national product	2,677	10,926	12,109
Import surplus	1,097	1,741	1,455
Total resources	3,774	12,667	13,564
Private consumption	1,850	7,165	8,100
Public consumption	758	2,379	3,554
Gross investment	1,166	3,123	1,910
Total uses of resources	3,774	12,667	13,564

SOURCE: State of Israel, Economic Planning Authority, *Israel Economic Development: Past Progress and Plan for the Future, Final Draft,* March, 1968, p. 9.

ductivity was aided by the work of the Productivity Institute of the Ministry of Labor, which in 1965–66 alone gave 185 courses to 5,500 persons in fields ranging from quality supervision to office mechanization. The existence in Israel of high-caliber institutions of applied science and technology made a significant contribution to the advancement of productivity. Technical know-how provided by many private American and other Western companies in the form of direct investment and licensing agreements also played an important role.

Historical Survey. Israel's economic achievements were all the more remarkable when viewed against the background of economic conditions prevailing in the early years after the establishment of the State in 1948. That period was marked by a costly war, mass immigration, and rampant inflation. Rationing and controls dominated the market, acute shortages of raw materials developed, the foreign trade gap widened, and foreign exchange reserves were exhausted. There was a sharp drop in the value of the Israeli pound (IL), accompanied by a loss of confidence in the stability of the economy.

Two bold and far-reaching economic stabilization programs, one launched in February, 1952, and the other a decade later, in February, 1962, had much to do with the recovery and growth of the economy. The two programs set the economy on the road to liberalization. They greatly reduced direct governmental controls over domestic economic activities and foreign trade and replaced them mainly with indirect fiscal and monetary policies, in line with trends in advanced Western countries. The 1952 program established a multiple exchange rate system to discourage imports and encourage exports and foreign investments. It also curbed the money supply and credit, froze basic wages, and abolished price controls and the cost-plus accounting method for government contracts. The 1962 program replaced the multiple exchange rate system built around an official rate of IL1.80 to the dollar with a unified exchange rate of IL3 to the dollar. It reduced tariff and administrative restrictions on imports to expose local industry to foreign competition, and it also included measures to stabilize prices, wages, and taxes and to encourage domestic saving.

The 1962 program was launched at a time of rapid expansion of the economy: GNP grew at an average annual rate of 11 per cent in the period 1960–64. But domestic prices and production costs rose at the same time, reducing the competitiveness of Israeli products in foreign markets. Strong demand in the local

market kept the rate of growth of exports down, while the rise in income caused imports to climb sharply. The import surplus reached a peak of $572,000,000 in 1964. The continuation of these trends would have rapidly depleted Israel's foreign exchange reserves, with the economy sliding back to the critical conditions of the early years rather than moving ahead toward eventual self-support.

At the end of 1964 the government therefore decided to introduce a policy of economic restraint known as *mitun*. This policy, which was applied in varying degrees until the early months of 1967, was reflected in a reduction of State-financed investment (especially in construction), a slower rate of expansion in public civilian consumption expenditures, and higher taxes. In September, 1966, a comprehensive economic reform program was adopted to take advantage of the slowdown in order to effect basic changes in the structure of the economy. The main goal of the program was to shift the employment of labor and the investment of capital from production for local consumption to production for export. Another major goal was to lower production costs by enhancing productivity and by stabilizing incomes, thus improving the competitive position of exports. The program involved export incentives but not devaluation. On Nov. 19, 1967, however, following the devaluation of the pound sterling, Israel devalued its currency from IL3.00 to IL3.50 to the dollar.

These policies represented a deliberate attempt by the government to slow down the economy in order to achieve certain specific objectives. But they reinforced trends, some originating externally and others operating within the economy, that had developed during the period 1965–67. The resulting recession was more severe than had been anticipated. The mainspring of the slowdown was the decline in population growth, which was due largely to a drop in immigration. Immigration, which had averaged 55,000 annually in the years 1961–64, fell to 20,000 annually in 1965–67; net immigration (immigration less emigration) declined even more drastically, to an average of 9,700. The decline affected investments in immigrant housing and public services as well as other investments designed to supply the additional demand for goods and services of newcomers. Net foreign investment also fell, from record highs of $162,600,000 in 1963 and $156,700,000 in 1964 to $91,800,000 in 1965 and $82,500,000 in 1966. The completion of a number of large development schemes, among them the Jordan-Negev National Water Carrier Project, the port of Ashdod, the Dead Sea Works, the five-year highway program, and new power stations, intensified the recession in construction, transportation, and industry.

The main thrust of the recession was felt in investment, the most volatile and crucial of the three components of total demand (see Table 1). Investment spending rose by 23 per cent in 1964, leading to a large expansion in productive capacity; but it fell by 2 per cent in 1965, 18 per cent in 1966, and 26 per cent in 1967 (in constant prices). Private consumption spending grew at a progressively slower pace, partly because the demand for dwellings and appliances by most households with sufficient income had been met during the earlier boom years; and, as noted above, government current consumption spending (for general administration and social services) was deliberately allowed to increase only moderately. Aggregate demand, or total spending by households, businesses, and government, had thus slackened off considerably. GNP grew by 8.2 per cent in 1965, 1.0 per cent in 1966, and 2.2 per cent in 1967. Unemployment rose from 3.6 per cent in 1965 to 10.4 per cent in 1967, when the average number of unemployed totaled 96,000.

In the second half of 1967 and in 1968 employment and output rose as economic activity showed strong signs of revival. The recovery began even before the *Six-day War and was strengthened by rising governmental expenditures for defense purposes.

Capital Imports. The single most significant fact about Israel's economy was its continued ability to obtain growing sums of outside capital well in excess of its huge import surplus. During the period 1950–67, Israel received $9,300,000,000 from abroad, of which $1,900,000,000 was repaid. Of the net capital imports of $7,400,000,000, about $6,400,000,000 was used to finance the import surplus of goods and services and $944,000,000 to build up foreign exchange balances; the remainder is accounted for by short-term capital movements and errors and omissions.

Unlike many developing countries which were forced to rely on only one or two major sources of external capital (e.g., aid from a major power or international institutions), Israel had recourse to a fairly wide variety of sources, as shown in Table 2. But no less significant than the magnitude and varied sources of the capital influx was the fact that more than half of gross capital imports, or two-thirds of net capital imports, consisted of unilateral transfers not requiring repayment. The transfer payments came from three sources: world Jewry, the German government, and the United States government.

The largest single sum, $1,735,000,000, came from transfers by national institutions (mainly the *Jewish Agency) and direct transfer payments to numerous educational, health, welfare, and other nonprofit institutions in Israel; these transfers were based on contributions by Jews in Western countries, mostly United States Jewry. Institutional transfers averaged $90,000,000 during the years 1960–66, as compared with almost $80,000,000 annually in the 1950s; they reached a record level of $324,000,000 in 1967. Their importance was decisive during the first years of independence, when the economy needed foreign exchange to absorb large numbers of immigrants. Private or personal transfers totaled $885,000,000. This source included remittances and merchandise gifts from relatives abroad, goods brought by im-

migrants, pensions from abroad, and similar items. Personal transfers averaged $28,000,000 in the 1950s but rose to $75,000,000 annually during the years 1960–67.

Total transfer payments received from the Federal Republic of Germany reached $1,965,000,000: $1,190,000,000 in the form of restitutions to individual Israelis and $775,000,000 in reparations to the Israeli government. The restitutions, which were paid in cash, consisted of nonrecurrent payments and annual pensions, the nonrecurrent payments constituting the larger part. Payments started in 1954, when they amounted to only $6,100,000; they rose steadily to a record high of $139,000,000 in 1963, ranging from $100,000,000 to $140,000,000 annually in the years 1960–67. Total receipts surpassed original estimates and were expected to remain at a high level in the late 1960s and early 1970s but to drop steeply once the lump-sum payments had been completed; annual pensions would continue as long as the recipients were alive. German reparations, which were paid mostly in goods, started in 1953 and ended in 1965. Their share in total capital imports was relatively high, especially from 1955 to 1959; they averaged $75,000,000 to $80,000,000 annually until 1961 but tapered off sharply thereafter.

United States government grants, which totaled $320,000,000, began in 1951 and were terminated in 1962. They were an important source of funds during the period 1951–55, when more than two-thirds of the total was extended.

Of the five specific nonrepayable sources, German reparations and United States grants, both of which were particularly important in the 1950s, came to an end. In contrast, institutional and personal transfers and German restitutions were at a considerably higher level in the 1960s than in the 1950s.

*State of Israel bonds were by far the single most important source of repayable capital. The bonds were first issued in 1951, when the State had not as yet established a reputation for credit worthiness that would facilitate a large-scale flow of long-term loans or private investment. From 1951 until the end of 1967, bond sales totaled $1,260,000,000, of which $486,000,000 had been redeemed (about half of this sum consisted of early redemptions in Israeli pounds for specific purposes such as contributions, private investments, and tourist outlays). Bonds played an essential role in financing economic development during the period 1951–59, when foreign exchange was scarce. Gross receipts were higher in the 1960s than in the 1950s, but with the start of regular redemptions in dollars in 1963 net average annual receipts ($23,100,000) were smaller in 1963–66 than in any other period. As in the case of institutional transfers, bond sales increased sharply in 1967, reaching an all-time high of $232,300,000, or more than twice the annual level in the previous two years.

United States government loans, which totaled $650,000,000, were of three types: loans for food surpluses, development loans, and credits from the Export-Import Bank of the United States. The largest component, about half of the total, consisted of loans for agricultural surpluses, mostly repayable in Israeli currency. In 1966 the terms of payment were amended: one-fourth of the Food for Peace sales was to be financed on a dollar credit basis for 20 years at 2.5 per cent interest, and the remaining three-fourths was to be repaid in local currency into the counterpart funds. These funds had been used by the United States government largely to extend grants or loans repayable in Israeli currency (for 30 years at 3.5 to 5 per cent interest).

Until 1962 development loans were also repayable in Israeli currency, over periods ranging from 10 to 40 years at interest

TABLE 2. CAPITAL IMPORTS BY MAJOR SOURCES, 1950–67
(In millions of dollars)

Source	Amount
Unilateral transfer payments	*4,905*
World Jewry	*2,620*
Institutional transfers	1,735
Personal transfers	885
West German government	*1,965*
Reparations	775
Personal restitutions	1,190
United States government grants	320
Long- and medium-term loans	*3,362*
Israel bonds	1,260
United States government loans	650
World Bank loans	92
Other loans	1,360
Foreign investments (net)	*1,000*
Grand total	9,267

SOURCE: State of Israel, Economic Planning Authority, *Israel Economic Development: Past Progress and Plan for the Future, Final Draft,* March, 1968, pp. 168–70.

rates of 3.5 to 5.25 per cent. These soft-currency loans closely resembled outright grants, and some studies have classified them as unilateral transfers. Interest rates were low, annual repayments were small, and repayments accumulated locally and could be reborrowed. However, the terms of these loans specified repayment either in dollars or in local currency linked to the dollar, at the option of the United States government. The third type of United States lending consisted of $150,000,000 in Export-Import Bank loans, repayable in dollars (this figure does not include the first Export-Import Bank loan, granted in 1949 in the amount of $100,000,000).

Starting in 1961, Israel also received loans from the International Bank for Reconstruction and Development (World Bank); through the end of 1967, $92,000,000 was disbursed to finance the expansion of the Dead Sea Works and the road network, construction of the Ashdod port, and the lending operations of the Industrial Development Bank of Israel. The residual item in Table 2, amounting to $1,360,000,000, covers a large number of loans from foreign governments, commercial banks, and investment companies. Most of these loans were for relatively modest amounts with a medium term of payment. The total also includes credits granted by West Germany beginning in 1966 under the agreement to establish diplomatic relations between Israel and Germany: these annual loans, extended at favorable terms, represented a new source of long-term capital.

The third major category of capital imports, net foreign investments, totaled $1,000,000,000. Foreign investments were particularly important in the period 1960–66, when they averaged more than $100,000,000 annually, as compared with yearly averages of less than $30,000,000 in the 1950s. The enactment of the Law for the Encouragement of Capital Investments as far back as 1950 and its periodic liberalization played an important role in attracting such a large flow of private capital despite serious geopolitical and economic obstacles.

A summary of the three main categories of capital imports shows that during the years 1950–67 world Jewry provided well over $4,500,000,000 (including the bulk of bond purchases and foreign investments), the German government more than $2,000,000,000 in restitutions, reparations, and credits, and the United States government nearly $1,000,000,000 in loans and grants. All other sources accounted for the remaining $1,800,000,000.

Not only did the steady flow of foreign capital cover the entire trade deficit, but, especially in the 1960s, it also left a comfortable margin that was used to build up foreign exchange reserves. During the years 1960–67 net capital inflow averaged $561,000,000 annually, as compared with an annual average import surplus of $459,000,000 (see Table 3). Foreign exchange holdings rose from $4,300,000 at the end of 1953 to $944,000,000 at the end of 1967 ($753,000,000 after deducting foreign deposits in Israel's banking system). Net holdings in 1967 reached a level equivalent to the amount needed to finance imports of goods and services for more than six months. But the spectacular rise in reserves was accompanied by a parallel increase in foreign indebtedness, from $409,700,000 at the end of 1954 to $1,556,000,000 at the end of 1967. About half of the debt consisted of Israel bonds (which mature in 12 years in the case of savings bonds and 15 years in the case of coupon bonds), and much of the rest of long-term loans. The growth of, the external debt constantly increased the repayments of principal

TABLE 3. BALANCE OF PAYMENTS SUMMARY FOR SELECTED YEARS
(In millions of dollars)

	1952	1961	1966	1967
Imports of goods and services	− 393.1	− 843.5	− 1,277.1	− 1,355.7
Exports of goods and services	86.5	397.9	832.2	918.4
Import surplus	− 306.6	− 445.6	− 444.9	− 437.3
Unilateral transfers, net	191.2	346.3	291.9	522.2
Long- and medium-term capital, net	114.9	186.5	183.7	257.5
Total transfers and capital	306.1	532.8	475.6	779.7
Foreign reserves and gold	− 2.4	− 94.9	19.0	− 215.9
Other short-term capital, net	3.9	10.3	− 22.9	− 12.3
Errors and omissions, net	− 1.0	− 2.6	− 26.8	− 114.2

SOURCES: For 1961, 1966, and 1967, Bank of Israel, *Annual Report, 1967* (in Hebrew), p. 36; for 1952, Central Bureau of Statistics, *Statistical Abstract of Israel, 1962*, p. 330; Nadav Halevi and Ruth Klinov-Malul, *The Economic Development of Israel*, Frederick A. Praeger, New York, 1968, pp. 296–97.

and interest, from $9,000,000 and $10,000,000, respectively, in 1955 to $200,000,000 and $50,000,000 in 1966.

Economic Goals and Economic Problems. Israel's ability to obtain sizable funds from diverse sources has sometimes been interpreted as an overdependence on outside aid. Some critics have gone so far as to argue that once the unilateral receipts dwindled and the loans fell due, the economy would face possible collapse. Israel indeed received substantially more aid than the vast majority of developing nations. According to a United Nations study, Israel received $113.20 per capita in net long-term capital and official donations in 1961; this figure was exceeded only by the $151.70 received by Puerto Rico. All underdeveloped countries combined received only $4.70 per capita. These figures must be related to three basic questions: (1) Was the massive aid used effectively? (2) Was the trend toward a lessening of dependence on foreign assistance? (3) Was economic policy geared toward the goal of economic independence?

The consensus of foreign observers is that Israel used aid intelligently and efficiently to absorb mass immigration and expand the country's productive capacity. This assessment was succinctly summed up in 1964 by David E. Bell, then administrator of the U.S. Agency for International Development (AID): "Israel has had extensive help from the United States and Europe, but above all it has had the kind of strong and sensible leadership which has been able to make the most out of its own resources, plus those obtained from outside."

A number of key indicators show that the reliance on capital imports was reduced, at least in relative terms. Exports of goods and services paid for 65 per cent of imports in 1966 and 68 per cent in 1967, as compared with only 22 per cent in 1952 (see Table 3). The share of the import surplus in total resources available to the economy declined steadily, from an annual average of 18.7 per cent in 1950–54 to 16.4 per cent in 1955–59 and to 14.6 per cent in 1960–64; there was a further decline to

11.5 per cent in 1965–67. The share of domestic savings (defined as gross investment less import surplus) in the financing of investment rose from 25 per cent in 1950–54 to 38 per cent in 1955–59 and to 45 per cent in 1960–66; the share of capital imports fell correspondingly.

The basic goal of Israel's economic policy was to continue these trends until the country attained economic independence by reducing the import surplus to a level that would no longer require long-term capital imports. A four-year plan covering the period 1968–71, prepared by the Economic Planning Authority at the direction of the Ministerial Committee on Economic Planning, envisaged a reduction in the import surplus to $400,000,000 in 1971, an amount equivalent to 6.4 per cent of total resources. This target would be achieved by a large increase in exports (15 per cent annually), with imports scheduled to rise more moderately (9 per cent annually). Exports were expected to cover almost 80 per cent of imports in 1971. A longer-range forecast set the import surplus at $200,000,000 by 1978, an amount equivalent to 2 per cent of total resources; the share of exports was expected to rise to more than 95 per cent of imports. This trade deficit would be covered by institutional and personal transfers, but even without unilateral receipts the achievement of this target may be regarded as economic independence.

The main hope for closing the trade gap rested on a steady expansion of industrial production and exports along competitive lines. In the early phase of the country's development, agriculture received the highest priority. By 1966 agriculture supplied more than 75 per cent of the food requirements of a population of 2.6 million, as compared with about 50 per cent for a population of less than 1 million in 1949. But farming reached a point near saturation because most of the existing water potential was being utilized. In the mid-1950s emphasis began to be shifted to manufacturing. The share of industry in the total number of employed persons rose from 21.9 per cent in 1955 to 25.3 per cent in 1966, while the ratio of the work force engaged in farming dropped from 17.6 to 12.6 per cent.

Despite rapid expansion, the basic problem of Israel's industry remained its high costs in comparison with those prevailing in international markets. The high costs were linked to the structure of industry, which was characterized by small plants, a large variety of products, a high protective tariff, and a limited degree of competition. These structural conditions resulted from the fact that output was geared mainly to local consumption. In the 1960s the government therefore gave special encouragement to industries which had a relative advantage in export markets. One category included industries based on local mineral and agricultural raw materials, with agricultural fertilizers and industrial chemicals as the main products. Another major category covered industries producing goods that contained any of the following features: a high component of skilled labor and research, a low transportation component, high quality, original design, and nonstandard character (e.g., electronic and optical products, pharmaceuticals, high fashion, equipment and machinery of various kinds, and products of science-based industries).

The rise in exports depended not only on competitive prices but also on access to Israel's major markets, particularly the European Economic Community (EEC; Common Market). The European Common Market bought almost 30 per cent of Israel's exports in the period 1963–66; with the rest of Western Europe, it constituted Israel's nearest trading partner. After more than five years of negotiations, a trade agreement was signed with the Common Market, but its effect on exports was limited. In 1966 Israel formally applied for associate membership in order to obtain terms equivalent to those extended to countries that competed with it. But as of 1968 the EEC had not consented to enter into an association agreement with Israel, mainly because of the desire to maintain its European character. *See also* EUROPEAN COMMON MARKET AND ISRAEL.

A fundamental premise of the four-year plan and of economic policy is that domestic saving must rise steadily so as to finance a growing share of investment. Saving amounted to 10 per cent of GNP in 1966 and to 4 per cent in 1967. But it would have to rise to 14 per cent in 1971 and to 24 per cent in 1978 to enable local sources to finance, respectively, 67 per cent and 92 per cent of gross investment in these years. This could be accomplished only if the rise in private and public consumption were curbed. Living standards, as measured by real per capita private consumption, should not advance by more than 3 per cent annually instead of 5 to 6 per cent as in the period 1955–65. As David *Horowitz, Governor of the *Bank of Israel, stated: "We don't want to reduce living standards or even to stop them from rising. We just want to limit ourselves to the rate considered satisfactory in industrialized countries abroad."

In addition to reduction of the import surplus, the Cabinet set forth four goals to guide the Planning Authority in the preparation of the plan: an annual rate of economic growth of 7 to 9 per cent; full employment; narrowing of disparities in living standards by improving the lot of the less privileged groups; and dispersal of the population from the coastal districts to development areas in the Southern, Northern, and Jerusalem Districts. But the experience of Israel's economy had shown that all these goals could not be attained at the same time; the attainment of one or more goals almost invariably meant sacrificing others.

The basic conflict was between economic growth and economic independence. Economic growth generates strong pressure for increased imports and retards the expansion of exports, thus making the economy more dependent on capital imports. This was the case until 1965. On the other hand, a significant reduction in the import surplus can be attained only by slowing down economic growth and maintaining a fairly high level of unemployment. The recession of 1965–67 dramatically illustrated this goal conflict. The import surplus, which generally rose from year to year, decreased by the very substantial amount of $135,000,000 between 1964 and 1967. But the price paid for this impressive gain was a virtual standstill in the GNP growth rate and a rise in unemployment to an alarmingly high level. The recovery of output and employment in 1968 confronted the economy once again with the problems of a rising import surplus and inflation.

Another major conflict existed between the goal of price stability and such goals as economic growth, full employment, and economic independence. Most of the years of Israel's existence were marked by persisting inflation. Price increases were particularly steep in the early years, doubling between 1951 and 1953. In the period 1955–66 prices rose by 5.4 per cent, as compared with 1.8 per cent in the United States, 2 to 5 per cent in European countries, and 10 to 30 per cent in many Latin American countries. The huge import surplus and, to a lesser extent, the government's fiscal, monetary, and price policies prevented inflation from being far more severe; the goal of greater price stability was thus accomplished mainly by sacrificing the goal of economic independence.

The basic cause of inflation in Israel was excess demand; that is, aggregate demand, or total spending by households for consumption, by businesses for investment, and by the government for both consumption and investment, exceeded the capacity of the economy to supply goods and services. Contributing to this type of inflation, which is known as demand-pull, was the rise in income due to full employment as well as to restitution payments and private transfers from abroad. Government financing of the Development Budget by converting foreign exchange receipts and by borrowing from the banking system was also inflationary throughout most of the period. Another cause of inflation was the rise in labor costs (wages and fringe benefits) in excess of productivity. The dominant position of labor, the difficulty of dismissing redundant and inefficient labor, very high social benefits, and the long-established system of linking wages to the cost-of-living index in all branches of the organized economy were the institutional factors that explained this type of inflation, which is known as cost-push. (On the other hand, the labor federation cooperated with the government in attempts to stabilize wages and prices.) Cost inflation was particularly important in periods of unemployment, such as 1952–53 and 1965–66; prices rose by 8 per cent in each of the two latter years despite the weakening of aggregate demand. The year 1967 was unusual in Israel's history: neither demand nor cost inflation made itself felt, with prices rising by only 2 per cent.

What further exacerbated these goal conflicts was the constant rise in the defense burden, both in relative and in absolute terms. Defense spending accounted for 50 per cent of government consumption expenditures and for about 11 per cent of total resources. The defense burden was relatively higher in Israel than in almost any other country, including the United States, which spent 9.4 per cent of total resources on defense in the period 1955–64. Annual defense expenditures in Israel (excluding local purchases) grew by 16 times between 1952 and 1966; they rose sharply in the 1960s, reaching a record of $629,000,000 in the fiscal year 1968–69. The real cost to the economy was not fully reflected by these data. It included, among other things, loss of production due to annual reserve duty by a large segment of the labor force and the cost of border settlements established on the basis of national security rather than economic feasibility. The purchase of arms abroad and the expansion of military industries at home were particularly important elements in the total defense burden.

Economic System and Role of Government. One of the main features of Israel's economic structure was its development as a mixed economic system. The economy consisted of three sectors: public, cooperative, and private. The public sector included government enterprises and corporations, local authorities, and national institutions such as the Jewish Agency and the *Jewish National Fund. The cooperative, or labor, sector included economic enterprises owned by and affiliated with the *Histadrut (General Federation of Labor). The private sector embraced all economic units not covered in the two other sectors, including most of the economic activities of the Arab population.

According to a study by the Falk Institute for Economic Research in Israel, the public and Histadrut sectors each accounted for about 20 per cent of net domestic product and

employment in the period 1953–60, with the remaining 60 per cent attributable to the private sector. In no other Western country did the socialized or nonprivate sectors play as prominent a role as in Israel. However, as in most other countries, government activities were concentrated in the fields of electricity and water (100 per cent of total production) and transportation and communications (40 per cent of the total). The share of government in other fields was relatively minor, even though more than 75 public-sector companies were represented in almost every economic branch. The 2,000 enterprises of the Histadrut sector contributed about one-third of the net product of agriculture. construction, and transportation and communications; one-fifth that of mining and manufacturing; one-sixth that of trade and services; and one-tenth that of banking, finance, and real estate. The private sector's main areas of economic activity were in banking, finance, real estate, trade, and services (80–90 per cent of total production); mining and manufacturing (73.5 per cent); agriculture (about 67 per cent); and construction (more than 50 per cent).

Despite the extensive socialization of the economy, the government's economic policy was flexible and pragmatic. The declared policy of the government was to give equal opportunities to all three sectors and to encourage mixed ownership of companies organized by the public sector. The Histadrut, foreign private investors, and local investors (including financial institutions, pension funds, and households) participated to the extent of one-fourth in the equity of government companies.

Although the government accounted directly for only one-fifth of production and employment, its impact on the economy was wide-ranging. The State was responsible for about half of all investment, granting sizable loans from the Development Budget to private and Histadrut undertakings. It exerted considerable influence on the economy through fiscal and monetary policies, extensive social services, controls over imports and foreign exchange, and subsidies to consumers and producers. Total public-sector expenditures on general, economic, social, and other services ranged from 40 to 50 per cent of GNP in the first half of the 1960s; this was one of the highest ratios for a non-Communist country.

The government's role was also felt in the area of economic planning. A number of ministries, among them Agriculture, Commerce and Industry, Development, and Transport, were engaged in sectoral planning for many years. But overall planning assumed importance only after the establishment of the Economic Planning Authority in 1962. The Authority's main task was to formulate, in cooperation with the various ministries and the Bank of Israel, long-term development plans and annual forecasts for the economy as a whole, including recommendations for government policy on wages, prices, budgets, saving, investment, and the balance of payments. Administratively the Authority was a part of the Prime Minister's Office, but functionally it was an arm of the Ministerial Committee on Economic Planning. It operated as a coordinating, advisory, and research institution dealing with broad goals and targets (similar to agencies found in Western Europe) rather than as a decision-making planning commission of the type prevalent in Communist or collectivist systems.

The government's deep involvement in economic development and social welfare reflected the ideology of the Israel labor parties, which had dominated all coalition Cabinets since the establishment of the State. In pursuance of this ideology it had to give consideration to economic factors such as the size and composition of immigration, the steady flow of foreign capital to the public sector, and the country's limited natural resources.

O. REMBA

ECUADOR, ZIONISM IN. Massive Jewish immigration to Ecuador began in 1938 and reached its climax in 1939. During World War II and the first two postwar years, the population of the Ecuadorean Jewish community reached 4,000 persons, its maximum. After 1946–47 there was practically no Jewish immigration; instead, there was a wave of emigration, mainly to the United States. In 1967 the Jewish population of Ecuador was 2,000 (in a total population of 5,508,000), with 1,000 living in Quito, 150 in Guayaquil, and the rest scattered in small places.

In 1939 the Jews of Ecuador began to organize communal institutions, the most important of these being the Asociación de Beneficencia Israelita, a welfare institution in Quito, and the Centro Israelito (Jewish Center), in Guayaquil. The programs of these organizations included Zionist activities, but in 1941 the Federación Sionista del Ecuador (Zionist Federation of Ecuador) was established as an independent institution dedicated exclusively to Zionist work, including propaganda, education, and fund-raising campaigns.

As of 1968 the Zionist Federation of Ecuador had its headquarters in Quito and a branch office in Guayaquil. It had committees for cultural affairs, for the *Jewish National Fund, and for the *Keren HaYesod (Palestine Foundation Fund). It also dealt with Israel bonds (see STATE OF ISRAEL BONDS). The *Women's International Zionist Organization (WIZO) of Ecuador (250 members in 1966) was formed at about the same time as the federation, as were a number of Zionist youth organizations and the Liga Femenina Pro-Israel.

Until 1963 the Federación Sionista maintained a professional office staff, which handled internal matters and relations with the leadership of Zionist organizations throughout the world. Because of the decrease in the Jewish population of Ecuador, the Federación was obliged to reduce its staff and abolish its permanent office, which was replaced by a Board of Directors and an honorary secretary. There was talk of a merger of the office of the Zionist Federation with that of the Asociación de Beneficencia Israelita and *B'nai B'rith. In Guayaquil the activities of the Federación were handled by the Israeli Consulate in that city, in collaboration with a group of directors.

M. WEISER

EDELSTEIN, JAKOB. *Po'ale Zion leader in Czechoslovakia (b. Gorodenka, Galicia, Austria, 1906; d. Auschwitz, 1944). The founder of an organization of Socialist Zionists and of *Tarbut in Czechoslovakia, Edelstein became one of the leading Zionists in that country and was a member of the Executive Committee and deputy chairman of the Zionist Federation. He also served as the executive of the Czechoslovak *HeHalutz and was a leading member of the local League for Labor Palestine.

With the exception of the year 1934, when he was active on behalf of *Keren HaYesod (Palestine Foundation Fund), Edelstein was director of the Prague Palestine Office (see PALESTINE OFFICES) from 1932 until it was closed during World War II. After the occupation of Czechoslovakia, he made every effort to aid his fellow Jews, continuing his selfless activity in the ghetto of Theresienstadt, where he and his family were held prior to their deportation to Auschwitz.

O. NEUMANN

EDER, EDITH LOW. Educator and Zionist leader, and the wife of Montague David *Eder (b. London, 1874; d. there, 1944). She taught school in London and in Manchester, where she first became active as a speaker and organizer for the labor movement. Settling in London, she became a leading member of the Fabian Society and wrote articles for women's magazines on social, educational, and literary subjects.

After she became the second wife of Montague David Eder, she accompanied him in 1918 to Palestine, where she became interested in Zionism. She investigated the conditions under which the women pioneers lived and worked, and subsequently, with Mrs. Israel M. Sieff (see SIEFF, REBECCA D. M.) and Mrs. Chaim Weizmann (see WEIZMANN, VERA CHATZMAN), she founded the *Women's International Zionist Organization (WIZO). At the time of her death, she was a member of the WIZO Executive and honorary vice-president of the Federation of Women Zionists of Great Britain and Ireland.

Mrs. Eder's last visit to Palestine occurred in 1937. In 1939 she was a member of a delegation of 200 women that went to the House of Commons to protest the *White Paper of 1939. She was the only one permitted to speak on that occasion.

EDER, MONTAGUE DAVID. Psychoanalyst and Zionist leader in England (b. London, 1866; d. there, 1936). An early disciple of Sigmund Freud, Eder was the first practitioner of psychoanalysis in Great Britain. He was an active member of the International Council of Israel *Zangwill's *Jewish Territorial Organization (ITO). During World War I he participated in the movement for the recruitment in England of a Jewish battalion (see JEWISH LEGION). In 1918 he joined the *Zionist Commission in the dual capacity of medical officer and representative of the ITO. While in Palestine, he became a convinced Zionist and thereafter devoted himself fervently to Zionist work. In 1921 he became a member of the Zionist *Executive, holding this post until 1923 and then again from 1925 to 1928. From 1930 to 1932 he was president of the Zionist Federation of Great Britain and Ireland (see GREAT BRITAIN, ZIONISM IN). Throughout his Zionist activities Eder was one of Chaim *Weizmann's most loyal followers.

EDERSHEIM, HENRI. Attorney and Zionist leader in the Netherlands (b. The Hague, 1885; d. Auschwitz, 1943). A brother of Karel J. *Edersheim, he founded the Dutch Zionist Students' Organization and headed (jointly with Leonard Salomon *Ornstein) the organization office of the 8th Zionist Congress (The Hague, 1907). He was chairman of the Amsterdam branch of the Dutch Zionist Federation and honorary editor of the Zionist weekly *De Joodse Wachter* from 1912 to 1920 and again in 1939. An active speaker and the author of Zionist pamphlets, Edersheim served as vice-chairman of the Dutch Zionist Executive (1924–27). He was arrested and deported by the Nazis in 1942.

EDERSHEIM, KAREL J. Attorney and Zionist leader in the Netherlands (b. The Hague, 1893). A younger brother of Henri *Edersheim, he helped establish *Jewish National Fund headquarters in The Hague in 1920. An ideological disciple of Nehemia *de Lieme, Edersheim served as chairman of the Dutch Zionist Executive (1927–30) and was named honorary representative of the *Jewish Agency in the Netherlands in 1945. In 1948 he served briefly as the ad hoc representative of the State of Israel in the Netherlands.

EDUCATION IN ISRAEL. This article describes (1) the development of Jewish education in Palestine until 1948 and (2) education in Israel since the establishment of the State.

HISTORICAL BACKGROUND

Prior to the coming of the *First 'Aliya in 1882, Jewish educational institutions in Palestine consisted almost entirely of such religious schools as Heders, Kuttabs (religious elementary schools of the Oriental Jews), Talmud Toras, and *Yeshivot, as in the other Jewish communities of the Middle East, North Africa, Eastern Europe, and other areas where modern Jewish schools had not been developed at that time.

1882–1918. Subsequent decades saw the establishment, both in towns and in the new settlements, of a variety of modern kindergartens, elementary schools, and trade schools. Most of the new schools were founded by Jewish philanthropic organizations from other countries, such as the *Alliance Israélite Universelle (which had established the Mikve Yisrael Agricultural School in 1870), the *Anglo-Jewish Association, and the *Hilfsverein der Deutschen Juden (founded in 1901), which developed wide-ranging educational activities in Palestine. These schools did not differ from those the organizations founded in other countries; that is, the medium of instruction was a foreign language, with *Hebrew occupying a secondary position. For these organizations Palestine was then just another country, and they never envisaged Jewish education there as the basis of a new Jewish life. The teachers came from the home countries of the respective organizations and taught in their native languages. Side by side with these institutions there developed schools of a national-Hebraic type, founded by the Zionist pioneers and representing the ideals of the Jewish renaissance. Such schools received support from the *Hoveve Zion movement and the *World Zionist Organization (WZO).

At an early stage, under the influence of Eliezer *Ben Yehuda and his disciples, Jewish subjects began to be taught in Hebrew in the schools administered by the foreign philanthropic organizations, but it was only in the schools of the modern settlers that attempts were made to teach secular subjects in Hebrew as well. In 1889 the elementary school of Rishon L'Tziyon became the first all-Hebrew school in the country. By 1908 all schools in the new settlements had adopted Hebrew as their only language of instruction. All-Hebrew schools also existed in the cities, and the language made increasing headway in the schools maintained by the foreign Jewish organizations. In 1906 a high school where Hebrew was the sole language of instruction was opened in Jaffa (later it was transferred to Tel

Athletic field outside a high school in Tel Aviv. [Israel Information Services]

Aviv; *see* HERZLIYA HIGH SCHOOL), and three years later a Hebrew High School was founded in Jerusalem.

The Hebraization of the schools continued despite immense difficulties: the skepticism of parents with regard to the revival of Hebrew; the opposition of many of the French assimilated officials who administered the settlements of the *Jewish Colonization Association (ICA); and the objective problems posed by Hebrew, which was not yet adequate to serve as the language of instruction for sciences and other secular subjects.

A major part in the development of modern Hebrew education in the country was played by the Merkaz HaMorim (Central Committee of Teachers). This was the executive body of the Hebrew Teachers Association of Palestine (later called Histadrut HaMorim), which had been founded in 1903 by 60 educators teaching in Hebrew in the schools of the country. Though the Merkaz HaMorim did not control any schools during the first years of its existence, it exerted a dominant influence on all school systems in the country. In 1906 it published a suggested curriculum for elementary schools and in 1910 established a board of examining teachers. It also published Hebrew textbooks and other Hebrew educational literature.

In 1913 the Merkaz HaMorim was in the forefront of the *Language War. Toward the end of that year, under the leadership of the Merkaz, teachers and students withdrew from the schools of the Hilfsverein, which opposed instruction in the Hebrew language. The students were accommodated in newly established all-Hebrew schools, which were administered by a Va'ad HaHinukh (Education Committee) composed of members of the Hebrew Teachers Association and representatives of other public bodies. The budget of the schools was guaranteed by the WZO; part of the funds was raised by the local population. During World War I the Va'ad HaHinukh took over several other Hebrew schools, because the societies or private persons who supported them could no longer do so.

1918–48. In 1918 the *Zionist Commission arrived in Palestine. It established a Department of Education that assumed control over the schools of the Va'ad HaHinukh. The WZO set itself the task of organizing a unified Hebrew system of education and of providing elementary education through the medium of Hebrew to all Jewish children in the country. This goal was to be achieved by expanding the schools of the Va'ad HaHinukh and by absorbing schools founded and maintained by other organizations. In the first postwar years all schools of the Hilfsverein, some schools of the Alliance, and the schools established by the *Palestine Jewish Colonization Association (PICA) in the settlements passed to the jurisdiction of the Department of Education. Thus a Jewish national school system came into being. The WZO maintained the system until 1929, when it was taken over by the *Jewish Agency.

Gradually the Jewish Agency reduced its financial allocations for education, and increasing obligations devolved on the organized Jewish community (*K'nesset Yisrael) in Palestine. In 1932 the *Va'ad L'umi (National Council) assumed full responsibility for the administration of the national school network, while the Jewish Agency continued to contribute modest annual grants for its maintenance. More than 80 per cent of the educational budget of the Va'ad L'umi was covered by contributions from the local Jewish authorities (councils of Jewish cities and settlements) and by tuition fees. Less than 20 per cent came from the British Mandatory government (*see* MANDATE FOR PALESTINE) and the Jewish Agency (see Table 1).

The British administration in Palestine enabled the Jewish

Children at school in a kibbutz. [Histadrut Foto-News]

A class in carpentry. [Israel Information Services]

national school system to enjoy a large measure of autonomy. The British provided only a small part of the budget of the Jewish school system. According to article 14 of the mandate, each community was assured the right to maintain its own schools for the education of its own members in its own language, while conforming to educational requirements of a general nature.

When the Department of Education was established by the Zionist Commission, religious Hebrew schools, which had been founded and supported by the *Mizrahi, became affiliated with it. Thus the new national school system came to consist of two "trends," general and religious, each of which enjoyed a wide measure of autonomy in the hiring of teachers and the development of curricula. In the early 1920s the Labor Zionist movement (*see* LABOR ZIONISM) began to organize its own educational institutions, in kibbutzim and moshavim and later also in the various towns. In 1926 the WZO recognized the labor schools as a separate trend (the labor trend), and in 1938 these schools were included in the centralized administrative network of the Va'ad L'umi.

TABLE 1. FINANCING OF THE JEWISH NATIONAL SCHOOL SYSTEM IN PALESTINE
(In Israeli pounds)

Source	1942–43 IL	Per cent	1944–45 IL	Per cent
Palestine government	92,741	11.5	127,082	8.5
Jewish Agency	46,500	5.7	116,760	7.9
Va'ad L'umi (general funds)	3,000	0.3	4,000	0.3
Deficit to be met by Va'ad L'umi Education Department	16,286	2.0	37,721	2.5
Local authorities and local Jewish communities	326,173	40.0	556,000	37.3
School fees	305,000	37.0	584,000	39.2
Unclassified	30,300	3.5	64,000	4.3
Total	820,000	100.0	1,489,563	100.0

SOURCE: Moshe Avidor, *Education in Israel,* Jewish Agency for Israel, Youth and HeHalutz Department, Jerusalem, 1957, p. 26.

The differences in program between the three trends reflected the different outlooks of the major Zionist parties that supported them—the General Zionists (*see* GENERAL ZIONISM), Mizrahi, and the labor parties. The schools of the general trend followed a national Zionist orientation, emphasizing the development of Hebrew culture and appreciation of national values. The Mizrahi networks offered a religion-oriented program stressing the inculcation of religious beliefs and the observance of ritual, while the labor schools devoted considerable time to the study of practical subjects and social studies. The Jewish national school system comprised kindergartens, elementary schools, high schools, vocational schools, and teachers training colleges (see Table 2).

Remaining outside the Jewish national school system were the schools of the *Agudat Israel, which had not become associated with the WZO and was not a member of the K'nesset Yisrael. The curriculum of its schools was religion-centered, a large part of the school time being devoted to Jewish religious studies. The schools of the Alliance Israélite Universelle, private kindergartens, and private religious schools also remained outside the system.

T. PRESCHEL

EDUCATIONAL DEVELOPMENT IN ISRAEL

After the independence of Israel, education in the country was governed by two basic pieces of legislation: the Free and Compulsory Education Law (1949) and the State Education Law (1953). Under the 1949 law all children between the ages of 5 and 14 had to attend school (one year of kindergarten, followed by eight years of elementary education). Elementary schooling was free. The 1949 law also required boys and girls aged 14 to 17 who had not completed their elementary education in Israel, and who had accepted employment, to attend schools for working youth during the afternoon and evening hours. As of 1968 these courses also were free. Secondary education was not compulsory.

The 1953 law was designed to put an end to a system, in existence for three decades, that had linked the schools closely with various political organizations. It provided for a unified public school system with two parallel trends, State schools and religious State schools. All schools in Israel gave basic compulsory courses in Bible and Jewish values. However, in contrast to the State schools, which emphasized Toda'a Y'hudit (Jewish consciousness), the religious State schools were, in the words of the 1953 law, "observant of Orthodox precepts as to their way of life, curriculum, teachers and inspectors." In these institutions time was set aside for prayers, and character education was based on the traditional Orthodox point of view. The 1953 law also provided for "recognized" schools (independent religious schools, or Hinukh 'Atzma'i), which were not "official" but received partial financial support from the State. This status was granted to a number of schools, chiefly those of Agudat Israel.

Administration. Education within the purview of the law, including the curricula of both State and religious State schools as well as the training of elementary school teachers, was under the direct supervision of the Ministry of Education and Culture. The Minister of Education and Culture, as a member of the Cabinet, was responsible to the *Knesset. In 1968 the State of Israel was divided into six school districts: Jerusalem, Tel Aviv, Haifa, Southern, Central, and Northern.

Students and Teachers. In 1967–68 there were 774,399 students on all levels of education in Israel, including 82,909 in Arab schools (see Table 3). The students were distributed in 5,356 educational institutions, with 26,274 female and 16,019 male teachers.

(The figures in this article do not report either East Jerusalem,

TABLE 2. NUMBERS OF TEACHERS AND PUPILS IN INSTITUTIONS OF THE JEWISH NATIONAL SYSTEM

School year	Kindergartens Teachers	Pupils	Elementary schools Teachers	Pupils	Secondary schools Teachers	Pupils	Vocational schools Teachers	Pupils	Teachers training colleges Teachers	Pupils	Total, all institutions Teachers	Pupils
1920–21	127	2,713	305	8,368	63	992	10	532	28	225	533	12,830
1925–26	107	3,036	412	10,770	69	1,365	31	779	35	293	654	16,243
1930–31	177	5,000	544	15,031	86	1,489	45	513	45	500	897	22,533
1935–36	238	6,398	1,002	29,472	149	2,603	29	738	40	490	1,458	39,701
1940–41	228	6,211	1,569	44,818	382	6,307	39	539	78	817	2,296	58,692
1941–42	267	7,398	1,510	46,690	474	7,335	41	609	75	775	2,367	62,807
1942–43	308	8,485	1,638	49,181	528	7,846	47	603	94	624	2,615	66,739
1943–44	410	11,049	2,175	51,672	567	8,929	65	734	107	720	3,324	73,104
1944–45	469	12,490	2,422	55,471	613	9,527	41	1,067	107	886	3,652	79,441

SOURCE: Colonial Office, *The System of Education of the Jewish Community in Palestine,* H. M. Stationery Office, London, 1946, p. 102.

TABLE 3. PUPILS IN EDUCATIONAL INSTITUTIONS, BY TYPE OF INSTITUTION

Type of institution	1948–49	1951–52	1956–57	1960–61	1964–65	1965–66	1966–67
All pupils	140,817	326,387	470,751	599,962	711,295	731,455	757,220
Educational system	134,887	315,126	443,618	562,814	654,720	669,392	683,889
Academic institutions	1,635	3,686	5,842	10,836	18,389	21,756	26,714
Other institutions	4,295	7,575	21,291	26,312	38,186	40,307	46,617
Hebrew education, total	129,688	294,084	432,069	548,147	643,730	659,359	679,743
Educational system	127,470	288,921	414,374	522,046	599,123	609,934	620,070
Kindergartens	25,406	63,556	73,218	74,995	82,885	85,541	87,565
Primary schools	91,133	185,407	285,926	361,707	397,921	395,901	392,562
Schools for handicapped children	....	3,236	4,783	8,111	10,989	11,316	11,485
Schools for working youth	....	10,780	11,341	7,744	4,443	4,374	4,733
Postprimary schools, total	(10,218)	24,985	36,506	66,636	97,837	106,551	116,253
Secondary schools	6,411	12,936	14,888	30,015	46,661	49,628	53,577
Secondary evening schools	....	1,433	2,766	4,202	2,851	2,456	2,346
Continuation classes	1,048	2,304	5,792	7,587	10,420	10,951	11,092
Vocational schools	2,002	4,315	6,380	11,560	25,441	31,239	35,234
Agricultural schools	....	2,788	5,148	5,598	6,929	6,564	7,062
Other postprimary schools	....	....	....	4,485	1,455	1,422	2,540
Preparatory classes to teachers training colleges	757	1,209	1,532	3,189	4,080	4,291	4,408
Teachers training colleges	713	957	2,600	2,853	5,048	6,251	7,466
Academic institutions	1,635	3,686	5,842	10,836	18,389	21,756	26,714
Other institutions	583	1,477	11,853	15,265	26,213	27,669	32,959
Arab education, total	11,129	32,303	38,682	51,815	67,565	72,096	77,477
Educational system	7,417	26,205	29,244	40,768	55,597	59,458	63,819
Kindergartens	637	3,299	3,610	5,546	7,528	7,845	8,230
Primary schools	6,766	22,293	24,659	33,379	46,121	49,349	52,820
Schools for handicapped children	....	....	....	....	10	7	37
Schools for working youth	....	185	80	89	99	213	244
Postprimary schools, total	14	428	853	1,277	1,721	1,901	2,280
Secondary schools	14	428	853	1,086	1,405	1,558	1,846
Vocational schools	....	....	....	....	215	217	261
Agricultural schools	....	....	....	47	65	93	173
Other postprimary schools	....	....	....	144	36	33	....
Teachers training colleges	....	....	42	117	118	143	208
Other institutions	3,712	6,098	9,438	11,047	11,968	12,638	13,658

SOURCE: Central Bureau of Statistics, *Statistical Abstract of Israel,* Jerusalem, 1967, p. 525.

which came under Israeli jurisdiction following the *Six-day War of 1967, or territories formerly under Jordanian administration on the *West Bank.)

Financing. The budget of the Ministry of Education and Culture was the second largest item in the Israel National Budget. In 1967–68 it amounted to IL386,400,000, plus IL80,600,000 for institutions of higher learning and IL18,000,000 for school construction.

Preschool and Kindergarten Education. Children between the ages of 3 and 4 might be enrolled in nursery schools sponsored by the municipalities or by organizations such as the Mizrahi Women's Organization, *Mo'etzet HaPo'alot, and the *Women's International Zionist Organization (WIZO). Since nursery education was not compulsory, it was subject to tuition fees, ranging as of 1968 from IL3 to IL36 per month (depending on the financial circumstances of the family) in municipal nurseries to IL34 to IL45 per month in nonpublic institutions. Kindergartens, in which attendance was compulsory for all children between the ages of 5 and 6, were run by various religious and public organizations. No tuition was charged.

Elementary Education. All children between the ages of 6 and 14 were required to attend the elementary schools nearest their homes. Kibbutzim maintained their own educational institutions in or near the settlements. Classes were conducted six days a week, with school hours ranging from 24 per week in grade 1 to 32 in the higher grades. The curriculum included the Bible, Hebrew language and literature, history, geography, sciences, mathematics, manual training (woodworking, home economics, agriculture), art, music, and physical education. In some elementary schools English and French were taught. During the early months of grade 8, all children except new immigrants were required to take a Seker (achievement test) that helped determine their eligibility for scholarship aid (graded tuition) in secondary schools. There was no tuition fee for the eight grades of elementary school, but as of 1968 the local municipalities levied a small yearly school tax to cover medical and psychological services, dental care (for kindergarten pupils only), insurance, psychological services, and textbooks for the first three grades. The tax varied in each community and with each grade; in Jerusalem it was IL20 for kindergarten and grades 4–8 and IL32 for grades 1–3. A tax reduction was given when more than one child in a family was enrolled in school.

In the late 1960s the main efforts in elementary education were directed toward closing the "cultural gap" in Israel. A Center for Aiding Schools with a Preponderance of Culturally Deprived Children (mainly in development areas with large immigrant populations) was set up by the Ministry and entrusted with solving this problem. The principle guiding the operation of the center was a differential approach to education, affording equality in educational opportunities for all children. The program endeavored to compensate for the initial handicap of culturally deprived children by offering them a longer school day and an extended school year. The extra time was utilized for additional instruction, supervised reading and homework, and social and art activities. Adaptation of textbooks, the addition of audio-visual equipment, and special in-service training for teachers working in such schools were also part of the concentrated effort to close the gap. Another important experiment in this problem area was the Interclass Grouping Method, which provided three-level instruction (below-average, average, and advanced) in Hebrew, English, and arithmetic. The remaining subjects were offered within the conventional classroom framework. The method was tried out in grades 6, 7, and 8.

Secondary Education. Like the elementary schools, secondary schools in Israel (grades 9–12, ages 14–18) were either religious or secular, depending on the composition of the student population served by the institution. As of 1968 most of the schools were operated by municipalities and organizations such as the Ministry of Labor and *ORT. All were under the supervision of the Ministry of Education and Culture. There were three types of secondary institutions: academic high schools, vocational high schools, and agricultural high schools.

Academic High Schools. Schools of this type (50 per cent of the secondary schools) had a four-year curriculum, which included Hebrew language and literature, the Bible and Talmud, history, geography, civics, English, French, or Arabic, mathematics and sciences, and miscellaneous minor subjects including physical education. Academic high schools offered a choice of several curricula: humanities, social sciences, mathematics and physics, Oriental studies, and biology. Homework averaged several hours per day. In high schools adhering to the religious trend, greater emphasis was placed on the Bible and Talmud.

To be accepted by institutions of higher learning graduates of academic high schools had to pass the Bagrut (State matriculation examination), a comprehensive test covering their 12 years of education. Since as of 1968 secondary education in Israel was neither compulsory nor free and, therefore, neither selective nor uniform in quality, the Bagrut examination was the only guarantee of an adequate standard of instruction. Students took the Bagrut examination in their high school specialty as well as in general subject matter. At the end of 1966–67, 10,732 high school students took this examination. In certain subjects research papers might be substituted for the Bagrut examination. Students who had completed the required 12 years of study but did not wish to take the Bagrut examination received a Certificate of Completion of Twelve Years of Study. This diploma was intended to discourage dropouts in the higher grades of the secondary schools.

Vocational High Schools. The course of study at vocational high schools was open to both boys and girls and, depending on the curriculum, varied in length from two to four years. About

26 hours per week were devoted to the humanities (Hebrew, the Bible, history, civics, and English), mathematics and sciences, technical subjects, and such minor subjects as physical education. An additional 18 hours were devoted to shopwork in the chosen trade. The vocational courses offered included electronics, automobile mechanics, woodworking, home economics, refrigeration, printing, drafting, and office practice. Final certificates were awarded to students who completed a four-year course. Students completing a two- or three-year course received leaving certificates, which were necessary to qualify them as apprentices or craftsmen in particular trades.

Agricultural High Schools. Most agricultural high schools offered a three-year curriculum, with approximately 30 hours per week for humanities, mathematics, sciences, agricultural subjects, and physical education and 24 hours for farmwork. Such schools generally provided dormitory facilities for their students. Graduates of four-year curricula might take the Bagrut examination. Graduates of the standard three-year curriculum received a completion certificate, as did graduates of a two-year course who had had two years of farming experience.

As of 1968 annual tuition fees in secondary schools ranged from IL875 to IL1,025, depending on the type of school and the grade attended. Under the graded tuition system, tuition was adjusted to parental means and the number of children in a family who were in school or in the army at the time. To qualify for tuition adjustments for the first year of academic high school, the student had to pass the Seker given in grade 8 of elementary schools. Students in vocational or agricultural schools or in grades 11 and 12 of academic high schools were eligible for scholarship aid regardless of the results of their Seker examinations. In 1968 students living in one of the *development towns and new immigrants during their first two years of residence in Israel were exempt from tuition fees, and 50 per cent of all secondary school students received free tuition.

A special Postelementary Education Authority, established in 1964, was responsible for the development of comprehensive schools in development areas, taking in all elementary school graduates living in a given area and offering two-, three-, and four-year vocational, academic, and agricultural curricula. In this type of school, students could move from curriculum to curriculum according to achievement or inclination. These schools provided for the intensive integration of students from different social strata and national backgrounds. The Authority was also responsible for the implementation of the graded tuition system and for enrichment programs for gifted students, especially for those from culturally deprived homes. In addition to a secondary boarding school, special day centers for the gifted were maintained throughout the country.

Arab Education. The language of instruction in all Arab schools in Israel was Arabic. Since existing textbooks became obsolete after the establishment of the State, a complete new set of Arabic textbooks for all subjects in elementary and secondary schools was issued by the Ministry of Education and Culture. Special stress was put on the development of vocational education, in-service training for teachers, and revision of syllabi and curricula. As a result of the special attention given to the education of Arab girls, the percentage of Arab school-age girls attending school in Israel rose from 15 under the mandate to 75 in 1968. *See also* ARABS IN ISRAEL.

Independent Schools. The status of independent schools was granted to a number of educational institutions, chiefly the schools of the Agudat Israel movement and private schools.

Agudat Israel. The educational institutions of Agudat Israel were recognized nonofficial schools. The elementary schools of the movement, 125 of which were in operation in 1966–67, had a combined enrollment of 25,101 (1967), or roughly 5.5 per cent of the entire elementary school population, and received 85 per cent of their budget from the Ministry of Education and Culture. Three-quarters of their curriculum was identical with the core curriculum of the State and religious State schools; the rest was devoted to religious subjects. The system also maintained a number of secondary schools and teacher training institutions.

Private Schools. There were two categories of private schools: foreign and local. As of 1968 the status of foreign schools, especially that of schools belonging to the Christian ecclesiastical organizations and missionary societies, had not yet been defined by law. While the 1953 law made special provision for the non-Jewish population, it did not cover private schools where non-Jews studied or private schools attended by Jewish pupils. The temporary solution thus far was to refrain from prosecuting parents whose children attended schools which had not been granted recognition and which therefore violated the 1949 and 1953 laws. In 1968 there were 30 such elementary and secondary schools.

The local schools belonged to resident religious communities (Muslim, Roman Catholic, Protestant, and Greek Orthodox). They accepted supervision and financial aid from the Ministry of Education and Culture, and their pupils were beneficiaries of the graded tuition system. In 1968, 20 such so-called community schools operated in Israel.

Higher Education. Higher education in Israel in 1968 was autonomous, and any recognized and duly accredited institution was free to conduct its academic and administrative affairs as it saw fit. In 1968 there were five recognized institutions of higher learning in Israel: the *Hebrew University of Jerusalem, the *Technion, *Tel Aviv University, *Bar-Ilan University, and the *Weizmann Institute of Science. Other institutions of higher learning were the New Bezalel School of Arts and Crafts in Jerusalem (*see* BEZALEL SCHOOL), the Israel Academy of Music in Tel Aviv, the Negev Institute for Higher Education in B'er Sheva' (in conjunction with the Hebrew University and the Technion), and the *Haifa University Institute (courses conducted in conjunction with the Hebrew University).

A Council for Higher Education was established by an act of the Knesset in 1958, with the function of counseling, coordinating, and accrediting institutions of higher learning. The Council could make recommendations for the establishment of new institutions, the expansion of existing ones, and government contributions to the budgets of institutions of higher learning. (In 1968 the government met almost 50 per cent of the total budget of higher education in Israel.) The Minister of Education and Culture was the Council's ex officio chairman.

Teacher Training. In 1968 Israeli schools offered training programs for elementary and secondary school teachers. Some 40 schools prepared teachers for the elementary schools. These schools, to which students were admitted on completion of grade 12 of high school, were organized along lines of the three major trends (state, religious State, and independent religious) and offered three-year courses. A number of institutions prepared students for teaching in specialized subjects such as art, music, physical education, and home economics. Special teachers training colleges also educated men and women for positions in kibbutzim and immigrant villages. Training for secondary school teachers was offered at Tel Aviv University, the Hebrew University, and Bar-Ilan University. Elementary school teachers were eligible for one year of study leave during their entire term of service; secondary school teachers and superintendents were entitled to this leave once in every eight years.

Adult Education. In the late 1960s five independent bodies cooperated in an extensive and variegated adult education program throughout Israel: the Cultural Department of the Ministry of Education and Culture, the *Histadrut, the *Israel Defense Forces, the Jewish Agency, and the universities.

In addition to regular programs in advanced education, Hebrew instruction for adults, extension services, elementary and secondary education for adults, and various study circles, a crash project to eliminate illiteracy was launched in 1963. It called for the eradication of illiteracy by attacking the problem on three levels: large metropolitan areas, immigrant towns, and rural settlements. Volunteers and professionals joined in teaching reading and writing to illiterates, who in the mid-1960s comprised 12.5 per cent of Israel's adult Jewish population.

In a class by itself, and a unique contribution in the field of adult education, was the Israeli-developed *Ulpan, an institution especially designed for the teaching of Hebrew to immigrant professionals.

Education in the Army. In the late 1960s the Israel Defense Forces played a vital role in almost all phases of education in Israel. The army had its own Education Department, complete with textbook publication and testing and evaluation services. It offered elementary, secondary, and vocational education and adult education courses. Intensive Hebrew courses were offered for new immigrant soldiers. The army also contributed to the solution of the teacher shortage problem by training female soldiers as teachers in conjunction with the Ministry of Education and Culture and by releasing after basic army training those of them who volunteered to work in schools in development areas.

Educational Television. An educational TV pilot project was initiated in the late 1960s by the Rothschild Foundation. A special committee of the Ministry of Education and Culture was responsible for the planning and presentation of the programs. The broadcasts were transmitted through an open-circuit system to grades 7, 8, and 9 in 30 schools.

Educational and Vocational Guidance. In the mid-1960s a countrywide Scholastic Test was administered to students at the end of grade 8. It served to guide parents and teachers in the choice of secondary education and vocational orientation to be followed by graduates of elementary schools. A National Institute for Educational Counseling and Vocational Guidance aided graduates of elementary schools in their choice of further studies or in the selection of appropriate professions.

Educational Planning. In view of rapid technological developments, the cultural gap between the old-timer and the newcomer segments of the population, and the shortage in academic manpower, educational planning came into its own in recent years. Both government and private research institutions tackled the problems and supply and demand of scientists, engineers, physicians, teachers, and others, and the findings were correlated with the standard and with the end product of instruction. In the late 1960s the Ministry of Labor, the Szold Institute–National Institute for Research in the Behavioral Sciences, the *National Council for Research and Development, and the Council for Higher Education were all engaged in surveys and follow-up studies pertaining to educational planning with a view to solving present and future problems of quality and quantity in leadership and academic personnel. A public commission for the study of problems connected with the extension of the Free and Compulsory Education Law was set up in 1963.

International Cooperation. Israel, a young nation, helped other emerging nations to help themselves. The Ministry of Education and Culture, in conjunction with the Division for International Cooperation of the Ministry of Foreign Affairs, offered numerous training courses for educators, administrators, youth leaders, social workers, and other educational personnel from developing countries. In the first 10 years following the initiation of this program in 1954, almost 6,500 persons graduated from these courses.

A Center for the Promotion of Jewish Consciousness was established by the Ministry of Education and Culture with the aim of strengthening awareness among Israeli youth of the history and heritage of the Jewish people, as well as of stressing relationships between all segments of the Jewish people throughout the world. The program was gradually introduced into all levels of education, not as a subject per se but integrated into suitable subject matter, such as history, literature, and geography.

EF'AL. Home for the aged near Tel Aviv, on the highway leading to Lod Airport. Founded in 1950. Population (1968): 250.

EFROS, ISRAEL ISAAC. Poet, author, and educator (b. Ostrog, Russia, 1891). Efros attended the Yeshiva of Mir and, after arriving in the United States in 1905, the Rabbi Isaac Elchanan Theological Seminary (later part of Yeshiva University) in New York. He was subsequently educated at New York University (B.A., 1913) and Columbia University (M.A., 1914; Ph.D., 1915). In 1918 he founded the Baltimore Hebrew College and Teachers Training School, of which he remained dean until 1928. That year he joined the faculty of the University of Buffalo as professor of Hebrew, serving in this position until 1941. From 1941 to 1955 he was professor of Hebrew at Hunter College in New York and professor of Jewish philosophy and Hebrew literature at the Dropsie College for Hebrew and Cognate Learning in Philadelphia. In 1955 he moved to Israel to become the first rector of *Tel Aviv University, a position he held until 1959, when he became honorary president.

A Hebrew poet of stature, Efros also wrote books on Jewish philosophy. In 1948 he edited an English translation of the poetry of Hayim Nahman *Bialik (2d ed., 1965). He translated into Hebrew Shakespeare's *Hamlet* (1942), *Timon of Athens* (1953), and *Coriolanus* (1959), for which he received the Tschernichowsky Award in 1961. He was the recipient also of the LaMed Poetry Prize (1942, 1954), the Brenner (1962) and Milo Prizes for poetry, and the Henrietta Szold Award "for advancing higher education in Israel." His wife, Mildred Blaustein Efros, wrote several educational works for *Hadassah, including *The Story of Zionism* (1952).

EGGED (bus cooperative). *See* COOPERATIVES IN ISRAEL.

EGLON. *See* TELL EL-HESI.

EGYPT, ZIONISM IN. The history of active Zionism in modern Egypt spans five decades, during which Egypt was first under British occupation (until 1914), then a British protectorate (1914–22), and finally a kingdom (1922-53). It began with the founding of a Zionist group in Cairo in 1897, the year the 1st Zionist *Congress met in Basle, and ended when, with the establishment of the State of Israel, the Zionist movement in Egypt was declared illegal.

Before the *Mandate for Palestine: 1897–1920. The first Zionist organization in Egypt was founded in Cairo in February, 1897, by Joseph Marcou *Baruch, a native of Constantinople who had moved to Egypt in 1896. This group, which was named the Bar Kokhba Society, started out with 7 members. By 1900 it had a membership of 60; one year later, it boasted an enrollment of 300. Its leaders included Jacques Harmalin, who served as president, and Joseph Leibowitz, who was secretary. Most of the members were Jews of Italian, Spanish, and Eastern European provenance; some had been drawn to the movement for ideological reasons, while others had been motivated by philanthropic sentiments. In 1900 Bar Kokhba was joined by B'ne Zion, a young people's society that had an initial membership of 15 and met for *Hebrew courses once a week. The following year, a Zionist school for boys and girls, Bet Sefer Tziyoni, was established in Cairo. It attained a peak enrollment of 290, but before long it was forced to close for lack of funds.

During the first decade of the 20th century Egypt received a substantial influx of Jewish immigrants who had left Russia as a result of the *Kishinev pogrom and the Russo-Japanese War. The newcomers contributed considerably to the further growth of Zionism among Egyptian Jewry.

On the eve of World War I Zionists were active not only in Cairo but also in Alexandria, Port Said, and Tanta. In Cairo the Ahavath Sion society, which had been in existence under other names since 1905 and had a membership of 35, disseminated Zionist information and formed young people's groups for Jewish studies and the discussion of Zionist issues. B'ne Zion continued to be active, working chiefly among Egyptian-born and Yemenite Jews and setting up Hebrew courses. According to a report made at the 9th Zionist Congress (Hamburg, 1909), Zionist efforts were hampered by the heterogeneous character of Egyptian Jewry: Zionist information had to be issued in four languages, Hebrew, French, Arabic, and Yiddish. In 1912 a French-language Zionist newspaper, *La Renaissance Juive,* was founded. Overall Zionist leadership was largely in the hands of a central committee consisting of Norman *Bentwich, Asher Bloom, Jacob Caleff, and S. Hasamsong.

During World War I, Egyptian Zionist groups assisted Jewish refugees who had come to Egypt after being expelled from Palestine by the Turks. They gave an enthusiastic reception also to the *Jewish Legion. The Jewish religious communities, which had previously held themselves aloof from Zionism, began to cooperate with the movement and helped counteract the anti-Zionist propaganda that was beginning to appear in the Arab press (*see* ANTI-ZIONISM).

Years of Growth and Activity: 1920–36. Zionist activity in Egypt received a powerful impetus from the developments that culminated in the decision of the *San Remo Conference (1920) to award the Palestine Mandate to Great Britain. In 1921 there were five Zionist societies in Cairo and one each in Alexandria, El-Mansura, Tanta, and Port Said. These groups raised funds, disseminated pro-Zionist information, and engaged in Hebrew studies. The total number of *Shekel (membership fee) contributors in Egypt that year was 2,000. There were two Zionist weeklies, *Israel* (published from 1920 to 1937 by Albert Mosseri in French, Spanish, Hebrew, and

English) and *La Revue Sioniste* (French). *Mizrahi and the *Women's International Zionist Organization (WIZO) also were active in Egypt in the 1920s. In Cairo and Alexandria there were Maccabee societies which, though not officially Zionist, tended toward Jewish *nationalism.

In March, 1929, the provisional committee that had supervised Zionist activities in Cairo for some years was replaced by a permanent committee, with Alex Green as president, Samy Goldstein and Daniel Saporta as vice-presidents, and Leon Bassan as treasurer. The committee conducted campaigns for the *Jewish National Fund and *Keren HaYesod (Palestine Foundation Fund) and helped set up Bet Ha'Am, a Jewish social center, in Cairo. The Cairo branches of the Union Universelle de la Jeunesse Juive and the Mo'adon 'Ivri (Hebrew Club) worked with young people. In the early 1930s Cairo was visited by a number of world Zionist leaders, including Prof. Selig *Brodetsky, Nahum *Sokolow, and Vera Chatzman *Weizmann.

The center of Zionist activity in Egypt in this period was Alexandria, where in 1932 an audience of more than 1,200 assembled to hear a speech by Sokolow. Other visitors who spoke in Alexandria in 1932-33 were Mrs. Ariel Bension, Meir *Dizengoff. Meir *Grossman, and Mr. and Mrs. Israel Moses *Sieff. Mrs. Bension formed a committee to raise funds for Keren HaYesod, particularly among middle-income people. In January, 1932, a Zionist library with books in French, Yiddish, and Hebrew was organized. In the cultural field the Hebrew Club organized a weekly series of Hebrew debates, and Hattehiah (HaT'hiya, "Revival"), the League of Jewish Youth, ran a Hebrew course.

A branch of *B'rit Trumpeldor (Betar) was established. Many young people wanted to emigrate to Palestine, but difficulty in obtaining *immigration certificates allowed only a few to do so.

Nazi Era, World War II, and Establishment of the State of Israel: 1936–48. Beginning in the mid-1930s, Zionist activity in Egypt increasingly had to contend with anti-Zionist agitation instigated by the growing Arab nationalist movement. In 1937 Egypt opposed the Palestine *partition proposal. That year saw a number of anti-Zionist demonstrations, which took the form of attacks on the Jewish population. On Nov. 2, 1937, the 20th anniversary of the issuance of the *Balfour Declaration, a delegation of Muslims called at the British Embassy in Cairo to protest the declaration. During April and May, 1938, there were anti-Zionist demonstrations all over Egypt. On April 29–30, students of al-Azhar University, the Muslim center of higher education, held a hunger strike to protest the partition proposal and staged a parade with 2,000 marchers in the streets of Cairo. On May 13, students attempted to attack Harat al-Yahud, the Jewish quarter of Cairo, but were repulsed by police guards. The police arrested individuals distributing leaflets urging a boycott of Egyptian Jews for "supporting the Zionists." That spring, Prime Minister Mohammed Mahmud Pasha promised Chief Rabbi Chaim Nahum Effendi that agitators found placing anti-Zionist posters on the streets of Cairo would be severely punished. On the other hand, on May 30, 40 members of the Egyptian Parliament, backed by Minister of Education 'Ali Allonba Pasha, appealed to Egyptian Jewry to repudiate Zionism.

The *White Paper of 1939, which restricted Jewish immigration to Palestine and the sale of Palestinian land by Arabs to Jews, was welcomed by most of the Arab world. However,

certain circles in Egypt and elsewhere voiced opposition to the land sale restrictions, fearing that these would curb Arab commercial enterprise. One of the newspapers expressing such reservations was the Egyptian Arabic-language daily *al-Misri.*

On July 7, 1939, a bomb was planted in a Cairo synagogue, along with an Arab warning to the Zionists, but the bomb failed to explode.

During World War II the Egyptian press and government came out against Zionism with increasing bluntness. In March, 1944, Egypt's Arab press, encouraged by the shelving of the Palestine resolution in the U.S. Congress (*see* UNITED STATES OF AMERICA: RELATIONS WITH ZIONISM AND ISRAEL), urged greater Arab solidarity against efforts to set up a Jewish State in Palestine. *Al-Balagh,* the official organ of the Egyptian Cabinet, demanded increased efforts, particularly in the economic field, to "prevent the Zionists from dominating any markets in the Middle East." In August, 1944, Hassan Nashat Pasha, Egypt's Ambassador to Great Britain, stated at a meeting of the Intergovernmental Committee on Refugees that the "main aim of the Committee should be to take the homeless back to their former countries and homes, where they should be guaranteed rights of citizenship and safety of life and property." Obviously, this statement implied that the Jewish "homeless" should not be permitted to go to Palestine after the war.

At the session of the UN General Assembly held late in 1946, which formulated a constitution for the International Refugee Organization (IRO), Egypt, which had become the leader of the *Arab League the year before, proposed an amendment clearly directed against Jewish immigration to Palestine. Resettlement of refugees, the draft amendment stated, should "in no case be imposed on a sovereign nation or run counter to the freely-expressed wishes and aspiration of a majority of the indigenous population of trust or non-self-governing regions or territories." The proposed amendment was defeated and replaced by a compromise amendment (sponsored by the United States) calling on the IRO to "give due weight, among other factors, to any evidence of genuine apprehension or concern" felt in regard to resettlement plans "by the indigenous population" of the non-self-governing country in question.

Meanwhile, in Egypt itself the Arab boycott against "Zionist" goods was rigorously enforced. "Jewish" goods in transit to overseas countries were impounded, and the loading of Jewish goods in Egyptian ports was forbidden.

In 1946 the Egyptian government began to contemplate steps against organized Zionism in Egypt. That year a bill was introduced in the Egyptian Chamber of Deputies making it an offense punishable by life imprisonment to establish or assist in establishing a "Zionist organization." "Zionist" was defined as "any attempt to transfer Jewish immigrants to Palestine, or any attempt to establish a Jewish State there or to obstruct measures to fight such [an] attempt."

On Nov. 25, 1947, while the United Nations debate on the Palestine partition resolution was in progress, Mohammed Hussein Heykal Pasha, head of the Egyptian delegation to the United Nations, threatened: "The lives of a million Jews in Muslim countries would be jeopardized by partition . . . if Arab blood is shed in Palestine, Jewish blood will necessarily be shed elsewhere in the world despite all the sincere efforts of the government concerned to prevent reprisals."

The establishment of the State of Israel and the *War of Independence gave the Egyptian government a pretext for harsh anti-Jewish measures. Jews in large numbers were arrested, attacked, and robbed although Zionism in Egypt and other Arab countries was at no time engaged in subversive activities. Indeed, Zionism in that area considered itself a spiritual, philanthropic movement that did not conflict with the duties of citizenship.

The final attack on Zionism in Egypt came long after Zionist activity had ceased there. On Nov. 20, 1956, Pres. Gamal Abdel Nasser passed Law 329, which in effect deprived all Zionists of Egyptian citizenship. Article 1 of the law stipulated that "neither Zionists, nor those against whom a judgment has been handed down for crimes of disloyalty to the country or for treason, may be considered Egyptian nationals." The citizenship of all Jews naturalized in Egypt after Jan. 1, 1900, was subject to reexamination, and only those who could prove to the Minister of the Interior that they had never been Zionists were secure against denaturalization. As of 1968, Egypt had only 2,500 Jews, in a total population of more than 30 million. Two decades earlier their number was 90,000.

G. HIRSCHLER

EGYPTIAN JEWS IN ISRAEL. Prior to World War II the Jewish population of Egypt numbered 80,000, concentrated in Cairo and Alexandria. Egyptian Jews began to migrate to Palestine in small numbers in 1936; the years that followed saw a limited *'Aliya (immigration) of young people who joined *Halutz (pioneer) and underground groups in Palestine.

With the creation of the State of Israel in May, 1948, hundreds of active Zionists were interned and many others were put under police surveillance. Following the cease-fire agreements after the Israel *War of Independence, a wave of Jewish emigration from Egypt (via France) to Israel began. After the *Sinai Campaign, Egyptian Jews were again jailed and exiled. Some remained in Europe; others migrated to the United States or to Israel.

Emigration brought 35,570 Egyptian Jews to Israel up to 1961. A small number settled in moshavim (see MOSHAV) and kibbutzim (see KIBBUTZ); the great majority congregated in such suburbs as Bat Yam and Holon (outside Tel Aviv), 'Akko and Kiryat Hayim (outside Haifa), and B'er Sheva'. Because of their command of languages and their adaptability, they played an active role in the tourist, hotel, banking, and aviation industries and in the *civil service. The generally successful adaptation of Egyptian Jews and their integration into the country were reflected in the fact that the "elite" of the community included lawyers, accountants, and police officials.

See also KARAITES IN ISRAEL.

S. KOHEN-SIDON

EHRENPREIS, MARCUS (Mordechai). Rabbi, author, and early political Zionist (b. Lvov, Galicia, Austria, 1869; d. Stockholm, 1951). Ehrenpreis received his religious training in Galicia and his secular education in Berlin and at the University of Erlangen (1895). He was rabbi in Croatia from 1896 to 1900, Chief Rabbi of Bulgaria from 1900 to 1914, and Chief Rabbi of Sweden from 1914 until his death.

He became active in *Hoveve Zion affairs in the late 1880s and helped organize the 1st Zionist *Congress (1897), to which he and Herzl jointly issued the invitations and at which he spoke on the Hebrew language and literature. Ehrenpreis sought to introduce the spirit of modern Europe into Hebrew literature. In later years he wrote in Swedish, translating Yiddish and Hebrew writings and editing books and anthologies about Jews and Judaism, including a selection of Herzl's writings. His

autobiography, *Osterlandets Sjal* (1926), was translated into English (*The Soul of the East*, 1928) and Hebrew (*Ben Mizrah L'Ma'arav*, 1953).

EICHMANN TRIAL. Trial of Adolf Eichmann, Nazi official, on charges of crimes against the Jewish people, war crimes against humanity, and membership in criminal organizations. The trial, which began in Jerusalem on Apr. 11, 1961, lasted 14 weeks. The judges were Moshe *Landau (presiding), Benjamin Halevy, and Itzhak Raveh. Gideon M. *Hausner, the Attorney General of Israel, led the prosecution, and attorney Robert Servatius, of Cologne, appeared for the defense. On Dec. 11, 1961, the court found Eichmann guilty as charged and sentenced him to death. Eichmann made an appeal to the Supreme Court of Israel, which was heard in March, 1962, and rejected on May 29, 1962. Eichmann applied immediately to the President of the State of Israel (see PRESIDENCY OF ISRAEL) for clemency but was refused, and his death sentence was carried out on May 31, 1962.

The trial unfolded the tragedy of European Jewry, which had been destroyed by Nazi Germany. In a systematic program of extermination, to which the Nazis referred as the *Endlösung* (final solution) to the Jewish problem, more than 6 million Jews had been put to death. The execution of the program had been entrusted to the Gestapo (secret police). As the head of the Gestapo's Jewish Department, Eichmann had been the "competent authority" in the "final solution" and had personally supervised all its phases, from the marking of all Jews with a yellow badge through the "ghettoization" of most European Jews, the murder of about 1.5 million Jews in Nazi-held Polish and Soviet areas by special paramilitary units, and, finally, the roundup of all European Jews in the German sphere of influence for deportation to certain designated areas, mostly in Poland, where death camps had been set up for them. The property of the deported Jews was seized and confiscated, an operation likewise superintended by Eichmann's department.

After the collapse of Germany in 1945, Eichmann went into hiding and in 1950 escaped to Argentina, where he lived under the assumed name Ricardo Klement. In May, 1960, he was tracked down by Israeli volunteers, who captured him in Buenos Aires and brought him to Israel. When the government of Argentina lodged a complaint against Israel with the Security Council of the United Nations, Israel apologized for the breach of Argentinian law by Eichmann's captors but insisted on the right of Israel, as the Homeland of Eichmann's victims, the Jewish people, to try him under its Punishment of Nazis and Their Collaborators Law, which had been enacted as early as 1950. Although the Security Council ruled that Israel was to make reparation for the violation of Argentina's sovereignty, it also decided that Eichmann should be brought to justice for his crimes. In the end, Argentina accepted Israel's apology as "reparation" and dropped its earlier request that Eichmann be returned to Argentina.

At the beginning of the trial the counsel for the defense argued that the trial was null and void by virtue of Eichmann's illegal arrest. The Attorney General cited precedents of numerous American and British court rulings in support of his argument that the court was not concerned with the manner in which the defendant had been brought to the bar of justice. Moreover, the Attorney General informed the court that no other country had required Eichmann's extradition, for all countries had acknowledged Israel's right to try the man

Trial of Adolf Eichmann in 1961. Eichmann stands in the glass booth on the left. [Israel Information Services]

responsible for the tragedy of the Jewish people. Insofar as crimes against humanity were concerned, the Attorney General argued, all civilized nations were entitled and, indeed, duty-bound to try the perpetrators. The objections were overruled, and the trial was permitted to proceed.

The prosecution called 112 witnesses. Some of these had personally observed Eichmann in the performance of his "duties" at various places; others, survivors of the death camps, were able to relate some of the events which they had lived through and which could be directly linked to Eichmann's activity. The prosecution further collected and submitted to the court nearly 1,400 documents, most of which were either signed by the accused or emanated from his department. The collection and compilation of the written evidence was particularly difficult since Eichmann's department, under his personal supervision, had destroyed its archives when it became clear that Germany would collapse. As a result, documentary evidence for the trial had to be reconstructed from other archives of the Third Reich that were still available, mainly those of the German Foreign Office, which had been salvaged at the last moment by the advancing American forces. This source of documentation enabled the prosecution to present to the court Eichmann's activities in most Nazi-occupied countries or in countries that had been Germany's allies (e.g., Slovakia, Hungary) and had aligned their policy with the German anti-

Jewish measures. In all these places Eichmann's department had had representatives directly responsible to him. Eichmann's complicity in the massacre of millions of Jews in the Nazi-occupied sectors of Poland and the Soviet Union was established both by virtue of his central position in the extermination program and by documents salvaged in Poland. The systematic work of the Nazi destruction of the Jewish communities in Germany itself was proved by producing the files of a local Gestapo office in Düsseldorf that had been discovered by the Israeli prosecution.

The main impact of the trial, however, was provided by the personal testimony of witnesses from many lands and from all walks of life, each of whom related his own experience, thereby bringing to the court fragments of the shattering story that had been pieced together by the prosecution. It was due to this extensive canvas of proof, expressed in human terms, that the trial of Eichmann became the trial of the entire holocaust. Those witnesses who had had direct dealings with Eichmann described his callous indifference to the Jews and to their suffering, his cunning, and his unflagging zeal in rounding them up and sending them to their destruction. Among the witnesses was a German pastor who had attempted to plead with Eichmann for the Jews.

Eichmann's role in the destruction of Hungarian Jewry was related in great detail, for in Hungary Eichmann had had to act in great haste and openly, in contrast to his customary remaining in the background. It was in Hungary, in 1944, that he was first catapulted into notoriety. It was there that he negotiated with the Jewish leaders a scheme of exchanging Jews for trucks to be supplied to Germany by the Western Allies.

Eichmann's defense was that he had been only a small cog in the German machinery, that he had acted only under orders, and that he was therefore, at least legally, not guilty. Eichmann occupied the witness stand for a whole month and called 16 witnesses in his defense (6 of these were then in prison for war crimes in Germany, Austria, and Italy). All the defense witnesses, including those to whom, at the insistence of the defense counsel, the Attorney General had promised safe-conduct, were examined abroad. None of the defense witnesses agreed entirely with Eichmann's modest version of his role. There was ample evidence that he had enjoyed very wide powers in Jewish affairs and that he had always acted with extraordinary zeal, frequently going beyond the instructions given him from higher quarters. Moreover, it was proved that he continued to exercise control over the fate of the Jews even inside the death camps.

In its long verdict the court considered all the legal problems involved and surveyed the various phases of Nazi Germany's anti-Jewish measures in order to establish Eichmann's place in the program and the extent of his responsibility. The court found that, according to the evidence adduced, Eichmann had been at the head of those engaged in carrying out the "final solution" and that his responsibility extended to all its phases. It found that he had shown zeal and efficiency in all his activities, which went beyond mere routine obedience to orders. Accordingly, Eichmann's plea that he had only been obeying orders "from above" was rejected as unfounded in law and unjustified by the facts of the case.

The trial revealed the involvement of the entire hierarchy of officials of Nazi Germany in the "final solution." It was established that almost every link in the chain of the German administration, including the army and the huge S.S. apparatus, had had its assigned share in the crime.

The evidence submitted regarding Jewish resistance in the ghettos and death camps revealed that, under the circumstances, the very existence of a Jewish underground was a surprising phenomenon, since the Jews lacked the prerequisites that had been available to other groups under the Nazi yoke. The Warsaw ghetto revolt, the culmination of the Jewish resistance movement, was described in the course of the trial. An attempt was made to correct the notions current concerning the Jewish councils of elders installed by the Nazis. It was proved that in many instances the individuals who had served on these bodies had not been collaborators motivated by personal gain but loyal Jews who had made a supreme effort to save Jewish lives. Eventually, all of them, too, had been exterminated by the Nazis along with all other Jews.

Evidence was also produced on the efforts of some gentiles in occupied Europe to save individual Jews by hiding them or by helping them escape, in striking contrast to the Great Powers, which had failed to come to the rescue of the Jews. It was proved that Jews could have been taken in by Great Britain and the United States but that these countries had deliberately closed the door on these possibilities. Even the urgent pleas of the Jewish leaders that the Allies bomb the railroad lines to Auschwitz had been ignored.

The trial evoked worldwide interest and was covered by hundreds of correspondents, writers, historians, and lawyers from all parts of the globe. The proceedings were televised, and tapes were carried daily on many broadcasting networks throughout the world, especially in the United States.

Before the trial began, there was controversy among statesmen, writers, and lawyers on whether or not it was proper for Israel, the home of Eichmann's victims, to try Eichmann. As the trial proceeded in strict adherence to all rules of procedure and as its testimony was unfolded, however, most of the critics changed their views and frankly admitted that Israel was giving Eichmann a fair trial. Most legal reviewers and writers upheld the Israeli legal approach. Books and articles in many languages were written about the trial. There were also widespread repercussions on the international scene, particularly in Germany. The trial had a strong impact on the young *Sabra generation, for which it proved to be of great educational significance. Years after its conclusion the effects of the trial were still being felt in Israel.

G. HAUSNER

EIN. *See* 'EN.

EINSTEIN, ALBERT. Physicist and active supporter of Zionism (b. Ulm, Germany, 1879; d. Princeton, N.J., 1955). Born of an assimilated family and educated in Switzerland, Einstein prepared four scientific papers that gained him international fame before he was 26. In 1914, having taught at the Universities of Bern, Zurich, and Prague, he was named professor of physics at Berlin University and director of the Kaiser Wilhelm Institute for Physics.

In 1916 he published the extended version of his theory of

Golden Book of the Jewish National Fund being presented to Albert Einstein in 1929, on his 50th birthday. In the foreground (left to right) are Dr. Emanuel Neumann, Dr. Einstein, Rabbi Z'ev Gold, and Miss Henrietta Szold. [Zionist Archives]

relativity, which revolutionized the foundations of the exact sciences and paved the way for signal advances in atomic physics. He donated the manuscript of the theory of relativity to the *Hebrew University of Jerusalem. In 1921 he received the Nobel Prize for his contributions to theoretical physics. After Hitler's rise to power in 1933, he settled permanently in the United States, where, working at the Institute for Advanced Study in Princeton, he became known as the country's foremost scientist. In time, his name became a synonym for genius in the popular language. It was Einstein who first brought the military potential of atomic energy to the attention of Pres. Franklin D. *Roosevelt, in a letter dated Aug. 2, 1939.

Einstein was never a practicing Jew from the religious point of view. But when, in 1920, the German Zionist leaders Kurt *Blumenfeld and Felix Rosenblüth (Pinhas *Rosen) sought support for Zionist aims from men prominent in cultural and public life, they decided to approach Einstein, who was widely revered for his honesty, humility, and humanitarianism. Blumenfeld explained to the scientist that Zionism sought to give the Jew a sense of inner security and freedom. After listening to a talk by Blumenfeld before a small group, Einstein declared that he opposed nationalism but now favored the Zionist cause.

In 1921 Chaim *Weizmann asked Blumenfeld to request Einstein to accompany Weizmann on a visit to the United States to raise funds for the *Keren HaYesod (Palestine Foundation Fund) and the Hebrew University. At first Einstein declined the invitation, but Blumenfeld finally persuaded him to go, arguing that if Einstein was truly serious in his interest in Zionism, he had to honor the wishes of the president of the *World Zionist Organization. Einstein and Weizmann were subsequently to become close friends. When the Hebrew University was established in 1925, Einstein became a member of its Board of Governors, remaining on the board until his death. In 1932 the university opened the Albert Einstein Institute of Physics.

Although Einstein considered Palestine "the embodiment of the reawakening spirit of the Jewish nation," he did not support political Zionism. Testifying before the *Anglo-American Committee of Inquiry in Washington on Jan. 11, 1946, he said that he opposed the creation of a Jewish State since he had never been "for a political state," but he urged that most of the Jewish refugees from Nazi-held Europe be brought to Palestine. He felt that the Arabs would not oppose Jewish *immigration to Palestine unless they were incited to do so. At the hearing, he charged that there would be no peace between Jews and Arabs in Palestine as long as the British ruled the country and said that the administration of Palestine should be international. In his writings on Zionism he tended to favor a binational state in Palestine.

After the State of Israel was established, however, Einstein became its fervent admirer and felt greatly honored when, after Weizmann's death in 1952, he was invited to stand for election to the *Presidency of Israel. He refused the invitation, giving as his reason that "scientific problems are familiar to me, but I have neither the natural capacity nor the necessary experience to handle human beings."

Einstein's views on Zionism and Palestine are set down in *Speeches and Letters about Zionism*, translated and edited by Leon *Simon (1931); *The Arabs and Palestine*, a reprint of articles written by Einstein and Eric Kahler in the *Princeton Herald* in April, 1944, to refute the pro-Arab views expressed by Dr. Philip K. Hitti of Princeton University before the Foreign Affairs Committee of the U.S. House of Representatives in February, 1944, during hearings on the Wright-Compton resolution on Palestine; *Out of My Later Years* (1950); *The World as I See It* (originally *Mein Weltbild*, 1934; English translation, 1949; later German edition, 1953); and *Ideas and Opinions by Albert Einstein* (1954).

EISENBERG, AARON. Pioneer of the *Hoveve Zion movement (b. Pinsk, Russia, 1863; d. Rehovot, 1931). As a youngster, Eisenberg founded a Hoveve Zion group in Pinsk. In 1886 he settled in Palestine, where he first worked as a stonecutter and later was a winegrower in Rishon L'Tziyon. His home in Rishon L'Tziyon served as the center for Jewish laborers and members of the *B'ne Moshe (Sons of Moses) order. Subsequently he settled in Rehovot, of which he was a founder.

Eisenberg was one of the most prominent leaders of the new settlements in the era before World War I. He helped establish new settlements and was active in a variety of social, cultural, and economic institutions. After the war he was a member of the Va'ad Z'mani (Provisional Council) of the Jews of Palestine and served on the Advisory Committee for Settlement Affairs of the Zionist *Executive.

EISENSTADT, Y'HOSHU'A. *See* BARZILAI, Y'HOSHU'A.

'EKRON. *See* MAZKERET BATYA.

'ELABUN. Christian Arab village in eastern Lower Galilee. Population (1968): 1,300.

EL 'AL. National air carrier of Israel. The decision to establish a national airline was one of the very first to be taken by the new State of Israel following its *Declaration of Independence. The purpose of the early establishment of El 'Al (Upward) was to ensure that Israel, surrounded as it was on three sides by neighbors who continued to maintain a formal state of war with the new State and blockaded it, should have an air link to the outside world. One of its first tasks was the airlifting of immigrants from all parts of the world to Israel.

El 'Al was incorporated on Nov. 15, 1948, and commenced scheduled operations between Israel and Rome and Paris in mid-1949. In 1950 scheduled services were extended to Athens, Vienna, Zurich, and London, in Europe, and to Nairobi and Johannesburg in Africa, and were begun between Tel Aviv and New York via various European gateways. In 1951 services to Nicosia, Istanbul, Brussels, Amsterdam, Teheran, Frankfurt on the Main, and Munich were added. Over the years more stops

A Boeing 707 jet aircraft of the El 'Al fleet. [El Al Israel Airlines]

were scheduled: Copenhagen, Geneva, Nice, Constanța, and Bucharest. By 1968 El 'Al routes linked 22 cities in 18 countries spread over four continents.

All El 'Al personnel, from flight crews and cabin attendants through ground staff, mechanics, and fitters to business office personnel, are trained at the company's school at its Lod headquarters, where its modern equipment includes flight simulators for the Boeing aircraft. In 1968 the company employed more than 2,800 persons in Israel and other countries. All airframe and engine maintenance was carried out at the Lod base on an equalized-maintenance basis worked out by El 'Al engineers as most suitable both mechanically and economically under the line's route structure, whereby aircraft generally left Israel in the morning and returned to base in the evening, so that equipment was available for maintenance work during the night hours. This system ensured a rate of daily utilization that was among the highest in the world.

Pure jet services were begun in January, 1961, and on June 15, 1961, El 'Al inaugurated the first nonstop service between New York and Tel Aviv, offering what was then the world's longest nonstop scheduled commercial flight—5,760 statute miles. In 1968 the El 'Al fleet consisted of five Boeing 707 jet aircraft and two Boeing 720B jets, in addition to three leased aircraft. El 'Al was to receive two additional jet transports in 1969 and the first of two Boeing 747s in 1971. The airline also decided to purchase two American supersonic transports, for delivery in the next decade.

All food served aboard El 'Al aircraft is prepared in accordance with Jewish dietary laws. Religious observance of the Sabbath and Jewish holidays restricts the use of El 'Al aircraft to 306 scheduled days a year, as no El 'Al planes leave or arrive at Lod on the Sabbath or on major Jewish holidays. Despite these blank days, El 'Al's average daily utilization, spread over the entire year, still amounts to 10.9 hours for 707s and 9.3 hours for 720Bs, as against an industry average of 10 hours per day. This record has been achieved by tight scheduling, maximum efficiency, and a minimum of delays and cancellations.

The company's balance sheet for the 1967–68 fiscal year showed a net profit of IL5,600,000. El 'Al emerged as the highest hard-currency earner ($63,000,000) of any single Israeli company. In 1967–68 El 'Al carried 364,360 passengers on 3,872 flights. Airline projections indicated that by the mid-1970s the airline would be carrying 921,000 of a total of 1,853,900 passengers to and from Israel.

El 'Al's first general manager was Arye Abraham *Pincus, subsequently chairman of the *Jewish Agency. He served with El 'Al from 1949 to 1956. In 1968 Mordecai Ben-Ari was president of the airline, and Transport Minister Moshe *Carmel was chairman of the board of directors.

EL-'ARISH SCHEME. Proposal for a Jewish settlement at Wadi el-'Arish, in Sinai. In the fall of 1902 Herzl met with Joseph *Chamberlain, then Colonial Secretary of Great Britain, and discussed the possibility of autonomous Jewish settlements in various parts of the British Empire. When Herzl proposed El-'Arish, Chamberlain approved but added that it would be necessary to secure the assent of Lord Lansdowne, the Foreign Secretary, and of the Earl of *Cromer, Britain's Consul General in Egypt. Lansdowne received Herzl's plan favorably and asked for a detailed memorandum, but he indicated that a final decision would have to come from both Lord Cromer and the Egyptian government.

At Lord Cromer's request, Herzl dispatched a special commission to investigate El-'Arish. It was headed by Leopold *Kessler, a South African Zionist and engineer. Its members were Col. Albert E. W. *Goldsmid, who was to report on the land; Selig E. *Soskin, an agricultural expert; Hillel *Joffe, who was to study the problems of climate and hygiene; and the architect Oskar *Marmorek, who was to investigate building and housing problems and to serve as the secretary of the commission. The Egyptian government was represented on the commission by the Chief Inspector of the Egyptian Survey Department, Thomas H. S. Humphreys. While the survey was in progress, Humphreys worked feverishly to enlist financial support and to influence key Anglo-Egyptian officials. The report of the commission, when released, showed that El-'Arish would be suitable for settlement if water could be brought to the area.

On May 11, 1903, the Egyptian government, believing that water from the Nile River could not be spared for the project, turned the plan down. Cromer also had second thoughts and rejected the scheme, claiming that the Egyptian government did not favor it, that the irrigation experts insisted the plan was unsound, and that it would be unwise to add to the main problems already involved in the administration of Egypt. Undaunted, Herzl continued to press British officialdom. On July 16, 1903, he received notification that the Foreign Office considered the El-'Arish scheme unfeasible, and at the 6th Zionist *Congress, held in August of that year in Basle, he reported on the failure of his efforts.

After Herzl's death (1904), David *Wolffsohn, in his capacity as president of the *World Zionist Organization, instructed Leopold J. *Greenberg on Feb. 4, 1906, to renew negotiations with the British government concerning El-'Arish. David *Lloyd George, who by that time was a member of the government as President of the Board of Trade, received Greenberg on February 12 and offered to forward a statement on the Sinai (El-'Arish) colonization scheme to Sir Edward Grey, the British Foreign Secretary. Four days later, Greenberg sent Lloyd George a lengthy memorandum, but a few days thereafter tension developed at the borders of Sinai between Britain and Turkey. This led to the appointment of a joint delimitation commission for defining the borders and forced an indefinite postponement of any serious Zionist-British negotiations on the El-'Arish scheme.   J. ADLER

EL-ASSIFA. *See* EL-FATAH.

ELAT. Port on the Gulf of Elat. The southernmost city of Israel, it is named for the ancient city of Elat (Elath), which was situated nearby. Population (1968): 11,000.

Ancient Elat is mentioned in the Bible as one of the places through which the Israelites passed in the course of their wanderings in the desert. It was from there and from nearby 'Etzyon Gever that King Solomon sent a fleet to Ophir (I Kings 9:26, I Chronicles 8:17–18). An attempt by King Jehoshaphat to emulate Solomon's enterprise failed, for "the ships were broken" at 'Etzyon Gever (I Kings 22:49–51, II Chronicles 20:35–37). Azariah, King of Judah, "built Elath, and restored it to Judah" (II Kings 14:22, II Chronicles 26:2). Later Retzin, King of Aram, took the place and expelled the Jews (II Kings 16:6).

In the Hellenistic period, Elat was a Nabatean port. It was of considerable commercial and military importance in Roman and Byzantine times. In the 7th century of the Common Era, some of

Philip Murray House, cultural center in Elat. [Israel Information Services]

the Jewish tribes that had fled from Arabia as a result of persecutions by Mohammed settled in Elat. The prosperous settlement was destroyed by the Crusaders in 1116. Later in the 12th century Elat was a small townlet inhabited by Arabs, but from the 14th century on it was completely deserted. Excavations carried out to the east of the present city have yielded remains of Nabatean and later settlements. The exact site of Biblical Elat has not been identified to date.

During the British *Mandate for Palestine (1917–48) a small police post existed on the site of Elat. The place was reached by the *Israel Defense Forces in March, 1949, and soon thereafter steps were taken to develop it as a port city. Initial growth was slow: by 1956 Elat had a population of only 800. Following the *Sinai Campaign, which removed the Egyptian blockade from the Gulf of Elat, the town expanded at a greater pace. The seaport was used for the shipment of exports to Africa and the Far East; crude oil, brought by tankers, was fed into the 16-inch pipeline running from Elat to the refineries in Haifa. In 1957 Elat was declared a municipality.

In the summer of 1968 the *Mekorot Water Company began construction of a 42-inch Elat–Ashk'lon pipeline (total length, about 175 miles). Linked to the existing 16-inch pipeline leading to the Haifa refinery just north of Zikim, the new line was designed to carry 60 million tons of oil annually. By 1969 it was expected to be able to handle 19 million tons, of which 14 million

were to be exported and the rest to be refined in Haifa. The cost of the first stage of construction was estimated at $62,000,000.

Elat's industrial enterprises include a water desalination plant (Zarchin process), a diamond-polishing plant, a fish cannery, and a factory making jewelry from semiprecious stones found in the neighborhood. Elat, which can be reached by a highway as well as by planes of the Arkia Aviation Company (*see* AVIATION IN ISRAEL) operating several flights daily, has developed into a popular tourist center. Water-skiing and excursions in in glass-bottomed boats in the waters of the gulf are special attractions. Points of interest in the city include the Elat Marine Museum, founded by Yirmiyahu *Halpern, and the Philip Murray House, a cultural center built by the *Histadrut (General Federation of Labor) and named for the American labor leader. Ephraim Levy, an immigrant from Egypt, became mayor in 1966.

ELAT (AKABA, 'AQABA), GULF OF. Israeli name for the northeastern arm of the Red Sea, derived from the port of Elat at the head of the gulf. The gulf is bounded by Israel, Jordan, Saudi Arabia, and the United Arab Republic (Sinai Peninsula). Its length is 117 miles; its breadth at the widest point, 9 miles. The maximum depth is 1,080 feet. The water has a high salt content and a relatively high temperature, and the gulf abounds in marine life.

At the mouth of the gulf lie the islands of Tiran and Sanafir, which belong to Saudi Arabia. Tiran is ancient Yotva, where an autonomous Jewish settlement existed in the early Middle Ages.

Recent History. At the end of 1949 Egypt (since 1958, the United Arab Republic) set up guns at Sharm el-Sheikh, on the southern tip of the Sinai Peninsula, commanding the Strait of Tiran and the mouth of the gulf. Unarmed merchant ships were fired on, stopped, searched, and turned back. It was the beginning of a blockade of Elat that lasted for seven years. The debate on Israel's complaints in the UN Security Council brought no results. One of the main objectives of the *Sinai Campaign of 1956 was the removal of this Egyptian blockade of Elat. When, under pressure by the United Nations, Israeli forces withdrew from Sinai, they did not abandon the Sharm el-Sheikh area until their places had been taken by the UN Emergency Force (UNEF), which was to ensure that passage through the strait remained open. In May, 1967, after the UNEF had been withdrawn at the request of the United Arab Republic, Egyptian forces reoccupied Sharm el-Sheikh and reimposed the blockade on Elat.

In justification of its blockade, the Egyptians' main argument was that the strait at the mouth of the gulf, being less than 9 miles wide, fell within the 12-mile limit of Egyptian territorial waters and that consequently they were entitled to control it. Israel's point of view, supported by the United States, Great Britain, and other major seafaring powers, was that a strait leading into a gulf bordered by different states was an international waterway. In the *Six-day War of 1967, Israel occupied the Sinai Peninsula, thereby breaking the blockade of Elat.

ELATH (EPSTEIN), ELIYAHU. Israeli diplomat and president of the *Hebrew University of Jerusalem (b. Showsk, Ukraine, Russia, 1903). Elath attended the University of Kiev and was active in the Zionist youth organizations *Tz'ire Zion and *HeHalutz in Russia. Settling in Palestine in 1925, he worked as an agricultural laborer in Rehovot and B'er Ya'akov until 1928 and as a construction worker in Transjordan in 1929–30.

Eliyahu Elath.
[Israel Information Services]

He also studied at the Hebrew University. Awarded a fellowship at the American University of Beirut in 1930, he traveled in the desert for eight months with Bedouin tribes, studying their life and customs. From 1934 to 1945 he was the head of the Middle and Near East Division of the Political Department of the *Jewish Agency, and from 1945 to 1948, director of the Agency's

Political Department in Washington. In that capacity he initiated the formalities for obtaining the recognition of Israel by Pres. Harry S *Truman.

From 1948 to 1950 Elath was Israel's Ambassador to the United States, serving simultaneously as a member of the Israeli delegation to the United Nations. From 1950 to 1959 he was Ambassador in London, and from 1959 to 1962 chairman of the Board of Governors of the Afro-Asian Institute for Labor Studies and Cooperation in Israel. He was elected president of the Hebrew University in 1962 and served until 1968.

An expert on the Middle East and the Arabs, Elath contributed numerous studies and articles to political and sociological journals. His works include *The Bedouins: Their Life and Customs* (1933) and *The Population of Transjordan* (1934), both published in Hebrew.

ELAZARI-VOLCANI, YITZHAK AVIGDOR (Isaac Wilkansky). Israeli agronomist and Zionist leader (b. Aishishok, Lithuania, 1880; d. Rehovot, 1955). He studied at the Yeshiva of Telšiai, the University of Bern, and agricultural colleges in Berlin and Königsberg. In 1908 he settled in Palestine, where he became active as a leader in the *HaPo'el HaTza'ir party. Elazari-Volcani was one of the pioneers who laid the foundation for Israel's modern agricultural industry. He served as director of the Ben Shemen and Hulda farms and as chief adviser on agriculture to the Palestine Office (*see* PALESTINE OFFICES) of the *World Zionist Organization (WZO) in Jaffa (1909–19). He was also a member of the *Zionist Commission and of the Zionist delegations that went to London and Paris for the negotiations leading to the conferment of the *Mandate for Palestine on Great Britain.

In 1921 he helped found, and then directed, the agricultural research station of the WZO in Tel Aviv, which was eventually moved to Rehovot. He held this position until 1951, when the station (now known as the *Volcani Institute of Agricultural Research) was taken over by the Israeli Ministry of Agriculture. He played an important role in the founding of the *Hebrew University Faculty of Agriculture in 1940, serving as chairman and as professor of agricultural economics until 1947. In addition, he was for many years a director of the *Jewish National Fund and a member of the Executive Committee of the *Histadrut (General Federation of Labor).

Elazari-Volcani published numerous articles, pamphlets, and studies on agricultural problems, practical and ideological (national) versus private settlement, and hired labor as opposed to *self-labor, as well as a collection of essays entitled *BaDerekh* (On the Way, 1918).

EL-BURJ. *See* DOR.

ELDAD (SCHEIB), ISRAEL. Publicist (b. Podvolochisk, Galicia, Austria, 1910). Eldad studied at the Hebrew High School in Łódź, the Vienna Rabbinical Seminary, and the University of Vienna. Subsequently he taught at Hebrew educational institutions in Poland. A leader in *B'rit Trumpeldor (Betar), the Revisionist youth movement, he contributed philosophical, literary, and political articles to the Hebrew and Yiddish press in Poland.

Settling in Palestine in 1941, Eldad taught at a Tel Aviv high school. He joined the *Lohame Herut Israel (Lehi), edited its publications *Hazit* and *HaMa'as*, and soon was considered the intellectual leader of the movement. In 1944, while attempting to escape arrest by British police, he fell and suffered a spinal injury. Encased in a cast, he was held in the Jerusalem Prison and at the Latrun detention camp.

In 1946 Eldad was brought to a Jerusalem hospital for the removal of his cast. There he was liberated by his friends. After the establishment of the State he launched the monthly *Sulam* (Ladder), in which he sharply criticized Israeli government policies and various facets of Israeli life and culture and advocated the establishment of a true Malkhut Yisrael (kingdom of Israel) through the liberation of the entire Land of Israel as defined in the Bible.

ELECTED ASSEMBLY. *See* ASEFAT HANIVHARIM.

EL-FATAH (al-Fatah). Arab terrorist organization founded in 1959 in Damascus, Syria, for the purpose of "liberating Palestine." Its name means "the Conquest." Its activities consisted of making raids into Israeli territory, carrying out attacks and sabotage, planting mines, and so on. The military arm of el-Fatah, called el-Assifa (al-Assifa, "storm troopers"), was originally estimated to have 200 active members. Beginning in 1965 el-Fatah raiders mostly used Jordanian territory on the east bank of the Jordan River as the base for their incursions into Israel and the Israel-held area on the west bank. Israel forces vigorously retaliated. At first King Hussein of Jordan tried to curb el-Fatah's activities, but subsequently he actually endorsed them. El-Fatah units became completely free to roam the country, cross the Jordan for raids into Israel, and return under the protective fire of the regular Jordanian Army.

Following the *Six-day War of 1967, el-Fatah emerged as the leading Arab terrorist organization. Early in 1969 it joined forces with the Palestine Liberation Organization (PLO). Headed by Yasir Arafat, it has headquarters in Amman, Jordan, and training camps in Jordan, Syria, Lebanon, and Iraq. Volunteers go through rigorous tests and training; trainees include children below the age of 12. El-Fatah has received support from a number of Arab governments, has developed considerable propaganda activity in the Western world, including the United States, where it has worked also through Arab students, and has gained support from Communist-front groups, New Left student radicals, and some extremist, revolutionary Negro organizations.

See also TERRORIST ORGANIZATIONS, ARAB.

ELIASBERG, MORDECAI. Rabbi, writer, and guiding spirit of the *Hoveve Zion movement (b. Chaikishok, Kaunas District, Lithuania, 1817; d. Bauska, Latvia, 1889). After engaging in business in Riga, Eliasberg became rabbi of Zesmir in 1851 and of Bauska in 1861. He wrote articles on the interrelationship and interdependence of the land and people of Israel. Under the influence of Zvi Hirsch *Kalischer's *D'rishat Tzi'yon*, he became active in the Hoveve Zion movement, disseminating its ideas in Orthodox circles and becoming a member of its Advisory Board in 1887. Eliasberg sought cooperation between religious and secularist Jews and advocated the appointment of spiritual leaders for Palestine settlers, study seminars for farmers, and the establishment of investment companies, banks, and industries in Palestine. In 1888 he decided to permit Jewish settlers in Palestine to work the soil during the Sh'mita (sabbatical) year, a decision that involved him in heated controversy with rabbinical authorities in Palestine and elsewhere. His writings include *T'rumat Yad,* a collection of rabbinic responsa (1875), and a study, *Sh'vil HaZahav* (The Golden Path), published posthumously in 1897 by his son, which discusses Jewish *nationalism and contemporary problems of Jewish settlement in Palestine.

ELIASH, MORDECAI. Israeli diplomat (b. Uman, Ukraine, Russia, 1892; d. London, 1950). He studied law in Russia and attended the University of Berlin and Oxford University. Settling in Jerusalem in 1919, he served there as secretary of the *Zionist Commission until 1921. Thereafter he entered private law practice. As legal adviser to the *Va'ad L'umi (National Council), he appeared before a number of commissions, including the *Shaw and *Peel Commissions of 1929 and 1936, the *Anglo-American Committee of Inquiry in 1946, and the *United Nations Special Committee on Palestine in 1947. In 1948 he was a member of the Israeli delegation to the United Nations. In 1949 he was named the first Israeli Minister to the United Kingdom, a position he held until his death.

ELIFELET. Village (moshav) in eastern Upper Galilee. Settled in 1949, mostly by *Yemenite Jews, and affiliated with *T'nu'at HaMoshavim. Population (1968): 360.

ELIOT, GEORGE (pseudonym of Mary Anne, or Marian, Evans). Novelist and non-Jewish precursor of Zionism (b. Warwickshire, England, 1819; d. London, 1880). A country girl of lower-middle-class origin, she was destined to take her place among the great English precursors of the Zionist idea. *Daniel Deronda* (1876) was her last novel. She had already won acclaim with *Mill on the Floss* and *Silas Marner*. *Daniel Deronda* has been described as her greatest novel and as a work of almost Tolstoyan proportions and qualities. In it she shows great insight into Jewish life and hopes and accurately forecasts the force which political Zionism was to become in the years ahead. One of her heroes, the spokesman for Jewish national aspirations, says:

> There is a store of wisdom among us to found a new Jewish polity, grand, simple, just like the old—a republic where there is equality of protection. . . . Then our race shall have an organic center, a heart and a brain to watch and guide and execute; the outraged Jew shall have a defense in the court of the nations. . . . And the world will gain as Israel gains.

George Eliot depicts two types of Jew, one who tries to escape from his Jewishness and another who, like her hero, acknowledges his identity and is proud of it. Daniel Deronda is filled with pride when he discovers his Jewish parentage. He resolves to learn as much as possible about his people and to rescue them from oppression through a return to their ancient Homeland. The religious Zionism of the scholar Mordecai, his demand to "revive the organic center," gives the book an oddly prophetic character, although Zionist sentiments were already in the air at the time. George Eliot's characterization helped stimulate the Zionist renaissance by influencing such personalities as Eliezer *Ben Yehuda, the father of modern Hebrew.   H. PINNER

ELISHAMA'. Village (moshav) in the Sharon Plain. Settled in 1951 by immigrants from Tripoli and affiliated with *T'nu'at HaMoshavim. Population (1968): 560.

ELITZUR (sports organization in Israel). *See* SPORTS AND PHYSICAL EDUCATION IN ISRAEL.

ELKOSH. Village (moshav) in western Upper Galilee. Settled in 1949 by *Yemenite Jews and affiliated with *T'nu'at HaMoshavim. Population (1968): 490.

ELMALEH, ABRAHAM RAPHAEL (Avraham Raphael Al-maliah). Leader of *Sephardim, author, and journalist (b. Jerusalem, 1885; d. there, 1967). After teaching in Jerusalem, he served as principal of Jewish schools in Constantinople and Damascus, in which capacity he did much to further Hebrew as a living language. Returning to Palestine in 1914, he was for a time director of the Anglo-Palestine Bank branch in Gaza (*see* BANK L'UMI L'YISRAEL) and later a teacher in Jaffa. In 1916 he was exiled by the Turkish authorities to Damascus, where he remained until 1918.

After the British conquest of Palestine, Elmaleh was head of the press office of the *Zionist Commission from 1919 to 1921. An active participant in the community organization of Palestine Jewry, he was a member of the *Asefat HaNivharim (Elected Assembly), the *Va'ad L'umi (National Council), on the Executive of which he later served, and the Jerusalem Municipal Council. Elmaleh served on the Executive Committee of the *World Federation of Sephardi Communities. In the period between World Wars I and II, he frequently traveled abroad on Zionist and Sephardi missions. Following the establishment of the State of Israel, he was a member of the First *Knesset.

Elmaleh edited numerous publications, including the newspaper *HaHerut* and the scholarly monthly *Mizrah UMa'arav,* and contributed to Hebrew, French, Arabic, Spanish, and Ladino periodicals. He compiled Hebrew-French and Hebrew-Arabic dictionaries and wrote numerous books and articles on the history and life of the Jews in the Near East and North Africa and on Sephardi leaders. Elmaleh also translated a great number of literary works into Hebrew.

ELON. Village (kibbutz) in western Upper Galilee. Founded in 1938 by members of *HaShomer HaTza'ir. Affiliated with the *Kibbutz Artzi Shel HaShomer HaTza'ir. Population (1968): 585.

ELOT. Village (kibbutz) north-northeast of Elat. Founded in 1962 and affiliated with the *Kibbutz M'uhad.

EL-QUDS. *See* JERUSALEM.

ELROI. *See* KIRYAT TIV'ON.

EL SALVADOR, ZIONISM IN. In 1968 the Jewish population of El Salvador was 300 in a total population of a little more than 3 million. A Zionist group had existed in San Salvador, the capital of the country, since 1943. In 1945 it was formally constituted as the Organización Sionista de El Salvador, with a membership of 35. The first president of the organization was Ernesto Liebes (1945–51). He was succeeded by Carlos Bernhard (1951–55), Enrique Guttfreund (1955–57), Carlos Bernhard (1957–65), and Pierre Cahen (1965–   ). In 1968 the organization had 60 members. A chapter of the *Women's International Zionist Organization (WIZO), which was founded at the same time as the men's organization, had 85 members.

The activities of the Zionist Organization included lectures, film presentations, distribution of informative material, contact with Zionist institutions in Israel and other countries, and financial support of the El Salvador–Israel Cultural Institute (founded in 1956), which had 130 members (mainly non-Jews) in 1968. The Institute presented Israeli films, displayed the work of Israeli and local artists, and organized lectures on Israel and exhibitions of Israeli stamps, photographs, radio programs, and so on.

In the period 1962–64 an Israeli teacher couple, who were in charge of the Jewish School in neighboring Guatemala, conducted once-a-month weekend courses in Judaism and Zionism for Jewish youths and a Bible course for adults. In 1965 a Hebrew-language course was organized by an Israeli teacher living in El Salvador. Beginning in 1963 a number of Salvadorean Jewish children attended summer camps organized annually by the Federation of Jewish Communities of Central America and Panama with the collaboration of the *Jewish Agency. Four members of the organization settled in Israel.

C. BERNHARD

ELUSA. *See* HALUTZA.

ELYAKHIN. Rural settlement in the Sharon Plain. Established in 1950. Population (1968): 1,750.

ELYAKIM. Village (moshav) in Samaria. Settled in 1949 by *Yemenite Jews and affiliated with *T'nu'at HaMoshavim. Population (1968): 640.

EL YAM (Israeli shipping company). *See* SHIPPING IN ISRAEL.

ELYASHIV. Village (moshav) in the Sharon Plain. Founded in 1933 by *Yemenite Jews and affiliated with the *Hitahdut HaIkkarim (Farmers' Federation). Population (1968): 360.

EMANCIPATION. Term applied, particularly in the modern Western world, to the removal of civic, political, and economic restrictions imposed on Jews.

Political History. Emancipation implied equality before the law, the right of equal participation in political life, and freedom to choose one's place of residence and to enter any profession, including civil service. Emancipation was an outgrowth of a number of trends and developments in modern states, such as the concept of religious tolerance, expressed in the separation of church and state, the American Revolution of 1776, and the French Revolution (1789–91) with its slogan "Liberty, Equality, Fraternity."

The newly independent United States of America and postrevolutionary France were the first countries to accord equal rights to Jews. The reaction following the Revolution of 1848 brought a temporary reversal, but subsequently the unification of Italy (1861), the reorganization of the Austro-Hungarian Monarchy (1867), and the establishment of the German Empire (1871) were all accompanied by legislation providing for the emancipation of the Jews. The growing separation of church and state in Europe in the second half of the 19th century further helped bring full emancipation to Jews of Great Britain and elsewhere in Europe. The Ottoman Empire passed legislation to that end (designed to benefit both Jews and Christians) in 1839 and 1859. When the European powers met in Berlin (Congress of Berlin, 1878) to discuss the future of Turkey and the Balkan states, they incorporated in the constitutions of the new states provisions guaranteeing equal rights for Jews.

The Russian Revolution of 1917 abolished all religious discrimination, and in the succession states set up in Central and Eastern Europe following World War I Jewish equality was established as a basic constitutional principle (which, however, was fully carried out only in Czechoslovakia). Similar principles were imposed also on the Arab states that were given independence after the war. However, the trend was reversed by the Nazi take-over in Germany in 1933, followed by German domination of much of Europe. After the establishment of the State of Israel in 1948, the Arab states, too, curtailed the rights of their Jewish inhabitants. In the Soviet Union and its satellite nations Jews and their institutions have variously been the victims of discrimination and persecution.

Emancipation and the Jewish Community. Emancipation was widely hailed by Jews as the dawn of a new day of universal tolerance and human brotherhood, in which eventually all barriers that separated men from one another would be broken down. This initial response found expression in widespread *assimilation and in the philosophy of "classic" Reform Judaism, which stressed the ethical message and "mission" of Judaism, playing down those features that distinguished the Jewish religion from other faiths. As for the age-old hope for a Return to Zion, it was reinterpreted (not only by Reform Jews) as a yearning for the advent of a "spiritual Jerusalem," a Messianic age for all mankind.

With the resurgence of the spirit of nationalism and super-patriotism in the post-Napoleonic era, emancipation proved to be a divisive factor, in that Jews of one country would find themselves differing from Jews in other lands when they wholeheartedly took the side of their "fatherland." On the other hand, it served a unifying function in that Jewries enjoying the benefits of emancipation would make every effort to obtain the same rights for their brethren elsewhere (e.g., the efforts of Sir Moses *Montefiore on behalf of Jewry in Tsarist Russia and the work of the *American Jewish Committee).

The resurgence of Jew hatred in the form of modern "racial" *anti-Semitism, culminating in the rise of Hitler, brought disillusionment to those who had pinned their hopes on emancipation and prompted the Jews to put renewed emphasis on their Jewish identity. This change in attitude also contributed to the growth of modern political Zionism.

Emancipation and Zionism. The relationship between emancipation and Zionism has been complex. The precursors of the Hibbat Zion movement (*see* HOVEVE ZION) rejected emancipation as promoting assimilation and therefore working against the Return to Zion. Such early spokesmen of modern Zionism as Leo *Pinsker and Herzl, the founder of political Zionism, pointed to the emergence of modern anti-Semitism as proof that emancipation had not fulfilled its promise. They urged the Jews to seek full civil and political rights through "auto-emancipation" in a Homeland of their own.

After Herzl's death, however, when it became clear that the realization of Zionist aims was still distant and, at any rate, would not provide a complete answer to the "Jewish problem," the Zionist movement in the *Diaspora incorporated in its platform the concept of *Gegenwartsarbeit,* or work for the betterment of the civic status of the Jews in Diaspora lands and for Jewish participation in the political life of the countries in which they lived. At the Paris Peace Conference following

World War I, the Zionist movement, in addition to pressing the claim for a Jewish National Home in Palestine, cooperated with non-Zionist bodies to demand cultural, social, and political rights for Jews throughout the Diaspora and special nationality-group or "minority" status (*see* AUTONOMY, JEWISH) for Jews in countries with large concentrations of Jewish population.

In retrospect, it might be said that emancipation actually made a contribution to Zionism and to the rise of the State of Israel in that the sense of human dignity emancipation instilled in the Jews helped prepare them intellectually and psychologically to press claims not only for equal rights but also for the right to a Homeland of their own.

I. KOLATT

'EMEK, THE. *See* JEZREEL VALLEY.

'EMEK HEFER. *See* HEFER VALLEY.

'EMEK YEZRE'EL. *See* JEZREEL VALLEY.

'EMEK Z'VULUN. *See* Z'VULUN VALLEY.

EMERGENCY COMMITTEE FOR ZIONIST AFFAIRS.

Coordinating body of American Zionist organizations, founded in 1939 and subsequently renamed American Emergency Committee for Zionist Affairs (January, 1942), American Zionist Emergency Council (fall, 1942), and American Zionist Council (1949).

EMERGENCY COMMITTEE FOR ZIONIST AFFAIRS

In the closing days of the 21st Zionist *Congress in Geneva, on the brink of World War II (August, 1939), Chaim *Weizmann and his colleagues in the *World Zionist Organization (WZO) authorized the setting up of a special Emergency Committee in the United States. This committee, which was to consist of a group of prominent leaders of the *Zionist Organization of America (ZOA) and of representatives of other main American Zionist organizations—*Hadassah, Labor Zionists (*see* PO'ALE ZION IN AMERICA), and *Mizrahi—was to have two purposes: (1) to have in the then neutral United States a body that could assume the authority and functions of World Zionist leadership to the extent that the activities of the World Zionist *Executive in London and Jerusalem might be restricted by wartime conditions; and (2) to bring home to the American public, Jewish and non-Jewish alike, and to American political leaders, the needs of the Jews as a people and the role of Palestine in the future of world Jewry. The latter function was considered a vital necessity in view of the role the United States could be expected to have in the eventual peace settlement.

The first meetings of the committee, initially named the Emergency Committee for Zionist Affairs, took place in New York in September and October, 1939. The committee included Louis *Lipsky, Stephen S. *Wise, Solomon *Goldman (then president of the ZOA), Abba Hillel *Silver, and Robert *Szold. The voting membership of the full committee came to include 24 American Zionist leaders, representing the national executives of their respective organizations. By 1940 the committee was further strengthened by the active participation of Nahum *Goldmann, who had come to the United States as a representative of the World Zionist Executive, and of Emanuel *Neumann, who had returned from Palestine.

American Zionist Council delegation visiting Pres. Dwight D. Eisenhower at the White House on Mar. 23, 1953. The members of the delegation (left to right) are I. L. Kenen, Rabbi James G. Heller, Mrs. Rose Halprin, Louis Lipsky, Rabbi Irving Miller, Rabbi Jerome Unger, and Rabbi Mordecai Kirshblum. [Zionist Archives]

At first the Emergency Committee was led by a Presidium consisting of Louis Lipsky, Stephen S. Wise, and Solomon Goldman, who was later replaced by Robert Szold. In 1942–43 Wise served as chairman. In October, 1940, an Office Committee was constituted, consisting initially of Leon *Gellman, Solomon Goldman, Edmund I. *Kaufmann, Louis Lipsky, Mrs. Tamar de Sola *Pool, Abba Hillel Silver, Robert Szold, and David Wertheim. This committee was subsequently renamed the Executive Committee.

In the beginning, practical conditions militated against the somewhat ambitious program envisioned by some members of the Emergency Committee. The budget, tentatively set at $20,800 for the first half of 1940, was inadequate. Separate office premises in New York were not rented until August, 1940, when a full-time secretary, Arthur *Lourie, was engaged. Some American Zionist leaders were at first reluctant to commit themselves to vigorous public activity for the Zionist cause, for many still hoped that a just solution to the "Palestine problem" would eventually be found by the British Mandatory power within the framework of the *Mandate for Palestine. The work of the committee was also hindered by two troublesome issues, the problem of leadership and the basic question of its character. Was the committee to function primarily as a group representing the World Zionist Organization or as an organ and agent of the American Zionist organizations, subject to their close scrutiny and approval?

From the outset the Emergency Committee had the benefit of information, advice, and assistance of World Zionist leaders such as Chaim Weizmann, David *Ben-Gurion, Kurt *Blumenfeld, Eliyahu *Golomb, Chief Rabbi Isaac H. *Herzog, and Georg Landauer, who were in the United States at various times during the war. The presence of these men at meetings enabled the committee to keep abreast of developments in London, Jerusalem, and elsewhere.

*White Paper of 1939. As early as the fall of 1939 the committee began a campaign against the White Paper of 1939, which imposed severe restrictions on the development of the Jewish National Home and, in fact, called for a virtual end of Jewish *immigration there by April, 1944. On Nov. 24, 1939, Solomon Goldman, Lipsky, and Wise, in an interview with Lord Lothian, British Ambassador to the United States, warned him that the Zionist movement would work to prevent the implementation of the plan. Early in 1940 the committee advocated the organization of mass meetings throughout the United States to protest British restrictions on land purchase in Palestine. Although none of these efforts yielded concrete results, they aroused public interest in the plight of Jewish refugees from Nazi oppression and helped direct attention to the inevitable link between the refugee problem and an equitable solution of the Palestine problem.

Jewish Army. During 1940 and 1941 the Emergency Committee also sought to extend support for the proposal submitted by the *Yishuv (Jewish population of Palestine) to the British authorities for the organization of a Jewish military unit to fight alongside the Allied forces. In March, 1941, a delegation of the committee, headed by Stephen S. Wise and including Gedalia *Bublick, Rabbi Israel *Goldstein, Hayim *Greenberg, Edmund I. Kaufmann, Louis Lipsky, Emanuel Neumann, and Tamar de Sola Pool, called on Lord Halifax, the British Ambassador to the United States. In addition to their oral representations, they handed him a memorandum expressing Jewish interest in a British victory over the Axis Powers but also opposition to the White Paper, and urging the organization of a Jewish military force to be accorded a status similar to that of military units supplied by Great Britain's other allies.

Since the United States was still formally neutral at the time, it was not until January, 1942, a month after the United States had entered the war, that the committee adopted a resolution to press public opinion and United States government circles "to secure the right to form a Jewish army, mobilized and organized in Palestine, to be composed, first, of the nucleus of Palestinian Jews who have already enlisted or will enlist; and second, of other Jews in the world who may be legally free to enlist in such an army that shall fight under Allied command for the survival of the Jewish people and the preservation of democracy." The committee then made a financial appropriation to initiate a campaign to win American favor for the project. *See also* JEWISH BRIGADE.

Jewish Splinter Groups. Beginning in 1940 the Emergency Committee fought against the activities of splinter groups, such as committees and organizations set up by the *Bergson group and Revisionist elements (*see* REVISIONISTS), which pressed for radical action on the Palestine problem. In a

number of publications, including *A Warning to the Zionists of America,* the Emergency Committee urged Zionists throughout the United States to mobilize public opinion behind "accredited" Zionist groups and to withhold support from splinter organizations that acted contrary to official Zionist policy and could only serve to confuse the public regarding the aims of World Zionism. These controversies consumed considerable effort and energy.

Department of Public Relations and Political Action. In January, 1941, the Emergency Committee set up a Department of Public Relations and Political Action, under the direction of Emanuel Neumann, who was assisted for a time by David W. Petagorsky. Neumann developed a variety of activities designed to win the support of public opinion for the Zionist cause. One of his first acts was to revive the *American Palestine Committee, which he had initially organized in 1932. By April, 1941, that committee had been reestablished with the help and advice of Justice Louis D. *Brandeis and Senators Robert F. Wagner (Democrat, New York) and Charles F. McNary, who had been the Republican candidate for the Vice Presidency in 1940. In a matter of months the American Palestine Commit-

Mass meeting in honor of the State of Israel, Madison Square Garden, New York. [Zionist Archives]

Rally in honor of Israel Independence Day in 1949, Madison Square Park, New York. [Zionist Archives]

tee had a membership of 700, including 3 Cabinet members, 68 senators, 200 members of the House of Representatives, and many others prominent in various walks of life. Its first dinner, in April, 1941, was presided over by Sen. Alben W. Barkley (Democrat, Kentucky) and addressed by prominent speakers, including Chaim Weizmann and Maj. Victor *Cazalet, M.P. Its membership eventually grew to 15,000 men and women throughout the country, most of them molders of public opinion, who helped to generate an atmosphere of interest, goodwill, and sympathy for the Zionist program.

By December, 1942, on Neumann's initiative, Rabbis Philip Bernstein and Milton Steinberg had approached a number of Christian clergymen, who then organized the Christian Council on Palestine, spearheaded by Henry R. Atkinson and Reinhold Niebuhr. The membership of this group, initially numbering 400, eventually grew to 2,400. Together with the American Palestine Committee it sponsored a lecture bureau (the Club Program Service) that aroused interest in the Palestine problem on the part of community, college, church, and women's clubs and provided effective lecturers for audiences to which Jewish speakers were not likely to have ready access. The activities of these organizations, spreading throughout the country, became an important factor in gaining the support of Christian America. The two groups merged in 1946 as the American Christian Palestine Committee.

An International Christian Conference for Palestine was convened in the United States in November, 1945. There were representatives from 30 countries including those that had constituted their own pro-Palestine committees. This conference resulted in the formation of a *World Committee for Palestine, headed by Sir Ellsworth Flavelle of Canada.

Relations with the U.S. Department of State. Although support for the Zionist cause was forthcoming in increasing measure from many individuals prominent in American public and political life, it was much more difficult to enlist the aid of the executive branch of the United States government, notably the U.S. Department of State. The Department tended to regard Palestine and its problems as a British affair not to be tampered with by departments of the United States government. Even before the United States entered World War II, many American diplomats, both in the Middle East and in Washington, urged the administration to prevail on American Zionists to modify their aims by forgoing the rights assured them by the *Balfour Declaration and the Mandate for Palestine. This sacrifice on the part of the Zionists, it was argued, would forestall an Arab revolt against the British and would thus be a definite contribution to the defeat of the Axis Powers.

In April, 1941, therefore, Adolf A. Berle, Jr., who was then Assistant Secretary of State, conferred with Neumann and suggested that the Zionists seek an accommodation with the Arabs by renouncing their political aims in Palestine and, moreover, that they consent to the evacuation of a large part of its Jewish population, in return for vague promises of a haven elsewhere and a kind of "Vatican City" in Palestine. His suggestions were rejected by the Zionist leadership.

When Britain, that spring, announced its intention to help organize an Arab federation but made no mention of the Palestine problem, the Emergency Committee made representations to the U.S. Department of State. The State Department, it was felt, should insist that the British government keep it informed of all developments bearing on the future of Palestine and should, in turn, be persuaded to consult with responsible Zionist leaders before consenting to any change affecting the political status of Palestine. In an interview with Neumann, Under-secretary of State Sumner Welles showed a sympathetic attitude. The matter was pursued further by Wise and Goldmann, who saw Welles and other United States officials from time to time with reference to the Palestine problem and also to discuss the question of a separate Jewish military force and the persecution of the Jews in Nazi-held Europe.

Other Activities Prior to United States Entry into the War. In addition to its contacts with the Department of State, the Emergency Committee at various times made representations directly to the British Embassy concerning deportations of refugees landing in Palestine; discussed the most effective means of communicating with Palestine in case of a Nazi invasion of the area; made contacts with non-Muslim groups in the United States (Lebanese Christians, Free French, and pro-Syrian groups) that were interested in the Middle East; and considered ways of obtaining the cooperation of non-Zionist Jewish organizations.

AMERICAN EMERGENCY COMMITTEE FOR ZIONIST AFFAIRS

With the official entry of the United States into the war and the lessening of the threat of loss of contact with World Zionist headquarters due to Nazi military action, the Emergency Committee endeavored to regroup its forces for an expanded program on the American scene. As the extent of the Nazi programs for the extermination of European Jewry became known, this phase of Zionist activity assumed crucial importance.

Expanded Program, 1942–43. In January, 1942, the committee adopted bylaws and, to emphasize the American aspect of its work, changed its name to American Emergency Committee for Zionist Affairs. Wise was chairman, and Robert Szold became treasurer and chairman of the Budget Committee. The members of the Office Committee included also Israel Goldstein and Louis E. *Levinthal (ZOA), Tamar de Sola Pool and Rose *Halprin (Hadassah), David Wertheim (Po'ale Zion), Leon Gellman (Mizrahi), Gedalia Bublick (alternate for Mizrahi), and Solomon Goldman, Hayim Greenberg, Rose Gell *Jacobs, Louis Lipsky, and Abba Hillel Silver, members at large.

*"Struma" Incident. The sinking of the "illegal" immigrant ship "Struma" in the Black Sea early in 1942 with all its passengers on board symbolized the appalling tragedy of of European Jewry. The Emergency Committee arranged memorial services for the victims and sent protest cables to Pres. Franklin D. *Roosevelt and Prime Minister Winston S. *Churchill. However, the committee organized no public demonstrations condemning Britain for the "Struma" tragedy because the British Embassy had warned that such activities would be regarded as a "declaration of war" against the British government.

Biltmore Conference. In view of the continued British intransigence on the Palestine issue and grim reports from Nazi-held Europe, there was a hardening of the mood of the Yishuv and of large sections of the Zionist movement. There was also a growing necessity to promulgate a definitive plan for the postwar solution of the Palestine problem and to press persistently for the acceptance of the plan by the Jewish world and by the embattled democracies. The plan, it was felt, would have to cease speaking in the nebulous terms of a "National Home" and instead set forth the Jewish claim to an independent Jewish State as part of the peace settlement. Normally such a change in declared Zionist policy would have required the approval of a World Zionist Congress, but under wartime conditions it was impossible to convene such a meeting.

Accordingly, the Emergency Committee decided to hold an extraordinary conference in New York to coincide with a visit of Chaim Weizmann. Meyer W. *Weisgal was in charge of the preliminary arrangements. The conference was held at the Biltmore Hotel on May 9–11, 1942, with the participation of Weizmann, Ben-Gurion, and American Zionist leaders. It brought together nearly 600 Zionists from all parts of the United States and adopted a series of resolutions that came to be known as the *Biltmore Program and, after approval by the Inner *Actions Committee in Palestine, became the program of the World Zionist Organization. The program proposed that "the gates of Palestine be opened; that the *Jewish Agency be vested with control of immigration into Palestine and with the necessary authority for upbuilding the country, including the development of its unoccupied and uncultivated lands, and that Palestine be established as a Jewish Commonwealth integrated in the structure of the new democratic world." The adoption of this program gave a renewed and powerful impulse to Zionist political efforts.

Discussions with Non-Zionists. During 1942–43 serious efforts were made to secure the political cooperation of the *American Jewish Committee, an outstanding non-Zionist organization. In a series of discussions with a subcommittee of the American Jewish Committee, substantial progress was made toward agreement, including the acceptance of the Jewish Commonwealth proposal. When, however, news of the intended recommendations of the subcommittee was leaked, the chairman of the American Jewish Committee, Maurice Wertheim, who personally favored agreement with the Zionists, found it necessary to retreat in order to avoid a threatened split in his organization. The American Jewish Committee then published its own statement, which fell short of the Zionist position.

*American Jewish Conference. Once the demand for a "Jewish Commonwealth" had been adopted by the great majority of the Zionist movement, the Emergency Committee was eager to have it approved and accepted by the whole of American Jewry. To further this purpose and to deal with other aspects of the peace settlement, the committee set about convening an American Jewish Conference, which met in New York from Aug. 29 to Sept. 2, 1943.

In the midst of preparations for this conference, Wise and Goldmann reported that officials of the U.S. Department of State and "other influential people in Washington" had requested that the conference be postponed. The request was accompanied by a warning that noncompliance would compel the American and British governments to issue a joint declaration urging their respective citizens to refrain from public agitation of the Palestine issues for the duration of the war. After anxious deliberation the Emergency Committee decided to hold the conference as scheduled. The threatened declaration did not materialize.

The conference was a complete success. Following a stirring address by Silver, the conference passed a resolution calling for a Jewish Commonwealth, which was approved by the overwhelming majority of delegates representing all important national Jewish organizations as well as local Jewish communities throughout the country. The only group at the conference that was definitely opposed to the Biltmore Program was the American Jewish Committee, which had agreed to participate only after lengthy negotiations and withdrew from the conference when the Jewish Commonwealth resolution was adopted. However, the overwhelming majority that adopted the decision enabled the Emergency Committee and its associated Jewish organizations to speak in the name of the American Jewish community.

Opposition from Jewish Organizations. Starting late in 1942, the Emergency Committee turned its attention to two newly founded Jewish groups opposed to the aims of the Zionist movement, though for widely different reasons. One was *Ihud, formed in Palestine, which called for a binational (Arab-Jewish) state in that country; the other was the American Council for Judaism, a small but vociferous group of anti-Zionists, with influence in certain American circles, formally launched in 1943 (see ANTI-ZIONISM).

With regard to Ihud, a resolution was proposed at a meeting of the committee opposing Ihud's views and activities but declaring the willingness of the Jewish people to cooperate with the Arabs. Failing unanimous approval, however, the resolution was not adopted. As for the American Council for Judaism, the committee at first acted with restraint, advising Zionist groups to keep a watchful eye on Jewish anti-Zionist activity in their localities. At a later stage the committee began to counter the council's propaganda in the press, over the radio, and on lecture platforms and eventually initiated an organized campaign against the council's efforts.

H. PARZEN

AMERICAN ZIONIST EMERGENCY COUNCIL (AZEC)

As the war progressed, it was increasingly felt that not enough was being done to win the United States for the Zionist cause. At the same time, reports indicating the full extent of the destruction of European Jewry made an unprecedented program of political action seem more imperative than ever. Important elements within the Emergency Committee itself became increasingly unhappy with its own performance. It appeared to be less a closely meshed committee than an ambassadorial conference of sovereign organizations, and it lacked the strong personal leadership enjoyed during World War I by the Provisional Executive Committee for General Zionist Affairs under the vigorous chairmanship of Louis D. Brandeis (*see* UNITED STATES OF AMERICA, ZIONISM IN).

Late in 1942 both Neumann and his assistant, Petagorsky, resigned in protest against the inadequacies of the committee. In addition, there was considerable prodding for change from World Zionist headquarters. In the end, Weizmann proposed that Abba Hillel Silver be drawn in more fully and entrusted with the direction and leadership of a reorganized body, competently staffed and with an adequate budget at its disposal.

In the fall of 1943 the committee was reorganized as the American Zionist Emergency Council, with Silver as co-chairman of the council and chairman of its Executive Committee. An eloquent orator and a dynamic personality, he had been chairman of the *United Palestine Appeal and now brought his skills and experience to bear on reshaping the political arm of the American Zionist movement. A budget of $500,000 was adopted, and an expert professional staff was engaged, including Henry Montor as executive director (later succeeded by Harry Shapiro). Some 14 subcommittees were constituted, including Finance and Personnel, Community Contacts, American Palestine Committee, Publications, Intellectual Mobilization, Contact with Jewish Religious Forces, Christian Clergy, Special Functions, Research, Press and Radio, Economic Resources, Contact with Labor Groups, Contact with Allied Postwar Groups, and Postwar Political Planning.

The functioning of these committees and their staffs under Silver's leadership caused a great forward surge in the activities of the council throughout the country. Hundreds of local emergency committees were formed and carried on an intensive campaign of education. Every possible means was employed to secure the support of public opinion. Press, pulpit, and radio were utilized. Public demonstrations were held from time to time, and thousands of lectures and speeches were delivered before Jewish and, especially, non-Jewish groups. At various times the White House and the Department of State as well as the offices of many congressmen were inundated by letters and telegrams calling for action by the government.

In Washington a branch office of the Emergency Council was set up late in 1943, under the direction of Leon I. Feuer. He was succeeded in 1945 by Benjamin *Akzin, a specialist in international law. The function of this office was to maintain contact with the Department of State, the British Embassy, and envoys of foreign countries. Its staff members also visited congressmen, distributed Zionist literature, and cooperated with delegations sent to Washington by local groups.

Palestine Resolution. Early in 1944 an additional step was devised to place the dual problem of the survivors of Nazi persecution and the future of Palestine on the national agenda of the American people. Resolutions in support of Jewish aspirations in Palestine were introduced into both houses of Congress: the Wagner-Taft resolution in the Senate and the Wright-Compton resolution in the House of Representatives. Timed to coincide with the approaching deadline set by the British White Paper of 1939 for the termination of Jewish immigration into Palestine, they were intended to break the official silence in Washington on the Palestine problem. Through its Washington bureau and local emergency councils, the AZEC canvassed congressional opinion, distributed pertinent material, and effected contacts with the appropriate congressional committees.

Silver conferred with members of the Foreign Relations Committee of the Senate and met no objections. At the hearings of the House of Representatives in February, 1944, the Zionist position was presented by Silver, Wise, Neumann, Israel Goldstein, Herman Shulman, Louis Lipsky, Z'ev (Wolf) *Gold, David Wertheim, Judith G. *Epstein, and James G. *Heller. Despite the favorable attitude of congressional leaders, intervention from the Departments of State and War on "military" grounds blocked the passage of the resolution. In response to strong public resentment President Roosevelt, after a meeting with Silver and Wise (Mar. 9, 1944), authorized the two Zionist leaders to issue a public statement in his name to the effect that "the American Government has never given its approval to the White Paper of 1939 . . . and that when future decisions are reached, full justice will be done to those who seek a Jewish National Home."

On May 23–24, 1944, a national conference of local emergency committees, representing 130 communities from 38 states, was held in Washington to launch a nationwide movement in favor of the resolutions. The AZEC organized a great rally in Madison Square Garden, New York, the first of many mass demonstrations that were to take place at critical moments of the struggle for a Jewish State. In June, Lipsky, Neumann, and Shulman called on members of the government, including Secretary of State Cordell Hull, who assured them that the United States had made no commitments in oil negotiations with the Arabs that might in any way affect the status of the Jewish National Home and its future.

That summer the Zionist political front shifted to Chicago, where the national conventions of the Republican and Democratic parties were being held. Intensive efforts by the AZEC representatives at these conventions brought about the adoption of unequivocal Jewish Commonwealth planks in the platforms of both parties. President Roosevelt affirmed his support of the Palestine plank in the Democratic platform. His unequivocal message to the convention of the ZOA in October, 1944, to that effect had been preceded by a pro-Zionist declaration from the Republican presidential candidate, Gov. Thomas E. Dewey.

In the light of all these statements and a further statement from the War Department that the "military objections" to the Palestine resolutions no longer existed, the resolutions were revived. On Dec. 11, 1944, however, Secretary of State Edward R. Stettinius appeared before the Senate Foreign Relations Committee and argued against the resolution. As a result, the measure was tabled by a bare majority.

The continued opposition of the administration precipitated serious policy disputes within the American Zionist Emergency Council. Some Zionist leaders, willing to rely on Roosevelt's promise of support at some future date, opposed further action that might prove embarrassing to the President or incur his hostility. Silver and his supporters, on the other hand, felt that every effort should be made to induce the administration to withdraw its opposition. The proponents of these two views adopted conflicting procedures. While Silver was pressing for a change in the administration's attitude, other Zionist leaders were assuring public officials that they would not seek action against Roosevelt's wishes, In the end Silver was forced to resign from his positions in the American Zionist Emergency Council (Dec. 20, 1944).

The controversy spread throughout American Zionism. Silver's supporters, led by Neumann and by Harry L. Shapiro, the executive director, and Harold P. Manson, director of public relations, who had resigned with Silver, formed the American Zionist Policy Committee with headquarters in New York. This group was officially headed by Charles J. Rosenbloom, treasurer of the United Palestine Appeal. The committee sent out literature to ZOA districts and to local emergency committees in support of Silver's policy, and its members took to the public platform in many cities. In the meantime, the AZEC, under Wise, pursued a quiet approach. In January, 1945, Wise called on Roosevelt, shortly before the latter's departure for the Yalta Conference, urging the President to bear in mind his commitments regarding Palestine. Less than three months later, Roosevelt was dead.

The subsequent disclosure of Roosevelt's secret correspondence with King Ibn Saud appeared to vindicate Silver's more militant approach, and in July, 1945, Silver was recalled to his former positions in the Emergency Council, bringing back with him the officials who had resigned out of sympathy with his stand. Eventually, in December, 1945, the Palestine resolution, though in a somewhat modified form, was discussed once again in Congress and after a full debate in the Senate was adopted by an overwhelming majority. The resolution was also adopted shortly thereafter by the House of Representatives.

San Francisco Conference. Although the AZEC as such was not represented at the San Francisco Conference (Apr. 25–June 26, 1945) at which the UN Charter was drawn up, a number of its members were on hand, working through the Jewish Agency and the American Jewish Conference. They were concerned to preserve intact the internationally secured rights of the Jewish people with respect to Palestine through the contemplated world organization. Months earlier the AZEC had conducted a nationwide campaign for the Biltmore Program, demanding that the doors of Palestine be opened wide to Jewish immigration even before the final decision was reached on the political future of the country. Mass rallies calling for a Jewish Commonwealth had been sponsored throughout the country, and although it was known that the San Francisco Conference would make no decision on Palestine, the AZEC issued literature to the press corps and to the delegates, including "The Jewish Case," a statement specifically directed to the delegations.

Potsdam Conference and After. Before leaving for the Potsdam Conference at the end of the war (July 17–Aug. 2, 1945), Pres. Harry S *Truman received a pro-Zionist petition on Palestine signed by 32 governors and a round-robin letter to the same effect over the signatures of 197 representatives and 41 senators. Although nothing of consequence with reference to Palestine occurred in Potsdam, a new chapter was opening in Anglo-American relations on that subject. On the one hand the new British Labor Government, which took office that summer, showed no disposition to rescind or modify the 1939 White Paper. On the other hand, President Truman received a report from his personal emissary, Earl G. Harrison, who had closely examined the condition of Jewish refugees in the displaced-persons camps and had recommended the early transfer of 100,000 homeless Jews to Palestine. The President thereupon,

in September, 1945, addressed a request to that effect to the British government — the first such concrete step to be taken by any American government. When this request went unheeded, the AZEC took further action.

Silver and Wise met with Truman on Sept. 29, 1945; and the council organized a mass rally in Madison Square Garden (September 30), with 22,000 filling the huge hall and another 45,000 persons outside. This rally was followed by an open-air demonstration in Madison Square Park (Oct. 24, 1945), for which 250,000 persons turned out. At the same time the American Jewish Trade Union Committee for Palestine requested the labor leader Sidney Hillman, who was then in Europe, to join a delegation to lodge a protest with the British Foreign Office in London.

By the latter part of 1945 the intensive activity of the AZEC and the forces allied with it had won over the great majority of American Jews. An opinion poll conducted by Elmo Roper in November of that year indicated that 80.1 per cent of American Jews supported the idea of a Jewish State in Palestine. Only 10.5 per cent were opposed to that program, while 9.4 per cent were undecided or did not express themselves.

*Anglo-American Committee of Inquiry, 1945–46. Although Silver considered this body simply another British device to delay immigration of Jewish refugees to Palestine and therefore declined to appear before it, he did not oppose the appearance of AZEC representatives at the hearings held by the Committee in Washington. A steering committee of the AZEC was constituted, with Neumann as chairman, to plan the presentation of the Zionist case. In due course testimony was given by Wise, Neumann, Gold, Hayim Greenberg, Judith Epstein, and Robert Szold. Other pro-Zionist statements were delivered by Henry *Monsky, for the American Jewish Conference; Rabbi Irving *Miller, for the *American Jewish Congress; and Walter C. *Lowdermilk and Abel Wolman, on behalf of the Commission on Palestine Surveys. Joseph M. Proskauer appeared for the American Jewish Committee. Among other persons testifying was Albert *Einstein, who urged the complete withdrawal of the British from Palestine.

When the report of the Anglo-American Committee was issued late in April, 1946, it was found to contain a number of positive recommendations, including the immediate transfer of 100,000 Jewish "displaced persons" to Palestine and the virtual abrogation of other provisions of the White Paper. However, its long-range recommendations were not satisfactory from a Zionist point of view, since it provided that Palestine should become neither a Jewish nor an Arab state. In releasing the report, President Truman issued a statement that drew an important distinction between the recommendations calling for the immediate abrogation of the negative and restrictive aspects of the White Paper, which he favored, and the long-term recommendations for the political future of Palestine, which he said required further study.

*Morrison-Grady Plan. Following the British government's rejection of the recommendation of the Anglo-American Committee, Truman appointed a Cabinet Committee on Palestine and Related Problems (June, 1946). The result of discussions between the deputy members of the Committee, led by Henry F. Grady, and a corresponding British group was a new British proposal that came to be known as the Morrison-Grady Plan. Calling for the cantonization of Palestine, with quite a small area marked for the Jews, it would have put an end to hopes for an independent Jewish State. This elicited immediate and energetic action by the AZEC. On July 14, 1946, almost 5,000 members of the Jewish War Veterans converged on Washington in a protest march against British policy in Palestine. The veterans' parade and the meetings of their representatives with President Truman, Under-secretary of State Dean Acheson, and British Ambassador Lord Inverchapel were widely reported in the press and over the radio. The demonstration contributed further toward the mobilization of American public opinion in support of Zionist demands. In the end Truman declined to give American sanction to the Morrison-Grady Plan.

Following the arrest of Jewish Agency leaders and other prominent Jews in Palestine in the summer of 1946, the council issued a statement of solidarity with the Jewish Agency. The British Consulate in New York was picketed, and a mass demonstration of protest was held in Madison Square Park, on July 2, 1946.

Zionist Political Actions Committee. Prior to the national elections of 1946 AZEC launched another nationwide program to demonstrate American Jewry's concern over the future of Palestine and its basic dissatisfaction with the record of the administration in Washington on the issue. A special Zionist Political Actions Committee was formed with Bernard A. *Rosenblatt as chairman, Louis *Segal as treasurer, and Rabbi Mordecai *Kirshblum as secretary to conduct a program of mass education. On Oct. 4, 1946, President Truman made public part of a letter he had sent to British Prime Minister Clement R. Attlee, to the effect that "substantial immigration into Palestine cannot wait a solution to the Palestine problem and . . . should begin at once." In his public statement Truman referred to the Jewish Agency's readiness to negotiate for a Jewish State in a part, rather than the whole, of Palestine, as had been reported by Nahum Goldmann. Truman considered that the differences between the Morrison-Grady Plan and the latest Jewish Agency proposal for *partition were not so great that they could not be bridged, and he added that "a solution along these lines would command the support of public opinion in the United States."

On Oct. 9, 1946, the AZEC issued a statement urging the President "to make full use of the influence and authority of his high office to the end that effective action be taken without delay, in fulfillment of the spirit of his statement. Nothing can satisfy the public conscience save the early movement of displaced and homeless Jews into Palestine, the prompt cessation of assaults on Jewish refugees, and a halt to the brutal repression practiced in Palestine."

On October 25, Secretary of State James F. Byrnes made a public statement denying that the State Department was not giving its full support to the Palestine policy of the United States, as set forth by President Truman. Three days later, in view of the unabated insistence of American Zionists on concrete action by the United States, Truman issued the text of a letter he had sent to King Ibn Saud. In this letter, which was a complete and straightforward defense of his position, he declared: ". . . it is only natural . . . that this Government should favor at this time the entry into Palestine of considerable numbers of displaced Jews in Europe, not only that they may find shelter there, but also that they may contribute their talents and energies to the upbuilding of the Jewish National Home." He further asserted his conviction that "responsible Jewish leaders do not contemplate a policy of aggression against the Arab countries adjacent to Palestine."

*United Nations Special Committee on Palestine (UNSCOP). In mid-February, 1947, fruitless talks between the representatives of the Jewish Agency and British Foreign Secretary Ernest *Bevin and his associates ended with a statement by Bevin that the Palestine problem would be referred to the United Nations. Within three days (February 17) the AZEC convened in Washington a conference of 650 leaders of local emergency councils throughout the country, at which Neumann reported on the collapse of the London talks. The meeting adopted resolutions calling upon the United States to champion the Zionist cause before the United Nations and urging that the Jewish Agency be represented at its hearings. Subsequently many meetings with important civic and political leaders were held throughout the United States. Petitions were circulated for signature, and special approaches were made to Democratic and Republican national leaders.

By this time Abba Hillel Silver was chairman of the American section of the Jewish Agency and in that capacity presented the Zionist case before the United Nations (May 8, 1947). At the same time he remained chairman of the AZEC and continued to direct the mobilization of American public opinion. Thus, in July, 1947, the dramatic chapter of the immigrant ship *"Exodus 1947" was the occasion for a bitter protest meeting of 20,000 persons in Madison Square Garden under the auspices of the AZEC.

This situation continued during the entire critical period (1947–49) when the United Nations was preoccupied with the Palestine problem. While official representations and contacts with delegations of various governments were in the hands of the American section of the Jewish Agency, the AZEC played its part by giving its fullest support to those efforts, especially insofar as the United States government was concerned. Its political activities were particularly intensive prior to the General Assembly's vote on Nov. 29, 1947, conferring international sanction on the establishment of a Jewish State in a part of Palestine. Similarly the Emergency Council reacted energetically after the reversal of United States policy in March, 1948, when spokesmen for the government argued in favor of an international trusteeship over Palestine in place of partition. It gave massive expression to public indignation at the administration's reversal. On Apr. 4, 1948, an estimated 50,000 members of the Jewish War Veterans paraded down Fifth Avenue in New York to protest the State Department's turnabout. Similar parades were held in Chicago, Boston, and Los Angeles, while 250,000 demonstrators denounced the administration at a rally in Madison Square Park.

When the State of Israel was proclaimed on May 14, 1948, the President of the United States immediately announced its de facto recognition, while Silver, in the last of his appearances before the United Nations, said: "Thus there has been consummated the age-old dream of Israel to be re-established as a free and independent people in its ancient Homeland." It is generally acknowledged that the intensive activity developed by the AZEC in the late 1940s and the continuing pressure exercised on the United States government by millions of Jews and non-Jews played a considerable part in shaping the final outcome.

AMERICAN ZIONIST COUNCIL (AZC)

In 1949, the State of Israel having been recognized by many nations and admitted to membership in the United Nations, the AZEC was reorganized as the American Zionist Council

(AZC), a permanent organization with greater emphasis on its more normal Zionist functions. It was headed by Louis Lipsky and composed of the 14 national Zionist organizations in the United States, as follows: the Zionist Organization of America; Hadassah; Labor Zionist movement, including *Farband, *Pioneer Women, and Po'ale Zion; *Religious Zionists of America, including Mizrahi Women, HaPo'el HaMizrahi, and HaPo'el HaMizrahi Women; American Jewish League for Israel; *B'nai Zion; Progressive Zionist League (*HaShomer HaTza'ir); United Labor Zionist party (*Ahdut 'Avoda and Po'ale Zion); and United Zionists-Revisionists of America.

From 1949 to 1954 the council continued its educational work in the Jewish community while it carried on a program of information and public relations among congressmen and other officials and public opinion molders on the vexing issue of the United States arms embargo against Israel. It also engaged in educating the American public and mobilizing support on other issues affecting Israel and its relations with the Arabs and in counteracting hostile activities such as the continuing anti-Zionist program of the American Council for Judaism.

In 1954 Rabbi Irving Miller succeeded Lipsky as chairman. The council discontinued its distinctly political activities but continued an information program designed to bring Americans a better understanding of Israel, the country's role in the Middle East, and developments in the area as they affected the interests of Israel and the United States. Another part of the council's program was directed toward the American Jewish community, with stress on adult Jewish education and culture, the *Hebrew language, and Zionist youth work.

A further reorganization took place in 1963–64 under the new chairman, Rabbi Max *Nussbaum. The council's program was now concentrated largely on coordinating Zionist policy throughout the country. Its aims were defined as the enrichment of Jewish community life and the strengthening of the cultural and spiritual approach between the American Jewish community and Israel. Local councils continued to implement the national program.

A further reassessment of collective Zionist responsibility emanated from the National Zionist Planning Conference in May, 1964, which placed greater emphasis on the strengthening and building of a meaningful Jewish life in the American Jewish community, on the involvement of Zionists in all communal endeavors affecting Jewish communities, and on strengthening the concepts of Jewish peoplehood and Jewish unity. Zionists were urged to take roles of responsibility in Jewish education in the United States and to pay special attention to the deepening of Jewish commitment among Jewish youth. At the same time the conference resolved that it would work "in undiminished fashion for the welfare, the security and progress of the people of Israel." The promotion of *'Aliya (immigration to Israel) was accepted as a cardinal task of Zionism.

Efforts to carry out these resolutions were begun in 1965 and expanded in 1966. In January, 1967, Rabbi Israel *Miller was elected chairman of the AZC. His administration was marked by the outbreak of the *Six-day War of 1967, which deeply stirred the American Jewish community and moved thousands of young persons to volunteer their services to the State of Israel. The AZC cooperated with the American section of the Jewish Agency in helping give orderly direction to all efforts to aid Israel, including the important matter of 'Aliya.

The 27th Zionist Congress (Jerusalem, 1968) adopted resolutions designed to change the organizational structure of the World Zionist Organization by the establishment of Zionist federations in all countries. The AZC took note of these resolutions and constituted a committee to work out appropriate forms for the implementation of that program in the United States.

R. HERSHMAN

EMERGENCY COMMITTEE TO RESCUE THE JEWISH PEOPLE OF EUROPE. See BERGSON GROUP.

EMIGRATION FROM ISRAEL. See IMMIGRATION TO PALESTINE AND ISRAEL.

EMUNIM. Village (moshav) in the southern coastal plain. Founded in 1950 and affiliated with *T'nu'at HaMoshavim. Population (1968): 390.

'EN (Ein). Hebrew word, meaning "well" or "fountain," that forms the first part of numerous place names in Israel, as in 'En HaKerem (Well of the Vineyard).

'EN AL-ASAD. Druze village in Upper Galilee (see DRUZE COMMUNITY IN ISRAEL). Population (1968): 352.

'ENAN. See MALHA.

'ENAT. Village (kibbutz) east of Petah Tikva. Founded in 1925 and affiliated with the *Ihud HaK'vutzot V'haKibbutzim. Population (1968): 520.

'EN AYALA. Village (moshav) on the Carmel coast. Founded in 1949 and affiliated with T'nu'at HaMoshavim. Population (1968): 326.

'EN DOR. Village (kibbutz) on the border of the Jezreel Valley and eastern Lower Galilee. Founded in 1948 and affiliated with the *Kibbutz Artzi Shel HaShomer HaTza'ir. The village was named for the Biblical 'En Dor (Joshua 17:11, I Samuel 28:7), which is believed to have been situated in this area. Population (1968): 545.

'EN ES-SAHLA. Arab village in Samaria. Population (1968): 392.

'EN GEDI. Village (kibbutz) on the site of ancient 'En Gedi, in the Judean Desert on the west shore of the Dead Sea. Founded in 1953 and affiliated with the *Ihud HaK'vutzot V'haKibbutzim.

ENGEL, YOEL. Composer (b. Berdyansk, Russia, 1868; d. Tel Aviv, 1927). One of the initiators of the Jewish musical renaissance movement in Russia and a cofounder of the Jewish Folk Music Society there, he lectured on the Jewish folk song in Russia and collected tunes in various communities. In 1922 he went to Berlin, where he founded a publishing house for Jewish music. Two years later, he settled in Palestine.

Engel is regarded as the pioneer of Hebrew song. He set to music the poems of the early classics of modern Hebrew and became known especially for his music for the HaBimah Theater's production of An-Ski's *Dybbuk* (see THEATER IN

A guard at the kibbutz 'En Gedi, on the Dead Sea. [El Al Israel Airlines]

ISRAEL). His children's songs are widely sung in Israel. The Tel Aviv Municipal Council established in his honor the Engel Prize, which is awarded annually to musicians and composers of special merit.   P. GRADENWITZ

'EN GEV. Village (kibbutz) on the east shore of Lake Kinneret. Founded in 1937 and affiliated with the *Ihud HaK'vutzot V'haKibbutzim. Established during the period of the *Arab riots of 1936–39, 'En Gev was one of the *"stockade and tower" settlements. The settlers had to cross the lake by boat to reach the site. At a later stage a road was built. During the *War of Independence, the kibbutz was heavily attacked by the Syrians. The settlers resisted heroically and threw back the invaders. A large concert hall constructed at 'En Gev has become an important center for musical activity in Israel.

ENGLAND, ZIONISM IN. *See* GREAT BRITAIN, ZIONISM IN.

'EN HA'EMEK. Village in Samaria. Founded in 1944 by *Kurdish Jews. Population (1968): 320.

'EN HAHORESH. Village (kibbutz) in the Sharon Plain. Founded in 1931 and affiliated with the *Kibbutz Artzi Shel HaShomer HaTza'ir. Population (1968): 570.

'EN HAKEREM ('En Karem). Urban quarter in Jerusalem, formerly an Arab village west of the city. It was abandoned by its inhabitants during the *War of Independence and subsequently resettled with new immigrants and incorporated in Jerusalem. On a nearby height stands the *Hebrew University–*Hadassah Medical Center.

According to Christian tradition, John the Baptist was born in 'En Karem. Various Christian denominations have built churches and monasteries there in his memory.

'EN HAMIFRATZ. Village (kibbutz) in the Z'vulun Valley. Founded in 1938 and affiliated with the *Kibbutz Artzi Shel HaShomer HaTza'ir. Population (1968): 580.

'EN HANATZIV. Village (kibbutz) in the Bet Sh'an Valley. Founded in 1946 and named for Rabbi Naphtali Tz'vi Y'huda *Berlin, who was known as "the Natziv." Affiliated with HaPo'el HaMizrahi (*see* MIZRAHI). Population (1968): 352.

'EN HAROD. Village (kibbutz) in the eastern Jezreel Valley. Founded in 1921. In 1959 the kibbutz split, and some of its settlers established 'En Harod B in the neighborhood. 'En Harod A and B are affiliated, respectively, with the *Ihud HaK'vutzot V'haKibbutzim and the *Kibbutz M'uhad. Population (1968): A, 690; B, 760.

'EN HASH'LOSHA. Village (kibbutz) in the western Negev. Founded in 1950 and affiliated with Ha'Oved Ha Tziyoni.

'EN HASHOFET. Village (kibbutz) in Samaria. Founded in 1937 and named for U.S. Supreme Court Justice (Heb., *shofet*) Louis D. *Brandeis. Affiliated with the *Kibbutz Artzi Shel HaShomer HaTza'ir. Population (1968): 590.

'EN HAT'KHELET. Urban quarter of northern N'tanya, situated on the Mediterranean shore. Founded in 1939.

'EN HOD. Artists' village on Mount Carmel. Founded in 1954. Population (1968): 30.

'EN IBRAHIM. *See* UMM AL-FAHM.

'EN 'IRON. Village (moshav) in the Sharon Plain. Founded in 1934 and affiliated with *T'nu'at HaMoshavim. Population (1968): 190.

'EN KAREM. *See* 'EN HAKEREM.

'EN KARMEL. Village (kibbutz) on the Carmel coast. Founded in 1947 near 'Atlit, it was transferred to its present site after the *War of Independence. Affiliated with the *Kibbutz M'uhad. Population (1968): 405.

'EN MAHIL. Arab village in eastern Lower Galilee. Population (1968): 2,730.

'EN RAFA. Arab village in the Judean Mountains. Population (1968): 350.

'EN SARID. Rural community in the Sharon Plain. Founded in 1950. Population (1968): 520.

'EN SHEMER. Village (kibbutz) in the Sharon Plain. Founded in 1927 and affiliated with the *Kibbutz Artzi Shel HaShomer HaTza'ir. Population (1968): 545.

ENTEEN (ENTIN), JOEL. Drama and literary critic, journalist, educator, and leader of *Labor Zionism (b. Minsk District, Russia, 1875; d. New York, 1959). A traditional Jewish and a secular education complemented each other in Enteen's intellectual development. In 1891, after a year in Moscow, he settled in New York, where he threw himself into the incipient Jewish labor movement, serving it as organizer, teacher, lecturer, and writer. He worked at various trades while studying and then became a professional newspaperman. Intensely interested in the theater and greatly influenced by Jacob Gordin, he joined the latter in forming literary and dramatic clubs that served as training schools for some of the most celebrated Jewish actors. He translated into Yiddish a number of Russian, Polish, and German plays. Many of his literary essays appeared in book form. He also edited textbooks for modern Jewish schools.

Entertaining Zionist sympathies from his early youth, Enteen joined the *Po'ale Zion party and soon became one of its outstanding spokesmen. Early in World War I, he called a meeting that laid the foundation for the People's Relief Committee. He was a founder and vice-president of the *Farband (Labor Zionist fraternal order) and a founder and former dean of the Jewish Teachers Seminary (now the Jewish Teachers Seminary and People's University).

C. B. SHERMAN

ENTERTAINMENT IN ISRAEL. A wide variety of cultural and artistic events and entertainment facilities is available in Israel to suit all tastes and to reach audiences in many languages. In considering the cultural activities of Israel, one must remem-

ber that the population is homogeneous neither in language nor in intellectual level; the majority of the population, furthermore, derives from countries of varying cultural backgrounds. The circumstance that there are few cultural elements common to all sections of the population leaves room for various influences to set their imprint on the cultural scene.

No form of art can influence or mold mass culture to the extent that the *theater can. An audience desiring a more spiritual and personal artistic experience can find satisfaction at the many concerts presented by Israel's excellent symphony orchestras (*see* MUSIC IN ISRAEL). Devotees of the plastic arts can enjoy the many showings of Israeli artists as well as special exhibits of masterpieces by the world's greatest artists (*see* ART IN ISRAEL).

Various governmental bodies and public institutions play an important role in shaping Israel's cultural life by sponsoring lectures and symposia and by bringing artistic programs to cities, towns, villages, and settlements throughout the country. The limited geographical area makes it possible to bring these cultural programs even to small villages and thus to reach the majority of the country's settlements. The main artistic events, whether privately sponsored or partially subsidized by institutions, are concentrated in the three major cities, particularly in Tel Aviv. These cities are also the centers for light entertainment. With the exception of army entertainment troupes, which provide light evening programs for Israeli soldiers guarding the border areas, the various types of entertainment are the products of private initiative. Thus, the nightclubs and evening programs reflect the taste of the Israeli public more faithfully than do the

An artist at his easel in the 'En Hod colony. [Israel Information Services]

A sidewalk café in Tel Aviv. [Israel Government Tourist Office]

more serious cultural events, for their backers seek to attract the largest possible audiences in order to make a profit.

Motion pictures provide by far the most popular and least expensive type of entertainment. It is estimated that annual attendance at motion-picture houses totals 50 million. This number does not include the nonpaying audiences in kibbutzim, army camps, and various educational institutions. Both standard box-office attractions and avant-garde European films are popular. The great popularity of motion pictures is less surprising when one recalls that there was no regular television programming in the country until 1968. The television station which began operating late in 1965 was still experimental and emphasized educational programs.

After evening performances the cafés fill with people drinking tea or eating ice cream, depending on the season and their country of origin. The warm climate encourages the consumption of cold soft drinks. The cafés reflect the Mediterranean climate in the style of their furnishings; gaily colored lightweight chairs line the sidewalks of the bustling streets, providing comfortable seats for the patrons to view the scene. The main shopping thoroughfare of Tel Aviv, the center of Israel's cultural and social activities, is lined with beautiful display windows and dotted with elegantly decorated or casually bohemian cafés.

The city's promenade extends along the shore front, from the Israel National Opera in the south to the magnificent hotels grouped in the north. Strung along the promenade are tiny, noisy cafés, providing meals, Turkish coffee, popular music, and singing in a warm, friendly atmosphere.

Many popular restaurants and cafés have been opened in the picturesque neighborhoods of Jaffa with their tumbledown houses and old mosques. Nightclubs are housed on many of the narrow streets in vaulted rooms with walls of hewn stone. The smoky cafés exude an easygoing charm and honest *joie de vivre*, qualities which more elegant and snobbish places of entertainment frequently lack. This explains why many of these popular little cafés keep a table "reserved for domestic tourists," for the aristocracy of Israeli society who often come "slumming" for an hour or two. Unfortunately for those who appreciate an authentic atmosphere, modern entertainment has invaded these places, too, and singing groups from the United

States and France threaten to usurp the place of the charming Greek, Turkish, and Sephardi melodies formerly heard. Nonetheless, if one is sensitive to the beauty of folk culture, one can still find enjoyment in these cafés.

Night life in Israel is as varied as it is anywhere else in the world. There are many nightclubs which provide shows of international talent. Most of the entertainers come from other countries. A typical program may include a dance number performed by three Swedish girls dressed as Bukharan boys, a Dutch "professor" of astrology attempting to tell the future from the stars of the Israeli skies, a couple of French singers presenting a medley of songs from many nations while doing acrobatics, and an international striptease artist doing her turn to the sound of music recorded somewhere in London or Paris. But there is no show without Israeli songs in Yemenite style and Yiddish jokes. The international character of the Israeli nightclub is further enhanced by the audience, which represents almost all the countries of the world.

Of still greater interest are the nightclubs which seek to present shows on a higher cultural level and in an authentic native style. One of the best of these is the Omar Khayyam, in Jaffa. The club is housed in a charming old Arab building with thick walls. It blends popular Middle Eastern charm and a European bohemian atmosphere with a commendable degree of success. On this club's tiny stage one may generally find Israeli folk singers with specialized repertoires that have both audience appeal and artistic merit. Sometimes the evening turns into a happy social gathering that embraces both patrons and waiters, or even into a jam session. Not far from the Omar Khayyam is the Hammam Theater Club, housed in an old

Folk singing in an Elat nightclub. [Israel Government Tourist Office]

abandoned Turkish bathhouse. The club, overlooking the shore front, is the focal point for young recognized artists who present original and fresh entertainment on its simple stage. Sometimes the show rises above the level of mere entertainment in its artistic merit or thoughtful content. Evenings of literary and political satire often end as lively parties. Other evenings feature literary parodies, singing trios, or comedy troupes performing in Yiddish.

While Tel Aviv, the city of commerce, parties the night away, the port city of Haifa goes to bed early like a workers' settlement. Jerusalem, the capital of Israel, prides itself on its own particular type of entertainment. Its cultural life is increasingly dominated by the students and faculty of the *Hebrew University of Jerusalem. The student center is Hillel House, from which the *Israel Broadcasting Service presents evening programs of serious discussion. But the student center for entertainment is found in the heart of Jerusalem, in a narrow old stone house called the Bacchus Club. This club was originally formed by students who wanted to prove that they did not lag behind the denizens of Paris's Left Bank as far as drinking wine was concerned. However, to the sorrow of those defending the bohemian reputation of Israeli students and to the joy of those seeking a quiet cultural evening, the wine cellar soon became a social club, in whose dark, narrow interior such avant-garde plays as Genêt's *The Blacks* and Jarry's *King Ubu* are presented in English by an enthusiastic group of amateurs of varied national origin. These plays, presented with lighting from portable spotlights and scenery of cardboard and gaily colored rags, have been so successful that the group has been invited to appear throughout the country. When the Bacchus stage is not in use, quiet evenings of poetry and song are presented by the students there.

The Tzavta (Togetherness) Club in Tel Aviv is a private-membership club frequented by students and young artists who attend the scheduled evening discussions on social and political problems, the cabaret performances of a literary or political nature, theater-in-the-round and other experimental theatrical productions, showings of unusual films, or evenings of community singing.

Mention must be made of the nightclubs of Elat, on the northern shore of the Red Sea. In these clubs local sun-tanned residents, wealthy tourists from distant lands, and tall, blue-eyed Swedish beatniks mingle in friendly fashion. The emphasis is on sociability, and most of the programs consist of folk songs sung to soft guitar accompaniment.

In conclusion, it must be noted that new troupes are constantly being formed, additional nightclubs and discothèques appear, and unknown and enthusiastic groups of young people seek to achieve recognition in the glare of the spotlights.

E. SHAVITT

ENTIN, JOEL. *See* ENTEEN, JOEL.

'EN TZURIM. Village (kibbutz) in the Judean Plain. The kibbutz was founded in 1949 by the members of a kibbutz with the same name that had existed in the Judean Mountains and had been occupied and destroyed by the Transjordan Arab Legion during the *War of Independence. Affiliated with Ha-Po'el HaMizrahi (*see* MIZRAHI). Population (1968): 320.

'EN VERED. Village (moshav) in the Sharon Plain. Founded in 1930 and affiliated with *T'nu'at HaMoshavim. It includes Bet HaNa'ara. Population (1968): 459.

'EN YA'AKOV. Village (moshav) in western Upper Galilee. Founded in 1950 and affiliated with *T'nu'at HaMoshavim. Population (1968): 271.

'EN YAHAV. Village (moshav) in the central Negev near the Jordanian frontier. Founded in 1951 and affiliated with *T'nu'at HaMoshavim.

EPSTEIN, ELIAS MAURICE. Journalist (b. Liverpool, England, 1895; d. Tel Aviv, 1958). After years of Zionist activity in his native land, Epstein went to Palestine in 1919 as a staff member of the *Zionist Commission. In the same year he became the editor of the newly established English-language publication *Palestine Weekly*. He served also as a correspondent for numerous newspapers, including general and Jewish publications in Great Britain and publications of the *Zionist Organization of America (ZOA). In addition, he held posts in the head office of the *Jewish National Fund in Jerusalem, on whose behalf he paid frequent visits to English-speaking countries. From 1936 to 1948 he edited the *Palestine Review*.

Epstein, who was prominently affiliated with the General Zionists, was in the last years of his life director of ZOA House in Tel Aviv. In 1964 a collection of his writings under the title *Jerusalem Correspondent, 1919–1958* was published in Jerusalem.

EPSTEIN, ELIYAHU. *See* ELATH, ELIYAHU.

EPSTEIN, ITZHAK. Zionist writer, educator, Hebrew linguist, and Palestine pioneer (b. Lyuban, near Bobruisk, Russia, 1862; d. Jerusalem, 1943). Epstein grew up in Odessa and at an early age joined the *Hoveve Zion movement. In 1886 he went to Palestine as one of a group of six administrators to work in the settlements supported by Baron Edmond de *Rothschild. After spending five years in Zikhron Ya'akov and Rosh Pina in this capacity, he taught school in Safed and Rosh Pina. In 1901 he published a textbook, *'Ivrit b''Ivrit*, in which he initiated a new method for the study of Hebrew through the speaking of Hebrew alone. It was the first of several books and numerous articles that he published on educational subjects.

Epstein went to Switzerland in 1902 to study modern educational methods at the University of Lausanne. In 1909 he became principal of a Hebrew school in Salonika, Greece, where he remained until 1915. He then returned to Switzerland to complete his doctoral studies in education and literature. Returning to Palestine in 1919, he served as principal of Levinsky's Women Teachers Seminary in Tel Aviv until 1923. He then moved to Jerusalem, where he became supervisor of schools administered by the Zionist movement. An advocate of Arab-Jewish cooperation, Epstein helped found *B'rit Shalom but later resigned from the organization.

EPSTEIN, JUDITH G. Zionist leader and pioneer of *Hadassah, the Women's Zionist Organization of America (b. Worcester, Mass., 1895). She began her Zionist activities after World War I. From 1928 to 1934 she was national secretary of Hadassah and later served as national vice-president and chairman of the building fund of the Hadassah-University Hospital in Jerusalem. As national president of Hadassah from 1937 to 1939, she headed its delegation to the Zionist Congresses of 1937 and 1939 (*see* CONGRESS, ZIONIST). From 1940 to 1968 she was a member of the *Actions Committee of the *World Zionist Organization.

In addition to her positions and work in Hadassah, Mrs. Epstein was active in the Zionist movement generally as a prominent member of the American Zionist Emergency Council (*see* EMERGENCY COMMITTEE FOR ZIONIST AFFAIRS) and as a lecturer on Zionism and Israel.

Judith G. Epstein.
[Hadassah]

EPSTEIN, ZALMAN. Hebrew journalist and early Zionist (b. Lyuban, near Bobruisk, Russia, 1860; d. Ramat Gan, 1936). After receiving a religious and a secular education, Epstein was active in the Hibbat Zion movement (*see* HOVEVE ZION) in Odessa and wrote for the Hebrew press. From 1890 to 1900 he was Moshe Leib *Lilienblum's assistant on the Central Secretariat of Hibbat Zion in Russia. In 1925 he settled in Palestine.

For almost two generations Epstein contributed articles to the Hebrew press and wrote numerous pamphlets stressing the urgency of continuing the religious tradition of the Jews, explaining Zionism, and emphasizing the value of the Hebrew language. In 1935 he published (in Hebrew) a volume on Lilienblum and the history of Hibbat Zion in Russia, *M. L. Lilienblum and His Thinking on Religion and the Renascence of the Jewish People in the Land of Its Fathers.*

G. KRESSEL

ERETZ YISRAEL (Land of Israel). Hebrew name for Palestine, derived from the Bible.

EREZ. Village (kibbutz) in the southern coastal plain. Founded in 1949 by members of *Palmah (commando units) and affiliated with the *Ihud HaK'vutzot V'haKibbutzim.

ERLANGER, MICHAEL. Leader of the *Hoveve Zion movement in France (b. Wissembourg, France, 1827; d. Paris, 1892). After receiving a religious and a general education, he went to Paris at the age of 17 and worked in a business firm. Later he became the manager of a firm in Alexandria, Egypt. There he met Dr. Albert Cohen, who was passing through the city on his way to Jerusalem to establish, on behalf of the Rothschilds, a hospital and school, and accompanied him to Palestine. He also helped Charles *Netter establish the agricultural school of Mikve Yisrael. In 1877, after Cohen's death, Erlanger was appointed administrator of charities of the French Rothschilds. He was active in the *Alliance Israélite Universelle and served as vice-chairman of the Consistoire Centrale des Israélites de France.

In his capacity as administrator of the Rothschild charities, Erlanger rendered much assistance to the early Jewish colonies in Palestine. The *Kattowitz Conference of Hoveve Zion (1884) elected him treasurer of the movement. He also served as liaison man between the Hoveve Zion and Baron Edmond de *Rothschild. In 1891 Erlanger participated in the negotiations of the Hoveve Zion with the Alliance Israélite Universelle and with Baron Maurice de *Hirsch, and attended a conference called in Berlin to render assistance to émigrés from Russia.

I. KLAUSNER

ESHBOL. Village (moshav) in the northern Negev. Founded in 1955 and affiliated with *T'nu'at HaMoshavim. Population (1968): 424.

ESHEL HANASI. Agricultural school in the northern Negev. Founded in 1952 and named for Chaim *Weizmann, President *(nasi)* of Israel. Population (1968): 328.

ESHKOL (SHKOLNIK), LEVI. Israeli labor leader and Prime Minister (b. near Kiev, Russia, 1895; d. Jerusalem, 1969). In Vilna, where he attended high school after having received a traditional education, he came in close contact with Zionist and Socialist ideas, particularly those of Aharon David *Gordon. There, too, he joined *Tz'ire Zion, which later merged with *HaPo'el HaTza'ir. Arriving in Palestine in 1914, he worked as an agricultural laborer and was elected to the agricultural workers' council in Petah Tikva. He was chosen a member of a group that set out to cultivate the lands of Kalandia ('Atarot). Forced to leave Kalandia soon after the outbreak of World War I, the group went to Rishon L'Tziyon to operate one of the old Rothschild farms on a collective basis. Although HaPo'el HaTza'ir opposed having Palestinian Jewish units fighting on the Allied side, Eshkol joined the *Jewish Legion in 1918.

Eshkol participated in the founding convention of the *Histadrut (General Federation of Labor) in 1920 and in the First *Asefat HaNivharim (Elected Assembly) of the *Yishuv (Jewish population of Palestine), and he attended every Zionist *Congress beginning with the 12th (Karlovy Vary, 1921). In 1921, along with Eliyahu *Golomb and David Hacohen, he was sent to Vienna to purchase arms to defend Jewish settlements against Arab attack. In the 1920s he spent some time in Lithuania to recruit pioneers for Palestine on behalf of HaPo'el HaTza'ir. During that period he went to Moscow (1927) to attend a cooperative congress. Long an advocate of labor unity, he was assigned various administrative positions in the *Mapai party, which was founded in 1930. By this time he had devoted considerable time to the study of economics and accounting methods, which was to serve him well in his subsequent career.

When the Nazis gained control in Germany, Eshkol headed the Settlement Department of the Palestine Office in Berlin for three years (*see* PALESTINE OFFICES). He organized immigration and the transfer of funds from Germany to Palestine, using the money to set up various economic and settlement projects, among them 'Amidar, Shikun, Nir, and the *Mekorot Water Company (of which he was director general for many years). His main interest throughout this period centered on agriculture and irrigation. At the same time he was active in the High Command of *Hagana, serving as its chief financial administrator and as one of its arms procurement experts. After the establishment of the State of Israel he became Director General of the Ministry of Defense. He was one of the founders of Israel's ordnance and arms industry.

In 1949 Eshkol became head of the Land Settlement Department of the *Jewish Agency and in this capacity coordinated the settlement of the masses of new immigrants arriving in Israel. He planned the construction of hundreds of new agricultural settlements throughout the country. From 1950 to 1952 he served as treasurer of the Jewish Agency. Meanwhile, in October, 1951, he was named Minister of Agriculture and Development. He helped promote the oil industry and the exploitation of mineral resources in the Negev and the Dead Sea. In June, 1952, he became Minister of Finance, a post in which he was responsible for the implementation of the reparations agreement with West Germany (*see* GERMAN-ISRAEL AGREEMENT). He directed reparations funds mainly to the development of industry and the establishment of Israel's merchant marine. Eshkol represented the *government of Israel at international conferences of the World Bank and the International Monetary Fund.

On the retirement of David *Ben-Gurion from the government in June, 1963, Eshkol succeeded him as Prime Minister and Minister of Defense. Shortly after he assumed office, a rift developed between the two men because Eshkol refused to reopen the Lavon affair as requested by Ben-Gurion. Early in 1965 Eshkol succeeded in his plan of bringing about an alignment between his party, Mapai, and the left-wing *Ahdut 'Avoda. Ben-Gurion and his followers strongly objected to this

Levi Eshkol.
[Israel Information Services]

alignment, and when the national Mapai Convention approved it, a split occurred with Ben-Gurion forming a new party, *R'shimat Po'ale Israel (Rafi). In the *Knesset elections of November, 1965, however, Eshkol was returned with a substantial plurality.

Eshkol visited the United States in June, 1964, and again in 1968 for talks with Pres. Lyndon B. Johnson. He also called on Pres. Charles de Gaulle in France and Prime Minister Harold Wilson in England, and he toured Africa. His term of office saw the establishment of diplomatic relations with West Germany (1965) and the inauguration of Israel's first jet engine manufacturing plant, in Bet Shemesh (1969).

In the last days of May, 1967, as the crisis arising from the withdrawal of United Nations troops from the Egyptian border area and the blockade of the Gulf of Elat imposed by President Nasser was reaching a climax, Eshkol found himself with a divided Cabinet. In response to public clamor he enlarged the Cabinet by coopting representatives of *Gahal (Herut-Liberal bloc) and appointing Moshe *Dayan of Rafi Minister of Defense. At the head of a Government of National Unity, Eshkol led Israel through the *Six-day War. Early in 1968 he reached an agreement with Rafi and Ahdut 'Avoda to effect their merger with Mapai in a united *Israel Labor party.

Some of Eshkol's many articles appeared in a book, *Hevle HaHitnahlut* (The Pangs of Settlement, 1958). In 1964 he received an honorary Ph.D. degree from the *Hebrew University of Jerusalem for his "major role in the administration and economic strengthening of the State."

G. KRESSEL

ESHTA'OL. Village (moshav) in the Jerusalem corridor. Settled by *Yemenite Jews in 1949 and affiliated with *T'nu'at HaMoshavim. Population (1968): 320.

ESRA. German *Hoveve Zion society, founded in Berlin on Jan. 26, 1884. Its aim was to support the Jewish colonies in Palestine and to shield new immigrants who were without means from the influence of Christian missionary societies. During the first two years of its existence, the group had about 2,000 members; its income, however, was small, as the annual membership dues were only half a (German) mark. In 1886 the society was reorganized. The number of members increased, and branch societies were established. The Berlin branch, which gained a most active worker in young Willy *Bambus, expanded greatly. The society gave valuable support to the settlement of Y'sud HaMa'ala and also assisted Petah Tikva and Mishmar HaYarden. In the 1890s the activities of the society expanded as a result of Bambus's organizational efforts and the help of Dr. Heinrich *Loewe, Dr. Jehuda Holzmann, and Isaac *Turoff, who toured Germany and established new branches. In 1897 Turoff, one of the society's founders, was appointed its secretary. By 1899 Esra had almost 5,000 members and a yearly income of 16,300 marks.

The society assisted in the settling of five Esra workers near Rehovot. At first, it provided them with supplementary farms, but later it set them up as independent farmers. Esra also helped settle workers in Motza, near Jerusalem; participated in the founding of the workers' settlement of Kastina (B'er Tovya); and aided the Hoveve Zion society of Tarnów, Galicia, in establishing the settlement of Mahanayim. The society aided in the sale of Palestine wines and brought the agricultural produce of the settlements to the 1896 Berlin Exhibition of Trade and Industry, which was afterward shown also in Breslau, Hamburg, Cologne, and Frankfort on the Main.

Taking part in the international activities of the Hoveve Zion movement, Esra assisted in setting up in Paris a Central Committee for all Hoveve Zion groups. The leaders of the society

Settlers at work in the seed nursery of Eshta'ol. [Israel Information Services]

were not in complete accord with the views of the political Zionists and demanded the continuation of settlement activities. In 1899 Esra initiated a conference in Frankfurt of Hoveve Zion societies from Germany, Russia, England, Galicia, France, and Denmark. The conference, which was attended also by delegates of the *Alliance Israélite Universelle and of Kolel Hod (*see* HALUKKA), decided to aid industry in the cities of Palestine, provide work opportunities for immigrants dependent on charity, and support religious education in the country. From 1899 on, Esra supported the settlers of B'ne Y'huda, east of Lake Kinneret. It also aided the *Bezalel School, the Hebrew Teachers Seminary of Jerusalem, and the Kiryat Sefer Agricultural School, founded by Israel *Belkind. In 1912, Esra assisted the immigration of *Yemenite Jews to Palestine. During World War I, the society provided substantial aid to farmers and agricultural workers in the country by granting them loans. It also supported the Pasteur Institute established by Dr. Arye *Beham.

With the growth and consolidation of the *World Zionist Organization and its institutions, Esra, like Hoveve Zion groups in other countries, gradually lost its influence and importance.   I. KLAUSNER

ETAN. Village (moshav) in the Lakhish region. Founded in 1955 and affiliated with HaPo'el HaMizrahi (*see* MIZRAHI). Population (1968): 475.

ETANIM. Center for State health institutions in the Jerusalem corridor. Opened in 1952. Population (1968): 200.

ETERNAL PEOPLE. *See* 'AM 'OLAM.

ETHNIC GROUPS AND PROBLEMS IN ISRAEL. The Jewish population of Israel, numbering close to 2.5 million in 1970, was composed of immigrant groups and their Israel-born descendants who had come from about 100 countries. In the course of their long sojourn in those countries, the Jewish communities had acquired enough of the demographic, social, cultural, and even physical characteristics of the peoples among whom they lived to develop considerable differences among themselves. Thus, the large-scale *Ingathering of the Exiles in Israel in 1948–52 brought together what in effect was a number of disparate ethnic groups, each of which brought along its own traditions and cultural physiognomy. After their arrival in Israel, they were thrown into close proximity with other, often greatly dissimilar groups and found themselves faced with problems for which their experiences in their countries of origin had not prepared them.

On the basis of its ethnic origin, the *Yishuv (Jewish population of Palestine) is usually divided into three major groups: the *Ashkenazim of Europe and the Americas, of whom a large part spoke Yiddish; the *Sephardim of the Balkans and the Near East, who spoke Ladino; and the so-called *Oriental Jews, consisting of such groups as the Arabic-speaking Jews of Yemen, Syria, Iraq, and North Africa, the Persian-speaking Jews of Iran and Afghanistan, and the Aramaic-speaking Jews of Kurdistan. In addition, there are the Jews from outside the Middle East proper, such as the Jews of India and Ethiopia.

Irrespective of this threefold classification, which has historical validity, the non-Ashkenazi communities have often been lumped together under a single denomination, on the basis of certain superficial similarities which seem to characterize them, particularly when contrasted with the Ashkenazim. The generic term used in this case has been "'Edot HaMizrah" (communities of the East). These communities themselves have shown a tendency to consider their position in Israel that of an underprivileged element, which consequently has certain common interests as opposed to those of the Ashkenazim. This dichotomy is occasionally reflected in official Israeli statistical publications, which group together Jewish immigrants from Europe and the Americas, on the one hand, and those from Asia and Africa, on the other. This division, of course, does not entirely coincide with the Ashkenazi-Eastern division, since it places the Sephardim from Greece, other Balkan countries, and Italy in the European and American group, while in actuality many of these Sephardim not only regard themselves as belonging to the Eastern group but have assumed the position of leaders and spokesmen of all the non-Ashkenazi Jews in Israel. In common parlance, Israelis refer to each other as either "Ashkenazim" or "Sephardim," the latter term being used synonymously with 'Edot HaMizrah. By 1968 the Afro-Asian group outnumbered the Euro-American (see table below), but the proportion of immigrants who had arrived prior to the establishment of the State was greater among the Ashkenazim.

It was inevitable that the differences in economic, social, educational, and cultural standards which characterized the countries of origin of the Ashkenazi Jews, on the one hand, and those of the Oriental Jews, on the other, and which had left their mark on the Jewish communities themselves should persist after the migration of these communities to Israel. As far as the Oriental Jewish communities were concerned, these differences manifested themselves in what appeared to be a cultural lag. Economically, the lack of skills useful in a modern, technolog-

ically oriented country such as Israel forced most of the Oriental Jewish immigrants into the less remunerative occupational fields.

Demographic Differences. Closely related to economic status was the demographic picture. The Oriental Jews (that is, those who had come to Israel from Asia and Africa, and their descendants) differed from their European- and American-born brethren in all their demographic traits. The median age of the Asian- and African-born immigrants on Dec. 31, 1968, was 33.2 years, while that of the European- and American-born immigrants was 49.7 years. Although the latter constituted 51.4 per cent of all immigrants, the number of those under 14 years of age among them was only 20,956 (about 25 per cent), as against 63,095 (about 75 per cent) among the Asian- and African-born immigrants. In other words, the Afro-Asian sector of the immigrant population was substantially younger than its European- and American-born counterpart. Another demographic difference was that the Asian-African group married at a higher rate and at a younger age than the European-American group.

In 1966, the Asian- and African-born Jewish population of Israel amounted to 652,391, as against 716,873 of Euro-American origin. Yet in 1965, 7,691 of the men contracting marriages had been born in Asia and Africa and only 5,017 in Europe and the Americas. That is to say, in both absolute and relative figures, more Asian- and African-born men married than did men of European and American birth. Both the average and median ages of Asian- and African-born bridegrooms and brides were about 2 years lower than the corresponding ages of European- and American-born bridegrooms and brides.

A significant difference in birthrates existed between the two groups. In 1968, of the Jewish families whose head was European- or American-born, only 11.3 per cent had three or more children, whereas of the Jewish families whose head was Asian- or African-born, 47.9 per cent had three or more children.

In 1967, 8,897 children were born to Jewish immigrant mothers who themselves had been born in Europe and the Americas, as against 29,148 for mothers born in Asia and Africa, although the number of mothers in the latter category was smaller than that in the former. To put it differently, the average number of children per married Jewish women aged between 40 and 49 was 2.2 for the European- and American-born group, as against 6.1 for the Asian- and African-born group. These figures indicate that the fertility of the Asian- and African-born Jewish women was almost three times as high as that of the European- and American-born Jewish women.

To these differences must be added the differences in annual death rates. Between 1963 and 1965 deaths averaged 11.5 per 1,000 for Jews born in Europe and the Americas as against 6.6 per 1,000 for Jews born in Asia and Africa. By deducting the death rates from the birthrates, we find that in 1964 the average annual rate of natural increase for the Jewish immigrant population that had come from Europe and the Americas was 10.6 per 1,000, whereas that for the Jewish immigrant population that had come from Asia and Africa was 42.7 per 1,000, or four times as high.

Thus, the average "Oriental" Jewish family was much larger and much younger than the average "Ashkenazi" family. Barring unforeseen changes resulting from immigration, it could thus be predicted that the Oriental half of the Jewish *population of Israel would rapidly become an increasing majority.

POPULATION OF ISRAEL, DEC. 31, 1968

	European and American origin	Asian and African origin	Total
Immigrants	702,445	661,772	1,364,217
Israel-born, first generation	401,725	494,385	896,110
Israel-born, second generation (estimated)	80,505	94,000	174,505
Total	1,184,675	1,250,157	2,434,832

Economic Status. This sector of Israel's population, however, still labored under the disadvantages caused by the lower level of educational attainment and skills it had brought from its countries of origin in Asia and North Africa. Consequently, the employment picture emerging from the tables of the official *Statistical Abstract of Israel* (1969) indicated a larger concentration of immigrants from Europe and the Americas in professional, scientific, technical, and related occupations; administrative, executive, managerial, and clerical work; and work as traders, agents, and salesmen. Immigrants from Asia and Africa were more numerous in farming, fishing, and related work; transport and communications; construction, mining, and quarrying; work as craftsmen; production processes and related occupations; and employment in services and in athletics and recreation. Lack of skills always goes hand in hand with underemployment: between 1961 and 1968 the percentage of immigrants from Asia and Africa registered at the labor exchanges was consistently and considerably higher than that of immigrants from Europe and the Americas.

The lower educational and skill level of the Asian- and African-born Jewish population of Israel is reflected also in its lower earnings. In 1968–69 the net average annual income of an urban employee's family whose head had been born in Asia or Africa was IL 9,802 ($2,800), as against IL 12,973 ($3,706) for a household unit whose head had been born in Europe or the Americas, although the former was, as we have seen, much larger than the latter.

This differential in income level was correlated with a differential in food intake. The immigrants from Asia and Africa consumed about the same number of calories daily (a little below 3,000) and the same amount of iron as the European- and American-born, but their diet included somewhat fewer proteins and less calcium, vitamin A, riboflavin, and ascorbic acid. (For a detailed treatment of the differences between the income levels and consumption patterns of the Afro-Asian and Euro-American sectors of Israel's Jewish population, *see* STANDARD OF LIVING IN ISRAEL.)

A similar disparity was found in housing. In 1968, only 14.4 per cent of the long-established settlers and 19.9 per cent of new immigrant European and American families had one room for two or more persons; the corresponding figures for Asian and African families (45.3 per cent and 55.8 per cent, respectively) indicated that the latter group lived under far more crowded conditions.

Education. The gap in skills and income was closely correlated, and largely rooted in, a gap in the educational level. Although Israel made great and successful efforts to narrow this gap, by 1968 much of it was still in evidence. Whereas the number of primary and secondary school teachers born in Europe and the Americas increased considerably from 1963–64 to 1966–67 (6,284 and 11,558, respectively), that of teachers born in Asia and Africa grew only from 2,797 to 4,198. Primary education is compulsory in Israel, and all children aged 6 to 14 of all communities must attend school. Although postprimary education is not compulsory, a high percentage of children aged 14 to 17 attend school. Of every 1,000 such children whose fathers or who themselves had been born in Europe and the Americas, 436 attended general high schools and 222 vocational and agricultural schools during the scholastic year 1968–69. The corresponding figures for children who had been born in Asia or Africa or whose fathers had been born on these continents

were 143 and 239, respectively. While there was thus still a considerable gap, the percentage of Asian and African children attending postprimary schools was increasing steadily.

In 1967–68 higher educational institutions enrolled 3,178 students who had been born (or whose fathers had been born) in Asia and Africa and 21,111 students who had been born (or whose fathers had been born) in Europe and the Americas. Here, therefore, the gap was still very large: only a small percentage of the Asian and African students who completed their secondary education went on to college. Of the Jewish population aged 14 and above, 27.8 per cent of those born in Asia and Africa had nine or more years of schooling, as against 53.6 per cent of those born in Europe and the Americas. Put differently, children of Afro-Asian origin made up 59.3 per cent of the primary school population in 1966–67, with 45.3 per cent of the total number of pupils in the ninth grade (aged 14–15), 18.9 per cent in the twelfth grade (aged 17–18), 12.6 per cent of all undergraduate students enrolled in universities, and 7.6 per cent of graduate students (based on 1965–66 figures). This progressively declining rate of attendance is reflected in the relatively low average educational level of the Afro-Asian group.

Cultural and Social Differences. Differences existed also in what may be called cultural consumption. In motion-picture attendance the difference was slight: in 1965 the adult Jewish population born in Asia and Africa attended an average of 18 performances, and the adult Jewish population born in Europe and the Americas, 22 performances. In reading habits the difference was marked: in 1965, among Jewish adults who had come from Asia and Africa, 34.3 per cent read books and 48.8 per cent newspapers; among the European and American immigrants, 60.7 per cent read books and 88.3 per cent newspapers.

As one would expect in a situation of social tension which always accompanies the presence, side by side, of two or more socioeconomically disparate populations, the crime and delinquency rates of the underprivileged groups were higher than those of the more privileged populations. Between 1951 and 1963 the annual rate of adult convictions per 1,000 of the specified population was 3.8 for Jews born in Europe and the Americas, 11.5 for those born in Asia, and 20.4 for those born in Africa (*see* CRIME IN ISRAEL). In 1966–67 the social welfare bureaus of Israel rendered assistance to 33,702 persons born in Europe and the Americas, as against 75,905 persons born in Asia and Africa.

Changes in Status. As the data cited above (all taken from the *Statistical Abstract of Israel* for 1969) indicate, even 15 years after the great mass immigration from the Middle East to Israel had subsided, there were still considerable disparities between the Afro-Asian and the Euro-American contingents of the country's Jewish population. The gap between the two population elements had undoubtedly narrowed, but the very fact that it had not yet been eliminated caused tension and recrimination between them. In complaining about what they had not yet achieved, the Afro-Asians tended to overlook what they had achieved: what immigration into and settling in Israel had meant to them. The fact is that by all objective standards the Afro-Asians were better off in Israel than they had been in the Arab and other Middle Eastern countries from which they had come. They received superior medical and health services, their life expectancy had increased, they got more and better education, they enjoyed full political rights, they were being integrated into the economy of the country, they received social insurance and other social service benefits, and their children increasingly intermarried with those of the Euro-Americans and native Israelis.

Yet people tend to judge their situation in relation to the present rather than the past environment. Thus the historical fact that in comparison with the past the Afro-Asians were better off did not counterbalance for them the more immediate fact that they were still worse off than the Euro-Americans in Israel. The resulting sense of dissatisfaction with their progress was reinforced by the feeling which the Oriental Jews had about the attitude of the economically, culturally, and politically dominant Ashkenazi element. They felt that the Ashkenazim discriminated against them because they regarded the Afro-Asians as backward and, for the same reason, expected them to assimilate to the Ashkenazi way of life and values as rapidly and as completely as possible.

While a lack of relevant surveys and public opinion studies makes it impossible to give precise data about the actual attitudes of the Ashkenazim toward the Oriental Jews, it cannot be doubted that the cultural distance that divided those enculturated in a Euro-American environment from those who had undergone the same process in Afro-Asian societies created a feeling of estrangement between the two elements and a definite preference for associating with persons of similar background and mentality. An important consequence of this tendency was the emergence, in the underprivileged groups, of a sense of being scorned and discriminated against by the Ashkenazim. In their home countries, despite their political insecurity and the occasional anti-Semitic outbreaks, the Oriental Jews could and did feel superior to the non-Jewish majority population because they were better educated, more urbanized, better placed economically, and, in countries which were under European domination or influence (as in Syria, Lebanon, Iraq, and North Africa), closer culturally to the Europeans than were the Muslim majority. In all these respects their relative positions became reversed with their settlement in Israel: here they were more poorly educated, less urbanized, worse off economically, and farther removed from the Western cultural pattern than were the Euro-American or Ashkenazi Jews. This abrupt deterioration in *relative* position could not be compensated for by the actual improvement in their economic, social, and cultural situation.

Outlook. By the late 1960s most of the Afro-Asian Jews in Israel had been in the country for about 20 years. In the course of this period their objective situation had improved, but this process was accompanied, as it usually is, by more vociferous and impatient demands for further improvement. At about the same time, the earlier Ashkenazi demand for a complete "merging of the communities," which was merely a euphemism for the assimilation of the Oriental Jews to the Ashkenazim, had been largely superseded by the ideal of cultural pluralism, under which each ethnic group in Israel would be encouraged to preserve a considerable part of its own cultural heritage. The emerging Israeli culture was no longer envisaged monolithically but rather as the sum total of numerous subcultures, each of which was accepted as making its specific contribution to the total picture.

At the same time, the numerical relationship of the two halves of Israel reached a turning point: in the second half of the 1960s the Orientals achieved numerical preponderance over the Ashkenazim, which made the latter's leadership aware of the need to give the Oriental Jews a greater voice in the country's political, economic, and cultural affairs.

The gradual narrowing of the gap between the two halves of Israel was shown also by the slow but steady increase of intermarriage between the two groups. In 1955, 9.8 per cent of the Asian- and African-born bridegrooms married European- and American-born brides; in 1964, 13.6 per cent. In 1955, 13.4 per cent of the European- and American-born bridegrooms married Asian- and African-born brides; in 1964, 16.8 per cent. There was thus a definite trend toward an actual biological "merging of the communities," which, in turn, reinforced the trend toward the reduction and ultimate elimination of the economic and cultural gap between the two groups.

R. PATAI

'ET LIVNOT (Polish Zionist faction formed in the 1920s). *See* POLAND, ZIONISM IN.

ETTINGER, AKIBA JACOB. Agronomist and blueprinter of the agricultural colonization of Palestine (b. Vitebsk, Russia, 1872; d. Tel Aviv, 1945). Ettinger studied agronomy at the Universities of St. Petersburg and Bonn and from 1898 to 1911 headed the *Jewish Colonization Association (ICA) projects in the Jewish Pale of southern Russia. From 1911 to 1913 he was agricultural consultant in the ICA settlements of Argentina and Brazil. Ettinger first visited Palestine in 1902 on behalf of the *Hoveve Zion movement and studied the economic condition of the settlements there. In 1914 he settled in Palestine.

From 1918 to 1925 Ettinger headed the Land Settlement Department of the Zionist *Executive, and his blueprint for settlement was accepted in 1921 by the 12th Zionist *Congress (the first to be held after World War I). He was instrumental in the settlement of the Jezreel Valley and other areas in the 1920s. From 1926 to 1936 he headed the Land Acquisition Department of the *Jewish National Fund and traveled abroad for various Zionist institutions. Ettinger wrote several books and articles describing his experiences in agricultural settlements of Jews in Palestine and other countries, among them (both in Hebrew) *The Carmel* (1931) and *With Hebrew Agriculturists in Our Land* (1945).

G. KRESSEL

ETZEL. *See* IRGUN TZ'VAI L'UMI.

'ETZYON BLOCK (Gush 'Etzyon). Site of former Jewish settlements in the Judean Mountains between Jerusalem and Hebron, taken over by Jordan (*see* TRANSJORDAN) in the *War of Independence. The settlements, which were situated close to one another, were K'far 'Etzyon, Massu'ot Yitzhak, and 'En Tzurim, all of HaPo'el HaMizrahi (*see* MIZRAHI), and R'vadim, of *HaShomer HaTza'ir. The settled area was named Gush 'Etzyon ('Etzyon Block) for K'far 'Etzyon, which, founded in 1943, was the oldest of the settlements.

Soon after the outbreak of Arab-Jewish hostilities, the Arabs launched a heavy attack on K'far 'Etzyon. This attack was repelled. Then, in January, 1948, a platoon of 35 members of *Hagana sent as reinforcements to the settlers was killed by Arabs. In March, a convoy which had broken the Arab siege of the block and had brought supplies and reinforcements to the settlements, was attacked on its return journey. On May 4, the Arab Legion, supported by trucks and irregular infantry forces from neighboring Arab villages, attacked the block. The attackers were repelled, but a week later they attacked again. The settlers, outnumbered and ill equipped, put up a heroic resistance. Finally, on May 14, 1948, after two days of desperate fighting, the 'Etzyon Block fell. Many of the settlers were killed during the fighting; the rest were taken prisoners by the Arab Legion. The surviving settlers subsequently founded the new settlements of Massu'ot Yitzhak, 'En Tzurim, and R'vadim in the Darom and Nir 'Etzyon on Mount Carmel.

As a result of the *Six-day War of 1967, the entire area of the 'Etzyon Block again came under Israeli control. In September, 1967, an advance party of pioneers, members of the 'Etzyon Block Sons' Association, returned to K'far 'Etzyon to set up an outpost of the Nahal pioneer training corps there.

EUROPEAN COMMON MARKET AND ISRAEL. In January, 1958, the European Economic Community (EEC; European Common Market, or Inner Six) became effective under the Treaty of Rome (1957). Soon thereafter, the Israeli authorities undertook comprehensive studies of the consequences and potentialities of the new organization for Israel's economic development. The members of the EEC—France, West Germany, Italy, the Netherlands, Belgium, and Luxembourg—have an aggregate population of 180 million whose 1967 output totaled $400,000,000,000. While Israel obviously is not a major consideration for the EEC, relations with the EEC are of considerable importance to Israel. In the absence of normal communications with neighboring Arab states, the EEC members are among the closest and most directly accessible countries with which Israel enjoys normal relations. In addition to geographical proximity, the EEC members show similar types of demand, methods of production, and ways of life and government. This relationship is reflected in the fact that in the mid-1960s almost 30 per cent of Israel's exports went to EEC countries, which in turn supplied about 28 per cent of its imports (see the accompanying table). Israel's trade balance with these countries (except for the Netherlands and Belgium) was in deficit, and this partly explains its desire to improve the situation.

Israel's commercial relations with the EEC countries are to some extent predetermined and not interchangeable, since substitute trade with North America and other parts of the world is limited either by the high cost of transportation, or (as in the case of the Communist countries) by political factors, or (as in the case of most African countries) by a demand structure that militates against Israeli products. In addition to this lack of alternatives is the consideration that an eventual

ISRAEL'S TRADE WITH THE EEC
(In millions of dollars and percentage of total trade)

Year	Imports		Exports	
		Per cent		Per cent
1961	$181	31	$ 63	26
1962	150	24	72	26
1963	157	23	107	30
1964	242	29	104	28
1965	202	24	122	28
1966	201	24	143	28
1967	160	29	185	24
1968	169	26	319	29

adherence of the United Kingdom and the other countries of the European Free Trade Association (EFTA; Outer Seven)—Austria, Switzerland, Portugal, Sweden, Norway, and Denmark—to the EEC will create a common market for all non-Communist European countries. In that case, Israel's dependence on Western Europe will be still greater, since more than half of its foreign trade will be conducted with that market. Israel's endeavor to obtain some sort of formal relationship with the EEC results from the provision of the Treaty of Rome that requires the eventual elimination of all customs barriers between member countries and the erection of a unified barrier against third parties that in some cases is higher than the tariffs existing previously in individual EEC countries. This situation places Israel at a disadvantage not only vis-à-vis the EEC members but also vis-à-vis countries such as the North African nations, Greece, Spain, and Turkey, which have obtained associate membership and preferential status with the EEC.

Informal talks beginning in 1960, followed by formal negotiations, led in July, 1964, to an agreement whereby a limited number of Israeli industrial products were given some tariff concessions, while the problem of citrus exports (see CITRUS INDUSTRY IN ISRAEL) was postponed until arrangements would have been completed with other Mediterranean citrus-exporting countries. This agreement, though of minor economic significance, was viewed by Israel as a political achievement and as a first step toward the development of fuller cooperation. The agreement expired in July, 1967. Prior to that date Israel again raised the question of associate membership, particularly in view of the fact that the EEC common external tariff was to become effective in July, 1968, and that Israeli exports to the EEC tended to decline. For a number of reasons, the EEC did not respond favorably to Israel's application for associate membership but preferred a less formal relationship, such as a customs union or a free trade zone. Even such an arrangement would at first be restricted to industrial products, since the inclusion of agricultural products would raise the question of discrimination against other Mediterranean countries.

The principal objection to Israel's expedient accommodation by the EEC was the desire to maintain the organization's European character and its political and economic cohesion, which were considered to form the basis for a United States of Europe. A non-European country such as Israel, with no share in the Western defense system, would tend to dilute the EEC structure. Moreover, a series of important problems precluded the EEC's preoccupation with Israel's application. Among them were the admission of the United Kingdom, a tariff agreement with the United States, and the collective association of a number of formerly French-controlled African countries. Moreover, there was resistance on the part of individual countries to a comprehensive arrangement wholly favorable to Israel. Not only did the Arab countries protest Israel's move for a link with the EEC, but there was considerable opposition by the Mediterranean members and their protégés and associates whose products competed with those of Israel: Italy, Spain, Greece, and the North African countries. Although most of these objections were related to the political context, the economic case against Israel's association rested on the country's desire to have the EEC share responsibility for its large trade deficit and its need for large-scale investment while it was still involved in a conflict with its neighbors and was not as yet prepared to remove reciprocally restrictions on the importation of EEC industrial products. This situation resulted in Israel's arguments for a favorable arrangement being mainly defensive, with emphasis on the serious consequences of exclusion. In view of Israel's difficulty in substituting trade relations with other parts of the world for those with the EEC, the significance of the Israeli market potential for EEC members and the possibility of retaliation against EEC imports in case of nonaccommodation did not appear to be fully convincing.

J. O. RONALL

EVANS, MARY ANNE (Marian). *See* ELIOT, GEORGE.

EVEN. Hebrew word, meaning "stone," that forms part of a number of place names in Israel, as in Even Y'huda (Stone of Judah).

EVEN M'NAHEM. Village (moshav) in western Upper Galilee. Founded in 1960 and named for Arthur Menahem *Hantke. Affiliated with *T'nu'at HaMoshavim.

EVEN SAPIR. Village (moshav) in the Jerusalem corridor. Founded in 1950 by *Yemenite Jews and named for Ya'akov HaLevi Sapir, scholar and author of the travel book *Even Sapir,* who visited Yemen in 1859. Affiliated with *T'nu'at Ha-Moshavim. Population (1968): 420.

EVEN SH'MUEL. Rural center in the Darom. Founded in 1956. Even Sh'muel serves the villages (moshavim) of Etan, No'am, Shalva, 'Uza, R'vaha, Zavdi'el, Ahuzam, and Vardon. Population (1968): 140.

EVEN Y'HUDA. Rural community in the Sharon Plain. Founded in 1932 by *B'ne Binyamin, an organization of the sons of veteran settlers, it is named for Eliezer *Ben Yehuda. Since the establishment of the State of Israel it has absorbed a large number of new immigrants and has grown considerably. It includes Hadasim. Population (1968): 3,980.

EVEN YITZHAK (Gal'ed). Village (kibbutz) in Samaria. Founded in 1945 by immigrants, mostly from Germany, and named for Yitzhak Hochberg, a prominent South African Zionist. Affiliated with the *Ihud HaK'vutzot V'haKibbutzim. The village is also known as Gal'ed ("cairn"; Genesis 31:47) in memory of comrades of the settlers who had perished in Europe. Population (1968): 251.

'EVRON. Village (kibbutz) in western Upper Galilee. Founded in 1945 and affiliated with the *Kibbutz Artzi Shel HaShomer HaTza'ir. Population (1968): 450.

A Byzantine church found at 'Evron is dated by inscription (C.E. 415) and contains a remarkable mosaic pavement.

EXECUTIVE, ZIONIST. Executive organ of the *World Zionist Organization (WZO), also called (to 1921) Inner *Actions Committee (AC), charged with the implementation of the decisions of the Zionist *Congress and the *Zionist General Council (Greater Actions Committee) and with the transaction of current affairs of the WZO, which it represents externally. It is responsible to the Congress and to the General Council. The Executive represents the leadership of the movement, whereas the Council represents local Zionist organizations and parties.

The development of relations between the Executive and the General Council reflects the changing structure and representative character of the WZO. During Herzl's lifetime there was no clear-cut, formal distinction between the Zionist representative bodies on the one hand and the executive organ on the other. The General Council (Greater Actions Committee), which was composed of the representatives of the Zionist Organization in the various countries, was considered the leading organ of the movement. The actual direction of the movement, however, was in the hands of five members of the Greater Actions Committee who lived in the same area and constituted the Inner Actions Committee. After Herzl's death an attempt was made to restore the preponderance of the General Council, but it failed because of the dispersion of its members in different countries.

In the constitution of the WZO adopted by the 8th Zionist Congress (The Hague, 1907) the General Council was declared the executive body of the movement, responsible to the Congress. It was to have a membership of no less than 21 and no more than 60; 3 to 7 of these members composed the Inner Actions Committee. However, the chairmen of the WZO and the Inner Actions Committee were elected by separate votes of the Congress and thus were granted an independent status. At the 10th Zionist Congress (Basle, 1911) the membership of the General Council was reduced to 25. The pre-World War I period marked the peak of the AC's influence in the WZO.

The headquarters of the WZO was located in the city where the president of the WZO resided. Until 1905 it was in Vienna, from 1905 to 1911 in Cologne, and thereafter in Berlin.

The 12th Zionist Congress (Karlovy Vary, 1921) consolidated the organizational structure of the WZO. The Zionist Executive (replacing the Inner AC) was declared the executive organ; it was to be composed of 9 to 15 members. Those members who resided in Palestine formed the Palestinian branch, with its seat in Jerusalem; all the others formed another part of Executive, which until 1948 had its seat in London. The Executive was elected by the Zionist Congress, which also determined its seat. Gradually all the functions of the Executive were assigned to its Jerusalem Office, with the London branch handling political activities in general and negotiations with the British government, which until 1948 was the mandatory power, in particular (*see* MANDATE FOR PALESTINE).

The Greater AC consisted of the members of the Executive, three members of the Financial and Economic Council elected by the Congress, one representative each of the *Jewish Colonial Trust, *Jewish National Fund, and *Keren HaYesod (Palestine Foundation Fund), and 25 members elected by the Congress. The Greater AC was given an independent Presidium, but it was usually convened by the Executive, which had become the more influential organ. However, the Greater AC was given authority in budgetary matters. With the growth of the Zionist movement subsequent Congresses elected larger Greater Actions Committees.

When the expanded *Jewish Agency was established in 1929, it was at first decided that half the members of the Agency's Executive were to be members of the Zionist Executive; the other half were to be non-Zionists. However, this arrangement was short-lived owing to insufficient interest on the part of the non-Zionists, which resulted in a reduction of their representation in the Jewish Agency Executive. Beginning in 1931 the Executive was based on a coalition of the principal Zionist parties, a practice continued ever since.

After the 1936–39 *Arab riots, a new Inner AC was established as an intermediate body between the Executive and the Greater AC, in order to keep the representatives of the main Zionist parties in touch with the Executive. All its members resided in Palestine, and during World War II it served as a substitute for the General Council. The first Congress after the war (Basle, 1946), elected a Greater AC consisting of 77 members and 21 "virilists" (the Zionist term for individuals not representing a party but elected because of their own merits). Subsequently the number of members fluctuated. After the establishment of the State of Israel almost all the members of the Executive named to the Israeli Cabinet resigned from the Executive and were replaced by other representatives of the Zionist parties. The new constitution of the WZO adopted in January, 1960, provided that the Council (the Greater AC) consist of 96 members representing the parties proportionately and entitled to vote, to be elected by the Congress, as well as members serving in an advisory capacity only.

The 26th Congress (December, 1964–January, 1965) determined that the number of members in the Zionist General Council, belonging to Zionist parties, be 107; in addition, it elected 22 delegates-at-large. The Council holds at least one session a year. The 26th Congress also passed a resolution calling for election to the Executive of a number of prominent Zionists not affiliated with any one Zionist party and of one representative each of the Sephardi community (see SEPHARDIM) and the *Women's International Zionist Organization (WIZO).

I. KOLATT

EXILE. See DIASPORA; GALUT.

"EXODUS 1947." Ship bearing "illegal" immigrants (see ILLEGAL IMMIGRATION) to Palestine under *Hagana auspices in 1947. Originally named "President Warfield," the ship was purchased by Hagana emissary Z'ev (Danny) Shind for the transportation of immigrants. It was first intended for Eastern Europe but was sent instead to the French port of Sète on the Riviera. In the space of a week 4,553 Jews were brought to Sète from displaced-persons camps in Germany, 1,800 by two trains and the rest in trucks. Aid was obtained from French officials, who facilitated entry despite the doubtful validity of the South American visas held by some of the Jews or the lack of all proper documentation in the case of others. In spite of a transport workers' strike, French truck drivers allowed the convoy to pass. On July 10, 1947, the ship received its passengers. Capt. Yitzhak (Ike) Rabinowitz was in charge of the vessel and Yosef Harel (Hamburger) in charge of the refugees. Both men were Hagana (*Palmah, or commando) emissaries working with 'Aliya Bet (illegal immigration) in Europe under Shaul Avigur in Paris. The American chief officer was Bernard Marks, 24, of Cincinnati, Ohio. A British plane, violating French air space, discovered the ship. Pressure on the French authorities resulted in an order to detain the ship, which, however, sailed through the narrow harbor entrance without a pilot, after having run aground twice and freed itself under its own power. After the ship had left territorial waters, the cruiser H.M.S. "Ajax" and several British destroyers escorted it to Haifa.

On July 18, "Exodus 1947" was attacked and then boarded by the British. In the battle with the unarmed immigrants, who used weapons such as tin cans and sticks to prevent the boarding, three men—Mordecai Burstein, 23, a former Polish inmate of a displaced-persons camp in Germany; Hirsch Jakubovitz, a teen-age refugee from Poland; and William Bernstein, 23, a member of the U.S. Naval Reserve who was chief mate of the ship— were killed. The next day members of the *United Nations Special Committee on Palestine (UNSCOP) witnessed the transfer of the refugees to three British transports, which were to take the Jews back to Europe in accordance with a special decision made by Ernest *Bevin, the British Foreign Secretary, and against the advice of Sir Alan Gordon *Cunningham, the British *High Commissioner for Palestine. On July 29, the French

"Illegal" immigrants aboard the Hagana ship "Exodus 1947." [Zionist Archives]

authorities at Port-de-Bouc, though ready to accept those willing to land, refused to force the refugees to leave the ship. Only 130 sick people and pregnant women disembarked. The rest of the refugees, led by elected leaders from their midst, refused to land. After 24 days at Port-de-Bouc, the three British ships sailed for Hamburg, where they arrived on September 8 and 9. Two of the transports landed their refugee cargo without resistance, but the passengers of the third ship, under the leadership of Mordechai Rosmann, offered resistance. Demonstrations and protests all over the Jewish world found response in non-Jewish public opinion, objecting to the cruelty of forcing Jews back to Germany.

Of the refugees, 2,800 were sent to Poppendorf and 1,400 to Amstau, both in the British zone of Germany. Later, camps were established for them at Wilhelmshaven and Emden. In November, 1947, most of the inmates were smuggled south into the American zone. They were given priority in illegal transports, and by early 1948 most of the physically fit had reached either Palestine (with forged visas) or Cyprus (*see* CYPRUS, DETENTION CAMPS IN). The last of the "Exodus" refugees reached Palestine on Sept. 7, 1948.   Y. BAUER

EYAL. Village (kibbutz) in the Sharon Plain. Established in 1949 and affiliated with the *Kibbutz M'uhad.

EYTAN, WALTER. Israeli diplomat (b. Munich, 1910). Eytan studied at Oxford University, receiving a master's degree in 1934, and subsequently became a lecturer in literature there. Settling in Palestine in 1946, he was principal of the *Jewish Agency's Public Service College in Bet HaKerem, Jerusalem (1946–48), and Director General of the Israeli Ministry of Foreign Affairs (1948–59). In 1960 he was appointed Israeli Ambassador to France.

Eytan was head of the Israeli delegation to the armistice negotiations at Rhodes in 1949 (*see* ARMISTICE AGREEMENTS), and he represented Israel at the Lausanne Conference later that year and at the Atoms for Peace Conference in Geneva in 1955. He wrote *The First Ten Years: A Diplomatic History of Israel* (1958).

'EZER. Village center in the Ashk'lon area. Founded in 1966. Population (1968): 28.

EZRA, NISSIM. *See* CHINA, ZIONISM IN.

'EZUZ. Village (kibbutz) in the western Negev. Founded in 1956.

EZ-ZIB. *See* AKHZIV.

F

FAMILY IN ISRAEL. The contemporary Israeli family can trace its antecedents in part to the ancient Jewish culture of the Biblical and Talmudic periods. The detailed and all-embracing religious laws and regulations governing personal and family relationships (as later codified in the Shulhan 'Arukh) preserved a unity of basic structure, custom, and morality throughout the Jewish communities of the *Diaspora.

The pioneers who settled in Palestine in the early 1900s attempted to revolutionize the traditional pattern to a point where legal marriage ceremonies were frowned on in some of the early kibbutz settlements. With the passage of time and especially after the establishment of the State of Israel and the mass *immigration of traditional Middle Eastern Jews, however, certain aspects of traditional Jewish family life were strengthened. As in the period of the British *Mandate for Palestine (1917–48), so after independence jurisdiction in all matters of matrimony, divorce, and other issues pertaining to the rights and obligations of husband and wife remained in the hands of the rabbinical courts. While this state of affairs was accepted as natural by the Orthodox and by the newcomers from the Muslim orbit, it became a source of tension among those who favored the secularization of matters of personal status and particularly the abrogation of features of Jewish religious law which they regarded as anachronistic in a modern state, for example, the levirate ritual (Halitza), marriage prohibitions applicable to Kohanites (the descendants of Aaron), and the regulations pertinent to the remarriage of the 'Aguna (a woman whose husband is missing but has not been proved dead to the satisfaction of Jewish legal requirements).

Despite these time-honored regulations which determine the legal framework of the Israeli family, the structure and functioning of the family in modern Israel show many variations. These are the result of the ideological patterns of the pioneer immigrants prior to 1948 and the specific cultural matrices and historical experiences of the many ethnic groups that arrived in Israel after the founding of the State.

Although disparate in substance, both the religious laws based on tradition and the new secular laws associated with democratic processes have encouraged acculturation and the emer-gence of a new Israeli pattern. Notable illustrations of the latter group of laws are the Women's Equal Rights Law (1951), the laws establishing compulsory elementary education for boys and girls and compulsory army service for both sexes, and the legal prohibition of polygyny and child marriages, which were practiced in certain Jewish communities in Muslim countries.

Family types in the 1960s ranged from the Ashkenazi ultra-Orthodox religious family (*see* ASHKENAZIM) through the Middle Eastern patriarchal family, the democratic family of the Ashkenazi veteran pioneers, and the isolated nuclear family of European refugee origin to the unique family pattern typical of kibbutzim. However, all these types are in a process of change.

ULTRA-ORTHODOX FAMILIES IN CLOSED COMMUNITIES

Despite sharp differences in religiopolitical affiliations, such communities as Me'a Sh'arim, the religious enclave in B'ne B'rak, and Kiryat Sandz have in common a characteristic family pattern. From the point of view of their material traits (housing, furniture, use of modern means of transportation) these families may be regarded as variants of modern Israeli society, but their

A Polish family in Israel. [Zionist Archives]

313

A Bukharan family in Israel. [Israel Information Services]

family life is a direct survival of the Eastern European Jewish *shtetl* (small town).

The men are readily recognizable by their long black coats (*kapote,* or *halatin*), long side curls (*peyot*), and large round-brimmed black hats or fur-trimmed shtreimels. The women try to follow current fashions to some extent but preserve certain standards of modesty, such as full-length or three-quarter sleeves, high necklines, and longish hemlines. The head, which is often shaved after marriage, is always covered by a headkerchief or a wig (*sheitel*).

Marriages are arranged through intermediaries, with minimal contact between the prospective bride and groom prior to the wedding. Emotional factors such as attraction or romantic love are considered transient and hence not a suitable basis on which to build one's future. Early marriage is encouraged, for women because childbearing is considered their prime function and for men because it is felt that they can concentrate wholeheartedly on their religious studies only after their basic physical and material needs have been met within the sanctity of the home and in accordance with religious precepts.

Women do not receive a higher education; the most advanced study usually open to them is teacher training. Since the ultra-Orthodox woman has low expectations of companionship or romance, she is unlikely to be disappointed in her marriage. The culture in which she moves is a declared male-dominated one, and the role of the wife is prescribed by custom based on religious law so as to preserve the status quo without change. Her rewards are motherhood and the indirect, subtly conveyed approval of her husband if she maintains a smoothly functioning household with a large number of children. Her prestige depends primarily on her husband's status in the religious hierarchy or on his reputation as a Talmudic scholar. His status is in no way adversely affected by his living on financial grants (*see* HALUKKA) so that he can devote all his time to study. A larger grant adds to the wife's prestige among her women friends because it enables her to live on a higher material standard.

Children are extremely important in the ultra-Orthodox family because of the religious significance of progeny and the fact that child care is the dominant activity and sphere of influence of the women. Pregnancy soon after marriage is considered ideal, and infants are expected to be breast-fed. Under Israeli law children of both sexes must attend school until the age of 14 and follow a standard curriculum of study. But in the ultra-Orthodox community primary stress is put on religious instruction beyond that offered by government-run religiously oriented public schools. In the schools maintained by these communities the sexes are strictly segregated and given different types of religious instruction. The high schools for boys are on the Yeshiva pattern (*see* YESHIVOT IN ISRAEL), some of them including vocational training or courses for the State graduation examination. The children dress like the adults of their community and have no contact with children outside their circle.

Social activities are always linked with religious ritual and, except on strictly family occasions, the sexes stay apart. Sports, the radio, motion pictures, and secular literature are regarded as demoralizing influences and hence are forbidden.

The ethnic composition of these communities includes third- and fourth-generation Israeli-born families of Eastern and Central European descent and immigrants, particularly from Poland and Hungary. At least several hundred individuals have either been born in the United States or lived there for some time.

It seems that this type of family structure is capable of functioning with little strain provided the members keep strictly to their own kind. Tensions, particularly intergeneration ones, erupt when families of this type attempt to live as part of the mainstream of contemporary Israeli society and to adhere at the same time to the community's own unbending code of behavior.

TRADITIONAL JEWISH FAMILIES FROM THE MUSLIM WORLD

Immigrants from Asia and North Africa increased the representation of Middle Eastern Jews in Israel's population from about 15 per cent in 1948 to more than 50 per cent in 1967. Whereas all these so-called Oriental communities shared a certain similarity of family structure and functioning, differential exposure to Westernization prior to their coming to Israel had already begun to effect some changes.

Another factor influencing the rate and type of change in their family structure was their mode of immigration to Israel. The wholesale evacuation of the Jewish communities of Iraq, Kurdistan, Yemen, and Libya brought entire families intact to Israel. Immigration from Morocco, Iran, and Turkey, on the other hand, was intermittent and consisted not only of extended families but also of parts of families and single adult males.

The traditional Middle Eastern Jewish family, like its Muslim counterpart, was extended, endogamous, patriarchal, patrilineal, patrilocal, and occasionally polygynous. Oriented toward the past, it stressed the desirability of a large number of children. Women married at a very early age. There was a distinct dichotomy between the male and female roles, with strong emphasis on premarital chastity for women, which led to restrictions on the movements and functioning of women in the general community.

The typical Middle Eastern extended family included the father and mother, unmarried sons and daughters, and married sons with their wives and children. The outstanding feature of this traditional type of family structure was the emphasis on family loyalty and interdependence. The individual was related to society as a member of a family in which he submerged his private ambitions. His reward was emotional security coupled with certainty of the family's protection and support at all times. The role and status of each member was defined in strict detail. Higher status and authority went to the males, particularly the head of the household and the eldest son. Females had a lower status but gained a measure of indirect power through motherhood. Marriages were arranged, the main factor determining suitability of marriage partners being family status, which, in turn, depended on wealth, education, and moral reputation. The bride's beauty and modesty were also valued. Marriages between cousins or other close relatives were preferred because they further consolidated family ties. The household functioned as an economic unit. Leisure-time activities were family-centered, and frequent family gatherings on Sabbaths, holidays, and ritual occasions formed the content of social life.

In Israel this traditional family pattern was exposed to the dominant ideal of the egalitarian family, which held out the promise of freedom of expression and individual advancement. Objective conditions, such as government-sponsored housing projects designed for the nuclear family, accelerated the breakdown of the extended family. In the 1960s the evolving patterns were far from clear-cut, but certain general trends, as well as particular ones along ethnic lines, could be noted.

The Moroccan family was fast moving toward modernity. Tensions eased because most parents encouraged not only their sons but also their daughters to learn new trades and were tolerant about religious observance. However, individual immigrants from Morocco who had come to Israel without their families experienced considerable difficulty in adjustment, a circumstance that resulted in certain types of asocial behavior (see CRIME IN ISRAEL; ETHNIC GROUPS AND PROBLEMS IN ISRAEL).

Within the community of *Yemenite Jews, traditional family patterns persisted to a greater extent, particularly among those who settled in cooperative smallholders' villages (see MOSHAV). However, conflicts tended to arise when the rate of acculturation within a family was uneven. If the head of the household failed to make an adequate vocational adjustment in Israel, his wife would frequently have to accept employment in domestic service, thus hastening her own adaptation to modern life but also accentuating the husband's loss of prestige. An additional problem for the father was his inability to fulfill in Israel his traditional role of supervising the education of his sons, because he lacked knowledge of the secular subjects taught at modern Israeli schools.

A marked change in the traditional Middle Eastern family in Israel was brought about by the opportunity given daughters to obtain an education and hence greater independence, mobility, and increased freedom of choice in the selection of a marriage partner. Army service also contributed its share to the emancipation of the Oriental Jewish girl, as did the spreading practice of family planning. The number of sons following the occupations of their fathers declined considerably, while the rate of intermarriage between Oriental and Ashkenazi Jews increased.

By and large, the low-earning unskilled or semiskilled occupations were filled by this section of the Israeli community. Forty-five per cent of the mothers were illiterate. The low educational level of the Oriental parent generation was a serious handicap for their children, many of whom were disappointed with their parents since, unlike Ashkenazi parents, they could not help them in their future careers.

To some extent, the community of *Iraqi Jews was an exception. A relatively higher percentage of both males and females in this group had received a modern education and professional training in Iraq prior to their arrival in Israel.

ASHKENAZI OLD-ESTABLISHED FAMILY IN URBAN AND SEMIRURAL AREAS

The patterns of families of this type differed before and after the establishment of the State.

Pre-State Ashkenazi Family (1882–1948). From 1882 to 1904 the immigrant groups were composed largely of families. From 1904 to 1924, however, the pioneering movement was typified by peer groups of young unattached adults who formed their family ties in Palestine, thus giving rise to the indigenous phenomenon of independent nuclear families closely linked to the political and underground liberation movements of the time.

These organizations, which were built on strong ties of loyalty, comradeship, and solidarity, served as substitutes for the extended-kinship-group relationships typical of the parent generation in Eastern Europe.

The Zionist and particularly the Socialist ideologies of the period gave expression to a rebellion against the traditional Eastern European *shtetl* way of life, which the younger generation considered oppressive. Especially the intense emotional ties which encouraged lasting interdependencies of family members, each with his own ascribed role and status, had come to be felt as burdensome rather than supportive.

In Palestine traditional patterns were deliberately cast aside. New roles were assumed by both men and women, resulting in changed relationships between husband and wife and between parents and children. Men and women worked side by side at manual tasks. Children were encouraged to be physically tough and emotionally independent. Their major social activities, like those of their parents, took place outside the home, within peer-group youth movements. Family relationships tended to be egalitarian, and the younger generation had freedom in the choice of a marriage partner.

The home was no longer the fortress in the traditional sense, and the needs of the conjugal family often had to be subordinated to national aims. Academic pursuits, religious observance, and economic success with their accompanying social manifestations did not command particular respect. The moral value of simple, austere living was stressed, and the ideal adult male figure was the pioneer who devoted himself to the upbuilding of the Jewish Homeland.

Post-State Ashkenazi Family (after 1948). The establishment of the State of Israel with its network of government institutions replacing voluntary pioneer organizations, and the sudden growth of population due to mass *'Aliya (immigration), which was followed by rapid industrial expansion and urbanization, had a marked effect on the family patterns of the old-established Ashkenazi family. With the passing of time, this nuclear family had become two- or even three-generational. Although married children set up independent households, strong ties based on mutual support, financial as well as emotional, were maintained between the generations. There seemed to be a definite trend, led by the second generation, toward more family-centered activities. Friendship patterns also changed, with cultural, occupational, and neighborhood ties replacing politicoideological identifications.

The pre-State stress on the moral value of simplicity gave way to a growing desire for a higher standard of living. Most striking, however, was the changed attitude toward academic studies and achievements. Relegated to the background during the pioneering period, these accomplishments were now encouraged by parents. Many who had dedicated their youth and early manhood to the struggle for a Jewish State returned to school in their middle years. There is continuity, however, in that the old pattern of pioneering has taken on the new form of volunteering for the most dangerous defense tasks whenever deemed necessary.

ISOLATED FAMILY OF POST-WORLD WAR II EUROPEAN REFUGEES

Between 1948 and 1953 Israel received a total of 340,000 immigrants from Europe who had suffered in one way or another from Nazi persecution. More than half of them had been subjected to direct and prolonged hardship in concentration camps, slave labor gangs, or ghettos. Many had spent the war years in constant flight or in hiding in forests or bunkers. These immigrants were survivors—in some cases, the sole survivors—of families truncated by deportation. Once in Israel, they showed an overriding desire to rebuild their personal lives within reconstituted nuclear families and to acquire some material comforts after the years of deprivation they had suffered.

Their emphasis on the welfare and material aspirations of the small nuclear family led to a general dissociation from the values of communal and pioneering endeavors. At the same time there was a revival of the traditional Eastern European attitude of respect for book learning, particularly among adults whose own studies had been cut short by the war. These parents made enormous sacrifices, taking on extra hours of work, to finance the higher education of their children.

Intense preoccupation with the advancement of the family unit, together with the therapeutic effects of human dignity regained in Israel. was a primary factor contributing to the satisfactory functioning of these families despite their traumatic past. Nevertheless, 20 years after the war there were still evidences of mental-health problems in survivor families, a marked feature being overanxiety about the health and future of the children. A special variant of parent-child conflict became evident between the survivors of the Nazi holocaust and their *Sabra children, who frequently rejected the image of their parents as helpless victims of the Nazis and exaggerated their self-image as "strong, independent Sabras."

Among the holocaust survivors were some 50,000 orphaned children who had been brought to Israel under the auspices of *Youth 'Aliya between 1945 and 1951. By the mid-1960s the large majority of these had married. Their family and social life was far less isolated than that of the adult survivors. They maintained friendships with other members of the Israeli youth groups in which they had been educated and also married into Israeli families. Some remained in the kibbutzim where they had been sent on their arrival in Israel.

KIBBUTZ FAMILY

The kibbutz family expresses the very quintessence of the moral, social, and economic values implicit in the ideologies of the pioneering era. The kibbutz family of the 1960s can be defined as an institutional couple relationship sanctioned by the State, the law, and ceremony, emphasizing love, affection, and emotional security, in which the socialization of the child and economic cooperation between spouses are minimized.

The communal basis of the kibbutz society made possible the realization of new forms of family structure and interpersonal relationships. The ideal pattern was nonexploitative companionship and a love-oriented marriage relationship. Its implementation was facilitated by a shared economy, equality between the sexes, and communal housekeeping services such as kitchen, dining, and laundry facilities. Husband and wife shared living quarters, but the children lived apart from their parents with their own age groups in the children's quarters, where they were cared for by kibbutz members assigned for this purpose. In a small number of kibbutzim the children shared their parents' quarters, but there, too, they were cared for by other kibbutz members during their parents' working hours. The children joined their parents at the close of the working day and remained with them until bedtime. Relieved of all other domestic chores, the parents were free to devote their entire attention to their children during those hours.

In the 1960s the kibbutz methods of socialization of children were the subject of controversy both inside and outside the kibbutz. Numerous studies are available on the subject, but none yields evidence of any attenuation of affective parent-child relationships.

The kibbutz family has been affected by changing life-styles in Israeli society. It has become more individualized, and the role of the children's houses and the use of communal facilities for leisure-time activities are gradually declining, with the parents' room becoming the focal point for these recreational pursuits.

With their formal equality fully ensured by the social structure, the women of the kibbutz in the 1960s tended to revert to the traditional "feminine" occupations, such as child care, education, and service branches, and to devote their free time to homemaking activities for their own individual families.

The younger kibbutz generation of both sexes showed an increasing interest in academic studies and professional opportunities. When individual aspirations clashed with communal considerations, tension arose.

Like the old-established urban family, the original nuclear kibbutz family has also widened. The kibbutz is one of the few areas of modern society where two or three generations of families are often concentrated in one close-knit community, with special provisions for aged parents who have come to Israel to join their children.

FAMILY AMONG THE RELIGIOUS MINORITIES

Muslim *Arabs form about 70 per cent of this group: 20 per cent are Christian Arabs, and the rest Druzes (see DRUZE COMMUNITY IN ISRAEL). The *War of Independence and the establishment of the State of Israel brought about considerable change within the Muslim Arab community. After an initial period of disorientation, however, the patterns reconstituted themselves basically along traditional lines, with modernization becoming evident but still peripheral.

In the 1960s the most important aspects of the individual's life were still carried on within, and were determined by, the extended family. Some 90 per cent of this group lived in villages, where the patriarchal head of the family still wielded decisive authority. He was the owner of the family's property, land, and labor. Although polygyny was prohibited by Israeli law, marriages took place in accordance with traditional and religious precepts and came under the jurisdiction of the Muslim religious courts. The parents chose brides for their sons according to a standard scale of preference. Cousins were considered the most desirable, next came members of the same clan, and then girls from the same village. Girls not meeting these qualifications were last in the scale. Since the bride price paid by the father of the groom to the father of the bride was extremely high, the sons had to wait their turn. Of the small group of young men who entered the modern professions, some married women of their own choice. By this display of independence they gained the admiration of their educated contemporaries but forfeited their status within their traditional community. Such defiant behavior was considered dangerous because of the extensive code of rules and customs associated with maidenly virtue. A man attempting to flirt with a girl could be assaulted by her brothers or cousins, and elopement or adulterous behavior could lead to the killing of the girl and the young man.

New phenomena in the Arab community were the joining of the urban labor force by men and the rising level of formal education for girls. However, the traditional family sanctioned by Muslim law and custom and linked to land tenure remained intact, its viability demonstrated by the low divorce rate and by the fact that the Muslim rate of natural increase in the 1960s was one of the highest in the world.

RECAPITULATION AND OUTLOOK

The features common to the ultra-Orthodox family, the traditional Jewish family from the Muslim orbit, and the family of religious minority groups were relatively early marriage (in the early 1960s the median age in these groups was about 25 years for grooms and about 21 years for brides), a large number of children (about four to six per couple among the ultra-Orthodox Ashkenazim and the Oriental Jews and more among the Arabs), and a relatively low rate of divorce (about 0.4 per 1,000 among the Oriental Jews and Arabs). In contrast, the Ashkenazi old-established family, the isolated family of the post-holocaust European refugees, and the kibbutz family were characterized by relatively late marriage (in 1962 the median age in these groups was 27.2 years for grooms and 24.6 years for brides), a small number of children (about two per married couple), and a relatively high rate of divorce.

In the 1960s a perceptible trend toward greater homogeneity was evinced by the various family types. There was a slow but steady increase in intermarriage between European (Ashkenazi) and Middle Eastern Jews. There also were indications that improvements in educational and economic standards would bring a decrease in the number of children born to Oriental Jewish couples. The kibbutz family showed a tendency toward more conventional development, while the Oriental Jewish family tended to assimilate to the European pattern.

P. PALGI

FARBAND (Labor Zionist Fraternal Order). American Zionist educational and mutual-benefit organization formed at a convention held in Rochester, N.Y., in 1912, after the ground had been laid in 1908. Among its first leaders were Samuel Bonchek, Mayer L. Brown, and David *Pinski.

It applied for and received its charter from the Insurance Department of New York State in 1913. The organization, which was then known as the Jewish National Workers Alliance (it received its present name in 1950), set itself a twofold purpose. It sought to provide its members with the benefits and services usually offered by the more advanced American Jewish fraternal bodies. At the same time, oriented as it was toward a Labor Zionist philosophy, it aimed to participate in movements seeking to enhance the status of the Jewish people, to build the Jewish National Home and a labor society in Palestine, and to strengthen and democratize Jewish group life in the United States and Canada. Starting out with a few hundred members, the Farband grew to a body of 40,000 members by the end of 1969, with $22,000,000 worth of insurance in force and nearly $8,000,000 in assets. It supplied its membership with modern life insurance, health and death benefits, and social services.

In the area of community concern, the Farband contributed to Jewish endeavors in Israel, to the rise and development of the State of Israel in general and to the labor sector in particular. It pioneered in establishing Yiddish schools in the United States and Canada and in the founding of the Jewish Teachers Seminary. Its cultural activities included adult education courses, choral societies, dramatic clubs, and lecture forums, and it published pamphlets and books in Yiddish, Hebrew, and

English. The Farband participated in the formation of the People's Relief Committee during World War I, and it founded the Labor Zionist Committee for Relief and Rehabilitation during the Nazi period and World War II. It also had a share in the founding of the *American Jewish Congress in 1918 and of the *American Jewish Conference in 1944, and was active in the struggle for civil rights and in other liberal causes in the United States and Canada. Its national secretary for 40 years was Louis *Segal. In 1969 Samuel Bonchek was president and Jacob Katzman national secretary.

C. B. SHERMAN

FARBSTEIN, DAVID ZVI. Jurist, veteran Zionist, and political leader (b. Warsaw, 1868; d. Zurich, 1953). Educated in Switzerland, Farbstein was one of the earliest pioneers of Zionism in that country and helped Herzl organize the 1st Zionist *Congress (1897), to which he reported on the economic situation of world Jewry. He was also active in political life and was elected to the Swiss National Council as a leader of the Social Democratic party. At the same time he was active in Jewish communal affairs.

In 1937 Farbstein delivered an address at the 40th jubilee assembly held in Basle in commemoration of the 1st Zionist Congress. He was the author of many papers on jurisprudence as well as Zionism. His German pamphlet *Der Zionismus und die Judenfrage, ökonomisch und ethisch* (Zionism and the Jewish Problem, from the Economic and Ethical Viewpoints) was published in 1898.

FARBSTEIN, Y'HOSHU'A HESHEL. *Mizrahi leader (b. Warsaw, 1870; d. Jerusalem, 1948). Farbstein joined the *Hoveve Zion movement and became an early adherent of political Zionism. He attended the 1st Zionist *Congress in 1897 and almost all subsequent Congresses. Deeply involved in Zionist and Polish-Jewish activities, he was a prominent leader of the Mizrahi movement. He served as president of the Polish Mizrahi (1918–31) and of the Warsaw Jewish Community (1926–31) and as chairman of the Association of Jewish Merchants in Poland. He was also a member of the Warsaw Municipal Council (1916–26) and a deputy to the Polish Sejm (1919–30).

Farbstein served as deputy president of the Zionist Greater *Actions Committee and for many years was a member of the Central Committee of the Mizrahi World Movement. Following his election to the Zionist *Executive, he settled in Jerusalem in 1931 and headed the Department of Trade and Industry for two years. Later he was for several years president of the Jerusalem Jewish Community and in 1945 was elected honorary president.

FARMERS' FEDERATION OF ISRAEL. See HITAHDUT HAIKKARIM.

FASHIONS IN ISRAEL. See CLOTHING IN ISRAEL.

FASTLICHT, ADOLFO. Zionist leader in Mexico (b. Przemyśl, Galicia, Austria, 1905; d. Mexico City, 1964). He was president of the Zionist Federation and of the *B'nai B'rith in Mexico and served as the first honorary Israeli Consul in that country. Fastlicht was the organizer and vice-president of the Instituto México-Israel and the cofounder and honorary president of the Mexico-Israel Chamber of Commerce. He was also a delegate to the 24th Zionist *Congress (1956) and

a member of the Board of Governors of the *Hebrew University of Jerusalem.

E. WEINFELD

FASUTA. Arab village in the 'Akko area. Population (1968): 1,430.

FAUNA OF ISRAEL. See ANIMAL LIFE IN ISRAEL.

FAYSAL I. See FEISAL I.

FEDAYEEN (Fedayin). Arab squads organized by Colonel Nasser in 1954 as a guerrilla force of 1,000 men, active in Israel in 1955 and 1956. The name means "self-sacrificers." Trained in the Gaza Strip, then under Egyptian control, the fedayeen made frequent nocturnal incursions into Israel, killing, stealing, and destroying. Following the *Sinai Campaign of October, 1956, the stationing of the UN Emergency Force along the border between Israel and Egypt (including the Gaza Strip) put an end to these fedayeen incursions. From the late 1960s on, the anti-Israel terrorist activities were expanded and taken over by other organizations. See TERRORIST ORGANIZATIONS, ARAB.

FEDERATION OF AMERICAN ZIONISTS. See ZIONIST ORGANIZATION OF AMERICA.

FEIGENBAUM, ARYE. Ophthalmologist and founder of the first Hebrew-speaking association of physicians in Palestine (b. Lvov, Galicia, Austria, 1885). He received a traditional education and studied at the University of Lvov and in Germany. In 1913 he became head of the ophthalmological department of the Nathan and Lina Straus Health Center in Jerusalem and inaugurated a campaign against trachoma. In 1922 he assumed the directorship of the department of ophthalmology at the Hadassah-University Hospital in Jerusalem, serving in that post until his retirement in 1959. He also lectured at the Henrietta Szold–Hadassah School of Nursing and was a professor of ophthalmology in the Medical School of the *Hebrew University of Jerusalem. In 1913 Feigenbaum helped found the first Hebrew-speaking association of physicians in Jerusalem. He was also the founder and chairman of the Palestine (Israel) Ophthalmological Society, and he wrote an ophthalmology textbook and edited several medical journals.

FEISAL (FAYSAL) I. King of Iraq (b. Taif, Hejaz, 1885; d. Bern, Switzerland, 1933). Feisal was the third son of Husayn ibn 'Ali, Sherif of Mecca and later King of the Hejaz, and the younger brother of 'Abdullah, King of *Transjordan. During World War I he commanded Arab Bedouin tribesmen who harassed the Turkish troops in the Arabian Desert. In June, 1918, Gen. Edmund H. H. *Allenby suggested to Chaim *Weizmann, who was then in Palestine with the *Zionist Commission, that the Commission approach Feisal for at least a tentative agreement on the Zionist program. As commander in chief of the Arab Army, Feisal had great influence not only in Arabia but also with the British authorities. Accordingly, Weizmann met Feisal near 'Aqaba, and Feisal agreed to foster friendly relations between Jews and Arabs and to cooperate at the postwar peace conference. Further discussions and negotiations took place between Feisal and Weizmann and other Zionist leaders, and they agreed on close collaboration.

In January, 1919, Feisal signed with Weizmann the so-called

Feisal-Weizmann Agreement. The agreement opened by stressing the racial relatedness and the ancient ties between the Arab and Jewish peoples, and emphasized that the best way to achieve their national goals was through close cooperation in developing the Arab State and Palestine. Paragraph 2 stated that, following the peace conference, a commission authorized by both sides would determine the final borders between Palestine and the Arab State. Paragraph 3 provided that "in the establishment of the Constitution and Administration of Palestine all such measures shall be adopted as will afford the fullest guarantees for carrying into effect" the *Balfour Declaration. Paragraph 4 stated that "all necessary measures shall be taken to encourage and stimulate the large-scale immigration of Jews into Palestine, and as quickly as possible to settle Jewish immigrants upon the land through closer settlement and intensive cultivation of the soil. In taking such measures, Arab peasants and tenant farmers shall be protected in their rights, and shall be assisted in forwarding their economic development." Paragraph 5 provided that all inhabitants of the country would enjoy equal rights and freedom of religion. Paragraph 6 stated that places holy to Muslims would remain under Muslim supervision. According to paragraph 7, the economic commission that the Zionist Organization planned to send to Palestine to study the country's economic possibilities would·be placed at the disposal also of the Arab State, and the *World Zionist Organization would help the Arab State financially to develop its natural resources and economic possibilities. Paragraph 8 stipulated that both sides were to act in full harmony at the peace conference on matters contained in the agreement. The final paragraph (9) provided that differences of opinion between the two parties would be submitted for adjudication to the British government. Feisal added a condition to the effect that he would be bound by the agreement only if the Arabs were to obtain the independence he had requested in a memorandum to the British Foreign Secretary. If changes occurred, he would not be bound by the agreement.

On Mar. 1, 1919, the French newspaper *Matin* published an interview with Feisal in which he revealed an anti-Zionist attitude. His secretary, however, promptly disavowed the interview. A meeting was arranged between Feisal, who was the leader of the Hejaz delegation to the Paris Peace Conference, and Felix *Frankfurter, who was a member of the Zionist delegation (see COMITÉ DES DÉLÉGATIONS JUIVES). On March 3, Feisal wrote a letter to Frankfurter, stating in part:

> We Arabs, especially the educated among us, look with the deepest sympathy on the Zionist movement. Our deputation here in Paris is fully acquainted with the proposals submitted by the Zionist Organization to the Peace Conference and we regard them as moderate and proper. We will do our best, insofar as we are concerned, to help them through: we will wish the Jews a most hearty welcome home.

The letter concluded:

> I look forward, and my people with me look forward, to a future in which we will help you and you will help us, so that the countries in which we are mutually interested may once again take their place in the community of civilized peoples of the world.

In May, 1919, Feisal returned to Syria. He convened an All-Syrian Congress, which opened in June. On July 2, the congress declared in a statement to the American (King-Crane) Commission of Inquiry (see KING-CRANE REPORT) its demand for an Arab Syria extending from the Taurus Mountains in the north to 'Aqaba in the south and its opposition to the "pretensions of the Zionists" and to "Zionist migration to any part of our country." In an appearance before the Commission, Feisal echoed the spirit of this statement.

In the fall of 1919 Feisal was in London. On October 3, the *Jewish Chronicle* published an interview in which he was quoted as considering Palestine an integral part of Syria and warning of the danger of Jewish-Arab clashes in Palestine because of Zionist extremist designs to establish a Jewish State there. In a subsequent meeting with Sir Herbert *Samuel and Zionist leaders, Feisal claimed that he had been misunderstood by the interviewer and reiterated his readiness to cooperate with the Zionists.

In March, 1920, the All-Syrian Congress proclaimed Feisal King of United Syria (i.e., Syria and Palestine). On July 25 of that year, however, Damascus was occupied by the French and Feisal took flight. Passing through Haifa, he met with Montague David *Eder, the chairman of the Zionist Commission. Feisal requested the diplomatic assistance of the Zionist Organization, which Eder could not promise him, for the Organization could not afford to become involved in a conflict with the French because of Feisal. After a year of exile in London, Feisal became King of Iraq, occupying the throne until his death. During this period he no longer took an active part in Palestine affairs.

T. PRESCHEL

FEISAL-WEIZMANN AGREEMENT. *See* FEISAL I.

FEIWEL, BERTHOLD. Writer and Zionist leader (b. Pohořelice, Moravia, Austria, 1875; d. Jerusalem, 1937). Feiwel was one of the first men to convey to the assimilated Western public the tenderness and intimacy of Eastern European folklore and religiosity and to translate Yiddish poetry into German. Having attended, as a young man, the 1st Zionist *Congress (1897), he became convinced that Zionism required not only political activity and organization but also a strengthening of popular feeling, closeness to the masses with their immediate needs, and cultural effort. As a man of considerable literary talent he was called to join the editorial staff of *Die *Welt*, but at the 5th Congress (1901) he was one of the founders of the opposition *Democratic Faction, together with Chaim *Weizmann, Leo *Motzkin, Martin *Buber, and others.

Later Feiwel was one of the founders of the German-Jewish publishing house Jüdischer Verlag in Berlin (1902), where the first books of the so-called Jewish Renaissance in the West appeared under his editorship. Among these were the *Jüdischer Almanach* and *Junge Harfen* (Young Harps, 1902–08), which contained also poetry written by Feiwel himself. A strong impression was made by his translation of the mediocre Yiddish poetry of Morris Rosenfeld.

Feiwel subsequently entered a banking business and spent World War I in Switzerland. From there he moved to London, where he joined Weizmann's circle of policy makers in the crucial years after the war. For some time he played an important role in the Zionist leadership in London, and was Weizmann's literary adviser. From 1919 to 1926 Feiwel was executive director of *Keren HaYesod (Palestine Foundation Fund). Because of prolonged illness he later retired and spent his last years in Palestine.

R. WELTSCH

FELDMAN, ABRAHAM. Physician and Zionist worker in Peru (b. Romania, 1925). In 1938 he emigrated to Peru, where he became president of the local Maccabi organization, *B'rit Trumpeldor (Betar, 1939), and *Revisionists (1945). From 1953 to 1955 he was in charge of *Jewish National Fund activities and youth work, and from 1958 to 1960 he served as president of the Zionist Organization of Peru. Feldman, a professor of medicine at the University of Lima, was also chairman of the Board of Directors of the León Pinelo Jewish Day School.

Y. I. HASSON

FELLAH (plural, Fellahin). Arabic term denoting a man who derives his livelihood from agricultural work regardless of whether he owns land. The Arabic term for land cultivated by the fellah is *falha.* Both terms are used in Israel today: *fellah* for any Arab villager and *falha* for extensively cultivated unirrigated field crops.

FELSENTHAL, BERNHARD. Rabbi, author, and early Zionist in the United States (b. Münchweiler, Bavarian Palatinate, Germany, 1822; d. Chicago, 1908). Felsenthal settled in the United States in 1854, served in several Reform congregations, and was a founder of the Jewish Publication Society of America (1888) and of the American Jewish Historical Society (1892). He became a Zionist before the advent of Herzl. In the early 1890s, he wrote articles about Jewish settlement efforts in Palestine. "The Palestine Memorial" (*Reform Advocate,* Mar. 20, 1891) dealt with a petition ("What shall be done for the Russian Jews?"), of which he had been a signer and which had been presented to Pres. Benjamin Harrison, asking for an international conference to consider the return of Palestine to the Jews. In a Hebrew article published in *HaPisga* (Nov. 6, 1891), Felsenthal discussed the future of *Hebrew as a living language. In "The Palestine Question" (*Jewish Voice,* Apr. 14, 1893), he opposed Jewish settlement efforts in Argentina at the expense of similar endeavors in Palestine.

Felsenthal denied that there was any incompatibility between Zionism and Reform Judaism (*see* ANTI-ZIONISM; REFORM JUDAISM AND ZIONISM). Though an adherent of the Reform Jewish "mission of Israel" theory, he held that a model Jewish State in Palestine would be a much more efficacious force for good among men than many millions of unorganized individuals scattered all over the world. He was active in early Zionist efforts in Chicago and was honorary vice-president of the Federation of American Zionists (*see* ZIONIST ORGANIZATION OF AMERICA) from 1903 until his death. Selections from his writings and a biographical sketch were published by his daughter, Emma Felsenthal, under the title *Bernhard Felsenthal, Teacher in Israel* (1924).

FEUERRING, ISAAK. Banker and Zionist leader (b. Zborov, Galicia, Austria, 1889; d. Jerusalem, 1937). Educated in Germany, Feuerring in 1912 became one of the founders of the Herzl Bund, a German Zionist movement of young businessmen. An active member of the Executive of the Zionist Organization of Germany, he was a delegate to several Zionist Congresses (*see* CONGRESS, ZIONIST) and served as both chairman and co-chairman of their Budget and Finance Committees. As a General Zionist (*see* GENERAL ZIONISM), he favored the encouragement of individual initiative and private investment.

Feuerring headed an international organization dealing in minerals and owned a pyrite mine in Norway. In 1934 he left Berlin to settle in Palestine, where he founded the General Commercial Bank, which later became the Feuchtwanger Bank. Part of his estate was used to found Bet Yitzhak, a middle-class agricultural settlement of Jews from Central Europe.

FEUERSTEIN, AVIGDOR. *See* HAMEIRI, AVIGDOR.

FICHMAN, YA'AKOV. Hebrew poet and critic (b. Beltsy, Bessarabia, Russia, 1881; d. Tel Aviv, 1958). Until 1912 he lived in various cities of Russia and, under the influence of Hayim Nahman *Bialik, wrote sensitive lyric poetry. As a literary critic he became known for his delicate style and his intimate reflections on the lives and works of the authors with whom he dealt. In 1912 he settled in Palestine. From 1914 to 1919 and again from 1922 to 1925 he was in Europe, participating in various literary enterprises. In Palestine, where he served as editor of the literary magazines *Moledet, Ma'abarot,* and *Moznayim,* he became a most influential literary figure.

In his Palestinian poetry, particularly in the book *P'at Sade* (Corner of the Field, 1945), Fichman depicts in a tranquil vein the scenic beauty of the country. In addition to books of essays on the masters of Hebrew and world prose and poetry, he wrote several textbooks on Hebrew literature.

H. LEAF

FIFTH 'ALIYA. Wave of Jewish *immigration that reached Palestine between 1929 and 1936 (according to some authorities, 1939). During this period a total of 188,000 Jews entered Palestine legally. More than 12,000 others immigrated "illegally," that is, without official permission or with tourist permits (*see* ILLEGAL IMMIGRATION). The Jewish population of Palestine grew from 160,000 to 400,000, increasing the percentage of Jews within the total population of the country from 17.7 to 30.6.

The Fifth 'Aliya began with the economic recovery that followed the depression of 1927–28 (*see* FOURTH 'ALIYA). Between 1929 and 1931 there were only 14,300 immigrants, and there were 4,100 emigrants. A large proportion of the immigrants came from the ranks of the pioneer youth movements; only 12 per cent came with "capitalist" certificates. In 1932 and 1933 the character of the 'Aliya began to change because of the worsening of the worldwide economic crisis, the tightening of immigration restrictions in countries throughout the world, and Hitler's rise to power in January, 1933—developments that were accompanied by increasing economic and governmental pressures on Jews throughout Eastern and Central Europe and by a sharp rise in *anti-Semitism. Between 1933 and 1936, 164,000 Jews arrived in Palestine as legal immigrants; emigration practically ceased. The percentage of immigrants arriving with capitalist certificates rose to 25. Of the immigrants, 24,000 were citizens of Germany; this figure does not include the many Jews with Polish and Lithuanian papers or the "stateless" individuals who left Germany for Palestine.

The Fifth 'Aliya brought a large volume of capital into Palestine; between 1932 and 1936, £P33,500,000 was transferred to the country, as compared with £P3,600,000 brought in by various fund-raising organizations. About half the money was invested in construction, £P7,000,000 in industry, and £P6,000,000 in agriculture, particularly citriculture (*see* CITRUS INDUSTRY IN ISRAEL). Citrus exports rose from 2.5 million crates in 1931 to 6 million in 1936 and to 15.3 million late in 1939.

The immigration of German Jews left its mark on the Fifth

'Aliya both quantitatively and qualitatively. The 18th Zionist *Congress (Prague, 1933) set up a central office for the settlement of German-Jewish immigrants in Palestine. An agreement was reached between the *Jewish Agency and the German government with regard to the transfer of funds belonging to Jews emigrating to Palestine (see HA'AVARA). In February, 1934, the first group of young people to be brought out of Germany by *Youth 'Aliya arrived in the country.

Mainly urban in character, the Fifth 'Aliya led to a phenomenal growth in the population of Palestine's cities. The population of Tel Aviv tripled, to 150,000, and the city expanded. The Jewish population of Haifa reached 50,000; the modern port of Haifa was opened late in 1933. Jerusalem's Jewish population increased by 50 per cent, to 76,000, and the Rehavia section of the city was expanded.

Urban expansion brought industrial development, for which the skills and the capital brought by the Fifth 'Aliya were primarily responsible. The number of workers employed in industry tripled, reaching 30,000. Production of electricity rose from 9 million kilowatt-hours in 1931 to 66 million (of which 19 million were for industrial use) in 1936. This period, too, saw the establishment and growth of Palestine Potash, Ltd. (see DEAD SEA WORKS COMPANY, LTD.), which brought about 1,000 Jewish workers to the Dead Sea and the desert region. The development of industry and its role in immigrant absorption helped change previously held Zionist concepts of settlement methods and of Palestine's absorptive capacity.

By contrast, the development of the agricultural sector lagged during the Fifth 'Aliya. Settlement was concentrated in the coastal plain and in the Sharon, which became areas with a Jewish majority. In these areas German immigrants established a new type of smallholders' settlement, engaging in intensive cultivation, poultry farming, and so on. Efforts were focused also on the rehabilitation of settlements hit by the *Arab riots in 1929 (B'er Tovya, Motza, Hulda, and Ramat Rahel) and on the Thousand Families Settlement Plan, a large-scale project for the settlement of workers in kibbutzim and moshavim and their employment in the orange groves of nearby settlements. A planned, comprehensive program to settle the Hefer Valley in the heart of the Sharon area was also begun. The large influx of immigrants and capital was not utilized for the penetration of remote areas of the country.

With the Fifth 'Aliya, the Zionist movement and migration to Palestine became central factors in the life of the Jewish people the world over, with Palestine providing a haven for Jewish victims of economic and political oppression in Eastern and Central Europe. During that period Palestine absorbed most of the Jewish migration; in 1935 more than 80 per cent of Jewish migrants settled in Palestine. As a result, the status of the Jewish community of Palestine underwent a striking change. While Jews still made up only one-third of Palestine's total population, they became a dominant factor in the country in terms of age range, for 60 per cent of the Jews were of working age (15 to 49 years), as compared with 43 per cent of the Arab population. In certain areas, such as the large urban centers and the coastal strip, the Jews constituted a majority of the population and owned the greater part of the land.

These developments alarmed the Arabs. The Arab nationalist movement, which had had only a limited appeal prior to August, 1929, now opened a campaign to halt Jewish immigration, prohibit further land purchases by Jews, and achieve the creation of an independent Palestine government in which the Arabs would have a majority. In April, 1936, Arab riots broke out in Jaffa; they developed into a general uprising against British rule and plans for a Jewish National Home. Signs of an economic crisis in the Jewish community of Palestine had begun to appear late in 1935 in the wake of the Italo-Ethiopian War, but it was these Arab riots that played a critical role in the decrease of Fifth 'Aliya immigration. In 1937 the number of Jewish immigrants dropped to 10,536.

Prior to 1936 each wave of immigration had brought basic changes in the social and political structure of the *Yishuv (Jewish population). With the Fifth 'Aliya, the last to be labeled by a number, the Yishuv became a consolidated society that underwent no additional essential changes until the mass immigration (1949–51) that followed the establishment of the State of Israel.　　　　　　　　　Y. SLUTSKY

FIGHTERS FOR THE FREEDOM OF ISRAEL. See LOHAME HERUT ISRAEL.

FINANCE IN ISRAEL. Under this heading the following subjects will be dealt with: currency, the banking system, public finance, investment, and the balance of payments.

Currency. Israel's basic unit of currency is the Israeli pound (Heb., Lira Yisr'elit), subdivided into 100 agorot (singular, agora), which in August, 1948, replaced the Palestine pound. Until the formation in 1954 of the *Bank of Israel, the currency issue was entrusted to the Anglo-Palestine Bank Ltd. (see BANK L'UMI L'YISRAEL). In 1968 notes of $\frac{1}{2}$, 1, 5, 10, and 50 pounds and coins in denominations of 1, 5, 10, 25, and 50 agorot were in circulation. On Apr. 30, 1969, Israel's money supply (demand deposits and cash in circulation) totaled 3,056,900,000 Israeli pounds, while notes and coins in circulation totaled 1,204,800,000 Israeli pounds.

Israel's money supply increased at a faster rate than the gross national product (GNP). During the period 1955–62 the real GNP rose by an annual average of 9 per cent, and during 1962–64 the rate reached 11 per cent. Subsequently it slowed down. The rise in the money supply is shown in Table 1. The disparity of

TABLE 1. ISRAEL MONEY SUPPLY, 1949–66
(Annual average, in millions of Israeli pounds)

Year	Cash in circulation	Demand deposits	Total	Percentage change
1949	38	86	123	....
1950	56	113	170	38.2
1951	82	142	224	31.8
1952	102	146	247	10.3
1953	120	170	290	17.4
1954	141	221	362	24.8
1955	165	230	395	9.1
1956	201	264	465	17.7
1957	230	328	558	20.0
1958	249	393	642	15.0
1959	267	457	724	12.8
1960	287	532	820	13.2
1961	339	630	970	18.3
1962	380	746	1,126	16.1
1963	491	983	1,474	30.9
1964	582	1,097	1,679	13.9
1965	657	1,242	1,899	13.1
1966	751	1,257	2,008	5.7

the increases in the GNP and the money supply was due primarily to public deficit financing and to the conversion of the capital inflow into local currency. Both measures were needed to provide funds for the absorption of mass *immigration during the early 1950s. The rapid increase in the money supply created the inflationary pressures that have beset Israel's economy throughout the country's independent existence and have necessitated periodic devaluations of the national currency.

The international value of Israel's currency since the independence of the country has depreciated from an exchange rate of $4.00 to $0.28, or by 93 per cent (since November, 1967, 3.50 Israeli pounds equal U.S.$1.00). Beginning in September, 1949, devaluations became necessary in order to adjust the international parity of the national currency to a realistic relationship to other currencies, particularly to meet the exigencies of the country's foreign trade.

Foreign exchange controls in Israel are administered by the Department of Foreign Exchange of the Ministry of Finance, under the responsibility of the Comptroller of Foreign Exchange in cooperation with other government agencies, and are carried out through authorized banks. Controls are in effect for both current and capital transactions; they have recently tended toward relaxation.

Israel is a member of the International Monetary Fund, the International Bank for Reconstruction and Development (World Bank), the International Development Association, and the International Finance Corporation.

Banking System. *See* BANKING IN ISRAEL.

Public Finance. The public sector in Israel includes the central government, the local authorities, and the national institutions. For specific purposes it is proper to include in the public sector some important nonprofit organizations that are engaged in activities similar to those of the public sector; moreover, a considerable contribution to the GNP is made by the *Histadrut (General Federation of Labor), a collective but nonpublic group of enterprises and institutions.

Among the various groups of the public sector the most important is the central government, which provides 70 per cent of the total revenue of the public sector and 50 per cent of that sector's purchases of goods and services. This represents one of the highest ratios of public economic activity in the non-Communist world. The local authorities enjoy considerable autonomy but depend on the central government for about 20 per cent of their revenue and therefore are responsive to the government's economic policy. The national institutions include the *Jewish Agency and its subsidiaries, the *Jewish National Fund, and the *Keren HaYesod (Palestine Foundation Fund). They are financed up to 80 per cent by transfers from abroad, and their main function is to contribute to the financing of immigration, the settlement of immigrants, and agriculture. The nonprofit organizations in 1966 included more than 5,000 legally autonomous institutions, although the 13 largest ones accounted for 70 per cent of the total expenditure. Like the national institutions, some of the nonprofit organizations are financed from abroad.

The Ministry of Finance prepares the central government budget for the fiscal year, which begins on April 1. The *Knesset approves the budget. The budget proposals for 1967–68 and 1968–69 showed a total revenue of 3,900,000,000 and 3,800,000,000 Israeli pounds, respectively, while total expenditure amounted to 6,000,000,000 and 5,400,000,000 pounds, leaving substantial deficits. Frequently, the government must submit supplementary budgets, either owing to unforeseen events such as the *Six-day War of 1967 or, more often, to overestimated revenue. Development, defense, debt repayment, and education are the principal expenditure items of the central budget. (For revenue items, *see* TAXATION IN ISRAEL.) A separate document, the Israel National Budget, is prepared annually by the Minister of Finance, the Office of the Prime Minister, and the Bank of Israel. It is a narrative summary of the course of the economy during the previous year and a forecast of the economy during the forthcoming year.

At the end of March, 1967, Israel's public debt totaled approximately 7,500,000,000 Israeli pounds, of which 40 per cent was repayable in foreign exchange.

Investment. Israel's progress since independence is mainly the result of the continued strong expansion of domestic consumption and investment. A high level of investment is required to provide the growing labor force with the capital equipment necessary for production. Gross investment (at current prices) between 1962 and 1969 rose from 2,120,000,000 to 3,400,000,000 Israeli pounds. Major sectors of private investment include industry and construction, as well as trade and business services. Large public-sector investments are being made in agriculture, transportation, housing, and public services. Histadrut through its holding company, Hevrat Ha'Ovdim, operates, often on a cooperative basis, about 25 per cent of Israel's industrial plants and maintains a high level of investment, prominently in heavy industries and construction with a considerable degree of vertical integration among Histadrut affiliates. Although this concentration has to some extent mitigated the problem of competition with private enterprise, there are points of friction between the cooperative and private sectors, particularly resulting from the strong economic and political position of the labor sector.

Direct foreign investment has concentrated on industries, including textiles, plastics, paper, tires, and tourism. In 1966 net foreign direct investment totaled $74,200,000, as compared with $82,700,000 in 1965. The Israeli government encourages investment aimed at developing the country's industrial potential, exploiting natural resources, improving the balance of payments, and absorbing immigrants. Investments approved by the Investment Authority are subject to the 1959 Law for the Encouragement of Capital Investments, which provides for remittance of profits, withdrawal of capital, tax concessions, and accelerated depreciation. Israel has an investment guaranty agreement with the United States that covers convertibility, expropriation, war, and extended risks.

Since 1935 there has existed in Tel Aviv a stock exchange, which began as a securities clearinghouse but now operates as a separate entity. In the beginning, trading was concentrated on bonds; the public interest in stocks began in the late 1950s and rose particularly after the devaluations of 1962 and 1967. There are about 50 members of the stock exchange, half of which are banks. The issue and trade in securities have been developed mainly through the banks, which act as underwriters, dealers, and brokers, and banks have therefore maintained the major share in current stock exchange transactions. Newly issued equities and securities must be approved by a securities authority. There is a wide field for developing the securities trade in Israel, mainly in respect of supervising new issues and providing adequate information to the stockholders. Since the mid-1960s Israeli investors have shown a preference for bonds that is reflected in the ratio of stocks to bonds traded at the stock

TABLE 2. TEL AVIV STOCK EXCHANGE, 1963–66
(Annual volume of securities trade)

	Millions of Israeli pounds			Percentage		
	Bonds	Shares	Total	Bonds	Shares	Total
1963	45.4	236.1	281.5	16.1	83.9	100
1964	72.8	222.2	295.0	24.7	75.3	100
1965	103.8	91.3	195.1	53.2	46.8	100
1966	131.9	59.3	195.2	69.0	31.0	100

TABLE 3. NEW SECURITY ISSUES, 1964–66
(Millions of Israeli pounds)

	Bonds	Shares
1964	218.6	107.8
1965	148.8	9.2
1966	414.1	4.2

TABLE 4. ISRAEL'S BALANCE SHEET, 1949–66
(Billions of dollars)

Imports	8.5	
Exports	3.3	
Deficit	5.2	
		Percentage
Foreign exchange reserves	0.6	12.0
German payments	1.5	29.0
United States grants	0.4	7.5
United States loans	0.4	7.5
Israel government bonds	1.0	19.0
Contributions and private investment	1.3	25.0
Total	5.2	100.0

TABLE 5. ISRAEL'S BALANCE OF PAYMENTS, 1963–66
(Millions of dollars)

	1963	1964	1965	1966
Exports of goods	337	350	405	503
Imports of goods	598	731	730	833
Trade balance	−261	−381	−325	−330
Services (net)	−144	−147	−160	−195
Transfers	347	335	330	306
Capital inflow	168	212	222	187
Gold and foreign exchange	515	545	643	621
External debt (long-term)	880	968	1,100	1,300

exchange. Tables 2 and 3 summarize recent activities of the Tel Aviv Stock Exchange.

Balance of Payments. Israel's balance of payments has consistently shown a substantial deficit owing to the fact that the country's import requirements exceed its exports, which in 1967 covered slightly more than half of imports. The deficit has been made up by contributions from world Jewry, foreign aid and borrowings, mainly from the United States, and German reparation and restitution payments (*see* GERMAN-ISRAEL AGREEMENT). Table 4 summarizes these developments during the period 1949–66.

During the 1960s the Israeli authorities inaugurated a new economic policy. Recognizing that the previous high level of capital imports could not continue indefinitely, they established among their principal aims the integration of Israel's economy with that of the rest of the world and the strengthening of the balance of payments. In the past, the trade gap had persistently widened, although there had been temporary factors which had influenced its size from year to year. A major objective of the new policy therefore was to reduce the deficit on goods and services so as to make the country less dependent on capital inflow. Since imports were likely to continue to increase, it could not be expected that the net balance of services would show substantial improvement in the near future, despite an increase in tourism. The reduction in the deficit would therefore have to come through increased exports. Moreover, with the end of mass immigration, the resources devoted to the absorption of immigration would be decreased. In addition, the government had adopted a policy of restraint with regard to other investment expenditure. Table 5 summarizes balance-of-payments developments during recent years.

Effects of the Six-day War. The Six-day War of 1967 struck Israel in the second year of an economic recession brought about by government measures designed to offset some of the undesirable effects of the rapid economic development of previous years, namely, inflation and a widening trade gap. There were indications that some of these objectives were about to be achieved: the country's GNP in 1966 and 1967 rose by 1 and 2.2 per cent respectively, as compared with the previous increase of more than 10 per cent. Early in 1967, however, unemployment, idle production capacity, and a decline in

investment forced the authorities into a reflating policy that gained momentum after the Six-day War. Increased defense needs (as reflected in budget increases), the occupied territories, and the replenishment of depleted stocks contributed to the resumption of increased economic activity. During 1968 the GNP again rose by 12 per cent, but price increases were kept in check, partly through higher subsidies, although with the result of a widening trade gap, which by the end of 1969 amounted to $606,000,000, as compared with $330,000,000 in 1966 and $217,000,000 in 1967. Heavy foreign exchange outlays, mainly for defense, by the end of 1969 reduced the country's international reserves to $367,000,000, as compared with $621,000,000 in 1966 and $715,000,000 in 1967 (the last-mentioned figure reflects worldwide contributions and the unprecedented sales of *State of Israel bonds during the May crisis and the Six-day War).

J. O. RONALL

FINEMAN, HAYIM. Educator and pioneer of American *Labor Zionism (b. Obolon, Russia, 1886; d. Philadelphia, 1959). Brought to Philadelphia by his parents at the age of four, Fineman was probably the first American-educated intellectual to join the Labor Zionist movement. His activities assumed national proportions in 1904, when he helped found the American Po'ale Zion party (*see* PO'ALE ZION IN AMERICA). He served as its national secretary in 1906 and again from 1920 to 1921 and as its president from 1947 to 1948. In 1912 he was among the organizers of the *Farband (Labor Zionist fraternal order) and in 1923 was a founder of the *Histadrut Campaign, which he served as Philadelphia chairman for many years. He was a delegate to a number of Zionist Congresses (*see* CONGRESS, ZIONIST) and a member of the Central Committee of Po'ale Zion until his death. In 1953 he was elected to the Presidium of the *Actions Committee of the *World Zionist Organization. Fineman was coeditor with Hayim *Greenberg of the **Jewish Frontier,* a Labor Zionist monthly he helped bring into being. For more than four decades, he was a professor of English literature at Temple University in Philadelphia.

C. B. SHERMAN

FINKELSTEIN, LOUIS. Rabbi and scholar in the United States (b. Cincinnati, 1895). After obtaining his Ph.D. degree from Columbia University (1918) and his rabbinical degree from the Jewish Theological Seminary of America (1919), he served as rabbi of Congregation Kehilath Israel in New York (1919–31). Joining the faculty of the Jewish Theological Seminary in 1920 as an instructor in Talmud, he became Solomon Schechter professor of theology in 1931, assistant to the president of the seminary in 1934, provost in 1937, president in 1940, and chancellor in 1951. In 1968 he was given the title of chancellor and president of the faculties.

The author and editor of numerous scholarly works on the Bible, rabbinic literature, Jewish history, and Jewish philosophy, Finkelstein contributed articles to a number of periodicals, including the *New Palestine.* Although not officially active in Zionism, he played a prominent role in the support of Israeli cultural projects. It was on his initiative that the seminary acquired the *Schocken Institute for Jewish Research, in Jerusalem. He visited Israel repeatedly on behalf of the seminary.

Louis Finkelstein.
[Jewish Theological Seminary of America]

In 1952 he conceived the plan of an American Student Center in Jerusalem to serve students of the seminary spending a year of study in Israel and to help build understanding between American Jewry, Israel, and the Middle East in general. The center was dedicated in 1962. Finkelstein served as a member of the Board of Directors of the American Friends of the *Hebrew University of Jerusalem and was a founder of the *America-Israel Society.

See also CONSERVATIVE JUDAISM AND ZIONISM.

FINKELSTEIN, SIGMUND. Journalist, writer, and Zionist leader (b. Lvov, Galicia, Austria, 1886; d. Jerusalem, 1959). Finkelstein studied law at the University of Lvov and did post-graduate work in Vienna and London. A Zionist from his youth on, he was active in organizing Zionist high school and university students and was a member of the Zionist Central Committee of Galicia. He edited the Polish-language Zionist periodical *Moriah* and was a regular contributor to the Zionist weekly *Voskhod* and to the *Togblat,* a Yiddish-language daily which appeared in Lvov.

In 1914 Finkelstein went to Vienna, where he continued his literary and communal activities. He was a member of the Central Committee of the Zionist Federation of Austria, editor of *Die Stimme,* and a contributor to a variety of periodicals. In Palestine, where he settled in 1938, he helped found the Hitahdut 'Ole Austria (Association of Immigrants from Austria; *see* AUSTRIAN JEWS IN ISRAEL). Finkelstein was the author of *Stürmer des Ghetto* and *Schicksalsstunden eines Führers.* The latter, a book on Herzl, also appeared in translation in other languages.

N. M. GELBER

FINLAND, ZIONISM IN. The Jewish community of Finland, which has always been small (in 1968 it numbered 1,700 in a total population of 4.6 million), had its first contact with Zionism in the 1880s through the *Hoveve Zion, but it was only after the advent of Herzl that Finnish Jews began to participate in the movement. Yiddish journals and lecturers visiting from Russia spread the Zionist idea among them, and soon a number of small Zionist societies were formed in the Finnish-Jewish communities. A local *Jewish National Fund committee was organized and received generous contributions. The *Jewish Colonial Trust, founded in 1903, aroused much interest in Finland, with many buying its shares.

The Zionist conference held in Helsinki in 1906 (*see* HELSING-FORS CONFERENCE) gave a strong impetus to the Zionist movement in Finland. As a result of the conference, the small Zionist societies of Finland grew rapidly to include almost all the Jews of the country. The first Zionist periodical in Finland, *Kadimah,* was launched in this period.

The Finnish Jews were given full citizenship rights in January, 1918. This achievement resulted in important developments in many spheres. The long-cherished hope for a Jewish day school in Helsinki was realized. The employment of teachers from Palestine brought close contact with the *Yishuv (Jewish population of Palestine). Many former pupils of the school settled in kibbutzim. In 1920 the Finnish Zionist movement joined the *World Zionist Organization. Finland was represented, for the first time, at the 17th Zionist *Congress in 1931 by Benjamin Nemeschansky-Nemes, one of the Zionist pioneers in the country.

When Israel's independence was proclaimed in 1948, a completely equipped military hospital was dispatched to the *Magen David Adom and the Jewish community of Helsinki sent a number of Tora scrolls to the *Israel Defense Forces. Jewish youths, many of whom had participated with distinction in the Finnish-Russian wars of 1939–40 and 1941–44, enlisted in the Israel Defense Army. Although only 27 in number, they represented 2 per cent of the Jewish population in Finland. By 1968 a total of more than 100 persons from Finland had settled in Israel, representing 6 per cent of the Jews in Finland.

Funds transferred from Finland to Israel between 1920 and 1964 amounted to almost $1,000,000. On a per capita basis, this was one of the highest contributions in the world. To enable the Finnish 'Olim to acquire land and build their own homes, a loan fund, Kupat Milve, of $10,000 was established in 1950.

Jewish girl scouts in Finland about 1935.[YIVO Institute for Jewish Research]

The *Women's International Zionist Organization (WIZO) was introduced into Finland in 1920. From 1957 on, the Finnish WIZO maintained a home for 50 children in Shaviv, near Herzliya. Each child at the home had his own "godparent" in Finland who contributed regularly to his support.

J. WEINSTEIN

FIRST 'ALIYA. Wave of Jewish *immigration that reached Palestine between 1882 and 1904. Most of the immigrants of this period came from Russia, Romania, and Galicia (then part of Austria); many had been inspired by the *Hoveve Zion movement. The difference between the old *Yishuv and these immigrants was that the latter were pioneers, seeking to rebuild the Jewish nation by setting up farms and agricultural villages outside the four "holy cities" of Jerusalem, Safed, Tiberias, and Hebron.

The pogroms and persecution which the Jews of Russia and Romania suffered in 1881–82 resulted in the start of large-scale Jewish emigration from Eastern Europe, but only 2 per cent of the emigrants of the time went to Palestine. From the outset the Turkish authorities opposed and forbade Jewish immigration into Palestine because they considered it a threat to their control over the country. Nevertheless, 'Aliya was continued under the protection of foreign consuls, who on occasion were given rewards for their help. Herzl criticized these methods, which he called infiltration.

The initial thrust of the First 'Aliya occurred between 1882 and 1884. The immigrants during these years were mainly families with limited financial means and members of the *Bilu movement. The early settlements of Rishon L'Tziyon, Rosh Pina, Zikhron Ya'akov, 'Ekron, and Y'sud HaMa'ala and the Bilu settlement of G'dera date from this period. Petah Tikva, which had been abandoned in 1881, was resettled. The immigrants' lack of funds, farming skills, and knowledge of conditions in Palestine soon led to an economic crisis that threatened the very survival of their projects. Baron Edmond de *Rothschild came to their rescue, sending to Palestine administrative officials and agricultural experts who developed a new field of agriculture: grape growing and wine making (*see* WINE INDUSTRY IN ISRAEL). The Rothschild administration also bought additional land to enlarge existing settlements and create new ones. In order to safeguard the infant settlements

and protect them from Turkish misrule, it exerted its influence with the central government in Constantinople. However, the regime it instituted in the Jewish settlements was characterized by paternalism and, at times, by inefficiency.

The second influx (1890–91), which came from Russia, led to sizable acquisitions of land in Palestine. Despite hindrances on the part of the Turkish authorities, these years saw the establishment of Rehovot, Hadera, and Mishmar HaYarden and the rise of a new class of farm workers in the villages, who in 1896 went out on their own to found the settlements of B'er Tovya (with help from Hoveve Zion in Russia) and M'tula (with the aid of the Rothschild administration).

With the transfer of the settlements from the baron's guardianship to the *Palestine Jewish Colonization Association (PICA), settlement of Lower Galilee was begun. Between 1901 and 1904 Sejera, Mes'ha (K'far Tavor), Milhamya (M'nahemiya), Yama (Yavn'el), and Bet Gan, all based on dry farming, were founded.

In the opening years of the 20th century the settlements, particularly those of Judea, where the cultivation of vineyards and citrus was prevalent (*see* CITRUS INDUSTRY IN ISRAEL), resorted to the employment of a considerable number of hired laborers from surrounding Arab villages. In some settlements Arab watchmen were employed. This employment was due to the lower wages paid to Arab laborers, their familiarity with farming, and the shortage of Jewish labor. The first form of Jewish self-defense in Palestine originated in Petah Tikva, where Abraham *Schapiro organized a group of Jewish watchmen to guard the settlement.

At a conference of representatives of the Jewish communities and moshavot (*see* MOSHAVA) held in Zikhron Ya'akov in the summer of 1903, M'nahem M. *Ussishkin made an unsuccessful attempt to form an overall organization of Jews living in Palestine. The First 'Aliya was also the pioneer of cooperative economic enterprises, in the field of citrus and wine marketing (*see* COOPERATIVES IN ISRAEL).

By the close of the First 'Aliya, a total of 350,000 dunams of land (*see* DUNAM) had been purchased by Jews; of this land, 92,000 dunams were east of the Jordan River. More than 20 agricultural settlements had been built, with a total population of 720 families, comprising more than 6,000 persons. In 1905 the four largest settlements were Zikhron Ya'akov (population, 1,100), Petah Tikva (880), Rosh Pina (800), and Rishon L'Tziyon (760). In these settlements about 28,000 dunams were planted in vineyards, and 1,400 in fruit-bearing trees (almond, olive, citrus). Of the 50,000 Jews who were then living in Palestine, about 10,000 belonged to what had come to be called the new Yishuv. In addition to the 6,000 who established their homes in the new settlements, the new Yishuv comprised about 1,000 Jews in Jerusalem and Haifa and most of the 3,000 Jews in Jaffa, which also developed considerably during the First 'Aliya. All members of the First 'Aliya, unlike those of the old Yishuv, were productive and self-supporting.

The First 'Aliya also saw the beginnings of the struggle over the cultural and spiritual character of the Yishuv. There were clashes between the rabbis of the old Yishuv in Jerusalem and the pioneers over the question whether, under Jewish law, the land might be worked during the sabbatical (Sh'mita) year of 1889, and over the use of the *Hebrew language for secular purposes.

In 1903 the Hebrew Teachers Association was formed. It

played an important role in the evolution of the Yishuv's educational patterns. It was in the settlements of the First 'Aliya that Hebrew evolved as a spoken tongue and that the earlier schools with Hebrew as the medium of instruction were established. These settlements were also nuclei of Jewish self-government, in that each of them managed its affairs by a democratically elected governing committee. *See also* EDUCATION IN ISRAEL; YISHUV, SELF-GOVERNMENT IN THE.

Notwithstanding the paternalistic regime of the Rothschild officials, the settlements succeeded in developing local self-government in such internal affairs as education, health services, religious needs, law enforcement, and real estate transactions as well as in organizing men to guard them against marauders. In recapitulation, it may be said that the First 'Aliya laid the economic and social foundations on which succeeding immigration waves were able to build.

Y. SLUTSKY

FISCAL SYSTEM OF ISRAEL. *See* FINANCE IN ISRAEL.

FISCHER, JEAN. Zionist leader in Belgium (b. Cracow, Poland, 1871; d. Antwerp, 1929). Fischer settled in Belgium in his youth and became prominent in the diamond industry in Antwerp. An early Zionist, he was a leading advocate of political Zionism. For many years he was a member of the board of directors of the *Jewish Colonial Trust. At the 11th Zionist *Congress (Vienna, 1913) he was elected to the *Actions Committée.

During World War I Fischer was one of the directors of the *Jewish National Fund head office in The Hague. He served as president of the Zionist Federation of Belgium, was a member of the Central Consistory of Belgian Jewry, and founded the Comité Belgique-Palestine, a Belgian pro-Palestine committee. After a visit to Palestine, Fischer published *Das heutige Palästina*

(Palestine of Today, 1908). K'far Yona, founded in 1932, was named for him.

FISCHER, MAURICE. Israeli diplomat (b. Antwerp, 1903; d. Switzerland, 1965). The son of Jean *Fischer, he settled in Palestine in 1930 and took an active part in the country's agricultural development. During World War II he served with the Free French forces. He was the representative of the *Jewish Agency in Paris from 1947 to 1948 and Israel's first Ambassador to France, from 1948 to 1953. Fischer served as Israeli Ambassador to Turkey from 1953 to 1956 and as Assistant Director General of the Ministry of Foreign Affairs from 1956 to 1961, when he became Ambassador to Italy, a position he held until his death.

FISHING IN ISRAEL. Fishing on the part of the modern *Yishuv (Jewish population) dates to the early 1920s, when members of the *Third 'Aliya who had engaged in fishing formed cooperatives and began to fish in Lake Kinneret (Sea of Galilee) and the Jordan River. These pioneer fishermen were not successful, and their cooperatives did not last. Individual fishermen, however, operated in Lake Kinneret.

Development of the Industry. In the 1930s fishing in Lake Kinneret began to expand with the formation of the kibbutzim of 'En Gev and Ginnosar along its shores. Several fishing cooperatives were formed along the Mediterranean shore. These fishermen sailed as far as the shores of the Red Sea, but a lack of anchorages and sheltered harbors for their boats led to the disintegration of most of the cooperatives.

In the 1930s and 1940s the fishing cooperatives of G'lil Yam, Mishmar Yam, HaHotrim, 'En HaYam, Sa'ar, S'dot Yam, Ma'agan Mikhael, and Palmahim were founded, mostly by nuclei of Palestinian youth groups that sought to "conquer the sea." They developed new methods of fishing in Lake Kinneret

FISHING IN ISRAEL

Year	Trawling		Shoreline and shallow-water fishing		Lake fishing		Red Sea fishing	Hatcheries	Deep-sea fishing	Total	
	Number of boats	Catch, in tons	Number of boats	Catch, in tons	Number of boats	Catch, in tons	Catch, in tons	Catch, in tons	Catch, in tons	Catch, in tons	Value, in thousands of Israeli pounds
1948	5	111	77	16	44	141	. . . . .	2,435	. . . . .	2,703	1,085
1949	15	646	77	252	48	397	. . . . .	2,938	. . . . .	4,233	1,505
1950	23	1,092	155	786	78	707	. . . . .	4,013	. . . . .	6,600	2,302
1951	23	929	212	1,071	81	927	. . . . .	3,904	. . . . .	6,831	2,859
1952	22	953	228	1,045	99	1,046	. . . . .	4,449	. . . . .	7,493	5,561
1953	23	1,286	219	938	90	781	. . . . .	4,652	. . . . .	7,657	7,895
1954	22	1,480	197	999	86	989	. . . . .	5,773	. . . . .	9,241	9,571
1955	27	1,518	213	952	86	895	. . . . .	7,338	. . . . .	10,703	11,661
1956	26	1,391	213	1,090	94	1,031	. . . . .	6,708	. . . . .	10,220	12,065
1957	27	1,550	209	1,244	83	1,328	. . . . .	7,567	. . . . .	11,689	16,032
1958	29	1,809	238	2,028	82	1,030	65	7,701	. . . . .	12,633	17,852
1959	27	1,952	275	2,280	76	1,011	55	7,917	. . . . .	13,215	18,370
1960	25	1,274	317	2,425	76	1,485	172	8,482	. . . . .	13,838	19,276
1961	19	992	315	1,850	74	1,223	927	9,205	727	14,924	20,789
1962	18	830	325	2,318	67	1,161	1,030	9,236	1,806	16,381	24,809
1963	17	707	292	1,827	76	1,410	563	10,055	2,932	17,494	29,907
1964	15	615	302	2,094	76	1,325	645	10,408	3,642	18,730	32,756
1965	18	761	328	2,149	78	1,333	686	10,199	4,385	19,513	35,347
1966	18	638	352	2,147	97	1,713	714	9,454	9,846	24,512	47,005
1967	17	741	373	1,886	87	1,835	572	8,773	8,051	21,858	38,409

Fishermen mend nets on Gaza beach. [Israel Information Services]

and the Mediterranean, based generally on techniques used in Italy and Yugoslavia. This period also saw the formation of Nahshon, a fishing enterprise founded by the *Histadrut (General Federation of Labor).

The opening of the port of Tel Aviv in 1936 helped the fishing industry. That year also saw the formation of the Maritime Department of the *Jewish Agency and a planned effort to use the resources of the sea. During World War II and the years of the Nazi holocaust, the Jewish fishermen of Palestine participated in the Yishuv-wide undertaking of smuggling illegal immigrants into the country (*see* ILLEGAL IMMIGRATION). Many ships and large numbers of fishermen played important roles in this effort.

Deep-sea Fishing. With the establishment of the State of Israel, a Fishing Division was formed in the Ministry of Agriculture. Its initial activities were expanded, trawlers were added to the fishing fleet, a modern sardine industry was begun in the Mediterranean, and improvements were made in sea fishing. In the 1960s deep-sea fishing was started; oceangoing ships were built that netted fish, froze them, and brought the catch back to Israel.

In 1968 Israel had six ships for deep-sea fishing. One of them, the "Dagit," was employed in catching tuna with floating hooks, a method developed by the Japanese, who were virtually the only ones to use it. The Israeli boat worked in cooperation with the Japanese and within the framework of a Japanese firm. The other five ships, owned by two Israeli firms, Yona and Atlantic, used nets. Yona's "Hiram" was the largest ship of the Israeli deep-sea fishing fleet. It employed 43 workers, of

whom 23 were Israelis. In 1967 it netted 3,000 tons of fish. Yona's other boat, the "Yam Suf," employed 25 workers, 14 of whom were Israelis. These boats worked in the Atlantic, near the west and south coasts of Africa. The Atlantic company owned three deep-sea fishing ships, which also were active on the west coast of Africa.

The home base of these ships was Haifa, but because of the great distance from the fishing area catches as a rule were sent by refrigerator boats to ports near the area. The crews of the boats were composed mainly of Israelis and natives of the countries near whose shores the boats operated. Yona also employed two small vessels for fishing in areas not far from Israel. The "Nitzan" and "LaMerhav" were active in the Red Sea, opposite the Ethiopian coast, and unloaded at Elat.

A fishing industry was begun in the Gulf of Elat and the Red Sea. Special attention was given to oceanographic research, which had been started by the Maritime Department of the Jewish Agency. After the establishment of the State of Israel, an oceanographic research station, working in cooperation with the *Hebrew University of Jerusalem, was set up in Haifa.

Fish Hatcheries. The fish hatchery industry, begun during the mandatory period (*see* MANDATE FOR PALESTINE), developed after the independence of Israel. The Yishuv welcomed the new industry, which developed a local food supply that was important to the country's economy both in normal times and in periods of emergency. In addition, the hatcheries brought some relief to the arid landscape of Palestine and helped turn malarial swamps and salt-soaked lands into places of beauty.

Breeding and Artificial Ponds. This industry began modestly. The first artificial pond was dug in Nir David; it measured 20 by 20 meters. The second, because it was unusually large, covering 1 acre, was called Kinneret. Following Israel's independence, the growth of the fishponds was marked. In 1948–49 they covered an area of 15,000 dunams (3,750 acres; *see* DUNAM);

A fishing boat on Lake Kinneret. [Trans World Airlines]

by 1966–67 they extended over 59,000 dunams (14,750 acres). The fish-breeding industry was a leading factor in the agricultural development and economic stabilization of the Bet Sh'an Valley; there, after a hopeless struggle against swamps, salt-soaked earth, a cruel climate, and malaria, the swamplands, the salt water, and the relatively small labor force were utilized for the creation of artificial fishponds. Despite a lack of know-how and difficulties in adjustment, the industry soon became self-supporting, and it was apparent that local climatic conditions favored its development, which was also aided by high protective tariffs.

After a brief initial period, the industry expanded, and many farms dug artificial ponds, which soon checkered the fields and became an integral part of the Israeli landscape. Israel became a leader in fish breeding in artificial ponds. It made important contributions to the science of fish breeding and was the first to do so in an international framework.

In nearly three decades of fish breeding, Israel gathered broad scientific and technical knowledge. In the 1960s two new varieties of fish, the tilapia and the mullet, were bred and developed in importance, both in ponds and on the market. Attempts were made to adapt new varieties of fish to the ponds so as to meet all the requirements of local fish consumption and also to provide for its expansion in both quantity and variety.

Results of scientific research were made available to the hatcheries from their inception, at first by the Maritime Department of the Jewish Agency, with the help of the Hebrew University, and in the 1960s by the well-known fish-breeding experimental station in Dor and the laboratory for fish diseases in Jerusalem and Nir David, which made impressive contributions to the industry.

Consumption and Production. In 1968 the annual consumption of fish in Israel was 22 pounds per person, of which the local fishing industry provided 16 pounds. Imports supplied 6 pounds of salted fish and fillets. Israel's deep-sea catch had begun to supply fillets, and it was anticipated that local production would soon meet consumer demand, just as the sardine-canning industry had met the requirements of local consumption and thus eliminated the need for imports. In 1968 the fishing industry employed 1,673 persons, and the hatcheries about 900. The industry had anchorages in Lake Kinneret, a fishing anchorage at the mouth of the Kishon River, a fishing port at 'Akko, and unloading privileges and the use of services at the ports of Ashdod, Jaffa, and Elat.

S. TAL

FISHMAN, ADA. *See* MAIMON, ADA.

FISHMAN, Y'HUDA LEB HAKOHEN. *See* MAIMON, Y'HUDA LEB HAKOHEN.

FLAG, ZIONIST AND ISRAELI. Soon after its inception, the Zionist movement adopted a flag of its own, consisting of a white field with two blue horizontal stripes and the *Magen David (Shield of David) in its center. The flag is said to have been designed by David *Wolffsohn, who had been inspired in the choice of colors by the tallith (prayer shawl).

Actually, however, flags of the same colors and design had been used as Jewish banners even before that time. One such flag was displayed in 1885 in Rishon L'Tziyon to celebrate the third anniversary of that settlement, and another in 1892 by the B'nai Zion Educational Society in Boston. Even earlier, the German-

The blue-and-white Israeli flag. [Israel Information Services]

Jewish writer Ludwig August Frankel, in a poem included in his *Ahnenbilder* (1864), had spoken of the blue and the white of the tallith as the colors of the Jewish people. When the State of Israel was established, the Zionist flag became its official banner and was declared so by a proclamation of the Provisional Council of State on Oct. 28, 1948. The Flag and Emblem Law of 5709 (1949), enacted by the *Knesset on May 24 of that year, provided for the protection of the dignity of the flag.

In his *Jewish State, Herzl had proposed a white banner with seven golden stars, symbolizing the seven-hour working day he envisaged. However, such a flag was never used by the Zionist movement.

T. PRESCHEL

FLEG (FLEGENHEIMER), EDMOND. Novelist, playwright, poet, and exponent of Jewish renaissance (b. Geneva, 1874; d. Paris, 1963). Raised in a formally observant but assimilated family, Fleg was indifferent to Judaism during his formative years. He studied at various universities in Europe, including the Sorbonne. Under the impact of the *Dreyfus affair he began to return to his discarded Judaism, a development he described in *Pourquoi je suis juif*, 1927 (*Why I Am a Jew*, 1929). After attending the 3d Zionist *Congress (Basle, 1899), he conceived an interest in the Zionist idea. In 1914 he joined the French Foreign Legion. Becoming a French citizen two years later, he entered the French civil service in Paris and continued his studies at the École Normale Supérieure.

After visiting Palestine in 1931, Fleg wrote *Ma Palestine* (*The Land of Promise*, 1935), in which he demonstrated the compatibility of French patriotism and Western culture with Jewish values. Fleg had considerable influence on French-Jewish literature. With the historian Jules Isaac, he was one of the

Edmond Fleg.
[Zionist Archives]

principal initiators of a movement for Christian-Jewish fellowship. His writings include a considerable number of books on Jewish subjects. Fleg was an officer of the French Legion of Honor (1937) and a laureate of the Académie Française.

S. HUBNER

FLEISCHMANN, GISI. *Women's International Zionist Organization (WIZO) leader (b. Bratislava, Slovakia, Hungary, 1892; d. Auschwitz, 1944). The daughter of an Orthodox family, she took an active interest in Jewish affairs from her early youth. In the early 1920s she joined the Zionist movement and in 1925 was one of the founders of WIZO in Slovakia, of which she later became chairman. Under her leadership, the Slovakian WIZO grew into a strong organization. In 1940 she became a member of the Executive of the Zionist Organization of Slovakia (*see* CZECHOSLOVAKIA, ZIONISM IN).

After the dismemberment of Czechoslovakia in 1938 she devoted herself to aiding Jewish refugees and promoting Jewish emigration. She was local representative of the *American Jewish Joint Distribution Committee in Slovakia and of *HICEM (an international Jewish agency for the regulation of Jewish migration). When the Judenzentrale (Center for Jewish Affairs) was established, she took charge of its Emigration Department. She developed a widespread rescue activity, often at great personal risk, and took a prominent part in negotiations with the Nazis for the stoppage of the deportation of Jews. She was arrested several times, the last time in October, 1944. She was briefly held at a concentration camp in Sered and then deported to Auschwitz, where she was killed.

O. NEUMANN

FLEXNER, BERNARD. Lawyer and Jewish communal worker in the United States (b. Louisville, Ky., 1865; d. New York, 1945). After receiving an LL.B. degree from the University of Louisville (1898), Flexner practiced law. He joined his friends Louis D. *Brandeis and Julian W. *Mack in their Zionist efforts, remaining a member of the *Zionist Organization of America while Brandeis was its honorary president (1918–21) and participating in the *London Zionist Conference of 1920.

A member of the American Jewish delegation to the Paris Peace Conference (*see* COMITÉ DES DÉLÉGATIONS JUIVES), Flexner

served as liaison man between the Zionists and the *American Jewish Joint Distribution Committee (JDC); he was a member of the latter's Executive and chairman of its Committee on Medical Affairs. When the JDC organized its Reconstruction Committee under the chairmanship of Herbert H. *Lehman, he became its vice-chairman. Flexner devoted his attention and energies to the economic development of Jewish Palestine. In 1925 he helped found the Palestine Economic Corporation in New York (*see* PEC ISRAEL ECONOMIC CORPORATION), serving as its president until 1931. He also organized the Central Bank of Cooperative Institutions in Palestine and was a member of the Board of Trustees of Palestine Endowment Funds, Inc., to which Brandeis bequeathed a substantial part of his estate. In 1929 Flexner was elected a non-Zionist member of the Council of the *Jewish Agency.

FLIMAN, AMELIA KIBLINSKY DE. Educator, journalist, Zionist leader in Chile (b. Buenos Aires). She studied philosophy and humanities in Chile. Active in the Zionist movement from 1935 on, she contributed to the publications *Mundo Judío* and *Idishe Vort*. Within the Zionist Federation of Chile she directed the *Keren HaYesod (Palestine Foundation Fund) campaign for seven years, and she directed the *Jewish National Fund (JNF) for five years. Subsequently she served as director of the Immigration Department of the JNF and was active in behalf of the *Hebrew University of Jerusalem. In 1958 she founded the Merkaz L'Tarbut Israel (Cultural Center) in Santiago for cultural activities and the teaching of Hebrew. She was an active member of *Po'ale Zion. In 1963 she was elected president of the Zionist Federation (the first woman to hold that office), and the next year she served as a delegate to the 26th Zionist *Congress.

FLORA AND VEGETATION OF ISRAEL. The term "flora" is defined as the plant population peculiar to an area. The term "vegetation" refers to the natural associations and divisions of

Agave flourishes on Mount Carmel. [Israel Information Services]

An olive tree in Upper Galilee. [Israel Information Services]

plants according to their habitats, such as forest, meadow, and savannah. The flora and vegetation of Israel and of the cis-Jordanian parts of Jordan (Palestine) are discussed here as a single entity, because physically there is a continuum in the distribution, form, and life of plants in every cross section from the Mediterranean Sea to the Jordan River.

Abundance of Flora. The unique geographical position of Palestine as a bridge between Asia and Africa and its varied *climate are the main factors that contribute to the abundance of Palestine's flora, which with that of Transjordan comprises 718 genera with 2,250 species of vascular plants: pteridophytes (horsetails and ferns), gymnosperms (Ephedrae and conifers), and angiosperms (monocotyledons and dicotyledons). This abundance is due partly to human alteration of the vegetation during thousands of years of civilization by the destruction of natural plant formation and by the introduction of cultivated and adventitious species (weeds).

Phytogeography. Five plant, or phytogeographical, elements are represented in Palestine.

1. *Eurosibero-Boreoamerican Element.* This element is represented by about 15 species, most of which are hydrophytes (water plants). These species, for which water habitat serves as a niche, are broadly distributed in the Northern Hemisphere. They include water ferns, water lilies, and reeds, as well as some weeds in dry and irrigated fields. The other four elements are each represented by many species and occupy definite territories in Palestine (see accompanying map).

2. *Mediterranean Element.* This element covers central and northern Palestine north of the Gaza-'Arad line, from the Mediterranean Sea to the watershed along the mountains of Judea and Samaria and to the Syrian border of Galilee. In the

north the Mediterranean region is connected with the same region in Lebanon and Syria. The Mediterranean element contributes almost all the woody species to the forest and the maquis (the dense bush formation typical of the Mediterranean region, similar to the chaparral of southern California) of the region. Most of these are sclerophyllous (bearing hard and relatively thick leaves) evergreen species such as the oak (*Quercus calliprinos*), the mastic pistachio (*Pistacia lentiscus*), the carob tree (*Ceratonia siliqua*), the heath or strawberry tree (*Arbutus andrachne*), the Aleppo pine (*Pinus halepensis*), and the juniper (*Juniperus oxycedrus*). Other tree species of the region are deciduous; among these are the Tabor oak (*Q. ithaburensis*), the pistachio (*P. palestina*), the *Styrax officinalis*, the Judas tree (*Cercis siliquastrum*), and, from the rose family, the thorny trees *Crataegus azarolus* and *Sorbus trilobata* and the wild plum (*Prunus ursina*).

Human activities have left only small remnants of true forests, among them the Aleppo pine woods on rendzina *soils, mainly on Mount Carmel. More common on terra rossa soil are small woods of the oak *Q. calliprinos* in Galilee, Samaria, and Judea around the sacred places. The only large forest in Israel is a mixed forest of Tabor oak and *S. officinalis* on the hills between Haifa and Nazareth. Two other woods of Tabor oaks have remained, one near the sources of the Jordan (see illustration) and one in the Sharon Plain. Large woods of Tabor oaks of the Sharon Plain were cut during World War I.

Afforestation is accomplished mainly with Aleppo pine, which does not need deep soil and has a high growth rate. In the foothills carob trees have also been planted. The rest of the non-cultivated areas in the mountains and hills are well covered with thick maquis of varied composition of the sclerophyllous species listed above. Owing in large part to the charcoal production and heavy grazing that have been common in Palestine for generations, these tree species in the maquis are mainly in the form of trunkless bushes.

Sacred forest of Quercus ithaburensis *and* Pistacia atlantica, *near the sources of the Jordan.* [Plant Life of Palestine, *by Michael Zohary, New York, The Ronald Press Company, 1962. Courtesy of the publishers.*]

Arctotis *growing wild in Galilee.* [Israel Information Services]

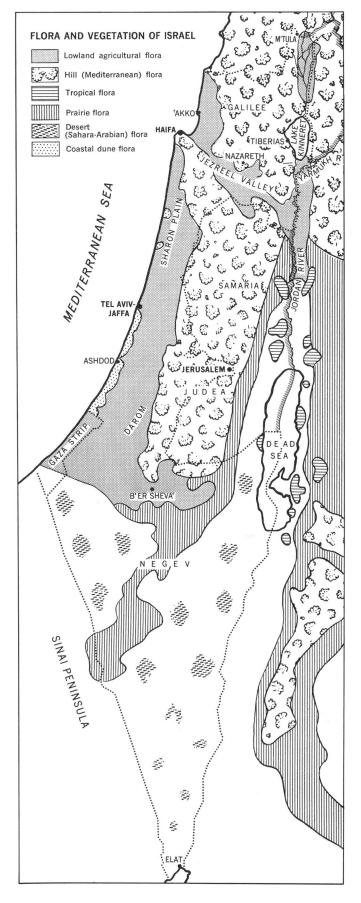

In addition to the woody species, the Mediterranean region is rich in many thorny and inedible species, which form the garigue, or *gariga* (bush formation of medium height), and the *batha* (low bush formation). The thorny burnet *(Poterium spinosum)*, of the rose family, is widespread in the Mediterranean region, forming thick, impenetrable *bathas*. Perennial grasses are found throughout the region. Their part in the vegetation has probably been underestimated, for in regions where grazing has been stopped they seem to take over new and larger areas. A large group of perennials, the bulbous plants, adds to the beauty of the country. The squill *(Urginea maritima)* produces its tall white inflorescences before the rains come and the leaves appear. Later on in the winter and spring the anemone *(Anemone coronaria)*, turban buttercup *(Ranunculus asiatica)*, tulip *(Tulipa oculus-solis)*, cyclamens, irises, and many other species give color to the natural vegetation. Other parts of the Mediterranean region are cultivated and have their specific weeds.

3. *Irano-Turanian Element.* The Irano-Turanian region adjoins the Mediterranean region on the south and east. This region, though narrow, is of considerable importance, since it is part of a continuous strip of land that runs from the Atlas Mountains to central Asia. In Palestine the Irano-Turanian region consists of steppe or desert and is characterized by low rainfall (4 to 12 inches). The only true tree of this element is the Atlantic pistachio *(P. atlantica)*, which is found singly or, at best, in a park formation with trees 150 feet apart and low vegetation between them. On the eastern slopes of Lower Galilee and

Zygophylletum dumosi *plant community, hammada, in the Negev.* [Plant Life of Palestine, *by Michael Zohary, New York, The Ronald Press Company, 1962. Courtesy of the publishers.*]

Samaria the thorny jujube *(Zizyphus lotus)* grows to a considerable size but mostly as a trunkless bush. Other plant species of this element are thorny composites, perennial grasses, white wormwood *(Artemisia herba-alba)*, and many of the beet family, such as the thorny *Noea mucronata* and the leafless *Haloxylon articulatum* and *Anabasis haussknechti*. These are adapted to the desert environment mainly by their high salt tolerance, extensive root systems, and variety of methods to reduce transpiration (water loss through the plant) during the long, dry summer.

4. *Saharo-Sindian Element.* Such mechanisms are common also in the other phytogeographical element of Palestine deserts, the Saharo-Sindian. This element covers the rest of Palestine in the east and south and also penetrates the sand dunes along the Mediterranean shore. It consists of some large bushes that grow in sandy habitats, including the white broom *(Retama roetam)* and the saxaul tree *(Heloxylon persicum)*, but mainly of low bushes that spread farther and farther from each other with the drop in rainfall. The most common low bushes are *Zygophyllum dumosum* and *Anabasis articulatum* on the hammadas (rocky and gravelly soilless plateaus) of the central and southern Negev (see illustration) and single-seeded wormwood

Stand of Hyphaene thebaica, *near Elat, southern ʻArava Valley.* [Plant Life of Palestine, *by Michael Zohary, New York, The Ronald Press Company, 1962. Courtesy of the publishers.*]

(A. monosperma), *Haloxylon salicornicum*, *Calligonum comosum*, and *Thymelaea hirsuta* on sandy soils.

5. *Sudanian Element.* The fifth phytogeographical element is the Sudanian, with about 40 species growing in oases and along watercourses in the ʻArava Valley, in the central Negev, and around the Dead Sea. Acacia species form savannah formations along dry watercourses as they do in eastern Africa. A rare species of this element is the dichotomous Sudanian palm *(Hyphaene thebaica;* see illustration) that grows near Elat. Other rare species grow in the oasis of ʻEn Gedi. The famous Christ's-thorn jujube *(Zizphus spina-christi)* is a large tree belonging to this element.

See also FORESTRY IN ISRAEL.   M. NEGBI

FOERDER, YESHAYAHU (Herbert). Chairman of the *Bank L'umi L'Yisrael (b. Charlottenburg, Berlin, 1901). Foerder attended the Universities of Freiburg and Heidelberg and received his doctorate in laws from the University of Königsberg in 1923. From 1924 to 1926 he was secretary of the Zionist Organization of Germany. Settling in Palestine in 1933, he was a cofounder of *RASSCO (Rural and Suburban Settlement Company) and its managing director from 1933 to 1957.

In 1948–49 Foerder served as Food Comptroller in Israel's Ministry of Supplies and in 1949–50 was managing director of the housing company ʻAmidar Ltd. Elected to the *Knesset in 1949 as a deputy of the *Progressive party, he served until 1957, when he resigned to become chairman of the board of directors of the Bank L'umi L'Yisrael.

FOLK MUSIC IN ISRAEL. The *Ingathering of the Exiles brought to Israel individuals, tribes, and peoples from many countries and regions, each contributing a rich heritage of ritual, customs, and folklore to the Israeli scene. The first ʻAliyot (*see* IMMIGRATION TO PALESTINE AND ISRAEL) from the Eastern European countries imported folk songs from the ghettos, later adapting Hebrew words to the original Yiddish melodies. Subsequent waves of immigrants, from the Central and Western European countries, had their own musical taste and background. The voice of the Near East was hardly heard prior to the immigration from Yemen and other countries of Asia and North Africa, which brought what can be termed an "Eastern-Mediterranean" musical idiom. The collecting, recording, and transcribing of this ancient material have fascinated the musicologists and attracted the composers of modern Israel, whose style is often influenced by what they regard as the genuine Israeli folklore—consisting, in fact, mainly of the Mediterranean and Near Eastern traditions.

Unlike nations which have been living on their own soil for many centuries, Israel has no genuine "anonymous" folk song; her folk songs have been written and composed by authors whose names are known, but these names are being forgotten and their songs have become folk songs in the real sense of the term. The earliest popular Palestinian Hebrew song was "Hava Nagila," composed in 1918 by Abraham Z. *Idelsohn, who wrote the words and used strains of a Hasidic melody. Later creators of popular songs were Yoel *Engel, Shalom Postolsky, Menashe Ravina, Yedidya Admon (Gorodchov), Emanuel Amiran (Pugatchov), Mordecai Zeira, Moshe Wilensky, Matityahu Shelem, Yehuda Sharett, Nahum Nardi, Daniel Sambursky, Nissan Cohen Melamed, David Zahavi, Emanuel Zamir, Naomi Shemer, and Sarah Levy.

P. GRADENWITZ

FOOD IN ISRAEL. In Israel the traditional dishes of the communities of *Ashkenazim, *Sephardim, and *Oriental Jews are being adapted to local products, climate, and tastes. The years of austerity which followed the birth of the State of Israel taught the population how to make the best of the simplest foods. Later, increased agricultural output introduced a more luxurious trend into cooking, so much so that culinary contests became a feature even of the Government Tourist Corporation. Owing to local demand no less than to tourist needs, hotels and restaurants in Israel are constantly at work improving their culinary standards. The limitations of Kashrut (Jewish dietary laws) have been overcome by the creativeness of Israeli chefs, who turn out kosher beef stroganoff, *pareve* (nonmilk) ice cream, and kosher chow mein which are hardly distinguishable from the nonkosher combinations.

Sabbath and Festival Dishes. While the *Sabra type of Israeli cuisine features a variety of salads, for breakfast as well as for lunch and dinner, and takes into account such local factors as climate (salt herring for breakfast replaces the taking of salt pills), the dishes traditionally associated with the Sabbath and Jewish festivals still occupy an important place. The Sabbath law forbidding the kindling of fire keeps many of these dishes on Israeli tables. The Ashkenazi *cholent* (like the Sephardi *dafina*), which cooks overnight for the Sabbath, still survives in Israel under the Hebrew name *hamim* (literally, "hot food"), with chick-peas frequently replacing the beans. Potatoes have taken the place of the dumpling familiarly known as *knaidel* in Europe and as *kouklas* in North Africa (which latter some presume to be the origin of the *kugel*).

On Rosh HaShana (Jewish New Year), Ashkenazim in Israel serve carrot *tzimmes*, which, golden and coin-shaped, symbolize prosperity. The Sephardim and the Jews from the Middle East place the head of a sheep or of a fish on their festive tables as reminders that the Jewish people should be at the head and not the tail of the nations.

Sukkot (Feast of Tabernacles) meals in Oriental families feature *sarmis*, a dish of chopped meat and rice rolled in grape leaves from the vineyards of Judea. Ashkenazim in Israel use the European cabbage leaf instead of the grape leaves and call the dish *holiptzes*. Families of Polish descent serve *fluden*, or *fladen*, on Simhat Tora; this is a layer cake made with many fruits, either fresh or dried. Persian families have rose-flavored or rose-decorated desserts on that holiday.

Latkes, a dish of grated raw potatoes mixed into a batter and fried, has yielded first place among Hanukka foods to *sufganiyot*, or filled doughnuts.

The fruits and fruit dishes that mark Tu Bish'vat (the New Year of the Trees) in the *Diaspora are everyday fare in Israel, where fresh fruit and fruit soups are almost daily fare in most homes.

About 20 different Purim delicacies are known in Israel by the name *ozne Haman* (Haman's ears). Some of these are twirly fried doughs; others resemble the familiar Hamantashen (filled baked pastry).

The same variety is found in the *haroset* mixture, which is one of the symbolic foods on the Passover Seder plate. Whereas European Jews make *haroset* from apples, almonds, cinnamon, and wine, Yemenite Jews use a mixture of dates and figs with ginger and chili pepper added and North African Jews use an almond mixture to which they add pine nuts, egg yolks, and spices. The native Israelis mix several of these concoctions together, the end product being a "mincemeat" mixture of wine,

cinnamon, and almost every fruit in season. As for *maror*, the "bitter herbs" of the Seder ritual, the Middle Eastern Jews do not use horseradish but bitter lettuce.

Western Jews in Israel mark Shavu'ot (Pentecost) with blintzes (crêpes filled with cottage cheese), knishes (pastries filled with cheese and baked), and cheesecakes, while families from the Mediterranean area serve *borekas*, "Mount Sinai cakes," and yogurt salads.

Everyday Fare. The *felafel, hummus* (a paste of pounded chick-peas with spices), and *tehina* (an oily paste of sesame seeds) of the Middle East have come to be regarded as typically Israeli. The *kreplach* and *varenikis* of Eastern Europe have become less popular and, instead of being homemade, are turned out by machine. Along with such dairy products as yogurt and sour cream, cheeses—from cottage cheese to Roquefort to salt goats' cheese—have assumed an important place in the Israeli menu. The Sephardi *hamindas* (eggs cooked for 24 hours) have become popular throughout Israel. Along with rice and chick-peas, the cracked wheat known as *burghul* is the main cereal of the Middle Eastern communities. The *kasha* (buckwheat groats) of Eastern Europe and the *mamalige*, a cornmeal mush of Romanian Jewry, are passing from the Israeli culinary scene. Couscous, a semolina grain dish among North African immigrants, seems to have come to Israel to stay.

Israel has an almost endless variety of breads, ranging from *pampalik* to *pita*, from pumpernickel to *shibolet*, and from rye to *halot*. Candies and sweets include the standard delicacies from the world over, but many Israeli housewives still turn out the *tayglach* (bits of dough cooked in special syrups), *mohnlach* (poppyseed confections), and *pomerantzen* (candied orange rinds) of Eastern Europe. Jews from Middle Eastern countries have brought to Israel candied nuts and various kinds of toasted seeds.

M. LYONS BAR-DAVID

FOREIGN AID PROGRAM OF ISRAEL. Israel became an active participant in international assistance activities in 1958 with the establishment of a Division for International Cooperation in the Ministry of Foreign Affairs. Since then it has developed a varied and widely respected program, involving at one

A Nigerian student learns to inoculate poultry at a Histadrut kibbutz. [Histadrut Foto-News]

An expert teaches the science of viticulture in an Israeli vineyard.
[Israel Information Services]

In Africa, an Israeli agricultural adviser confers with youthful farmers. [Israel Information Services]

time or another some 90 developing countries in the Middle East, other parts of Asia and Africa, and South America. As a small nation that still requires external capital for its own development, Israel has concentrated mainly on technical assistance rather than transfers of capital. Moreover, as a matter of principle as well as a matter of financial necessity, Israel's program is organized as a cooperative venture in which its partners share a large part of the financial burden.

History. Contacts of the *Histadrut (General Federation of Labor) and *Mapai (Israel Labor party) with Asian and African labor leaders in the early 1950s paved the way for the evolution of the Israeli foreign aid program. Burma, the first Asian country to establish diplomatic relations with Israel, also became its first cooperation partner, as early as 1954. Under the leadership of David Hacohen, the former director of the Histadrut construction company Solel Bone and Israel's first Ambassador to Burma, Israeli experts were sent to advise the economic branch of the Burmese Army in a variety of nonmilitary tasks, while in the military sphere Israel provided training for Burmese Air Force ground crews and army technicians. These programs were followed by a variety of projects in agriculture and joint ventures in shipping and construction.

In Africa cooperation programs began in 1957, with Ghana's independence. Fraternal relations between the Histadrut and the Ghanaian Trade Union Congress led to the assignment of Israeli advisers and to trade union–oriented training programs in Israel, while a variety of technical assistance projects was initiated at the governmental level. Joint-venture partnerships were established in 1958 between Solel Bone and the Zim–Israel Shipping Company, Ltd., and Ghanaian government agencies.

Principles. From its own experience as a still-developing society and as a country until recently dependent on external assistance for economic survival, Israel has shaped the principles and characteristics that govern its program of international cooperation. In part out of necessity and in part out of conviction, Israel has placed major emphasis on the provision of training services. It has found this type of assistance to be the most suitable and economical use of its limited resources. Israelis believe, moreover, that their experience qualifies them particularly well for the preparation and training of development-oriented and -motivated manpower. Thus, in addition to

bringing to Israel as many as 2,000 persons annually for training, numerous Israeli experts in developing countries devote much of their effort to training activities. Ideally, Israel favors so-called integrated projects, in which training in Israel or other countries is combined with the services of technical assistance experts, so that the trainees can speedily replace the experts and establish an independent operational capability. This pattern was applied to Israel's first agricultural assistance project in Burma, in which Burmese Army veterans were brought to Israel for training and on their return to Burma worked with an Israeli agricultural team in a new settlement scheme. With some modifications, the approach has since been followed in many other countries.

As a rule, Israel has adopted an open-door policy in responding to requests for training or expert services. Though quite sensitive to the political significance of its cooperation program, Israel does not attach political strings to it. A number of countries that do not maintain full diplomatic relations with Israel, among them Iran, India, and Malaysia, have nevertheless benefited from some aspects of Israel's cooperation program. Similarly, in the economic sphere Israel has extended assistance in branches of the economy such as citriculture that are at least potentially competitive with its own interests.

The personal involvement of trainees and Israeli experts is considered an essential element in Israel's cooperation programs. In accordance with this precept, much stress is laid on practical fieldwork, demonstrations, and direct participation at all levels of the development process. Israelis believe there is no greater stimulus to this process than the example of those who lead it. Inherent in this sense of personal involvement and commitment emphasized in the Israeli programs are a willingness to work hard and face up to difficulties, a capacity to improvise, and a well-developed social consciousness. The emphasis Israel places on developing these attitudes lends its programs a special quality.

Israelis also stress the importance of mutual benefit in their cooperative programs with other nations. Not that they expect or require specific quid pro quos in their cooperation activities, but they do contend that developing nations can learn from one another and that Israel can and does benefit from its cooperation activities. While the returns to Israel in terms of developmental know-how are difficult to define, there seems to be little doubt that the programs have greatly promoted Israel's self-respect, helped break through the ring of isolation and hostility around the country, and laid the basis for friendly international relations with most of the developing world.

Scope and Character of the Foreign Aid Program. In the late 1960s Israel has been spending about $6,000,000 annually from governmental and nongovernmental sources on its technical cooperation program. The actual volume of activity generated by these funds, however, is estimated at two to three times the level of Israel's own annual expenditures. This multiplier effect results mainly from the unusually high ratio of financial participation by Israel's cooperation partners in project activities and to a lesser extent from international organization cosponsorship of Israeli training programs. The financial participation of cooperating governments often extends to assuming a large share of the salaries of visiting experts, and international organization cosponsorship involves the assumption of such costs as international travel and out-of-pocket expenditures for the operation of training facilities.

Although Israel's primary emphasis is on technical cooperation, it has also extended, in the period 1960–66, some $20,000,000 to $25,000,000 in short- and medium-term loans or credits. Such capital transfers have usually been made in conjunction with or in support of Israel-sponsored joint commercial ventures or technical cooperation activities. Israeli loans or credits have been extended to the African countries of Sierra Leone, Nigeria, Ghana, Liberia, Ivory Coast, and Tanzania, and Israel has also invested some $3,000,000 in bonds of the Inter-American Development Bank to promote development in Latin America.

Israel's technical assistance efforts include most of the non-Communist developing nations except the *Arab League countries and certain others that have refused cooperation with Israel out of deference to Arab sensitivities. The greatest concentration of Israeli activity has been in Africa south of the Sahara. Of the approximately 1,800 experts who carried out some 3,500 assignments in 1960–66, more than two-thirds worked in Africa. The rest were active in Asia, the Mediterranean area, and Latin America. A similar ratio was apparent among those who came to Israel for training (see Table 1).

Professionally, Israeli activity has been quite varied, including training programs or expert services in everything from poultry husbandry, youth development, and rural regional planning to medicine, business administration, and management or to the establishment of national lotteries. The primary focus has been on agriculture, cooperation, and youth development for national service or on settlement in the backward areas of developing countries (see Table 2).

Compared with the thousands of experts and training opportunities provided every year by the major industrial countries and international organizations, Israel's effort is comparatively small. However, it is one of the largest and best-organized programs set up by a developing country, and it compares favorably with programs developed by many of the industrial countries. Because of the limitations on the manpower and financial resources that can be devoted to the cooperation program, Israel has had to be increasingly selective in responding to requests for assistance. Unlike some of the large industrial countries, it has established no permanent assistance missions abroad, and about one-fourth of its experts have been provided for short-term assignments of less than a year's duration. Similarly, in its training activities, Israel emphasizes specially prepared training courses of three to four months' duration, or even shorter programs of the seminar type, rather than longer-term academic studies. Most of those involved as experts or instructors in the Israeli cooperation activities are borrowed for their assignments from other jobs in the Israeli government or from the cooperative and private sector. Israeli officials do not favor a career service for their program, even though the present system makes recruitment more difficult and at times causes a certain amount of discontinuity. They believe that no

TABLE 1. FOREIGN ASSIGNMENTS OF ISRAELI EXPERTS AND NUMBER OF FOREIGN TRAINEES IN ISRAEL, BY GEOGRAPHIC AREA AND YEAR, 1958–66

Geographic area	Total*	1958	1959	1960	1961	1962	1963	1964	1965	1966
Assignment of experts:										
Total	3,476	40	80	163	280	395	544	698	636	640
Africa	2,485	25	51	122	211	265	424	528	453	406
Asia	345	15	25	31	44	52	43	39	44	52
Latin America	270	...	2	3	11	19	37	73	55	70
Mediterranean area†	376	...	2	7	14	59	40	58	84	112
Trainees in Israel:										
Total‡	12,627	137	213	672	1,250	1,621	2,272	2,446	2,267	1,749
Africa	6,640	59	75	291	876	899	1,231	1,363	1,032	814
Asia	2,167	71	109	309	267	197	199	224	376	415
Latin America	1,467	2	11	37	17	137	289	399	342	233
Mediterranean area†	2,059	5	18	35	90	346	545	428	354	238

SOURCE: Leonard Laufer, *Israel and the Developing Countries: New Approaches to Cooperation,* Twentieth Century Fund, New York, 1967, p. 76.
*The number of experts who served abroad was smaller, since many experts carried out several assignments during the period. The actual number of experts, by area, were: total, 1,815; Africa, 1,261; Asia, 180; Latin America, 144; Mediterranean area, 230. The actual number of trainees who arrived in Israel was also smaller, since some long-term trainees spent more than one year in Israel. The number of trainees arriving, by area, were: total, 9,074; Africa, 4,482; Asia, 1,163; Latin America, 1,281; Mediterranean area, 1,853.
†Includes Cyprus, Iran, Malta, Turkey, and Yugoslavia.   ‡ Totals include 295 trainees from other areas, not shown in annual figures by area.

TABLE 2. ISRAELI EXPERTS SERVING ABROAD AND TRAINEES ARRIVING IN ISRAEL, BY FIELD OF SERVICE OR TRAINING AND GEOGRAPHIC AREA, 1958–66

Field of service or training	Geographic area				
	Total	Africa	Asia	Latin America	Mediterranean area*
Experts:					
Total	1,815	1,261	180	144	230
Agriculture	523	261	73	75	114
Youth organization	256	234	4	17	1
Engineering	64	42	10	2	10
Medicine and health	202	173	26	3	.....
Education	106	102	1	3	.....
Cooperation	24	21	.....	3	.....
Management	63	46	10	4	3
Construction and building	65	49	5	1	10
Social work	23	22	.....	.....	1
Miscellaneous	489	311	51	36	91
Trainees:					
Total †	9,074	4,482	1,163	1,281	1,853
Agriculture	2,264	805	213	553	673
Cooperation and trade unionism	1,048	664	162	138	73
Community development	712	493	124	17	27
Youth leadership	529	285	42	165	34
Health and medicine	265	211	21	6	22
Commerce, transport, finance, and industry	156	37	9	1	107
Study tours and seminars	1,622	537	238	198	503
Individual academic studies	230	102	60	26	35
Miscellaneous	2,248	1,348	294	177	379

SOURCE: Leonard Laufer, *Israel and the Developing Countries: New Approaches to Cooperation,* Twentieth Century Fund, New York, 1967, p. 77.

*Includes Cyprus, Iran, Malta, Turkey, and Yugoslavia.

†Totals include 295 trainees from other areas.

Israeli engaged in the program should ever be in a position where he may be suspected of wishing to perpetuate his job, and they contend that performance might suffer if people were too long removed from their professional pursuits and from their Israeli environment.

Perhaps the most outstanding characteristic of Israel's cooperation program is its predominant orientation toward the essentials of nation building. By utilizing the experience in rebuilding a Jewish Homeland and forging a modern nation, the Israeli program seeks to promote a sense of national unity, national pride, social consciousness, human dignity, and the worth of labor, including manual labor, in the process of national construction. On the practical level these elements are expressed in an undogmatic, pragmatic approach, a willingness to improvise and experiment, a sense of urgency and commitment, and a dogged determination to succeed. This identification with the essentials of the nation-building process perhaps

accounts more than any other quality for the receptivity to Israeli cooperation programs and constitutes an exceptional contribution to the art of development assistance.

Agricultural Cooperation and Pioneering. There is no set pattern for Israeli assistance in agriculture, except that many of the larger Israeli-aided projects combine agricultural pursuits with some features of cooperative enterprise. However, Israeli forms of collective settlement such as the *kibbutz are rarely if ever used as models, and even less collectivist patterns, such as the smallholders' settlements (*see* MOSHAV), have had to be considerably modified when tried abroad. Frequently Israeli advisers work with military services or paramilitary organizations in developing programs of agricultural training and settlement, modeled broadly after the Nahal pioneering program of the Israel Defense Army. This has provided many of the new African countries, especially, with an opportunity to promote agricultural pursuits and stimulate pioneering among their younger generation.

An example of an agricultural program is a center in Togo at which 120 members of Togo's Agricultural Pioneer Youth are trained each month in the principles and practices of cooperative agriculture; subsequently, the young farmers return to their villages, where they farm cooperatively for three years, after which they are ready to establish new cooperative villages. In another project, a demonstration farm for the development of industrial crops in Cambodia is guided by Israeli experts, working as part of an international team developing the Mekong River delta; a related irrigation system is being developed in conjunction with a Japanese dam construction team. Yet another approach has been taken in Venezuela, where a training center has been established for professional agricultural personnel, economists, and engineers involved in rural regional planning and development; several new settlement areas are being developed and supervised by personnel from the center, and experimentation in new techniques of supervised agricultural credit and village rehabilitation is going on.

Youth Development. The major purpose of Israel's many cooperation projects involving youth is to stimulate concepts of national service and national unity and to promote an interest in agriculture and agricultural settlement so as to slow the prevailing drift from the countryside to overcrowded cities. Israelis with experience as leaders of Israel's own Gadna' organization (*see* ISRAEL DEFENSE FORCES) or other Israeli *youth movements have organized national youth movements as important supplements to the countries' formal educational establishments. The National Youth Movement in Costa Rica, for example, which was organized in 1965, has trained a volunteer leadership corps and established youth clubs in many outlying villages where for the first time young people are brought together for competitive sports, social activities, and discussions of current problems. In the Ivory Coast the Israeli-aided Youth and Work Movement combines supplementary education for school dropouts with a sports and scouting program. For boys of military age there is the National Service, also advised by Israelis, which concentrates on agricultural training and settlement; for girls between 16 and 18 years of age, a Women's National Service has been established. After 6 to 12 months of training by selected Ivory Coast instructors and a team from the Women's Army of the Israel Defense Army, the young graduates return to their villages as teachers and "agents of change."

Social Welfare. Cooperation programs in social welfare and related sectors have utilized Israel's considerable achievements in the organization of social services, health care, labor, and cooperative services. Examples are a school for social workers organized in Kenya and initially staffed entirely by Israeli instructors, a hospital in Ethiopia directed by an Israeli physician, and bus cooperatives in Peru organized with the help of advisers from Israel's Egged bus cooperative. Attempts in several African countries to organize multipurpose labor federations along the lines of Israel's Histadrut have had only limited success, because political and social conditions in Africa differ greatly from those that had given rise to the Histadrut. Nevertheless, the philosophy and strength of Israel's trade union and cooperative movement continue to attract many visitors and students from developing countries.

Joint Ventures. While joint industrial and business ventures between foreign enterprises and local companies or governments of developing countries are not new, Israel's approach in this sphere is somewhat different. The Israeli goal is to create new enterprises of definite developmental value that operate along commercial lines and are under the control of the respective countries. The Israeli partner usually provides up to 49 per cent of the capital and, initially, most of the executive personnel, but control rests with the host government, which provides more than half the capital and which under the contract can buy out the Israeli partner after five years. Until then the Israeli partner provides managerial and other types of backstopping and trains local personnel so that they can operate without external assistance. This was the pattern which enabled Ghana in 1958 to establish a National Construction Company in partnership with the Histadrut's Solel Bone construction enterprise and with its own Black Star Shipping Line in conjunction with the Zim–Israel Shipping Company. Joint enterprises were also established in Burma, Nepal, Ivory Coast, Sierra Leone, Niger, and Nigeria.

Short Training Programs. Israel conducts widespread training programs both in its own country and abroad. Although there is some difference between on-the-spot courses conducted in the developing countries themselves and training in Israel, the emphasis in both types is on short, highly concentrated courses for middle-level personnel. The average short course in Israel lasts about three months; that abroad, even less. Within Israel primary responsibility for the conduct of short-term training has been delegated by the Ministry of Foreign Affairs to various other ministries or public institutions. The Ministry of Agriculture conducts most agricultural training and has set up its own Foreign Training Department; the Ministry of Defense through its Gadna'/Nahal Department takes charge of youth development and leadership courses and has also provided military training to various African nations; the Productivity Institute of the Ministry of Labor has a Foreign Department that is responsible for training in management and public administration. In addition, there are special institutes devoted exclusively to foreign training activities, among them the Afro-Asian Institute for Labor Studies and Cooperation, the Latin American Center for Cooperative and Labor Studies, and the Mount Carmel International Training Center for Community Services. The language of instruction in most of the courses is English, French, or Spanish, but at times special courses have been arranged in such languages as Turkish, Persian, and Portuguese.

The Foreign Training Department of the Ministry of Agriculture, the largest of the Israeli training institutions, often conducts several courses at the same time. Its schedule of courses includes agricultural cooperation, extension services, poultry husbandry,

Israeli engineers advise in the construction of a hospital in Africa. [Israel Information Services]

irrigation, agricultural planning, arid-zone agriculture, fisheries, and fertilizers. In addition, it supervises many individual training programs in specialized subjects, which are arranged at the request of various countries. Despite the great variety of instruction offered, there are some common themes. These are to bring trainees closer to the so-called grass roots by enabling them to talk, work, and even live with Israeli counterparts and to promote a sense of pride in and dedication to agricultural pursuits as vital elements of the development process of their own countries. The Latin American Center for Cooperative and Labor Studies follows a similar approach in its agricultural cooperation courses but concentrates on cooperative agriculture and agroindustry associated with the Histadrut-affiliated settlements and Histadrut industry.

The Afro-Asian Institute for Labor Studies and Cooperation, sponsored jointly by the Histadrut and the Israel government, is Israel's best-equipped center devoted to the training of people from developing countries. It accommodates up to 60 students at one time and has a 12-man professional staff. As its name implies, the institute specializes in various aspects of labor organization and cooperative enterprise as practiced in Israel within the integrated Histadrut complex of trade unions, settlement movements, marketing organizations, financial and welfare institutions, and industry. By combining in its training the trade union and cooperative elements as they are combined in the Histadrut, the institute hopes to stimulate an awareness of the close and natural affinity between the two as well as of the potential benefits to development from such an integrated labor-cooperative movement.

Emphasis on cooperation as a key tool for development also characterizes the various courses in community development and related subjects organized by the Mount Carmel International Training Center for Community Services, in Haifa, and the pioneering and youth leadership training conducted under Ministry of Defense auspices. The Mount Carmel Center specializes particularly in the role women can play in the development of their countries and incorporates such subjects as health, nutrition, literacy, and crafts in its curriculum. Youth and pioneering training, on the other hand, stresses the ways and means of mobilizing the capacities and energies of young people, including young soldiers, for constructive nation-

A class at the Afro-Asian Institute for Labor Studies and Cooperation. [Histadrut Foto-News]

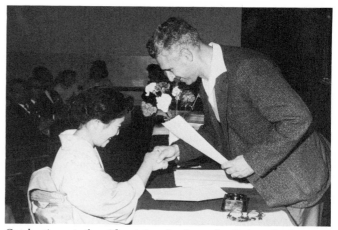

Graduation at the Afro-Asian Institute for Labor Studies and Cooperation. [Histadrut Foto-News]

building activities. A course in youth leadership, for example, normally includes a study of world youth movements, including Israel's Gadna' workshops and discussions on problems of young people, techniques of organizing and operating youth and pioneering movements, observation and participation in pioneering activities of Israel's Gadna' and Nahal organizations, sports and cultural activities, and handicrafts.

On-the-spot courses in the developing countries themselves began as a distinct training activity in 1962, as a means of stretching Israeli manpower and financial resources. Their scope and magnitude are shown in Tables 3 and 4. Although there is some overlap with courses offered in Israel, such as those in agricultural cooperation, extension, and public administration, many of the subjects taught are more technical, as, for example, courses for construction foremen or in first aid. There are obvious limitations to the impact of on-the-spot courses, which cannot utilize the Israeli environment to convey attitudes and experiences. On the other hand, these courses offer direct contact with the environment and conditions of the country for which they are designed.

Academic and Vocational Programs. Israel's long-term academic and vocational training programs for students from developing countries are on a much smaller scale than the short-term training programs. Between 1958 and 1966 some 400 students received such training, compared with more than 8,500 who came to Israel for short-term instruction. The most important of the long-term programs are a six-year medical course,

conducted initially in English for about 70 students from 18 countries at the *Hebrew University–Hadassah Medical School in Jerusalem, and an agricultural engineering program for a similar number of students at the Haifa *Technion. In addition, a postgraduate course in comprehensive rural planning is offered at the Rehovot Settlement Study Center, which is affiliated with the Hebrew University. Two- and three-year vocational and nursing education programs in English and Hebrew were conducted until 1965 but are no longer offered.

Rehovot Conferences. One of Israel's more original contributions to development thinking and philosophy has been the so-called Rehovot movement, which began in 1960 under the auspices of the Israeli government and the *Weizmann Institute of Science. The underlying goal of the movement is to bring together leading world scientists and statesmen or professional leaders of developing countries for a discussion of major questions of development. The resulting dialogue has a twofold purpose: to expose the scientific community directly to the thinking and aspirations of the developing world and, in turn, to stimulate the political leaders of the developing countries to learn and appreciate the views of the foremost professional authorities. The First Rehovot Conference, held in 1960 and devoted to the role of science in the advancement of new states, was attended by 120 distinguished participants from 40 countries. It was the forerunner of the UN Conference on the Application of Science and Technology for the Benefit of the Less Developed Areas, held in Geneva in 1963. Subsequent Rehovot conferences have dealt with comprehensive rural planning, fiscal and monetary policies, and health problems of the developing world.

TABLE 3. PARTICIPANTS IN ON-THE-SPOT COURSES,
BY FIELD OF STUDY AND CONTINENT, 1962–66

	Africa	Asia	Latin America	Total
Health and medicine	2,060	..	...	2,060
Agriculture	155	..	...	155
Cooperation	419	..	521	940
Home industry	.....	28	...	28
Management, finance, and local government	815	39	...	854
Building	200	..	...	200
Total	3,649	67	521	4,237

SOURCE: *Israel's Programme of International Cooperation,* Ministry of Foreign Affairs, Jerusalem, 1967, p. 83.

TABLE 4. PARTICIPANTS IN ON-THE-SPOT COURSES, 1962–66

	1962	1963	1964	1965	1966	Total
Africa	285	172	262	2,615*	315	3,649
Asia	...	...	25	28	14	67
Latin America	...	...	145	141	235	521
Total	285	172	432	2,784	564	4,237

SOURCE: *Israel's Programme of International Cooperation,* Ministry of Foreign Affairs, Jerusalem, 1967, p. 83.
*Includes nearly 2,000 participants in a series of itinerant first-aid courses held in Niger.

It is evident that Israel's program of cooperation with developing countries has already made a notable contribution to these nations. At the same time, it has opened the doors to friendship and other fruitful relationships between Israel and the majority of the developing world.

The following list contains the names of the countries to which Israel sent experts and from which it received trainees from 1958 to 1966: *Mediterranean area*—Cyprus, Iran, Malta, Turkey, and Yugoslavia; *Africa*—Botswana, Burundi, Cameroon, Central African Republic, Chad, Congo (Brazzaville), Congo (Kinshasa), Dahomey, Ethiopia, Gabon, Gambia, Ghana, Guinea, Ivory Coast, Kenya, Lesotho, Liberia, Malagasy Republic, Malawi, Mali, Mauritius, Niger, Nigeria, Rwanda, Senegal, Sierra Leone, Tanzania, Togo, Uganda, Upper Volta, and Zambia; *Asia*—Burma, Ceylon, Nepal, Philippines, Singapore, and Thailand; and *Latin America*—Argentina, Bolivia, Brazil, Chile, Colombia, Costa Rica, Dominican Republic, Ecuador, Guatemala, Jamaica, Peru, Surinam, Trinidad and Tobago, and Venezuela. In addition, trainees were sent to Israel from the following countries: *Mediterranean area*—Greece, Portugal, and Spain; *Africa*—Angola, Mozambique, Portuguese Guinea, Rhodesia, Somalia, South West Africa, and Swaziland; *Asia*—India, Indonesia, Korea, Laos, and Malaysia; and *Latin America*—El Salvador, Guyana, Haiti, Honduras, Mexico, Nicaragua, Panama, Paraguay, and Uruguay.

L. LAUFER

FOREIGN RELATIONS OF ISRAEL. Israel's foreign policy is predicated on five basic characteristics of the country, which in one way or another influence its attitude toward other countries and toward events in any part of the globe. First and foremost, Israel is located in the ancient Homeland of the Jewish people, in the Middle East at the crossroads of three continents, an area which since antiquity has been focal to the interests not only of its inhabitants but also of outside powers, in fact, of the major powers of their times.

Second, in this area Israel is surrounded by Arab countries which, although divided among themselves and distinct from each other in outlook and in economic and political structure, are united in their hostility toward the Jewish State and in their avowed desire to see it disappear.

Third, as a Jewish State, Israel has a legitimate interest in the welfare of Jewish communities in other countries and in the establishment and maintenance of close links with them in all fields of endeavor. The attitude of any government toward the Jewish community living within its boundaries thus cannot be divorced from the relations between that government and the *government of Israel. At the same time, the government of Israel has made it abundantly clear that it does not ask for or expect political allegiance from any but its own citizens and, conversely, that its policies are determined by the duly elected representatives of the citizens of the State alone.

Fourth, all the successive Cabinets of the State of Israel have been consistent in their desire to establish and maintain friendly relations with all countries regardless of their constitutions or form of government. However, the fact that Israel is a parliamentary democracy, which has safeguarded its democratic institutions jealously even in times of emergency and war, cannot but determine a closer affinity with the group of democratic countries, sometimes loosely referred to as the free world.

Fifth, although Israel is located in Asia and has been making

determined efforts to cultivate its relations with other countries on that continent and the adjoining one of Africa, its economy is predicated to a large and increasing extent on close relations with the countries of Western Europe; hence the consistent endeavor, which has become more emphatic in recent years, to find a form of association with or membership in the European Economic Community (*see* EUROPEAN COMMON MARKET AND ISRAEL).

HISTORY

Although the State of Israel was created in 1948, its foreign relations date back several decades. From its inception the Zionist movement conducted diplomatic activity as one of its primary functions. In fact, the inception of such activity and the development of political thinking were among Herzl's principal contributions to the development of Zionist thought and organization.

In the mandatory period (*see* MANDATE FOR PALESTINE), the main foci of political activity were in London as the seat of the mandatory government and in Jerusalem. Even during that period, however, the United States came increasingly to the fore because of the importance of its Jewish community and its weight on the international scene. In the years following World War II, with relations between the mandatory government and the *Yishuv (Jewish population of Palestine) strained, Jerusalem hamstrung in its possibilities, and, on the other hand, Great Britain depending more and more on the United States, the major emphasis shifted to the latter power. It was the Political Department of the *Jewish Agency that in 1947 organized and conducted the successful struggle at Lake Success, which resulted in the adoption by the United Nations of the *partition resolution. This struggle was a cooperative effort of Zionist leaders in Israel and the *Diaspora.

First Years of the State. In the early months of 1948, when a nucleus for the government for the future State was set up in the abandoned Templar village of Sarona, near Tel Aviv, one building was set aside for the future Ministry of Foreign Affairs. Even as warfare raged throughout the country (*see* WAR OF INDEPENDENCE), with the British government nominally still in charge of law and order and some officials of the new State detained in besieged Jerusalem, this nucleus, under the direction of Moshe Shertok (later *Sharett), then head of the Political Department of the Jewish Agency, took charge of the incipient State's foreign relations. Sharett was aided by a secretary and a personal assistant.

It was from here that on May 15, 1948, cables went out to all the capitals of the world asking for recognition of the newly established State. Events moved fast. Communications were difficult. Thus, it was to a large extent on his own initiative that the self-styled "Agent, Provisional Government of Israel" in Washington asked on May 14 for recognition of his government by the government of the United States. While the UN General Assembly was still debating the Palestine problem, Pres. Harry S *Truman took the historic decision of granting de facto recognition to the provisional government of Israel. The second country to recognize Israel was Guatemala (May 15), and the third the Soviet Union (May 18). Within a few days, 5 Eastern European and 5 Latin American countries had followed suit. At the beginning of August, 1948, however, no more than 15 countries had recognized Israel.

At the time Great Britain refused to extend recognition. Its communications were stubbornly directed to the "Jewish

Authorities in Tel Aviv" and were rejected with equal stubbornness. It was only toward the end of the fighting, early in 1949, that Great Britain and France extended recognition to Israel. By Feb. 1, 1949, the number of countries recognizing Israel had risen to 33, corresponding exactly to the number that had voted for Israel's independence in the General Assembly but including several countries that were not members of the United Nations. By Mar. 1, 1949, the number had risen to 45, and by early April it was 53. Some countries gave de jure recognition; others, de facto recognition only. Many stipulated that the question of *boundaries, an important attribute of statehood, was not prejudiced by recognition.

With the battle for recognition won, the next logical step for Israel was to seek admission to the United Nations. Symbolically, on Nov. 29, 1948, the first anniversary of the partition resolution, Israel submitted its application. Although supported by both the United States and the Soviet Union (a unanimity that was a unique feature of Israel's early political struggles, to be repeated, inversely, seven years later after the *Sinai Campaign), Israel's application failed. When Israel tried again, early in 1949, after the signing of the armistice agreement with Egypt (see ARMISTICE AGREEMENTS), the Security Council changed its attitude and, with only Egypt opposing and Great Britain abstaining, recommended the admission of Israel to full membership. The General Assembly approved the resolution in May, 1949, almost exactly one year after the establishment of the State.

Throughout this first year, the United Nations (the Security Council and the General Assembly) was engaged almost continuously in considering the "Palestine problem." The first and second truces, the abortive mediation effort, and the signing of armistice agreements have been described elsewhere. It was only in July, 1949, after lengthy negotiations, that the last of those agreements (with Syria) was signed. Syria had been the only Arab country which, at the end of hostilities, still occupied territories allotted to Israel under the partition plan. Although persuaded to evacuate those territories, it persisted in demanding that they be declared demilitarized zones, whose nature and status were left deliberately vague in the agreement, resulting in interminable incidents and debates in subsequent years. See also UNITED NATIONS AND PALESTINE-ISRAEL.

Armistice Agreements. As stated in their preambles, these were considered a temporary measure, a step toward establishment of a permanent peace. By a resolution of the UN General Assembly of December, 1948, the Palestine Conciliation Commission, consisting of representatives of Turkey, France, and the United States, was constituted "to take steps to assist the governments and authorities concerned to achieve a final settlement of all questions outstanding between them"—even at that time the word "peace" was avoided in order not to give offense to Arab sensitivities. Specifically, the Conciliation Commission was instructed to find solutions for the problems of Jerusalem and refugees. The Commission did not interpret its mandate to include bringing Israeli and Arab representatives together under one roof; it met separately with the Israelis, on the one hand, and with Arabs (representatives of all Arab countries), on the other. This procedure no doubt contributed to the inefficacy of the Commission. By bringing all Arabs together as one party, it discouraged moderates from speaking openly; by meeting separately with Israelis and Arabs, it prevented a free exchange of views. Hostilities having been terminated, Arab governments saw no overwhelming reason for accommodating themselves to

the existence and reality of the State of Israel or of reaching any agreement with it. As a result, the peace conference, which was opened in Lausanne in April, 1949, failed. The Palestine Conciliation Commission, though still officially in existence in 1968, has been ineffectual ever since.

Early in 1948 the first blueprint for a Ministry of Foreign Affairs and a Foreign Service was prepared. As a first step it envisaged the establishment of four Israeli legations, in London, Washington, Paris, and Moscow, in view of the importance of these capitals; and of "passport control offices" in Hamburg, Frankfurt, Vienna, and Bucharest, for the issuance of visas to meet the urgent needs of Jewish displaced persons and refugees. A second phase was to be the establishment of posts in Shanghai, Prague, Ankara, Teheran, and Warsaw and of passport offices in Aden, Algiers, and Trieste; a third, the setting up of posts in Stockholm, Rio de Janeiro, Bombay, Brussels, Rome, Johannesburg, Montreal, and Melbourne. There were considerable deviations from this plan from the very start of its implementation.

Relations with the Soviet Union. The government of Israel, with the full support of the *Knesset (Parliament), declared from the very beginning that it would maintain friendly relations with all countries regardless of the nature of their regimes. The unanimity of the United States and the Soviet Union in 1948, despite the growing rift between them in the cold war, was considered a major asset. However, relations with the Soviet Union were to deteriorate rapidly. Whether as a result of the overwhelming reception prepared by Russian Jewry for Mrs. Golda *Meir, Israel's first Minister to Moscow, which may have shocked Moscow's rulers into the realization that relations with Israel could not be separated from the "internal" Jewish problem of the Soviet Union; or as a result of Israel's vote on the Korean issue in 1951, which represented its first deviation from the policy of "nonidentification" followed to that point; or as most observers are inclined to believe, chiefly because of the changing circumstances in the Middle East and the concomitant shift in Soviet interests—the Soviet Union soon abandoned its support for Israel, which was then no longer engaged in war against a Western colonial power. In the fall of 1953, while the infamous "doctors' plot" (see SLANSKY TRIAL) was being hatched in Moscow, the explosion of a small bomb in the garden of the Soviet Embassy in Tel Aviv, presumably the action of an *agent provocateur*, was used as a pretext for a break in diplomatic relations. Though renewed some months later following a promise from Israel not to grant bases to any powers bent on aggression against the Soviet Union, relations between Israel and the Soviet Union never again became as cordial as they had been in the first months of the existence of the State. With British influence in Arab countries receding, new openings presented themselves for Soviet policy in the Middle East; the Egyptian-Czechoslovak arms deal in 1955 only set the seal on a trend which had been evident for quite some time before.

Bandung Conference. As relations with the Soviet Union were cooling, the 1954 Bandung Conference, the first conference of independent Asian and African states, demonstrated the tenuousness of Israel's diplomatic position among the new states of Asia and Africa. Israel was not invited to the conference for fear that the Arabs might decide to boycott it, and a resolution was adopted which, though calling for a peaceful settlement of the Palestine question, supported the rights of Arabs in Palestine. By that time, Israel already had close relations with Burma, one of the sponsors of the conference, and consular missions in other Asian countries, but these were of no avail.

Relations with Egypt and the Arab States. Egypt's newly gained confidence, which was based to a large extent on the knowledge of unconditional Soviet support in the United Nations and elsewhere, no doubt encouraged Colonel Nasser to increase *fedayeen operations against Israel, to persist in preventing passage of Israeli ships and Israel-bound cargo through the Suez Canal, and ultimately to nationalize the canal. The subsequent Sinai Campaign, though successful militarily, found Israel almost completely isolated diplomatically. Not only the Soviet Union supported Nasser's government; practically all Asian and African governments opposed Israel, to a large extent because of their opposition to the Anglo-French expedition, which they considered an act of colonialism; the United States government also took exception to the operation and joined the Soviet Union in condemning Israel. Thus, the government of Israel was compelled to withdraw from the Gaza Strip and the Sinai Peninsula, on the "understanding" that freedom of navigation through the Strait of Tiran would be maintained and offensive actions from the Gaza Strip against Israel prevented—an understanding that was put to the test, and found wanting, 10 years later.

The years following the Sinai Campaign were marked by determined efforts on many diplomatic fronts. Relations with its immediate neighbors still constituted Israel's foremost security and foreign relations problem, but on this particular front no breakthrough was evident. Pres. Habib Bourguiba of Tunisia became the first Arab leader openly to denounce the traditional Arab attitude toward Israel, insisting that the Arabs accept reality. Since he was far removed from the scene, however, the impact of his words could not change the basic situation. On the contrary, from the time of the first Arab summit conference in 1961, it became evident that Arab policies were geared to preparations for another round against Israel, to be opened whenever and wherever Arabs would consider themselves militarily ready for such a venture. The inauguration of the Jordan-Negev *National Water Carrier Project by Israel in 1964, an event which had been openly declared as constituting a *casus belli,* evidently found Arab rulers still unwilling to take the leap; the diversion of the Jordan headwaters, which had been decided upon earlier by the Arabs as a substitute for war, was successfully thwarted by Israel within the framework of legitimate self-defense undertaken in the course of frequent incidents along the Syrian border.

Foreign Aid Missions. These years coincided with the "winds of change" in Africa. Previously, Israel had established diplomatic relations with Liberia and Ethiopia and also with Ghana, when the Gold Coast Colony was established as an independent state under that name. Now Israeli diplomacy worked hard to keep pace with the fast-moving events on the African continent. Within three years the number of Israeli missions in African states had increased from 3 to 21, and ultimately almost all the non-Arab independent African states came to maintain cordial and friendly relations with the State of Israel.

The idea of international cooperation, of sharing Israel's know-how and experience with other developing countries, which was first debated in the context of Israeli-Burmese relations, became one of the mainsprings of Israel's foreign relations during the years of Mrs. Golda Meir's service as Foreign Minister. The Foreign Ministry's Division for International Cooperation, jointly with departments of other ministries,

dispatched experts and invited students from more than 60 countries, and Israel came to occupy a place on the map of international cooperation out of all proportion to its size and population. The fact that Israel's relations with many Asian, African, and Latin American countries withstood the persistent pressures of Soviet and Arab policies is due in great measure to the positive and constructive contribution of its *foreign aid program.

***Eichmann Trial.** While relations with Latin American countries developed satisfactorily, beginning with the period before the establishment of the State when Israel enjoyed overwhelming support at the United Nations, an unfortunate although inevitable hiatus occurred in relations with Argentina, after the capture of Adolf Eichmann on Argentinian territory. Though by no means condoning Nazi activity, the government of Argentina resented the intrusion of Israeli agents into its territory and recalled its Ambassador to Israel. Relations were reestablished after a short interval, however, and have since been consistently cordial.

The capture of Eichmann, illustrating as it did Israel's continuing concern with the sufferings of the Jewish people in the recent past and its refusal to forgive and forget Nazi crimes, highlighted the simultaneous development of relations with Germany after a great deal of heart searching and acrimonious debate. Beginning with the reparations agreement negotiated in 1952 (*see* GERMAN-ISRAEL AGREEMENT), economic relations were followed by diplomatic contacts, which in turn brought about the establishment of full diplomatic relations in 1965. When the first Ambassador of the Federal Republic of Germany presented his credentials in Jerusalem, he was met by demonstrations, which at times became violent; upon leaving his post three years later, his last act in office was to lower the fence around the embassy, signifying his certainty that such demonstrations would not be repeated.

Before the outbreak of the *Six-day War of 1967, the State of Israel, with about 400 representatives abroad, maintained some 100 missions on all continents. Israel was represented in practically every capital of the Western Hemisphere and of both Western and Eastern Europe, in most non-Arab capitals of Africa, and in non-Muslim capitals of Asia. It was this network, diligently established in the course of 19 years, that enabled Israel to withstand successfully the determined onslaught of Soviet and Arab diplomacy following the Six-day War.

FOREIGN RELATIONS IN 1967-68

The more than 20 years that have passed since the establishment of the State of Israel have not witnessed any basic change in the attitude of the neighboring Arab countries toward Israel. The decisions adopted at the 1967 Khartoum Conference of Arab heads of state, to wit, no negotiation with Israel, no recognition, and no peace, were but an echo of the statements of the representatives of the same governments in the UN General Assembly prior even to the adoption of the resolution on the partition of Palestine: a Jewish State was not to be established in Palestine or in any part of it; violence would be used to prevent its establishment.

Arab belligerency has varied in intensity, shifting emphasis from one weapon to another, transferring its spearhead from time to time—from Damascus to Cairo and back—but it has been consistent in its aim, sometimes framed euphemistically as "peace with justice in Palestine," meaning the return of Palestine to its Arab inhabitants (otherwise known as "de-Zionizing"

Israel), but often termed more bluntly and brutally as driving the Jews into the sea. While paying lip service to all United Nations resolutions and decisions against aggression, the Arab governments maintain that the existence of Israel is an act of aggression in itself and thus any action against it is not only permissible but obligatory. Israel is to be branded an outcast in international law.

This basic attitude of the neighboring Arab governments toward Israel has not changed. After three disastrous wars, there is open incitement and agitation for another one, accompanied by active steps toward the reequipment and retraining of Arab armed forces, particularly those of the United Arab Republic (UAR).

While formally accepting a political solution, either through the good offices of the United Nations emissary or through other channels, Arab governments have been accelerating the organization, financing, training, and support of terrorist activities. The presence of an Israeli military government in considerable areas of the West Bank of the Jordan, the Gaza Strip, and the Sinai Peninsula has been considered an auspicious circumstance for the propagation of guerrilla warfare; however, the vast majority of the Arab population of these Israel-administered areas has been reluctant to give aid and comfort to guerrilla fighters. Thus terrorist operations after the Six-day War have reverted to their prewar character of acts directed and supported from across the borders and concentrated to a large extent along the border areas. *See also* TERRORIST ORGANIZA-TIONS, ARAB.

Suez and Arab Boycott. Ironically, the UAR's declaration of a blockade of the Strait of Tiran and its attempt to prevent passage of Israeli shipping en route to Elat, in addition to its consistent refusal to allow such shipping to pass through the Suez Canal, has brought about a situation in which the Suez remains closed to the shipping of all nations while the Strait of Tiran is open to all. Thus, the UAR's maintenance of the right of blockade in Tiran and refusal of passage through Suez had become theoretical by 1968. The government of Israel insists that free navigation through the Suez Canal for ships of all nations, including Israel, must be guaranteed in any eventual peace treaty. That right is inherent in the Constantinople Convention of 1888 and was explicitly confirmed by the UN Security Council in 1951, before the Soviet veto had become available to Egypt; however, a test case attempted by Israel in 1954 (the passage of the "Bat Galim") resulted merely in the confiscation of the ship with scant and totally ineffectual international reaction.

Arab governments maintain their boycott of Israeli goods and continue to threaten with boycott companies in other countries that maintain commercial ties with Israel (*see* ARAB BOYCOTT OF ISRAEL). While the boycott policy has scored some success, on the whole it has failed in its objective. Israel's economy has been making considerable progress through the years, and the boycott has in fact served as an incentive to develop the country's own industries. When faced with a determined stand by international corporations, the sponsors of the Arab boycott have consistently backed down; the most notable example is the abolition of the boycott against Western oil companies, which was decreed shortly after the Six-day War.

For many years the distribution of the waters of the Jordan River was a central issue in Israel-Arab relations. Although Arab technicians had accepted the formula proposed by Eric Johnston, it was rejected by their governments on the ground that any agreement would imply recognition of the existence of the State of Israel. Nevertheless, both Israel and Jordan proceeded independently to carry out their parts of the plan. Israel's project had to be changed when the UN Security Council in 1953 called for a "temporary" cessation of work undertaken in the demilitarized zone pending an "urgent" investigation. Since that investigation has never been terminated, the starting point was moved south to Lake Kinneret. Arab plans to thwart Israel's Jordan-Negev project by diverting the Jordan's headwaters prior to their entry into Israeli territory came to naught, and in 1964 the project was inaugurated without publicity and without major reaction.

Aftermath of the Six-day War. Along with the reequipment of their armed forces and the waging of terrorist warfare, the major effort of Arab governments and their allies in the wake of the Six-day War has been directed toward a political battle, designed to isolate Israel and minimize support for its policies and satisfaction of its needs.

The various forums of the United Nations and its specialized agencies have been utilized for this political battle. There the Arabs have enjoyed a tremendous advantage: there are 15 Arab votes in the United Nations, which are easily united on anything concerning Israel; the Soviet Union and its satellites have come unwaveringly to support Arab policies, and a number of Muslim countries in Asia and Africa are automatically aligned on the side of the Arabs, as are some neutralist countries, first and foremost among them India. Thus, while Israel can count on only its own vote, the Arabs from the outset can count on more than 40 votes. The new realities created after the Six-day War have supplied Arab political warfare with a number of themes, which are fully exploited, including the existence of an Israeli military government and the creation of a new refugee problem.

Parallel with political warfare there has been a considerable increase in propaganda warfare, again not merely directed by Arab governments and the *Arab League against Israel but also supported decisively by the Soviet Union and the propaganda machine at its disposal and by various elements in Western countries, most of which are linked with political and economic interests in the Arab states. An effort is made to present Israel as an expansionist, colonialist country, the stooge or cat's-paw of neoimperialism, or as the Prussia or Sparta of the Middle East, while presenting Arab terrorism as "resistance" or comparing the terrorists with the partisans of World War II.

The reunification of Jerusalem in the wake of the Six-day War has provided Arab political warfare with a convenient steppingstone. A strange alliance, consisting of Arabs, Communists, and elements affiliated with Christian interests in the *holy places, has been formed—an alliance which cannot possibly agree on a unified, positive approach to the problem but which has been able to agree on negation of and opposition to Israeli measures that are designed to unify the city.

Simultaneously, the ever-present problem of the *Arab refugees is being exploited to the full. While there is a growing realization that the problem cannot be solved unless there is a will on the part of the Arab governments to solve it, within the framework of an overall peace settlement—in other words, while there is a growing conviction that Israel's basic attitude toward the problem is correct in political terms—the natural sympathy for the victims of the war is often exploited and directed against Israel, the supposed originator of their plight.

Speaking shortly after the acceptance of Israel as a member

of the United Nations, Israeli Foreign Minister Moshe Sharett stated:

> The storm which has been raging around us will not soon be stilled. Nor do we hold the certainty in our hearts that it will not break out anew, with greater violence. Our vital interest is in a comprehensive peace soon, and we are duty-bound to lend our best efforts to its achievement. But with all our striving for peace, we must not lose patience if it tarries in coming. If destiny has so decreed it we are strong enough to wait with composure.

Twenty years later Israel's attitude remained the same. Israel was determined to adhere to the cease-fire and to maintain the cease-fire lines agreed upon following the Six-day War, unless and until they were replaced by secure and agreed-upon boundaries within the framework of a peace treaty with its neighbors. As of 1968, no public position had been taken as to the demarcation of such boundaries, except that they would not be identical with the armistice lines agreed upon following the War of Independence. These lines, which were never more than temporary lines based on military considerations of the moment and had never constituted political boundaries, as Arab spokesmen consistently pointed out, had ceased to exist, along with the whole structure of the armistice agreements, as a result of Arab aggression in May and June, 1967.

Israel and the United States. The problems facing Israel in its relations with its neighbors are very closely linked not only with the problems of its security but with its very existence as a State and the survival of its inhabitants. The same problems therefore also deeply affect the trend and content of Israel's relations with other countries and, first and foremost, with the major powers. Close ties have existed between Israel and the United States of America from the inception of the State. The United States has consistently declared the preservation of the security, integrity, and sovereignty of the State of Israel to be one of the objectives of its Middle Eastern policies. Formal expression of this concern was given in the Tripartite Declaration of May, 1950, issued by the United States, Great Britain, and France. This declaration, although referring to all countries of the region, has generally been interpreted as being particularly relevant to Israel. However, the sovereignty and integrity of Israel have never been the only objectives of the United States in the area. Within the framework of the global confrontation with the Soviet Union, the United States has an interest in maintaining positions in the Middle East apart from Israel. In a more immediate local context there are vast oil interests as well as interests connected with communications and defense; thus, there never has been complete identity of outlook on every problem between Israel and the United States.

The United States government was instrumental in bringing about the withdrawal of Israeli forces from the shores of the Suez Canal and from Sinai following the Sinai Campaign in 1956; at the same time, it declared the Strait of Tiran to be an international waterway through which free and innocent passage of ships of all nations should be permitted. However, when the UN Emergency Force (UNEF) evacuated its positions at the behest of President Nasser and a blockade was declared by the UAR government in the Strait of Tiran on May 29, 1967, the United States government was unable to give practical effect to its declared position. It was this realization, more than any other, which brought about the decision of the Israeli Cabinet to reopen the strait through the efforts of its own armed forces

early in June, 1967. Israel made it clear from the outset that it did not ask or expect American soldiers to fight for it; at the same time, the firm stand taken by Pres. Lyndon B. Johnson against any intervention by the Soviet Union was no doubt decisive in the effort to maintain the local character of the conflict at the time.

Soon after the Six-day War, President Johnson stated the five principles that were to govern American policy in the Middle East in the postwar period. The gist of these principles was that an overall solution must be found for the Middle Eastern problem by the countries directly concerned and that the United States was to support the sovereignty and territorial integrity of all nations in the Middle East and to maintain freedom of navigation in international waterways in that as in any other region. These principles generally coincide with those of Israel's own attitude toward the problems of the region and have been consistently followed. Nevertheless, American attitudes have differed from those of Israel on certain important details, including the status of Jerusalem. American sympathy and backing, rooted in the overwhelming support by public opinion in the United States, continues to be an important asset in Israel's foreign relations; at the same time, its limitations must not be underestimated or overlooked. Its 20-year history has convinced Israel that it can rely only on itself for the vital problems of its security and must take all necessary steps to maintain its deterrent capacity and, should that fail once more, its capacity of dealing a decisive blow to potential enemies. *See also* UNITED STATES OF AMERICA: RELATIONS WITH ZIONISM AND ISRAEL.

Israel and the Soviet Bloc. Following the Six-day War, the Soviet Union and all countries of the Soviet bloc, with the remarkable exception of Romania, broke diplomatic relations with Israel. This was the second time that a break had occurred. Relations with the Soviet Union had been established immediately after the independence of the State, when Soviet political support in the United Nations and elsewhere and the supply of arms from Czechoslovakia were important elements in Israel's struggle for survival. Soon thereafter, however, relations began to deteriorate. It became evident that the Soviet Union found it convenient to support Israel only as long as Israel was engaged in a struggle against the British government's position in Palestine; once that struggle was over, Soviet policy veered increasingly toward support of the Arabs.

The Egyptian-Czechoslovak arms deal, concluded in 1955 with the evident blessing of the Soviet Union, symbolized the new policy that included the following features: a growing flow of arms from the Soviet Union toward the so-called revolutionary Arab governments, first and foremost among which were Egypt (United Arab Republic) and, later, Syria and Iraq; consistent Soviet support for Arab anti-Israel policies at the United Nations, including an automatic veto in the Security Council whenever a resolution was introduced which Arab governments did not consider favorable to them; and the employment of Soviet propaganda machinery in the cause of propaganda warfare designed to present Israel as a colonialist phenomenon, notwithstanding the fact that the Soviet Union had lent its determined support toward its creation.

Since the Six-day War and the disastrous defeat of the Soviet protégés, the Soviet physical presence in the Middle East has increased. The Soviet fleet in the Mediterranean has been augmented, and its ships have paid frequent courtesy calls at Arab ports, in some of which they enjoy all the facilities and services normally associated with the concept of a naval base. Soviet bombers have similarly flown courtesy missions to various Arab countries. The similarity of Arab and Soviet policies has become increasingly evident. At the same time it may be assumed that the Soviet government endeavors to restrain the UAR and Syria from engaging in another round of all-out warfare, not because of any sympathy with Israel but because of doubt in the ability of Arab armed forces, reequipped though they have been, to overcome the determined *Israel Defense Forces.

Israel's relations with the Soviet Union have always been influenced by its interest in the fate of the Jewish minority in the U.S.S.R., which, estimated at 3 million persons, is the second largest in the world. Although from time to time it has been intimated that an improvement in relations between Israel and the Soviet Union could be achieved if Israel abandoned its interest in the fate of that minority, the government of Israel has been unable and unwilling to purchase this improvement at such a price. Israel's spokesmen have consistently raised their voices in protesting discrimination against the Jewish minority in the Soviet Union, the denial of rights granted to other minorities, such as the free practice of religion and customs, the teaching of traditions, and associations for cultural purposes. Israel has called for the right of free emigration and reunification of families torn apart by World War II. At the same time, it has been quick to detect and decry manifestations of *anti-Semitism, which abounded in Stalin's time and have since by no means disappeared. *See also* RUSSIA: RELATIONS WITH ZIONISM AND ISRAEL.

Israel has had no diplomatic relations with other countries of the Soviet bloc since the Six-day War. Yugoslavia, which has reverted to a satellite status in this respect, has also broken off diplomatic relations with Israel. Commercial relations, which had begun to develop, have been simultaneously paralyzed. The notable exception is Romania, which has not only maintained its diplomatic relations but has refused to brand the State of Israel as an aggressor and has been active in promoting economic, political, and cultural ties with Israel ever since. An important trade convention was signed with Romania in 1968.

Israel and France. Israel's relations with France, cordial but by no means particularly close during the first years of the State, reached a climax of cordiality in the late 1950s. Overall considerations of French policy coincided with general sympathy for a country besieged by its neighbors. France became the major supplier of armaments for Israel, particularly for the Israel Air Force. Following the Sinai Campaign, France insisted that any withdrawal of Israeli forces must be accompanied by a guarantee for free navigation in the Gulf of Elat. This close cooperation came to an abrupt end in June, 1967. Pres. Charles de Gaulle joined with those who branded Israel an aggressor and demanded the unconditional withdrawal of Israel forces. Meanwhile, he imposed an embargo on the sale of French planes to Israel, at the same time continuing the sale of armaments to Algeria and Lebanon, both of which participated in the war against Israel, and publicly declaring his readiness to sell arms to Iraq as well. At a press conference in November, 1967, President de Gaulle, for the first time, made remarks about the Jewish people which could not but encourage anti-Semitic sentiments in his country and elsewhere. *See also* FRANCE: RELATIONS WITH ZIONISM AND ISRAEL.

Relations with Other Western Countries. In this area it can be said in a general way that there is sympathy for Israel and a desire for its strengthening, side by side with a desire and perhaps also a need to consider political, economic, and strategic interests in Arab countries. The historic relations between Great Britain and the Middle East, including those with Palestine and the Zionist movement, have contributed to making diplomatic exchanges with that country particularly intense. On the whole, it can be stated that British-Israeli relations have developed satisfactorily. At the same time, after the Arab countries broke off diplomatic relations with Great Britain under the pretext (subsequently admitted to be false) that the British had participated in the Six-day War, Great Britain engaged in an effort to renew such relations, simultaneously showing particular concern for the reopening of the Suez Canal. *See also* GREAT BRITAIN: RELATIONS WITH ZIONISM AND ISRAEL.

After a long period of agitation and soul searching, aided by the fulfillment of the reparations agreement, the government of West Germany established diplomatic relations with Israel in 1965. Despite the obvious burden which the recent past had imposed on the development of relations between the two countries, relations have since been developing satisfactorily. Other Western countries, notably the Netherlands, Australia, Canada, Italy, and the Scandinavian nations, manifested sympathy for Israel in the period immediately preceding the Six-day War and understanding and support, although never unqualified, in the subsequent political struggle.

Spain, Ireland, and Portugal still do not maintain diplomatic relations with Israel. Whereas Israel was reticent at first about establishing relations with Spain because of the links between General Franco's regime and the Axis Powers prior to and during World War II, later overtures were rejected by the Spanish government, which has consistently been cultivating the Arab countries to gain support for its policies in Africa and Gibraltar. Nevertheless, certain economic and cultural links have been developed. Relations with Portugal have been maintained at the consular level; Israel has found itself at variance with Portuguese colonial policies.

Special importance has been attached to relations with non-Arab countries in the eastern Mediterranean and the Middle East. In spite of their inferior formal status, links with Greece, Turkey, and Iran have become increasingly close and substantive. An embassy has been in existence in Cyprus since the island obtained its independence.

Israel and Latin America. Warm relations have existed with the countries of the Latin American bloc, a number of which were among the sponsors of the State of Israel in 1947. Israel has been in a position to compensate some of them for their consistent support and interest with an increasing measure of economic and technical cooperation. Although opinions may differ on specific issues and particularly on Jerusalem, where as Catholic countries they have a particular interest, Israel maintains diplomatic relations with all countries of the Western Hemisphere. These relations are not exceeded in warmth and intensity by those with countries in any other region. Many leading Latin American statesmen have visited Israel, and the President of Israel and ministers of the State have been received in Latin American countries with genuine sympathy.

Relations with Asian and African Nations. For a great variety of reasons, Israel's path on the continent of Asia on which it is located has been particularly difficult. In addition to Arab countries, there are non-Arab Muslim countries which, irrespective of their private attitudes toward Arab governments, particularly that of the UAR, have refused to establish diplomatic relations with Israel and have been inclined to support the Arabs in international forums. Nevertheless, Israel has succeeded in establishing diplomatic relations with 13 Asian countries and, while not receiving enthusiastic support, has at least been able to balance some of the otherwise predominant pro-Arab interest and sentiment.

A particular effort has been made to maintain and strengthen relations with the new countries of the African continent, often even before these countries have received their official independence. A large part of Israel's constructive efforts in international cooperation has been directed toward Africa and with singular success. African leaders have visited Israel, and Israeli leaders have returned their visits. The fact that Cairo and other Arab capitals are located on the African continent and that the UAR is an African country, participating in all African gatherings, must be taken into account in assessing Israel's achievement. To mention only one facet, at the 1967 emergency session of the UN General Assembly 18 of the 30 African countries refused to support the Indian-Yugoslav resolution, which would have called for the unconditional withdrawal of Israeli forces, and thus brought about its rejection.

For reasons connected primarily with the existence of a large and distinguished Jewish community in the Republic of South Africa, Israel maintains diplomatic relations with that country. At the same time, as a Jewish State Israel has found it imperative consistently to oppose apartheid in all its forms. For the same reason, Israel has not given recognition to the Ian Smith regime in Rhodesia.

Summary. In 1968 Israel maintained diplomatic relations with 94 countries and was recognized de facto or de jure by 14 others. This number included 6 Eastern European countries and Guinea, which broke off relations in 1967 but with which Israel maintained indirect relations through the good offices of the missions of other countries. In 75 of these countries Israel maintained permanent missions, and in 19 it was represented by non-resident representatives. Israel was also represented in 4 non-self-governing territories. Altogether, in 1968 Israel had 64 embassies, 6 legations, 5 other diplomatic missions, 14 consulates general, and 6 consulates. Of these missions, 12 were located in Asia and Oceania, 29 in Africa, 22 in Western Europe, 1 in Eastern Europe, 13 in North America, and 17 in Central and South America.

Israel is a member of all 13 specialized agencies of the United Nations. Although it is frequently faced with Arab attacks in these agencies, it has devoted a major and increasing effort to constructive participation, particularly in the field of cooperation with developing countries and development in general and in the field of human rights, which is of particular and vital interest to the Jewish State.   N. LORCH

FOREIGN TRADE OF ISRAEL. As in other small countries with few natural resources and limited domestic markets, foreign trade is a major component of Israel's total economy. Imports of goods and services form a significant percentage of the country's available resources. In 1950 imports at current prices and official exchange rates (both of which imply some distortion) constituted 20 per cent of Israel's available resources; by 1969 this figure had risen to 31 per cent. More impressive still was the increase in the percentage of exports during the same period, from 2.5 to 18 per cent.

Merchandise Account: Direction and Composition. Israel's foreign trade is oriented toward the West. The United States

Bananas readied for export in the kibbutz Y'hi'am. [Israel Information Services]

and Western Europe supply about 80 per cent of Israel's imports and buy about the same proportion of its exports. In 1967 the United States was Israel's largest single trading partner, taking about 17 per cent of Israel's exports and supplying about 25 per cent of its imports. The share of the European Economic Community (EEC), or Common Market (the Benelux countries, France, West Germany, and Italy), in the same year was 24 and 27 per cent, respectively, and that of the European Free Trade Association (EFTA; Austria, Denmark, Norway, Portugal, Sweden, Switzerland, and the United Kingdom) was about the same (24 and 27 per cent). Consequently, trade relations with the Communist countries and the underdeveloped world have remained negligible, and the expectation that Asian and African markets would present an important field for the expansion of Israel's foreign trade has thus far not been borne out by experience. As a result of this past performance, Israel ascribes particular significance to a close association with the EEC. Under an agreement for trade expansion reached in 1964, Israel obtained tariff reductions on some Israeli products of minor export importance; major items such as oranges, eggs, tires, and plywood were excluded. Negotiations on the preferential admission of citrus fruit were inconclusive, and in October, 1966, Israel formally applied for associate membership in the EEC. The 1964 trade agreement expired in 1967, but its provisions were still maintained in effect. As of early 1970, Israel had not yet obtained association with the EEC, but the EEC had concluded a preferential five-year trade agreement with Israel.

During the 1950s the Israel authorities believed that bilateral trade and payments agreements with other countries would provide additional trading volume and relieve the country's shortage of foreign exchange. But since most partners to these agreements were countries in a similar position, this expectation proved futile and occasionally even caused difficulties, such as the freezing of funds in Turkey. To some extent, however, the system of bilateral agreements continued, although the number of such agreements declined from 17 in 1956 to 10 at the beginning of 1968, including an agreement concluded with Romania early that year. Of Israel's trade agreement partners in 1968, five were Communist countries (Bulgaria, Hungary, Poland, Romania, and Yugoslavia); the others were Brazil, Ghana, Greece, Portugal, and Turkey.

The composition of Israel's exports is shown in Table 1. The fact that citrus and diamonds constitute relatively large portions of total exports seems to corroborate the observation that exports to the less highly developed countries are negligible, since such countries obviously do not represent markets for products usually associated with higher standards of living.

TABLE 1. ISRAEL'S EXPORTS BY MAJOR COMMODITY GROUPS, 1949–66
(In millions of dollars and percentage of total)

	Citrus and other agricultural products	Per cent of total	Diamonds	Per cent of total	Other industrial products	Per cent of total
1949	$ 20.4	71.33	$ 5.2	18.18	$ 3.0	10.49
1950	18.3	52.14	8.8	25.07	8.0	22.79
1951	19.1	42.63	11.7	26.12	14.0	31.25
1952	19.6	44.04	11.2	25.17	13.7	30.79
1953	22.2	39.43	12.7	22.56	21.4	38.01
1954	38.4	43.79	15.6	17.79	33.7	38.43
1955	36.2	40.72	20.6	23.17	32.1	36.11
1956	48.1	43.85	24.7	22.52	36.9	33.64
1957	57.5	40.84	35.5	25.21	47.8	33.95
1958	62.3	45.08	34.3	24.82	41.6	30.10
1959	60.4	34.22	45.2	25.61	65.9	37.34
1960	66.0	31.38	56.4	26.82	82.9	39.42
1961	70.9	30.36	65.3	27.97	97.3	41.67
1962	78.4	28.89	83.9	30.91	109.1	40.24
1963	102.1	30.29	104.0	30.85	131.0	38.86
1964	86.1	24.50	118.2	33.63	147.2	41.88
1965	104.2	25.67	131.7	32.44	170.1	41.90
1966	114.8	24.08	164.7	34.54	197.3	41.38

Services Account. Like the merchandise trade (visibles) account, the services (invisibles) account of Israel's balance of payments shows a considerable and persistent deficit, which in 1966 amounted to $133,500,000. Table 2 indicates that Israel government activities abroad and the service cost of foreign credits are the major debit positions, while transportation and tourism have become substantial foreign exchange earners, mainly as a result of the country's expanding merchant marine and air services.

Foreign Trade Regulations. Israel's foreign trade is subject to extensive government regulation. Importers of goods, which in 1966 represented slightly more than half of total imports, must be approved as importers by the government, and many imports

TABLE 2. ISRAEL'S IMPORTS AND EXPORTS OF SERVICES, 1966
(In millions of dollars and percentage of total)

	Debit		Credit		Balance
Transportation	$102.5	19.8%	$156.7	40.7%	$ 54.2
Foreign travel	48.8	7.9	59.1	15.4	10.3
Insurance	53.0	10.7	51.3	13.3	− 1.7
Capital servicing	118.6	23.4	48.2	12.5	− 70.4
Government, not elsewhere specified	135.5	26.6	25.0	6.5	−110.5
Miscellaneous	60.1	11.6	44.7	11.6	− 15.4
Total	$518.5	100.0%	$385.0	100.0%	$−133.5

are subject to licensing. The list of goods importable under automatic approval has been growing and in 1967 accounted for about 40 per cent of total imports. Some basic food products are imported exclusively by or for the account of the Israel government. In recent years the policy has been to expose manufacturing industry to greater foreign competition. The protection previously granted to local production (Totzeret Ha'Aretz) by quantitative restrictions has been replaced by fiscal protection. An import license carries the authorization to acquire foreign exchange for payment. Most exports do not require licenses. For some commodities such as wines, antibiotics, and cotton yarns, however, export licensing is maintained for quality control. Export proceeds in foreign exchange must be surrendered to authorized banks or kept in special accounts. The Israel authorities are endeavoring to promote exports through an elaborate system of general and specialized incentives. There are special funds to provide inexpensive credit for exporters, as well as the refund of various taxes, fees, and insurance premiums. Exports are also promoted by the cartelization of specified industrial branches, such as textiles, plywood, and leather, and by outright subsidies.

1965 Recession. While the policy of restraint (mitun) initiated by the government in 1965 had many recessionary effects on Israel's domestic economy, it produced salutary results in foreign trade. The trend became discernible in 1965 and gained momentum during 1966–67. The narrowing of the trade gap in this period, shown in Table 3, was the result of both declining imports and increasing exports. This development was interrupted by the *Six-day War of 1967 and the resultant recovery, which led to a slowdown in exports and a reexpansion of imports during the second half of 1967 and the first months of 1968. Under these circumstances the promising results of the mitun period, which pointed to a greater degree of economic independence, may have been an exercise in frustration.

Customs Tariff. Customs duties represent a substantial portion of Israel's government revenue. During the 1964–68 period customs revenue amounted to an average of 12.5 per cent of annual budgetary income. Israel's customs tariff includes both

TABLE 3. ISRAEL'S TRADE BALANCE, 1949–66
(In millions of dollars)

	Imports (net)	Exports (net)	Trade deficit	Exports as percentage of imports
1949	$253.1	$ 28.6	$224.5	11.30
1950	298.8	35.1	263.7	11.75
1951	379.8	44.8	335.0	11.80
1952	323.1	44.5	278.6	13.77
1953	281.9	56.3	225.6	19.97
1954	295.8	87.7	208.1	29.65
1955	333.6	88.9	244.7	26.65
1956	367.0	109.7	257.3	29.89
1957	432.1	140.8	291.3	32.59
1958	421.5	138.2	283.3	32.79
1959	426.5	176.5	249.9	41.38
1960	495.6	211.3	284.4	42.64
1961	583.9	239.1	344.8	40.95
1962	626.2	271.4	354.8	43.34
1963	663.5	338.3	325.2	50.99
1964	815.4	351.5	463.6	43.11
1965	812.0	406.0	406.0	50.00
1966	810.6	476.8	333.8	58.82

TABLE 4. ISRAEL'S IMPORTS (GROSS) BY ECONOMIC DESTINATION, 1949–66
(In millions of dollars and percentage of total)

	Consumer goods	Per cent of total	Raw materials	Per cent of total	Investment goods	Per cent of total	Fuel and lubricants	Per cent of total	Unclassified goods	Total imports
1949	$81.0	32.0	$ 82.3	32.5	$ 71.6	28.3	$15.2	6.0	$3.0	$253.1
1950	77.7	26.0	95.6	32.0	101.6	34.0	22.4	7.5	1.5	298.8
1951	97.5	25.7	140.4	37.0	106.2	28.0	35.3	9.3	0.4	379.8
1952	74.3	22.5	119.5	36.2	88.1	26.7	40.4	12.2	8.0	330.3
1953	59.1	21.0	127.4	45.2	64.1	22.7	31.3	11.1	· · ·	281.9
1954	52.9	17.9	149.1	50.4	62.5	21.1	31.3	10.6	· · ·	295.8
1955	51.3	15.4	172.1	51.6	76.7	23.0	33.0	9.9	0.5	333.6
1956	57.2	15.6	172.5	47.0	103.7	28.3	32.9	9.0	0.7	367.0
1957	50.0	11.6	211.9	49.0	116.0	26.8	53.5	12.4	0.7	432.1
1958	53.1	12.6	211.4	50.2	114.4	27.1	42.0	10.0	0.6	421.5
1959	48.6	11.4	233.2	54.7	112.9	26.5	34.7	8.1	0.8	426.4
1960	40.7	8.3	284.0	57.9	123.2	25.1	34.9	7.1	0.3	490.8
1961	44.2	7.7	317.9	55.4	177.5	30.9	34.2	6.0	0.4	574.2
1962	50.3	7.9	373.5	58.9	170.9	26.9	40.1	6.3	0.4	634.5
1963	57.9	8.6	429.5	63.8	141.7	21.0	44.5	6.6	· · ·	673.6
1964	81.4	9.7	512.0	61.1	197.5	23.6	46.6	5.6	· · ·	837.5
1965	83.9	10.1	516.2	61.8	181.2	21.7	53.3	6.4	· · ·	834.6
1966	88.1	10.6	546.3	65.7	139.1	16.7	58.2	7.0	· · ·	831.7

NOTE: Table may include a statistical discrepancy.

ad valorem and specific duties, as well as duties combining ad valorem and specific rates. Duties are imposed at rates ranging from 5 to over 100 per cent, but most are between 10 and 60 per cent. Most of the basic food commodities, raw materials, and machinery for industry and agriculture are exempt from customs duty. Materials used in the manufacture of export products are subject to a customs refund. In 1962 an import tariff liberalization policy was begun, since in many cases tariff policy had become important as a protective measure for Israel's domestic industries.

*Arab Boycott. The results of the Arab boycott are difficult to assess, and Israeli presentation of its effects has not been unequivocal. Undoubtedly the closure of the Suez Canal to Israeli shipping has been a substantial burden to Israel in terms of shipping expense and as an obstacle to foreign trade and shipping expansion. At the same time, exclusion from neighboring markets must have stimulated trade relations with overseas areas and familiarized Israeli importers and exporters with the conditions of the world's larger markets. Whether Israeli products would be competitive in Middle Eastern markets remains a moot question, since many Arab countries have undergone considerable industrial development and Israel's (or Palestine's) past experience of almost monopolistic exports during World War II and shortly thereafter can no longer serve as a yardstick. On the other hand, it seems quite possible that Arab imports into Israel (which would have formed an integral part of mutual trade relations) would have substantially affected Israel's production and price structure.

Foreign Trade and Economic Policy. The salient feature of Israel's foreign trade is the substantial excess of imports over exports, as shown in Table 3. In the past this persistent trade deficit has been covered by capital imports, mainly of an unrequited and unilateral nature, such as United States grants and loans, German reparation and restitution payments, Israel government bond sales, and charitable contributions. But the anticipated decline in unilateral capital imports makes an early improvement in Israel's trade balance imperative. Since a

reduction in imports would curtail production and employment, import substitution through expanded local production seems more important than import restriction. Moreover, a widening base of local production would increase the earning power needed to pay for imports. In fact, there has been a marked shift from the importation of consumer goods to that of capital goods and industrial materials, as reflected in Table 4. Consequently, as indicated in Table 3, a steadily rising percentage of imports has been paid for by exports. Between 1949 and 1966 this figure rose from 11.3 to 58.8 per cent.

The task of improving the goods and services deficit continues to require a major effort. The recent narrowing of the trade gap occurred during a period of slow domestic growth, declining investment, and rising unemployment. Indications are that imports will increase again as growth resumes and the heavy defense expenditure continues. Important considerations, therefore, are the need to prevent an excessive rise in imports and the maintenance of the export potential. The question of export competitiveness is particularly significant for industrial exports. In the case of citrus, Israel is a rather efficient producer for the European market (see CITRUS INDUSTRY IN ISRAEL); in the case of diamonds (see DIAMOND INDUSTRY IN ISRAEL), more than 80 per cent of diamond export value is accounted for by the import cost of the rough stones and the equipment needed for cutting and polishing. Under these circumstances local cost cannot add substantially to the export price. For other industrial products, however, the import component averages 60 per cent, and here domestic inflationary pressures have greatly affected the country's export potential.

J. O. RONALL

FORESTRY IN ISRAEL. The long history of Palestine is a history of deforestation. During centuries of neglect the forests were almost completely destroyed by overgrazing, soil erosion, forest fires, wars, and invasions. With the beginning of Jewish resettlement, tree planting became part of the Zionist work of rebuilding the landscape of Israel. Jews from Russia first planted

Pine seedlings tended at a nursery. [Israel Information Services]

eucalyptus in swampy areas for drainage. The *Jewish National Fund made afforestation one of its major activities and began to plant conifers in the Herzl Forest at Hulda and at Ben Shemen.

Afforestation in Israel comprises protective and productive forests with multiple-use benefits to the population. The forests protect the soil from erosion, fix shifting sand dunes, and produce timber for various uses, thus making Israel less dependent on imports. They beautify the landscape and provide recreation grounds. Afforestation also provides employment for newcomers.

As an integral part of the overall planning for effective land use, different types of forest are planted. In the hill country, on heavily eroded mountain terra rossa and rendzina *soils, conifer forests are planted during the rainy season (December–February) in pits at a density of about 3,000 trees per hectare. Tending entails hoeing during the first two years. Subsequent operations are pruning and periodic selective thinning. The rotation is estimated at 45 to 50 years. The main species used is the native Aleppo pine *(Pinus halepensis)*, whose mean

A new forest near Tiberias. [Israel Information Services]

annual increment is 3 cubic meters per hectare. Other species employed in afforestation are *Pinus brutia*, the Mediterranean cypress *(Cypressus sempervivens)*, and, on a limited scale, stone pine *(Pinus pinea)* and Canary pine *(Pinus canariensis)*.

In the lowlands and valleys eucalyptus trees are planted at a density of 800 to 1,200 trees per hectare. The main species is *Eucalyptus camaldulensis*. The trees are managed as coppice with an average rotation of 7 to 10 years. The annual increment varies between 5 and 15 cubic meters per hectare, depending on the quality of the soil and the amount of rainfall. The highways and roads of Israel are lined mainly with eucalyptus trees. *Acacia cyanophylla* saplings and *Tamarix articulata* cuttings have been used for fixing coastal and inland dunes.

In the arid Negev, shelter belts of eucalyptus, tamarisks, and acacias have been planted to provide shelter for crops and grazing animals. Small woodlots have been planted near settlements to provide some greenery and shade, and trees have been planted along wadis (*see* WADI) to protect the soil from erosion. To ensure its survival, each tree is individually irrigated during the first and second summers after planting.

The Department of Forests is part of the Land Development Authority of the Jewish National Fund. It is headed by a director, who is assisted by the heads of the Divisions of Management and Natural Forests. As of 1966 the country was divided into four districts and the department managed 60,000 hectares of forests, of which 30,000 were natural scrub. By 1968 a total of 20 million trees had been planted in Israel. They were grouped in several major forest units, of which the most important were the *B'nai B'rith Martyrs', the Jerusalem Peace, the John F. Kennedy Peace, the Lyndon B. Johnson, the Harry S *Truman, and the Chaim *Weizmann Forests.

The Fibers and Forest Products Research Institute, under the authority of the Ministry of Agriculture, was concerned with research in various phases of forestry and the utilization of home-grown timber. The Society of Israeli Foresters, which had 400 members in the 1960s, organized lectures, field trips, and meetings and published a professional journal, *La Ya'aran*.

J. KAPLAN

FOURTH 'ALIYA. Wave of Jewish *immigration that reached Palestine between 1924 and 1928. Half of the immigrants of this period came from Poland, having been forced to leave that country by an economic crisis there and high taxation, aimed particularly at the Jews. (The Fourth 'Aliya was often slightly referred to as the "Grabski 'Aliya" after the Prime Minister associated with Poland's anti-Jewish fiscal policies.) Because the United States, which formerly had received large masses of Eastern European Jews, instituted immigration restrictions based on national origin (Immigration Act of 1924), many Jews who might otherwise have gone to the United States moved to Palestine instead. In addition to immigrants with pioneering aspirations, this 'Aliya brought a considerable number of persons of moderate means, businessmen and craftsmen who hoped to pursue the same types of work in Palestine.

The first phase of the Fourth 'Aliya (spring, 1924–spring, 1926) was characterized by economic prosperity. In these two years a total of 62,000 Jewish immigrants arrived in Palestine; 11,500 Jews left the country. The second phase (1926–28) saw an economic slump, resulting in a sharp drop in immigration, with emigration exceeding immigration for the first time (5,200 immigrants; 7,200 emigrants).

The period of prosperity was due to the boom in construction of housing for the newcomers, most of whom settled in the urban areas. During those years the Jewish population of Jaffa and Tel Aviv grew from 20,000 to 52,000, that of Jerusalem from 34,000 to 51,000, and that of Haifa from 6,500 to 15,000. The Jewish population of Palestine swelled from 90,000 to 155,000, increasing the percentage of Jews within the total population of the country from 13.3 to 17.7. In Tel Aviv alone £P 1,800,000 was invested in construction between 1924 and 1926, and 45 per cent of the city's labor force was engaged in building. Many stores, workshops, restaurants, and small hotels were built, and speculation in building lots and apartment housing spread.

The principal cause of the severe economic crisis that struck the Fourth 'Aliya in 1928 was the inability of agriculture and industry in Palestine to absorb so large an immigration wave. The situation was aggravated by the outgrowth of economic instability in Europe; Poland, faced with inflation, put restrictions on the transfer of funds by emigrants, with the result that the flow of private capital, which constituted the bulk of new capital coming into Palestine, declined very considerably. By the summer of 1928, 8,500 Jews in Palestine, half of them in Tel Aviv, were unemployed, and many left the country. A number of enterprises engaged in construction and immigrant settlement went bankrupt.

The private Jewish agricultural sector, on the other hand, continued its steady development. The acreage of orange orchards, in particular, expanded from 12,000 dunams in 1924 (see DUNAM) to 45,000 in 1928. The older plantation moshavot (especially Petah Tikva) and the newer moshavot (K'far Saba, Ra'anana, Magdiel, Herzliya, and Karkur) expanded both in population and in plantation area. There was an increase also in the number of Jewish workers employed in these settlements; the new settlements employed only Jewish labor from their inception. During the economic crisis many workers drifted to the older settlements, where they formed temporary communes (Havurot) to tide them over the lean years. Some of these Havurot developed into nuclei of pioneers who settled in the vicinity of various moshavot and in time set up permanent kibbutzim and moshavim (see KIBBUTZ; MOSHAV). From time to time there were clashes between the workers and the farm owners over the use of non-Jewish labor in the orchards. See also JEWISH AND ARAB LABOR.

The period of the Fourth 'Aliya also saw attempts at settlement by private groups outside the area of the moshavot. Thus the *American Zion Commonwealth expanded its activities and by 1926 had purchased 120,000 dunams of land. This organization established the town of Herzliya, but its attempt to found a town, 'Ir Yezr'el, in the heart of the Jezreel Valley (on the site of present-day 'Afula) ended in failure. In and around the large towns new quarters were built, particularly in the three main cities. Ramat Gan, in the vicinity of Tel Aviv, developed into an urban center.

The Fourth 'Aliya made a significant contribution to the development of industry, small and medium; while some enterprises failed, most of the others grew and expanded. During this period the foundation was laid for a modern and ramified textile industry, with the Lodzia knitting plant the largest of its kind. See also INDUSTRY IN ISRAEL.

Another effort at group settlement in Palestine was made by Hasidim headed by the rabbis of Yablonov (Jablonów), Galicia, and Kosienice, Poland, who bought 20,000 dunams of land in the Z'vulun Valley. But this group, too, was soon faced with bankruptcy and survived only with the help of the official fund-raising institutions. See also HASIDIC JEWS IN ISRAEL.

The large-scale pioneering efforts of the workers came to a halt early in the Fourth 'Aliya. The labor movement was shaken by the rift in the *G'dud Ha'Avoda V'haHagana 'Al Shem Yosef Trumpeldor late in 1926 and by the liquidation of Solel Bone, the construction contracting company of *Histadrut (General Federation of Labor), in 1927. Between the latter part of 1926 and April, 1928, thousands of unemployed workers had to receive welfare aid from the Zionist *Executive. In 1928 the Jewish national institutions and the British Mandatory government (see MANDATE FOR PALESTINE) joined forces to set up a public works program (swamp drainage, highway construction, etc.), which gradually put an end to unemployment. In this period eight settlements—K'far Y'hoshu'a, Sarid, 'Ayanot, HaSharon, G'vat, K'far Barukh, S'de Ya'akov, and Mishmar Ha'Emek—were founded in the Kishon Block.

With the beginning of the Fourth 'Aliya a debate developed within the Zionist movement over settlement methods in Palestine. Middle-class groups in Palestine as well as in the *Diaspora wanted to see financial support shifted from labor settlements to settlements founded in urban and rural areas by middle-class groups with private capital investment. This trend was reflected in the rise of new political parties (e.g., 'Et Livnot in Poland) and in the development of the Revisionist movement (see REVISIONISTS).

Despite the difficulties with which it had to cope, the Fourth 'Aliya made an important contribution to the development of the Yishuv and of Zionism. It was during this period that Palestine first became a significant factor in Jewish migration. In contrast to the 10,300 who went to the United States in 1925, 34,400 Jews migrated to Palestine that year and most of them remained there. The economy of the Yishuv (citriculture, industry, craft enterprises) expanded. That period also saw the beginnings of the two distinct economic systems of the country, the Histadrut sector and the private-enterprise sector.

Y. SLUTSKY

FOX, ISRAEL SOLOMON. Physician, public servant, and Zionist leader in Great Britain (b. Cracow, Poland, 1896). The son of the editor of the Hebrew weekly *HaMaggid, he founded the Jewish Students' Association at the University of Liverpool and later became chairman of Liverpool's Zionist Central Council. In 1933 he settled in London, became a member of the *Board of Deputies of British Jews, and was elected chairman of the Zionist Federation (see GREAT BRITAIN, ZIONISM IN) and later its vice-president. He was active in establishing Jewish day schools in England and served as chairman of the Jewish Day Schools Committee, president of the Synagogue Council of the Zionist Federation, and chairman of the editorial boards of the Zionist quarterly Gates of Zion and of the Zionist Year Book. Dr. Fox was sheriff of Chester County in 1931 and mayor of the city of Chester in 1932.

J. FRAENKEL

FRAENKEL, JOSEF. Zionist researcher and author (b. Ustryzki Dolne, Galicia, Austria, 1903). Fraenkel participated in the inaugural meeting of Agudat HaNo'ar Ha'Ivri (Hebrew Youth Organization) but in 1925 joined the *Revisionists. He attended Zionist Congresses (see CONGRESS, ZIONIST) as a delegate and was secretary of the Austrian section of the *World Jewish Congress. After Hitler's annexation of Austria in 1938, he became correspondent of the *Jewish Telegraphic Agency in Prague. He was a delegate of the *Jewish State party to the 21st Zionist Congress in Geneva (1939) and from there went to London, where he became chairman of the party.

Fraenkel was cofounder and chairman of the Nahum *Sokolow Society, cofounder of the Unity group, and honorary secretary to the *Council of Continental Zionists and the Jacob Ehrlich Society. In 1940 he became honorary secretary of the Association of Jewish Journalists and Authors. He was instrumental in convening the World Conference of Jewish Journalists that met in Jerusalem in 1960. Among Fraenkel's writings are numerous studies of Zionist leaders and other subjects.

FRANCE: RELATIONS WITH ZIONISM AND ISRAEL.
The interest of France in the Levant dates from the 16th century. From the middle of the 18th century on, France maintained an active interest in Egypt, Syria, and Palestine. The so-called capitulations, by which the Turkish government ceded certain rights to France, made France the official protector of Christian pilgrims in Palestine. France's early concern for Palestine was motivated in part by religious considerations: the only Roman Catholic power among the nations vying for supremacy in the region (which was then part of the vast but weak Ottoman Empire), France developed considerable missionary activity in Syria and Lebanon and regarded itself as the protector of the Christian *holy places in neighboring Palestine. From the end of the 19th century on, France's attitude to Palestine (and, subsequently, to the State of Israel) was determined variously by rivalry with the British Empire and, after World War II, by efforts to preserve its interests and to maintain a certain influence in the Arab countries.

EARLY VIEWS
The first official French support for the "restoration of Israel" dates from the last years of the 18th century.

Napoleon's Proclamation. At the time of his military campaign in Egypt (1798–99), Napoleon Bonaparte, eager for the support of the Jews of the Middle East in his plans of conquest, proclaimed that he would favor "the restoration of Jerusalem to its ancient glory." But following his defeat near Acre ('Akko) in 1799, he said no more about the subject. As Emperor of the French (1804–14), he was more concerned with the integration and assimilation of his Jewish subjects than with helping them establish a homeland of their own.

"The restoration of Jerusalem" did not again become a subject of wide discussion in France until the reign of Napoleon III (1852–70). His rule was marked by a rise in French prestige in the Levant (notably the construction of the Suez Canal by the French diplomat and engineer Vicomte Ferdinand-Marie de Lesseps) and also by a growing interest in influential British circles in the reconstitution of the Jewish Homeland (see GREAT BRITAIN: RELATIONS WITH ZIONISM AND ISRAEL).

Laharanne. In 1860 Napoleon's private secretary, Ernest Laharanne, published a brochure entitled *The New Problem of the Orient: Reestablishment of Jewish Nationality.* Laharanne, a Roman Catholic, considered the solution of the Jewish problem through Palestine one of the most important tasks France might accomplish in the Levant. Pointing out the great cultural benefits the Jews, based in Palestine, would be in a position to confer

on the entire Levant, he called on France to help the Jews realize their dream of the restoration of their Homeland and urged the Jews to work for the rehabilitation of Palestine "under the egis of France, the Emancipator." Laharanne was extensively quoted in the writings of Zionist forerunners such as Moses *Hess. "Do you still doubt," Hess wrote in *Rome and Jerusalem* (1862), "that France will help the Jews to found colonies which may extend from Suez to Jerusalem and from the banks of the Jordan to the coast of the Mediterranean? . . . France will extend the work of redemption also to the Jewish nation. . . . Frenchmen and Jews! It seems that in all things they were created for one another."

Napoleon III. On Feb. 6, 1866, the London *Morning Herald* reported that Napoleon III had granted an interview to Paris Jewish communal leaders to find out "how far there yet lingered in the Jewish mind a belief and desire that they might become repossessed of their native country." The interview seems to have had no far-reaching consequences, but if it indeed took place, it probably came about through the influence of Jean-Henri Dunant (1828–1910), the founder of the International Red Cross, who was greatly respected at the French Court. The noted humanitarian, who was to share with Frédéric Passy the Nobel Peace Prize in 1901, was an early Christian advocate of Jewish settlement in Palestine. In a letter to the editor of the London *Jewish Chronicle* (published on Dec. 13, 1867), he appealed to the Jews to give their support to a committee formed in Paris for the colonization of Palestine, for which he, Dunant, had obtained the patronage of no less a person than the Empress Eugénie. He envisioned the formation of an international society that would establish business enterprises, a seaport, and a railroad in Palestine, reconstruct the holy places, and create European colonies in the Holy Land. These colonies were to be administered by the society under the nominal authority of the Sultan and neutralized diplomatically on the pattern of Dunant's native Switzerland. Such an arrangement, Dunant pointed out, would also end the conflict among the Great Powers over the holy places. Even more important, these colonies would serve a valuable function by spreading Western civilization to Turkey and the "far east." Although his bold scheme received little support, Dunant later took an interest in the activities of the Zionists and, in fact, attended the 1st Zionist *Congress (Basle, 1897) as a visitor.

Bourgeois. Like Dunant, the social philosopher Léon V. A. Bourgeois (1851–1925), an early advocate of the League of Nations and Prime Minister of France in 1895–96, stressed the cultural potential of a Jewish Homeland in Palestine. In a letter to Baroness Bertha von Suttner (published by the baroness in 1899), Bourgeois attacked *anti-Semitism as "opposed to culture" and then set forth his views on Zionist aspirations. While it was self-evident that the first purpose of the Jewish Homeland was to "bring relief to a persecuted and unfortunate people," he wrote, "a nation newly reconstituted, full of energy and composed of such intelligent, capable and talented elements" could be expected to bring about "an increase in the general work of culture."

Pre-World War I Decades. During this period, the French government had scant use for Zionist political aspirations. After the British had taken control of Egypt in 1882, France clung all the more tenaciously to its interests in Syria and Palestine, where it had large capital investments and owned valuable harbor and railway concessions. Along with certain circles in Great Britain, France suspected that the Zionists were working with the pro-German elements that had abetted the rebellion (1908) of the nationalist Young Turks, who were attempting to shore up the tottering Ottoman Empire, and that the Zionists would favor a German foothold in Palestine. The circumstance that many of the Zionist leaders had been raised or educated in Germany and that the proceedings of Zionist Congresses were then conducted largely in German only served to deepen these suspicions. In November, 1913, Max *Nordau, in an interview with Foreign Minister Stéphen Pichon shortly before Pichon left the Cabinet, protested "the slander that we [the Zionists] are German agents and the advance guard of German influence." In that interview Nordau indicated to Pichon, as he also had to such other French statesmen as Aristide Briand and Paul Painlevé, that he favored French influence in Constantinople on behalf of the Jews and even a French protectorate over Palestine. According to his biographers Anna and Maxa Nordau (*Max Nordau*, Nordau Committee, New York, 1943), Nordau at the time felt that political Zionism should seek only the support of France because, in his view, the Jewish mentality was more akin to the Latin spirit.

COMPETITION FOR PALESTINE, 1914-48

After Turkey's entry into World War I on the side of the Central Powers, France, Great Britain, and Russia, acting on the assumption that the war in the east would end with the collapse of the Ottoman Empire, made plans for dividing Turkey's Asian territories among themselves.

France's Claims. France immediately marked out its claim to Syria, which it understood to include all Palestine. But the frontiers of French control in the area were placed in question by a letter (Oct. 24, 1915) from the British High Commissioner in Cairo, Sir Henry McMahon, to Husayn, Sherif of Mecca (see MCMAHON CORRESPONDENCE), roughly defining the area in which Great Britain would be prepared to recognize and support an independent Arab state or confederation of states. With Russia already claiming Constantinople and the Straits, France and Britain felt pressed to come to an agreement with regard to their own spheres of influence in the Asian part of the Ottoman Empire. The initial result of French-British bargaining on the partition of the Ottoman territory in the Middle East was the *Sykes-Picot Agreement (January, 1916). In these negotiations Britain was represented by Sir Mark *Sykes, M.P. (1879–1919), and France by François-Georges Picot (1870–1951).

Under the terms of the agreement the area subsequently demarcated as Palestine was partitioned into British, French, and international zones, with France receiving Galilee from a line north of Acre to the Sea of Galilee (Lake Kinneret). Having considered all Palestine as its preserve, France was none too happy with the arrangement but had to acquiesce in it under pressure from the British, who had been playing the dominant role in the military campaign against Turkey, and in the knowledge that Orthodox Russia would not countenance Roman Catholic expansion in the Holy Land. The Sykes-Picot Agreement did not take Zionist aspirations into account; in fact, the Zionists were not even aware of its existence until it was made known to Chaim *Weizmann by Charles Prestwich *Scott of the *Manchester Guardian*.

Pro-Zionist Views. The French government's indifference to Zionism did not mean that the Zionists had no influential friends. They received some encouragement from the Socialist leader Jules Guesde, who had joined René-Raphaël Viviani's National Government as a Minister of State in 1914–15.

Another noted Socialist, Gustave Hervé, came out in his paper, *La Guerre Sociale* (Feb. 12, 1915), for the restoration of the Jews to Palestine. In his opinion, this was to be done under the egis of France. "Let us see," he wrote, "that Palestine falls to the share of the French Republic. France has given the Jews human dignity. Today she must do more—she must make the Jewish nation revive." Hervé had even introduced Vladimir *Jabotinsky to Foreign Minister Théophile Delcassé. However, the French statesman and his government had then been indifferent to Zionism, at least in part because the movement was not to the liking of the Syrian Christians and the pro-Catholic group working for France in the Levant.

Basch Mission. In the spring of 1916 the French government learned officially that the sympathies of organized Zionism, particularly American Zionism, were important for the Allied cause. Late in 1915 the government had first received disturbing reports from the French Embassy in Washington that Jews in the United States, which was then still neutral, tended to sympathize with the Central Powers, not so much because of any admiration for the Germans but because of outrage at Tsarist Russia's treatment of the Jews. The French government, therefore, in November, 1915, sent an emissary to the United States to learn at first hand whether these reports were true and, if so, what could be done to influence American Jewry in behalf of the Allied cause. The emissary chosen was Prof. Victor-Guillaume *Basch of the Sorbonne, who, on his return in the spring of 1916, made a personal report to Pres. Raymond Poincaré. His mission had yielded no perceptible results in the United States, but Basch felt that American Jewry might be favorably impressed by an Anglo-French assurance that when the time came for a peace settlement, the two governments would work for the redress of Jewish grievances and would take an interest in the future of the Jews in Palestine. The Zionist movement in the United States, he pointed out, was steadily growing in strength and influence, and should not be ignored by the French and British governments in their efforts to bring the United States into the Allied camp.

While Basch was in the United States, the French government approved the setting up of a Comité de Propagande Français auprès des Juifs Neutres (Committee for French Propaganda among Jews in Neutral Countries). Presided over by Georges Leygues, chairman of the Foreign Affairs Committee of the Chamber of Deputies (and Prime Minister in 1920), the committee included a number of well-known Jews, among them Basch himself and Jacques Bigart, secretary of the *Alliance Israélite Universelle, which soft-pedaled its anti-Zionist attitude when it became obvious that this might injure the Allied cause. This French group worked closely with the Conjoint Foreign Committee in Great Britain to influence Jewish opinion in neutral countries in favor of the Allies.

French-British Discussions. The British government, having had second thoughts about the Sykes-Picot Agreement, began searching for ways and means of bringing the whole of Palestine under British control. From various quarters, military and others, it was urged on the British that it was essential for the protection of imperial interests to have a friendly buffer state northeast of the Suez Canal. The progress of British arms against the Turks and their conquest of southern Palestine in 1917 made this problem very urgent. It was then that Sir Mark Sykes, acting for the Foreign Office, approached Zionist leaders in London and urged them, *inter alia,* to secure the approval of the French government for Jewish settlement of

Palestine. On Feb. 8, 1917, Sykes introduced Nahum *Sokolow to Picot. Picot bluntly told Sokolow that 95 per cent of the French people were strongly in favor of the annexation of Palestine by France. Still, Picot consented to receive Sokolow alone at the French Embassy the next day. In that interview Picot reminded Sokolow that France had always championed the cause of small nations and hence was naturally inclined to take an interest in Zionism. On the other hand, he warned that if the Zionists were to represent themselves as one of the small peoples pressing for liberation, they would meet with strong resistance from the Jews of France.

In view of Picot's attitude, Sykes and the Zionists decided that first priority should be given to obtaining French sympathy for Zionist aims as such. This strategy could be counted upon in the long run to strengthen Britain's claim to Palestine. To this end, Sokolow was sent to Paris with the encouragement of Picot, who hoped that the visit would help wean the Zionists from their exclusive reliance on Britain. On Apr. 9, 1917, Sokolow was received at the Quai d'Orsay. Among those present at that conference, in addition to Picot himself, was Jules Cambon, Secretary-General of the French Foreign Ministry. The meeting took place under the impact of a previous declaration from Sykes to Picot that Britain would press its claims in Palestine and that there could be no hope for order in the Middle East if Allied arrangements for Palestine ran counter to the wishes of the Zionists.

On May 25, 1917, Sokolow was received by Prime Minister Alexandre Ribot and, later in the day, by Jules Cambon. In response to Sokolow's request, Cambon, on June 4, wrote him the following letter, the first official pro-Zionist statement to be made by any of the Great Powers:

> You were good enough to present the project to which you are devoting your efforts, which has for its object the development of Jewish colonization in Palestine. You consider that, circumstances permitting, and the independence of the Holy Places being safeguarded on the other hand, it would be a deed of justice and of reparation to assist, by the protection of the Allied Powers, in the renaissance of the Jewish nationality in that Land from which the people of Israel were exiled so many centuries ago.
>
> The French Government, which entered this present war to defend a people wrongly attacked, and which continues the struggle to assure the victory of right over might, can but feel sympathy for your cause, the triumph of which is bound up with that of the Allies.
>
> I am happy to give you herewith such assurance.

This letter was not made public, but Arthur James *Balfour was to use it at a meeting of the British War Cabinet (Oct. 4, 1917) as evidence that the French could be expected to agree to the statement that was to become known as the *Balfour Declaration. Contrary to Balfour's expectations, however, France ignored the declaration completely when it was issued.

In a speech to the Chamber of Deputies (December, 1917) after the capitulation of Jerusalem to the forces of Gen. Edmund H. H. *Allenby, Stéphen Pichon, who had again become Foreign Minister, stated that Palestine would be ruled neither by the British nor by the French but by an international administration. Moreover, in a report submitted to the French Senate on Dec. 31, 1917, on a petition dealing with French-Arab relations, Zionism was described as *une utopie dangereuse* (a dangerous utopia). About two months later, however, Pichon was to adopt, at least on paper, a more cooperative stand on the

Balfour Declaration and the promises it contained. In January, 1918, Sokolow was in Paris again. He met with Jules Cambon (February 4) and with Baron Edmond de *Rothschild, on whose help he had been able to rely throughout. Rothschild suggested to Georges Clemenceau, who had become Prime Minister in November, 1917, and with whom the baron had been on friendly terms, that France would be wise to match the British commitment to the Zionists with a similar assurance. At Clemenceau's request, Pichon received Sokolow on Feb. 9, 1918. The result of the interview was the following communiqué issued for publication:

> Monsieur Sokolow, representing the Zionist Organizations, was received this morning at the Ministry of Foreign Affairs by Monsieur Stéphen Pichon, who was happy to confirm that there is complete agreement between the French and British Governments in matters concerning the question of a Jewish establishment [*un établissement juif*] in Palestine.

The communiqué was followed a few days later by a letter (dated Feb. 14, 1918) from Pichon to Sokolow:

> As arranged at our meeting on Saturday, the 9th of this month, the Government of the Republic, with a view to defining its attitude towards Zionist aspirations looking to the creation of a national home for the Jews in Palestine, has published a communiqué in the press.
>
> In sending you this text, I am particularly glad to take this opportunity to congratulate you on the generous devotion with which you are working for the realization of the hopes of your co-religionists, and to thank you for your zeal in making known to them the sympathy aroused by their efforts in the countries of the Entente, and especially in France.

Although the French were to claim at the London and San Remo Conferences two years later (*see* SAN REMO CONFERENCE) that they had never officially endorsed the Balfour Declaration, this statement was taken by the Zionists as France's ratification of the British commitment.

Paris Peace Conference. At the end of 1918 Clemenceau, during a visit to London, came to a private agreement with Prime Minister David *Lloyd George whereby France was to accept British control over Palestine. Clemenceau seems to have been persuaded by Lloyd George's arguments (which were reiterated at the Paris Peace Conference) that the British had overthrown the Ottoman Empire virtually alone, with almost no help from the French, that international governments tended to lead to trouble, and that all the inhabitants of Palestine, Arabs and Zionists, appeared to favor a British Mandate in preference to French control.

At the meeting of the Council of Ten (Supreme Council) of the Paris Peace Conference (February, 1919), a Zionist delegation (including André *Spire) and a French non-Zionist spokesman (Sylvain Lévi) were given a hearing. After the hearing, André Tardieu, one of the French representatives on the Council, reportedly stated that France would not oppose a League of Nations *Mandate for Palestine with Great Britain as the mandatory. Nevertheless, France did not give up Palestine without stiff resistance, first at the Inter-Allied Conference in London (Feb. 12, 1920) and subsequently in San Remo (April, 1920). Alexandre Millerand, a Socialist turned rightist and nationalist after World War I who had become Prime Minister in 1920, had strong views on French interests in the Levant. In London and again at San Remo, the French stated their willingness to accept a British Mandate for Palestine, but only with special reservations as regarded the holy places. However, Lloyd George's counterargument that there was no room for dual control in Palestine eventually carried the day and the Mandate for Palestine was finally awarded to the British in San Remo. France was given the Mandate for Syria proper and Lebanon.

Between the Wars, 1920–39. During the period between the two world wars French public opinion generally favored Zionist aims. In 1926 a French committee of friends of Zionism, the France-Palestine Committee, was founded; it was followed in 1928 by a French-Palestinian Chamber of Commerce. Both organizations were headed by prominent French parliamentarians, mostly non-Jews. Under the Radical party leader Justin Godard, the France-Palestine Committee sought to aid the Jewish National Home through work with the *Jewish National Fund and *Keren HaYesod (Palestine Foundation Fund). The honorary presidency of the France-Palestine Committee was held by Pres. Gaston Doumergue (1863–1937). Other well-known members were Louis Barthou, Aristide Briand, Édouard Herriot, and Paul Painlevé, all of whom served at various times as Prime Ministers of France, and prominent scholars and intellectuals, among them the physicist Paul Langevin.

World War II and the Struggle for the Jewish State, 1939–48. Throughout the war French Zionists were active in the resistance movement as well as the Free French movement, and formed warm friendships with the leaders of the French underground (see FRANCE, ZIONISM IN). Because of these friendships, as well as French sympathy for the plight of the remnants of European Jewry and annoyance with the British for having helped edge them out of Syria during the war, France placed no obstacles in the way of the early postwar work of the *Jewish Agency and the *Hagana. These branches of the Zionist movement in France were left free to organize "*illegal" immigration, to purchase arms, to set up training camps, and even to start a broadcasting station near Paris. After the liberation the French authorities showed a friendly attitude to illegal Jewish immigration to Palestine and to Zionist aspirations in general. The plight of the passengers of the *"Exodus 1947" aroused widespread outrage and sympathy in French public opinion. Those refugees who were willing to disembark were offered asylum in France.

When the Palestine problem was brought before the United Nations, France, notwithstanding very strong pressures from Algeria, Morocco, and Tunisia, then French possessions, voted for the establishment of a Jewish State in Palestine (Nov. 29, 1947).

FRANCE AND THE STATE OF ISRAEL, 1948–

France's early official relationship with the Jewish State was marked by caution and reluctance to incur Arab displeasure. The French government waited until Jan. 19, 1949, to extend de facto recognition to Israel. De jure recognition did not come until May 21, 1949. When Israel's first application for membership in the United Nations (Nov. 29, 1948) failed to obtain a majority vote in the Security Council, France was one of the five nations that abstained from the voting. However, she supported Israel's second application both in the Security Council (Mar. 4, 1949) and in the General Assembly (May 11, 1949). French diplomatic representatives in Israel were Édouard-Félix Guyon (1949–53), Pierre-Eugène Gilbert (1953–59), Jean A. A. Bourdeillette (1959–66), and Bertrand de la Sablière (1966–68). In 1968 Francis Huré was appointed Ambassador of France. Israel was represented in France by Maurice *Fischer

(1949–53), Ya'akov Tzur (1953–59), and Walter *Eytan (1959–   ).

Soon after the establishment of the State, certain Catholic circles in France urged the French government to get early agreements with Israel to safeguard the status of French religious institutions in that country. Negotiations were opened, and agreements satisfactory to both sides were reached in 1951. On Jan. 30, 1950, Roger Garreau of France, then chairman of the UN Trusteeship Council, announced a "compromise" plan for Jerusalem, whereby the city would remain divided between Israel and Jordan as it had been at the end of the *War of Independence; only the *Western Wall (Wailing Wall) and the Christian holy places would be internationalized. However, this plan was rejected by both the countries immediately concerned.

France was a member of the UN Palestine Conciliation Commission as well as of the Advisory Commission for the UN Relief and Works Agency for Palestine Refugees in the Near East (UNRWA). On May 25, 1950, France joined the United States and the United Kingdom in the Tripartite Declaration, which aimed to maintain the status quo in the Middle East. While stating opposition to an arms race between Israel and the Arab states, the parties to the agreement conceded that both sides needed to maintain a certain level of military force to assure internal security and legitimate self-defense. All applications for arms and war materials were to be considered in the light of these principles.

In November, 1950, France and Israel signed a trade agreement, but the large French-owned enterprises that operated in the Middle East showed no eagerness to make investments in Israel. The Israeli government, on its part, did little in the beginning to foster close contacts with France. This was especially true in the cultural sphere. Israeli leaders, many of whom had received their education in Britain or the United States, tended to look to those countries rather than to France.

Rapprochement. Rapprochement between France and Israel was given impetus by France's growing troubles with the Muslim world, particularly Egypt, where the Cairo Radio was inveighing against the French. In time, increasing numbers of French journalists, writers, trade unionists, and politicians paid visits to Israel. Cultural contacts were established between the two countries; in the early 1950s a French cultural center was opened in Tel Aviv, and the Association France-Israël, a nonsectarian group, started a public information program intended to improve relations with Israel. At the UN Security Council France joined with the United Kingdom and the United States to introduce a resolution (Aug. 16, 1951) calling on Egypt to end its blockade of the Suez Canal to Israeli shipping.

As the Algerian independence movement became increasingly troublesome for France, it began to show an interest in acquiring Israel as a potential ally. French Ambassador Pierre-Eugène Gilbert, who took up his post in Israel in 1953, and Shim'on *Peres, Director General of Israel's Ministry of Defense, cooperated closely in matters involving the strengthening of the defense of Israel. Israel began to receive French tanks and Ouragan and Mystère II fighter jets. Following the arms agreement between Czechoslovakia and Egypt in the fall of 1955, France showed willingness to sell arms to Israel. That year, too, an accord was signed between the two countries enabling France to make use of a process discovered by Israeli scientists for the production of heavy water. Even before Egypt's nationalization of the Suez Canal in July, 1956, French arms deliveries to Israel were increased (beginning with 1955) to include French Mirage IV jets and heavy tanks.

On Oct. 10, 1956, a Franco-Israeli agreement was signed, setting terms for additional arms deliveries, air squadron assignments, and supplies to Israel's troops in the Sinai Peninsula. On October 16, the British approved the inclusion of Israel in the planned Anglo-French operation in Egypt. From October 22 to 24, Premier David *Ben-Gurion was in France for secret conferences with high French government officials, in which Israel was promised French air cover against possible Egyptian bombing raids on its towns and cities. On Oct. 29, 1956, Israel launched its *Sinai Campaign; Britain and France started their attack two days later.

In spite of the failure of the Suez operation, the French press in the months that followed had only praise for Israel and its lightning campaign. French politicians of all parties, except the Communists (who, in keeping with the Soviet party line, had come to consider Israel a tool of the "imperialists"), neutralists, and left-wing intellectuals (who disapproved of the war), vied with one another in praising Israel. The French government continued its stanch support of Israel. In a message to the European Conference of Solidarity with Israel, organized by Keren HaYesod in Paris (March, 1957), Premier Guy Mollet pledged continued French aid for the "small and yet most threatened member state of the United Nations." Also early in 1957, despite its own financial difficulties, France granted Israel a loan of $30,000,000, which was increased to $45,000,000 by that August.

At the United Nations, Foreign Minister Christian Pineau consistently defended Israel's stand, particularly against the Afro-Asian proposal (Jan. 9, 1957) demanding Israel's immediate and unconditional withdrawal from the Sinai Peninsula. It was Pineau who drew up the "understanding" with the United Nations and the United States, in accordance with which Israel finally withdrew its forces from the Gaza Strip and from the mouth of the Gulf of Elat ('Aqaba). Late in March, 1957, after Israel had completed its withdrawal from the Gaza Strip, Pineau told the French Parliament that if Israel were to reenter the area as a result of the resumption of *fedayeen activities against its borders and citizens, France would consider that action justified and would support Israel. In a message to the Women's Division of the *American Jewish Congress early in May, Premier Mollet stated: "It is important that world opinion realize that the very principles of international law are involved in the settlement of problems facing Israel, be it that of the free passage of its ships through the Suez Canal, the free navigation in the Straits of Tiran and in the Gulf of 'Aqaba or, even more so, in the general peace settlement in the Near East to which it is entitled."

De Gaulle Era. Even before his return to power (he became Premier in 1958 and President of France the following January), Gen. Charles de Gaulle had frequently expressed sympathy for Israel. Members of the De Gaulle Cabinet favoring continued close cooperation with Israel included Guy Mollet, André Malraux, the Catholic Pierre Pflimlin, and Jacques Soustelle (who was then president of the Association France-Israël).

The years 1958 and 1959 saw cultural exchanges between France and Israel, including the opening of a French culture center in B'er Sheva' and visits of Jewish and non-Jewish school youngsters to France. A French-Israeli cultural agreement was reached to which the French attributed great importance because it provided for the greatly increased teaching of French in Israeli schools. Much was actually achieved in this area, and at the same time nine chairs of Hebrew were established at various universities in France. At the same time, Israel's exports to France continued to rise and began to include industrial as well as agricultural products. In the late 1950s a French corporation built Haifa's subway line. The leading spirit in the group that financed the construction of the large Elat-Haifa pipeline was the second Baron Edmond de *Rothschild. The Renault Automobile Corporation, which had canceled its contract with the Kaiser-Frazer plant in Israel in October, 1959, to escape an Arab boycott, resumed the relationship in the early 1960s. In 1961 a number of ships built for Israel in French shipyards were launched. Israeli leaders were given cordial receptions in France. In August, 1958, Golda *Meir went there for talks with De Gaulle and Foreign Minister Maurice Couve de Murville.

The pro-Israel activities of non-Jewish groups and individuals in the early and middle 1960s were of great significance. In the French Senate there was Amitié France-Israël (France-Israel Friendship), headed by André Monteuil, a former Cabinet Minister and leader of the Christian Democratic party. A corresponding group in the Chamber of Deputies was headed by Raymond Schmittlein, a former Cabinet Minister, Vice-Chairman of the Chamber, and one of the leaders of the Government party. These two committees, which promoted friendly relations between France and Israel, included several hundred senators and deputies of every political party (even some Communists).

The Alliance France-Israël, whose founder and director general was Sh'lomo Friedrich, a prominent Zionist, had among its members some of the foremost men of France. Gen. Pierre Koenig, a World War II hero, was its president; André Monteuil, Diomède Catroux (a prominent member of the Government party), and Raymond Schmittlein served as vice-presidents.

The Ligue Internationale contre le Racisme et l'Anti-Sémitisme (International League against Racism and Anti-Semitism) and the Comité d'Anti-Diffamation Interraciale (Interracial Anti-Defamation Committee), the two organizations set up in France to combat racism and anti-Semitism, were conducting a campaign against Arab anti-Israel agitation.

Public demonstrations of France's friendship for Israel and the Zionist movement included the naming of a Paris square near the Israeli Embassy Place d'Israël and an official ceremony in 1962 at the Hotel Ritz, in which a tablet was unveiled by Maurice Weil, vice-president of the Paris Municipal Council, to commemorate Herzl's stay at the hotel. In June, 1960, Premier Ben-Gurion arrived in Paris on an extended official visit. At a luncheon tendered Ben-Gurion a year later in the Élysée Palace (June, 1961), De Gaulle referred to Israel as "our friend and ally."

De Gaulle's initial efforts in the early 1960s to effect a rapprochement with the "Third World," including the United Arab Republic (UAR; Egypt) and Syria (Algeria left the French fold permanently in 1962), did not at first affect his good relations with Israel. Even after France had resumed diplomatic relations with the UAR and De Gaulle had received King Hussein (Husayn) of Jordan (October, 1963), French arms shipments to Israel continued. By the mid-1960s, however, it was obvious that French officials were showing a certain sympathy for Arab grievances against Israel. At the United Nations France displayed a reserved attitude toward Israel which occasionally amounted to hostility. These developments were probably responsible for Israeli Premier Levi *Eshkol's private visit to France from June 28 to July 10, 1964. During his visit, Eshkol conferred with Premier Georges Pompidou, Foreign Minister Couve de Murville, Defense Minister Pierre Messmer, and President de Gaulle. De Gaulle again frequently referred to Israel as France's "friend and ally," and Israel's proposals for cooperation with French scientists in oceanography and arid-zone research met with great interest.

The critical weeks preceding the *Six-day War of 1967 showed that Israel's reservoir of goodwill in French public opinion was still intact. Jewish organizations were joined in their public demonstrations by nonsectarian political associations such as the Committee for French Solidarity with Israel (founded by General Koenig) and the French Assemblage for Israel (led by the Gaullist politician Jean-Claude Servan-Schreiber, who was of Jewish descent). Financial contributions poured in, volunteers offered their services, and pro-Israel statements were made by many political groupings, with the notable exception of one leftist faction and of the Communists, who had consistently opposed Israel as an ally of the United States and who were now following the Moscow line.

Six-day War. In view of these overwhelming public demonstrations of pro-Israel sentiment, Israel and its friends were dismayed when President de Gaulle told Israeli Foreign Minister Abba *Eban, who had come to Paris (May 24, 1967) to ask French assistance after the UAR's blockade of the Gulf of Elat, that De Gaulle would not approve military action on the part of Israel against the UAR. He would not permit Israel to be destroyed, but he would consider the country that fired the first shot to be the guilty party in the conflict.

At a Cabinet meeting on June 2, 1967, De Gaulle declared that "France is in no way involved . . . with any of the states concerned. . . . That state which will be the first to resort to force will have neither her approval nor her support." France no longer considered itself bound by its 1957 affirmation of the international status of the Gulf of Elat. The next day the Israeli Embassy in Paris was informed that France had placed an embargo on all arms deliveries to all countries in the Middle East. After the Six-day War this was restricted to Mirage jet fighters.

On June 8, 1967, France voted for the cease-fire resolution of the UN Security Council. It subsequently supported the resolution submitted by Yugoslavia calling for the withdrawal of Israeli forces from Arab territory but not the Soviet resolution, which was couched in even harsher terms. Foreign Minister Couve de Murville declared in the French National Assembly that although France had been on friendly terms with Israel, it had close relations also with the Arab states; he reiterated this view on June 14, 1967, at the NATO Conference in Luxembourg. At a Cabinet meeting on June 21, 1967, De Gaulle condemned Israel for having started the fighting.

The government's anti-Israel stance was resented by French public opinion, even in Gaullist circles. Gaullist Finance Minister Michel Debré attempted to bend De Gaulle's views in a direction more favorable to Israel. Even some of France's left-wing intellectuals refused to believe that Israel was a puppet of American imperialism. While initially constituting the bulk of France's pro-Arab element, many of this group subsequently attempted to moderate the brutality of Arab anti-Israel invective. Jean-Paul Sartre, the philosopher and writer, originally sym-

pathized with President Nasser, but his statements in Tel Aviv and Jerusalem after visits to the UAR and Israel (March, 1968) indicated a modification of his views. A sector of the traditionally anti-Semitic right wing, which had sided with Israel in 1956, once more championed the Israeli cause against the Communists, but most of the extreme anti-Jewish right, particularly the students in that faction, were outspoken in their support of the Arabs. Generally, however, while Israel's attitude had given rise to some controversy, Frenchmen agreed that De Gaulle's analysis of the Middle Eastern situation prior to the outbreak of the war had not been realistic. De Gaulle's radical turnabout seemed to have been motivated by anti-Americanism and by considerations of pure political expediency, as well as by the desire to make France a factor in any settlement in the Middle East.

De Gaulle's Press Conference. A number of statements made by De Gaulle at a press conference in Paris on Nov. 27, 1967, caused widespread dismay among Jews and non-Jews alike, for they were interpreted as an official "green light" for anti-Semites to express their views, which had been taboo in France since World War II. In his reply to a query about the Middle Eastern situation, De Gaulle resurrected the question of the place of the Jew in French society and of the compatibility of Zionist sympathies and loyalty to the French fatherland. He violently attacked Israel for its policies in the Arab territories it had occupied during the Six-day War. "During the Suez Campaign," he said, "we witnessed the appearance of a warrior State determined to get larger, doubling its population by immigration and, in order to enlarge it, using any possible occasion." Referring to the Jews as *"un peuple d'élite, sur de lui-même et dominateur"* (an elite people, sure of itself and domineering), he wondered whether, once "gathered on the site of their former grandeur," they might not transform their "very touching" hope, "Next year in Jerusalem," into the vaulting ambition of a conqueror. De Gaulle specifically charged Israel with using Nasser's blockade of the Gulf of Elat as an excuse to launch the Six-day War. These statements were in sharp contrast to the views expressed by De Gaulle in an interview soon after the Sinai Campaign in 1956. At that time De Gaulle had advised Israel to fight for its freedom of navigation and had told Ambassador Ya'akov Tzur to tell Ben-Gurion that even if Israel were forced to withdraw its troops from Egyptian territory, "she would never lose the immense gains she made in international prestige or her strengthened position in the Middle East that resulted from the war."

De Gaulle's statements met with violent protests from every sector of French public opinion. The French press rejected his "incredible attitude" *(Aurore)* and asserted that there was "an unpleasant smell of anti-Semitism" in his remarks *(Le Monde)*. Raymond Aron, an eminent sociologist at the Sorbonne, a Jew but not a Zionist, set forth his protest in a small book, *De Gaulle, Israël et les juifs* (De Gaulle, Israel and the Jews). De Gaulle's reply to his critics, who included former Israeli Prime Minister David Ben-Gurion and French Chief Rabbi Jacob *Kaplan, was not calculated to allay the misgivings he had aroused. In his reply to Ben-Gurion (Dec. 30, 1967), De Gaulle said that although he would never have permitted the annihilation of the State of Israel, which he still considered "a friend and ally," he was convinced that Israel had "exceeded the bounds of moderation when she ignored the warnings of the Government of the French Republic . . . and by force of arms occupied Jerusalem, and Jordanian, Egyptian and Syrian territory. . . ."

In a 15-minute private talk with Chief Rabbi Kaplan at the 1968 New Year's reception at the Élysée Palace, De Gaulle replied to a question from Kaplan that he, De Gaulle, saw "no conflict at all" between the duties of French Jews as citizens of France and their special sympathy for Israel. However, it was noted that he spoke of special sympathies for "the people and the soil" but made no mention of the State of Israel.

De Gaulle's stand was warmly praised by the Arabs; French oil interests in Algeria were untouched, and the French gained important oil concessions in Iraq after a visit (December, 1967) from a high-ranking Iraqi delegation to France. Meanwhile, however, Israel continued to receive military supplies from France, all except for the 50 Mirage V jets which it had ordered before the official 1967 embargo and paid for since. In 1968, however, De Gaulle clamped a total embargo on all arms deliveries to Israel, including spare parts of jets. In general, he adopted the Soviet pro-Arab policy, demanding that Israel unconditionally withdraw from all occupied territories and that a solution agreed upon by the Big Four be imposed on Israel and the Arab countries.

G. WEILL

FRANCE, ZIONISM IN. Zionism was the subject of considerable debate in France as early as the 1860s. In response to pro-Zionist statements by various non-Jewish writers (*see* FRANCE: RELATIONS WITH ZIONISM AND ISRAEL), the *Archives Israélites,* a Jewish periodical edited by Isadore Cahen, became a forum for heated controversy (1864). Lazar Lévy-Bing, a banker in Nancy who was to become a member of the French National Assembly in 1871, maintained that there was no conflict between the desire for the restoration of Palestine to the Jewish people and the patriotic sentiments of Jews living in France.

The Jews of 19th-century France were profoundly influenced by the spirit of *assimilation and endeavored to become part of a national and cultural entity that was regarded as representing the best in European civilization. Thus, the *Revue des Études Juives* (1882) said of Leo *Pinsker's *Autoemancipation:*

The first departure of French Jewish youths for Palestine after World War II. [YIVO Institute for Jewish Research]

"The persecution of the Jews in Russia has inspired in the author the fanciful notion to seek the emancipation of the Jews through the establishment of a Jewish State" (p. 298). In *Les prophètes d'Israël* (1892) the Orientalist James Darmesteter wrote: "By breaking the barriers separating Christian and Jew, the French Revolution put an end to the history of the Jewish people. Since September 28, 1791, there has been no more room for a history of the Jews in France; today, there is room only for a history of French Judaism" (p. 189). Théodore Reinach, a French-Jewish historian, asserted: "In exchange for liberty and equal rights Israel abandoned its dream of political restoration; it has ceased to be a nation, or to wish to be restored to nationhood, and remains only a religious group" (*Histoire des Israélites depuis leur dispersion,* Paris, 1884, 1910, p. xiii). "The French Jews," the poet André *Spire (see below) explained, "could not imagine that one might hope for a solution [to the Jewish problem] by means other than a gradual change for the better in human nature. . . . They were convinced that the Jews in other lands would find salvation, like themselves, in the triumph of the principles of [the French Revolution of] 1789" (*L'Écho Sioniste,* Oct. 4, 1912, pp. 67–69).

This attitude explains why not only Herzl's initial overtures to prominent French Jews but also the principles of Zionism met largely with skepticism, indifference, and even outright rejection.

The *Alliance Israélite Universelle, which was founded by French Jews in 1860 to assist Jews and to defend their civil and religious rights the world over, was the first Jewish organization in France to extend practical assistance to the Jewish community of Palestine. After a visit to Palestine in 1868, Charles *Netter (1826–82), one of the founders of the Alliance, convinced Adolphe Crémieux (1796–1880), then the president of the organization, of the necessity for initiating and supporting educational and philanthropic projects in that country. The result was the founding of the Mikve Yisrael Agricultural School near Jaffa in 1870 and of other schools in the large towns of Palestine.

The first Zionist pioneers in Palestine received generous support from Baron Edmond de *Rothschild, who, beginning in the 1880s, supported the new settlements and sent agricultural experts to train the new farmers. However, Rothschild was motivated primarily by philanthropic considerations and did not join the Zionist movement. The *Jewish Colonization Association (ICA), which, though incorporated in England, conducted its activities from Paris, earmarked most of its funds for Jewish agricultural settlements in Argentina and other *Diaspora countries, leaving very little for the purchase of land in Palestine.

In 1881 Russian-Jewish students in France formed a group they named "The Eternal Jew," and in 1886 they founded B'ne Zion, which bought 120 dunams of land (*see* DUNAM) in Wadi al-Hanin in 1890. Other groups developed, and some native-born French Jews joined their ranks. Student groups were formed in Paris, Montpellier, and elsewhere. In 1890 an attempt was made to set up in Paris a Central Committee representing *Hoveve Zion groups from all over the world.

Early Beginnings, 1897–1919. It was while in Paris as correspondent for the Vienna *Neue Freie Presse* that Herzl, under the impact of the *Dreyfus affair, conceived the idea of modern political Zionism and wrote his *Jewish State,* which was published in 1896. Max *Nordau, Herzl's close associate and vice-president of the early Zionist Congresses (*see* CONGRESS,

ZIONIST), lived in France from 1880 until the outbreak of World War I. Among the early Zionists in France were the biologist Dr. Alexander *Marmorek, his brothers Oskar (see MARMOREK, OSKAR) and Isidore, the writer Bernard *Lazare, defender of Dreyfus, Miss Miriam Schach, a Paris high school teacher, and the sculptor Samuel Friedrich *Beer. Although Chief Rabbi Zadoc *Kahn rejected political Zionism, he used his moral influence with Baron Edmond de Rothschild and with the Jewish Colonization Association, of which he was a director, to support Jewish settlement in Palestine. He also gave encouragement and help to Herzl.

The delegation from France to the 1st Zionist Congress (Basle, 1897) consisted of Jacques and Blanche Bahar, Samuel Friedrich Beer, Joshua Heshel *Buchmil, Boris Katzmann, Abraham *Ludvipol, Joseph Mirkin, Max Nordau, Moïse Padua, Miriam Schach, Moshe Schornstein, and Dr. Eugène Valentin. In 1899 Alexander Marmorek founded the newspaper L'Écho Sioniste, which appeared from 1899 until 1905 and again from 1912 to 1914. In 1916 it reappeared under the title Le Peuple Juif and remained in existence until 1921.

The majority of France's native-born Jews, however, continued to be indifferent to Zionism. Most of them rejected the concept of Jewish *nationalism and considered themselves Frenchmen in every respect, professing the Jewish religion or merely Jewish descent. On the other hand, Zionism had an appeal for the Jewish immigrants from Eastern European countries who had found a refuge in France. The newcomers duplicated in France the Zionist groups they had left behind in their native countries. For a long time, announcements of Zionist affairs were printed in both French and Yiddish.

The first meeting of the Fédération Sioniste de France (Zionist Federation of France) was held on Oct. 12, 1901, with Alexander Marmorek in the chair (he was to remain president until his death in 1923) and Victor Jacobsohn as vice-chairman. In 1903 the federation sponsored a ball in Paris, at the end of which Max Nordau, who at the time supported the *East Africa scheme, narrowly escaped assassination by a student from Russia. On July 23, 1904, the federation held a memorial meeting for Herzl, who had died a few days before. By the eve of World War I the federation had eight constituent groups: five in Paris (Assidas Zion, Mebassereth Zion, Atereth Zion, a Zionist women's society, and a students' society), one in Nice, and two (Association Sioniste and Société Sioniste de Tunis) in Tunis. The *Jewish National Fund (JNF) began small-scale activities in France soon after the 5th Zionist Congress (Basle, 1901).

Non-Jewish supporters of Zionism at the time included the statesman Léon V. A. Bourgeois (1851–1925) and the noted writer Émile Zola (1840–1902). These men equated liberalism with an active struggle for the rights of victims of oppression everywhere, and they interpreted Zionism as a political means for that purpose. In 1915 a group of Jewish and non-Jewish intellectuals including Charles Andler, the economist Charles Gide (1847–1932), Alphonse Lods, the statesman Marius Moutet, the historian Charles Seignobos (1854–1942), Nahum *Slouschz, André Spire, and Emanuel Weill founded the Ligue Franco-Sioniste (Franco-Zionist League) in Paris.

André Spire, the French-Jewish poet, had become interested in Jewish problems as early as 1904 under the influence of Israel *Zangwill and had attended the 11th Zionist Congress (Vienna, 1913). In 1917, together with his friends Roger Lévy (who was to serve as secretary to Chaim *Weizmann in 1919) and the poet Henri Franck, he founded the nonsectarian Ligue des Amis du Sionisme (League of the Friends of Zionism). The original members of this new organization, of which Maurice Vernes, professor at the École des Hautes-Études, was president, included academicians such as Richard Bloch, Ferdinand Brunot, Julien Cain, Louis Eisenmann, Jules Isaac, François Monod, Miriam Schach, Gabriel Séailles, and Jean Wahl; statesmen such as Albert Thomas (1878–1932); writers such as Edmond *Fleg, Henri Hertz (1875–1965), Gustave Kahn, and Aimé *Pallière; clergymen such as Bishop Lacroix and the Reverend Roberty; Baruch Hagani, long-time editor of Le Peuple Juif; and Dr. Armand Bernard, brother of Bernard Lazare. Spire, who was secretary-general of the Ligue, founded its publication, La Palestine Nouvelle (The New Palestine).

As a member of the staff of André Tardieu, High Commissioner of France to the United States and French plenipotentiary at the Paris Peace Conference, Spire was able to render valuable service to the Zionist cause. Tardieu, who later was to serve briefly as Prime Minister of France, had first become acquainted with Zionism through Justice Louis D. *Brandeis. In February, 1919, Tardieu requested Spire to represent the Zionists of France at a session of the Council of Ten (Supreme Council) of the peace conference to which Zionist and other Jewish leaders were invited to present their views on the future of Palestine.

On Feb. 27, 1919, Sokolow, Spire, M'nahem M. *Ussishkin, and Chaim Weizmann, who represented the Zionist movement, and Sylvain Lévi, then president of the Alliance Israélite Universelle, were given a hearing by the Council of Ten, which included Arthur James *Balfour and Lord Milner for Great Britain, Tardieu and Stéphen Pichon for France, Robert Lansing and Henry White for the United States, and Baron Sidney Sonnino for Italy. At the hearing Lévi, representing the Alliance, expressed disagreement with the Zionist view. After praising the work of Zionism from the moral point of view, since it had uplifted the Jewish masses and oriented them toward Palestine, he said that Palestine was too small to accommodate millions of Jews. He suggested, however, that the Jews might be allowed to create communities of their own in those localities in Palestine where they represented a majority of the population. This statement aroused intense indignation among the Zionists but had no influence on the Allied Powers assembled in Paris.

Between the Two World Wars, 1920–39. The period between the two world wars saw a slow growth of Zionist activity in France. In November, 1920, a Zionist group of college students was organized in Paris. In the summer of 1921 a *Mizrahi group was established with headquarters in Strasbourg.

The Jews of Alsace-Lorraine, many of whom were Orthodox, were more receptive to Zionism than their coreligionists in the rest of France. In 1917 the students of the region founded in Strasbourg a Zionist youth movement, later known as HaTikva, that was to supply Palestine with the bulk of French 'Olim (immigrants) prior to 1939. In November, 1925, Léopold Metzger, a Strasbourg attorney, with the help of Robert Lévy-Dreyfus (who in 1949 became Israeli Consul in Strasbourg) founded the Union Régionale des Sionistes de L'Est de la France (Regional Union of the Zionists of Eastern France), which was to retain its separate identity until 1941. The union was by far the strongest Zionist organization in pre-1939 France, its membership in Alsace, Lorraine, and Belfort being larger than the total membership of the Fédération Sioniste. The young people brought to the union idealism and organizing skills that had long been lacking in the Paris organization. They founded a weekly, *Le Juif* (later, *La Tribune Juive*). From 1919 to 1926 the Strasbourg Jewish National Fund Commission took over the functions of the Paris JNF office. It published an information bulletin, *La Terre Promise* (the Promised Land), founded in 1919.

In 1923 Mrs. Richard Gottheil (whose husband was then a visiting professor in Strasbourg) founded, with her sister Léonie, the Union des Dames Juives (Union of Jewish Women), a pro-Zionist group. The union's overemphasis on philanthropic endeavors led to the organization, by Mrs. Claire Braunberger, of Ghalei (G'dud Ha'Ovdot L'Eretz Israel, or Group of Women Workers for the Land of Israel), which subsequently merged with the *Women's International Zionist Organization (WIZO).

It was at a meeting in Strasbourg in 1923 that the Association of French Rabbis stressed the importance of Jewish settlement in the Holy Land and favored the creation of a Zionist society free of partisan or nationalist doctrines so that all the Jews of France would be able to see their way clear to taking part in the rebuilding of Palestine. Despite this appeal, however, the official representative organizations of French Jewry (consistories and religious communities) did not come out in favor of Zionism.

Aimé Pallière, an advocate of Judaism, lectured to various Jewish communities in France to propagate the idea of a Jewish National Home and to emphasize the importance of the Jewish National Fund. In 1926 the Paris headquarters of the JNF was reorganized by Joseph Fisher-Ariel (later Israel's Ambassador to Belgium). JNF receipts for the period 1937–39, including funds raised in Algeria, totaled 2,372,037 francs.

French Jewry accepted Weizmann's invitation to participate in the worldwide Jewish conference held in Zurich in August, 1929, for the purpose of enlarging the *Jewish Agency. At that conference the non-Zionists of France were represented by Léon *Blum, Robert Bollag, and Dr. Léo Zadoc-Kahn, of Paris, and by Dr. Henri Lévi, of Strasbourg. Blum was to serve for several years as a representative of French Jewry on the Agency's Council.

The Coordinating Committee of Zionist Organizations, founded in 1937, embraced the entire French Zionist spectrum, from General Zionists (*see* GENERAL ZIONISM) through the Left *Po'ale Zion, with the exception of the *Revisionists. The president of the committee was Léonce Bernheim (d. 1944), an attorney and brother-in-law of Edmond Fleg. In the 1930s the following Zionist organizations were active in France:

Left Po'ale Zion. Founded in 1922, it included a number of workers' mutual-aid societies and athletic clubs. A splinter group, Left Po'ale Zion Activists, was organized in 1935.

Revisionists. The World Union of Zionists-Revisionists was founded in Paris in 1925.

*Po'ale Zion–*Hitahdut.* With 14 branches all over France and a total membership of about 400, this organization included a League for Labor Palestine and the Jewish People's League, a mutual-aid society formed in 1937.

Organisation Sioniste de France. General Zionist organization formally established in 1933.

Mizrahi. Mizrahi in France had a small congregation, Yavne, and a library that published a Yiddish-language bulletin, *Pariser Yidishe Tzeitshrift,* in 1936.

Jewish State Party. Founded in 1936, it had 150 members in Paris.

Women's International Zionist Organization (WIZO). It was founded in 1935.

There were also a Sephardi Zionist Organization, with 250 members; a Zionist group of refugees from Nazi Germany, with a membership of about 100; and a Territorialist organization, founded in 1935 (*see* JEWISH TERRITORIAL ORGANIZATION).

In the same period branches of many Zionist youth movements were formed, including Bleu-Blanc (Blau-Weiss; General Zionist); B'rit HaKana'im (Jewish State party); *D'ror (Right Po'ale Zion); *HaShomer HaTza'ir; *HeHalutz, which in 1939 had 300 members and three Hakhsharot (training farms; *see* HAKHSHARA) in the provinces; Revisionist youth groups; *Tz'ire Mizrahi and HaPo'el HaMizrahi; the Youth Federation of Labor Palestine; and *HaNo'ar HaTziyoni. In 1937 the Éclaireurs Israélites de France (EIF), an influential pro-Zionist scouting movement founded in 1922 by Robert Gamzon (Robert Castor; 1906–61), joined French Zionist youth groups to form the Fédération de la Jeunesse Sioniste et Pro-Palestinienne (Federation of Zionist and Pro-Palestine Youth of France). This federation, with 47 constituent organizations and a total membership of 5,000 in France and French North Africa, coordinated Zionist youth work. In 1946 the EIF was to found N've Ilan, the first French *kibbutz in Palestine.

A branch of the *B'rit 'Ivrit 'Olamit (World Hebrew Federation) was founded in 1938. Its Hebrew-language courses were attended by more than 100 students, mostly from Zionist youth organizations. *'Aliya from France before World War II was small. During the period immediately preceding the war, more than 90 per cent of the 'Olim from France were refugees from Nazi Germany.

World War II and Nazi Occupation, 1939–45. When France was overrun by the Nazis, Zionists played an important role in Jewish life and in the underground resistance movement. Most of the Jewish organizations that had had headquarters in Paris transferred their centers of activity to the southern sector, known as unoccupied, or Vichy, France.

In September, 1940, the JNF, directed from Lyon by Joseph Fisher-Ariel, resumed its activities and carried on an educational program. Thanks to an arrangement with JNF headquarters in Geneva, it was able throughout the war to distribute mimeographed information bulletins, providing a welcome source of news when there was no access to foreign newspapers. In 1941 Fisher-Ariel called a secret conference in Lyon at which an overall Zionist leadership, embracing all Zionist groups in the country, was set up under the chairmanship of Léonce Bernheim. In 1942 a Va'ad HaHinukh (Education Committee) was created; it was concerned primarily with the promotion of the study of the Hebrew language. The Office des Oeuvres Pro-Palestiniennes (Office of Pro-Palestine Projects) supported local Zionist efforts in Limoges and Toulouse and set up training-farm centers in Belmont, in Haute-Vienne; Gilland, in Haute-Garonne; and Chamy, in Tarn-et-Garonne.

At a secret meeting held in Vichy in December, 1941, the Mouvement de la Jeunesse Sioniste (MJS; United Zionist Youth Movement) was created, embracing all French Zionist youth movements regardless of political tendency. Directed by Simon Lévitte and Jules Jefroykin, the MJS published an underground bulletin and organized courses in Jewish history and literature, the history of Zionism, and the geography of Palestine. At its first general meeting, held in Montpellier in May, 1942, the MJS decided to take an even more active part in the work of the resistance movement. Accordingly, it began to smuggle Jewish refugees, particularly children, across the border into neutral Switzerland and Spain and aided the armed resistance.

A French Zionist newspaper of May 2, 1952. The headline reads: "Jews the World Over Celebrate the Fourth Anniversary of the Proclamation of the State of Israel. [Zionist Archives]

In 1942 a group of young Zionists in Toulouse organized the Armée Juive (AJ; Jewish Army). Placed under the orders of Zionist leadership, this group helped hide children in friendly homes in France, distributing adolescents among various fighting units and smuggling young people into Spain, from where they enlisted in Gen. Charles de Gaulle's Free French forces or went on to Palestine. The AJ also maintained contacts between the Fédération des Sociétés Juives de France (Federation of Jewish Associations of France) and the Jewish communities of Switzerland, Spain, and Portugal. Eventually, the AJ became a combat unit, taking the name Organisations Juives de Combat (OJC; Jewish Fighting Forces). When the Éclaireurs Israélites de France was disbanded by the Vichy government, the organization placed itself under the orders of the OJC. In January, 1944, Gilbert Bloch (d. 1944), Robert Gamzon, and Marc Hageneau (d. 1944) organized the Black Mountain Maquis (underground fighters), later known as the Marc Hageneau Company, which liberated the towns of Castres and Mazamet in August, 1944.

A nucleus of members of the Paris WIZO, led by its secretary-general, Juliette Stern (1893–1963), devoted its energies to the rescue of adults and children from the occupied zone and particularly to the placement of Jewish children with Christian families. The Oeuvre de Secours aux Enfants (OSE; Child Rescue Project), which carried on its work in Paris, as well as in the internment camps and principal cities of unoccupied France, made use of the OJC escape routes, bringing 52 children across the Pyrenees into Spain, where they were received by representatives of the *American Jewish Joint Distribution Committee (JDC) and taken to Palestine.

After World War II, 1945–67. Following the liberation of France from Nazi occupation, the attitude of French Jewry developed markedly in favor of Zionism. After the end of the war, HaShomer HaTza'ir, HeHalutz, *Histadrut (General Federation of Labor), Mizrahi, Po'ale Zion, and *Youth 'Aliya

established their continental European headquarters in Paris. Paris was also a center for the activities of the *Hagana and the *Irgun Tz'vai L'umi.

In 1947 the Union Sioniste Française (French Zionist Union) was formed in order to unite all French-speaking Zionists of France proper and French North Africa, regardless of party affiliation, for the purpose of giving moral and political support to the work of the Jewish Agency. For a time, the presidency of this organization was held by André Blumel, a distinguished jurist and one-time member of Léon Blum's office staff.

During the six-month period following the adoption of the United Nations *partition resolution, French Jewry raised considerable amounts of money for Jewish Palestine. Between November, 1947, and May, 1948, a campaign for funds for the Hagana organized by Lazare Rachline (d. 1968) brought in more than 2,000,000 francs. When Chaim Weizmann arrived in Paris shortly after accepting the Presidency of the provisional government of Israel, he was given a warm reception.

In 1950, 63,248 Shekels (membership fees; *see* SHEKEL) were sold in France for the 23d Zionist Congress (Jerusalem, 1951). That same year Aide à Israël (Aid to Israel) joined with the newly established Fonds Social Juif Unifié (United Jewish Social Fund) to campaign jointly as L'Appel Unifié (United Appeal). Baron Guy de Rothschild, then the president of the Consistoire Centrale des Israélites de France, the official religious body of French Jewry, was elected chairman of the United Appeal's Board of Directors. The campaign took place in 1950; in the Department of the Bas-Rhin it was continued throughout the ensuing years, and in 1967 (after the May crisis) it was resumed all over France under the name Fonds de Solidarité avec Israël (Israel Solidarity Fund). Presidents of Aide à Israël between 1950 and 1968 were Dr. Benjamin Weill-Halle and Raymond Weill-Vallier.

In the early 1950s Zionist activity in France revolved around three main organizations, the Fédération Sioniste de France, the Fédération des Sociétés Juives de France, and the Paris office of the Jewish Agency. The Fédération Sioniste was opened to individual membership for a time but without particular success. In time the Jewish Agency transferred to the Fédération Sioniste such functions as Zionist education and the Economic Department, which advised the owners of small French businesses who wished to trade with Israel. Community centers in which Jewish social and cultural activities were carried on became bases for pro-Zionist work. In the fall of 1957 the first *Ulpan course for adults in France was opened at Fontainebleau.

Notable work was done by the French WIZO, which as of 1967 had 10,800 members, with 29 chapters in the Paris metropolitan area and 67 in the provinces. The aim of WIZO in France was to foster Jewish home life through educational and cultural activities. The fortnightly WIZO bulletin *Revue de la WIZO*, with a circulation of 17,100, also reached French-speaking WIZO groups in Belgium, Luxembourg, Switzerland, Greece, Spain, Portugal, South America, Canada, and Israel.

The influx of Jewish immigrants to France from North Africa following the war with Algeria and the secession of Tunisia and Morocco infused new vitality into *B'ne 'Akiva and HaShomer HaTza'ir in France. In the 1960s Oded, a students' group consisting mostly of young people from North Africa, was organized with the object of interesting French-educated university students in 'Aliya to fill Israel's need for individuals with academic training.

By the 1960s all leading Jewish organizations and institutions in France, except for the Communists and a small number of Bundists (*see* BUND), were Israel-oriented. Among them were such communal organizations as the Consistoire Centrale; the Consistoire de Paris; the Alliance Israélite Universelle; the Conseil Représentatif des Juifs de France (CRIF; Representative Council of French Jewry), which, originally set up as an underground organization during the Nazi era, included all the Jewish factions in the country; the Organization of Jewish War Veterans; and the Organization of Former Jewish Deportees. Almost all synagogues in France sponsored pro-Israel activities. In 1966 Chief Rabbi Jacob *Kaplan was honorary president of Mizrahi–HaPo'el HaMizrahi and participated officially in all major Zionist efforts in the country.

*Six-day War of 1967 and Its Aftermath. The wholehearted support of all French Jewish groups for Israel was demonstrated particularly during the crisis of May and June, 1967. On May 26, 1967, a Comité de Coordination des Organisations Juives en France (Coordinating Committee of Jewish Organizations in France) was created. Headed by Guy de Rothschild, this central body, composed of some 30 major organizations, had an executive office, a permanent staff, and a Financial Action Committee consisting of representatives of all the Jewish organizations engaged in raising funds for Israel. It published an information bulletin (of which 19 issues appeared by March, 1968), with comments on political events, and a press digest. The Fonds de Solidarité avec Israël, the emergency campaign launched by the Financial Action Committee, brought in 20,000,000 francs ($4,000,000) within a few weeks. Pro-Israel demonstrations were held on May 31 and during the days that followed in Paris and throughout the country.

As of 1968 the following Zionist or pro-Israel organizations were active in France: *Ahdut 'Avoda–Po'ale Zion; Amitié France-Israël; *B'rit Halutzim Datiyim (Bachad); B'rit Herut-HaTzohar; B'rit 'Ivrit 'Olamit; *B'rit Trumpeldor (Betar);

Cercle Ahavat Zion; Cercle Ben-Zvi; Cercle Bernard Lazare, ideologically close to *Mapam; Chambre de Commerce France-Israël; Federation of Physicians and Opticians; Fédération Sioniste de France; Friends of Israel; Friends of the *Hebrew University of Jerusalem; Independent General Zionist Organization; Jewish National Fund; *Keren HaYesod–Appel Unifié pour Israël (Aide à Israël); *Magen David Adom; Mapam; *Pioneer Women; Po'ale Zion–Hitahdut; *Professional and Technical Workers' 'Aliya (PATWA); Religious Zionist Organization Mizrahi–HaPo'el HaMizrahi; Va'ad Lema'an Ha-Hayal, a women's organization belonging to the Federation of Jewish Knitwear Manufacturers that aided Israeli soldiers; WIZO; the Workmen's Home (ideologically close to Ahdut 'Avoda–Po'ale Zion); Youth 'Aliya; and the Zionist Organization of France (General Zionists).

Youth organizations included B'ne 'Akiva (Mizrahi); D'ror (Ahdut 'Avoda); Éclaireurs Israélites de France (a scouting organization); HaNo'ar Ha'Ivri (Independent Zionists); HaNo'ar HaTziyoni (General Zionists); HaShomer HaTza'ir and Mishmar (Mapam); HeHalutz; Ihud HaBonim (*see* HABONIM; *Mapai); and Tora V'Tziyon (religious organization for the education of refugee children and youths).

The following Zionist and pro-Zionist periodicals were published in France in 1968: (in French) *Amitiés France-Israël* (since 1953), a monthly with a circulation of 5,000; *Cahiers Bernard Lazare*, an organ of Mapam; *Perspectives France-Israël*, a Zionist Revisionist quarterly, published by the Alliance France-Israël; *Revue de la WIZO* (since 1947), a bimonthly with a circulation of 17,100; *Revue Encyclopédique Juive* (since 1967), a bimonthly; and *La Terre Retrouvée* (since 1928), which merged in 1964 with *La Tribune Sioniste*, a weekly with a circulation of 10,000; and (in Yiddish) *Arbeiter Vort* (since 1943), a biweekly organ of Ahdut 'Avoda–Po'ale Zion; *Di Naye Shtimme* (since 1962), a biweekly organ of the General Zionist party with a circulation of 2,500; *Unzer Veg* (since 1946), a Mizrahi weekly with a circulation of 8,500; *Unzer Vort* (since 1945), the only Zionist daily in Europe, published by Mapai; and *Zionistishe Shtimme*, an organ of the Independent General Zionist Organization.

G. WEILL

FRANK, JOSEPH NAHUM. Zionist leader and insurance executive (b. Manchester, England, 1906). At the age of 12, he joined Canadian *Young Judaea, then under the leadership of Dov *Joseph. He became national president of Canadian Young Judaea in 1934 and from then on was a member of the Executive Board of the Zionist Organization of Canada (ZOC; *see* CANADA, ZIONISM IN). From 1944 to 1946 he served as national president of the Zionist order *HaBonim, from 1942 to 1950 as chairman of the Executive of the Montreal *United Palestine Appeal, in 1953 as first chairman of the National Executive of the *State of Israel Bonds, and in 1964 as vice-president of Canada-Israel Securities, Ltd. Frank attended the Zionist Congresses (*see* CONGRESS, ZIONIST) of 1951, 1956, and 1960 and was a member of the First National Canadian Mission to Israel in 1960. After serving for several years as national treasurer of the ZOC, he was elected president of the organization in 1962.

B. FIGLER

FRÄNKEL, ABRAHAM HALEVI. Mathematician and faculty member of the *Hebrew University of Jerusalem (b. Munich, 1891; d. Jerusalem, 1965). He studied at German universities and subsequently taught at the Universities of Marburg and Kiel. From 1929, when he settled in Jerusalem, until his retirement in 1959, he was a professor, and from 1938 to 1940 rector, of the Hebrew University. A mathematician of international fame, Fränkel was the author of numerous mathematical and philosophical treatises. He was active in the *Mizrahi movement in Germany and served as a delegate to the 12th Zionist *Congress (1921). In Israel, he was prominently associated with numerous communal endeavors and was a member of the Presidium of the *Asefat HaNivharim (Elected Assembly).

J. STAVI

FRANKEL, LEE KAUFER. Social worker and Zionist sympathizer in the United States (b. Philadelphia, 1867; d. Paris, 1931). Frankel was one of the earliest American-born and American-educated full-time professional social workers in Jewish communal service. In 1909 he joined the Metropolitan Life Insurance Company, inaugurating a health care and education program for policyholders. By 1924 he was second vice-president of the company, a position he held until he died.

A member of the *American Jewish Committee from its inception, Frankel was deeply concerned about the plight of Eastern European Jewry in World War I. When the *American Jewish Joint Distribution Committee (JDC) was founded, he became a member of its Executive, serving for the rest of his life. In 1922 he headed a survey commission sent by the JDC to Eastern Europe. In 1927 he was chairman of a commission sent to Palestine under the auspices of the *Jewish Agency to study conditions in that country. This study contributed to the reorganization of the Jewish Agency, in connection with which Frankel was appointed a non-Zionist member of its Council.

FRANKENBURGER, PAUL. See BEN-HAIM, PAUL.

FRANKFURTER, FELIX. Associate justice of the Supreme Court of the United States (b. Vienna, 1882; d. Washington, 1965). Frankfurter was brought to New York as a child in 1894. After his graduation from Harvard Law School in 1906, he became Assistant U.S. Attorney for the Southern District of New York under U.S. Attorney Henry L. Stimson. When Stimson became Secretary of War in 1911, Frankfurter went to

Felix Frankfurter.
[Zionist Archives]

Washington as his assistant. In 1914 he became professor of administrative law at Harvard Law School, holding this position until his appointment as associate justice of the U.S. Supreme Court in 1939. He retired from the Supreme Court in 1962. A close friend and adviser of Pres. Franklin D. *Roosevelt, Frankfurter made significant contributions to legal literature and produced notable opinions in many areas of American law. An outspoken liberal in his political views, he was a founder of the American Civil Liberties Union and took an active part in many civil liberties cases.

During World War I and immediately thereafter, Frankfurter was associated with Justice Louis D. *Brandeis in American Zionist leadership and served on the Provisional Executive Committee for General Zionist Affairs in the United States (*see* UNITED STATES OF AMERICA, ZIONISM IN). In 1919 he was legal adviser to the Zionist delegation at the Paris Peace Conference (*see* COMITÉ DES DÉLÉGATIONS JUIVES). There he collaborated closely with Chaim *Weizmann in his negotiations with Emir Feisal, the Arab leader, with whom he met. The understanding reached in these negotiations on Arab-Jewish cooperation in Palestine was confirmed in a letter addressed by Feisal to Frankfurter (for the text of the letter, *see* FEISAL I). After the resignation of the Brandeis administration, Frankfurter withdrew from active participation in American Zionist leadership. However, he remained deeply interested in World Zionist affairs, visited Palestine several times, was elected an alternate member of the Consultative Political Council of the Zionist *Executive in 1937, and became a member of the Board of Directors of the American Friends of the *Hebrew University of Jerusalem in 1938.

His many writings include *Mr. Justice Brandeis* (edited by Frankfurter, 1932) and *Felix Frankfurter Reminisces* (1960).

FREEDOM MOVEMENT. See HERUT.

FREIER, RECHA. Social worker and originator of the idea of *Youth 'Aliya (b. Norden, Germany, 1892). The daughter of a writer and teacher, she studied at the University of Munich and subsequently worked as a teacher. Early in 1932 Mrs. Freier, then engaged in folklore research in Berlin, where her husband was a rabbi, was disturbed by the anti-Jewish discrimination in employment of the depression period and conceived the idea of bringing young people and children in large groups to Palestine and arranging for their settlement in kibbutzim. Georg Landauer, a member of the Zionist *Executive, suggested that she get in touch with Henrietta *Szold, then director of the Department of Social Welfare of the *Va'ad L'umi (National Council) in Jerusalem. Since Miss Szold's first reaction was negative, Mrs. Freier herself began to raise funds for her project and, on Jan. 30, 1933, the day Hitler took office, established the Society for Youth 'Aliya in Berlin. In May, 1933, she went to Palestine and persuaded Miss Szold to take charge of Youth 'Aliya.

Returning to Germany in July, Mrs. Freier, aided by Jüdische Jugendhilfe (Jewish Youth Aid), organized prospective Youth 'Aliya wards into groups, taught them Hebrew, and prepared them and their parents for the separation that lay ahead. She traveled to England and the Balkans to speed the departure of Jewish youths from Nazi-held lands. In 1941 she herself settled in Palestine, where she continued her educational and social work for poor children.

A student of music, Mrs. Freier also wrote poetry and plays, and in 1957 she founded the Israel Composers Fund. She published *Let the Children Come: The Early History of Youth 'Aliya* (1961).

FREIMAN, ARCHIBALD JACOB. Zionist leader and businessman in Canada (b. Virbalis, Lithuania, 1880; d. Ottawa, 1944). In 1901 he was elected to the Zionist National Council of Canada. In 1912 he became vice-president, and in 1919 chairman, of the Provisional Executive of the Federation of Zionist Societies, and thus head of the Zionist movement in Canada. For 23 years, from 1921 to 1944, he served as president of the federation, the name of which was changed in 1923 to Zionist Organization of Canada (ZOC; *see* CANADA, ZIONISM IN).

Under Freiman's leadership the ZOC made great progress and attained increasing objectives in successive annual campaigns, with Freiman himself setting an example as the most generous contributor in Canada. Freiman fought against the merging of Zionist appeals with combined campaigns, believing that step to threaten the integrity and identity of the Zionist cause. He readily lent his leadership to all communal, civic, and patriotic causes.

Founder and president of A. J. Freiman Ltd., a leading commercial firm in Ottawa, he was also president of Adath Jeshurun Congregation of Ottawa for 25 years. A settlement in Israel, Bitan Aharon, in the Hefer Valley, was named in his honor as a tribute from Canadian Jewry.

B. FIGLER

FREIMAN, LAWRENCE. Businessman and Zionist leader in Canada (b. Ottawa, 1909). The son of Archibald and Lillian *Freiman, he succeeded his father in 1944 as president and general manager of A. J. Freiman Ltd. He was president of the Ottawa Jewish Community Council in 1948–49 and chairman of the *United Jewish Appeal from 1951 to 1958. Freiman first visited Palestine in 1934, and in 1953 he attended a Conference on the Economy of Israel held in Jerusalem.

Freiman was national secretary and then president (1958–62, 1964) of the Zionist Organization of Canada (ZOC; *see* CANADA, ZIONISM IN). In 1959 he was chosen Citizen of the Year by the *B'nai B'rith of Ottawa. In 1960 he was a member of the First National Canadian Mission to Israel. Freiman received the honorary degree of LL.D. from Ottawa University in 1958. A *Nahla in the western Negev was established in his honor by the Jewish community of Ottawa.

B. FIGLER

FREIMAN, LILLIAN. First president of Canadian *Hadassah (b. Mattawa, Ont., 1885; d. Montreal, 1940). The wife of Archibald Jacob *Freiman of Ottawa, she was appointed chairman of Hadassah for Canada in January, 1919, by the Federation of Zionist Societies of Canada. That year, as head of the Helping Hand Fund campaign, she toured Canada, raised $200,000 (the largest sum realized to that date by a Zionist campaign), and organized many Hadassah chapters.

At the first convention of Canadian Hadassah, in 1921, she was elected president, a position she held until her death. Mrs. Freiman was honored by King George V with the Order of the British Empire for her services on behalf of war veterans. A settlement, Havatzelet HaSharon, in the Hefer Valley of Israel, was named in her honor.

B. FIGLER

FRENCH REPORTS. Two reports published on Dec. 12, 1931, and Apr. 20, 1932, respectively, by Louis French, British-appointed Director of Development, on the future development of land settlement in Palestine. In July, 1931, the British Man-

datory government (*see* MANDATE FOR PALESTINE) appointed French, a former Chief Secretary of the Punjab, Director of Development. Following the recommendations of the *Shaw Commission and the *Hope-Simpson Report, French was charged with the registration of dispossessed Arabs, the preparation of a plan for their resettlement, and the relieving of Arab congestion in the hilly areas of Palestine. At the same time he was to investigate methods of facilitating Jewish colonization and of putting uncultivated land to use. He also was to study proposals for the extension of agricultural credits and plans for drainage, irrigation, and other means of land improvement. In this way it was hoped that the conflicting Arab and Jewish claims could be reconciled.

However, French received cooperation neither from the Arabs nor from the Jews. The Arabs demanded advance assurance that the development scheme would not be based on the principles laid down in the *MacDonald letter addressed to Chaim *Weizmann. The Jews were apprehensive lest the restrictions on land purchase envisaged in the Shaw and Hope-Simpson reports be put into effect.

The findings made public in the French Reports seemed to justify the Zionist contention that Jewish land purchases did not displace Arab cultivators. Only 664 Arab families were defined as landless, and only a few Arabs requested the proposed governmental assistance in their resettlement. However, French criticized Jewish settlement in the hill areas.

The development proposals made by French were not intended to improve the lot of the fellahin (*see* FELLAH) by ameliorating their farming practices and improving their living conditions. Rather, they pointed toward restrictive legislation and recommended the passage of an Occupying Tenants Ordinance to guarantee the inalienability of a minimum holding for every cultivator. Since both parties rejected the proposals contained in the reports and since the British government itself was not inclined toward large-scale development, French resigned at the end of 1932.

I. KOLATT

FREUND, MIRIAM KOTTLER. Communal worker, writer, lecturer, and Zionist leader in the United States (b. New York, 1906). She studied at Hunter College (B.A., 1925) and New York

Miriam K. Freund.
[Hadassah]

University (M.A., 1928; Ph.D., 1936). As a teacher and lecturer at schools in New York City, she developed a particular interest in youth activities. Mrs. Freund played a leading role in

American Zionist youth activities from the early 1940s on. In 1945 she helped found the Intercollegiate Zionist Federation of America (*see* AMERICAN ZIONIST YOUTH COUNCIL), and in 1948 she became a founding director of the Brandeis Youth Foundation.

Mrs. Freund was *Hadassah's national vocational education chairman (1948–53), *Youth 'Aliya chairman (1953–56), and national president (1956–60). She made numerous trips to Israel to study and deal with health, youth, and vocational education problems of concern to Hadassah and to confer with Israeli *government officials. She was a delegate to the 24th, 25th, and 26th Zionist Congresses (1956, 1960–61, and 1964–65; *see* CONGRESS, ZIONIST) and served as editor of the *Hadassah Magazine* (1967–   ).

FRIEDBERG, ABRAHAM SHALOM. Hebrew writer (b. Grodno, Russia, 1838; d. Warsaw, 1902). While working first as a watchmaker and then in business, Friedberg began to contribute to Hebrew periodicals and anthologies. He was one of the early adherents of the *Hoveve Zion movement and urged Jewish settlement in Palestine. In 1883 he joined in St. Petersburg the editorial staff of *HaMelitz,* which under his influence came to support the Hoveve Zion. Three years later he settled in Warsaw, where he worked for *HaTz'fira.*

Friedberg's main contributions to Hebrew literature were historical stories and novels, some of which were translations or adaptations. His *Zikhronot L'Vet David* (Reminiscences of the House of David, 1893–97) was very popular. He also wrote a history of the Jews of Spain (1893) and translated scholarly works, including Moritz *Güdemann's *Geschichte des Erziehungswesens* (HaTora v'HaHayim, 3 vols., 1896–99).

FRIEDEMANN, ADOLF. Lawyer, author, and Zionist leader (b. Berlin, 1871; d. Amsterdam, 1933). Friedemann joined the Zionist movement at its inception and soon became an intimate of Herzl, whom he accompanied to Egypt in 1903. From 1902 to 1920 Friedemann was a member of the Greater *Actions Committee of the *World Zionist Organization, and also served on the board of the *Jewish Colonial Trust. His publications include *Reisebilder aus Palästina* (Travel Impressions of Palestine, 1904), *Das Leben Theodor Herzls* (1914), and *David Wolffsohn* (1916).

FRIEDENWALD, AARON. Ophthalmologist and early Zionist leader in the United States (b. Baltimore, 1836; d. there, 1902). After receiving his degree in medicine from the University of Maryland in 1860, Friedenwald spent two years in Europe specializing in diseases of the eye. Returning to Baltimore in 1862, he opened a practice the following year. In 1873 he became the first professor of diseases of the eye and ear at the newly founded College of Physicians and Surgeons in Baltimore, a position he held until his death. He was the first president of the Maryland Ophthalmological Society and was elected president of the Medical and Chirurgical Faculty of Maryland in 1890.

Friedenwald's activities in Jewish communal life were varied and extensive. In 1886 he helped found the Jewish Theological Seminary Association, the forerunner of the Jewish Theological Seminary of America. He was a founder also of the American Jewish Historical Society and a founder and vice-president of the Jewish Publication Society of America. In 1888 he became the first president of the Baltimore branch of the *Alliance Israélite Universelle.

An early and articulate advocate of the *Hoveve Zion movement, Friedenwald served for several years as vice-president of the Federation of American Zionists (*see* ZIONIST ORGANIZATION OF AMERICA). He and his wife visited Palestine in the summer of 1898. The author of several works on general medicine, Friedenwald also wrote a study entitled *Jewish Physicians and the Contributions of Jews to the Science of Medicine* (1897).

FRIEDENWALD, HARRY. Ophthalmologist and Zionist leader in the United States (b. Baltimore, 1864; d. there, 1950). The eldest son of Aaron *Friedenwald, he was graduated from Johns Hopkins University in 1884 and received his degree in medicine from the Baltimore College of Physicians and Surgeons in 1886. After spending two years in Berlin, he returned to Baltimore and established his practice there in 1890. In 1894 he was appointed associate professor of ophthalmology and otology at the Baltimore College of Physicians and Surgeons; in 1902 he became a full professor, serving in that capacity until his retirement in 1929. In 1933 he was Doyne lecturer at the Ophthalmological Congress in Oxford. He was president of the American Ophthalmological Society in 1936 and 1937.

In the early 1890s Friedenwald joined the Hevras Zion, a pre-Herzlian Zionist group in Baltimore. From 1904 to 1910 he was president of the Federation of American Zionists (*see* ZIONIST ORGANIZATION OF AMERICA). He attended the 6th (Basle, 1903), 7th (Basle, 1905), 10th (Basle, 1911), and 16th (Zurich, 1929) Zionist Congresses (*see* CONGRESS, ZIONIST). In 1911 he made the first of many visits to Palestine. During World War I he was a member of the Provisional Executive Committee for General Zionist Affairs and in 1919 served as acting chairman of the *Zionist Commission in Palestine. While in Palestine with the Commission, he was a member of the Executive Committee of, and medical adviser to, the *American Zionist Medical Unit. A childhood friend of Henrietta *Szold, he aided and encouraged her in her work with *Hadassah. During the years following World War I he became chairman of the Palestine Committee of the *American Jewish Congress, and a member of the Council of the Palestine Economic Corporation (*see* PEC ISRAEL ECONOMIC CORPORATION). In 1925 he was named to the Advisory Committee of the *Hebrew University of Jerusalem and helped interest Jewish physicians in the United States in raising funds for the institution. In 1936 he

Harry Friedenwald.
[Zionist Archives]

attended the founding conference of the *World Jewish Congress in Geneva and drafted its declaration of principles.

Active in Jewish communal and educational work, Friedenwald was an authority on the contribution of Jews to medicine and wrote *The Jews and Medicine* (1944) and *Jewish Luminaries in Medical History* (1946). He accumulated one of the largest collections of books and manuscripts on the history of medicine among the Jews, which he presented to the library of the Hebrew University. He edited *Life, Letters and Addresses of Aaron Friedenwald* (1906). His own biography, *Vision,* by Alexandra Lee Levin, appeared in 1964. A tract of land near Hadera, which he purchased and later donated to the *Jewish National Fund, was named Ya'ar Shalom (Forest of Peace – Friedenwald); it became the site of housing for 100 Yemenite families.

Friedenwald's son, Jonas Stein Friedenwald (1897–1955), a Baltimore ophthalmologist, lectured at the Hebrew University in 1936 and returned to Palestine in 1945 to help establish the university's Medical School.

J. DIENSTAG

FRIEDLAENDER, ISRAEL. Scholar, educator, and author (b. Kovel, Russia, 1876; d. near Mogilev, Russia, 1920). After receiving the traditional rabbinical ordination (S'mikha) in Warsaw, Friedlaender went to Berlin to study at the University of Berlin and the Hildesheimer Rabbinical Seminary. In 1900 he obtained his Ph.D. degree from the University of Strasbourg, where he also taught for a time. In 1903 he went to the United States to become professor of Biblical literature and exegesis at the Jewish Theological Seminary of America. A distinguished Arabist, Friedlaender was the author of various studies on the history of Muslim sects and Judeo-Arabic literature.

Friedlaender's philosophy of Judaism derived in great part from that of *Ahad Ha'Am, whom he deeply admired and whose works he translated into German. His marriage to the daughter of the Zionist leader Herbert *Bentwich further identified him with the Zionist movement. In an essay, "Zionism and Religious

Israel Friedlaender.
[Jewish Theological Seminary of America]

Judaism," published in the *New York Evening Post* (Dec. 12, 1917), he stressed the religious aspects of the possibility of Jewish resettlement in Palestine opened by the *Balfour Declaration, holding that once on its historic soil and free from ghetto confinement and alien influences, the people of Israel would be able to fulfill its historic purpose as a potent factor in the religious life of all mankind. On the other hand, he disagreed with the view that Judaism would not be able to survive outside Palestine and formulated the concept of "Diaspora plus Palestine, religion plus nationalism."

Friedlaender was not a mere theoretician but a dynamic force in the practical work of the Zionist movement. He was the first president of *Young Judaea and a member of the Provisional Executive Committee for General Zionist Affairs in the United States, the Federation of American Zionists, and, subsequently, the *Zionist Organization of America.

During World War I, in November, 1917, the American Red Cross decided to send a commission to the Middle East to provide relief for war sufferers. The *American Jewish Joint Distribution Committee (JDC) nominated Friedlaender to participate in the commission. However, when the appointment was announced, Richard *Gottheil and Stephen S. *Wise issued statements to the press charging that Friedlaender had been pro-German prior to the United States entry into the war and that he represented pro-German elements of the community. A storm ensued, and in the end Friedlaender resigned his appointment.

Since Friedlaender was a member of the Executive of the JDC, he urged that he be sent to Russia on a relief mission. He left the United States on Jan. 20, 1920. Three months earlier, in November, 1919, he had received an invitation from the *World Zionist Organization to attend a conference of Jewish scholars in Switzerland, scheduled for June 14–16, 1920, to draw up plans for the *Hebrew University of Jerusalem. On his way to Eastern Europe he met Chaim *Weizmann in Paris and was offered a position on the university faculty.

On July 5, 1920, he was murdered by brigands wearing the uniforms of Soviet Russia in a village near Mogilev.

H. PARZEN

FRIEDMANN, PAUL. Zionist precursor (b. Königsberg, East Prussia, 1840; d. ca. 1900). A scion of an old Jewish family, Friedmann was a convert to Christianity. Troubled by the plight of Russian Jewry, he studied the Jewish problem and came to the conclusion that emigration and colonization were the solution. Since the Turkish Sultan constantly placed obstacles in the way of colonization in Palestine, Friedmann decided to found a Jewish settlement in the vicinity of Palestine, in what once was Biblical Midian. In 1891 he published a pamphlet in Berlin, *The Land of Madian* ("Madian" is the Arabic form of Midian). He considered Midian, with an area estimated at 9,000 square miles, suited for colonization. With the knowledge and consent of the authorities in London, Berlin, Vienna, and Cairo, he organized an expedition composed of persons mostly from Russia, with a few from Galicia, and chartered a steamer which he named "Israel" and which brought the group to Suez on Dec. 1, 1891. From Suez the pioneers proceeded to Sharm Moyeh, on the tip of the Sinai Peninsula, to begin colonization. But after a short time the project collapsed because of internal strife and external political difficulties. Friedmann, who was a wealthy man, spent about £25,000 on his Midian project.

J. FRAENKEL

FRIEDMANN-YELLIN, NATHAN. Engineer and Israeli political leader (b. Grodno, Russia, 1913). Friedmann-Yellin studied at the Warsaw Institute of Technology, graduating as an engineer. Active in *B'rit Trumpeldor, the Revisionist youth movement (*see* REVISIONISTS), he was a member (1937–38) of the Central Committee of the Polish Revisionist party and the editor (1938–39) of *Die Tat,* a Yiddish daily published by the *Irgun Tz'vai L'umi in Warsaw. During World War II he escaped from German-occupied Poland and after arduous wanderings arrived in Palestine, where he joined the *Lohame Herut Israel, the underground group also known as Lehi and Stern group. Arrested by the British in 1942, he escaped in 1943 with 20 fellow Lehi members from the detention camp in Latrun through a tunnel they had dug, and took over the leadership of Lehi's armed struggle against the British administration in Palestine. From the passage of the United Nations *partition resolution of November, 1947, until the establishment of the State, he joined in the fight against attacks by Arab irregulars. Lehi fought Arab irregulars who attacked the *Yishuv (Jewish Community of Palestine).

Following the assassination of Count Folke *Bernadotte (September, 1948), for which a group calling itself Hazit Ha-Moledet (Fatherland Front) claimed responsibility, Friedmann-Yellin and other Lehi members were arrested. He was tried and sentenced to eight years' imprisonment but was freed in the general amnesty issued in February, 1949. While he was still in prison, former members of Lehi submitted a list of candidates, headed by Friedmann-Yellin, for election to the *Knesset. He was elected and represented the Lohamim (Fighters) party in the First Knesset (1949–51). In 1958 he initiated the short-lived Semitic movement, which aimed at reaching an understanding between Israel and the Arabs.

FRISCH, DANIEL. Businessman and Zionist leader in the United States (b. Târgu-Frumos, Romania, 1897; d. New York, 1950). In 1920 Frisch went to Palestine and worked briefly in Rishon L'Tziyon. That year he moved to Cleveland, where he taught Hebrew. Then, in 1921, he moved to Indianapolis, where he attended classes at the Extension Division of Indiana University from 1922 to 1925 and established himself in business in 1933. Between 1925 and 1937 he was chairman of the Board of Education of the Jewish Education Society of Indianapolis. He was elected president of the Indiana State Division of the *Zionist Organization of America (ZOA) in 1929 and president of the Indianapolis Zionist District in 1936. In May, 1949, he was elected president of the ZOA.

His administration, which lasted only nine months, emphasized cultural relations between American Jewry and the State of Israel. It was on his initiative that the ZOA erected the ZOA House in Tel Aviv as a cultural and civic center and as a center for Israeli-American activities. The house was subsequently named for him.

FRISCHMANN, DAVID. Hebrew and Yiddish writer, editor, and translator (b. Zgierz, near Łódź, Russian Poland, 1860; d. Berlin, 1922). After traditional schooling in a Heder and private instruction in Western languages, literature, and science, Frischmann studied philosophy and the history of art at the University of Breslau from 1890 to 1895. Meanwhile, in 1886–87, he served as assistant editor of *HaYom,* the first modern Hebrew daily (St. Petersburg), and in 1888 became one of the principal staff members of the *Ahiasaph publishing company in Warsaw. He was also editor of two Hebrew weeklies, *HaDor* (Cracow, 1901–04) and *HaZ'man* (St. Petersburg, 1903), and of *Hajnt,* a Yiddish daily (Warsaw, from 1908). In 1911 he became editor in chief of the Stybel publishing house in Warsaw and, after 1918, of its quarterly publication *HaT'kufa,* which he managed until his death.

Frischmann's main contribution to modern Hebrew writing was his effort to improve Hebrew literary standards. For 40 years he called for greater purity of language and inveighed

against the florid style of contemporary Hebrew literature. As illustrations of good literature, he translated into Hebrew many of the best works of European fiction, poetry, philosophy, and science. Most of his own short stories centered on the conflict between modernity and tradition, life and law, East and West, and the true and the false. In general, his themes were taken from the contemporary scene, folklore, the Bible, and Jewish history. His style was a blend of Biblical and modern Hebrew. His poetry—lyric poems, historical ballads, love songs, elegies, and dramatic verse—was an instrument in his campaign against superstition and bigotry. His feuilletons were sharp and satirical criticisms of contemporary issues and events.

The first anthology of Frischmann's works appeared in 4 volumes (*K'tavim Nivharim,* 1899–1906); it was followed by a 16-volume jubilee edition (1914). A 10-volume Hebrew anthology was published by his widow (1929–39). There was also a 7-volume Yiddish collection (Łódź, 1909, 1914; Warsaw, 1927).

FROSTIG, MOSHE. Zionist leader in Poland and member of the Polish Parliament (b. Żółkiew, Galicia, Austria, 1885; d. San Remo, Italy, 1928). Frostig was one of the founders of the Galician Zionist high school students' organization *Tz'ire Zion, of which he eventually became leader (1906–08). He was an important publicist whose writings had considerable influence on the development of Galician Zionism. From 1907 to 1909 he was editor of the monthly *Moriah* and from 1909 to 1926 editor in chief of the Lvov Yiddish daily *Lemberger Togblat.* After this paper was discontinued, he edited the newly established *Der Morgen.*

Between 1912 and 1914, Frostig devoted himself to organizing the Jewish merchants in Galicia. During World War I he set out for the United States, but the ship on which he sailed was intercepted by the British and, being an Austro-Hungarian subject, Frostig was interned as an enemy alien. From 1910 until his death he was a member of the Central Committee of the Zionist Organization of Galicia. He served in the Polish Sejm (Parliament) from 1922 to 1928.

N. M. GELBER

FRUCHT, BERNHARD. Zionist leader in Austria (b. Bukovina, Romania, 1918). Active in the Zionist movement from 1933 on, Frucht became a member of the *B'rit Trumpeldor (Betar) youth organization. In 1948 he was in Czechoslovakia, working with the *Irgun Tz'vai L'umi and the Revisionist party there (*see* REVISIONISTS). Some time after the Communist take-over of Czechoslovakia, Frucht settled in Austria, where he became active in the Revisionist party of Vienna, representing the party in numerous overall organizations. In 1949 he was elected to the Executive of the Herut (Revisionist) group and was its vice-president in 1966. In 1962 he became vice-president and treasurer of the Zionist Federation of Austria (*see* AUSTRIA, ZIONISM IN). He served as acting president of the federation for about one year.

FRUG, SIMEON. Poet (b. Bobrovy-Kut, Russia, 1860; d. Odessa, 1916). Frug, who has been regarded as the most important Jewish national poet in the Russian language, made his debut in 1880 with the publication of some poems in the Russian-Jewish weekly *Rassviet.* Subsequently he settled in St. Petersburg, where he developed an extensive literary activity, contributing to publications in both Russian and Yiddish. The themes of his poetry were the misery and sorrow of the

Jewish people and their hope and yearning for redemption. Frug also wrote ballads based on Biblical and Talmudic motifs and legends, as well as stories and feuilletons. He had a great influence on Russian-Jewish youth, whom he inspired with the ideals of Jewish *nationalism. Some of his Yiddish and Russian poems were set to music and became quite popular. Shortly before his death he wrote a number of Hebrew poems. He also prepared a Russian edition of *Sefer Ha'Agada* by Hayim Nahman *Bialik and Y'hoshu'a *Rawnitzky. Frug spent the last years of his life in Odessa, where he had moved in 1909 because of ill health. The major part of his Russian poetry was translated into Hebrew, and some of his works into other languages as well.

FRUMKIN, ARYE LOEB. Rabbi and early Palestine pioneer (b. Kelmė, Lithuania, 1845; d. Petah Tikva, 1916). While in Palestine in 1871, Frumkin began a monumental work on the lives of the rabbis and scholars of Jerusalem *(Toldot Hakhme Y'rushalayim)*. He described his impressions of the country in *Massa' Even Sh'muel* (1871). In 1874 the first part of his great work appeared in Vilna. Later he served for several years as a rabbi in a town near Kaunas.

After the Russian pogroms of 1881, Frumkin advocated the emigration of Russian Jews to Palestine and visited Germany to persuade German Jewry to support the establishment of Jewish settlements there. The Berlin Jewish philanthropist Emil Lachmann gave him funds to set up a farm, and in 1882 Frumkin went to Palestine and purchased land in Petah Tikva. A year later he settled there permanently. He urged the original settlers, who had abandoned Petah Tikva and established themselves in nearby Y'hud, to return. Frumkin built the first house in Petah Tikva and established a Talmud Tora and a Yeshiva.

Differences with Lachmann and persecution by the Turkish authorities, resulting from a false accusation brought against him by his enemies, forced him to leave the country. In 1894 he went to London, where he opened a wine store. In 1911 he returned to Palestine and devoted himself to the completion of *Toldot Hakhme Y'rushalayim,* which was published by Eliezer Rivlin after Frumkin's death. Frumkin's other works include commentaries on the Book of Esther and the Passover Haggada. He also published the *Siddur of Rabbi Amram Gaon* from a manuscript.

FRUMKIN, ISRAEL DOV. Palestinian Hebrew journalist and public figure (b. Dubrovno, Mogilev District, Russia, 1850; d. Jerusalem, 1914). Brought to Palestine by his parents at the age of nine, he married the daughter of Israel Beck, founder of *Havatzelet,* the second modern Hebrew newspaper to be started in Jerusalem, which first appeared in 1863. When the paper was revived in 1870, after publication had been stopped in 1864, Frumkin began to contribute articles to it and soon became editor in chief, continuing in that position for 40 years. He invited Eliezer *Ben Yehuda from Paris to help him in the editing of the paper. At first a bitter critic of the old *Yishuv (Jewish population of Palestine) and of the *Halukka (religious charity) regime, he changed his views after the arrival of the first group of modern pioneers in 1882, becoming an outspoken opponent of the *Hoveve Zion movement and subsequently also of Herzl. In addition to journalistic articles, he published Hebrew translations of German belletristic works. An anthology of Frumkin's best works, together with a monograph on the author, appeared in 1954.

G. KRESSEL

FÜNN, SAMUEL JOSEPH. Hebrew writer and pioneer Zionist (b. Vilna, Russia, 1818; d. there, 1890). Educated in Vilna, he was one of the leaders of that city's *Haskala (Jewish Enlightenment) movement. He helped establish a model Jewish school in Vilna, taught Hebrew, and aided Dr. Max Lilienthal in his endeavors to establish schools and spread "enlightenment" among the Jews of Russia. Fünn was coeditor of the literary miscellanies *Pirhe Tzafon* (1841, 1844) and from 1860 on edited the weekly *HaKarmel.* He published studies in Jewish history and began the publication of a biographical dictionary of Jewish sages and personalities and of a dictionary of the Bible and the Talmud. Fünn was active in communal affairs in Vilna and supported the Palestine settlement activities of Chaim *Lorje and Rabbi Zvi Hirsch *Kalischer. When the *Hoveve Zion movement came into being, he became the leader of the Vilna group. Elected president of the movement at the *Druskenik Conference (1887), he served as a mediator between the religious and the nonobservant elements in the Hoveve Zion.

I. KLAUSNER

FUREYDIS. Arab village in the Hadera area. Population (1968): 2,690.

G

GA'ASH. Village (kibbutz) in the Sharon Plain. Founded in 1951 and affiliated with the *Kibbutz Artzi Shel HaShomer HaTza'ir. Its name is Biblical. Population (1968): 372.

GABEL, HEINRICH. Parliamentarian and Zionist leader in Austria (b. Lvov, Galicia, Austria, 1873; d. Vienna, 1910). Gabel studied and practiced law in Lvov. A pre-Herzlian Zionist, he served on the editorial board of *Przyszlosc* (The Future), the first Galician Zionist weekly in the Polish language. He helped build the Zionist Organization of Galicia, attended Zionist Congresses (*see* CONGRESS, ZIONIST), and was a member of the Greater *Actions Committee. An advocate of the pursuance of nationalist Jewish policies in the *Diaspora, Gabel was elected to the Austrian Reichsrat in 1907 as the representative of the Jewish nationality group from the electoral district of Buczacz (now Buchach), Galicia. He served in that capacity until his death.

GADISH. Village (moshav) in the Jezreel Valley. Founded in 1956 and affiliated with *T'nu'at HaMoshavim. Population (1968): 446.

GADNA' (Israeli youth battalions). *See* ISRAEL DEFENSE FORCES.

GADOT. Village (kibbutz) in eastern Upper Galilee. Founded in 1949 and affiliated with the *Kibbutz M'uhad.

GAHAL. Israeli parliamentary bloc. In 1965 the *Herut and *Liberal parties, while retaining their independent party organizations, combined to form a parliamentary bloc, Gush Herut-Liberalim, or Herut-Liberal bloc (abbreviated Gahal). That same year they put up a joint list for elections to the *Knesset, the municipal councils, and the *Histadrut (General Federation of Labor). Gahal obtained 26 seats in the Knesset, polling more than 21 per cent of the votes in the parliamentary election and 15.2 per cent of the votes in the Histadrut election. It also gained representation on all city and town councils. In the 1969 elections it again obtained 26 seats in the Knesset.

Gahal joined the Government of National Unity formed on the eve of the *Six-day War of 1967. It was represented in the Cabinet by two Ministers without Portfolio, M'nahem *Begin (Herut) and Joseph *Saphir (Liberal party). The organ of the bloc in 1969 was *Ha Yom*, a daily established in 1966, replacing *Herut* and *HaBoker*.

GAL'ED. *See* EVEN YITZHAK.

GALICIA, ZIONISM IN. *See* AUSTRIA, ZIONISM IN; POLAND, ZIONISM IN.

GALILEE. Northernmost section of Israel, lying north of the transverse valleys of Jezreel and Bet Sh'an. In its narrow sense it comprises only the hilly lands between the coastal plains of Z'vulun and 'Akko and the Jordan Valley, divided into mountainous Upper Galilee and hilly Lower Galilee by a steep scarp running along the edge of the valley of Bet Kerem.

Upper Galilee. Upper Galilee is the highest part of Israel, reaching a peak of 3,961 feet in Mount Meron (Arab., Jermak). From this central dome, which is deeply dissected by the tributaries of the Kesiv River, it gradually slopes toward the west and north, with the northernmost spurs lying within the territory of Lebanon. The western slopes are separated from one another by steep, narrow valleys. The ridges of Upper Galilee receive the highest rainfall in Israel (up to 40 inches), and their slopes are covered with dense natural vegetation of degenerated forest (maquis). The eastern part consists of a series of basaltic plateaus, separated from one another by very steeply incised rivers and towering above the Hula Valley. On a separate knoll, which rises to more than 3,000 feet above Lake Kinneret, lies the town of Safed, which was the area's only urban center in the 1960s. In contrast to western Galilee, the eastern parts are covered with sparse vegetation, but wide areas have been reforested in recent decades.

Throughout history, Upper Galilee was a remote part of the country, lacking roads or urban centers and providing shelter for religious or national minorities: Jewish communities held out here even in the late Middle Ages, and in the 1960s its western parts held the main concentration of the *Druze community in Israel. After the creation of the State of Israel a large part of Upper Galilee's Arab population remained in their homes, while new Jewish immigrants settled in a number of new villages. Its economy, hampered by poor roads, shallow soils, and lack of water for irrigation, was based mainly on the cultivation of fruits and tobacco, which provided only scant income for its settlers.

Lower Galilee. This part of Galilee consists of a large number of interior basins, separated from each other by hilly ranges, which reach an average elevation of about 1,800 feet. The highest peak is Mount Tabor (1,929 feet), which forms a round, isolated hill on the southern extremity. The eastern part of Lower Galilee is covered with a thick layer of basalt and descends in steps toward Lake Kinneret. Throughout history, its wide valleys offered not only fertile soils but also wide lanes for communication from the coast (especially the port of 'Akko) to Lake Kinneret and the Jordan Valley and thence to Transjordan and Damascus.

An ancient center of agriculture and communications, Lower Galilee contains many historic sites and formed the center of Jewish settlement after the destruction of the Second Temple. Later, it was densely settled by Muslim Arabs, but around

Nazareth there is a cluster of Christian villages. Recent Jewish settlement took place only in the eastern parts, and after its inclusion in the State of Israel its central sector came to hold the largest concentration of the Arab minority in the country. Within its Arab parts lies the main concentration of olive cultivation in Israel. Its agriculture, handicapped by lack of water for irrigation, is confined mainly to grain. Its urban center is Nazareth. On its western edge lies the town of Kiryat Tiv'on, which is actually a dormitory suburb of Haifa; new *development towns are Migdal Ha'Emek on its southern fringe and the planned town of Karmiel in the north. To the east of Galilee are the *Gaulan Heights, occupied by Israel after the *Six-day War.

Y. KARMON

GALILEE, SEA OF. *See* KINNERET, LAKE.

GALILI, ISRAEL. *Ahdut 'Avoda leader (b. Brailov, Ukraine, Russia, 1910). Galili was taken to Palestine at the age of 4. After graduating from school, he went to work and at the age of 14 founded the labor youth organization HaNo'ar Ha'Oved. After organizing the first agricultural settlement group of the

Village of K'far Hittim, in Lower Galilee. [Israel Government Tourist Office]

organization, he helped found the kibbutz Na'an, of which he remained a member thereafter. At an early age he joined *Hagana and, rising in its ranks, became a member of its com-

Israel Galili.
[Zionist Archives]

mand and deputy commander in chief. In the provisional government of Israel (1948) he served as Deputy Minister of Defense.

A leading member of Ahdut 'Avoda, Galili was a delegate to the 19th Zionist *Congress (Lucerne, 1935) and to subsequent Congresses, and served in the *Knesset from its inception. In 1966 he became a member of the Cabinet without portfolio, a position he still held in 1969.

GAL'ON. Village (kibbutz) in the Darom. Founded in 1946 and affiliated with the *Kibbutz Artzi Shel HaShomer HaTza'ir. Population (1968): 350.

GALUT. Hebrew term, meaning "exile," applied to the state of the Jewish people living in dispersion. *See* DIASPORA; ISRAEL AND THE DIASPORA; NEGATION OF THE DIASPORA.

GALUT NATIONALISM (Diaspora Nationalism). Concept of Jewish nationalism in the *Diaspora. Crystallizing into a philosophy of Jewish national existence late in the 19th century, it left its mark on all present-day Jewish movements, including those negating Jewish continuity in the Diaspora. Taking many forms, undergoing numerous modifications and revisions, accepted in full by some, in part by others, and rejected by still others, Galut nationalism gave rise to several Jewish parties, influenced the local activities of various Zionist groups, and supplied the ideological basis of the Bundist program of cultural autonomy (*see* AUTONOMY, JEWISH; BUND). Galut nationalism also reinforced the *Po'ale Zion concepts of linking the building of a Jewish State in Palestine with the political and social struggles of the Jewish masses the world over. In addition, it stimulated Jewish cultural and literary efforts in Yiddish, Hebrew, and other languages. What all the varieties of Galut nationalism (which never became an important organized force in Jewish life) had in common was the recognition that the Jews of the world constituted a people or nation bound together by a common history, shared experiences, and a common culture. As a people, the Jews stood in need of creating for themselves social and cultural conditions that would enable them to retain their distinctive identity in the midst of the non-Jewish majorities of the countries where they lived.

Two names stand out in the ideological foundation of Galut nationalism: Simon *Dubnow, the historian, and Chaim *Zhitlowsky, the Jewish theoretician of socialism. Dubnow

formulated his theories in a series of letters he began to publish in 1897. According to him, Jewish national development had been creative and morally superior precisely because the Jews constituted a spiritual rather than a territorial entity: ". . . and this people, after passing through the stages of its tribal nationalism, ancient culture, and political territory, was able to establish itself on the highest level, the spiritual and historical-cultural, and succeeded in crystallizing itself as a spiritual people that draws its lifeblood from a natural or intellectual 'will to live.'"

Though basically a secularist, Dubnow regarded the Jewish religion as the greatest manifestation of the Jewish creative genius. However, he also attributed decisive survival value to the other products of Jewish creativity which in their totality shaped the course of Jewish history through the ages. Structurally, he regarded Jewish collective life as resting on autonomous Jewish communities. "Autonomy, as a historical postulate," he considered to be "the inviolable right of every national individuality."

Chronologically, Zhitlowsky may be said to have preceded Dubnow. Vague hints of Galut nationalism can be found in his very first work, published in 1887. More is contained in his essay *A Jew to Jews* (1892). His theories both paralleled and differed from those of Dubnow. Whereas Dubnow insisted that a people achieved spiritual fulfillment only to the extent to which it transcended the mere normality of territorial nations, Zhitlowsky was primarily concerned with equating the status of the Jewish people with that of normal nations. He wanted the Jewish people to regulate its economic, social, and cultural life as if it had already attained normal statehood. It was Dubnow's contention that "a Jew may be a son of the Jewish faith potentially or actually, or he may be without a religion at all; but exit from Judaism by acceptance of the Christian religion means exit from the Jewish nation." Zhitlowsky, on the other hand, claimed that it was possible to be a Christian by faith and a Jew by nationality. To Dubnow, Hebrew and Yiddish were like the two legs of a person; but while Hebrew was a natural leg, Yiddish was a wooden leg grafted onto the Jewish national body after the amputation of one of the natural legs. To Zhitlowsky, the father of Yiddishism, Yiddish was the center of modern Jewish culture; it was the cornerstone of the Jews' survival as a progressive people. The complete failure of their autonomist theories notwithstanding, both forms of Galut nationalism—Dubnow's among the Jewish middle classes and Zhitlowsky's in the ranks of the Jewish labor and Socialist movement—were powerful instruments in the struggle against assimilationist views.

C. B. SHERMAN

G'ALYA. Village (moshav) in the Darom. Founded in 1948 by immigrants from Bulgaria and affiliated with *T'nu'at HaMoshavim. Population (1968): 398.

GAN. Hebrew word, meaning "garden," that forms part of a number of place names in Israel, as in Gan HaDarom (Garden of the South).

GAN HADAROM. Village (moshav) in the Darom. Founded in 1953 and affiliated with the *Ihud Haklai. Population (1968): 275.

GAN HASHOMRON. Village in the vicinity of Hadera. Founded in 1934 by immigrants from Germany. Population (1968): 327.

GAN HAYIM. Village (moshav) in the Sharon Plain. Founded in 1935 and named for Chaim *Weizmann. Affiliated with *T'nu'at HaMoshavim. Population (1968): 220.

GANNE 'AM. Village (moshav) in the Sharon Plain. Founded in 1934. Population (1968): 183.

GANNE TIKVA. Township south of Petah Tikva. Founded in 1953. Population (1968): 2,990.

GANNE Y'HUDA. Village (moshav) south of Petah Tikva. Founded in 1951 and affiliated with the *Ihud Haklai. Population (1968): 580.

GANNE YOHANAN. Village (moshav) in the Darom. Founded in 1950 by immigrants from Romania and Poland and named for Johann (Yohanan) *Kremenetzky. Affiliated with *T'nu'at HaMoshavim. Population (1968): 340.

GANNOT. Village (moshav) east of Tel Aviv. Founded in 1953 and affiliated with the *Ihud Haklai. Population (1968): 240.

GANNOT HADAR. Village in the Sharon Plain. Founded in 1954. Population (1968): 95.

GAN SH'LOMO. Village (kibbutz) in the Darom. Founded in 1927 and named for Solomon (Sh'lomo) *Schiller. Affiliated with the *Ihud HaK'vutzot V'haKibbutzim. Population (1968): 265.

GAN SH'MUEL. Village (kibbutz) in the Sharon Plain. Named for Sh'muel *Mohilever and affiliated with the *Kibbutz Artzi Shel HaShomer HaTza'ir. As early as 1896 the planting of a citrus grove was begun on the site (see CITRUS INDUSTRY IN ISRAEL). Later, a group of laborers who worked in the grove settled there. The present kibbutz was established in 1927. Population (1968): 700.

GAN SOREK. Village (moshav) in the Judean Plain. Founded in 1950 and affiliated with *T'nu'at HaMoshavim. Population (1968): 122.

GAN YAVNE. Village in the Darom. Founded in 1931. Population (1968): 2,840.

GAN YOSHIYA. Village (moshav) in the Sharon Plain. Founded in 1949 and named for Josiah C. *Wedgwood. Affiliated with *T'nu'at HaMoshavim. Population (1968): 235.

GARBER, MICHAEL. Lawyer and Zionist leader in Canada (b. Lithuania, 1892). A member of the Executive Board of the Zionist Organization of Canada (ZOC) from 1919 on, Garber was national chairman of the *Jewish National Fund of Canada from 1941 to 1944, national vice-president of the ZOC for a number of years, one of its three copresidents from 1944 to 1946, and its president from 1956 to 1958. He visited Israel several times.

In 1919 he took a leading part in the organization of the Canadian Jewish Congress. He was active in the congress after it reconvened in 1934 and served as chairman of the Dominion Executive. In 1962 he was elected president of the congress.

Garber was at one time lecturer in Talmud at McGill University. A prominent barrister, he was a member of the Councils of the Bar of Montreal and of the Province of Quebec from 1952 to 1954. He was the first Jew to serve as alderman of the city of Westmount, Que.

B. FIGLER

GAS PRODUCTION IN ISRAEL. *See* PETROLEUM AND GAS PRODUCTION IN ISRAEL.

GASTER, MOSES. Rabbi and scholar (b. Bucharest, 1856; d. near Abingdon, England, 1939). Gaster studied at the Jewish Theological Seminary of Breslau and the University of Leipzig. In 1881 he was appointed a lecturer at the University of Bucharest, a post he held until 1885, when he was expelled from the country because of his protests against the persecution of Jews. He then settled in England, where he lectured at Oxford University and, in 1887, was chosen Haham of the London Sephardi community, serving in that capacity until his retirement in 1918. A noted authority in Romanian philology and literature, folklore, and many branches of Jewish knowledge, he was the author of numerous studies in these fields and was prominently associated with various learned societies and institutions.

A leading member of the *Hoveve Zion in his native Romania, Gaster organized meetings that were addressed by Laurence *Oliphant, and he helped establish the Jewish settlement of Zamarin (Zikhron Ya'akov) in Palestine. He joined political Zionism at its very beginning, chairing the first large meeting in Whitechapel, London, addressed by Herzl (July 13, 1896). His speeches and writings gave great impetus to the movement.

After the 1st Zionist *Congress (Basle, 1897), Gaster published a letter in the London *Times* explaining Zionism. In 1898 he helped found the English Zionist Federation (later, Zionist Federation of Great Britain and Ireland). He was a prominent figure at Zionist Congresses, serving as vice-president at several of them. During the controversy over the *East Africa scheme, he became an outspoken opponent of Herzl.

During World War I, Gaster took a leading part in the talks and negotiations with British statesmen that led to the issuance of the *Balfour Declaration. He was one of the speakers at the great demonstration held at Covent Garden in December, 1917, which expressed gratitude to the British government for the declaration. In his speech he declared that what Jews wanted in Palestine was an autonomous Jewish Commonwealth in the full sense of the word.

J. FRAENKEL

GAT. Village (kibbutz) in the Darom. Founded in 1942 and affiliated with the *Kibbutz Artzi Shel HaShomer HaTza'ir. Population (1968): 435.

GA'TON. Village (kibbutz) in western Upper Galilee. Founded in 1948 and affiliated with the *Kibbutz Artzi Shel HaShomer HaTza'ir. Population (1968): 255.

GAT RIMMON. Rural community near Petah Tikva. Founded in 1926. Population (1968): 175.

GAULAN (GOLAN) HEIGHTS. Region east of the Hula Valley, the upper reaches of the Jordan River, and Lake Kinneret. The Gaulan Heights are part of a larger geographical unit, which was known in antiquity as Bashan and in modern

Children of new immigrants out for a walk at Gat Rimmon in 1949.
[Zionist Archives]

times as Hauran. It is characterized by wide expanses of lava, which erupted through fissures or from volcanic cones in connection with the formation of the Jordan Rift Valley. This volcanic cover assumes different shapes according to the consistency of the material and the process of eruption, ranging from an impenetrable maze of boulders in the Trachonitis district to wide, level areas of deep, fertile soil.

Along the center of the basalt region of southern Syria, which stretches for about 60 miles from north to south and from east to west, runs a trough of fertile level land, the Hauran proper. Along this trough extends the main axis of the area, the road and railway from Damascus to Dar'a and Amman, the ancient King's Highway and the medieval Darb el-Hajj (Pilgrims' Route). The Gaulan Heights rise gently to the west of this trough but descend steeply toward the Hula Valley and Lake Kinneret in scarps with relative elevations of about 2,000 feet. The highest part of the Gaulan is in the northwest, where it abuts the slopes of majestic Mount Hermon; here the plateau reaches a general level of about 3,000 feet above sea level. It slopes gradually to the south and east to 1,000 feet above sea level in its southern sector. Its southern boundary is sharply defined by the deeply incised valley of the Yarmukh River, whose bottom lies about 600 feet below sea level. Its eastern boundary is defined approximately by the valley of the Rukkad River, which flows from north to south and joins the Yarmukh in a steep ravine. This valley defines approximately the cease-fire boundary of 1967 between Israel and Syria. Within these boundaries the area has a length of about 40 miles from north to south and a width of about 10 miles from east to west.

The Gaulan Heights also possess the general character of a level plateau, but the area is mostly strewn with basaltic boulders. Only a few favored areas are covered with a deep layer of volcanic dust, which forms a fertile, easily worked soil. From the general level of plateau a great number of volcanic cones rise to relative heights of 200 to 1,000 feet. The highest is Tel Abu Nida (3,950 feet, or as high as the highest mountain in Israel).

Although the Bashan was famous in antiquity for its fertility, most of the Gaulan Heights area must be cleared of rocks before the land can be cultivated. Thus settlements persisted only in the areas of deep soils, and most of the land was used by the Bedouins for grazing. The sparse population increased at the end of the 19th century, when Circassians—Muslim refugees from the margins of the Caucasus—were settled here by the Turkish authorities to form semimilitary border villages. The Circassians founded a considerable number of villages which subsisted on grain cultivation and cattle grazing, and they also established the only urban settlement of the area, the small town of Quneitra.

After the *War of Independence, the Gaulan, which previously had formed an important link between Syria and Egypt via Palestine, became a dead-end zone and soon was turned into a military area, whose string of heavy fortifications overlooked and menaced the Jewish settlements in the Jordan Rift below. During the *Six-day War of 1967, the area was abandoned by the Arab and Circassian population, except for a few hundred people, who remained in Quneitra. The only people left in the Israeli-occupied parts of the Gaulan Heights were about 5,000 Druzes, who lived in five villages at the northern end of the territory, which actually forms part of the slopes of Mount Hermon.   Y. KARMON

GAZA STRIP. Southernmost section of the coastal plain of former Palestine. The Gaza Strip is 25 miles long and varies in width from 4 miles in the north and center to 8 miles in the south. It consists of the territory which was held by Egyptian forces at the end of the *War of Independence in 1948.

The western half of the strip is occupied by sand dunes and the southeastern section by barren hills of sandstone or chalk covered with loess. Thus, the area suitable for agriculture is restricted to a narrow central belt, 2 to 3 miles wide, which becomes broader only around the town of Gaza. This belt is intensively cultivated with the aid of irrigation from a rich underground water horizon. Most of it is utilized for citrus groves, which are equal in area to about one-quarter of Israel's citrus plantations (*see* CITRUS INDUSTRY IN ISRAEL). The fruit has been exported mainly to Eastern Europe. The rest of the belt serves for intensive vegetable growing.

History. The Gaza area was incorporated in the Second Jewish Commonwealth by the Hasmonean rulers and since then has continuously had a Jewish population along with other ethnic groups. At the end of the British Mandate (*see* MANDATE FOR PALESTINE), the Gaza Strip had about 70,000 inhabitants, mostly Arabs. To these were added, in 1948, approximately 200,000 *Arab refugees. From then until June, 1967, Egypt ruled the strip by virtue of the Israel-Egypt armistice agreement of Feb. 24, 1949, except for a few months during 1956–57, when Israel occupied it in the *Sinai Campaign. Egypt did not, however, claim sovereignty over this territory, describing it merely as "Egyptian-controlled"; nor did it grant its inhabitants permission to migrate to Egypt: the law applicable was that of Mandatory Palestine, of which the area was a part. In the 1960s there still was a stiff customs barrier with Egypt.

Politically, the Gaza Strip served Egyptian interests through the so-called All-Palestine government proclaimed in Gaza on Sept. 20, 1948, under Cairo's auspices, with Hajj Amin *al-Husayni, former mufti of Jerusalem, as president of the "Palestine National Assembly." The Gaza regime was to serve more as a counterbalance to 'Abdullah, then King of Transjordan,

The main street and shopping center in Gaza, the largest town in the Gaza Strip. [Israel Information Services]

than as a genuine home for the refugees. Though recognized by four Arab states, the Gaza government soon disintegrated and moved to Egypt. Thereafter, the Gaza Strip served as a strategic advance base for hit-and-run guerrilla raids against Israel by Egyptian-trained *fedayeen. It was briefly occupied by Israeli forces during the Sinai Campaign and then became the center of Egyptian intelligence work in Israel. Beginning in 1964 the area served as an official training base for Ahmed Shukairi's "Palestine Liberation Army," composed of refugees, whose stated purpose was the destruction of Israel.

Although water in the strip is plentiful and, except in the southern part, vegetables and fruit are abundant, the area has not been economically viable to sustain so large a population. The refugees have been housed in specially erected camps, fed by the UN Relief and Works Agency for Palestine Refugees in the Near East (UNRWA) and schooled by the UN Educational, Scientific and Cultural Organization (UNESCO). These and other United Nations agencies, however, have done little to solve the refugee problem by programs of reeducation or resettlement.

The Gaza Strip was conquered by Israel after heavy fighting on June 5 and 6, 1967. According to the census undertaken by Israel in September, 1967, the strip had about 350,000 in-

habitants, of whom one-half were refugees. Owing to the shortage of space, the whole population lived in five large urban concentrations (Gaza, Jebeliya, Deir el-Balah, Khan Yunis, and Rafa) and some smaller refugee camps. The main town is Gaza (population, 120,000), which serves as the center of administration and commerce. It also possesses a roadstead, which is utilized for the export of citrus and for most imports, but mainly for those of UNRWA.

Y. KARMON AND J. M. LANDAU

GAZIT. Village (kibbutz) in eastern Lower Galilee. Founded in 1948 and affiliated with the *Kibbutz Artzi Shel HaShomer HaTza'ir. Population (1968): 414.

GAZZALIN. Bedouin tribe in the B'er Sheva' region. Population (1968): 43.

G'DERA (Gedera). Township in the Darom. Founded in 1884 by members of *Bilu. Population (1968): 5,100.

G'DUD HA'AVODA V'HAHAGANA 'AL SHEM YOSEF TRUMPELDOR. Pioneering group active in Palestine during the 1920s. For reasons of security, the word "*Hagana"

(Defense) was omitted from the name of the group, which was usually referred to as G'dud Ha'Avoda (Labor Battalion). The battalion was initiated in Palestine by a group of Joseph *Trumpeldor's followers who were among the earliest contingents of the *Third 'Aliya to arrive from Russia after World War I. Whereas the immediate objective of this organization was to find employment for its own members and to secure work for the thousands who were arriving after them, its long-range aim was to transform the workers of Palestine into one great "commune" open to all and based on the common ownership of property and "equality as consumers." Each member of the battalion agreed to accept unconditionally the work assignments scheduled for him. The earnings of the individual or of the unit (P'luga) to which he belonged went to the central treasury of the battalion, which assumed the responsibility of providing for the maintenance of all members on a basis of equality, independently of the quality or quantity of the work performed.

Development. The prospects opened by the *Balfour Declaration, on the one hand, and the social radicalism engendered by Russia's October Revolution, on the other, gave impetus to the movement, determined its ideology, and shaped its organizational pattern. At first, central control enforced by a common treasury and strict egalitarianism were accepted as axiomatic. An avant-garde group that considered itself the elite of the entire *Halutz (pioneer) movement, the battalion negated all other forms of agricultural settlement, considering the K'vutza (see KIBBUTZ) the only proper form of social and economic organization. At the battalion's first conference, held in Migdal in 1921, its program was defined as ". . . the upbuilding of the Land through the creation of a general commune of the workers of Palestine." Unlike the K'vutza, which derived its revenue from, and subsisted on, the land allocated to it, the battalion collected the income of the K'vutzot affiliated with it as well as the wages earned by the P'lugot working as hired-labor groups in towns and colonies. This was to serve as a prototype, a miniature society, which would expand into the great commune destined eventually to draw in all the workers of Palestine.

At first the battalion operated as a contractor securing public-works jobs for its members. Its first undertaking was the construction of a highway from Tiberias to Migdal. A camp was set up to provide living quarters, food, and services; as the group moved to another place, the camp organization could follow it. It was in this camp that the social pattern of the battalion evolved. In September, 1921, K'far Gil'adi, a K'vutza in Upper Galilee, joined the battalion. When the *Jewish

A view of G'dera about 1925. [Zionist Archives]

National Fund acquired huge tracts of land in the eastern Jezreel Valley, the battalion moved in to occupy the land, establishing two settlements there, 'En Harod (Sept. 22, 1921) and Tel Yosef (Dec. 14, 1921). In 1922 the P'luga of masons operating in Jerusalem established the settlement of Ramat Rahel at the southern approaches to the city. Thus the battalion was based on four K'vutzot permanently established on the land and engaged in farming and on numerous P'lugot working as hired-labor units and often moving from place to place as new work became available. At times, particularly beginning in 1923, some of the P'lugot were unemployed and had to be maintained by the central treasury.

Membership was open to all. Although there was always a hard core of devotees, enrollment fluctuated. There were in all Palestine at one time or another 44 P'lugot, and the total number of persons who at one time or another were members of the battalion was about 2,500. At its peak, in 1925, it had 665 members, men and women. The stoppage of immigration from the Soviet Union deprived the battalion of its principal source of manpower. Many new arrivals who joined left soon after acquiring a trade or receiving other employment. For many, membership in the battalion was a transitional stage, but even those who did leave cherished a sense of loyalty to the traditions of the battalion.

Disintegration. The hard core of several hundred determined members which shaped the development of the battalion later brought about its disintegration. The first symptom of trouble was resentment at excessive centralism in general and at the common treasury in particular. The economic crisis in 1925 and unemployment in many P'lugot strained the resources of the treasury, and many K'vutzot objected to the treasury's diverting funds allocated by the *World Zionist Organization for the construction of the settlements and using them particularly for the maintenance of P'lugot affected by unemployment. In February, 1926, the first crisis occurred in 'En Harod and Tel Yosef, when the proponents of autonomy concentrated in the former K'vutza and all the adherents of centralism moved to the latter. Gradually the debates of autonomy versus centralism moved into the wider sphere of politics. The battalion conference of 1926 revealed the existence of a pronounced leftist trend and even of a clandestine Communist group. It turned out, too, that the Hagana groups within the battalion had come under the influence of the leftist elements. Finally, in December, 1926, the battalion split into two wings, the rightist and the leftist, the latter becoming openly pro-Communist (see COMMUNISTS IN ISRAEL). By 1927 the leftist wing had disintegrated and some of its leadership and adherents left for Russia, where it established a K'vutza, Voja Nova, in the Crimea, which, however, was disbanded two years later. The rightist wing disintegrated in 1929, when its four K'vutzot joined the federation of kibbutzim known as the *Kibbutz M'uhad.

In many respects the battalion represented the elite of the Third 'Aliya, embodying its most radical and far-reaching ambitions. It attested to the flowering of Russian-Jewish revolutionary youth and attracted the most adventurous elements of the Halutz movement; the fact that its ambitions went far beyond its capacity to achieve them was a reflection of the great hopes cherished by the post-World War I generation.

S. Z. ABRAMOV

GE'A. Village (moshav) in the Darom. Founded in 1949 and affiliated with *T'nu'at HaMoshavim. Population (1968): 200.

GEDALYA, HAYIM. *See* GUEDALLA, HAYIM.

GEDERA. *See* G'DERA.

GEFEN. Village (moshav) in the Lakhish region. Founded in 1955 and affiliated with HaPo'el HaMizrahi (*see* MIZRAHI). Population (1968): 395.

GELBER, EDWARD ELISHA. Zionist leader and attorney in Canada (b. Toronto, 1903). A graduate of the Jewish Theological Seminary of America, New York, and of Osgoode Hall, Toronto, Gelber was a member of the Ontario bar and of the bar of Palestine, where he practiced law from 1935 to 1939. For six years he was vice-president of the Zionist Organization of Canada (ZOC), representing it at international conferences. He was copresident (with Samuel E. Schwisberg) of the ZOC from 1950 to 1952 and president from 1952 to 1956. On his retirement from this office he settled in Jerusalem.

During his residence in Canada, Gelber held leading offices in the Canadian Jewish Congress, the American Friends of Israeli Institutions, the Associated Hebrew Schools of America, the American Association for Jewish Education, the National Hillel Commission, the Training Bureau for Jewish Communal Services, and the Keren HaTarbut. He was a member of the Board of Overseers of the Jewish Theological Seminary of America, a governor of the *Weizmann Institute of Science, and chairman of the Executive Council of the *Hebrew University of Jerusalem. The Jewish community of Toronto established a *Nahla (tract of land) in his honor in the western Negev.

B. FIGLER

GELBER, NATHAN MICHAEL. Historian of Zionism (b. Lvov, Galicia, Austria, 1891; d. Jerusalem, 1966). Prominently associated with Zionist activities from his youth in Galicia onward, Gelber was active in local Zionist student organizations while studying at the Universities of Vienna and Berlin. After World War I he became secretary-general of the Zionist Federation of Austria and later edited Zionist periodicals in Vienna. In 1930–31 he was editor of the Zionist daily *Nowe Slowo* in Warsaw. Subsequently he went on missions on behalf of the *Keren HaYesod (Palestine Foundation Fund). In 1933 he settled in Palestine, where he worked in the head office of the Keren HaYesod until 1948.

Gelber contributed historical essays, especially on the Jews of Poland and on Zionism, to numerous periodicals, and he published many books in these fields, including *On the Prehistory of Zionism* (in German, 1927); *The Balfour Declaration and Its History* (in Hebrew, 1939); *The History of the Jews of Brody* (in Hebrew, 1955); and *The History of Zionism in Galicia* (in Hebrew, 2 vols., 1958). He also contributed to encyclopedias and to books commemorating the Jewish communities of Europe destroyed in the Hitler era.

GELLMAN, LEON. Leader in the *Mizrahi movement (b. Yampol-Volynsk, Russia, 1887). He received a secular and a religious education. In 1910 he emigrated to the United States, where he served as principal of Hebrew schools in St. Louis from 1911 to 1917. Gellman helped organize the Mizrahi movement in the United States on the eve of World War I and was its first honorary secretary. He was vice-president (1930–35) and president (1935–59) of the Mizrahi Organization of America. In 1949 he was elected chairman of the Mizrahi–

HaPo'el HaMizrahi World Movement. He was also a deputy member of the Executive of the *Jewish Agency from 1948 to 1953 and a member of the Presidium of the Zionist *Actions Committee.

For many years Gellman was editor and publisher of the *St. Louis Jewish Record*. He edited Mizrahi publications in the United States, contributed to periodicals, and wrote several books. In 1949 he settled in Israel.

J. STAVI

GENACHOWSKI, ELIYAHU MOSHE. Leader in the *Mizrahi movement (b. Grajewo, Russian Poland, 1903). He received a traditional Jewish education and studied at Yeshivot. In 1923 he participated in the founding of the *Halutz (pioneer) movement of Mizrahi in Poland. From 1926 until 1933, when he settled in Palestine, he resided in Belgium, where he organized the *Tz'ire Mizrahi, founded the League for Religious Labor, and served as vice-president of the Zionist Federation of Belgium. From 1933 until 1946 he was on the Central Committee of the Mizrahi World Movement. He was a member of the *Knesset from 1949 until 1955. His publications include *Ki Tavo'u el Ha'Aretz* (1936), on Mizrahi's activities in Palestine; and selections from the writings of Rabbis Mordecai *Eliasberg (1947) and Yitzhak *Nissenbaum (1948).

GENERAL COUNCIL OF THE ZIONIST ORGANIZATION. *See* ZIONIST GENERAL COUNCIL.

GENERAL FEDERATION OF LABOR. *See* HISTADRUT.

GENERAL ZIONISM. In the first decade of the Zionist movement (1897–1907), General Zionism was in a sense synonymous with Zionism itself. Although there were a variety of views, there were no political parties in the movement. The year 1907 may be regarded as a turning point: in it the religious *Mizrahi and the Socialist *Po'ale Zion crystallized as political parties within the Zionist movement. The great majority of Zionists were affiliated with neither of the two political parties and constituted an undefined and unorganized element; in default of a better definition they were then referred to as General Zionists. It was this element, which until 1925 was largely in control of the *World Zionist Organization (WZO), that provided the movement with its most outstanding leaders and was responsible for its political activity and material progress.

Early Years: 1907–29. In trying to define their program, the General Zionists considered themselves to be concerned exclusively with the task of realizing the *Basle Program. This task implied the promotion of Zionism in the *Diaspora, political activity for securing Jewish rights in Palestine, and provision of the necessary financial means for the Zionist movement and its activities in Palestine. The General Zionists regarded themselves as a middle-of-the-road, liberal, and democratic movement within the Zionist movement. They did not elaborate a program of their own for the economic or social development of the Jewish Homeland, nor were they concerned, as the Mizrahi and Po'ale Zion were, with establishing institutions or initiating economic projects in Palestine for their followers.

There was another definition, quite prevalent in the Zionist vocabulary, that was of a negative character. The WZO was composed, according to its statutes, of "*separate unions" and "territorial federations." A separate union was a political party, such as Po'ale Zion or Mizrahi, that had a particular ideology in addition to the Basle Program. It was organized on an international scale, its members were bound by party discipline, and its policies were determined by a world conference and directed by a central office. A territorial federation, in contrast, was a general organization of Zionists in a particular country and was confined to that country. Its program was the Basle Program. Consequently, a Zionist who did not belong to a separate union was automatically a member of a territorial federation, regardless of his particular convictions. The Zionists who were members of a territorial federation were referred to as General Zionists, and the territorial federation became a general depository for all Zionists who did not belong to any separate union. Thus, General Zionism became a composite of many views but not an ideological entity. Between Zionist Congresses (see CONGRESS, ZIONIST) each separate world union, being a political party, crystallized its policies and demands for action at the next Congress; but the territorial federations, with no permanent ties between them, came to the Congresses strong in numbers but divided, without a united program for action. The heterogeneous composition of General Zionism inevitably resulted in a process of dissipation of energies which eventually led to its decline. Thus, in 1921, 73 per cent of all delegates to the 12th Zionist Congress were General Zionists, whereas the Labor Zionists constituted only 8 per cent. Ten years later, at the 17th Congress (Basle, 1931), the General Zionists were split into three groups, together comprising 53 per cent of the delegates, while Labor Zionist representation had increased to 29 per cent. Thereafter, the decline of the General Zionists continued, though at a slower pace, and was reflected in the composition of subsequent Zionist Congresses.

Prewar Decade: 1929–39. At the 16th Congress (Zurich, 1929), Dr. Isaac *Schwarzbart, a Zionist leader in Galicia, began organizing the General Zionists, but only a minority could be brought together. Negotiations with a number of territorial federations continued, and on the eve of the 17th Zionist Congress (Basle, 1931), the First World Conference of General Zionists met with the following groups participating: group A (those committed to Chaim *Weizmann's political program); group B (those critical of that program as well as of the economic policy pursued by the WZO in Palestine); and the *Radical Zionists, led by Itzhak *Grünbaum and Nahum *Goldmann. At this conference delegates from 34 countries established the World Union of General Zionists. Dr. Isaac Schwarzbart was elected first president of the World Union, whose central office was established in Cracow, Poland. This experiment, however, was short-lived. At the Second World Conference, in 1935, the World Union of General Zionists split into two distinct units: group A, which supported the Weizmann policy vis-à-vis Great Britain and followed a prolabor line in economic and social policy in Palestine; and group B, which was critical of Weizmann's political approach and regarded the massive support allocated by the Zionist budget to labor institutions in Palestine as detrimental to private initiative in general and to the middle class in particular. One of the issues in Palestine was the question of attitude toward the *Histadrut and the intention of General Zionists B to set up a separate workers' organization. Instead of devoting all their efforts, as the other Zionist parties did, to the development of institutions of their own in Palestine and supporting their followers there, the two groups expended their energies on internal controversy. It was not surprising,

therefore, that at the 19th Zionist Congress (Lucerne, 1935), the two General Zionist groups secured only 35 per cent of the delegates, while the labor parties increased their representation to 35 per cent.

The General Zionists A drew their support mainly from the General Zionists in Great Britain, a part of the *Zionist Organization of America (ZOA), *Hadassah, the General Zionists of South Africa and Germany, and a considerable section of the Zionists in Poland. In Palestine the General Zionists A were supported by Ha'Oved HaTziyoni, a Histadrut-affiliated group of General Zionists from Poland and Romania, and by *'Aliya Hadasha, an organization of German Jews who had arrived in large numbers after the rise of Hitler in 1933. The General Zionists B drew their strength similarly from Poland, particularly from Galicia, which was their European stronghold, from the majority of the Zionist Organization of America, especially after its leadership passed to Abba Hillel *Silver, and from the Organization of General Zionists in Palestine. In other European countries, the two groups had their followers. Throughout their existence both groups devoted their principal efforts to the furtherance of Zionism in the Diaspora, to the political struggle for Jewish rights in Palestine, and, first and foremost, to raising the funds needed for the upbuilding of the Jewish National Home. Neither group paid much attention to its own particular interests or devoted means or efforts to support its adherents in Palestine.

As a result of the holocaust of World War II, General Zionists B almost entirely disappeared from the European continent. During this period the ZOA experienced a remarkable revival when, headed by Abba Hillel Silver and Emanuel *Neumann, it led American Jewry in the struggle for a Jewish State.

Final Years of the Mandate: 1946–48. At the 22d Zionist Congress (Basle, December, 1946), the first to be held after World War II, a new attempt to reunite the General Zionists resulted in a *World Confederation of General Zionists, with Israel *Goldstein as chairman. A Fund for Constructive Enterprises was established and confirmed by the *Actions Committee of the WZO. This fund was to derive its finances from the *United Palestine Appeal in the United States, united Israel campaigns in Great Britain, Canada, South Africa, and Latin American countries, and separate fund-raising efforts in other countries. It was to finance or support private housing and other enterprises, agricultural development, cooperatives, kibbutz industry, agricultural training, education, immigrant absorption, and personal loans, and the relatively few institutions founded by General Zionist groups in Palestine.

The guiding idea of General Zionism of every shade was the supremacy of the national interest over any party or class interest. This liberal and rather vague principle was difficult to put into action when ambitions of groups, classes, and vested interests clashed in everyday life in Palestine. The General Zionists, who, unlike other parties, were predominantly Diaspora-based and -oriented, avoided intimate involvement in the conflicts and problems arising from the upbuilding of a new land and a new society. Their central idea generally remained in the realm of the abstract, inasmuch as most General Zionists failed to appreciate that the realization of an idea needs organized strength in numbers, means, and positions of influence.

One of the main bones of contention between the A and B groups was the attitude toward Weizmann's policy vis-à-vis

Great Britain as the mandatory power (*see* MANDATE FOR PALESTINE). In general, group A continued to support his pro-British orientation even after he declared, at the 17th Zionist Congress (1931), that the creation of a Jewish majority in Palestine was not an essential aim of Zionism. Group B, on the other hand, advocated a firmer policy vis-à-vis Great Britain and regarded the attainment of a Jewish majority as a *sine qua non* on the road to the fulfillment of Zionist aspirations. Certain elements within group A, particularly many German Zionists, viewed with favor the possibility of setting up a binational state in Palestine if that step would secure Jewish-Arab understanding. Group B rejected this idea, remaining completely united in its support of the Jewish State principle as laid down in the *Biltmore Program with the approval of both groups of General Zionists. At the 22d Congress in 1946, a coalition of delegates of the ZOA and other group B delegates, led by Abba Hillel Silver, and of *Mapai delegates, led by David *Ben-Gurion, succeeded in defeating a proposal supported by Weizmann calling for acceptance of an invitation from the British government to reopen negotiations for an Anglo-Zionist agreement on Palestine. This was one of the factors that prevented Weizmann's reelection to the presidency of the WZO. The reason advanced for the rejection of the proposal was the refusal of the British to agree that the principle of Jewish statehood must serve as a basis for the negotiations. Group A supported Weizmann's stand.

Stated in very general terms, the social and economic program of General Zionism called for freedom of economic initiative for individuals and groups, though always subject to the general national interest and with a wide range of welfare state services taken as axiomatic. The General Zionists advocated the elimination of social conflicts by arbitration or, at least, compulsory mediation of labor disputes in essential industries and services. They supported trade unions as an essential element in a democratic society. Until the elimination of the general, religious, and labor "trends" in the public school system in Palestine and, later, in Israel (*see* EDUCATION IN ISRAEL), the General Zionists advocated their abolition and the removal of party control and influence from the educational system. They always took a positive attitude toward religion and tradition, regarding these as integral parts of the national culture. At the same time, they opposed the imposition by law of religious practices and restraints and called for changes that would remove some of the personal hardships resulting from the rigid application of Halakhic rules, especially in matters of marriage and divorce. They further called for the adoption of a codified bill of rights and consistently adhered to democratic principles and procedures. In the field of social policy, they urged that the main social services to which persons in a progressive society were entitled, such as education, medical aid, and employment, be provided for all citizens by the state rather than by political parties or quasipolitical organizations that extended these services to their members only. Finally, they urged that the citizen's economic dependence on a bureaucracy and, in particular, on political parties and institutions be eliminated as impinging on individual liberty.

General Zionist Party in Israel: 1948——. One might think that the political and social philosophy accepted by the General Zionists as axiomatic would have made for unity and cohesion. Soon after the creation of the State of Israel, however, serious controversies arose. The application of general prin-

ciples, not in the abstract, as was the case in the Diaspora, but to the concrete reality of an actual State, revealed differences of opinion that tore General Zionism asunder and made all attempts at reunification short-lived and futile. The splits that occurred after 1948 were due largely to the divergent attitudes and policies of the Israeli affiliates of the General Zionist movement, that is, the *Progressive party in Israel, which was supported by the General Zionists A in the Diaspora, and the General Zionist party in Israel (since 1961, the *Liberal party), which was supported by the General Zionists B in the Diaspora.

The first split, which did not at that point disrupt the unity of the World Confederation of General Zionists, occurred when the General Zionists, on the eve of the elections to the First *Knesset (1949), divided into two independent political parties, the one adopting the name General Zionist party and the other calling itself the Progressive party. It was deep-seated differences in backgrounds and attitudes, rather than matters of principle, that created a gulf between these groups. The General Zionists in Israel, on the whole, were old-time Palestinians, members of the middle class and of the economically better-off elements, who were most sensitive to what they regarded as Histadrut and government encroachments on the middle class and curtailment of private initiative. The members and supporters of the Progressive party, in contrast, were more recent immigrants to Israel. Many were refugees from Nazi Germany, while others belonged to Ha'Oved HaTziyoni, originally a *Halutz-oriented organization consisting primarily of arrivals from Poland and Romania. The latter, largely workers with a sprinkling of kibbutz settlers, regarded affiliation with the Histadrut as a cardinal plank in their platform and cooperation with the Israeli labor parties, particularly with Mapai, as their constant policy. They maintained strong internal discipline and, relying on a number of economic and educational institutions as well as on several kibbutzim they had established, were able to assert their influence in the party. Before long, Ha'Oved HaTziyoni became the dominant element in the Progressive party. Unlike the General Zionists, the Progressives, by reason of their previous Zionist activity in the Diaspora, had a better political background and were more articulate than their rivals.

The first confrontation between the General Zionists and the Progressives concerned an issue that Ha'Oved HaTziyoni considered paramount, that all party members who were workers and employees generally must join the Histadrut. In contrast, the General Zionists, who regarded the Histadrut as a political organization aiming at establishing socialism in Israel, rejected the principle of compulsory membership and instead allowed their members to join either the Histadrut or a separate union which the General Zionists then supported. This was an insurmountable obstacle, making any understanding between the two parties impossible. Psychologically, too, the members of Ha'Oved HaTziyoni, who were largely employees, were reluctant to coexist in one party with members who were also employers or purported to represent employers. Hoping to build their future strength on converts from other labor groups, the members of Ha'Oved HaTziyoni, and with them the Progressives in general, developed a pro-Histadrut orientation that made cooperation between their group and the General Zionists within the framework of one political party both irksome and tenuous.

General Zionism and the Diaspora: 1948–68. The split occurring within the ranks of the General Zionists in Israel in 1948 caused tension within their World Confederation. In October, 1950, the leaders of the ZOA issued a statement of policy expressing sympathy with the General Zionist party in Israel. This step contributed to the tension that appeared at the Second World Conference of the Confederation, held in Jerusalem in August, 1951. The crisis did not lead to a break, however, and an uneasy unity was maintained. Nevertheless, the reestablished unity was short-lived. Elements in the ZOA, including those who were in sympathy with the Progressives in Israel, objected to the 1950 statement of policy in favor of the General Zionists and demanded its rescission. Failing to carry with them a majority of the ZOA, they advanced the principle that the World Confederation of General Zionists and its constituent organizations throughout the Diaspora take no stand for or against the General Zionists in Israel or the Progressives, on the ground that such an identification amounted to interference in Israeli politics. The proponents of the 1950 statement, on the other hand, argued that their sympathy for the General Zionists in Israel did not constitute interference, for only Israeli citizens could determine the policies of their party and participate in the political life of Israel. The ZOA majority leaders contended that it was not only the right but even the duty of a Zionist to express his views on social, economic, and cultural developments in Israel, as these not only had a bearing on Jewish communities in the Diaspora but also related to Diaspora Jews as potential settlers. They further pointed out that all other world confederations within the WZO operating in the Diaspora, such as the Labor Zionists and Mizrahi, supported their adherents in Israel, who, like the General Zionists and Progressives, were also members of political parties on the Israeli scene. In 1957 the opponents of the 1950 declaration under the leadership of Louis *Lipsky, one of the outstanding leaders of American Zionism, formed a separate organization called the *American Jewish League for Israel. Their followers were relatively few, and in time some of them returned to the fold of the ZOA.

At the World Conference of the World Confederation of General Zionists held in Jerusalem in 1956 simultaneously with the 24th Zionist Congress, a split between the two groups was avoided by means of an agreed upon compromise to the effect that the Confederation become merely a coordinating body with two autonomous affiliates. Its functions would be (1) to bring together for political purposes the representatives of the two groups at the Congresses and meetings of the Actions Committee and (2) to determine the allocations of the Fund for Constructive Enterprises among the various projects in Israel founded by them. Each of the two formations within the Confederation party was to be autonomous in carrying out its activities. The 1956 arrangement was in fact a recognition of the split in the ranks of the General Zionists and of the de facto existence of two confederations of General Zionists under one roof.

The de facto split was soon formalized. In March, 1958, a conference summoned by Israel Goldstein and Rose *Halprin met in London and constituted itself a separate World Confederation of General Zionists, with a platform "affirming the principle that there shall be no identification of the movement with any political party within the State [of Israel]." As a result, the Progressive party in Israel was excluded from that Confederation. Goldstein and Mrs. Halprin were elected cochairmen.

The same year the General Zionists, led by Dr. Neumann, met in Israel and formed a World Confederation using the same name as that of the rival organization. Their program stressed the independence of General Zionist formations in the Diaspora, expressed their sympathy for the General Zionist party in Israel, and laid down the principle that General Zionists who were citizens of Israel had the right to associate with like-minded Zionists the world over in order to implement mutual Zionist purposes and policies. The two confederations thus formed with identical names were distinguished by reference to their leaders: one confederation was led by Neumann, and the other by Mrs. Halprin and Goldstein.

In Israel the two General Zionist groups, the General Zionist party and the Progressive party, pursued different policies. From the formation of the first government following the election of the First Knesset in January, 1949, the Progressive party, except for a short period, was always part of a Mapai-dominated coalition government. In the Knesset elected in 1949 it had 5 deputies (in a total membership of 120). In the next election (1951) it was represented by a similar number. It always adhered to the view that it could best serve the interests of General Zionism by joining a Mapai-dominated government even though it could never threaten governmental stability by its withdrawal from the coalition. Until 1961 it was represented in the government by Pinhas *Rosen, who was Minister of Justice. In the Histadrut elections, Ha'Oved HaTziyoni, the Progressive party labor wing, averaged between 3 and 4 per cent of the votes cast. The other General Zionist group, numerically larger than the Progressive party, was, except for the short period 1952–55, in opposition to the government. Its attitude was that a change in economic and social policy, which in the opinion of both parties was essential for the development of the Jewish State, could not be brought about by participation as a minority group in a coalition government and that, consequently, it could serve the interests of General Zionism by acting as an opposition party until such time as the General Zionists, with the support of other groups, could form an alternative government.

Despite these divergencies, attempts were made to reunite the two Israeli parties and thus pave the way for the reestablishment of unity in the General Zionist camp in the Diaspora. In 1952 the General Zionist party in Israel decided to form within its ranks a labor group that would join the Histadrut and function there as the General Zionist labor wing, thus reversing its previous policy, which the Progressives had resented. Such a group was formed and participated in the Histadrut election in 1956. By taking this step, the General Zionist party removed a serious obstacle to rapprochement with the Progressives. At their national convention in N'tanya in 1954, the Progressives had considered a proposal made by the General Zionists for a merger of the two into one political party. The proposal was actively supported by Dr. Nahum Goldmann, who spoke on its behalf at the convention. This attempt at reunion had been defeated by a small majority, which was spearheaded by Ha'Oved HaTziyoni.

A successful attempt to merge the Israeli parties was made at the end of 1960. Several circumstances encouraged the willingness of the Progressives to consider such a merger. By the end of 1960 the Lavon affair threatened to split Mapai. The Progressives, excluded from the World Confederation of General Zionists led by Rose Halprin and Israel Goldstein, were isolated on the Zionist scene. As a result of these efforts, the General Zionists and the Progressives merged in April, 1961, into one party, the Liberal party of Israel, and under that name stood for election to the Knesset in 1961, electing 17 deputies, as against the 14 seats won by the two parties in the preceding election (1959).

Following the reunion in Israel, attempts were made to reunite the two confederations of General Zionists. In March, 1963, however, the Goldstein-Halprin Confederation, in accordance with its policy not to admit an Israeli party, rejected the proposal for reunion. In July, 1963, pursuant to a joint call of the Confederation led by Dr. Neumann and the Liberal party of Israel, a conference was held in Israel. It decided to assume the name *World Union of General Zionists to mark the distinction between the two groups. The members of the former Progressive party were now part of the World Union of General Zionists, while the rival Confederation had no affiliate in Israel.

But even this limited union of General Zionists in Israel was short-lived. While the merger of the General Zionist party and the Progressive party succeeded and former distinctions were gradually becoming obliterated, an external development again disrupted the ranks of Israeli General Zionists. In 1965 Prime Minister Levi *Eshkol, the leader of Mapai, seeking to strengthen and unite the labor parties, succeeded in forming an alignment between his party, Mapai, and the left-wing *Ahdut 'Avoda. This alignment, advocating a more pronounced Socialist policy, proposed to put up a joint list of candidates for the Knesset and Histadrut elections that were to be held that year. Under pressure of public opinion calling for an alignment of non-Socialist elements, the Liberal party considered a proposal made by *Herut that both parties, while retaining their independence, form a parliamentary bloc and put up a joint list of candidates to the Knesset election. Since the majority of the Liberal party was in favor of the proposed bloc, the minority, consisting of most of the former Progressives, withdrew, formed a new party named the Independent Liberal party, and contested that election. The Herut-Liberal bloc (*Gahal) elected 26 representatives in the Knesset, of whom 11 were members of the Liberal party. The Independent Liberals secured 5 seats.

While separated from the Liberal party as of 1965, the Independent Liberal party remained in the World Union of General Zionists and was represented on the Executive of the *Jewish Agency. Following the 27th Zionist Congress (Jerusalem, June, 1968), the Independent Liberal party withdrew from the World Union of General Zionists, and because of the small number of its delegates to the Congress it lost its seat on the Executive of the WZO. After 1968 there were thus three General Zionist formations: the World Union of General Zionists, presided over by Neumann, which included as its Israeli affiliate the Liberal party of Israel; the World Confederation of General Zionists, presided over by Rose Halprin and Israel Goldstein; and the Independent Liberal party, which was affiliated with neither group.

Like other groupings within the Zionist movement, General Zionism as a school of Zionist thought was a product of the Diaspora. However, unlike the other groupings, which early in their development promoted close ties with Palestine and established institutions and positions of influence there, the General Zionists concentrated their efforts on the furtherance of Zionism in the Diaspora and on raising funds for the upbuilding of Palestine. Their liberal outlook and their reluctance to engage in partisan controversies with other parties were not conducive to organizational strength and discipline. Their effective confrontation with Palestine took place only after the establishment of the State, when the field was already dominated by others. They were prepared neither organizationally nor ideologically for united action in Israel, and their recurrent divisions were the expressions of a search for ways and means of making a liberal outlook applicable to a new society in which the various kinds of collectivism were already firmly entrenched. Nevertheless, the two General Zionist parties, despite the lack of an institutional base and of adequate means, maintained on the whole their numerical strength in Israel and persisted in their efforts to elaborate a meaningful liberal program that would appeal to the emergent Israeli society.

In most Diaspora countries the General Zionists of both wings remained, on the whole, the dominant force in the Zionist movement not only numerically but also with respect to fundraising activities and political action in support of Israel as well as other Zionist endeavors. At the 27th Zionist Congress (1968) their combined strength was approximately 180 delegates, or about one-third of the Congress. They were represented in the World Zionist Executive (Jewish Agency) by four members—the same number as Mapai, the largest party in Israel.

S. Z. ABRAMOV

GEOGRAPHY OF ISRAEL. The State of Israel comprises the largest part of the geographical and historical entirety of western Palestine. Its political *boundaries as demarcated in the *armistice agreements of Rhodes (1949) were in the main identical with the international boundaries of the former British *Mandate for Palestine, with certain restrictions in demilitarized zones. Only the boundary between Israel and the Hashemite kingdom of Jordan in the center of the country was different: the largest part of the Central Highlands was within Jordanian territory, while a narrow strip of land, the Jerusalem corridor, connected the Israeli sector of Jerusalem with the coastal plain. Also, the Gaza Strip, which had formed part of Mandatory Palestine, was outside Israel. Within these boundaries the area of Israel is 7,954 square miles, compared with the 10,152 square miles of the mandate.

Although small in size, Israel shows a large variety of landscape, owing to sharp differences in *climate and the proximity of the Great Rift Valley to the Mediterranean, which causes substantial variations in elevation over short distances. Thus a number of geographical units can be clearly discerned within the boundaries of Israel. The most important dividing line is drawn by climate; it runs from east to west at a line starting at the southern edge of Israel's Mediterranean shore and passing through B'er Sheva' to the shore of the Dead Sea. South of this line is the arid Negev, which comprises almost two-thirds of the State's area, while north of it lie regions enjoying the Mediterranean type of climate with winter rains sufficient to raise at least winter crops without irrigation. Each of these climatic regions is again subdivided by topographic variation.

NORTHERN ISRAEL

The northern, or Mediterranean, part of Israel is divided into three main geographical units, each of which runs as a narrow strip from north to south.

Coastal Plain. The western unit, the coastal plain, is widest in the south (about 20 miles) and narrows in the north to a mere 4 miles. The coast itself is mainly level: in the center it is accompanied by a wide belt of sand dunes. In the north the coast becomes rocky and is indented by small coves. The only bay is Haifa Bay, which has been developed into the principal seaport of the country. The coastal plain inland is mainly level, with some undulating hills of red sandy loam and some narrow ridges of limy sandstone in the west. It is covered by various kinds of alluvial soils: in the south mainly by loess with a gradual transition to calcareous soils, mixed with sand and loam; in the center mainly by red sandy loam; and in the north by dark river-alluvium soils. Many small rivers, which drain the mountains, once formed large swamps, but these were completely drained by the 1960s. An underground horizon of fresh water provides water for irrigation except in the south, where the loess soils prevent the formation of the horizon.

The combination of level deep soils with availability of water for irrigation has turned the coastal plain into the main area for Jewish settlement and into the main concentration of population. The development of ports and the growth of most of the older settlements into small industrial towns have turned it also into the most urbanized part of Israel. Although the coastal plain occupies only 15 per cent of the State's total area, 77 per cent of Israel's population lived here in the 1960s.

Highlands. The main part of the settled area is occupied by the highlands, which reach an average width of 25 to 30 miles. This sector consists mainly of slightly folded mountains, built of limestones and dolomites, which attain an average height of 2,300 to 2,600 feet. Whereas the mountains are only slightly disturbed in the south and center, faulting is strong in the north, creating a number of small intermontane basins surrounded by steep slopes and elevated hills. It is here that the highest mountain of Israel, Mount Meron (3,961 feet), is located. Another outcome of the faulting is the occurrence of volcanic material, especially basalt, mainly in the eastern fringe of the northern mountains, which are also visited by earthquakes. Faulting created also the main transverse valley of the country, the Jezreel Valley, and its continuation, the Harod and Bet Sh'an Valleys. It divides the highlands into two main parts: the Northern Highlands–Galilee, subdivided into Upper and Lower Galilee; and the Central Highlands, consisting of Samaria in its northern half and Judea in its southern half. The Central Highlands lie mainly in Jordan.

As the highlands in Israel are rocky and mostly have shallow soils, their agricultural potential is much smaller than that of the coastal plain and their population is much sparser. The Arab population of Israel, which throughout history always preferred the highlands, is almost completely concentrated in Galilee and on the fringes of Samaria.

Jordan Valley. The easternmost part of the country is the Jordan Valley, which lies partly within Israel. Although it is nowhere wider than 6 miles, it has such unusual scenic and climatic types that it adds much variety to Israel's landscape. Except for the Hula Valley (250 feet above sea level), it lies below sea level. Its most important feature is Lake Kinneret (686 feet below sea level). After a few miles the Jordan River, which flows out of the southern end of the lake, becomes deeply entrenched in the valley bed of marl and forms the boundary between Israel and the kingdom of Jordan. In the 1960s settlement in the Jordan Valley was fairly dense, and its agriculture specialized in subtropical plantations.

THE NEGEV

Altogether, the nonarid parts of Israel in the 1960s contained 96 per cent of the country's population, although they comprised only one-third of its area. In the Negev, including B'er Sheva', about 100,000 people lived in six urban concentrations; the agricultural population centers consisted of six small collectives (*see* KIBBUTZ). Although the landscape of the Negev is determined by its arid character, there are wide varieties of topographical features, the most peculiar ones being large erosion craters called Makhteshim. In the southern Negev, in the vicinity of Elat, there is the only occurrence of plutonic and metamorphic rocks such as granite, porphyry, and gneiss. The Jordan Valley is continued within the Negev by the rift valley called 'Arava, which starts at the Red Sea and, after ascending to a watershed 709 feet above sea level, drops to the lowest spot on the surface of the earth, the Dead Sea (1,296 feet below sea level).

Although the Negev was still sparsely settled in the 1960s, it showed some promising features for the future. The region holds the main mineral deposits of Israel (copper, phosphates, potassium, gypsum, fireclay, glass sand, bromine) and, through the port of Elat, provides Israel with a gateway to the Red Sea and thus to East Africa and the Far East.

For a discussion of the areas occupied by Israel after the *Six-day War of 1967, *see* GAULAN HEIGHTS; GAZA STRIP; SINAI; WEST BANK.

Y. KARMON

GEPSTEIN, SH'LOMO. Israeli architect and writer (b. Odessa, Russia, 1882; d. Tel Aviv, 1961). He studied architecture in St. Petersburg and at an early age began to contribute to the Zionist press (*Yevreiskaya Zhizn, Yevreiskiy Narod, *Rassviet*) and to the Russian *Jewish Encyclopedia*. In 1917 he was elected to the Central Committee of the Russian Zionist Organization. After leaving Russia, he became editor in chief (1922–24) of *Rassviet*, which had been transferred from Russia to Berlin.

In 1924 Gepstein settled in Palestine, where he worked as an architect and town planner while continuing his journalistic activities. One of the founders of the Revisionist movement, he served on the Central Committee of the Palestinian branch of the party (*see* REVISIONISTS). He was elected to the Second and the Third *Asefat HaNivharim (1925, 1931). In 1929 he served as assistant editor of the daily *Do'ar HaYom*. He also wrote for *HaBoker, *HaMashkif, *Herut, and several professional journals. In 1948 he was on the Central Committee of the *Herut movement.

Gepstein wrote a Hebrew biography of Vladimir *Jabotinsky (1941) and was prominently associated with the publication in Hebrew of Jabotinsky's collected writings.

I. BENARI

GERI (GERING), YA'AKOV. Industrialist and former Israeli Cabinet member (b. Shadi, Lithuania, 1901). Geri studied and practiced law in Johannesburg, South Africa. Settling in Israel in 1935, he became prominent in various enterprises. He was chairman of the board of directors of Africa-Palestine Investments, Ltd., the Ata Textile Company, the Israel Land Development Company, and other concerns. Although not a member of any political party, he served as Israel's Minister of Commerce and Industry in 1950–51.

GERMAN-ISRAEL AGREEMENT (Luxembourg Agreement). Restitution agreement between the State of Israel and the Federal Republic of Germany, ratified by the lower house (Bundestag) of the West German Parliament in Bonn on Mar. 18, 1953, and by the upper house (Bundesrat) two days later. This treaty, which went into operation on Apr. 1, 1953, obligated the

Federal Republic of Germany to pay to the State of Israel, over a period of 12 to 14 years and in kind, the countervalue of $822,000,000. Of this amount, $107,000,000 was to be turned over by Israel to the Conference on Jewish Material Claims against Germany, representing 23 Jewish organizations. Under the terms of the agreement, payments were to be made in 14 annual installments. In addition, Germany undertook to pass an Indemnification Law covering compensation payable to individual victims of the Nazi persecutions who had suffered imprisonment, mutilation, and loss of profession or property, and a law restoring property seized by the former Third Reich and other bodies. This undertaking was the result partly of a deep inner urge felt by large segments of the German people to atone for the horrors of the Hitler period and partly of the desire of the new German leadership to rehabilitate Germany in the eyes of the world.

Claims of Israel. The negotiations leading to the Luxembourg Agreement began in a request addressed by Chaim *Weizmann in behalf of the *Jewish Agency to the governments of the United Kingdom, the United States, the Soviet Union, and France, demanding "that the Jewish people also should be allotted a proper percentage of reparations, to be entrusted to the Jewish Agency for Palestine." The claim of the State of Israel to function as the legal recipient of German restitution funds was based largely on the fact that of the nearly 200,000 Jewish displaced persons who had been located within the German borders at the end of World War II, 130,000 had emigrated to Palestine-Israel.

In a note dated Jan. 16, 1951, addressed to the four Allied occupation powers, the Israeli government criticized the meager and unsatisfactory restitution and indemnification legislation which then existed and expressed interest in an urgent solution of the problems stemming from Israel's absorption of the majority of the Jewish displaced persons. In a second note, dated Mar. 12, 1951, Israel laid down the basis for Jewish claims against Germany:

> The amount to be claimed must be related, on the one hand, to the losses suffered by the Jewish people at the hands of the Germans, and on the other, to the financial cost involved in the rehabilitation in Israel of those who escaped or survived the Nazi regime.... Israel can base its claim only on the expenditure in connection with the resettlement of the Jewish immigrants from the countries formerly under Nazi control. Their number is estimated at about 500,000 which would involve an overall expenditure of 1.5 billion dollars.

A series of exchanges between Israel and the three Western powers followed. (The U.S.S.R. remained silent and never acknowledged Israel's representations.) The answers received made it clear, by implication, that a settlement could be achieved only through direct negotiations between Israel and Germany. This confronted world Jewry with a dilemma. The bitter memories of the Nazi regime had created strong feelings of revulsion against any form of contact with Germany. While no formal relationships existed between Jews and Germans, some Jewish organizations in the United States and Great Britain had established contact with liberal groups in Germany. One of the first prominent Germans to acknowledge his country's responsibility to pay for the crimes committed against the Jews was Dr. Kurt Schumacher, chairman of the Social Democratic party. Chancellor Konrad Adenauer, Schumacher's outspoken political opponent on most major issues, was of like mind on the question of restitution.

In February, 1951, the Bundestag debated the problem of restitution and indemnification. Prof. Carlo Schmid, spokesman for the Social Democratic party, suggested that Germany propose to the Allies that the Jews recognize Israel as the legal heir to all heirless Jewish property and indemnification claims. On Aug. 30, 1951, Erich Lüth, director of the Hamburg State Press Office, and his friend Rudolf Küstermeier, editor in chief of *Die Welt*, published articles under the title "We Beg Israel for Peace." On Sept. 27, 1951, in a speech before the lower house in Bonn, Chancellor Adenauer said:

> Unspeakable crimes were perpetrated in the name of the German people which imposed upon them the obligation to make moral and material amends, both as regards the individual damage the Jews have suffered and as regards Jewish property. With regard to the extent of the reparations—huge problems in view of the immense destruction of Jewish assets by the National Socialists—it will be necessary to consider that limits are set on Germany's ability to pay by the bitter necessity of providing for innumerable war victims and caring for the refugees and expellees.

On Oct. 25, 1951, 22 Jewish organizations (a 23d joined later) established the Conference on Jewish Material Claims against Germany, headed by Dr. Nahum *Goldmann, who met with Chancellor Adenauer on Dec. 6, 1951, in London. Following a lengthy discussion, Chancellor Adenauer confirmed in writing that the "German Federal Government saw in the problem of reparation above all also a moral duty and regarded it as an obligation of honor for the German people to do everything possible to repair the injustice done to the Jewish people." Moreover, the Chancellor accepted as a basis for negotiations the claim of $1,500,000,000 which the government of Israel had formulated in its note of Mar. 12, 1951.

Negotiations. The first talks opened in The Hague on Mar. 12, 1952, and ended in the first week of April without practical results. Certain German banking interests were seeking to link the German-Israeli negotiations in The Hague with the settlement of Germany's prewar commercial debts, which were being negotiated in London at the same time. When the debt conference was resumed in London, Hermann Abs, chief of the German delegation, insisted that any financial obligations to Israel would depend on the outcome of the conference. Thereupon the chief German delegates, Prof. Franz Böhm and Dr. Otto Küster, resigned in protest.

The restitution agreement caused a deep crisis of conscience in the *Diaspora countries and even more so in Israel. Large segments of the Israeli population felt that it was morally wrong to accept "blood money" from the Germans. When the issue of direct negotiations with the Bonn government came before the *Knesset (Jan. 7, 1952), it provoked a heated discussion in the press and public opinion. The opposition centered in a wide assortment of parties: *Herut, *Mapam, and some of the General Zionists (see GENERAL ZIONISM), as well as the *Communists. The Knesset debate took place against the background of a violent demonstration in immediate proximity to the building. On January 9, the Knesset approved the government's request for authorization to begin direct negotiations with the Bonn regime by a vote of 61 to 50, with 5 abstentions (4 members were absent).

On May 28, 1952, Chancellor Adenauer met Dr. Goldmann in Paris and assured him that a concrete German offer would be forthcoming. On June 9, at the urgent invitation of the Chancellor, Dr. Goldmann flew to Bonn with Felix Shinnar and Noah *Barou, chairman of the European section of the *World Jewish Congress. In addition to Chancellor Adenauer, the German representatives were Secretary of State Walter Hallstein, Assistant Secretary Herbert Blankenhorn, the banker Hermann Abs, Prof. Franz Böhm, and Dr. Abram Frowein, an official of the German Foreign Office.

The meeting led to a tentative agreement, which was incorporated in the German-Israel Agreement on the following day. On September 10, the agreement was signed in Luxembourg by Chancellor Adenauer for Germany, Foreign Minister Moshe *Sharett for Israel, and Dr. Goldmann for the Conference. From September, 1952, to March, 1953, the Arabs tried in vain to block the agreement by threats of an *Arab boycott against Germany. Because of a difference of opinion within the German Cabinet, ratification was delayed. Strong statements by Erich Ollenhauer of the Social Democratic party, Walter Freitag of the trade unions, and others broke the deadlock, and the lower house ratified the agreement on Mar. 18, 1953.

Implementation. The implementation of the agreement constituted a significant contribution to the economic development of Israel, coming as it did at a time when the State was in great need of foreign exchange. Until the end of 1964, a total of DM3,450,000,000 (approximately $815,000,000) was paid to Israel in goods or cash; of this, DM450,000,000 was allocated to the Conference on Jewish Material Claims against Germany in accordance with the terms of the agreement.

Deliveries from Germany helped the mechanization of Israel's agricultural production. The kibbutzim, always short of manpower, received large-scale shipments of German machinery, which enabled Israel's *agriculture to reach a stage of modernization then unknown in many European countries. German reparations helped bring about similar advances in Israel's *industry. The diversification and large production capacity of Israel's industry were due, to a considerable degree, to German reparation supplies. Likewise, the building of a considerable merchant marine would have been entirely impossible without the reparations. Until the end of 1964, 60 ships, totaling 450,000 gross tons, were built and delivered under the terms of the agreement. Additional tonnage, ordered for delivery between 1958 and 1962, included a 45,000-ton tanker, one of a series of eight with a total tonnage of 200,000. A drydock, essential for repair of the growing Israeli merchant marine, was also supplied under the reparations agreement (see SHIPPING IN ISRAEL).

*Transportation between Haifa and Tel Aviv was improved by modern fast trains supplied under the agreement. The inadequate telephone service was improved by the importation of new German equipment. New power stations supplied by Germany enabled Israel's agriculture, irrigation, and industry, all of which depend on electric current, to increase substantially. The growth of the cities and the founding of new settlements, too, were facilitated by the increased supply of electricity. Germany also paid for the supply of fuel oil, which is used in Israel to generate electric power (see ISRAEL ELECTRIC CORPORATION, LTD.).

Ten years after the signing of the agreement, all concerned agreed that it had helped cover 15 to 20 per cent of Israel's import needs. DM1,650,000,000 was delivered for various goods, and DM750,000,000 was paid to oil companies in the sterling area. The last payment under the agreement was made by Germany in 1965.

K. GROSSMANN

GERMAN JEWS' AID SOCIETY. See HILFSVEREIN DER DEUTSCHEN JUDEN.

GERMAN JEWS IN ISRAEL. Beginning in the 15th century there was an almost uninterrupted, although very limited, movement of Jews from Germany to Palestine. Those who came included pilgrims as well as settlers. In the 19th century the birth of the *Hoveve Zion movement and the growing political interest of Germany in the Near East intensified the contacts between German-Jewish circles and Palestine, motivated by national-religious as well as philanthropic interest. A number of German Jews were prominently associated with the communal activities of the then-small Jewish population of Palestine.

Among the early immigrants who reached Palestine before World War I were Dr. Arthur *Ruppin, who later directed the colonization work of the *World Zionist Organization, Dr. Arthur Yitzhak *Biram, founder of the Reali High School in Haifa, and Dr. Wilhelm Bruenn, a medical practitioner who settled in the malaria-infested village (moshava) of Hadera. Following World War I there was some immigration of German Jews, consisting mainly of academicians and pioneers. The rise of Nazism in Germany caused a mass emigration of German Jews to Palestine. It was estimated that about 60,000 German Jews entered the country between 1933 and 1941.

The absorption of German-Jewish mass immigration in Palestine involved socioeconomic as well as cultural problems. The immigrants, mostly middle-class and professional people, were ill prepared for life in a land that was just being developed. Their adjustment necessitated the acquisition of new skills and, in many cases, adaptation to physical labor and to new forms of economy. Deeply rooted in German culture, they had much greater difficulty in acculturation than the newcomers whose mother tongue was Yiddish and who had always lived in an intensely Jewish environment.

General Influence. The German-Jewish immigrants contributed significantly to the upbuilding of a modern economy and society in Palestine. Though many of the individual immigrants arrived with very limited resources or with no means at all, the German-Jewish *'Aliya as a whole, through the *Ha'avara (capital transfer) arrangement, brought large capital funds into the country, a good deal of which was invested in industrial as well as agricultural development.

Under the influence of the German-Jewish immigrants, cities and towns changed their appearance, architecture followed new paths, retail trade was modernized, and numerous new industrial enterprises and workshops were established. Although not all the last-named proved successful, they helped pave the way for subsequent larger industrial developments. While the majority of the immigrants from Germany settled in urban areas, many of them turned to agriculture. A number of successful settlements along cooperative lines were established by German immigrants who in Germany had belonged to the middle class and were middle-aged at the time of their arrival in Palestine. These settlements, such as Ramot HaShavim, Ramat Hadar, K'far Sh'maryahu, Bet Yitzhak, Nahariya, and Shave Tziyon, largely constructed with means supplied by the settlers themselves, were based on rather small holdings, averaging 2 to 5 acres, on which model poultry farms were established. In others, the intensive cultivation of vegetables and flowers was successfully practiced in addition to poultry raising. In some instances, the German settlers specialized in maintaining rest homes, while Nahariya eventually developed into a summer resort. The experience gained in the establishment of these subsequently prosperous settlements was put to use by the *Jewish Agency and the State authorities when the necessity arose for settling larger masses of immigrants on the land. German-Jewish youths participated prominently also in the *kibbutz movement and founded several new communal settlements.

After it had mastered the difficulties of cultural integration, the numerically large group of German-Jewish intelligentsia was able to put its imprint on the cultural, scientific, and artistic life of the country. It brought new ideas and methods to the field of education and took a prominent part in the establishment and extension of secondary and higher educational institutions. German-Jewish scientists made significant contributions to the growth of scientific, and especially medical, research. Others advanced painting and sculpture (see ART IN ISRAEL), were pioneers in the field of *music, and exerted some influence even on the Hebrew-language *theater. Jews from Germany were active in Hebrew journalism, and some of them became well-known Hebrew authors (see LITERATURE, MODERN HEBREW AND ISRAELI). The progress of the German-Jewish immigrants in political life was slower, but eventually they came to occupy important positions in that area also.

Individual Contributions. The large number of German Jews who have contributed significantly to the life and culture of the country and have held prominent positions in State and national institutions include Sh'lomo Yoseph *Burg, Peretz (Fritz) *Bernstein, Giora (Georg) *Josephthal, Peretz *Naphtali, and Pinhas *Rosen, who attained Cabinet rank; Siegfried *Moses and Yitzhak (Ernst) Nebenzahl, who came to occupy the position of *State Comptroller; Kurt *Blumenfeld, Arthur *Hantke, Georg Landauer, Arthur Ruppin, and David Werner *Senator, who headed national organizations and institutions; Arthur Yitzhak Biram and Siegfried Lehman, who were pioneers in education; and Helene Hanna Thon and Siddy Wronsky, who worked in the field of social organization.

Ludwig Strauss and Max *Brod, outstanding German-language writers, as well as Jacob *Steinhardt and Hermann *Struck, famous graphic artists, settled in Palestine. Gertrud Kraus and Yosef Millo (Passovsky) became prominent in the theater and the *dance, as did Leo Kestenberg in music. Azriel *Carlebach was one of Israel's foremost publicists. Moshe Wallach, founder and for many years director of the Sha'are Zedek Hospital in Jerusalem, Bernhard *Zondek, international medical authority, Elias Auerbach, and Max Marcus contributed to the progress of the health services and medicine. Moshe Smoira, Hayim *Cohn, and Alfred Witkon (Witkovsky) were Supreme Court justices.

Alexander Baerwald, Max Hecker, Richard *Kaufmann, and Markus Reiner were outstanding architects; Walter Moses and Reuben Hecht were prominent in industry; and Aron *Barth and Yeshayahu *Foerder were active in banking and financial development. Distinguished scientists and scholars included Martin *Buber, Max Eitingon, Abraham Halevi *Fränkel, Julius Guttmann, Isaac Heinemann, Heinrich *Loewe, Erich Neumann, Gotthold Weil, David Ernst *Bergmann, Fritz Baer, Samuel Hugo *Bergmann, Samuel Sambursky, Gershom *Scholem, and Ernst *Simon.

In the 1960s the Hitahdut 'Ole Germania V'Austria (Association of Immigrants from Germany and Austria), afterward the Irgun 'Ole Merkaz Europa (Organization of Immigrants from Central Europe), was the major organization of German and Austrian Jewish immigrants in Israel. Its work included aid for immigrants and widespread social and cultural activities.

K. LOEWENSTEIN

GERMANY: RELATIONS WITH ZIONISM AND ISRAEL.
A study of the relations between Germany and post-Herzlian Zionism (for the Herzlian period, see HERZL, THEODOR) and the State of Israel lends itself naturally to division into five periods: pre-World War I (1905–14), World War I (1914–18), the Weimar regime (1919–32), the Nazi era (1933–45), and the years following the independence of Israel (1949———). Between May, 1945, and May, 1949, there was no German government.

Pre-World War I, 1905–14. After Herzl's death (1904), the Central Office of the *World Zionist Organization (WZO) along with the editorial office of Die *Welt, the official organ of the WZO, was moved to Germany, where it remained, de jure and de facto, until the end of World War I. At first, the office was in Cologne, the residence of David *Wolffsohn, Herzl's successor. When Otto *Warburg succeeded Wolffsohn in 1911, Zionist headquarters was moved to Berlin, where Warburg lived. The Palestine Office of the WZO, which was set up in Jaffa in 1908, was headed by a German Zionist, Arthur *Ruppin.

Despite the location of World Zionist headquarters in Germany and the key roles played by German Zionists in the movement during this period, relations between the German government and the Zionist movement were minimal at first. During Wolffsohn's presidency, the Zionist Organization was controlled by the "political" faction, which considered its major task to be the achievement of a recognized political-legal status in Palestine. The political Zionists were opposed by the "practical" Zionists, among them Chaim *Weizmann (see PRACTICAL ZIONISM). In fact, however, the Wolffsohn presidency was not an era of great political activity. Aside from Wolffsohn's visits to the Russian Prime Minister, Pyotr Arkadyevich Stolypin, and to Constantinople in 1908 nothing was accomplished. In 1909, however, pressure exerted by the practical Zionists, particularly the Russian group (M'nahem M. *Ussishkin, Vladimir *Jabotinsky, and Yehiel *Tschlenow), which expected that Zionism would benefit from the 1908 Revolution of the Young Turks, brought renewed political activity in the form of the creation of a Political Bureau in Constantinople. The victory of the practical Zionists and the election of their candidate, Otto Warburg, to the presidency (1911) also gave added impetus to political action. This was due partly to general political developments and partly to Warburg's position as one of the chief scientific advisers to the German Imperial government on German colonies in Africa and Australasia.

Kaiser *Wilhelm II, who was highly susceptible to personal pressure, was subjected to two opposing influences with respect to Zionism: Grand Duke Friedrich of Baden, Herzl's friend and an enthusiastic pro-Zionist, on the one hand, and Chancellor Bernhard von Bülow, who was skeptical about Zionism, on the other. The formulation of the Reich's policy toward Palestinian affairs was also influenced by the German Embassy in Constantinople and the consuls in Palestine (Jerusalem, Jaffa, and Haifa).

The Zionist Political Bureau, opened in 1909 in Constantinople, had high ambitions but limited financial means. The Zionist Organization opened a local bank, the Anglo-Levantine Banking Company, and published a newspaper with a definite pro-Turkish orientation, Le Jeune Turc, to which a number of well-known Young Turk journalists contributed. The representative of the Zionist Organization in Constantinople until 1915 was Victor *Jacobson, who also was manager of the bank. Richard *Lichtheim became his assistant in 1913 and director of the Political Bureau early in 1915. This office was very active in the period before World War I, which was also the high mark of German penetration of Turkey and of the rise of the German Empire as the European power of decisive influence in Constantinople. The construction of the Constantinople-Baghdad railroad (which was not completed) opened the Ottoman Empire to widespread German economic infiltration. The arrival in June, 1914, of a large German military delegation headed by Gen. Otto Liman von Sanders emphasized German influence in the military sphere.

In these prewar years the Zionist Organization was generally pro-Turkish in its policies. In both the Italo-Turkish War (1911) and the Balkan Wars (1912–13), *Die Welt* took a stand that was pro-Turkish, which under the circumstances often meant pro-German. Victor Jacobson went even further: he suggested the creation of a Jewish brigade to aid Turkey in its war against Italy, the dispatch of a Jewish medical mission to the Tripoli front, and the organization of a Jewish fund-raising campaign for the benefit of Turkey. A sharply anti-British article by a Turkish journalist appeared in *Le Jeune Turc*. However, the conspicuously anti-British position, which was calculated to arouse German sympathies, provoked a negative reaction in the Zionist leadership: as in Herzl's days, the basic international orientation of the WZO was directed at Britain. On Dec. 10, 1911, Nahum *Sokolow informed Wolffsohn very clearly that "we must prepare now or in the very near future to establish contacts and relationships with the Government of England."

Not long thereafter, however, direct contact was established between the German authorities and the WZO, not because of the general international situation but as a result of an internal Jewish conflict. At the end of 1913 the so-called *Language War broke out in Palestine. The Zionist Organization and the *Hilfsverein der Deutschen Juden had been partners in the creation of the *Technion in Haifa. The Zionists insisted that the language of instruction at the Technion be Hebrew; the Hilfsverein group, which was imbued with German patriotism, insisted that first place be given to German.

At first the German Embassy in Constantinople and the German consuls in Palestine sided with the Hilfsverein. The Consul General in Jerusalem described the battle in the *Yishuv for the supremacy of the Hebrew language as a plot of "Russian revolutionaries" and as a "Jewish-Russian conspiracy" against German interests. (At the time, about half the Jews in Palestine were of Russian origin.) The German newspaper *Osmanischer Lloyd*, published in Constantinople and considered the organ of the German Embassy there, printed anti-Zionist and pro-Hilfsverein articles and news reports.

As a result of the Language War, Zionism incurred the ill will of German diplomatic circles and of the German Foreign Ministry, for the Germans definitely aspired to spread German language and *Kultur* throughout the Middle East. In addition, it was known that most of the Jews in Germany were anti-Zionists. "The mood in the German consulates in Palestine and in the embassy here," Richard Lichtheim wrote to the Zionist Office in Berlin in January, 1914, "is against us to such an extent that we are afraid of real trouble."

Repercussions of the clash between the Hilfsverein and the Zionist Organization soon reached the Foreign Ministry in Berlin. Working on behalf of the Hilfsverein were Paul Nathan and James Simon (the latter was close to Wilhelm II), while Otto Warburg was the principal defender of the Zionist position. It must be noted that the Foreign Ministry in Berlin showed greater understanding of Zionism than did the German diplomats in Turkey. This was due in part to the international character of the Zionist movement. In the tense atmosphere that prevailed on the eve of World War I, German policy was sensitive to international forces, and one may surmise that this played a part in the compromise which was reached between the Zionist Organization and the Hilfsverein in February, 1914, a compromise that, in fact, constituted a Zionist victory.

The serious talks held during those months between the Zionist Political Bureau in Constantinople and the staff of the German Embassy developed into a basic and comprehensive discussion of the essence of Zionism and Zionist aspirations. Richard Lichtheim succeeded in converting one anti-Zionist, Gerhard Muthius, Counselor of the Embassy, into a stanch friend of the movement. Lichtheim's arguments were that the Zionist Eastern European Jews could help promote German trade in Russia and other Eastern European countries and that, in general, the Jews who returned to their Homeland would constitute a political and spiritual force to be reckoned with. Muthius was most impressed by the latter argument.

World War I, 1914–18. World War I brought an unexpected impetus to relations between Germany and the Zionist Organization. In November, 1914, Turkey entered the war on the side of Germany and Austria-Hungary. At the meeting of the Zionist *Executive in Copenhagen in December, 1914, the Zionist movement decided to remain strictly neutral. As a result, World Zionist headquarters was allowed to remain in Berlin, but an additional office, headed by Leo *Motzkin, was opened in neutral Copenhagen (*see* COPENHAGEN BUREAU, 1915–18). Sokolow and Tschlenow went to work in England; Sh'marya *Levin was authorized to continue Zionist activities in the United States. Victor Jacobson and Richard Lichtheim were in Constantinople, but Jacobson, a Russian citizen and hence an enemy alien in Turkey, was declared *persona non grata* by the Turkish government. He left Turkey, and Lichtheim remained the sole Zionist representative there until 1916, when he was joined by Arthur Ruppin, who had been exiled from Palestine by Ahmed *Jamal Pasha. To avoid having to take an official stand on the events of the war, the official Zionist publication *Die Welt* ceased to appear. During the first year of the war, many Zionists believed that Germany would emerge victorious. The Russian Zionists, who hated the Tsarist regime as strongly as the other Jews of Russia did, also hoped for a German victory. Of the leaders of the Zionist movement at the time, only three had pro-British sentiments: Weizmann and Vladimir Jabotinsky, who openly avowed their attitude, and Aaron *Aaronsohn, who could not take an open stand because he lived in the Ottoman Empire until the end of 1916. For a long time these three labored outside the official Zionist framework.

The Zionist Organization was concerned mainly with assuring the survival of the Palestine community of approximately 85,000 Jews, about half of whom were Russian citizens and therefore enemy aliens within the Ottoman Empire. Actual power in Palestine was held by Jamal Pasha, a member of the ruling triumvirate of the Young Turks and the commander of the Turkish forces that controlled Syria and Palestine. Although

Jamal Pasha was not an enemy of Zionism, he was ready to sacrifice the Yishuv since he had doubts about its loyalty to the Ottoman government. Concern in Zionist circles turned into real alarm when information about the expulsions and massacre of the Armenians began to leak out early in 1915. In response to this threat, the effort to aid Palestine was reorganized in the following manner: the main task of fund raising was assumed by the Jews of the United States, the transfer of funds being left to the government in Washington, while the political and physical welfare of the Yishuv was to be safeguarded by German Zionists through intercession with the German government. Thus, German and American Zionists worked hand in hand until April, 1917, when the United States entered the war on the side of the Allies. From that time on, the welfare of the Jewish population of Palestine was the responsibility of the German Zionists, who were aided by funds coming from neutral countries.

Ever since the beginning of the war, the attitude of the German government toward the Zionist movement and its work in Palestine had been one of sympathy, which was not affected even by the renewal of anti-Zionist pressure by the Hilfsverein group (Ephraim Cohen in Palestine and Paul Nathan in Berlin). Contacts between the Zionist Office in Constantinople and the German Embassy remained close. Victor Jacobson, a Russian citizen, was supplied with German papers to enable him to travel freely through European countries, both neutral ones and allies of the Central Powers. The German diplomatic pouches in Constantinople and in the consulates in Palestine were placed at the disposal of the Zionist Organization and its representatives, so that they were able to correspond with Palestine without the knowledge of the Turkish authorities. The representatives of the WZO in Palestine and Constantinople were permitted to use the official couriers of the German Embassy. The Germans could, of course, read the material sent by the Zionists, but the Zionists used this circumstance as an indirect means of bringing to the attention of the Germans information and propaganda which they could not comfortably have transmitted directly to the Germans. In this way Lichtheim reported early in 1916 on the extent of the Hejaz rebellion against Turkey, information which the Ottoman authorities had withheld from their German allies. As a kind of unofficial condition for the unhampered continuation of these Zionist activities, it was understood that the Central Office of the Zionist Organization would remain in Berlin. The Zionists both in Germany and in the anti-German states saw nothing wrong with this; it did not prevent them from continuing Zionist political activity also among the Allies, particularly in London and Washington.

Through German-Zionist cooperation, the three German ambassadors in Constantinople—Baron Hans von Wanggenheim (until 1916), Count Paul Wolff-Metternich zur Gracht (1916), and Count Johann-Heinrich von Bernstorff (1917-18)—became pro-Zionist, and they frequently took the initiative in supporting the interests of the Yishuv. Count von Bernstorff aided the Zionists unintentionally at first, when he served (until 1917) as German Ambassador in Washington. He then transmitted to the Foreign Ministry in Berlin information and reports on the American reaction to the persecution of the Jews in Palestine and the gratification of American Jewry at German efforts on behalf of the Yishuv. He transmitted directly to Wanggenheim copies of his reports to the Foreign Ministry in Berlin. An unofficial link in this chain, a link whose value should not be minimized, was Dr. Isaac Straus, a Zionist from Munich. Straus was sent in 1914 by the German government to the United States, where he acted as Bernstorff's private adviser in Washington and had access to the material received at the German Embassy. The Counselor and Chargé d'Affaires at the German Embassy in Constantinople during the second half of the war was a relatively young diplomat, Constantin von Neurath. At first anti-Zionist (and perhaps even anti-Semitic), he later turned pro-Zionist. Twenty years later, however, he had another change of heart and became Hitler's Foreign Minister.

Zionist activities in Berlin were aimed at the issuance of official instructions from the German Foreign Ministry to German representatives in Turkey to use their influence with the Turkish authorities to protect the Yishuv. Such orders were, in fact, issued in November, 1915, in a secret document that asked the German consuls in Turkey to support legitimate Jewish activities and to encourage Jewish settlement. Palestine was not mentioned specifically, but the reference was obvious. The directive was carried out faithfully by consuls and officials, some of whom were personally anti-Zionist and anti-Jewish.

German assistance to the Yishuv consisted mainly of intervention with the Turks to prevent the mass expulsion of enemy alien Jews from Palestine, to protect Jewish and Zionist enterprises, particularly economic institutions, from looting or confiscation, to prevent Turkish seizure of aid funds from abroad, and to obtain the reversal of Turkish death sentences in Palestine. As a rule, German intervention was successful. In their clashes with Jamal Pasha, the Germans usually had the upper hand, and they were forced to intervene frequently, for Jamal Pasha had recourse to anti-Jewish measures time and again. Sometimes he found good reasons for so doing. For instance, certain Jewish and Zionist enterprises, such as the *Alliance Israélite Universelle and the Anglo-Palestine Company (see BANK L'UMI L'YISRAEL), were registered in enemy states (France and Great Britain, respectively). Nonetheless, German pressure (and until 1917, American pressure as well) enabled these institutions to continue their work in Palestine. While at times German intervention was not completely successful in preventing anti-Jewish measures by the Turks, it at least softened their effects. Although Jews were expelled from Jaffa in April, 1917, the decree to expel them from the settlements in Judea and the Sharon Plain was revoked. Similarly, the Turkish authorities were restrained in the campaign of vengeance which they had planned against the Yishuv after the discovery of the *Nili spy ring in October, 1917. In some cases the German authorities worked through senior German officers in Palestine, particularly Generals Erich von Falkenhayn and Friedrich Kress von Kressenstein, on whose help the Turks were greatly dependent.

The main reason for Germany's stand was the realization that the Zionist movement was an international political body. Germany understood "international Jewry" to include not only the Jews of the United States but particularly the 6 million Jews in the Russian Empire, who, it was anticipated, would play an important role in the development of German commerce and influence after the war. From this point of view, the Zionist political progress with the Allied Powers (especially in London) strengthened the Zionist position in Berlin. On July 2, 1917, the Zionist Executive handed the German Foreign Ministry a memorandum describing the good prospects for Zionist aspirations in the Western capitals. The *Balfour Declaration was issued four months later. On the other hand, the Zionists did not put pressure upon the German government to issue a political declaration in favor of a Jewish Palestine as long as Berlin would be unable to obtain Turkey's agreement to such a statement. Baron von Wanggenheim was able to state, in clear conscience, that "we do not intend to sign a treaty with the Zionists" or to support a "Zionist state."

While the German attitude was motivated in part by the humanitarian impulse to save a civilized settlement from Levantine despots, the importance of such considerations should not be exaggerated. When Henry *Morgenthau, the American Ambassador to Constantinople, turned to Baron von Wanggenheim with a request to initiate joint activities to protect the Armenians, the German Ambassador replied, "I can do nothing. Be glad I am helping you to protect the Jews." Wolff-Metternich attempted to work on his own initiative to put a stop to the Armenian massacres, but he was blocked by a sharp reaction from the Turks, who requested that he be transferred from Constantinople.

After the issuance of the Balfour Declaration, the Zionist Executive in Berlin entered into negotiations with the German government to issue a pro-Zionist statement concerning the future of Palestine. The Germans found it difficult to do anything against the will of the Turkish government, but finally, on Jan. 5, 1918, an official German pronouncement appeared, which read:

> As regards the aspirations in Palestine of Jewry, especially Zionists, we welcome the recent statement of the Grand Vizier Talaat Pasha, expressing the Turkish Government's intention, in accordance with the friendly attitude they have always adopted towards the Jews, to promote a flourishing Jewish settlement within the limits of the capacity of the country, local self-government corresponding to the country's laws, and the free development of their civilization.

In the latter part of 1918, when it became apparent that Germany was losing the war, Zionist attempts to influence the Berlin government slackened, but with a view to Germany's postwar status efforts to obtain support from influential political circles continued. The theoretical basis for this activity is explained in Kurt *Blumenfeld's article in the *Preussische Jahrbücher* of 1915, entitled "Zionism as a Problem of German Policy in the War." Blumenfeld suggested German-Zionist cooperation in the economic development of Turkey, the furthering of German culture throughout the Ottoman Empire, and other steps. He stressed the absolute independence of the Zionist movement. In 1918 Zionist efforts at influencing German public opinion resulted in the creation of a pro-Palestine committee, the German Palestine Committee, which included such leading public figures as Col. Carl Franz von Endres, the military writer; Matthias Erzberger, the head of the Catholic Center party; Dr. Adolf Grabowsky, a sociologist; the economist Werner Sombart; and academicians such as Adolf Weber and Max Weber. The committee published a series of monographs, the most comprehensive being written by Otto Eberhardt, an educator. One of Eberhardt's arguments in favor of a Jewish State (or National Home) in Palestine was that its creation would obviate the migration of Jews from Eastern Europe into Germany.

Weimar Regime, 1919-32. After its defeat in World War I, Germany remained outside the sphere of world politics until 1925, when it was admitted to the League of Nations. The Zionist Organization of Germany forbade its members to assume political posts in the Weimar government and attempted to establish a nonpartisan German front for Zionism. Late in 1926 the German Palestine Committee was reconstituted, with German statesmen and public figures from many groups attending its conferences. Some of these men, such as Count von Bernstorff and Siegfried von Kardorff, were long-established friends of Zionism; others, such as Prof. Carl Heinrich Becker, Minister of Culture and Religion, and Konrad Adenauer, then mayor of Cologne, were newcomers to pro-Zionist ranks. Supporters of Zionism were found in many groups, with the exception of the extreme right and the Communist party; many of the pro-Zionists, among them Eduard Bernstein and Joseph Bloch, were nonorthodox Social Democrats and "liberal" Conservatives.

With the rise of *anti-Semitism and the strengthening of Nazism in the German public in the early 1930s, the representatives of the Zionist movement in Germany sought to obtain a strong declaration from the German government against Nazi anti-Semitic provocations by stressing the influence of Zionists upon the governments of various nations. Chancellor Heinrich Brüning evaded the request, nor were the Zionists successful in their attempts to obtain governmental support of emigration to Palestine as a constructive outlet for internal pressures. Before long the Weimar Republic collapsed, and on Jan. 30, 1933, Hitler became Chancellor of Germany.

Nazi Era, 1933-45. The history of the attitude of the Nazi regime toward Zionism may be divided into two distinct periods, the years preceding World War II (1933-39) and the war years (1939-45). During the first period the Nazi government actually encouraged Jewish emigration from Germany, including migration to Palestine. In 1933 an agreement was signed with the Zionist "transfer" organization to handle the funds of the emigrants (*see* HA'AVARA). In 1934 an official directive (which was intended to be secret but was published by mistake) was issued to all the authorities in the Reich, ordering them to encourage the activities of the Zionist Organization and the Zionist youth groups insofar as they served to further Jewish emigration. This decree specifically stated that transfer activities and the agricultural *Hakhshara of the pioneering organization *HeHalutz "are in the interest of the [German] State."

The Arab *riots of 1936-39 led to a reversal of the Nazi attitude toward Zionism. Nazi agents vied with Fascist Italy in joining with extremist Arab nationalist groups. German non-Jewish residents of Palestine began to participate in Arab terrorist and political activities. In 1938 the *Völkischer Beobachter*, the official Nazi party organ, took an extreme pro-Arab and anti-Zionist stand. Nevertheless, it did not come out in opposition to Jewish migration to Palestine.

On Jan. 1, 1939, the Nazi authorities disbanded all Jewish groups, including the Zionist Organization. The Reichsvertretung der Deutschen Juden (National Representative Council of German Jews) was also dissolved, but a short time later permission was granted for its reconstitution as the Reichsvereinigung für Auswanderung und Fürsorge der Juden (Reich Union for Jewish Emigration and Welfare). About half the Jews of Germany left the Reich before the war began; approximately 70,000 to 80,000 of them went to Palestine.

After the outbreak of war in September, 1939, Jews were prevented from leaving Germany and Nazi-occupied countries. In 1940 the Nazis began to deport Jews to concentration camps in Poland, which in 1941-42 became death camps. The decision to destroy the Jews was urged on the Nazis by Hajj Amin *al-Husayni, the former mufti of Jerusalem, who arrived in Germany in 1941. He was promised that if the Nazis were to conquer Palestine, the Jews of that country, too, would be wiped out. A close relationship developed between the Reich and the extreme Arab nationalists. Army units of Arab and Muslim volunteers were formed within the Nazi armed forces. The Nazi regime thought so highly of the Nazi-Arab pact that as late as November, 1944, German paratroopers were flown to Palestine to carry out acts of sabotage and to assist anti-Jewish and anti-British Arab groups. These paratroopers were captured by the British forces.

Relations between Germany and Israel, 1949———. From the spring of 1945 to the spring of 1949 there was no German government. In 1949 two separate German states, one in western Germany, supported by the Western Powers, and one in the east, supported by the Soviet Union, were formed. East Germany has treated Israel with consistent hostility: it has not paid reparations for Jewish property stolen by the Nazi government, and it consistently has sided with the Arab governments in their disputes with Israel. East Germany has maintained the most extreme anti-Israel policy within the Communist bloc.

The Federal Republic of Germany has attempted to conciliate and indemnify Israel for losses sustained in the Nazi holocaust. The 1951 reparations agreement (*see* GERMAN-ISRAEL AGREEMENT) and the decision of the Bonn government to pay reparations to individual Jews who suffered at the hands of the Nazi regime reflected this attitude. During the years immediately following the reparations agreement, Israel refused to establish normal political relations with Bonn. The memory of the holocaust was still fresh, and there was a general lack of confidence in the sincerity of German repudiation of Nazi crimes. As a result of the reparations and payments, however, commercial relations were expanded, and by the mid-1960s West Germany was third among the nations trading with Israel. At the end of 1957 Israel was ready to enter into military-commercial agreements with Bonn, with Israeli-manufactured uniforms and light armament being shipped to the German Army in return for a supply of German arms and equipment to the Israeli Army. However, Israeli public opinion was opposed to this cooperative undertaking, which many interpreted as Jewish approval of German rearmament. Nevertheless, in July, 1958, the government policy was approved in the *Knesset by a vote of 57 to 54. In the spring of 1960 Prime Minister David *Ben-Gurion of Israel met Chancellor Konrad Adenauer of West Germany in New York, where they reached agreement concerning German financial aid after the completion of the reparations payments.

The discovery of West German technical experts working in the United Arab Republic (UAR) on the development of lethal weapons of aggression aroused a storm of protest in Israel in 1963. The Knesset passed a unanimous protest vote. In actual fact, the experiments of the experts failed. At the end of 1964 West German newspapers published details of a secret Israel-German agreement for the shipment of German arms, including armored vehicles, to Israel on easy terms. The secret nature of the agreement aroused dissatisfaction in both Israel and Germany. As a result, the Bonn government announced the cancellation of the agreement and simultaneously asked for a normalization of political relations, through reciprocal diplomatic recognition and the exchange of ambassadors. Diplomatic recognition was effectuated in 1965; it was followed by the breaking of diplomatic relations with Bonn by various Arab governments, including that of the UAR. In 1966

an agreement was reached for a favorable long-term loan to Israel by the German government.

During and after the *Six-day War of 1967, the Bonn government assumed a friendly attitude toward Israel, without taking an official position on Israeli-Arab problems. Public opinion also was pro-Israel. The federal government has consistently supported Israel's admission to the European Common Market as an associate member, but because of French opposition such admission had not been effected as of 1969 (*see* EUROPEAN COMMON MARKET AND ISRAEL).

E. LIVNEH

GERMANY, ZIONISM IN. German Zionism developed within a largely assimilated Jewish community. It represented, on the one hand, a reaction to *assimilation and its inadequacy in the light of the persistence of *anti-Semitism and, on the other, a search for a solution of the problem of the Eastern European Jewish *Diaspora in the wake of the Russian pogroms of the 1880s. Zionism in Germany was generally a movement of the young, long before it was conceived in those terms elsewhere, and basically it remained so until 1933. With the advent of Nazism, there was a rise in Zionist membership, but even after 1933 the movement did not win a majority of German Jews.

Despite its relatively small membership, however, the Zionist movement in Germany came to have a considerable impact on German Jewry as well as on World Zionism as a whole. After the death of Herzl, World Zionist headquarters was transferred from Vienna to Germany (first to Cologne and then to Berlin), remaining there until World War I.

Early Beginnings. The first pre-Zionist society in Germany was the *Colonisations-Verein für Palästina (Settlement Society for Palestine), which was founded in Frankfurt on the Oder by Chaim *Lorje for the purpose of establishing a large Jewish agricultural settlement in Palestine and of encouraging and assisting individual Jewish agriculturists there. However, the society ceased to exist in 1864.

In the 1860s, after the appearance of Zvi Hirsch *Kalischer's *D'rishat Tziyon* (1861), a book that advocated Jewish settlement in Palestine, small groups in Germany rallied around such men as Rabbis Elijah *Gutmacher, Azriel *Hildesheimer, and Isaac *Rülf for the purpose of practical action to rebuild Palestine. In 1864 Kalischer founded in Berlin a Central Committee for Palestine Colonization. Two years earlier (1862), Moses *Hess, in his Zionist classic *Rome and Jerusalem*, had propounded a Zionism based not so much on religion as on the nationhood of the Jews.

Most of the Jews in Germany, however, had little use for nationalist theories, for they were convinced that, despite temporary setbacks, the promise of *emancipation was well on the way to fulfillment. Still, a small number were brought closer to the concept of Jewish nationhood by the rise of modern political and social anti-Semitism and by reports of the anti-Jewish excesses of Tsarist Russia.

In 1880 Gustav G. *Cohen, a wealthy merchant in Hamburg, wrote a brochure entitled *Die Judenfrage und die Zukunft* (The Jewish Problem and the Future), in which he proposed the revival of the Jewish nation in Palestine, but it did not appear in print until 10 years later. In 1883 a group of Orthodox Jews led by Naftali Zvi Hirsh *Hildesheimer, son of Azriel Hildesheimer, founded the *Esra society to raise funds for Jewish settlement in Palestine. However, it could gather no more than 115,000 marks during all the 25 years of its existence. That same year saw the publication of a Zionist pamphlet, *Aruchas Bass Ammi* (The Healing of the Daughter of My People), by Rabbi Isaac Rülf. Also in the early 1880s, Moses Moses, a merchant, and Selig Freuthal, a teacher, launched a small Zionist magazine, *Der Colonist* (The Settler), in Kattowitz, Prussia (now Katowice, Poland), and helped prepare for the *Kattowitz Conference of the European *Hoveve Zion movement (1884). A group in Berlin, including a number of Jews from Eastern Europe, published a nationalist and Palestine-oriented monthly, *Serubabel*, which appeared from 1886 to 1888. It resumed publication in 1890 under the editorship of Albert Katz, who had come to Germany from Russia and who, in one of his advertising circulars, wrote that *Serubabel* would demonstrate the fact of Jewish nationhood and promote the national heritage of Judaism without entering into religious controversies.

In 1889 Russian-Jewish students in Berlin organized the Russian-Jewish Academic Association to counteract the Russian Association, an older students' group whose membership consisted almost entirely of assimilationist Jews. Among the members of the new group were the future Zionist leaders Victor *Jacobson, Sh'marya *Levin, Joseph *Luria, Leo *Motzkin, and Nachman *Syrkin and, later, Selig *Soskin and Chaim *Weizmann.

In 1891 Max *Bodenheimer, a young lawyer in Cologne, published a brochure *Wohin mit den russischen Juden?* (Whither the Russian Jews?), in which he described the tragic situation of Eastern European Jewry and urged Jewish settlement in Palestine or Syria as a solution. Two years later Bodenheimer, together with David *Wolffsohn, later Herzl's trusted lieutenant, founded the Cologne Association for the Furtherance of Agriculture and Handicrafts in Palestine. Among the others who were drawn to the concept of modern Jewish nationhood were Dr. Moritz Rahmer, a rabbi in Magdeburg and editor of the *Israelitische Wochenschrift,* and his pupil Heinrich *Loewe. In 1892 Loewe, with Willy *Bambus, founded the pre-Herzlian Zionist society *Jung Israel in Berlin. Also founded in Berlin that year was the Jüdische Humanitätsgesellschaft (Jewish Humanities Society), which aimed to win German-born university students for the Zionist idea. Among its founders were Max Bodenheimer, Adolf *Friedemann, the brothers Robert and Arthur *Hantke, Ernest-Eliakim *Kalmus (a medical student), Edmund Landau, Walter Munk, and Dr. Max Oppenheimer. In 1894 Dr. Moshe Wallach settled in Jerusalem, where he opened the Sha'are Zedek Hospital.

In 1895 Loewe, the German-born members of Jung Israel, and several members of the Humanitätsgesellschaft, who felt that their organizations had not been sufficiently outspoken in their Zionist stand, founded the Jewish Students' Association, whose official aim was the cultivation of Jewish "self-respect." Its first Presidium consisted of Walter Munk, first chairman; Robert Hantke, second chairman; Ernest-Eliakim Kalmus, secretary; Theodor *Zlocisti, treasurer; and Heinrich Loewe, officer in charge of athletics and fencing. It was Loewe, too, who, seizing on the "muscle Jewry" concept set forth by Max *Nordau at the 2d Zionist *Congress (1898), helped found the Bar Kokhba athletic group, from which the Maccabi sports movement later evolved.

In 1893, when Nathan *Birnbaum's Jewish magazine *Selbst-Emanzipation ceased publication, the Berlin Zionists launched the weekly *Jüdische Volkszeitung* under Birnbaum's nominal editorship. After one year, this paper, too, was discontinued and supplanted by *Zion* (1895), under Heinrich Loewe's editorship.

The Russian-Jewish Academic Association in Berlin in 1890. [Zionist Archives]

In 1896 Loewe left for Palestine, and Birnbaum moved from Vienna to Berlin, where he issued in the same year a brochure entitled *Jüdische Moderne*. In 1897-98 a semimonthly magazine was published in Berlin under the same title, and, also in 1897, Willy Bambus became editor of *Zion*.

From 1896 to 1914. The reaction of the majority of German Jewry to Herzl's **Jewish State*, the blueprint of political Zionism that appeared in 1896, was negative. Even many early Zionists, among them Willy Bambus and Adolf Friedemann, felt impelled at first to oppose him because they considered Zionism too dangerous a political force. They resented the fact that in his book Herzl did not speak exclusively in terms of Palestine as a Jewish Homeland or envision Hebrew as the language of the projected Jewish State. A few months later, however, a group of young Herzlian Zionists was formed in Berlin, and David Wolffsohn of Cologne went to Vienna to make Herzl's acquaintance. As early as May, 1896, Max Bodenheimer invited Herzl to deliver an address in Berlin, but Herzl declined the invitation because he feared that the opposition to his aims would be too strong.

In March, 1897, a delegation of Berlin Zionists, consisting of Willy Bambus, Nathan Birnbaum, Moses Moses (Kattowitz), Osias *Thon, and Isaac *Turoff (representing Esra), called on Herzl in Vienna to discuss plans for a Zionist publishing house. Because of lack of funds, this project could not be carried out. Herzl took the opportunity, however, to discuss plans for the 1st Zionist Congress. He suggested Zurich as the site of the Congress, but later the Viennese Zion society suggested Munich instead. When the Jewish Religious Community of Munich made an official protest against having the Zionist Congress take place in its city, however, the committee appointed by Herzl to prepare the Congress chose Basle.

In July, 1897, the Executive Committee of the Association of Rabbis in Germany published a declaration in many German newspapers rejecting Zionism. Herzl countered with his famous article against the **Protestrabbiner (Die *Welt*, July 16, 1897). Earlier that year Max Bodenheimer, Fabius *Schach, and David Wolffsohn had founded the Nationaljüdische Vereinigung Köln (National Jewish Association of Cologne), which adopted political Zionism. The association pledged itself to the promotion of Jewish settlement in Syria and Palestine, to the advance-

A delegation of the Zionist Organization of Germany at the jubilee of Grand Duke Friedrich of Baden in 1902. From left to right: Alfred Klee, M. Kaufman, Max Bodenheimer, Julius Moses, Adolf Friedemann, Rudolf Schauer. [Zionist Archives]

ment of Jewish education and tradition, including the study of the Hebrew language, and to the improvement of the social and cultural position of the Jews.

A conference held in Bingen on the Rhine on July 11, 1897, marked the beginning of organized political Zionism in Germany. It was attended by, among others, Max Bodenheimer, Elieser Rubinsohn, Fabius Schach, Gustav Wolff, and David Wolffsohn (all of Cologne), Leo Eastermann (Berlin), Hermann *Schapira (Heidelberg), and Rudolf Schauer (Bingen). The conference decided to form the Nationaljüdische Vereinigung für Deutschland (National Jewish Association of Germany). The second conference of German Zionists was held during the 1st Zionist Congress (Basle, Aug. 29–31, 1897), at which Hermann Schapira submitted his plan for the creation of a *Jewish National Fund.

Under the impact of the Congress, the German delegates decided to organize the Zionists of Germany as part of the *World Zionist Organization (WZO). Thus, on Oct. 31, 1897, the Zionist Organization of Germany (Zionistische Vereinigung für Deutschland, or ZVFD) was founded in Frankfurt on the Main. Its leadership was entrusted to a Central Committee consisting of Max Bodenheimer as chairman, David Wolffsohn as treasurer, and Lipman Prins, Rabbi Isaac Rülf, Fabius Schach, and Hermann Schapira. That same year Heinrich Loewe founded the Zionist Association of Berlin, of which he became president.

In 1898 Herzl finally went to Berlin to bring his program before the wealthy Jews of that city. That year Willy Bambus and Adolf Friedemann were elected delegates to the 2d Zionist Congress by a Berlin group that opposed Herzl. While Friedemann eventually became one of Herzl's most devoted disciples, Bambus later quit the political Zionist scene altogether.

Among the leaders who acquired prominence in German Zionist circles in the period 1896–1914 were Julius Becker (editor of the *Jüdische Rundschau* for several years), Kurt *Blumenfeld, Sammy *Gronemann, George *Halpern, Arthur Hantke, Hans Gideon Heymann, Karl Jeremias, Ernest-Eliakim Kalmus, Alfred *Klee, Max Kollenscher, Eduard Leszynsky (Hantke's law partner), Richard *Lichtheim (editor of *Die Welt* in 1911–13 and later political representative of the Zionist movement in Constantinople), Julius Moses, Franz *Oppen-

heimer, Arthur Pelz, Aharon *Sandler, Hugo Hillel *Schachtel, Fritz Sondheimer, Elias Straus, Davis *Trietsch, Otto *Warburg, Arnold Wiener (Kattowitz), and Max Wollsteiner (Berlin).

An important factor in the development of Zionism in Germany was the presence there, for considerable periods of time, of Russian and Austrian Zionists. Sh'marya Levin, Leo Motzkin, and Selig Soskin acted as intermediaries between the Zionist organizations of Germany and Russia until World War I.

In 1902 Martin *Buber, Berthold *Feiwel, Ephraim Moses *Lilien, and Davis Trietsch founded in Berlin the Jüdischer Verlag, which was to be a leading Zionist publishing house for many years. This group strove for a Jewish cultural renaissance in line with the ideals of *Ahad Ha'Am (*see* CULTURAL ZIONISM) and opposed those who, like Max Bodenheimer, Adolf Friedemann, and Franz Oppenheimer, tended to regard Zionism primarily as a practical, "philanthropic" solution for the problem of the persecuted Jews of Eastern Europe. The philanthropic view was also increasingly opposed by a younger group, whose most important spokesman was Kurt Blumenfeld, the first party secretary of the ZVFD. However, the influence of the "practical" Zionists (as distinct from the proponents of "political" Zionism) such as Franz Oppenheimer, Selig Soskin, Davis Trietsch, and Otto Warburg was by no means insignificant. The development of the economic institutions of Palestine was due in no small measure to their initiative. Gradually, the upper hand in German Zionism was gained by the supporters of *Synthetic Zionism, combining political, cultural, and practical work on behalf of Palestine.

In 1902 the Zionist movement took over the *Israelitische Rundschau,* a Berlin weekly which, renamed the *Jüdische Rundschau* (Jewish Review), was the official organ of Zionism in Germany until 1938. It played a prominent role in bringing Zionism to the notice of German-speaking Jewry and discussed Zionist issues on a high literary and intellectual level. Its first editor was Heinrich Loewe.

During the early 1900s a number of prominent German Zionists, including Adolf Friedemann, Eduard Leszynsky, Richard Lichtheim, and Heinrich Loewe, visited Palestine. Arthur *Ruppin went there to set up (1908) the Palestine Office in Jaffa (*see* PALESTINE OFFICES), of which he became director. By 1910, 20 Jews from Germany, including professional men such as the physicians Elias Auerbach and Wilhelm Bruenn, Arthur *Biram, an educator, Joseph *Treidel, an engineer, and Dr. Louis Weinberg, a lawyer, had settled in Palestine (*see* GERMAN JEWS IN ISRAEL).

Since opposition to Zionism was unabated and the early outcry of the *Protestrabbiner* was followed also by opposition from extreme Orthodoxy as well as from the assimilationists, particularly the Centralverein Deutscher Staatsbürger Jüdischen Glaubens (Central Union of German Citizens of the Jewish Faith), the Zionist movement in Germany devoted a large part of its efforts to propaganda and ideological debates with the Centralverein and the official Jewish religious communities.

The Bund Jüdischer Corporationen (BJC) and (after 1902) the Kartell Zionistischer Verbindungen (KZV), which joined forces in 1914 as the *Kartell Jüdischer Verbindungen (KJV), strove for the support of Jewish university students. A number of students' groups were organized, one after the other: Organization of Jewish Students (Verein Jüdischer Studenten, Breslau and Munich, 1900; Charlottenburg, 1901; Strasbourg and Freiburg, 1903; Marburg, 1906); Makkabäa (Breslau,

1901–03; the first Jewish students' society to accept the *Basle Program); Hasmonea (Berlin, 1903); Techiah (Cöthen, 1903; the first group to organize vacation study courses on Palestine); Jordania (Munich, 1906); and Ivria (Freiburg, 1907).

Between 1908 and 1912 Germany was third in membership strength in the World Zionist Organization, trailing only Russia and the United States, as shown by annual *Shekel payment figures. The number of Shekel contributors in Germany was 4,790 for 1909–10, 7,836 for 1910–11, and 5,176 for 1911–12. Jewish National Fund drives in Germany yielded good results and showed a rapid and steady increase.

In 1904 the Zionist Organization of Germany set up a head office in Berlin (Bleibtreustrasse), headed by Arthur Hantke, Eduard Leszynsky, and Emil Simonsohn. Max Bodenheimer remained chairman until 1910, however, and continued to live in Cologne. In 1906 the Berlin office was moved to larger premises in the western sector of the city. In 1910 Arthur Hantke became chairman of the ZVFD (he held this office until 1920, when he joined the Zionist *Executive in London), and in 1911 World Zionist headquarters was transferred from Cologne to Berlin, to a large new office at 8 Sächsischestrasse, which housed the ZVFD, the editorial offices of *Die Welt*, and the Inner *Actions Committee. In 1924 the ZVFD acquired a building of its own at 10 Meineckestrasse.

By 1912 the ZVFD had a membership of 8,400, including women and young people, mostly from middle-income groups. The leadership consisted mainly of intellectuals and professional men—lawyers, writers, journalists, economists, and physicians. Eventually, it was joined also by the *Mizrahi, which was led by Dr. Aron *Barth, his brother Lazarus Barth, Rabbi Nehemia Anton *Nobel, Hermann *Pick, Hermann *Struck, and Oskar Wolfsberg (Y'sha'yahu *Avi'ad-Wolfsberg).

The platform drawn up at the 13th German Zionist Convention, held in Posen (now Poznań) in May, 1912, called on every Zionist individual to make *'Aliya (immigration to Palestine) a part of his life's plan. At the same time the Zionists took a stand in the debates then going on concerning the role of Jews in German life (for example, the view of Werner Sombart, a German political economist, who urged the Jews to abstain from claiming all their civic rights).

During the years immediately preceding World War I the Zionists continued their ideological arguments with the official Jewish communities, insisting that the latter should serve not only the purely religious concerns but also the secular and national interests of their members. This era also saw endeavors on the part of the Zionists to win over nonpolitical Jewish youth groups, the beginnings of the Blau-Weiss (Blue-White) youth movement (founded by Dr. Adalbert Sachs in 1913), and a showdown in the relations between the Zionists and the anti-Zionists (the anti-Zionist resolutions of the Centralverein in 1913 and the founding of the Anti-Zionist Committee in 1914). Another controversy was that involving the *Hilfsverein der Deutschen Juden in connection with the language of instruction to be used in Hilfsverein-operated schools in Palestine. *See also* LANGUAGE WAR; T'KHELET-LAVAN.

World War I. At the meeting of the Actions Committee in Copenhagen in December, 1914, it was decided that the Central Office of the WZO should remain in Berlin with Otto Warburg, Arthur Hantke, and Victor Jacobson in charge, while other members of the Executive should proceed to European capitals to explain the Zionist position. Neutrality vis-à-vis the belligerents was the cornerstone of Zionist policy. Contacts be-

tween the Berlin office and Zionists in other countries were effected from an office set up in neutral Copenhagen (*see* COPENHAGEN BUREAU). The Central Office in Berlin concerned itself with the protection of the *Yishuv (Jewish population of Palestine) under Turkish military rule. About half of the Jews in Palestine at the time were Russian subjects and hence in danger of deportation or internment as enemy aliens. Working through the Zionist Office in Constantinople, directed by Richard Lichtheim, who enjoyed the support of the German Embassy in the Turkish capital, the Zionist Executive in Berlin rendered valuable service in protecting these Jews from Turkish persecution. Assistance was financial as well as political. Efforts were made to gain the sympathy of the German government for the Zionist cause. In his capacity as Counselor to the German Embassy in Washington, Dr. Isaac Straus, a Munich Zionist, was able to aid Zionist efforts in Berlin and Constantinople. Subsequent negotiations by the Zionist Executive in Berlin with the German Foreign Office resulted in a promise by the German government to give what protection it could to the Yishuv.

German pro-Palestine efforts were guided by the desire to gain the favor of world Jewry, particularly that of the Jews of the United States, which at first was neutral. During the war years the German ambassadors to Turkey and other German

Headquarters of the Zionist Organization of Germany, 10 Meineckestrasse, Berlin. [Kurt Blumenfeld, *Erlebte Judenfrage*, Deutsche Verlags-Anstalt, Stuttgart, 1962]

diplomatic officials repeatedly interceded with the Turkish government to permit Russian Jews to remain in Palestine and to protect the Jews and Zionist institutions of Palestine from persecution by the military regime of Ahmed *Jamal Pasha. The representative of the World Zionist Organization in Constantinople obtained permission to use the German diplomatic pouch for communicating with Berlin headquarters and the Jaffa Palestine Office. In November, 1915, the German consuls in Palestine received official instructions to protect the interests of the Jews there. Toward the end of the war the German government created a special Department of Jewish Affairs in the Foreign Office.

A number of German Zionists joined the *Komitee für den Osten (Committee for the East), which was set up to represent the interests of the Jews residing in German-occupied sectors of Eastern Europe. These first contacts with the masses of Eastern European Jewry made a profound impression, and the opportunity afforded Jewish soldiers serving in the German Army on the eastern front to become acquainted with their coreligionists in Eastern Europe led many young German Jews to turn to Zionism.

After the issuance of the *Balfour Declaration, a German statement of sympathy with Zionist aspirations was promised. However, German efforts to induce the Turkish government to issue a pro-Zionist declaration were fruitless, and it was only close to the end of the war, when Turkey was nearing collapse, that a rather vague pro-Zionist statement came forth.

During the war the German Palestine Committee, a pro-Palestine committee that included leading German statesmen as well as non-Zionists and politically prominent non-Jews, was formed in Berlin. This committee carried on useful propaganda in support of Zionism, which came to the notice of Great Britain, then in the midst of its negotiations with the Zionist leaders.

From 1918 to 1933. The postwar social upheavals in Germany, the repercussions of the Russian Revolution, and increasingly close contacts between the Zionists in Germany and the pioneer workers in Palestine helped turn many young German Zionists to Socialist ideas. At the 1918 Zionist Convention in Berlin a strong current of opinion developed in favor of a Socialist program in Palestine. Considerable activity was started by *HaPo'el HaTza'ir, which rallied around Hayim *Arlosoroff, who was in charge of *HeHalutz headquarters in Berlin for a time. Arlosoroff and Yosef *Sprinzak, who also lived in Berlin for a period, represented an anti-Marxist Socialist trend supported by the intellectual circle associated with the *Jüdische Rundschau*, which from 1919 on was under the editorship of Robert *Weltsch. The Marxist trend was represented by the *Po'ale Zion.

In 1920 the Socialist and radical nationalist trends were countered by the founding of the *Binyan Ha'Aretz group by a number of older Zionists, including Alfred Klee, Max Kollenscher, Karl Lewin, and Gotthold Weil, who, like Louis D. *Brandeis in the United States, held that the time for ideological bickering was past and that all Jews, regardless of political opinion, should unite in the work of rebuilding Palestine. To counteract the influence of the Binyan Ha'Aretz group, a National Unity Bloc was formed by Kurt Blumenfeld, Arthur Hantke, Fritz Löwenstein, and Egon Rosenberg. The bloc ran for the May 13–17, 1921, convention in Hannover, won the election, and made Felix Rosenblüth (Pinhas *Rosen) chairman. The defeat of the Binyan Ha'Aretz (closely paralleling that of the Brandeisists at Cleveland that year) disappointed its sup-

porters, and to all practical purposes the group ceased to function in 1922. In subsequent years, its members joined one or the other of the opposition groups that arose between 1921 and 1933. Kollenscher formed the Independent Zionists in 1929.

In the dispute between Weizmann and Brandeis over economic policy (1920; see UNITED STATES OF AMERICA, ZIONISM IN), the great majority of German Zionists sided with Weizmann and began an active campaign for the *Keren HaYesod (Palestine Foundation Fund). Although the number of Shekel contributors in Germany prior to 1933 never exceeded 20,000, the total contributions from Germany to Keren HaYesod in the late 1920s ranked third among all the countries participating.

Upon the resignation of Dr. Arthur Hantke, Alfred Klee and Felix Rosenblüth became joint chairmen of the ZVFD (1920–21); Rosenblüth alone served as chairman from 1921 to 1923, when Dr. Alfred Landsberg was elected. He was replaced in turn by Kurt Blumenfeld (1924–33). It was Blumenfeld who, in 1921, had persuaded Albert *Einstein to go to the United States with Weizmann on behalf of Keren HaYesod. During his term as president, Blumenfeld endeavored to get large gifts for Keren HaYesod from wealthy individuals, to gain support for the Zionist cause from German Jewry's religious and intellectual leadership, and to disseminate the message of Zionism among the young. After 1920 the following German Zionist leaders served as members of the Executive of the WZO: Hayim Arlosoroff, Lazarus Barth, George Halpern, Arthur Hantke, Hermann Pick, Felix Rosenblüth, Arthur Ruppin (by then in Palestine), and Julius *Simon (by then in the United States).

The decade preceding the Nazi take-over was a period of growth for the Zionist youth movement in Germany. Students' groups and Zionist sports and athletics clubs such as the hikers' movement (Wanderbewegung) developed apace. The collapse of Blau-Weiss in 1925 was offset by the rise of the Socialist Zionist–oriented B'rit Ha'Olim Young Jewish Hikers' Club and other youth groups. The *Halutz (pioneer) movement had taken root in Germany but produced little 'Aliya at the time.

Meanwhile, the leaders of the ZVFD were engaged in debate with the spokesman of the Jüdische Volkspartei (Jewish People's party), which had been founded in 1919 by Georg Kareski, Alfred Klee, Max Kollenscher, and Heinrich Loewe. This party drew its support from Zionists, conservative religious elements, and postwar Eastern European immigrants and strove to win the Jewish religious communities for the Zionist cause. Their endeavor was crowned with success in 1928, when Kareski was elected president of the Berlin Jewish Community.

The political disputes within the WZO over the British stand on Arab-Jewish relations set off considerable controversy within the ZVFD as well. As early as 1921, Martin Buber presented a resolution on the Arab problem in the name of HaPo'el HaTza'ir. In 1929 Robert Weltsch and Moritz Bilesky drafted a memorandum suggesting that the World Zionist movement reformulate its objective as aiming at a binational Arab-Jewish State in Palestine under British rule rather than a Jewish State (see B'RIT SHALOM). The debate reached its climax at the convention held in Jena that year. The majority of Zionists in Germany always backed the moderate and pro-British political line adopted by Dr. Weizmann and his associates, and were among his stanchest supporters in the major controversies that occurred during Weizmann's presidency of the WZO. The projected broadening of the *Jewish Agency to include non-Zionists, as propounded by Weizmann, was approved by the

Debatte im Oberhaus

Einzelnummer 0,25 Goldmark

JÜDISCHE RUNDSCHAU

Erscheint jeden Dienstag u. Freitag. Bezugspreis bei der Expedition monatlich 2,— Goldmark, vierteljährlich 5,75 Goldmark. Auslandsabonnements werden in der Währung der einzelnen Länder berechnet. Anzeigenpreis: 8 geep. Nonpareillezeile 0,50 G. M. Stellengesuche 0,25 G. M.	Redaktion, Verlag und Anzeigen - Verwaltung: Jüdische Rundschau G m b H., Berlin W15, Meinekestr. 10. Telefon: J 1 Bismarck 7165-70. Anzeigenschluß Dienstag und Freitag nachmittags 4 Uhr Redaktionsschluß Sonntag und Mittwoch nachmittag.	Postscheck - Konten: Berlin 173 92, Basel V 9355, Belgrad 680 32, Brüssel 394 33, Budapest 596 93, Danzig 1973, Haag 140 470, P-ag 594 10, Riga 4155, Straßburg 164 30, Warschau 190 708, Wien 156 030 Bank Konten: Dresdener Bank, Depositen Kasse Berlin, Kurfürstendamm 52, Rumänische Kreditbank, Cernauti (Rumänien); Anglo Palestine Co. in Haifa, Jerusalem, Tel-Aviv
Nummer 27	**Berlin, 4. IV. 1933**	ח' ניסן תרצ"ג	**XXXVIII. Jahrg.**

Der Zionismus erstrebt für das jüdische Volk die Schaffung einer öffentlich-rechtlich gesicherten Heimstätte in Palästina. „Baseler Programm.“

Tragt ihn mit Stolz, den gelben Fleck!

Der 1. April 1933 wird ein wichtiger Tag in der Geschichte der deutschen Juden, ja in der Geschichte des ganzen jüdischen Volkes bleiben. Die Ereignisse dieses Tages haben nicht nur eine politische und eine wirtschaftliche, sondern auch eine moralische und seelische

ist eine nationale Frage, und um sie zu lösen, müssen wir sie vor allem zu einer politischen Weltfrage machen, die im Rate der Kulturvölker zu regeln sein wird."

Man müßte Seite um Seite dieser 1897 erschienenen Schrift abschreiben, um zu zeigen Theodor Herzl war

gedacht. Wir nehmen sie auf, und wollen daraus ein Ehrenzeichen machen.

Viele Juden hatten am Sonnabend ein schweres Erlebnis. Nicht aus innerem Bekenntnis, nicht aus Treue zur eigenen Gemeinschaft, nicht aus Stolz auf eine

Headline in the Jüdische Rundschau, *Apr. 4, 1933: "Wear the Yellow Badge with Pride."* [YIVO Institute for Jewish Research]

majority of German Zionists, for they themselves had found it expedient to work with non-Zionists in behalf of Keren HaYesod.

Despite internal disagreements, the ZVFD remained, by and large, an overall roof organization for Zionist activity in Germany. It included also the Orthodox Mizrahi movement.

The Revisionist movement (*see* REVISIONISTS) was started by Vladimir *Jabotinsky in Berlin in 1923, and its leaders soon included Georg Kareski and Georg Lichtheim. The secession of the Revisionists from the WZO in 1935 had no marked repercussions. The Po'ale Zion, led by Alfred Berger, also stayed out of the ZVFD but maintained close relations with the latter.

In addition to those already mentioned, Zionist leaders in the 1920s and 1930s included Georg Gerson, Nahum *Goldmann, George Joseph *Herlitz, Sally Hirsch, Gustav Krojanker, Hermann Lelever (president of Maccabi), Martin *Rosenblüth, and Moshe Smoira. Several active Zionists held public office in the Weimar Republic; Herman Badt was a ministry executive (*Ministerialdirektor*), and Hans *Goslar was press chief in the Prussian government. The German Zionists, by reason of their talent for organization, their intellectual attainments, and competent leadership, not only were an important political and moral factor in German Jewry but exerted considerable influence on the WZO.

From 1933 to 1938. On Jan. 30, 1933, Adolf Hitler became Chancellor of Germany. The assimilationists were soon disabused of their illusion that only "suspicious characters" would suffer at the hands of the Nazis and that eventually German Jewry as a whole would find a way of coexisting with the new regime. On Apr. 1, 1933, Joseph Goebbels, the Minister of Propaganda, announced a countrywide boycott of Jewish business firms and professional services. The boycott was the occasion for an article by Robert Weltsch in the *Jüdische Rundschau* of Apr. 4, 1933, under the headline "Wear the Yellow Badge with Pride," calling on German Jewry to bear its fate with dignity and to work for the cause of Jewish nationhood and the future of the Jewish people in Palestine. A few days before, Hermann Goering, as Minister of the Interior,

had ordered the Jewish organizations of Germany to act to scotch the "atrocity stories" being circulated abroad about Nazi anti-Semitic excesses. A delegation of three—two Zionists (Richard Lichtheim and Martin Rosenblüth) and one representative of the Centralverein (Ludwig Tietz)—was dispatched to London for this purpose. The three men succeeded in communicating the true state of affairs without being found out by the Nazis.

In its early days the Nazi regime considered mass emigration rather than mass murder the most effective way of rendering Germany *judenrein* and hence tended to tolerate the Zionist Organization as a movement promoting Jewish emigration. A great many Zionists, including Kurt Blumenfeld, soon left for Palestine. The ZVFD centered its efforts on preparing its members, particularly the young, for 'Aliya and vocational readjustment in Palestine. Important work along these lines was done by Georg Landauer, organizer and head of the Palestine Office of the ZVFD, who became Arthur Ruppin's chief coworker in the German section of the Jewish Agency. He cooperated closely with Henrietta *Szold in *Youth 'Aliya, which had first been proposed by Mrs. Recha *Freier, the wife of a Berlin rabbi. The *Ha'avara project was set up for the transfer of German-Jewish assets to Palestine. Despite the risks involved, the Zionist leaders still remaining in Germany maintained their contacts with the World Zionist movement and other international Jewish organizations. A delegation of German Zionists attended the 19th Zionist Congress (Lucerne, 1935).

Martin Buber and Ernst *Simon helped actively in the development of Jewish schools and adult education programs after the Jews were barred from German cultural and educational facilities. In the fall of 1933, the Zionists and the Centralverein joined to form the Reichsvertretung der Deutschen Juden (National Representative Council of German Jews) to defend the interests of all the Jews of Germany, regardless of party affiliation. Rabbi Leo Baeck was chairman of the Executive Board, and Siegfried *Moses, who had succeeded Blumenfeld as president of the ZVFD, was vice-president. Among the other Zionist members of the Reichsvertretung was Rabbi Jacob

*Hoffman, a leader in the Mizrahi movement. Zionists were prominent also in the Zentralausschuss für Hilfe und Aufbau (Central Committee for Help and Reconstruction), which, founded in 1933 and incorporated in the Reichsvertretung in 1935, dealt with the social, economic, and emigration problems of German Jewry.

By 1937 the situation of the Jews in Germany had deteriorated to such an extent that only delegates (and no visitors) were permitted to leave Germany to attend the 20th Zionist Congress in Zurich. The pogroms of November, 1938, put an end to organized Zionist activity in Germany. That month, the Gestapo occupied Zionist headquarters. The Palestine Office was incorporated in the Reichsvereinigung für Auswanderung und Fürsorge der Juden (Reich Union for Jewish Emigration and Welfare), which had taken the place of the Reichsvertretung. By the outbreak of World War II, about 60,000 German Jews had succeeded in reaching Palestine. But a substantial number of Zionist workers refused to leave Germany as long as any Jews were left there, and some gave their lives for the rescue of their fellow Jews.

From 1945 to 1967. At the end of World War II there were in Germany 188,000 Jews, more than 170,000 of whom were inmates of concentration camps. The majority of them were not German Jews but Jews from German-occupied territories in Eastern Europe. During the period immediately following the war, two main centers for Zionist activities developed in Germany: one in the British occupation zone at Bergen-Belsen and the second in the American occupation zone in Munich. Beginning in 1945 many displaced persons emigrated to Israel, either legally or as illegal immigrants (*see* ILLEGAL IMMIGRATION). Then came the mobilization period when young Jews went to Israel to take part in the struggle for the Jewish State. After the creation of the State legal emigration of displaced persons began. Between July, 1947, and the end of 1950, a total of 120,766 Jews emigrated via Germany to Israel.

When the displaced-persons camps closed, no further basis for Zionist activities seemed to exist in Germany. Late in 1949 the Executive of the World Zionist Organization decided to discontinue all organizational activities in Germany. In July, 1954, however, leaders of the Jewish communities in Germany met at Düsseldorf and reestablished the Zionist Organization of Germany. The keynote address at this meeting was delivered by Hayim *Yahil, Deputy Chairman of the Israeli mission in Germany. This was followed in the next month by the founding of a chapter of the Zionist Organization in West Berlin. Within a year chapters were established also in Frankfurt on the Main, Cologne, Stuttgart, Munich, Hannover, Hamburg, and Regensburg. In March, 1955, the first United Israel Campaign in Germany was launched. The Keren HaYesod and Jewish National Fund resumed their fund-raising activities. The former raised over $80,000, held its first conference in Düsseldorf in November, 1955, and established headquarters in Frankfurt. In March, 1956, the Zionist Organization of Germany held its first nationwide gathering in Cologne. That year, 6,996 Sh'kalim were sold in 128 German cities for the 24th Zionist Congress, to which Karl Marx of Düsseldorf and Heinz Galinski and Carl Busch of Berlin were elected delegates.

In 1956–57 the Magbit campaign raised over $125,000, and the Jewish National Fund extended its activities. The birthdays of Herzl and Hayim Nahman *Bialik were observed, as was Israel *Independence Day. In 1958 the Friends of the *Hebrew University of Jerusalem established a German branch with local chapters in Berlin, Hamburg, Düsseldorf, and Munich. Its national conference was held in Frankfurt in March of that year. An impressive public celebration of Israel's 10th anniversary took place on May 16, 1958, in the Parliament of North Rhine–Westphalia at Düsseldorf, which was attended by many high German officials.

In 1960 new Zionist groups were founded in Nürnberg and Straubing, a German section of the *Women's International Zionist Organization (WIZO) was set up, a Zionist Club was inaugurated in Frankfurt, and a number of German-Jewish youngsters went to Israel, while others attended a Zionist pioneer camp in Neuberg, Austria. The 100th anniversary of the birth of Herzl was celebrated in all the Jewish communities of West Germany. That year West German Jews raised sizable sums for the Keren HaYesod, the Jewish National Fund, and Youth 'Aliya, amounting to a total of approximately $190,000. The membership of the Zionist Organization reached 1,000 (of a total of only 24,000 Jews registered with Jewish communities in West Germany). In the years that followed, the collections increased to $200,000 and membership to 1,200.

In East Germany, under Communist rule, no Zionist activity was permitted.   K. GROSSMANN

GERSON-KIWI, EDITH (Esther). Israeli musicologist (b. Berlin, 1908). Receiving her doctorate from the University of Heidelberg in 1933, she settled in Jerusalem in 1935. She taught musicology and the history of music at the Tel Aviv Music Teachers College and at the Rubin Academy of Music in Jerusalem. Beginning in 1950, she was in charge of the phonographic archives of Jewish and Oriental music at the *Hebrew University of Jerusalem. A member of the Board of Directors of the International Musicological Society, she was a guest lecturer in various European countries and in the United States and contributed to musicological journals and encyclopedias, especially on the music of the Oriental Jewish communities and on problems of comparative musicology.

GESHER. Village (kibbutz) in the Jordan Valley. Founded in 1939 and affiliated with the *Kibbutz M'uhad. During the *War of Independence, the settlement withstood heavy attacks by Iraqi troops, but most of its buildings were destroyed. Population (1968): 355.

GESHER B'NOT YA'AKOV. Bridge over the Jordan River in Upper Galilee and frontier outpost between Israel and Syria. It derives its name from an Arab legend according to which

A view of Gesher in 1952. [Zionist Archives]

A view of the kibbutz Gesher HaZiv. [Israel Information Services]

this was the site where the daughters of Jacob (B'not Ya'akov) crossed into the country. For centuries the bridge, a link in the highway leading from Galilee to Damascus, was a busy thoroughfare and, because of its strategic importance, the site of many battles. In 1918 heavy fighting took place here between the advancing British forces and the retreating Turks. With the defeat of the latter, the road to Damascus was opened to the British.

In July, 1946, *Hagana, as part of a countrywide action of sabotage against bridges linking Palestine with neighboring countries, blew up the bridge. In the *War of Independence the Syrians used the bridge to enter the country and occupy Mishmar HaYarden, but they later withdrew in accordance with the Israel-Syria armistice agreement (*see* ARMISTICE AGREEMENTS).

GESHER HAZIV. Village (kibbutz) in western Upper Galilee. Founded in 1949 and named for a nearby bridge dynamited by the *Hagana in June, 1946, during which action 14 members of Hagana lost their lives. The settlement was established by former members of the kibbutz Bet 'Arava north of the Dead Sea, which was abandoned during the *War of Independence and subsequently destroyed by the Transjordan Arab Legion. The village is affiliated with the *Ihud HaK'vutzot V'haKibbutzim. Population (1968): 328.

GEULA. *See* G'ULA.

GEVA'. Village (kibbutz) in the Jezreel Valley. Founded in 1921 and affiliated with the *Ihud HaK'vutzot V'haKibbutzim. Population (1968): 510.

GEVA' KARMEL. Village (moshav) on the Carmel coast. Founded in 1949 by North African immigrants and affiliated with *T'nu'at HaMoshavim. Population (1968): 430.

GEVAT. *See* G'VAT.

GEVERKSHAFTEN CAMPAIGN. *See* HISTADRUT CAMPAIGN.

GEVIM. Village (kibbutz) in the Darom. Founded in 1947 and affiliated with the *Ihud HaK'vutzot V'haKibbutzim. Population (1968): 179.

GEZER. Village (kibbutz) southeast of Ramle. Established in 1945 and affiliated with the *Ihud HaK'vutzot V'haKibbutzim. Population (1968): 49.

Gezer was first inhabited by cave dwellers in the Chalcolithic period; the rough wall on top of the mound is their work. The city itself began in the early Bronze period, when the caves were converted into burial places and a "high place" with steles was erected. In the middle Bronze period an inner wall was added, and a tunnel dug to reach a spring at the foot of the mound. In the late Bronze period the city prospered, as evidenced by Egyptian and Aegean influences. When King Solomon took possession of Gezer, a new wall with a fortified gate was built. From the Israelite age dates the famous Gezer Calendar, a limestone tablet with a list of agricultural activities arranged by months. After the fall of Judea (586 B.C.E.) Gezer continued to exist, as shown by cuneiform contracts remaining from the Assyrian and Neo-Babylonian periods. In Hellenistic times Gezer was a Seleucid stronghold until Simon the Hasmonean captured it and built a palace and a fortress.

GHETTO FIGHTERS. *See* LOHAME HAGETA'OT.

GIBTON. Village (moshav) in the Darom. Founded in 1933. Population (1968): 170.

GID'ONA. Village (moshav) in the Jezreel Valley. Founded in 1949 and named for Gideon, Judge of Israel (Judges 6–8), who assembled his soldiers not far from there before going to war against the Midianites. Population (1968): 139.

GIL'ADI, ISRAEL. Early Palestinian pioneer (b. Kalarash, Bessarabia, Russia, 1886; d. Tiberias, 1918). Gil'adi went to Palestine in 1905 and worked as a farmhand. He helped found *HaShomer (1907), the Jewish guardsmen's organization, and

Mount Gilboa. [Israel Information Services]

was one of its leaders and officers. Gil'adi bore the brunt of HaShomer's problems in 1917–18, when it was persecuted by the Turkish military authorities. He planned and organized the founding in Upper Galilee of the HaShomer settlement K'far Gil'adi, which bears his name.

GILAT. Village (moshav) in the northern Negev. Founded in 1949 and affiliated with *T'nu'at HaMoshavim. The name is derived from Isaiah 35:2. Population (1968): 555.

GILBERT, JENNIE Z. Zionist leader and communal worker in Ireland. Successively honorary secretary, vice-president, and chairman of *Tora va'Avoda (Religion and Labor), she was president of the Mizrahi Federation of Ireland (*see* MIZRAHI), vice-president of the Mizrahi Women's Organization of Great Britain and Ireland, chairman of the Shekel Board of Ireland (*see* SHEKEL), and honorary secretary of the Hebrew Speakers' Circle. In 1960–61 she served as a delegate from Ireland to the 25th Zionist *Congress.

GILBOA, MOUNT. Northeastern spur of the Samaria Mountains, forming a limestone plateau that reaches elevations of approximately 1,500 feet. While the top of the plateau is almost level, it descends steeply to the north and east into the Harod and Bet Sh'an Valleys, which lie several hundred feet below sea level. Numerous springs at the foot of Mount Gilboa provide water for irrigation of the valleys. The boundary between Israel and Jordan runs along the top near the edge. Although the Jordanian part, which is level, is densely settled, there are only two Israeli border settlements on the crest.

Y. KARMON

GIMZO. Village (moshav) southeast of Lod. Founded in 1950 and affiliated with the *Po'ale Agudat Israel. The village is named for Gimzo, which is mentioned in the Bible and the Talmud and is believed to have been situated on the site.

GINNATON. Village (moshav) east of Lod. Founded in 1949 by immigrants from Bulgaria and affiliated with *T'nu'at HaMoshavim. Population (1968): 244.

GINNEGAR. Village (kibbutz) in the Jezreel Valley. Founded in 1922 and affiliated with the *Ihud HaK'vutzot V'haKibbutzim. Population (1968): 400.

GINNOSAR. Village (kibbutz) on Lake Kinneret. Founded in 1937 and affiliated with the *Kibbutz M'uhad. Population (1968): 427.

GINSBOURG, BENJAMIN. Physician and Zionist leader in France (b. Valensole, Department of the Basses-Alpes, France, 1897). In 1927 Benjamin Ginsbourg settled in Reims, where he was *Jewish National Fund commissioner until 1937. After World War II he founded the first Jewish physicians' association in France, whose program consisted of mutual aid, pro-Israel work, and combating *anti-Semitism. He became secretary-general of the organization and was editor in chief of a medical journal.

In 1954, with André Blumel, a lawyer, and Henri Bulovka, Ginsbourg founded a left-wing pro-Israel organization under the name Cercle Bernard *Lazare, which was closely linked with *Mapam ideologically but had no official ties with the party. It was, however, closely linked with the left-wing United Socialist party of France. Ginsbourg himself was a member of Mapam, representing the movement at various Zionist gatherings in France.　　　　　　　　　　　　　　　　S. KLINGER

GINZBERG, ASHER ZVI. See AHAD HA'AM.

GIV'AT. Hebrew word, meaning "hill of," that frequently appears as the first part of a compound place name in Israel, as in Giv'at Brenner (Hill of Brenner).

GIV'AT 'ADA. Village in the Hadera area. Founded in 1903. Named for Adélaïde, wife of Baron Edmond de *Rothschild. The settlement expanded greatly in 1952 and 1953 through the absorption of new immigrants. Population (1968): 1,330.

GIV'ATAYIM. Town between Tel Aviv and Ramat Gan. It was formed by the amalgamation of several suburbs, the oldest of which was Sh'khunat Borokhov, founded in 1922. Population (1968): 40,900.

GIV'AT BRENNER. Village (kibbutz) in the Darom. Founded in 1928 and named for Yoseph Hayim *Brenner. Affiliated with the *Kibbutz M'uhad. It is one of the largest settlements, with an economy based on agriculture and industrial enterprises. It maintains one of the larger rest houses in the country. Population (1968): 1,520.

GIV'AT HASH'LOSHA. Village (kibbutz) in the Petah Tikva region. Founded in 1925 and affiliated with the *Kibbutz M'uhad. Population (1968): 510.

GIV'AT HAVIVA. Educational institution of the *Kibbutz Artzi Shel HaShomer HaTza'ir and *HaShomer HaTza'ir, at the foot of the Samaria Mountains. Founded in 1951 and named

The industrial quarter of Giv'at Brenner. [Zionist Archives]

A view of Giv'at Hayim A and Giv'at Hayim B. [Zionist Archives]

for Haviva Reik, the parachutist who, during World War II, was dropped into Czechoslovakia, captured by the Germans, and executed (see PARACHUTISTS, PALESTINIAN JEWISH). An institute for the training of youth leaders, a social research center, and the Institute for Jewish-Arab Studies form parts of Giv'at Haviva.

GIV'AT HAYIM A. Village (kibbutz) in the Sharon Plain. Founded in 1932 and named for Hayim Victor *Arlosoroff. Affiliated with the *Kibbutz M'uhad. Population (1968): 705.

GIV'AT HAYIM B. Village (kibbutz) in the Sharon Plain. Established in 1952 near Giv'at Hayim A after the original settlement split. Affiliated with the *Ihud HaK'vutzot V'haKibbutzim. Population (1968): 690.

GIV'AT HEN. Village (moshav) in the Sharon Plain. Settled in 1933 and named for Hayim Nahman (HeN) *Bialik. Affiliated with *T'nu'at HaMoshavim. Population (1968): 232.

GIV'ATI. Village (moshav) in the Darom. Founded in 1950 and affiliated with *T'nu'at HaMoshavim. Population (1968): 345.

GIV'AT KOAH. Village (moshav) in the Petah Tikva region, near the foothills of the Judean Mountains. Founded in 1950 and affiliated with *T'nu'at HaMoshavim. The village is named in memory of 28 (numerical value of the Hebrew letters in "Koah") members of the *Israel Defense Forces who fell in this sector during the *War of Independence. Population (1968): 371.

GIV'AT NILI. Village (moshav) in Samaria. Founded in 1953 and named for the *Nili organization. Affiliated with *Herut. Population (1968): 208.

GIV'AT 'OZ. Village (kibbutz) in the Jezreel Valley. Founded in 1949 and affiliated with the *Kibbutz Artzi Shel HaShomer HaTza'ir.

GIV'AT SHAPIRA. Village (moshav) in the Sharon Plain. Founded in 1958 and named for Hermann *Schapira. Affiliated with the *Hitahdut HaIkkarim. Population (1968): 107.

GIV'AT SH'MUEL. Township south of B'ne B'rak. Founded in 1942 and named for Samuel *Pineles. Population (1968): 4,470.

GIV'AT Y'ARIM. Village (moshav) in the Jerusalem Mountains. Founded in 1950 and affiliated with *T'nu'at HaMoshavim. Population (1968): 500.

GIV'AT Y'SHA'YAHU. Village (moshav) in the Judean Plain. Founded in 1958 and named for Y'sha'yahu *Press. Affiliated with Ha'Oved HaTziyoni. Population (1968): 127.

GIV'OLIM. Village (moshav) in the northern Negev. Founded in 1952 and affiliated with HaPo'el HaMizrahi (*see* MIZRAHI). Population (1968): 207.

GIV'OT ZEID. Village in the Jezreel Valley. Founded in 1943 and named for Alexander Zeid, a member of *HaShomer, who was killed in this locality in 1938. Population (1968): 90.

GLASS, CIRO. Lawyer and Zionist leader in Italy (b. Fiume, Hungary, 1901; d. Palermo, Italy, 1928). After moving to Florence in 1919, he began to take an interest in Jewish life and Zionism and soon became a moving spirit in Jewish life, exercising a growing influence on the youth of Florence, then the center of Jewish life in Italy. From 1924 on, he was successively president of the Italian *Jewish National Fund, the Italian *Keren HaYesod (Palestine Foundation Fund), and the Italian Zionist Federation. He founded and directed Casa Editrice Israel, a publishing enterprise.

G. ROMANO

GLICKSON, MOSHE YOSEPH. Journalist and editor of *Ha'Aretz* (b. Golynka, Russia, 1878; d. Tel Aviv, 1939). Glickson received a Yeshiva and a university education and was active in the student Zionist movement, opposing acceptance of the *East Africa scheme. From 1907 to 1911 he served on the Secretariat of the *Hoveve Zion movement in Odessa and after 1912 on the editorial board of *Ha'Olam*. In 1917 he moved to Moscow, where he edited the Hebrew weekly *Ha'Am* (later a daily). After the collapse of the Tsarist regime, he edited, in Hebrew, the first uncensored publications of the Zionist movement in Russia (*'Olamenu* and *Massu'ot*, 1917).

In 1919 he settled in Palestine, where he wrote for various

newspapers. From 1922 to 1937 he was editor of the liberal democratic daily *Ha'Aretz*. The ideologist of the General Zionist party (*see* GENERAL ZIONISM) and of the youth group *HaNo'ar HaTziyoni, he occupied an eminent centrist position in the *Yishuv (Jewish population of Palestine). Glickson wrote a book on *Ahad Ha'Am (1927) and translated various works of German philosophy into Hebrew. Anthologies of his articles appeared in 1939 and 1963.

G. KRESSEL

G'LIL YAM. Village (kibbutz) in the Sharon Plain. Founded in 1943 and affiliated with the *Kibbutz M'uhad. Population (1968): 310.

GLITZENSTEIN, HENRY. *See* GLYCENSTEIN, HENRYK.

GLUSKIN, Z'EV. Director of economic and colonizing institutions of the Hibbat Zion (b. Slutsk, Russia, 1859; d. Tel Aviv, 1949). In 1881, after spending his early youth in business, Gluskin settled in Warsaw, where he became active in the Hibbat Zion (Love of Zion) movement (*see* HOVEVE ZION) and headed the secret order *B'ne Moshe (Sons of Moses). He helped organize the M'nuha V'Nahala settlement society, which built the village of Rehovot, and *Ahiasaph, a publishing company for Hebrew and Yiddish books of Zionist content. He also organized the Carmel Mizrahi Company and, after settling in Palestine in 1906, served as a director of the *G'ula land purchase society, the Winegrowers' Association, and various other economic and colonizing institutions. Glushkin's *Memoirs* (in Hebrew) were published in 1946.

G. KRESSEL

GLYCENSTEIN, HENRYK (Henry Glitzenstein). Sculptor and Zionist (b. Turek, Russian Poland, 1870; d. New York, 1942). Educated at Yeshivot in Poland, he began to sculpt while still a youth in Łódź. With the backing of Samuel Hirszenberg, the noted Jewish painter, who was then living in Łódź, he went to study at the Academy of Art in Munich, where he soon received awards and aroused the interest of the art world. He then won a scholarship from the Berlin Academy of Art, which enabled him to continue his studies in Italy. Glycenstein's works include "Messiah," "Destiny," "Cain and Abel," "Wanderer," and "Nostalgia for the Homeland." His entire artistic output expressed in plastic form the Zionist aspiration of the Jewish people. The Glycenstein Museum, which was opened in Safed in 1952, was named for him.

A. ALPERIN

GOLAN HEIGHTS. *See* GAULAN HEIGHTS.

GOLD, Z'EV (Wolf). Rabbi, lecturer, and *Mizrahi leader (b. Szczuczyn, Russian Poland, 1889; d. Jerusalem, 1956). Arriving in the United States in 1907 shortly after receiving S'mikha (traditional rabbinic ordination), he served as rabbi in various American communities, in which he organized Jewish schools and community institutions. A founder of the Union of Orthodox Rabbis in the United States, Gold helped arrange the first Mizrahi convention in 1914 and traveled extensively to establish groups and raise funds. In 1924 he settled in Palestine, where he served as a "circuit-riding" rabbi for scattered settlements. He returned to the United States to serve as president of Mizrahi from 1931 to 1934 and then, in 1935,

Giv'ot Zeid in 1954. [Zionist Archives]

went back to Palestine to head the organization's World Center. In 1940 he realized an old dream, the establishment of an agricultural Yeshiva in K'far HaRo'e.

During World War II Gold lived in the United States. In 1946 he became a member of the Executive of the *Jewish Agency. He was a member of the Jewish delegation to the United Nations in 1947 and advocated the establishment of a Jewish State before the Foreign Affairs Committee of the U.S. House of Representatives. A member of the Provisional Council of State when the State of Israel was created, he briefly headed the Jerusalem Development Committee of the Jewish Agency and in 1951 became chairman of its Department of Religious Education and Culture in the Diaspora. In 1955 he was elected president of the Mizrahi–HaPo'el HaMizrahi World Movement.

G. BAT-YEHUDA

GOLDBERG, ABRAHAM. Hebrew and Yiddish journalist and Zionist leader (b. Brest Litovsk, Russia, 1881; d. Warsaw, 1934). Goldberg began his literary career in 1901 in the Hebrew newspapers *HaTz'fira, HaMelitz, and HaTzofe. In 1906 he became one of the editors of the Yiddish daily newspaper Dos Tagblat and later of Hajnt, both published in Warsaw. He was editor in chief of Hajnt for many years after World War I, remaining on the staff of this leading Zionist Yiddish newspaper until his death. One of the principal spokesmen and proponents of the Zionist cause in Poland, Goldberg was cofounder of the group of Radical General Zionists (see RADICAL ZIONISTS) in Poland, whom he represented at several Zionist Congresses (see CONGRESS, ZIONIST).

A. ALPERIN

GOLDBERG, ABRAHAM. Zionist leader and writer (b. Yarmolintsy, Russia, 1883; d. New York, 1942). Goldberg received a traditional Jewish education. While still a youngster he founded a Zionist youth group in his birthplace and later was active in Zionist affairs in Berdichev, where he taught Hebrew. Settling in the United States at the age of 18, he worked in a garment factory in New York and became active in the trade union movement. In 1903 he helped found the first *Po'ale Zion group in the United States. A supporter of the *East Africa scheme, he was prominently associated with the Socialist-Territorialists (see JEWISH TERRITORIAL ORGANIZATION) but soon returned to the Zionist fold. In 1908 he became a member of the governing board of the Federation of American Zionists. He also assumed the editorship of the Zionist Yiddish weekly Dos Yidishe Folk. In 1911 he helped found the *B'nai Zion fraternal order, serving as its first secretary.

During World War I Goldberg helped organize relief projects for European Jewry, participated in the founding of the *American Jewish Congress, and was active in organizing the American *Jewish Legion. After the war he became a member of the Political Committee of the *Zionist Organization of America. He played a significant role, together with Louis *Lipsky, in the controversy between the Brandeisists and the supporters of Chaim *Weizmann's policies in 1921, and in the presentation and passage of the 1922 joint resolution of the U.S. Congress favoring "the establishment in Palestine of a National Home for the Jews" (see LODGE-FISH RESOLUTION).

A spokesman for American Zionism at Zionist Congresses (see CONGRESS, ZIONIST), Goldberg was the most popular Zionist propagandist of his day and served for many years as a member of the Zionist *Actions ,Committee. He served as Chaim

*Weizmann's emissary, traveling to various Jewish communities to explain the idea of the enlarged *Jewish Agency, and in 1937 became a member of its Administrative Committee. He was also a leader of the Hebrew-language movement in the United States.

An author of note, Goldberg contributed articles to Yiddish newspapers and periodicals and also to Hebrew and English publications. Collections of his Hebrew and Yiddish writings were published in book form. His Pioneers and Builders (biographical studies and essays) was published after his death, in 1943.

GOLDBERG, BORIS (Dov). Industrialist and writer (b. Šakiai, Suwałki District, Russian Poland, 1866; d. Tel Aviv, 1922). He was the youngest brother of Itzhak Leib *Goldberg. After studying at German universities and graduating as a chemical engineer, he settled in Vilna and established a factory there.

A Hovev Zion (see HOVEVE ZION) from his youth, Goldberg became an early adherent of Zionism. He was a founder of the Central Committee of Russian Zionists (1905) and opened the conferences of Russian Zionists in Helsingfors (1906), The Hague (1907), and Hamburg (1909). Goldberg was among the early advocates of practical work in Palestine (see PRACTICAL ZIONISM) and at the 8th Zionist *Congress (The Hague, 1907) was elected to the Greater *Actions Committee, on which he served for many years. He was prominently associated with Zionist periodicals, serving as a member of the editorial board of *Ha'Olam, and wrote on Jewish problems and on Zionism.

During World War I Goldberg traveled on Jewish and Zionist missions to Copenhagen, London, and the United States. After the Russian Revolution, he was chosen chairman of the Palestine Committee of the Central Committee of Russian Zionists and was among the leaders in convening an All-Russia Jewish Congress. In 1919 he represented Russian Jewry on the *Comité des Délégations Juives to the Paris Peace Conference. In 1920 he became director of the Department of Trade and Industry of the Zionist *Executive in London and participated in the founding of the *Keren HaYesod (Palestine Foundation Fund). The following year he settled in Tel Aviv, where he established the Silicat brick factory. Wounded in Jaffa during the *Arab riots of May, 1921, he went to Berlin for treatment but died shortly after his return to Palestine. His will instructed his family to give a tithe of his estate to the *Jewish National Fund.

A. ALPERIN

GOLDBERG, ISRAEL. See LEARSI, RUFUS.

GOLDBERG, ITZHAK LEIB. Citrus grove owner in Palestine, supporter of Hebrew literature, and Zionist leader (b. Šakiai, Suwałki District, Russian Poland, 1860; d. Switzerland, 1935). He joined the *Hoveve Zion movement in his early youth and organized the *Druskenik Conference in 1887. Goldberg participated in the 1st Zionist *Congress in Basle in 1897 and became a cofounder of the Russian Zionist Organization. He was one of the first large contributors to the *Jewish National Fund and other Zionist funds, backed the establishment of Hebrew publishing houses, and financed the publication of *Ha'Olam, the central Hebrew organ of the *World Zionist Organization in Vilna. In 1916 he bought land on Mount Scopus and donated it to the Jewish National Fund for the campus of the *Hebrew University of Jerusalem.

In 1918 Goldberg left Russia, and in 1920 he settled in Palestine. There he established many industrial and agricultural enterprises and founded the Hebrew daily *Ha'Aretz, which he supported for many years. His son, Binyamin Z'ev Goldberg, named for Theodor (Binyamin Z'ev) Herzl, was murdered while defending the *Yishuv (Jewish population of Palestine) in the *Arab riots of 1929. Goldberg memorialized his murdered son by establishing in Tel Aviv a cultural center and a city park named for him. He willed half of his estate to the Jewish National Fund for the founding of cultural institutions and for other cultural purposes.

A. ALPERIN

GOLDBLOOM, JACOB KOPPEL. Hebrew teacher and Zionist leader (b. Kletsk, Minsk District, Russia, 1872; d. London, 1961). An adherent of the *Hoveve Zion movement from his early youth, he continued to serve the movement after his arrival in London in 1892. After meeting Herzl in 1896, he became a political Zionist and began to organize Zionist societies in Whitechapel, the ghetto in London's East End. An eloquent orator, he brought the message of Zionism to large numbers of Jews and participated in the founding of the English Zionist Federation (later, Zionist Federation of Great Britain and Ireland). He was vice-president of the federation in 1916–17 and president from 1920 to 1940. From 1940 to 1945 he was executive director of the *Jewish National Fund in Canada.

Goldbloom attended every Zionist *Congress from 1900 until the end of his life and was a member of the Presidium of several Congresses and of the Zionist *Actions Committee. From 1936 to 1938 he was chairman of the *World Confederation of General Zionists.

A Hebrew teacher by profession, Goldbloom founded (1901) in London a Talmud Tora where the language of instruction was exclusively Hebrew. He was chairman of the British branch of the *B'rit 'Ivrit 'Olamit (World Hebrew Federation) and was prominently affiliated with Zionist and Hebraist educational enterprises.

J. FRAENKEL

GOLDMAN, SOLOMON. Rabbi, Hebrew scholar, and Zionist leader in the United States (b. Kozin, Ukraine, Russia, 1893; d. Chicago, 1953). Brought to the United States by his parents

Solomon Goldman.
[Zionist Archives]

at the age of seven, he received a traditional Jewish education at the Rabbi Isaac Elchanan Theological Seminary in New York and later studied at the Jewish Theological Seminary of America and Columbia University. After his ordination, he served congregations in New York, Cleveland, and Chicago.

Goldman became prominent in Jewish life as well as in the public life of the larger community of Chicago. His major activity was the propagation of Jewish education and culture in various strata of the Jewish population by his writing and lectures. He became a leader in numerous Zionist and general Jewish organizations. After holding a number of offices in the *Zionist Organization of America (ZOA), he served as its president from 1938 to 1940. He headed the ZOA delegation at the 21st Zionist *Congress in Geneva in 1939. Goldman published many books on Judaica, Zionist problems, and Jewish and Hebrew literature.

See also CONSERVATIVE JUDAISM AND ZIONISM.

A. ALPERIN

GOLDMANN, NAHUM. President of the *World Jewish Congress and former president of the *World Zionist Organization (b. Vishnovo, Russia, 1894). He was raised in Frankfurt on the Main, where the home of his parents was the meeting place of leading Zionists and journalists. At the age of 15, Goldmann started to publish articles under the pen name Ben-Koheleth and to make speeches at Zionist meetings. As a law student at the University of Heidelberg (1912-14), he joined the *Kartell Jüdischer Verbindungen. In 1913 he visited Palestine and presented his impressions in *Eretz Israel—Reise-Briefe aus Palästina* (Letters from Palestine, 1914).

During World War I he headed a desk for Jewish affairs at the Foreign Ministry in Berlin. In his essay "The World Cultural Significance and Task of Judaism" he endeavored to interest Germany in the establishment of a Jewish Homeland in Palestine. He joined with other Zionist leaders in efforts to persuade the German government to intervene in Constantinople to keep the Jewish settlements in Palestine from being harmed.

Returning to his studies in Heidelberg in 1919, he received his doctorate in law in 1920. In 1919 he published a brochure, *The Three Demands of the Jewish People* (namely, the right of the Jews to Palestine, minority rights for Jews in *Diaspora countries, and civic equality for Jews).

In 1920 Goldmann, together with Jacob *Klatzkin, founded in Heidelberg the *Freie Zionistische Blätter*, a magazine independent of party alignments, for the discussion of Zionist ideology. This magazine, which featured articles by such authors as Moshe *Beilinson, (Samuel) Hugo *Bergmann, and Arnold Zweig, appeared at irregular intervals during 1921. In 1923 Goldmann moved to Berlin, where he and Klatzkin founded the Eschkol publishing house and began publishing the *Encyclopedia Judaica*, of which 10 volumes in German and 2 in Hebrew appeared before Hitler came to power and publication had to be suspended.

Goldmann attended every Zionist *Congress from 1921 on. At the 13th Congress (Karlovy Vary, 1923) he joined the Radical Zionist faction (*see* RADICAL ZIONISTS). At the 14th Congress (Vienna, 1925) he opposed the enlargement of the *Jewish Agency as suggested by Chaim *Weizmann. He favored an extended Agency with powers limited to problems pertaining to the economic upbuilding of Jewish Palestine and with no jurisdiction in political matters. When the expansion of the Jewish Agency was decided upon in 1929, however, he yielded to the majority and associated himself more closely with the Agency's work. At the 17th Zionist Congress (Basle, 1931) he formulated and presented a resolution of the Political Committee, deploring Weizmann's statement in an interview with the *Jewish Telegraphic Agency that questioned the necessity of ensuring a Jewish majority in the population of Palestine.

In March, 1932, Nahum *Sokolow (who had succeeded Weizmann as president of the WZO) and Goldmann conducted a successful *Keren HaYesod (Palestine Foundation Fund) campaign in the United States. In 1933, a few days before the Gestapo began looking for him, Goldmann left Germany at an urgent call to the sickbed of his father in Tel Aviv, and from there he went to Geneva.

In numerous speeches, in many countries, Goldmann consistently advocated a concept of Zionism as a revolutionary movement, both politically and spiritually. In the United States, Stephen S. *Wise asked Goldmann to prepare the framework of the World Jewish Congress (WJC), which was established in August, 1936, as an overall representation of Jews in all countries organized democratically along pro-Zionist lines for the protection of Jewish civic, political, and religious rights. Goldmann was elected chairman of the Administrative Committee. After the Nazis assumed power, Goldmann and his associates in the Congress embarked on a vigorous program of political and diplomatic activity to call the attention of the democracies to the fate of German Jewry, and also sought to mobilize Jews the world over against the Nazi regime and to organize an effective economic boycott of Nazi Germany.

Goldmann took a leading role in the formulation of the WJC's program of postwar Jewish demands. In 1949 he became acting president, and in 1953 president, of the WJC. After the death of Leo *Motzkin (1933), Goldmann had succeeded him as president of the *Comité des Délégations Juives, which later merged with the WJC.

Between 1935 and 1939 Goldmann served as political representative of the WZO at the League of Nations in Geneva. His new duties involved also the problem of refugees and negotiations with League's High Commissioner for Refugees. At the 1937 Zionist Congress, he advocated the *partition of Palestine in order to attain a "viable Jewish State."

Early in World War II, Goldmann left Europe for America to continue his work and his struggle against Nazi Germany in New York. He acted as representative of the Jewish Agency in Washington, directing its political work. He participated in the formulation of the *Biltmore Program (1942) and was one of the main advocates of the idea of the establishment of a Jewish State in part of Palestine.

At the end of the war he obtained the support of the United States government for the proposal of Jewish statehood in partitioned Palestine. He negotiated for several months with Ernest *Bevin, then the British Foreign Secretary, in an effort to get Great Britain to agree to this program. When the British government handed over the Palestine issue to the United Nations, he negotiated with many governments, including that of the United States, to obtain their support.

After the establishment of the State of Israel, Goldmann stressed the continued importance of the World Zionist Organization, stating that "the view that the Zionist program has been fulfilled by the proclamation of the State is wrong and illusory." In the discussions about the status and future of the World Zionist Organization, he defended it against attacks from various groups, including David *Ben-Gurion and his followers.

In 1949 Goldmann became chairman of the American section of the Jewish Agency Executive and, in 1956, president of the World Zionist Organization and chairman of the Zionist *Executive, serving as president until 1968. His main efforts were directed toward Jewish unity, in accordance with his view that

"the Jewish State cannot exist without world Jewry, and the survival of the Jewish people without the State is even less feasible."

In October, 1951, after consultation with the Israeli government, Goldmann invited a number of Jewish organizations to establish the Conference on Jewish Material Claims against Germany (see GERMAN-ISRAEL AGREEMENT) and later, after Noah *Barou had prepared the ground, established his first contact with German Chancellor Konrad Adenauer in London. The negotiations with Germany, which he conducted, led to the

Nahum Goldmann.
[World Jewish Congress]

agreement signed in Luxembourg between Chancellor Adenauer on behalf of West Germany, Foreign Minister Moshe *Sharett on behalf of Israel, and Goldmann on behalf of the Claims Conference. This agreement was the basis for the payment of $822,000,000 to Israel and of many millions of dollars to individual victims of Nazi persecution, both as indemnification for survivors of the Nazi period and as restitution of lost property. For many years Goldmann conducted negotiations with the West German government concerning further legislation for the benefit of Nazi victims. As president of the Executive Committee on Jewish Claims against Austria (1953), he also conducted negotiations with the Austrian government.

In New York, where he lived until 1964, he established the *Conference of Presidents of Major American Jewish Organizations, for the purpose of taking united action in matters concerning Israel, and from 1954 to 1959 served as chairman of this body. In 1964 he established his main residence in Jerusalem and became a citizen of Israel. That year, after the Memorial Foundation for Jewish Culture had been established at his suggestion, he became president of the foundation.

In the spring of 1970 wide attention was aroused by the report of a possible meeting between Goldmann and Egypt's President Nasser. Considerable controversy was caused by the views expressed by Goldmann on Israel's foreign policy.

Goldmann wrote numerous essays in various languages. Many of his speeches were published, several of them in a Yiddish and Hebrew collection entitled *In the Generation of Destruction and Regeneration* (1964). The first two volumes of his biography were published by Jacob Draenger in 1956 (in French) and 1959 (in German). His autobiography was published in 1969 in New York.

GOLDSMID, ALBERT EDWARD WILLIAMSON. Anglo-Jewish leader and advocate of Jewish *nationalism (b. Poona, India, 1846; d. Paris, 1903). Scion of a noted Jewish family, he returned to the Judaism his parents had abandoned. Brought up in England, he embarked on a military career and rose to the rank of lieutenant colonel and finally to the post of chief of staff of the 6th Division in the Boer War. Goldsmid visited Palestine in 1883 and became a zealous advocate of the renaissance of Hebrew as a living language. He was one of the founders of the *Hoveve Zion movement in England, organizing it along military lines and serving for more than a decade as its "chief."

In 1892 Goldsmid obtained a year's leave of absence from the army and went to Argentina to reorganize Baron Maurice de *Hirsch's agricultural settlements. On his return he resumed leadership in the Jewish community and was among the key persons approached by Herzl when he first introduced political Zionism to the English scene. In 1898 Goldsmid convened the Clerkenwell Conference that led to the establishment of the Zionist Federation of Great Britain and Ireland. Later he participated in the expedition that surveyed the possibilities of an autonomous Jewish settlement in Sinai (see EL-'ARISH SCHEME). The Jewish Lads Brigade, founded by Goldsmid for the physical and spiritual training of British Jewish youth, was still in existence in 1969.

E. LEHMAN

GOLDSTEIN, ALEXANDER. Zionist writer, orator, and propagandist (b. Minsk, Russia, 1884; d. Jerusalem, 1949). He began his literary career and Zionist work while still a student at the University of St. Petersburg. The author of many articles on Zionism and other Jewish subjects, he translated Mordekhai Z'ev Feierberg's Hebrew novels into Russian. Goldstein was a member of the Central Committee of Russian Zionists until the Russian Revolution of 1917, playing a prominent part in all the conferences of the Russian Zionists. He was also active in Russian-Jewish political life and represented the Ukrainian Jews in the *Comité des Délégations Juives at the Paris Peace Conference. One of the organizers of the *Keren HaYesod (Palestine Foundation Fund) in London in 1920, he devoted all his efforts from then on to campaigns for the fund in Jewish communities throughout the world.

A. ALPERIN

GOLDSTEIN, ANGELO. Lawyer and Zionist leader in Czechoslovakia (b. Prague, 1890; d. Tel Aviv, 1947). The son of a rabbi, Goldstein practiced law in Prague and joined the Zionist movement prior to World War I. He rose rapidly in Zionist ranks, serving as an alternate member of the Zionist *Actions Committee, representing the General Zionist party (see GENERAL ZIONISM), from 1931 to 1939. In 1931 he became one of the representatives of his country's Jewish party in the Czechoslovak Parliament, succeeding his friend and mentor, Ludwig *Singer. During his term (he served until 1939), Goldstein sponsored much legislation dealing with Jewish issues and fought against anti-Jewish laws and pro-Nazi members of Parliament. In 1933 he engaged in a fistfight on the floor of Parliament with a German nationalist who had called for a struggle against the Jews and the "Jewish spirit."

Settling in Palestine in 1939, Goldstein opened a law practice in Tel Aviv. During a brief visit to Czechoslovakia in October, 1946, he obtained from Pres. Eduard Beneš a statement reiterating his support of the establishment of a Jewish State in Palestine.

GOLDSTEIN, ISRAEL. Rabbi, author, and Zionist leader in the United States (b. Philadelphia, 1896). An alumnus of the University of Pennsylvania, Columbia University, and the Jewish Theological Seminary of America, he served as rabbi of Congregation B'nai Jeshurun in New York from 1918 to 1960, when he became rabbi emeritus. Active in the Zionist movement from his youth on, Rabbi Goldstein served as pres-

Israel Goldstein.
[Jewish National Fund]

ident of *Young Judaea (1930–33), president of the *Zionist Organization of America (ZOA; 1943–45), honorary president of the *Jewish National Fund (1944——), president of the *World Confederation of General Zionists (1946——), member of the Executive of the *Jewish Agency (1948——), member of the Board of Governors of the *State of Israel Bonds Organization (1951——), and world chairman of the *Keren HaYesod (Palestine Foundation Fund)—United Israel Appeal (1961——). He was chairman of the Western Hemisphere Executive of the *World Jewish Congress from 1949 to 1960 and president of the *American Jewish Congress from 1951 to 1958.

In 1947 Goldstein served as a member of the Political Advisory Committee of the *World Zionist Organization to the Zionist delegation at the United Nations. He was chairman of the Jewish Restitution Successor Organization beginning in 1950 and a member of the Presidium of the Conference on Jewish Material Claims against Germany (see GERMAN-ISRAEL AGREEMENT) beginning in 1951.

Goldstein was one of the founders of Brandeis University in Waltham, Mass., in 1946. He was a member of the Board of Governors of the *Hebrew University of Jerusalem (1950——) and of the *Weizmann Institute of Science and president of *B'rit 'Ivrit 'Olamit (World Hebrew Federation).

From 1961 on Goldstein resided in Israel, where a chair in Zionism and the history of the *Yishuv (Jewish population of Palestine) was established in his name at the Hebrew University. He was the author of several books on the history of the Jews in America and on the problems of Judaism, Zionism, and the State of Israel.

See also CONSERVATIVE JUDAISM AND ZIONISM.

GOLDSTEIN, PERETZ. *See* PARACHUTISTS, PALESTINIAN JEWISH.

GOLOMB, ELIYAHU. One of the founders and leaders of the *Hagana (b. Volkovysk, Russia, 1893; d. Tel Aviv, 1945). Golomb went to Palestine to study at the *Herzliya High School of Tel Aviv, where he was the oldest member of the first graduating class. He urged his fellow graduates to pioneer in land settlement and to become active in the labor movement.

At the outbreak of World War I he was engaged in securing arms for *HaShomer. After the British conquest of Judea (1917), he also was prominent in the campaign for voluntary enlistment in the *Jewish Legion, in which he served from 1918 to 1920. He then continued his work in agriculture and helped found the Hagana, which he headed until his death. During World War II he directed the *illegal immigration movement into Palestine. His articles on defense, which appeared in anthologies in 1950 and 1954, were printed in the labor press. Golomb was a brother-in-law of Moshe *Sharett, Shaul Avigur, and Dov *Hos.

G. KRESSEL

GOLUCHOWSKI, COUNT AGENOR VON. Austrian statesman (b. Lvov, Galicia, Austria, 1849; d. there, 1921). Goluchowski held the position of Minister of Foreign Affairs in the Austro-Hungarian Monarchy from 1895 to 1906, and it was in this capacity that he received Herzl in April, 1904. Herzl described his long conversation with Goluchowski as "an important and perhaps consequential discussion." Goluchowski evinced an earnest interest in Zionism and advised Herzl to work in England for a parliamentary expression of opinion in favor of Palestine as a Jewish Homeland.

GOMBEROFF, LEÓN ITSCOVICH. Lawyer, journalist, and Zionist leader in Chile (b. Buenos Aires, 1908). After his graduation from law school in 1934, Gomberoff founded the León Jaffe Zionist Center and was president of the Jewish Youth Center. He was the director of the weekly *Mundo Judío* (Jewish World) and the founder of the magazine *Nosotros.* Gomberoff served as president of the Zionist Federation of Chile for eight terms. He was a delegate of *Po'ale Zion (*Mapai) to the Zionist Congresses of 1956 and 1960–61 (see CONGRESS, ZIONIST). In 1969 he was advisory director of the Zionist Federation of Chile, vice-president of the Jewish Club, and director of the Jewish bank and national insurance company La Israelita.

GONEN. Village (kibbutz) in eastern Upper Galilee. Founded in 1951 and affiliated with the *Ihud HaK'vutzot V'haKibbutzim.

GOODMAN, PAUL. Historian and author (b. Tartu, Estonia, 1875; d. London, 1949). Goodman served for 50 years as secretary to the London Spanish and Portuguese Congregation. He became a Zionist after he heard Herzl speak in London in 1896. One of the founders of the Zionist Federation of Great Britain and Ireland (see GREAT BRITAIN, ZIONISM IN), he occupied important positions in the British Zionist movement. During World War I he was a member of the Zionist Political Advisory Committee established in London by Chaim *Weizmann and Nahum *Sokolow.

After the formation of the *World Union of General Zionists (1931) Goodman participated in the regular deliberations of that body, and after the establishment of the *World Confederation of General Zionists (1935) he served as honorary treasurer of its European Executive. In 1939 he was a delegate to the *St. James Conference in London.

Goodman was editor of the London *Zionist Review* (1920–26, 1934–38) and of the *Gates of Zion* (1946–49). In addition to shorter tracts on Zionism, he wrote *Zionism in England* (1929; rev. ed., 1949) and edited the volumes *Zionism: Problems and Views* (with Arthur I. Lewis, 1916); *The Jewish National Home*

The kibbutz Gonen in 1957. [Israel Information Services]

(1943); and *Chaim Weizmann: A Tribute on his Seventieth Birthday* (1945).

GORDON, AHARON DAVID. Ideological leader of the Jewish workers' movement in Palestine during the *Second 'Aliya (b. Podolia, Russia, 1856; d. D'ganya, 1922). Gordon grew up in a rural atmosphere that had a lasting influence on his life. After

Aharon David Gordon.
[Zionist Archives]

studying at home and then in Vilna, he worked as a clerk and in educational extension activities for 20 years. At the age of 48 he settled in Palestine as a farmhand. He worked in Petah Tikva, Rishon L'Tziyon, and 'En Ganim. From 1912 on, he worked in new settlements in Galilee and finally settled in D'ganya.

His philosophy of the religion of labor, which idealized labor and particularly the tilling of the soil as an ultimate ethical value in which one could discover the essence of both Jewish and universal values, became a cornerstone of the Palestinian non-Marxist labor movement. Gordon regarded physical labor as the basis of human existence. While culture was the acme of human achievement, the distance that had developed between cultured man and nature, the source of his very existence, was detrimental to human life. Man must return to nature and give expression to his closeness to nature by physical labor and especially by tilling the land, which must become the property not of individuals but of the community as a whole.

An anthology of Gordon's works appeared posthumously and was reprinted in the 1950s. Bet Gordon (District Museum for Nature and Agriculture), in D'ganya, and the *Gordonia youth movement, which was active between the two world wars, were named for him.

See also LABOR ZIONISM.

G. KRESSEL

GORDON, DAVID. Hebrew publicist (b. Podmerecz, near Vilna, Russia, 1831; d. Lyck, East Prussia, Germany, 1886). He was educated in a Yeshiva in Vilna but also studied secular subjects. After serving for some time as a teacher in a small town in Lithuania, he emigrated to England. In 1858 he became assistant editor of the Hebrew weekly *HaMaggid*, to which he had contributed since its launching in 1856, and settled in Lyck (now Ełk, Poland). He took an active part in the shaping of the paper and became its actual editor before officially assuming that title in 1880. One of the first to support the *Colonisations-Verein für Palästina (Settlement Society for

Palestine) and to write enthusiastic reviews of *D'rishat Tziyon* by Zvi Hirsch *Kalischer and *Rome and Jerusalem* by Moses *Hess, Gordon tirelessly advocated the establishment of Jewish agricultural settlements in Palestine.

With the spread of the *Hoveve Zion movement in Russia in the early 1880s, Gordon, who had contributed greatly to its rise, became one of its leaders. *HaMaggid* served as the mouthpiece of the movement, devoting a special column and later even a separate supplement, *Ahavat Zion* (Love of Zion), to pro-Palestine propaganda and work. In 1884 Gordon was chosen by the Hoveve Zion societies of Russia to present Sir Moses *Montefiore with an album prepared by them on the occasion of his 100th birthday. While in Western Europe, Gordon met local Jewish notables and reported on his mission to the first Hoveve Zion conference, held toward the end of that year in Kattowitz (*see* KATTOWITZ CONFERENCE).

GORDON, SAMUEL LOEB (known as ShaLaG, from his initials). Hebrew poet, educator, and Zionist writer (b. Lida, Russia, 1865; d. Tel Aviv, 1933). He published his first Hebrew poems, *Kinor Y'shurun* (three pamphlets), from 1891 on and subsequently contributed poems to most of the Hebrew periodicals of the late 19th century.

Gordon worked in Palestine as a teacher from 1898 to 1901. He returned to Warsaw in 1901, established a modern Hebrew school there, and worked as an educator and writer. In 1924 he went back to Palestine, residing there until his death. From 1901 to 1905 he edited numerous Hebrew periodicals for children and young people, as well as an educational monthly, *HaPedagog* (Cracow, 1903–04). One of the pioneers of modern Hebrew and Zionist education, which he helped promote with his school manuals and writings, Gordon published many textbooks and school editions of the Bible with his own commentaries. These, which began to appear in Warsaw in 1912, were widely used in subsequent decades in the Hebrew schools of Palestine and Israel.

GORDON, Y'HUDA LEIB. Foremost Hebrew poet of the *Haskala (Jewish Enlightenment) period (b. Vilna, Russia, 1831; d. St. Petersburg, 1892). His philosophy of Jewish adjust-

Y'huda Leib Gordon.
[Zionist Archives]

ment to modern times was best expressed in his famous slogan, "Be a Jew in your tent and a man [of the world] outside." In a series of satirical and realistic narrative poems he criticized the inflexible application of Jewish law by the rabbis of his time.

In his historical poems he attributed the loss of Jewish statehood to the leadership which had stressed the spiritual over the worldly aspects of life. Gordon's vigorous personality emerges in his prose as well as in his poetry. His essays and articles encompass a variety of scholarly and timely topics. His short stories combine realism and satire.

After the Russian pogroms of 1881, Gordon realized that the ideas of the Enlightenment, which favored the socioeconomic integration of the Jews into their environment, were completely out of touch with reality. In short but very effective poems he called for unity and pointed to the solution of the Jewish problem through emigration. Although sympathetic to the cause of the Return to Zion, he did not fully identify himself with the movement because he doubted its practicality. As a poet, novelist, publicist, editor, and scholar, Gordon left his mark on his generation and contributed greatly to the advancement of the Hebrew language and literature.

H. LEAF

GORDONIA, Pioneer scouting youth movement named for Aharon David *Gordon. Founded in 1924 in Poland, it spread to other countries. The movement, which was identified ideologically with *HaPo'el HaTza'ir in Palestine and with *Hitahdut–*Tz'ire Zion in the *Diaspora, aimed at educating youth for pioneering and life in communal settlements. Its graduates established many settlements.

Prior to World War II the movement had branches in Eastern European countries, Austria, Belgium, the United States, Argentina, and Palestine, with a combined membership of 34,000. As a result of amalgamation with kindred youth movements, it eventually became part of Ihud HaBonim (see HABONIM) and its Israeli counterpart, *HaNo'ar Ha'Oved V'haLomed.

GORELIK, SH'MARYA. Writer (b. Poltava District, Ukraine, Russia, 1877; d. Tel Aviv, 1942). In 1891 he settled in Vilna, where he began his literary career in 1899. Gorelik was first a follower of the *Bund (Jewish Socialist Workers party), but in 1905 he became a Zionist and began to contribute journalistic and literary articles to the Zionist press. He also toured Russian-

and contributed numerous articles to the Jewish press in Europe, North America (which he visited in 1923–24), and Palestine.

A. ALPERIN

GOREN. Village (moshav) in western Upper Galilee. Founded in 1950 and affiliated with *T'nu'at HaMoshavim. Population (1968): 319.

GORT, 6TH VISCOUNT (John Standish Surtees Prendergast Vereker). British soldier and *High Commissioner for Palestine (b. London, 1886; d. there, 1946). Educated at Harrow and Sandhurst, he was chief of the Imperial General Staff from 1937 to 1939, commander in chief of the British Field Force in France in 1939–40, and Governor and commander in chief of Gibraltar in 1941–42 and of Malta from 1942 to 1944. He served as High Commissioner for Palestine from Oct. 31, 1944, to Nov. 21, 1945.

Lord Gort arrived in Palestine at the peak of tension, after the assassination of Lord *Moyne and the attempt on the life of Sir Harold *MacMichael. Like his predecessors, he was unable to carry out a policy of his own but had to deal with local issues arising from the British Palestine policies. He established relations with Jewish and Arab leaders. To him was attributed the decision to permit the return to Palestine (February, 1945) of those illegal Jewish immigrants who in 1940 had been deported to the island of Mauritius (see MAURITIUS CAMPS). He impressed both Jews and Arabs as a sincere and straightforward administrator, and, within the limitations of the policy set for him, tried to improve relations with the *Yishuv (Jewish population). Although during his short term of office major Jewish resistance to the British anti-Zionist policy was developing, the end of World War II and the victory of the Labor party in Great Britain resulted in a postponement of decisive action and kept Palestine in a state of expectation.

Lord Gort resigned because of ill health just as the Jewish resistance movement began to develop activity. He was succeeded by Sir Alan Gordon *Cunningham.

I. KOLATT

Sh'marya Gorelik.
[YIVO Institute for Jewish Research]

Jewish cities and villages to propagate Zionism. During World War I he lived in Switzerland. In 1918 he settled in Berlin, where he wrote for the *Jüdische Rundschau. He emigrated to Palestine in 1933. Gorelik wrote several books in Yiddish and German

Lord Gort is greeted on his arrival in Palestine, Oct. 31, 1944, by Moshe Sharett. [Zionist Archives]

GOSLAR, HANS. Public servant in Germany and leader in the *Mizrahi movement (b. Hannover, Germany, 1899; d. Bergen-Belsen, 1945). He was active in the Social Democratic party and after World War I became head of the Press Department of the Prussian government, holding this position until the Nazis' rise to power.

Goslar was introduced to Zionism by Hermann *Struck. During World War I, under the impact of his meetings with the Jewish masses of Eastern Europe, where he served with the German Army, he became strictly Orthodox. He joined the Mizrahi in 1919 and subsequently played a leading role in the movement as a member of its German Executive and European Central Committee. Active also in the Berlin Jewish community, he was elected to the Jewish Community Council in 1928 and became prominent in welfare activities.

In 1935 Goslar emigrated to the Netherlands. In 1944 he was deported to the concentration camp of Bergen-Belsen, where he died of starvation shortly before the liberation. Goslar was the author of several books on Jewish problems.

S. HUBNER

GOTTHEIL, GUSTAV. Rabbi, teacher, writer, and one of the founders of the Zionist movement in the United States (b. Pinne, Posen Province, Germany, 1827; d. New York, 1903). After studying in Halle and Berlin, he became assistant to the rabbi of the Reform synagogue in Berlin in 1855 and obtained his own pulpit at the Reform synagogue in Manchester, England, in 1860. In 1873 he went to the United States, and after serving for some time as assistant rabbi, became rabbi of Temple Emanu-El in New York. One of the first Reform rabbis in the United States to join Herzl's Zionist movement, Gottheil was elected vice-president of the Federation of American Zionists (*see* ZIONIST ORGANIZATION OF AMERICA), founded in 1898. The Gustav Gottheil Lectureship in Semitic Languages at Columbia University was established by his friends and admirers in honor of his 75th birthday.

GOTTHEIL, RICHARD JAMES HORATIO. Scholar in Semitics and Zionist leader (b. Manchester, England, 1862; d. New York, 1936). Son of Rabbi Gustav *Gottheil, he taught

Richard Gottheil.
[Zionist Archives]

Semitic languages at Columbia University from 1886 until his death. From 1896 on he was also director of the Oriental Division of the New York Public Library.

In October, 1897, a conference of American *Hoveve Zion

and Zionist societies held in New York elected Gottheil chairman. Thereafter he headed the committee that prepared the constitution of the Federation of Zionists of New York City and Vicinity (December, 1897). At the First Annual Conference of American Zionists (July, 1898), he was elected president, serving until 1904. In 1902 the CCNY (City College of New York) Zionist Society elected him honorary president.

In 1900 he toured the American Middle West to strengthen the Zionist movement there. Gottheil attended the 2d and other Zionist Congresses (*see* CONGRESS, ZIONIST) and was a member of the Greater *Actions Committee and of the Council of the *Jewish Colonial Trust. At the 3d Zionist Congress (1899) he read a report on the progress of Zionism in the United States.

Gottheil carried on an extensive correspondence with Herzl, to whom he reported frequently and in detail about his efforts to organize, spread, and strengthen the Zionist movement in the United States. He was opposed to any involvement of the Zionist movement in American politics, and insisted that the Federation of American Zionists be the only Zionist body in the United States recognized by the World Zionist Organization.

The author of many scholarly works, he wrote the first comprehensive work on Zionism in English (*Zionism*, 1904).

GOTTLIEB, JOSHUA HESCHEL. Zionist leader, writer, publicist, and essayist (b. Pinsk, Russia, 1882; d. there, 1941). Gottlieb studied in Switzerland, where he was active in student Zionist groups. He was editor of the *Lodzer Morgenblat*, the Zionist Jewish daily published in Łódź, Russian Poland, from 1912 to 1914; of *Dos Yidishe Folk*, the central organ of the Zionist Organization in Poland, published in Warsaw until 1918; and of *Hajnt*, the Warsaw daily Zionist newspaper on whose staff he served until 1934, when he joined the other Warsaw Yiddish daily, *Der Moment*.

As a leader in the Polish Zionist movement, Gottlieb was head of 'Et Livnot, a group of General Zionists (*see* GENERAL ZIONISM; POLAND, ZIONISM IN), representing the group at many Zionist Congresses (*see* CONGRESS, ZIONIST) prior to World War II. From 1935 to 1938 he represented the Jews of Warsaw in the Polish Parliament. He died in a Soviet prison.

A. ALPERIN

GOTTLOBER, ABRAHAM BER (pseudonym, Mahalalel). Poet of the Hibbat Zion idea (*see* HOVEVE ZION), Hebrew and Yiddish writer, journalist, historian, and leader of the *Haskala (Jewish Enlightenment) movement (b. Staro-Konstantinov, Russia, 1811; d. Białystok, Russian Poland, 1899). He was active in several Russian-Jewish communities as a teacher and educator and published many volumes of poetry in Hebrew and Yiddish. In Odessa he studied the life and history of the Karaites. After the pogroms of 1880, he published a series of pro-Zionist poems and songs, appealing to the Russian Jews to return to their ancient Homeland. The most popular of his songs were "Nes Ziona" and "Asire HaTikva." After a long and fruitful literary career, he died blind and destitute.

GOVERNMENT CORPORATIONS IN ISRAEL. A significant feature of Israel's economic structure is the prevalence of government economic activity. This prevalence is reflected in the fact that in the late 1960s more than 200 corporations subject to direct government control operated in the country. These corporations are legal entities in whose management

TABLE. 1. TOTAL DIRECT GOVERNMENT INVESTMENTS IN CORPORATIONS, IN LOANS AND SHARES, MAR. 31, 1967
(In thousands of Israeli pounds)

Economic branch	Loans	Per cent	Shares	Per cent	Total	Per cent
Agriculture, forestry, and fisheries	6,926	0.3	2,300	0.2	9,226	0.3
Mines and quarries	54,051	2.3	130,274	13.1	184,325	5.4
Manufacturing (industry and crafts)	77,127	3.1	78,103	7.8	155,230	4.5
Building (including public works)	616,833	25.5	67,048	6.7	683,881	20.0
Electricity, water, and sanitary services	722,031	30.0	173,433	17.4	895,464	26.2
Trade	10,728	0.4	40,733	4.1	51,461	1.5
Trade banks	872,542	36.1	310,893	31.2	1,183,435	34.7
Transportation, haulage, storage, and communications	53,518	2.2	177,806	17.8	231,324	6.7
Public and commercial services	2,991	0.1	5,846	0.6	8,837	0.2
Private services	....	....	615	0.1	615	0.2
Miscellaneous	....	....	9,622	1.0	9,622	0.3
Total	2,416,747	100.0	996,673	100.0	3,413,420	100.0

either the central government, or a government-owned corporation, or a local authority has a share. Excluded from this category are departmental operations such as posts, telegraph and telephone, and the railways; statutory bodies such as the *Bank of Israel and the Port Authority; and corporations controlled by the Jewish national institutions and *Histadrut-affiliated enterprises.

Government corporations are engaged in a wide range of activities including agriculture, mining, industry, public utilities, construction, transportation, trade, finance, and other services. Most corporations, although initiated and controlled by the government, are not necessarily fully owned by it. The most important partners of the government are the *Jewish Agency, the *Bank L'umi L'Yisrael, the Industrial Development Bank of Israel, the Israel Discount Bank, and Hevrat Ha'Ovdim (a Histradrut-owned holding company). In 1967 the central-government equity investment in these corporations was about IL1,000,000,000 ($333,000,000). In addition, the government is continually making available to these corporations, at preferential terms, substantial loans amounting to a multiple of its equity investment (see Table 1). Indications are that the trend toward proliferation of government corporations is rising: during 1967 public investment in such corporations rose by 19 per cent over 1966 and included the formation of six new corporations. Details of selected corporations are shown in Table 2.

While government corporations in the 1960s absorbed about 20 per cent of the gross national investment, their contribution to the gross national product (GNP) and to employment was only in the 5 to 6 per cent range. In exports, however, government corporations exceeded their share in the GNP and employment: their sales abroad of goods and services represented about 20 per cent of total exports.

The legalities of the initiation, operation, status, and supervision of government corporations had not been defined as of 1968. The corporations are subject to the (Amended Palestine Government) Companies Ordinance, which applies to all corporations but is inadequate on many counts for government corporations. A recommendation of the *State Comptroller to enact legislation on government corporations (which as of 1968 had not been followed) specified various problems requiring legislative solutions. These problems included procedures for the initiation and formation of government corporations; authority to form, organize, control, and supervise them;

ways and means to ensure government control of the corporations' operations and development planning; and uniformity of reporting, accounting, auditing, and budgeting. In 1968 there was a considerable diversity in these matters, but a general pattern that could be seen in most cases showed that the formation of a government corporation was usually initiated by one of the ministries concerned with economic affairs (Finance, Commerce and Industry, Development, Labor, Transport, Housing, Tourism) if such an establishment was indicated and a budgetary allocation was available. The *Knesset took no part in sanctioning the formation of, or investment in, a govern-

TABLE 2. SELECTED GOVERNMENT CORPORATIONS
SHOWING BALANCE SHEET TOTAL*
(In millions of Israeli pounds)

Corporation	Assets	Year of formation
Mining:		
Dead Sea Works Company	293	1952
Israel Oil Prospectors Corporation	59	1959
Naphtha Petroleum Corporation	40	1956
Israel National Oil Company	33	1958
Industry:		
Fertilizers and Chemicals, Ltd.	112	1946
Haifa Refineries	90	1959
Israel Shipyards	29	1959
Construction:		
'Amidar Ltd.	643	1949
Housing and Development for Israel	200	1961
Water and electricity:		
Israel Electric Corporation	771	1923
Mekorot Water Company	867	1937
Tahal	336	1952
Transportation:		
Zim–Israel Shipping Company	361	1945
El 'Al Israel Airlines	189	1949
Oil Lines	61	1959
Finance:		
T'fahot mortgage bank	939	1961
Industrial Development Bank of Israel	796	1957
Maritime Bank	476	1962
Israel Bank of Agriculture	290	1951
Tourist Industry Development Corporation	65	1957

*Assets are taken from latest available balance sheet.

ment corporation but was restricted to expressing its views (ex post) through the budgetary process.

As far back as 1959 the Ministry of Finance established a Bureau of Government Corporations, which in 1961 was reconstituted, renamed Government Corporation Authority, and vested with powers to control the corporations. The Authority is guided by a Council consisting of the directors general (the permanent top civil servants in each ministry) of the various economic ministries under the chairmanship of the Director General of the Ministry of Finance. Although the Authority lays down guidelines for the management of the corporations, there seem to be basic deficiencies in their structure and performance that are reflected in the frequent critical comments of the State Comptroller on their organizational and operational methods.

The considerations that prompted the government's investments in, and continued financial assistance for, these corporations are controversial. Advocates of governmental economic enterprise, motivated mainly by political ideologies, claim that many development activities in which the corporations are engaged often exceed the financial capabilities of the private sector. Moreover, some projects are not expected to yield reasonable profits within the foreseeable future or are not attractive to private investors for some other reason, such as insecurity in border areas. Some private companies were taken over by the government when their shareholders were unable to mobilize additional funds for expansion or decided to liquidate their holdings in Israel. Although the reasoning of the advocates of public enterprise sounds convincing in respect to infrastructural development, its validity becomes questionable if applied to production and service industries. Here it would seem that private initiative was deliberately excluded by the government, which preempted the field.

Ordinary criteria of profitability obviously cannot apply to government corporations engaged in long-term infrastructural development or to those which subordinate their profit considerations to policy decisions that adversely affect them. Profits of government corporations before taxes in 1966–67 amounted to about 7.5 per cent of their total equity; the government's income from dividends distributed by these corporations amounted to about 4 per cent of equity held by the government, but profitability to the government was still lower because of substantial government lending to these corporations at preferential terms. These figures are not necessarily conclusive but seem to indicate that the formation of government corporations should be limited to cases in which they clearly serve the public interest. As investments they have not been rewarding.

J. O. RONALL

GOVERNMENT OF ISRAEL. The powers and duties of the executive branch of the State of Israel were defined by the Law and Administration Ordinance of 1948, promulgated by the Provisional Council of State immediately following the *Declaration of Independence, and the Transition Law enacted by the First *Knesset on Feb. 14, 1949, and subsequently amended. It was only on July 13, 1968, that the Knesset enacted a law entitled Basic Law: the Government, which provides the legal basis for the functioning of the executive branch. This law, with the basic laws already enacted, such as the Basic Law: the President of the State and the Basic Law: the Knesset, is intended, with other laws to be enacted eventually, to be incorporated in the future Constitution of the State of Israel.

The Basic Law: the Government. This law defines the government as the executive branch of the State and provides that Jerusalem be its permanent seat. The government is responsible to the Knesset, and its responsibility extends to the actions of every one of its members. It stays in office as long as it enjoys the confidence of the Knesset. The government is composed of a Prime Minister and a number of ministers. The Prime Minister must be a member of the Knesset, but a minister may be a nonmember. A minister is generally placed in charge of a ministry, that is, a government department, but there may also be ministers who are not in charge of ministries, that is, ministers without portfolio.

A new government is formed after the previous government has resigned or a new Knesset has been elected. After consulting with the leaders of the parties, the President of the State (see PRESIDENCY OF ISRAEL) charges a member of the Knesset with the task of forming a government; if that person fails to form a government within 21 days, the President may either extend the term for another 21-day period or request another member of the Knesset to form a government.

When a government has been formed, the Prime Minister designate presents it to the Knesset, announces its policy, and indicates the distribution of the ministries among its members. Once the Knesset has voted confidence in the government and the Prime Minister and the other ministers have taken the oath of office, the government is deemed to be duly constituted.

The function of the Prime Minister is not merely to preside at meetings of the Cabinet but also to represent it, to coordinate the activities of the ministries, and, in general, to formulate the policies of the government. Unless the government decides otherwise, he takes charge of any department whose minister is temporarily absent. He may also assume permanent responsibility for a ministry. Thus, David *Ben-Gurion during his term of office as Prime Minister was also Minister of Defense; Moshe *Sharett was also Minister of Foreign Affairs; and Levi *Eshkol, until the end of May, 1967, was also Minister of Defense. The resignation of the Prime Minister or his death, unlike that of other ministers, entails the resignation of the entire government.

The government may, with the approval of the Knesset, redistribute the ministries among its members, coopt a minister to the government, unify two ministries into one or divide a ministry into two, thus forming a new ministry, or abolish a ministry and transfer its functions to another ministry. A single minister may be in charge of more than one ministry.

With the approval of the government, a minister may appoint a member of Knesset as deputy minister and define the scope of his activities. The minister may dismiss a deputy he has appointed. When a minister resigns, the deputy he has appointed is deemed to have resigned with him. The Knesset must be notified of the appointment of a deputy, but its approval is not required. Thus far the right to appoint a deputy has been exercised by the Ministers of Defense, Finance, Commerce and Industry, Development, and Religious Affairs.

To assure the normal functioning of the government the law provides that when a government resigns or a new Knesset is elected, the existing government remains in office until a new government has been duly constituted. The deliberations of the government on the defense of the State, its foreign relations, and any other matter that the government regards as essential are secret. Section 29 of the Basic Law grants the government residuary powers. It provides that "the government is authorized on behalf of the State and subject to law to perform any act,

Meeting of the first elected government of Israel in 1949. From left to right: Golda Meir, Zalman Shazar, B'khor Shitrit, E. Maimon (stenographer), Dov Joseph, Eliezer Kaplan, Moshe Sharett, David Ben-Gurion, Z'ev Sharef (secretary), Pinhas Rosen, David Remez, Moshe Shapira, Rabbi Yitzhak Meir Levin, Rabbi Y'huda Leb Maimon. [Zionist Archives]

the performance of which is not imposed by law on another authority."

Coalition Governments. All Israeli governments from 1948 on were coalition governments, consisting of representatives of several parties. The need for a coalition government was a consequence of the multiplicity of parties encouraged by the proportional system of representation, with the result that no single party succeeded in obtaining a majority in the Knesset. *Mapai and, since 1968, the *Israel Labor party, being the largest, formed the central force of all coalition governments and effectively controlled them. Because of the need to secure the support of a substantial majority of the Knesset, however, ministerial portfolios had to be given also to small parties, with the result that the Cabinet was quite large and ministries had to be subdivided or new ones created to afford portfolios to a large number of ministers. Except for a brief interval, the National Religious party was Mapai's constant and close partner in all coalition governments; without this party's support it was almost impossible for Mapai to form a government without compromising its economic policy. The first Cabinet following the creation of the Knesset, formed on Mar. 10, 1949, had 12 ministers; the Cabinet formed on Dec. 23, 1959, had 16 ministers; and that formed on Jan. 12, 1966, had 18. When the Government of National Unity came into being in 1967, the number rose to 21, including 3 ministers without portfolio.

In general, the governments of Israel have enjoyed stability,

largely because of the dominant position of Mapai and the support given it by the National Religious party. The changes in government personnel from Knesset to Knesset have been none too numerous. Thus, in the first 22 years of its existence, Israel had only four Prime Ministers, three Foreign Ministers, and four Ministers of the Interior. There have been, on the whole, few Cabinet crises, for with a broad coalition the withdrawal of one party or another does not necessarily shake the stability of the government. Thus, in July, 1958, when the ministers of the National Religious party withdrew from the government in protest against the definition of "Who Is a Jew?" adopted by the Minister of the Interior, the government was able to carry on until the Knesset elections in the following year. The broadening of the government that took place at the end of May, 1967, resulted from vigorous public pressure to have a truly national government in the days preceding the *Six-day War. Thus, despite the multiplicity of parties and the need to form coalitions Israel has had governmental stability.

Ministries. As of 1970 the government of Israel is composed of the following ministries:

1. The Office of the Prime Minister is concerned with the coordination of the activities of the several ministries. It is assisted by a Cabinet Secretariat and maintains several specialized departments, such as the *National Council for Research and Development, the Central Bureau of Statistics, and the National Archives. The Prime Minister's Office also exercises

Members of the new Cabinet at the first session of the Fourth Knesset in 1959. From left to right: Moshe Dayan, Abba Eban, Levi Eshkol, Pinhas Sapir, Pinhas Rosen, Mordecai Bentov, Yisrael Barzilai. [Zionist Archives]

general supervision over the *Israel Broadcasting Service and the Government Press Bureau.

2. The Ministry of Finance (the Treasury) is the principal ministry charged with determining economic policy by means of the national budget, *taxation, and foreign exchange control. It initiates fiscal legislation in the Knesset and controls expenditures by other ministries. The Office of the Civil Service Commissioner functions within the framework of the Treasury. *See also* CIVIL SERVICE IN ISRAEL; FINANCE IN ISRAEL.

3. The Ministry of Defense is in charge of all the *Israel Defense Forces, including the navy and air force. It helps veterans become adjusted to civilian life by enabling them to acquire trades and skills. It is also concerned with the rehabilitation of war invalids. The Gadna' Department provides paramilitary training for boys and girls of the 14–18 age group. In addition, the Ministry maintains a Scientific Research Department and publishes a variety of periodicals and books.

4. The Ministry of Foreign Affairs maintains Israel's embassies, legations, and consular-level missions in all parts of the world. With nonresident missions included, the Ministry in 1968 maintained diplomatic relations with 84 nations. Most of the countries with which Israel maintains diplomatic relations themselves have diplomatic representatives resident in Israel. The Ministry is divided into eight regional departments and a number of functional departments, such as those concerned with protocol, information and press, research, economic affairs, cultural relations, international cooperation, and personnel. *See also* FOREIGN RELATIONS OF ISRAEL.

5. The Ministry of Health is in charge of preventive *medicine, supervises the country's hospitalization services and the training of nurses, sets medical standards, and coordinates medical services. A few of the country's hospitals are run directly by the Ministry. *See also* PUBLIC HEALTH IN ISRAEL.

6. The Ministry of Posts is in charge of the regular postal services. The telephone and telegraph services are departments of the Post Office. In addition, the Ministry operates a postal savings bank, maintains a secondary technical school for radio and telegraph operators, and runs a philatelic service.

7. The Ministry of Religious Affairs supervises the affairs of Israel's religious *communities, including the administration of the ecclesiastical courts, which exercise jurisdiction in matters of marriage, divorce, and personal status in general. *See also* RABBINATE OF ISRAEL

8. The principal task of the Ministry of Education and Culture is the maintenance and control of the system of compulsory education for children between the ages of 5 and 14. The school system of the Ministry is divided into schools with Hebrew and those with Arabic language of instruction. The Ministry also sets and controls the scholastic standards of secondary schools (14–18 age group) and helps finance them, and it maintains colleges for the training of teachers. In addition, it supervises private (including missionary) schools. In the field of culture, it encourages the setting up of public *libraries, affords assistance to theaters (*see* THEATER IN ISRAEL), supervises archeological excavations (*see* ARCHEOLOGY IN ISRAEL), and with the aid of local authorities promotes adult education. Through

the Council for Higher Education it supervises the academic standards of Israel's institutions of advanced study. *See also* EDUCATION IN ISRAEL.

9. The Ministry of Agriculture carries on research in most branches of farming and fisheries, offers guidance to farmers, and supervises the planning and distribution of water resources. Through marketing boards, it largely controls the production and marketing, as well as the prices, of many farm products. *See also* AGRICULTURE IN ISRAEL; FISHING IN ISRAEL; RURAL SETTLEMENT IN PALESTINE AND ISRAEL.

10. The Ministry of Commerce and Industry, in addition to supervising commerce and manufacturing, is the principal agency for the industrialization of the development areas (*see* DEVELOPMENT REGIONS; INDUSTRY IN ISRAEL). It also controls the Investment Center, which operates in pursuance of the Law for the Encouragement of Capital Investments.

11. The Ministry of Justice is in charge of planning and drafting legislation. The State Attorney's Department is in charge of public prosecutions, and other departments deal with the registration of companies, partnerships, trademarks, and patents. Land registries record transfers of real estate. The courts of law are under the administrative control of this Ministry. *See also* JUDICIARY IN ISRAEL.

12. The Ministry of Social Welfare, through its local offices, is concerned with social work among the underprivileged. It is entrusted with the supervision of juvenile delinquents. *See also* SOCIAL INSURANCE IN ISRAEL; SOCIAL WELFARE SERVICES IN ISRAEL.

13. The Ministry of Labor operates labor exchanges in accordance with the Employment Service Law of 1959 and maintains a department for the training of apprentices and unskilled workers. The Department of Public Works is in charge of road and bridge building and of the construction of public buildings. The National Insurance Institute, dealing with old-age pensions, workmen's compensation, and other social benefits, also comes under the control of this Ministry.

14. The Ministry of the Interior is in charge of municipal and other local governments (*see* LOCAL GOVERNMENT IN ISRAEL) and is responsible for town planning. It maintains a department for the registration of inhabitants and provides for the administration of national and local elections.

15. The Ministry of Transport administers the ports, airports, and railway system of the country. It supervises interurban public motor transport and operates the meteorological services. *See also* TRANSPORTATION IN ISRAEL.

16. The Ministry of Development is concerned primarily with exploitation of the natural resources of the Negev.

17. The Ministry of Housing superintends the construction of large-scale housing developments for the accommodation of immigrants and other persons of limited means. *See also* ARCHITECTURE AND TOWN PLANNING IN ISRAEL.

18. The Ministry of Police controls the Israel Police Force and administers the prisons. *See also* POLICE IN ISRAEL.

19. The Ministry of Tourism was formed in December, 1964. *See also* TOURISM IN ISRAEL.

20. The Ministry for the Absorption of Immigrants was formed in the summer of 1968.

S. Z. ABRAMOV

GOVRIN, 'AKIVA. Israeli labor leader and parliamentarian (b. Shpikov, Ukraine, Russia, 1902). Educated in Kiev and at the University of Berlin, Govrin was a cofounder of the pioneering movement *HeHalutz in the Ukraine. He settled in Palestine

in 1922. In 1925 he became general secretary of the Employees Union (union of clerks and professional people) of the *Histadrut (General Federation of Labor), which under his administra-

'Akiva Govrin.
[Israel Information Services]

tion became the largest trade union in Palestine. During the *Arab riots of 1929 he participated in the defense of Jerusalem, and during those of 1936–39 he was a member of the Tel Aviv *Hagana command. He was elected to the Histadrut Executive Committee in 1942 and served as a delegate to various international trade union congresses and World Zionist Congresses (*see* CONGRESS, ZIONIST).

Elected to the *Knesset in 1949, Govrin served until 1969. He served as Minister without Portfolio in 1963–64 and as Israel's first Minister of Tourism from 1964 to 1966.

B. EPSTEIN

GRADENWITZ, PETER (Emanuel). Israeli musicologist (b. Berlin, 1910). He settled in Tel Aviv in 1936 after receiving a doctorate from the University of Prague. The founder and director of a number of Israeli music publications, Gradenwitz contributed articles to musicological journals and encyclopedias, especially on early 18th-century symphonic music, contemporary trends, and music in Israel. In 1964 he served as president of the Israel Musicological Society. He was a guest lecturer in European countries and the United States and a correspondent for several radio stations. Gradenwitz was the author of *The Music of Israel* (1949), which also appeared in Spanish, German, and Hebrew editions; *Music and Musicians in Israel* (1959); *Approaches to the Music of Our Time* (in German, 1963); and historical works in Hebrew.

GRANOTT (GRANOWSKY), ABRAHAM. Zionist official and expert on agrarian policy (b. Faleshty, Bessarabia, Russia, 1890; d. Jerusalem, 1962). Granott attended the *Herzliya High School in Tel Aviv and then studied law and political economy in Switzerland. In 1919 he joined the staff of the head office of the *Jewish National Fund in The Hague. He continued to work for the Fund after the transfer of the head office to Jerusalem (1922) and for many years served as its managing director. In 1945 he became chairman of the board, and in 1960 president. From 1949 to 1951 he was a member of the *Knesset, representing the *Progressive party. He headed a number of public corporations and was on the Board of Governors of the *Hebrew University of Jerusalem and of the *Weizmann Institute of

Science. During the last years of his life he taught agrarian policy at the Hebrew University.

Granott wrote prolifically on land problems, contributing to the Hebrew press and periodicals, and published a large number of booklets and books, several of which were translated into other languages. Among his books that appeared in English are *Land Problems in Palestine* (1926), *Land Taxation in Palestine* (1927), *Land and the Jewish Reconstruction in Palestine* (1931), *The Fiscal System of Palestine* (1935), *Land Policy in Palestine* (1940), *The Land System in Palestine* (1952), and *Agrarian Reform and the Record of Israel* (1956). He also wrote literary essays, some of which were collected.

GRASOWSKI (GRAZOVSKI), Y'HUDA. *See* GUR, Y'HUDA.

GREAT BRITAIN: RELATIONS WITH ZIONISM AND ISRAEL.

The traditional love of the English people for the Bible, their belief in the prophets and the millennium, and their interest in the "Ten Lost Tribes" led them to view with sympathy the concept of the restoration of the People of Israel to the Holy Land. One result of this attitude was that in no other country did non-Jews write so much about this problem as in England. As early as 1621 Sir Henry Finch wrote a treatise entitled *The Restoration of the Jews*.

19th Century. The 19th century saw a formidable array of literature on the subject. Lord Byron's *Hebrew Melodies* (1814) were translated into Hebrew and Yiddish. Frequently recited by Jews the world over were these lines from his poem "O Weep for Those":

> The wild-dove hath her nest, the fox his cave,
> Mankind their country—Israel but the grave.

The reply to this lament can be found in Benjamin *Disraeli's novel *The Wondrous Tale of Alroy* (1833):

> You ask me what I wish: my answer is, the Land of Promise.
> You ask me what I wish: my answer is, Jerusalem.
> You ask me what I wish: my answer is, the Temple.
> All we have forfeited,
> All we have yearned after,
> All for which we have fought,
> Our beauteous country,
> Our holy creed,
> Our simple manners
> And our ancient customs.

In 1847 Disraeli published *Tancred*, which is considered the first "Zionist" novel. In another "Zionist" novel, *Daniel Deronda* (1874–76), by George *Eliot, the Zionist philosopher Mordecai expresses his fervent belief that a new Judea will arise again some day: "The vision is there; it will be fulfilled."

In 1840 Biblical and literary Zionism was joined by the first practical proposals to set up Jewish settlements in Palestine. Anthony Ashley Cooper (later 7th Earl of Shaftesbury) addressed a memorandum to Viscount Palmerston, the Foreign Secretary, seeking a "guarantee" or "protection" for the return of the Jews to the land of their ancestors. Five years later, George Hamilton Gordon, 4th Earl of Aberdeen, as Foreign Secretary, appointed James Finn British Consul in Jerusalem, with instructions to assist the Jews there and to protect them from persecution.

George Gawler, a former Governor of South Australia and a Christian forerunner of Zionism, considered it England's duty to help the Children of Israel establish Jewish settlements under British protection. He accompanied Sir Moses *Montefiore on one of his journeys to Palestine. Other Christian Zionists of that era were Edward *Cazalet and Col. Charles Henry *Churchill, who expressed similar views.

With the foundation of the Palestine Exploration Fund in London in 1865, interest in the restoration increased. The accounts of the fund's expeditions were published in its quarterly as well as in dozens of books, among them *The Land of Promise, or Turkey's Guarantee* (1875), by Sir Charles Warren, and *Tent Work in Palestine* (1878), by Claude Reignier Conder. These scholars believed in the Bible and the prophets and proposed Jewish settlement in Palestine. They addressed meetings, published articles and letters propagating the idea of a Jewish Palestine, and encouraged and assisted the *Hoveve Zion movement in England.

The name of Laurence *Oliphant will always be linked with the beginnings of Jewish settlement in Palestine. The author of *The Land of Gilead* (1880), Oliphant drafted a plan for a Jewish agricultural settlement, went to Haifa, and with Cazalet tried to obtain a firman from the Sultan in Constantinople authorizing Jewish settlement. He assisted Jewish settlers and persuaded the 1st Baron Rothschild (*see* ROTHSCHILDS: BRITISH BRANCH) to take an active interest in Palestine. The Prince of Wales (later King Edward VII) and the British government were sympathetic to his plans. In 1887 Oliphant helped purchase 2,100 dunams of land (*see* DUNAM), on which the colony B'ne Y'huda was founded.

Some Jews including Naftali Herz *Imber, the author of "*HaTikva," suspected that Oliphant's activities in behalf of Jewish settlement in Palestine were motivated by Christian missionary zeal. But when Imber convinced himself that this was not the case, he became Oliphant's secretary. Other British friends of Palestine, however, seemed to have been impelled by missionary motivation. A meeting of the Syrian Colonization Fund (which was founded by Jean-Henri Dunant in 1876) adopted (1891) the following resolution: "That it is the duty of all Christians to give practical aid to persecuted and suffering Jews, especially in the Holy Land, as approved by the late Lord Shaftesbury, President of the Society."

Early Political Zionism, 1890s–1914. Meetings of the Hoveve Zion were frequently addressed by Christian Zionists, among them Father *Ignatius, a Benedictine monk. "We English," Father Ignatius used to say, "venerate the Jews. We see in them the source of our best blessings in the sphere of politics, morals and religion. But even the Jews who, like those in England, are not exposed to brutal attacks, and the rich Jews who escape oppression—they, too, will be raised in the esteem of all the nations when they can refer to their own home country, their own government and their own State constitution."

At a mass meeting of the Hoveve Zion in London in 1891, Rev. Simeon Singer read a petition in English and Hebrew, in which the "Right Hon. the Lord Rothschild, Chief among the Remnant of Israel," was asked to bring this "Petition to the notice of The Most Noble the Marquess of Salisbury." The Hoveve Zion appealed to the British government to intervene in Russia, with a view to letting the Jews emigrate, and in Turkey, to gain permission for them to enter Palestine.

This political action in London raised the hopes of Jews everywhere that an era of miracles had dawned in which the age-old dream of a Jewish State would come true. William E. Gladstone, in a letter to Samuel Montagu, who had chaired the meeting, declared that he regarded any plan for the introduction of large numbers of Jews into Palestine with warm and friendly interest. On June 5, 1891, the Foreign Office wrote Lord Rothschild that Sir William White, the British Ambassador in Constantinople, would discuss the matter with the Sultan.

Soon afterward, the English Hoveve Zion, comprising 31 Hoveve Zion tents, 4 cadet tents, and 1 women's tent, sent a second petition to the Earl of Rosebery, the Foreign Secretary, with a request that it be conveyed to Sultan *'Abdul Hamid II. The Hoveve Zion wanted the right to acquire land in Palestine on which to settle "selected" persons. These individuals were to receive "certificates" from the Hoveve Zion, permitting them to work on the land, build houses, schools, and synagogues, dig wells, construct roads, and so on, without having to request special permission each time.

On Nov. 21, 1895, Herzl visited London for the first time. The following year, copies of his treatise The *Jewish State, in Sylvie d'Avigdor's English translation, were sent to a number of British statesmen including Gladstone and Joseph *Chamberlain. Before the 1st Zionist *Congress (Basle, 1897), British newspapers and weeklies published information and articles on Herzl and Zionism. Reports and commentaries on the Congress appeared in the Times, Morning Post, Echo, Westminster Gazette, Daily News, Daily Chronicle, Globe, Standard, St. James's Gazette, Morning Leader, Cosmopolis, Asiatic Quarterly Review, Contemporary Review, and other periodicals. The Daily Chronicle and Pall Mall Gazette supported the Congress and suggested the convocation of a European conference for the solution of the Jewish problem along the lines of Zionism. Magazines, too, devoted space to comments on Zionism, mainly favorable. Cosmopolis carried "Impressions of the Congress," by Israel *Zangwill; Asiatic Quarterly Review, Moses *Gaster's "Return of the Jews to Palestine and the Zionist Movement"; and the Nineteenth Century, Herbert *Bentwich's article "Philo-Zionists and Anti-Semites."

The Times published an article by Oswald H. Simon against the Congress and the Jewish State, with a reply by Gaster, who pinned his hopes on Zionism. In "The Basle Congress," published in the Contemporary Review (October, 1897), Herzl also refuted the views of Simon. Another article by Herzl, entitled "The Wandering Jew," appeared in the Daily Chronicle (Nov. 12 and 13, 1897).

The 4th Zionist Congress was held in London in 1900. In his opening speech, Herzl declared: "England, great England, freedom-loving England, overlooking all the seas, will understand and sympathize with the aims and aspirations of Zionism. From here the idea of Zionism will soar higher and further. Of this we may be sure." While in London, Herzl had interviews with Lord Salisbury's private secretary, Eric Barrington, and other Foreign Office officials. The British press printed friendly comments and exhaustive reports under the heading "Palestine for the Jews" and articles on the possible restoration of a Jewish State. The London Congress was first and foremost successful propaganda. Some British journalists and politicians had come to link the solution of the Jewish problem with the aims of Zionism.

The first major political action of the English Zionist Federation took place shortly after that Congress. Parliamentary candidates of all parties received circulars briefing them on political Zionism and asking them, if elected, to adopt a favorable attitude toward Zionism. Among these candidates were several statesmen who were, or were to become, Cabinet ministers. One of them was Arthur James *Balfour. Before the elections the Zionist Federation received 130 replies from candidates, almost all of them favorable; 31 of these candidates were elected. After the elections another 13 members of Parliament, among them a member of the Cabinet, replied, promising to support Zionism. Soon the number rose to 75, 24 of them from London, 32 from the provinces, 5 from Scotland, 6 from Wales, 7 from Ireland, and 1 from Burma.

Members of the House of Commons and the House of Lords were invited to take the chair or speak at Zionist meetings. The British press not only published reports of Zionist Congresses and Herzl's speeches in London but also covered interesting lectures on Zionism and reported on Herzl's audience in Constantinople. British statesmen, scholars, generals, admirals, and officials appeared at the Article Club on Nov. 20, 1901, to listen to Zangwill's address on Palestine. Lord Suffield, who presided, read a telegram from Herzl and added that he himself had always sympathized with the dream of a restoration of the Jewish State. Hall Caine and Bernard Shaw also spoke out on behalf of Zionism. Newspaper readers in England, more than those of any other country, were made familiar with the aims of Zionism.

On Mar. 21, 1902, the Salisbury Government appointed a Royal Commission on Alien Immigration, and thanks to the efforts of Leopold J. *Greenberg and Arnold White, author of The Modern Jew (1899), Herzl was invited to present his views on the Jewish question. This invitation was of historic significance, for it was regarded as tantamount to official recognition of the *World Zionist Organization (WZO). Herzl also had private interviews with the seven members of the Commission, including its chairman, Lord James of Hereford. Herzl's memorandum on Zionism was read to the Commission, and afterward members asked questions, which he answered in detail. The British public followed the sessions of the Commission with great interest. The Commission's report was not ready until August, 1903, when it was submitted to the new Balfour Government.

Herzl won over English politicians and writers to Zionism and negotiated with the Colonial Secretary, Joseph Chamberlain. With the approval of the British government, an expedition was undertaken to El-'Arish to investigate the area's suitability for Jewish settlement (see EL-'ARISH SCHEME). As the results were negative, Chamberlain offered the Zionist Organization an opportunity to establish an autonomous Jewish settlement in East Africa (see EAST AFRICA SCHEME) under British suzerainty. David *Lloyd George and Prime Minister Balfour took part in the debate on East Africa in the House of Commons. When a letter from Sir Clement Hill, head of the Protectorate Department of the Foreign Office, stating that Lord Lansdowne, the Foreign Secretary, "has studied the question with the interest which His Majesty's Government must always take in any well-considered scheme for the amelioration of the position of the Jewish race," was read at the 6th Zionist Congress (Basle, 1903), both the delegates in favor of the East Africa project and those opposed burst into cheers for England.

After the Turkish Revolution of 1908–09, when Turkey was drawing closer to Germany, British circles in Constantinople voiced their suspicions that powerful Jewish interests, including the Zionists, had allied themselves with Germany in order to undermine British interests in the Near East. These suspicions were based in part on the circumstance that German Jews happened to be the leaders of the Zionist movement at the time.

British misgivings were enhanced by pro-German articles in *Le Jeune Turc*, the subsidized organ of the Zionist Office in Constantinople, and by the activities of Alfred *Nossig (formerly a Zionist but disowned by the WZO in 1909), who arrived in Constantinople and proposed a settlement of Jews in Palestine and Asiatic Turkey, under the auspices of a German-Jewish organization founded by him, with headquarters in Berlin. In 1911–12 the London *Times*, through its Constantinople correspondent, frequently carried warnings about the supposed hostility of Zionism to Britain and the propaganda carried on among Turkish Jews by "German Zionist agents."

These charges were refuted in the *Times* (May 11, 1911) by David *Wolffsohn, president of the WZO, by Max *Nordau at the 10th Zionist Congress (Basle, 1911), and by Moses Gaster, who said at the 11th Congress (Vienna, 1913):

> [Zionism] is not a German movement. I wish you to understand this because it has been described as such in the English press, from *The Times* downward.... We are fighting everywhere to make it clear that we feel neither German nor English nor French nor Russian but ... solely and exclusively Jewish.

In the summer of 1912 Nahum *Sokolow, then a member of the Zionist *Executive, was sent to reestablish contact with British public opinion and government circles. Aware of the appeal of Zionism to Englishmen on Biblical grounds, he approached Rev. William H. *Hechler, Herzl's friend, and called on a number of leading Anglican clergymen, among them Bishop Thomas Edward Wilkinson, who had long superintended Anglican interests on the Continent and had met Herzl. After the outbreak of the Balkan Wars (1912–13) Sokolow was sent to England again, on his way to the United States. On Mar. 3, 1913, he called on several high officials of the Foreign Office, to whom he explained that Britain should support the Zionist cause not only on humanitarian grounds but in its own interest. Although he received no assurances of any sort from the Foreign Office, he left the meeting satisfied that the Zionist movement had reestablished official contact with the British government.

World War I, 1914–17. When Sokolow went to London again late in 1914, the Foreign Office excused itself from receiving him, explaining that it already had ample information on Zionism. However, leading men in the government itself had become interested in Zionism. Late in 1914 and early in 1915 Herbert *Samuel, then a member of the government, had explained Zionist aims to Foreign Secretary Sir Edward Grey and to David Lloyd George, and by January, 1915, Lloyd George was entertaining the idea of setting up a Jewish buffer state in Palestine to protect British interests in the Near East.

It was during these years that Chaim *Weizmann played a crucial role in gaining British sympathy for the Zionist cause. In 1914 he made the acquaintance of Charles Prestwich *Scott, editor of the *Manchester Guardian*, and through Scott he met Lloyd George, then Minister of Munitions, who enlisted Weizmann's scientific skills in the production of explosives, thus helping to make the scientist well known to the high officials with whom he subsequently was to negotiate on behalf of Zionism.

Zionist aims were ignored in the *Sykes-Picot Agreement of May, 1916, between Britain and France, which concerned the postwar partition of the Ottoman Empire, including Palestine. It was hoped that this agreement would pave the way for a joint Anglo-French attempt to woo the Arabs from the Turks and so lay the foundations for an Arab state or confederation of states. At the same time, British leaders were concerned about the war situation and were anxious to obtain the support of the United States. It was felt that a pro-Zionist statement by Britain would help win over many influential American Jews who reportedly had pro-German leanings. It would also gain for Britain the goodwill of Jews in neutral countries. This thinking on the part of Britain's leaders eventually led to the issuance of the *Balfour Declaration (Nov. 2, 1917), in which the British government promised to aid the establishment of a Jewish National Home in Palestine.

By 1917 Sir Mark *Sykes, the British signatory to the Sykes-Picot Agreement, had become sympathetic to the Zionist movement. From other considerations he had become convinced that the agreement was not in Britain's best interest.

Meanwhile, Herbert *Sidebotham, the military expert of the *Manchester Guardian*, and his Manchester friends had formed a British Palestine Committee in order to attract sufficient influential support to be able to press its pro-Zionist views on the British government. But though the committee was intended to be nonsectarian, all its members except Sidebotham were Jews. In January, 1917, the committee began to publish a weekly journal, *Palestine*, which carried on its masthead the aim of the committee: "to reset the ancient glories of the Jewish nation in the freedom of a new British dominion in Palestine." Meanwhile, too, Joseph *Trumpeldor had organized the *Zion Mule Corps and Vladimir *Jabotinsky the *Jewish Legion, both of which fought in the Near East on the side of the British.

Eventually the fact that British troops had conquered Palestine without French aid placed the British in a position where they could in effect bring France to nullify the Sykes-Picot Agreement and leave them in sole charge of Palestine.

J. FRAENKEL

THE MANDATE AND THE STATE

Southern Palestine, including Jaffa and Jerusalem, was under British control by the end of 1917. The rest of Palestine was in British hands by late September, 1918.

Balfour Declaration and Establishment of Mandate, 1917–22. The Balfour Declaration received widespread support from British public opinion: 33 privy councillors, more than 200 members of Parliament, 14 bishops of the Church of England, 8 bishops of the Roman Catholic Church, and the heads of several other religious denominations in the United Kingdom expressed their concurrence in the British statement of policy with regard to the Jewish National Home. The British press widely welcomed the declaration, and the three major political parties—Conservative, Liberal, and Labor—approved of it.

Early in 1918 the British government authorized the dispatch of a *Zionist Commission to survey the situation in Palestine and to prepare plans for the future. The Commission, headed by Chaim Weizmann, was accompanied by Maj. William Ormsby-Gore, M.P. (later Colonial Secretary and afterward Lord *Harlech), as political officer on behalf of the British authorities; he was assisted by Maj. James de Rothschild. Prior to the departure of the Commission (which arrived in Palestine on Apr. 4, 1918), Weizmann was received by King George V, a gesture that underlined the importance of his mission.

Whereas the British government was fully committed to the policy of facilitating establishment of the Jewish National Home, the military administration in Palestine paid little attention to the Balfour Declaration. It adhered strictly to the status quo, and some officials showed open hostility to Jewish aspirations; this attitude was not lost on the Arabs and precipitated developments that had a serious impact on the future of the National Home. After that time British policy ran in two parallel lines, support for Zionism on the one hand and encouragement of Arab nationalism on the other, with the latter gradually assuming priority.

A tug-of-war of sorts developed between the pro-Zionist elements of the British government in London and the *anti-Zionism within military administration circles in Palestine and in Cairo. An expression of the latter attitude was seen in the belated arrival of British troops on the scene in Jerusalem when an Arab mob attacked the Jews there during Passover of 1920 (see ARAB RIOTS IN PALESTINE). When a small group of young Jews tried to defend their neighborhood, they were promptly arrested. The leader of the self-defense unit, Vladimir Jabotinsky, received a sentence of 15 years at hard labor (the court verdict was quashed in due time).

On Apr. 24, 1920, the Supreme Council of the Paris Peace Conference (on which Britain was represented by David Lloyd George, Arthur James Balfour, and Lord Curzon), meeting at San Remo (see SAN REMO CONFERENCE), resolved that the Balfour Declaration be incorporated in the peace treaty with Turkey and that the *Mandate for Palestine be assigned to Great Britain. The way was opened for the termination of military rule in Palestine and its replacement by a civil administration.

On July 1, 1920, Sir Herbert Samuel (later Viscount Samuel) arrived in Palestine as the first *High Commissioner. The appointment of such a prominent man—a Jew and a well-known supporter of the Balfour Declaration—was considered a friendly gesture on the part of the British government toward the Zionist movement. Brig. Gen. Sir Wyndham *Deedes, who had a deep sympathy for the National Home, was named Chief Secretary of the Palestine administration.

These appointments created fresh hopes among the pro-Zionists. But early in 1921 Winston *Churchill, then Colonial Secretary, in an effort to solidify Britain's position with the Arabs, decided to detach the territory east of the Jordan from the area in which the National Home was supposed to be established. 'Abdullah, a son of Husayn, Sherif of Mecca, was appointed Emir of newly created *Transjordan. At the same time Churchill told an Arab delegation in Jerusalem that it was only right that the Jews should have a National Home. Reminding the Arabs that they had been liberated from the Turks by British forces, he rejected their demand for the stoppage of Jewish *immigration and for the creation of a government in Palestine by those who had lived there prior to 1914.

Following the Arab riots of May, 1921, a commission of inquiry was appointed (see HAYCRAFT COMMISSION OF INQUIRY). It found that the fundamental cause of the riots was Arab discontent and Arab hostility to the Jews "due to political and economic causes connected with Jewish immigration and with their conception of Zionist policy as derived from Jewish exponents." The one-sided report came as a shock to the *Yishuv (Jewish population of Palestine) and to the Jewish world. Various measures were taken by the Palestine administration to pacify the Arabs. Jewish immigration was temporarily suspended. Hajj Amin *al-Husayni, who was appointed mufti of Jerusalem in 1921, emerged as a violent opponent of both the Yishuv and the British administration. The interim report of the Palestine administration for the period from July 1, 1920, to June 30, 1921, contained a new formulation of the official British attitude to the National Home:

The policy of H.M. Government contemplates the satisfaction of the legitimate aspirations of the Jewish race throughout the

world in relation to Palestine combined with a full protection of the rights of the existing population. . . . The Zionism that is practicable is the Zionism that fulfils this essential condition. There must be satisfaction of that sentiment regarding Palestine—a worthy and ennobling sentiment which, in an increasing degree, animates the Jews of the world. The aspirations of these fourteen millions of people also have a right to be considered.

Soon afterward the popular press, which was controlled by Lords Northcliffe and Beaverbrook, started a violent campaign against the idea of the Jewish National Home. The Jewish pioneers were accused of being "Bolsheviks," and it was claimed that the "Zionist experiment" was costing the British taxpayer enormous sums of money. These were just a few of the stories spread by the reactionary British press at a time when the government was engaged in final negotiations connected with Britain's assumption of the Mandate for Palestine. At the same time an anti-Zionist campaign motivated by a mixture of pro-Arab sentiments, British isolationism, and *anti-Semitism was led by Sir William Joynson-Hicks, a Conservative, in the House of Commons and by Lords Islington and Sydenham in the House of Lords.

In a debate in the House of Lords on June 21, 1922, the Government was attacked for its pro-Zionist policy. Lord Balfour, who had just been inducted into the Upper House, rose in defense of the policy with which his name was identified, but the House of Lords adopted (60 to 29) a motion to postpone acceptance of the mandate. Although this decision had no practical effect (a motion to repeal the Balfour Declaration was heavily defeated in the House of Commons), it was an indication of the anti-Zionist feeling in certain upper circles of British society.

On June 30, 1922, the British government, under the authority of Colonial Secretary Churchill, published a White Paper that defined Jewish rights as follows (see WHITE PAPER OF JUNE, 1922):

Where it is asked what is meant by the development of the Jewish National Home in Palestine, it may be answered that it is not the imposition of a Jewish nationality upon the inhabitants of Palestine as a whole, but the further development of the existing Jewish community with the assistance of Jews in other parts of the world, in order that it may become a centre in which the Jewish people as a whole may take, on grounds of religion or race, an interest and a pride. But in order that this community should have the best prospect of free development and provide a full opportunity for the Jewish people to display its capacities it is essential that it should know that it is in Palestine as of right and not on sufferance.

On the other hand, the White Paper made it clear that whereas Jewish immigration must continue, "this immigration cannot be so great in volume as to exceed whatever may be the economic capacity of the country at the time to absorb new arrivals," that "the immigrants should not be a burden upon the people of Palestine as a whole," and that "persons who are politically undesirable" would be excluded from Palestine. It also stressed the intention of the British authorities to foster the establishment, by gradual stages, of a full measure of self-government in Palestine.

The White Paper included a letter from the Colonial Office to the WZO, requesting the latter to give "formal assurance" that it accepted the policy set forth in the statement and was prepared to conduct its own activities in conformity therewith, and a reply from Chaim Weizmann embodying a resolution of the Zionist Executive that contained the required assurance. The Executive considered the White Paper a serious whittling down of the Balfour Declaration. Since it was made clear to the Zionists that confirmation of the mandate would be conditional on their acceptance of British policy as set forth in the White Paper, however, the Executive sent the requested letter of acceptance (June 18, 1922), expressing the hope that whatever arrangement the British government would make with regard to Jewish immigration into Palestine would be in keeping with the spirit of the Balfour Declaration and assuring the British that the WZO would spare no effort to foster the "spirit of goodwill" which the British had agreed was the only sure foundation for the future prosperity of Palestine. On July 24, 1922, the Council of the League of Nations entrusted the administration of Palestine to Great Britain as the mandatory power.

Quiet Years, 1922–29. The years 1922–29 were a relatively tranquil period in the development of the Jewish National Home and in the political field. After accepting the League of Nations Mandate for Palestine, the British government made various attempts to secure the cooperation of the Arab leaders. The latter, however, rejected a proposed *Legislative Council in Palestine and opposed the organization of an Arab Agency that would have occupied a position analogous to that of the *Jewish Agency. As a result, the legislative as well as the executive functions in Palestine remained the sole prerogative of the High Commissioner.

The Conservative Government of Great Britain was defeated in the general election of November, 1923, and was succeeded by a Labor Government under James Ramsay *MacDonald, who had a first-hand knowledge of conditions in Palestine. On Feb. 2, 1924, James Henry Thomas, the new Colonial Secretary, stated in reply to a parliamentary question:

> H.M. Government have decided after careful consideration of all the circumstances to adhere to the policy of giving effect to the Balfour Declaration of 1917, under which Great Britain undertook to promote the establishment in Palestine of a National Home for the Jewish people, it being clearly understood that nothing should be done to prejudice the civil and religious rights of other communities in the country. This policy was embodied in the Mandate for Palestine, which was approved by the League of Nations.

A new general election in 1924 returned a Conservative Government under Stanley Baldwin. On Apr. 21, 1925, Leopold Amery, the new Colonial Secretary, made the following statement to an Arab deputation in Jerusalem:

> The question [of the Balfour Declaration] was considered first of all by the British Government which announced the Declaration; it was reconsidered by the Conservative Government which followed. . . . It has since been confirmed by a Government of quite a different party. It has also been examined by all the nations represented in the League of Nations. I am sure, therefore, that the gentlemen here do not really expect that the British Government could change its policy on this matter.

In his address to the 14th Zionist Congress (Vienna, 1925), Weizmann expressed his appreciation of the courteous and sympathetic hearing that was invariably given to Zionist representatives by the Colonial Office and other departments of the British government with which they were brought into contact. He added that during the preceding two years (1923–25) the Zionist movement had visibly risen in public esteem in Great Britain. The report of the Zionist Executive to the 15th Zionist Congress (Basle, 1927) stated that relations with the British

government had been satisfactory throughout. It added that although the representations of the Zionists were inevitably not always successful, they had received prompt and sympathetic consideration and the attitude of the Colonial Office on the whole had been friendly and helpful.

In 1926 an influential Parliamentary Palestine Committee was formed. It comprised about 75 members from all sections of the House of Commons, including two ex-prime ministers, Lloyd George and Ramsay MacDonald. On August 27, Lord Balfour, MacDonald, Lloyd George, Philip Snowden, Ethel Snowden, Lieut. Gen. Sir George McDonogh, Col. Josiah Clement *Wedgwood, Sir Wyndham Deedes, Blanche *Dugdale, and Herbert Sidebotham signed a letter to Weizmann, assuring him of their deep interest in the Zionist movement. In March, 1928, followed the establishment of a Palestine Mandate Society under the chairmanship of Lord Cecil of Chelwood. In 1928 Colonel Wedgwood, a stanch supporter of the Zionist movement, published his book *The Seventh Dominion*, advocating the view that Jewish Palestine should become an integral part of the British Empire.

Between 1922 and 1929 the Zionist movement had various misgivings about the policy of the mandatory power on concrete issues, but these controversies were conducted on the basis of the general policy adopted by the British government in Palestine, namely, adherence to the principles laid down in the Balfour Declaration and the mandate. From time to time attacks on Zionism were published in the British press, but these largely emanated from reactionary and pro-Arab circles; they did not affect the Palestine policy of the three major political parties and their sympathetic attitude to the Jewish National Home. On the Zionist side, Chaim Weizmann, who was president of the WZO during the period in question, followed a consistent policy of cooperation with the British government.

The Arab riots of 1929, followed by the report of the *Shaw Commission and the publication of the strongly anti-Zionist *Passfield White Paper (1930), came as a shock to the Jewish world and made the Palestine problem a controversial issue in British politics.

Prewar Decade, 1930–39. Leaders of the Opposition, including Lloyd George, Stanley Baldwin, Sir Austen Chamberlain, Leopold Amery, and Sir John Simon, from varying points of view attacked the Passfield White Paper as inconsistent with the mandate which Britain had been given over Palestine. More serious for the Government was the indignation within the Labor party in Parliament. Matters were brought to a head during the Whitechapel by-election, in which a Labor seat was endangered by the Government's White Paper. In addition, the anti-Zionist document was severely attacked in the *Times* by leading statesmen of all parties. On Nov. 17, 1930, the issue was the subject of a debate in the House of Commons in which a great deal of sympathy was expressed for the Zionist cause. Finally, Prime Minister MacDonald agreed to set up a committee of Cabinet ministers to discuss the situation with representatives of the Jewish Agency. Arthur Henderson acted as chairman and Malcolm MacDonald, the Prime Minister's son, as secretary; both were known as friends of Zionism.

The outcome of the Cabinet committee's discussions with the representatives of the Zionist movement was the publication on Feb. 13, 1931, of the *MacDonald letter to Weizmann. Although this document did not officially reject the Passfield White Paper, it explained away and negated its objectionable passages. The appointment of Sir Arthur *Wauchope as the new High Commissioner for Palestine (1931) did much to restore the confidence of the Yishuv in the Palestine administration. A situation of comparative tranquillity continued until 1933, the year of Hitler's advent to power.

Between 1933 and 1936 two tendencies were noticeable in Britain's attitude toward the Zionist movement. On the one hand, there was much sympathy for the Jewish victims of Nazism and support for increased Jewish immigration to Palestine. On the other hand, there was great concern about growing Arab resistance encouraged by Nazi and Fascist propaganda.

At the end of 1935 the High Commissioner announced a proposal for the establishment of a Legislative Council in Palestine, a project that had been rejected by the Arab leaders in 1922. The Jewish Agency leaders denounced the proposal on the ground that it would reduce the Jews to a minority status in their own National Home; they considered it an act of appeasement of Arab extremism. The Jewish point of view received much sympathy in parliamentary circles, especially in the Labor and Liberal parties, which were now the Opposition. While talks on the Legislative Council reached a deadlock, murderous attacks were launched by Arab terrorists on Jewish civilians in Jaffa. The riots soon spread throughout the country; there were assaults also on the British military and police. During the three years that followed (1936–39), the terrorists were assisted by mercenaries from Iraq and Syria and by funds and arms from Nazi Germany and Fascist Italy.

Although there was great sympathy in Britain for the Jewish victims of Arab terrorism, the deterioration of the international situation fostered a growing tendency in British government circles to meet Arab demands to limit Jewish immigration and to follow a policy of status quo in Palestine; this meant, in effect, to arrest further development of the Jewish National Home. The government had moved cautiously in order not to antagonize the pro-Zionist elements, but following the outbreak of the 1936 riots its policy in Palestine was moving toward a pro-Arab orientation.

In August, 1936, the British government appointed a Royal Commission under Lord Peel to investigate the causes of unrest and alleged grievances of Arabs and Jews. The *Peel Commission's report, which recommended the *partition of Palestine, was published in July, 1937. It aroused great controversy in Britain. During the parliamentary debate some members supported the principle of partitioning Palestine into two states, while others violently opposed it and urged the continuation of the mandate. The Zionist movement was engaged in the same controversy and was especially concerned with the problem of the territory to be allotted to the Jewish State.

In the two years preceding the outbreak of World War II it became obvious that the Government of Neville Chamberlain was determined to pursue a policy of appeasement, not only toward the Nazis but also toward the Arabs, and to ignore the provisions of the Balfour Declaration and the mandate. To gain time the government sent (1938) another commission to Palestine, the *Woodhead Commission, which reported that it had no concrete partition proposal to offer. In 1939 the British government called the *St. James Conference, during which it conducted talks separately with Arab and Jewish represent-atives. It was clear from the beginning that the negotiations were a mere formality because the government was determined to limit Jewish immigration and land purchase in Palestine. On Mar. 6, 1939, the London *News Chronicle* published the results of a survey made by the British Institute of Public Opinion on the question whether the British government should continue to permit Jews to settle in Palestine. The replies received showed that 60 per cent of those polled favored Jewish immigration into Palestine, 14 per cent opposed it, and 26 per cent had no opinion.

The *White Paper of 1939, which severely limited Jewish immigration and land purchase, opened a new chapter in the political history of Palestine. The document was denounced in strong terms by the Labor and Liberal parties; it was also condemned by a group of Conservative members of Parliament led by Winston Churchill. Opposition to the White Paper was strong in many organs of the press. Many British leaders opposed the Chamberlain policy of appeasement, compared it to the betrayal of Czechoslovakia, and denounced it as a breach of faith with the Jewish people. But the general climate of opinion in Europe a few months before World War II held out little hope for a change in the government's anti-Zionist policy.

World War II, 1939–45. On Aug. 29, 1939, a few days before the outbreak of the war, Weizmann wrote a letter to British Prime Minister Neville Chamberlain, declaring that the Jewish people would stand by Great Britain and fight on the side of the democracies. He also expressed the readiness of the Jewish Agency to enter into immediate arrangements for utilizing Jewish manpower, technical ability, and resources for the war effort. A letter of acknowledgment from Chamberlain, dated Sept. 2, 1939, expressed warm appreciation but agreed with Weizmann that "differences of opinion exist between the Mandatory Power and the Jewish Agency as regards policy in Palestine." It soon emerged that the British government intended to adhere to the provisions of the White Paper.

On Feb. 28, 1940, the government promulgated the *Land Transfer Regulations, which severely restricted the right of Jews to acquire land in Palestine. During a dramatic parliamentary debate (Mar. 6, 1940) a vote of censure against the Chamberlain administration was moved by the Labor Opposition. The Socialist spokesmen denounced the new regulations as "politically unwise, economically unsound and constitutionally unjust."

The resignation of the Chamberlain Cabinet and the formation of a new government headed by Winston Churchill (May 10, 1940) raised great hopes in both the Yishuv and the Zionist movement, but there was no change in the White Paper policy. During the war years the Jewish Agency tried to convince the British government that the restrictions on Jewish immigration to Palestine were causing the loss of many Jewish lives, but the government adhered to the status quo, promising that its policy would be reviewed after the war. Between 1940 and 1945 the British public was preoccupied with the prosecution of the war, and there was little chance for successful opposition to the official policies pursued by the coalition Government. There was great interest, however, in postwar aims.

Meanwhile, the Jewish Agency, anxious to have Jewry participate in the war effort under its own banner, made various approaches to the British government, drawing attention to the war potential of the Yishuv with its skilled labor and highly specialized experts in science and industry. However, the official response was lukewarm and dilatory. The proposal to organize a Jewish fighting force composed of Palestinian and non-Palestinian Jews found strong support in Britain, but the government, fearful of antagonizing the Arabs, viewed it with great hesitancy. It was not until Sept. 19, 1944, that an official announcement was made in London to the effect that the government had decided to accede to the Jewish Agency's request that a *Jewish Brigade be formed to take part in active operations. Speaking in the House of Commons on September 28, Prime Minister Churchill declared:

> I know there are vast numbers of Jews serving with our Forces and the American Forces throughout all the Armies, but it seems to me indeed appropriate that a special Jewish unit, a unit of that race which has suffered indescribable torments from the Nazis, should be represented as a distinct formation among the forces gathered for their final overthrow, and I have no doubt they will not only take part in the struggle but also in the occupation which will follow.

During its struggle for the establishment of the Jewish Brigade, the Jewish Agency had the support of many prominent British men and women. The Zionist cause sustained great losses during the war years through the deaths of Miss Eleanor Rathbone, M.P., Lord Wedgwood, Lord Snell, Lord Davies, and Col. Victor *Cazalet, M.P., all of whom had been stanch champions of Jewish aspirations in Palestine for many years.

By the summer of 1944, when there was every indication of a quick Allied victory, the Jewish Agency felt that the time had come to make its views on a settlement of the Palestine problem officially known to the British government. Prime Minister Churchill indicated to Weizmann that the issue would be dealt with at the end of the war with Germany. On May 25, 1945, the Jewish Agency submitted a second memorandum to the Prime Minister. On June 9, Churchill sent a reply to the effect that he saw no possibility of the Palestine question's "being effectively considered until the victorious Allies are definitely seated at the Peace Table." Soon after this exchange of correspondence the coalition Government came to an end and was succeeded by a Labor Government with Clement R. Attlee as Prime Minister and Ernest *Bevin as Foreign Secretary.

At first there were high hopes that the new Socialist administration would abrogate the provisions of the White Paper, for the Labor party had been strongly committed to support of the Zionist cause. Shortly before the general election of 1945 the annual conference of the Labor party had declared that "there is surely neither hope nor meaning in a 'Jewish National Home' unless we are prepared to let Jews, if they wish, enter the tiny land in such numbers as to become a majority. . . . The Arabs have many wide territories of their own; they must not claim to exclude the Jews from the small area of Palestine, less than the size of Wales. . . ." Much to the dismay of Jewish opinion as well as of many Labor supporters, however, it emerged that Foreign Secretary Bevin, who wielded great influence in the Cabinet, was determined to continue the White Paper policy.

Final Years of the Mandate, 1945–48. On Nov. 13, 1945, Foreign Secretary Bevin announced the appointment of an *Anglo-American Committee of Inquiry to study the Palestine problem and the situation of European Jewry. He made it clear that there would be no change in the restrictions on Jewish immigration and land purchase during the interim period. In reply to questions he said: "I am sure that this House [House of Commons] and Jewry as a whole, apart from the Zionist Organization, are anxious to see a final solution." He added: "The Arabs are meeting me very well, and I thank them for it. There is a great sense of responsibility, except for one small section among Jewry, and the Jews are not all Zionists." That same day the Jewish Agency declared in reply to Bevin's statement that the policy embodied in the White Paper and still enforced by the British government was "a violation of the Palestine Mandate."

A debate in the House of Lords on Dec. 4, 1945, followed by a debate in the House of Commons on Feb. 21, 1946, as well as various press comments showed that the majority of both Government supporters and the Conservative Opposition were prepared to back Bevin's policy. However, a sizable section of the Labor party and several Conservative members, headed by Winston Churchill, were opposed to the continuation of the White Paper.

The publication of the unanimous report of the Anglo-American Committee (May 1, 1946) led to renewed controversy on the Palestine problem in Parliament and outside it. The British government, under Prime Minister Attlee and Foreign Secretary Bevin, refused to carry out the report's recommendation to admit 100,000 Jewish refugees to Palestine forthwith. In the face of growing resistance activity in Palestine, it intensified the struggle against "*illegal immigration." On June 30, 1946, the Palestine administration arrested many leading figures of the Jewish Agency and the Yishuv. This unexpected step led to a stormy debate in the House of Commons on July 1. A section of the Labor party strongly attacked its own Government's policy, while several Conservatives urged stronger measures against the Yishuv. No vote was taken. It was clear that Bevin intended to continue his policy. In view of his powerful position in the Government and in the Labor movement and of the support he was receiving from a large majority of the Conservative party, he could afford to ignore the fairly strong opposition within his own party.

The Yishuv's resistance to Bevin's policy deeply divided British public opinion; the majority backed the government's policy, while the minority felt uneasy, especially in light of Jewish suffering in Europe and the situation of Jewish displaced persons in Germany, Austria, and Italy. Opposition to Bevin's policy was especially strong in the Labor and the Liberal parties, and Churchill and several of his friends remained true to their long-standing friendship for the Zionist cause—a point of view not shared by his own party.

On Attlee's insistence that his government wanted the United States to assume a share of responsibility and to supply military and financial assistance for the implementation of the recommendations of the Anglo-American Committee, Pres. Harry S *Truman set up a Cabinet committee, which in turn appointed a working body of alternates, chaired by Henry F. Grady, to develop the pertinent details with the British. The outgrowth of these deliberations was the *Morrison-Grady Plan, which called for the division of Palestine into Jewish and Arab provinces (cantons) under a federalized government. It was introduced in the House of Commons on July 31, 1946, by Deputy Prime Minister Herbert Morrison, and was eventually rejected not only by the Jews and Arabs but also by President Truman. During the parliamentary debate Churchill suggested that the Palestine problem be submitted to the United Nations, a course of action that was actually adopted six months later.

Late in January, 1947, a conference on the Palestine problem was opened in St. James's Palace, London, between eight Arab delegations and the British government. On January 29, six representatives of the Jewish Agency Executive—David *Ben-Gurion, Selig *Brodetsky, Nahum *Goldmann, Berl *Locker, Emanuel *Neumann, and Moshe Shertok (Moshe *Sharett)—met with Bevin and Colonial Secretary Arthur *Creech-Jones for an exchange of views. On February 7,

Bevin submitted to the Arabs and the Jewish Agency his plan for the settlement of the Palestine problem. Palestine was to be divided into two semiautonomous states, one Jewish and one Arab, subject to the overall authority of the British government. The areas to be included in each state were not defined, but it was specified that they need not be contiguous and would be determined by the majority of the population living in each district. Under this plan Jewish immigration to the Jewish sector, which had been limited to 1,500 persons a month, was to be raised to 4,000 persons a month for a period of two years, after which the High Commissioner could reduce immigration if, in his opinion, it exceeded the absorption capacity of the area. If, after five years, the Bevin Plan should prove unworkable, the Palestine problem was to be referred to the UN Trusteeship Council. The plan was rejected by the Jews and the Arabs (the latter wanted a completely independent Arab state and a complete cessation of Jewish immigration), and the conference ended in failure.

On Feb. 25, 1947, the government finally decided to submit the Palestine issue to the United Nations; this step came as a great relief to British public opinion. In the meantime, however, Bevin, backed by the government and especially by Prime Minister Attlee, continued the White Paper policy in Palestine and intensified the struggle against illegal immigration, which reached its climax in the tragedy of the *"Exodus 1947," whose passengers were forcibly removed from Palestine to Germany (July–August, 1947).

On Sept. 26, 1947, Colonial Secretary Creech-Jones made a statement before the Political Committee of the UN General Assembly outlining Great Britain's Palestine policy. While expressing its readiness to cooperate with the Assembly to the fullest possible extent, he made the following reservation: "The United Kingdom Government is ready to assume responsibility for giving effect to any plan on which agreement is reached between the Arabs and the Jews." He made it clear that if there was no such agreement, it would be necessary to provide for some alternative authority to implement the plan arrived at. He also stated that, in deliberations on any proposal to the effect that the British government participate with others in the enforcement of a settlement, the United Nations would have to consider not only whether the settlement would be fair but also whether, and to what extent, it could be carried out without military force. He announced that in the absence of a settlement the United Nations must count on the early withdrawal of British forces and British administration from Palestine.

On Nov. 29, 1947, the General Assembly approved (33 to 13, with 10 abstentions) the partition of Palestine, that is, the establishment of a Jewish State in part of the country. Britain refused to help implement the decision.

On Dec. 11, 1947, Creech-Jones announced in the House of Commons that the Palestine Mandate would be terminated on May 15, 1948. Foreign Secretary Bevin stated that Britain was under no obligation to change the immigration quota during the brief period remaining in which it would be responsible for Palestine. He also asserted that the enforcement of the United Nations decision would have to be left to others. He pointed out that the decision had been described by one of the parties as "illegal and unjust," a view backed by 13 negative votes and 10 abstentions, representing a Muslim world of 200 million, as opposed to between 10 and 20 million Jews.

First Decade of the State of Israel, 1948–58. Britain's negative attitude to the partition plan and the establishment of a Jewish

State was felt in Palestine throughout the transition period from December, 1947, to May 15, 1948, the day when the State of Israel came into being. British public opinion was sharply divided on the partition decision. There was widespread relief that the mandate had come to an end, but there were serious differences of opinion on the government's policy during the transition period. Whereas some members of Parliament and part of the press considered Bevin's approach correct, others deplored and condemned the policy of "neutrality" and lack of cooperation, which, it was thought, was unfair to the Jewish side and would inevitably lead to bloodshed in Palestine.

In reply to a parliamentary question, Bevin declared on June 9, 1948, that in the opinion of the government the recommendations voted by the UN General Assembly on Nov. 29, 1947, could not be construed as legally obligating Britain to recognize the new Jewish State. Pointing out that the United Nations resolution had instructed the Palestine Commission to carry out a detailed plan culminating in the establishment of a Jewish and an Arab State linked by an economic union and that almost no part of this plan had been executed, the Foreign Secretary made it clear that the government would judge the Jewish State's case for recognition on its own merits according to the accepted criteria of international law.

During the second half of 1948 there was increasing pressure on the British government to recognize the new State, but it was not until Jan. 29, 1949, that Bevin was finally compelled to give way and accord de facto recognition to Israel. On Apr. 27, 1950, the government extended de jure recognition.

For several years Britain's policy with regard to the Arab-Israel problem was governed by the Tripartite Declaration of May 25, 1950, adopted at a London conference of the Foreign Ministers of Britain, France, and the United States, which signified the determination of those nations not to permit any change of frontiers in the Middle East by military force. Following the events of 1956, which led to the *Sinai Campaign, the declaration lost a great deal of its significance, but it was never offically invalidated.

In 1951 Ernest Bevin was replaced by Anthony Eden (later Lord Avon) as Foreign Secretary. When Britain joined the Baghdad Pact (1955), in which Iraq but not Israel was a partner, Eden declared in the House of Commons that the agreement was "based on the concept of cooperation between equal partners, which it has been our purpose to establish generally in our relations with Middle Eastern countries." In his memoirs Eden stated that if the pact would bring new security to the Middle East, Israel also would benefit. In a speech delivered in London on Nov. 9, 1955, Eden, by then Prime Minister, called for a compromise adjustment between Israel's borders at the time and those assigned it under the United Nations partition resolution.

The Sinai Campaign of 1956 brought great changes in Britain's Middle East policy. Overnight the Conservative Government became friendly to Israel, while the Labor Opposition was critical of David Ben-Gurion's action against Egypt. It took a year for the Labor party gradually to revert to its friendship for Israel, making a clear differentiation between the motives behind the Anglo-French action at the Suez Canal and Israel's decision to fight for its survival. The isolation of Britain in the Middle East, which reached its climax with the coup d'état in Iraq (1958), led Harold Macmillan, who had become Prime Minister after the resignation of Sir Anthony Eden, to espouse an attitude of genuine neutrality toward Arab and

Jewish claims, placing Anglo-Israel relations on a basis of mutual understanding and friendship. This turning point in Britain's attitude toward Israel was fully reflected in Parliament and in the press, which had anticipated the Foreign Office in their positive attitude toward Israel. The Opposition parties, the Labor party led by Hugh Gaitskell and the Liberals, warmly welcomed the new policy toward Israel.

After Sinai, 1958–69. The years immediately following the Sinai Campaign (1958–63) saw an improvement in Anglo-Israel relations. The Labor party showed great understanding of Israel's position, although its left wing was still somewhat suspicious of Israel as a result of the Sinai Campaign. The Conservatives, especially the "Suez rebels," were highly critical of Egypt's President Gamal Abdel Nasser and friendly to Israel.

On May 14, 1963, Prime Minister Macmillan made a statement in the House of Commons that indicated a radical change in Britain's policy in the Middle East. He endorsed Pres. John F. Kennedy's statement to the effect that, should Israel or any of the Arab states appear to violate frontiers or armistice lines, the United States would take immediate action both within and outside the United Nations to prevent such violation. Macmillan clarified Britain's attitude as follows:

> Her Majesty's Government are deeply interested in peace and stability in this area and are opposed to the use of force or the threat of force there as elsewhere in the world. We are equally opposed to the interference by any country in the internal affairs of another, whether by the encouragement of subversion or by hostile propaganda. I cannot say in advance what action we would take in a crisis since it is difficult to foresee the exact circumstances which might arise. We regard the United Nations as being primarily responsible for the maintenance of peace in the area. If any threat to peace arises, we will consult immediately with the United Nations and will take whatever action we feel may be required.

This statement of British policy toward the Arab-Israel problem indicated further disengagement from the Middle East and a de facto annulment of the Tripartite Declaration, which had stressed active intervention in the area under certain circumstances. It signified the end of the formal understanding with France, while maintaining a close link with the United States. Finally, it made clear that the United Nations, and not Britain or any other country, was to be held responsible for the maintenance of peace in the Middle East.

When the Labor Government returned to power in October, 1964, it endorsed Macmillan's statement. The new Prime Minister, Harold Wilson, made it clear, as he had prior to the elections, that while he would strive for improved relations with the Arab states, he would not do so at the expense of Israel. This pledge, which was reiterated on a number of occasions by senior members of the Labor Government, became a guideline for Labor policy in the Middle East.

In the years that followed, Anglo-Israel relations were strengthened on the diplomatic level through the exchange of delegations, increased trade, cultural contacts, and tourism. Friendship for Israel had been removed from party politics and was shown by the leading figures and the rank and file of all the major political parties.

During the Middle East crisis of May, 1967, Britain's main concern was to safeguard free navigation through the Suez Canal and the Strait of Tiran, and it supported the efforts of the United States government to lift the blockade of the strait im-posed by Nasser. At the same time, Britain was anxious to prevent the outbreak of open warfare in the Middle East. The government was determined not to become directly involved in the conflict, but public opinion was strongly on the side of Israel. A day after the outbreak of the *Six-day War on June 5, Foreign Secretary George Brown declared in the House of Commons: "The Government's attitude—and the House will, I know, support me in saying this—is that the British concern is not to take sides but to ensure a peaceful solution to the problems of the area." This position was similar to that taken by the United States and a number of other Western governments.

Between June and November, 1967, British objectives at the United Nations were as follows: to achieve strict adherence to the cease-fire agreement; to extend help to the civilian victims of hostilities and to prisoners of war; to obtain Israel's consent for the return of the *Arab refugees who had fled as a result of the military operations; to oppose Israel's annexation of Arab territories under its control; and to promote agreement in the Security Council on a resolution dealing with the long-range settlement of the Arab-Israel conflict. The government and public opinion were greatly relieved by Israel's victory, but the Foreign Office under George Brown was anxious to maintain "neutrality." It indulged in a campaign of sympathy for the Arabs, especially on the problem of refugees and Jerusalem, appealing to Israel to pursue a policy of restraint and "magnanimity." Brown's policy was frequently criticized both in Parliament and the press.

On Nov. 22, 1967, the Security Council adopted the British-sponsored resolution on the Middle East. Thereafter the British government tried to promote agreement between the Arab states and Israel and to maintain genuine neutrality; it avoided blaming one side or the other for the difficulties of the Middle East situation. On Nov. 28, 1967, the Foreign Office, in reply to a communication from the *Board of Deputies of British Jews, explained British policy with regard to the Arab-Israel conflict as follows:

> In tabling the British draft resolution in the Security Council Her Majesty's Government had very much in mind the urgent need to make real progress on the ground towards a permanent settlement in the Middle East which alone could provide an assured and lasting guarantee for the security of Israel in the longer term. The recent breaches of the cease-fire have shown all too clearly that time is on no one's side and that in the absence of effective action by the Security Council renewed fighting is inevitable sooner or later with the likelihood of much greater destruction and loss of life..
>
> Naturally any resolution which had any likelihood of achieving the co-operation of both sides with the Secretary-General's representative, who is to go to the area in a conciliatory role, was bound to have elements in it not entirely to the liking of one side or the other. However, the text must be read as a whole. Israeli withdrawal is balanced by "termination of all claims or states of belligerency and respect for and acknowledgment of the sovereignty, territorial integrity and political independence of every state in the area and their right to live in peace within secure and recognized boundaries free from threats or acts of force." Furthermore, the necessity for guaranteeing freedom of passage through international waterways is also specifically mentioned. The resolution states the principles on which a settlement should be based but it does not call for Israel withdrawal in advance of acceptable arrangements to provide for Israel's security in accordance with the balancing provisions of the resolution set out above. . . .

As of mid-1969 Anglo-Israel relations could be described as normal and friendly; differences of opinion emerged from time to time, but this was inevitable in a relationship between two governments whose interests did not always coincide. British public opinion, with the exception of a vociferous pro-Arab group organized in the Council for the Advancement of Arab-British Understanding, showed a general appreciation for Israel's problems. The volume of trade between the two countries was on the increase; Israel was buying more goods from Britain than all the neighboring Arab countries combined. Negotiations on an Anglo-Israel cultural agreement had reached an advanced stage.

A Gallup Poll survey taken in February–March, 1969, showed that of every 59 Britons taking sides in the Arab-Israel conflict, 53 favored Israel and only 6 the Arab states as compared with 41 and 8, respectively, in January, 1969. On Mar. 24, 1969, Foreign Secretary Michael Stewart dealt with the question of whether a solution of the Arab-Israel conflict could be imposed by the four great powers. He said in the course of a House of Commons statement: "If by 'impose,' one means something that both sides, or even one side, bitterly hated but were told they must accept, I do not think that such a solution would work. . . . On the other hand, there is clearly the necessity to have some degree of very urgent persuasion by the Four Powers . . . a real solution, therefore, stands somewhere between 100 per cent free acceptance by the parties concerned . . . and 100 per cent imposition which is impossible."

S. LEVENBERG

GREAT BRITAIN, ZIONISM IN. Following a period of several decades during which certain Jewish circles evinced increasing interest in the idea of the Return to Zion and organized *Hoveve Zion groups and other proto-Zionist societies, political Zionism became established in Great Britain as a result of Herzl's visit to London in 1896. That year, disappointed by the lukewarm reception he had found among the more Anglicized Jews, Herzl decided to turn to the Jewish masses, and one of his first steps in this direction was his appearance at a mass meeting at the Workingmen's Club in London's East End (July 12, 1896). The meeting was chaired by Moses *Gaster, Haham (rabbi) of the London Sephardi community, and addressed by Ephraim *Ish-Kishor. These two men, together with Jacob *de Haas and Israel *Zangwill, became the earliest and most faithful lieutenants of Herzl in organizing the Zionist movement in Great Britain.

However, the wave of enthusiasm created by Herzl's appearance did not go beyond the immigrant element and the few young college graduates who had sprung from its midst. It did not affect circles that had political influence or were affluent enough to give the movement substantial financial backing. The London Hoveve Zion were, in fact, alarmed by the political methods Herzl outlined at their meeting of July 13, 1896, to which he was invited and which was chaired by Col. Albert E.W. *Goldsmid. They feared that Herzl's plans would cause Turkey to ban Jewish settlement work in Palestine, which at the time was the sole aim of the Hoveve Zion.

About a year later, when Herzl sent out invitations to the

Theodor Herzl with a group of friends in London in 1900. To the right of Herzl is his mother; to the left, Israel Zangwill. Seated on the ground in front of Herzl's mother is Col. Albert Edward Williamson Goldsmid. [Zionist Archives]

1st Zionist *Congress (Basle, 1897), the London Hoveve Zion declined to attend. Eight delegates from the newly organized Zionist societies in England accepted, however, among them Joseph *Cowen, a London manufacturer, Jacob de Haas, A. Ginsburg, a Liverpool Jew of Russian origin, Ephraim Ish-Kishor, Joseph *Massel, a Hebrew printer in Manchester, Solomon B. Rubinstein, a London lawyer, and Israel Zangwill.

Early Years. As it grew, the Zionist movement was subjected to criticism and opposition by lay and religious leaders of the community. Among its detractors were Lucien Wolf, the publicist and historian, and Israel Abrahams, the Jewish scholar. The Chief Rabbi, Dr. Hermann Adler, sounded a warning against "fantastic and visionary ideas" about the reestablishment of a Jewish State or a Jewish nation.

Several months passed before the British Hoveve Zion decided to join forces with the new Zionist societies. At a conference held at Clerkenwell Hall in North London on Mar. 6, 1898, 27 Hoveve Zion tents and 15 Zionist societies were represented. Colonel Goldsmid, who was in the chair, said that only two choices were open to British Jewry: *assimilation or Zionism. The conference adopted a Zionist program that can be summarized as follows:

1. The national idea is an integral part of the Zionist movement. The aim is to secure a legally safeguarded resettlement of the Jewish nation in Palestine.

2. As many Jews as possible should settle in Palestine.

3. A federation of Zionist societies should be formed.

4. Knowledge of the *Hebrew language should be diffused.

By the 2d Zionist Congress (Basle, August, 1898), there were 26 Zionist societies in Great Britain. They sent 15 delegates to Basle. Two months later (October, 1898), Herzl addressed the largest Jewish meeting ever to have been held in London.

The inaugural meeting to implement the formation of an English Zionist Federation took place in January, 1899. Sir Francis Abraham *Montefiore, a nephew of Sir Moses *Montefiore, took the chair and was elected president. Other officers were M. Umansky, Moses Gaster, Leopold J. *Greenberg, Herbert *Bentwich, Jacob de Haas, J. S. Loewy, and Joseph Cowen.

In 1899 Herzl, whose belief in Britain never wavered, brought about the registration of the first Zionist financial instrument, the *Jewish Colonial Trust, as a British corporation. The branches of the federation formed share clubs, whose members invested small sums in the "Zionist" bank. Although the Hoveve Zion looked askance at this pretentious move, its influence was waning, for its most prominent members were increasingly supporting the activities of the federation. It struggled on, but by the early years of the 20th century it had almost completely disappeared.

In June, 1899, Herzl was again in London, this time to address the first conference of the English Zionist Federation in St. Martin's Town Hall. At the 3d Zionist Congress (Basle, 1899), British Zionists were represented by 16 delegates.

The Zionist movement, now stabilized, continued to spread. The enthusiasm of the East End masses, combined with the organizing skill of British-born leaders such as Joseph Cowen, earned Herzl's commendation. In his *Diaries* Herzl called them *"meine braven englischen Jungens"* ("my gallant young Englishmen"). Herzl felt that the time had come to hold a Zionist Congress in London. "Political Zionism comes to London," he wrote in *Die *Welt*, "to introduce itself officially, so to speak, to the British Empire and to ask its moral support."

At the 4th Congress, held in London in August, 1900, the 38 societies of the English Zionist Federation were represented by 28 delegates. The proceedings of that Congress were sympathetically reported in the London and provincial press.

After the Congress the federation began its political activities. Parliamentary candidates of all parties received circulars on the aims of political Zionism, inviting their comments. Herzl described this as "the most intelligent action of our movement for a long time." Thus began a tradition of information work directed to British public opinion that was to continue throughout the association of Britain with the Zionist cause.

English Zionists were active and prominent in both the *East Africa scheme and the *El-'Arish scheme. Leopold *Kessler led the El-'Arish Expedition to investigate the suitability of the area for Jewish settlement, and Col. Albert E. W. Goldsmid was its secretary. Joseph Cowen and Leopold J. Greenberg supported Herzl's position on East Africa, while Rev. Jacob Koppel *Goldbloom, the erstwhile fervent Herzlian, led his East End Jews into the camp of opponents. The controversy and bitterness that these projects engendered took their toll of the young movement. The most formidable blow to its prestige was the secession of Israel Zangwill to form the *Jewish Territorial Organization in 1905. In 1907 the *Jewish National Fund was registered in London as a British corporation.

The years following Herzl's death (1904) saw a struggle between the English Zionist Federation and the *Order of Ancient Maccabeans. This "friendly society," which aided Jewish immigrants in England with loans, sick benefits, and pensions, had been founded in 1896 by Ephraim Ish-Kishor. When David *Wolffsohn was elected president of the *World Zionist Organization (WZO) in 1905, the order opposed him and, moreover, pressed for recognition by the Zionist Congress as a separate union, that is, a Zionist society independent of the English Zionist Federation (*see* SEPARATE UNIONS). To put an end to this disunity Wolffsohn addressed a letter to the 1910 conference of the Zionist Federation, stressing that the federation was the only recognized representative of the WZO in England. The following year the Order of Ancient Maccabeans agreed to become a constituent of the Zionist Federation.

The appearance of Chaim *Weizmann in England in 1904 gave new impetus to the movement, which in the meantime had suffered a serious decline. Weizmann first settled in Manchester (the center of Zionist activity was then in London) and gathered around him a group of young intellectuals such as Israel Moses *Sieff, Simon *Marks, Harry *Sacher, then a leader writer on the *Manchester Guardian*, and Leon *Simon, then in Leeds but on his way to becoming a distinguished civil servant, Hebrew scholar, and the translator of *Ahad Ha'Am. Sacher and Simon took over the Zionist monthly *Zionist Banner*, which was founded in 1910 by Joseph L. Cohen in Manchester, and in 1911 moved it to London and renamed it the *Zionist*.

The influence of the Manchester group gradually made itself felt. The year 1913 marks a turning point. The forces of Zionism in England had rallied and were consolidated. The controversy over East Africa had subsided. The Hoveve Zion had disappeared as a separate entity and merged with the Zionist movement. The Maccabeans had become a constituent of the Zionist Federation. Weizmann, who had long been known in the Zionist world, turned his attention to English Zionism and won the English Zionists to his "synthetic" and practical

A meeting of the English Zionist Federation on Nov. 2, 1918. At the right corner of the dais is Nahum Sokolow. Second to the left of him is Chaim Weizmann. [Zionist Archives]

approach (*see* PRACTICAL ZIONISM; SYNTHETIC ZIONISM). By 1914 he had become the vice-president of the federation. Its president was Joseph Cowen, who was by then committed to the Weizmann policy.

World War I and the Postwar Decade. World War I placed the Zionist Federation, then comprising 50 societies, in a key position. The Zionist *Executive could no longer operate as a central body, since its headquarters in Germany was cut off from the rest of the world. Weizmann, who by this time had established contact with British statesmen, was joined in London by Nahum *Sokolow, who as a member of the Zionist Executive officially represented the WZO. There was also the Provisional Executive Committee for General Zionist Affairs, located in New York and headed by Louis D. *Brandeis. At the same time Herbert *Samuel, then a Cabinet Minister, was endeavoring on his own to influence the British government in favor of a Jewish State in Palestine.

Representatives of the Executive Council of the Zionist Federation conferred with the Conjoint Foreign Committee of the *Board of Deputies of British Jews and the *Anglo-Jewish Association, with a view to securing a joint declaration of Jewish aims on Palestine. The negotiations were abortive, and the federation launched its own campaign, inviting signatures to a petition based on the *Basle Program. It obtained 77,039 signatures from a Jewish population of less than 300,000 and thus established that the leadership of British Jewry was out of touch with the views of the overwhelming mass of British Jews.

In January, 1916, an advisory committee was set up to direct Zionist political activity in England. It was composed of Nahum Sokolow and Yehiel *Tschlenow, members of the Executive of the WZO, and Moses Gaster, Chaim Weizmann,

Herbert Bentwich, and Joseph Cowen. The committee's work came to an end in January, 1917.

In February, 1917, Joseph Cowen voluntarily resigned from the presidency of the Zionist Federation to make way for Weizmann, who was elected in his place. In the early part of the year, Weizmann and his associates had gone far in their discussions with British political leaders. The federation provided the mass support while the official leaders of the community remained hostile and were indeed working against Zionism in influential circles. The struggle between these two elements took a dramatic turn when a letter appeared in the London *Times* over the signatures of the Board of Deputies president, D. L. Alexander, K.C., and Claude Montefiore, repudiating Zionist aims in the name of both the board and the Anglo-Jewish Association. Zionists were aroused. Reinforced by their petition, they challenged the president of the board and forced his resignation. He was replaced by Sir Stuart Samuel, who, though not officially an adherent of Zionism, was known to hold sympathetic views. The board itself endorsed the Zionist position. Lord Rothschild, an outstanding figure in British Jewry (*see* ROTHSCHILDS: BRITISH BRANCH), was honorary president of the Zionist Federation, and it was to him in this capacity that the *Balfour Declaration was addressed, on Nov. 2, 1917.

The Zionist Federation had played no small part in the achievement of this success. It had mobilized its members to petition their members of Parliament, write to the press, arrange meetings of information, and engage in many other activities. Thousands of pamphlets were printed and distributed. A new advisory political committee was set up in the fall of 1917, composed largely of persons connected with the Zionist movement of Britain. It included Ahad Ha'Am, Herbert

Bentwich, Joseph Cowen, Vladimir *Jabotinsky, Leopold Kessler, Simon Marks, Israel Sieff, Leon Simon, and Samuel *Tolkowsky.

The Balfour Declaration having been secured, the Zionist Federation began to grow rapidly, both in numbers and in influence in the community. It continued its task of organizing the Jewish community, but it was also conscious of its special role of bringing the knowledge of Zionism to the attention of the political leaders of the country and the non-Jewish population.

The *Zionist Commission, which went to Palestine in 1918, contained three Zionist Federation members, Joseph Cowen, Leon Simon, and Israel Sieff. In Palestine James de Rothschild and Edwin *Samuel were attached to the Commission. In 1919 the junior Zionist societies were federated in the Young Zionist Organization of the United Kingdom, and the Federation of Women Zionists of Great Britain and Ireland was formed.

The *San Remo Conference, convened in 1920 to discuss the future of Palestine, aroused violent opposition in a certain section of the British press, notably in Lord Beaverbrook's *Daily Express*. This influential newspaper adopted what was known as the "bag and baggage" policy to prevent Britain from accepting the *Mandate for Palestine. The federation then began a campaign to organize public opinion in favor of acceptance. Large numbers of pamphlets were issued, and a "monster petition" was organized.

The *London Zionist Conference of 1920 elected Weizmann president of the WZO and Sokolow chairman of the Zionist Executive. Thus London became the center of Zionist activities. The 12th Zionist Congress (Karlovy Vary, 1921) reelected Weizmann and confirmed London as the headquarters of the Zionist movement. From this time on the Executive of the WZO worked in close cooperation with English Zionist Federation. The work of propaganda conducted by a special committee of the federation never ceased. The *Arab riots of 1921 presented a new challenge. The federation issued 10,000 copies of an article by David *Lloyd George and of speeches favoring the British Mandate by such statesmen as Sir Wyndham *Deedes and Lord Milner.

The *Keren HaYesod (Palestine Foundation Fund), which had been established at the London Zionist Conference of 1920 and incorporated in 1921, had its head office in London until 1926, when it was transferred to Jerusalem. The Organization Department of the Zionist Executive was also located in London until its transfer to Jerusalem in 1936. The Political Department remained in London and was staffed by British Zionists (Leonard Jacques *Stein, Lewis Bernstein *Namier, Joseph Isaac *Linton).

By 1922 the Zionist Federation comprised 74 Zionist bodies (including 14 women's societies and 9 junior societies), 62 synagogues, and 40 friendly societies and similar bodies. In 1923 it took charge of the Keren HaYesod, for which it carried out an intensive campaign, raising £22,000 between December, 1923, and June, 1925. In the same period the Jewish National Fund raised almost £25,000. The federation's organ, the *Zionist Review* (founded in 1917), frequently gave expression to the authorized views of the WZO, with which the federation cooperated closely, especially in the political field. The Hebrew weekly of the WZO, *Ha'Olam*, was published in London for many years. The Young Zionists and the University Zionist Federation (which had become part of the Zionist Federation in 1924) published their own monthly, the *Young Zionist.* By the 1920s a great number of the leaders of British Jewry

had joined the ranks of the Zionist movement, and several of them took its helm. The writer Philip *Guedalla was president of the federation from 1924 to 1928, and Lord *Melchett from 1928 to 1930.

In the decade following World War I the federation organized several important mass meetings, which were addressed by, among others, Sir Herbert Samuel, Viscount Allenby (Edmund H. H. *Allenby), Sir Wyndham Deedes, and leaders of the World Zionist movement. The funds raised by the Keren HaYesod and the Jewish National Fund continued to increase. The work of the federation spread into so many areas that special committees had to be created to assist the Executive Council. By 1928 the following six committees were functioning: the Central Keren HaYesod Committee, the Synagogue Council, the Political Committee, the Teachers' Committee, the Education and Propaganda Committee, and the United Synagogue Central Keren HaYesod Committee.

Among the numerous meetings of this period, special mention must be made of the large meeting held on Oct. 22, 1928, to protest the incidents that had taken place at the *Western Wall in Jerusalem. Also in 1928, a joint deputation of Zionist representatives and spokesmen of the Board of Deputies of British Jews called on the *High Commissioner designate, Sir John *Chancellor, to present the views of British Jewry on British policy in Palestine. In addition, a mass demonstration was held in support of the plan to expand the *Jewish Agency. The name of the federation was changed to the Zionist Federation of Great Britain and Ireland.

M. ROSETTI

Development from 1929 to World War II. The formation of the expanded Jewish Agency (Zurich, 1929) brought about a rapprochement between the British Zionists and the non-Zionist spokesmen of Anglo-Jewry. The Board of Deputies of British Jews, whose president at the time was Sir Osmond d'Avigdor Goldsmid, became a constituent body of the Jewish Agency, a British section of which was formed in November, 1929. The political value of this development became evident in 1930, when, after the issuance of the *Passfield White Paper, the World Zionist leadership was supported by leaders of British Jewry in efforts to modify the restrictive policy embodied in the document. The *MacDonald letter (1931), addressed to Chaim Weizmann, which attempted to explain British policy vis-à-vis Palestine, was the result of these efforts. The British Zionists responded vigorously to the Arab riots of 1929. Deputations were organized and met with Sir John Chancellor, who was then in London. A mass demonstration, attended by 10,000 persons, took place at the Royal Albert Hall to protest the Arab atrocities. A Parliamentary Palestine Committee, with Barnett *Janner as honorary secretary, was formed. It was constantly furnished with material to enable it to champion the Zionist cause in Parliament.

In 1930 the federation organized numerous mass protest meetings against the suspension of certificates of *immigration to Palestine and the Passfield White Paper, arranged a large number of interviews with members of Parliament, and distributed many pamphlets. These activities, as well as the political and propaganda work of the federation, demonstrated the ability of British Zionists to aid the World Zionist movement and the *Yishuv (Jewish population of Palestine) in times of crisis by exerting influence on the British government circles that controlled the administration in Palestine.

The Revisionist movement (founded in 1925; see REVISIONISTS) transferred its central office from Paris to London in 1929. The Revisionist leaders Meir *Grossman, John M. *Machover, and M. Schwartzman had lived in London, and Grossman and Joseph *Schechtman were the editors of Der Naier Weg, the London Yiddish weekly of the Revisionist movement. Vladimir Jabotinsky, who had spent some time in London during World War I campaigning for the *Jewish Legion, settled in London in 1936 and directed the independent political activity of the *New Zionist Organization. During World War II Abraham Abrahams edited in London the Revisionist party organ, the Jewish Standard.

Following Hitler's rise to power in Germany (1933), British Zionists were deeply concerned over the fate of the German Jews. The Zionist Federation joined in forming the Central British Fund to aid German Jewry. Sir Herbert Samuel and Simon Marks visited the United States to coordinate British and American Jewish efforts on behalf of the refugees who soon began to leave Germany. Many of these refugees went to Palestine. There they were absorbed by the Yishuv, whose importance, and with it the importance of Zionism for world Jewry, was now brought home strongly to Anglo-Jewish leaders. The suffering of German Jewry and the ability of the Yishuv to serve as a haven for the refugees led to an upsurge of Zionist and Jewish awareness. This was the period in which the 2d Baron Melchett and his sister Eva, wife of the 2d Marquess of Reading, formally embraced the Jewish faith and became stanch supporters of the Zionist cause.

The Jewish refugees from Nazi and Fascist persecution who sought a haven in England reinforced the British Zionist movement. Under the leadership of its general secretary, Lavy *Bakstansky, the Zionist Federation became one of the best-organized and most effective bodies in Anglo-Jewry. The younger generation of Anglo-Jewry responded to the challenge by intensifying its Zionist activities. In 1935 the Association of Young Zionist Societies and the University Zionist Council merged to form the Federation of Zionist Youth. Several alumni of this federation, among them Abba *Eban and Avraham *Harman, were to become leading figures on the Israeli political scene. The Zionist Federation itself joined the *World Confederation of General Zionists.

Also in 1935, the Leeds Jewish Students' Federation, under the inspiration of Selig *Brodetsky, submitted a resolution to the annual conference of the Zionist Federation, urging "that a Jewish day school system—such as exists in many countries abroad—can and should be developed in this country." A number of Jewish day schools were already in existence in Great Britain at the time, but the type of educational institution envisioned by the Jewish Students' Federation, with stress on Zionism and Hebrew as a living language, did not emerge on the Anglo-Jewish scene until nearly two decades later. The *Tarbut organization expanded its Hebrew educational activities under the leadership of Rev. Jacob Koppel Goldbloom, Simon Rawidowicz (who later became professor of Hebrew literature and Jewish philosophy at Brandeis University), and Sir Leon Simon. Another significant development as Nazism spread in Europe was the increasing interest of British Zionist youth in *'Aliya (immigration to Palestine). In 1935 the David *Eder Farm was established by *HaBonim to train young people for pioneer work in Palestine.

Preoccupation with practical and cultural activities within the Jewish community did not divert the Zionist movement in Great Britain from its political work, which came to assume vital significance as it became obvious that the British government, in order to appease the Arabs, would repudiate the obligations it had assumed in the Balfour Declaration and in the mandate. To unify Zionist political work in Great Britain, the federation in 1938 invited the *Po'ale Zion and the *Mizrahi to participate in the Political Committee. Also in 1938, the monthly Zionist Review was converted into a weekly.

During the Arab riots of 1936–39 British Zionists cooperated closely with the leaders of the Jewish Agency, whose Political Department was led by Selig Brodetsky, Berl *Locker (from 1938), and Sh'lomo Zalman *Shragai. Among the leaders of the Yishuv who visited England during those years were David *Ben-Gurion, Itzhak *Ben Zvi (who represented the Yishuv at the coronation of King George VI in 1937), Eliezer *Kaplan, Berl *Katznelson, Golda Meyerson (Golda *Meir), David *Remez, Moshe Shertok (Moshe *Sharett), and Yosef *Sprinzak.

In February, 1939, London was the scene of the *St. James Conference, convened by the British government to find a solution to the Palestine problem. The Jewish delegation of the conference included a number of British Zionist leaders, among them Rev. Jacob K. Goldbloom, Chief Rabbi Joseph H. *Hertz, Lewis Bernstein Namier, Harry Sacher, and Leonard Jacques Stein (then honorary counsel to the Jewish Agency).

At the 21st Zionist Congress (Geneva, 1939), the last Congress to meet before World War II, the Zionists of Great Britain were represented by 15 delegates: 8 from the Zionist Federation, 3 from Po'ale Zion, 3 from the Mizrahi, and 1 from the *Jewish State party. The *White Paper of 1939, which restricted Jewish immigration and land purchases in Palestine, set off an intensive political campaign on the part of British Zionists, which had the support of a large majority of Anglo-Jewry and of many non-Jews from all walks of life.

World War II. During World War II the Zionist movement in Great Britain faced great difficulties. Many British Jews entered the armed forces, a large number of Jewish civilians were dispersed through evacuation from the cities to the countryside, and many Jewish refugees from Nazi-held Europe were interned as enemy aliens. Despite these hardships, added to the general disruption of communications and the massive air raids, Zionist work continued in England.

The Political Committee of the Jewish Agency became the nerve center of Zionist activity. Its members at the time were Selig Brodetsky, Mrs. Blanche *Dugdale (niece of Arthur James *Balfour), Joseph Linton (political secretary), Berl Locker, Lewis Namier, and Chaim Weizmann. Members of the Jewish Agency Executive in Jerusalem and New York came to London to participate in the deliberations of the committee.

One of the major problems facing the Jewish Agency during the first year of the war was the maintenance of contact with Palestine Jewry and the dissemination of reliable information about the Yishuv to Jewish and non-Jewish circles. For this purpose the Agency created a special Information Department, whose work was greatly aided by the Association for the Jewish National Home, founded by Sir Wyndham Deedes, former Civil Secretary of the Palestine administration and a stanch friend of the Zionist movement.

The Jewish Agency and the British Zionist movement cooperated closely in the campaign for the formation of a Jewish fighting force (see JEWISH BRIGADE). The Revisionists conducted their own campaign for a Jewish army. They were aided by Capt. Yirmiyahu *Halpern, who had started the *B'rit Trumpeldor (Betar) maritime training program in Civitavecchia, Italy (see ITALY, ZIONISM IN), and was then living in London. The Revisionist party remained active in England until the establishment of the State of Israel. The Palestine Labor Political Committee, established in 1940, kept in close touch with the British Labor party and international Socialist circles. Meanwhile, rescue work and assistance to the Jewish underground in Europe became a major concern of the Zionist movement in England, whose leaders endeavored to keep public opinion informed of the catastrophe that had befallen European Jewry.

The war changed the character of the Zionist Federation; in 1942 Po'ale Zion became one of its constituents. Also affiliated with the federation was the Jewish State party in England, of which Josef *Fraenkel had been elected president. Branches of the party were formed in Cardiff, Glasgow, and Liverpool. Some of its meetings were addressed by British statesmen such as Joseph Montague Kenworthy (see STRABOLGI, 10TH BARON) who favored the establishment of a Jewish State in Palestine. As veteran Zionist leaders moved on to greater responsibilities, new leaders came to the fore. Abraham Richtiger was a central figure in *Halutz (pioneer) youth work, and Oscar Phillips was the mainstay of *B'rit Halutzim Datiyim (Bachad). Zionists from the provinces rose to positions of national Zionist leadership.

The election of Brodetsky as president of the Board of Deputies of British Jews as early as December, 1939, was a great triumph for the Zionist cause and gave the Zionist movement increasing influence in Anglo-Jewish communal life. Elections to the board in 1943 further favored Zionist influence, though they were accompanied by strong attacks by non-Zionists and anti-Zionists on the leadership of the Zionist Federation. In 1944, after a dramatic debate, the board declared itself in favor of the establishment of a Jewish State in undivided Palestine, which, the board hoped, might find a place within the British Commonwealth.

Struggle for the Jewish State, 1945–48. With the end of World War II the Zionist movement in England turned its energies to the political struggle against the White Paper of 1939 and for the establishment of a Jewish State in Palestine. In August, 1945, London was the scene of a World Zionist Conference, the first such meeting since the outbreak of the war. Participants included leading Zionists from Palestine, the United States, and the liberated countries of continental Europe. At the conference Selig Brodetsky expressed gratification at the victory of the Labor party in the elections held in Britain several days before; he stressed the resolutions favoring the Zionist cause that the party had adopted in years past.

Foreign Secretary Ernest *Bevin's announcement that fall that he would not alter the White Paper policy caused dismay throughout Anglo-Jewry. On Dec. 2, 1945, the Zionist Federation held a "Palestine crisis" demonstration in London. In July, 1946, it organized a march to Trafalgar Square in London, to protest the arrest of leaders of the Jewish Agency and of Palestine's Jewish community. At the 1947 conference of the British Labor party, the delegate of the British section of Po'ale Zion, which was affiliated with the party, moved a resolution requesting the government to act in the spirit of the Labor party's preelection pledges on Palestine. In their efforts on behalf of Palestine, the Zionists had the full support of most of Anglo-

Jewry, which was shocked by the tragic reports from Europe and had come to realize that the future of the Jewish people depended on the fate of the National Home.

Within the Zionist movement itself these years were a time of intensive ideological discussions and intellectual ferment. Simon Rawidowicz was instrumental in the formation of a Jewish Unity Group, which aimed at creating a united Jewish front to the gentile world. One of the group's prominent members was Ignatz *Zollschan.

Development since the Establishment of the State of Israel, 1948———. Since the establishment of the State of Israel, British Zionists have continued active public relations work. Contact has been maintained with members of Parliament and other leaders of British public opinion. A number of Anglo-Israel Friendship Leagues have been set up in London and the provinces. *Bridge in Britain has enabled both Jews and (since 1961) gentiles to study in Israel.

The Zionist movement has maintained its influence in the Anglo-Jewish community. In 1949 Rev. Abraham Cohen, a veteran Zionist, was elected president of the Board of Deputies. His successors in that office—Barnett Janner, Abraham Moss, Solomon Teff, and Alderman Michael Fiddler—have all been stanch supporters of Israel. The most important committees of the board are chaired by Zionists; in 1969 Schneier *Levenberg headed the Israel Committee, and Sir Barnett Janner the Foreign Affairs Committee. Members of the Honorary Officers' Committee of the board are also Zionists; in 1968 they included Sir Samuel Fisher, Victor Mishcon (former chairman of the London County Council), and Harry Landy (a member of the Zionist *Actions Committee).

During the critical period immediately preceding the *Six-day War of 1967, Britain's entire Jewish community mobilized in support of the Jewish State. An audience of 10,000 attended mass rallies at Hyde Park and in the Royal Albert Hall, organized by the Zionist Federation. Communal leaders and Jewish intellectuals maintained close contact with members of Parliament. The Joint Palestine Appeal raised an emergency fund of £17,000,000. More than 10,000 Jews volunteered to go to Israel; some 2,000 actually went there.

'Aliya Activity. Although the number of British Jews who have actually settled in Israel is relatively small (see BRITISH JEWS IN ISRAEL), 'Aliya has had a high priority in the program of the Zionist organizations in Britain. For almost four decades there has been a Halutz *Hakhshara (agricultural training) farm (the David Eder Farm) near Horsham, Sussex. In 1948 the *Professional and Technical Workers' 'Aliya (PATWA) was founded to encourage and facilitate the 'Aliya of professional and technical workers.

The absorption of other British 'Olim (immigrants) was greatly aided by the Israel Office set up in Israel by the Zionist Federation in October, 1949. In 1969 Eric Lucas was director, and Moshe Dubsky deputy director. Both these men, as well as Lucas's predecessor, Sh'lomo Temkin, are 'Olim from Great Britain. In 1950 the Federation of Zionist Youth launched the *Sh'nat Sherut (Year of Service) program for young people willing to devote a year to work on the land in Israel. In 1969 its honorary president was Sir Barnett Janner. Also in 1950 the Zionist Federation helped form the *Anglo-Israel Chamber of Commerce to promote trade between the United Kingdom and Israel.

The Zionist Federation, the Mizrahi, and the Po'ale Zion each has its own 'Aliya Committee to study problems entailed

A demonstration of the Zionist Federation in London in 1947. [YIVO Institute for Jewish Research]

in the settlement of their members in Israel. The Federation of Women Zionists cooperates closely with HaBonim in these matters. In 1969 a Volunteers' Union was established in England with the main purpose of sponsoring 'Aliya among its members.

Educational Activities. One of the most important developments in British Zionism since the establishment of the State of Israel is the network of Zionist day schools sponsored by the Zionist Federation Educational Trust, which was set up for this purpose in 1953. The first Zionist day school, the Hillel House Kindergarten and Primary School, was established in London in 1954. By 1969 there were 11 Zionist day schools (in London, Edgware, Leeds, Glasgow, Westcliff, Liverpool, and Birmingham), with a combined enrollment of more than 3,500. These institutions differ from other Jewish day schools in Britain in that they emphasize the place of Israel in Jewish life and teach Hebrew as a living, modern language. Their religious orientation tends toward Orthodoxy.

Regular Hebrew-language programs have become a permanent feature in British Zionist cultural work. Hebrew seminars sponsored by the Educational Departments of the Jewish Agency and the Zionist Federation are popular. The Jewish Agency also sponsors Hebrew courses jointly with the London County Council. There is a special seminar for students. The Agency's Department of Religious Education and Culture sponsors special seminars for Orthodox participants. The British branch of the *B'rit 'Ivrit 'Olamit (World Hebrew Federation) arranges regular lectures in Hebrew. There is a Hebrew journal, *Tarbut*, published by the Zionist Federation.

Jewish Agency. In 1949 Schneier Levenberg was appointed the official representative of the Jewish Agency in London. In 1969 the Agency had the following departments functioning in England: Education and Culture, B'rit 'Ivrit 'Olamit, External Relations, Reference Section (library open to Jews and non-Jews interested in Israel and the Zionist movement), Publications, Sh'nat Sherut Movement, Unified Department for Immigration and Absorption, Youth and *HeHalutz, Department of Religious Education and Culture, and Children and *Youth 'Aliya Committee for Great Britain. In 1969 eight members of the Zionist Actions Committee and two "virilists" (persons chosen to the Zionist Executive on the basis of personal merit in Zionist work) were residing in England.

S. LEVENBERG

MAJOR ZIONIST ORGANIZATIONS ACTIVE IN GREAT BRITAIN

The following Zionist and pro-Israel organizations were active in Great Britain in 1969:

Zionist Federation of the United Kingdom of Great Britain and Northern Ireland. The federation consists of 530 affiliated societies and bodies: 402 Zionist societies, 124 synagogues, and 4 friendly societies and orders. The Zionist societies include 58 Po'ale Zion groups, including *Pioneer Women and Young Po'ale Zion; 187 societies affiliated with the Federation of Women Zionists; 8 *Mapam groups; 431 societies of the Federation of Zionist Youth; 29 groups of HeHalutz B'Anglia and HaBonim; and 5 *D'ror groups. Mizrahi–HaPo'el Ha-Mizrahi is not in the federation. In 1967 the Interuniversity Jewish Federation joined the Zionist Federation.

The official organ of the federation is the weekly *Jewish Observer and Middle East Review*, which has been in existence since 1952 as the successor of the *Zionist Review*. The first editor of the *Observer* was Jon Kimche. Maurice Samuelson was editor in 1969. The federation also publishes the *Zionist Year Book*, which has appeared annually since 1951. Since 1946 the Synagogue Council of the federation has published its own Hebrew and English quarterly, *Gates of Zion*. The work of the Zionist Federation is conducted by 20 committees that meet regularly. The highest organs of the federation are the principal honorary officers, the Honorary Officers' Committee, and the Executive Council elected by the annual conference.

The Synagogue Council of the Zionist Federation was established in 1917 as a result of an attempt made a year earlier by Nahum Sokolow, together with Rev. Jacob Koppel Goldbloom, to organize the synagogues affiliated with the federation in Great Britain in order to provide support for the forthcoming Balfour Declaration. Goldbloom served as its first chairman and later as its president. Among its other presidents were Moses Gaster and Sir Hermann Gollancz. In 1944 Paul *Goodman, the well-known Zionist author and historian, became chairman, and Joseph Litvin was appointed secretary. On Goodman's death in 1949, Isaac Solomon Fox, son of the editor of *HaMaggid*, was appointed chairman. On the death of Goldbloom, Isaac Solomon Fox assumed the presidency, and Moshe Lederman, president of the Federation of Synagogues, became chairman. In 1968 there were 120 synagogues affiliated with the Zionist Federation through the Synagogue Council:

65 in London and 55 in the provinces, with a combined membership of about 55,000.

The Synagogue Council is headed by a Council consisting of 30 delegates elected annually at a conference of representatives of all affiliated synagogues. It does not limit its activities to affiliated synagogues but preaches Zionism in every Jewish house of worship in Great Britain. It arranges functions of a semireligious character, publishes manifestos in Yiddish and English for Passover and the High Holidays, and informs synagogues of important Zionist developments.

Mizrahi–HaPo'el HaMizrahi Federation of Great Britain and Ireland. The Mizrahi movement first developed significant activity in Great Britain during World War I. Under the leadership of Israel Wolf Slotki, Chaim Sugarman, and Rabbi Israel Jacob Yoffe, all of Manchester, Mizrahi societies were formed in London and the provinces. The first Mizrahi conference, with Rabbi Yoffe in the chair, was held in Manchester in December, 1918. The 50 delegates who attended elected Rabbi S. J. Rabbinowitz of Liverpool honorary president, Chief Rabbi Joseph H. Hertz president, and Rabbi Victor Schonfeld, F. S. Spiers, and Rabbi Yoffe vice-presidents. Rabbi Schonfeld played an important role in the early development of Mizrahi schools in Palestine. Mizrahi originally adopted a resolution to join the Zionist Federation but withdrew from the federation several years later.

London rally protesting British policy in Palestine in 1947. [YIVO Institute for Jewish Research]

In 1955 Mizrahi and HaPo'el HaMizrahi merged. The constituent bodies of the Mizrahi–HaPo'el HaMizrahi Federation of Great Britain and Ireland are the Mizrahi Women's Organization and the youth groups HaMishmeret HaTz'ira, Bachad, and B'nei 'Akiva. The federation has published the fortnightly *Jewish Review* since 1946. Officers of the federation (1969) were former Chief Rabbi Sir Israel Brodie, honorary president; Haham Solomon Gaon, honorary vice-president; Arieh L. Handler, chairman; and Aba Bornstein, Jacob Braude, and Harry Landy, executive vice-presidents. Barry Mindel has been general secretary of the federation since 1942.

J. FRAENKEL

Mapam (Socialist Zionist Party of Great Britain and Ireland). The British branch of Mapam was founded in 1949 as a union of the Left Po'ale Zion, which had been politically active in Britain since 1920, and *HaShomer HaTza'ir, which first appeared in Britain in 1948. From 1948 to 1959 the views of this trend in British Zionism were expressed in the fortnightly *Labor Israel*, which eventually merged with *Israel Horizons* in New York. With the intensification of the cold war and the increasing Soviet hostility toward Israel the party suffered setbacks. One of the prominent members of Mapam was Sydney S. Silverman, M.P., who represented the party at the 24th Zionist Congress (Jerusalem, 1956). In 1956 Mapam was affiliated with the Zionist Federation.

Groups related to Mapam include the Friends of the Kibbutz and the Friends of Giv'at Haviva, founded in the 1960s, which support the school established in Giv'at Haviva for the promotion of understanding between Arabs and Jews.

I. B. D. MOSHE

Po'ale Zion. The largest Labor Zionist group in Europe (*see* LABOR ZIONISM) and one of the strongest in the *Diaspora, Po'ale Zion includes Pioneer Women and Young Po'ale Zion. It is in close touch with the British Labor party, with which it has been affiliated since 1916, and with the Zionist Federation, which it joined in 1942. First introduced into England by immigrants from Eastern Europe, it was inspired by the ideas of Yoseph Hayim *Brenner and Ber *Borochov, who were in London in the early part of the 20th century. The Po'ale Zion program includes the democratization of the Zionist movement, the improvement of the position of the working class through the class struggle, and support of the Jewish National Fund and the *Shekel (membership fee). During the early years of its existence, Po'ale Zion in England conducted widespread activity in Yiddish, organized trade unions, and attempted to secure the support of anti-Zionist Socialists such as members of the *Bund. In 1920 the Po'ale Zion World Movement opened a Political Office in London. Directed by Dov *Hos and Sh'lomo *Kaplansky, the office was very active in the 1920s and 1930s as the Yiddish-speaking nucleus of disciples was gradually augmented by British-born members. In 1937–38 the Palestine Labor Studies Group, with the participation of Abba Eban, Avraham Harman, Schneier Levenberg, Berl Locker, and Moshe *Pearlman, issued several publications including a series of 12 pamphlets on Labor Zionism.

After World War II, with the Labor Government in power, Po'ale Zion was in the thick of the struggle for the Jewish State. Its delegates made their Zionist views known at every annual conference of the Labor party. Relations between Po'ale Zion and the party were strained as the result of Ernest Bevin's anti-Zionist policies but resumed their former cordiality after the Labor Government had recognized the new Jewish State in 1949.

Po'ale Zion's fortnightly publication *Jewish Vanguard* first appeared in 1949. The movement also launched a Histadrut campaign, which subsequently became part of the Joint Palestine Appeal. In the 1960s the British Po'ale Zion created a nonsectarian Labor Friends of Israel, which included a number of leading Labor politicians in its ranks.

H. PINNER

Federation of Women Zionists of Great Britain and Ireland. From 1900 on the societies of the Zionist Federation of Great Britain and Ireland included a handful of women's groups. By 1917 there were 12 such groups, and a Ladies Committee was formed to stimulate propaganda and recruit women members. The leaders of this committee were Rebecca Doro Marks *Sieff, Vera Chatzman *Weizmann, and Romana Goodman, who were determined that Jewish women should have equal rights and opportunities within the Zionist movement. At a conference held in Manchester in 1918, the Federation of Women Zionists of Great Britain and Ireland was founded. The major tasks which this new body undertook were self-education in matters of Jewish and Zionist interest, the introduction of national consciousness in the Jewish home, and the practical work of setting up services to safeguard the welfare of the woman pioneer and her family in Palestine. This latter objective was taken very seriously, and a world organization of women Zionists was envisaged to achieve it.

In 1919 Henrietta Irwell and Lady Samuel, the wife of Sir Herbert Samuel, together with representatives of the women's Zionist groups and purely philanthropic movements such as the Cultural League for Palestine, joined forces to set up the *Women's International Zionist Organization (WIZO). The Executives of the Federation of Women Zionists and WIZO, though separate bodies, worked side by side until the head office of WIZO was transferred to Tel Aviv in 1948.

By 1933 WIZO was able to play a very substantial part in the rescue and care of many women, children, and young people who fled from Nazi oppression. It was responsible for the setting up of Whittingehame College, a farm training school, for about 200 young refugees. Through Rebecca Sieff, the federation obtained permission from the government to bring to England about 1,000 young Zionists from HeHalutz training farms in Germany, found homes for 1,000 young refugee children, and set up a domestic bureau to help find employment for such women as could escape from the Continent.

World War II was a difficult period for the federation in England since many of its members were evacuated with their families from the cities to the countryside. A special committee was set up to keep in touch with the evacuees and visit them in their temporary homes. Thanks to these efforts the federation not only held its own but was able to grow during the war. In addition to its organizational work, the federation gave strong support to the political struggle against the White Paper policy, joining in all rallies and demonstrations of the Zionist Federation and organizing impressive demonstrations on its own.

Besides supporting the great network of WIZO services for the woman and her family in Israel, the Federation of Women Zionists has established and maintained almost 100 WIZO projects of its own, founded either as a joint responsibility of the federation or by individual groups. The largest of these is the Jerusalem Baby Home and Child Center in Bet HaKerem, which in 1969 cared for 300 children in its wards and kindergartens, in addition to the many hundreds who attended its outpatient clinics and children's library. There are also prenatal and postnatal clinics for the women of Jerusalem. Other large institutions sponsored by the federation are the Women's Center and Youth Club in Ashdod, a day crèche in Katamon, and many other crèches, women's centers, youth clubs, playgrounds, and the like.

In 1969 the federation had 17,000 members in 190 branches and published the bimonthly *Jewish Woman's Review*. Officers included the Hon. Mrs. Michael Sieff, president; Mrs. Tina Bloch and Mrs. Miriam Sacher, vice-presidents; Mrs. George Webber, chairman; and Miss Rosalie Gassman (Mrs. Leonard Sherr), general secretary.   R. GASSMAN

Mizrahi Women's Organization of Great Britain and Ireland. Founded in 1945 as part of the World Mizrahi Women's Organization, this organization maintained in 1969 kindergartens, children's homes, girls' homes, and a mothercraft center in Israel and helped maintain 40 afternoon clubs and kindergartens. Among the officers in 1969 were Lady Brodie, honorary life president; Mrs. Immanuel Jakobovits, honorary president; Mrs. Isaac Cohen, Mrs. Isidore Epstein, Mrs. Solomon Gaon, and Mrs. Kopul Rosen, honorary vice-presidents; and Lady Wolfson, president.

Pioneer Women. Founded after World War II, the Pioneer Women (Women's Labor Zionist Organization of Great Britain) is affiliated with Po'ale Zion and with the *Mo'etzet HaPo'alot (Working Woman's Council of Israel). Its officers in 1969 included Mrs. Fania Jezierski, president; Mrs. Doris Samson and Mrs. Ruth Orbach, honorary vice-presidents; Mrs. Lilo Berkovitch, national chairman, and Mrs. Rosella Welan, general secretary.

MAJOR ZIONIST YOUTH MOVEMENTS ACTIVE IN GREAT BRITAIN

The following Zionist youth movements were active in Great Britain in 1969:

Achdut. This young couples' group, organized in 1967, is an affiliate of the Zionist Federation. It engages in cultural activity as the educational arm of the Joint Palestine Appeal and is pledged to the promotion of 'Aliya. In 1969 it had headquarters in London and Manchester. Its chairman was Norman Feingold.

Bachad. Founded in 1942 to promote Jewish religious education and provide agricultural and vocational training for Jewish youth, Bachad is an affiliate of the Mizrahi–HaPo'el HaMizrahi Federation of Great Britain and Ireland. Officers (1969) included former Chief Rabbi Sir Israel Brodie, life president; Chief Rabbi Immanuel Jakobovits and Haham Solomon Gaon, honorary presidents; Alexander Margulies, president; Sir Godfrey Davis and Sir Samuel Fisher, vice-presidents; Arieh L. Handler, chairman; and N. Dykierman, secretary.

B'nei 'Akiva. Founded in Britain in 1940, B'nei 'Akiva is the youth movement of Mizrahi–HaPo'el HaMizrahi. It stresses the value of a life of religious pioneering in Israel and encourages its members (ages 8–22) to plan to join religious kibbutzim in Israel. Neville King was general secretary in 1969.

D'ror Zionist Youth Organization. A Halutz movement founded in England in 1952 in association with *Ahdut 'Avoda, D'ror caters to young people between the ages of 10 and 19. It is the youth movement of the *Kibbutz M'uhad.

Federation of Zionist Youth. Formed in 1935 through a merger of the Association of Young Zionist Societies and the University Zionist Council, the federation caters to young people between the ages of 17 and 25. Its program consists of Jewish and Zionist education, fund raising, and 'Aliya. With its junior branch, HaFinjan (founded in 1960), the federation is affiliated with the Zionist Federation and with the World Confederation of General Zionists. Its chairman in 1969 was John H. Corre.

HaBonim. Founded in 1929 as a Jewish scouting movement with the aim of Hakhshara and eventual 'Aliya, HaBonim maintains several clubs and hostels in London and the provinces. Activities of this group, which caters to young people between the ages of 10 and $18\frac{1}{2}$, include scouting, camping, and Hebrew studies. Affiliated with the Zionist Federation, HaBonim became part of World HaBonim in 1951.

***HaNo'ar HaTziyoni.** Part of the General Zionist world youth movement, HaNo'ar HaTziyoni was founded in 1956 in association with the Federation of Zionist Youth for boys and girls between the ages of 9 and 20. Its adult patrons include Lavy Bakstansky, Isaac Solomon Fox, Sir Barnett Janner, Woolf Perry, and Donald Silk.

HaShomer HaTza'ir. HaShomer HaTza'ir, an affiliate of Mapam, was founded in Great Britain in 1940. It established the kibbutz Yagur in 1949. Other members joined the kibbutzim Zikim and Nahshonim.

HeHalutz B'Anglia (the Pioneer in England). This group was founded in 1935 by members of HaBonim between the ages of 17 and 25 who wanted to settle in Palestine as farmers or artisans and by unaffiliated individuals who wished to become members of *Histadrut (General Federation of Labor) as industrial or agricultural workers. Catering to young people between the ages of 16 and 28, HeHalutz B'Anglia maintains Hakhshara training farms in the United Kingdom. It is also responsible for the maintenance of the Herbert Samuel Educational Center at the David Eder Farm.

Members of HeHalutz B'Anglia were among the rescue groups that went from England to the Continent after World War II to work in displaced-persons camps, on illegal immigrant ships (*see* ILLEGAL IMMIGRATION), and in Cyprus (*see* CYPRUS, DETENTION CAMPS IN).

HeHalutz arranges for young people over the age of 18 to visit kibbutzim in Israel as working guests for periods ranging from 3 months to 2 years. It also maintains a Hakhsharat No'ar (youth Hakhshara) course in which boys and girls between the ages of $16\frac{1}{2}$ and 18 are given a grounding in agriculture, Hebrew, Jewish history and literature, the geography of Israel, and Zionism.

Interuniversity Jewish Federation of Great Britain and Ireland. This organization coordinates the activities of 80 Jewish and Zionist societies at colleges and universities throughout Britain. Representing 3,000 students, it is affiliated with the Zionist Federation and with the World Union of Jewish Students. It publishes an annual literary magazine, *Agora*.

***Tora va'Avoda (Tora and Labor).** This religious Zionist movement for young people between the ages of 18 and 30 is affiliated with the Mizrahi–HaPo'el HaMizrahi Federation of Great Britain and Ireland. Founded in 1919 as Young Mizrahi, it assumed its present name in 1937.

Young Mapam. This Socialist Zionist group was formed after the Six-day War of 1967 to organize young people between the ages of 18 and 30 who support the aims of Mapam. Its educational program is based on the Socialist Zionist approach and the promotion of 'Aliya.

Young Po'ale Zion. An educational and 'Aliya movement founded in 1938 and renamed in 1948, this organization is part of Po'ale Zion and has a center, Bet Berl, in northwest London. Its activities include Israeli folk dancing, Hebrew studies, weekend and summer seminars, and social functions. It has a high record of 'Aliya.

Zionist Youth Council. All Zionist youth movements in the United Kingdom are represented in a Zionist Youth Council, which meets regularly to discuss matters of common interest. In addition, there are a Joint Committee for Youth Affairs and many young people's committees to raise funds for Israeli institutions such as *Magen David Adom and Sha'are Zedek Hospital.

J. FRAENKEL

MAJOR FUND-RAISING ACTIVITIES

The principal Zionist fund-raising activities in Great Britain in 1969 were the following:

Jewish National Fund (JNF). The pioneers of JNF work in Britain, which was begun in 1902, were Louis Eisen, Phineas Horowitz, Leopold Kessler, Eli W. Rabbinowitz, M. Shire, and Leonard Jacques Stein. The first national conference of JNF was held in Manchester in 1918. Collections for 1919 totaled £18,000, which included £5,000 as a first installment of a gift of £25,000 from Sir Alfred Mond. In 1929 the JNF raised money for the Balfour Forest in Palestine. In 1933 it arranged the Anglo-Palestine Exhibition, which was opened by Prime Minister (James) Ramsay *MacDonald under the chairmanship of the Marquess of Reading.

During the presidency of Robert Solomon (1930–37) the King George V Memorial Forest was planted in Palestine. In 1938 the Fund sponsored a Palestine Fair and Exhibition, the Galilee Redemption Fund, and the Lady Fitzgerald Jewelry Fund. In 1941, when Gen. Erwin Rommel's Afrika Korps was almost at the gates of Palestine, the JNF, with Prof. Samson Wright as president, launched the Palestine Victory Campaign. The following year three noted non-Jewish Socialist leaders— Herbert Morrison, Anthony Greenwood, and Camille Huysmans—opened the Palestine Solidarity Campaign. In 1944 the JNF joined Keren HaYesod in establishing the Joint Palestine Appeal. After World War II and the establishment of the State of Israel the JNF enlarged its Youth and Education Department and created the Younger JNF Commissions, which numbered 41 in 1969 and worked through the JNF National Council of Younger Commissions (founded in 1958).

In 1969 JNF published the *JNF News* (included with the *Jewish Observer and Middle East Review*) and other pamphlets. Officers included Rosser Chinn, president; Lady Wolfson and Mrs. S. Gestetner, vice-presidents; and Hyman Joseph Osterley, executive director. Rev. Isaac Levy, O.B.E., had been director of the JNF since 1965.

Keren HaYesod. British Zionists played an important part in the development of Keren HaYesod, whose headquarters was in London during the early years of its existence (1920–26). British Zionists were instrumental in securing the first loan for the Keren HaYesod from Lloyds Bank in 1934, which lent prestige to the fund.

In 1933, after the Nazis came to power in Germany, the representatives of the Zionist Federation and prominent non-Zionists, led by the Rothschild group (New Court Committee),

agreed to launch a Central British Fund (later, Council for German Jewry). The British Keren HaYesod suspended its activities and placed its staff and machinery at the disposal of the new fund, with the proviso that £28,000 be made available to the British Keren HaYesod each year. In 1940 the needs in Palestine and the grave Jewish refugee problem in Britain itself made it necessary to reach a new agreement on a joint appeal for £400,000. It was resolved that £75,000 be allocated for Keren HaYesod and victims of Nazi oppression in Palestine. The new drive was launched in February, 1940, under the chairmanship of Anthony de Rothschild. A delegation from Palestine, consisting of Leib *Jaffe, Alexander *Goldstein, and Yosef *Baratz, arrived in England to help conduct the campaign; they were assisted by Israel *Cohen.

Late in 1940, when England was threatened with invasion, British Zionists decided to launch an independent Keren HaYesod campaign for £75,000. A special appeal drive was organized under the chairmanship of the Marchioness of Reading. A delegation from Palestine, consisting of Leib Jaffe, Manya *Wilbuschewitz-Shohat, and Theodore *Kollek, traveled about the country on behalf of the First War Appeal, which raised £90,000. The Second War Appeal (1942) raised £120,000; the Third War Appeal (1943), with the participation of Mrs. Archibald Silverman and Rabbi Irving *Miller from the United States, raised £240,000.

The Marks-Sieff and Sacher families played an outstanding role in the development of the Keren HaYesod and other Zionist fund-raising endeavors in Britain. Since 1944 the Keren HaYesod has been part of the Joint Palestine Appeal. In 1969 the officers of Keren HaYesod were Lord Sieff and the Marchioness of Reading, vice-presidents; Sir Barnett Janner, chairman; Ernest S. Frankel, treasurer; and Lavy Bakstansky, general secretary.

Joint Palestine Appeal (JPA). The Joint Palestine Appeal, which was founded by Sir Simon Marks (1st Baron Marks of Broughton) in 1944, is the combined fund-raising instrument of the JNF and Keren HaYesod and has a close working arrangement with the Jewish Agency. Since the establishment of the State of Israel, the JPA has raised more than £60,000,000 for the transportation and absorption of new 'Olim. Organized on a nationwide basis, the JPA works through regional and trade commissions. An annual conference sets quotas and policy. Between conferences the work is conducted through an Administrative Committee. JPA publishes a yearbook and has a weekly supplement in the *Jewish Observer and Middle East Review*. JPA claims some 30,000 subscribers, representing one out of every four Jewish families in Britain. Officers in 1969 included Chief Rabbi Immanuel Jakobovits, former Chief Rabbi Sir Israel Brodie, Haham Solomon Gaon, Lord Sieff, and Sir Isaac *Wolfson, honorary presidents; J. Edward Sieff, president; Hyam Morrison, chairman; Rosser Chinn and Michael M. Sacher, vice-chairmen; Lavy Bakstansky, director; and Alfred Klein, executive director.

S. LEVENBERG

OTHER FUND-RAISING BODIES

There are a number of other Zionist fund-raising bodies operating in Britain, of which the most important are the Friends of the *Hebrew University of Jerusalem, established in 1926; British Technion Society, established in 1951 to further the development of the *Technion in Haifa; *Weizmann Institute of Science Foundation, established in 1956; Friends of the *Bar-Ilan University, established in 1957; Friends of the Magen David Adom in Great Britain; Children and Youth Aliyah, established in 1933; Friends of the Anti-Tuberculosis League of Israel; Friends of the Art Museum in Israel, established in 1947; and Friends of the Midrasha in Pardes Hanna.

GREECE, ZIONISM IN. Organized Zionism in Greece had its beginnings in 1902, when Abraham Cohen of Larissa, in central Greece, founded a Zionist society. However, an official Zionist organization was not set up until 1911, when a *Po'ale Zion society was organized in Volos, in central Greece.

Early Years. In 1912 the constitution of the Zionist Organization was officially recognized by the Greek government. The first Zionist *Congress to be attended by representatives from Greece was the 11th (Vienna, 1913); the delegates were Moissis Coffina of Volos and David Florentin of Salonika (Thessalonike).

In 1915 a Zionist group called Ohave Zion was founded in Larissa. Another group, Erets Zion, was founded in Trikkala; and a third, Amele Zion, was organized in Ioannina, a northern Greek city with a large Jewish population. That same year, several Greek Zionist societies organized the Zionist League of Greece with headquarters in Salonika, which had the largest Jewish community in Greece at the time. (Salonika, like other parts of the Ottoman Empire, had had no Zionist societies because of governmental prohibition. It was only after 1913, when Salonika was annexed by Greece, that Zionist activity became legal.) Among the presidents of the Zionist League were Isaac Amarilio, Isaac Angel, and Asser Moissis.

The Greek government and church leaders joined the Zionists in welcoming the issuance of the *Balfour Declaration in 1917. In February, 1918, Foreign Minister Nikolaos Politis announced that his government favored the establishment of a Jewish National Home in Palestine. A similar statement was made that month by King Alexander in an audience he granted to the Pro-Palestine Organization of Greece. In June of that year, M. Simos, the Minister of Defense, conferring with Nissim David Levis, stated that Premier Eleutherios Venizelos and other members of his government would do their utmost to help the Zionist program. That September, Foreign Minister Politis announced his government's approval of a suggestion made by Chaim *Weizmann to the Greek representative in Egypt that a

A Zionist training farm in Athens. [YIVO Institute for Jewish Research]

Celebration of Israel Independence Day in 1952 by the Jewish community of Salonika. [YIVO Institute for Jewish Research]

volunteer corps for service in Palestine be recruited from among the Jews of Salonika. The project did not materialize because the war was drawing to a close.

Between the Two World Wars. In 1922 Patriarch Meletios, the head of the Greek Orthodox Church, declared that the Orthodox Church did not object to a Jewish National Home in Palestine.

The Zionist Federation of Greece had been organized by Asser Mallah in July, 1918. In the early 1920s, largely owing to the initiative of Moissis Coffina, the first Greek Jews left for Palestine. In 1937 they were to form their own community, a *moshav (cooperative village) in the Sharon Plain, under the name Tzur Moshe in honor of Coffina. In 1928 a Greek branch of the *Women's International Zionist Organization (WIZO) was founded on the initiative of Mrs. Rea Kanety. It was still in existence in the late 1960s.

In the early 1930s Greece indirectly aided prospective emigrants to Palestine by granting a 50 per cent fare reduction to groups of 25 or more Jews using Greek railways to travel to Greek embarkation ports on the way to Palestine and a reduction of 50 per cent in taxes on passage between Greece and Palestine. By 1935 economic conditions in Greece, particularly in Salonika, had deteriorated to a point at which emigration became a necessity for many. On May 26 of that year, many Jews applied to the Palestine Office in Salonika (*see* PALESTINE OFFICES) for *immigration certificates. That November, after complaints from the British Legation that Greece had become the center of an organization promoting the *illegal immigration of Jews into Palestine, the Greek government announced that henceforth no foreign Jew would be permitted to enter Greece for any purpose except by special permission of the Foreign Ministry. A month later, however, Premier Panayiotes Tsaldaris announced that, because of the damage it had caused to Greek business, this measure would affect only Jews from Germany and Poland.

World War II and After. World War II, which resulted in the annihilation of 65,000 Greek Jews, swept away all Zionist and other Jewish activities. Of the fewer than 10,000 Jews who survived the war in Greece, some 5,000 emigrated to Israel, the United States, Canada, and Australia. After the war the Zionist movement in Greece was revived. A Zionist youth organization was founded in 1945, but two years later it was forced to suspend its activities because the majority of its members had left for Palestine. In 1948 a Zionist Federation was founded.

Because of Arab pressure, Greece was the only European country which, as of the mid-1960s, had not extended de jure recognition to the State of Israel. In 1951, however, it sent a diplomatic mission to Israel, and the attitude of the Greek government and people was definitely friendly. Israel likewise maintained a diplomatic mission in Athens. Statesmen on both sides exchanged visits (Abba *Eban and Yigael *Yadin visited Greece, and Angelos Angeloussi, the Greek Minister of Public Works, visited Israel), and an active effort was made to promote trade and cultural exchanges between the two countries through trade fairs, lectures, and art exhibits. In the mid-1950s thousands of refugees from Romania and Egypt passed through Greece on their way to Israel and were given help by the Greek authorities.

Zionist Periodicals. The first Zionist organ, the monthly *Jewish Review*, was published in Athens by Moissis Haimis from 1909 to 1915. In 1916 another monthly, *Israel*, edited by Asser Moissis and Yomtov Yacoel, appeared in Trikkala. These two publications contributed much to the popularization of Zionism among Greek-speaking Jews.

From 1920 to 1922 *New Zion*, a biweekly, appeared in Salonika. Soon thereafter the Zionist Federation of Greece placed Isaac Kabelis in charge of a Greek-language supplement to the magazine *Jewish Rebirth*, which previously had been published in Ladino only. In 1925, under the sponsorship of the *B'nai B'rith of Salonika, another Zionist weekly, the *Jewish Tribune of Greece*, made its appearance in both Greek and French. In 1926 it ceased publication and its place was taken by another magazine entitled *Israel*, which appeared between 1931 and 1939.

Before World War II the *Voice of Israel* appeared under the editorship of Raphael Constantinis, who also published the *Jewish Home* between 1948 and 1962. From then until 1964 no Jewish periodicals were published in Greece. In 1964, however, the Zionist fortnightly *Jewish Review* began to appear as the sole official newspaper of the Jewish communities of Greece under the editorship of Marcel M. Yoel.

M. M. YOEL

GREEN, DAVID. *See* BEN-GURION, DAVID.

GREENBERG, AHARON YA'AKOV HALEVI. Writer, *Mizrahi leader, and Israeli public figure (b. Sokołów Podlaski, Russian Poland, 1900; d. Ayelet HaShahar, 1963). Having achieved unusual excellence in his Jewish studies at a very early age, Greenberg was appointed head of the Yeshiva established by the rabbi of Sokołów, Yitzhak Zelig Morgenstern. During World War I, while still in his teens, he organized relief projects for refugees and began to work for Zionism among the religious young people in his hometown. Moving to Warsaw, he joined the newly organized *Tz'ire Mizrahi (Mizrahi Youth) and soon became one of its leaders. He helped establish HeHalutz HaMizrahi (religious pioneer organization) and toured Poland to inspire Jewish youth to *'Aliya (immigration). He also edited the party organ and represented his organization in the Warsaw Palestine Office (*see* PALESTINE OFFICES).

In 1935 Greenberg settled in Palestine, where he joined the leadership of HaPo'el HaMizrahi, representing it at Zionist Congresses (*see* CONGRESS, ZIONIST) and in the *Actions Committee. In 1945 he went to the United States, where for several years he directed the activities of the League for Religious Labor in Palestine. With the establishment of the State of Israel, Greenberg was elected to the *Knesset, serving as a Deputy Speaker in the Fourth and Fifth Knessets.

D. TELSNER

GREENBERG, HAYIM. Essayist, lecturer, editor, and ideological leader of *Labor Zionism (b. Bessarabia, Russia, 1889; d. New York, 1953). His broad Jewish and general education and mastery of languages were acquired largely by self-instruction and extensive reading. At the age of 17, he was a delegate to the *Helsingfors Conference of Russian Zionists. A felicitous writer in Hebrew and Russian, he was also much in demand as a

The Jewish Home, *a Zionist fortnightly published in Athens from 1948 to 1962.* [YIVO Institute for Jewish Research]

speaker. After the Russian Revolution he was active on behalf of *Tarbut, the organization for the promotion of Hebrew language and culture. Arrested by the Bolsheviks because of his Zionist activities, he left Russia in 1921 and, after a brief stay

Hayim Greenberg.
[Zionist Archives]

in Kishinev (then Chişinău, Romania), made his way to Berlin, where he became one of the editors of *Ha'Olam*, Hebrew organ of the *World Zionist Organization.

Greenberg went to the United States on a mission for Tarbut in November, 1924, and remained there. As a leader of *Tz'ire Zion and the editor of its publication, he helped bring about a merger of his organization with *Po'ale Zion and became the acknowledged spokesman for Labor Zionism the world over. As the editor of the weekly *Yidisher Kemfer* and of the monthly *Jewish Frontier*, he raised these two publications to a high literary and ideological standard. His influence transcended party lines, and he was generally regarded as one of the important Zionist thinkers of his generation. His approach to social problems was guided by a humanist philosophy coupled with Jewish ethical ideals. To him Zionism was not a narrow nationalist movement but the fulfillment of the universal ideals of Judaism, and he viewed socialism not as an end in itself but as a means of achieving true democracy. Many of his essays, written in Yiddish, Hebrew, Russian, German, and English, are counted among the classics in Zionist literature. Elected to the Executive of the *Jewish Agency at the 22d Zionist *Congress in 1946, he subsequently headed its Department of Education and Culture until his death.

C. B. SHERMAN

GREENBERG, IVAN MARION. Anglo-Jewish journalist (b. London, 1896; d. there, 1966). The son of Leopold Jacob *Greenberg, he joined the staff of the *Jewish Chronicle* in 1925, becoming its editor in 1936. Like his father, he was a forceful champion of Jewish rights and a strong supporter of political Zionism. In the period following World War II he sharply criticized the British government's anti-Zionist policy and openly supported the Jewish armed resistance in Palestine. This outspoken stand led to disagreement with the directors of the paper and to his resignation from the editorship. Subsequently he joined the Zionists-*Revisionists and in his writing and speeches espoused the cause of the Jewish underground fighters. He was a delegate to the 22d Zionist *Congress (1946) and later served

as chairman of the United Zionists-Revisionists (1947) and of the *Herut movement (1949) of Great Britain.

GREENBERG, LEOPOLD JACOB. Anglo-Jewish journalist and early Zionist leader (b. Birmingham, England, 1861; d. London, 1931). An early follower of Herzl, Greenberg was a delegate to several Zionist Congresses and a cofounder of the Zionist Federation of Great Britain and Ireland (*see* CONGRESS, ZIONIST; GREAT BRITAIN, ZIONISM IN). He helped Herzl make political contacts in England, represented him in the negotiations with British authorities on the *El-'Arish scheme (1902), and later was the principal intermediary when the British offered a territory in East Africa for the establishment of a Jewish settlement (*see* EAST AFRICA SCHEME).

In 1907, when a group of Zionists acquired the *Jewish Chronicle*, he became its editor and served in that capacity until his death. In the paper he vigorously championed Jewish rights all over the world, incessantly drew attention to, and protested forcefully against, anti-Jewish measures and persecution in various countries, especially Tsarist Russia, and spoke up for Zionism. During World War I he supported the efforts of Vladimir *Jabotinsky to establish a *Jewish Legion, called on the British government to recognize the right of the Jews to Palestine, and helped promote talks between Zionist leaders and British officials. The lead article he wrote after the issuance of the *Balfour Declaration was distributed throughout the world by the British government's Information Service.

Faithful to Herzlian Zionism, Greenberg opposed all attempts to interpret the Balfour Declaration so as to weaken its original intent, and he frequently criticized official Zionist policy when he thought it compromised the Zionist ideal. He was also an outspoken opponent of the extended *Jewish Agency, which included non-Zionist elements.

GREENBERG, SIMON. Rabbi, educator, and communal and Zionist leader in the United States (b. Goroshin, Russia, 1901). Brought to the United States in 1905, Greenberg was educated there and at institutions of higher learning in Palestine. A leader of American Conservative Judaism, Rabbi Greenberg was a professor at the Jewish Theological Seminary of America in New York and at its branch in Los Angeles. An author of a number of religious books, he also outlined a plan for the reorganization of the Zionist movement. From 1966 on he was a member of the Executive of the *World Zionist Organization.

See also CONSERVATIVE JUDAISM AND ZIONISM.

A. ALPERIN

GREENBERG (TUR MALKA), URI ZVI. Hebrew and Yiddish poet (b. Bely Kamen, Galicia, Austria, 1895). A scion of illustrious Hasidic families, he published his first poems between 1912 and 1914 in *S'nunit*, *Der Yidisher Arbeter*, *HaShiloah*, and *Ha'Olam*. Drafted into the Austro-Hungarian Army in 1915, he served on the southern front. He was deeply shocked by the war atrocities and by the pogroms perpetrated by Poles in Lvov in 1918, in which his father's house was also destroyed. In 1920 Greenberg headed a group of young Yiddish writers in Warsaw in a revolt against traditional literary trends and founded a monthly, *Albatross*, which took a position favoring expressionism. He also published Hebrew poems in *HaT'kufa*.

In 1923 he left for Berlin. The next year he settled in Palestine, where he became the "poet of the Halutzim" (pioneers; *see*

HALUTZIYUT). His fiery poetry was published in *Kuntres*, *HaPo'el HaTza'ir*, and *Davar*. Later his work assumed an extreme nationalistic character, visualizing the destiny of the Jewish people in terms of the restoration of the kingdom of

Uri Zvi Greenberg.
[Zionist Archives]

Israel along Messianic lines and in total isolation from other civilizations. Dissatisfied with the slow pace of Zionist realization, Greenberg broke with the Socialist party and joined the *Revisionists under Vladimir *Jabotinsky. In *Hazon Ahad HaLigyonot* (Vision of a Legionnaire, 1928), he called for the establishment of a Jewish armed force. That same year, he published a lyrical work entitled *Anakreon 'al Kotev Ha'Itzavon* (Anacreon on the Pole of Gloom). Between 1931 and 1935 he edited the Revisionist Yiddish weekly *Die Velt* in Warsaw.

He returned to Palestine in 1936 and the next year published his great work, *Sefer HaKitrug V'haEmuna* (Book of Indictment and Faith), castigating Jewish self-restraint in the face of Arab atrocities (*see* HAVLAGA). The book had a considerable impact on Jewish youth. Greenberg supported the underground movements fighting the British in Palestine. His *R'hovot HaNahar* (Streets of the River, 1951) is a powerful poetic portrayal of the World War II holocaust.

Greenberg, who also excelled as a publicist, was twice awarded the Bialik Prize and the *Israel Prize for literature. He was a member of the First *Knesset (1949), representing the *Herut party.   J. NEDAVA

G'ROFIT. Village (kibbutz) in the southern Negev. Founded in 1963 and affiliated with the *Kibbutz M'uhad.

GRONEMANN, SAMMY. Lawyer, author, and Zionist leader (b. Strassburg, Germany, 1875; d. Tel Aviv, 1952). Gronemann studied law at Berlin University, attended the Hildesheimer Rabbinical Seminary, and subsequently entered legal practice. He joined the Zionist movement in 1897 and soon became one of the leading German Zionists. From 1901 on he was a delegate to all Zionist Congresses (*see* CONGRESS, ZIONIST). In 1907 he was elected to the Greater *Actions Committee, and from 1921 to 1946 he served as chairman of the *Congress Tribunal. Gronemann was also active in behalf of Russian Jewry. After the Russian pogroms of 1905 he participated in efforts to help Russian-Jewish emigrants.

Serving in the German Army in Eastern Europe during World

War I, he helped create the Vilna Truppe, an internationally famous Yiddish theater. He contributed articles on Zionism and jurisprudence to German and German-Jewish periodicals and in 1903 helped found a satirical Zionist monthly in Berlin. He was

Sammy Gronemann.
[Zionist Archives]

also the author of short stories and of Jewish comedies, which have been translated and performed on the Hebrew stage. In 1936 he settled in Palestine, where his memoirs, entitled *Memoirs of a Yekke* (1946), were published.

GROSSMAN, MEIR. Zionist leader and journalist (b. Temryuk, Russia, 1881; d. Tel Aviv, 1964). Grossman joined the Zionist movement in his early youth and in 1905 began his journalistic career in the Russian and Yiddish press. At the beginning of World War I he joined Vladimir *Jabotinsky's campaign for the formation of a Jewish battalion to fight as part of the British Army on the Palestine front. In 1915–16 he edited in Copenhagen and London the Yiddish biweekly *Di Tribune*, then the only mouthpiece of the activist trend in Zionism. After the Russian Revolution of March, 1917, he returned to Russia. In 1917–18 he edited *Oif der Wach* and *Der Telegraf* in Kiev and was elected a member of the Central Committee of the Zionist Organization of the Ukraine, a delegate to the Jewish National Council in the Ukraine, and a member of the Ukrainian Rada, the assembly that set up a Ukrainian government in April, 1917.

In 1919, with Jacob *Landau, Grossman formed the *Jewish Telegraphic Agency in London. In 1925 he was a founder, with Jabotinsky, of the World Union of Zionists-Revisionists (*see* REVISIONISTS), serving as its vice-chairman. In 1933, along with Richard *Lichtheim, Robert *Stricker, Selig Eugen *Soskin, and Ya'akov *Cahan, he formed the *Jewish State party, which remained within the *World Zionist Organization and of which he remained chairman until 1948, when the party merged with the Revisionist Union into the United Zionists-Revisionists.

In 1934 Grossman settled in Palestine, where he headed a bank for middle-income settlers for a time. At the outbreak of World War II he transferred his political and journalistic activities to New York. In 1948 he was elected to the Executive of the *Jewish Agency and placed in charge of the Economic Department. The next year, after the merger of *Herut and the Revisionist movement in Palestine, he left the Revisionist ranks and, in 1953, joined the General Zionist party (*see* GENERAL ZIONISM), which he represented in the Jewish Agency Executive from 1954 until 1961.

From 1910 on, Grossman contributed to leading Yiddish papers in Europe, the United States, and Palestine, including *Hajnt* and *Der Moment* in Warsaw and *Der Tog, Wahrheit,* and *Die Zeit* in New York. In Palestine he edited *'Iton M'yuhad* (1934) and *'Am uM'dina* (1950), founded Palestine's first English-language paper, the *Palestine Bulletin,* and contributed regularly to **HaBoker.*

I. BENARI

GRÜNBAUM, ITZHAK. Zionist and Jewish leader in Poland, publicist, historian, and Minister of the Interior in Israel's first Cabinet (b. Warsaw, 1879). Grünbaum grew up in Płońsk, Russian Poland, where he joined the Zionist movement as a high school student in 1898. As a law student at Warsaw University in 1901, he contributed articles to Yiddish and Hebrew periodicals. Grünbaum was a proponent of *Gegenwartsarbeit* (work on behalf of Jewish political rights in the **Diaspora) at the **Helsingfors Conference of Russian Zionists in 1906. He soon gained prominence and influence with Polish and Russian Zionists and became secretary-general of the Central Committee of Russian Zionists in Vilna in 1908. He also contributed articles to **Ha'Olam* and served temporarily as its editor.

In 1914 Grünbaum edited the Warsaw Yiddish weekly *Dos Yidishe Folk.* After the outbreak of World War I, he moved to St. Petersburg (Petrograd), where he edited the *Petrograder Togblat* in 1917. In 1918 he returned to Poland, where 'he developed widespread Jewish political and Zionist activities, resumed the editorship of *Dos Yidishe Folk,* and was for a time editor of the Hebrew daily **HaTz'fira.* In 1919 he was elected to the Polish Sejm (Parliament), in which he served until 1930. As a deputy to the Sejm, he was a member of the committee that drew up the Polish Constitution. A strong champion of the rights of Jews as a national minority group, he helped organize the minority bloc in the Polish elections of 1922. As a result, the minorities, including the Jews, succeeded in electing a large number of deputies. In the Sejm he spoke up vigorously against Polish anti-Jewish policies and also served as chairman of the Jewish Club.

Itzhak Grünbaum.
[Israel Information Services]

In World Zionist affairs Grünbaum became a leader of the **Radical Zionists, opposing the expansion of the **Jewish Agency. He held high office in the Polish Zionist Organization, serving as its president for several years.

An advocate of the secularization of Jewish life, Grünbaum clashed frequently with the religious parties. He was an organizer of **Tarbut, the movement for the promotion of the Hebrew language and culture in Poland.

In 1932 he left Poland for Paris. The following year he was elected to the Jewish Agency Executive and settled in Palestine. He headed the Agency's Absorption and Labor Departments and during World War II was chairman of the Agency's Rescue Committee. Grünbaum was among the Jewish Agency leaders who were arrested by the British in June, 1946. In the months preceding the establishment of the State of Israel, he initiated negotiations for cooperation between the **Hagana and the **Irgun Tz'vai L'umi.

Grünbaum was a signer of the **Declaration of Independence and, as a representative of the General Zionists (*see* GENERAL ZIONISM), Minister of the Interior in the provisional government, in which capacity he organized the first general elections. He submitted a party list of his own to the first **Knesset elections. Failing to be elected, he continued as a member of the Jewish Agency Executive. Subsequently he retired from active political life, resuming his literary career. His publications in book form include collections of Zionist essays, memoirs, and a history of Zionism. He was also editor of the *Encyclopedia of the Diaspora.*

A. ALPERIN

GRUNER, DOV. Palestinian underground hero (b. Kisvárda, Hungary, 1912; d. 'Akko Prison, 1947). Gruner received Yeshiva and technical training and in 1940 settled in Palestine. After working for some time with a **B'rit Trumpeldor (Betar) labor group, he joined the British Army, serving with the British forces for five years, including two in the **Jewish Brigade, and took part in the fighting in Italy.

On his release from the army he joined the **Irgun Tz'vai L'umi and participated in a raid on the Ramat Gan police station, in which he was seriously wounded and captured. Condemned to death, he could have saved his life by appealing the sentence, but he refused to do so since that would have implied recognition of the authority of the British judiciary in Palestine. While efforts were still being made to save his life, the British executed him.

GRÜNTHAL, JOSEPH. *See* TAL, JOSEPH.

GUARDIANS OF THE CITY. *See* N'TURE KARTA.

GUARDSMEN. *See* NOTRIM.

GUATEMALA, ZIONISM IN. The Jewish community of Guatemala was established close to 100 years ago by immigrants who came mostly from Germany. In 1967 the Jewish population, 90 per cent of whom lived in Guatemala City, numbered 1,500 in a total population of 4,575,000; the majority were **Ashkenazim. As of 1968 the community had three congregations: the Sociedad Centro Hebreo (Ashkenazim), Maguen David (**Sephardim), and the German-speaking community.

As of 1968 the Zionist Organization, created in 1947, was the leading Jewish body in Guatemala. Other functioning organizations were Maccabi; the **Women's International Zionist Organization (WIZO), with 250 members in 1966; the Committee for the Annual Magbit Campaign of the United Israel Appeal; the Club Deportivo Israelito (Jewish Athletic Club), which worked in close contact with the **Jewish National Fund; and the Jewish School (Colegio Guatemalteco Israelito), with

75 pupils, Jews and non-Jews, in 1966. In 1965 the Zionist Organization was instrumental in setting up a Jewish Central Community Organization in which every Guatemalan Jewish congregation and organization was represented. One of the purposes of this new central body was to improve Jewish education in general and disseminate the knowledge of Zionism in particular.

Because of its preoccupation with general Jewish communal tasks and problems, and also because of its support by the Guatemalan authorities, the Zionist Organization was recognized also as the spokesman of the Jewish community. In 1967 the Zionist Organization had a total membership of 98.

N. YUSSEF

GÜDEMANN, MORITZ. Chief rabbi of Vienna (b. Hildesheim, Germany, 1835; d. Baden, near Vienna, 1918). Güdemann studied at the Jewish Theological Seminary in Breslau and in 1862 accepted a pulpit in Magdeburg, Germany. In 1866 the Vienna Jewish Community elected him preacher. In 1892 he and Adolf Jellinek (1820–93) both received the title of chief rabbi. After Jellinek's death, Güdemann remained the sole chief rabbi of Vienna.

Before Herzl published *The *Jewish State*, he wanted to hear Güdemann's views of it, and, with Heinrich Meyer-Cohn (1855–1905), the two men met in Munich on Aug. 17, 1896, to read a draft of the manuscript. Herzl reports in his *Diaries* that at first the chief rabbi was fascinated by the idea of a Jewish State. Gradually, however, he grew cooler, and in April, 1897, he issued an anti-Zionist brochure, *Nationaljudentum* (National Judaism; published by Max Breitenstein, who had printed *The Jewish State*), in which he contended that Judaism was a religion and not a nationality. Herzl replied in an article entitled "Güdemann's National Judaism," in Josef Samuel Bloch's *Österreichische Wochenschrift* (Vienna, Apr. 23, 1897); and Max *Nordau did likewise in "A Dispute in the Temple" (*Die *Welt*, June 11, 1897).

A scholar of worldwide reputation, Güdemann was the author of books on a variety of Jewish subjects, among them a three-volume work, *History of Education and Culture of Occidental Jewry* (in German, 1880–88).

J. FRAENKEL

GUEDALLA (GEDALYA), HAYIM. Communal worker in England (b. 1815; d. London, 1904). Guedalla's birthplace is given as London by some authorities and as Jerusalem by others. The descendant of a noted Sephardi family (*see* SEPHARDIM), he received a general and a thorough Jewish education. Active in London Jewish communal life, he accompanied his relative Sir Moses *Montefiore on many of the latter's journeys and participated in his efforts to improve the situation of Palestine Jewry. In 1869 Guedalla influenced the Spanish government to readmit Jews to Spain.

In 1875, in his capacity as chairman of a group of holders of Turkish debentures, he suggested to the Turkish authorities that the empire's financial crisis could be resolved by selling land, especially in Palestine, for cash and in exchange for debentures. He intended in this way to acquire Palestine for the settlement of Jews. Guedalla appealed to fellow Jews in various countries to help him in his endeavors, propagated his ideas in writing, and disseminated reprints of some chapters of George *Eliot's *Daniel Deronda*, which was published at that time. The outbreak of the Russo-Turkish War of 1877 put an end to Guedalla's efforts.

Until the very end of his life he took an active interest in the welfare of Palestine Jewry, supporting religious institutions, especially those of the Sephardim.

GUEDALLA, PHILIP. Historian and essayist (b. London, 1899; d. there, 1944). A member of an old English Sephardi family, he was an elder of the Sephardic Synagogue in London, president of the Jewish Historical Society of England, and president (1924–28) of the English Zionist Federation (later the Zionist Federation of Great Britain and Ireland; *see* GREAT BRITAIN, ZIONISM IN). In 1927 Guedalla attended the 15th Zionist *Congress in Basle as the leader of the delegation from England.

Among his writings is a pamphlet, *Napoleon and Palestine* (1925), discussing Napoleon's offer to restore Palestine to the Jews.

J. LEFTWICH

G'ULA (Geula). Society founded in Warsaw in 1904 for the purchase of land in Palestine. G'ula (Redemption) also maintained an office in Odessa. After the British conquest of Palestine, it was registered as a Palestinian company with its seat in Tel Aviv. The society made large land purchases, serving individuals, various groups, and the *Jewish National Fund. Its directors in Palestine were Meir *Dizengoff, Bezalel *Jaffe, and Z'ev *Gluskin.

G'ULE TEMAN. Village (moshav) in the Sharon Plain. Founded in 1947 and affiliated with HaPo'el HaMizrahi (*see* MIZRAHI). Population (1968): 345.

G'ULIM. Village (moshav) of *Yemenite Jews in the Sharon Plain. Founded in 1945 and affiliated with *T'nu'at Ha-Moshavim. Population (1968): 480.

GUR (GRASOWSKI, GRAZOVSKI), Y'HUDA. Hebrew writer and lexicographer (b. Pogost, Minsk District, Russia, 1862; d. Tel Aviv, 1950). After studying at the Yeshiva of Volozhin, he lived in Vilna, where he helped found a youth group called Sha'alu Sh'lom Y'rushalayim (Seek the Peace of Jerusalem). In 1887 he settled in Palestine, where he first worked as a laborer and clerk. In 1889 he became a teacher in 'Ekron and later in Zikhron Ya'akov, Jaffa, and Mikve Yisrael. Beginning in 1902, he worked for the Anglo-Palestine Bank Ltd. (*see* BANK L'UMI L'YISRAEL), first in Beirut and later in Jaffa.

Gur contributed to the Hebrew press, wrote Hebrew textbooks, and translated works of world literature into Hebrew. He helped organize the Asefat HaMorim (1892), precursor of the Histadrut HaMorim (Teachers Association). Gur was also prominently affiliated with the secret order *B'ne Moshe (Sons of Moses) and served as secretary of its Jaffa chapter. With Joseph *Klausner and later with David *Yellin, he published small Hebrew dictionaries. His magnum opus, the large *Milon HaSafa Ha'Ivrit* (Dictionary of the Hebrew Language), first appeared in 1935. It has since been reissued in numerous editions. Gur was of great assistance in land purchases for Tel Aviv, Nes Tziyona, and the Jewish quarters of Haifa.

I. KLAUSNER

GUREYFAT. Bedouin tribe in the B'er Sheva' region. Population (1968): 275.

GUSH 'ETZYON. *See* 'ETZYON BLOCK.

GUSH HALAV. *See* JISH.

GUTMACHER, ELIJAH. Rabbi and precursor of Zionism (b. Borek, Russian Poland, 1796; d. Grätz, Germany, 1874). He received his training in Yeshivot in Silesia and studied under Rabbi 'Akiba Eger (1761–1837) in Posen (Poznań). At the age of 26 he became rabbi in Pleschen. Then, in 1839, he received a call from the community of Grätz (now Grodzisk, Poland), where he served until his death.

Influenced by Kabbalistic literature, Gutmacher held that the redemption of the Jewish people would be hastened if morally superior individuals were to restore to Israel the Shekhina (Divine Presence) which had departed from the Jewish people when it went into exile. Eventually, he came to believe that full moral perfection was unattainable outside the Land of Israel. The *Diaspora, he felt, was progressively contaminating the spirit of the Jewish people. At that time, he received from Rabbi Zvi Hirsch *Kalischer the manuscript of the latter's *D'rishat Tziyon*. He eagerly espoused Kalischer's plan to establish Jewish agricultural settlements in Palestine, considering this a major step toward the beginning of the redemption of Israel.

In 1860 Gutmacher attended a conference of rabbis called by Kalischer in Thorn (Toruń) to consider practical steps for the establishment of settlements in Palestine. With Kalischer, he was also prominent in the *Colonisations-Verein für Palästina and in the settlement society established later in Berlin. A noted Talmudist, Gutmacher was the author of novellae on the Talmud, responsa, and homiletical and exegetical works, some of which were printed.

T. PRESCHEL

GUTMAN, NAHUM. Israeli painter (b. Teleneshty, Bessarabia, Russia, 1898). The son of the poet and novelist who wrote under the pseudonym Simha *Ben-Zion, Gutman was brought to Palestine at the age of seven. He studied at the *Bezalel School. During World War I he served with the *Jewish Legion attached to the British forces in Palestine and thereafter continued his studies in Vienna. He is known chiefly as an aquarellist and an illustrator of books.

A. WERNER

GUTMANN, SIMHA ALTER. *See* BEN-ZION, SIMHA.

GUTTMAN, LOUIS. Sociologist (b. Brooklyn, N.Y., 1916). Educated at the University of Minnesota (B.A., 1936; M.A., 1939; Ph.D., 1942), Guttman taught at Cornell University (1945–50). In 1948 he founded Israel's *Institute of Applied Social Research and became its scientific director. In 1953 he also became professor of psychological measurement at the *Hebrew University of Jerusalem. He served as visiting professor at Michigan State University (1962–63) and the University of Michigan (1964–65).

G'VAR'AM. Village (kibbutz) in the Darom. Founded in 1942 and affiliated with the *Kibbutz M'uhad. Population (1968): 240.

G'VAT (Gevat). Village (kibbutz) in the Jezreel Valley. Founded in 1926 and affiliated with the *Kibbutz M'uhad. Population (1968): 625.

G'VULOT. Village (kibbutz) in the northern Negev. Founded in 1943 and affiliated with the *Kibbutz Artzi Shel HaShomer HaTza'ir.

GYMNASIA HERZLIYA. *See* HERZLIYA HIGH SCHOOL.

H

HA'AHDUT. First Zionist Socialist periodical in Palestine and mouthpiece of *Po'ale Zion. Founded in 1910 in Jerusalem, it first appeared as a monthly, becoming a weekly in 1911. It was devoted to the problems of the Jewish workers in Palestine and to the advancement of Jewish national interests in the country. Members of the editorial board included Itzhak *Ben Zvi, David *Ben-Gurion, Rahel *Yanait, Ya'akov *Zerubavel, Yoseph Hayim *Brenner, Alexander Hashin, and Aaron Reuveni. The paper was suspended by the Turkish authorities in 1915.

HA'ARETZ. Israeli daily newspaper. Founded as *Hadashot Ha'Aretz*, it first appeared on June 18, 1919, in Jerusalem, the first Hebrew daily to be published in Palestine after World War I. *Ha'Aretz* (The Land) went through frequent changes of editors and owners. Leading Hebrew writers, among them Eliezer *Ben Yehuda, Joseph *Klausner, and Vladimir *Jabotinsky, served either as editors or as major contributors. Moshe *Glickson edited the paper from 1922, after *Ha'Aretz* had been transferred to Tel Aviv, until 1937, when the paper was acquired by Sh'lomo Salman *Schocken.

In its first lead article *Ha'Aretz* promised "to communicate the national needs of the Jewish people in general and the *Yishuv in *Eretz Israel* in particular . . . , to serve as a bridge between various parts of the nation, between the *Diaspora and *Eretz Israel*, between East and West, and between the various parties, groups and classes of the Yishuv."

The program of the paper was restated in the 10,000th issue, in 1952, with the assumption of the editorship by Gershom *Schocken, its present editor: "*Ha'Aretz* strives to portray events in *Eretz Israel* and abroad, in the State of Israel, in the Diaspora and on the international scene. The paper aims to report on these events and to express the opinions which they provoke. It is this aim that has dictated one of the characteristics of the paper; namely, its complete independence of party affiliation."

The only Israeli morning paper not affiliated with any political party, *Ha'Aretz* is served by special correspondents in all major political centers. Its literary and economic supplements appear weekly. It is widely regarded as the best non-biased source of information on domestic and international affairs. The enlarged Friday edition includes a magazine.

In 1966 *Ha'Aretz*, which had started with a circulation of less than 1,000 at a time when only 50,000 Jews were living in Palestine, reported a weekday circulation of over 40,000 and a much larger one on Friday. This increase was almost exactly proportionate to the general growth of the Jewish population of Israel since 1919.

J. RUBIN

HA'ARETZ V'HA'AVODA. Periodical published by *HaPo'el HaTza'ir, the laborers' party in Palestine, from 1913 to 1918. The name means "Land and Labor." Starting as a summary and digest of the weekly *HaPo'el HaTza'ir*, it was directed toward pioneer youth in the *Diaspora. It claimed to be more in the nature of a gospel preaching the primacy of life and labor in the Land of Israel than a work of pure literature. After World War I, before *HaPo'el HaTza'ir* was revived, *Ha'Aretz V'ha'Avoda* served as an organ of the HaPo'el HaTza'ir party, taking up the challenge of changed conditions in Palestine and appealing to the youth in the Diaspora.

Ha'Aretz V'ha'Avoda had its counterpart in Germany in *Land und Arbeit*, which was published in 1918 by the followers of HaPo'el HaTza'ir in Germany, including Hayim Victor *Arlosoroff.

I. KOLATT

HAAS, JACOB DE. *See* DE HAAS, JACOB.

HA'AVARA. Arrangement for the transfer (Heb., *ha'avara*) of money by German-Jewish immigrants to Palestine during the early part of the Nazi era. When Hitler became Chancellor of Germany on Jan. 30, 1933, the German Jews who were then forced to leave the country were faced with strict currency controls in Germany, on the one hand, and with *immigration difficulties in Palestine, on the other. The mandatory authorities permitted only a limited number of quota immigrants without means but admitted "capitalists" with assets of at least LP 1,000 (equal to £1,000) without restriction. At first, Jewish emigrants from Germany could withdraw LP1,000 from their assets at the German Reichsbank. Soon, however, the German government ceased to make foreign exchange available for Jewish emigrants. Other ways had to be found to release their assets.

On Aug. 25, 1933, Eliezer Siegfried *Hoofien, then the general manager of the Anglo-Palestine Bank (now *Bank L'umi L'Yisrael), agreed with the German Ministry of Economics to use Jewish assets for the purchase of goods needed in Palestine. Known as the Hoofien transfer agreement, this arrangement formed the financial basis of an official Jewish emigration plan. In 1933 the Anglo-Palestine Bank established in Tel Aviv the Trust and Transfer Office Ha'avara Ltd., with a capital of LP100 (then $500). A corresponding body was set up in Berlin with the assistance of two leading Jewish bankers, Max Warburg, of M. M. Warburg, Hamburg, and Dr. Siegmund Wassermann, of A. E. Wassermann, Berlin. The Berlin company, known as Palästina Treuhandstelle zur Beratung Deutscher Juden, or Paltreu, assumed responsibility for negotiating with the German authorities the settlement of bills of German exporters and contracts with German Jews wishing to leave for Palestine.

At the 19th Zionist *Congress (1935) a number of delegates, especially those from the United States, charged Ha'avara with breaking the boycott of German goods. Arthur *Ruppin, Eliezer *Kaplan, Henrietta *Szold, and Georg Landauer, from Palestine, and representatives of the German Zionists refuted the charge and contended that the transfer arrangement was the only way of salvaging Jewish property and enabling Jews to immigrate to Palestine. The Congress approved of this arrangement and put Ha'avara under the control of the Zionist *Executive.

The Anglo-Palestine Bank transferred its interest in Ha'avara to the *Jewish Agency in Jerusalem, which appointed a board of directors representing Palestinian and German Jews. The operations of Ha'avara included the promotion of German exports to Palestine, against payment in blocked Jewish funds, and the creation of the highest possible number of "capital" lots of LP1,000 per immigrant. The Nürnberg laws of 1935 and the "Crystal Night" pogroms of November, 1938, sharply increased registration and payments into Ha'avara accounts.

The German Reichsbank ceased selling foreign exchange to Jewish emigrants and pooled its foreign exchange with the transfer receipts of Ha'avara. By early 1937 the Reichsbank had sold some 34,000,000 Reichsmarks in foreign exchange, an amount roughly equivalent to the total proceeds from "regular" German exports to Arabs and German gentiles in Palestine. From the very beginning, however, the Reichsbank refused the usual export subsidies for exports sold in "Ha'avara marks" to Palestine, and Ha'avara had to reduce the inflated prices by a corresponding discount, called "bonification," given to the importer in Palestine. A further complication in Ha'avara operations arose from the endeavor to avoid competition between German imports and locally produced goods as well as British imports. For this purpose, intricate financial arrangements were worked out which included the payment of premiums and long-term financing of German imports, particularly construction materials, partially paid through mortgages and bank guarantees. These arrangements made the importation of building materials possible to such an extent that at the outbreak of World War II considerable quantities of such materials were available in Palestine for the use of the Allied forces. Other Ha'avara projects helped bring into existence the German middle-class settlements, settlement companies such as *RASSCO, Pasa, and the *Mekorot Water Company and enabled corporations such as Nir Ltd., the Palestine Land Development Company, Lodzia, HaNote'a, 'Atid Navigation, Nehushtan, and many others to expand their operations.

Until 1938 German Jews, like emigrants elsewhere, were permitted to take with them their personal belongings and thus were able to transfer additional assets. Ha'avara also formed a credit system whereby tourists could visit Palestine before deciding to settle there.

Jews in Palestine could support relatives or friends in Germany through Ha'avara. In 1937 Siegfried *Moses, the former German Zionist leader and later the first *State Comptroller of Israel, agreed with the London holders of frozen credits in Germany to extend this support scheme through Ha'avara. Ha'avara's subsidiary in London, founded under the name Intria Ltd., for this purpose cooperated with Rothschild Frères in France, the Banque Lambert in Belgium, the Swiss Bank Corporation, the Basler Handelsbank in Switzerland, and the American Express Company in the United States.

When Ha'avara ceased operations at the outbreak of World War II in September, 1939, after almost six years, it had about 12,000 accounts, had dealt with 160 banks, and had handled yearly about 500,000 transactions. Most of the 50,000 Jews who left Germany between 1933 and 1939 used the services of Ha'avara. This number included children sent to Palestine ahead of their parents and war veterans and civil servants who had been forced to retire and whose pensions had been paid by the German authorities to Ha'avara for transfer to Palestine.

Ha'avara transferred a total of 140,000,000 marks from Germany, resulting in a net transfer of LP8,100,000, with an average loss of 30 per cent for the individual transferor. Fees for transfers were set by the board of directors, and for certain types of transfers were based on the transferor's financial status. The major part of these transfer fees paid for the import bonuses needed to reduce inflated German prices.

At the outbreak of World War II, Paltreu, after refunding undisbursed amounts, ceased operations. The working capital of Ha'avara still remaining in Germany was administered by the custodian of British property and thus escaped the general confiscation of Jewish assets. Liquidation of Ha'avara assets in Palestine was completed by 1940.

W. FEILCHENFELD

HABANI JEWS IN ISRAEL. The Habani community, an exotic Jewish community which had lived in the isolated Hadhramaut region near the southern coast of the Arabian Peninsula, was one of the groups brought to Israel by *Operation Magic Carpet. Although Sh'muel Yavne'eli of Palestine visited Yemen and Hadhramaut in 1922, it was not until 1943 that the *Jewish Agency office in Aden established contact with the Habani Jews. The first Jewish family from Haban arrived in Palestine in 1945. In 1950 the entire community moved to Israel via Aden, the great majority settling in Bareket, near Lod. Others live in K'far Shalom (Salameh), Hadid, and Nes Tziyona. In 1968 the total number was estimated at 500.

The Habani Jews, none of whom consider themselves descendants of Kohanim (the priestly class) or L'viyim (Levites), are pious; all the men speak, read, and write Hebrew. Most Habani Jews became farmers; others are laborers, artisans, and factory workers. A few continued to work as goldsmiths and silversmiths. The women, who had gone about veiled in Hadhramaut, adopted modern dress in Israel. Overcoming their traditional restraints, they engaged in work outside the home, on farms, in factories, and so on. The army (*see* ISRAEL DEFENSE FORCES) was an important factor in the integration of the younger Habani Jews into Israeli life. Still, the Habani community retained its identity, and only a very small percentage married outside the group.

A. MASHIAH

HABIMAH (HaBima). *See* THEATER IN ISRAEL.

HABOKER. Israeli daily newspaper, published in Tel Aviv from 1935 to 1966. According to a statement in the first issue, *HaBoker* (Morning) was founded by a group of private citizens with no party affiliation. A leading article by one of the founders, Meir *Dizengoff, the mayor of Tel Aviv, stated: "There is an urgent need for a newspaper which will not be enslaved by any specific political party, nor edited and directed by party orders. The general public needs a newspaper of its own. Such a paper must have only one task—to serve the people, and the people alone. This should imply service to all the people without distinction of class, for the furtherance of our spiritual, cultural and material values." Following Dizengoff's death, Yisrael *Rokah became the most influential member of the paper's governing group.

To the public *HaBoker* came to be identified with business and free-enterprise groups in the *Yishuv (Jewish population of Palestine). After these groups had formally joined the General Zionist party, *HaBoker* became that party's organ (*see* GENERAL ZIONISM). Regular news columns on local and international developments were supplemented by articles dealing with problems of the free-enterprise economy, its relationship with the collective sector, and issues involving social and tax legislation. A literary supplement furnished a review of cultural life and creativity in Israel.

Dr. Samuel Perlman, writer and educator, the first editor, was succeeded by Joseph *Heftman, who, in turn, was followed by Peretz *Bernstein, Jacob Grauman, and Gershon Tzifroni. In the 1960s *HaBoker*, initially one of Israel's three morning papers with the largest circulation, experienced a decline in readership, reporting a circulation of 12,350 in 1965. On Jan. 1, 1966, *HaBoker* ceased publication.

J. RUBIN

HABONIM. Village (moshav) on the Carmel coast. Founded in 1949 and affiliated with *T'nu'at HaMoshavim. Population (1968): 145.

HABONIM (Ihud HaBonim). Largest of the worldwide *Halutz (pioneer) youth movements of *Labor Zionism, encompassing more than 20,000 members. In Israel the movement is affiliated with the *Ihud HaK'vutzot V'haKibbutzim, to which the kibbutzim established by its graduates belong. By 1966, 22 kibbutzim had been established by HaBonim graduates. In some countries, such as the United States, Canada, Argentina, and Brazil, the movement was the youth affiliate of the adult Labor Zionist movement (*Ihud 'Olami–*Mapai). In other countries, such as Great Britain, South Africa, and Australia, it was the youth affiliate of the Zionist federation as a whole. Its Israeli counterpart was *HaNo'ar Ha'Oved V'haLomed.

The movement in its present form was the result of a series of amalgamations of Labor Zionist Halutz youth groups which had their roots in the very beginnings of Zionist Halutz endeavor. The precursors of the movement were known variously as *Gordonia, Young Po'ale Zion, Freiheit, *D'ror, and HaBonim. These movements encompassed thousands of members, were affiliated to a greater or lesser extent with the adult Labor Zionist movement, and educated their members toward affiliation with one or the other of the Mapai-oriented settlement movements in Israel. After World War II, a gradual amalgamation process due to the destruction of European Jewry in the Nazi holocaust, developments and realignments in the Israeli labor movement, and local conditions resulted in the crystallization of the various groups in one youth movement in the English-speaking countries called HaBonim and one movement in the Spanish- and French-speaking countries called Ihud HaNo'ar HaHalutzi. In the 1950s these two movements united to form Ihud HaBonim. It was this organization that established the 22 kibbutzim mentioned above. While each branch functions with complete independence in its own country, an elected World Secretariat in Israel is in charge of coordinating Israeli activities, such as the absorption of HaBonim graduates in the country, the selection of Sh'lihim (emissaries from Israel; *see* SHALIAH), and relations with World Zionist institutions.

In the United States and Canada the movement included groups in 23 cities (1966). It operated a network of nine summer camps, attended by about 1,500 children every summer. For 15 years Ihud HaBonim conducted a program called the Youth Workshop in Israel, which provided young people above the high school level with a year of work and study at a kibbutz in Israel. Over the years, more than 800 young people participated in the program and almost 35 per cent returned to Israel to take up temporary or permanent residence. Three kibbutzim in Israel, K'far Blum, Gesher HaZiv, and Urim, were established by Ihud HaBonim graduates from the United States and Canada, while hundreds of other American HaBonim graduates settled in moshavim. During the Israel *War of Independence, many American HaBonim members volunteered for work on immigrant ships and for the struggle in Israel itself.

Ihud HaBonim published magazines for young people (*Ha-Boneh* and *Furrows*) as well as a variety of educational materials. In 1966 it had about 3,000 members between the ages of 10 and 23, with the bulk of the membership between the ages of 15 and 19.

M. KEREM

HACOHEN, MORD'KHAI BEN HILLEL (Marcus Kahan). Author and Zionist leader (b. Mogilev, Russia, 1856; d. Haifa, 1936). Hacohen contributed to the Hebrew and Russian-Jewish press and was for a time secretary of the editorial board of *Rassviet*. With the rise of the *Hoveve Zion movement he published (1881) a call in the Hebrew periodical *HaMelitz* for emigration to Palestine. For several years he devoted all his time to business affairs but subsequently resumed his writing and his communal activities. In 1890 he attended the first general meeting of the *Odessa Committee of Hoveve Zion, and a year later he again visited Palestine, this time for the purpose of purchasing land there.

Hacohen was a delegate to the 1st Zionist *Congress in 1897 and was the only speaker to address it in Hebrew. He attended the first and second conferences of Russian Zionists, held in Warsaw (1898) and Minsk (1902), respectively. In 1907 he settled in Palestine. Hacohen was one of the founders of Tel Aviv and became its civic leader. In 1918 he was one of the founders of the Va'ad Z'mani (Provisional Council) of the Jews of Palestine.

Hacohen founded and was prominently associated with numerous educational, communal, and financial institutions in the country. He was also the founder and president of the Jewish Arbitration Court (Mishpat HaShalom Ha'Ivri).

In his more than 60 years of literary activity, which he pursued despite his many business and communal commitments, Hacohen contributed to numerous periodicals and papers and published a large number of books, including 'Olami (My World, 5 vols., 1927–29), memoirs; and Milhemet Ha'Amim (War of the Peoples, 5 vols., 1929–30), a diary of World War I.

I. KLAUSNER

HADANI, 'EVER. Hebrew writer (b. Zdoyzha, near Pinsk, Russia, 1899). At the age of 13 he went to Palestine, where he entered *Herzliya High School in Tel Aviv. In World War I he volunteered for the *Jewish Legion and later worked in Mahanayim and K'far Gil'adi. In 1924–25 he took training in cattle raising and dairy culture in the Netherlands and on his return to Palestine worked for the T'nuva cooperative's dairy industry (see HISTADRUT).

During World War II, Hadani was active on behalf of the Palestinian Jewish volunteers in the British forces. He was one of the first authors to portray the life of the *Halutz (pioneer) and the conquest of the wasteland in fiction. His novels Tz'rif Ha'Etz (The Wooden Shack, 1930) and Nahalulim (Brambles, 1935) portray the vision as well as the grim reality of the pioneers who, in the face of overwhelming obstacles, endeavored to build a new society.

Hadani also wrote several books dealing with the Return to Zion and the development of Jewish settlement in Israel. These include 'Am B'Milhamto (A People in Struggle, 1948 ff.), an account of Jewish war efforts and defense activities from World War I until the end of World War II; Hadera (1951), the story of the city of Hadera, published on the 60th anniversary of its founding; and B'Ruah Uv'Hayil (By the Spirit and by Strength, 1952), chapters from the history of the Jews of Palestine from the time of the expulsion from Spain until the present.

H. LEAF

HADAR 'AM. Rural community in the Sharon Plain. Founded in 1933. Population (1968): 183.

HADAR HAKARMEL. See HAIFA.

HADAR RAMATAYIM. See HOD HASHARON.

HADASIM. Youth village incorporated into Even Y'huda, in the southern Sharon Plain. Founded in 1947 by the Canadian Hadassah (affiliated with the *Women's International Zionist Organization, or WIZO).

HADASSAH. With a membership of approximately 318,000 in more than 1,350 chapters and groups throughout the United States and Puerto Rico, Hadassah, the Women's Zionist Organization of America, is the largest Zionist organization in the world.

Early History. Hadassah developed from a small study group that was part of a very limited United States Zionist movement called the Daughters of Zion. Very often groups of this type took additional names such as Rebecca or Deborah. The group that became Hadassah was called Daughters of Zion, Hadassah. Henrietta *Szold, who joined this group in 1907, went on to found the Hadassah organization. In 1910 Miss Szold urged her Hadassah circle to engage in health work among the Jews in Palestine, with headquarters in Jerusalem. With her mother she had just visited Palestine, where she found great infant mortality in Jerusalem and a need for nursing service in all areas. From this undertaking developed the idea of forming a national network of American Zionist women for these purposes. The motto adopted for the organization in 1914 was taken from Jeremiah 8:22: "The Healing of the Daughter of My People."

The first meeting called to discuss purposes was held at 8:00 P.M. on Saturday, Feb. 24, 1912, at Temple Emanuel-El, New York. The meeting notice was signed by Sophia Berger (later Mrs. Mohl), Henrietta Szold, Lotte Levensohn, Rosalie (Mrs. N. Taylor) Phillips, Gertrude Goldsmith (later Mrs. Bernard G. Rosenblatt), Emma (Mrs. Richard) Gottheil, and Mathilde (Mrs. Solomon) Schechter. The aim, as stated by the group, was to promote Jewish institutions and enterprises in Palestine and to foster Zionist ideals in the United States. On Mar. 7, 1912, the festival of Purim, officers and the Board of Directors were elected as follows: president, Henrietta Szold; vice-presidents, Mrs. E. W. Lewin-Epstein, Mrs. N. Taylor Phillips, and Mrs. Richard Gottheil; treasurer, Miss Nettie Illoway; corresponding secretary, Miss Rose Herzog; recording secretary, Miss Rachel Natelson; and directors, Miss Rebecca Aaronson (Mrs. Barnett Bridener), Mrs. S. P. Abelow, Miss Sophia Berger (Mrs. Mohl), Miss Gertrude Goldsmith (Mrs. Rosenblatt), Miss Rose Jayne (Mrs. D. Blondheim), Mrs. Solomon Schechter, Miss Alice *Seligsberg, Mrs. Mordecai Kaplan, Miss Sarah Kussy, Miss Lotte Levensohn, Mrs. Judah L. Magnes, Mrs. Cecil Ruskay, and Dr. Anna Wilner. Among other early leaders were Miss Jessie *Sampter and Miss Eva Leon.

The group was originally the women's group within the Federation of American Zionists, in which it had a great deal of autonomy. Hadassah terms of reference provided for an annual convention to decide policy; between conventions a Central Committee acted for the organization. When, after the *Balfour Declaration was promulgated (November, 1917), the Federation of American Zionists, which then changed its name to *Zionist Organization of America (ZOA), adopted a district plan (1918), each Hadassah chapter constituted a Zionist society within this structure. However, Hadassah maintained its own identity. Chapters met, conventions were held, and a School of Zionism led by Jessie Sampter was established to further the organization's program of education. The Central Committee was practically autonomous, and Hadassah had complete control over all funds raised for its Palestinian purposes.

From 1921 to 1926, because of ideological and practical differences with the ZOA, Hadassah became practically autonomous in other areas of its program, and during the years 1926–33 it achieved complete independence. Early in its history Hadassah had affiliated with the *World Zionist Organization (WZO), and after its withdrawal from the structural setup of the ZOA it maintained an independent affiliation.

Political Work. During World War II and the postwar period before the establishment of the State of Israel in 1948, Hadassah, with all other Zionist organizations and, in fact, with the Jewish people as a whole, was actively engaged in trying to bring about the development of the Jewish National Home in Palestine and to rescue the victims of the Nazi era. Hadassah's representatives testified at various hearings, including those of the *Anglo-American Committee of Inquiry and the *United Nations Special Committee on Palestine. They traveled throughout the United States, setting forth the reasons motivating the Jewish people toward the establishment of a Jewish State in Palestine and explaining the concern of Jews everywhere with that land. This work of informing Hadassah's membership and the community in general of the issues involved helped greatly to focus attention on the need for the Jewish Homeland and performed a valuable service in creating a favorable climate of opinion.

Health Programs. In 1913 Hadassah sent two American-trained nurses to Palestine. They set up a small welfare station in Jerusalem for maternity care and the treatment of trachoma, the eye disease that was then the scourge of the Middle East. With the outbreak of World War I, their work was terminated by the Turkish authorities. In 1918, an *American Zionist Medical Unit, sponsored by Hadassah, the ZOA, and the *American Jewish Joint Distribution Committee and comprising 45 physicians, dentists, and nurses, reached Palestine. Hospitals were subsequently opened in Jerusalem, Jaffa, Haifa, Tel Aviv, Safed, and Tiberias, marking the inauguration in Palestine of a comprehensive health program that was a major factor in making it possible for Israel to enjoy the highest health standard in the Middle East. Hadassah services were open to all who sought them, regardless of race, color, or creed.

As soon as municipal and central governments and other proper authorities are in a position to support and operate the projects initiated by Hadassah, they are turned over to such authorities. In this way, hospitals, day care centers, health stations, infant welfare stations, school luncheon programs, and playgrounds have been established and then given to the authorities. In 1939 Hadassah's first Medical Center was opened on Mount Scopus. Throughout World War II this Medical Center was used by the Allied authorities for research, diagnosis, and treatment in tropical medicine and military hygiene, as well as for regular disciplines. By the war's end, it had become the medical focal point not only for Palestine but for neighboring countries as well.

In May, 1948, as a result of an Arab ambush on the Scopus road in which Dr. Hayim *Yassky, director general of the Hadassah medical organization, and 74 of his colleagues and members of the *Hebrew University faculty were murdered while en route from Jerusalem to Mount Scopus, the Medical Center there was evacuated. Its buildings and those of the Hebrew University were left under guard of the Israel Army. When Mount Scopus was demilitarized, the road was placed under the protection of the United Nations. An Israeli police force was stationed in the Hadassah and Hebrew University institutions.

It was not until June, 1967, and Israel's victory in the *Six-day War, that the Mount Scopus facilities were returned to Hadassah. Immediately upon repossessing its installations on Mount Scopus, Hadassah began to plan for their use. The plans included the opening of a 60-bed rehabilitation pavilion for patients handicapped by incapacitating injuries, war wounds, heart disease, cancer, stroke, and so on, including physiotherapy and occupational therapy; the transfer to Mount Scopus, from Jerusalem's Russian Compound, of the School

of Physiotherapy, a joint operation of Hadassah, the Israel government, Malben, and *Kupat Holim (Sick Fund) under Hadassah administration; and the establishment of a Youth Center to accommodate Jewish young people from the United States and other countries who come to work and study in Israel. In addition, a 200-bed general hospital to service both the Arab and Jewish populations of East Jerusalem was to be established there. These buildings were under construction in 1968.

From 1948 until the opening of the Hebrew University–Hadassah Medical Center in 'En HaKerem ('En Karem) in 1961, Hadassah conducted its medical activities in five temporary hospitals in Jerusalem. It was in the midst of Israel's *War of Independence, while Jerusalem was under siege, that Hadassah began planning the Medical Center at 'En HaKerem and, together with the Hebrew University, the establishment of Israel's first medical school. The Hebrew University–Hadassah Medical School was opened in 1949 with a student body of 45. By 1968, with an eminent faculty and a student body of about 800, the Medical School, located at the Hebrew University–Hadassah Medical Center, already had given Israel a corps of expertly trained physicians. Graduates of the school constituted 90 per cent of the hospital resident physicians in Israel.

The Hebrew University–Hadassah Medical Center is located on a 300-acre site in the Judean Mountains, overlooking the

Hadassah nurses in Jerusalem outside the health station established in 1913. [Hadassah]

ancient town of 'En HaKerem. In 1968 it comprised a 650-bed teaching hospital with diagnostic and research laboratories; the Rosensohn Outpatient Clinics, which handle more than 250,000 patient visits annually; the Adolf and Felicia Leon Mother and Child Pavilion, comprising 57 obstetrical beds and 64 bassinets; the Henrietta Szold–Hadassah School of Nursing (founded in 1918) with complete housing and teaching facilities for 150 student nurses and a residence for graduate (unmarried) nurses; the John F. Kennedy Building, a tribute to the late President of the United States, which serves as Hadassah's tourist information center; a synagogue, which houses the world-famous stained-glass windows, depicting the Twelve Tribes, created for Hadassah by Marc *Chagall; and the Herman Dana Child Psychiatry Division. In addition, the center includes the buildings of the Hebrew University–Hadassah Medical School and the Hebrew University–Hadassah School of Dental Medicine, founded by Alpha Omega.

New facilities in the course of construction in 1968 at the Hebrew University–Hadassah Medical Center included the Siegfried and Irma Ullman Institute for Cancer and Allied Diseases to house Hadassah's Moshe Sharett Institute of Oncology; a trauma unit to deal with victims of injuries of various kinds; a burn unit to treat soldiers and civilians for burns; quarters for resident physicians and interns; a residence for physicians and other medical experts from other countries who visit the Medical Center; an additional nurses' residence; a new floor for public health work; and an additional department for pediatric ophthalmology.

A comprehensive fellowship program established in 1948 enabled more than 250 Hadassah physicians, nurses, and hospital administrators to receive specialized training at universities and hospitals in the United States and Europe. American medical authorities have also been sent to teach in Israel.

Although Hadassah turned over its health centers to the Jerusalem municipality, it retained the center at Kiryat HaYovel on the outskirts of Jerusalem. There Hadassah conducts a pilot-plant operation involving a new approach to curative and preventive medicine. This program stresses health work on a group basis and focuses on the needs of the individual as they involve his family, home, and community. It is a total program involving the whole family. At Kiryat HaYovel, Hadassah health teams provide a comprehensive program of preventive, diagnostic, and curative health services. Attention is paid to psychological factors as they affect the physical and mental health of the individual. This Hadassah center was cited by representatives of the World Health Organization and by agencies of other governments for adaptation in areas with problems similar to those found in Israel. Hadassah physicians there see an average of 22,000 patients annually; nurses see an average of about 45,000. Home visits are made as required.

In earlier years, Hadassah also conducted special programs, including school luncheons, child health and welfare centers, and playgrounds. All of these are now operated by the municipalities or the central government.

Hadassah became an important instrument for helping the newly developing Afro-Asian countries meet their needs for medical personnel and find solutions to their medical and public health problems. In 1968 Hadassah medical teams were at

Hebrew University–Hadassah Medical Center in 'En HaKerem. [Israel Information Services]

work in Liberia, Ethiopia, Sierra Leone, and Tanzania. Medical training was provided for students from African and Asian countries at the Hebrew University–Hadassah Medical School, and Afro-Asian nursing students were trained at the Henrietta Szold–Hadassah School of Nursing. *See also* FOREIGN AID PROGRAM OF ISRAEL.

Hadassah in the Six-day War. When Jordan attacked Israel on Monday, June 5, 1967, at 9:30 A.M., the first shells hit the Hebrew University–Hadassah Medical Center. The Medical Center suffered damage from four direct hits.

During the Middle East crisis that preceded the outbreak of hostilities, the Medical Center was placed on a war footing, ready to receive casualties. Prof. Kalman J. Mann, director general of the Hadassah medical organization, was placed in charge of all medical activities for Jerusalem and its environs. The Hebrew University–Hadassah Medical Center was declared a medical base and chief casualty clearing station for the area. Within two hours, civilian and military casualties began pouring into the Medical Center in increasing volume. By Thursday noon, June 8, Hadassah's medical staff had treated 985 patients, 50 of whom were Arab prisoners of war.

On Friday, June 9, 1967, following Israel's capture of East Jerusalem, the Hadassah flag was hoisted once more atop its battered hospital on Mount Scopus. After 19 years, Hadassah facilities on Mount Scopus were back in Hadassah hands.

After the Six-day War, the Arabs of East Jerusalem and the West Bank made increasing use of Hadassah's medical facilities, soon constituting a considerable percentage of patients treated for cancer (at the request of the UN Relief and Works Agency for Palestine Refugees in the Near East, or UNRWA), coronary diseases, and other ailments.

Special courses were arranged for Arab doctors from East Jerusalem and the West Bank at the Medical Center, so that they could be brought up to date on the latest developments in the different medical specialties. Arab students from East Jerusalem began applying for admission to the Henrietta Szold–Hadassah School of Nursing and to X-ray technician courses.

Hadassah-Israel Education Services. In 1942 Hadassah inaugurated a vocational education program in Palestine with the establishment of the Alice L. Seligsberg Vocational High School for Girls, in Jerusalem, and the Louis D. *Brandeis Vocational Center, in the Romema section of the city, which contains two schools for young adults, the Fine Mechanics and Precision Instruments School and the Printing School. Later a tool and die-making department, the first in Israel, was added. A separate floor in the building houses the new industrial electronics department, which was instituted at the request of the Ministry of Education and Culture to prepare for the advent of automation in Israel. In 1944 Hadassah opened its Vocational Guidance Institute in Jerusalem. In all schools and workshops, a high school academic curriculum was provided together with vocational training. In 1952 Hadassah and *Youth 'Aliya opened the Rural Vocational Guidance Center, N'urim, at K'far Witkin, which offered vocational training to young people from surrounding villages. At Hadassah-N'urim, the Rural Vocational Guidance Center at K'far Witkin, where a separate electronics building has been added, youth from *development towns, including Arab boys and girls, are given short-term courses in much-needed village skills, among them carpentry, care and maintenance of farm machinery, cooking, and child care.

In 1968 Hadassah adopted the name "Hadassah-Israel Education Services" for the nonmedical aspects of its education work in Israel and transformed the Seligsberg Vocational High School into a comprehensive high school for boys and girls, which includes grades 7 through 12, full academic courses, and opportunities for varied vocational training.

Youth 'Aliya. Through this youth immigration movement, under the auspices of the *Jewish Agency for Israel, Hadassah has helped resettle and rehabilitate in Israel nearly 135,000 Jewish youths from 80 lands. The principal agency in the United States supporting the program of Youth 'Aliya in Israel, Hadassah provides about 40 per cent of the budget needed for maintenance, education, and special projects.

Founded in 1934 by Recha *Freier and other courageous Jewish leaders in Germany and fostered by Henrietta Szold, founder of Hadassah, who became its director in Palestine, Youth 'Aliya has since then "graduated" tens of thousands. These graduates have subsequently become a valuable element and positive force in the development of their country, making contributions to agriculture, industry, teaching, the arts, the defense forces, the merchant marine, and the diplomatic service.

In 1968 there were some 12,000 wards in training in 267 Youth 'Aliya installations, kibbutzim, youth villages, and day centers, where they were being given academic and vocational education plus recreational and cultural activities. Ramat Hadassah Szold, once a reception center for all children accepted in Youth 'Aliya, offered in 1968 one- and two-year courses of special education to prepare those who had a low educational level for entry into the regular Youth 'Aliya program. The Eddie Cantor Memorial Workshop of the center stresses courses in carpentry and metalwork and prevocational training.

Youth 'Aliya, together with the Absorption Department of the Jewish Agency and the Israeli Ministries of Labor and Education and Culture, runs 17 day centers (mostly in development towns in the Negev and Galilee) to provide vocational education and training for civic responsibility for unemployed young people or those unable to continue their studies.

Activities in the United States. Hadassah provides education for creative Jewish living through study, discussion, and book review groups, forums, and institutes to equip members to understand the Jewish heritage and enrich their lives as Jews in the United States. Within this context, Hadassah has been responsible for the publication of a series of volumes, including *Guide to Palestine* (1918), edited by Jessie Sampter (rev. ed., 1933, under the title *Modern Palestine*); *The American Jew: A Composite Portrait* (1942), edited by Oscar I. Janowsky; *Great Ages and Ideas of the Jewish People* (1956), edited by Leo W. Schwarz; *Life and Letters of Henrietta Szold*, by Marvin Lowenthal; and *Woman of Valor: The Story of Henrietta Szold* (1961), by Irving Fineman. A history of Hadassah was being written in 1968 by Marlin Levin. Hadassah is a founding member of the World Jewish Bible Society and of the American section of the Society, and has embarked on an intensive new approach to Bible study, including Bible tours of Israel, study guides, and special courses. As a means of developing closer ties with Israel and Jews everywhere, Hadassah actively promoted the study of *Hebrew.

Early in 1965 Hadassah undertook a five-year publication program, to be carried out in cooperation with the National Foundation for Jewish Culture. A demographic study of Jews in the United States, *Jewish Americans: Three Generations in a Jewish Community* by Sidney Goldstein and Calvin Goldscheider (1968), is the first publication under Hadassah's sponsorship. Also undertaken by Hadassah in 1968 was a textbook and teaching syllabus on the Nazi holocaust by Irving Halpern. The aim of this program was to enlist outstanding younger scholars in an effort to give greater understanding to the place of the Jew in American life and his relation to world Jewry. An important medium in Hadassah's overall program is the *Hadassah Magazine*, published 10 times a year.

Hadassah's American Affairs Program provides information on political, social, and economic issues in the United States for Hadassah members, to enable them better to understand and defend their democratic heritage at home and abroad. Monthly kits are distributed to members, who are encouraged to participate in civic efforts and in activities designed to strengthen the United Nations, where Hadassah is an accredited nongovernmental organization.

The primary goal of Hadassah's Zionist Affairs Program is to advance Zionism as an integral part of Jewish thought and action. The program therefore is geared to execute three principal functions: education, public relations, and liaison with related overall organizations with which Hadassah is affiliated. Intensification of Arab propaganda on American college campuses impelled Hadassah to prepare a special briefing kit for college-bound high school graduates. Widely distributed, it was commended by other organizations as a major contribution toward solving an urgent problem. Hadassah is a member of the Coordinating Committee of Jewish organizations (founded in 1966), which acts as a clearinghouse for information on campus activities. Hadassah is represented in the WZO as a constituent member of the *World Confederation of General Zionists, a Zionist grouping that has no political affiliation with any party in Israel (*see* GENERAL ZIONISM). Hadassah also is represented on the Zionist General Council (*Actions Committee), where it has eight members and several alternates, and has a representative on the Executive of the Jewish Agency for Israel. On the question of *'Aliya, Hadassah cooperated with the Committee on Manpower Opportunity in Israel of the Jewish Agency and with its Israel 'Aliya Department and endorses the program of the Association of Americans and Canadians in Israel. Hadassah is a constituent member of the American Zionist Council (*see* EMERGENCY COMMITTEE FOR ZIONIST AFFAIRS) and of the *Conference of Presidents of Major American Jewish Organizations. It also is a member of the American Jewish Conference on Soviet Jewry. In 1970 Hadassah became a founding member of the American Zionist Federation.

Through its youth movement, HaShahar (The Dawn), Hadassah offers young people a varied program whose goals are enriched Jewish living in the United States, deeper understanding and acceptance of Zionism, and stimulation of active interest in Israel and its people. This youth program has four divisions: Junior Young Judaea for boys and girls between 9 and 11, Intermediate Young Judaea for those between 11 and 13, Senior Judaea for youths of high school age, and Ha-Magshimim (the Fulfillers) for high school graduates up to age 25. The programs, which are geared to the interest of each age division, include discussions, social activities, seminars, leadership training, and Israel work-study-travel institutes. In addition, through the Hadassah Zionist Youth Commission, Hadassah operates eight summer camps.

For many years prior to the establishment of HaShahar, Hadassah had been the sole sponsor of *Junior Hadassah, the Young Women's Zionist Organization of America, and

a cosponsor of *Young Judaea. Eventually Hadassah became the sole sponsor of Young Judaea. Following Hadassah's acceptance of this responsibility, Young Judaea and Junior Hadassah merged in 1967 to form HaShahar.

In 1967 Hadassah inaugurated a scholarship plan to enable American young people to study and work in Israel for one year. The objective of this plan was to reach young Jews who, without the incentive provided by these scholarships, might not go to Israel for this purpose. The first group of 30 scholarship winners, from different parts of the United States, left for Israel in 1968.

The national presidents of Hadassah from its foundation were Henrietta Szold (1912–21, 1923–26); Alice Seligsberg (1921–23); Irma *Lindheim (1926–28); Zip Falk *Szold (1928–30); Rose Gell *Jacobs (1930–32, 1934–37); Rose *Halprin (1932–34, 1947–52); Judith G. *Epstein (1937–39, 1943–47); Tamar de Sola *Pool (1939–43); Etta L. *Rosensohn (1952–53); Rebecca *Shulman (1953–56); Dr. Miriam *Freund (1956–60); Lola *Kramarsky (1960–64); Charlotte Stone *Jacobson (1964–68); and Faye Z. *Schenk (1968–   ).

H. GOLDBERG

HADERA (Hedera). City in the northern Sharon Plain. Founded in 1890 in a deserted swampy and dune-covered area by immigrants of the *First 'Aliya from Russia. The original settlers suffered heavily from malaria, and many of them died. At the initiative and expense of Baron Edmond de *Rothschild, eucalyptus trees were planted and drainage canals dug to eliminate the danger of malaria. In 1914 Hadera had a population of 1,100. With growth, Hadera's original rural character changed, and after World War I it developed into a considerable urban center. An important junction between Tel Aviv, Haifa, and the Jezreel Valley, it became the headquarters of a subdistrict, where, after Israel attained its independence, the *government established the local offices of various ministries.

Hadera's economy is based on agriculture, trade, and industry. The cultivated land extends over an area of about 50,000 dunams (12,500 acres), including 15,000 dunams planted with citrus and other fruit trees; 8,000 dunams with irrigated produce, chiefly potatoes and peanuts; 15,000 dunams devoted to sericulture; 1,000 dunams of fishponds; and 2,500 dunams of eucalyptus groves, which supply a substantial percentage of the country's timber. Larger industrial enterprises, mainly located in a special industrial zone, include the Alliance tire factory; the American-Israel paper mills, the only enterprise of its kind in the Middle East; and two factories for preserved vegetables and fruit, P'ri-Ze and P'ri-Ta'im.

In the course of archeological exploration, a number of pottery house-shaped ossuaries (bone containers), as well as a fine synagogue and the remains of an Arab caravansary, were found at Hadera.

Hadera's population, which was 1,250 in 1925 and 7,500 in 1948, had risen to 30,000 by 1968. Of the city's youths, 4,852 attended elementary schools, 1,012 high schools, and 941 trade schools. The municipality's budget in 1968 totaled IL 9,018,000. Dov Barzilai served as mayor.

HADHRAMAUT JEWS IN ISRAEL. *See* HABANI JEWS IN ISRAEL.

HADID. Village (moshav) east-northeast of Lod. Founded in 1950 and affiliated with HaPo'el HaMizrahi (*see* MIZRAHI). Population (1968): 388.

HADOAR. *Hebrew-language weekly published in New York. The only Hebrew-language weekly appearing in the *Diaspora, *HaDoar* (The Post) was founded in 1921 as a daily paper under the editorship of Mordecai Lipson, a Hebrew essayist and folklorist. It appeared as a daily for nine months and was then converted into a weekly under the editorship of Menahem *Ribalow, who served as its editor until his death in 1953. He was succeeded by Moshe Maisels ('Amishai), who was followed in turn (1959) by Moshe Yinon, with David Epstein as managing editor.

From its earliest beginnings *HaDoar* has encouraged the creative work of Hebrew writers, poets, scholars, and thinkers in the United States and other Diaspora countries as well as those in Israel. It has developed a devoted community of Hebrew readers in both the United States and other countries, among them men of letters, educators, rabbis, and communal leaders of diverse viewpoints, who regard *HaDoar* as an independent literary communal organ concerned solely with the future of the Jewish people and the advancement of Jewish culture.

HaDoar is the organ of the *Histadrut 'Ivrit of America and is published by the Hadoar Association, Inc., of which Boris Margolin is president and Rabbi Edward T. Sandrow chairman of the board.

D. EPSTEIN

HAFETZ HAYIM. Village (kibbutz) in the Darom. Settled in 1944 and affiliated with *Po'ale Agudat Israel. The settlement is named for the classic Talmudic treatise *Hafetz Hayim*, by Rabbi Israel Meir Kahan (1835–1933) of Radun, Poland (now Russia). Population (1968): 370.

In this kibbutz the Biblical law of Sh'mita, prescribing that the land be left fallow for one year every seventh year, is observed literally. The economic loss is partially offset by the use of hydroponics in growing vegetables.

HAGANA. Underground Jewish army, founded in Palestine in 1920 for the purpose of protecting Jewish life and property against attacks by Arabs (*see* ARAB RIOTS IN PALESTINE), and precursor of the *Israel Defense Forces. It functioned as a clandestine organization during the entire period of the British *Mandate for Palestine and was transformed into the Israel Defense Forces two weeks after the Proclamation of the State of Israel (*see* DECLARATION OF INDEPENDENCE). At times it was tolerated and even aided by the mandatory power. On other occasions, it was persecuted and openly attacked by the British authorities in Palestine. Hagana evolved from semiautonomous units formed in towns and settlements and charged with local defense against Arab attacks into a centralized military machine operating on a national scale in the service of the Zionist movement, eventually employed as a weapon in the fight against the British Mandatory power, and finally into a full-fledged army which repelled the Arab attack on the newly born Jewish State.

Formation and Early Development, 1920–35. As part of the *Yishuv (Jewish population of Palestine), the Hagana reflected the strains and stresses of its political life. Its formation and early development were accompanied by intra-Zionist debates. Vladimir *Jabotinsky advocated an official Jewish defense force subject to British command, while the leadership of the Yishuv, and particularly the *Ahdut 'Avoda (United Zionist Labor party), forerunner of *Mapai, was in favor of an unofficial and, if necessary, underground force independent of

the British authorities. At first the force was under the exclusive control of Ahdut 'Avoda; with the establishment of the *Histadrut (General Federation of Labor), it came under the control of the latter, although admission was open to all. In 1931 the non-Histadrut elements seceded from the Hagana and formed a separate force which remained independent until 1937, when, under the impact of the Arab riots of 1936–39, it merged with Hagana and was placed under the control of the Executive of the *World Zionist Organization. It was managed by a directorate composed of Histadrut and other elements on a footing of equality. Thus, the Hagana became *the* armed force of the Yishuv.

Hagana's first real account of itself was given in April, 1920, when 200 Jews in Jerusalem, hastily assembled and led by Jabotinsky and Pinhas *Rutenberg, put up resistance to Arab attackers. The more widespread Arab riots of May, 1921, found the Hagana unprepared, especially in Jaffa, where Jewish casualties were numerous. The Arab attempt on Nov. 2, 1921, to attack the Jewish quarter in the Old City of Jerusalem was effectively frustrated by a prepared defense of Hagana units. The comparative quiet that prevailed in Palestine from 1921 to 1929 left the Hagana in a state of stagnation; few joined its ranks, it lacked an enterprising leadership, and its stock of weapons was confined to pistols, rifles, and hand grenades, with a few machine guns.

The countrywide Arab riots of 1929 took the Hagana by surprise. While it succeeded in repelling Arab attacks in Jerusalem, Haifa, and the settlements and held its ground for over a week until the arrival of British troops, it failed to prevent the slaughter which took place in Hebron and Safed. The consequence was a far-reaching reorganization of Hagana. The clandestine importation of arms from abroad was increased, and a local arms industry was established to produce explosives, hand grenades, mines, and small-arms equipment. Local units were made part of a regional organization, and provision was made for employing units and arms outside their own localities. From passive defense (awaiting an attack behind barbed-wire barricades) Hagana shifted to defense in the field. Courses for local commanders were conducted, and planning began to assume a nationwide character. Girls were enlisted on an equal footing with men.

Arab Attacks, 1936–39. The riots of April, 1936, which gradually turned into an Arab revolt that continued intermittently until World War II, accelerated the transformation of the Hagana from local and largely autonomous units into a closely knit national army. At first Arab attacks were directed against Jewish settlements, but despite the continual repetition of these attacks over a widespread area, not a single Jewish settlement was abandoned. Gradually Arab tactics changed and were directed at the disruption of Jewish communications. The normal functioning of economic life was threatened with paralysis. Late in 1936, Hagana formed mobile units to ambush marauders and to surprise attackers in their villages. By 1937 a national scheme of defense had been evolved.

As the Arab Revolt developed from an anti-Jewish movement into one directed against both the Jews and the British, the mandatory government was compelled to cooperate with the Hagana by organizing a "legal" Jewish force, which to all intents and purposes was recruited and controlled by the Hagana. In 1937 a Jewish Settlement Police numbering over 1,000 was set up by the mandatory power; later it was enlarged by a Supernumerary Police (*see* NOTRIM) organized in 10 regiments, numbering by 1939 about 22,000, and armed with rifles

Hagana recruits on parade in a training camp near Tel Aviv in 1948. [Zionist Archives]

and submachine guns. These legal formations afforded facilities for training to thousands of Hagana members. The legal units took over the duties of guarding railways, harbors, bridges, and government installations.

In the spring of 1938 the British Army authorized Capt. Orde *Wingate to organize *Special Night Squads trained in night fighting; their daring attacks on Arab guerrilla bases contributed greatly to the suppression of the revolt. The Night Squads laid the foundation during World War II of the *Palmah battalions (Striking Forces) of the *War of Independence. During the three years of the Arab Revolt (1936–39), 52 new settlements, planned and protected by the Hagana, were founded throughout the country. In 1939 a General Staff was set up with a chief of staff, and departments were established for planning, operations, munitions, training, and intelligence. To provide the necessary funds, *Kofer HaYishuv, a fund-raising agency, was established in 1938. It existed until the establishment of the State of Israel and levied what amounted to a tax on the Jewish community. The munitions industry was enlarged, and underground arsenals for storing munitions were built in many settlements. A permanent medical unit was established and the general standard of training raised.

World War II, 1939–45. The anti-Zionist *White Paper of 1939, which aimed at freezing the development of the National Home, confronted not only the Zionist movement but also the Hagana with a major crisis. The Zionist Organization rejected the White Paper and laid plans for "*illegal" immigration, the establishment of new settlements outside the restricted area allocated to Jews by the White Paper, and the strengthening of the Hagana, which was put in charge of receiving illegal immigrants (Ma'apilim) on arrival. This had actually started in 1938, when 6,100 illegal immigrants had been brought in. By the end of September, 1939, 15,000 such illegal immigrants had reached the shores of Palestine.

The outbreak of World War II and the common effort against the threat of the Axis Powers brought about a suspension of the Anglo-Zionist conflict, and the Yishuv offered its cooperation to the British authorities. Thousands of young Jews, many of them members of Hagana, joined the Jewish units of the British Army and later the *Jewish Brigade. Hagana directed many of its members to join specialized units of the British forces, such as the Artillery Corps and the Royal Air Force. Early in the war, a working arrangement between the British intelligence service and that of the Hagana was established. In 1941 Hagana reconnaissance units spearheaded the British invasion of Vichy French–occupied Syria. The British trained Hagana members as parachutists to be dropped over Nazi-occupied Europe (*see* PARACHUTISTS, PALESTINIAN

JEWISH). Of these, 32 were sent on such missions in 1944; 7 were caught and executed. The others rendered valuable services to the Allied cause and succeeded in establishing contact with Jewish groups in Nazi-occupied territories. As the German menace to Egypt increased, the British trained Jewish commandos (Palmah) as part of a Jewish plan to concentrate the Yishuv in the north of the country in the event of an enemy invasion of Palestine, to hold out against the invader until the arrival of Allied reinforcements.

Following the Anglo-American invasion of North Africa late in 1942 and the elimination of the Nazi menace to the Middle East, the cooperation between Hagana and the British came to an end and the former reverted to its clandestine role. Disclosures of the acquisition of weapons by the Hagana and its activities on behalf of the Jewish *immigration brought about a number of clashes with the British authorities during the last two years of the war. With the end of the war and the adoption of the anti-Zionist policy of Ernest *Bevin by the Labor Government in 1945, open hostility to the British developed.

Illegal Immigration and Struggle with the British, 1945–47. From 1945 to 1947, the Hagana, no longer concerned with the Arabs, who had chosen to remain neutral in the conflict between the British and the Jews of Palestine, became the instrument of Zionist policy in bringing in and protecting illegal immigrants and undermining the general British position in the country. On Oct. 10, 1945, a Hagana unit attacked a British Army camp in 'Atlit, south of Haifa, overpowered the guards, and released 208 illegal immigrants detained there. The following month, British Coast Guard vessels engaged in the detection of immigrant ships were attacked and destroyed, as were army radar installations.

The rejection by the British government of the recommendation of the *Anglo-American Committee of Inquiry to admit 100,000 Jewish concentration camp survivors intensified Hagana activities, now operating as the Hebrew Resistance Movement, and in conjunction with the two dissident underground organizations, the *Irgun Tz'vai L'umi (IZL) and the *Lohame Herut Israel (Lehi), Hagana launched a series of nationwide attacks on military installations that challenged the authority of

Hagana Museum (Bet Golomb), in Tel Aviv. [Israel Information Services]

the British government in Palestine. This campaign reached its climax when 11 bridges connecting Palestine with neighboring countries were blown up during the night of June 17, 1946. The British retaliated and, in an attempt to smash the Hagana, carried out a nationwide raid on June 29 (Black Sabbath) in which about 3,000 persons were arrested. However, Hagana had obtained advance knowledge of the raid and thus emerged practically intact. It stopped all armed attacks on the British, but its work on behalf of the Ma'apilim continued unabated. By the end of 1947, the total number of illegal immigrants brought in by the Hagana alone amounted to more than 90,000. From the middle of 1946 on, the armed struggle against the British was carried on only by the Irgun and Lehi.

During this period, Hagana perfected its organization, extended its arms industry, and added to its ranks thousands of demobilized soldiers from the Jewish units in the British Army, including many seasoned officers. Thousands of young Jews in Europe and in the detention camps in Cyprus were trained by Hagana. An illegal broadcasting station was installed which, despite all attempts to suppress it, carried on its activities until the establishment of the State.

Establishment of the State, 1947–48. Following the *partition resolution of the UN General Assembly of Nov. 29, 1947, tension and, at times, clashes between the Hagana and the British continued until the withdrawal of the British forces on May 14, 1948. To frustrate the United Nations resolution, the Arabs of Palestine, aided by Arab volunteers from neighboring countries, particularly Syria, launched all-out attacks on Jewish towns and settlements. Hagana moved from the underground into the open. Until February, 1948, it had been subjected to considerable pressure on the part of Arab attackers; from then until May 14, 1948—the day of the Proclamation of the State—the Hagana took the offensive and established its authority over nearly the whole area allotted to the Jewish State and in some parts beyond it. With the Declaration of Independence, it was confronted by the armies of the neighboring Arab states. Officially, Hagana ceased to exist as of May 31, 1948, when the Israel Defense Forces were constituted by order of the provisional government.

Until 1929 Joseph *Hecht was head of the Hagana; following him, Eliyahu *Golomb, Shaul Avigur, Yohanan Rattner, Moshe *S'ne, and Israel *Galili were successively its commanders in chief. In 1944 Hagana had approximately 36,000 members, Palmah about 2,000 (3,000 by 1948). The Hagana had about 10,000 rifles and 100 mortars but neither artillery nor an air force.

S. Z. ABRAMOV

HAGOR. Village (moshav) in the Sharon Plain. Founded in 1949 and affiliated with *T'nu'at HaMoshavim. Population (1968): 322.

HAGOSHRIM. Village (kibbutz) in eastern Upper Galilee. Founded in 1948 and affiliated with the *Kibbutz M'uhad. The site was occupied from 1943 to 1948 by the moshav N'halim. Population (1968): 412.

HAHAM BASHI (Chief Rabbi). *See* RABBINATE OF ISRAEL.

HAHOTRIM. Village (kibbutz) south of Haifa. Settled in 1948 and affiliated with the *Kibbutz M'uhad. Population (1968): 305.

HAIFA. Seaport and second largest city in Israel. Population (1968): 215,000.

Archeologically, Haifa is relatively young, its oldest monuments going back only to the Turkish period, although its site is probably identical with that of the late classical Sycaminum (Heb., Shikmona). The earliest mention of ancient Haifa, which was situated north of the present center of the city, dates to the first centuries of the Common Era. A Jewish townlet, it was then the home of a number of Talmudic sages. In the latter part of the 11th century, Haifa was the temporary seat of the Gaonate (central rabbinical authority) of Palestine. In 1100 Jews and Arabs fought side by side to defend Haifa against the Crusaders. The conquerors massacred the local population.

During the era of Turkish rule in Palestine (*see* ISRAEL, HISTORY OF), Haifa was a small townlet inhabited by Muslims, Christians, and a few Jews. In about the middle of the 18th century, Dhaher el-'Amr, ruler of northern Palestine, razed Haifa but later had it rebuilt on its present site. Some Jews settled in the new town, but a significant Jewish community began to develop only in the early 19th century with the arrival of Jews from Morocco and Algeria. *Ashkenazim settled there in the 1870s. In 1875 there were about 500 Jews in Haifa.

The development of the township into a large urban center dates from the early 1900s. Its growth was sparked by the construction of the Haifa-Damascus railway in 1905, the building of the *Technion (Israel Institute of Technology) and the Hadar HaKarmel quarter in the years before World War I, and the influx of Jewish immigrants. Haifa was the scene, in 1921, of the founding conference of the *Histadrut (General Federation of Labor). The period between the two world wars saw the establishment of the Haifa-Lydda (Lod)-Egypt railway (1919), the construction of the Nesher cement factory, the Shemen Oil Company plant, and Haifa harbor, in the 1920s and early 1930s, the establishment of new Jewish residential neighborhoods (Ahuza on Mount Carmel) and of an industrial zone on Haifa Bay, the laying of the Iraq-Haifa oil pipelines, and the building of oil refineries.

During World War II, Haifa was an important base for the British Navy, and the city's heavy industry contributed greatly to the *war effort of the Yishuv. After Italy's entry into the war in 1940, Haifa was the target of enemy air attacks.

In 1944 Haifa had about 128,000 inhabitants, of whom 66,000 were Jews, most of them concentrated in the Hadar HaKarmel section of the city on the northern slope of Mount Carmel, overlooking Haifa Bay. After the United Nations *partition decision of November, 1947, the Arabs attacked the Jewish population and numerous clashes occurred. The Arab ranks were swelled by fighters from neighboring countries. On Apr. 22, 1948, immediately after the British forces had withdrawn from the city and before the Arabs had had time to readjust themselves to the new situation, *Hagana launched an of-

Lower Haifa, below Mount Carmel. [Israel Government Tourist Office]

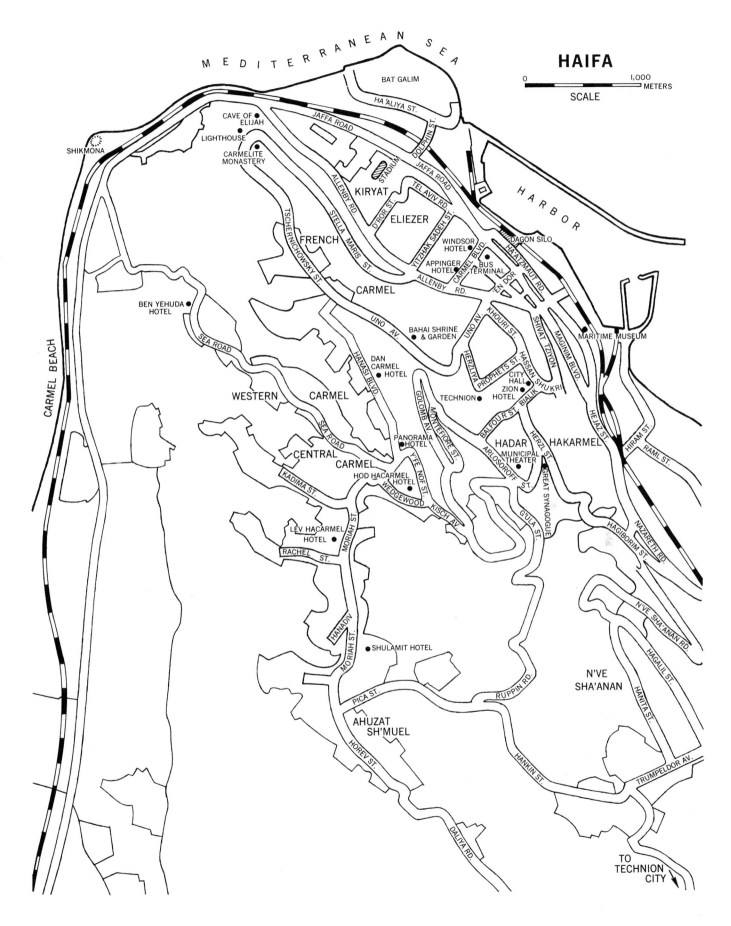

HAIFA

SCALE

0 _____ 1,000
METERS

MEDITERRANEAN SEA

BAT GALIM

HA 'ALIYA ST.

JAFFA ROAD

DOLPHIN ST.

HARBOR

CAVE OF
ELIJAH

LIGHTHOUSE

SHIKMONA

CARMELITE
MONASTERY

JAFFA ROAD

STADIUM

KIRYAT

ELIEZER

TEL AVIV RD.

D'ROR ST.

ALLENBY RD.

STELLA MARIS ST.

FRENCH

TSCHERNICHOWSKY ST.

YITZHAK SADEH ST.

WINDSOR
HOTEL

APPINGER
HOTEL

CARMEL BLVD.

BUS
TERMINAL

DAGON SILO

HA'ATZMAUT RD.

CARMEL

ALLENBY RD.

BEN DOR

BEN YEHUDA
HOTEL

SEA ROAD

UNO AV.

BAHAI SHRINE
& GARDEN

UNO AV.

KHOURI ST.

HERZLIYA

SHIVAT TZIYON

MAGINIM BLVD.

MARITIME MUSEUM

DAN CARMEL
HOTEL

HANASI BLVD.

PROPHETS ST.

HASSAN SHUKRI

WESTERN   CARMEL

GOLOMB AV.

TECHNION

CITY
HALL

ZION
HOTEL

BIALIK

BALFOUR ST.

HERZL ST.

HEJAZ ST.

HIRAM ST.

RAML ST.

PANORAMA
HOTEL

MONTEFIORE ST.

HADAR   HAKARMEL

CENTRAL

CARMEL

KADIMA ST.

Y'FE NOF ST.

HOD HACARMEL
HOTEL

WEDGEWOOD

KISCH AV.

MUNICIPAL
THEATER

ARLOSOROFF
ST.

G'ULA ST.

GREAT SYNAGOGUE

HAGIBORIM ST.

NAZARETH RD.

LEV HACARMEL
HOTEL

MORIAH ST.

RACHEL   ST.

N'VE SHA'ANAN RD.

HAGALIL ST.

HANITA ST.

N'VE
SHA'ANAN

HANADIV ST.

SHULAMIT HOTEL

PICA ST.

RUPPIN RD.

AHUZAT
SH'MUEL

HOREV ST.

HANKIN ST.

TRUMPELDOR AV.

DALIYA RD.

TO
TECHNION
CITY

CARMEL BEACH

fensive against Arab Haifa, which brought the city under Jewish control. Before the end of the fighting, the local British commander initiated a meeting between Jewish and Arab notables. The Arabs were asked to surrender, and despite repeated requests from the Jewish leaders that they remain, the great majority, obeying the call of the Arab military leadership, left the city by sea for 'Akko and Lebanon. Only a few thousand remained in Haifa.

After the establishment of the State, Haifa grew apace, and by 1968 it had a population of 215,000, of whom 11,700 were non-Jews. The city, which extends down to Haifa Bay and over Mount Carmel, became the center of Israel's heavy and chemical industries. On either side of the port area are the country's largest factories, a modern grain elevator, railway yards, and the headquarters of the *Israel Electric Corporation, Ltd. Among the many other industrial enterprises in the Haifa area are the Vulcan foundries, the Phoenicia glass factory, flour mills, and textile, equipment, and food-processing plants. The large oil refineries had been inactive for years following the stoppage of the oil flow from Iraq after the outbreak of the *War of Independence but were reactivated for the refining of oil brought to the country by tankers for local consumption. The deep-sea harbor constructed by the British in the early 1930s was expanded and improved by the Israeli government. An auxiliary port established at the Kishon Estuary became the base of Israel's navy and merchant marine.

Haifa is the seat of the Technion, which outgrew its original quarters in the center of the city and moved to a new large campus, Kiryat Technion, on the outskirts of Mount Carmel. In 1964 the *Haifa University Institute was opened, and a year later the cornerstone for its campus on Mount Carmel was laid. The Reali High School, one of the best-known high schools in the country, includes a special boarding school for students wishing to enter military academies after graduation. Of the city's youth, 38,320 attended elementary schools, 9,697 high schools, and 5,248 trade schools in 1968. There are more than 200 synagogues and houses of prayer in the city, the largest of which is the Central Synagogue in the Hadar HaKarmel quarter. Religious educational institutions include several *Yeshivot.

The municipality has made great efforts to attract writers and artists. *Karmelit*, a yearly miscellany published by Haifa writers with the assistance of the municipality, began to appear in 1953. The Haifa City Symphony Orchestra was founded in 1950, and the Haifa Municipal Theater (Teatron 'Ironi) opened in 1961 (*see* THEATER IN ISRAEL). Museums include the Maritime Museum, the Municipal Museum of Antiquities and Modern Art, the Ethnological Museum, and the Museum of Japanese Art. The city has several public gardens, parks, and playgrounds, as well as bathing beaches on the sea. In the beautiful Persian Gardens, situated on the ascent to Carmel, are the temple and tombs of the first leaders of the Bahai sect

Port of Haifa, seen from Mount Carmel.   [Israel Government Tourist Office]

Haifa at night, viewed from 'Akko across Haifa Bay.   [Israel Government Tourist Office]

(*see* BAHAI COMMUNITY IN ISRAEL). The cave of Elijah, at the foot of Mount Carmel, said to be the place where the prophet hid during his flight from Ahab, King of Israel, is a major pilgrimage site. The Carmelit cogwheel subway, which connects the port area with the top of Mount Carmel, was inaugurated in 1959.

In 1968 Haifa had a municipal budget of IL 102,000,000. Shabetai Levy was mayor of the city from 1940 to 1951. He was succeeded by Abba *Khoushi, who held this post until his death in 1969.

T. PRESCHEL

HAIFA UNIVERSITY INSTITUTE. Institution of higher education established by the Haifa municipality under the academic supervision of the *Hebrew University of Jerusalem. It was opened in 1964. In 1965 the cornerstone for its permanent campus on Mount Carmel was laid, and two years later the institute moved from temporary quarters to the first completed building. By 1968 the institute had 16 departments in the humanities and social sciences, more than 1,800 regular students, and a teaching staff of 250. Among its students are a steadily increasing number of Arabs and Druzes. A comprehensive preparatory course, given in English and Spanish, was started for foreign students in 1967–68.

HAJAJRE. Bedouin tribe in Lower Galilee. Population (1968): 306.

HAJIRAT. Bedouin tribe in Lower Galilee. Population (1968): 530.

HAKHAM BASHI (Chief Rabbi). *See* RABBINATE OF ISRAEL.

HAKHSHARA (plural, Hakhsharot). Training center to prepare prospective 'Olim (immigrants) for a pioneering life in Palestine. During the 1920s and 1930s, different types of Hakhshara farms were established, mainly in Poland, Lithuania, and Germany, by *HeHalutz youth organizations to train candidates for *immigration to Palestine in agriculture and craftsmanship. Some of the Hakhsharot were based on work on land owned by private farmers in the neighborhood; others operated their own farms. In the latter the problem of adequate return was acute. Hakhsharot also maintained cooperative workshops for the training of their members as artisans.

The Hakhshara social and cultural program included social education and the study of the *Hebrew language and culture. Later, the Hakhsharot added military training, an aspect stressed particularly by the *Revisionists. Group life was the rule in most of the Hakhsharot. Like HeHalutz in general, the Hakhsharot were supported by the *World Zionist Organization.

I. KOLATT

HAKIBBUTZ HA'ARTZI SHEL HASHOMER HATZA'IR
See KIBBUTZ ARTZI SHEL HASHOMER HATZA'IR.

HAKIBBUTZ HADATI (Kibbutz Dati). Federation of Orthodox Zionist kibbutzim in Israel (*see* KIBBUTZ), affiliated since its inception in 1934 with HaPo'el HaMizrahi (religious Zionist labor organization; *see* MIZRAHI).

Origins. The primary source of membership in the Kibbutz Dati was the German-Jewish Orthodox youth that gravitated toward the Bachad (*B'rit Halutzim Datiyim) organization. It was around Rodges, the first collective group of Bachad members to settle in Palestine at the end of 1929, that the religious Zionist kibbutz movement as a whole was to crystallize. Secondary sources of membership in the 1930s had their origins in Eastern Europe, chiefly in Poland, and among local Palestinian youth. Although as early as 1930 a collective group of religious Halutzim (pioneers; *see* HALUTZ) from Eastern Europe, known as Shahal, had been formed in Palestine, it was essentially after religious youth movements (HaShomer HaDati and *B'ne 'Akiva) had been founded in Eastern European countries that the religious kibbutz ideal in those countries received its organizational basis. At the same time, this ideal took root in the newly founded B'ne 'Akiva youth movement in Palestine. Of special importance in the growth of the Kibbutz Dati were the collective groups of religious *Youth 'Aliya graduates, from 1934 on trained for the most part in previously established religious kibbutzim.

Settlement and War Period. If the 1930s may be regarded as the formative years of the Kibbutz Dati, the 1940s may be considered its period of actual settlement. The latter period spans the years 1937–49, during which 12 groups founded kibbutzim, 10 before the establishment of the State and 2 afterward. Of the first 10 kibbutzim, 9 were settled beyond the then-existing geographical-political frontiers of the *Yishuv (Jewish population of Palestine), in three blocks of 3 settlements each: in the Bet Sh'an Valley, in the Hebron Hills, and in the Negev, around the Arab coastal city of Gaza. The peripheral location of these settlements stood out in bold relief in the *War of Independence, marking the Kibbutz Dati for a notable role, quite disproportionate to its size, in the fighting. A number of these settlements, commanding vital lines of Arab communication and blocking the invasion routes of the Arab armies, wrote some of the most heroic chapters in the history of the war. Special mention should be made of the stand of the three settlements of the 'Etzyon Block in the Hebron Hills, which protected the southern approaches to Jerusalem; of Tirat Tz'vi, in the Bet Sh'an Valley; and of B'erot Yitzhak and K'far Darom, in the Negev. By the end of hostilities 6 of these 9 settlements had been destroyed; of these 6, 5 were to be rebuilt later in other parts of the country.

At the end of 1966 the Kibbutz Dati consisted of 10 settlements. Since 1949, 3 of the original 12 had been converted into a *Moshav Shitufi type of village, while 1 new kibbutz had been formed and settled. The trend of physical development had shifted from external expansion to internal consolidation, so that almost all additional collective groups that were formed in religious Zionist youth movements, in Israel and in the *Diaspora, joined the existing kibbutzim. The accompanying table presents a summary of the origins and historical development of the Kibbutz Dati. The kibbutzim are listed in the order in which they were settled. The letter following the group name signifies the country of origin of most of the founding members: G, for Germany; P, for Poland; R, for Romania; H, for Hungary; C, for Czechoslovakia; Pa, for Palestine; E, for England; and I, for Israel.

ORIGINS AND DEVELOPMENT OF THE KIBBUTZ DATI

Kibbutz	Founding group	Date of group foundation	Date of settlement
Tirat Tz'vi	Rodges (part; G)	1930	
	Shahal (P, R)	1930	1937
	K'far Ya'avetz (G)	1935	
S'de Eliyahu*	K'vutzat Arye (G)	1936	1939
Yavne	Rodges (G)	1930	1941
B'erot Yitzhak	Ramat HaShomron (G)	1935	1943†
K'far 'Etzyon	K'vutzat Avraham (P)	1933	1943‡§
Massu'ot Yitzhak*§	Massu'ot (G, H)	1942	1945†
'En HaNatziv*	Emunim (G)	1939	1946
'En Tzurim	Birya (Pa)	1945	
	Palestine youth group (Pa)	1946	1946†
K'far Darom*§	N'tivot (G)	1946	1946†
Sa'ad	'Alumim (Pa)	1940	1947
Sh'luhot*	Sh'luhot (G)	1941	1948
Lavi	Gar'in Angli (E)	1948	1949
'Alumim	'Alumim (I)	1963	
	Urim (I)	1965	1966

* Founding group trained by Youth 'Aliya.
† Destroyed in War of Independence; resettled in 1949.
‡ Destroyed in War of Independence; resettled in 1950 and name changed to Nir 'Etzyon.
§ Converted to a Moshav Shitufi after 1949.

Ideology. Although the Kibbutz Dati adopted the communal form of living as an integral part of the Zionist kibbutz movement, it sought from its very beginning to effect a synthesis between this form of living and religion. On one level this synthesis found its expression in the religious ethic of brotherhood and social justice in interpersonal economic relations, coupled with *self-labor. This ethic had originally been propounded by the *Tora va'Avoda movement, founded in the 1920s as the ideological movement of HaPo'el HaMizrahi, but it was developed in the context of communal living principally by the Eastern European element in the Kibbutz Dati.

On a second level the synthesis was effected with the aim of creating a modern self-contained community governed by religious law. The goal sought was to reestablish the close link between religious law and Jewish community life which had been severed by the *emancipation, and this ideology was particularly propounded by the German element. By applying religious law to life in a viable community embracing and integrating the major social institutions, the religious kibbutzim sought to bridge the gap between this law and modern self-contained community life by means of the centralized authority and rational organization of communal living.

Thanks to its ability to control the total economic resources of the community, including the economic roles of its members, the kibbutz is in a position to bring into sharp focus on a community level the problems deriving from conflicts between the spheres of self-contained social life and religious law and to press for the solution of these problems on that level. A number of religious problems confronting the early settlers of the kibbutzim which have been satisfactorily solved—for example, the milking of cows and guard duty on the Sabbath—are examples of the success the Kibbutz Dati has attained in this area.

The Kibbutz Dati publishes its own monthly, which was named 'Amudim in 1954.   A. FISHMAN

HAKIBBUTZ HAM'UHAD. See KIBBUTZ M'UHAD.

HALEVY, JACOB. Educator and Zionist leader in England (b. Rishon L'Tziyon, 1898). He studied at the *Herzliya High School in Tel Aviv and then joined the *Jewish Legion. Settling in England, he became a cofounder of the University Zionist Federation and president of the Zionist Society in Brighton and Hove. He also became chairman of the Zionist Federation of Great Britain and Ireland (see GREAT BRITAIN, ZIONISM IN) and a member of the European Executive of the *World Union of General Zionists. In addition, he was active in the *World Jewish Congress, serving as chairman of its British section.

Halevy was a delegate to Zionist Congresses (see CONGRESS, ZIONIST) and the chairman of the *Sh'nat Sherut scheme, which was founded in 1950 to send young people to Israel for a year of service. He headed the editorial board of the *Jewish Observer and Middle East Review*.

                                                        J. FRAENKEL

HALPERN, GEORGE. Businessman, economist, and Zionist leader in Germany and Israel (b. Pinsk, Russia, 1878; d. Jerusalem, 1962). After attending the Universities of Vienna and Berlin and obtaining his doctorate in political economy from the University of Munich, Halpern became business correspondent for the *Frankfurter Zeitung* in Hamburg, where he was also president of the local *B'nai B'rith lodge. Between 1913 and 1921 he was associated with several oil companies in Germany.

Halpern's Zionist activities spanned 60 years. He participated in early Zionist Congresses (see CONGRESS, ZIONIST) with Herzl, and beginning with the 6th Congress (Basle, 1903), he attended every Congress through several decades. A founder of *Keren HaYesod (Palestine Foundation Fund), of which he was a director, he was elected to the Zionist *Executive in 1921. From 1921 to 1928 he was general manager of the *Jewish Colonial Trust in London. In 1921 he also became a member of the board of directors of the Anglo-Palestine Bank Ltd., continuing in that capacity with its successor organization, the *Bank L'umi L'Yisrael, and eventually becoming its honorary chairman.

After Halpern took up residence in Palestine in 1933, his principal business activity was the Migdal Insurance Co., Ltd., which he founded in 1934. He retired as general manager of the company several years before his death but continued as chairman of the board. He was also instrumental in the financing and founding of the Palestine Electric Corporation (see ISRAEL ELECTRIC CORPORATION, LTD.), serving as a member of its board of directors for many years and as board chairman from 1954 to 1956. Halpern was the author of *Jewish Workers in London* (in German, 1909).

HALPERN, Y'HIEL MIKHAEL. Early Zionist pioneer (b. Vilna, Russia, 1860; d. Safed, 1919). A grandson of Meir Leibush Malbim, the famous Bible commentator, Halpern was reared in Orthodoxy. From early youth he led an adventurous life, entertaining fanciful ideas for improving the world and helping his people. He spent much of his family's money on social experiments and was for a time associated with the Russian Social Revolutionists. After the Russian pogroms of 1881–82, he began to advocate the return of the Jews to their ancient Homeland. In 1885 he visited Palestine, and settled there in 1887. In Rishon L'Tziyon he organized the *Agudat Po'alim, the first Jewish workers' union in the country. Halpern supported the settlers' opposition to the administration of Baron Edmond de *Rothschild. He founded Nes Tziyona and helped found Hadera. In 1892 he returned to Europe and established an agency in Warsaw for the sale of Palestinian wines. He traveled throughout Russia organizing youth and Socialist Zionist workers' groups. Thus he was one of the initiators of *Po'ale Zion, whose name he coined.

Halpern was active also in organizing Jewish self-defense units in Russia and advocated the formation of a "people's legion," a paramilitary force in Palestine. Returning to Palestine in 1905, he laid the groundwork for the Jewish watchmen's organization *HaShomer. He served as a watchman himself and was wounded in clashes with Arab marauders. In pursuance of his idea of a people's legion he traveled to Ethiopia to recruit Falasha Jews. When the *Jewish Legion arrived in Palestine late in World War I, Halpern volunteered for service but was rejected because of his age.

HALPERN, YIRMIYAHU. Revisionist (see REVISIONISTS) leader (b. Smolensk, Russia, 1901; d. Tel Aviv, 1962). The son of Y'hiel Mikhael *Halpern, he was brought to Palestine in 1913, and aided in the defense of the Jews of the Old City of Jerusalem during the *Arab riots of 1920. Active in *B'rit Trumpeldor (Betar) in Palestine, he helped found the Hagana L'umit (forerunner of the *Irgun Tz'vai L'umi). In the 1930s he was in charge of military training for the World Betar movement. Himself a certified ship's captain, he advocated the education of Jewish youth for seamanship and became head of the maritime division of Betar. He organized the Jewish Marine League in various countries and founded (1934) and led the Betar Maritime School in Civitavecchia, in Rome. He was also world commander of *B'rit HaHayal, and during World War II he was active in both the United States and Britain in an effort to establish a Jewish army. He was also associated with the Hebrew Committee of National Liberation (see BERGSON GROUP). He returned to Israel in 1948 and lived for some time in Elat, where he studied oceanography and founded the Marine Museum.

Halpern contributed articles to newspapers and periodicals and wrote a number of books, including *T'hiyat HaYama'ut Ha'Ivrit* (The Renaissance of Jewish Seafaring, 1961) and *Avi, Mikhael Halpern* (1964), a biography of his father.

HALPRIN, ROSE. Zionist leader in the United States (b. New York, 1897). She attended Hunter College, Columbia University, and the Teachers Institute of the Jewish Theological Seminary of America. In 1914 she married Samuel W. Halprin, a businessman. From 1932 to 1934 and again from 1947 to 1952, Mrs. Halprin served as national president of *Hadassah, the Women's Zionist Organization of America. In 1934 she was delegated to serve as Hadassah's liaison officer to the Hadassah medical organization in Palestine and spent five years there with her family. In 1939 she was elected to the Zionist General Council (see ACTIONS COMMITTEE), on which she served until 1946.

In 1942 Mrs. Halprin became treasurer of the American Zionist Emergency Council (see EMERGENCY COMMITTEE FOR ZIONIST AFFAIRS), and from 1945 to 1947 she served as its vice-chairman. From 1943 to 1946 she also played an active role in the *American Jewish Conference, first as a member of its Secretariat and then as a member of its Executive Committee and as chairman of its Palestine Committee. In 1946 she was elected to membership in the American section of the Executive of the *Jewish Agency and served on its Finance Committee.

Rose Halprin.
[Hadassah]

From the establishment of the State of Israel until July, 1968, Mrs. Halprin continued to serve on the Jewish Agency Executive. From 1949 to 1954, at the request of Finance Minister Eliezer *Kaplan, she was chairman of a special interorganizational financial committee charged with mobilizing financial means to meet Israel's critical needs during the years of mass immigration.

Mrs. Halprin was acting chairman of the American section of the Jewish Agency Executive from 1956 to 1960. Elected chairman in April, 1960, she served in this capacity until 1963 and intermittently thereafter. Meanwhile, she continued as chairman of the Finance Committee, of the Department of Education and Culture, and of the Committee on Control and Authorization of Campaigns. She was also honorary vice-president of Hadassah, a member of the boards of the *United Jewish Appeal of Greater New York, the United Israel Appeal, the *American Zionist Youth Foundation, and the *Jewish National Fund, and a member of the Board of Directors of the American Friends of the *Hebrew University of Jerusalem. In addition, she was cochairman of the *World Confederation of General Zionists.   I. HAMLIN

HALUKKA. Organized collection of funds in the *Diaspora for distribution (Heb., *halukka*) among needy pious Jews in Palestine. For centuries Jewish communities in the Diaspora regarded it as their sacred duty to support those of their brethren in the Holy Land who devoted their lives to prayer and study; in a way, these subsidies were considered a continuation of the obligatory half-shekel contribution made by every Jewish individual for the maintenance of the Temple in Jerusalem. Just as the Temple service had been regarded as representing the entire people of Israel in its worship of the Lord, the pious Jews who spent their days at sacred studies in the Holy Land were seen as representing the Jewish people, praying for the peace and welfare of their brethren "in the presence of the Lord." Also, the support of the poor of the Land of Israel was regarded as a specific religious obligation.

For centuries the Jewish communities of Palestine sent emissaries to Diaspora Jewries to solicit funds for their scholars, pious students of the Law, and the poor. The emissaries, many of whom were themselves noted Talmudic scholars, were received with respect and frequently were able to infuse new life into communities where religion and study had declined. One of the most famous emissaries was Rabbi Hayim Yosef David Azulai (1724–1806), a prolific author, who traveled through North Africa and Europe and was respected by Jews and non-Jews alike. Among the first Halukka emissaries to America was Rabbi Moses Malki of Safed, who visited New York and Newport, R.I., in 1759.

In many countries one local resident was appointed to take charge of the collection and transfer of funds to the Holy Land. Such an individual, generally a famous rabbi or a wealthy, influential layman, had the title N'si Eretz Yisrael (Prince of the Land of Israel) conferred on him by the Palestinian Jewish communities.

Diaspora communities helped their members, especially the old, to settle in Palestine to live out the rest of their lives in prayer and study, thereby serving as "intermediaries before the Divine presence" for their brethren in the *Galut (exile). Whereas Diaspora communities contributed funds to a variety of institutions in the Holy Land, they were particularly concerned, as might be expected, with the welfare of their own countrymen who had settled there. Thus immigrants from various countries banded together to form their own communities and institutions (Kolelim), which obtained their financial support primarily from the Jewish communities in their lands of origin. In time, arrangements evolved whereby Jews in each Diaspora country or community regularly set aside funds for the maintenance of their own Kolelim in Palestine.

The administration of Halukka funds in Palestine was in the hands of *Sephardim until 1777, when the first Hasidic groups settled in the country (*see* HASIDIC JEWS IN ISRAEL). The 19th century saw the establishment of the Kolel P'rushim (composed of disciples of the Gaon of Vilna), Kolel Habad (Habad Hasidim), Kolel HoD (immigrants from Holland and Germany), and Kolelim from Warsaw, Grodno, Galicia, Bukovina, Hungary, and elsewhere. American Jews formed a Kolel in Palestine in 1895. In 1866 the Va'ad K'lali, a central committee of all Ashkenazi Kolelim, was formed (*see* ASHKENAZIM).

Most of the pious immigrants settled in areas of the Holy Land that were regarded as particularly sacred, that is, the four holy cities of Jerusalem, Hebron (the site of the tombs of the patriarchs), Safed (the center of scholars and Kabbalists), and Tiberias. In addition to supporting their members, some of the Kolelim built for them institutions and residential quarters. Contributions to Halukka by individuals were made in various forms, the most widespread being the Rabbi Meir Ba'al HaNes collection boxes, which are still found in many Orthodox Jewish homes.

Before the coming of the modern pioneers in the 1880s the Kolelim formed the major part of Palestine's Jewish population. In the 1960s they constituted only an extremely small segment of the population of the State of Israel.

T. PRESCHEL

HALUTZ (Pioneer; plural, Halutzim). Term used in the Zionist movement and in Israel to designate an individual who devoted himself to the ideals of upbuilding Jewish Palestine with physical labor, primarily in agriculture.

See also HALUTZIYUT.

HALUTZA (Elusa, Khalasa). Archeological site south-southwest of B'er Sheva'. Founded by the Nabateans, Halutza was in ancient times the principal city of the Negev. It prospered under the Byzantine Empire. The ruins yielded mainly inscriptions.

HALUTZIYUT (Pioneering). Term that evolved in the wake of the arrival of Halutzim (pioneers; singular, Halutz), starting with the *Third 'Aliya, and was used intermittently thereafter until the outbreak of World War II in 1939. In its broader sense it implied a return to the Jewish Homeland with the aim of pioneering in what was then the most arduous pursuit, settlement on the land, reclaiming the land and farming it under the most difficult conditions. It further implied the renunciation of material ambitions and of attractive opportunities of self-advancement in favor of hard physical labor with little expectation of material rewards. Halutziyut was, therefore, in many instances an act of selfless dedication to a cause, with the pioneer identifying his personal happiness with the attainment of a national and social ideal. It later came to be associated with the act of joining a *kibbutz (communal settlement), which was regarded as the highest level of Halutz self-fulfillment. In the final years of the mandatory era, service in the *Hagana and carrying out missions, such as aiding *illegal immigration, formed an additional aspect of Halutziyut.

Although representing only a minority within the totality of immigrants in the period from 1920 to 1939, the Halutz was the ideal type who left his imprint on the Jewish society that evolved in the National Home and in whom the *Yishuv (Jewish population of Palestine) and the Zionist movement took equally great pride. He was the person who totally, and with unflinching dedication, lived up to the Zionist ideal. He was praised and extolled in poetry and prose and was a dominant character in the literature and the art of the period.

After the foundation of the State of Israel, many of the functions performed on a voluntary basis by Halutzim were taken over by the State. Service in the army was no longer voluntary but became compulsory. Rural settlement and the cultivation of formerly unoccupied areas became largely the work of masses of immigrants who poured into the country after 1948 and whose needs were met by well-equipped governmental and other agencies. The meager means available to Halutzim were replaced by the considerable resources at the disposal of a sovereign State and the massive aid of world Jewry. Halutziyut in its original meaning was largely replaced by a healthy and constructive patriotism, expressed by the performance of such services as health and educational work in outlying parts of the country and work with new immigrants. Halutziyut in its classic form made a reappearance after the *Six-day War of 1967, when young men and women volunteered to settle outlying areas.   S. Z. ABRAMOV

HAMADYA. Village (moshav) in the Bet Sh'an Valley. Founded in 1942 and affiliated with the *Ihud HaK'vutzot V'haKibbutzim. Population (1968): 260.

HAMAGGID. First modern Hebrew weekly newspaper. *HaMaggid* (The Narrator) was founded in Lyck, East Prussia, in 1856 by Eliezer Lipman Silberman. Two years later, David *Gordon became editor, a post he kept until his death in 1886. Gordon thrust the weekly into active battle against *assimilation and made it an ardent advocate of the Return to Zion.

His articles, published in 1863 and 1869, had a very wide audience and far-reaching effects. In the course of time, *HaMaggid* became the only Hebrew paper to appeal to all Jewish factions throughout the world.

After the pogroms in Russia in the 1880s, all Zionist and pro-Palestine activities centered in *HaMaggid*, which became the unofficial spokesman for the *Hoveve Zion movement. After Gordon's death, the paper underwent many changes. It appeared in Berlin and then in Galicia, finally ceasing publication in 1903. Its issues are still the richest source of material on the history of the Hibbat Zion (Love of Zion) movement in Russia and Western Europe during the second half of the 19th century.   G. KRESSEL

HAMA'PIL. Village (kibbutz) in the Sharon Plain. Founded in 1945 and affiliated with the *Kibbutz Artzi Shel HaShomer HaTza'ir. Population (1968): 465.

HAMASHBIR HAMERKAZI (Central Supplier). See HISTADRUT.

HAMASHKIF. Israeli daily newspaper established in 1939 in Tel Aviv as the official organ of the Zionists-*Revisionists. From its inception, *HaMashkif* (The Observer) carried on its masthead the inscription "With the permanent participation of Z'ev (Vladimir) *Jabotinsky." Espousing the ideals of Jewish statehood and of an active struggle for its achievement, *HaMashkif* became a frequent target of repressive measures on the part of the British Mandatory administration (see MANDATE FOR PALESTINE). Although the editors used all possible devices to camouflage the paper's support of the *Irgun Tz'vai L'umi, existing emergency regulations enabled the British administration to close the paper whenever they deemed it advisable. Under the editorship of Jacob A. Rubin the paper changed its name several times until it was permitted to appear again under its original name, *HaMashkif*.

The struggle against the anti-Zionist policies of the British administration and against the official policy of the World Zionist *Executive, as well as the support of direct action against the British and of so-called *illegal immigration, endowed *HaMashkif* with the character of a fighting paper. After a very brief period under the editorship of Itzhak Gurion, the paper was edited by Jacob A. Rubin and, later, by Isaac Remba. The weekly Friday supplements carried articles by Jabotinsky, Abba *Ahimeir, Z'ev (Wolfgang) *von Weisl, and other leaders of the Revisionist movement. With the establishment of the State and the emergence of the daily *Herut*, *HaMashkif* lost ground and ceased publication.   J. RUBIN

HAMAT GADER. Group of springs near the entrance of the Yarmukh River into the Jordan. From 1948 on Hamat Gader was within the demilitarized zone between Israel, Jordan, and Syria. During the *Six-day War of 1967 it was occupied by Israel.

The hot springs were famous in Roman times and are often mentioned in the Talmud. Ruins of a Roman theater, dating from the 3d century of the Common Era, as well as remnants of an ancient synagogue, have been discovered on nearby hills. The various springs have differing temperatures.

HAMEIRI (FEUERSTEIN), AVIGDOR. Hebrew poet and novelist (b. Dávidháza, Hungary, 1890; d. Tel Aviv, 1970).

Hameiri received a secular and a broad Jewish education. While still in his teens, he began to write poetry in Hungarian and in Hebrew and was an active Zionist. After leaving school, he worked for the Hungarian and Hungarian-Jewish press but at the same time continued his Hebrew writing. In 1910 he edited *HaY'hudi*, a Hebrew weekly in Budapest. In 1912 the Hungarian Zionist Organization published his first collection of Hebrew poetry.

While serving as an officer in the Austro-Hungarian Army during World War I, Hameiri was wounded several times and taken prisoner by the Russians. After the Russian Revolution he was released from captivity in Siberia and took up residence in Odessa, where he worked for Hebrew publishing houses. In 1921, following the suppression of Hebrew by the Bolsheviks, he settled in Palestine, where he became one of the leading literary figures.

Hameiri wrote extensively on political and cultural problems in the Hebrew press and in his own monthly, *HaMahar* (Tomorrow), founded the satirical theater Kumkum (*see* THEATER IN ISRAEL), and translated works of Hungarian and other European literature into Hebrew. Temperamental and dynamic, he described the horrors of war, stressing particularly the fate of the Jew and his role as a historic scapegoat in *Tahat Shamayim Adumim* (Under Red Skies, 1925) and *HaShiga'on HaGadol*, 1929 (*The Great Madness*, 1952). His novels and short stories of Palestinian life, for example, *T'nuva* (1934–35), have a romantic and piquant touch. Hameiri received the Bialik Prize.

H. LEAF

HAMEIRI (OSTROWSKI), MOSHE. Rabbi and *Mizrahi leader (b. Karlin, near Pinsk, Russia, 1885; d. Tel Aviv, 1947). Brought to Palestine by his family when he was a child, he was educated at Yeshiva Torat Hayim in Jerusalem. He served as the rabbi of 'Ekron from 1912 to 1918.

After World War I Hameiri helped found the Mizrahi in Palestine, participated in the establishment of the *K'nesset Yisrael, and served as representative of Mizrahi in the *Asefat HaNivharim (the Elected Assembly of the Jewish population of Palestine) and in the Executive of the *Va'ad L'umi (National Council). In 1931 he became head of the Department of Community Organization of the Va'ad L'umi.

Hameiri represented Mizrahi at many Zionist Congresses (*see* CONGRESS, ZIONIST) and in 1946 was chosen a member of the Central Committee of the Mizrahi World Movement. A founder of the Mizrahi Teachers Seminary in Jerusalem, he taught Talmud at this institution from its inception (1920) until his death. His publications include books on the Talmud and a history of the Mizrahi in Palestine.   G. BAT-YEHUDA

HAMLIN, ISAAC. Labor Zionist leader in the United States (b. Komarin, Russia, 1891; d. Tel Aviv, 1967). In 1909 Hamlin settled in the United States. Taking up residence in Boston, he became New England secretary of the *Po'ale Zion party and was among the organizers and leaders of the People's Relief Committee for European Jews in World War I. He represented the Po'ale Zion party at the founding conference of the *American Jewish Congress in Philadelphia in 1918 and helped organize the *Jewish Legion. He was also a member of the group that founded the *Keren HaYesod in the United States, and served on its Board of Directors for many years.

In 1921 he was elected general secretary of the Po'ale Zion party in the United States. During his term of office he played

an active role in the founding of the American Labor party (1923; subsequently the Liberal party) and fought for the recognition of Po'ale Zion as part of it. In 1923, when at the call of David *Ben-Gurion the United Hebrew Trades of America and the Labor Zionist movement (*see* LABOR ZIONISM) decided to launch a fund-raising campaign on behalf of Israel's pioneers, Hamlin was elected national secretary and served in that capacity until 1955. Under his leadership $60,000,000 was raised for the institutions of the *Histadrut (General Federation of Labor). He was also instrumental in uniting the varied elements that made up the Histadrut movement, many of them Jewish trade union circles that had previously been indifferent or even opposed to Zionism.

Hamlin attended nearly all Zionist Congresses (*see* CONGRESS, ZIONIST) from 1926 on and was elected a member of the *Zionist General Council at the 24th Zionist Congress, held in Jerusalem in 1956. In 1955 he was invited by the Histadrut Executive Committee in Israel to take over the leadership of the American Histadrut Center in Tel Aviv, which was subsequently named for him. He served in this capacity until his death.

HANITA. Village (kibbutz) in western Galilee, on the Lebanese border. Founded in 1938 and affiliated with the *Ihud Ha-K'vutzot V'haKibbutzim. Population (1968): 389.

Kibbutz Hanita, in western Galilee. [Zionist Archives]

HANKIN, Y'HOSHU'A. Palestine pioneer (b. Kremenchug, Ukraine, Russia, 1864; d. Tel Aviv, 1945). In 1882 Hankin's father settled in Palestine and joined the founders of Rishon L'Tziyon. Young Y'hoshu'a worked on his father's farm and helped defend the settlement against Arab marauders. Father and son were among the leaders of the settlers' rebellion against the administration of Baron Edmond de *Rothschild, and in 1887 they left Rishon, moving to the *Bilu settlement of G'dera. Establishing close relationships with Arab peasants and landowners, Hankin was able to carry through land purchases for the purpose of expanding Jewish settlement. He was instrumental in acquiring the land for Rehovot and Hadera. Later he acted as purchasing agent for the *Jewish Colonization Association (ICA), the *Jewish National Fund, and the Palestine Land Development Company.

During World War I Hankin was exiled by the Turkish authorities to Anatolia. After the war he resumed his land-purchasing activities. In more than half a century of service as land buyer and planner of Jewish settlements, Hankin was instrumental in the acquisition and settlement of large tracts of land in the country, including the Jezreel Valley, becoming widely known as the Redeemer of the 'Emek.

HANNIEL. Village (moshav) in the Sharon Plain. Founded in 1950 and affiliated with *T'nu'at HaMoshavim. The village is named for Hanniel, son of Ephod, leader of the tribe of Manasseh (Numbers 34:23). Population (1968): 282.

HANO'AR HADATI. *See* B'NE 'AKIVA.

HANO'AR HA'OVED V'HALOMED. Israeli youth movement founded in 1959 through the merger of HaNo'ar Ha'Oved (Working Youth) and *HaT'nu'a HaM'uhedet (United Movement). In 1968 HaNo'ar Ha'Oved V'haLomed (Working and Studying Youth) had a membership of more than 100,000. The movement is an integral part of the *Histadrut (General Federation of Labor) and is composed of several sections, the chief of which are the Professional and Educational Sections. The former had in 1968 about 40,000 members who were employed in factories, workshops, offices, and elsewhere and were organized in professional sections. About one-fourth of the members were covered by the Law of Apprenticeship, which gave them the possibility of studying one day a week and thus of advancing in their professions. The section also maintained a network of evening elementary and high schools, which were attended by 10,000 youths. Cultural and educational activities in this section were directed by youth club instructors, who organized study evenings, theater groups, outings, and so on. Efforts were made to direct some of the youths to training for agricultural settlement or to cooperatives in cities. Several thousand members of the Professional Section belonged also to the Educational Section.

The Educational Section is divided into two subsections. Members of the first subsection are predominantly studying and working youths in new immigrant areas. In 1968 this subsection had a membership of about 24,000, organized in 170 branches, with activities conducted by instructors provided by the movement in cooperation with the Ministry of Education and Culture and the Youth and Absorption Departments of the *Jewish Agency for Israel. The instructors undergo special training. With the increase in the number of youths in new immigrant villages receiving a high school education, efforts have been made to select instructors from among them.

The second subsection of the Educational Section is composed of youths of the veteran Jewish population. This subsection had in 1968 about 17,000 members, organized in 65 branches. The educational activities are conducted along the lines of HaNo'ar Ha'Oved and HaT'nu'a HaM'uhedet, and it has retained the character of a pre-State youth movement. It is staffed by volunteers, mainly graduates of the movement, who served with Nahal (*see* ISRAEL DEFENSE FORCES) or are members of kibbutzim. The youths are educated in the spirit of the labor movement and *Halutziyut (pioneering). The graduates form settlement nuclei and enlist in Nahal. In 1966–67 the two subsections of the Educational Section furnished 22 settlement nuclei which served to strengthen various kibbutzim and to help in the establishment of new settlements.

Other sections of the movement were the B'ne Moshavim (9,000 members), B'ne HaKibbutz HaM'uhad, and B'ne HaIhud. As their names indicate, they comprised young people from the workers' settlements and kibbutzim. Several thousand Arab youths (2,000 working youths and 2,600 studying youths) were also organized in the movement. Great efforts were made to promote friendship between them and their Jewish comrades through the organization of joint meetings, study groups, and outings.

Y. SLUTSKY

HANO'AR HATZIYONI. Zionist *Halutz (pioneer) youth movement founded on May 25, 1931, at a conference held in Lwów (Lvov), Poland, at which representatives of the HaShomer HaL'umi, HaNo'ar Ha'Ivri, and HaNo'ar HaTziyoni movements from Belgium, Hungary, Iraq, Luxembourg, Palestine, Poland, Romania, and the United States resolved to unite under the name HaNo'ar HaTziyoni. In the years 1931–39 additional branches of the movement were established in Austria, Czechoslovakia, France, Latvia, and Lithuania, and, after World War II, in Argentina, Bolivia, Brazil, Canada, Chile, Costa Rica, Cuba, Great Britain, Mexico, Morocco, the Netherlands, Paraguay, Tunisia, and Uruguay.

HaNo'ar HaTziyoni is an integral part of the World Zionist movement. In Israel it is identified with the Independent Liberal party (*see* PROGRESSIVE PARTY IN ISRAEL); its members are also in the *Histadrut-affiliated Ha'Oved HaTziyoni. In the late 1960s the movement had 4,500 members in Israel and more than 8,000 in Europe, the Americas, and Africa.

The aims of HaNo'ar HaTziyoni include the achievement of harmony among the various social classes in Israel, the participation of Jewish youth in the upbuilding of the State of Israel, and the safeguarding of Israel's democratic character. It educates its members in a pioneering spirit and in the appreciation of social and national values, and it has consistently guided its members to the kibbutz way of life as the best means of furthering the best of human aspirations and, at the same time, of identifying with the welfare of the Jewish State.

During the era preceding the establishment of the Jewish State, HaNo'ar HaTziyoni participated in every joint endeavor of the *Yishuv (Jewish community of Palestine), including not only the work of rebuilding the land but also volunteer service in the British Army (during World War II), in *Hagana, *Palmah, and parachute units (*see* PARACHUTISTS, PALESTINIAN JEWISH), and in rescue missions to Europe after the war.

In the late 1960s HaNo'ar HaTziyoni had kibbutzim throughout Israel, which were composed of Sabras (natives of Israel; *see* SABRA) as well as immigrants from many diverse national and cultural backgrounds. These kibbutzim included 'En HaSh'losha, HaSol'lim, K'far Glickson, Me 'Ami, Nitzanim, Tel Yitzhak, and Usha. HaNo'ar HaTziyoni also maintained five youth villages, where 1,500 boys and girls from 48 countries received their education. These institutions are organized in the Y'sodot federation within the framework of institutions run by Ha'Oved HaTziyoni, which attends to their financial needs. Each institution has its specialized educational program. The Nitzanim Youth Village offers agricultural and nautical training. Alone Yitzhak and the Israel Goldstein Village in Jerusalem offer a program of academic studies; the Jerusalem village also offers vocational training, as does the Magdiel Vocational Institute. N've Hadassah is intended for the education of younger children.

Z. HASSON

HANTKE, ARTHUR MENAHEM. Zionist leader and official in Germany and Israel (b. Berlin, 1874; d. Jerusalem, 1955). Educated at the Universities of Berlin and Freiburg, Hantke opened a law practice in 1900. In 1893, while a student in Berlin, he joined the Jüdische Humanitätsgesellschaft, a pre-Zionist students' group. He attended the 5th Zionist *Congress (Basle, 1901) and most subsequent Congresses. In 1903 he was named to the Executive Committee of the *Jewish National Fund, an office he held until 1928. In 1905 he was elected to the Greater *Actions Committee of the *World Zionist Organization and that year also became president of the Zionist Organization of Germany (see GERMANY, ZIONISM IN), an office he held until 1920. He led the opposition to concentration on the political aspects of Zionism and favored emphasis on a program of practical settlement work in Palestine.

As a member of the Zionist *Executive from 1911 to 1920, Hantke played an important role in international Jewish and Zionist affairs during World War I. He represented the Zionists of Germany in organizations formed to aid Jews in German-occupied Eastern European areas and participated in efforts to secure equal rights for Romanian Jews when Romania signed a separate peace dictated by the Central Powers (May, 1918). He also prevailed on the German government to intercede with Turkey for the safety of Palestine's Jewish community. Anxious to keep the Zionist movement strictly neutral, he opposed the formation of a *Jewish Legion to fight alongside the Allies. However, he openly expressed gratification when the *Balfour Declaration was issued and used it to persuade the Central Powers to make a similar pro-Palestine declaration. He obtained a promise from the Foreign Minister of the Austro-Hungarian Monarchy that his government would commend the Zionist cause to the Turks. Similar declarations were obtained from Germany and Turkey, although by that time only the northern part of Palestine was left in Turkish hands.

Shortly after the war Hantke went to London to set up the Organization Department of the World Zionist Executive, but after the election of a new Executive at the *London Zionist Conference of 1920, he returned to Berlin, where he became director of the Central European Office of the newly established *Keren HaYesod (Palestine Foundation Fund). In 1921 he was elected vice-chairman of the Greater Actions Committee. Five years later he moved to Palestine to become director of the Jerusalem headquarters of Keren HaYesod, a position he held until a few months before his death. At the 23d Zionist Congress (Jerusalem, 1951) he was elected one of the three chairmen of the Board of Directors of Keren HaYesod.

HANUKKA. Festival celebrating the victory of the Maccabees over the Syrians in 164 B.C.E. that led to the restoration of religious freedom and national independence to Jewish Palestine. Hanukka (Dedication), which begins on the 25th of Kislev (some time in December) and lasts for eight days, is observed by the recital of thanksgiving prayers and the lighting of candles. The candles commemorate the miracle at the rededication of the Temple, when a small jar of oil, which had not been defiled by the heathen, burned for eight days in the Sanctuary's *Menora, allowing time for ritually pure oil to be prepared.

With the rise of modern Jewish *nationalism, the nationalist aspect of the festival, which had lost much of its significance after the destruction of the Temple and the ruin of the Jewish State, again became prominent. *Makkabäerfeiern* (Maccabees' celebrations), extolling the national struggle and military prowess of the Maccabees, first introduced by pre-Herzlian Zionists in Vienna, became permanent features of the activities of Zionist societies.

In Israel, Hanukka is celebrated publicly as both a religious and a national festival. Large Hanukka Menorot are lit in public squares and buildings, and torchlight parades are held. Since 1910, when they were instituted by the teachers and students of the *Herzliya High School, annual pilgrimages have been held to Modi'in, birthplace of the Maccabean revolt, where the traditional tombs of the Maccabees may be seen. In the 1940s, the Modi'in torchlight marathon was established. A Hanukka torch, lit at the tombs of the Maccabees, is carried by marathon runners to other parts of the country, where the flame is used to light other torches. During Hanukka thousands of young people make their way to M'tzada (Masada) on the Dead Sea, to climb the steep path to the remains of the fortress which was the last Jewish stronghold in the war against the Romans.

HA'OGEN. Village (kibbutz) in the Sharon Plain. Founded in 1947 and affiliated with the *Kibbutz Artzi Shel HaShomer HaTza'ir. Population (1968): 500.

HA'OLAM. Hebrew weekly, official organ of the *World Zionist Organization (WZO). The name, which means "The World," was a translation of *Die *Welt*, the first German-language organ of the WZO. Established in 1907 in Cologne, *Ha'Olam* was published in that city under the editorship of its founder, Nahum *Sokolow, until 1909. From 1909 until 1913 it appeared in Vilna and subsequently, until the interruption of its publication by World War I, in Odessa. Editors during *Ha'Olam's* publication in Russia were Y. S. Goldberg (1909–10) and Alter *Druyanow (1911–14).

Revived in London in 1919, *Ha'Olam* was published there until 1921, when its publication temporarily ceased. It appeared again in Berlin in 1923 and in 1924 returned to London; from there it moved to Jerusalem in 1936. From 1923 to 1948 it was edited by Moshe *Kleinman. It ceased publication in 1949.

HA'OLAM HAZE (magazine). *See* CANAANITES AND SEMITIC ACTION.

HA'ON. Village (kibbutz) on the eastern shore of Lake Kinneret. Founded in 1949 and affiliated with the *Ihud HaK'vutzot V'haKibbutzim.

HA'OVED HADATI. Religious workers' party, established in 1943 and affiliated with the *Histadrut, the General Federation of Labor in Israel, within which it fights for the rights and views of the religious workers. In the elections to the Histadrut held in 1960 it received 7,500 votes.

HA'OVED HATZIYONI. *See* PROGRESSIVE PARTY IN ISRAEL.

HAPO'EL (The Worker; sports organization in Israel). *See* SPORTS AND PHYSICAL EDUCATION IN ISRAEL.

HAPO'EL HAMIZRAHI. *See* MIZRAHI.

HAPO'EL HAMIZRAHI WOMEN'S ORGANIZATION. *See* MIZRAHI.

HAPO'EL HATZA'IR. Labor organization active in Palestine from 1905 to 1930. HaPo'el HaTza'ir (The Young Worker), whose full name was Histadrut HaPo'alim HaTz'irim B'Eretz

Yisrael HaPo'el HaTza'ir, was founded by young people who had come to Palestine with the *Second 'Aliya in protest against the *East Africa scheme and with the determination to demonstrate the possibility of practical work in the country. Many of the members had belonged to *Tz'ire Zion groups in Europe. In Palestine the young people kept themselves separate from the veteran workers, who were striving to establish themselves on the land with the help of *Jewish Colonization Association (ICA) or the *Odessa Committee. HaPo'el HaTza'ir regarded the "increase of the number of Jewish workmen in the country and their entrenchment in all fields of labor as a prerequisite for the realization of Zionism." In this program it saw a way of creating a Jewish majority in Palestine and giving the Jews the moral right to the land. HaPo'el HaTza'ir also demanded that its members devote themselves to the *"Conquest of Labor." As a consequence, it insisted on 'Avoda 'Ivrit (the exclusive employment of Jewish labor). In the first period of its activity (until about 1910), HaPo'el HaTza'ir opposed the establishment of labor settlements. It feared such settlements would draw Jewish labor away from the moshavot (private villages; see MOSHAVA), which were in need of hired labor and would then revert to the practice of hiring Arab labor.

Although HaPo'el HaTza'ir attracted mainly workers, particularly agricultural workers, it also had members and sympathizers among the intelligentsia, including writers and educators. It opposed all class and proletarian slogans and, unlike *Po'ale Zion, the other workers' organization in the *Yishuv (Jewish population of Palestine), opposed the concept of class struggle. HaPo'el HaTza'ir demanded the democratization of the Yishuv and advocated the dissemination of the *Hebrew language. Its organ, HaPo'el HaTza'ir (established in 1907), rallied many of the intellectuals of the Yishuv, was read also in the *Diaspora, and had great influence on young Zionists.

Prior to 1911 HaPo'el HaTza'ir sought also to establish various facilities for the farm workers, such as kitchens, laundries, and living quarters. That year nonparty associations of agricultural workers were founded in Judea and Galilee, and Ha-Po'el HaTza'ir wielded considerable influence in their midst. Mainly under the influence of Aharon David *Gordon, it stressed the concept of labor and attachment to the soil as a personal and national value. HaPo'el HaTza'ir urged the *World Zionist Organization (WZO) to engage in practical work in Palestine and, from about 1910 on, began to regard the formation of groups independently cultivating publicly owned land as an effective method of settlement and of creating a just society. In 1913 HaPo'el HaTza'ir, with Tz'ire Zion, formed a joint faction at the 11th Zionist *Congress in Vienna and thus increased its influence. Through its periodical Ha'Aretz V'ha-'Avoda it spread its ideas among the youth of the Diaspora. Its leaders, Joseph *Aronowicz, Isaac Wilkansky (Yitzhak Avigdor *Elazari-Volcani), Yosef *Sprinzak, and Nahum Twersky, became prominent in the Yishuv and in the Zionist movement.

During World War I HaPo'el HaTza'ir advocated loyalty to the Turkish authorities. Toward the end of the war most of its members opposed enlistment in the Jewish battalions fighting on the Allied side, fearing that such participation would cause the abandonment of labor positions in the country.

In 1919 *Ahdut 'Avoda (in full, Hitahdut Tziyonit-Sotzialistit Shel Po'ale Eretz Yisrael–Ahdut 'Avoda, or Zionist Socialist Union of the Workers of Palestine–Ahdut 'Avoda) was founded. This organization, which was both political and trade-unionist in character, was founded by Po'ale Zion and part of

the membership of the Agricultural Workers' Federation and was intended to serve as an all-embracing workers' organization. HaPo'el HaTza'ir refused to join Ahdut 'Avoda on the grounds that it was based on class ideology, was not sufficiently loyal to the cause of the Hebrew language, and formed part of the World Union of Po'ale Zion. HaPo'el HaTza'ir opposed all Socialist and class definitions, although its program included the Socialist principle of public ownership of the land and the means of production. Viewing national ownership of the land and "*self-labor" as the way to realize Jewish peoplehood, HaPo'el HaTza'ir demanded action on the part of the Zionist movement to expand agricultural settlement in Palestine. Its members were the initiators of the Moshav 'Ovdim (see MOSHAV). HaPo'el HaTza'ir influenced members of Tz'ire Zion to settle in Palestine as pioneers.

In April, 1920, HaPo'el HaTza'ir and its kindred organizations in the Diaspora established the Hitahdut 'Olamit Shel HaPo'el HaTza'ir UTz'ire Tziyon (see HITAHDUT), which became a constituent faction of the WZO. Within the WZO the Hitahdut advocated political moderation, sought agreement with the Arabs, and criticized Zionist leadership for insufficient action on *'Aliya, settlement, and reconstruction projects.

Late in 1920 HaPo'el HaTza'ir and Ahdut 'Avoda jointly established HaHistadrut HaK'lalit shel Ha'Ovdim Ha'Ivrim B'Eretz Yisrael (General Federation of Jewish Workers in Palestine and Israel; see HISTADRUT) for joint action in practical endeavors. The Histadrut was organized after direct general elections based on party slates had been held. Within the Histadrut, HaPo'el HaTza'ir formed a minority, with Ahdut 'Avoda constituting the majority faction. HaPo'el HaTza'ir opposed tendencies toward class radicalism and centralization and called for economic realism instead of expansionism. It sought to secure the independence of the workers through rural settlements in moshavim and K'vutzot (see KIBBUTZ), and its position toward the urban proletariat as a potential carrier of the ideology of class struggle was reserved. It initiated the establishment of workers' contract labor groups for employment on privately owned plantations and fought for the settlement of the workers in and near their places of employment. Among those actively involved in these endeavors was Levi Shkolnik (*Eshkol).

During the 1920s two separate trends emerged within HaPo'el HaTza'ir. One trend, led by Hayim Victor *Arlosoroff and Eliezer *Kaplan and supported by the leadership in Palestine and the movement in the Diaspora, sought to turn the party into a political and ideological movement, fighting for the realization of Zionism and the adoption of a kind of "people's socialism," in harmony with the spirit and the best interests of the Jewish people as a whole. A second trend opposed all ideological dogma and political activity, let alone affiliation with international Socialist groups. Led by the so-called Nahal group, its adherents sought to influence the Jewish people as a whole by living in model communities of agricultural self-labor in moshavim and K'vutzot.

In the late 1920s the first trend came to dominate the organization. After long hesitation, HaPo'el HaTza'ir supported the expansion of the *Jewish Agency as serving the best interests of Jewish settlement in Palestine. Late in 1929 political problems in Palestine and within the WZO, coupled with a lessening of emphasis on the class struggle in Ahdut 'Avoda, resulted in a merger between HaPo'el HaTza'ir and Ahdut 'Avoda into the Mifleget Po'ale Eretz Yisrael (*Mapai). In 1932 Hitahdut

Signpost at Har'el. [Zionist Archives]

merged with the World Union of Po'ale Zion and Zionists-Socialists, thus creating a united movement in the Diaspora.

I. KOLATT

HAQIQAT AL-AMR. Arabic-language weekly published in Israel. It began publication in Tel Aviv in March, 1937, in the midst of the *Arab riots in Palestine. Sponsored by *Histadrut (General Federation of Labor), *Haqiqat al-Amr* (The Truth of the Matter) proposed to explain to Arab readers the aims of the Histadrut and of Zionism.

The weekly appeared without interruption until 1960, when the Histadrut took over the Arabic daily *al-Yom* under the editorship of Michael Assaf (of the *Davar* editorial board) and Tuvia Shammush. *Haqiqat al-Amr* first appeared as a 4-page full-size paper and later was changed to a 16-page tabloid form. It included columns on Histadrut affairs, news and views of the life of the Jews and the Arabs, and world news. A literary column published original writings in Arabic and translations of stories from Hebrew, Yiddish, and other languages. In an attempt to expose the fallacies of Arab propaganda, the paper frankly explained the practical aims of Zionism in general and of the Jewish labor movement in particular. It also emphasized the ceaseless striving of the Jews for peace and their desire for mutual understanding with the Arabs in general and the Palestinian Arabs in particular. The highlights in the relationship between the two peoples and the two cultures, in the past and in the present, were described and emphasized.

The appearance of *Haqiqat al-Amr* was greeted by sharp opposition on the part of the leaders of the Arab nationalist movement and by the Arab laborers, nationalists as well as Communists. On several occasions the Court of the Arab Revolt judged and punished those who distributed the paper, and circulation declined sharply. Until the creation of the State of Israel, the paper was not sold nor could Arabs write for it under their own names.

After 1948 the contents of the weekly changed. New columns were added, including one designed for schoolchildren. The number of Arab writers signing their names to their contributions increased, and the paper was sold openly.

M. ASSAF

HAR'EL. Village (kibbutz) in the Jerusalem corridor. Founded in 1948 and affiliated with the *Kibbutz Artzi Shel HaShomer HaTza'ir.

HAR HATZOFIM. *See* SCOPUS, MOUNT.

HAR HAZETIM. *See* OLIVES, MOUNT OF.

HAR HERZL. *See* HERZL, MOUNT.

HARKAVI, ITZHAK. Educator and Zionist organizer in Latin America and Israeli public servant (b. Białystok, Russian Poland, 1915). In 1926 his family settled in Mosesville, the oldest of the agricultural settlements founded by Baron Maurice de *Hirsch in Argentina. While a law student at Santa Fé University, Harkavi was active in the *D'ror movement in Argentina and became a leader in Zionist youth movements. During World War II he headed the information service of the *Jewish National Fund in Argentina. He founded the Institute for Israeli Culture in Argentina and in 1950 was named South American representative of the Department of Education and Culture of the *Jewish Agency.

A leading figure in the League for Labor Palestine and secretary-general of the *Po'ale Zion party, Harkavi was elected to the Zionist *Actions Committee in 1951. A founder of the Supreme Zionist Council in Argentina, he served first as its secretary and then as its chairman (1951–54).

Harkavi was headmaster of the Bialik School in Buenos Aires and lecturer in Jewish history and sociology at the teachers training seminary there. Settling in Israel in 1954, he was selected secretary-general of the *Ihud 'Olami (World Union of Zionists-Socialists). He was Israel's Ambassador to Uruguay from 1960 until 1963, when he succeeded President-elect Sh'neur Zalman *Shazar as world head of the Jewish Agency's Department of Education and Culture.

His literary activities included the editorship of *Jerusalem*, a Spanish-language quarterly in Argentina, and Spanish translations of selected works of *Ahad Ha'Am and Ber *Borochov.

HARLAP, YA'AKOV MOSHE. Rabbi and author (b. Jerusalem, 1883; d. there, 1951). He received a traditional Jewish education from rabbis and Yeshivot in Jerusalem. A friend and disciple of Rabbi Abraham Isaac *Kook, Harlap boasted that he had never breathed the air of the *Diaspora. In *Echoes of Palestinian Life* (1912), he underscored the superlative quality of the Holy Land. The Diaspora differs from Palestine, he wrote, as slavery differs from freedom.

After the issuance of the *Balfour Declaration, Harlap advocated the formation of a central Yeshiva in Jerusalem and an organization of religious leaders to plan the spiritual foundations of the future Jewish Homeland. He taught at the Merkaz HaRav Yeshiva and in later years founded a Talmudical academy specializing in the study and interpretation of religious laws whose observance was dependent on residence in the Holy Land.

G. BAT-YEHUDA

HARLECH, 4TH BARON (William George Ormsby-Gore). British statesman and colonial affairs expert (b. Ireland, 1885; d. London, 1964). He was introduced to Zionism in 1916 while serving with the Arab Bureau in Cairo. In 1917 he joined the Secretariat of the British Cabinet and was concerned with the political activity that led to the *Balfour Declaration. The following year Ormsby-Gore acted as liaison officer between the British authorities in Palestine and the *Zionist Commission headed by Chaim *Weizmann. He was regarded as a friend of the Zionist cause, exerting his influence in its behalf. During his tenure as Secretary of State for the Colonies (1936–38) the British government released the report of the *Peel Commission, which recommended a *partition of Palestine.

J. ADLER

HARMAN, AVRAHAM. Israeli diplomat (b. London, 1914). The son of an ordained rabbi, Harman received a B.A. degree in jurisprudence from Oxford University in 1935. He first went to Palestine in 1938, but the next year he left for South Africa, where he headed the press and youth departments of the Johannesburg Zionist Association until 1940, when he settled in Jerusalem. That year he became head of the English section of the Youth and HeHalutz Department of the *Jewish Agency. Between 1942 and 1948 he was head of the English section of the Agency's Information Department.

Avraham Harman.
[Israel Information Services]

In July, 1948, Harman was appointed Deputy Director of the Press and Information Department of the Israeli Ministry of Foreign Affairs, a position he held until the following year, when he became Consul General in Montreal. In 1950 he moved to New York to head the Israel Office of Information there, serving also as Counselor to the Israeli delegation at the United Nations. In 1953 he was appointed Consul General in New York. Two years later he returned to Israel as Assistant Director General of the Foreign Ministry in charge of information services, a position he held until 1956, when he was named

head of the Information Department of the Jewish Agency and a member of the Agency's Executive in Jerusalem. In 1959 he was appointed Ambassador to the United States. America's support of Israel before and during the *Six-day War was due in no small measure to his efforts. In 1968 he resigned his post to become president of the *Hebrew University of Jerusalem.

HARTGLAS, MAXIMILIAN APOLINARY. Polish Zionist leader (b. Biała Podlaska, Russian Poland, 1883; d. Tel Aviv, 1953). Hartglas studied law at Warsaw University and subsequently engaged in private legal practice. A Zionist from his youth on, he was a delegate to the *Helsingfors Conference (1906) and to several Zionist Congresses (*see* CONGRESS, ZIONIST). In the period between the two world wars he held high positions in the Polish Zionist movement, including that of president of the Polish Zionist Organization. From 1919 until 1930 he was a deputy in the Sejm (Parliament) and in 1926 served as president of the parliamentary Jewish Club.

Escaping German-occupied Warsaw, he went in 1940 to Palestine, where he was active in the General Zionist movement (*see* GENERAL ZIONISM). After the establishment of the State he served as Director General of the Ministry of the Interior of the provisional government of Israel.

Hartglas contributed to Jewish, general, and professional periodicals. His publications included *Territory and Nation* (in Russian, 1906), dealing with Jewish national rights in the *Diaspora.

HARUTZIM. Village in the Sharon Plain. Founded in 1951. Population (1968): 590.

HARZFELD, ABRAHAM. Israeli labor leader (b. Stavishche, Ukraine, Russia, 1888). After studying at the Talmudic academies of Berdichev and Telšiai, Harzfeld settled in Vilna, where he joined the Labor Zionist movement. Arrested in 1908 by the Tsarist authorities because of his revolutionary activities, he was deported to Siberia two years later, but escaped in 1914 and arrived in Palestine that summer. After a brief period of agricultural work, he was put in charge of the labor exchange in Petah Tikva, which saw to the welfare of Jewish farm laborers. He established the first workers' free loan fund in Palestine. In December, 1917, after spending a year at Tel 'Adashim, a *HaShomer settlement in Galilee, he went to Damascus to aid Jewish deportees from Palestine who had been imprisoned by the Turkish authorities. Returning to Palestine in the fall of 1918, he was elected to the Executive of *Ahdut 'Avoda the following year.

On the establishment of the *Histadrut (General Federation of Labor) in 1920, Harzfeld represented the interests of Palestine's farm, moshav, and kibbutz labor vis-à-vis the *World Zionist Organization. A member of the Zionist *Actions Committee from 1921 on, he attended the 12th Zionist *Congress (Karlovy Vary, 1921) and all subsequent Congresses.

During the quarter century preceding the establishment of the State of Israel, Harzfeld played a leading role in the development of new agricultural settlements. In the 1930s he initiated a large-scale project to settle 1,000 families in the coastal plain (Thousand Families Settlement Plan), and between 1936 and 1947 he was a driving force behind the organization of the *"stockade and tower" settlements in the Negev and other parts of Palestine.

From 1949 until 1965 he represented *Mapai in the *Knesset. In 1963 he donated all his savings to the Science Development Company for scientific research in Israel. Harzfeld wrote numerous articles for the Israeli and foreign press. A biography of him by Simon Kushnir was published in an English translation (*The Village Builder*, 1967).

HASHAHAR (American Zionist youth organization). *See* YOUNG JUDAEA.

HASHAHAR (Hebrew periodical). *See* SMOLENSKIN, PERETZ.

HASHILOAH. Hebrew monthly magazine and leading literary periodical in Eastern Europe for about two decades. (Shiloah is the Biblical name of a well outside the Old City of Jerusalem.) The publication was founded in 1896 by *Ahad Ha'Am, who edited it for several years, first in Berlin and then in Odessa. The editorship was subsequently taken over by Joseph *Klausner and Hayim Nahman *Bialik. With a few interruptions, the magazine carried on until 1914. Subsequently several short-lived attempts were made to revive it, but it never regained its erstwhile importance. Its headquarters at various times was in Berlin, Odessa, Cracow, and Warsaw and, later, in Jerusalem. Among the contributors were the three leading poets Bialik, Saul *Tschernichowsky, and Zalman Shneour; other, lesser-known poets; some of the prose writers whose works were recognized as classics in Hebrew, including Mendele Mocher Seforim and Isaac Leb Peretz; and scholars, publicists, and literary critics, such as Ahad Ha'Am, Nathan *Birnbaum, Reuben *Brainin, Klausner, David Neumark, Hayim *Tchernovitz, and Hillel *Zeitlin.

Ahad Ha'Am's original idea was to confine the material published in the magazine to topics of strictly Jewish interest since presumably most of its readers had access to Russian and other languages. However, when Klausner took over the editorship, he changed this policy in accordance with his endeavor to foster both Jewish and general humanistic interest. Originally *HaShiloah* was financed by the tea magnate Kalonymus-Z'ev *Wissotzky. Later the *Ahiasaph company, which published *HaShiloah* as well as books, was formed. Although its circulation seldom exceeded 2,000, the magazine exerted a pronounced influence on the Hebrew literary scene. Because of its high literary standards, its cultivation of modern Hebrew prose, its hospitality to diverse viewpoints, and its devotion to the ideas of Jewish *nationalism, it was the greatest single ideological influence among the Hebrew-reading Jewish intelligentsia before World War I. For many years it carried the message of Ahad Ha'Am's philosophy of Jewish nationalism, and even after his relinquishing its editorship, *HaShiloah* remained for many years the forum for his teachings.

M. Z. FRANK

HASHOMER (Shomer). Self-defense organization of Jewish pioneers of the *Second 'Aliya, established in Palestine in 1909 to protect Jewish settlements there. It was founded by the Jewish farmhands in the colony of Sejera (now Ilanya), in Lower Galilee, most of whom were members of *Po'ale Zion and recent arrivals from Russia, where many of them had participated in the self-defense organization set up during the 1904–06 pogroms. The founders and leading members of HaShomer were Itzhak *Ben Zvi, Israel *Gil'adi, Israel *Shohat, and Alexander Zeid, with Shohat acting as the driving spirit and

Group of Shomrim in Rehovot. [Zionist Archives]

political mentor of the group throughout its existence. HaShomer entered into agreements with the committees of the several colonies in Lower Galilee, undertaking the protection of their property from Arab marauders in return for an annual fee. Each such colony, after having dismissed its Arab watchmen, was supplied with Shomrim (watchmen) who were always under the orders of the Central Committee of HaShomer. In 1911 the *Jewish National Fund, having made its first purchase in the Jezreel Valley by the acquisition of the land on which Merhavya was later established, invited HaShomer to take charge of the land to protect it against the encroachments of neighboring Arabs. Also in 1911, HaShomer first went outside Galilee, taking charge of guarding Hadera and later Rehovot. In 1912 it signed similar agreements with Rishon L'Tziyon and B'er Ya'akov. In the conditions of insecurity prevailing under Ottoman rule, HaShomer performed an essential service to the new *Yishuv (Jewish population of Palestine).

In the initial period, the total membership of HaShomer numbered about 30, and at no time did it exceed 100. Admission to membership was limited and subject to a long probation period. Qualifications included personal courage, excellence in horsemanship, and strict discipline. The aim of HaShomer was to protect the lives and property of the settlers, to inspire the Arabs with respect for the Jews, and at the same time to cultivate friendly relations with the Arabs and to learn their language and customs. Within a few years of its emergence, HaShomer had gained a reputation for courage, devotion, and integrity. It raised the prestige of the Jews in the eyes of the Arabs, and was a source of inspiration to Jewish youth in Palestine and in the *Diaspora. In its encounters with Arab marauders, HaShomer suffered many casualties.

While the work of the watchmen was carried on in the open without interference from the Turkish authorities, HaShomer's internal activities were conducted in secrecy. Although nearly all its members belonged to Po'ale Zion, HaShomer refused to accept the authority of the party or to render account to it or to the Palestine Office (*see* PALESTINE OFFICES) of the *World Zionist Organization. From documents published at a later date, it appears that its members regarded themselves as the nucleus of a future Jewish army. While refusing to accept the authority of the Yishuv, HaShomer claimed an exclusive right to guard the Jewish settlements. This exclusiveness brought the organization into conflict with the old settlements in Judea, from which it was forced to withdraw.

In the course of time it was considered necessary to assure the economic future of the members by settling them on the land. In 1913 the first HaShomer settlement was established in Tel 'Adashim; it was followed by K'far Gil'adi in 1916 and by Tel Hai in 1918.

Shortly after the outbreak of World War I, HaShomer proposed the establishment of a Jewish legion in the Turkish Army, but the offer was rejected by the Turkish authorities. HaShomer nevertheless persisted in its pro-Turkish orientation, which brought it into conflict with *Nili, the Jewish underground group that operated an intelligence service supporting the advancing British troops.

When the *Hagana was formed in 1920, HaShomer was requested to disband and merge with it. An acrimonious dispute broke out within the ranks of HaShomer, many of whose members claimed for HaShomer the exclusive right of controlling Jewish self-defense in Palestine. While officially deciding to disband, HaShomer maintained its own arsenal in K'far Gil'adi and exerted influence on Hagana members in *G'dud Ha-'Avoda V'haHagana 'Al Shem Yosef Trumpeldor. Some of the members of HaShomer developed leftist tendencies. It was only after the outbreak of the *Arab riots of 1929 that they turned their arsenals over to the Hagana.

The early history of HaShomer gave an example of Jewish heroism to the youth of the Diaspora. This was the first attempt to establish a Jewish armed force in Palestine. HaShomer is considered the forerunner of the Hagana.   S. Z. ABRAMOV

HASHOMER HADATI (Shomer Dati). *See* B'NE 'AKIVA.

HASHOMER HATZA'IR (Shomer Tza'ir). Jewish youth movement formed in 1913, when various local Zionist groups in Galicia (then under Austro-Hungarian rule) and Poland (then under Tsarist Russian rule) combined under the name HaShomer HaTza'ir. These groups had included the Jewish scout organization named HaShomer (after the self-defense organization *HaShomer in Palestine), which had been strongly influenced by the general boy scout movement in Europe and by the Wandervogel German youth movement that had revolted against militarism and parental and school discipline and emphasized the independence of youth. Also involved were the *Tz'ire Zion groups, which were deeply committed to Zionism and Jewish culture.

The educational system of HaShomer HaTza'ir was based on the K'vutza, a group of 10 to 20 youngsters under a young group leader (Madrikh), whose authority stemmed from his personal example. Each educational group was part of a local Ken (literally, nest), which was divided into three age sections: the youngest group (11–14), variously known as B'ne Midbar (Sons of the Desert), K'firim (Lion Cubs), B'ne M'tzada (Sons of Masada), or Kovshim (Conquerors); the middle group (14–16), known as Tzofim (Scouts); and the oldest group (17 and over), known as Bogrim (Adults), K'shishim (Elders), or Magshimim (Realizers). In addition to the scouting program, the educational content stressed history and the life of the *Yishuv (Jewish population of Palestine). By the earliest years, the pattern of individual self-fulfillment leading to *'Aliya (immigration) and settlement in a *kibbutz for all the older members of the youth movement became the model that has since been generally followed. The first Shomrim (as members of HaShomer HaTza'ir were called) left to settle in Palestine in 1919.

The first world convention of HaShomer HaTza'ir met in Danzig in the summer of 1924. In addition to representatives from several countries, delegates of the earliest HaShomer HaTza'ir kibbutzim in Palestine (Bet Alfa, founded in 1922, as well as Mishmar Ha'Emek, Merhavya, and 'En Shemer) participated. The membership of the world movement then totaled about 11,000. By that time training farms (*see* HAKHSHARA) had been established in the various countries for graduates of the youth movement in preparation for future settlement in kibbutzim.

The role of HaShomer HaTza'ir kibbutzim in Palestine became more decisive in the development of the world movement. The early 'Olim (immigrants) from the youth movement had played an active role in the founding of the *Histadrut (General Federation of Labor) in 1920, and Meir *Ya'ari (one of the leaders from Galicia), who was to become, together with Ya'akov *Hazan (one of the leaders from Poland), the active head and ideological mentor of the movement, was elected to its first Executive Committee, representing the "independents and new immigrants." Sh'lihim (emissaries; *see* SHALIAH) from the kibbutzim were sent to the various countries on educational and organizational missions. The establishment of the *Kibbutz Artzi Shel HaShomer HaTza'ir as the federation of HaShomer HaTza'ir kibbutzim in 1927 provided a focus for the world organization and greatly strengthened the mutual ties and purposes of the territorial organizations in the *Diaspora. By that time, the movement had spread to the United States, Canada, and Cuba as well as to Czechoslovakia, Bulgaria, and Belgium.

The second world convention took place in Danzig in September, 1927. The major issue was identification with the newly formed Kibbutz Artzi federation. The delegates from Latvia and Austria and, especially, the Soviet Russian movement (today concentrated in the kibbutz Afikim), which had virtually ceased to function because of suppression by the Soviet regime, opposed the establishment of ties with Kibbutz Artzi in favor of a general political and kibbutz unification in Palestine. To bridge the difference, the convention proclaimed Kibbutz Artzi Shel HaShomer HaTza'ir "the organic continuation of our movement in the Diaspora and its principal channel in Palestine." At this convention, too, the obligation of 'Aliya and life in a kibbutz for all adult members was formally adopted.

During the following period, while depression was spreading in the world and the Jewish communities were in ideological ferment, HaShomer HaTza'ir crystallized its Socialist Zionist ideological independence as a distinct trend in the World Zionist movement. From the end of 1928 on, a large number of arrivals from HaShomer HaTza'ir organizations throughout Europe reached Palestine. The first branches of HaShomer HaTza'ir in the towns of Palestine itself were formed in 1929. The world movement by this time numbered almost 40,000 members and had a network of Hakhshara farms, a widespread press in Hebrew and other languages, and its own publishing house.

The third world convention took place at Vrúty, Czechoslovakia, in September, 1930. By that time, members of HaShomer HaTza'ir from the Soviet Union, Latvia, and Austria had left the movement. By an overwhelming majority the convention "viewed Kibbutz Artzi as its *sole* path in Palestine." By August, 1935, when the fourth world convention met at Poprad, Czechoslovakia, HaShomer HaTza'ir numbered 70,000 members in 25 countries. The movement had spread to Germany, South

Africa, Yugoslavia, England, Egypt, and France. The shadow of Nazism was added to the persistent depression with widespread unemployment, breadlines, and *anti-Semitism.

When World War II started in 1939, many HaShomer HaTza'ir members in Poland and the Baltic countries pressed eastward into the Soviet territories in the face of the Nazi invaders. Vilna became a central point for these Shomrim. Cooperatives and training centers were organized, and groups of "illegal" immigrants to Palestine were formed and sent on their way (see ILLEGAL IMMIGRATION). Emissaries were sent back to Nazi-occupied Poland, where they helped organize and maintain Jewish youth groups and participated in armed resistance units in many cities, including Warsaw, where the HaShomer HaTza'ir units numbered 4 out of 22 fighting groups in the ghetto uprising and the overall commander was Mordecai *Anilewicz, a leader of HaShomer HaTza'ir. Members of HaShomer HaTza'ir played an active role also in the resistance in Vilna, Białystok, Sosnowiec, Będzin, Cracow, Rajcza, Tarnów, and other cities. In the other countries of Nazi occupation, the Shomrim fought in the resistance and tried to maintain their group identity. Particularly in Slovakia, as in other places, the Shomrim joined and organized partisan units. In Auschwitz, they took part in the underground.

After World War II, the scattered remnants of the movement began to gather together and call for 'Aliya to Palestine. They were active in illegal immigration and in the displaced-persons camps in Germany and Italy.

The political changes in Eastern Europe soon put an end to the work of the HaShomer HaTza'ir there, and those who could quickly found their way to Palestine. In Western Europe, the movement was renewed in Austria, Italy, Belgium, the Netherlands, Switzerland, France, England, and Germany, and it spread throughout North Africa. The movement also grew in North and South America and sent a steady stream of 'Olim who joined kibbutzim.

In 1946 HaShomer HaTza'ir formally became a political party in Palestine, and in 1948 it participated in the formation of *Mapam.

In 1958 the fifth world convention of HaShomer HaTza'ir took place at Giv'at Haviva, with delegates representing organizations in 24 countries. By far the largest group was now the Israeli movement. The focus of expansion and activity in the Diaspora was in South America.

Following the establishment of the State of Israel, nearly 4,000 members of HaShomer HaTza'ir settled in kibbutzim. Unlike other kibbutz movements, it insisted on *ideological collectivism (identity of doctrine, not only common action, among its members, espoused the cause of revolutionary socialism, welcomed the Soviet Union as the pioneer of the new social order, and denounced the Western powers for imperialist policies. Prior to 1948 it advocated an Arab-Jewish binational state. It consistently preached an Arab-Jewish rapprochement and closer relations with the Arab minority in Israel. In domestic policy it stressed the importance of the class struggle.

In some of the kibbutzim in the 1960s, the younger generation was showing signs of uneasiness because of the rigid Marxism and anti-Western orientation of its leadership. These tendencies became more pronounced when enthusiasm for the Soviet Union waned in the wake of Soviet wholehearted support of the Arabs before, during, and after the *Six-day War of 1967. The Kibbutz Artzi numbered 73 settlements in 1969.

Ideologically it was identified with the Mapam party, which in fact it dominated and whose principal mainstay it was.

A. SCHENKER

HASHOMER HATZA'IR ZIONIST YOUTH IN NORTH AMERICA.

In 1923 small, isolated groups of *HaShomer HaTza'ir were formed in North America by recent arrivals from Europe. After contacts had been established among the groups in New York, Boston, and Montreal, a national organization was formed in 1927, and Avraham Zeiger, who had been a leader in the Romanian HaShomer HaTza'ir, became the national secretary.

In the summer of 1928 the first summer camp was organized at Shadow Lake, N.Y. The 1929 national convention of the American HaShomer HaTza'ir adopted the obligation of *Halutziyut (pioneering) for its oldest age group. The news of the 1929 *Arab riots in Palestine led to the formation of the first organized nucleus of 70 members for settlement in a kibbutz, the Kibbutz 'Aliya Aleph. The members sent a group to work on a New Jersey farm, and in 1931 the first American HaShomer HaTza'ir 'Olim reached Palestine.

During the same year the *Kibbutz Artzi Shel HaShomer HaTza'ir (the federation of HaShomer HaTza'ir kibbutzim) dispatched Dr. Mordecai *Bentov, the first *Shaliah (emissary) to the movement. Bentov was followed by a steady stream of Sh'lihim (emissaries), including graduates of the American movement. The most noteworthy was Moshe Furmansky (a member of the kibbutz Mishmar Ha'Emek), who founded the publication first known as HaShomer HaTza'ir and later as Youth and Nation, and who was killed in 1948 in an attack on the kibbutz during Israel's *War of Independence.

With the help and encouragement of Justice Louis D. *Brandeis and Mrs. Irma *Lindheim, the second national president of *Hadassah, the first American kibbutz was established in the Hills of Ephraim in 1937 and named 'En HaShofet (the Well of the Justice) in honor of Justice Brandeis. At the time of its Cleveland Convention in 1937, HaShomer HaTza'ir had 8 branches (Kinim; literally, nests) in New York and others in 13 other cities of the United States and Canada. A permanent training farm (see HAKHSHARA), first established in Liberty, N.Y., was later moved to Hightstown, N.J. The second American kibbutz, K'far M'nahem, was established in the foothills of Judea late in 1937. The training farm continued to operate during World War II, and industrial training centers were set up in Baltimore, Toronto, Montreal, and New York in preparation for the establishment of a foundry and a die-casting plant in the movement's future kibbutz, Hatzor, the third American kibbutz.

After the war *'Aliya was resumed, to Hatzor in 1945; to the fourth American kibbutz, 'En Dor, in Lower Galilee, in 1947; to the fifth, Sasa, near the Lebanese border, in 1949; and to the sixth, Barkai, near the Jordanian border, in 1950. Members-to-be of 'En Dor and Sasa were among the Americans who manned the ships of the *illegal immigration, were interned by the British Navy at Cyprus with survivors of the displaced-persons camps, and fought with the *Hagana and *Palmah in Israel's War of Independence.

In the post-State period the 'Aliya nuclei dwindled. Slowly, the *HeHalutz training farms of the various youth movements closed for lack of candidates until only the HaShomer HaTza'ir–sponsored HeHalutz farm Shomria at Hightstown, N.J., remained. Instead of founding new kibbutzim, the next six kibbutz nuclei were Hashlamot (literally, completions) of four older kibbutzim (Gal'on, Nahshon, HaZore'a, and Barkai) that required a middle generation between the founders and their children. The thirteenth kibbutz nucleus of HaShomer HaTza'ir was organized in 1966. In 1967, following training at the farm, its members began to leave for Israel, particularly as volunteers during the period of *Six-day War. In May, 1968, the fourteenth kibbutz nucleus was organized.

In 1964 the movement established the HeHalutz Israel Institute as a seminar and conference center on the grounds of the training farm. The institute serves all Zionist youth organizations as well as Jewish centers and schools in the New York–New Jersey area.

A. SCHENKER

HASIDIC JEWS IN ISRAEL. Hasidic Jews are the adherents of Hasidism, the Jewish religious movement that became popular in Eastern Europe in the 18th century. The *immigration and settlement of Hasidic Jews in Palestine began in the middle of the 18th century, when several relatives and disciples of Rabbi Israel Ba'al Shem Tov (BeShT, 1700–60), the founder of Hasidism, settled in Jerusalem, Hebron, and Tiberias. Thereafter, individual Hasidim, mostly from Volhynia and Podolia, Russia, continued to arrive in Palestine, and in 1777 a large group led by Menahem Mendel of Vitebsk settled in Safed. Some members of this group later moved to Tiberias.

Early Years. One of the most famous Hasidic rabbis, Nahman of Bratslav, Russia, visited Palestine in 1798. His teachings had been suffused with deep longing for the Holy Land, and after his return he spoke of the great inspiration he received there. A group of Hasidim from Lyubavichi, Russia, settled in Hebron early in the 19th century. In 1830 Rabbi Avraham Dov of Auzuch settled in Safed and became the head of the Hasidic community in the town. In 1850 Moshe of Lebuv, a Hasidic rabbi, settled in Jerusalem with his sons and their families. Even before he went to Palestine, he had done much to support Hasidim living in the country. In 1869 Rabbi Hillel Moshe of Białystok, a disciple of the Gerer and Kotzker Rebbes (the rabbis of Góra Kalwaria, near Warsaw, and Kotsk), settled in the Old City of Jerusalem and rented three large courtyards. Rabbi Joseph Alter of Radovitsy, grandson of the first Gerer Rebbe, settled in Safed in 1873. Subsequently, numerous other members of this family settled in Palestine. In 1887 Rabbi Simha Bunim, son of Rabbi Yitzhak of Warka, Poland, settled in Tiberias with his large family but, failing to obtain a permit from the Turkish government, had to leave the city after three months. In 1906 he returned, settled in Jerusalem, and died in 1907 in Tiberias. In 1896 Yitzhak Friedman, rabbi of Buhuşi, Romania, planned to establish a settlement for 50 families and sent two emissaries to Palestine to buy land, but he died before the plan could be carried out.

Numerous other Hasidic rabbis, either alone or accompanied by relatives and followers, visited or settled in Palestine in the late 19th and early 20th century. The Hasidim founded Kolelim of their own (see HALUKKA) and maintained their own synagogues and institutions in Palestine. They were supported by fellow Hasidim in the *Diaspora.

Between the Two World Wars. The first Hasidic rabbi to visit Palestine after World War I was Abraham Mord'khai Alter, the Gerer Rebbe. He went there first in 1921. In 1924 he

went again, this time accompanied by relatives and numerous followers. Upon his return to Poland he urged his well-to-do followers to settle and invest in the country. After several other visits (in 1927, 1932, and 1937–38), the Gerer Rebbe settled in Jerusalem in 1940 and died there in 1948.

In 1924 two young Hasidic rabbis obtained land from the *Jewish National Fund for the purpose of establishing Hasidic settlements in the vicinity of Nahalal in the Jezreel Valley. Rabbi Yehezkel Taub of Yablonov (Jablonów), Galicia, founded the settlement of Nahlat Ya'akov, and Rabbi Yisrael Eliezer Hofstein of Kozienice, Poland, founded the settlement of 'Avodat Yisrael. A total of 110 families settled in the two villages, which soon thereafter merged into K'far Hasidim, a village which in 1968 had 410 inhabitants. An offshoot of this village, K'far Hasidim B, founded in 1950, had 215 inhabitants in 1968. K'far Hasidim A is famous for its Yeshiva. This Hasidic settlement had been inspired and aided by Rabbi Yeshayahu Schapira, scion of a famous Hasidic dynasty, who was a leader of the *Mizrahi.

Also in 1924, Polish Hasidim, jointly with other religious Jews from Poland, founded B'ne B'rak, near Tel Aviv, which developed into one of the major cities of the country and an important religious center. In 1926 a group of Polish Hasidim were the first settlers of K'far Ata.

The mass immigration engendered by the rise of Nazism in Europe brought many Hasidim and Hasidic leaders to the country. The latter included Rabbi Israel Friedman of Husiatyn (Gusyatin) and members of the dynasties of Sadagura (Sadgora), Bouyan, and Buhuşi.

World War II. Among the arrivals during World War II, in addition to the Gerer Rabbi, was Rabbi Aharon Rokeah of Belz, who had been saved from Nazi-occupied Galicia. In 1945

Hasidim dancing. [Israel Information Services]

Rabbi Barukh Hager of Vishnitz (Vishnevets) arrived. He established himself in Haifa, where he founded a Hasidic quarter and a Yeshiva.

After the Establishment of the State. Following the independence of Israel a larger number of Hasidic leaders and their followers came to settle in the new State. In 1949 Rabbi Hayim Meir of Vishnevets, the brother of Barukh Hager, arrived and built a Hasidic quarter and Yeshiva in B'ne B'rak. The same year Hasidim of Lyubavichi who had managed to escape from the U.S.S.R. established the village of K'far Habad, which by 1968 had about 1,440 inhabitants and contained several educational and vocational institutions.

The 1950s and 1960s saw attempts by Hasidic rabbis in the United States to establish residential quarters or institutions in Israel. The largest of these was Kiryat Sandz, a quarter in N'tanya founded by Rabbi Yekutiel Halberstam of Cluj (Klausenburg), Romania, a descendant of the rabbinic dynasty of Nowy Sącs (Neu Sandec, Sandzs), Poland. Kiryat Sandz was established in 1956, and in 1960 the rabbi himself moved there from Brooklyn, N.Y., with his family and about 50 of his followers.

In 1968 Kiryat Sandz had 1,000 inhabitants, one-half of whom had come from Eastern Europe and one-fourth from the United States. It maintained a home for the aged, an institution for children who had been brought to Israel by *Youth 'Aliya, and a maternity hospital. Under the influence of the rabbi, one of his Hasidim moved his diamond-polishing factory from New York to Kiryat Sandz together with his 200 employees and their families.

Following this example, the Rebbe of Bobov, Sh'lomo Halberstam, another descendant of the Nowy Sącs dynasty, built a settlement in Bat Yam near Tel Aviv, which he called Kiryat Bobov. The rabbi himself continued to maintain his court in Brooklyn, but many of his Hasidim, as well as others, settled in Kiryat Bobov, which in 1968 had a population of about 500. This group founded a bank with a capital of IL 1,000,000 to help investors establish industries in Kiryat Bobov.

The various Hasidic groups founded their own *Yeshivot. The Hasidim of Lyubavichi also maintained a network of educational institutions.

I. SCHEPANSKY

HASKALA. Hebrew term, meaning "enlightenment," coined in 1832 by Judah Jeiteles to denote the movement for the dissemination of modern European culture among the Jews. The Haskala movement began in Berlin about 1750 with the work of Moses Mendelssohn (1729–86), the German-Jewish philosopher and Bible commentator; his commentary on the Pentateuch (Biur) was completed by 1783, the year in which he also wrote his *Jerusalem*, an analysis of Judaism and a spirited advocacy of civil rights for Jews. Advocates of the Haskala believed that to achieve *emancipation the Jews had to become modernized and westernized, adapting themselves to the social customs and acquiring the intellectual values of the nations in which they lived. Modern European culture for the Jews of the mid-18th century largely meant German culture, which in fact most Maskilim (adherents of Haskala) endeavored to acquire, although Jews in other countries (notably in France, as a result of Napoleon's Sanhedrin) also began efforts to acquire the languages and cultures of their respective countries.

One aspect of the Haskala was that, in order to spread modern

culture, its proponents used the *Hebrew language for secular purposes. This resulted in the resurgence of the language as expressed in the publication of Hebrew journals (e.g., the quarterly *HaM'asseph*, 1784–1811) and books. Another effect of the Haskala was that it created a growing stratum of secularized Jews who had come under the influence of the political and social ideas of modern Europe and still retained their ties with Jewish historic traditions and Hebrew culture. It was from among the sons and grandsons of these Maskilim that the first leaders and Central and Western European followers of Zionism were recruited, beginning with Herzl himself. Without the emergence of such a stratum of Jews, who combined in themselves varying degrees of traditional Jewish and modern European orientation, the rise of political Zionism would have been impossible.

On the other hand, Haskala very frequently led directly to *assimilation, especially in those countries of Central and Western Europe in which the Maskilim, having become acquainted with the culture of their gentile environment, found it so attractive (not only because of cultural but also because of social and economic considerations) that they opted for it at the price of abandoning their own traditions, religion, language, and culture. Thus, it was the Haskala that was responsible for the development of that sector of the assimilated or semiassimilated Jewish population in Central and Western Europe as well as the United States which during the lifetime of Herzl and for a considerable period thereafter was opposed to Zionism (*see* ANTI-ZIONISM). It was this development from Haskala to assimilation that prompted Peretz *Smolenskin to denounce Haskala as a betrayal of Jewish identity.

R. PATAI

HASOL'LIM. Village (kibbutz) in western Lower Galilee. Founded in 1949 and affiliated with Ha'Oved HaTziyoni. Population (1968): 216.

HATIKVA. Anthem of the Zionist movement and national anthem of the State of Israel. The song, whose title means "The Hope," expresses the hope and yearning of the Jew for the Return to Zion. Written by Naftali Herz *Imber, either in 1878 in Iaşi, Romania, or in 1882, when the poet resided in Rishon L'Tziyon, it was first published in 1886 in Jerusalem. Before long its first verse was widely sung by the pioneers in Palestine, and the first settlers of Rehovot adopted it as their song. From Palestine "HaTikva," then known by its refrain, " 'Od Lo Avda" ("Our Hope Is Not Yet Lost"), spread to Europe, gaining ever-increasing popularity among Jewish nationalists and finally becoming the anthem of the Zionist movement. Though the protocols of the 8th Zionist *Congress (The Hague, 1907) were the first to record the singing of " 'Od Lo Avda" at the close of a Zionist Congress, it was sung on such occasions before then.

The tune of "HaTikva" has been said to have been adapted from a Moldavian folk melody by Sh'muel Cohen, a settler of Rishon L'Tziyon. The same melody seems to have been used by the Czech composer Bedřich Smetana for his *Vltava*. Musicologists have also pointed to the similarity between the tune of "HaTikva," an old Sephardi melody, and the German folk song "Fuchs, du hast die Gans gestohlen."

With the passing of time, the words of the refrain of "HaTikva" were changed to suit modern historical developments. With the rise of Israel, "HaTikva" became the national anthem

HATIKVA

The full text of "HaTikva." [Zionist Archives]

of the State. The full text of "HaTikva" is given in the accompanying illustration.

HAT'NU'A HAM'UHEDET (T'nu'a M'uhedet). Israeli youth movement whose full name was HaT'nu'a Hak'lalit Shel Ha-No'ar HaLomed HaHalutzi B'Eretz Yisrael (General Movement of Student Pioneering Youth in the Land of Israel). It was founded late in 1945 as a result of the merger of *Gordonia-Maccabi-HaTza'ir with a minority of Mahanot Ha'Olim, which had left that movement several months earlier in the wake of the split in *Mapai. HaT'nu'a HaM'uhedet was linked ideologically to Mapai and to the *Hever HaK'vutzot (later *Ihud HaK'vutzot V'haKibbutzim). In 1951 HaT'nu'a Ha-M'uhedet merged with *HaBonim, which was primarily active in Anglo-Saxon countries, and the shortened name of the movement was changed to HaBonim–HaT'nu'a HaM'uhedet.

The movement educated its members to become adherents of the Zionist Socialist movement and obligated its graduates to personal realization of its values within the framework of communal or workers' settlements. The movement had two banners, the blue-and-white Zionist flag and the red flag of socialism. Its emblem featured three ears of corn, a sickle, and the Shield of David (*Magen David) surrounded by olive leaves. Its organ was *Sh'demot* (Fields).

The movement admitted young people between the ages of 10 and 18, divided into four age groups. Education in the two lower age groups (10–12 and 12–14) was conducted along the lines of scouting. Summer camps and trips throughout the land were important elements. Graduates of the movement formed *Hakhshara training-farm nuclei, which in the pre-State period attached themselves to the framework of *Palmah (commando units) and received both agricultural and military training in its camps. After the establishment of the State, the Hakhshara nuclei were part of Nahal (Fighting Pioneer Youth; see ISRAEL DEFENSE FORCES).

In the first year of its existence the movement had 2,775 members. Its graduates helped establish 22 settlements in Israel. The first was Ma'ayan Barukh, founded in March, 1947. Among the others were Hamadya, Tzor'a, Yizr'el, Gevim, Rosh HaNikra, Nahal 'Oz, Yiftah, and S'de N'hemya. In 1958 Yotvata was established in the 'Arava, in the Negev. In the founding of many of these settlements, graduates of the movement cooperated with immigrant youth, chiefly from the ranks of HaBonim.

In 1958 the movement had 34 branches with a total membership of 7,500. Though it could boast considerable results in the field of training and had produced from four to six Hakhshara nuclei each year, there was a feeling of disappointment at the failure of the organization to wield greater influence among the masses of studying youth. During deliberations in 'En Gev in May, 1958, it was decided to unite the movement with HaNo'ar Ha'Oved. The merger agreement resulted in cooperation between the two movements in training and summer camping. In May, 1959, the unity conference of the two movements was held in Tel Aviv, and the new name HaHistadrut HaK'lalit Shel HaNo'ar Ha'Oved V'haLomed Ha'Ivri B'Yisrael (General Federation of the Hebrew Working and Student Youth in Israel) was adopted (see HANO'AR HA'OVED V'HALOMED).

Y. SLUTSKY

HATZAV. Village (moshav) in the Darom. Founded in 1949 by immigrants from Tripolitania and affiliated with *T'nu'at HaMoshavim. The name is derived from the urgineas (shrubby plants, *hatzav* in Hebrew) which grow in abundance in the neighborhood. Population (1968): 745.

HATZERIM. Village (kibbutz) in the northern Negev. Founded in 1946 and affiliated with the *Ihud HaK'vutzot V'haKibbutzim. Population (1968): 257.

HATZEVA. Village (moshav) in the Negev. Founded in 1965 and affiliated with *T'nu'at HaMoshavim.

HATZ'FIRA. Hebrew periodical which appeared, though not continuously, from 1862 to 1931. *Hatz'fira* (The Dawn) first made a brief appearance in 1862 as a Warsaw weekly with Haim Selig Slonimsky as editor, appeared in Berlin in 1874–75, and then resumed publication in Warsaw. Its initial aim was to disseminate general knowledge, particularly of the natural sciences. When Nahum *Sokolow joined the editorial staff (about 1885), he modernized the paper, improved its language and style, and attracted some of the finest Hebrew writers to its columns. Its attitude toward the *Hoveve Zion movement was cool at first, but after Sokolow's participation in the 1st Zionist *Congress (1897), *Hatz'fira* became an ardent spokesman of political Zionism, supporting Herzl during the debate over the *East Africa scheme.

In 1886 it became a daily newspaper. After ceasing publication in 1906, it reappeared in 1910, with Sokolow again assuming the editorship despite his important and active role in the Zionist movement. Closing once again during World War I, it became a weekly in 1917 and a daily in 1920. It suspended publication in 1921, reappeared in 1926 with Joseph Hayim *Heftman as editor, and then ceased publication in 1928, appearing again only briefly in 1931. The history of the newspaper is bound up to a large extent with the history of Polish Jewry, with important chapters in the development of Hebrew literature, and, in the early years of the 20th century, with the growth of political Zionism.   G. KRESSEL

HATZOFE. Israeli daily newspaper. Founded in Jerusalem on Aug. 4, 1937, it was at first published three times a week. In December, 1937, *HaTzofe* (The Observer) became a daily and was transferred to Tel Aviv. Its founder and first editor was Rabbi Meir *Bar-Ilan. The programmatic proclamation on the front page of the paper's first issue stated: "*HaTzofe* will strive to be a daily deserving of the name, informative and provocative, covering the daily events of the wide world in general and of our own world in particular;... it will be loyal to Jewish tradition, religious and national, and to everything sacred to us...."

HaTzofe serves as the mouthpiece of the Mizrahi–HaPo'el HaMizrahi World Movement (*see* MIZRAHI). In it, religious publicists have found, for the first time, a daily platform, while religious authors have welcomed its weekly literary supplement. For the first time in the history of rabbinic literature, discourses on religious subjects have found their way to thousands of readers, daily and weekly. While adhering to the pattern of the national religious ideology in its editorial policy, *HaTzofe* resembles other dailies in Israel insofar as the organization of its contents is concerned.

The paper has been edited consecutively by Y'hoshu'a *Radler-Feldman (Rabbi Binyamin), Mordecai *Lipson, Y'sha'yahu Bernstein, and Shabtai Don Yahya (Sh. Daniel), the present editor. In 1966 *HaTzofe* reported a circulation of 11,000.   J. RUBIN

HATZOHAR (Tzohar). Name of the Zionist Revisionist organization, composed of the initial letters of HaTziyonim HaRevizionistim (*see* REVISIONISTS).

HATZOR. Township in eastern Upper Galilee. Founded in 1953. Population (1968): 5,250.

North of the township is one of the most important archeological sites in Israel. Extensive excavations conducted by the James A. de Rothschild Expedition unearthed a large middle Bronze Age city (almost 200 acres in extent), which continued to flourish in the late Bronze Age. Hatzor was a Canaanite city with underground burials, a glacis with gates, three sanctuaries, and a craftsmen's quarter. One of the sanctuaries anticipated the plan of Solomon's Temple in Jerusalem. Solomon fortified Hatzor, erecting a casemate wall and gate, but the Israelite town was confined to the tell (mound) occupying the southwest corner of the site. King Ahab added a citadel and public buildings. In addition, an Israelite "high place" was excavated on the site.

HATZOR-ASHDOD. Village (kibbutz) in the Judean Plain. Founded in 1937 by pioneers who had founded G'vulot in the Negev. Affiliated with the *Kibbutz Artzi Shel HaShomer HaTza'ir. Population (1968): 535.

HAUSNER, DOV. Educator and Polish government official (b. Chortkov, Galicia, Austria, 1874; d. Tel Aviv, 1938). Hausner studied at the Universities of Vienna and Prague and at the Rabbinical Seminary in Vienna, where he joined the Zionist movement. Returning to Galicia, he taught religion in a Lvov high school and continued his Zionist activities. During World War I he served as chief rabbi of Russian-occupied Lvov and was a chaplain in the Austro-Hungarian Army on the Italian front.

Hausner was for several years head of the *Jewish National Fund in eastern Galicia, then part of Poland, and from 1921 to 1925 of the eastern Galician *Mizrahi, in which capacity he devoted himself to the expansion of the local religious-national school network. He was elected to the Sejm (Polish Parliament) in 1922. In 1927 he became Polish Commercial Attaché in Tel Aviv and in 1932 was appointed Consul. He returned to Poland in 1933 but settled permanently in Palestine two years later.

                                                    Y. RAPHAEL

HAUSNER, GIDEON M. Israeli jurist (b. Lvov, Galicia, Austria, 1915). Brought to Palestine in 1927, Hausner was graduated from the *Hebrew University of Jerusalem in 1940 and from the Jerusalem Law School in 1941. During the *War of Independence he was military prosecutor and then president of the Jerusalem Military Court. He engaged in private law practice from 1946 to 1960 and was lecturer in commercial law at the Hebrew University from 1956 to 1960. From 1960 to 1963 he served as Attorney General of the State of Israel and in that capacity was chief prosecutor at the *Eichmann trial, on which he wrote in *Justice in Jerusalem* (1966). In 1965 he was elected to the *Knesset as a representative of the Independent Liberals.

HAVAT HASHOMER. Educational institution in Lower Galilee. Founded in 1956. Population (1968): 240.

HAVATZELET HASHARON. Village (moshav) in the Sharon Plain. Founded in 1935 and affiliated with the *Ihud Haklai. Population (1968): 145.

HAVIV-LUBMAN, AVRAHAM DOV. Pioneer in Palestine and mayor of Rishon L'Tziyon (b. Hariczova, near Orsha, Mogilev District, Russia, 1864; d. Rishon L'Tziyon, 1951). Shortly after arriving in Palestine in 1885, Haviv-Lubman settled in Rishon L'Tziyon, where he engaged in farming until his death. Active in community affairs and in the farmers' association, he helped form the Winegrowers' Association and the Carmel Mizrahi Company. For many years, including those of World War I, he served as mayor of Rishon L'Tziyon. His writings about the history of the settlement (all in Hebrew) include *Rishon L'Tziyon* (1929 ff.), *Stories of Rishon L'Tziyon* (1934), and *Members of My Generation* (1946), biographies.

                                                    G. KRESSEL

HAVLAGA (Self-restraint). Term widely used at the time of the controversy which raged in the *Yishuv (Jewish population of Palestine) during the *Arab riots of 1936–39 as to whether the *Hagana should retaliate against the Arabs for acts of murder and terrorism or confine itself to repelling Arab attacks. The latter course had been the policy of the Hagana since its establishment in 1920 and was pursued consistently until about 1938. Whenever a Jew was murdered, it was the practice of the Hagana to try to apprehend the culprits and deliver them to the British Mandatory authorities for trial (see MANDATE FOR PALESTINE). Havlaga was effectively enforced, although a few instances of retaliation involving innocent Arabs did occur.

The widespread riots that had started in 1936 developed into a countrywide Arab revolt with indiscriminate attacks on Jewish settlements and urban quarters and on individual Jews. The attacks continued for months on end, placing a heavy strain on the Hagana, and the policy of Havlaga was challenged. It was widely felt that passive defense not only was encouraging further Arab aggression but also was discouraging the members of Hagana and having an adverse effect on public morale. However, the Yishuv leaders, with the active support of Chaim *Weizmann and David *Ben-Gurion, imposed the Havlaga line; they were convinced that deviation from the Havlaga policy would give an excuse to the mandatory power to treat the riots not as one-sided attacks by Arabs on Jews but as an Arab-Jewish internecine strife, thus invoking its duty to act as arbiter between the two sides rather than to maintain peace and carry out its obligations under the mandate. It was further contended that acts of retaliation would infuriate public opinion in Great Britain and prejudice the development of legal defense units, such as the Jewish Settlement Police and the Supernumerary Police (see NOTRIM), which were then in process of formation by the British authorities. It was also contended that indiscriminate retaliation was likely to strengthen the extremist elements among the Arabs and to drive the moderates to the guerrillas.

The intensification of the Arab revolt and the mounting total of Jewish casualties strained Havlaga to the limit. There were several instances of Hagana commanders' committing acts of retaliation on their own initiative. The situation was further aggravated by the emergence in 1937 of the *Irgun Tz'vai L'umi as a dissident military organization politically controlled by the *Revisionists. The Irgun advocated a policy of retaliation, and on several occasions its members bombed Arab localities in Haifa and Jerusalem, inflicting heavy casualties. The Havlaga line was somewhat modified when, in the summer of 1939, a punitive expedition of Hagana units claimed many victims at the Arab village Balad esh-Sheikh, near Haifa, in retaliation for a series of murders perpetrated by its inhabitants. On July 2, 1939, a Hagana order officially modified Havlaga policy: retaliation by way of indiscriminate murder or bombing was forbidden, but fighting units were authorized to pursue marauders into their villages.

The controversy over Havlaga terminated with the collapse of the Arab revolt and the outbreak of World War II. On the whole, the principle of Havlaga had been maintained in spite of the most difficult circumstances and the tremendous strain on Hagana's discipline.

S. Z. ABRAMOV

HAYCRAFT COMMISSION OF INQUIRY. Commission appointed by British *High Commissioner Sir Herbert *Samuel to investigate the *Arab riots of May, 1921, in Palestine. It was headed by Sir Thomas Haycraft, Chief Justice of Palestine.

In the report by the Commission, the immediate cause of the disturbance was stated to have been a Jewish Communist demonstration in Jaffa. However, the Arabs were charged with having started the riots. In establishing the remoter causes of the incidents, the Commission disagreed with the Zionist version which attributed the disturbances to the resentment of the Arab landlord (effendi) class, which was allegedly fearful

of losing its position in the country, and to the hostility of certain British officials toward the Jewish National Home policy. The Commission was of the opinion that the outburst had been brought about by Arab anxiety in face of a British pro-Zionist commitment, the promotion of Jews in public service, and Jewish competition in commerce and labor. It was critical of any interpretation of British obligations which claimed special rights for the Jews, denounced any idea of future Jewish domination of the country, and blamed Jewish representatives for advocating these ideas.

The Zionist representatives considered the report a concession to violence and an attempt to justify British restrictions on Jewish *immigration.

I. KOLATT

HAYIM GREENBERG INSTITUTE. Teachers institute in Jerusalem, founded in 1954 by the Department of Education and Culture of the *Jewish Agency for Israel and named in memory of Dr. Hayim *Greenberg, the American Zionist leader, teacher, and philosopher and first head of the department. The institute began as a special one-semester Israel study course with a small group of students from various American Hebrew teachers colleges. In 1958–59 its program was extended to a full year, and eligibility was enlarged to include students not currently enrolled in an American Hebrew teachers college. Such students receive special preparatory language training of the *Ulpan type before beginning regular studies.

The institute's purpose is to enable young men and women who are preparing to enter the field of Jewish education and community service to spend a year in Israel pursuing intensive studies in Judaica and Hebraica. Applicants admitted to the institute receive room and board and are responsible for their travel and personal expenses. The curriculum in 1966–67 included a wide selection of course offerings in four divisions: classical, contemporary, education, and arts. All studies were in the fields of Judaica and Hebraica. The number of American students in the 1966–67 academic year was 60 in a total enrollment of 160; most of the other students came from Latin America, and a few came from Europe.

HAYOGEV. Village (moshav) in the Jezreel Valley. Founded in 1949 by the settlers of Bet Eshel in the Negev, which had been destroyed during the *War of Independence. Affiliated with *T'nu'at HaMoshavim. Population (1968): 359.

HAYOM. Israeli daily newspaper, established in 1966 in Tel Aviv. Although formally founded as an independent daily, *Ha Yom* (The Day) was, in fact, to serve as the organ of *Gahal, the alignment of the *Liberal and *Herut parties. In this respect, it replaced the two party dailies, *Herut* of the Herut party and *HaBoker* of the Liberal party. The first editor, Gershon Hendel, was succeeded by Yitzhak Rager, with Hendel continuing as managing editor. The paper ceased publication in December, 1969.

J. RUBIN

HAZAN, YA'AKOV (Jacob Chasan). *Mapam and *HaShomer HaTza'ir leader (b. Brest Litovsk, Russia, 1899). He grew up in Warsaw and studied there at the Institute of Technology. He participated in the founding of HaShomer HaTza'ir and *HeHalutz in Poland and served in its leadership. Settling in Palestine in 1923, he helped found the kibbutz Mishmar Ha-'Emek (1926), of which he was still a member in 1968. With

Meir *Ya'ari, he was a founder and leader of the *Kibbutz Artzi Shel HaShomer HaTza'ir. Hazan played a leading role, too, in the HaShomer HaTza'ir party and subsequently in Mapam. A member of the Executive Committee of *Histadrut (General Federation of Labor), he represented HaShomer Ha-Tza'ir and later Mapam at Zionist Congresses (see CONGRESS, ZIONIST). A member of the *Knesset, representing Mapam from 1949 on, he was on its Foreign Affairs and Defense Committee. He was a member of the Board of Directors of the *Jewish National Fund and a member of the *Zionist General Council. He wrote *The Workers' Movement and the War* (in Hebrew, 1943) and many articles and pamphlets on labor problems.

HAZAZ, HAYIM. Hebrew novelist (b. Kiev District, Russia, 1898). His first stories appeared after World War I and depicted life in the small Jewish town in the throes of the Bolshevik Revolution. Combining stark realism with incisive satire, these stories are studies of character, revealing the thoughts and reactions of the Jewish Communists who tried to mold life in the "revolutionary" image.

In the 1920s Hazaz lived in Paris. In 1931 he settled in Palestine, where he became interested in the life and mores of of the *Yemenite Jews, about whom he wrote several novels, among them *HaYoshevet BaGanim* (1944) and *Yaish* (1947–52), some of which were translated and published in English (*Mori Sa'id*, 1956). His drama *The End of the Days* (1946) centers on the effects of the Shabbetai Tz'vi religious movement in the 17th century.

Hazaz' more recent works include sketches of the new settlements in the Lakhish region and of the underground struggle against British rule prior to the establishment of the State of Israel. He was awarded the Bialik and Israel Prizes.

H. LEAF

HAZORE'A. Village (kibbutz) in the Jezreel Valley. Founded in 1936 and affiliated with the *Kibbutz Artzi Shel HaShomer HaTza'ir. Population (1968): 610.

HAZOR'IM. Village (moshav) in eastern Lower Galilee. Founded in 1939 and affiliated with HaPo'el HaMizrahi (see MIZRAHI). Population (1968): 300.

HEALTH SERVICE IN ISRAEL. See MEDICINE IN ISRAEL; PUBLIC HEALTH IN ISRAEL.

HEB ABU SIYAH. Bedouin tribe in Lower Galilee. Population (1968): 346.

HEB BATUF. Bedouin tribe in Lower Galilee. Population (1968): 387.

Members of the kibbutz HaZore'a. [Zionist Archives]

HEBREW. Semitic language in which most of the Bible, the Mishna, parts of the Talmud, and much of rabbinic and secular Jewish literature have been written. Hebrew is the official language of the State of Israel.

Like all Semitic languages, Hebrew is written from right to left, and its alphabet was originally a notation system of 22 consonants only. Occasionally vowels were indicated by the use of the *vav* for *o* and *u* and of the *yod* for *i* and more rarely for *e*, which practice was later expanded. In the 8th century scholars in Tiberias developed the system of full vocalization employing lines below, and dots either above or below, the consonants. This system was eventually accepted by all Jewry, facilitating the reading of Hebrew. When the first printed copies of the Bible were produced (15th cent.), some were vocalized. The manuscript scrolls of the Pentateuch used in the synagogue service, however, remained unvocalized. Most books and newspapers printed in Israel are unvocalized; to facilitate reading, there is a tendency to use the *matres lectionis vav* and *yod* more frequently than was the case in any previous period in the history of the Hebrew language. For children and persons learning Hebrew (primarily new immigrants), vocalized Hebrew-language textbooks, newspapers, and books are produced.

Among the Hebrew consonants in Biblical times there were several laryngeals (*he het, 'ayin,* and the *aleph,* the so-called glottal stop) as well as emphatic consonants distinguished both in pronunciation and in writing from their nonemphatic counterparts (*tet-tav, qof-kaf, sade-samekh*). The difference between the *qof* and *kaf* disappeared in the Ashkenazi sector of Jewry (*see* ASHKENAZIM), in which both the *tet* and the *qof* became nonemphatic, while the *sade* became an affricate, *tzade*. The old pronunciation was, however, retained by the *Sephardim and *Oriental Jews, each of whose communities has its own variety of traditional Hebrew pronunciation.

The colloquial Hebrew of Israel combines features of the Ashkenazic and Sephardic pronunciation. From the former it has retained the affricative *tzade* as well as the disregard of the difference between the *tet* and *tav* (both of which are pronounced like the *tav*); between the *qof* and *kaf* (both pronounced *kaf*); between the *het* and *khaf* (both pronounced *khaf*); and between the *aleph* and *'ayin* (both pronounced like a glottal stop). From the latter it took the pronunciation of both the *patah* and the *qametz gadol* as *a*; of the *holam* and the *qametz qatan* as *o*; and the fricative variant of the *tav* (without *dagesh qal*) as *t* (in the Ashkenazic *s*).

History. Until the Babylonian Exile (586 B.C.E.), Hebrew was the sole language of the Jews. Following the Exile, the Jews began to make wide use of Aramaic, a language closely related to Hebrew and popular throughout the Middle East. Aramaic was used also, along with Hebrew, during the Second Commonwealth. Hebrew remained in use even after the destruction of the Second Temple (C.E. 70) and the Bar Kokhba revolt (ca. C.E. 135). The Mishna, Tosefta, and various Midrashim, both Halakhic and Aggadic, were composed in Mishnaic, or post-Biblical, Hebrew, which is simpler in style than the Hebrew used in the Bible.

When persecution and anti-Jewish legislation enacted by the Christian Roman emperors disrupted organized Jewish communal life, a further decline of spoken Hebrew ensued, even in scholarly circles in which it had always been widely used. This is reflected in the fact that the Jerusalem Talmud, which was completed about C.E. 400 and which records discussions of the academies of Palestine, was written in Western Aramaic.

In Babylonia, which then emerged as the main center of Jewry, Aramaic had replaced Hebrew much earlier; the Babylonian Talmud was composed in Eastern Aramaic. Similarly, in other *Diaspora countries the Jews adopted the languages of their host peoples and ceased to speak Hebrew even among themselves.

Nevertheless, Hebrew continued to be the principal language in Jewish literature. In it were written most of the works produced by Jews in both Palestine and the Diaspora from the Middle Ages to the dawn of the modern era: Biblical and Talmudic commentaries, codes of religious law, rabbinic responsa, Kabbalistic books, homiletic literature, religious and secular poetry, historical works, stories, and even works on philosophy, medicine, astronomy, and other sciences. Since every Jew was familiar with Hebrew from the prayer book, the Bible, and other religious literature, a Jew writing in Hebrew in one country could be sure that he would be read and understood by Jews in other lands.

Even during the golden age of Spain (10th–12th cent.), the only period during the Middle Ages when Jews fully participated in the cultural life of their Muslim neighbors and when many Jews wrote their works in Arabic, the greater part of Jewish literature was written in Hebrew. Important works written by Jewish authors in Arabic were soon translated into Hebrew to make them accessible to Jews in Christian countries.

The golden age was the period most productive of studies in Hebrew grammar and of Hebrew translations of works by non-Jewish savants. Jews translated numerous scientific and other books from Arabic. After the decline of Arab culture and the rise in Europe of Scholasticism, which employed Latin as its literary vehicle, Jews began to translate scientific works from that language into Hebrew. Authors and translators began to enrich the Hebrew language by coining new terms and constructing new word forms.

Nor was the use of Hebrew confined to literary works. Although the Jews of the Middle Ages spoke the languages of their host peoples, many of them could read and write only in Hebrew. For this reason, Hebrew was used by individuals and communities alike in everyday transactions. Communal regulations and record books were written in Hebrew, and so was all official correspondence between Jewish communities. Individuals used Hebrew for personal letters and bookkeeping.

Inevitably, Hebrew as the main medium of Jewish literary activity came to have a forceful influence on the colloquial languages evolved and used by the Jews in the Diaspora. Judeo-German, Judeo-Spanish, Judeo-Italian, Judeo-Arabic, Judeo-Persian, and other tongues are replete with Hebrew expressions and turns of phrase. These Jewish colloquial languages never attained the importance of Hebrew in the eyes of the Jews. In literature they were generally used only in books intended for women or for men not proficient in Hebrew. As the language of the Bible and of prayer and as the language used by the Jewish people when it still dwelled on its own soil, Hebrew was considered the sacred tongue. Throughout the centuries Jewish writers never ceased to praise its beauty and to advocate its study.

Moreover, even during the Middle Ages Hebrew was not confined to the written word. Jewish travelers and traders visiting countries whose language they did not know were able to converse with local Jews in Hebrew. Rabbis and teachers preaching in distant communities addressed their audiences in Hebrew. Jewish groups from different countries settling side by side in the same city communicated in Hebrew. Teachers intent on widening the Hebrew knowledge of their pupils spoke to them in Hebrew, and religious leaders used Hebrew to add solemnity to certain occasions and declarations.

*Haskala (Enlightenment). Such was the status of Hebrew until the 18th century, which saw the beginnings of Haskala and *emancipation. Both these movements brought about far-reaching changes in the cultural physiognomy of Jewry. The Maskilim (those engaged in Haskala) used Hebrew as a medium for bringing the spirit and culture of modern Europe to the Jews of the ghetto.

In the countries of Central and Western Europe, Haskala did not produce great Hebrew literary values of its own. It served merely as a bridge for the Jew to the culture and civilization of his non-Jewish environment. Thus, the Haskala era in these countries did not last long. Having adopted the dominant culture and having been accepted into European society, the Jews soon discarded many of their traditional values, including the cultivation of the Hebrew language.

The situation in Eastern Europe was different. There large, compact masses of Jews lived surrounded by people who themselves had barely been exposed to the European Enlightenment and who were unwilling to regard the Jew as their equal. Although Haskala had a great impact also on Eastern European Jewry, the Jewish masses were not easily swayed to renounce their cultural and religious heritage. A fierce battle ensued between proponents of the old and the new. In view of continued persecution and unabating *anti-Semitism, Maskilim eventually began to wonder whether they had been right in urging their fellow Jews to give up their own ways and to assimilate to their neighbors (*see* ASSIMILATION).

The Haskala literature of the East reflected the spiritual struggles and soul searching of the period that gave rise to Jewish *nationalism. This period also saw the appearance of the first Hebrew works of modern Jewish scholarship and the rise of the first Hebrew newspapers. This literature contributed much to the enrichment of the Hebrew language.

Jewish nationalism, born in Eastern Europe of the disillusionment with Haskala, was spearheaded by Peretz *Smolenskin. At first he advocated a spiritual nationalism, criticizing the assimilationist tendencies of the Haskala and stressing adherence to the cultural heritage of the Jewish people and of Hebrew, a chief component of that heritage. After the Russian pogroms of the early 1880s, however, Jewish nationalism became Palestine-oriented, urging the return to the ancient Homeland.

Hebrew in the *Yishuv. When the pioneers of the *First 'Aliya arrived in Palestine in the 1880s, it seemed only natural that they adopt Hebrew as their vernacular. In the first place, Hebrew was the language associated from time immemorial with the land of Palestine. Second, Hebrew would serve as the natural medium of communication between the Ashkenazi pioneers who spoke Yiddish and European languages and the Sephardi "old-timers" whose languages had been Ladino and Arabic. They also adopted much of the Sephardic pronunciation of Hebrew for everyday use.

The man most prominently associated with early efforts to revive the Hebrew language was Eliezer *Ben Yehuda, who arrived in Palestine in 1881 and immediately embarked upon the promotion of Hebrew as a spoken language. At first Ben Yehuda encountered ridicule from skeptics who did not believe it was possible to revive the language, as well as opposition

from some extreme Orthodox circles that objected to the "profanation" of the "sacred tongue" by using it for everyday purposes.

The revival of Hebrew involved also serious practical difficulties because of the vocabulary gap between a language which for many centuries had been used only as a literary vehicle and the requirements of daily life. For centuries, Hebrew writers and translators had formed new Hebrew words. Following in their tradition, Ben Yehuda and his collaborators set out to broaden the language, coining new words on a large scale, mostly based on roots already existing in the language. Ben Yehuda himself contributed significantly to the new vocabulary, searching in the Hebrew literature of all ages for little-known expressions that could be invested with new life and laying down rules for new word formation. He founded (1890) the Va'ad HaLashon Ha'Ivrit (Hebrew Language Council, which after the establishment of the State became the Akademiya LaLashon Ha'Ivrit, or *Hebrew Language Academy) for the major purpose of creating a modern Hebrew terminology and usage.

Despite great initial difficulties, Hebrew made swift headway in Palestine. Under the leadership of devoted and enthusiastic teachers all-Hebrew nursery schools and elementary schools were established in the new settlements. Some time later all-Hebrew educational institutions also came into being in the cities. Even the schools run by Jewish philanthropic organizations from other countries, in which a European language was generally dominant, came to give more time to the teaching of Hebrew or instruction in Hebrew (*see* EDUCATION IN ISRAEL).

In 1913 the question of the language of instruction to be used at the Haifa *Technion unleashed the violent dispute that became known as the *Language War. The struggle, which ended with the victory of the Hebraists, resulted in a large-scale extension of the all-Hebrew school network. In 1921 the British Mandatory administration (*see* MANDATE FOR PALESTINE) recognized Hebrew as one of the three official languages of the country.

During the period between the two world wars the autonomous Jewish community in Palestine invested great efforts in fostering the use of Hebrew and took appropriate steps to prevent the entrenchment of any language used by immigrants (especially Yiddish) that might impede the progress of Hebrew or challenge its supremacy.

Modern Israel. When the State of Israel attained its independence (1948), Hebrew became its official language. By that time Hebrew had become so deeply rooted in the community that even the influx (1948–52) of hundreds of thousands of persons who did not know the language did not endanger its dominant position. However, the mass immigration represented a great educational challenge, to meet which the *government of Israel initiated large-scale projects, including the establishment of Ulpanim (language-teaching centers; *see* ULPAN), the issuance of publications (newspapers, etc.) in simple elementary Hebrew, and the introduction of broadcasts designed especially for learners, to impart the language to the newcomers.

Hebrew in the Diaspora. Almost simultaneously with the efforts to revive Hebrew as a spoken language in Palestine, Hebrew-speaking circles and groups sprang up in the Diaspora, especially in Eastern Europe, inspired by the expanding *Hoveve Zion movement. Hoveve Zion also inspired the establishment of the Hebrew Heder M'tukan (modern Heder), where, in addition to religious teachings, some secular subjects, Hebrew literature, and Hebrew language were taught and where the 'Ivrit b''Ivrit (all-Hebrew) method of instruction was used. This education was not confined to boys; similar educational institutions for girls were established. In the United States the first all-Hebrew school was established in Brooklyn, N.Y., in 1893, by Sundel Hirsch Neumann (1860–1934).

The birth of political Zionism and the progress of Hebrew in the Yishuv added impetus to the Hebraist movement in the Diaspora. In 1903, at the time of the 6th Zionist *Congress in Basle, Hebraists founded 'Ivriya, a worldwide organization for the dissemination of Hebrew. At the First World Conference in The Hague in 1907, 'Ivriya declared its aim to be the revival of Hebrew and discussed the feasibility of making Hebrew the "official" language of Diaspora Jewry. In subsequent years two other international Hebrew conferences were held (Berlin, 1909; Vienna, 1913).

The championship of Hebrew by the Zionists aroused strong opposition from the Yiddishists, mainly followers of the *Bund and other leftist-oriented Jewish groups, who rejected the Jewish national renaissance in Palestine and advocated Jewish cultural and national autonomy in the Diaspora with Yiddish as the "official" language. At a conference of Yiddishists held in Czernowitz (now Chernovtsky) in 1908, some speakers sharply attacked Hebrew, calling it a dead language. The conference adopted a resolution declaring Yiddish a national language of the Jews. However, the attacks of the Yiddishists did not impede the progress of Hebrew, and many Yiddish writers and Yiddish newspapers themselves condemned the Czernowitz Conference.

The period between the two world wars saw the establishment of numerous kindergartens, elementary and secondary schools, and teachers training institutes where Hebrew was taught or spoken, as well as the institution of modern Hebrew language courses for youths and adults in many countries, mainly in Eastern and Central Europe. A dominant role in the dissemination of Hebrew and in the establishment of Hebrew schools was played by the *Tarbut organizations, which set up networks of Hebrew educational institutions, published their own textbooks and Hebrew pedagogical literature, and also engaged in other Hebrew cultural activities.

In Russia Tarbut activities were short-lived, for in the 1920s the Communists, incited by Jewish members of the party, suppressed all Hebrew studies. During the short period in which Hebrew activities were permitted in the Soviet Union, Hebrew educational institutions and a Hebrew press flourished, and HaBimah, the famous Hebrew theater ensemble (now in Israel), was born.

In 1922 a Tarbut world center, Merkaz L'Iny'ne Tarbut, was founded in Berlin. In 1931 the *B'rit 'Ivrit 'Olamit (World Hebrew Federation) was established in the same city.

The establishment of the State of Israel and the subsequent tightening of relations between the State and Jewish communities strengthened the Hebrew movement in the Diaspora. Jewish schools began to devote more time to modern Hebrew, and numerous new institutions for the teaching of Hebrew to adults came into being. At many of these, the language was taught by instructors brought from Israel for the purpose. Thousands of youths and adults participated in study programs, which included prolonged visits to Israel and attendance at educational institutions there. Under the impact of the creation of the State, some communities in the Diaspora even adopted the Sephardi pronunciation for prayers. Being the official language of Israel, Hebrew was recognized as a foreign language and taught also at numerous non-Jewish educational institutions.

See also LITERATURE, MODERN HEBREW AND ISRAELI.

T. PRESCHEL

HEBREW COMMITTEE OF NATIONAL LIBERATION. *See* BERGSON GROUP.

HEBREW LANGUAGE ACADEMY (Akademiya LaLashon Ha'Ivrit).
Institution established in 1953 by the *government of Israel to conduct research into the history and development of the *Hebrew language. The academy is the supreme authority for modern Hebrew terminology, usage, and spelling.

The academy had its origins in the Va'ad HaLashon Ha'Ivrit (Hebrew Language Council), founded in 1890 by Eliezer *Ben Yehuda for the purpose of establishing the proper orthography for renascent Hebrew, determining its pronunciation, and coining new terms to meet the demand for an expanded vocabulary. The Va'ad ceased activities after a short time, but it was reorganized in 1904 with the help of the Hebrew Teachers Association of Palestine.

Initially composed of philologists, the Va'ad came to include writers and poets as well. Presidents of the Va'ad from its inception and until its dissolution with the establishment of the academy were Eliezer Ben Yehuda, David *Yellin, Aaron *Mazia, Hayim Nahman *Bialik, Naphtali Herz *Tur-Sinai, and Joseph Gedalia *Klausner.

The Va'ad HaLashon and its successor, the Hebrew Language Academy, have both published a large number of specialized and technical dictionaries, *L'shonenu* (a quarterly journal established in 1928), and *L'shonenu La'Am* (a periodical), as well as extensive studies on the Hebrew language. A separate publication is devoted to the academy's proceedings. In 1966 work on the *Historical Dictionary of the Hebrew Language,* one of the great projects of the academy, was in progress. Tur-Sinai, who had been president of the academy since its founding, still held that office in 1966.

HEBREW LANGUAGE ASSOCIATION OF AMERICA. *See* HISTADRUT 'IVRIT OF AMERICA.

HEBREW LITERATURE. *See* LITERATURE, MODERN HEBREW AND ISRAELI.

HEBREW PRESS. More than the Jewish press in any other language, the Hebrew press had a uniquely Zionist orientation. To all intents and purposes the term "Hebrew press" was synonymous with "Zionist press." The *Hebrew language in itself formed a direct link with Palestine and the Return to Zion. Even during the *Haskala period, when the Hebrew press was concerned with Enlightenment, which it then regarded as the primary solution to the Jewish problem, it was preparing the ground, unawares, for Hibbat Zion (*see* HOVEVE ZION) and Zionism, for the written Hebrew word as such evoked memories of the lost Homeland and longing for its restoration. The key periodicals during the *Haskala period, *HaMaggid* and *HaShahar*, were among the first to rebel against the quasiassimilationist connotations of Haskala (*see* ASSIMILATION) and to support Hibbat Zion. The leaders of the Hebrew press during three generations—David *Gordon, Peretz *Smolenskin, Alexander *Zederbaum, *Ahad Ha'Am, and Nahum *Sokolow

An issue of HaMelitz, *an early Hebrew newspaper published in St. Petersburg.* [YIVO Institute for Jewish Research]

—were also leaders of Hibbat Zion and the Zionist movement.

The antinationalist and anti-Zionist positions (*see* ANTI-ZIONISM) frequently expressed in the Jewish press in various languages during the 19th century were rarely found in Hebrew periodicals. Where they did occur, they reflected the views of extreme Orthodoxy or of the extreme left. The gradual decline of the Hebrew press in Europe, even as it flourished in Palestine, demonstrates the organic link between the Hebrew press and the Jewish Homeland.

The Hebrew press first developed in Western Europe, particularly within the borders of late-18th-century Germany. From there it spread to Austria proper and Galicia and, in the course of the 19th century, became rooted in Eastern Europe—Lithuania, Russia, and Poland—which had masses of Hebrew readers. There it flourished until World War I, and its growth in the East paralleled its decline in Western Europe.

During the first century of its existence (1750–1856) the Hebrew press consisted of annuals and of periodicals appearing at irregular intervals. Current events occupied only a small place in its columns, which were devoted mainly to scholarship and literature. Although the Hebrew press, in the generally accepted sense of the term, was not born until 1856, with the appearance of *HaMaggid*, the first Hebrew newspaper, the previous century had played an important role in that it saw the evolution of Hebrew from a "holy tongue," used only for prayer and sacred studies, into a living, modern language capable of expressing current news and thought.

The Hebrew press made its appearance in Palestine in 1863, only seven years after its birth in Europe. Its development was uninterrupted, and it reached its zenith at a time when it had almost completely disappeared in Eastern Europe.

Contemporary Hebrew publications outside Israel maintain close ties with the Jewish State and reflect Israeli news and views. But today it is only in Israel that there is a comprehensive Hebrew press, ranging from daily newspapers to magazines and journals dealing with every facet of life and culture and catering to every element of the reading public.

By World War II the Hebrew press had reached fourth place in circulation of Jewish newspapers and other periodicals in the world, ranking after the English-language, German-language, and Yiddish-language Jewish press. In 1969 the Hebrew press was second only to the Anglo-Jewish press and constituted more than one-fourth of the world Jewish press in all languages combined. In numbers of daily newspapers the Hebrew press stood first (Yiddish was second).

Early Beginnings, 1750–1856. The appearance of the first Hebrew periodicals in Germany was an outgrowth of the endeavors of the Haskala. These early journals were influenced by the German periodicals of the late 18th century, which were devoted to literature, philosophy, and sociology. Moses Mendelssohn's journal, *Kohelet Musar*, appeared about 1750. From then through 1856 a varied group of periodicals appeared at irregular intervals. Content was often determined by frequency (or infrequency) of appearance. Unable to keep pace with current events, these periodicals dealt with them only in a very general manner. On the other hand, they devoted a good deal of space to literary and scientific topics which were not time-bound. In the course of time, these topics developed into belles lettres (poetry and prose, original and in translation, generally from the German and from other languages via German), studies in Biblical, Talmudic, and medieval literature, linguistic research, historical-biographical studies, editions of old manuscripts together with introductory material and commentaries, reviews of developments in Hebrew literature, Judaica in various languages, general literature, and so on.

These endeavors laid the foundations for the development of the Hebrew press and, more important, helped the Hebrew language evolve into one capable of reflecting contemporary life and, eventually, to refute assimilationism and expound modern Jewish *nationalism.

Emergence of the Hebrew Newspaper, 1856–86. The three decades between 1856 and 1886 saw the emergence of a Hebrew press patterned on the contemporary general press. Its aim was to provide news of current developments and editorial comment. At first the news was presented in a most primitive fashion. Since the Hebrew press had no news services or reporters of its own, the information it printed was copied, with considerable delay, from the general press or from Jewish periodicals published in other languages. By the 1880s, however, a modern Hebrew press had come into existence, complete with news coverage, editorials, and various columns. Jewish literature and scholarship occupied a disproportionate place in the early Hebrew press, because the readers were particularly interested in these subjects and had been accustomed to look to the general press for news of current events.

By this time the Hebrew press had all but disappeared in Western Europe. In Eastern Europe, except for Galicia, which was then part of Austria, Jewish journalism had been muzzled by Tsarist Russian censorship. This censorship cramped the style even of the Hebrew periodicals published outside the Tsarist Empire, since these papers were circulated throughout Russia and were censored. Literature found "objectionable" would either be deleted by the censors or be kept from circulation in Russia. Thus, during the period of its growth in Tsarist Russia, the Hebrew press was not able to express itself freely on contemporary affairs. For this reason, it often had to resort to hints and innuendos which the readers understood very well. Contemporary references might be enveloped in many layers of metaphor harking back to medieval liturgical poetry, which only a discerning eye could properly interpret.

From its very beginnings until the 1880s, the Hebrew press saw Haskala as the panacea for the suffering of the Jewish people in Europe. The more the intellectual horizons of the Jews expanded, it was held, the easier it would be for them to enter the world of the non-Jews among whom they lived. At the same time it was implied, directly or indirectly, that the anti-Jewish prejudices of the gentiles were caused by the fact that the Jews had refused to give up their distinctively Jewish ways. As these distinctive Jewish traits disappeared, it was claimed, the gap between the Jews and the other nations would narrow.

Detachment from Jewish distinctiveness and the gradual adaptation to the non-Jewish milieu was the leitmotiv of both the Hebrew and the non-Hebrew press, with one basic difference. The Hebrew press could not, by its very nature, preach this line so zealously, for the written Hebrew word as such conjured up memories that could not be eradicated. Thus the Hebrew press was the first to rebel against the aims of Haskala and to turn to Jewish nationalism and, later, to Zionism. It was in the Hebrew rather than in the non-Hebrew Jewish press that the first rabbis

to preach Hibbat Zion (e.g., Zvi Hirsch *Kalischer) found a platform.

At the time the Orthodox non-Hebrew press (in Germany, for instance) did not differ in essence from its Reform counterpart in its attitude toward the Return to Zion. It opposed the assimilationist, nonreligious connotations of Haskala but shared with Reform the belief that better understanding between Jews and their gentile neighbors would put an end to anti-Jewish prejudices. The Western European Orthodox viewpoint was expressed in the motto devised by its foremost advocate, Samson Raphael Hirsch (1808–88), *"Tora 'im derekh eretz"* (Tora with secular education). Palestine was viewed either in terms of a miraculous, Messianic redemption, which it would be sin for mere human beings to hasten, or as an object of philanthropic support. It never occurred to adherents of these views that they could hasten redemption by going to Palestine themselves to rebuild the Jewish Homeland.

The fulsome praise the Hebrew press bestowed upon the Tsarist regime should, naturally, not be accepted at face value. It was the one way to ensure that the Tsarist government would permit Hebrew newspapers to circulate in the Russian Empire.

The rejection of Haskala and the growing trend toward nationalism in the 1860s and 1870s was intensified in the 1880s, when anti-Jewish pogroms erupted in southern Russia. The attitude of the Hebrew press toward Jewish nationalism was generally positive, and if here and there some opposition was expressed, it was only in the sense of an appeal for prudence and against overhasty action. It is interesting to note that two Hebrew papers, *HaMelitz* and *HaL'vanon*, which took opposing sides on the issue of religious reform (*HaMelitz* taking the Liberal view and *HaL'vanon* reflecting the Orthodox attitude)

Modern Hebrew newspapers and magazines on sale in Jerusalem. [Israel Information Services]

later collaborated as advocates of Hibbat Zion, *practical Zionism, and *'Aliya (*immigration to Palestine).

A major event in the early history of the Hebrew newspaper was the appearance of the first Hebrew-language Socialist paper. Edited by A. S. Lieberman and a group of his friends, it was first called *HaEmet* and later renamed *Asefat Hakhamim*. The preaching of cosmopolitanism in the Hebrew language was a novel phenomenon; it was to recur, in somewhat different guise, in Communist Hebrew papers published in Israel (*see* COMMUNISTS IN ISRAEL).

Modern History in the Diaspora, 1886– . This period began with a milestone in the history of the Hebrew press, the appearance of the first Hebrew daily, *HaYom*, edited by Y'huda Leib Kantor (St. Petersburg, 1886). For the first time the Hebrew press was faced with the challenge of keeping abreast of daily events. This enterprise required entirely new techniques. Exact forms of expression had to be found, and the plague of rhetoric and flowery phraseology had to be overcome. Because of the nature of the Hebrew language, rhetoric could never be eliminated entirely, but it was no longer used as a stylistic device; it was employed only to provide exact expressions to fit the subject. The triumvirate that guided *HaYom* consisted of Kantor, Y'huda L. Katzenelson (known by his pseudonym, Buki ben Yogli), and David *Frischmann. Although the paper ceased publication after two years (according to some sources, it had to suspend publication because it had reservations about Zionism), it can be said that it marked the beginning of a new era in Hebrew journalism. In any event, two nationalist periodicals, *HaMelitz* and *HaTz'fira, subsequently followed its example and also became dailies.

The mid-1880s saw a flowering of Hebrew newspapers and magazines that lasted until World War I. These publications nurtured the Hibbat Zion movement, their editors being among its active leaders. The idol of the Hebrew press at this time was Nahum Sokolow, one of the builders of the Hebrew press for almost two generations and later president of the *World Zionist Organization. The flourishing press led to the growth of Hebrew literature in Eastern Europe, and together the two modes of expression inspired three generations of pioneers to go to Palestine to rebuild the Jewish Homeland. The two giants of Hebrew literature, Hayim Nahman *Bialik and Ahad Ha'Am, among others, appeared for years in the pages of the Hebrew press.

The 1905 Revolution in Russia slowed the development of the Hebrew press, but not for long; the Hebrew press continued to flourish in Russia until the Revolution of 1917. The few months between the onset of the 1917 Revolution and the Bolsheviks' seizure of power and prohibition of the Hebrew language were a very rich period in the history of the Hebrew press in Russia. Thereafter, with but few and rare exceptions, the Hebrew language fell silent in Soviet Russia. Guided by the notorious Yevsektzia, the Soviet officials soon understood the link between the Hebrew language and Zionism and banned both in Communist Russia.

World War I dealt a severe blow to the Hebrew press throughout the *Diaspora. The formation of the newly independent nations and the isolation from Soviet Russia curtailed the circulation of the Hebrew press in Poland. *HaTz'fira*, the single Hebrew daily that existed in Poland between the two world wars, had to struggle for its existence and finally ceased publication several years before the Nazi holocaust. The Hebrew weekly that appeared from then almost until World War II

did so with the greatest of difficulty and only with the support of a Yiddish paper, *Hajnt*. However, Hebrew yearbooks and periodicals devoted to literary, artistic, and social affairs as well as to current events flourished and enjoyed a wide circulation.

The modern Hebrew press in the United States, England, and elsewhere in the West was an offshoot of the Hebrew press in Eastern Europe, having been imported by immigrant intellectuals and writers imbued with love for the Hebrew language. These periodicals reflected the change in milieu, but their essential character remained unchanged. The first Hebrew paper in the United States, *HaTzofe Ba'aretz HaHadasha*, had appeared as early as 1871. Two attempts were made to establish a Hebrew daily in the United States: *HaYom* (Moshe Goldman, 1909) and *HaDoar (Mordecai *Lipson and a group of writers, 1921–23). In general, however, these publications appeared sporadically. *HaDoar* later became a weekly and still appeared as such in 1970. In England the weekly *HaY'hudi* appeared from 1897 to 1913; thereafter only ad hoc periodicals were published. Similar developments occurred in other countries on a smaller scale. At present, *HaDoar* and several professional journals in education, Jewish studies, and other fields are published in the United States, making North America, with a total of about 20 Hebrew periodicals, second only to Israel in the size of its Hebrew press.

Hebrew Press in Palestine. The Hebrew press in Palestine developed quite differently from that in the Diaspora, for although non-Hebrew Jewish newspapers appeared in Palestine, the Hebrew press was *the* press of the *Yishuv (Jewish population of Palestine), from the beginning. In 1863 *HaL'vanon* and then *Havatzelet* began to appear in Jerusalem. Each represented a distinct group within the heterogenous Jewish community in Palestine; each defended its position by sharp attacks on the other. Both printed literary and scholarly articles, but they also dealt with the practical problems of the Yishuv, a fact that lent these papers special significance even in their infancy. Both papers ceased publication after one year. *HaL'vanon* later appeared again outside Palestine; *Havatzelet* reappeared in Jerusalem seven years later.

Unlike the Hebrew press in the Diaspora, the Hebrew newspapers in Palestine, even those not affiliated with a specific political party, always represented specific interests. The Palestinian Hebrew press differed from the Hebrew press in the Diaspora even when it supported Haskala. In Palestine, Haskala was supported by Hasidim who rallied around *Havatzelet* (*see* HASIDIC JEWS IN ISRAEL). These were pious Jews (as were the majority of the Maskilim, or adherents of Haskala, in other countries), whose concern with Enlightenment was expressed not in terms of accommodation with the gentile world but in terms of reforms in Jewish education, the establishment of a public library in Jerusalem, and the study of Arabic and other languages. *HaL'vanon* and *Havatzelet* both shared the goal of making the Yishuv productive and played a role in the establishment of Petah Tikva, the "mother of moshavot," by members of the old Yishuv. Although Hebrew at the time was not yet the everyday language of the Yishuv, it was the natural language of the Yishuv, as it were, for it was the only language common to the Jews who had come to Palestine from Yemen, Russia, and other Diaspora countries. Thus the Hebrew press in Palestine came to play an important unifying role.

The Hebrew press in Palestine was ahead of its counterparts in the Diaspora in the quality of its editorial comment, for from its inception it had to deal with concrete realities, responding to and interpreting the everyday problems of the Yishuv, its heterogeneous internal viewpoints, and its relationship to the Diaspora and to the world at large. Dealing with daily realities was one of the outstanding attributes of the Hebrew press in Palestine from its inception.

The history of the Hebrew press in Palestine can be divided into three stages: prior to 1880, 1881–1918, and 1918–48.

Prior to 1880. The seventh and eighth decades of the 19th century saw the beginning of modern Jewish immigration to Palestine and the establishment of the first agricultural settlements there. Attempts were made to publish newspapers in Ladino and Yiddish, but these were short-lived. During this period, despite the divisions within the Yishuv, all the newspapers were basically Orthodox in religious orientation. As mentioned before, even the Haskala had an approach different from that in the Diaspora countries.

1881–1918. A new era in Palestinian journalism began with the arrival in 1881 of Eliezer *Ben Yehuda, who became associated with Israel Dov *Frumkin's *Havatzelet.* Ben Yehuda had supported political Zionism from its inception, whereas *Havatzelet* strongly opposed Herzl and joined with the religious anti-Zionists abroad. Nonetheless, Frumkin, the editor of *Havatzelet* and an active community leader, maintained close contacts with the religious groups in the new settlements. After several years, Ben Yehuda, a product of Russian Haskala and European culture, found the Jerusalem paper confining. He sought to create a modern newspaper such as he had known in France, and in 1884 he founded *HaTz'vi.* Here, for the first time, a secular viewpoint was introduced into the Palestinian press. The old Yishuv and its newspapers closed ranks and united against Ben Yehuda's paper, which was supported by the new immigrants and came to be their organ. *HaTz'vi* was banned, and Ben Yehuda himself was once jailed, a move that incurred the wrath of Hoveve Zion in the Diaspora toward the old Yishuv.

Since the Hebrew language as it was then did not meet the needs of a modern newspaper, Ben Yehuda had to create new words and concepts, particularly when he began to translate from French literature. Some of his innovations grated on the ears of such Hebrew philologists as Yehiel Mikhel *Pines and Hayim Nahman Bialik. Moreover, his introduction of spoken Hebrew into the home necessitated the creation of new words for everyday use.

Changing their names as their Ottoman permits expired, Ben Yehuda continued modernizing his newspapers always along the lines of what he had seen in France. Eventually he reached a point where a weekly no longer sufficed. In 1908 he and his son Itamar *Ben Avi began to publish *HaTz'vi* (later *Ha'On*), the first daily paper in Palestine. This was the period of the Young Turk Revolution, and the Yishuv was naturally eager for daily news reports.

The early 20th century marked the beginning of the *Second 'Aliya, which established newspapers of its own. The immigrants of that period did not find that Ben Yehuda's papers expressed their goals, particularly after he supported the *East Africa scheme. Nor were the journalistic devices of Itamar Ben Avi to their liking. The first publication of the Second 'Aliya to appear was *HaPo'el HaTza'ir* (in stencil in 1907, and in print in 1908); this was followed by *Ha'Ahdut* (1910), which was supported by *Po'ale Zion. The press of the old Yishuv began to decline, to be replaced by other periodicals and dailies. By the outbreak of World War I several dailies were appearing in Palestine, in addition to various periodicals dedicated to scholarly research,

culture, and literature (e.g., the anthologies of Abraham Moshe Luncz; *Ha'Omer* of Simha *Ben-Zion, in which Sh'muel Y. *Agnon's work first appeared) and children's papers, agricultural journals, and so on. This wide variety of publications in Hebrew was unique to Palestine.

The years immediately preceding World War I were the formative years of the modern daily press in Palestine. Each newspaper reflected its own partisan interests, but all shared certain common, basic concerns: the Hebrew language, Hebrew culture and literature, and, of course, Zionism.

1918–48. A new era began after the war, with the 'Aliya from Russia of the key figures in the Hebrew literature and press. In 1919 these newcomers took over the daily *Ha'Aretz (which originally had appeared as an organ of the British military regime) and invited Ben Yehuda and his son to join them. But these were men of two very different worlds, and in 1919 Ben Yehuda, his son, and a group of native-born writers formed a second daily, *Do'ar HaYom, which in its very first issue expressed for the first time what later came to be known as the "Canaanite" viewpoint (*see* CANAANITES AND SEMITIC ACTION). Both *Ha'Aretz* and *Do'ar HaYom* were originally published in Jerusalem, but when *Ha'Aretz* was moved to Tel Aviv in 1923, Tel Aviv began to develop into the focal point of Palestinian journalism. Soon Jerusalem, for 60 years the journalistic center of the country, was left with only a few extreme Orthodox papers.

These two dailies were quite different from each other. *Ha'Aretz* was democratic and liberal, styled after the best Hebrew literature and journals in Russia; *Do'ar HaYom* was the paper of the native-born Palestinian Jew, the farmers and groups close to the British bureaucracy and the Arabs.

As the Hebrew press began to die in Poland, the last Eastern European country to have a Hebrew press, Palestine became the focal point of the Hebrew press. New dailies began to appear, reflecting the views of the various political parties. *Davar* (1925) belonged to the *Histadrut (General Federation of Labor). There were a Revisionist press (*see* REVISIONISTS), a General Zionist press (*see* GENERAL ZIONISM), and an Orthodox press, and there were papers representing factions within the Histadrut. The press showed steady improvement, both in technical aspects and in style and expression. Its development was a most important factor in the renaissance of the Hebrew language, literature, and culture. Even the extreme Orthodox papers adopted modern techniques to promote their objectives.

Hebrew Press in the State of Israel. The establishment of the Jewish State found in Palestine a modern press, ranging from extreme Orthodox to Communist (the Communist press had been underground during the mandatory era). All except the extreme right and left shared a common foundation, as had been most apparent during the Yishuv's struggle against the British in the 1940s. It was then common for Hebrew newspapers to be banned by the British authorities, and each paper shared this fate at one time or another. When one paper was closed down, another would appear in its place.

More recent developments in the Hebrew press include the appearance of mass-circulation evening papers (*Y'di'ot Aharonot* and *Ma'ariv; the individual most responsible for this development was the gifted journalist Azriel *Carlebach); papers in simple vocalized Hebrew for new immigrants, often with translations of difficult words in several languages; and illustrated periodicals for entertainment. Unique to Israel is the appearance of local Hebrew periodicals, particularly in the agricultural community, which are almost unknown outside the settlements that publish them. Many hundreds of such publications appear in kibbutzim, moshavim, and other forms of settlement (mostly in stencil) as well as in cities, towns, and villages. Many of these periodicals have appeared for dozens of years and provide valuable material concerning the history and development of the Yishuv and its various internal groupings.

In 1969 there were 14 Hebrew dailies in Israel. *Ha'Aretz, Davar, *HaTzofe, *'Al HaMishmar, *LaMerhav, *Kol Ha'Am, HaModi'a, *HaYom,* and *Omer* (vocalized) are morning papers; *Y'di'ot Aharonot* and *Ma'ariv* are afternoon papers; *Hadashot HaSport* is a sports paper; and *Sha'ar Kalkala* and *Yom Yom* deal with economic affairs. In the same year *HaYom* ceased publication, and *Kol Ha'Am* became a weekly. There has been a marked improvement in the appearance and content of the papers during the two decades of the State's existence, but they all have retained past traditions in that they have avoided yellow journalism. All the papers naturally have in common the love of *Eretz Yisrael. Since the *Six-day War of 1967 the Communist paper, *Kol Ha'Am,* has joined this common front. The current topic of concern among the newspapers is the struggle for the security of the State. The censorship of the mandatory period no longer exists, but the press has willingly accepted certain governmental restrictions concerning the publication of information that might be potentially dangerous to the State's security.

Other developments in recent years include the wide circulation achieved by afternoon papers that present news in a lighter fashion yet on a high journalistic level; the control of the press by a younger generation of writers, among them children of the original journalists, and the growing number of women writers; the appearance of illustrated magazines, mainly weeklies; and, for the first time in the history of the Hebrew press, pornographic periodicals.

The Hebrew press has rendered outstanding service in the three wars since the creation of the State. Correspondents in military service sent news from the battlefronts to the papers and to the Kol Yisrael radio network (*see* ISRAEL BROADCASTING SERVICE). The vast literature that appeared, particularly after the Six-day War, was written mainly by journalists.

The period of Israel's existence has also been a period of large-scale immigration, and the contribution of the non-Hebrew press that has appeared since the last third of the 19th century must not be overlooked. In 1969 there were 9 non-Hebrew daily papers and other publications appearing in Israel in Yiddish, Arabic, Hungarian, Bulgarian, English, Romanian, French, Polish, and German. As the immigrants adapt to the culture and language of the country and as the younger generation grows up, however, these periodicals will have outlived their usefulness.

One may estimate that since the publication of the first Hebrew periodical several thousands of Hebrew publications have appeared throughout the world, but only a small fraction have had a long life-span. The oldest publications still appearing in 1969 are *HaPo'el HaTza'ir* (weekly, 62 years), the two Israel dailies *Ha'Aretz* (50 years) and *Davar* (44 years), and the American *HaDoar* (weekly, 48 years). *HaTz'fira,* which with some interruptions appeared for almost 50 years, *HaMaggid* (47 years), *HaMelitz* (43 years), *Havatzelet* (more than 40 years), and the various Ben Yehuda newspapers (more than 30 years) are no longer in existence.

The largest collections of Hebrew publications, particularly those which appeared in Palestine, are to be found in the *Jewish National and University Library in Jerusalem and the Zalman Pevsner Collection, now in *Tel Aviv University.

See also LITERATURE, MODERN HEBREW AND ISRAELI.

G. KRESSEL

HEBREW UNIVERSITY OF JERUSALEM.

Largest institution of higher learning in Israel. In the mid-1960s the university comprised Faculties of Humanities (consisting of the Institute of Jewish Studies, the Institute of Asian and African Studies, and general humanities), Social Sciences (Eliezer *Kaplan School of Economics and Social Sciences), Law, Science, Agriculture, Medicine, and Dental Medicine; a School of Pharmacy, a School of Education, a Graduate Library School, a School of Home Economics, and the Paul Baerwald School of Social Work; the Jewish National and University Library; the Magnes Press; and the Adult Education Center. The university was also responsible for the academic affairs of the *Haifa University Institute, run by the Haifa municipality; and for studies in biology and the humanities at the Negev Institute for Higher Education, situated in B'er Sheva'.

Campus. The Hebrew University was opened in 1925 on Mount Scopus, one of the hills surrounding Jerusalem, and remained there until 1948, when, during the *War of Independence, Mount Scopus became inaccessible, forming a Jewish enclave in Arab territory. During the *Six-day War of 1967, Mount Scopus was liberated by the *Israel Defense Forces and restored to the university, which thereupon embarked on planning for its future use.

In the meantime a new campus was built at Giv'at Ram, to the west of Jerusalem. By 1967 this campus housed all the university's institutions except the Faculties of Agriculture, Medicine, and Dental Medicine and the School of Pharmacy.

The Faculties of Medicine (Hebrew University–Hadassah Medical School) and Dental Medicine (Hebrew University–Hadassah School of Dental Medicine, founded by the Alpha Omega fraternity) form part of the Medical Center at 'En HaKerem ('En Karem), one of the western suburbs of Jerusalem, built since the mid-1950s. The Medical Center is a joint undertaking of the university and *Hadassah; in addition to the two medical faculties, it includes the Hadassah-University Hospital, other Hadassah medical institutions, and the Julius Jarcho Medical Library. The university's School of Pharmacy, which in 1970 was still accommodated in provisional premises in the city of Jerusalem, was eventually also to have its home in the Medical Center. The Faculty of Agriculture is situated in Rehovot, south of Tel Aviv on the coastal plain.

Student Enrollment and Faculty. In 1969–70 the student body numbered 15,316 (about one-third women), of whom 14,366 were graduates and undergraduates and 950 were research students working for their doctorates. Of the graduates and undergraduates, 4,500 were in the Faculty of Humanities, 3,200 in Social Sciences, 850 in Law, 1,920 in Mathematics and Science, 430 in Agriculture, 536 in Medicine, 182 in Dental Medicine, 158 in Pharmacy, 260 in the Paul Baerwald School of Social Work, and 75 in the Graduate Library School. (Students in the School of Education are included in the Faculty of Humanities.) The major proportion of the students had received their secondary education in Israel. The number of students from other countries has steadily increased; in 1969–70 they numbered some 3,200, of whom about half were from the United States and the others from some 50 other countries including Asian and African developing nations. The number of

Buildings on the Giv'at Ram campus of the Hebrew University. [Israel Information Services]

Israeli Arab and Druze students (*see* ARABS IN ISRAEL; DRUZE COMMUNITY IN ISRAEL) was 200. The academic staff numbered some 2,000, a large proportion of whom were graduates of the university.

Degrees. The Hebrew University offers courses leading to the degrees of bachelor, master, and doctor. By summer, 1969, it had awarded 19,416 degrees, as follows: 9,010 bachelors (B.A., B.Sc., B.Sc.Agr., LL.B., B.S.W.), 5,691 masters (M.A., M.Soc.Sc., LL.M., M.Sc., M.Sc.Agr., M.Pharm., M.P.H.), 1,220 doctors of philosophy (Ph.D.), 1,153 doctors of medicine (M.D.), 150 doctors of dental medicine (D.M.D), and 18 doctors of laws (Dr.Jur.).

Teaching and Research. The Hebrew University is a teaching and a research institution. Both the circumstances which brought the university into being and its location in Israel have been major factors in determining the scope and character of its work. Intended from the beginning to serve not only as the university of Israel but as that of the Jewish people as a whole, it has set as one of its goals the promotion of Hebrew and Jewish culture throughout the world. It thus assigns special importance to Jewish scholarship, and its Institute of Jewish Studies is today the central seat of Jewish learning.

The geographical situation of the university and the natural conditions of Israel and the region of which it forms part are reflected in many aspects of its work. In the experimental disciplines studies are carried out, *inter alia*, on the diseases and the general medical problems of the area, on problems (geological, botanical, etc.) relating to arid zones, on the exploration for water, oil, and minerals, on aspects of local agriculture, on the fauna and flora of the Middle East, and on the exploitation of local natural resources for industry.

Israel's position in the heart of the Middle East also led the university as early as 1926 to set up a School of Oriental Studies in which the main emphasis was on Islamic civilization and Arabic and other Middle Eastern languages and literatures. Following developments on the world stage in recent years, the school expanded its curriculum to include Asian and African studies as well, and in 1962 it was accordingly renamed the Institute of Asian and African Studies.

In 1960 the university set up an Authority for Research and Development to encourage and foster research as well as to help secure funds for the purpose. In 1967 Hebrew University scientists were engaged in some 2,500 research projects on overseas and local grants received through the authority, the amount involved exceeding IL 12,000,000. Most of the grants came from outside Israel, among the main sources being various agencies of the United States government, the Ford and Rockefeller Foundations, and the World Health Organization.

In 1964 the university set up the Yissum Research Development Company to handle the industrial byproducts of research and to provide a centralized service both to the university's scientists and to Israel.

Jewish National and University Library. See separate article under this title.

Magnes Press. The Hebrew University Press (renamed the Magnes Press in 1949) was established in 1929 with the aim of publishing original Hebrew works and Hebrew translations of ancient and modern classics. In 1954, to make the research work done at the university accessible to scholars in other countries, publication was begun in English of *Scripta Hierosolymitana*, containing studies in various fields at the university. and this has been followed by the publication from time to time also of other works in English.

From its inception to 1968 the Magnes Press has published more than 550 books dealing with Jewish studies, Oriental studies, philosophy, education, mathematics, science, bibliography, and other subjects; 42 volumes of *Kiryat Sepher*, the bibliographical quarterly of the Jewish National and University Library; 37 volumes of *Tarbiz*, a quarterly for Jewish studies; 20 volumes of *Scripta Hierosolymitana*; and 6 volumes of *Textus*, the annual of the Hebrew University Bible Project and the first international journal to be devoted entirely to study of the Bible text.

Adult Education Center. This institution organizes and directs extramural courses of study on the university level in the towns and villages of Israel. In cooperation with other bodies it also sponsors a number of permanent institutions, such as an evening college in Tel Aviv, a teachers training college in B'er Sheva', and regional schools for adults. In 1967, following the Six-day War, the center cooperated with the Jerusalem municipality and the Ministry of Education and Culture in organizing extramural classes for the study of Hebrew by Arab residents of East Jerusalem, in which several hundred students are enrolled. At the same time, the center organized extramural courses in Arabic, which are at present attended by large numbers.

Harry S *Truman Research Institute on Mount Scopus. Established in honor of the former President of the United States, who was responsible for America's action as the first country to recognize the State of Israel, the center was in the course of formation in 1968. It was to be dedicated to studies aimed at achieving international cooperation and amity. Its various programs were to be directed to seeking out the historic sources of international tension and studying them with a view to their elimination as possible sources of conflict and war. The building for the center, originally planned as part of the Giv'at Ram campus, was being erected on the university's old campus on Mount Scopus.

History. The origins of the Hebrew University go back to the 1880s, when with the rise of the Jewish national movement the need was felt for a Jewish university which would serve as a focus for the scientific and cultural aspirations of the Jews of Palestine and at the same time provide a center

Campus of the Hebrew University at Giv'at Ram. [Israel Information Services]

from which the Jewish people could make its own specific contribution to world knowledge. It was also considered necessary in view of the fact that many young Jews were excluded from the universities of Eastern and Central Europe.

The first voice raised in favor of a Jewish university was that of Hermann *Schapira, professor of mathematics at the University of Heidelberg, who in 1897, at the 1st Zionist *Congress, proposed the establishment of such an institution. The proposal was sympathetically received, but the *World Zionist Organization was at that stage still too young for undertakings of such a nature. Four years later, at the 5th Zionist Congress, Chaim *Weizmann put forward a similar proposal, also without practical results. The idea of a Jewish university in Palestine, however, began to receive increasing support from leading Zionists, notably *Ahad Ha'Am. In 1902 Weizmann, Martin *Buber, and Berthold *Feiwel published a pamphlet, *Eine jüdische Hochschule* (A Jewish College), stressing the need for a Jewish university and detailing a plan for its organization and financing. When the 11th Zionist Congress met in 1913, it listened attentively to the arguments of Weizmann and also of M'nahem M. *Ussishkin, who had joined the ranks of the university proponents, and it eventually resolved that immediate steps be taken toward the establishment of a Hebrew University in Jerusalem.

With the adoption of that resolution the Hebrew University began to take shape. Special committees were formed in Berlin (where the Zionist Organization was then centered), London, and Jerusalem to deal with its implementation. The Russian Zionists gave their support to the idea, and the *Hoveve Zion organization of Odessa and Itzhak Leib *Goldberg of Vilna (later of Tel Aviv) contributed substantial sums for the purchase in 1918 of the Gray Hill estate on Mount Scopus, which was to form the nucleus of the university campus.

Further action was halted by the outbreak of World War I, and it was not until 1918 that the foundation stones of the university could be laid. This was followed during the next few years by the establishment of three research institutes: one for chemistry, set up through the efforts of the London committee; another for microbiology, which owed its existence to the American Jewish Physicians' Committee, formed in 1921; and the third for Jewish studies, for whose creation the Jerusalem committee was responsible.

On Apr. 1, 1925, the university was formally opened at a ceremony attended by a galaxy of distinguished visitors from all over the world. Dr. Weizmann, as president of the World Zionist Organization, presided, and the chief inaugural address was delivered by the Earl of *Balfour, author of the *Balfour Declaration. Others participating in the program were Sir Herbert (later Viscount) *Samuel, the first *High Commissioner for Palestine, Hayim Nahman *Bialik, the Hebrew poet, and Chief Rabbi Abraham Isaac *Kook.

As the university expanded its curriculum, enrollment increased. Under the leadership of Dr. Judah L. *Magnes new departments were set up, and with the financial assistance of Jews throughout the world the once-barren ridge of Mount Scopus was in due course covered with an array of imposing buildings.

The academic staff was small to begin with, its members hailing mostly from Eastern and Central Europe. With the advent of Nazism and later of *anti-Semitism in Italy under Mussolini, several scores of refugee scholars and scientists made their way to Jerusalem, forming an accretion of intellec-

tual talent of great importance to the university. After the establishment of the State of Israel, the faculty was enlarged by the addition of personnel from the United States, Canada, England, and South Africa, but it was largely the graduates of the university itself who began to fill academic posts.

From the beginning the university's influence was felt throughout the country. Its medical research contributed appreciably to raising health standards. Research conducted in its laboratories benefited agriculture and industry. The university provided teachers for the rapidly growing school population, and its scholars played a major role in adapting the ancient Hebrew language to modern requirements.

By the end of 1947 the university was firmly established as the major institution of higher learning in the country and was receiving increasing recognition in academic circles abroad. The number of students had risen to 1,000 and that of the faculty to 190. Large-scale plans for expansion were under way, but before these could be carried out, the War of Independence intervened. Mount Scopus was cut off from the rest of the country. Overnight, the university's buildings and facilities, the library, and the major part of the scientific equipment were no longer accessible to students and faculty. Nevertheless, in the shortest possible time the university was functioning again, in makeshift provisional premises in the city, gradually acquiring new books and scientific apparatus to replace what it had lost.

Despite the difficulties under which it labored, the university's progress during the next few years was more rapid than ever before, for it now had to serve the needs of the newly created State of Israel, to train the personnel of which there was a serious dearth in every sphere, and to help accelerate the scientific development of the country. By 1953 the university was scattered in 50 rented buildings throughout Jerusalem. Conditions of work were difficult in the extreme, and it became imperative to build new premises. The result was the campus at Giv'at Ram and the Medical Center at 'En HaKerem.

Organization and Administration. The supreme authority of the university is vested in the Board of Governors, an international body which includes men distinguished both in academic and in public life, leading members of the societies of Friends of the Hebrew University, and representatives of the *government of Israel and the World Zionist Organization. The board exercises ultimate control in matters of major policy, elects the president and vice-president, determines financial policy, and approves the annual budget.

The president of the university is head of the administration, directing the work of the university in accordance with the powers conferred on him by the Board of Governors. Eliyahu *Elath was president of the university from 1961 to 1968, when Avraham *Harman was elected.

The Executive Council is the representative in Israel of the Board of Governors and is responsible for the conduct of university affairs between the annual meetings of the board. It appoints a Permanent Committee, which is responsible for the conduct of the day-to-day affairs of the university.

The Senate is the supreme academic body of the university. It enjoys academic autonomy and is responsible for the maintenance of academic standards. It elects the rector as its chairman and as the academic head of the university. In 1970 the office of rector was held by Jacob Katz.

The university is financed by subsidies from the Israeli government and by funds raised by the societies of Friends of the

Hebrew University throughout the world. Such societies exist in the United States and Canada, Great Britain, continental Europe, Central and South America, Australia, New Zealand, South Africa, and Israel itself.

The American Friends of the Hebrew University was chartered in 1931. With headquarters in New York and several regional chapters, it had in 1968 about 10,000 members and was the university's prime source of outside assistance. It includes in its organizational structure an Office of Academic Affairs, which conducts a one-year study program for American college students at the university and an English-language summer session at the university, as well as programs involving scholarships, fellowships, faculty exchanges, and other activities designed to create a "cultural bridge" between the university and the academic community of the United States.

In 1970 Samuel Rothberg was president of the American Friends of the Hebrew University and chairman of the university's Board of Governors. Prof. Milton Handler was chairman of the Board of Directors and Joseph M. Mazer chairman of the Executive Committee.

M. GITLIN

HEBREW WRITERS' ASSOCIATION IN ISRAEL. *See* AGUDAT HASOFRIM HA'IVRIM B'YISRAEL.

HEBRON (Hevron). Town south-southwest of Jerusalem, situated in the Judean Mountains, in the kingdom of Jordan. One of the oldest cities in the world, it played an important role in the early history of the Israelites as the residence of the Biblical patriarchs and as King David's capital before the conquest of Jerusalem. Hebron, or Kiryat Arba', as it was also called, is mentioned as one of the localities where the returning exiles from Babylonia settled. From that time on, until the era of the Crusaders, there seems always to have been a Jewish community in Hebron.

The small Jewish community which existed there at the end of the Middle Ages experienced some growth in the 18th century and continued to grow throughout the 19th century. In 1820 the first Ashkenazi community was established there by Habad Hasidim (*see* HASIDIC JEWS IN ISRAEL). In 1895 there were about

Muslim sanctuary above the cave of Machpela, traditional burial place of the Jewish patriarchs, in Hebron. [Israel Government Tourist Office]

1,400 Jews in the city, or 10 per cent of the total population. This number decreased in the years immediately following. After the *Arab riots of 1929, during which many Hebron Jews were killed, the Jews left the city. In 1931 some families returned, but they left again during the Arab riots of 1936.

According to tradition, Abraham, Isaac, and Jacob and their wives, Sarah, Rebecca, and Leah, are buried in the cave of Machpela in Hebron. According to the Talmud, the cave was also the last resting place of Adam and Eve. The traditional site of the cave, over which a Muslim mosque was erected, is one of the most sacred shrines of the country and has been a place of pilgrimage over the centuries (*see* HOLY PLACES IN ISRAEL). After the *War of Independence, Jews from Israel had no access to the cave of Machpela until the *Six-day War of 1967, during which the city of Hebron was occupied by the *Israel Defense Forces.

HECHALUTZ. *See* HEHALUTZ.

HECHAVER (Zionist student organization). *See* HEHAVER.

HECHLER, WILLIAM H. British clergyman and early Zionist sympathizer (b. South Africa, 1845; d. London, 1931). Born of German parents, he completed his studies for the Protestant ministry and, on the recommendation of the British court, became tutor to Prince Ludwig, son of Friedrich, Grand Duke of Baden. While in this post, he met the Grand Duke's nephew, the future Emperor *Wilhelm II of Germany. Following Prince Ludwig's premature death, Hechler served in the ministry in England. In 1882 he took part in a meeting of Christian notables in London that discussed the possibility of settling Jewish refugees from Romania and Russia in Palestine. He subsequently visited Russia to help Jewish pogrom victims. In 1884 he wrote a treatise entitled *The Restoration of the Jews to Palestine According to the Prophets*, in which he predicted, on the basis of certain ancient prophecies and Biblical passages, that Palestine would be returned to the Jewish people in about 1897–98.

In 1885 Hechler became chaplain to the British Embassy in Vienna, a position he held until 1910. While in Vienna, he learned from Saul Raphael *Landau of Herzl's *Jewish State*, and, on Mar. 10, 1896, he paid a call on the Zionist leader. Hechler became Herzl's devoted friend and introduced him to Grand Duke Friedrich. The meeting that followed, Herzl's first contact with royalty, paved the way for subsequent interviews with other rulers such as Wilhelm II.

Hechler introduced Herzl also to other political figures. He was a guest at the 1st Zionist *Congress (Basle, 1897), attended subsequent Congresses, and continued to support the Zionist movement after the death of Herzl.

HECHT, JOSEPH. *Hagana leader (b. Bykhov, Russia, 1894). Settling in Palestine in 1914, he volunteered for the *Jewish Legion in 1918. During the *Arab riots of May, 1921, he organized the defense of Mikve Yisrael. Later, he was appointed to the Executive Committee of Hagana as the representative of the *Histadrut (General Federation of Labor). He became the de facto head of Hagana, serving in that capacity until the middle of 1931. Hecht set up the first arms caches of Hagana and organized a central leadership course. During the Arab riots of 1929 he directed the defense of the *Yishuv (Jewish population of Palestine). In 1938 he was in charge of the security of the workers who erected the Teggart Wall (a barbed-wire fence) on the border between Palestine and Syria and Lebanon to prevent the infiltration of Arab marauders.

Y. SLUTSKY

HECHT, REUVEN. Political scientist, businessman, and Zionist leader (b. Antwerp, 1909). While a student at the Universities of Munich, Berlin, and Heidelberg, he joined the Zionist student organization *Kartell Jüdischer Verbindungen in Germany. A cofounder and member of the Executive of Yavne v'Yodefeth (World Union of Zionist Revisionist Students), he was active in the Revisionist organizations of Switzerland, France, and Belgium (see REVISIONISTS) and in the arrangement of *illegal immigration to Palestine. During World War II he was a member of the Hebrew Committee of National Liberation and of the Executive of the United Zionists-Revisionists.

Hecht became associated with the shipping and storage business in Palestine in 1936–39 and again in 1948. In 1950 he received a government concession for silo enterprises in the *ports of Israel. The next year he formed Dagon Bate Mamgurot l'Yisrael, Ltd., in Haifa.

I. BENARI

HEDERA. See HADERA.

HEFER VALLEY ('Emek Hefer). Central section of the Sharon Valley in the coastal plain of Israel and its lowest part. With a width of 10 miles from the sea to the Jordanian border, it forms the narrow neck of the State of Israel. Formerly known as Wadi Hawarith, it consisted of sand dunes in the west and of large swamps (of the Alexander River and its tributaries) in the center and east. Until its acquisition by the *Jewish National Fund in 1929, the Hefer Valley was occupied mainly by Bedouins. After the drainage of its swamps it became one of the most fertile regions of Israel, yielding oranges, bananas, vegetables, and dairy products. Its center is the town of N'tanya, a seaside resort and site of light industry.

Y. KARMON

HEFTMAN, JOSEPH HAYIM. Poet, journalist, and editor of *HaBoker (b. Brańsk, Russian Poland, 1888; d. Tel Aviv, 1955). Heftman's first poems were printed in *HaTz'fira. After helping to found the youth organization *HeHalutz, he became the editor of its organ. He went to Palestine in 1920, representing HeHalutz at the founding convention of the *Histadrut (General Federation of Labor) in December, 1920, and subsequently (1921) served as secretary to the *Va'ad L'umi (National Council) and to Nahum *Sokolow when the latter visited Palestine. Heftman composed the anthem of the *Third 'Aliya, "Anu Nihye HaRishonim" ("We Will Be the First").

Returning to Poland in 1922, he became active in the Federation of General Zionists ('Al HaMishmar) and revived the defunct HaTz'fira, remaining its editor in chief almost until the end of its existence. In 1934 he settled in Palestine. He first edited *Do'ar HaYom and then served as editor in chief of HaBoker (from 1935 until his death). Heftman was a founding member of the Israel Journalists Association, which he headed until his death. An anthology of his writings appeared in 1956.

G. KRESSEL

HEFTZI-BAH. Village (kibbutz) in the eastern Jezreel Valley. Founded in 1922 and affiliated with the *Kibbutz M'uhad. The name is derived from Isaiah 62:4. Population (1968): 500.

HEHALUTZ (Hechalutz). World organization of Jewish youth which trained its members for pioneering work and self-defense in Palestine. The name means "The Pioneer."

Early Development. The first attempt to establish a pioneer organization was made by the *Bilu group. In the early 1900s, M'nahem Mendel *Ussishkin advocated the formation of groups of young people pledged to go to Palestine and work there for a period of three years. At the same time attempts were made to organize pioneer groups in southern Russia (HeHalutz and Biluim Hadashim) and in the United States. From time to time, appeals for the *immigration of pioneers would also come from the Jewish workers in Palestine. On the whole, however, the immigration of pioneers at the time of the *Second 'Aliya was an individual affair, not preceded by group activities in the *Diaspora.

During World War I, David *Ben-Gurion and Itzhak *Ben Zvi were active in the United States in the establishment of a pioneer movement whose members were to go to Palestine when they could be asked to do so. These were among the first volunteers for the American contingent of the *Jewish Legion.

Also during World War I, HeHalutz developed into a mass movement in Russia. In various localities young Jews organized for the purpose of studying Hebrew and acquiring agricultural skills to prepare them for emigration to Palestine. The movement was broadened upon the outbreak of the Russian Revolution of 1917. Early in 1918 representatives of HeHalutz groups from Russian cities met in Kharkov and laid the foundation for an all-Russia HeHalutz. The Kharkov Conference debated the character of HeHalutz: was it to serve as an advance guard and embrace only those who were ready to engage in pioneer work, or should it organize all workers emigrating to Palestine? This debate was to occupy the movement for several years.

In the spring of 1918, Joseph *Trumpeldor joined HeHalutz. His accession gave great impetus to its work. At a meeting of HeHalutz representatives it was decided that the movement should be nonpolitical and be open to all youths above the age of 18 who regarded Hebrew as their national language and who were preparing themselves for work in Palestine. In January, 1919, a HeHalutz conference, held in Moscow with representatives from 23 groups participating, elected Trumpeldor president. The seat of the movement was subsequently transferred from Moscow to Minsk, and Trumpeldor went to Palestine to make preparations for the settlement of the HeHalutz pioneers. At that time Halutzim (pioneers; see HALUTZ) from Russia began to make their way to Palestine via the Black Sea and the Caucasus. Trumpeldor's death in Tel Hai in March, 1920, was a great blow to the movement, for which his heroic personality had become an inspiring symbol.

Movement in the Soviet Union. With the consolidation of the Soviet regime, the new rulers of Russia and especially their Jewish underlings opened a drive against HeHalutz, despite the fact that the movement was not officially proscribed and that in many localities its members took part in the efforts of the Soviet authorities to rehabilitate those Jews who had been displaced economically. The HeHalutz conference of October, 1920, stressed the importance of training prior to emigration to Palestine, and the establishment of training squads was begun. The growth of the movement alarmed its opponents, and in January, 1922, all delegates to the third HeHalutz conference were arrested. The movement was subsequently torn by a debate between those who demanded a measure of adaptation to the ideology dominant in the Soviet state so that He-Halutz might achieve official recognition and those who wanted HeHalutz to remain nonpolitical. In April, 1923, the leadership determined that the movement would regard itself as part of the international Jewish proletariat and that, recognizing the necessity of class war, it would fight capitalism in all its forms. It also resolved that the communal settlement was the only way of life to which HeHalutz would direct its members. These decisions produced a rift in the movement, and in August, 1923, after official approval for the HeHalutz statutes had been received, the organization split into the "legal" Halutz Ma'amadi-Kibbutzi and the "illegal" Halutz L'umi-'Amlani.

The legal HeHalutz established branches throughout the Soviet Union with the exception of White Russia and the Ukraine, struggled openly with the Jewish Communists, issued a central publication (*HeHalutz*), and established the training farms of Tel-Hai in the Crimea and Zangen (Yiddish, Ears of Grain) near Moscow. The illegal HeHalutz conducted its activities underground. Of its training farms, Mishmar in the Crimea and Bilu in White Russia became known. The crisis of the Jewish small towns and the news of prosperity in Palestine brought an increase in membership. By the end of 1925 the two factions had a combined membership of about 14,000. However, the movement was hampered by the economic crisis which gripped Palestine in 1925; the dissolution of the *G'dud Ha'Avoda V'haHagana 'Al Shem Yosef Trumpeldor, which had been the finest achievement of the Russian HeHalutz; and growing persecution and arrests by the Soviet authorities, which in 1928 withdrew the permit they had granted HeHalutz. Thousands of Halutzim and members of Zionist youth movements were held in prison and sent to exile in Siberia and Central Asia. Some of them, after years of suffering, were permitted to emigrate to Palestine, but even this emigration was stopped in the early 1930s. Attempts to conduct activities of HeHalutz underground continued until the end of 1934.

International Development. Concurrently with HeHalutz in Russia, pioneer movements came into being in Poland and Lithuania and, on a smaller scale, in Romania, Latvia, Germany, Austria, and Czechoslovakia. The many Russian Halutzim who passed through these countries on their way to Palestine strengthened the local movements and in some countries formed the majority of local membership in those years. In August, 1921, the First World Conference of HeHalutz convened in Karlovy Vary, Czechoslovakia, on the occasion of the 12th Zionist *Congress. It decided to establish an international HeHalutz organization within the *World Zionist Organization. The Congress approved the organization as an independent movement devoted to the training of prospective immigrants. The Second World Conference of HeHalutz was held in Berlin in December, 1922.

The further development of HeHalutz was shaped by three factors: (1) the political and economic position of the Jews in the various countries; (2) the possibilities of emigration to and settlement in Palestine; and (3) the educational activities of pioneering youth movements, whose graduates were to join HeHalutz. In periods of crisis in the Diaspora and of prosperity in Palestine, HeHalutz was swamped by "pioneers" who had received no Zionist education and many of whom left the movement when Zionism went through a period of decline. HeHalutz made great efforts to direct and unite the youth movements. In the early 1920s it even established a youth movement of its own, HeHalutz HaTza'ir. Efforts at unification

failed. In 1926 the movement was forced to recognize the right of *HaShomer HaTza'ir to establish its own training centers within the framework of HeHalutz. In 1930 it conferred similar rights on the pioneering youth movement *Gordonia.

The Third World Conference (Danzig, 1926) established the guiding principles of HeHalutz: manual labor, Hebrew language and culture, liaison with the *Histadrut (General Federation of Labor), and participation in the Diaspora activities of Labor Palestine. Those years saw the development of the permanent organizational pattern of HeHalutz. The S'nif (branch) organized members 18 years of age and over, training them for work and settlement in Palestine. From the S'nif members went to a kibbutz *Hakhshara (training group), where they lived a communal life, engaged in manual work, and waited for their turn to emigrate to Palestine. A general meeting of the kibbutz would select the prospective immigrants after a period of training, the length of which was determined by the number of immigration permits at the disposal of the movement at the time.

World HeHalutz outside Russia had a membership of 16,350 in 1926, 23,000 in 1930, 89,500 in 1935, and 70,000 to 75,000 in 1939. At various periods, 20 to 25 per cent of the members were at training centers. Between 1919 and 1939 about 45,000 members (including those from Russia) settled in Palestine. They constituted one-third of all worker immigrants of those years.

In the late 1920s, with the rise of the influence of emissaries from the Palestinian *kibbutz movement, a process of division began in HeHalutz. Graduates of HaShomer HaTza'ir were affiliated with the *Kibbutz Artzi Shel HaShomer HaTza'ir; those of Gordonia, with *Hever HaK'vutzot; and former members of HeHalutz HaTza'ir and other Halutz youth movements (Freiheit, HaShomer HaTza'ir–Netzah, *HaBonim, etc.), as well as Halutzim who came from no particular youth group, with the *Kibbutz M'uhad. Outside the general framework of HeHalutz stood HeHalutz HaMizrahi (*Mizrahi Pioneer) and HeHalutz HaTziyoni HaK'lali (General Zionist Pioneer). The divisions within HeHalutz prevented the calling of a world conference of the movement in the 1930s.

Movement in Poland. After the suppression of the Halutz movement in Russia, the movement in Poland came to occupy the central place in the world organization, and its members constituted the great majority of the world membership. In Poland, more than anywhere else, HeHalutz was a mass movement only some of whose members came from Zionist youth movements. Consequently, its membership was subject to considerable fluctuation. Between 1919 and 1923 HeHalutz in Poland was strongly influenced by the stream of Halutzim from Russia and the Ukraine, who constituted an entity of their own. Much importance was attached, especially in the early years, to agricultural training with peasants, on estates or on farms established by HeHalutz, of which the one at Grochów, near Warsaw, became a permanent institution. The desire to assure the fulfillment of the task of the movement by its members even after their emigration to Palestine led to the formation of compact training groups, whose members lived together on a communal basis and, after settling in Palestine, sought to concentrate in kibbutzim of their own. In such a manner pioneer training was organized in five territorial districts: Klosova (Volhynia), Shaharia (Polesie-Vilna), Tel-Hai (Białystok-Grodno), Borochów (Łódź, Silesia), and Grochów (central Poland). In the 1930s the training group of HaShomer HaTza'ir and Gordonia established its own associations within the framework of HeHalutz. The Galician HeHalutz had its own organization, in which Halutzim from the youth movements of HaShomer HaTza'ir and Gordonia had a decisive influence.

HeHalutz branches conducted Zionist propaganda activities and Hebrew-language courses. Under the direction of emissaries from Palestine, seminars for HeHalutz guides and workers were held. Between 1927 and 1931, when Zionism was at a low ebb, HeHalutz proved to be a tower of strength to the movement in the Diaspora, supplying the majority of all immigrants to Palestine. During the period of prosperity in Palestine in the 1930s, HeHalutz expanded and embraced tens of thousands. The existing training facilities were not able to absorb all those who wanted to join. Groups of prospective pioneers went in search of training places in cities and villages. Hundreds of Hakhshara kibbutzim were then established, including some large ones with 200 to 300 members (Łódź, Vilna). The trainees lived under appalling conditions of poverty and lack of space, with insufficient nutrition and one bed for two or three persons, but the knowledge that persistence even in the face of these hardships could ultimately bring them to Palestine kept up their morale. From 1936 on, following the outbreak of *Arab riots in Palestine, military instruction was given to HeHalutz training groups by emissaries of the *Hagana. In the same years, under the pressure of the Halutzim, an "illegal" Halutz immigration (see ILLEGAL IMMIGRATION) to Palestine was begun, and until the outbreak of World War II about 6,000 Halutzim, mostly from Poland, were brought into the country. Toward the end of the 1930s, when there was a decline in the membership of HeHalutz, the influence of the respective groups formed by graduates of the youth movements increased still further and HeHalutz actually became a federation of a variety of groups.

Movement in Other Countries. In Romania and the Baltic countries, HeHalutz was even more greatly concerned with pioneer training. On the whole, only persons who were undergoing actual pioneer training were regarded as members of HeHalutz. Also in these countries the influence of the Russian Halutzim was felt in the early 1920s. In Romania the majority of members of HeHalutz were graduates of HaShomer HaTza'ir and Gordonia. They were concentrated mainly in Bessarabia and Bukovina. Training farms existed in Bălți (now Beltsy; Massada), Iași, Galați, and Floriana, near Bucharest.

In Lithuania, HeHalutz maintained a training farm, Kibbush, and also concentrated its members in small groups on estates in the Memel (Klaipeda) district, where pioneer training was conducted on an intergroup basis. In Latvia, where HeHalutz drew its membership from graduates of the youth movements, the Halutzim received their training at five permanent training centers.

In Germany, prior to the rise of Nazism, the members of a small Halutz movement received their training on peasant farms and were loosely organized in an organization named Herut. With the rise of the Nazi regime, the Halutz movement grew and came to embrace large masses, including people who had had no previous Zionist education at all. The members of *B'rit Halutzim Datiyim (Bachad; Association of Religious Pioneers) also participated in the activities of HeHalutz. The efforts of HeHalutz were integrated with the general activities to help German Jewry, and the movement received much support from Jewish aid organizations in Germany and abroad. Training centers for Halutzim were established in Germany

as well as in France, the Netherlands, Yugoslavia, Denmark, Sweden, and England. Halutzim from Germany also joined Halutz training centers in Poland. In 1935 HeHalutz in Germany instituted a training program for members of the 14–17 age group, who with their practical training received a Hebrew and Zionist education. That year, about 4,500 Halutzim from Germany underwent training, one-third of them in centers outside the country.

In the 1930s, nuclei of Halutz movements were established in Austria, Czechoslovakia, England, the United States, Syria, and Egypt.

Development in World War II. With the outbreak of World War II, thousands of Halutzim tried to make their way to Palestine. A large number was concentrated in Vilna, which was then temporarily under Lithuanian rule. About 1,000 of them reached Palestine. In Soviet-occupied Poland, the Baltic states, and Bessarabia, the movement was liquidated, and many of its members were arrested and exiled to various parts of the U.S.S.R. In the German-occupied territories, HeHalutz continued its activities underground. After the Jews had been placed in ghettos, HeHalutz established training groups which became the focal points of its activities. The movement embraced large numbers of youths, who found in their Halutzic groups a substitute for the homes they had lost. The groups found work for them and provided them with food. Meetings and gatherings were held, and a variety of underground literature and periodicals was published. HeHalutz was practically a federation of movements consisting of cells (*D'ror, in which were merged the youth organizations affiliated with the Kibbutz M'uhad, HaShomer HaTza'ir, Gordonia, *HaNo'ar HaTziyoni, *'Akiva, and Mizrahi). The members kept in touch with one another through a coordinating committee. Contact between the ghettos was maintained by emissaries, who went about disguised as non-Jews. Contact was also maintained with central HeHalutz headquarters in Geneva and with the kibbutz movement in Palestine. The Halutz groups rendered aid to various sectors of the ghetto population, especially to intellectuals.

When the Nazi plans for the mass extermination of Jews became known, the Halutz movement recognized the necessity of resistance. It debated the question whether Halutzim should escape from the ghettos and join the guerrilla bands, organized at the time especially in eastern Poland, or whether they should remain in the ghettos to arouse the Jews to passive and active resistance against the Germans. A collection of weapons was begun, and liaison was established with non-Zionist groups (*Bund, Communists) as well as with anti-Nazi circles outside the ghettos. Halutzim played a leading role in the Jewish resistance movement and were among the founders of the Jewish Fighting Organization in Poland. Mordecai *Anilewicz, commander of the Warsaw ghetto revolt, was a member of HaShomer HaTza'ir. Of the 22 fighting units of the ghetto, 12 were recruited from Halutz youth groups. Halutzim led revolts also in other ghettos. After the suppression of the revolts, many of them found their way to guerrilla groups.

In the United States, the Halutz movement increased in strength during World War II. A clandestine Halutz movement was established in Iraq. Many Halutzim, especially from Romania, arrived in Palestine aboard "illegal" ships.

Development in the Postwar Years. With the end of the war, the Halutz movement resumed its activities in Europe. It became the backbone of the large-scale operation of moving hundreds of thousands of survivors from country to country (*B'riha) and of organizing their "illegal" immigration to Palestine. The leaders of the movement were survivors of the prewar HeHalutz and emissaries from the settlement movements in Palestine. The training centers of HeHalutz, which came into being in Poland, Romania, Germany, Hungary, Italy, and other countries, served as transit stations for tens of thousands on their way to ports of illegal emigration. While waiting for their turn to emigrate, the people received hasty agricultural or vocational training, studied Hebrew, searched for relatives, and helped in locating Jewish children sheltered in Christian homes and monasteries where they had been hidden during the war. Prospective immigrants also received premilitary training. HeHalutz activities were aided greatly by international and Jewish relief organizations (UN Relief and Rehabilitation Administration, International Refugee Organization, the *American Jewish Joint Distribution Committee, *ORT).

Immediately after the war, there was a tendency among Halutz youth to establish a unified movement. Nonparty organizations, such as Partizanim-Hayalim-Halutzim and No'ar Halutzi M'uhad, came into being, and an attempt was made to establish common training centers for all groups. This tendency sprang from the wartime conditions which had obliterated all party distinctions and differences. It was also encouraged by the soldiers of the *Jewish Brigade, who contributed much to the rebuilding of the movement. Before long, however, separatist tendencies, nurtured by the emissaries from Palestine, again gained the upper hand, and HeHalutz once more became a federation of different Halutz movements: Gordonia-Maccabi-HaTza'ir, D'ror-Borochów, HaNo'ar HaTziyoni-'Akiva, Ha'Oved, HaShomer HaTza'ir, No'ar Halutzi M'uhad (HaBonim), *Po'ale Agudat Israel, Partizanim-Hayalim-Halutzim, and *Tora va'Avoda. *B'rit Trumpeldor (Betar) was not affiliated with the framework of HeHalutz.

With the Communist seizure of power in Eastern Europe, the Halutz movements, after transferring a considerable part of their membership beyond the borders, discontinued their activities. Especially hard hit was the movement in Romania, where there was still a large Jewish population. HeHalutz branches were closed, and their leaders were arrested, tried on spurious charges, and sentenced to long terms of imprisonment (1949).

In Italy a consolidated entity represented the Halutz movement. Many Halutzim waited for their turn to embark on "illegal" ships. Between 1945 and 1948, 260 Halutzim groups, numbering about 21,000, passed through Italy. They constituted two-thirds of all immigrants who sailed from that country. HeHalutz maintained 75 training centers in Italy, in which a total of 8,650 Halutzim underwent training in 1947.

The organized Halutz groups performed a vital task in encouraging and giving direction to the masses of homeless survivors. They also led political activities such as demonstrations for the right of Jews to emigrate to Palestine. The organizers of B'riha and of illegal immigration relied on them to keep order and discipline in the displaced-persons camps, on the illegal ships, and in Cyprus (see CYPRUS, DETENTION CAMPS IN). Early in 1949, with the conclusion of mass emigration from Central and Eastern Europe, this historic task of the Halutz movement was completed.

Y. SLUTSKY

HEHALUTZ B'ANGLIA (The Pioneer in England). *See* GREAT BRITAIN, ZIONISM IN.

HEHALUTZ HAMIZRAHI. *See* B'NE 'AKIVA.

HEHAVER (Hechaver). Zionist student organization founded in March, 1912, in Bern, Switzerland, at a meeting of Jewish students from Russia. HeHaver societies soon came into being at various universities in Western Europe as well as in Russia, where the movement was illegal. The headquarters of the movement was in Berlin; there its organs, *Yevreiski Student* (in Russian) and *HeHaver* (in Hebrew), were published. At the time of its third general convention, held in Heidelberg in June, 1914, HeHaver had 700 organized student members.

During World War I HeHaver continued its illegal work in Russia. At the beginning of the 1917 Revolution it cooperated with *Tz'ire Zion, but when the latter evolved into a political party, HeHaver decided to continue as a General Zionist organization (*see* GENERAL ZIONISM). In February, 1917, the Sixth HeHaver Convention was held in Petrograd. It declared the aim of the movement to be the "preparation of cadres of a Zionist activist intelligentsia." It also decided to support Maccabi, the Zionist sports organization, and to admit mature high school students to membership. Following the Communist Revolution, HeHaver again became illegal and many of its members were arrested.

In the early 1920s the organization resumed its legal activity and the publication of *Yevreiski Student* (seven issues; March, 1922–May, 1923), but the Yevsektzia (official Jewish section of the Communist party) soon began to harass it and denounce it to the Soviet authorities. Persecution by the authorities and the arrest of its members caused HeHaver to decide on a merger with similar organizations: the Association of Zionist Students of the Ukraine and Kadima of Byelorussia. The decision was ratified by the HeHaver Convention in Leningrad, and the merger was carried out in March, 1924. The united body was called the United All-Russia Organization of Zionist Youth (Russian initials, EVOSM).

Y. SLUTSKY

HEKHAL SH'LOMO. Center for religious activities in Jerusalem, erected with funds donated by Sir Isaac *Wolfson of London in memory of his father, Solomon Wolfson. It was

Hekhal Sh'lomo, Jerusalem. [Israel Government Tourist Office]

Oil spurts from a drilling at Heletz. [Israel Information Services]

dedicated in 1958. The imposing building, situated in the center of Jerusalem, is the seat of the Chief *Rabbinate of Israel and of the Rabbinical Court of Appeals (*see* JUDICIARY IN ISRAEL). It also houses a synagogue, the Central Rabbinical Library (housing about 50,000 volumes), a Museum of Religious Articles, a Department of Religious Information, and the Institute for Halakhic Research and the Study of Jewish Music.

Activities taking place at Hekhal Sh'lomo include study courses, public lectures, and conferences and gatherings devoted to Jewish religion, law, and tradition. The center also organizes and directs funds for the support of *synagogues, *Yeshivot, and Jewish religious endeavors in the country. Publications by the center in 1970 included a monthly bulletin on religious life in Israel and a yearbook, *Shana B'shana*. The officers of Hekhal Sh'lomo in 1970 were Chief Rabbis Yitzhak Rahamim *Nissim and Issar Y'huda *Unterman, Sir Isaac Wolfson, Hayim Moshe *Shapira, Minister of the Interior and Health, Zerah *Wahrhaftig, Minister of Religious Affairs, Nahum Z. Williams, and Maurice A. Jaffe.   A. PECHENIK

HELETZ. Village (moshav) in the Darom. Founded in 1950 and affiliated with *T'nu'at HaMoshavim. In 1955 oil was discovered in the vicinity of the settlement. Population (1968): 520.

HELLER, JAMES GUTHEIM. Rabbi, composer, and Zionist leader in the United States (b. New Orleans, 1892). A graduate of Tulane University and the University of Cincinnati (M.A.,

(1914), Heller was ordained by the Hebrew Union College (1916), served briefly as a chaplain with the United States Army in France during World War I, and held pulpits in Philadelphia (Knesseth Israel, 1916–18), Little Rock (1919–20), and Cincinnati (Isaac M. Wise Temple, 1920–52).

For a time, Heller was professor of musicology at the Cincinnati Conservatory of Music, from which he received the degree of Mus.D. in 1935, and composed a number of works, including several pieces of synagogue music. From 1941 to 1943 he was president of the Central Conference of American Rabbis.

Active in Zionism from his youth, Heller was chairman of the *United Palestine Appeal (1941–46), vice-president of the *Zionist Organization of America (1943–45), and national president of the Labor Zionist Organization of America (*see* PO'ALE ZION IN AMERICA; 1952–54). From 1954 to 1965 he served as chairman of community relations for the *State of Israel Bonds Organization. He wrote numerous articles for the *New Palestine* and a book, *Isaac M. Wise: His Life, Work and Thought* (1965), in which he devoted a chapter to Wise's attitude toward Zionism.

HELSINGFORS CONFERENCE. Third conference of Russian Zionists, held from Dec. 4 to 10, 1906 (Nov. 21 to 27, 1906, in the Russian calendar), in Helsingfors (Helsinki), in the Grand Duchy of Finland. It could not be held in Russia itself because of the suspicious attitude of the Russian government toward the Zionist movement and because of the Tsarist restrictions on freedom of speech. The conference, which was attended by about 80 delegates from 56 localities, was presided over by Yehiel *Tschlenow. Discussion centered on the three programmatic speeches, by Tschlenow (general survey of problems), Boris *Goldberg (practical work in Palestine), and Itzhak *Grünbaum (Zionism and political activity in Russia).

Resolutions of the conference included a call to the *World Zionist Organization to engage in planned practical activity in Palestine (which had already been approved by the 7th Zionist *Congress, 1905) parallel with its political endeavors. To promote settlement work the conference recommended the establishment of a Palestine institute to study conditions in the country, guide settlement activities, and render assistance to individuals as well as groups interested in living and working in Palestine or in investing capital there. Other recommendations along these lines included the establishment of a network of institutions to aid Jewish workers in Palestine and the founding of an agricultural bank.

With regard to the participation of Zionism in political activities within Russia, the conference adopted resolutions formulated by a committee headed by Vladimir *Jabotinsky and calling for the democratization of the Russian state, the granting of full and equal rights to the Jewish population, the assurance of fair representation for minority groups in all elections, the recognition of Russian Jewry as a separate nationality group with autonomous national rights, the convening of a Jewish national assembly for the purpose of creating a national organization in Russia, the right to use the two Jewish languages (Hebrew and Yiddish) in public life, and the right to observe the Saturday Sabbath in lieu of the compulsory Sunday rest. Nonetheless, there were Zionist leaders who at the conference and afterward criticized this decision on political as well as tactical grounds. They branded it a departure from basic Zionist ideology, which, they claimed, called for the concentration of all efforts on Jewish settlement in Palestine.

At the Fourth All-Russia Zionist Conference, which met at the time of the 8th Zionist Congress in August, 1907, at The Hague, far-reaching amendments of the Helsingfors resolutions were demanded. In the end, however, the conference adopted the Helsingfors resolutions in their entirety.

T. PRESCHEL

HEMED. Village (moshav) southeast of Tel Aviv. Founded in 1950 by Orthodox ex-servicemen and affiliated with HaPo'el HaMizrahi (*see* MIZRAHI). Population (1968): 495.

HEN (HeN). Abbreviation of the Hebrew words Hel Nashim, or Women's Army (*see* ISRAEL DEFENSE FORCES).

HEPTAPEGON. *See* TABGHA.

HEREV L'ET. Village (moshav) in the Sharon Plain. Founded in 1947 by ex-servicemen of World War II and affiliated with the *Ihud Haklai. Its name, "From Sword to Ploughshare," is derived from Isaiah 2:4. Population (1968): 249.

HERLITZ, GEORGE JOSEPH. Director of the Central Zionist Archives in Jerusalem (b. Oppeln, Germany, 1885; d. Jerusalem, 1968). Educated in both Jewish and general studies, Herlitz received his doctorate in 1909. That same year he was

elected to the Presidium of the Zionist student organization *Kartell Jüdischer Verbindungen in Berlin, serving in that capacity until 1916. In 1911 he began working in the General Archives of German Jewry. He became vice-chairman of the Zionist Association of Berlin in 1919. That year Arthur *Hantke invited him to organize the archives of the *World Zionist Organization (*see* LIBRARIES AND ARCHIVES, ZIONIST). In 1933 he moved to Jerusalem with the archives, which he continued to head until his retirement.

From 1920 to 1930 Herlitz and Dr. Bruno Kirschner edited the *Jüdisches Lexikon*. From the 17th Zionist *Congress (Basle, 1931) until the 23d (Jerusalem, 1951), with the exception of the 18th, Herlitz served as secretary of the Congress Presidium, and from 1927 to 1930 he participated in the Zionist *Actions Committee meetings as recording secretary. He wrote many articles about German Jewry and Zionist history. In 1949 he published *Das Jahr der Zionisten* (The Year of the Zionists), and in 1964 *Mein Weg nach Jerusalem* (My Road to Jerusalem), his memoirs.

N. M. GELBER

HERRMANN, HUGO. Editor, author, and Zionist leader in Czechoslovakia and Israel (b. Moravská Třebová, Moravia, Austria, 1887, d. Jerusalem, 1940). Raised in an assimilated, pro-German environment, Herrmann studied philology at the Universities of Vienna and Prague. During his student days he developed an interest in Zionism and became a leader of the Prague *Bar Kokhba student Zionist organization. Between 1909 and 1912 he was secretary of the Zionist Organization of Bohemia. He then went to Berlin, where he edited the *Jüdische Rundschau until 1914. After serving as an officer in the Austro-Hungarian Army in World War I, he founded (1919) in Moravská Ostrava the *Jüdisches Volksblatt*, which he edited until 1922. Subsequently he was the director of the *Keren HaYesod (Palestine Foundation Fund) in Czechoslovakia, a position he held until he settled in Palestine in 1934.

Herrmann wrote a large number of essays, brochures, and books on Palestine and Zionism. His Zionist writings include *Palästinakunde* (1935), a handbook on Palestine, and *Keren HaYesod: The Beginning of a Jewish Public Treasury* (1939). Among his other writings is *In Jenen Tagen* (In Those Days, 1938), an autobiography. Herrmann also participated in the organization of Zionist Congresses (*see* CONGRESS, ZIONIST) between the two world wars.

HERRMANN, LEO. Secretary-general of *Keren HaYesod (b. Lanškroun, Bohemia, Austria, 1888; d. Tel Aviv, 1951). In 1908–09 Herrmann was president of *Bar Kokhba, the Zionist student organization of Prague. Between that year and 1910 he was instrumental in organizing public meetings on Jewish national and general issues which brought to Prague such men as Felix Salten, Martin *Buber, Jacob Wassermann, Berthold *Feiwel, and Aaron *Aaronson and was thus able to elevate Bar Kokhba to the level of a spiritual Zionist center.

Herrmann's speeches and articles appeared in the *Jüdische Volksstimme* (Brno), the *Jüdische Zeitung* (Vienna), and *Selbstwehr* (Prague). Some of his reminiscences are recorded in the volume *Prag Virushalayim* (Prague and Jerusalem), published in 1953 in his memory. Becoming editor of *Selbstwehr* in 1910, Herrmann fashioned it into a literary and political Zionist weekly of high standards. In 1913 he was appointed secretary of the Zionist *Executive in Berlin. At the time of the *Language War (1913–14) he wrote a pamphlet, *Der Kampf um die hebräische Sprache* (The Struggle for the Hebrew Language). During World War I (1914–19) he was editor of the *Jüdische Rundschau*.

In 1919 the Secretariat of the Zionist Executive was transferred from Berlin to London, and Herrmann continued to serve as its secretary. With the establishment of the Keren HaYesod (Palestine Foundation Fund) in 1920, he was made its secretary-general and continued to serve in that capacity after the organization's headquarters was moved to Jerusalem (1926) until his death.

N. M. GELBER

HERSHBERG, ABRAHAM SH'MUEL. Writer (b. Kolno, Łomża District, Russian Poland, 1859; d. Białystok ghetto, 1943). An adherent of the *Hoveve Zion movement, he worked closely with Rabbi Sh'muel *Mohilever. When an economic crisis forced him to close his textile factory in Białystok in 1899, he spent 18 months traveling in Palestine. He recorded his impressions in *Mishpat HaYishuv HeHadash B'Eretz Yisrael* (1901) and *B'Eretz HaMizrah* (1910). On his return to Białystok, he devoted himself to cultural and literary affairs. He contributed to numerous Hebrew and Yiddish periodicals and wrote Jewish historical studies. He also helped found the Hevrat Tora (Tora Society) in his city and lectured there on Judaism and Jewish history. From 1913 to 1914 he edited the *Białystoker Togblat*. He was killed in World War II.

Y. RAPHAEL

HERTZ, JOSEPH HERMAN. Chief Rabbi of the United Hebrew Congregations of the British Empire (b. Rebrin, Slovakia, Hungary, 1872; d. London, 1946). Brought to New York at the age of 12, he was graduated from the Jewish Theological Seminary of America in 1894 and held a pulpit in Syracuse, N.Y., from 1894 to 1898. He then became rabbi of the Witwatersrand Old Hebrew Congregation in Johannesburg, South Africa, where he served until 1913, when he was appointed Chief Rabbi.

As ecclesiastic head of British Jewry, Hertz was an advocate of enlightened Orthodoxy. He was a stanch upholder of Jewish rights, spoke out against the persecution of Jews on the Continent, and aided Jewish refugees in Britain. In the period between the two world wars he was the leading personality in Jewry's fight against the calendar reform which might have imperiled the observance of the Sabbath.

An early Zionist, Hertz was a cofounder of the South African Zionist Federation (see SOUTH AFRICA, ZIONISM IN). During World War I he was concerned in the efforts to make the British government support the Jewish national aspirations in Palestine. In May, 1917, he published in the London *Times* a protest against a statement by the Conjoint Foreign Committee of the *Board of Deputies of British Jews and the *Anglo-Jewish Association, which had appeared in that paper a few days earlier and expressed objection to the aims of political Zionism.

Hertz was one of a small group of prominent Jews who were consulted by the British government prior to the issuance of the *Balfour Declaration. His statement that the proposed declaration would mark an epoch in Jewish history and would be received with joy by the overwhelming majority of British Jewry carried much weight with the British Cabinet.

Hertz was associated with many facets of the work of Jewish

reconstruction in Palestine and did not hesitate to criticize British anti-Zionist policies. In 1925 he attended the opening of the *Hebrew University of Jerusalem and became a member of its Board of Governors. He served as president of the Mizrahi Organization of Great Britain and Ireland (see GREAT BRITAIN, ZIONISM IN; MIZRAHI) and headed a variety of educational and cultural Anglo-Jewish organizations. Hertz was the author of a number of books, including commentaries on the Pentateuch and the Daily Prayer Book. His anthology, *A Book of Jewish Thoughts* (1917), was printed in numerous editions and translated into several other languages.

J. FRAENKEL

HERUT. Village (moshav) in the Sharon Plain. Established in 1930 and affiliated with *T'nu'at HaMoshavim. The name, meaning "freedom," was adopted in memory of Judea's struggle for freedom in the 2d century of the Common Era under the leadership of Bar Kokhba. Population (1968): 372.

HERUT (newspaper). Official daily organ of the *Herut party. The paper, which made its first appearance on Rosh HaShana Eve, 1948, was a continuation of the underground publication of the *Irgun Tz'vai L'umi. It bore on its masthead the slogans of the party it represented: "For an Undivided Motherland; for the Ingathering of the Exiles; for Social Justice; for the Freedom of the Individual."

The leading writers and publicists of the Revisionist movement (see REVISIONISTS) either joined the editorial staff or became permanent contributors. Among them were Uri Zvi *Greenberg, Abba *Ahimeir, Z'ev (Wolfgang) *von Weisl, Michael Berchin, and Joseph *Schechtman. A weekly article by M'nahem *Begin, head of the party, expounded Herut's official position on problems of Israel's foreign and internal politics. Literary and economic supplements appeared weekly.

Jacob A. Rubin served as the first editor of *Herut*. In 1957 Isaac Remba became editor. In 1966 *Herut* ceased publication. It was succeeded by *HaYom, which represents the views of Gahal (Herut-Liberal bloc).

J. RUBIN

HERUT (full name, T'nu'at HaHerut, or Freedom Movement). Israeli political party founded by the *Irgun Tz'vai L'umi in 1948 after the Proclamation of the State of Israel and the dissolution of the Irgun. Although Zionist Revisionist in outlook and origin (see REVISIONISTS), it ignored the Revisionist movement in Israel and its leadership and set up an independent party. The elections to the First *Knesset in 1949 were contested by the two groups independently. In 1949, after prolonged negotiations, Herut became an integral part of the World Union of Zionists-Revisionists (B'rit Herut-HaTzohar). In the elections to the First Knesset it secured 14 seats.

Aims. Herut advocates the unification of Eretz Yisrael within its historic boundaries and the promulgation of a written constitution for the State of Israel. The party favors a self-supporting national economy based on private initiative, free competition, and replacement of the prevailing system of economic sectors (comprising *Histadrut-controlled economy, State-controlled enterprises, and privately managed enterprises) by an integrated national economy, subordinated to one legal code. Its program urges the separation, in both theory and practice, of the economic enterprises of the Histadrut (General Federation of Labor) from the purely trade union functions of the federation and the transfer of commercial, industrial, financial, and other enterprises owned by the Histadrut to workers' co-operatives set up for that purpose. It wishes to encourage private initiative in all fields of the national economy without restrictive supervision.

Herut's fiscal policy envisages the termination of the special tax privileges enjoyed by Histadrut enterprises and by the kibbutzim, while allowing for special tax relief and other benefits to border settlements.

Herut stresses the right of workers to form trade unions of their own choice and advocates State-owned medical service and unemployment insurance. Rejecting the practice of strikes as a means of settling conflicts between labor and capital, it advances the principle of compulsory national arbitration in vital industries and services between disputes. It demands the dissolution and nationalization of existing sick funds (see KUPAT HOLIM; KUPAT HOLIM L'OVDIM L'UMIYIM) and their amalgamation into a State Health Service.

In the area of *immigration and immigrant absorption, Herut advocates the creation of social, economic, and political conditions conducive to immigration from the countries of the free world. Relief funds contributed by world Jewry and intended for the absorption of new immigrants are to be devoted exclusively to this purpose, including vocational training and guidance for immigrants and their integration in the life of the country. Herut urges political efforts to obtain reparations for confiscated property of immigrants from Arab countries.

Developments in the 1960s. In 1963 the Herut Conference decided to form in the Histadrut a Herut faction under the name T'khelet-Lavan (Blue-White). In 1965 T'khelet-Lavan concluded an electoral agreement with the liberal faction in the Histadrut, Irgun Ha'Ovdim (Workers' Organization), and the two factions obtained 15.2 per cent of the votes, returning 122 of the 801 delegates to the Histadrut Conference.

In 1965 Herut entered into a parliamentary and electoral bloc with the *Liberal party, under the name Gush Herut-Liberalim (*Gahal), to participate in elections to the Knesset and the Histadrut. The Gahal slate received 26 (15 Herut, 11 Liberal) of the 120 Knesset seats. In the 1969 Knesset elections it also received 26 seats.

The supreme governing body of Herut is the biannual conference elected by direct representation in the branches. The conference elects the chairman of the movement and the Central Committee, which, in turn, nominates the Executive. The T'khelet-Lavan faction, representing Herut in the Histadrut, was headed by Arye *Ben Eliezer, Deputy Speaker of the Knesset. Among the leaders of Herut are Yohanan *Bader, M'nahem *Begin (chairman of the Central Committee), Hayim Landau, and Ya'akov *Meridor. Herut representatives sit on municipal councils and in the *World Jewish Congress. Affiliated with Herut are *B'rit Trumpeldor (Betar), a youth organization, B'rit Nashim Herut, a women's association, and Ahdut Israel, an autonomous religious association.

The Herut movement maintained in the 1960s 14 rural settlements, most of them border villages, including M'vo Betar Nordiya, and Bar Giyora, as well as youth farms in B'er Ya'akov and Herzliya. The movement published magazines and newspapers in various languages, among them the daily *Herut (until 1966, when it was replaced by *HaYom), in Hebrew; El Hurriya, a weekly in Arabic; La Liberté, a weekly in French; Freiheit, in German; and papers in Hungarian, Romanian, Polish, Yiddish, and other languages.

At the 1966 convention of Herut a controversy arose, as a result of which three members of the Knesset seceded from Herut. In 1967 they and their followers, led by Sh'muel Tamir and Eliezer Shostak, general secretary of the *Histadrut Ha-'Ovdim HaL'umit, formed a new political grouping, HaMerkaz HaHofshi (Free Center). It received 2 seats in the 1969 Knesset elections.

I. BENARI

HERZBERG, ABEL L. Attorney and Zionist leader in the Netherlands (b. Amsterdam, 1893). He was chairman of the Dutch Zionist Students' Organization in Amsterdam and, later, of the Amsterdam branch of the Dutch Zionist Federation. In 1931 he became a member, and from 1934 to 1939 was chairman, of the Dutch Zionist Executive. He was active as a speaker and writer for the Zionist cause. Returning from Bergen-Belsen after World War II, he became known also in non-Jewish circles for his writings and addresses in behalf of the State of Israel.

HERZL, THEODOR. Father of political Zionism and founder of the *World Zionist Organization (b. Pest, Hungary, May 2, 1860; d. Edlach, Austria, July 3, 1904). Raised in a well-to-do, conservative family, Herzl may have heard in his youth about the proto-Zionist ideas of Rabbis Judah S. H. *Alkalai and Joseph *Natonek and about a relative of his who had settled in Jerusalem and died there; but in general his education was in the spirit of the German-Jewish enlightenment then prevailing. He attended a Jewish elementary school and subsequently a public high school in his native city. In 1878, after the death of his only sister Pauline, he moved to Vienna with his parents and entered the Law School of the university of that city. In 1881 he joined Albia, a German student fraternity, but resigned two years later in protest against its anti-Semitic attitude (see ANTI-SEMITISM). This protest was not an accidental outburst. The Jewish problem had engaged Herzl from at least 1882, when he read Karl Eugen Dühring's anti-Semitic book Die Judenfrage als Rassen- Sitten- und Culturfrage (The Jewish Problem as a Question of Race, Morals, and Culture), and he returned again and again to the Jewish problem in renewed efforts to find a solution for it.

Herzl's birthplace on Tabak Street in Budapest (at left, next to the synagogue). [Zionist Archives]

In 1884 he completed his law studies but shortly afterward abandoned the legal profession, devoting himself entirely to literature. From 1885 on he published feuilletons and short stories characterized by a delicate style and penetrating observations on the fate of man in the modern world. These were favorably received, and selections from them appeared in a series of books: *Neues von der Venus* (News about Venus, 1887); *Buch der Narrheit* (Book of Folly, 1888); *Philosophische Erzählungen* (Philosophical Stories, 1900); and *Feuilletons* (2 vols., 1903). He also wrote a number of plays, several of which were successfully performed in Vienna, Berlin, Prague, and many other places, including New York. In these plays he dealt—sometimes in serious and sometimes in humorous vein—with the problems of contemporary society. The most important of them were *Tabarin* (1884; successfully performed in New York, November, 1885); *Seine Hoheit* (His Highness [the Money], 1885); *Wilddiebe* (The Poachers, jointly with H. Wittmann, 1888); *Was wird man sagen?* (What Will They Say?, 1890); *Prinzen aus Genieland* (Princes from the Land of Genius, 1892); *Die Glosse* (The Gloss, 1895): *Das neue Ghetto* (The *New Ghetto, 1894; 1898); *Unser Käthchen* (Our Katie, 1899); *Gretel* (1899); and *Solon in Lydien* (Solon in Lydia, 1904).

In 1889 Herzl married Julie Naschauer (1868–1907). The union was not a happy one, partly because of his wife's inability to understand Herzl's aspirations and partly because of Herzl's uncommon attachment to his parents, especially to his mother, and later, his consuming devotion to his Zionist work. There were three children: Pauline (1890–1930), Hans (1891–1930), and Margarethe, called Trude (1893–1943).

From October, 1891, until July, 1895, Herzl served as Paris correspondent of the *Neue Freie Presse*, a liberal and influential Viennese daily. He took a great interest in the social and national problems of France, with particular attention to French parliamentary life. A small selection of his writings on this topic appeared in book form under the title *Das Palais Bourbon* (1895). The increase of anti-Semitism in France served to deepen Herzl's interest in the Jewish problem. His first article on the subject, entitled "French Anti-Semites," appeared in the *Neue Freie Presse* in 1892. About a year later he spoke of the Jewish problem as a social question to be solved either by having the younger generation baptized *en masse* in an organized effort or by having them all join the Socialist movement. But he soon realized the futility of these ideas, and in his play *Das neue Ghetto*, which he wrote in the fall of 1894, in an attempt to stimulate free public discussion of the Jewish problem by presenting it on the stage, he rejected *assimilation and conversion as effective means to the attainment of the desired end: mutual tolerance and understanding between Jews and gentiles.

The Dreyfus trial, which opened in Paris at this time and which Herzl attended as a journalist, further clarified his views (*see* DREYFUS AFFAIR). The humiliating ceremony at the École Militaire (January, 1895) in which the innocent Jewish captain was stripped of his rank and drummed out of the army, to the accompaniment of the cries of the mob, "Death to the Jews," convinced him that the only solution to the Jewish problem would be a Jewish exodus from countries infested with anti-Semitism and the concentration of the Jews in their own territory.

In May, 1895, he asked Baron Maurice de *Hirsch, the leading Jewish philanthropist of his time, for an interview to

Herzl in Basle. [Zionist Archives]

discuss the Jewish problem. However, their conversation on June 2, which was the beginning of Herzl's Zionist activity, yielded no practical results. During this period Herzl worked on the details of his plan, at first in the form of a written "Address to the Rothschilds," in which he aimed to impress upon the international Jewish banking family that its vast fortune could be preserved only by dedicating it to the financing of his plan (which Herzl unfolded in detail) of the settlement of the Jews in a state of their own. However, the plan was never presented to the Rothschilds in this form.

In July, 1895, after having been released at his own request from his post in Paris, Herzl returned to Vienna, where he became feuilleton editor of the *Neue Freie Presse*. On August 17, Herzl met in Munich with Dr. Moritz *Güdemann, chief rabbi of Vienna, and Heinrich Meyer-Cohn, a Berlin banker and member of *Hoveve Zion, and read to them his "Address to the Rothschilds." Güdemann was deeply impressed at first but later retreated from, and finally even expressed publicly his opposition to, Herzl's plan. Herzl was also not successful in his attempts in Vienna, Paris, and London during the second half of 1895 to persuade Jewish leaders to make a serious study of his plan. The only important result of his talks was that he won over Max *Nordau, who placed his reputation, his forceful pen, and his oratorical talents at the service of Herzl and Zionism.

Convinced that he must present his project directly to the public, he reworked his "Address to the Rothschilds" into a treatise entitled *Der Judenstaat* (The *Jewish State), which was published in Vienna in February, 1896. In that same year Hebrew, English, French, Russian, and Romanian translations appeared. In his treatise Herzl analyzed the Jewish question and suggested the establishment of a Jewish State as its only solution. As the first step he envisaged the securing of the political basis; as the second, the organized mass *immigration of Jews into their new country.

The book set off a variety of reactions. The majority of the Jews of Western Europe, from the extreme assimilationists to the extreme Orthodox, rejected Herzl's basic premise and his practical project of a Jewish State. Even some of the Hoveve Zion of Western and Eastern Europe regarded his plan as too far-reaching. Many of the Hoveve Zion, however, as well as the Zionist students of Austria and other countries, hailed Herzl's ideas with enthusiasm. Thus, within a short period, Herzl became the leader of a political movement, which adopted the name Zionist movement. Through his contacts with the Hoveve Zion and the Jewish masses, especially those of Eastern Europe, Herzl came to recognize that only Palestine had the power of attraction necessary for the establishment of the Jewish State, although in his *Judenstaat* he had not yet regarded it as the only possibility.

He began political action at once. Through the good offices of Rev. William H. *Hechler, Herzl received an audience on Apr. 23, 1896, from Grand Duke Frederick I of Baden, who from then on was a warm supporter of Zionism. That June Herzl went to Constantinople, where Philip Michael de Newlinski, a Polish and Austrian diplomatic agent, arranged an audience for him with the Grand Vizier. Herzl proposed to the Vizier that the Jews would undertake to straighten out the precarious financial situation of Turkey in return for an independent Jewish Palestine. When this proposal was rejected, Herzl substituted a request for permission for the establishment of a Jewish State in Palestine as a Turkish dependency. From 1898 on, Herzl tried to obtain a *Charter for the establishment of a systematically organized large Jewish settlement in Palestine enjoying internal autonomy and the right of self-defense.

While Herzl received an enthusiastic welcome from the Jews of many lands, he failed to win the support of the leaders of Anglo-Jewry, of the British Hoveve Zion, and of the Executive of the *Jewish Colonization Association (ICA). Baron Edmond de *Rothschild, on whose attitude the stand of the communal leaders and of the Hoveve Zion of Western Europe largely depended, rejected Herzl's plan in a decisive interview in Paris on July 18, 1896, giving as his reason the impossibility of organizing the Jewish masses. This setback contributed to Herzl's decision to organize the Jewish masses in behalf of the Jewish State in Palestine. On Mar. 6, 1897, a preliminary meeting of representatives of Hoveve Zion societies from Germany, Austria, and Galicia decided at the suggestion of Herzl to convene a general Zionist *Congress. Herzl's success in convening the Congress as the "National Assembly of the Jewish People" despite opposition even from many adherents of Hoveve Zion was due to his tireless energy and unusual powers of persuasion. To spread the Zionist idea Herzl founded *Die Welt*, a weekly, the first issue of which appeared on June 4, 1897. It was financed personally by Herzl, who was its chief editor.

The 1st Zionist Congress, which met in Basle, Aug. 29–31, 1897, formulated the program of Zionism (see BASLE PROGRAM) and established the World Zionist Organization as the political instrument of the "Jewish people on the way" to its state. Herzl presided over these sessions as well as the next five Congresses, and was elected president of the Zionist Organization, a post he held until his death.

From that time on, despite a heart ailment aggravated by overwork, and opposition from outside the movement and from within, Herzl persistently strove to attain two principal aims: (1) the establishment of a Homeland for the Jewish people in Palestine with the permission of the Great Powers and of Turkey, to be achieved through diplomatic negotiations; and (2) the development of the Zionist Organization into a force to be reckoned with in political and financial negotiations with the outside world and into an instrument capable of carrying out the work of settling Palestine.

Shortly after the 1st Congress, Herzl laid the groundwork for a bank with a founding capital of £2,000,000 as a financial basis for his negotiations with the Turkish government. He assumed that after the successful completion of his negotiations, those financial institutions which would be needed for the development of the country and for the organization of emigration and settlement would be established as subsidiary companies of the bank. At the 2d Congress (Aug. 28–31, 1898) a resolution calling for the establishment of the bank was passed, and the decision was acted on in March, 1899. The bank, with headquarters in London, was named the *Jewish Colonial Trust; in 1903 a subsidiary company, the Anglo-Palestine Bank, was opened in Jaffa (see BANK L'UMI L'YISRAEL). Since the great Jewish banks, whose owners opposed political Zionism, did not participate in the enterprise, the Zionist Organization was able to raise only £250,000, a larger sum than had ever been raised by a Zionist association before but small in comparison with the important part Herzl expected the bank to play in his plans. His inability to gain the sympathy and active support of wealthy Jews proved the greatest impediment in Herzl's political work and was perhaps the main cause of his failure to achieve his aim during his lifetime despite partial political successes.

In September, 1898, shortly after the Congress, Herzl, through the mediation of the Grand Duke of Baden, succeeded in winning the sympathy of the German emperor *Wilhelm II for Zionism. In September, the Emperor notified Herzl through Philipp zu Eulenburg, the German Ambassador to Vienna, that he was ready to receive Herzl in audience in Jerusalem during his forthcoming visit to Palestine. Wilhelm first received Herzl in Constantinople (Oct. 18, 1898) and told him that he was willing to commend the Zionist movement to the Sultan and to assume patronage of the Settlement Company for Palestine and Syria, which Herzl planned to establish.

In Palestine, Herzl was enthusiastically greeted by the Jewish settlers of Mikve Yisrael, Rishon L'Tziyon, Nes Tziyona, and Rehovot. In Mikve Yisrael the German Emperor and his entourage stopped to greet Herzl. However, Herzl's official interview with the Emperor, which took place on Nov. 2, 1898, in the latter's tent near Jerusalem, did not yield the results Herzl had expected. This was due mainly to Count Bernhard von Bülow, Germany's Foreign Minister, who, in turn, was influenced by the opposition of Jewish banking circles to Zionism and by the antagonism displayed by influential Jews in Germany and the majority of Jewish newspapers and journalists. Although the Emperor stated in his reply to Herzl's address that he looked with favor on the efforts of the Zionist movement to resettle Palestine and even promised to study the matter further, he gave no further attention to the movement during the remainder of Herzl's life.

Herzl's personal political efforts in Constantinople also brought no positive results. On the recommendation of Arminius *Vámbéry, who was very close to the Imperial court, Sultan *'Abdul Hamid II granted an audience to Herzl on May 17, 1901, and requested him to submit to him in writing proposals for Jewish financial aid to Turkey. However, Herzl was unsuccessful again in persuading the Jewish financiers to put the needed funds at his disposal, with the result that no progress was made in the negotiations.

In the middle of February, 1902, Herzl was again invited to Constantinople. He stayed there as the guest of the Sultan but was not granted a second personal interview. He was offered permission to set up isolated Jewish settlements in various parts of the Ottoman Empire, particularly in Mesopotamia, but since Palestine was explicitly excluded, Herzl rejected the offer. That July Herzl was invited to Constantinople once again, but the negotiations brought him no closer to his aim.

As a result, Herzl decided to shift the center of his political activity to Great Britain, whose importance to Zionism he had realized from the very beginning. For this reason, he had envisaged the establishment of the Zionist financial institutions as companies registered in Great Britain. In order to gain the sympathy of British statesmen and of the British public, Herzl convened the 4th Zionist Congress (1900) in London. With the aid of Leopold J. *Greenberg, the Jewish journalist who had become his faithful lieutenant, he established contact with the British government. Invited to London in June, 1902, to testify as an expert before a Royal Commission appointed to investigate the immigration of aliens (meaning Jews) into England, Herzl conferred with Lord Rothschild, head of the British branch of the banking house (see ROTHSCHILDS: BRITISH BRANCH). Lord Rothschild, though opposed to the plans for

Jewish settlement in Palestine, showed an interest in the settlement of Jews in territories of the British Empire. In his testimony before the Royal Commission Herzl indicated that the problem of large-scale Jewish immigration to England would be solved if the British government were to set aside a strip of territory for the establishment of an autonomous Jewish settlement. He stated that while the aim of Zionism as formulated in the Basle Program was to establish an autonomous Jewish settlement in Palestine, the Zionist movement, in view of the urgency of the problem, would consider itself obligated to try also other means of aiding the Jewish victims of oppression. The following day Herzl informed the chairman of the Commission in a private conversation that the areas he had in mind for settlement were Cyprus and the Sinai Peninsula, territories adjacent to Palestine and governed by Britain, which had been called to his attention years before by Davis *Trietsch. In view of the breakdown of negotiations with the Turkish government, Herzl thought it proper to confer with the British for the granting of a Charter for Jewish settlement in these territories, which were considered as belonging historically to Palestine. He believed that in this way he would soon be able to start colonization activities, which were being demanded by an ever-increasing number of Zionists in view of the lack of progress in the political arena. He hoped, too, that the establishment of the Jews in a territory adjoining Palestine would induce the Turkish government to grant concessions there.

In an interview with Herzl on Oct. 22, 1902, Joseph *Chamberlain, the British Colonial Secretary, rejected the idea of a Jewish settlement in Cyprus but favored Herzl's plan with

Herzl en route to Palestine in 1898. With him are David Wolffsohn, Moritz T. Schnirer, and Max Bodenheimer. [Zionist Archives]

regard to the Sinai Peninsula, going so far as to commend it to Lord Lansdowne, the British Foreign Secretary. As a result of these talks, Herzl was requested by the British Foreign Office on Dec. 18, 1902, to send an investigation commission to the Sinai Peninsula. He was promised that if the report of the commission should prove favorable, the British government would commend the plan to the Egyptian government. The commission found that settlement in Sinai and in El-'Arish was feasible, if the Egyptian government were to agree to channel considerable quantities of Nile water to these regions (*see* EL-'ARISH SCHEME). Following protracted negotiations conducted by Herzl, Leopold J. Greenberg, and Col. Albert Edward Williamson *Goldsmid with Lord *Cromer, the British High Commissioner in Egypt, and the Egyptian government, Cromer and the Egyptians rejected the plan, whereupon the British withdrew their support.

On May 20, 1903, Greenberg, in a talk with Chamberlain, again brought up the proposal of a Jewish settlement in Cyprus, but Chamberlain was of the opinion that the island was not suitable for an autonomous Jewish settlement. He referred instead to a territory in East Africa, as he had already done in his talk with Herzl on Apr. 23, 1903, at which time Herzl had rejected it (*see* EAST AFRICA SCHEME). However, under the impact of the *Kishinev pogrom, Herzl saw himself justified in continuing the negotiations based on Chamberlain's suggestion. Political, practical, and tactical considerations contributed to this decision. Herzl believed that if in this way the ties between the Zionist Organization and England were to be strengthened, England would come to recognize the Jews as a nation in the political sense and would eventually assist in the realization of the Zionist program. Herzl also believed that the East Africa plan would induce Turkey to make greater concessions with regard to Palestine lest it lose the aid of Jewish capital. Finally, Herzl saw in this plan a means of transforming the frantic flight of the Jews from Russia into an organized immigration movement to a country that could serve as a base of sorts for the center which eventually would rise in Palestine.

At the same time, however, Herzl continued his direct efforts for Palestine. On Aug. 5, 1903, he went to Russia to plead for the Jews there and to obtain Russia's support in Constantinople for the Zionist demands regarding Palestine. He was received twice by Baron Vyacheslav K. von Plehve, the Russian Minister

Herzl's study in Vienna. [Zionist Archives]

of the Interior, who promised him that his government would commend Zionism to the Sultan. On this journey Herzl was enthusiastically greeted by the Jewish masses of Russia, particularly in Vilna. While Herzl was in Russia, Greenberg received the British government's declaration of Aug. 14, 1903, that if an investigating commission sent out by the Zionist Organization were to find an area in East Africa suitable for Jewish settlement, the British government would authorize the establishment there of an autonomous Jewish settlement ruled by a Jewish governor under the British Crown.

With the consent of the *Actions Committee of the Zionist Organization, Herzl submitted the East Africa proposal to the 6th Zionist Congress (Basle, Aug. 23–28, 1903). Although he made it clear in his opening address that the proposal in no way changed the ultimate aim of Zionism, the project aroused bitter opposition, especially among the delegates from Russia. When the Congress nevertheless decided to establish a committee to advise the Inner Actions Committee with regard to the sending of the investigating commission to East Africa, the opponents of the plan walked out of the hall. By reassuring the dissidents that he had not for a moment abandoned his efforts for Palestine, Herzl was able to prevent a split in the movement.

After that Congress, Herzl continued his negotiations for Palestine with the Great Powers. He corresponded with Von Plehve, who sent instructions to the Russian Ambassador in Turkey. Herzl himself submitted new suggestions to the Turkish government. In January, 1904, he had talks with the Pope, King Victor Emmanuel III of Italy, and the Italian government without positive results. At the same time he continued his negotiations with the British government in a vain attempt to revive the Sinai scheme. The vehement struggle of the Zionist opposition, led by M'nahem M. *Ussishkin, Yehiel *Tschlenow, and *Ahad Ha'Am, against him made it difficult for Herzl to abandon the East Africa project openly. At the initiative of Ussishkin, who was in Palestine at the time of the 6th Congress, the Russian members of the Actions Committee met in November, 1903, in Kharkov (*see* KHARKOV CONFERENCE) and decided, among other things, to send a delegation to Herzl, demanding from him a written promise to abandon the East Africa project and any other scheme for the establishment of a Jewish settlement outside Palestine. Herzl refused to see the delegates as a formal delegation and to receive their ultimatum. After several months of struggle and polemics in the Zionist press and at public meetings, Herzl decided to convene the Greater Actions Committee to clarify the controversy. The meeting, which took place on Apr. 11–12, 1904, in Vienna, was stormy, but Herzl ultimately succeeded in reassuring the opposition and thus preserving the unity of the Zionist Organization.

The incessant strain and struggles further weakened Herzl's ailing heart. Immediately after the meeting he was forced to go to Franzensbad for a cure. His condition did not improve, however, and he returned to Vienna. He then went to Edlach, a resort, where he died of pneumonia on July 3, 1904, at the age of 44, leaving his family without means since he had spent all his personal funds for the Zionist cause.

Herzl's majestic appearance, dignified bearing, and striking personality impressed all those who knew him. Those who worked with him were profoundly affected by his vision, broad political outlook, organizational abilities, and devotion to his idea. After his death he became a legend in the Jewish world,

Page from a letter by Herzl. [Zionist Archives]

and before long the results of his activities became apparent. The Jews were recognized as a nation, and a new period in Jewish history began. Herzl forged the Zionist movement, which before him had been small and weak, into an effective instrument, and with the creation of the Zionist Organization gave it the form of a political body, which a world power such as Great Britain recognized as the authorized representative of the Jewish people. This laid the groundwork for the *Balfour Declaration and the establishment of the State of Israel.

As a thinker Herzl analyzed the Jewish problem clearly and deeply. In his *Jewish State* and especially in *Old-New Land* (1902), he foresaw events in Jewish life that actually came to pass years later. His writings contain dark prophecies concerning the future of European Jewry. Herzl urged the development of Palestine by means of science and technology, advocated tolerance in all areas, including Arab-Jewish relations, and strove to found a new society in Palestine based on the cooperative principle. The motto of *Old-New Land*— "If you will it, it is no fable"—became the slogan of the Zionist movement. Herzl's *Diaries* and Zionist writings are the prime sources for the early history of the movement he brought into

being and led until 1904. His achievements are in no way diminished by those shortcomings which provoked criticism from his contemporaries, namely, his lack of familiarity with Jewish tradition and his failure to recognize the importance of the *Hebrew language in the rebirth of the Jewish people.

In his will he asked to be buried near his father in Vienna until such time as the Jewish people would transfer his remains to Palestine. In August, 1949, his remains were reinterred on Mount Herzl in Jerusalem (see HERZL, MOUNT). Tammuz 20, the Hebrew anniversary of his death, is observed as a day of remembrance in Israel and by Zionists throughout the world, who continue to revere his name as that of the father of the Jewish State. Many original manuscripts of his writings and his voluminous correspondence are preserved in the Central Zionist Archives in Jerusalem. A museum with exhibits depicting his life in documents and pictures and containing the original furniture of his study in Vienna has been set up on Mount Herzl near the tomb.

A. BEIN

HERZL, MOUNT (Har Herzl). Hill on the western outskirts of Jerusalem, the last resting place of Theodor Herzl, whose remains were brought there from Vienna in 1949. Several other prominent Zionist leaders are also buried there. Nearby are the Herzl Archives, containing books and documents relating to Herzl, and the Herzl Room, a replica of his study in Vienna, containing his original furniture and library. On the northern slope of the hill is a military cemetery.

HERZL FOREST. Forest in Hulda, planted in 1905 and named for Theodor Herzl. Herzl House, the cultural center of Hulda, is located in this forest.

HERZL INSTITUTE. *See* THEODOR HERZL INSTITUTE.

HERZLIYA. City in the southern Sharon Plain, on the Mediterranean coast. Founded in 1924 by the *American Zion Commonwealth and named for the founder of political Zionism. In the period between 1948 and 1968, Herzliya's population increased from 5,000 to 35,600.

The city's economy is based on agriculture, especially citrus growing, as well as on industry and tourism. A popular holiday and health resort, Herzliya has a fine bathing beach and luxury hotels. Its educational institutions include two high schools, an *ORT vocational school, and a music school.

HERZLIYA HIGH SCHOOL (Gymnasia Herzliya). First Hebrew high school in Palestine, founded in 1905 in Jaffa on the initiative of Yehuda *Metman-Kohen, Hayim *Bograshov (Boger), and Ben-Zion *Mossinsohn. Its program was to provide the students, through the sole medium of *Hebrew, with a secular and a Jewish education. The establishment of the Gimnasiya 'Ivrit of Jaffa, as the institution was first named (it was subsequently renamed for Herzl), produced great enthusiasm among Jewish youth in Russia and in other countries, and many came to study at the school. In 1911 the number of students reached 300; by 1914 it was 800.

After a visit to the school, David *Wolffsohn praised its achievements and made an appeal for its support to the 8th Zionist *Congress (1907). Jacob *Moser, a judge from Bradford, England, pledged himself to provide the institution with a building of its own. In 1909 the Ahuzat Bayit quarter, which later became Tel Aviv, was established, and the *Jewish National Fund donated land for the school on its outskirts. The Ottoman government accorded the school official recognition in 1913.

The experiment to teach all subjects in Hebrew proved a success. The school published the first Hebrew textbooks in mathematics, physics, chemistry, geography, geology, and natural sciences and coined a new Hebrew terminology in these fields. Herzliya's method of teaching the Bible, which was tinged with Biblical criticism, gave rise to a prolonged controversy. From 1910 to 1914 the Hebrew periodicals *HaShiloah and *Ha'Olam frequently carried articles criticizing or defending the school's approach to Bible instruction. The students of the school took a very active part in the *Language War.

Herzliya suffered greatly during World War I. Financial support from abroad ceased. Hundreds of students from Russia were cut off from their parents and remained without means. The directors of the school were expelled from the country, and older students were recruited into the Turkish forces. A handful of teachers struggled hard to keep the school open. When the population of Tel Aviv was expelled by the Turkish authorities, the teachers and 120 young students moved to Sh'feya, where they encamped in a forest. Suffering from hunger and persecuted by the authorities, they nevertheless continued their studies under the open sky.

After the occupation of the country by the British in 1917, the school was reopened and continued to play a major role in the education of the Jewish youth of the country. It was the birthplace of various youth groups which subsequently spread throughout the country, such as the scout movement, T'nu'at HaHugim, a *Halutz (pioneer) movement, and G'dud Magine HaSafa, devoted to the defense of Hebrew. In those years Herzliya also ran an agricultural course in cooperation with the agricultural school of Mikve Yisrael.

For many years there were 12 grades for students from 6 to 18 years of age. In 1954, however, the school transferred the 6 lower grades to the municipality of Tel Aviv. In 1967 Herzliya had 1,000 students. The higher grades were divided into five curricula: literary, bilingual, mathematical-physical, mathematical-electrical, and biological.

B. BEN YEHUDA

HERZL PRESS. Publishing house of the *Jewish Agency for Israel–American Section, founded in 1956 for the purpose of publishing books and pamphlets dealing with Zionism, modern Israel, and related subjects. Among the important works published by the Herzl Press are *The Complete Diaries of Theodor Herzl* (5 vols., with notes, 1960), *The Herzl Year Book* (Essays in Zionist History and Thought, 6 vols., 1958–65), *The Zionist Idea* (ed. by A. Hertzberg, 1959), and *John F. Kennedy on Israel, Zionism and Jewish Issues* (1965). The Herzl Press also publishes a pamphlet series, first called the Herzl Institute Pamphlets (1958–61) and subsequently Seven Star Books (1961–   ). By 1970 the press had published more than 100 titles. The chairman of the Herzl Press since its foundation has been Emanuel *Neumann; its editor since 1957, Raphael *Patai.

HERZOG, ISAAC HALEVI. Chief Rabbi of Israel (b. Łomża, Russian Poland, 1888; d. Jerusalem, 1959). Educated in Leeds, England, where his father served as rabbi, Herzog showed unusual academic ability at an early age. After his ordination at the age of 20, he studied at the Universities of London and

Paris, receiving his doctorate from the University of London for research on the topic "The Dyeing of Purple in Ancient Israel." His wide interests encompassed law, philosophy, and social studies. He knew 12 languages.

Isaac Halevi Herzog.
[Zionist Archives]

From 1916 to 1919 Herzog held a pulpit in Belfast. Called to Dublin in 1919, he became Chief Rabbi of the Irish Free State in 1925. Because of his reputation and his friendship with Prime Minister Eamon de Valera permission for ritual slaughtering was granted in Ireland. Always a Zionist, he was a founder of the *Mizrahi movement in England. Elected Chief Rabbi of Palestine in 1936, he sought to strengthen the religious institutions and extend the jurisdiction of the rabbinical courts (*see* RABBINATE OF ISRAEL). During the period of the British *Mandate for Palestine, he attended the *St. James Conference in London (1939) and testified before the *Anglo-American Committee of Inquiry and the *United Nations Special Committee on Palestine.

During World War II, Herzog enlisted the cooperation of the governments of Great Britain, the Soviet Union, and Japan to rescue rabbis and Yeshiva students from Poland and Lithuania and was in contact with the Vatican, the Greek Orthodox Church, and various governments in an effort to save Jewish refugees. After the war he spent six months visiting refugee camps in Europe, encouraging the survivors and arranging for thousands of children who had been hidden in convents and Christian homes during the war to be returned to the Jewish fold.

His writings include Halakhic novellae, responsa, and *The Main Institutions of Jewish Law* (2 vols., 1936–39). The settlement of Massu'ot Yitzhak (founded in 1946) in the 'Etzyon Block was named for him. Destroyed in the *War of Independence, it was rebuilt in another location.

His son Chaim Herzog (b. Belfast, 1918) held high positions in the *Israel Defense Forces, including that of chief of staff of the Southern Command (1957–59) and head of Intelligence (1959–62). During the *Six–day War of 1967 he was appointed first military governor of the West Bank. Herzog's younger son, Jacob David Herzog (b. Dublin, 1921), was Israel's Ambassador to Canada from 1960 to 1963. In 1966 he became Director General of the Prime Minister's Office.

G. BAT-YEHUDA

HESS, MOSES. Pioneer of modern socialism, social philosopher, and forerunner of Zionism (b. Bonn, Germany, 1812; d. Paris, 1875). Although given a Jewish education by his grandfather, he did not show interest in Jewish problems until relatively late in life. Instead, he became deeply involved in the rising Socialist movement. Karl Marx and Friedrich Engels acknowledged that they learned much from him during the formative years of the movement, though Hess eventually broke

Moses Hess.
[Zionist Archives]

with them because he was unwilling to accept their under-emphasis of the role of ethical values in social processes. Hess lived in Germany, France, Switzerland, and Belgium, where he pursued a fruitful literary career. He was the author of philosophical and scientific books and of a variety of tracts, and contributed articles to numerous newspapers.

The Damascus blood accusation of 1840 first evoked Jewish national sentiment in Hess, but it was only in 1862, in his German book *Rome and Jerusalem*, that he became an out-spoken advocate of Jewish *nationalism. In this work he con-ceived of the solution of the Jewish problem as part of universal human progress. He saw mankind as an evolving body in which each nation constituted an organ performing a definite function. The function of Judaism as a religion of history and of the Jewish people as a nation in possession of "a special talent for social revelations" was to bring into harmony all the forces making for human advancement and thus usher in the era of the "eternal Sabbath." However, the Jews would be able to fulfill this function only as long as they were living on their own soil and giving expression to the spirit of Judaism in the form of literature and institutions.

To be able to resume their task, the Jews had to become a nation again on their ancestral soil. Any attempt to regenerate Judaism in the *Diaspora, whether through philanthropic ef-forts or through religious reforms, was foredoomed to failure. Hess was convinced that the return of the Jews to their Home-land and their political rebirth were not utopian dreams. He was sure that the restoration of Jewish statehood, which would have its beginning in the establishment of Jewish settlements in Palestine, would be aided by France, for he believed that the restoration of Jewish nationhood not only enjoyed the sympathy of the French people but also was in France's own best interest from the political point of view. Moreover, Hess was certain that not only the French but also Christians in many other lands would want to see a renaissance of the Jewish people.

As for the Jews themselves, Hess felt that they, particularly the pious masses in Eastern Europe, deeply yearned for Zion and that even the Jews in the West were not altogether indif-ferent to such hopes. If these sentiments were to be aroused for practical action, there would be no lack of Jewish labor, capital, and talent to carry out the pioneering work in Palestine.

While Hess was working on his *Rome and Jerusalem*, Rabbi Zvi Hirsch *Kalischer's *D'rishat Zion* appeared. Hess welcomed Kalischer's call for the establishment of a society for the coloni-zation of Palestine and viewed it as proof of his claim that pious Jews and modernists would unite to reestablish the Jewish nation in Palestine.

Hess was thus a forerunner of political and *cultural Zionism in general and of Socialist Zionism in particular. His book elicited little response during his lifetime, but it has since been recognized as a major classic in Zionist literature.

Originally buried in Deutz, near Cologne, his remains were transferred to the State of Israel.

C. B. SHERMAN

HEVER. Rural center in the Jezreel Valley, serving the settle-ments of D'vora, Barak, and Adirim. Founded in 1958. Popu-lation (1968): 20.

HEVER HAK'VUTZOT (League of K'vutzot). Organization of K'vutzot (collective settlements or communes; *see* KIBBUTZ), founded in Palestine in 1931 and consisting of the smaller col-lectives (originally called K'vutzot as distinct from the larger kibbutzim, a distinction in terminology, which, however, soon became obsolete). A basic endeavor of the K'vutzot was to retain their character as small, intimate groups.

In 1934 the Hever HaK'vutzot united with the settlements of *Gordonia. Later the Hever HaK'vutzot was joined by K'vutzot established by Maccabi HaTza'ir and *HaNo'ar HaTziyoni youth movements. In 1950 Hever HaK'vutzot embraced 43 K'vutzot with a total population of more than 11,000. Most of its members identified ideologically with *Mapai. Its central financial instrument was the Keren HaK'vutzot, founded in 1935, and its publications included a quarterly, *Niv HaK'vutzot*, and a weekly, *Niv LaNo'ar*.

In 1951, following the split in the *Kibbutz M'uhad, the dissident minority of the latter, together with the Hever HaK'vutzot, formed the *Ihud HaK'vutzot V'haKibbutzim.

HEVRAT HAKHSHARAT HAYISHUV. Land-purchasing and development company in Israel. It was founded in 1908 by the *World Zionist Organization after the opening of the Palestine Office in Jaffa (*see* PALESTINE OFFICES) under the direc-tion of Arthur *Ruppin and registered the following year in England as the Palestine Land Development Company, a limited liability company with a share capital of £50,000. After the establishment of the State of Israel, the name of the company was changed to Israel Land Development Company. The main purpose of the enterprise was to purchase land in Palestine for the *Jewish National Fund (JNF) and private investors. It was to act as a central land-purchasing agency to check land speculation, deal with obstacles imposed by Turkish laws governing land transfers, and obviate random and unsystematic purchases of scattered tracts of land, concentrating instead on the acquisition of large, connected tracts for purposes of settle-ment.

The first chairman of its board of directors was Otto *War-burg; Arthur Ruppin was the first managing director. Ruppin was later succeeded by Ya'akov *Thon, who shared the posi-tion with Y'hoshu'a *Hankin until the latter's resignation in 1941. Ruppin remained on the company's board of directors as governor for many years. During the period preceding the establishment of the State of Israel, the board included such prominent Zionists as Joseph *Aronowicz (of the Workers'

Bank), Max *Bodenheimer, M. L. Braudo, Isaak *Feuerring, Itzhak L. *Goldberg, George *Halpern, Arthur *Hantke, Victor *Jacobson, Eliezer *Kaplan, Berl *Katznelson, Johann *Kremenetzky, Heinrich Margulies, Isaac *Naiditsch, Kurt Ruppin, Harry *Sacher, David Werner *Senator, Israel *Sieff, Moshe *Smilansky, Yehiel *Tschlenow, M'nahem M. *Ussishkin, and Chaim *Weizmann. In the 1930s Adolf *Böhm of Vienna and Joseph *Rufeisen of Moravská Ostrava acted as advisers for work outside Palestine.

The company developed the land it purchased, making it ready for all types of settlers. Once initial improvements (roads, water supply) had been made, the large tracts were divided into parcels for individual settlers, who could obtain advice from the company's professional agriculturists and gardeners. In an effort to attract private capital, the company organized plantation companies (Ahuzot; see AHUZA SOCIETIES) in other countries and proceeded to lay out citrus plantations for Jewish purchasers living outside Palestine (see CITRUS INDUSTRY IN ISRAEL). The company then managed the plantations until the trees bore fruit and the owners settled in the country. It established a farm on land leased from the JNF on Lake Kinneret for the training of agricultural workers.

During the first 25 years of its existence, the company bought 125,000 acres of agricultural land and about 3,700 acres of land in urban areas. The company's first land purchase was made in 1909 in the Jezreel Valley; at that time it bought 2,375 acres for the settlement of Merhavya. In 1922, aided by the JNF, it purchased 15,750 acres in the region, providing land for such settlements as Nahalal, 'En Harod, Tel Yosef, K'far Y'hezk'el, and Balfouriya. The first major land purchase in the Sharon Plain was made in 1912. In an effort to encourage interest in farming among Jerusalem's Jewish population, the company bought land in nearby Kiryat 'Anavim and 'Atarot. One of its main undertakings was the Hula concession, which was sold to the JNF after the establishment of the State of Israel. The company had a share also in the growth of Tel Aviv, and in Haifa it bought the land that eventually became the Hadar Ha-Karmel section. After World War I the company established a town planning department, which was the first of its kind in Palestine.

More than 90 per cent of the land purchased by the company from the Arabs had belonged to large landed proprietors. Arab tenants received compensation in the amount of twice the annual income of a *fellah family. In nearly every case the fellahin were able to transfer their work to other places and to use the compensation received from the company to pay off their debts.

Following the establishment of the State of Israel, the company centered its activities mainly on urban development and redevelopment. In the late 1960s it owned land in and near the principal cities for residential, commercial, industrial, and recreational development. It offered other companies and private investors both in Israel and in other countries the chance to participate in joint enterprises in various types of profit-yielding investments. In the late 1960s it controlled resort hotels in Herzliya-on-Sea, the Sharon Hotel, the Sharonit Hotel, the Rimon Inn in Safed, and Gale Kinneret in Tiberias. Founders' shares were held by the *Jewish Agency and *Keren HaYesod with preferential voting rights but no preference over ordinary shareholders in the distribution of profits. Paid-up capital reserves as of June, 1967, exceeded IL20,000,000. Board members in 1968 included A. Ashbel, chairman; Arye Leon

*Dultzin, governor; Shalom Peretz Doron, managing director; and Israel *Goldstein, Herman Hollander, Kurt Ruppin, David Tanne, Jacob *Tsur, and Moshe Ussoskin. The company has its headquarters in Jerusalem and branch offices in Tel Aviv and Haifa.

G. HIRSCHLER

HEVRAT HA'OVDIM (Society of Workers). See HISTADRUT.

HEVRON. See HEBRON.

HIBBAT ZION. Village (moshav) in the Sharon Plain. Founded in 1933 and affiliated with *Hitahdut HaIkkarim. Population (1968): 303.

HIBBAT ZION (Love of Zion). See HOVEVE ZION.

HICEM. Emigration association, set up in 1927 jointly by HIAS (Hebrew Immigrant Aid Society), ICA (*Jewish Colonization Association), and EMIG-DIRECT (an office organized in Prague to assist Jewish emigration from Europe, especially Russia).

HIGH COMMISSIONER FOR PALESTINE. Title of the head of the British Mandatory government of Palestine. The powers and duties of the High Commissioner were defined by (1) His Majesty's orders-in-council relating to Palestine; (2) the commission issued to the High Commissioner under His Majesty's sign manual and signet; (3) the instructions given to him for the purpose of executing the provisions of the *Mandate for Palestine under His Majesty's sign manual and signet, or by order-in-council, or by His Majesty through one of his principal secretaries of state; and (4) the laws and ordinances in force in Palestine. All His Majesty's officers, civil and military, and all other inhabitants of Palestine were required and commanded by the Palestine Order-in-Council (1922) to be obedient, aiding and assisting the High Commissioner.

Executive Council. The High Commissioner was assisted by an Executive Council composed of the Chief Secretary, the Attorney General, and the Treasurer, who were styled ex-officio members; and such other persons holding office in the public service of Palestine as were appointed by him, pursuant to His Majesty's instructions, the latter being styled official members. The Executive Council could not conduct business unless it had been duly summoned by authority of the High Commissioner, who was required by the royal instructions to attend and preside over all its meetings unless prevented by illness or other grave cause.

The High Commissioner was required by the royal instructions, in the exercise of the powers and authorities granted to him by His Majesty's orders-in-council, to consult with the Executive Council in all cases, excepting only those which were of such a nature that, in his judgment, it would materially prejudice His Majesty's service if the Council were to be consulted thereupon, or were too unimportant to require its advice, or were too urgent to allow sufficient time for its advice to be given. In all such urgent cases the High Commissioner was obligated, at the earliest practicable time, to communicate to the Council the measures which he had adopted and the reasons thereof.

The High Commissioner alone was authorized to submit questions to the Executive Council for its advice or decision.

However, if he declined to submit a question to the Council when so requested in writing by any member, such member could ask that his written application, together with the High Commissioner's answer, be recorded in the minutes.

The High Commissioner could act contrary to the advice of the members of the Executive Council, if in any case he deemed it right to do so, but he had to report such cases to the King at the earliest opportunity, along with the reasons for his action. In every such case any member of the Executive Council could require that any advice or opinion he had given on the matter be recorded in detail in the minutes.

Promulgation of Ordinances. The High Commissioner had full power and authority, without prejudice to the powers inherent in, or reserved by, the Palestine Order-in-Council to His Britannic Majesty, and subject to any limitations prescribed by royal instructions given directly or through a Secretary of State, and after consultation with the Advisory Council, to promulgate such ordinances as were necessary for the peace, order, and good government of Palestine. However, no ordinance could be promulgated which restricted complete freedom of conscience and the free exercise of all forms of worship, save insofar as was required for the maintenance of public order and morals, or which tended to discriminate in any way between the inhabitants of Palestine on the ground of race, religion, or language, or which was in any way repugnant to, or inconsistent with, the provisions of the mandate. Furthermore, no ordinance concerning matters dealt with specifically by the provisions of the mandate could be promulgated until a draft had been communicated to and approved by a Secretary of State, with or without amendment. Every ordinance promulgated by the High Commissioner was subject to veto by His Majesty within one year of the date of its promulgation. Certain classes of ordinances could not be promulgated by the High Commissioner unless he had previously obtained instructions thereupon from one of His Majesty's principal secretaries of state. Those included ordinances relating to immigration, divorce, Palestine currency, or the issue of bank notes; ordinances the provisions of which seemed inconsistent with obligations imposed on His Majesty by treaty or by the mandate; and ordinances interfering with the discipline or control of His Majesty's forces by land, sea, or air.

Appointment of Public Officials. Subject to the direction of the Secretary of State, the High Commissioner could appoint, or authorize the appointment of, such public officers of the government of Palestine under such designations as he thought fit and prescribe their duties. Unless otherwise provided by law, all such public officials held their offices during the pleasure of the High Commissioner, who, subject to instructions given to him, could, on what seemed to him sufficient cause, dismiss or suspend from office any person holding any public office within Palestine or, subject as aforesaid, take such other disciplinary action as seemed to him desirable.

Courts. The High Commissioner could, by order, define the districts and subdistricts in which magistrates' courts, and the districts in which district courts, were to be established. He could establish such land courts as were required and such separate courts for the district of Beersheba (B'er Sheva') and for such other tribal areas as he thought fit. He could also, by ordinance, define the offenses in addition to offenses punishable by death with regard to which the Court of Criminal Assize established by the Palestine Order-in-Council should have exclusive jurisdiction and prescribe the constitution of the Supreme Court established by the Palestine Order-in-Council. He also approved rules made by the Chief Justice of Palestine for regulating the practice and procedure of the Supreme Court and of all other civil courts established in Palestine, and no sentence of death could be enforced until confirmed by him. The High Commissioner could also pardon or reprieve any offender condemned to death if it appeared to him expedient so to do, on the advice of the Executive Council, but in all such cases he had to decide either to extend or to withhold a pardon or reprieve according to his own deliberate judgment, whether the members of the Executive Council agreed or not, but recording in the minutes of the Executive Council a detailed statement setting forth his reasons in case his decision ran counter to the judgment of the majority of the members.

The High Commissioner could also grant a pardon to any accomplice in any offense committed within Palestine or for which the offender could be tried there, if that individual gave information and evidence leading to the conviction of the principal offender. He could also grant to any offender convicted of any offense in any court within Palestine a pardon, either unconditional or subject to lawful conditions, or any remission of the sentence passed on such offender, or any respite of the execution of such a sentence, for such period as he thought fit, and remit any fines, penalties, or forfeitures which accrued or became payable by virtue of the judgment of any court in Palestine.

The jurisdiction of the Muslim, Jewish, and Christian religious courts established and exercising jurisdiction at the date of the Palestine Order-in-Council (Sept. 1, 1922) was defined by that order-in-council, but the High Commissioner was authorized by ordinance or order to make changes in the constitution and jurisdiction of those courts.

The High Commissioner could also, with the approval of the Secretary of State, prescribe by regulation the noncontentious measures which a foreign consul in Palestine might take in relation to the personal status of nationals of his state.

No action could be brought against the government of Palestine or of its departments except with the previous written consent of the High Commissioner, and the civil courts could exercise no jurisdiction in any proceeding whatsoever over the High Commissioner or his official or other residence or his official or other property.

Where an offender convicted before any court in Palestine was sentenced to imprisonment, the High Commissioner, if he considered it expedient, could direct that the sentence be carried out in some part of His Majesty's dominions, outside the United Kingdom, provided that the government thereof would accept the individual for that purpose.

Deportation. Where it was shown by evidence on oath to his satisfaction that any person was conducting himself in such a manner as to endanger peace and good order in Palestine, or was seeking to foment enmity between the people of Palestine and the mandatory, or was intriguing against the authority of the mandatory in Palestine, the High Commissioner, if he thought fit, could order that person to be deported from Palestine to such place as he directed, in some part (if any) of His Majesty's dominions to which the person belonged or the government of which consented to the reception of persons so deported, or to some place under the protection of His Majesty, or in the country out of His Majesty's dominions to which that person belonged. Whenever any person was deported from Palestine by order of the High Commissioner, the High Commissioner had to report immediately to the King, through a principal secretary of state, his order, the grounds for it, and the measures taken to enforce it.

Public Lands. All rights in, or in relation to, any public lands, that is, lands in Palestine subject to the control of the government of Palestine by virtue of treaty, convention, agreement, or succession and all lands acquired for the public service or otherwise, were vested in, and could be exercised by, the High Commissioner for the time being in trust for the government of Palestine. All mines and minerals of every kind and description whatsoever, in, under, or on any land or water, whether the latter were inland rivers or seas or territorial waters, were vested in the High Commissioner subject to any right subsisting at the date of the Palestine Order-in-Council of any person to work such mines or minerals by virtue of a valid concession.

The High Commissioner could make grants or leases of any such public lands or mines or minerals, or permit such lands to be temporarily occupied, on such terms or conditions as he thought fit, subject to the provisions of any ordinance. Such grant or disposition had to be in conformity either with some order-in-council or law or ordinance in force in Palestine or with such instructions as were addressed to the High Commissioner under His Majesty's sign manual and signet, or through a Secretary of State, for the purpose of executing the provisions of the mandate. Before disposing of any vacant or waste lands belonging to the government of Palestine, the High Commissioner, according to royal instructions, had to have them surveyed and have such parts reserved, as he thought necessary, for roads or other public purposes. The High Commissioner could not purchase for himself directly or indirectly any such lands without His Majesty's special permission given through one of His Majesty's principal secretaries of state.

Transjordan. Article 25 of the Mandate for Palestine provided that in the territories between the Jordan and the eastern boundary of Palestine as ultimately determined the mandatory should be entitled, with the consent of the League of Nations, to postpone or withhold application of such provisions of the mandate as he considered inapplicable to existing local conditions and to make such provisions for the administration of the territories as he considered suitable to those conditions, provided that no action should be taken which was inconsistent with certain specified provisions of the mandate.

Article 86 of the Palestine Order-in-Council provided that the order should not apply to such parts of the territory in Palestine to the east of the Jordan and the Dead Sea as were defined by order of the High Commissioner and that, subject to the provisions of article 25 of the mandate, the High Commissioner could make such provision for the administration of any territories so defined as aforesaid as might be prescribed with the approval of the Secretary of State. In the exercise of that power the High Commissioner made the Palestine Order-in-Council 1922 (Boundaries) Order 1922, which came into force simultaneously with the Palestine Order-in-Council of Sept. 1, 1922, and provided that the Palestine Order-in-Council of 1922 should not apply to the territory lying east of a line drawn from a point 2 miles west of the town of 'Aqaba in the Gulf of 'Aqaba (Elat) up the center of the Wadi 'Araba, the Dead Sea, and the Jordan River to the junction of the latter with the Yarmukh River, thence up the center of the Yarmukh River to the Syrian frontier.

Blue Book. Under the royal instructions the High Commissioner was required to forward to His Majesty punctually from year to year, through one of His Majesty's principal secretaries of state, the annual book of returns or reports, commonly called the Blue Book, relating to the revenues and expenditure, defense, public works, legislation, civil establishment, pensions, population, schools, holy sites and antiquities, rate of exchange, imports and exports, agricultural produce, manufacturing, the immigration of Jews and the welfare of the Arab population, and other matters more particularly specified in the said Blue Book with reference to conditions in Palestine and having regard to His Majesty's obligations as the mandatory of Palestine in accordance with Article 22 of the Covenant of the League of Nations.

Departure from Palestine. Except in the cases provided for in the Palestine Order-in-Council, the High Commissioner was not allowed for any reason whatever to leave Palestine without having first obtained leave from His Majesty under the sign manual and signet or through one of the principal secretaries of state.

H. E. BAKER

CONDUCT OF THE OFFICE

It was customary for the High Commissioner to take an annual vacation in the United Kingdom and also to return there from time to time for consultation with the Colonial Office. Several High Commissioners appeared before the Permanent Mandates Commission of the League of Nations at Geneva to give additional information in person where needed when the British government's annual report on Palestine was being considered. Some of the High Commissioners would visit the neighboring Middle Eastern countries, especially Egypt, either on leave or on duty. If the High Commissioner was to be absent for any length of time, an officer administering the government would be appointed; if the absence was to be for a few days only, a deputy would be named. The only constitutional limitation on the deputy's authority was that he had no power to grant pardons. In exceptional circumstances either of these two temporary assignments would be entrusted to the Chief Secretary.

Until Transjordan acquired independence in May, 1946, the High Commissioner for Palestine was always the High Commissioner for Transjordan as well. He would be represented at Amman by a Resident and kept in close touch with Emir (later King) 'Abdullah, official visits to Amman and Jerusalem being frequently exchanged.

The High Commissioner was also titular commander in chief, but the actual conduct of military operations and control of the garrison were vested entirely in the general officer commanding, acting under direct instructions from the War Office in London, except during the period from 1924 to 1932, when Palestine was an air force command and the garrison was under the control of an air officer commanding, acting under direct instructions from the Air Ministry. Political problems were often involved in military decisions, and there was close cooperation not only between military headquarters and the High Commissioner's Secretariat but also between the general officer commanding and the High Commissioner in person, especially when the latter was himself a distinguished soldier, as in the case of Field Marshals Lord Plumer (Herbert Charles Onslow *Plumer) and Lord *Gort.

Social Leadership. The considerable constitutional authority vested in the High Commissioner gave him a strong position of leadership in the Palestine community. He did a great deal of official entertaining. Important visitors from abroad would sign the visitors' book kept at the entrance to Government House or present letters of introduction and promptly be invited to lunch or dinner.

But visitors apart, the High Commissioner almost uninterruptedly acted as host to residents of Palestine, including his own British senior civilian staff, British naval, military, and air force officers, the consular corps, nonofficial British residents (missionaries and businessmen), and leading Palestinians. On such occasions as the annual investitures on New Year's Day or the King's birthday, several hundreds would be invited, making it possible for members of all communities and sects to meet on neutral ground and to get to know the senior members of the mandatory government. Receptions of that kind had value in helping weld together a particularly divided society.

It was a heavy drain on the time and energies, and even on the purse, of the High Commissioner, but he rarely accepted hospitality in Jerusalem except from members of his Executive Council or in military messes. A life of semiseclusion was held necessary to maintain the dignity of his office. He did, however, accept invitations to open bazaars and to distribute prizes at schools, with appropriate speeches; this permitted him to keep in touch with the nonofficial community. His social contacts with the rural population and with notables of the smaller towns were much less formal.

Political Leadership. There was no vestige of representative, much less of responsible, government. Public policy was determined by the British. A good deal of the political responsibility and leadership thus fell on the High Commissioner personally, and it was essential for him to keep close watch on political developments. Copies of all important political reports and intelligence summaries were at his disposal, supplemented by information on the state of public opinion obtained in conversation with leading Palestinians and members of the civil service in touch with local affairs, particularly the district administration. His frequent visits to the villages and smaller towns all over Palestine were a valuable source of information which was wisely exploited, especially by Sir Arthur *Wauchope.

Administrative Leadership. All administrative problems of major importance were referred to the High Commissioner personally for decision. The volume of reference varied with different High Commissioners. Some, such as Lord Plumer, preferred to delegate authority to the permanent staff and to remain primarily the King's representative; others, like Sir Herbert *Samuel, kept the reins firmly in their own hands. The manner in which administrative problems reached the High Commissioner also varied. Sir Arthur Wauchope chose to see life at first hand and spent most of his time on tour; Sir Harold *MacMichael was more withdrawn and dealt with most questions on paper.

At any rate, a certain amount of official business had to be put formally to the High Commissioner. He was expected by the Colonial Office to sign personally all dispatches addressed to it, and he had to read all the principal papers concerned with each. As head of the Executive Council, he was present at all its weekly meetings: as a matter of fact, the Council could not meet in the absence of the High Commissioner or officer administering the government. He was also chairman of the Advisory Council, which met less frequently and was largely a formal body.

All instructions emanating from the Secretariat were issued in his name: "I am directed by the High Commissioner to inform you that. . . . " To the civil service he was thus the fount of authority, and for heads of departments this authority was supplemented by the periodic interviews each had with him to discuss departmental affairs. Any member of the public who had a matter of public or private importance to discuss could usually see the High Commissioner personally, if his application was submitted through the proper channels and if all resources at lower levels had been exhausted.

On tour the High Commissioner was even more accessible. Petitions would frequently be pressed into his hand as he walked through a village. Any peasant with a grievance could, by planting himself in his path, secure a summary hearing. A visit to a village much resembled a medieval royal progress and gave tremendous satisfaction to the inhabitants, who liked to feel that they could, when in trouble, appeal directly to the highest authority in the land. There was much Muslim and Jewish tradition behind this feeling, which was particularly strong in regard to the exercise of justice. The power of pardon was expressly conferred on the High Commissioner and was frequently exercised by him on the advice of the Attorney General and occasionally of the judges themselves.

The post was not an easy one for the Colonial Office to fill, principally because of the onerous political responsibility attaching to it. Of Palestine's seven High Commissioners, only two (Sir John *Chancellor and Sir Harold MacMichael) were career appointments. Palestine was rather exceptional in the type of man appointed to govern it. Of the other five, four were professional soldiers and one a former Cabinet minister. It is rare for Cabinet ministers to accept colonial appointments in peacetime, for their future lies so much in British politics and not overseas. But the imagination of David *Lloyd George, the Prime Minister who personally selected his former Cabinet colleague, Sir Herbert Samuel (later Viscount Samuel), for the post, coupled with Sir Herbert's interest in Palestine and the Jewish problem and his strong sense of public duty, was responsible for this very unusual nomination.

The appointment of the four soldiers (Lord Plumer, Sir Arthur Wauchope, Lord Gort, and Sir Alan *Cunningham) is more easily explicable. The Palestine of the mandate was a disturbed area in which troops frequently had to be used to protect one section of the population against the other, the government from either section, or both.

The titles and dates of appointment of the seven High Commissioners are as follows:

Rt. Hon. Sir Herbert Samuel, P.C., G.B.E.	
(later Rt. Hon. Viscount Samuel, P.C.,	
G.C.B., O.M., G.B.E.)	July 1, 1920
Rt. Hon. Field Marshal Baron Plumer,	
G.C.B., G.C.M.G., G.C.V.O., G.B.E.	Aug. 14, 1925
Lieut. Col. Sir John Chancellor,	
C.C.M.G., G.C.V.O., D.S.O.	Nov. 1, 1928
Lieut. Gen. Sir Arthur Wauchope,	
G.C.B., G.C.M.G., C.I.E., D.S.O.	Nov. 20, 1931
Sir Harold MacMichael, K.C.M.G., D.S.O.	Mar. 3, 1938
Field Marshal Viscount Gort, V.C., G.C.B.,	
D.S.O., M.V.O., M.C.	Oct. 31, 1944
Gen. Sir Alan Gordon Cunningham,	
G.C.M.G., K.C.B., D.S.O., M.C.	Nov. 21, 1945

VISCOUNT SAMUEL

HIGHER EDUCATION IN ISRAEL. In 1970 the network of higher educational institutions in Israel comprised the following schools (in alphabetical order): *Bar-Ilan University, in Ramat Gan; *Haifa University Institute; *Hebrew University of Jerusalem; Negev Institute for Higher Education, in B'er Sheva'; New Bezalel School of Arts and Crafts (see BEZALEL SCHOOL), in Jerusalem; School of Physiotherapy, in Jerusalem; *Technion (Israel Institute of Technology), in Haifa; *Tel Aviv University; and *Weizmann Institute of Science, in Rehovot. The total number of students attending these institutions on a full-time or part-time basis in the 1967–68 academic year was 31,624, and the academic staff numbered 3,749. Supervision of these schools, including accreditation, recognition of degrees granted, and the like, was in the hands of the government-appointed Council for Higher Education.

HILDESHEIMER, AZRIEL. Rabbi, scholar, and communal worker in Central Europe (b. Halberstadt, Germany, 1820; d. Berlin, 1899). Educated at Yeshivot and at the Universities of Berlin and Halle (Ph.D., 1844), he became secretary and a leading figure in the Orthodox community of Halberstadt, where he taught Talmudic subjects. From 1851 to 1869 he served as rabbi in Kismartón (Eisenstadt), Hungary, where he established a religious school and rabbinical seminary that included secular studies in its curriculum. Both the ultra-Orthodox and the Reform adherents protested vehemently, and he was excommunicated and reported to the authorities, who sought to close the school.

Becoming rabbi of the Orthodox Adat Yisrael Congregation in Berlin in 1869, he established a coeducational religious school and a rabbinical seminary which gave instruction also in secular studies and which he staffed with the finest teachers, raising funds for its maintenance and serving as its head until his death. He sought to build a similar school in Jerusalem but was unable to do so because of local opposition.

Hildesheimer organized welfare campaigns for Jews throughout the world and supervised the allocation of most of the funds going to Palestine from the Austro-Hungarian Jewish community. The land on which G'dera was built and orchards near Tiberias were purchased and registered in his name. In addition to articles about contemporary problems and Palestine and polemical writings against the Reform movement, he published a number of Jewish scholarly studies.

G. BAT-YEHUDA

HILDESHEIMER, NAFTALI ZVI HIRSH. Lecturer and editor (b. Kismartón, Hungary, 1855; d. Berlin, 1910). The son of Rabbi Azriel *Hildesheimer, he studied Jewish subjects at home and classical languages and ancient history at the University of Berlin (Ph.D., 1880). He was appointed lecturer in history and geography at the Hildesheimer Rabbinical Seminary. From 1883 on he edited the *Jüdische Presse* and published research articles about Palestine. He helped found *Esra, a society to aid Palestinian settlers, and advocated a central organization for *Hoveve Zion groups and Jews throughout the world for the settlement of Palestine. Later, he broke with the movement on the question of political Zionism. Hildesheimer actively fought *anti-Semitism in Germany, sponsored educational services in Palestine, and played a prominent role in Jewish cultural institutions.

Y. RAPHAEL

HILF. Bedouin tribe in Lower Galilee. Population (1968): 490.

HILFSTEIN, HAYIM. Physician and Zionist leader (b. Cracow, Poland, 1877; d. Tel Aviv, 1950). A Zionist from his youth on, Hilfstein helped found the pre-Herzlian Zionist movement in Galicia. He served as president of the Zionist Organization, the *Keren HaYesod (Palestine Foundation Fund), and the *Jewish National Fund of western Galicia.

In the period between the two world wars, Hilfstein, a well-known physician in Cracow, devoted much time to Jewish educational affairs and, with Osias (Y'hoshu'a) *Thon, founded a network of Jewish high schools in Galicia. After the Nazi occupation of Poland he was arrested and sent to a concentration camp. Following his liberation, he settled in Palestine.

N. M. GELBER

HILFSVEREIN DER DEUTSCHEN JUDEN (German Jews' Aid Society). German-Jewish philanthropic agency, founded in 1901 in Berlin for the purpose of promoting the spiritual, moral, and economic welfare of the Jews, especially in Eastern Europe and the Oriental countries. Its founders were Rabbi H. Horowitz, Eugen Landau, Paul Nathan, Carl Leopold Netter, James Simon, and Berthold Timendorfer. The organization rendered generous aid to survivors of pogroms and to victims of war, floods, famine, and other disasters in Eastern and Southern European Jewish communities. Prior to World War I, it brought influence to bear on the governments of Romania, Russia, Finland, and other countries to mitigate anti-Jewish legislation and discrimination, and it engaged in other defense activities. The Hilfsverein was also very active in emigrant aid, counseling and extending financial assistance to hundreds of thousands of Jewish emigrants from Eastern Europe who passed through Germany on their way to America. In the educational sphere, it both maintained and subsidized Jewish schools, helped Jewish students at German universities, and promoted their professional training.

Between 1903 and 1918, the Hilfsverein developed a wide educational program in Palestine directed by Ephraim Cohn-Reiss. It took over the *Lämel School in Jerusalem and established a teachers training college, which was attached to it. At one time, the Hilfsverein also maintained 11 kindergartens, 5 boys' and girls' schools, a high school, a business school, a girls' home, a course for rabbis, and a kindergarten teachers training course. It subsidized four Talmud Toras, an evening school, a library, and an eye clinic.

The Hilfsverein also initiated the establishment of the *Technion in Haifa and of the Reali High School attached to it. The suggestion was made by Paul Nathan, the funds were provided by Jacob H. *Schiff, James Simon, and Kalonymus-Z'ev *Wissotzky, and the land was furnished by the *Jewish National Fund. In October, 1913, when the facilities were near completion, the representatives of the Hilfsverein on the Board of Governors of these institutions adopted a resolution that all scientific and technical subjects at both the Technion and the Reali High School be taught in the German language. This stirred up a storm of protest in Palestine and led to the so-called *Language War, during which numerous teachers and students left the institutions of the Hilfsverein and established Hebrew-language schools.

After the British conquest of Palestine, the facilities of the Hilfsverein were turned over to the occupation authorities, and the schools were taken over by the *World Zionist Organization.

With the rise of Nazism in Germany, the Hilfsverein concentrated its activities on the needs of German Jewry. Its major task remained migration, with advice and material assistance given solely to Jews who wanted to leave Germany. The organization was officially abolished in 1939 but continued to function as part of the Reichsvereinigung der Juden in Deutschland (Union of Jews in Germany) during World War II.

T. PRESCHEL

HIRSCH, BARON MAURICE DE. Philanthropist (b. Munich, 1831; d. Ógyalla, Hungary, 1896; buried in Paris). The son of a German-Jewish family of bankers with a tradition of philanthropy, Hirsch received a religious education. In 1855 he married Clara (1833–99), daughter of Raphael Jonathan Bischoffsheim, a member of the Belgian Senate. After spending some time in Munich and Brussels, the couple settled in Paris. Hirsch laid the foundations of his wealth by establishing a Belgian bank and by engaging in railway construction in Russia, Hungary, and Turkey. The large-scale enterprise in Turkey, involved as it was in international politics, made his name well known all over Europe.

After the death of his only son Lucien in 1887, Hirsch, assisted by his wife, turned to philanthropic projects. Earlier, he had made generous contributions to the *Alliance Israélite Universelle for primary and vocational education in the Near East. In 1891 he set up a foundation in Vienna for schools in Galicia and Bukovina and the Baron de Hirsch Fund in New York for aid to Jewish immigrants in the United States.

On Sept. 11, 1891, the London *Times* published the bylaws of the *Jewish Colonization Association (ICA), founded by Hirsch with an initial capital of £2,000,000 "to assist and promote the emigration of Jews from any part of Europe and Asia" and to "establish colonies in various parts of North and South America and other countries." He later increased the capital to nearly £10,000,000. London became the headquarters of the ICA, which extended its activities mainly, but not solely, to Eastern Europe, engaging in colonization work in several countries but concentrating on Argentina. Believing that the Russians would continue to oppress the Jews, Hirsch sought to aid in the rescue of the Russian Jews by resettling 200,000 to 300,000 of them.

Baron de Hirsch.
[YIVO Institute for
Jewish Research]

About nine months before the publication of his *Jewish State*, on June 2, 1895, Herzl met Baron de Hirsch and attempted to win him over to his newly conceived idea of political Zionism. The meeting was inconclusive. When Hirsch died 10

months later, Herzl wrote in his *Diaries*: "[Hirsch's] participation could have helped our cause to success tremendously fast. . . . his death is a loss to the Jewish cause. Among the rich Jews he was the only one who wanted to do something big for the poor. . . . It seems to me as though our cause has grown poorer this day. For I still kept thinking of winning Hirsch over to the plan."

After the death of Baron de Hirsch, his widow continued his charitable work. The ICA helped individual settlers in Palestine, assisted educational institutions, established a training farm and settlements, and, in 1900, took over the administration of the settlements founded by Baron Edmond de *Rothschild.

J. FRAENKEL

HIRSCHMANN, IRA ARTHUR. Business executive and communal worker in the United States (b. Baltimore, 1901). Early in 1944 Hirschmann was appointed special representative of the newly created War Refugee Board, attached to the United States Embassy in Ankara.

After the war, as special Inspector General of the UN Relief and Rehabilitation Administration (UNRRA), Hirschmann visited displaced-persons camps in Germany to study and help improve conditions there. Later, he visited refugee camps in Arab countries, met with a number of Arab leaders, including Gamal Abdel Nasser, made recommendations for the rehabilitation of Arab refugees, and was named consultant to the UN Relief and Works Agency for Palestine Refugees in the Near East (UNRWA).

In 1949 Hirschmann received the One World Award. He wrote three books: *Life-Line to a Promised Land* (1946), an account of the year he spent in Turkey; *The Embers Still Burn* (1949), a record of his work in displaced-persons camps; and an autobiography, *Caution to the Winds* (1962). He was a contributor to the anthology *Nazism: An Assault on Civilization* (1934).

HISSIN, HAYIM ISSER. *See* CHISSIN, HAYIM ISSER.

HISTADRUT (General Federation of Labor). Labor organization in Israel. Its full name is HaHistadrut HaK'lalit shel Ha'Ovdim Ha'Ivrim B'Eretz Yisrael (General Federation of Jewish Workers in the Land of Israel). In 1966 the 10th Conference of the Histadrut resolved to eliminate the word "Jewish" from the official title.

HISTORY

The Histadrut was founded in Haifa in 1920, but its ideological and organizational character was derived primarily from the members of the *Second 'Aliya (1904–14). Although a general federation of workers in Palestine was not formed at that time, regional organizations such as the Federation of Judean Workers, the Workers' Committee of Galilee, and the Workers' Federation of Samaria were established.

Formation and Early Years. The first attempt to form a general labor federation was made in 1914, with the creation of the United Commission of Palestinian Workers. This organization was short-lived because of the opposition of the political parties *HaPo'el Hatza'ir and *Po'ale Zion, which continued to maintain their own organizations and services for their members. *Ahdut 'Avoda, a political party formed in 1919, encompassed the majority of Palestine's labor force, but HaPo'el HaTza'ir did not join it. With the advent of the *Third 'Aliya (1919–23), efforts to unite all the workers of Palestine were intensified. They culminated in the founding conference of the Histadrut, which was held in December, 1920, in the courtyard of the Haifa *Technion.

Participating in the elections to the founding conference were 4,433 voters. Of the delegates elected, 37 represented Ahdut 'Avoda; 26, HaPo'el HaTza'ir; 6, recently arrived workers (*HaShomer HaTza'ir, *HeHalutz, Young Zionists, and so on); 6, the Socialist Workers party (*Communists); and 2, independent groups. The deliberations and resolutions of the conference centered on the close links of Palestine's labor force with Zionism and with the rebuilding of the country, support of Jewish *immigration and aid to immigrant absorption, and nurturing of the *Hebrew language and Jewish culture. These principles were coupled with a firm attachment to socialism, which was viewed as the goal to be attained. The opening resolutions adopted by the conference read:

> It is the aim of the United Federation of all the workers and laborers of Palestine who live by the sweat of their brows without exploiting the toil of others, to promote land settlement, to involve itself in all economic and cultural issues affecting labor in Palestine, and to build a Jewish workers' society there.

Following the conference, the various trade and economic organizations hitherto maintained by the political parties were gradually absorbed by the Histadrut.

The first economic enterprise founded by the Histadrut was the Bureau for Public Works, a building organization formed to secure contracts for the construction of houses and roads and to provide employment for recent arrivals. The Agricultural Workers' Federation focused its attention first on securing work in the moshavot and later also on settling working people on land. The agricultural settlement program undertaken by the *World Zionist Organization (WZO), especially in the Jezreel Valley in the early 1920s, absorbed nearly 1,000 recent arrivals in newly established moshavim and K'vutzot.

To strengthen ties with Jewish labor organizations in the United States, a Histadrut delegation visited the United States for the first time in the summer of 1922. The delegates, Yosef *Baratz, Berl *Katznelson, and Manya *Wilbuschewitz-Shohat, sought to sell shares in the Bank HaPo'alim (Workers' Bank), the Histadrut's first financial institution.

The first workers' census in Palestine, held in September, 1922, showed that, of the 16,608 workers then in Palestine, 8,394 were members of the Histadrut and that about 75 per cent of the new immigrants had joined the organization. Soon after the 1st Histadrut Conference, the Central Cultural Commission was formed to help propagate the Hebrew language and promote adult education. All schools established in the workers' settlements were supervised by the commission. The Second 'Aliya had laid the foundations for the organization of working women, the first conference of working women having been held in 1911. After the establishment of the Histadrut, *Mo'etzet HaPo'alot (Working Women's Council) was formed to consolidate the organizational and social activities of working women in both rural and urban areas.

The 2d Histadrut Conference was held in Tel Aviv from Jan. 7 to 20, 1923. At this conference, 6,581 voters elected 127 delegates, of whom 69 represented Ahdut 'Avoda, 36 HaPo'el HaTza'ir, 6 *G'dud Ha'Avoda V'haHagana 'Al Shem Yosef Trumpeldor, and 4 HaShomer HaTza'ir. The rest were chosen from small splinter groups, including the Communists. The agenda of the conference included economic problems; the establishment of the Hevrat Ha'Ovdim (Society of Workers), an umbrella corporation for the varied economic enterprises owned by the Histadrut; the promotion of housing projects for urban workers; and the organization of Solel Bone (Paver-Builder), a contracting corporation for road and housing construction. After the conference work was begun on Sh'khunat Borochov.

Development in the 1920s and 1930s. The beginning of the *Fourth 'Aliya (1924) marked a period of expansion and full employment, particularly in building construction. By the end of 1925, however, a serious economic crisis was affecting Palestine, and Solel Bone was forced into bankruptcy. There was considerable unemployment, urgent public works were organized by the WZO and the government of Palestine, and direct relief had to be offered in some instances. Only in mid-1928, as the country slowly emerged from the economic slump, did the situation improve and immigration resume.

The first attempt to organize an Arab-Jewish trade union was made among the railroad, postal, and telegraph workers (all government employees). To serve the needs of Arab workers the Histadrut began in 1925 to publish a periodical in Arabic. *See also* JEWISH AND ARAB LABOR.

The Histadrut was also concerned with the organization of working youth and arranged vocational training for them. In 1924 local groups were amalgamated to form the Histadrut HaNo'ar Ha'Oved (Federation of Working Youth) as an integral part of the Histadrut, with the aim of providing "economic protection for working youth, improvement of their living conditions, vocational training, employment for new members, educational opportunities and organizational recognition." The first conference of working youth, held in September, 1924, confirmed the nonpartisan basis of the organization and set the age for membership between 13 and 18. The Working Women's Council also embarked on a program of vocational training. The farms and clubs that it created for its members filled an important function in Palestine in the 1920s.

In addition to encouraging the land settlement projects of the WZO, the Histadrut sought to increase the number of Jewish workers in the old-established settlements, which employed large numbers of Arab workers, who received lower wages and were more accustomed to tilling the soil than Jewish workers. When Jewish farmers refused to employ only Jewish farmhands, conflicts sometimes occurred. The Histadrut sought to strengthen the position of hired labor in the settlements by facilitating, with the financial assistance of the WZO, the establishment of *auxiliary farms. To promote land settlement, the Histadrut formed Nir Ltd., a corporation concerned with this problem.

After many organizational difficulties, the years 1926 and 1927 saw the formation of the *T'nu'at HaMoshavim, the *Kibbutz M'uhad, and the *Kibbutz Artzi Shel HaShomer HaTza'ir. (The settlement projects of G'dud Ha'Avoda joined the Kibbutz M'uhad in 1929.) Meanwhile, T'nuva, an agency to market the farm produce of the working settlements, was formed in 1924. In 1926 Yakhin, a contracting office for agricultural work, was established. It played an important role in promoting the use of Jewish labor in the moshavot and later undertook the task of attracting Jewish capital from other countries for investment in citrus planting (*see* CITRUS INDUSTRY IN ISRAEL).

Histadrut's founders at the Haifa Convention in 1920. Among the delegates are Itzhak Ben Zvi and his wife, Yosef Sprinzak, and Berl Katznelson. [Histadrut Foto-News]

As the activities of Histadrut gradually expanded in many directions, a Members' Tribunal was formed to adjudicate disputes between the members. In 1927 HaS'ne Corporation, which eventually became one of the largest insurance concerns in Israel, was formed. The outstanding achievement of Histadrut in the cultural field was the founding of the daily newspaper *Davar* in 1925, under the editorship of Berl Katznelson. *Davar* evolved into a publishing outlet for Histadrut. In 1925 the workers' theater Ohel was formed (*see* THEATER IN ISRAEL); its actors were drawn mainly from labor circles. HaPo'el, a sports association, was established to further various types of sports activity (*see* SPORTS AND PHYSICAL EDUCATION IN ISRAEL).

The 3d Conference of the Histadrut was held in Tel Aviv in July, 1927. The 17,036 voters who participated elected 201 representatives: Ahdut 'Avoda, 108; HaPo'el HaTza'ir, 54; Left Po'ale Zion, 14; kibbutzim list, 8; left-wing bloc, 8; left-wing opposition, 4; *Revisionists, 2; and nonaffiliated, 3. David *Ben-Gurion, who was secretary-general of the Histadrut from 1920 on, reported that the Histadrut had 25,000 members, or 75 per cent of the Jewish labor force in Palestine. New institutions were established, among them the Central Comptroller's Commission, centers for cooperatives and housing, and the B'rit Po'ale Eretz Yisrael, a joint trade union which included Arab as well as Jewish workers.

In 1928, on the initiative of the leaders of the Histadrut, members of the Socialist International in Europe formed a Committee for Labor Palestine, headed by leading Socialists,

among them Léon *Blum, Émile Vandervelde, and Edouard Bernstein. The Congress for Labor Palestine, which was held in Berlin in 1930 and attended by outstanding leaders of European socialism, demonstrated its friendship for the Histadrut and for the Palestinian workers' movement. It also had an impact on labor parties in Europe.

From the slump of the late 1920s, Palestine rose to prosperity in the early 1930s, particularly as the rate of immigration from Germany increased. The citrus-growing area was expanded, unemployment declined, and additional labor was sought. As immigration rose in 1932–33, about 12,000 new members joined the Histadrut. Opportunities for employment increased with the arrival of immigrants from Germany, some of whose capital was channeled to Histadrut agricultural projects. This period saw the expansion of T'nuva and of HaMashbir HaMerkazi as the principal purchasing agency of the Histadrut-affiliated moshavim and kibbutzim. Growing numbers of workers, drawn by the promise of better economic opportunities, moved from the countryside to urban areas. As Arabs, including Arabs from Syria, began to fill available jobs in the expanding economy, it became necessary to safeguard the position of the Jewish agricultural workers in the moshavot. This problem was complicated by the clash with the Revisionists, who, repudiating socialism, set up their own labor organization, *Histadrut Ha'Ovdim HaL'umit. In 1934, seeking to avoid a head-on collision, David Ben-Gurion and Vladimir *Jabotinsky signed a working agreement for a just apportionment of employment opportunities, the safeguarding of proper working conditions, and the improvement of relationships among the workers. However, a Histadrut referendum rejected the agreement.

The outbreak of Italo-Ethiopian hostilities in September, 1935, had an adverse effect on Palestine. Economic depression created considerable unemployment, and it became necessary to draw on the Unemployment Fund created by the Histadrut and other institutions. To relieve the crisis the Histadrut, with the aid of the WZO, sponsored the settlement of about 500 families on land.

In the 1930s Solel Bone was reestablished. As the sole recipient of Histadrut building projects as well as those of the WZO, it soon emerged as the largest contracting firm in Palestine. Its position was further strengthened by very substantial building contracts secured from the British Army during World War II.

The 4th Histadrut Conference met in Tel Aviv in two sessions, one in February, 1933, and the other in February, 1934. The 22,341 participating voters elected 201 delegates: *Mapai, 165; Left Po'ale Zion, 16; HaShomer HaTza'ir, 16; *Yemenite Jews, 2; religious Socialists, 1; and General Zionist Youth (see GENERAL ZIONISM), 1. With the merger of Ahdut 'Avoda and HaPo'el HaTza'ir in 1930, Mapai became the majority Histadrut party and thereafter effectively controlled it. The conference dealt with the labor problems of an expanding economy in the areas of housing, cooperative ventures, and culture. Following this conference, the Center for Education and Culture was established. In 1932 a Labor Archives was created to engage in research and in the collection of material pertaining to the Jewish labor movement.

World War II and the Struggle for Statehood. The Histadrut's 5th Conference met in Tel Aviv in April, 1942, during World War II. Of its 125,793 members, 88,198 voted for the following delegates: Mapai, 278; HaShomer HaTza'ir and the Socialist League, 77; Left Po'ale Zion, 17; Ha'Oved HaTziyoni, 14; and Po'ale Zion, left-wing, and Marxist groups, 6. The delegates of the proletarian list (Communists) were eliminated. The conference dealt mainly with problems pertaining to enlistment in the armed forces and the struggle against the British Mandatory government (see MANDATE FOR PALESTINE). It adopted the demands of the Zionist movement for a Jewish State in Palestine after the war, as embodied in the *Biltmore Program. This program was opposed by HaShomer HaTza'ir.

Throughout the period of *illegal immigration and the anti-British activity of *Hagana (1939–47), the facilities, institutions, and personnel of the Histadrut were placed at the service of the struggle for 'Aliya and Jewish statehood. Histadrut offices were often the clandestine centers of underground activity.

At the 6th Histadrut Conference, which met in three sessions lasting almost a year, from November, 1944, to October, 1945, 106,302 voters elected the following delegates: Mapai, 216; HaShomer HaTza'ir, Socialist League, and Left Po'ale Zion, 83; Ahdut 'Avoda (splintered from Mapai), 71; new immigrants, 2; Ha'Oved HaTziyoni, 12; *Ha'Oved HaDati, a religious workers' group, 4; Yemenites, 2; and Po'ale Ha'Am, 1. The conference was devoted to a critical evaluation of intra-Histadrut policies and the establishment of national trade unions. This led to the formation of national unions of workers engaged in construction, printing, metalwork, baking, weaving, and woodworking and of social workers and sailors. After

the establishment of the State of Israel, a Federation of Government Employees was formed to replace the Federation of Railroad, Postal, and Telegraph Workers, which was dissolved. The conference also considered the problem of the employment of hired labor in cooperatives affiliated with the Histadrut, which posed the question: Can members of the Histadrut, organized in cooperatives, employ hired labor? The decision calling for the elimination of hired labor was adopted but not implemented. In fact, hired labor spread from urban cooperatives to moshavim and kibbutzim.

In 1942 Histadrut founded the publishing house 'Am 'Oved, of which Berl Katznelson served as editor in chief. It eventually published hundreds of books in all fields of literature and the sciences. In 1947 a school was initiated to provide seminars and courses for Histadrut members. A similar institution was established in the Jordan Valley to honor the memory of Katznelson, who died in 1944. By the establishment of the State of Israel in 1948, Histadrut had 184,000 members.

Development under the State of Israel. Because of Israel's *War of Independence, the 7th Histadrut Conference was not convened until May, 1949, in Tel Aviv. The 139,007 voters chose the following representatives: Mapai, 286; *Mapam, a merger of HaShomer HaTza'ir, Ahdut 'Avoda, and Left Po'ale Zion, 172; Ha'Oved HaTziyoni, 19; Maki (Israel Communist party), 13; and Ha'Oved HaDati, 11. The convention discussed the invitation extended to the Histadrut to participate in the Communist-oriented World Federation of Trade Unions. The opposition to participation in this body carried the day, and after lengthy discussion Histadrut joined the International Confederation of Free Trade Unions in 1953.

The 8th Histadrut Conference, held in Tel Aviv in March, 1956, represented more than 552,000 members, of whom 410,451 voted for the following representatives: Mapai, 463; Ahdut 'Avoda and Left Po'ale Zion (which had broken away from Mapam), 117; Mapam, 101; Ha'Oved HaTziyoni, 42; Maki, 33; Union of General Zionist Workers, 30; and Ha'Oved HaDati, 15. Most of the discussion at this conference centered on the relationship between the Israeli government and Histadrut, trade union and cooperative activities, the role of Arab workers in the Histadrut, and wage scale policies. Ben-Gurion defined the relationship between the Histadrut and the State of Israel. He asserted that the Histadrut would have

Histadrut headquarters, Tel Aviv. [Israel Information Services]

to relinquish those social, cultural, and political activities which it had performed prior to the founding of the State but which were actually governmental functions. Its task now was to concentrate on trade union and cooperative endeavors and to organize the labor force in order to help promote the welfare and development of the State. This policy initiated a debate that has not been settled. Solel Bone, Histadrut's largest economic institution, was reorganized late in 1958. The Histadrut Savings and Loan Funds were merged with the Bank HaPo'alim. Resolutions for the gradual elimination of hired labor in Histadrut cooperatives in towns and villages were again adopted.

Of the 635,464 members of Histadrut, 504,687 voted for the election of representatives to the 9th Histadrut Conference (which met in Tel Aviv in February, 1960) as follows: Mapai, 444; Ahdut 'Avoda and Po'ale Zion, 136; Mapam, 112; Ha-'Oved HaTziyoni and Progressive list, 46; Union of General Zionist Workers, 28; Maki, 22; and Ha'Oved HaDati, 14. Attention was focused on reorganization of the cooperative and business enterprises of Histadrut, participation of workers in the management of Histadrut industrial concerns, and acceptance of Arab workers in the Histadrut. Objection to the participation of workers' representatives employed in Histadrut-owned industries was raised by the managerial element of Histadrut industries. Although approved in principle, worker participation in the management of the enterprises was not implemented.

In September, 1965, elections were held for the 10th Conference; 669,270 of Histadrut's 862,019 members voted. Since the preceding conference the party structure within Histadrut had changed. Histadrut members belonging to *Herut (T'khelet-Lavan faction) and workers belonging to the *Liberal party had united to form one bloc, and a splinter group headed by Ben-Gurion that seceded from Mapai formed a new political party, *R'shimat Po'ale Yisrael (Rafi). Before the 1965 elections, Mapai and Ahdut 'Avoda–Po'ale Zion had formed an alignment and entered the elections on a joint list. The election results were as follows: Mapai and Ahdut 'Avoda alignment, 50.88 per cent; *Gahal (the anti-Socialist bloc, which appeared for the first time), 15.20; Mapam (left-wing Socialists), 14.51; Rafi, 12.11; Independent Liberal party, 4.43; Communist party, 1.58; and New Communists, 1.29.

The following have served as secretary-general of the Histadrut: David Ben-Gurion (from its creation to 1935), David *Remez (1935–45), Yosef *Sprinzak (1945–49), Pinhas Lavon (1949–50, 1956–61), Mord'khai *Namir (1950–56), and Aharon Becker (1961–   ). In late 1966 Histadrut had 1,533,135 members, of whom 100,603 were Arab workers. Since its formation Histadrut has been the largest organization in the *Yishuv (Jewish population of Palestine) and in the State of Israel, its membership comprising a majority of the country's population.

ORGANIZATION AND POLICIES

According to the latest Histadrut constitution (November, 1964), the General Conference is the highest Histadrut authority, and its resolutions are binding on all Histadrut members and institutions. The conference chooses a Histadrut Council, reflecting the relative party strength at the conference, which exercises authority between conferences. The Council, in turn, elects an Executive Committee, a Members' Tribunal, and a Central Comptroller's Commission. The Executive Committee carries out all Histadrut decisions and is responsible to the General Conference and to the Council. It supervises and has authority over all Histadrut institutions. The Executive Committee chooses a Secretariat responsible for the transaction of Histadrut affairs. There has been almost no change in the program of the Histadrut since its creation except for the addition of a provision that membership is open to every worker in the country, regardless of religion, race, nationality, or political affiliation. At the conference election in 1965 a resolution was passed committing the Histadrut to the realization of socialism in Israel.

Labor Policies. By the end of 1966 Histadrut membership included more than 62.32 per cent of Israel's Jewish population. Only about 50,000 workers were still not affiliated with any organization. Histadrut was concerned mainly with trade union problems, full employment, safeguarding of the wage earners' *standard of living, and adjustment of wage policies to the general economic policy of the government. It helped raise the wages of Arab workers from the low pre-State level to that enjoyed by Jewish workers and to accord them the same fringe benefits.

The achievements of Histadrut have been many and varied, and they have left their mark on every aspect of Israel's life. Often strikes broke out against the wishes of Histadrut. Between 1960 and 1967 there were numerous strikes in which large numbers of workers were involved, the predominant majority being strikes in Histadrut-owned and government-owned enterprises. In nearly all cases the strikes were declared against the wishes of the Histadrut. These strikes brought to the fore the question of the compatibility of the Histadrut's role of proprietor and manager of enterprises with its role as protector of workers' rights in these enterprises.

Because of the paramount position of the Histadrut, on the one hand, and the relative weakness of the employers, on the other, it was Histadrut that in fact determined wage policy and employment conditions for the entire Yishuv. Both full employment and security of tenure were the guidelines of the Histadrut. Dismissals of incompetent employees and of superfluous personnel became nearly impossible and caused considerable immobility of the labor force. The principle of first in, last out operated against new immigrants and seriously hampered the healthy development of many enterprises and services.

With the rise in price levels following the outbreak of World War II, the Histadrut succeeded in obtaining the agreement of the Palestine government to the payment of a cost-of-living allowance, which was added to the basic wage and represented the increase in the price level. A mechanism was set up to determine periodically changes in the index of prices, and wages were adjusted accordingly.

The policy of periodic addition of a cost-of-living allowance to the basic salary continued after Israel came into being and became an integral part of wage policy. With the rapid rise in prices in the wake of an inflationary spiral that became pronounced from 1950 on, the policy of automatic salary increases applied on a national scale caused a number of problems. Before long, the amount of wage increases representing the higher index of prices was far in excess of the basic wage. As the cost-of-living allowance was calculated on a fixed maximum wage, the increases that followed nearly obliterated the wage differential, which in Palestine and in Israel was among the lowest in the world. This resulted in considerable unrest among skilled labor and professional and trained personnel, who found themselves not far from the bottom of the salary scale. Professional groups then attempted to form independent unions and pursue a wage policy that at times conflicted with the Histadrut policy and led to numerous strikes.

Labor-management relations were based on collective agreements negotiated by Histadrut with the Israeli Manufacturers Association. Whatever salary increases were sanctioned by these agreements were adopted by the government and by the Histadrut for their respective employees. The Minister of Labor was authorized by law to impose the terms of agreement, collectively negotiated in a certain industry, on enterprises not affiliated with the Israeli Manufacturers Association, thus assuring a uniform wage system on a national scale. Although possessing sufficient power to impose its policies on employers, the Histadrut exercised restraint in pressing for higher wages. It generally tried to adjust its policy to the anti-inflation policies of the government. It was also mindful of its own interests as the proprietor of numerous industries and services and as the employer of thousands of wage earners.

The Histadrut trade unions by special arrangement included non-Histadrut groups such as HaPo'el HaMizrahi (see MIZRAHI), *Po'ale Agudat Israel, and *HaNo'ar Ha'Oved V'haLomed. The largest national trade unions were the Union of Civil Servants (manual laborers and clerical workers employed in municipal and public enterprises, with 120,000 members in 1967), the Union of Construction Workers (60,000 members), the Federation of Government Employees (manual laborers and clerical workers, 45,000 members), and the Teachers Association (37,000 members).

Other Activities. Histadrut also encompassed mutual-aid institutions, the largest being *Kupat Holim (Sick Fund), which provided, with very substantial government assistance, medical aid to the great majority of the population. Mish'an, which provided social services for needy members, had a budget of more than IL 10,000,000 in 1966–67 and served some 60,000 Histadrut members. It maintained homes for the aged and children's institutions. The funds of Dor L'Dor and Matziv provided old-age pensions and survivors' benefits for widows and orphans. In 1968 these three bodies were merged.

In the 1960s the widespread economic and financial activities of Histadrut were centralized in Hevrat Ha'Ovdim, the holding company of all Histadrut enterprises, which had a far-reaching influence on the country's economy. In 1966 Histadrut institutions employed some 209,860 workers. The Histadrut thus emerged as the single largest employer of labor and by far the largest business concern, controlling manufacturing companies, banking, insurance companies, suppliers of goods and services, transportation, urban and interurban shipping and aviation, housing, and real estate.

In 1966 the income of the seven Histadrut pension and benefit funds was IL 381,000,000 (IL 308,500,000 in 1965). Nearly the entire income of Histadrut funds was invested in government bonds and in financing the economic enterprises of the Histadrut. This enabled the latter to enjoy extensive credit facilities unavailable to other concerns because of government policy of restricting bank credits.

Histadrut's Political Department cultivated contacts with workers' movements throughout the world, particularly with the emergent independent African nations. In 1960 the Afro-Asian Institute for Labor Studies and Cooperation was formed to coordinate Histadrut activities in Africa and Asia; it attracted hundreds of students from the two continents each year. The Department for Arab Affairs was concerned with the economic situation of the Histadrut's Arab members and formed an Arabic publishing house that produced books, a daily paper, *al-Yom, and educational material. The Center for Education and Culture sponsored thousands of lectures, motion-picture showings, courses, seminars, adult education institutes, and vocational schools and engaged in extensive projects of adult education.

The 1965 administrative budget of the Histadrut Executive Committee was about IL 50,000,000. This sum did not include the budget of the mutual-aid institutions or those of the economic enterprises. In 1968 the Histadrut imposed a tax on its members to finance the political parties represented in the Histadrut.

Status. From modest beginnings, Histadrut grew to become the most powerful organization in Israel. Through its control of the Histadrut, Mapai was at all times able to dominate political life. The Histadrut combined in its ranks hired labor with self-employed persons such as farmers in moshavim, members of kibbutzim, small-scale artisans, members of transport cooperatives, and others who generally did not employ labor. In addition, it was the largest single employer of labor. This unusual combination of diverse social elements and strata made the Histadrut a unique institution in the world. Its growth was largely made possible by the extensive material assistance, direct and indirect, afforded it by the WZO and its financial agencies and by the role it played in encouraging land settlement and in pursuing a policy of welcoming immigrants and aiding their settlement.

G. KRESSEL

HISTADRUT (GEVERKSHAFTEN) CAMPAIGN (National Committee for Labor Israel). Organized in 1923 under the sponsorship of the United Hebrew Trades (Faraynikte Yidishe Geverkshaften) of New York and formally launched at a mass meeting held at Cooper Union on Feb. 13, 1924, the Histadrut Campaign, originally named the National Labor Committee for Organized Jewish Labor in Palestine, popularly known in its early years as the Geverkshaften Campaign, and subsequently adopting its present name, espoused the following aims: (1) to give all possible financial and moral aid to the undertakings of the *Histadrut (General Federation of Labor) in Palestine, particularly those designed to encourage, absorb, and integrate new working immigrants; (2) to serve as a link between organized labor in Israel and organized labor in the United States and Canada; and (3) to win the support of American organized labor and of all liberal groups for the State of Israel.

From its beginning to the end of 1967, the campaign raised a total of $73,000,000 for labor causes in Palestine and later in Israel. No less than 1,400 projects in Israel, including hospitals, vocational schools, cultural and sports centers, old-age homes, and synagogues, were either established with its help or received substantial contributions from it. Through the American Histadrut Trade Union Council, organized in 1945, the American Federation of Labor, the *Congress of Industrial Organizations, the united AFL-CIO (see AMERICAN FEDERATION OF LABOR–CONGRESS OF INDUSTRIAL ORGANIZATIONS), and their affiliated local, national, and international unions gave substantial economic, moral, and political support to the Histadrut and to the cause of Zionism in general. In addition to the Trade Union Council and the various divisions engaged in fund raising, the Histadrut Campaign organized and maintained the American Histadrut Cultural Exchange Institute. The campaign also sponsored a camping program to enable American youngsters of high school and college age to spend their summers in work, study, and recreation in Israel. The Tourist Department of the Histadrut Campaign facilitated visits to Israel by Americans of modest means. The campaign built up a mass following among all segments of the American Jewish community, and its educational work extended to all sections of the United States and Canada.

C. B. SHERMAN

HISTADRUT HA'OVDIM HAL'UMIT. Israeli non-Socialist labor organization, founded in Jerusalem in 1934 as a non-party trade union. Its members, numbering 76,000 in 1966, uphold the idea of a Jewish State within the historic boundaries of the Land of Israel.

Histadrut Ha'Ovdim HaL'umit (National Workers Federation, or NWF) opposes the compulsory unification of Israeli trade unions in a single labor organization and advocates the right of Israeli workers to form free professional organizations. It rejects the Socialist contention that the class struggle and strikes constitute the only effective weapons in the defense of labor interests and considers compulsory national arbitration in all conflicts between labor and capital the only constructive method of regulating relations between employers and employees. In the field of economic endeavor, the NWF favors workers' cooperative enterprises instead of the establishment and ownership of economic enterprises by trade unions, as practiced by the *Histadrut (General Federation of Labor) in Israel. It advocates the introduction of a State Health Service instead of the existing system of professional, party, and private health organizations. The NWF has adopted as Labor Day the 20th of Tammuz, the anniversary of the death of Herzl; it flies only the national flag (*see* FLAG, ZIONIST AND ISRAELI) and has adopted "*HaTikva" as its sole anthem.

The supreme organ of NWF is the triennial Convention elected by its members, which nominates a Council of 71 members, an Executive, a Control Committee, and a Court of Honor. In 1966 the Executive was headed by Eliezer Shostak, M.K., general secretary of the NWF.

As a trade union, the NWF is divided into professional sections, charged with the protection and promotion of the interests of members engaged in various occupations. Among the services provided by the NWF to its members, the most important is the National Workers' Sick Fund (*Kupat Holim L'Ovdim L'umiyim). The Agricultural and Colonization Department of the NWF operates 14 agricultural settlements in Israel. Other social services include an unemployment fund, a general insurance fund, a special insurance fund for building and agricultural workers, a mutual-aid fund (Kupat 'Amal), a housing construction company, business centers in the development areas, synagogues, and kindergartens, as well as dispensaries of the National Workers' Sick Fund.

The federation controls the construction cooperatives Merkaz Ha'Avoda and Mossad and the Bri-On Company, which is responsible for the maintenance of convalescent and rest homes and of recreation centers. Attached to it is HaNo'ar Ha'Oved HaL'umi (National Labor Youth Organization), which maintains clubs, conducts vocational training, and organizes cultural and sports activities in urban and rural centers, especially among the new immigrants. The federation publishes two monthly magazines: *Hazit Ha'Oved HaL'umi* (National Workers' Front), for its adult members; and *Lapid* (Torch), for its youth organization.

In the *Diaspora, the federation is supported by Leagues for National Workers and Leagues for the National Workers' Sick Fund, whose function is to give financial assistance to the trade union institutions and to supply them with books and with medical, agricultural, and athletic equipment. In 1966 the Friendship League of the NWF operated in the United States, the Latin American countries, Europe, and South Africa.

I. BENARI

HISTADRUT 'IVRIT OF AMERICA (Hebrew Language Association of America). Organization founded in 1916 and devoted to the cultivation and dissemination of the *Hebrew language and Hebrew literature. The Histadrut 'Ivrit, whose headquarters is in New York, is the authorized American branch and affiliate of the *B'rit 'Ivrit 'Olamit (World Hebrew Federation).

During the first decade of its existence, it sought to promote the Hebrew language by a variety of projects and activities, especially the publication of books and periodicals and the organization of Hebrew-language courses. The Histadrut 'Ivrit has been associated with *HaDoar, a Hebrew-language newspaper which first appeared in 1921 as a daily, almost since its establishment. In 1922 *HaDoar* became a weekly, and it has appeared without interruption from that time on.

In the 1920s the Histadrut 'Ivrit established 'Ogen, its own publishing house, which, in addition to many books, issued for a number of years the *Sefer HaShana LIhude Amerika* (American Hebrew Year Book). Histadrut 'Ivrit also published *Niv* (founded in 1939), an illustrated quarterly magazine written and edited by junior members of the organization, and, since 1959, *LaMishpaha* (For the Family), an illustrated monthly in vocalized Hebrew.

Histadrut 'Ivrit established Masad (an independent entity since 1958), the first Hebrew summer camps for children and youth; sponsors the annual Hebrew Month, which focuses attention on the Hebrew language in Jewish schools and in the family; and established the Hebrew Academy for writers and scholars, which had its own publication, *P'rakim* (Chapters). In 1939 the Histadrut 'Ivrit also instituted the Hebrew Arts Foundation, which in 1952 founded the Hebrew Arts School for Music and the Dance in New York.

Among the founders of the Histadrut 'Ivrit were Eliezer *Ben Yehuda, David *Ben-Gurion, Itzhak *Ben Zvi, Reuben *Brainin, and Sh'marya *Levin. Its leaders have included Alexander Mordecai *Dushkin, Israel I. *Efros, Abraham *Goldberg, Samuel Kalman Mirsky, Menahem *Ribalow, and Abraham Spicehandler. In 1969 it was headed by Judah L. Pilch, president.

HISTORY OF ISRAEL. *See* ISRAEL, HISTORY OF.

HISTORY OF ZIONISM. *See* ZIONISM, HISTORY OF.

HITAHDUT. Abbreviated name of the Hitahdut 'Olamit Shel HaPo'el HaTza'ir UTz'ire Tziyon (World Union of *HaPo'el HaTza'ir and *Tz'ire Zion), a Labor Zionist party (*see* LABOR ZIONISM) that existed from 1920 to 1932. The rapprochement between the Eastern European Tz'ire Zion and the Palestinian HaPo'el HaTza'ir had its beginnings in the years prior to World War I. At the 8th Zionist *Congress (The Hague, 1907), Joseph *Aronowicz and Eliezer *Shohat, delegates of HaPo'el HaTza'ir, met with the delegates of Tz'ire Zion and decided to set up a joint office to serve both movements. On the eve of the 11th Congress (Vienna, 1913) the Central Committee of HaPo'el HaTza'ir asked the Tz'ire Zion societies in Russia to elect Palestinian HaPo'el HaTza'ir members as delegates to the Congress. The response was positive, and 14 Palestinian HaPo'el HaTza'ir delegates were elected in Russia, in addition to the 3 delegates elected by HaPo'el HaTza'ir in Palestine. At the Congress the two organizations formed a unified faction of 37 members. They also held a joint conference, at which it was decided that Tz'ire Zion was to maintain constant contact with HaPo'el HaTza'ir and to support the latter's activities in Palestine.

During World War I, a *Halutz (pioneer) wing evolved within the Tz'ire Zion movement, and *HeHalutz groups affiliated with Tz'ire Zion came into being. In that period groups of HaPo'el HaTza'ir and its sympathizers were organized also in Central Europe. Among the active members of HaPo'el HaTza'ir in Germany was Hayim *Arlosoroff. A similar circle, rallying around Samuel Hugo *Bergmann and Max *Brod, was founded in Prague. These circles advocated a populist, or humanitarian, socialism (as opposed to Marxist socialism). Close to this ideology was the youth movement *HaShomer HaTza'ir, which came into being during the war in Vienna and Galicia.

After the war it was decided to draw Tz'ire Zion and HaPo'el HaTza'ir even closer together, and a world conference of both organizations was convened in Prague in March, 1920. The conference, which was attended by 60 delegates, heard programmatic speeches by Aharon David *Gordon and Eliezer *Joffe. It proclaimed as the aim of the united movement the creation in Palestine of a free Hebrew society, built on *self-labor, without either exploiters or exploited. The name adopted for this movement was Hitahdut.

Very soon, however, the Soviet Russian branch of the movement split as a result of the decision of the Tz'ire Zion Council, which met clandestinely in Kharkov in May, 1920, to change the name of the movement to Zionist Socialist party (ZS). A minority decided to continue with the name Tz'ire Zion–Hitahdut. Similar divisions occurred within the Tz'ire Zion in other European countries, between those who remained faithful to the Hitahdut and those who organized themselves into the Zionist Socialist party (these included the Tz'ire Zion of Poland). The members of the Zionist Socialist party who settled in Palestine joined the *Ahdut 'Avoda. In the *Diaspora they joined (1925) the Right *Po'ale Zion.

In the Soviet Union the Tz'ire Zion–Hitahdut party, joined by General Zionist youth groups (see GENERAL ZIONISM), could develop only clandestinely. In May, 1922, the party held a conference in Kiev, at which it formulated a program aiming at "building a new society based on social justice." The platform consistently refused to employ the term "socialism." The conference confirmed the Russian name of the party, the Zionist Laborite party. On the 11th day of the conference the delegates were placed under arrest, but they continued their deliberations in prison. Twelve of those arrested were sentenced to two years' imprisonment; after some time they were "deported" to Palestine. Until 1926 the party maintained an underground printing press, which published leaflets and booklets.

In the wake of the separation of the Zionist Socialist party and the Zionist Laborite party, there occurred (at the end of 1923) a split in HeHalutz. The Zionist Laborite party, which in 1923 joined the World Hitahdut, gave its support to and identified itself with the illegal HeHalutz, the Halutz L'umi-'Amlani (National Pioneer Laborite Organization). Also under the influence of this party were the United Association of Zionist Youth in Russia and the Laborite HaShomer HaTza'ir. Between 1922 and 1930 about 3,000 members or sympathizers of the party immigrated to Palestine, and many others were arrested and exiled. Beginning in 1924, the movement maintained a delegation in Palestine, which represented it vis-à-vis the official institutions of the *World Zionist Organization (WZO). Some members of the movement returned illegally to the U.S.S.R. as emissaries of the movement and were arrested by the Soviet authorities. In September, 1934, the members of the last Central Committee were arrested in Moscow, and thus the party ceased to exist as an organized party. Nevertheless, many of its members, even in prison and concentration camps, remained loyal to the movement.

Outside the Soviet Union, the movement continued to develop, especially in Poland, Romania, Lithuania, and Latvia. The largest and best-consolidated countrywide organization was that of eastern Galicia.

The central theoretical-ideological problem of the party was the definition of its attitude toward socialism and the international Socialist movement. In Poland (after a minority had left and joined the Zionists–Socialists) the party disassociated itself from all Socialist tendencies, but such tendencies were strong in Lithuania, Latvia, Romania, and Germany. In August, 1926, the third conference of the Hitahdut was held in Berlin. This conference, with Hayim Arlosoroff as its central figure, drafted the program of the party, which declared that the aim of the Hitahdut was the creation of a free Hebrew working society in Palestine. This society was to serve as a national center, based on a Socialist public economy, freed from all forms of exploitation, and permeated by the Hebrew labor culture. At this conference the party was finally given its official name: World Zionist Labor Party Hitahdut (of HaPo'el HaTza'ir and Tz'ire Zion).

The Hitahdut adopted a positive, active attitude toward the *Hebrew language. It was among the chief supporters of the *Tarbut organization and a chief defender of Hebrew-language schools against the attacks of the Yiddishists.

In the mid-1920s, when HaShomer HaTza'ir began to evolve a leftist ideology that supported communism, Hitahdut found it necessary to establish a Zionist Halutz youth movement that remained true to the original aims of the party. The new organization, called *Gordonia, was established first in eastern Galicia (1925) and later in Poland, Romania, Lithuania, and other countries. It was organizationally independent, but the party devoted great effort to it and party members shaped its ideological stature.

The unification in Palestine of HaPo'el HaTza'ir and Ahdut 'Avoda in 1930 to form the Mifleget Po'ale Eretz Yisrael (*Mapai) confronted the Hitahdut with the problem of parallel unification with Po'ale Zion (ZS). The differences between the two parties in the Diaspora were greater than the differences between their counterparts in Palestine. Po'ale Zion (ZS) appeared in Jewish public life as a Socialist party which advocated the class struggle and stressed its separateness from the general Zionist movement. Hitahdut, on the other hand, advocated at most a "populist socialism," was opposed to the class struggle, and cooperated with the general Zionist movement. Hitahdut opposed the activities of Poʻale Zion (ZS) in the field of Yiddish education in the Diaspora. Poʻale Zion did not oblige its members to recognize the Jewish national flag. Hitahdut demanded of them the recognition of both the flag of the "class" (i.e., the red flag) and that of the Jewish nation. In the end, the position taken by the party in Palestine was decisive. Hitahdut participated in the First Congress for Labor Palestine, which was held in Berlin in September, 1930; it was represented there by 36 delegates in a total of 188. In Lithuania and Latvia the local branches of Tzʻire Zion–Hitahdut and Poʻale Zion (ZS) united without waiting for a world conference to effect unification. At the 17th Zionist Congress (Basle, 1931) the delegates of Hitahdut, together with those of Mapai, Poʻale Zion, and HaShomer HaTzaʻir, formed a joint labor faction.

In August, 1932, a joint conference of both parties, held in Danzig, decided to establish one party called Ihud Bʻrit HaPo-ʻalim HaYʻhudim HaSozialistit Poʻale Zion (Mʻuhadim ʻim Z.S.) UMifleget HaʻAvoda HaTziyonit HaʻOlamit Hitahdut or, in brief, Ihud (or *Ihud ʻOlami). The conference proclaimed as the aim of the new party the establishment of "a Jewish-Socialist workers' society in Palestine" and stressed the party's affiliation with the Socialist International. Ihud recognized the equality of Hebrew and Yiddish for educational and cultural activities in the Diaspora. It ruled that all national organizations that conducted schools in Hebrew or in Yiddish should guarantee to the minority of their membership the right to form schools in the other Jewish language.

Within a few years the unification was accomplished in all countries of the Diaspora with the exception of central Poland and western Galicia, where negotiations between the two parties continued without agreement until World War II. In particular, the language question and the national flag remained in dispute. In 1930 the party had 3,000 members in Poland proper and the same number in western Galicia. Only after the Nazi holocaust, in June, 1947, did the remnants of the two parties unite.

Y. SLUTSKY

HITAHDUT HAIKKARIM (Farmers' Federation of Israel).
The first steps to organize the farmers of the *Yishuv (Jewish population of Palestine) were taken at the beginning of the 20th century. The year 1903 saw the organization of the first association among the farmers of some of the settlements. This group, which was called the Association of Agricultural Settlements in Judea, failed after a few years, and a second attempt was made in Rishon L'Tziyon in 1913. This time the farmers, again of the Judea area, organized the Union of the Settlements. During World War I, under a strict Turkish law prohibiting Jewish autonomy, the organization ceased to exist. Four years after the British conquest of Palestine, in 1922, the third and successful attempt took place, this time through the initiative of the local farmers' organization in Petah Tikva. The new group was called Hitahdut HaIkkarim, or Farmers' Federation of Israel.

The Farmers' Federation represents the *moshava, or private village, in which each farmer owns his own land, buildings, equipment, and livestock. Membership in the Farmers' Federation does not call for association with any particular political party or social ideology, nor does the federation attempt to organize moshava residents into formal political units. In 1968 the Farmers' Federation comprised local branches in all the moshavot in Israel, totaling approximately 7,000 to 8,000 families. The federation's share in the various branches of agriculture in 1968 is indicated in the accompanying table.

AREA DEVOTED TO BRANCHES OF AGRICULTURE
(In dunams)

Branch	All Israel	Hitahdut HaIkkarim
Plantations	638,000	299,000
Citrus	453,000	199,000
Vineyards	100,000	63,000
Vegetable and commercial crops	280,000	60,000
Deciduous fruit	46,000	9,000
Almonds	23,000	21,500

The federation is governed by a Council elected by the representatives of the branches at a triennial meeting. The Executive Board consists of the heads of the various committees; and the president of the federation presides over the board. The federation, through its economic departments and marketing boards, assists its members in matters of taxation, labor relations, municipal councils, organization, public relations, and settlements. It also publishes a monthly. In 1968 the president of the federation was Tzʻvi H. Izakson; the director general, Yitzhak Ziv-Av.

The financial and economic institutions of the Hitahdut are the Farmers' Mortgage Company, the ʻAmir Supply Company, and the ʻAmir-Biaf Marketing Company. These are under the guidance of the Farmers' Holding Company. The Hitahdut also maintains an agricultural secondary school in Pardes Hanna, established in the late 1930s.

Cooperatives. The Hitahdut constantly stimulates local co-operation among producers without, however, forcing individual farmers to participate in such programs. The cooperative is regarded not as the ideological but as the economic backbone of the Hitahdut. The first cooperative, Pardes (literally, "citrus grove"), was established in 1900, years before the new forms of settlement (kibbutz, moshav) came into being. The organized efforts of the citrus planters have had a decisive influence on marketing methods in both the export and the domestic trade. Eventually private merchants found it necessary to join the central body of the citrus cooperatives, the Pardes syndicate, accepting its authority in matters of general policy.

Pardes and the Agudat HaKormim (Winegrowers' Association), set up in 1906, were the first to export agricultural produce cooperatively. Some time later the wine cellars of Rishon L'Tziyon and Zikhron Yaʻakov, established by Baron Edmond de *Rothschild, were transferred to the Winegrowers' Association. See also WINE INDUSTRY IN ISRAEL.

The Farmers' Federation has an audit union, called HaIkkar (Cooperatives' Cooperative), sometimes referred to as a central cooperative society. In addition to auditing the books of the member cooperative societies, HaIkkar advises them on financial and managerial problems. About 80 cooperatives are members of HaIkkar. They cover all branches of agriculture, planting, water supply, and so on.

Y. ZIV-AV

HODESS, JACOB.
Yiddish and Anglo-Jewish journalist (b. Vainutas, Lithuania, 1885; d. Jerusalem, 1961). Hodess went to England as a youth and served on the editorial boards of several Yiddish newspapers and Anglo-Jewish periodicals.

From 1924 to 1948 he was the editor of *New Judea*, which was the official organ of the World Zionist *Executive. After settling in Israel, he continued its publication under the name *Zion, Incorporating New Judea* (1949–52). Hodess was also acting secretary of the Zionist Executive in London (1929–39) and London editor of Palcor, the Zionist news agency (1939–49).

HOD HASHARON. Township in the Sharon Plain. Created through the amalgamation of the settlements Hadar Ramatayim, Magdiel, and Ramat Hadar, the oldest of which (Magdiel) was founded in 1924. Population (1968): 12,400.

HODIYA. Village (moshav) in the Darom. Founded in 1949 by immigrants from India (Heb., *Hodu*) and affiliated with *T'nu'at HaMoshavim. Population (1968): 403.

HOFFMAN, HAYIM. *See* YAHIL, HAYIM.

HOFFMAN, JACOB. Rabbi, scholar, and *Mizrahi leader (b. Pápa, Hungary, 1881; d. Tel Aviv, 1956). Ordained rabbi at the Yeshiva of Bratislava, he subsequently received a Ph.D. degree from the University of Vienna. He early became active in the religious Zionist movement, attending the first international convention of Mizrahi in 1904. During World War I he served as chief Jewish chaplain in the southern theater of operations of the Austro-Hungarian Army. In 1922 Hoffman was elected chief rabbi of Frankfort on the Main, where he founded a Yeshiva that encouraged its students to acquire a higher secular education. Hoffman soon was regarded as the leading spokesman for Mizrahi in Central and Western Europe.

When the Nazis came to power in Germany, he was chosen to serve on the seven-man Reichsvertretung der Deutschen Juden, the only Orthodox Jew on this board, which acted as German Jewry's official representative body before the Nazi government. In 1937 his public criticisms of the Nazi leadership resulted in his arrest by the Gestapo and his deportation to Austria. In 1938, while on a mission in the United States on behalf of German-Jewish relief, he was elected rabbi of Congregation Ohab Zedek in New York, a position he held until his retirement in 1953. While in New York, he was vice-president of the Mizrahi Organization of America (*see* RELIGIOUS ZIONISTS OF AMERICA), chairman of the Va'ad HaHinukh HaHaredi (Committee for Religious Education), and a member of the Executive of *Keren HaYesod. He published a number of scholarly works. In 1954 he moved to Tel Aviv, where he became head of the Central Committee of the National Religious party.

G. BAT-YEHUDA

HOFIT. Rural community in the Sharon Plain. Founded in 1955. Population (1968): 310.

HOGLA. Village (moshav) in the Sharon Plain. Founded in 1933 and affiliated with T'nu'at HaMoshavim. Population (1968): 184.

HOLIDAYS IN ISRAEL. *See* SABBATH AND HOLIDAYS IN ISRAEL.

HOLON. City south of Tel Aviv. Founded in 1940 by the merger of several residential neighborhoods, the first of which had been established in 1933. The name Holon, derived from

A view of Hogla in 1955. [Zionist Archives]

the Bible, was chosen because of the sand (Heb., *hol*) dunes on which the city was built. In 1950 Holon was granted municipal status. Population (1968): 75,900.

The Lodzia textile plant, founded by immigrants from Łódź, Poland, played an important role in the early development of Holon. In 1945 Holon had about 5,000 inhabitants; by 1948 the population had grown to 7,000. After the establishment of the State of Israel, the city expanded rapidly. Its hundreds of factories and workshops made it an important industrial center. Its products include textiles, metal and leather goods, furniture, glassware, foodstuffs, plastics, and building materials.

Holon is the center of the *Samaritans of Israel. A separate neighborhood in the city houses more than 200 Samaritans, or about half the Samaritan population of Israel (the other half live in Nablus, near Mount G'rizim, which is their religious center). In 1968 there were in the city 24 elementary schools with a total enrollment of 12,049, 5 high schools with a total enrollment of 1,742, and 2 trade and technical schools with a total enrollment of 1,074. The municipal budget in 1948 was IL 282,000, of which IL 84,000 was earmarked for development. By 1968 the regular budget had grown to IL 21,500,000 and the development budget to IL 4,830,000. Pinhas Eylon was mayor in 1968.

HOLY LAND. *See* PALESTINE.

HOLY PLACES IN ISRAEL. Each of the three monotheistic religions—Judaism, Christianity, and Islam—has had its holy places in Palestine-Israel, sites associated with their respective religions and usually including religious buildings as well. Many of these sites are in or near Jerusalem, and their care has frequently been a matter of fierce controversy among the different *communities and, in the case of the Christian sites, particularly among the various churches. One of the causes of the Crimean War (1854–56), which was fought between the Russians on one side and Turkey, France, and Great Britain on the other, was a dispute between the Orthodox (Greek and Russian) and the Roman Catholic Churches about their respective rights to the Church of the Nativity in Bethlehem. From that time on the question of the holy places has been one of the unsettled problems of European diplomacy.

Mandatory Period. The British *Mandate for Palestine, approved by the Council of the League of Nations in 1922, included two articles on the subject. All responsibility in connection with the holy places and religious buildings and sites in Palestine—including that of preserving existing rights, of securing free access to the sites, and of protecting the exercise of the right to worship while at the same time assuring the requirements of public order—was assumed by the mandatory, which was responsible solely to the League in all related matters. Nothing in the articles was to be construed as preventing the mandatory from entering into arrangements with the Palestine administration for the purpose of enforcing the provisions.

A special commission was to be appointed to study, define, and determine rights and claims in connection with the places and rights relating to the different religious communities. After the confirmation of the mandate, the British government made a resolute attempt to form such a commission, with a proposed membership of five Christians, three Jews, and three Muslims. The attempt failed because of the suspicious attitude of each community toward the others. In the case of the Christian holy places, the administration was guided by the record of the rights and practices compiled by Ottoman officials prior to the British occupation of the country. That record of the status quo was treated as Holy Writ. There was no serious trouble in connection with the holy places during the 30 years of British administration. The time-honored Easter ceremonies in the Church of the Holy Sepulchre were maintained, and the agreement of the contending churches to carry out the necessary repairs on the building was obtained by the British administration. The Roman Catholic Franciscans were permitted to erect new churches on the Mount of Olives, in the Garden of Gethsemane, and on Mount Tabor in Galilee.

*Western Wall. The one serious trouble during the period of the mandate concerned the right of worship by Jews at the outer Western (Wailing) Wall of the Temple of Solomon and Herod, the Kotel Ma'aravi, in Jerusalem. The right of the Jews to pray at this corner of the most holy area of the Temple ruins had been established ever since the destruction of the Temple in the 1st century of the Common Era, but after the Muslim conquest of Palestine it had been limited and restricted. The Muslims regarded the site of the former Temple as a holy place because, according to their tradition, it was from there that Mohammed had ascended to heaven. On that ground they had built the Dome of the Rock over the place of the altar, converting a former Christian basilica into al-Aqsa Mosque, the third most holy site of their faith. Attempts by Jewish groups and individuals to get the Muslim authorities in Palestine to agree to the sale of the pavement in front of the Wall and the buildings around it, so as to allow more space and comfort for Jewish worshipers, broke down. In September, 1928, a disturbance in the previously amicable relations between the Jews and Arabs occurred when the beadle of the informal Jewish congregation that had gathered for prayer at the Wall placed chairs there on the Eve of the Day of Atonement and affixed a screen, by means of a bolt in the pavement, to separate the men from the women. This act, considered a breach of the status quo, drew immediate protest from the Arabs, and the beadle was ordered by the district commissioner to remove

Western (Wailing) Wall in Jerusalem. [Zionist Archives]

the screen before services began that day. When he objected that he could not do this on the Holy Day, a British police officer was sent by the commissioner to remove the screen. Passions were quickly stirred on both sides. After serious outbreaks of *Arab riots all over the country, the British government obtained the approval of the Council of the League of Nations for the appointment of an ad hoc international commission to investigate problems of religious rights at the Western Wall. The report of the Commission, published in June, 1931, found that the Wall and the pavement were Muslim property. The Wall was a sacred site for Muslims, but the pavement was not; both, however, were holy places for the Jews. The latter could not claim exclusive rights to the pavement, but the Commission considered that "there was a right *sui generis*, the basis of which is an ancient custom." The Commission confirmed the action taken by the Palestine government as to the manner of worship and the appurtenances which the Jews might bring to the Wall. The British government issued an order-in-council (a legislative act), defining the rights and conditions laid down by the Commission and imposing penalties for violations.

Following the occupation of the Old City of Jerusalem by the Jordanian forces in 1948, the Jews were deprived of access to the Wall despite the provision of the 1949 armistice agreement with Jordan whereby access to the holy places was to be assured. Nineteen years later, following the *Six-day War of 1967, when Israel gained control of the Old City, the old and dilapidated small houses facing and flanking the Wall were removed and a spacious paved square was created in front of it. Since that time, thousands of religious visitors and tourists have thronged the square daily, and communal prayers are held there at all hours of the day.

Other Holy Places. The 1947 resolution of the United Nations concerning the *partition of Palestine into Jewish and Arab states, with an international trusteeship for Greater Jerusalem, including Bethlehem and 'En HaKerem, stressed the importance of the protection of religious sites and of free access to them for worship. Because of violent Arab protests, the provisions of the resolution concerning Jerusalem remained a dead letter. Israel, on the other hand, made it clear that it would welcome the appointment of a UN High Commissioner to safeguard all the holy places of the three religious communities. Failing such action, owing to the refusal of the Arabs to negotiate, Israel took steps through the Ministry of Religious Affairs to protect Christian and Muslim holy places and religious buildings in its territory. These included Mount Zion and 'En HaKerem, the birthplace of John the Baptist, in Jerusalem; Nazareth, Capernaum, and other sites of the ministry of Jesus, in Galilee; and the cave of Elijah, at Haifa. Israel was also in control of the site shared by the three communities on Mount Zion, which comprised the reputed tomb of King David, holy to Muslims and Jews alike, and the Chamber of the Last Supper, which is holy to Christians. During the mandate era entry to the tomb chamber was reserved to Muslims. From 1948 on it was open to all. Mount Zion became a place of religious pilgrimage in Israel. The tomb of Rachel, on the road between Jerusalem and Bethlehem, was within Arab territory, as were the grave of Simeon the Just and the Mount of

Church of the Holy Sepulchre, in Jerusalem. [Israel Government Tourist Office]

Dome of the Rock, on the site of Solomon's Temple, in Jerusalem.
[Israel Government Tourist Office]

Olives Cemetery, until 1967. On the other hand, archeologists excavated the famous burial ground of Bet Sh'arim near Haifa, where Rabbi Judah HaNasi, the compiler of the Mishna, is buried. Maintenance of the holy places of the three religious communities in Israel is the responsibility of the Ministry of Religious Affairs.

The principal holy places of the three communities include the following sites:

Jewish. The Western Wall of the Temple, in the Old City of Jerusalem; the tomb of David, on Mount Zion in Jewish Jerusalem; the grave of Simeon the Just, in a suburb of Jerusalem; the tombs of the patriarchs Abraham, Isaac, and Jacob, in Hebron; the tomb of Maimonides, in Tiberias; and the graves of the mystics at Meron, in northern Galilee, near Safed.

Muslim. The Haram ash-Sharif (Noble Sanctuary) of Jerusalem, which includes the al-Aqsa Mosque and the Dome of the Rock; the Haram (Sanctuary) of Hebron, which covers the tombs of the patriarchs Abraham, Isaac, and Jacob; and the cave of Elijah, at Haifa.

Christian. The Church of the Holy Sepulchre and other churches and monasteries in the Old City of Jerusalem; the Garden of Gethsemane, on the Mount of Olives; the Church of the Nativity, in Bethlehem; the Church of the Annunciation, in Nazareth; the ancient synagogue in Capernaum; and the Mount of the Beatitudes, at the northern end of the Sea of Galilee (Lake Kinneret).

Following the Six-day War of 1967 and the unification of Jerusalem, the *Knesset passed the Holy Places Bill, which ensures full access to the holy places and prohibits all desecration or violation of them. This law also created a legal basis for self-supervision by the various religious communities of their holy places.

N. BENTWICH

HOMA UMIGDAL. *See* "STOCKADE AND TOWER" SETTLEMENTS.

HOOFIEN, ELIEZER SIEGFRIED. Israeli banker, economist, and public servant (b. Utrecht, Netherlands, 1881; d. K'far Sh'maryahu, 1957). The son of the communal rabbi of Utrecht, Hoofien attended business school in Amsterdam and worked as a public accountant in that city from 1903 to 1909, when his friend Jacobus *Kann recommended him for the position of director at Zionist headquarters in Cologne. In 1912 he left Cologne to settle in Palestine, where he was appointed assistant general manager of the Anglo-Palestine Bank Ltd. (forerunner of the *Bank L'umi L'Yisrael). He was joint general manager of the bank from 1919 to 1923, general manager from 1924 to 1947, and chairman of the board of directors of the bank from 1947 until his death.

Under Turkish rule during World War I Hoofien, as a national of a neutral country, organized a committee for the distribution of aid sent to the *Yishuv (Jewish population of Palestine) from abroad and arranged for the issue of provisional bank notes for the Yishuv's needs. In 1917 and 1918 he was the representative of the *American Jewish Joint Distribution Committee (JDC) for Palestine. In 1923 he was a founder of the Tel Aviv–Jaffa Chamber of Commerce, the first such organization in Palestine, of which he was honorary president at the time of his death. In the 1930s he helped set up the *Ha-'avara project to transfer German-Jewish assets to Palestine.

After the establishment of the State of Israel, Hoofien served as Economic Coordinator in the Prime Minister's Office in 1948–49. When the *Bank of Israel was established, he was named chairman of its Advisory Committee.

Hoofien was awarded the Order of the British Empire in 1925 and the Order of Orange-Nassau in 1931. For many years prior to the establishment of the State of Israel he was Netherlands Consul in Tel Aviv. He contributed numerous articles on economic problems to the Israeli and foreign press.

HOPE-SIMPSON REPORT. Report on economic conditions in Palestine from the point of view of protecting the rights of the Arab population (*see* ARABS IN ISRAEL). Submitted to the British government by Sir John Hope-Simpson in August, 1930, it was published in October, 1930, simultaneously with the statement of policy called the *Passfield White Paper.

Sir John Hope-Simpson, a retired civil servant in India and a member of the League of Nations commission for the resettlement of Greek refugees, was appointed by the British government as a direct consequence of the *Shaw Commission's recommendation; it was his task to prove the extent to which Arab complaints were justified.

Hope-Simpson spent only two months in Palestine, during which he was preoccupied mainly with the influence of Jewish *immigration and settlement on the Arab population and with problems of development. He considered the country predominantly agricultural and discounted its industrial potentialities. From this point of view he found that, under existing conditions in the Arab villages and existing Zionist policies, there was no room for newcomers.

His estimate of arable land (6,544,000 dunams; *see* DUNAM) was 40 per cent lower than that reached by Jewish experts. Accordingly, he found not only that there was no surplus of land but that, taking 130 dunams per family as the minimum for a decent standard of living, the actual Arab rural population suffered from an acute shortage of land. The only vacant lands seemed to Hope-Simpson the unutilized lands held by the Jewish institutions.

The Arab farmer was found to be living under deplorable conditions: he suffered from shortages of land and capital and from rising rents, heavy taxes, and bad crops. He was also in debt and was forced to pay high rates of interest on his loans. The tenant farmer was not protected from eviction, and once evicted, he could not find work. The Jewish national institutions were accused of causing Arab unemployment by their adherence to the principle that Jews in Palestine employ Jewish labor only. To Hope-Simpson the solution seemed to lie in developing intensive agriculture and changing the structure of the Arab village. He recommended large-scale irrigation, partition of jointly held lands in the Arab villages, introduction of new crops, promotion of education, and encouragement of rural cooperation. Once these reforms were introduced, he reasoned, there would be room for another 20,000 families. He recommended putting a stop to the immigration of Jewish labor until the problem of Arab unemployment would have been resolved. *See also* JEWISH AND ARAB LABOR.

As against these recommendations it was pointed out by the Jewish leadership that since the Jewish economic sector employed only Jewish labor, the Arabs would gain nothing by a cessation of immigration of Jewish laborers. In fact, the expenditure of Jewish capital might well eventually result in a demand for Arab services. But Hope-Simpson did not believe that a growing market created by immigrants would advance industrial production. He found labor too expensive for a competitive textile industry. Only a slow growth of small-scale industry using local products seemed possible to him, and even in this field he criticized the replacement of traditional Arab crafts by Jewish enterprises.

The Passfield White Paper policy was based on this report.

I. KOLATT

HORA. The most popular folk dance of Israel. A round dance, the Hora is known in all Balkan countries. The Palestinian Jewish version of the Hora was created in 1924 by Barukh Agadati, a Romanian-born actor who had immigrated to Palestine in 1910. Tel Aviv's Ohel Theater introduced the dance into the settlements of the Jezreel Valley and Galilee, and it spread throughout the country. In the course of time, the form of the Hora Agadati, as the first Palestinian Jewish version was known, underwent several changes. Expressing the temperament and verve of the pioneering spirit of the Halutzim (pioneers; *see* HALUTZIYUT), the Hora also incorporated influences from the past, notably the deep feeling and soulfulness of the Hasidim. Many Israeli composers created Horas, which became popular also in Zionist youth movements all over the world.

See also DANCE IN ISRAEL; THEATER IN ISRAEL.

HOROWITZ, DAVID. Israeli economist and public servant (b. Drogobych, Galicia, Austria, 1899). Educated in Lvov and Vienna, Horowitz joined the Zionist youth movement *Ha-Shomer HaTza'ir. In 1920 he went to Palestine with a group of Halutzim (pioneers; *see* HALUTZIYUT) and became one of the leaders of *G'dud Ha'Avoda V'haHagana 'Al Shem Yosef Trumpeldor. In 1923 he joined the Executive Committee of the *Histadrut (General Federation of Labor). Between 1927 and 1932 he was a free-lance journalist and lecturer. In 1932 he was appointed economic adviser and secretary of the *American Economic Committee for Palestine, Inc., a position he held until 1935, when he became director of the Economic Department of the *Jewish Agency.

Between 1946 and 1948 Horowitz was assigned responsible tasks in presenting the Jewish case to the *Anglo-American Committee of Inquiry and the *United Nations Special Committee on Palestine (UNSCOP) and served on the Jewish delegation to the United Nations at Lake Success. From 1948 to 1952 he was Director General of the Israeli Ministry of Finance. In 1950 he headed an Israeli delegation that went to London to negotiate with the British government on British and Israeli claims resulting from the termination of the *Mandate for Palestine.

In 1954 Horowitz was named the first Governor of the *Bank of Israel. As of 1967 he was also Israel's representative in the International Bank for Reconstruction and Development (World Bank), chairman of the Board of Directors of the Eliezer *Kaplan School of Economics and Social Sciences (from 1953), and a member of the Council for Higher Education. Horowitz published a number of works dealing with the economic problems of Palestine and Israel, including *Aspects of Economic Policy in Palestine* (1936), *Jewish Colonization in Palestine* (1937), *Economic Survey of Palestine* (1938), and *State in the Making* (1953).

HORSHIM. Village (kibbutz) in the Sharon Plain. Founded in 1955 and affiliated with the *Kibbutz Artzi Shel HaShomer HaTza'ir.

HORWICH, BERNARD. Businessman, communal worker, and early Zionist leader in the United States (b. Poniemon, Lithuania, 1861; d. Chicago, 1949). After working in Germany, Horwich went to Chicago in 1880 and engaged in business. In 1898, at the urging of his brother Harris, who had been to Palestine, he organized the Chicago Zionist Organization No. 1, the Chicago section of what later became the *Zionist Organization of America (ZOA). Horwich was president of the group from 1898 to 1901 and treasurer from 1912 on. He also founded, with Leon *Zolotkoff, the Order Knights of Zion, of which he was the first grand master.

Horwich attended the 5th Zionist *Congress (Basle, 1901) and seven other Congresses. He was an early member of the Greater *Actions Committee. After his partial retirement from business in 1927, he paid a visit to Palestine, and in 1939–40 he was a member of the ZOA National Administrative Council. He published an autobiography, *My First Eighty Years* (1939).

HOS, DOV. Labor leader and public servant in Palestine (b. Orsha, Russia, 1894; d. near Bet Lid, 1940). Settling in Palestine in 1906, Hos studied at the *Herzliya High School in Tel Aviv until 1913 and then worked in D'ganya until the following year. In 1915 he joined the Turkish Army. With the British advance on Palestine and the issuance of the *Balfour Declaration in 1917, however, he deserted from the Turkish Army and joined the *Jewish Legion to fight on the side of the British.

After the demobilization of the legion in 1919, Hos participated in the founding of *Ahdut 'Avoda and the *Histadrut (General Federation of Labor) in 1920. He undertook several missions abroad on behalf of the Palestine labor movement. In 1922 he was in Berlin, and in 1927–28 in the United States, on behalf of the Histadrut. At the end of 1928 he was sent to London as the political representative of the Histadrut and the World Union of *Po'ale Zion. Remaining in England until 1931, he studied at the London School of Economics and represented Palestinian Jewish labor at several conferences of the British Labor party and the International Federation of Trade Unions, seeking the support of organized labor for Zionism. He established close personal ties with leaders of British labor. His outstanding linguistic ability enabled him to establish close contacts with other European labor circles as well.

From 1925 to 1927 Hos was a member of the Tel Aviv Municipal Council, and in 1936 he became deputy mayor of Tel Aviv, holding this office until his death in an automobile accident. A leading figure in *Hagana, he stressed the need for adequate Jewish self-defense. In 1941 the first gliding school for Jewish aviators in Palestine was named for him.

HOSEN. Village (moshav) in western Upper Galilee. Founded in 1949 and affiliated with *Herut. Population (1968): 256.

HOVEVE S'FAT 'EVER (Lovers of the Hebrew Language). Organization in prerevolutionary Russia for the propagation of spoken *Hebrew. Before World War I the society had more than 60 branches all over the Russian Empire, mainly in the so-called Jewish Pale, namely, Poland, Lithuania, White Russia, and the Ukraine. More than twice that number of applications were posted with the reluctant Tsarist Russian authorities, who at first exacted the condition that Hebrew should not be spoken except for "didactic" purposes. In 1912 the main branch of the society, in St. Petersburg, presented the opera *Samson and Delilah* in the Hebrew translation it had commissioned. By that time a number of branches in the provinces, especially in the Ukraine, were operating Hebrew kindergartens. The society held regular literary meetings and annual celebrations, which included performances by its own choirs.

The main branch in St. Petersburg was incorporated in 1907, but it had been anticipated by a society with similar aims and a similar name (Agudat Hoveve S'fat 'Ever). There had been earlier, individual attempts to organize Hebraists in Russia on a local level, and still other such societies existed outside the country. The Hoveve S'fat 'Ever paved the way for the more ambitious and more comprehensive *Tarbut, which came into being at the end of World War I and embraced a much larger number of adherents. It was wiped out by the Bolshevik regime.

M. Z. FRANK

HOVEVE ZION (Lovers of Zion). Movement that came into being in 1882, as a direct reaction to the widespread pogroms in Russia in 1881, for the purpose of encouraging Jewish settlement in Palestine and achieving a Jewish national revival there. Its founders had been influenced by Rabbi Zvi Hirsch *Kalischer, Rabbi Nathan Friedland, David *Gordon, and others and by the struggle of the Balkan nations for independence. Thus, Eliezer *Ben Yehuda wrote in 1879 that if the Jews were to survive as a people, a Jewish National Home would have to be created in Palestine. The growth of the movement was prompted also by the unfavorable conditions under which the Jews of Eastern Europe lived. Pogroms and the denial of civil rights in Russia, and persecution and economic pressures in Romania, led to Jewish emigration from these countries and strengthened the concept of settlement in the Land of Israel. The movement drew its supporters from Russia, which then had the largest Jewish population, and it also gained a strong and active following among the Jews of Romania. Smaller Hoveve Zion groups were established in Austria-Hungary, England, and the United States. As the pioneer Jewish Palestine

settlement organization, the Hoveve Zion can be considered the founders of the modern *Yishuv (Jewish population of Palestine) as well as the forerunners of Herzlian Zionism. It was from their ranks that the Zionist movement in Eastern Europe drew its leadership. Pro-Palestine groups and initiatives, unrelated to any political vision of a Jewish revival in Palestine, appeared also in France and Germany (*see* FRANCE, ZIONISM IN; GERMANY, ZIONISM IN).

Russia. The idea of Jewish national redemption in Palestine had spread among the Jews of Russia long before the emergence of Herzl's political Zionism. As early as 1860 and again in 1871, David Gordon published in the Hebrew paper *Ha-Maggid* (The Narrator) a series of articles in which he discussed the basic principles of Jewish *nationalism in connection with the renaissance of Palestine. A powerful voice was that of Peretz *Smolenskin, whose monthly, *HaShahar* (The Dawn), published in Vienna beginning in 1868, combated both Orthodoxy and *assimilation, extolled the *Hebrew language, and fervently espoused the Palestine idea. His *'Am 'Olam* (Eternal People), which appeared in 1873, had a powerful impact on the Jewish intelligentsia. Smolenskin got an enthusiastic reception from student groups in St. Petersburg and Moscow. Moshe Leib *Lilienblum, a regular contributor to *HaShahar*, published a widely read brochure, *The Rebirth of the Jewish People in the Land of Its Ancestors*, and to the end of his life remained in the forefront of the struggle for Palestine. After the pogroms of 1889, Leo (Leb) Levanda, who had been an ardent advocate of "Russification" for years, became a firm supporter of the Palestine solution of the Jewish problem.

Probably the most searching analysis of the Jewish situation was given in 1882 in a German-language pamphlet entitled *Autoemancipation* and subtitled "An Admonition to My Brethren by a Russian Jew." It was written by Dr. Leo *Pinsker, an Odessa physician, who, like Levanda, had previously been an advocate of assimilation but had drastically revised his views after the pogroms. Pinsker eloquently pleaded for the establishment of a Jewish nation in America or Palestine "to permit the settlement of some millions." This indecision as to the territory to be chosen did not last long, for under the influence of Lilienblum, Pinsker became a convinced supporter of Palestine. Translated into Russian, the brochure influenced a far wider circle than any previous advocacy of the cause of Jewish national renaissance.

The response of Jewish youth was particularly enthusiastic. A group of 25 Jewish students of Kharkov University adopted as its motto the call of the prophet Isaiah, "Bet Ya'akov L'khu V'nelkha ("O House of Jacob, come ye and let us go forth"), and adopted the name *Bilu, composed of the initial letters of the verse. The aim of the members was to go to Palestine at once as pioneers and to dedicate their lives to the realization of the national ideal. They toured the Russian-Jewish communities and recruited 500 adherents from among their fellow students and others. The seat of the Bilu committee was transferred from Kharkov to Odessa, and a delegation was sent to Constantinople, where it entered into negotiations, albeit unsuccessfully, for the purchase of land in Palestine. Despite this setback, the first group of 14 Biluim (Bilu-immigrants) landed in Jaffa in June, 1882. They founded the settlements Rishon L'Tziyon (1882) and G'dera (1884).

The cumulative effect of the numerous appeals was the emergence of a dynamic movement called Hibbat Zion (Love of Zion). Clandestine groups of Hoveve Zion, headed mostly by professional men, communal leaders, and rabbis, were formed in numerous Jewish centers. The first Hoveve Zion conference, held at Kattowitz on Nov. 6–12, 1884, was attended by 34 delegates from Romania, Germany, England, France, and Russia, with the Russians playing the dominant role (see KATTOWITZ CONFERENCE). Pinsker presided, and Rabbi Sh'muel *Mohilever, the editor of HaMelitz, Alexander *Zederbaum, the historian, Shaul Pinhas *Rabinowicz (Shepher), Leon *Chasanowitsch, and others were the guiding spirits of the gathering. It was decided to extend financial assistance to the Biluim and other settlers; headquarters was established in Odessa, where Pinsker was also president of the local Hoveve Zion society.

A second conference was held in 1887 at Druskenik, with the participation of Meir *Dizengoff (who was to become mayor of Tel Aviv) and M'nahem M. *Ussishkin, who later played a leading role in the World Zionist movement (see DRUSKENIK CONFERENCE). Two years later, by which time some 80 groups were in existence, another conference was held in Vilna, attended by delegates from 35 societies. The year 1890 saw the legalization by the Russian government of the Society for the Support of Jewish Agriculturalists and Artisans in Palestine and Syria, with headquarters in Odessa. The society, chaired by Pinsker until his death in 1891 and popularly known as the *Odessa Committee, assisted in the establishment of the settlements Rehovot and Hadera, acquired land for Jewish colonization, and helped support schools in the settlements.

The small-scale, practical, and predominantly philanthropic activities of the Hoveve Zion were of indisputable help to the struggling early settlements in Palestine. They were, however, subjected to trenchant criticism by a leading member of the Odessa Committee, *Ahad Ha'Am. The secret order *B'ne Moshe (Sons of Moses), created and headed by Ahad Ha'Am, attracted the elite of the Hoveve Zion. The monthly *Ha-Shiloah, founded by Ahad Ha'Am in 1896, exercised a decisive influence on the intellectual outlook of the Hebrew-reading public.

J. SCHECHTMAN

Poland. The spread of *Haskala (Enlightenment) among the Jews of Poland and Russia alarmed the religious elements, which declared war on the bearers of Enlightenment. In 1860 Rabbi Zvi Hirsch Kalischer of Thorn (Toruń) and Elijah *Gutmacher of Grätz (Grodzisk) stressed the need for a great Jewish ideal to draw the masses away from the influence of the *emancipation movement; they called a conference of Jewish notables and rabbis in Thorn, at which they established a society for settlement in Palestine and laid the foundation of the Hoveve Zion movement. The initial response to this conference came mainly from German Jewry, but the Jews of Poland and Russia also began to identify themselves with the Hibbat Zion movement as a result of the anti-Jewish riots that swept Russia in 1880 and of the pogrom in Warsaw in 1881. That same year the Jews of Suwałki established Y'sud HaMa'ala, a society to support settlement in Palestine. In 1882 a similar organization was formed in Międzyrzec, and later societies were established in other cities as well. At first the membership comprised mainly Jews who had migrated from Lithuania to Poland, but Polish Jews soon became active also.

Hibbat Zion groups were scattered throughout Poland. For a long time the Warsaw group, founded in 1883, served as the center of the organization. Its activities, which were illegal, were channeled through various synagogues. In Warsaw it was the Ohel Moshe Synagogue, named for Sir Moses *Montefiore. Among the active members in Warsaw were Shaul Pinhas Rabinowicz, Israel *Jasinovsky, Leib Davidson (the grandson of Rabbi Hayim Davidson of Warsaw), Z'ev *Gluskin, Jacob Moses Meirson, and, for a time, Dr. Ludwig Zamenhof, the creator of Esperanto. Active members in Białystok included Rabbi Sh'muel Mohilever and Dr. Joseph *Chasanovich; in Vilna, Samuel Joseph *Fünn and Leo Levanda; and in Grodno, Bezalel and Leib *Jaffe. Groups also existed in Łódź, Zgierz, and Kattowitz (Katowice).

The headquarters of Hibbat Zion in Warsaw maintained contact with groups outside Poland and Russia. The program adopted by the early Hibbat Zion and Sh'erit Yisrael groups in Warsaw stated: "We have reached the conclusion that only through the spread of agriculture among the Jews in the Holy Land, and the strengthening of love for Eretz Yisrael among all Jews, can the Jews become a united, vital and self-respecting people."

The Hibbat Zion movement did not succeed in attracting the masses, for large and powerful groups—Hasidim and assimilationists, the wealthy and the intelligentsia—were arrayed against it. During its early years Nahum *Sokolow and Isaac Leb Peretz were among those who opposed it. Sokolow viewed its activities directed at *immigration to Palestine as potentially injurious to welfare work on behalf of local Jewish communities, which were then at a low ebb economically as well as spiritually. As editor of *HaTz'fira, Sokolow was among the main advocates of aid to local Jews and frequently criticized Hibbat Zion activities. Despite his doubts, however, he participated in the 1st Zionist *Congress (Basle, 1897) at Herzl's invitation. He returned from the Congress impressed by Herzl's personality, and immediately became one of the main proponents of Zionist thought and action.

At the time, Hoveve Zion activities centered mainly in fund raising for the purchase of land in Palestine, where Polish Jews founded the settlements Y'sud HaMa'ala and 'Ekron, lent support to Petah Tikva, and in later years helped establish Rehovot and Hadera. In 1884 the Warsaw headquarters initiated an international conference of Hoveve Zion. While visiting Warsaw and Białystok, David Gordon, the publisher of HaMaggid, sent an open letter to the leaders of Hoveve Zion in which he explained the need for the conference. To this letter the Warsaw group attached a plan for a unified organization. Thirty-five delegates attended the conference, which took place in Kattowitz in November, 1884, after preliminary talks held the previous year.

At the conference, Dr. Leo Pinsker voiced the concept "rejection of the *Diaspora" (see ISRAEL AND THE DIASPORA) and stressed the movement's obligation to aim at Jewish renascence through labor, particularly agricultural labor, in Palestine. It was decided to allot 10,000 francs for Petah Tikva and 2,000 rubles for Y'sud HaMa'ala and, after some debate, to support the Bilu settlements. To develop industry in Palestine, the delegates pledged investments totaling 18,000 rubles. They formed an organization named the Montefiore Association (Mazkeret Montefiore) after Sir Moses Montefiore, in the hope that the latter would help support it financially. This hope did not materialize, and the organization lacked the financial means to develop the projects. Despite the mood of excitement and optimism that pervaded the conference, it was not successful in arousing widespread activity among the masses. The conference established two centers: one in Odessa, headed by Pinsker and Moshe Leib Lilienblum; and one in Warsaw, headed by Israel *Jasinovsky. They were joined by Rabbi Mohilever, Leo Levanda, and others.

In 1887 the Druskenik Conference was held near Vilna, with the participation of many Orthodox rabbis and laymen. It decided to petition the Russian authorities to extend official recognition to the movement. In 1889 Ahad Ha'Am's B'ne Moshe found support among the Polish Hoveve Zion groups. The Jeshurun Society, which was formed in Warsaw and became the center for these groups, was instrumental in establishing Rehovot and founded the *Ahiasaph Hebrew publishing company.

Simultaneously, groups of Dorshe Zion (Seekers of Zion) were formed and aided practical settlement work in Palestine. Their members included a number of wealthy men. The group in Pinsk, which counted 40 families, raised 10,000 rubles to buy land and in 1891 sent emissaries to Palestine for that purpose. Similar groups were formed in Międzyrzec and Białystok. The rabbi of Kotsk joined the latter together with 13 Hasidic families. Less affluent supporters formed "clubs of 1,000," comprising 1,000 families each, with each family paying 40 rubles a year for five years in an effort to raise the funds necessary for their settlement in Palestine.

A. REISS

Romania. In 1872 Benjamin F. Peixotto, a Romanian Jew who at the time was the American Consul in Bucharest, proposed the transfer of all Romanian Jews who suffered from civil disabilities and persecution to the United States. This plan was rejected by the *Brussels Conference of large Jewish organizations, but Rabbis Hayim Zvi *Sneersohn, Zvi Hirsch Kalischer, and Judah Solomon Hai *Alkalai and others endorsed the idea of settling Romanian Jews in Palestine. A settlement society, founded in Moineşti in 1875, sent emissaries to Palestine to purchase land, but they were prevented from reaching their destination by the Russo-Turkish War.

The arrival in Romania in 1880 of Eleazar *Rokeah, an emissary from the Jewish community of Safed, led to the formation of a Palestine settlement society in Bucharest. However, the society, which comprised 100 families, was unable to obtain funds. In Iaşi, then the largest Jewish community in Romania, Rokeah founded a Palestine settlement society and a journal, *Jezreel*, devoted to the dissemination of its ideas. Dr. Karpel *Lippe became chairman of the society. Similar societies were formed elsewhere. The Moineşti society sent one of its founders, David Shub, to Palestine to purchase a tract of land near Ja'uni from the Jews of Safed.

Late in 1881 a conference of all Palestine settlement societies in Romania, called by the Bucharest group, convened with 51 delegates representing 36 societies. It was presided over by Samuel *Pineles of Galaţi. The conference decided on immediate emigration to Palestine. The first transport, consisting of 100 families, was scheduled to leave in the spring of 1882. The Central Committee, whose seat was in Galaţi, invited Laurence *Oliphant, who had been chosen to administer the Mansion House Fund for the relief of persecuted Jews in Russia and was then visiting Lvov in connection with his work, to come to Romania. On the occasion of his visit, a conference of all colonization societies convened in Iaşi, on May 4, 1882, received substantial financial pledges from wealthy Iaşi Jews,

chose a delegation to purchase land in Palestine, and authorized Oliphant to intercede in Constantinople for permission to Jews to settle in Syria. In Bucharest, too, a large meeting was held, with Oliphant's participation. After arriving in Constantinople, Oliphant invited two representatives of the Bucharest settlement society, and the latter submitted to the American Consul a petition that he take action to obtain permission for Romanian Jews to settle on government-owned land in Syria and to purchase land. When the permission thus obtained excluded Palestine, the representatives, as residents of former Turkish territories conquered and annexed by the Romanians, requested protection from their former government. They were received in audience by the Sultan, the Prime Minister, and the Minister of the Interior, and their request seemed about to receive favorable consideration when the occupation of Egypt by Great Britain and France caused a postponement.

In July, 1882, the Galaţi Central Committee, which did not approve of the activities of the representatives in Constantinople, sent another delegation to Palestine to purchase land. A group of 30 wealthy young Jews also sent emissaries, including Eleazar Rokeah, to Palestine to purchase land. These attempts ended in failure. Later, members of the Moineşti society actually settled on the land they had bought from the Safed Jews and established the village Rosh Pina. They were joined by several pioneers from other Romanian cities. Some of the latter sought other settlement sites and founded Zamarin (later Zikhron Ya'akov), south of Haifa. With the acquisition of this tract, additional groups of immigrants left Romania to settle in Palestine.

The movement in Romania continued to spread. Youth groups and women's societies came into being. *HeHalutz, a society for prospective Palestine settlers without means, was established. In December, 1882, youth groups named for Oliphant held a countrywide conference and elected a Central Committee of their own. At their second conference, in April, 1883, they merged with the Galaţi committee. The Zion Society, organized in 1873 by Benjamin F. Peixotto along the lines of the American *B'nai B'rith, included in its program the establishment of a colony in Palestine for its members. In October, 1883, the Zion Society held a special conference devoted to the problems of settlement in Palestine.

Since the Galaţi committee had difficulty in raising funds, the financial position of Rosh Pina and Zamarin became precarious. In February, 1883, the committee sent Karpel Lippe to Paris to seek the support of the *Alliance Israélite Universelle. He received promises but no actual help.

The colonies were eventually saved from starvation and disintegration by Baron Edmond de *Rothschild. On Sept. 16–17, 1883, a convention called by the Galaţi committee accepted Rothschild's conditions and agreed to the transfer of the colonies to his administration. Many Romanian-Jewish families applied to Rothschild's representative for permission to join the existing colonies, but their request was refused. Only a few families who were already in the country were permitted to join Rishon L'Tziyon and 'Ekron. The Palestine settlement movement in Romania, which strove to solve the problem of the country's Jewish population by emigration, began to disintegrate. Local committees and colonization societies dissolved, and the Central Committee itself disbanded in 1885.

In that year a society for colonization in Cyprus (*see* CYPRUS PROJECT) was formed in Piatra-Neamţ. Twenty-five families from this town and some from Bacău emigrated to the island, but their attempt to settle there encountered insuperable difficulties. The emigrants scattered, the majority going to Palestine or Alexandria, while a minority returned to Romania.

In 1887 the Dorshe Zion society was organized in Iaşi, and similar groups sprang up in other cities. In the early 1890s a movement for the settlement of Palestine was revived in Romania, inspired by the achievements of the Russian Hoveve Zion. The societies adopted the same name, and on Apr. 11, 1893, held a convention in Galaţi. A Central Committee, with headquarters in Galaţi, was elected. By the summer of 1894, 26 such societies were active in Romania. Samuel Pineles resumed his activities, becoming the head of the Galaţi committee.

At that time a group of 80 families from Romania and 10 from Bulgaria organized the 'Ezra MiTzar society with a center in Iaşi. In 1893, 'Ezra MiTzar bought 18,000 dunams (see DUNAM) in the Gaulan from the Paris Palestine Committee, set up by Rothschild in 1892 for the resale of land he had purchased in Transjordan. In 1894 the Central Committee of the Romanian Hoveve Zion bought 11,000 dunams on easy terms of payment from the Paris committee. In addition, it received 10,500 dunams of rocky land free of charge. All societies contributed to the payment of annual installments.

In the fall of 1895, 4 Romanian members of 'Ezra MiTzar, joined by a Bulgarian, settled in Palestine. These were followed several months later by 7 other members with their families. Five or six, who were in a financial position to do so, began to build small houses in the village of Sahm el-Jaulan in Transjordan; the rest returned to Romania. Although they warned their friends not to migrate prematurely, soon 16 more families from Romania and 7 from Bulgaria arrived in Palestine. Despite the difficulties they encountered, several more families arrived from Romania in May, 1896.

With the blessing of the rabbi of Buhuşi, two men were sent to Palestine in the summer of 1896 to purchase land in Galilee or Transjordan for 50 families, but after the rabbi's death the project was abandoned. The settlement in Transjordan came to an end when the Governor of Damascus sent soldiers to drive the settlers out. Baron de Rothschild refunded to the societies the money they had invested in the purchase of the land.

The first two conventions of the Romanian Hoveve Zion movement were held in 1895 and 1896, respectively. The first, attended by delegates from 19 societies, debated propaganda methods and settlement problems. The Central Committee got in touch with the Paris Palestine Committee in order to purchase land. The principal item on the agenda of the second convention was Jewish settlement in Transjordan.

I. KLAUSNER

Austria. In Vienna the *Ahavat Zion society was formed by Dr. Reuben *Bierer in 1882 to aid Russian immigrants to Palestine. Its ranks included both Orthodox Jews (Rabbi Sh'lomo Binyamin Spitzer) and "enlightened" Jews (Peretz Smolenskin and many students). When Rabbi Spitzer was elected chairman, the students, including Bierer, Nathan *Birnbaum, and Moritz Tobias *Schnirer, seceded, forming their own group, *Kadimah (in 1882), and Ahavat Zion soon disbanded. The purpose of Kadimah was to fight assimilation, promote Jewish consciousness, and work for the settlement of Palestine. The first practical step toward pro-Zionist propaganda was taken by Nathan Birnbaum, who in 1885 commenced

publishing a fortnightly (in German) called *Selbst-Emanzipation* (Self-emancipation, a title obviously chosen in reference to Leo Pinsker's brochure *Autoemancipation*, 1882), aimed at the advancement of the "national, social, and political interests of the Jewish race." Birnbaum's ideas exerted great influence, especially in Galicia (then part of Austria), where the Jews were fighting both Jewish assimilationists and the nationalist demands of the Poles, Ukrainians, and Ruthenians.

Contact was soon established with Hoveve Zion groups in other countries, and in 1885 a Hoveve Zion group named Zukunft ('Atid) was formed in Vienna. That same year saw the foundation in Vienna of Admath Jeschurun (later known as the Zion society), another Hoveve Zion group, aiming at the establishment of settlements in Palestine. Among the active members of the association were Adolf Schramek, president, Rudolf Feldbaum, Herz Fischler, Moses Heilpern, Oser *Kokesch, Lazar Rathaus, Abraham *Salz, Moritz Tobias Schnirer, Josef Schwarz, Aaron Weil, and Wilhelm Wenig. Also in 1885, a young women's group, Miriam, was founded on the initiative of Miss Sabine Karmel. This group held meetings and sponsored talks on Jewish history, Jewish settlement in Palestine, and "Jewish national problems." These groups, which included a Hebrew-speaking club in Vienna, were soon joined by other clubs and students' associations in Vienna and throughout Austria. Many leaders in the Zionist movement were alumni of the groups.

In 1881 a group was formed in Przemyśl, in Galicia. The Israelitische Allianz in Podgaytsy (Podhajce) raised funds for Russian refugees and sought to channel all subsidies to immigrants to Palestine. A short-lived group in Cracow, headed by Rabbi Simon Schreiber (Sofer), a member of the Austrian Parliament, supported settlers in Rosh Pina. In Lvov, Dr. Bierer and Dr. Joseph Koback worked for Palestine. In 1883 the latter founded a club for Hebrew studies, which later became known as Zion. Other Hoveve Zion groups existed in Tarnów, Drogobych, Stryy, Borislav, and Stanislav. The Hoveve Zion of Galicia, however, did not think in terms of immigration and settlement. In 1893 the Zion society in Lvov held a national conference at which it was decided to establish a Jewish National party to protect the political interests of the Jews. That year a central Zion society was also formed in Austria-Hungary, and a similar political party was established.

J. FRAENKEL

Great Britain. In 1884 Kalman (Charles) Wollrauch formed a Hoveve Zion group in London, which was affiliated with the Central Committee in Odessa. Its members were mainly of Russian and Polish origin. Two of the thirty-six delegates attending the Kattowitz Conference in 1884—Zerah Barnett and Charles Wollrauch—came from England. It was at this conference that Dr. Leo Pinsker, who was in the chair, proposed the establishment of an association (Maskeret Montefiore) to honor Sir Moses Montefiore, the British philanthropist and supporter of Jewish settlement in Palestine, on his 100th birthday. On Mar. 13, 1885, the Chevra Hoveve Zion–L'Maskereth Moshe (Hevra Hoveve Zion L'Mazkeret Moshe) was established in London "to colonize the Holy Land of our fathers by Jewish toil." However, this society was not able to collect substantial amounts for Palestine settlement, and its activities were hardly noticeable.

In 1887 Russian immigrants founded in Whitechapel a Kadimah group whose main activity consisted of lectures on

Palestine and discussions on Jewish affairs. Only after the appearance of the Kamenitzer Maggid (Hayim Zundel Maccoby) at a Kadimah meeting on Feb. 1, 1890, was there a noticeable growth in the Hoveve Zion movement in England. Leaders of the established Jewish community joined the movement and petitioned the British government to help ease Turkish restrictions on immigration to Palestine, but they were unsuccessful in achieving British intervention.

The Hoveve Zion movement of Britain had two outstanding leaders, Elim Henry *d'Avigdor, who advocated "Palestine as a real political State," and Col. Albert Edward W. *Goldsmid, who strove for a "resuscitated Jewish State." Hoveve Zion groups were set up in London, Leeds, Manchester, Birmingham, Cardiff, Sheffield, Edinburgh, and Glasgow. The leading event of the British Hoveve Zion was a meeting on May 23, 1891, in the Great Assembly Hall, London, attended by an audience of 4,000—the largest crowd seen in Whitechapel to that time.

Although the activities of Hoveve Zion in England aroused public interest and received much newspaper publicity, they did not develop as the organizers had hoped. The organization suffered a succession of crises. The death of D'Avigdor in 1895 was a serious setback. Colonel Goldsmid could be persuaded only with great difficulty to continue as "chief" of the English Hoveve Zion. This was the state of affairs until Herzl appeared on the Jewish scene and created an enthusiastic following in England.   J. FRAENKEL

United States. The Hibbat Zion movement, which began in the early 1880s, was part of the spiritual baggage brought to the United States by Russian-Jewish immigrants. The first Hoveve Zion society was formed in New York in 1882, and other societies soon followed in Boston, Baltimore, Philadelphia, and other cities. By 1890 there were eight branches affiliated with the New York group. In Chicago, Bernard *Horwich organized a Zion Society in 1896. The Yiddish press, which was founded at about this time, began to play a leading role in spreading the idea of Jewish nationalism and the restoration of Zion.

Some of the men most prominent in the Hoveve Zion groups were Dr. Joseph I. *Bluestone; Aaron S. Bernstein, the editor of a Hebrew weekly; Alexander Harkavy, the Hebrew and Yiddish lexicographer; Rabbi Aaron Wise; Rabbi Gustav *Gottheil; Joseph H. Cohen; Hyman Aaron Medalie; Dr. Moses Mintz; Adam *Rosenberg; and Meyer London. The Zionist idea was preached by Rabbi Bernhard *Felsenthal of Chicago, Dr. Marcus Jastrow and Rabbi B. L. *Levinthal of Philadelphia, and Rabbi Benjamin Szold and Dr. Aaron *Friedenwald of Baltimore.   S. CAPLAN

Other Countries. In 1882 Russian-Jewish students founded the Nir Society in Zurich, Switzerland. Four Hoveve Zion groups in Serbia and Bosnia became affiliated with the Odessa center in 1885.

Herzl. The appearance of Herzl's *Jewish State and the convening of the Zionist Congress in Basle (1897) brought the Hoveve Zion face to face with the problem of political Zionism. Baron Edmond de Rothschild, who had always minimized the political goals of settlement in Palestine, refused to meet with Herzl. Nonetheless, the majority of the Hoveve Zion did support the new movement, though insisting that settlement activities be continued even before political authorization was ob-

tained from the Turkish government. The French and British Hoveve Zion groups would not participate in the Zionist Congresses, however, and a separate British Zionist Federation was created in 1899 (see GREAT BRITAIN, ZIONISM IN). The Hoveve Zion groups maintained their Central Committee, but its influence and activities were minimal and were overshadowed by the work of the *World Zionist Organization in the political, financial, and educational spheres. Although the *Esra society in Germany continued to function, as did the Odessa Committee in Russia (as the only group having government recognition), the Zionist movement under the dynamic leadership of Herzl in effect engulfed almost all the Hoveve Zion and became a continuation of that movement in a modified form.

                                                       I. KLAUSNER

HUBERMAN, BRONISLAW. Violinist and founder of the Palestine Orchestra (b. Częstochowa, Russian Poland, 1882; d. Corsier-sur-Vevey, Switzerland, 1947). A student of Joseph Joachim, Huberman traveled widely and published articles and

Bronislaw Huberman.
[Zionist Archives]

pamphlets on musical questions as well as on political and cultural-political problems, including the *Pan-Europa* (Pan-European) idea. Visiting Palestine for the first time in 1929, he started planning the foundation of a first-class music organization for the country. When Hitler came to power, Huberman assembled first-desk orchestra players from the major orchestras in Eastern and Western Europe and invited them to Palestine, thus saving the lives of many persecuted artists. In 1936 he founded the Palestine Orchestra (now the *Israel Philharmonic Orchestra) in Tel Aviv. Arturo Toscanini agreed to conduct the opening concert. Huberman continued to work for the advancement of "his" orchestra, which, contrary to his wishes, was long known as the Huberman Orchestra. His writings and collections are now in the Hekhal HaTarbut (Culture Hall) in Tel Aviv, at the Central Music Library, in the same building as the Israel Philharmonic. The street on which the library is located is named for Huberman.

                                                   P. GRADENWITZ

HUKOK. Village (kibbutz) in eastern Lower Galilee. Founded in 1945 and affiliated with the *Kibbutz M'uhad. Population (1968): 231.

HULATA. Village (kibbutz) in the Hula Valley, in eastern Upper Galilee. Founded in 1937 on the shores of Lake Hula and moved to its present site in 1946. Affiliated with the *Kibbutz M'uhad. Population (1968): 392.

Drainage project in the Hula Valley. [Israel Information Services]

HULA VALLEY. Northernmost part of the Jordan depression, bounded on the west by the steep slopes of the Naphtali Mountains of Upper Galilee and on the east by the volcanic slopes of the Gaulan Heights of Syria. Situated at an elevation of 300 feet above sea level, it is 13 miles long and 5 miles wide. Its southern edge is formed by a volcanic sill through which the Jordan River breaks in a steep gorge. In the north of the valley the sources of the Jordan combine to form the main river, which bears the name Jordan from that point on and passes through the center of the valley. In ancient times the blocking of the Jordan outlet by rockfall (near the bridge of B'not Ya'akov) caused the flooding of large parts of the valley and the formation of a huge papyrus swamp, whose deepest part formed Lake Hula, 5 square miles in extent and 6 to 9 feet deep. The area was so malarious that few people could survive there. In the 19th century it was settled by the semi-nomadic Ghwarna tribes, which raised buffaloes and cultivated some rice and other grains but suffered severely from malaria.

In 1934 the *Hevrat Hakhsharat HaYishuv obtained a concession for the drainage of the area. However, although Jewish settlement started in 1939, drainage operations had to be postponed because of World War II and the *War of Independence and did not begin until after the consolidation of the State of Israel. Drainage works carried out between 1951 and 1958 resulted in the complete elimination of the swamps and the lake. The whole of the reclaimed area and its fringes were turned into irrigated land and came to be one of the most fertile regions in Israel. Owing to a combination of hot summers and cool winters, the valley specializes in the cultivation of deciduous fruits, especially apples, together with subtropical summer crops, such as cotton or even rice. The lower parts are utilized for fishponds (comprising 40 per cent of all fishpond areas in Israel). In the 1960s the urban center of the valley was the town of Kiryat Sh'mona, where the processing industries for the products of the valley were concentrated and which provided manpower for seasonal agricultural work.

Y. KARMON

HULDA. Village (kibbutz) in the Lod area. Founded in 1930 and affiliated with the *Ihud HaK'vutzot V'haKibbutzim During the *War of Independence Hulda was an important

base for the Israeli forces in their battles to free the road to besieged Jerusalem. Population (1968): 296.

An earlier settlement of the same name was located nearby. Originally formed in 1907, it was attacked in the 1929 *Arab riots. The handful of settlers and some members of *Hagana heroically defended the small, isolated settlement in what was then an otherwise completely Arab-populated area, but they were forced to abandon it when the British did not come to their aid. In the Arab attack Efrayim Czisik, the commander of the defenders, was killed.

HUNGARIAN JEWS IN ISRAEL. Jews from Hungary, including territories that were assigned to other countries after World War I, first came to the Holy Land as early as the 16th century. Following the Turkish occupation of central Hungary in 1526, the Turks moved 20 Jewish families from Buda to Safed, where they soon were assimilated to the Sephardi Jews (*see* SEPHARDIM). Early in the 19th century, Moses Sopher, the rabbi of Pressburg (now Bratislava), was instrumental in the settlement of several hundreds of his students and disciples in Jerusalem. Following the collapse of the 1848–49 Hungarian uprising against Austria, in which the Jews of Hungary took an active part, a number of Jewish freedom fighters escaped to Palestine. Later in the 19th century, many religious Jews went from Hungary to Jerusalem, Safed, Tiberias, and Jaffa to live on charity made available to them by the Hungarian Kolel (*see* HALUKKA).

In 1878 Joshua *Stampfer, David Guttmann, and several other Hungarian Jews who lived in the Hungarian Houses (Bate Ungarn) in the Me'a Sh'arim section of Jerusalem, maintained by the Hungarian Halukka, founded Petah Tikva, the first moshava (agricultural settlement) in Palestine. Although they were soon compelled to abandon their village, their attempt remains of historical significance. Today Hungarian Jews are represented in large numbers in numerous newly founded kibbutzim and moshavim.

In 1921 there began an *'Aliya (immigration) of young engineers from Budapest, motivated by Zionist conviction as well as by the so-called White Terror which swept Hungary after the ouster of the short-lived Communist regime of Béla Kun. Among them were Árpád Gut, who built the Nesher cement factory in Haifa, and Prof. Joseph Breuer, who headed the drainage of the Jezreel Valley. From 1924 to 1939 the 'Aliya from Hungary was considerable, reaching its peak in 1939, when many Hungarian Jews living in the successor states left for Palestine.

From 1919 to 1948 more than 10,000 Hungarian Jews immigrated legally, and there were also 1,300 Ma'apilim (illegal immigrants; *see* ILLEGAL IMMIGRATION). From 1948 to 1955 another 15,000 came, while as a result of the Hungarian Revolution of 1956 about 5,000 Hungarian Jews settled in Israel. Since then, the Hungarian government has allowed between 50 and 200 Jews to emigrate annually. By 1961 more than 30,000 Hungarian Jews had immigrated to Palestine-Israel. It is estimated that in 1966 there were in Israel 190,000 Jews whose mother tongue or whose parents' mother tongue was Hungarian. This figure included Hungarian-speaking Jews from Yugoslavia, Romania (Transylvania), Czechoslovakia, and Austria.

The first three professors at the *Hebrew University of Jerusalem were Hungarians: Andor Fodor taught chemistry; Michael Guttmann, Talmud; and Samuel Klein, Palestinology.

They were joined in 1927 by Michael Fekete, professor of mathematics. The first Ph.D. degree awarded by the university (1936) was to a Hungarian, Raphael *Patai. Subsequently, Y'hezk'el Kutscher, Saul Patai, and Y'sha'yahu Tishby joined the faculty, and many more Hungarian Jews are now among the lecturers and student body. The situation is similar at *Bar-Ilan and *Tel Aviv Universities and at the Haifa *Technion, where Joseph Breuer taught after completing his work as head of the Jezreel Valley drainage project.

Avigdor *Hameiri was one of the first Hebrew poets and novelists to settle in Palestine (1921). Ephraim Kishon is a successful humorist and playwright. Joshua Bar-Yoseph is well known as a novelist, and Itamar Krest, as a translator. Numerous Hungarian-Jewish newspapermen in Israel, such as David Gil'adi (*Ma'ariv), Hanna Zemer (*Davar), Y'huda Edelstein (*HaBoker), Mord'khai Avi-Shaul (*Kol Ha'Am), and Barukh Beer (*Ha'Aretz), write only in Hebrew. Others, such as Thomas Lampel, Alexander Gervai, Dan Ofry, Hillel Danzig, Valery Stark, and Naphtali Krausz, write in Hungarian as well as in Hebrew. Y'huda Marton is in charge of foreign broadcasts at the *Israel Broadcasting Service. Ernő *Marton was the editor of the Hungarian daily *Uj Kelet.

In the fine arts, Yosi Stern, a teacher at the *Bezalel School, achieved great popularity with his scenes of Jerusalem, as did Mord'khai Levanon. The uncontested leaders in cartoons and caricatures are Dosh (Károly Gardos), Samuel Katz, and Zeev (Jacob Farkas). Among the well-known painters of Hungarian origin are Stephan Alexander, Béla Bán, David Gilboa, László Keleti, Moshe Levanon, Stephan Adler, Edvin Salamon, Blanka Tauber, Stephan Rodan, and Stephan Mokadi.

In the *theater, Hanna Meron and Batya Lancett are recognized stars. Also well known are Miriam Nevo and Abraham Rónai, János Kristof is active as a stage director.

Jews of Hungarian descent are also outstanding in the field of music. Lóránt Fenyves was the original first violinist of the *Israel Philharmonic Orchestra; Ödön *Partos is an outstanding cellist; the pianist Vera Lengyel, the husband-and-wife team László Vince (cellist) and Ilona Vince (pianist), and the violinists Ilona Fehér and Alexander Tal are among the well-known performing artists. Emy Peer, Marta Aczél, and Sigmund Rosenfeld are members of the Israel National Opera, and László Pataky is an influential music critic.

Jews of Hungarian origin outstanding in Israeli commerce, industry, and foreign trade are too numerous to be mentioned by name. They played an active role in the development of Israeli shipping; many of them are ships' officers. Their representation among the officers of the *Israel Defense Forces is impressive. They work in governmental and municipal offices and in the diplomatic service. In 1966 five of them were members of the *Knesset.

The Association of Immigrants from Hungary is a constituent of the World Federation of Hungarian Jews. It has its center in Tel Aviv and 15 chapters throughout Israel. Its president in 1965 was the veteran novelist Illés Kaczér; its secretary, Tibor Farkas. In addition, there are so-called Landsmannschaften, comprising immigrants from various localities, such as Ungvár (Uzhgorod), Kassa (Košice), and Budapest. The General Zionists (see GENERAL ZIONISM) among the Hungarian 'Olim (immigrants) founded the B'ne Herzl society; the *Mapai members, the Golden Age Club. Hungarian Jews also founded the Nordau Lodge of *B'nai B'rith.

T. FARKAS

HUNGARY, ZIONISM IN. Hungarian Zionism developed in a community that was generally hostile to it. Both the Orthodox Jews of Hungary and the rapidly developing "Neolog" congregations, whose membership was inclined toward *assimilation, vigorously opposed the idea of Jewish *nationalism. Nevertheless, the publication in 1896 of Herzl's *Jewish State aroused some interest in Hungarian Jewry, and in 1897 seven Hungarian Jews from five cities participated in the 1st Zionist *Congress.

Beginnings. Also in 1897, following the 1st Congress, several local Zionist organizations were established in a number of cities, including Budapest, the capital, Pozsony (Bratislava), Kolozsvár (Cluj), Nagyszombat (Trnava), Kassa (Košice), and Szabadka (Subotica). A year later, at the 2d Zionist Congress, it was reported that Hungary had 32 Zionist groups. On the national level, the movement was launched in the spring of 1902, when a provisional national Zionist committee was established. The committee included János *Rónai, Béla *Österreicher, and Samu *Bettelheim, who were reelected to their positions at the 1st Hungarian Zionist Conference, held in Pozsony in 1903. In the same year the *Jewish National Fund was established in Hungary, and in 1904 *Mizrahi held its First World Conference in Pozsony.

Pre-World War I Decade. At the 7th Zionist Congress (1905) it was reported that a number of Orthodox rabbis in Hungary had issued a proclamation against Zionism. The assimilationists accused the Zionists of lack of patriotism, and in 1908 the issue of patriotism formed the subject of a debate in the Hungarian Parliament. To ease matters, David *Wolffsohn, president of the *World Zionist Organization, visited Budapest in 1908 and was received by the Hungarian Minister of the Interior, Count Gyula Andrassy. The latter, while expressing friendship for Zionism, would not grant approval of the statutes of the Zionist Organization in Hungary, as was required by law.

Makkabea, the Zionist students' organization, was established in 1903, and it soon emerged as a center of Zionism in Hungary. Led by such men as Niszon *Kahan, Mózes *Bisseliches, Áron Schönfeld, and Lajos *Dömény, Makkabea engaged in effective propaganda and produced some of the ablest leaders of the local Zionist organizations. It was under the auspices of Makkabea that the first Zionist organ, the Zsidó Néplap (Jewish People's Paper), was launched in 1905. The paper, however, was short-lived, and in 1907 Ármin Bokor, its editor, started a second Zionist weekly, Zsidó Élet (Jewish Life), with the collaboration of Leo Singer, but this, too, was discontinued in the same year. Zsidó Szemle (Jewish Spectator), the organ of the Hungarian Zionist Organization, made its appearance on Jan. 1, 1911; it was first a monthly, then a fortnightly, and finally a weekly. It became an influential forum, especially under the editorship of József *Schönfeld, who had translated Herzl's Jewish State into Hungarian and remained editor of the weekly for 20 years.

Another periodical, Mult és Jövő (Past and Future), devoted to Jewish culture, literature, and art, played an important role in arousing interest in Jewish Palestine even among the "assimilated" Hungarian Jews. Founded (1911) and edited by Joseph *Patai, this magazine reached a wider range of readers than the Zionist papers and was influential in gaining numerous followers for Zionism.

The Hungarian Zionist Organization pioneered in the physical education of youth by establishing the VAC (Vívó és Atlétikai

Club, or Fencing and Athletic Club), in 1906. Kadimah, the first Jewish boy scout movement, was established in 1911, by Lajos Dömény. The famous HaKoah sports club of Vienna was founded on the pattern of the VAC with the help of Hungarian Zionist organizers.

At the 10th Hungarian Zionist Conference, held in Kassa in 1910, Mizrahi seceded from the Hungarian territorial Zionist Organization. This action brought about a decline in the movement, with the result that several groups ceased functioning altogether.

In 1912 a branch of the *Jewish Territorial Organization was founded in Hungary. Following a period of sharp feuding between the Territorialists and the Zionists, the former sent an invitation to Israel *Zangwill, founder and head of the Jewish Territorial Organization. In July, 1913, Zangwill went to Budapest, where he delivered a speech on Jewish nationalism. The Territorialist movement, however, had few followers.

Hungarian Zionist conventions took place every year. In 1913 the Hungarian delegation to the 11th Zionist Congress in Vienna consisted of 10 delegates. Early in 1914 David Wolffsohn revisited Budapest with Sh'marya *Levin.

World War I and the Postwar Decade. During World War I there was practically no Zionist activity in Hungary except for the publication of the *Zsidó Szemle* and *Mult és Jövő*. Following the war, which resulted in the annexation by Czechslovakia, Romania, and Yugoslavia of about two-thirds of Hungary's prewar territory, the Hungarian Zionist movement lost contact with the Zionist groups that flourished in the detached provinces of Burgenland, Slovakia, Subcarpathian Ruthenia, Transylvania, and Croatia-Slavonia. The prewar leadership, elected in 1913, resigned owing to internal discord, and the new temporary committee appointed in 1919 could not start functioning because of the unsettled political conditions. During the short-lived Communist regime of Béla Kun (1919) the new committee was dissolved and the publication of *Zsidó Szemle* prohibited. Following the Romanian occupation of Budapest, however, the Zionist weekly resumed publication (September, 1919).

Banquet of the Hungarian Zionist Organization in honor of Kurt Blumenfeld in Budapest in the late 1920s. From left to right: József Schőnfeld, Mózes Bisseliches, Lipót Osztern, an unidentified woman, Mrs. Hansi Bisseliches, Kurt Blumenfeld, two unidentified women, Ignác Friedmann, and Mrs. Niszon Kahan.
[Andrew Freeman]

With the restoration of normal conditions Zionist work was resumed, and at the *London Zionist Conference of 1920, Hungary was represented by three delegates, one of whom, Béla Österreicher, was elected to the *Actions Committee. In 1921 the Hungarian Zionist Organization had a membership of 5,000, organized in local groups in the capital and 17 other towns. The Zionist Women's Union had 700 members. A National Committee of seven headed the central office. A Halutz (pioneer) organization (*see* HALUTZIYUT) trained young people and taught them *Hebrew. At the Palestine Office (opened in 1919; *see* PALESTINE OFFICES) several thousand persons were registered as prospective emigrants, and in the first half of 1921, 103, among them 20 engineers, actually left for Palestine.

In the early 1920s the so-called Friedrich Decree prohibited the organization and operation of associations whose bylaws had not been formally approved by the authorities, and consequently the Hungarian Zionist Organization had to suspend its activities. In 1926 the Zionists again asked for the legalization of their bylaws, but this was denied because of opposition to Zionism on the part of the leaders of the Jewish Congregation of Pest and the National Bureau of Hungarian Jews. Finally, in 1927, the bylaws of the Hungarian Zionist Organization were approved by the government, mainly as a result of pressure brought to bear by the World Zionist leadership.

Also in 1927, owing largely to the initative and leadership of Joseph Patai, the Pro-Palestine Association of Hungarian Jews was established, primarily for the purpose of mobilizing the widest possible strata of Hungarian Jewry (including the assimilationists who refused to join the politically tinged Zionist Organization) in support of the rebuilding of a Jewish Homeland in Palestine. The foundation of this association represented a major breakthrough in making interest in and support of Jewish Palestine accepted by the elite of Hungarian Jewry. Its leadership was soon joined by Baron Adolf Kohner, Court Councillors Károly Baracs and Ferenc Székely, Chief Government Councillor Ignác Friedmann, and Professors Bernát Alexander, Gyula Donath, Bernát Heller, and Ignác Pfeiffer.

By 1929 the Hungarian Zionists were able to report to the Zionist Congress a marked upsurge in the movement in Hungary. Youth groups and *HeHalutz pioneering groups were organized, the membership increased, and, on the basis of Shekels (membership fees; *see* SHEKEL) sold, Hungary was entitled to send two delegates to the Congress. At the founding conference of the expanded *Jewish Agency, which took place immediately following the Congress, Hungarian Zionists were represented by Joseph Patai and non-Zionists by Chief Rabbi Immanuel Löw, of Szeged, and Ferenc Székely, who were elected to the Council of the Jewish Agency. Chief Rabbi Gyula Fischer, Ignác Friedmann, Emil Makai, and Prof. Lajos Török, all of Budapest, were elected deputy members.

Pre-World War II Decade. In the decade preceding World War II, Zionism made gradual headway in Hungary, although the opposition of the established Jewish leadership had by no means been entirely overcome. On the contrary, the official heads of the Jewish Congregation of Pest maintained their opposition to Zionism, as illustrated by the statement of its chief rabbi, Simon Hevesi: "There is no ground for, nor inclination to, Zionism among Hungarian Jews. This is the historically formed opinion of Hungarian Jewry, and there is no reason to depart from it." Nevertheless, the movement grew, and by 1933 all Zionist groups and organizations found in other Central and Eastern European countries had their branches or counterparts in Hungary. Next to the adult groups there were affiliated youth organizations, such as Maccabi, Aviva-Barissia, *HaNo'ar HaTziyoni, *B'rit Trumpeldor, No'ar Mizrahi, and *HaShomer HaTza'ir, with a total membership of some 2,000. In 1931, 40 Halutzim received training on a *Hakhshara farm. From 1930 on there existed a *B'rit 'Ivrit 'Olamit group which took charge of Hebrew-language instruction. At two schools, the Jewish High School (Gymnasium) of Debrecen and the Jewish Women Teachers Seminary in Miskolc, Hebrew was taught as a living language. At public functions arranged by the Hungarian Zionist Organization jointly with the Pro-Palestine Association, numerous foreign visitors appeared, among them Prof. Selig *Brodetsky of London, Dr. Nahum *Goldmann, Miss Nadia Stein, secretary of the *Women's International Zionist Organization (WIZO), and several German and Viennese Zionist leaders.

The Hungarian-Jewish press, with the exception of unswervingly anti-Zionist *Egyenlőség* (Equality), became pro-Zionist. By 1937, 17 local Zionist groups were functioning, with a total membership of 3,600, and WIZO had 1,200 members.

Although few in numbers, Zionists achieved a degree of influence in intellectual and literary circles. Among the leading writers and scholars championing the Zionist cause were men like Mózes *Richtmann, Lajos *Simon, János Rónai, Samu Szilágyi, Bernát *Singer, Herman Bokor, Ottó *Komoly, Ernő *Marton, and Mihály *Salamon.

New blood was infused into the Zionist movement after the reannexation in 1939 of some of the pre-World War I border areas of Hungary, which contained a strong minority of Jews, many of them Yiddish-speaking, who were imbued with a deeper sense of Jewish national consciousness. Also, the influence of the Zionist leaders tended to increase with the exacerbation of the anti-Semitic measures (*see* ANTI-SEMITISM) adopted in Europe in general and in Hungary in particular.

The last national conference of Hungarian Zionists took place in March, 1939. It was attended by 300 delegates representing all shades of Zionism organized in 41 constituent groups. Dr. J. Miklós, first elected president in 1937, was reelected. In 1939 the Hungarian government prohibited the publication of all Jewish periodicals with the exception of *Mult és Jövő*, which continued to appear, although in a reduced size, until close to the German occupation of Hungary in March, 1944.

World War II. Following the incorporation of Austria and Czechoslovakia (1938–39) into Germany, and especially after the outbreak of World War II, Hungary became a haven for thousand of refugees from Nazi-occupied Europe. The work and scope of the Zionists in Hungary acquired new dimensions. The imperatives of the time required not only the rescue of the refugees and, wherever possible, their transfer to Palestine but also the preparation of the Hungarian Jewish masses themselves for all eventualities.

In Hungary itself the situation gradually deteriorated, first through the adoption of a series of anti-Jewish laws and then by acts of violence. The severity of the laws notwithstanding, most of the Jews were able to survive until the German occupation. Mass brutalities began only after the Nazi drive against the Soviets in June, 1941. The massacre of Jews in Nazi-occupied Poland and Russia began concurrently with the slaughter of 18,000 to 20,000 "alien" Jews who had been rounded up in Hungary and forcibly "repatriated" to Galicia in the summer of 1941. This first mass action against Jews by Hungarians was followed by the killing of 700 to 1,000 Jews at

Ujvidék (Novi Sad), in the Bácska (Bačka), in January, 1942, and the atrocities perpetrated against the thousands of labor battalion draftees in the Ukraine.

Although the Zionists were severely restricted during the World War II years, having been virtually outlawed in the provinces, they took the initiative in trying to persuade the assimilationist "legitimist" leadership to abandon the traditional, outdated strategy and to adopt tactics better suited to the extraordinary conditions created by the war. They undertook a vigorous campaign to bring about the establishment of a unified representation of Hungarian Jewry in order to overcome the divisive element inherent in factionalism and to establish close contacts with Jewish organizations abroad. The latter became especially imperative in December, 1941, when the American representative of the *American Jewish Joint Distribution Committee left Hungary, cutting off the community's last official link with world Jewry.

The same month the Transylvanian Zionist leaders, including Dr. József Fischer, Dr. Rezső Rudolf *Kasztner, and Dr. Ernő Marton, convened a meeting of Hungarian-Jewish parliamentarians in Budapest for the purpose of considering reports on the annihilation of the Jews in Nazi-occupied Europe and of planning the unified defense of Hungarian-Jewish interests. The meeting achieved no tangible results. The advent of the war, the influx of ever-increasing numbers of refugees from neighboring Poland and Slovakia, and the aggravation of the situation in Hungary itself compelled the Zionists to mobilize their available resources to meet the recurring emergencies. At first haphazard and diffuse, the rescue and relief operations were placed on a more systematic basis in January, 1943, when the Zionist emissaries from Palestine operating in Istanbul urged the establishment of a branch of the Va'adat 'Ezra V'Hatzala (Help and Rescue Committee) in Budapest. Heeding this call, the leaders of the Zionist groups and parties of Budapest met and decided on the establishment of such a branch under the chairmanship of Ottó Komoly.

Before the German occupation of Hungary in March, 1944, the primary responsibility of the Help and Rescue Committee revolved around the saving of Jews from Nazi-occupied Europe through the organization of an elaborate network of human contraband operations, the "legalization" of the refugees who had reached Hungary (15,000 by November, 1943), and the maintenance of *'Aliya (immigration) to Palestine.

The activity of the Zionists gathered momentum during the second half of 1943, when it became increasingly apparent that the Hungarian government under Prime Minister Miklós von Kállay was searching for a way to extricate itself from the war against the Allies. The appointment of Aladár Szegedy-Maszák, a political moderate, as head of the Political Division of the Foreign Ministry (July, 1943) afforded the Zionists an opportunity of crystallizing their views. These were included in a memorandum jointly prepared and submitted by Ottó Komoly, Ernő Szilágyi, Ernő Marton, Rezső Rudolf Kasztner, and Hillel Danzig, demanding, among other things, that the Zionist movement be legalized and permitted to publish its own weekly. The conciliatory mood of the time was also reflected by the memorandum which the Zionists prepared on the specific request of the Foreign Ministry and submitted to the Allies through their "friends" in Istanbul. It contained a request that, in view of the Hungarian government's positive attitude toward the Jews and its search for an honorable way out of the war, Budapest be spared from bombing.

Public lecture on Palestine by Protestant Bishop Dezső Balthazár on Mar. 1, 1933, organized by the Pro-Palestine Association of Hungarian Jews. At the dais, from left to right: Niszon Kahan, Lipót Osztern, Ignác Friedmann, Ignác Pfeiffer, Bishop Balthazár (standing), Rabbi Arnold Kiss, and Joseph Patai.
[Andrew Freeman]

The high hopes attached to the changing position of the government came to a sudden end on Mar. 19, 1944, when German troops occupied the country. One of the official pretexts given for the occupation was "the unrestricted presence of some 1 million Jews as a concrete menace to the safety of German arms in the Balkan Peninsula."

With the occupation and the subsequent preparing of the deportation machinery by the Eichmann *Sonderkommando*, the main concern of the Zionists was to try to save what they could and, above all, to stall for time, in the hope of the "imminent" arrival of the Soviet forces. Therefore, in addition to intensifying their rescue work, they entered into negotiations with the Germans. This maneuver was motivated not only by their desire to delay the deportations by dragging out the negotiations but also by the fact that the Jewish leadership had been informed by the Hungarian pro-German authorities that they had to "meet the demands of the Germans."

The Jewish population was ignorant of the extermination of Jews then in full swing. Though there was some ill-defined plan for the organization of a resistance movement, it came to nothing, primarily because the men in the 20–48 age group were in the labor battalions and the Palestinian Jewish *parachutists of Hungarian origin, including Hanna *Szenes, who were to provide not only the psychological boost but also military leadership, were captured soon after their landing. Bluffed and misled by the Germans, the Jewish negotiators could not prevent the rounding up and deportation of the Jews from the provinces. Nevertheless some 1,700 Jews were saved through the so-called Bergen-Belsen transports, and from 15,000 to 20,000 Jews at Strasshof, Austria, where they had been "laid on ice" pending the outcome of the ill-fated Joel *Brand mission to Istanbul, which carried a German offer of saving Jewish lives in exchange for sending Germany much-needed equipment.

Although the mass-resistance plans did not materialize, some of the most memorable pages in Hungarian-Jewish history were written during this period, primarily by Zionists, who, often disguised as Storm Troopers or Hungarian soldiers, served as couriers between the provincial communities and Budapest and saved thousands of lives through the mass produc-

tion and clandestine distribution of false identity documents and the rescue of helpless victims from prisons, death marches, or execution places.

Postwar Years. After the liberation early in 1945 the attention of the Zionists centered on rehabilitation, reconstruction, and the revitalization of the movement. During the early phase of the postwar period the Zionists, like the surviving Jewish community as a whole, enjoyed both the sympathy and the support of the governmental authorities and managed to revive their activities.

With the gradual elimination of the democratic parties and the transformation of Hungary into a Communist dictatorship, the Zionist movement was also gradually suppressed. The Communist party's thesis concerning Zionism and the Jewish question was stated as early as Apr. 11, 1946, by Eric Molnár, a leading ideologist and then Minister of Public Welfare: "There are two solutions to the Jewish problem in Hungary, a reactionary and a progressive one. The reactionary solution is Zionism. . . . The progressive solution is the complete social amalgamation of Jews. In the course of democratic development and by the defeat of reactionary forces, anti-Semitism will cease to exist. The distinctiveness of Jews will also cease to exist."

Ironically, shortly after this statement of policy, two vicious anti-Jewish incidents took place at Kunmadaras and Diósgyőr in May and July, 1946, respectively, which claimed the lives of a number of Jews who had survived the Nazi concentration camps. Both were condoned, if not instigated, by Communists and were aimed to a large extent at increasing the popularity of the party among anti-Semitic elements by organizing drives against "black-marketeers." The infiltration of mass organizations by Communist agents and their consequent split into "democratic" and "reactionary" factions, with the latter soon to be eliminated, also affected the Jewish organizations. With the founding of the National Association of Jews, a fellow-traveler organization, on July 8, 1946, the influence of the legitimate Jewish organizations, including the Zionist, was gradually reduced. Mihály Salamon, the head of the Hungarian Zionist Organization, noting the suppression of political independence and freedom, offered his resignation at the national convention of Mar. 14, 1948. His successor, Mózes Bisseliches, one of the original founders of the movement, was given the unenviable task of amalgamating the Zionists with the regime-supported organization for the purpose of creating a single-list electoral slate for the election of the leaders of the Jewish Community of Pest.

After a brief lull during the establishment of the State of Israel in May, 1948, which was sympathetically viewed by the Soviet Union and its allies for reasons of their own, the climate soon changed and a concerted drive against Zionism began. Again taking their cue from the Soviet Union, the Hungarian regime launched a vicious campaign against "cosmopolitanism" and Zionism, identifying the Zionists as agents of imperialism and reaction. Following the example already set in the Soviet Union, Poland, and Romania, the Hungarian Communists established a so-called Committee for the Liquidation of the Hungarian Zionist Organization. In the name of the committee, Dr. Galos, its secretary-general, issued the following statement toward the end of March, 1949:

> The National Committee of the Hungarian Zionist Organization, at its meeting of Mar. 13, 1949, passed the following unanimous resolution: whereas with the establishment of the State

of Israel the main objective of the Organization has been attained, and whereas normal diplomatic relations exist between Hungary and Israel, the National Committee has decided to terminate the activities of the Hungarian Zionist Organization. The Organization, its subdivisions, and local groups have terminated their activities in accordance with the above resolution.

The drive against cosmopolitanism and Zionism was intensified during the Rajk trial of September, 1949, when some of the accused were identified as having been agents of imperialism and of the U.S. Secret Service. During the campaign of the early 1950s against bourgeois class enemies and the deportation from the capital and other larger cities of "nonproductive elements," Jews again were subjected to treatment reminiscent of the Nazi era.

The situation changed considerably for the better after the death of Stalin and the introduction of the "new course." With the normalization of political and economic life, the Jewish community regained considerable autonomy in the cultural and religious spheres. Zionism, however, continued to be identified as a bourgeois, reactionary force that was totally incompatible with the new order being built in the country.

Although Zionism had ceased being a viable political movement affecting the Jewish masses of Hungary, its international implications continued to influence both the Jews and the People's Democratic regime. In the wake of the Revolution of October–November, 1956, many of the Jews, among them undoubtedly a considerable number of latent Zionists, fled the country and settled in Israel and elsewhere in the free world. With the return to normalcy, Hungary continued to follow, albeit occasionally reluctantly and, thus far at least, always moderately, the leadership of the Soviet Union in its dealings with Zionism and Israel. During the 1960s it echoed the pro-Arab position of the Soviet bloc and broke off diplomatic relations with Israel in the wake of the *Six-day War of 1967. However, it refused to emulate the Soviet Union and some of the other bloc nations in their campaigns against Israel and "Zionist imperialism" abroad and the Jewish community at home.   R. L. BRAHAM

HURFEISH. Arab village in western Upper Galilee. Population (1968): 1,510.

HUSAYNI, HAJJ AMIN AL-. *See* AL-HUSAYNI, HAJJ AMIN.

HUSAYNI CLAN. *See* AL-HUSAYNI, HAJJ AMIN; ARAB HIGHER COMMITTEE; ARABS IN ISRAEL.

HUSHI, ABBA. *See* KHOUSHI, ABBA.

HUSSEIN I. *See* TRANSJORDAN.

HUZAYL. Bedouin tribe in the B'er Sheva' region. Population (1968): 3,510.

HYAMSON, ALBERT MONTEFIORE. Historian and British civil servant (b. London, 1875; d. there, 1954). During World War I he participated in the Political Committee that was in charge of Zionist policy in England, and from 1917 to 1919 he was joint editor of the London *Zionist Review*. In November, 1917, he became head of the Jewish Section in the British Ministry of Information.

In 1921 Hyamson was appointed Assistant Director of Immigration in the Palestine administration, and in 1926 Director, in which capacity he served until 1934. His service proved a disappointment to the *Yishuv, for he zealously carried out British government policy, interpreting harshly the *immigration laws. As a consequence, he was regarded as responsible for some of the restrictive immigration measures.

Hyamson later became an advocate of a binational Arab-Jewish state and subsequently was active in the "Freeland" Territorialist movement. He was the author of many books, including *British Projects for the Restoration of the Jews* (1917), *Palestine: The Rebirth of an Ancient People* (1919), and *Palestine under the Mandate, 1920–1948* (1950).

I

I'BLIN. Arab village in western Lower Galilee. Population (1968): 3,120.

IBTHAN. Arab village in the Sharon Plain. Population (1968): 388.

IBTIN. Arab village in the Haifa region. Population (1968): 620.

ICA. *See* JEWISH COLONIZATION ASSOCIATION.

IDELSOHN, ABRAHAM ZVI. Musicologist and composer of Jewish music (b. near Libau, Latvia, 1882; d. Johannesburg, South Africa, 1938). Idelsohn studied music in Königsberg, London, Berlin, and Leipzig and became cantor at the Regensburg synagogue in 1903. In 1905 he settled in Jerusalem. There he taught music and founded an Institute for Jewish Music in 1910 and a Jewish School of Music in 1919. He collected, recorded, and transcribed the songs of Jewish communities in the Near East and in Eastern Europe, and between 1914 and 1932 published his monumental 10-volume *Thesaurus of Hebrew-Oriental Melodies*. His *History of Jewish Music* appeared in Hebrew in 1924 and in English five years later. In 1921 he brought his collections to Germany. The next year he went to the United States, where he taught at the Hebrew Union College in Cincinnati from 1924 to 1934. After suffering a paralytic stroke, he was taken to join relatives in Johannesburg.

Apart from his musicological work, which has become basic material for all further studies (copies of his recordings are kept in the phonographic archives of the *Hebrew University of Jerusalem), Idelsohn found time to compose songs (including "Hava Nagila"), publish songbooks for school and home, and compose synagogues services and *Jephtah*, a Biblical opera.

P. GRADENWITZ

IDEOLOGICAL COLLECTIVISM. Philosophy of communal life in the ideological sphere, which was developed in *HaShomer HaTza'ir kibbutzim and became a basic concept of the *Kibbutz Artzi Shel HaShomer HaTza'ir, formed in 1927. This unique philosophy holds that the kibbutz is not only an economic and social partnership but an ideological partnership as well. After discussions among its members, the kibbutz establishes its ideological and political stand, which then is binding on its entire membership.

Other kibbutzim formed in the 1920s did not obligate their members to accept binding ideological formulations or one specific political position. The Kibbutz Artzi, which grew out of the close social integration of the HaShomer HaTza'ir youth movement, however, assumed that kibbutz collectivism had to be based on a broad, shared ideological outlook. This viewpoint also assumed that the Kibbutz Artzi would have a point of view and activity of its own in the political sphere, although it did not define itself as a political party. It identified itself with Marxism and laid down its own premises with regard to Zionism, socialism, and kibbutz life.

The HaShomer HaTza'ir kibbutzim with memberships of Russian and Latvian origin did not accept this principle, which the Kibbutz Artzi embraced at the time it was formed, and therefore did not join it. They were opposed to separate political action on the part of the kibbutz body and insisted on political activities only within the framework of the wider labor party (at first, *Ahdut 'Avoda; after 1929, *Mapai). Ideological collectivism was criticized within the labor movement in Palestine for placing limitations on the individual's freedom of thought and for causing a separation of the kibbutz sector of HaShomer HaTza'ir from the general labor movement.

In the 1930s and 1940s ideological collectivism led to the increasing politicization of the Kibbutz Artzi. In 1936 the Socialist League, a political party close in spirit to the Kibbutz Artzi, was formed among urban workers; in 1946 the two groups joined to form the HaShomer HaTza'ir party. The new party upheld the ideological collectivism of the kibbutzim but placed political matters under the jurisdiction of the broader party. The attachment to ideological collectivism, including the Marxist viewpoint, was carried over to the *Mapam party, which was formed in 1948.

Ideological collectivism was subjected to great strains in the 1950s and 1960s as a result of the actions of the Soviet Union during the *Slansky trial (1952), the trumped-up charges against Jewish doctors (1952–53), and Soviet policy toward the State of Israel (from 1955 through the *Six-Day War of 1967). Leftists on the one hand and anti-Communists on the other protested against the ideological hypotheses of the leadership of the Kibbutz Artzi. However, it had become clear in other kibbutz groups that the existence of different political viewpoints within one kibbutz entity added to the difficulties of collective living and frequently caused divisions in the group.

I. KOLATT

IDF. *See* ISRAEL DEFENSE FORCES.

IGNATIUS, FATHER, O.S.B. (Joseph Leycester Lyne). English monk and superior at Llanthony Abbey, Wales, and supporter of Zionism (b. London, 1837; d. Camberley, England, 1908). In 1860 he became curate of St. Peter's, Plymouth, where he established a community of brothers. In 1869 he founded a Benedictine monastery and established the Abbey of Llanthony.

As a result of a vision he had in his youth about the Jewish people, he came to consider the Jews the "sacred race" and to believe in their ultimate return to Palestine. Whenever he saw a Jew with beard and sidelocks in Whitechapel, he would bow and bare his head. A passionate orator who drew large crowds, Father Ignatius addressed meetings of the *Hoveve Zion movement and of the Zionist Federation of Great Britain and Ireland. *Die *Welt* published a letter by him on July 2, 1897.

At a meeting held in Whitechapel in April, 1900, Father Ignatius declared that it had been prophesied that the Jewish people would return to Palestine and that "the God who helped at the crossing of the Red Sea would see that His promise was fulfilled." Moses *Gaster, who presided, called him "one of the great apostles of our movement among the non-Jewish public."

J. FRAENKEL

IHUD. Palestinian Jewish group advocating an Arab-Jewish binational state in Palestine. The *Peel Commission, which the British government had appointed in 1936 to investigate causes of the troubles in Palestine, where the Arabs were in revolt against the British administration, reported in the summer of 1937 that the plan for a binational commonwealth, in which Jews and Arabs would have equal rights, was no longer practicable. The Commission proposed, instead, a *partition of the country into a minuscule Jewish state, an autonomous Arab state, and an area remaining under the British *Mandate for Palestine. The followers of the *B'rit Shalom group, who included Judah L. *Magnes, Martin *Buber, Hayim *Kalwariski-Margolis, and Arthur *Ruppin, opposed the idea of partition. They still believed that cooperation between Jews and Arabs was possible and right. Two years later, the British Statement of Policy in Palestine, known as the *White Paper of 1939, rejected the idea of partition and proposed the creation of an independent Palestine after five years, with an Arab majority that would have the power to limit Jewish *immigration. The Jewish reaction was to resist the White Paper and to demand a Jewish State, while at the same time fully participating in the Allied war effort. Magnes felt that a determined effort should be made to avert a head-on collision between Arabs and Jews. Jointly with Buber, Moshe *Smilansky, and the heads of the leftist youth movement *HaShomer HaTza'ir, he formed in 1942 Ihud (Unity), a society advocating the combination of Jews and Arabs in a self-governing undivided Palestine. A small group of Arabs, including a member of the Husayni family

(the family of Hajj Amin *al-Husayni, mufti of Jerusalem, the archenemy of the Jews and of England), joined Ihud, but these men were murdered by Arab extremists, one after the other.

The society issued pamphlets in Palestine's three official languages and *Ner*, a monthly paper. The main controversy and the issue of Jewish-Arab cooperation centered in the volume of Jewish immigration to be permitted. The Arabs wanted a limit which would assure them majority status in Palestine for years ahead. The delegates of HaShomer HaTza'ir would not agree. At the end of World War II, Ihud held out for negotiation with the Arabs. In 1946 Magnes and Buber appeared before the *Anglo-American Committee of Inquiry, which had been appointed by the governments of Britain and the United States to consider the problems of a haven for the survivors of the Nazi holocaust in Europe, immigration to Palestine, and the future of the country. Ihud continued its efforts in behalf of the binational solution in 1947. Magnes also testified before the *United Nations Special Committee on Palestine (UNSCOP), but with little effect. He pleaded for a system of complete parity of Jews and Arabs in government and administration and for parity of numbers, with restrictions on Jewish immigration once parity had been attained. He also urged that Palestine be neutralized as Switzerland was and that the Jews be represented as a national entity at the United Nations.

When, in November, 1947, the UN General Assembly adopted by a majority vote the resolution in favor of partition and civil strife followed, Magnes made an attempt to move American opinion in favor of a period of trustee administration. When this failed, he and Ihud, while accepting the fait accompli of the Jewish State, pressed for the establishment of a Semitic confederation including Israel, again to no avail because of Arab intransigence.

N. BENTWICH

IHUD HABONIM (Labor Zionist Youth). *See* HABONIM.

IHUD HAKLAI (Agricultural Union). Organization of middle-class agricultural settlers with headquarters in Tel Aviv. A nonpolitical organization of farmers working their own family farms, it assists its members in establishing and consolidating their farmsteads and helps organize economic and social life in middle-class agricultural settlements. In 1968 it represented 3,500 smallholdings, or a total of 52 settlements with a population of 15,000.

Institutions connected with Ihud Haklai and serving its membership include Tene, a cooperative for the marketing of agricultural produce; the Tene Noga dairies; and Haspaka, a central supply cooperative. Also affiliated with the organization are a number of professional associations of agriculturists, such as associations of cattle breeders, poultry farmers, and vegetable growers. In 1968 the organization published a monthly, *HaMeshek HaHaklai* (The Agricultural Farm).

IHUD HAK'VUTZOT V'HAKIBBUTZIM (Union of K'vutzot and Kibbutzim). Organization of collective villages in Israel, founded in 1951 by a merger of the *Hever HaK'vutzot and the dissident *Mapai-oriented minority of the *Kibbutz M'uhad. While officially the organization was not affiliated with any political party, most of its members belonged to Mapai.

The union, which rejects the principle of *ideological collectivism, is governed by a National Convention, two-thirds of whose members are delegates from the kibbutzim belonging to the union while one-third are elected by the general membership. The central financial agency of the union is the Keren HaIhud (Union Fund). The union maintains a teachers seminary called Bet Berl after Berl *Katznelson. In 1966 the union comprised 76 communes with a total population of 24,533.

IHUD 'OLAMI (World Union of Zionists-Socialists). Union of the Jewish Socialist labor confederation *Po'ale Zion (united with the Zionist Socialist Federation) and the Zionist labor party *Hitahdut. It was the product of a number of mergers that had taken place in the Labor Zionist ranks (see LABOR ZIONISM). Prior to the establishment of the State of Israel, its aim was to "create an autonomous commonwealth in Palestine as the Jewish National Home based on the principles of cooperativism, Jewish labor, and Hebrew culture." Subsequently, it became the world body of all Labor Zionist groups that identified their aims with those of *Mapai insofar as the building of Israel was concerned. As such, Ihud 'Olami constituted the largest single faction within the *World Zionist Organization, in which it played a leading role, as well as in the *Jewish Agency.

From its center in Tel Aviv, it coordinated the activities of its affiliated groups in world affairs, represented them in the Socialist International, and published periodicals and books of general interest. It served as the link of its constituent groups with Mapai in Israel and as a channel for the exchange of views, sharing of experiences, mutual aid, and cooperation in action among Po'ale Zion groups in the *Diaspora. Its

governing bodies were elected at world conferences to which all affiliates sent delegates. The world conference held in July, 1964, in Tel Aviv was attended by representatives of Po'ale Zion groups from 24 countries. Yitzhak Korn served as general secretary.

C. B. SHERMAN

IKSAL. Arab village in the Jezreel Valley. Population (1968): 3,000.

ILANOT. See KADIMA.

ILANYA. Village (moshav) in eastern Lower Galilee. Founded in 1902 and affiliated with the *Ihud Haklai. The village was first called Sejera after an Arab village in the neighborhood. The present name is a Hebrew translation of *sejera*, the Arabic word for "tree." Population (1968): 180.

During the *Second 'Aliya the settlement was a center of the Jewish labor movement in the country. In it were founded HaHoresh (1907), a workers' cooperative, which set itself the task of training Jewish agricultural laborers; and *HaShomer (1909), a self-defense organization. During the *War of Independence Ilanya withstood many Arab attacks.

ILLEGAL IMMIGRATION. From the 1880s to 1948 some of the Jewish *immigration to Palestine was classed as illegal owing to restrictions imposed on such immigration first by Turkish and later by British authorities. See B'RIHA.

Illegal immigrants arriving at Tel Aviv in 1939. [United Israel Appeal]

Early Period. Under the Turks, an entry permit was often difficult to obtain, and there were instances of immigrants' being turned back to Russia by the authorities in Constantinople. Subterfuges were employed, sometimes accompanied by bribery, to manage entrance into Palestine. With the establishment of British rule after World War I, the number of illegal immigrants (Ma'apilim) decreased considerably, though individuals and groups sometimes entered the country surreptitiously through Lebanon or posed as tourists and then remained in the country. However, there was no organized illegal immigration movement at the time. Generally speaking, in the 1920s there were more numerous possibilities of legal entry than there were prospective immigrants. This situation changed with the advent of the economic crisis of 1929, which brought an increase in the number of prospective immigrants. At first, British immigration policy was relatively liberal. Nevertheless, the relative prosperity of Palestine during the time of the worst economic and political crises elsewhere led a number of persons to enter the country illegally, posing as tourists, especially during the Maccabia sports rally and similar events in the early 1930s (see SPORTS AND PHYSICAL EDUCATION IN ISRAEL). Small groups also crossed the Lebanese border from Beirut via K'far Gil'adi in the north of Palestine.

In July, 1934, a group of young Halutzim (pioneers; see HALUTZIYUT) from Poland arranged for the sailing of the "Velos" from Greece to Palestine with 350 people on board. The organizers of the operation, kibbutz members from Palestine, were acting against the express wish of the *Jewish Agency and the *Histadrut (General Federation of Labor), which at that time saw no reason to jeopardize their good relations with the

In 1947 a British boarding party intercepts immigrants arriving illegally at Haifa. Most of the refugees were later sent to Cyprus.
[Zionist Archives]

British, since immigration certificates were being given out quite liberally. In August, 1934, several leading *Revisionists in Vienna organized the sailing of the "Union." When this ship reached Palestine, most of the immigrants aboard were caught and arrested by the British. The "Velos" sailed again in September but was intercepted and turned back. From then until 1937 there was no illegal immigration by sea to Palestine at all, and there were only isolated cases of border crossings from Lebanon. In 1935 there were 62,000 legal immigrants; it was therefore felt there was no point in antagonizing the British government.

Prewar Years. In 1937 illegal immigration was resumed, again with the support of the Viennese Revisionists. It was continued, on a larger scale, by the Revisionists in Poland and Czechoslovakia. In April, and again in September, 1937, small groups of immigrants—69 persons in all—were brought to Palestine. In January, 1938, the illegal immigration of Halutzim started again. This time, the Histadrut and, much later on, the Jewish Agency gave their unofficial blessing. From then until September, 1939, illegal immigration proceeded apace in three main streams: that of the Revisionists, that of the Histadrut-Halutzic immigration, and that of private individuals and political groups organizing sailings on their own responsibility.

Beginning with the Nazi annexation of Austria in March, 1938, immigration to Palestine took on the character of a rescue operation. The Revisionists placed special emphasis on the immigration of young people who would be under military discipline, with the older family element paying for the transportation of these younger persons as well.

Immigration operations carried on by the Histadrut were separate from those conducted by the *Hagana, and in the fall of 1938 a center for illegal immigration (Mosad L'Aliya Bet) was founded under the Histadrut, which was joined by non-Histadrut parties during World War II. The so-called private illegal immigration was run by a diversified range of persons: idealistic benefactors with no particular political affiliation (such as Baruch Confino of Bulgaria), individuals who had been removed by the Revisionists from immigration affairs because of a suspicion of unethical practices, and various youth movements that worked together for specific operations. Occasionally, the Mosad L'Aliya Bet and the Revisionists would use each others' ships for their clientele. The "evacuation" plan of Vladimir *Jabotinsky, which consisted in the proposed transfer of 100,000 Jews in 10 ships from Poland via Romanian ports so as to force Britain's hand in Palestine, was not implemented, partly because the Revisionists lacked the financial resources but mainly because of the outbreak of World War II. On the coast of Palestine, Hagana and *Irgun Tz'vai L'umi groups were responsible for receiving the immigrants in secret landings, with Hagana usually taking charge of the "private" ships as well as those of the Mosad. The most accurate count of pre-World War II illegal immigration was 41 ships (16 each by the Mosad and the Revisionists and the rest private) and 15,500 immigrants (of whom the Revisionists brought about 5,300, the Mosad 5,000, and private ships 5,200).

World War II. Illegal immigration continued to take place throughout the war years, and British immigration policy continued to be restrictive, although from 1942 on there was an unofficial understanding that Jews who managed to reach Istanbul would be allowed to proceed to Palestine. By that time, however, the chances of reaching Istanbul were very small, and the British seem to have sabotaged all efforts to secure Turkish or neutral ships for these voyages. Until the end of 1944, 26 vessels attempted the journey from Romanian and Bulgarian ports, and some smaller craft organized by the Mosad got 850 Greek Jews to Asia Minor. Of these 26 vessels, 5 were sunk, among them the *"Struma" (Feb. 24, 1942, with 769 people on board) and the "Mefkura" (August, 1944). Earlier, in November, 1940, in Haifa harbor, the Hagana sank the *"Patria," a French ship which the British had intended to use for the deportation to Mauritius of those refugees who had managed to get to Palestine. Some 280 persons were drowned through a miscalculation of the amount of explosives necessary to damage the ship sufficiently to prevent her from sailing. Of the 21 vessels whose passengers eventually got to Palestine, 11 were Mosad ships, 2 had been chartered by the Revisionists, and 8 had been chartered by private groups and individuals. Altogether, some 16,500 persons sailed for Palestine on these ships.

Postwar Years. After the war, several months passed before illegal immigration started again, this time via Italy, where the first large groups of displaced persons arrived in July, 1945. Under Yehuda Arazi in Italy and later under Shaul Avigur, the commander of Mosad L'Aliya Bet, who set up headquarters in Paris in 1946, Mosad operations increased. Between August, 1945, and the end of that year, only a few more than 1,000 persons came on Mosad boats. In 1946, however, 22,365 persons arrived, and in 1947 a total of 41,261 immigrants came. By May 14, 1948, the day Israel's independence was proclaimed, more than 69,000 persons had come by ship, though after August, 1946, most of the ships had been intercepted by the British and brought to Cyprus, where some 56,000 persons were interned (these are included in the grand total above). In all that time the *Bergson group (former Revisionists) brought in just one ship, the "Ben Hecht," with 599 passengers aboard (March, 1947). Thus, between 1934 and 1948, a grand total of just over 100,000 Jews had been brought "illegally" by sea either to Palestine or to Cyprus (from where they came to Israel after the establishment of the State). About 81,000 were brought in Mosad boats and over 9,000 in Revisionist ships; among the latter, wide publicity was given to the steamer "Zakaria," which carried 2,400 immigrants (February, 1940).

Mosad L'Aliya Bet remained formally independent of the Hagana, but with the beginning of World War II it became, for all practical purposes, subject to the control of the Political Department of the Jewish Agency Executive in Jerusalem. Avigur, the head of Mosad, had been the head of the Hagana (with Eliyahu *Golomb) in the 1930s, and there was, in fact, interchangeability of personnel between the two allied organizations. Mosad members were all Hagana people assigned to that duty by their commanders, and in the 1945–48 period they were largely recruited from the naval branch of the *Palmah, Hagana's Striking Forces. Ports of embarkation included various points on the coast of Italy; Port-de-Bouc and small places near Marseille in France; small fishing harbors near Šibenik, Yugoslavia; Constanţa, Romania; and Varna, Bulgaria. Funds came, directly or in a roundabout way, from the *American Jewish Joint Distribution Committee and the Jewish Agency. French Gaullists and Socialists, Italians of various political hues, and liberals and Communists in the countries of Southern and Eastern Europe tended to support the movement for political reasons.

During the war, the Mosad also began to bring people into northern Palestine over the land route, mainly from Iraq, Syria, and Lebanon, where anti-Jewish feeling was rampant. Between 1942 and the end of the war in 1945, 3,740 persons were brought

to Palestine by that route, and 4,948 between 1945 and 1948, making a total of 8,688 immigrants brought to Palestine by land. In addition, immigrants were brought in by means of fictitious marriages with Palestinian Jewish soldiers in Europe and with the use of forged passports or passports made out to others than those bearing them. In two instances, immigrants came in by air. Between 1945 and 1948 the Mosad brought more than 9,500 persons into Palestine by these means. The total number of illegal immigrants is therefore in the neighborhood of 120,000, or about 15 to 20 per cent of the then Jewish population in Palestine (about 640,000 in May, 1948), depending on whether or not one includes the Cyprus internees.

Y. BAUER

'ILUT. Arab village in western Lower Galilee. Population (1968): 1,470.

IMBER, NAFTALI HERZ. Hebrew poet and author of "*HaTikva" (b. Zolochev, Galicia, Austria, 1856; d. New York, 1909). Imber began to write Hebrew poetry at an early age. After living in Lvov, Vienna, and Romania, he went to Constantinople, where he met Laurence *Oliphant. In 1882 he went to Palestine as Oliphant's secretary. During his stay in the country he contributed to the local Hebrew press and published his first collection of poetry, *Barkai* (Jerusalem, 1886). In 1887 he returned to Europe and the following year went to England. Imber soon became fluent in English and began to write in this language. He also wrote poetry in Yiddish. In 1892 he went to the United States, where he contributed to Hebrew, Yiddish, and English periodicals. In 1900 his brothers published in Zolochev (Złoczów) a second collection of his poetry, *Barkai HeHadash*. In 1905 he issued in New York another collection, under the title *Barkai HaShlishi*.

Naftali Herz Imber.
[Zionist Archives]

One of the first poets of the Jewish national renaissance, Imber expressed in his poems the sorrow of generations over the desolation of the Homeland. He called upon the Jewish people to return to its Homeland and reconquer and rebuild it, and he hailed the work of the early pioneers. His "HaTikva" was very popular with the early pioneers and eventually became the anthem of the *World Zionist Organization and the State of Israel. Another poem of his that was popular with the pioneers was *Mishmar HaYarden* (The Watch of the Jordan).

IMMIGRANTS' CAMPS. *See* IMMIGRATION TO PALESTINE AND ISRAEL.

IMMIGRANTS' VILLAGES (Mosh've 'Olim). Villages in Israel of a type that came into existence soon after the establishment of the State. By 1966 more than 275 such villages had been established.

Mosh've 'Olim were planned settlements that were not initially independent. Established as part of a countrywide program for the settlement and cultivation of deserted or previously uninhabited areas within the State, they were built under the auspices of, and administered and serviced by, a number of quasi-governmental and governmental agencies, with central responsibility vested in the country's chief settlement authority, the Land Settlement Department of the *Jewish Agency. The villages were planned and established on the model of the *moshav, or smallholders' cooperative settlement, a pre-State type of modern farming community organized on a cooperative but not collective basis.

While the settlers of the moshavim were motivated by the pioneering ideology of *Labor Zionism and most of them also had considerable agricultural training, the settlers of the Mosh've 'Olim were new immigrants, most of whom initially had little or no understanding of the principles and underlying ideology of the moshav organization. The majority of these new immigrants came from non-European countries and had previously lived in traditional societies. Some were from remote villages in which they had engaged in peasant agriculture and handicrafts; a large number of families had been petty craftsmen and traders in small towns and predominantly preindustrial cities. Few of the immigrants had been reached by Zionist organizations prior to the creation of the State, and many had come from regions just beginning to be affected by the spread of Western technology, education, and democratic modes of government.

In view of the background of these immigrants, the administration of village affairs, unlike that in the moshav, was not initially in the hands of the settlers. Instead, the settlement authorities employed teams of village workers to administer the villages, supervise their development, and teach the settlers the agricultural and civic skills necessary for their new way of life. These teams ideally consisted of a social worker or village manager, one or more agricultural instructors, and a woman instructor in home economics.

Therefore, by definition, the Moshav 'Olim until the 1960s was a transitional type of village, officially viewed by the settlement authorities as a temporary phase of the moshav, necessitated by the unpreparedness of the new immigrants for scientific small farming and life in modern cooperative institutions. As the settlers learned new skills and adapted themselves to Israeli conditions and institutions, it was expected that the differences between the Moshav 'Olim and the moshav would gradually disappear.

Many of the immigrants' villages established within the first five years after the founding of the State were hastily planned and imposed considerable hardships on the settlers, who were often hurriedly recruited and included families unable or unwilling to endure such hardships. Furthermore, moshav organization calls for adaptation to a special way of life as well as to farming as a vocation. The strains of such adaptation were not lessened by the frequent placement of families from different countries and of very divergent backgrounds in one settlement. This occurred partly because of the policy of the "merging of exiles" and partly because families were often settled together in the order of their arrival, recruitment, and the places available in a village. Political factors also were involved, since each village was affiliated with a federation of settlements linked with a national political party, with the central office of the federation exercising extensive powers in the moshav. The federations carried out recruitment and, in doing so, could cut across other ties which united or divided the immigrants. Established under these conditions, villages seethed with dissidence, and many communities experienced a considerable turnover in population as dissatisfied families left and were replaced by others.

Mosh've 'Olim established after 1955 were characterized by much more careful planning carried out according to the principle of regional settlement. Clusters of villages, each settled by people of similar background, were built around rural centers, where services originally provided separately for each village were centralized, improving their quality and efficiency of operation and affording to people of different backgrounds an opportunity to mingle, without living together in the same village. Such clusters of villages, in turn, were linked to the services of a nearby urban center which usually processed industrial crops grown in the villages. The most prominent example of such a regional settlement project is that of the Lakhish region. *See also* DEVELOPMENT REGIONS.

Although by the mid-1960s the initial physical hardships of settlement had been greatly mitigated in the Mosh've 'Olim established after 1955, the immigrant settlers did not passively adapt themselves to the way of life planned for them. Conflicts between settlers and instructors remained frequent, as the latter sought to implement village development goals to which the former did not subscribe. The settlers themselves were frequently embroiled in disputes with each other. A turnover in instructor personnel as well as in settlers could add to initial village instability.

Nonetheless, most families who remained in the Mosh've 'Olim adapted themselves to modern small farming and to basic moshav institutions, while land settlement policy became somewhat more flexible in the implementation of these institutions. After 1960 no new Mosh've 'Olim were set up, and by the late 1960s all Mosh've 'Olim had been transformed into regular moshavim.

D. WILLNER

IMMIGRATION TO PALESTINE AND ISRAEL. The immigration (*'Aliya; literally, "ascent") of Jews from the *Diaspora countries to Palestine and (after May 14, 1948) Israel—the *Ingathering of the Exiles—was the principal objective of the Zionist movement. Prior to the politically motivated Zionist immigration effort, however, there was throughout Jewish history a steady trickle of Jewish immigrants to Eretz Yisrael, the Holy Land in which it was one of the foremost precepts of Jewish religion to live and die. These immigrants augmented and strengthened the nucleus of Jewish population that had remained in Palestine following the destruction of the Second Jewish Commonwealth by Titus in C.E. 70, under Roman, Byzantine, Arab, Crusader, Mameluke, and Turkish rule.

In the late 15th and in the 16th century some of the Jews expelled from Spain began to settle in the four holy cities of Palestine: Jerusalem, Hebron, Safed, and Tiberias. In the early 16th century the Jewish population of Palestine was estimated at no more than 5,000. By the middle of the 19th century the population had grown to about 12,000, and by 1882 to about 24,000.

Since 1882 both the absolute and the relative sizes of immigration have shown great variation. On the whole, immigration has tended to increase from period to period, and in all eras it has had a wavelike aspect, largely because of the following factors: (1) changing political and economic conditions in the Diaspora; (2) the changing influence of ideological factors conducive to immigration, such as Zionism, religion, socialism, and pioneering, on the various classes of the Diaspora communities; (3) changing policies in various countries regarding emigration (assets and property) in general and regarding Jewish emigration in particular, especially in Eastern Europe and the Arab countries; (4) changing immigration policies in Ottoman- and, later, British-controlled Palestine and Israel and in other countries absorbing Jewish immigrants; and (5) changing political and economic conditions in Palestine and Israel.

In the days of Turkish rule the immigrants came from many countries, but during and after the era of the British *Mandate for Palestine immigration became virtually cosmopolitan, with almost every Jewish community in the Diaspora represented among the immigrants to Israel. Although the attraction of Israel was felt throughout the Jewish world, the intensity of participation by the various communities, as measured by yearly rates of immigration to Israel per 1,000 Jewish inhabitants of each country, varied considerably from country to country and from year to year.

The tendency to immigrate to Israel was evident throughout the mandatory and independence periods in the Jewish communities of the Balkans, Asia, and Eastern Europe. In particular, the communities of Bulgaria, Iraq, and Yemen were transplanted almost in their entirety to Israel in the first period after independence. Central Europe had high rates of emigration to Palestine after the Nazi persecution, and North Africa had high rates in the independence period. Western Europe, the Americas, and Oceania retained low rates during both the mandatory and the State periods. As a rule, the Soviet Union and countries in the Soviet orbit severely limited the emigration of Jews following World War II, so that in the 1960s the future of immigration to Israel depended largely on immigration from the Western countries and on a possible change in the emigration policy of the U.S.S.R.

Sex and Age Distribution. Unlike most international migrations due mainly to economic factors, Jewish immigration to Palestine and Israel was generally well balanced with regard to sex. Only in very difficult periods, as during the *Third 'Aliya in 1919–23, the waves of *illegal immigration in the 1940s, and the wave before the *War of Independence in 1948, did the proportion of men considerably outweigh that of women.

The age structure of the immigrants in the mandatory period differed from that of the State period. Because of selection, immigration in the mandatory period was very irregular in its age distribution; it included a very high proportion of young people and was strongly at variance with the age distribution of their communities of origin. The high proportion of persons in young working ages was a considerable asset to the economic, social, and political development of the Zionist enterprise.

During the State period most of the immigrants were of nonselective types and reflected the structure of their communities of origin. Since selected waves of this period were also more regularly distributed than those of the mandatory period, the overall distribution of immigration of the State period was much more regular. This immigration had a much

An immigrant reception center in 1939. [Keren HaYesod]

higher proportion of children, a somewhat higher proportion of old people, and a total proportion of people in dependent ages to those in working ages higher than that of the mandatory period.

R. BACHI

HISTORY OF IMMIGRATION SINCE 1882

Jewish immigration to Palestine between 1882 and 1939 was divided into five 'Aliyot, or immigration waves. During World War II (1939–45) immigration was partly legal and partly illegal. From the end of the war to May 15, 1948 (the establishment of the State of Israel), most of the immigrants came illegally. On the establishment of the State, free mass immigration started on an unprecedented scale, resulting in an increase in the percentage of world Jewry living in Palestine (and, later, in Israel) from 0.2 in 1850 to 17 at the end of 1967. During the 29 years of the British Mandate for Palestine, Jewish immigration to Palestine totaled 452,158, while the number of Jewish immigrants arriving in Israel between May 15, 1948, and Dec. 31, 1965, reached 1,227,000. The total Jewish population of Israel in September, 1968, was 2,415,500.

*First 'Aliya, 1882–1903. The First 'Aliya consisted of groups organized by the *Hoveve Zion and *Bilu movements in Russia and Romania, as well as of a considerable number of individual pioneers. This period brought to Palestine some 25,000 immigrants, who laid the foundations of the new *Yishuv (Jewish population of Palestine) and established Palestine's first Jewish agricultural settlements.

*Second 'Aliya, 1904–14. The second wave of immigration brought into the country young pioneers from Russia, many of them disillusioned by the new wave of pogroms that followed the 1905 Revolution. The total number of Jewish immigrants during this period was about 40,000. Since the Turkish authorities prohibited Jewish immigration into Palestine, the immigrants arrived as "pilgrims," with temporary permits, remaining in the country without legal authorization to do so. A considerable number left Palestine, being unable to adjust themselves to the new land. The majority were without means.

The outbreak of World War I in 1914 interrupted immigration to Palestine. Nevertheless, small groups of pioneers made their way into the country after the issuance of the *Balfour Declaration in 1917, while hostilities were still in progress.

Third 'Aliya, 1919–23. The Third 'Aliya brought mainly young Halutzim (pioneers; *see* HALUTZIYUT) from the centers of Jewish life in Russia, Poland, and Romania. During this period immigration was administered and assisted by the Executive of the *World Zionist Organization in Palestine. In 1920 the British and Palestine governments issued the Immigration Ordinance, which provided for the admission of immigrants by immigration certificates divided into five categories: A I, persons of independent means (owning at least 1,000 Palestine pounds); A II, persons belonging to the liberal professions or artisans (this category was practically abolished in 1921); A or B III, students with assured means of support; C, persons ready for employment (labor category); and D, dependents of residents of Palestine.

This system remained in force, with minor modifications, during the entire British Mandatory period and served as the basis for regulations and restrictions of Jewish immigration issued by the mandatory government. In 1925 the mandatory authorities issued a revised Immigration Ordinance, whereby authority to approve immigration certificates was vested in a Chief Immigration Officer in Jerusalem instead of the British consulates, as it had been before. For the labor category, the semiannual schedule of certificates to be approved individually by the *Jewish Agency remained in force. Further modifications (mainly restrictions) were enacted as ordinances in 1929, 1932, and 1938–39 (*see* WHITE PAPER OF 1939).

Statistics of immigration during the Third 'Aliya period, according to information on file with the Palestine Zionist *Executive, are given in Table 1. The immigrants came mainly from Russia (13,363), Poland (9,158), and Romania (1,404), with smaller numbers from Lithuania, Germany, the United States, and other countries.

TABLE 1. IMMIGRANTS OF THE THIRD 'ALIYA*

Year	Number
1919	1,806
1920	8,223
1921	8,294
1922	8,685
1923	8,093
Total	35,101

*Figures included 4,932 tourists who remained in Palestine.

*Fourth 'Aliya, 1924–32. The members of the Fourth 'Aliya were mainly middle-class immigrants who left Poland in the wake of economic measures adopted by the Polish government against the Jewish middle class. The number of immigrants during this period, according to official government statistics, is shown in Table 2.

Children of new immigrants meet with their counselor in 1939. [Keren HaYesod]

TABLE 2. IMMIGRANTS OF THE FOURTH 'ALIYA

Year	Number
1924	12,856
1925	33,801
1926	13,081
1927	2,713
1928	2,178
1929	5,249
1930	4,944
1931	4,075
1932	9,553
Total	88,450

*Fifth 'Aliya, 1933–39. The severe persecution of the Jews in Germany created a new era in Palestine immigration, which developed into a Jewish exodus from all the countries of Central Europe. This period, too, saw the beginning of *Youth 'Aliya. Of the total of 215,000 immigrants in this 'Aliya (see Table 3), 44,419 came from Germany.

TABLE 3. IMMIGRANTS OF THE FIFTH 'ALIYA

Year	Legal	Tourists and illegal	Total
1933	27,862	2,465	30,327
1934	38,244	4,115	42,359
1935	58,050	3,804	61,854
1936	27,910	1,807	29,717
1937	9,855	681	10,536
1938	11,441	1,427	12,868
1939	16,405	11,156	27,561
Total	189,767	25,455	215,222

World War II, 1939–45. These were the years when Jewish life came to a tragic end in Germany, Poland, and other Nazi-occupied countries all over Europe. Immigration to Palestine continued under the most difficult conditions, both legally, on the basis of the immigration certificates issued by the British Mandatory government of Palestine under the schedule of the 1939 White Paper, and illegally, with the Ma'apilim (illegal immigrants) either sailing directly for Palestine or going to neutral ports in Turkey where they received certificates. Immigration during World War II is shown in Table 4. "Illegal" immigration was hampered by disasters to refugee ships (see Table 5), which cost the lives of thousands of refugees.

The desperate efforts to rescue Jewish children from Nazi-occupied territories continued throughout the war, and 16,617 certificates were allocated by the Jewish Agency in the period 1939–45 for this purpose. During these years 15,329 children and adolescents arrived in Palestine on Youth 'Aliya certificates. Most of the youngsters came from Germany and Austria (6,766), Poland (2,608), Romania (2,841), and Hungary (670).

After World War II, 1945–48. The extensive movement of Jewish displaced persons in the years immediately following the war created a severe immigration problem. The influx of survivors from concentration camps in Poland, Romania, and other countries and some 200,000 Jewish returnees from the U.S.S.R. filled refugee camps set up in the liberated areas

TABLE 4. IMMIGRANTS, SEPTEMBER, 1939–DECEMBER, 1945

Year	Legal	"Illegal"	Total
1939*	4,092	4,330	8,422
1940	4,547	3,851	8,398
1941	3,647	2,239	5,886
1942	2,194	1,539	3,733
1943	8,507	. . . . .†	8,507
1944	14,464	. . . . .†	14,464
1945	12,751	370	13,121
Total	50,202	12,329	62,531

*September—December.
†No figures are given because all refugees from Romania, etc., received immigration certificates on their arrival in Istanbul and thus reached Palestine as "legally authorized" immigrants. During this period 310 Jewish "illegal" immigrants were deported from Palestine.

TABLE 5. REFUGEE SHIP DISASTERS

Year	Ships	Deaths
1939	"Danube," at Kladovo	1,160
1940	"Salvador," off Turkish coast	230
1940	"Patria," off Haifa	about 280
1942	"Struma," off Istanbul	769
1944	"Mefkura," off Istanbul	430
	Total	2,869

in Germany and Italy to serve as transit stations for refugees on the way to Palestine, which at that time was still almost hermetically closed to immigrants. The *American Jewish Joint Distribution Committee provided health and welfare assistance, and the Jewish Agency furnished rehabilitation and cultural help for those registered as prospective immigrants and awaiting transportation to Palestine. Despite the restrictions of the Palestine government regulations under the White Paper policy, 120,000 displaced Jews reached Palestine during the period 1945–48.

The "temporary" regulations imposed in January, 1946, provided for a monthly quota of 1,500 immigrants. The 43,500 certificates allocated under this arrangement were used mainly for refugees intercepted en route or detained in camps in 'Atlit and Cyprus (see CYPRUS, DETENTION CAMPS IN). In addition, 17,000 refugees arrived illegally.

The figures for total immigration to Palestine during the period between the end of World War II and May 15, 1948, are shown in Table 6. Between Jan. 1, 1945, and May 15, 1948, a total of 83,807 illegal immigrants arrived in Palestine. This figure includes "illegal" immigrants stranded in camps on Cyprus and groups of immigrants who infiltrated by land (7,500), or who arrived on boats clandestinely, without being registered at all. Of these, 65 ships of the "'Aliya Bet fleet" brought 69,878.

Jewish immigration by countries of origin in the period 1919–48 is shown in Table 7, and that by ethnic groups in the period 1882–1948 in Table 8.

After Independence, 1948–   . With the establishment of the Jewish State, free 'Aliya began under the auspices of the government of Israel. Between May 15, 1948, and Dec. 31, 1966,

TABLE 6. IMMIGRANTS IN POSTWAR PERIOD

Year	Immigrants registered	Illegal immigrants	Total
1946	7,850	9,910	17,760
1947	7,290	14,252	21,542
1948*	2,109	15,065	17,174
Total	17,249	39,227	56,476

*January 1–May 14.

1,231,023 Jews arrived in Israel. Between May 15, 1948, and the end of 1952 entire Jewish communities were transplanted to Israel. Among these countries were Yemen, 45,288; Iraq, 122,380; Iran, 29,660; Bulgaria, 37,892; Yugoslavia, 7,683; Czechoslovakia, 18,241; Poland, 103,996; Romania, 122,652; Morocco-Tunisia-Algeria, 52,852; Libya, 31,628; China, 2,250; and Aden, 3,190. In all, immigrants came to the new State of Israel from 70 countries. In addition to the sea route, the Jewish Agency organized accelerated immigration by airlift from Yemen, Iraq, and elsewhere (see OPERATION 'EZRA AND NEHEMIA; OPERATION MAGIC CARPET).

The government of Israel established consulates in the countries of emigration or transit to endorse visas, while the offices of the Jewish Agency arranged transportation by sea and air and care of the immigrants en route, and saw to the absorption of the immigrants after their arrival in Israel. During the period of mass immigration (1948–52) most immigrants were placed on arrival in temporary immigrants' camps until more permanent accommodations could be built for them. Statistics of free immigration to Israel from May 15, 1948, to 1966 are summarized in Table 9.

H. BARLAS

EMIGRATION FROM ISRAEL

As in every country of large-scale immigration, in Israel, too, some immigrants found adjustment so difficult that they decided to reemigrate. Added to these were Israel-born citizens who, for personal or economic reasons, left the country permanently. There were waves of emigration during the economic slump of the late 1920s and during the period of depression and disillusionment preceding the *Six-day War of 1967.

Most of the emigrants came from the ranks of those who had arrived in Israel after 1948: in the years 1948–51 this group constituted 67.5 per cent of all emigrants; in 1952–61, 60.9 per cent; and in 1962, 52.7 per cent. As to the origin of the emigrants, of those leaving in the years 1948–51, 24.6 per cent had been born in Asia and Africa, 65.6 per cent in Europe and the Americas, and 9.7 per cent in Israel. Of those leaving in the years 1952–61, 15 per cent had been born in Asia and Africa, 63.7 per cent in Europe and the Americas, and 21.2 per cent

TABLE 7. JEWISH IMMIGRATION, 1919–MAY 15, 1948, BY PRINCIPAL COUNTRIES OF ORIGIN

Country	1919–23	1924–31	1932–38	1939–45	1946–48*	Total, 1919–48
Poland	9,158	38,605	89,307	15,928	17,129	170,127
Romania	1,404	4,063	10,538	8,935	16,165	41,105
Germany	469	997	35,855	14,247	1,383	52,951
U.S.S.R.	13,363	14,911	5,486	784	262	34,806
Czechoslovakia	112	409	3,903	8,260	4,110	16,794
Hungary	291	312	1,335	3,691	4,713	10,342
Turkey	478	1,303	2,179	4,196	121	8,277
Bulgaria	328	1,209	1,121	3,220	11,199	17,077
Morocco-Tunisia-Algeria	51	30	94	281	568	1,024
Yemen	184	2,511	7,035	4,703	133	14,566
Total	25,838	64,350	156,853	64,245	55,783	367,069

*To May 15, 1948, only.

TABLE 8. PRE-STATE 'ALIYOT, 1882–1948, BY ETHNIC GROUPS

Period	Years	Ashkenazi Jews*	Sephardi and Oriental Jews*	Not known	Total number of immigrants
First 'Aliya	1882–1903 †	24,000	1,000	. . . . .	25,000
Second 'Aliya	1904–1913 †	38,000	2,000	. . . . .	40,000
Third 'Aliya	1919–1923	29,000	2,400	3,783	35,183
Fourth 'Aliya	1924–1931	64,000	9,800	7,813	81,613
Fifth 'Aliya	1932–1939	170,000	15,600	39,185	224,785
World War II 'Aliya	1940–1945	25,000	15,500	13,609	54,109
Postwar 'Aliya	1946–1948 ‡	29,300	5,100	11,986	46,386
Total	1882–1948	379,300	51,400	76,376	507,076

*Calculated on the basis of known countries of origin.
† Unofficial estimates.
‡ To May 15, 1948, only.

in Israel. Of those leaving in 1962, 18.3 per cent had been born in Asia and Africa, 51.3 per cent in Europe and the Americas, and 30.4 per cent in Israel. In the 1960s there was a marked decrease in the emigration of Asian- and African-born residents of Israel, a slight decrease in that of the European- and American-born, and a marked increase in that of the Israel-born, many of them *Sabra youths who complained of a lack of incentives and challenges in Israel. In 1967, 196,000 Israelis living abroad had declared themselves emigrants. Table 10 compares the statistics of immigration to and emigration from Israel.

TABLE 9. JEWISH IMMIGRANTS TO ISRAEL, MAY 15, 1948–DEC. 31, 1966, BY CONTINENT OF ORIGIN

Year	From Europe and Americas	From Asia and Africa	Percentage of total from the four continents		Not known	Total
			From Europe and Americas	From Asia and Africa		
1948	77,032	12,931	85.6	14.4	11,856	101,819
1949	123,097	110,780	52.7	47.3	5,199	239,076
1950	84,638	83,296	50.4	49.6	1,471	169,405
1951	50,204	123,449	28.9	71.1	248	173,901
1952	6,647	16,725	28.4	71.6	3	23,375
1953	2,574	7,760	24.9	75.1	13	10,347
1954	1,966	15,493	11.3	88.7	12	17,471
1955	2,562	33,736	7.1	92.9	5	36,303
1956	7,305	47,617	13.3	86.7	3	54,925
1957	39,763	29,361	57.5	42.5	609	69,733
1958	14,428	11,490	55.7	44.3	1	25,919
1959	15,348	7,635	66.8	33.2	4	22,987
1960	16,684	6,801	71.0	29.0	2	23,487
1961	24,564	22,004	52.7	47.3	3	46,571
1962	12,793	46,677	21.5	78.5	3	59,473
1963	19,028	43,054	30.7	69.3	4	62,086
1964	30,362	21,831	58.2	41.8	. . . . . .	52,193
1965	15,025	13,476	52.7	47.3	. . . . . .	28,501
1966	7.537	5.914	56.0	44.0	. . . . . .	13,451
Tourists settling, 1948–67	15,642	10,806	59.1	40.9	. . . . . .	26,448
Total, 1948–66	567,199	670,836	45.8	54.2	19,436	1,257,471

TABLE 10. JEWISH EMIGRATION FROM AND IMMIGRATION TO ISRAEL

Year	Number of emigrants (est.)	Number of immigrants	Emigration rate*	Immigration rate†	Percentage of emigrants to immigrants
1948‡	1,040	101,828	1.5	177	1.02
1949	7,207	239,576	8.0	266	3.01
1950	9,463	170,249	8.6	154	5.56
1951	10,057	175,095	7.6	132	5.74
1952	13,000	24,369	9.1	17	53.35
1953	12,500	11,326	8.5	8	110.36
1954	7,000	18,370	4.7	12	38.10
1955	6,000	37,478	3.9	24	16.01
1956	11,000	56,234	6.8	35	19.56
1957	11,000	71,224	6.4	41	15.44
1958	11,500	27,082	6.4	15	42.46
1959	9,500	23,895	5.2	13	39.75
1960	8,500	24,510	4.5	13	34.68
1961	7,330§	47,638	3.3	25	15.39
1962	7,644§	61,328	3.3	30	12.46
1963	10,866§	64,364	4.5	30	16.88
1964	9,121§	54,716	3.6	25	16.67
1965	7,941§	32,939	3.0	14	23.94
1966	7,793§	15,730	2.9	15	49.64

*Per 1,000 population.   ‡ May 15–December 31.
†Per 1,000 Jewish population.   §Includes Jewish and non-Jewish emigrants.

In the 1960s the prevalent attitude in Israel toward emigrants tended to be one of resentment. They were called Yordim (descenders), in contrast to immigrants, for whom the Hebrew term is 'Olim (ascenders). Emigration from Israel (Heb., *y'rida*, "descent") is considered an act bordering on disloyalty, an evasion of Jewish national duties and responsibilities.

The attitude of the Yordim to Israel, on the other hand, remained in general positive. Although some of them were critical of Israel, mainly in order to justify their emigration, most showed continued interest in what went on in Israel, and many devoted all or part of their time of work for various Israeli and Zionist causes.

The year 1968 saw a considerable increase in the number of emigrants returning to Israel: 1,479 in the first nine months of 1968, as compared with 393 for all of 1967 and a few dozen for 1966. This development was attributed to patriotic sentiment aroused by the Six-day War and to economic incentives offered to returning emigrants.

R. PATAI

INBAL DANCE THEATER. *See* DANCE IN ISRAEL.

INDEPENDENCE DAY OF ISRAEL (Yom Ha'Atzmaut). Holiday celebrated annually on the 5th of Iyar to commemorate the Proclamation of the State of Israel on May 14, 1948 (Iyar 5, 5708). Celebrations are ushered in by a torch-lighting ceremony at Herzl's tomb on Mount Herzl. Festivities include special prayers, athletic events, street dances, pageants, music festivals, and the awarding of the *Israel Prize for outstanding contributions in various fields. The chief event of the day, until 1969, was a military parade. It has become the custom for the President of the State (*see* PRESIDENCY OF ISRAEL) to receive representatives of the diplomatic corps at his official residence on Independence Day.

The preceding day, Remembrance Day, is dedicated to the memory of those who fell in the *War of Independence and in defense of the country. On that day memorial prayers are recited in the synagogues, memorial lights kindled, services conducted in military cemeteries, and memorial parades held in military camps. A two-minute silence is observed.

In 1949 the *Knesset enacted the Independence Day Law, making Independence Day an official holiday and a compulsory day of rest. If the 5th of Iyar falls on a Sabbath, Independence Day is celebrated on the 3d of Iyar; if it falls on a Friday, it is celebrated on the 4th of Iyar.

INDEPENDENT LIBERAL PARTY. *See* PROGRESSIVE PARTY IN ISRAEL.

INDIA, ZIONISM IN. The early history of the Jews in India is obscure. However, this much is clear: of the three communities that form the bulk of Indian Jewry, the Baghdad Jews, the

Tanks parade during the celebration of Yom Ha'Atzmaut in 1959. [Keren HaYesod]

Street dancing in Haifa on the anniversary of independence in 1968. [Keren HaYesod]

Cochin Jews, and the B'ne Israel, the last named were the earliest Jewish settlers in the country.

The origin of the B'ne Israel is unknown. For centuries they had no contact with other Jewish communities, and their religious practices deviated considerably from those of other Jews. In the 18th and 19th centuries, under the influence of teachers from Cochin and Baghdad, a religious revival took place, and since then the B'ne Israel have conformed to traditional Jewish practice.

The Cochin Jews, so called because of their settlements in Cochin and vicinity on the Malabar Coast, in southwest India, were divided into two groups: the "White Jews," who had a lighter complexion, and the "Black Jews," who were brown. While the White Jews were descended from Jewish immigrants, it has not been established whether the Black Jews were the offspring of Jews who had married native women or the descendants of native groups that had embraced Judaism. According to their own tradition, the Cochin Jews were the descendants of the Judean captives exiled by Nebuchadnezzar in 586 B.C.E.

The Baghdad Jews began arriving in India early in the 19th century and established communities of their own.

In 1966 there were about 16,000 Jews in India in a total population of over 470 million. The great majority were B'ne Israel; several thousand were Baghdad Jews, and several hundred were Cochin Jews. The latter were mostly White Jews, most of the Black Jews having left for Israel.

Early Years. In 1897 Herzl invited the leaders of the B'ne Israel of Bombay to attend the 1st Zionist *Congress. This invitation remained unanswered, and it was not until the issuance of the *Balfour Declaration in 1917 that the Jews of India began to show an interest in Zionism. The Bombay Zionist Association was founded in 1920. Zionism in India received added stimulus by the visit of Israel *Cohen, general secretary of the *World Zionist Organization, who was then on a Zionist mission to Australia and the Far East. It was only appropriate that he should visit Bombay, the city containing the majority of India's 25,000-strong Jewish community. Cohen was the first among many subsequent emissaries for the *Jewish National Fund. Another was Emanuel *Olswanger, who enjoyed the high esteem of India's Jews.

In 1933 the first representative sent by the *Jewish Agency arrived in Bombay. Hebrew-language classes and groups for the study of Palestinography, Jewish history, and Hebrew songs and dances were organized, as was a group preparing for Halutzic (pioneer) *'Aliya (immigration; *see* HALUTZIYUT). This created a precedent for the establishment, after World War II, of a *Hakhshara training farm in a village near Bombay.

The first *HaBonim youth group was founded in 1935 in Bombay; it was followed by branches in Calcutta and Cochin. The Bombay branch of the *Women's International Zionist Organization (WIZO) was formed in 1938.

The cultural and fund-raising activities of the Bombay Zionist Association led to the founding of the *Jewish Advocate*, which, with the *Jewish Tribune*, disseminated news and views of the Zionist and Jewish scene. Of considerable interest was a letter in 1939 from Jawaharlal Nehru (later Prime Minister of India) to the *Jewish Advocate*, stating that if the ruling British power withdrew, the Jews and Arabs in Palestine would be able to solve their political problems together.

World War II and After. During World War II, Zionist activities received added impetus from the arrival of Jewish soldiers in the British Army and European refugees with a Zionist background.

In 1943 the *Jewish Advocate* launched a vigorous press campaign to counteract the anti-Zionist propaganda generated by a conference in Bombay of the All-India Muslim League, the body which was to found the new state of Pakistan in 1947. This was one of the few manifestations of *anti-Semitism in

Group of B'ne Israel in Bombay in 1927. [Zionist Archives]

India, which as a rule had shown complete tolerance of, and respect for, Judaism and the Jewish community.

In 1947 Nehru convened the First Asian Relations Conference in New Delhi, at which delegates from the nationalist movements of various colonial territories discussed problems arising from their dependent status. A delegation from the *Yishuv (Jewish population of Palestine) was invited to this historic conference, at which much Arab hostility to Israel was evident.

Emigration from India to Israel commenced on a large scale in 1949 and resulted in the settlement in Israel of about 10,000 Indian Jews. Most of them were B'ne Israel. At the 26th Zionist Congress (1964–65) in Jerusalem, the B'ne Israel were represented for the first time by two delegates. In 1950 the Zionist Federation of India, consisting of Zionist associations in Bombay, Calcutta, Poona, Ahmadabad, and Cochin, was formed.

India accorded de facto and de jure recognition to Israel in 1950, and in 1952 an Israel Consulate was set up in Bombay. India, however, has maintained no diplomatic or consular representation in Israel and has on all occasions supported the Arab states against Israel. The consulate, together with the Bombay Zionist Association and the latter's monthly organ, the *Indo-Israel Review* (launched in 1958), did valuable public relations work for Israel. Previously a privately sponsored monthly, *India and Israel* (1948–52), had been devoted to strengthening the ties between the two countries. The India-Israel Friendship League, whose membership included prominent Indians, was set up in New Delhi in 1964.

See also INDIAN JEWS IN ISRAEL.   P. S. GOURGEY

INDIAN JEWS IN ISRAEL. In 1968 there were about 13,000 Jews of Indian origin in Israel. Some 5,000 of these belonged to the B'ne Israel, indigenous to western India (in and near Bombay); about 3,000 were Cochin Jews, from the Malabar Coast and south India; and about 5,000 were Arabic-speaking Jews whose parents had originally migrated from Baghdad to India. Many of them lived in the *development towns, particularly those of southern Israel; others, in the three main cities of Tel Aviv, Jerusalem, and Haifa, while some settled in kibbutzim and moshavim (*see* KIBBUTZ; MOSHAV). Although many of them were employed as unskilled laborers, quite a few had professional qualifications and held clerical positions.

The large-scale emigration of Jews from India began in 1949

Immigrants from Cochin, India, arriving in Israel in 1954. [Zionist Archives]

Immigrants from India engaged in agriculture in Israel. [Keren HaYesod]

with the organization by the *Jewish Agency of special direct charter flights from Bombay to Lod, because the Suez Canal was blocked by the Egyptians to all shipping destined for Israel. The *'Aliya from India, Burma, Singapore, and other parts of Southeast Asia had idealistic, social, and economic motivations. Among Jewish youths from Bombay who left a *Hakhshara training farm outside the city to join the *Mahal volunteer unit in Israel's *War of Independence were Abe Nathan, who later was to become known for his "peace with Nasser" flight, and Capt. Nissim Sampson, who settled in D'ganya. Emanuel *Olswanger of Jerusalem, the linguist, scholar, and great friend of the B'ne Israel of India, proved most helpful with the absorption problems encountered by Indian Jews in Israel. In the summer of 1949 the Jewish Agency took steps to set up a moshav for Indian immigrants at Julis, east of Ashk'lon. To further this scheme of settlement and to represent the interests of the immigrants from India, the Hitahdut 'Ole Hodu (Association of Immigrants from India) was organized.

Immigration from India proceeded smoothly until 1951, when a number of B'ne Israel, finding adaptation to kibbutz life difficult and unable to secure employment in B'er Sheva', staged a sit-down strike outside the Jewish Agency offices and demanded to be taken back to India. After their arrival in India, however, they were unable to regain their former posts, and in December, 1954, most of them (33 families) returned to Israel and finally settled down. A new moshav, called K'far 'Ofer and composed mainly of Jews from Iraq and India, was formed near Haifa in 1952. There were also Indian Gar'inim (nucleus groups) in Ma'ayan Tz'vi and Tirat Tz'vi. A number of young people also went to Israel under the auspices of *Youth 'Aliya.

In 1954 and 1955 Jewish families from the Malabar Coast of southwestern India, near Cochin, arrived in Israel, a large group of them settling down at two moshavim. Ta'oz and M'sillat Tziyon, on the road between Jerusalem and Tel Aviv. They were the most Orthodox element in Indian Jewry; many of them were farmers, and their integration into Westernized and industrialized Israeli society was exemplary.

In 1961 Sephardi Chief Rabbi Yitzhak R. *Nissim issued directives instructing rabbis to examine the descent of B'ne Israel Jews wishing to marry outside their own community, apparently on the ground that the legitimacy of their descent was in doubt since it was not certain whether their ancestors had observed the Jewish marriage and divorce laws. The ensuing conflict led to mass demonstrations and hunger strikes (1964) that received considerable popular support. A special session of the *Knesset was convened on Aug. 17, 1964, at which indignation was expressed at the action of the rabbinical authority. The Rabbinate was finally forced to alter its policy, and no further complaints were brought to public attention.

P. S. GOURGEY

INDUSTRY IN ISRAEL. Modern industry in Palestine began under adverse conditions. The lack of raw materials, of power and capital resources, and of industrial techniques presented obstacles to the introduction of industrial processes; in addition, the ideological trends prevalent among the early Zionist settlers stressed agriculture as the primary means toward Binyan Ha'Aretz (the upbuilding of the land) and thus militated against industrial efforts. Before 1918 modern industry consisted of the wineries in Rishon L'Tziyon and Zikhron Ya'akov and of a number of small mills and workshops, among which those of the German (Templar) settlers were prominent (see TEMPLARS). Most of these enterprises were actually handicraft undertakings such as potteries, tanneries, and carpet-weaving and glassblowing shops in Gaza, Hebron, Jaffa, Jerusalem, and Ramle. About 80 per cent of them had fewer than four employees.

MANDATORY PERIOD

The British Mandatory administration of Palestine (see MANDATE FOR PALESTINE) was reluctant to promote industrialization. Its tariff system was designed to provide revenue rather than promote industries; banks were skeptical of industrial ventures; and the lack of a modern infrastructure led to failures among the early industrial pioneers and confirmed the critical attitude of the authorities, the banks, and a good part of the public. In 1924 Jewish immigrants from Poland initiated a change, for they included persons with industrial experience (mainly in textiles) and some financial means. They formed a number of enterprises, but the 1926 economic crisis in Poland deprived them of their financial backing and industrial progress slowed down. Nonetheless, their ventures created a shift in public opinion that induced the *World Zionist Organization to provide some financial facilities for industry, and the mandatory government began gradually to adjust its fiscal policy to the needs of local industry.

The growth of industry was slow but steady, and between 1921 and 1930 the number of persons employed in industry grew from 5,000 to almost 11,000 (see Table 1). It was during the 1920s and the early 1930s that some of Palestine's larger industrial establishments were formed, among them the Nesher portland cement factory, the Shemen Oil Company, and the Phoenicia Glass Company, in Haifa; the Ata spinning and weaving mill, in K'far Ata; and the Lodzia textile plant, in Tel Aviv. These enterprises were founded by private capital. The Palestine Electric Cooperation, Ltd. (see ISRAEL ELECTRIC CORPORATION,

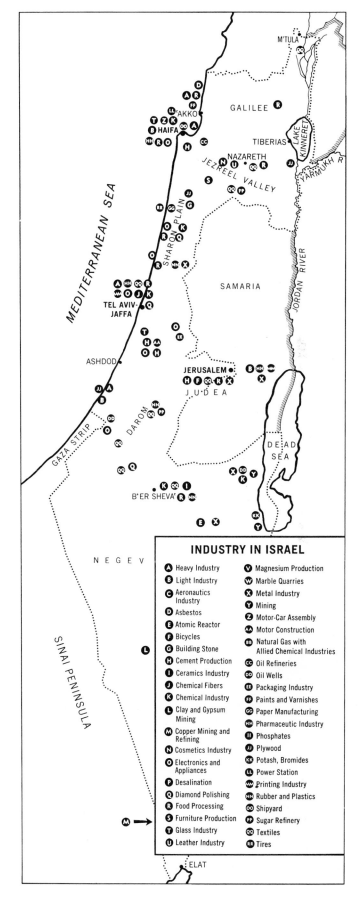

TABLE 1. INDUSTRY IN PALESTINE, 1921–42

	1921	1930	1939	1942
Number of establishments	1,850*	624†	1,212†	2,489†
Persons employed	4,750	10,968	17,795	36,577
Capital invested (in thousands of Palestine pounds)	600	2,234	5,635	14,191

*Industrial and handicraft.
†Industrial only.

LTD.) received an initial investment from Zionist institutions, but the bulk of its capital was provided by British investors. The modern flour mill built in Haifa in the early 1920s included an investment from Baron Edmond de *Rothschild. Many workshops were established in this period, and some of them developed into sizable factories in the course of years.

The events in Germany in 1933 and subsequently in Austria and Czechoslovakia brought about the second major phase in Palestine's industrialization. The Jewish immigrants from Central Europe created a larger and more sophisticated market and included industrialists with capital, know-how, and experience. Industrial investment rose steeply, to £7,000,000 between 1933 and 1939, more than doubling the investment of the period 1918–33. Tools and equipment imported in the years 1933–39 from Germany, from which capital could be exported only in kind, may have been in excess of immediate needs, but it became an important reserve to draw on for the industrial expansion that took place during World War II.

This period saw the introduction of new branches of industry: cotton spinning, diamond polishing (see DIAMOND INDUSTRY IN

Pipe- and tube-manufacturing plant near 'Akko. [Israel Information Services]

Paper mill in Hadera. [Israel Information Services]

ISRAEL), plate glass making, and the beginnings of the rubber and plastics industry. The expanding citrus plantations (*see* CITRUS INDUSTRY IN ISRAEL) became the base for modern food processing and essential oils manufacturing, and the establishment of a cast iron plant inaugurated the country's heavy industry. Outside the Jewish sector, oil refineries were constructed in Haifa by the Iraq Petroleum Company, and a modern Arab-owned spinning mill and several cigarette factories were established.

The dislocations and disruptions of supply channels caused by World War II, which limited Palestine to its own resources, resulted in a broadening of the industrial base, the establishment of new industries, and the extension of existing plants. This rapid growth made Palestine an important supply source for the needs of the Allied armed forces stationed in the Middle East and for the countries of the region. To cope with the sudden demand, the existing industrial potential was exploited to the fullest, and of the many new plants that were set up, some, such as metal, precision instruments, and chemical plants, were new to the country. Although some of the wartime enterprises were bound to disappear with the end of the war, Palestine's industrial sector accumulated adequate reserves for postwar reequipment and modernization, trained a competent labor force, and developed considerable ingenuity to cope with the difficulties of postwar readjustment. Despite the rising political tension and disorders that preceded the *partition of Palestine, industrial activity remained at a high level.

See also WAR EFFORT OF THE YISHUV.

J. O. RONALL

DEVELOPMENT AFTER INDEPENDENCE

The development of Israel's industry since the establishment of the State has been influenced by a diversity of factors, all of which, however, have pointed in the same direction. The dynamic growth of the population followed by a rapid increase in local consumption, on the one hand, and the availability of large investment credits coupled with a fiscal policy designed to facilitate new industries, on the other, have led to an increase in industrial investment and to a rise in production capacity. Other factors which have contributed to this development are protective tariffs on imports, the efforts by both manufacturers' and workers' organizations to raise productivity, and the promotion of exports. The resulting expansion of Israel's industry may be gauged by the fact that the value of its production increased tenfold in constant prices between 1949 and 1966.

Trends in Industrial Development. Industrial development during the first years of the State was marked by a number of characteristic tendencies. One of these was the manufacture of finished products, leading very often to the importation of semifabricated and even of mainly manufactured goods for finishing. In certain industries this practice was necessitated by the absence of local raw materials or the lack of skilled labor. Later, a growing concentration of investments in the complete production of finished articles resulted in the establishment of enterprises for the production of raw materials and of heavy industries which were financed both by *government funds and by private investments. Other significant features were the erection of numerous small factories and, at the same time, a growing centralization in other industries.

The government made continual attempts to counter the inflationary tendency of the local market. The most important measures affecting Israel's industry were the economic programs and the currency devaluations of 1952 and 1962, as well as the devaluation of 1967 (see ECONOMY OF ISRAEL; FINANCE IN ISRAEL).

The years between 1953 and 1956 were marked by a tendency to shift to the production of goods better adapted to the requirements of consumers, who had begun to demand higher quality. Moreover, producers were forced to seek foreign markets as outlets for their goods. Industrial production, classified by official statistics in seven principal groups (food, metals, electrical appliances, leather goods, chemical goods and pharmaceuticals, textiles, and footwear), continued to expand. It included several new branches such as factory equipment, agricultural machinery, electric motors, spare parts for the assembly of electrical machinery, refrigerators, watches, pipes, electric light bulbs, ceramics, and glassware. The production of potash was resumed, while the extraction of phosphates and the manufacture of superphosphates were increased. Several industrial products based on agricultural raw materials were developed, particularly sugar beets for the new sugar refineries and cotton for the spinning mills serving the textile industry.

The devaluations of February, 1962, and November, 1967, which provided, respectively, for unified rates of exchange of IL3 and IL3.50 to $1, did not bring significant benefits to many export industries, whereas the customs tariff introduced under the import liberalization policy provided ample protection for the local market. The excessive protection granted to production for the home market and the inadequate rate of exchange allowed for exports led to a misallocation of labor and capital. Investments destined for the domestic market received preference over investments oriented chiefly toward the foreign market, even when the cost of the dollar saved on the production of import substitutes was higher than the cost of the value-added dollar from exports.

There was, however, a difference in the effect on the general price level between the earlier policy of administrative import restrictions (quotas and licenses) and the new system of fiscal import protection (tariffs). With the partial removal of import barriers, fiscal protection was likely to hold down prices in the long run, provided import prices did not change and tariffs were not raised.

Output per man rose by 4 to 5 per cent yearly, indicating a continuation of the trend toward rising productivity. The annual growth rate of output per man in industry ranged between 5 and 6 per cent, compared with 2 to 3 per cent in the 1950s. The increase no doubt reflected both the higher capitalization of local industry and technological advances.

Industrial Investments. The trend and nature of industrial investments in Israel were governed by local needs, which to a large extent comprised consumer goods, the sale of which was often artificially stimulated by rapidly rising purchasing power.

The choice of investments was also affected by the professional qualifications of the immigrants, who naturally wished to avail themselves of machinery brought from their countries of origin or who possessed funds earmarked for certain categories of merchandise. Over the years, industrial investments showed a marked tendency toward selective fields, as directed by the government on the basis of statistical data relating to certain spheres of production or of economic plans drawn up by teams of experts. In planning industrial investments, the government confined itself to granting licenses for the importation of machinery, extending long-term credits from the Development Budget, authorizing purchases of foreign machinery (either from loans or through German reparations), granting fiscal relief for the benefit of approved enterprises, and allowing nonresident investors to repatriate profits in foreign currency.

Ownership. The share of the private sector in total industrial investments (see Table 2) has undergone many fluctuations. From 50 per cent in 1951–52, it dropped to 35 per cent in 1953 and then rose to over 70 per cent in 1960. It should be noted, however, that an increasingly important part of private investment has consisted of capital loaned to private investors from State-controlled sources.

Growth of Production. The total gross revenue of industry in 1966–67 in current market prices, including direct taxes and excluding subsidies, was IL6,237,000,000. The production of leading industrial products rose in the period 1950–66 as shown in Table 3. The production of electricity rose from 500 million kilowatt-hours in 1960 to more than 4.5 billion in 1966.

TABLE 2. ESTABLISHMENTS AND EMPLOYED PERSONS IN INDUSTRY BY TYPE OF OWNERSHIP, 1965 CENSUS

Type of establishment	Employed persons	Establishments
Single owners	44,451	16,096
Partnerships	26,995	417
Private companies	99,582	2,853
Public companies	31,122	221
Cooperative societies	14,973	1,169
Others	12,406	340
Total	229,529	21,096

TABLE 3. OUTPUT OF LEADING INDUSTRIAL PRODUCTS, 1950 AND 1966

Product and unit of production	1950	1966
Crude petroleum (million liters)	0	216
Natural gas (million cubic meters)	0	95
Copper ore (metric tons)	0	10,300
Phosphate rock (metric tons)	0	400,000
Preserved fruit (metric tons)	1,000	35,000
Jam (metric tons)	3,700	4,500
Citrus concentrates (million liters)	1	12
Natural citrus juice (million liters)	20	35
Unrefined oils (million liters)	0	15
Refined oils (million liters)	12	34
Cotton yarn (metric tons)	8,000	23,000
Worsted yarn (metric tons)	900	2,900
Stationery and printing paper (metric tons)	0	20
Tires (metric tons)	0	13,000
Storage batteries (units)	0	108,000

Planning. Several attempts have been made to plan industrial investments. The establishment in 1953 of an Economic Advisory Office was an important step in this direction. The Office comprised a team of outstanding experts in many fields, including industrial production. United Nations and United States aid missions have also lent technical assistance to various Israeli industries.

After the Economic Advisory Office closed down in 1956, a special Department of Industrial Planning was established. The Economic Planning Authority and the Planning Department of the Ministry of Commerce and Industry have undergone numerous experiments in reorganization. Technological research has been carried out by the *National Council for Research and Development of the Prime Minister's Office, which has devoted particular attention to the chemical research of quarries and the Dead Sea deposits.

Dynamic development interferes with the accurate planning of production, not only because it sets so rapid a pace but also because regular trends are lacking. A sudden short-lived influx of new immigrants, for instance, may leave in its wake an excess of productive capacity in industries which furnish immigrants with housing and primary consumption goods.

Industrial Exports. The value of industrial exports, including diamonds, rose from $28,500,000 in 1949 to $503,000,000 in 1966. The most striking increases in exports, in both absolute and relative terms, were achieved by the following branches of industry. Exports of mine and quarry products advanced at a very rapid rate owing to a rise in prices and an increase in volume. The two principal products of this industry are copper cement and potash. The absolute growth of copper-cement exports was due partly to an expansion of productive capacity, but the volume of production depended largely on a chance factor, the richness of the ores mined. The growth of potash exports was limited by the productive capacity of the potash works. The accelerated expansion of such exports reached a peak as a result of investments which were still in progress, but the rate would no doubt decline after their completion. Another leading export was plywood.

The products principally responsible for a large increase in textile exports were cotton yarn and synthetic yarn. The export of cotton yarn was made possible by surplus productive capacity, which was subsidized, as in the other textile and clothing branches, by a higher effective rate of exchange than that applicable to most other industries. Synthetic-yarn sales were different in character. Here there was a rising world demand, with indications that the supply was unable to keep pace with it.

Garment exports developed very sluggishly in the 1960s. Whereas the annual export increment between 1958 and 1961 had averaged 40 per cent, it dropped to a mere 8 per cent in 1962. A recession in 1963 was not offset by increases in the period 1964–66. Raincoats, bathing suits, and knitted goods accounted for more than two-thirds of total clothing exports. The only item to show a constant, though slow, increase was apparel made from imported cotton, which constituted the remaining third of the exports.

Israeli exports amounted to 11.3 per cent of imports in 1949 and to 58.8 per cent in 1966. Exports totaled $27 per capita in 1949 and $181 in 1966. The trade deficit per capita was $214 in 1949 and $127 in 1966.

Labor Force. Israel's relative advantage in industry was due to the skills of the individual Israeli. Israel had at its disposal a local labor force of great adaptability and potential as well as substantial inventive qualifications to form individual patterns of industrial production.

According to the trade and industry census of 1965, the leading industrial branches in the preceding five years were manufactured electric, electronic, and mechanical equipment, in which the labor force grew by 150 to 250 per cent. In the textile field, the most important place was taken by woven materials and knitted products, which jointly accounted for 46 per cent of the labor force in the textile industry. The labor force of the garment industry showed an increase of more than 60 per cent, while the increase of employment in the diamond industry reached a figure of 256 per cent in five years.

L. BERGER

INGATHERING OF THE EXILES (Kibbutz Galuyot). The concept that the exiled Jewish *communities scattered in the *Diaspora will be gathered into the Land of Israel was originally a religious one and as such formed the subject of a prophecy of Ezekiel (34:13). Following the destruction of the Second Jewish Commonwealth in C.E. 70, the idea of the Ingathering became closely linked to the belief in the future coming of the Messiah who would be instrumental in bringing it about. When political Zionism began its work for a return to Palestine, some Orthodox Jewish circles objected because they still adhered to the belief that only the Messiah could restore the exiles to the Land of Israel. The Ingathering of the Exiles became an important concept in Zionism, and after the establishment of the State of Israel it was given legal expression in the Law of *Return and was partly realized in the form of the *immigration of Jewish individuals and groups from about 100 countries. In several cases this immigration amounted to a near-total evacuation of entire Jewish communities from countries such as Iraq and Yemen in which they had resided since ancient times, resulting in their complete transfer to Israel.

See also OPERATION 'EZRA AND NEHEMIA; OPERATION MAGIC CARPET.

INSTITUTE OF APPLIED SOCIAL RESEARCH. Research institution founded in 1949 with the aid of a grant from the Israeli government. It developed from a volunteer group of the *Hagana (underground defense army) and was officially established under the leadership and direction of Louis *Guttman and others. At first under the Ministry of Defense, it worked for two years under the auspices of the Prime Minister's Office and in 1955 became an independent nonprofit organization. The institute's purpose is to plan and carry out research projects in social psychology and related disciplines; to supply government offices and other public and private institutions with research material and to advise them in the above-mentioned fields in an attempt to direct and improve their operations; to cooperate with organizations in Israel and other countries that are engaged in these and related fields; to raise the level of research in Israel in these fields and to maintain its professional standards; and to receive contributions, grants, and payments from individuals and organizations that wish to encourage the work of the institute or to benefit from its services.

Research projects have been commissioned by various government departments, public bodies, and academic institutions in Israel and other countries and by private commercial and industrial organizations. Research grants have been awarded by foundations and government institutions in Israel and the United States to individual staff members for projects in which they are interested. The work of the institute has covered a wide variety of topics in both theoretical and applied social science. By 1967 more than 350 research projects had been carried out by the institute.

The American Committee for Social Research in Israel, Inc., was founded in 1951 to help further the work of the institute. The committee includes scholars, foundation officials, business executives, and community leaders.

INTERCOLLEGIATE ZIONIST FEDERATION OF AMERICA (IZFA). *See* STUDENT ZIONIST ORGANIZATION.

INTERMARRIAGE IN ISRAEL. *See* POPULATION OF ISRAEL.

INTERNATIONAL CHRISTIAN CONFERENCE FOR PALESTINE. *See* WORLD COMMITTEE FOR PALESTINE.

INTERNATIONAL CULTURAL CENTER FOR YOUTH IN JERUSALEM. Nonsectarian cultural and educational institution. The International Cultural Center for Youth in Jerusalem (ICCY) grew out of the desire of a group of Christians and Jews in Scarsdale, N.Y., in 1941, to assist in the rescue and rehabilitation of youth from the bombed areas in London and, later, of Jewish children who had survived the Hitler terror. Allied in 1944 with Children to Palestine, Inc., a Massachusetts organization of Christian men and women under the leadership of the late Dr. Samuel A. Eliot, it worked under the aegis of *Youth 'Aliya to bring a measure of normalcy to the young survivors of the war, who were helped to build a new life in the Jewish Homeland. It has since evolved into an autonomous project concerned with the furtherance of better international and interhuman relations through youth. A group of American citizens of all faiths, aided by prominent persons from other countries, have lent their talents and means to the realization of this vision.

In 1960 ICCY launched its first major pilot project, the International Youth Center in Jerusalem, and appointed an Advisory Council headed by Moshe *Kol. In the 1960s the youth center organized exhibits and programs on the culture and life of many countries, including the developing nations of Africa and Asia. It conducted special programs and workshops for Jewish and Arab youth and initiated meetings with young people from foreign countries. It commemorated special events recommended by the UN Educational, Scientific and Cultural Organization (UNESCO) and celebrated the national holidays of other countries, whose representatives participated in the festivities. It presented to Israeli audiences interpretations of life and culture in South America and Europe and a realistic view of the United States of America. Officers in 1970 were Spyros D. Skouras, honorary chairman; Mrs. Murray Silverstone, president; Mrs. Hiram B. D. Blauvelt, first vice-president; Alice Topp Lee, treasurer; and Leslie Whelan, chairman, International Public Relations.

IRAN, ZIONISM IN, AND RELATIONS WITH ISRAEL. Jews have lived on Persian territory since the days of Cyrus the Great (6th cent. B.C.E.). For two centuries after the conquest of Babylonia by Cyrus (538 B.C.E.), Palestine itself was a province of Persia. For 25 centuries the Jews were scattered throughout Persia, the principal Jewish communities being in cities such as Hamadan, Isfahan, Kermanshah, Shiraz, Teheran, and Meshed (where, from 1839 on, the Jews lived as Marranos). In 1968 the Jewish population of Iran (Persia officially adopted

the new name in 1935) was about 80,000, in a total population of 25 million.

During the 19th century a large number of Jews from Persia emigrated to Palestine, most of them settling in Jerusalem, where they established a colony of Persian-speaking Jews (*see also* IRANIAN JEWS IN ISRAEL). Contacts with this colony, the rebirth of Jewish life in Palestine brought about by early Zionist pioneers, and an increasingly liberal spirit manifest in Persian public life (Persia was granted a constitution in 1906) helped produce a cultural and national revival also among the Jews of Persia.

The year 1917 saw the foundation of a Society for the Promotion of the Hebrew Language; this was followed a year later by a Judeo-Persian and *Hebrew printing press in Teheran. In 1918 the society published a textbook for modern Hebrew, *Sefer Hizuk S'fat 'Ever* (Book for the Promotion of the Hebrew Language). Written by Sh'lomo ben Kohen Tzedek, a Jewish communal leader and Persian government official, the book concluded with the Hebrew and Persian texts of "*HaTikva." In 1920 the society published *The History of the Zionist Movement* (in the Persian language in Hebrew characters), by 'Aziz ben Yona ('Azizullah) Na'im, which presented a survey of the Zionist movement and its activities in Palestine and quoted liberally from the Psalms and the Book of Isaiah. Also in the 1920s the society published *HaG'ula*, a Persian-language Jewish periodical edited by Na'im, and *HaHayim*, the organ of the Jewish renaissance movement, which carried Persian translations, by Na'im, of some of the poems of Hayim Nahman *Bialik.

Zionism in Iran. Organized Zionism in Persia had its beginnings in 1919, when Sh'lomo ben Kohen Tzedek and 'Aziz ben Yona Na'im (serving as president and secretary, respectively) founded the Comité Central de l'Organisation Sioniste en Perse in Teheran. This overall body, which had 18 branches in the main cities of Iran, sold some 3,500 shekels (*see* SHEKEL) for the 12th Zionist *Congress (Karlovy Vary, 1921; for which, however, the Persian delegation arrived too late) and collected considerable sums of money for the *Keren HaG'ula (Redemption Fund) between 1919 and 1922. In the late 1920s the leadership of the Comité Central included Samuel J. Rokhsar, chairman, Soleiman Bostenai, comptroller, Anayatollah Sapir, general secretary, Farajollah Hakim, head of the *Jewish National Fund Department and cashier, and Mirza Agha Rahimzadeh, head of the Emigration Department.

Central Council of the Zionist Organization in Persia. [Zionist Archives]

The late 1920s saw a decline in Zionist activity in Persia. Both Kohen Tzedek and Na'im left the country (Kohen Tzedek was to return in 1936). The Persian government abrogated freedom of assembly and showed a hostile attitude also toward Zionism. As a result, Zionist meetings were forbidden and Zionist newspapers closed down. Sh'muel Y'hezk'el Hayim, who represented the Jewish community in the Majlis (Parliament) from 1922 to 1924, headed a new Zionist organization from 1922 until his arrest in 1926. He was executed five years later.

Nevertheless, Jewish nationalist activity in Persia did not cease. In 1930 a new Jewish school, Coresh (named for Cyrus the Great), was founded in Teheran; its curriculum included the teaching of modern Hebrew with the aid of new textbooks such as *Sefer HaMathil* (1933–34), modeled on texts then in use in the *Yishuv (Jewish community of Palestine). In the decade preceding World War II the Jewish community of Iran was visited by a number of travelers from Jerusalem, including Itzhak *Ben Zvi.

During World War II the Zionist Organization of Iran gave shelter to many Jewish refugees in Teheran. M. Karmenian of Teheran founded a B'ne Zion youth group and published Persian translations of Jewish history texts and Zionist literature. In 1942 a Palestine Office (*see* PALESTINE OFFICES) was opened in Teheran with the primary purpose of aiding Iranian Jews desiring to settle in Palestine. Although Iranian law did not permit the opening of such an office, the authorities tolerated its existence and did not hamper its work. Thus the director of the Palestine Office was able to maintain close contact with the *Jewish Agency in Jerusalem.

In the 1960s the Zionist Organization of Iran, with its center in Teheran, effectively assisted the work of Sh'lihim (emissaries; *see* SHALIAH) sent from Israel to Iran on behalf of *'Aliya (immigration) and Zionist education. From time to time it organized groups of young people to visit Israel and explore the possibilities offered those planning to settle in the country. The organization also sent delegates to the Zionist Congresses. All the elementary and secondary Jewish schools maintained by the *Alliance Israélite Universelle, the Otzar HaTora, and the Cyrus Society stressed Hebrew studies in their curricula.

Iran's Relations with Israel. Iran was one of the 11 nations represented on the *United Nations Special Committee on Palestine (UNSCOP). After the State of Israel was established, Iran accorded de facto recognition to the new republic (March, 1950) and established a consulate in Israel. The consulate was closed a year later, when Premier Mohammed Mossadegh nationalized Iran's oil industry and sought Arab friendship. Nevertheless, except when the Iranian government briefly closed the Teheran office of the Jewish Agency (April–May, 1953), it made no attempt to restrict 'Aliya from or Zionist activity in the country. Although as of 1969 Iran and Israel still had no official diplomatic ties, relations between them were good and Iran was one of the countries to which Israel sent technical experts and and from which it received trainees within the framework of its *foreign aid program.   H. MIZRAHI

IRANIAN JEWS IN ISRAEL. The longing of the Jews in Persia (since 1935, Iran) to return to Zion was particularly strong in times of troubles and persecution. The poetry and song of Persian Jewry reflected love of Jerusalem and yearning for the Messiah. Such an emotional climate encouraged the emergence of many pseudo Messiahs who instilled false hopes in the masses.

Male members of an Iranian family at their home in Bet Shemesh. [Keren HaYesod]

Throughout the years, scattered Jews braved the dangers of desert travel to reach Jerusalem, but it was not until 1886, following the example of Mulla Aharon Cohen, that a group of Jews migrated from Shiraz to Jerusalem. These early settlers were stone quarriers, stonecutters, and shepherds. The Sephardi community (*see* SEPHARDIM) helped them obtain land in Shevet Tzedek, a shantytown section known as Sh'khunat Pahim (Tin Town) from the sheets of tin used as walls for primitive shelters. A few years later the settlers acquired additional land in the vicinity and built a new section called N've Tzedek.

The lyric poet Mulla Hayim El'azar gave impetus to the migration of Teheran Jews when he settled in Jerusalem in 1895 as Hazzan (cantor) of the Persian community. Many tales are told of his devotion to the Holy Land and the sacrifices he made to live there.

In March, 1839, a pogrom took place in Meshed, the holy city of Shi'ite Islam. The survivors were forcibly converted to Islam, but they secretly remained faithful to Judaism. When their community leaders were compelled to make the pilgrimage to Mecca, they invariably included a stay in Jerusalem in their journey. After the issuance of the *Balfour Declaration, many Jedid al-Islam (new Muslims) from Meshed moved to Palestine. In 1922 the wealthy 'Azizullayoff and Aminov families settled in Jerusalem, introducing the carpet trade to Palestine. Immigrants came also from Hamadan and other Persian cities, settling mainly in N've Tzedek. By the 1930s there were about 2,000 Meshed Jews in Jerusalem, accounting for almost one-half of all Iranian Jews in the city.

Communal Organizations. In 1900 the Persian Jews of Palestine formed their first communal organization, Ohave Zion, to serve the welfare needs of the community and to provide education for the children. Its representatives participated in the assembly of Palestinian Jews held in Zikhron Ya'akov in 1902. Agaian Ya'akov HaKohen and Mashiah ben Nisan Levi, both of Meshed, raised funds for a community synagogue and Talmud Tora. The synagogue was subsequently built in the Bukharan quarter of Jerusalem, where most of the Meshed Jews were settled.

Following the issuance of the Balfour Declaration, a General Committee of the Persian Jewish Community in Jerusalem was elected to represent the community, supervise its property and institutions, raise funds for social welfare, maintain a

Iraqi Jew in Israel. [Keren HaYesod]

cemetery, and, in general, improve the lot of its members. In 1919 an Association of Persian Youth was formed. It established a synagogue, sponsored courses in Jewish and general studies, and expanded social welfare activities among the new immigrants.

Iranian-Jewish Community in Israel. Between 1919 and May, 1948, a total of 3,632 Jews emigrated from Iran to Palestine. However, owing to natural increase, their number reached 7,275 by 1926 and 16,000 by 1935. Following the creation of the State of Israel, immigration increased considerably: between May, 1948, and 1952, a total of 25,972 Iranian Jews arrived. Between 1953 and 1960 about 14,000 came. According to the 1961 census of Israel, there were in the country 37,433 Jews who had been born in Iran and another 22,465 whose fathers had been born in Iran. Exact figures for subsequent immigration and natural increase are unknown, but the total number of Iranian Jews in Israel in 1966 may be estimated at 75,000. Many of them settled in Ma‘abarot (*see* MA‘ABARA) near Pardes Hanna, N'tanya, Tel Mond, and B'er Sheva‘ before moving to permanent dwellings, mainly in agricultural settlements.

The Iranian-Jewish community in Israel retained the Persian tongue as its colloquial, but it also produced Hebrew poets like N'horai Mizrahi, prose writers like Moshe ‘Oved and Avraham ‘Amitzur, scholars like ‘Ezra Zion Melamed, and many teachers and educators.

H. MIZRAHI

IRAQ, ZIONISM IN. Until the end of World War I Iraq formed part of the Ottoman Empire, and Zionist activity within it was therefore illegal. Although no Zionist groups could thus be organized in Iraq, interest in the Holy Land remained alive in its 2,500-year-old Jewish community, as manifested by a steady trickle of immigrants to Palestine even before the war.

In 1919 Aharon Sassoon of Baghdad initiated a Zionist society that gained legal recognition from the British Mandatory government of Iraq in 1921. Its official name was the Mesopotamian Zionist Committee; Sassoon served as president and Yoseph Eliyahu Gabbai as vice-president. The leaders of the committee carried on extensive Zionist propaganda work in Iraq, including Kurdistan, organized fund raising, and encouraged *‘Aliya (immigration) to Palestine. They established a youth club, the Society of the Youths of the Sons of Yehuda, and set up branches in Basra, Khaneqin, ‘Amara, and Erbil. The Iraqi Zionists sent a delegate to the 13th Zionist *Congress (Karlovy Vary, 1923). By 1925 the society had 1,000 members.

In 1923 a *Keren HaYesod (Palestine Foundation Fund) committee was organized in Baghdad. From 1920 to 1940 the Jews of Baghdad donated nearly £40,000 to the *Jewish National Fund, in addition to which Ezra Sasson Suheik gave £80,000 and Eliezer Kaddouri £10,000 for the establishment of a village, K'far Y'hezk'el, in the Jezreel Valley. In 1929, when Zionism was declared illegal in Iraq, the Ahi‘ever society was founded for the purpose of distributing *Hebrew books in the Jewish community. In 1929–30 a Maccabi sports organization functioned in Baghdad, and the Hebrew Youth Organization there published Hebrew pamphlets.

All this activity went on despite the most unfriendly attitude displayed by the Iraqi authorities. In 1924, after a visit to Baghdad, Judah L. *Magnes reported that the authorities objected to all Zionist activity. Nevertheless, contact with the *Yishuv was maintained and Palestinian Jewish teachers were engaged in the Baghdad Hebrew schools. Under the guidance of Sh'lihim (emissaries from the Yishuv; *see* SHALIAH), Jewish youth groups were organized, undertook Zionist educational work, prepared themselves for ‘Aliya, and organized *illegal immigration. All these activities were headed by young members of the community. Several hundred young Jews were thus enabled to leave Iraq and reach Palestine.

When Iraq obtained its independence (1932), the government embarked on a course of official suppression of Zionist activities. Study of the Hebrew language and Jewish history in schools was forbidden. The Palestinian Hebrew teachers were expelled; in several schools even the Bible had to be taught in Arabic. Schools of the Jewish community in Baghdad, as well as private Jewish schools, were closed down. Thus Zionism was forced to go underground.

In 1934, when the Iraqi government closed down the Baghdad office of the *Jewish Agency, the T'nu‘at HeHalutz HaBavlit, a Zionist youth organization, was founded. Among its aims was the organization of Jewish self-defense and illegal emigration from Iraq for the purpose of reaching Palestine. These activities took place clandestinely, led by youth Sh'lihim. Within a short time the movement had 16 chapters in Baghdad, Basra, ‘Amara, and other Iraqi cities, with some 2,000 members, aged 15 and over. It distributed two Hebrew and two Arabic mimeographed monthly bulletins among its members and founded and maintained a Zionist library.

In 1936, when the *Arab riots broke out in Palestine, the Iraqi government intensified its persecution of Zionism and

Zionists. Leaders of the Jewish community were arrested and tried, among them Aharon Sassoon, who, however, managed to leave Iraq and settled in Jerusalem.

Anti-Jewish and anti-Zionist propaganda was intensified after the outbreak of World War II, culminating in a pogrom (June 1–2, 1941) in which some 170 Jews were killed and about 800 injured in Baghdad. The pogrom, the first of its kind in Iraq, shocked Iraqi Jewry. Hundreds of Jews left for India. Others went to Palestine, but owing to the limited number of immigration certificates available to Iraqi Jewry only a few of the emigrants were able to enter the country legally, while several hundred succeeded in reaching it illegally.

Following this outbreak, various Jewish self-defense organizations were active in Baghdad for differing periods of time. In 1944 these were expanded into a united organization that had its branches in several sections of the city as well as in other towns of large Jewish concentration. The young members were trained in intensive courses. Another important activity was the *B'riha, the organization of escape, which helped some 10,000 Iraqi Jews to reach Palestine.

After the independence of Israel (1948), the Zionist movement in Iraq was, in addition to being illegal, subject to persecution. Many Jews were charged with Zionist activities, and in September, 1948, a prominent Jew, Shafiq 'Adas, was hanged.

Early in 1950 the government of Iraq allowed its Jewish residents to leave the country on condition that they relinquish their Iraqi citizenship and leave behind their property and possessions except for personal belongings and petty cash. The number of Jews who left Iraq in 1950 and 1951 exceeded 120,000, and during the years that followed a small trickle persisted (*see* OPERATION 'EZRA and NEHEMIA). Thus the bulk of the Iraqi-Jewish community settled in Israel. In 1968 about 2,500 Jews were left in Iraq, in a total population of a little over 7 million. Their position was precarious, as evidenced by the hanging of several Jews, accused of spying for Israel, early in 1969.

H. J. COHEN

IRAQI JEWS IN ISRAEL. Early in 1950 the Jewish community of Iraq readily accepted the offer of the Iraqi government to allow every Jew who wanted to leave the country to do so on condition that he renounce his citizenship and undertake never to return to Iraq. The wave of government-inspired persecution of Iraqi Jews undoubtedly contributed to their eagerness to leave the country, in which their ancestors had lived since the Babylonian Exile of 586 B.C.E.

Once begun, the airlift known as *Operation 'Ezra and Nehemia ran smoothly, and by May, 1951, more than 95 per cent of the Jews of Iraq had been brought to Israel. A few thousand went to Europe, the United States, or the Far East, but some of these, too, made their way to Israel in due time. It is estimated that in 1968 there were only 2,500 Jews remaining in Iraq.

In Israel, the more than 122,000 immigrants from Iraq encountered difficulties. They were faced by a new environment that differed greatly from their old life in Iraq. Problems caused by the new language, the differences in patterns of work and in housing, and the necessity of living in Ma'abarot (transit villages; *see* MA'ABARA) for some time made for trouble, friction, and bitterness. Precisely at that difficult period of transition, Iraqi-Jewish families had to see their boys and girls enter the Israeli Army. Townsmen who had lived mainly in Baghdad had to adjust themselves to village life. People accustomed to traditional

crafts had to be fitted into the regimented patterns of a modern industrial society. In several cases, families which had not engaged in agriculture for several centuries returned to the soil with surprisingly little effort. The few thousand Jewish villagers of northern Iraq (mainly *Kurdish Jews) became farmers in Israel with little difficulty.

The Jewish community of Iraq which came to Israel included more than 1,000 teachers, 100 physicians, and a sizable number of engineers, lawyers, journalists, and professional persons. In 1968, 18 years after Operation 'Ezra and Nehemia, one could find Iraqi Jews integrated into Israeli society everywhere, in banks, in commerce, in government posts, and in the *Histadrut (General Federation of Labor). Iraqi Jews occupied many positions in the Arab departments of Israeli government offices and also formed the bulk of the staff of the Arabic Section of the *Israel Broadcasting Service and of *al-Yom, the only Arabic-language daily in the country. Iraqi-Jewish students at the *Hebrew University of Jerusalem constituted the largest Oriental group in that institution. The Jewish community of Iraq was producing many chartered accountants and auditors every year. Iraqi Jews were also making headway both in banking and finance and in the development of the export trades.

One of the principal changes that took place within the

Iraqi immigrants arrive in Israel in 1951 as part of Operation 'Ezra and Nehemia. [Keren HaYesod]

A family of Iraqi Jews in Israel. [Zionist Archives]

community was in the position of women. Iraqi-Jewish women, whose life during the past centuries had followed the confining patterns of Muslim society, found emancipation in Israel. Jewish girls of Iraqi origin became equal partners with their brothers and parents in all walks of life. In the family itself, the old patriarchal rule weakened, and increasing numbers of young Iraqi Jews broke away from the traditional extended family and found their places independently in the economic and social life of the country.

I. BAR-MOSHE

IRELAND, ZIONISM IN. Jews have lived in Ireland since the Middle Ages. These were Jewish congregations in the country in the 17th and 18th centuries, but modern Jewish communal life had its origins in congregations founded during the 19th century. In 1970 there were about 3,700 Jews in the Republic of Ireland in a total population of nearly 3 million, almost all of whom lived in the capital, Dublin; the rest resided in Cork. Belfast, in Northern Ireland, had another 1,400 Jews.

The history of Zionism in Ireland began toward the end of the 19th century with the founding of a *Hoveve Zion group by immigrants from Russia; it met at the Camden Street Synagogue. Members of this group were the first supporters of the Dublin Commission of the *Jewish National Fund (JNF), which was founded in 1901 by Jacob Elliman, an immigrant from Lithuania, a stanch supporter of traditional Judaism and an ardent Zionist. The first chairman of the Dublin Commission, which became the focus of all Zionist work in Ireland, was Simon Cornick. After a few months he retired in favor of Elliman, who headed the commission for many years. In 1937 the commission was reorganized with Elliman as life president.

The oldest existing Zionist women's group in Ireland was the Dublin Daughters of Zion, founded in 1900 by Esther Barron. Its first chairman, Rose Leventhal, guided the group for 40 years. She was succeeded by Ethel (Mrs. W. A.) Freedman, who continued in office for 11 years, and by Annie (Mrs. P. H.) Glass, who held this position in 1966. Later, with the establishment of the Federation of Women Zionists of Great Britain and Ireland and of the *Women's International Zionist Organization (WIZO), the Daughters of Zion became affiliated with these organizations and throughout the years were active in welfare work as well as on behalf of WIZO projects in Israel. By 1966 there were six Zionist women's groups in Dublin, one in Cork, and three in Belfast. Their activities were coordinated

by a Regional Council of Women Zionists, with headquarters in Dublin.

In 1907 the Dublin branch of the *Order of Ancient Maccabeans, the Mount Carmel Beacon, was founded. In the 1920s the Dublin Jewish Debating Society was formed. It became affiliated with the Federation of Zionist Youth of Great Britain and Ireland. Later, it became the Tel Hai Beacon, a junior branch of the Order of Ancient Maccabeans.

The *Mizrahi Organization in Ireland was formed in the 1920s. Its first honorary president was Rabbi Isaac H. *Herzog, then Chief Rabbi of Ireland. Young Mizrahi, organized in 1927, was renamed *Tora va'Avoda in 1951. In 1945 *B'ne 'Akiva, the *Halutz (pioneer) Mizrahi youth group, was organized in Dublin, and a year later the Dublin Mizrahi Women's Organization was founded and led by Jennie Z. *Gilbert. Mizrahi and B'ne 'Akiva groups existed also in Belfast. All Mizrahi groups were organized within the framework of the Mizrahi–HaPo'el HaMizrahi Federation of Ireland. *HaBonim groups were formed in 1929.

In the 1930s, following a visit by Vladimir *Jabotinsky, a Zionist Revisionist branch was established. Prominently affiliated with the group, as well as with the world Revisionist movement (see REVISIONISTS), was Robert Briscoe, Irish leader and member of the Irish Parliament, who later became the first Jew to be lord mayor of Dublin.

In 1941 the Dublin Younger Commission of the JNF was organized. The Children's and *Youth 'Aliya Group was formed in 1946, and its Younger Committee in 1961. A Society of Friends of the *Hebrew University of Jerusalem was established in 1948. The Joint Palestine Appeal was launched in Ireland in 1951.

In 1951 a need was felt to coordinate the activities of all Zionist groups, and the autonomous Zionist Council of Ireland was represented independently at the Zionist *Congress. Liaison was maintained with the Zionist Federation of Great Britain and Ireland in London (see GREAT BRITAIN, ZIONISM IN). The Zionist Council maintained the Hebrew Speakers' Circle and a Hug 'Aliya (founded in 1963).

Considering their small numbers, the Jews of Ireland have an impressive record of Zionist activity. During the Israel *War of Independence, a number of Irish-Jewish youths served as volunteers in the *Israel Defense Forces. Many young Irish Jews, including professional persons and kibbutz members, have made Israel their permanent home.

J. Z. GILBERT

IRGUN IMAHOT 'OVDOT (Organization of Working Mothers). *See* MO'ETZET HAPO'ALOT.

IRGUN K'FARIM SHITUFIYIM (Organization of Communal Villages). *See* K'far Shitufi.

IRGUN TZ'VAI L'UMI (Etzel). Palestinian Jewish military organization (also called Hagana Bet) formed in 1931 and headed by Abraham Tehomi (Silber), a Revisionist whose underground alias was Gideon, as a nonparty group, organized on a purely military basis and trying to stress military training and discipline. In its early years civilian backing was provided by a broadly based board consisting of representatives of all non-Socialist parties in the *Yishuv: the General Zionists (see GENERAL ZIONISM), *Mizrahi, *Revisionists, and the *Jewish State party. The rank and file of the organization consisted overwhelmingly of members of *B'rit Trumpeldor (Betar) and young Revisionists, but the Revisionist movement had at that stage no decisive influence over the body.

On Dec. 5, 1936, an agreement was signed in Paris between Vladimir *Jabotinsky and Tehomi, under which Tehomi was appointed commander of Etzel by the president of the *New Zionist Organization, and was to lead it in the spirit of the the latter's instructions.

In 1937 Tehomi reached an agreement with *Hagana (the self-defense organization of the Yishuv) for the merger of the two defense bodies. This led to a split in Etzel (April, 1937); fewer than one-half of its 3,000 members followed Tehomi's lead, while the majority reasserted the independent existence of an Irgun Tz'vai L'umi.

Etzel asserted that only active retaliation would deter the Arabs. Its ideology, based on the teachings of Jabotinsky, was built on the principle that armed Jewish force was the prerequisite for the Jewish State and that every Jew had a natural right to enter Palestine. Irgun's first commander was Robert Bitker, who was succeeded by Moshe Rosenberg and then by David *Razi'el. Its symbol was a hand holding a rifle over the map of Palestine, including *Transjordan, with the motto "Rak Kakh" ("Only Thus"); its anthem was "Hayalim Almonim" ("Unknown Soldiers").

Prewar Years. The *Jewish Agency strongly denounced Irgun's "dissident activities," which the British administration countered by suppression and mass arrests. Sh'lomo *Ben Yosef, a member of Betar, was the first Jew to be hanged in Palestine (June 8, 1938), for an attack on an Arab bus.

Until May, 1939, Irgun's activities were limited to retaliation against Arab attacks. After the publication of the British *White Paper of 1939, the British Mandatory authorities became Irgun's main target. Another major field of activity was the organization of 'Aliya Bet (*illegal immigration) and helping "illegal" immigrants land safely. A most secret British intelligence report compiled by the Jerusalem Criminal Investigation Department on May 19, 1939, stated that the Revisionists (Irgun's parent body) were "at present organizing illegal immigration by far on the biggest scale."

World War II. With the outbreak of World War II, Irgun announced the cessation of anti-British action and offered its cooperation in the common struggle against Nazi Germany. Its commander in chief, David Razi'el, was killed in Iraq in May, 1941, while leading Irgun volunteers on a special mission for the British. Razi'el's successor was Ya'akov *Meridor, who in turn was replaced by M'nahem *Begin in December, 1943. From 1944 to 1948, the most critical period in Etzel's activities, it was commanded by Begin.

In January, 1944, Irgun declared that the truce was over and that a renewed state of war existed with the British, who had "taken into consideration neither our loyalty nor our sacrifices." Roused to anger by the horrifying news of the mass extermination of European Jewry and by the British refusal to give sanctuary in Palestine to escapees from Nazi terror, Irgun demanded the liberation of Palestine from foreign (i.e., British) occupation. Irgun's attacks were directed against government institutions (immigration, land registry, and income tax offices, police and radio stations, etc.). Intensified British repressive measures, which included the deportation to Eritrea in East Africa of 251 "terrorists or accomplices in terrorist activities," reached their peak after the assassination, in November, 1944, in Cairo of Lord *Moyne by members of *Lohame Herut

Israel (Lehi). In these efforts official Jewish bodies actively cooperated with the British.

Postwar Resistance Movement. Limited cooperation was established in the late fall of 1945 between Irgun, Lehi, and Hagana with the formation of the Hebrew Resistance movement. Each organization retained its separate identity and its own command, but no operations were to be undertaken without authorization or assignment by the High Command of the resistance movement. The first concerted action took place on the night of Oct. 31–Nov. 1, 1945, when railway lines and bridges were blown up in 153 places throughout Palestine.

Cooperation between the three resistance forces lasted, with occasional setbacks, until August, 1946. Relations became strained when, after the June 29, 1946, searches carried out by the British (the so-called Black Sabbath), the Jewish Agency leaders decide to postpone further action. Three weeks later, on July 22, Etzel blew up the British Army headquarters and the Secretariat of the Palestine government in the King David Hotel in Jerusalem. The British disregarded the warning given them half an hour in advance to evacuate the building; as a result, 91 persons were killed and 45 injured. Kol Yisrael, Hagana's radio station (see ISRAEL BROADCASTING SERVICE), denounced "the heavy toll of lives caused by the dissidents' operation." Irgun, while deploring the casualties, insisted that it had acted on instructions of the resistance command. A final break followed Hagana's acceptance of the Jewish Agency's cease-fire decision; Irgun continued widespread anti-British activities. The attacks grew in frequency and strength. The attackers penetrated even the heavily fortified security zones which the British had established in the principal cities for the protection of the administration and its personnel. On May 4, 1947, an Irgun commando force smashed its way

Irgun fighters transfer to the Israel Defense Forces after the Proclamation of the State of Israel in 1948. [Zionist Archives]

into the 'Akko fortress (*see* 'AKKO PRISON) in what the British press described as the "greatest jail break in history."

Late in 1946 the British sentenced two young Irgun soldiers to prison terms and floggings. After one of the boys had been flogged, Etzel retaliated by seizing some British officers and flogging them. On April 16 the British executed four members of Irgun in 'Akko Prison: Dov *Gruner, Mordecai Alkahi, Y'hiel Dresner, and Eliezer Kashani. About a week later, Meir Feinstein of the Irgun and Moshe Barzani of Lehi committed suicide in Jerusalem's Central Prison just before they were due to be executed. In July the Irgun took two British sergeants as hostages to prevent the execution of three of their members who had been sentenced to death. A year earlier the kidnapping of several British officers had brought about the commutation of two death sentences. This time, after searching in vain for the two sergeants, the British executed in 'Akko Avshalom Haviv, Ya'akov Weiss, and Meir Nakar. Subsequently the Irgun executed the two sergeants.

In 1946 Etzel numbered some 3,000 men, and in 1948 some 5,000, including all formations down to the youth guards. According to Irgun's commander, however, no more than 20 to 40 persons were on full-time service at any given time. The rest continued their ordinary day-to-day pursuits but were available whenever they were called upon. The actual struggle was conducted by the Assault Force, which used highly trained small units even for major actions and based the actions largely on the factor of surprise.

Actions of 1947–48. When, after the United Nations *partition decision of Nov. 29, 1947, organized Arab bands launched murderous anti-Jewish attacks, Irgun vigorously counterattacked at Haifa, Tiran, Yas'ur, Jerusalem, and Y'hudiya and later at Ramle. The capture, on Apr. 10, 1948, of the village of Deir Yassin by Irgun-Lehi forces, which resulted in 240 Arab civilian casualties, was utilized by the Arab leadership for atrocity propaganda and considerably intensified and panicked mass flight on the part of the Arab population. The Irgun-Lehi attack unit, consisting of 100 men, sustained 41 casualties, 4 of them fatal. *Background Notes on Current Themes,* published by the Information Division of Israel's Ministry of Foreign Affairs on Mar. 16, 1969, states unequivocally that the battle for Deir Yassin "was an integral inseparable episode in the battle for Jerusalem," and that prior to the attack "a warning was broadcast in Arabic to civilian, noncombatant inhabitants to withdraw from the danger zone as an attack was imminent." Some 200 villagers did come out, and were taken unharmed to safety by the Jews.

The March, 1948, session of the Zionist *Actions Committee had approved a temporary arrangement maintaining Irgun's separate existence but made its operational plans subject to prior approval by the Hagana command. On Apr. 25, 1948, Irgun forces, disregarding Hagana's objections, launched an offensive against Jaffa and took the Manshiye quarter. On April 28 Hagana joined Etzel, and on May 13 Jaffa surrendered.

When the State of Israel was proclaimed on May 14, Irgun announced that it would disband and transfer its men to the *Israel Defense Forces. For several weeks, however, until full integration into the army was completed, Irgun formations continued to function as separate units which were recognized as such in the operational orders of the army frontline and brigade commanders.

On June 20, 1948, a cargo ship, the "Altalena," purchased and equipped in Europe by Irgun and its sympathizers, and carrying 800 volunteers and large quantities of arms and ammunition, reached Israel's shores. Irgun demanded that 20 per cent of the arms be allocated to its still independent units in Jerusalem, but the Israeli government ordered the surrender of all arms and of the ship. When the order was not complied with, government troops opened fire on the ship, which consequently went up in flames off Tel Aviv.

In the Jerusalem area Irgun units stopped the Egyptian attack on Ramat Rahel. On July 16–17, they broke through the Old City wall but were ordered to withdraw by the Hagana command, since the Jerusalem truce started on the morning of the 17th. On Sept. 1, 1948, the remaining units disbanded and joined the Israel Defense Forces.

Recognition. With the passing of time, bitterness against the "dissident" underground organizations, the Irgun and Lehi, gradually disappeared and their service to the cause of Jewish statehood was fully recognized. Whereas only service with the Hagana counted in computing pension and severance payments to Israeli civil servants from 1948 to 1961, the *Knesset, in December, 1961, instructed the Civil Service Commission to consider service in Irgun and Lehi on the same basis as service in Hagana. In April, 1966, the honor guard at the kindling of the War of Liberation Memorial Torch in Jerusalem for the first time included veterans of the Irgun and Lehi alongside the Hagana veterans. In November, 1968, Pres. Zalman *Shazar presented the State Fighters Ribbon to representatives of all organizations and groups that had participated in the struggle for the Jewish State, including representatives of *Nili, the *Jewish Legion, Irgun, and Lehi. The award was also given to Prof. Eri Jabotinsky, son of Vladimir Jabotinsky, to Mrs. Abraham Stern, widow of the late Lehi leader, and to the father of Moshe Barzani, the Lehi fighter who had committed suicide along with Meir Feinstein of the Irgun.   J. SCHECHTMAN

IRRIGATION. *See* AGRICULTURE IN ISRAEL.

'ISAFIYA. Druze village in the Haifa region. Population (1968): 3,760.

ISH-KISHOR (SPINDELMAN), EPHRAIM. Zionist pioneer, Hebrew teacher, Yiddish writer, and newspaper editor (b. Suwałki District, Russian Poland, 1863; d. Jerusalem, 1945). Ish-Kishor spread the ideas of the *Hoveve Zion movement in England, where he edited (1891) *Die Yidishe Nazionalzeitung.* He fought *Territorialism, especially Baron Maurice de *Hirsch's efforts for Jewish settlements in South America. An early adherent of Herzl, he helped him found the first Zionist society in London, attended the 1st Zionist *Congress (1897), and was for years active in the leadership of British Zionism. Later, Ish-Kishor lived in the United States, where he continued his Zionist activities. In his old age, he took up permanent residence in Palestine.   J. LEFTWICH

ISH-SHALOM, MORD'KHAI. Deputy mayor of Jerusalem (b. Varniai, Lithuania, 1902). Ish-Shalom was active in the pioneering organization *HeHalutz in Lithuania. In 1923 he settled in Palestine, where he worked on road-building projects. He was elected on the *Mapai slate to the Jerusalem Municipal Council, serving from 1935 to 1950. In 1955 he became a deputy mayor and in 1959 mayor of the city, a position he held until 1965. As of 1969 he was again a deputy mayor of Jerusalem.

ISRAEL (Yisrael). Name used in such compound forms as Land of Israel (Heb., Eretz Yisrael), People of Israel (Heb., 'Am Yisrael), and State of Israel (Heb., M'dinat Yisrael), derived from the Biblical name Israel, given to Jacob after he had wrestled with the angel (Genesis 32:29). The designation Children of Israel (Heb., B'ne Yisrael) is a common Biblical name for the Hebrews who entered Egypt under Jacob, left it under Moses, conquered Canaan under Joshua, and lived in the Land of Israel under their judges and kings. After the death of King Solomon (ca. 930 B.C.E.), his realm split into two states, a northern one, called the kingdom of Israel, and a southern one, the kingdom of Judah.

The name Israel was adopted as the official designation of the Jewish State by the leaders of the *Yishuv (Jewish population of Palestine) shortly before the *Declaration of Independence (May 14, 1948), which specified that the Jewish State was to be called Israel.

ISRAEL, HISTORY OF. The history of the area that forms the territory of the modern State of Israel can be divided into five major periods: (1) prehistory; (2) the period from the settlement of the Israelite tribes to the end of the Second Commonwealth (13th cent. B.C.E.–C.E. 70); (3) Palestine under the Romans, Byzantines, Arabs, Crusaders, Mamelukes, and Turks (70–1882); (4) the period of the new Yishuv (1882–1948); and (5) the State of Israel (1948–   ).

PREHISTORY

Among the important sites attesting to the emergence of *Homo sapiens sapiens* (contemporary modern man) in the Middle Paleolithic period (Old Stone Age) are the Mount Carmel caves in which Dorothy Garrod and Theodore McCown discovered remains of the early and middle Mousterian cultures along with several dozen human skeletons, or rather parts of skeletons. These skeletal remains, whose age was established by carbon 14 as dating from 30,000 to 35,000 B.C.E., are remarkable in their variability. The human fossils, found in the lower levels of the Tab'un Cave, are of a type similar to the Swanscombe-Steinheim type of *Homo sapiens steinheimensis* (the ancestral stock from which, in all probability, Neanderthal man, or *Homo sapiens neanderthalensis*, evolved). In the upper levels of the cave were found remains of genuine *Homo sapiens sapiens* as well as of other types with mixed Neanderthal and modern traits.

One of two evolutionary processes or a combination of both can account for these finds: either the Mount Carmel population represented the hybridization of Neanderthals with a population of modern *Homo sapiens*, both having originated separately elsewhere; or a basic Neanderthal population was evolving in the area into modern man; or evolutionary divergence and hybridization were occurring simultaneously. In any case, following the period of Carmel man a *Homo sapiens sapiens* type became dominant in Palestine and elsewhere in Southwest Asia and, according to one theory, spread from there westward into Europe, carrying with him his paleolithic traditions.

Some 20,000 years later, upper paleolithic culture in Palestine developed into mesolithic (Middle Stone Age) culture, represented by the Natufian assemblage in the upper levels of the Mount Carmel caves and in rock shelters, dating from about 9000 B.C.E. The Natufians also lived in round stone-walled houses with plastered bell-shaped pits beneath the floors in which they stored the surplus from their intensive foraging—the earliest men known to do so. They buried their dead carefully,

believed in life after death and other religious tenets, and clearly represented a transitional stage from hunting and food gathering to the cultivation of cereals.

One of the places where Natufian culture evolved into neolithic (New Stone Age) culture was Jericho, where Kathleen Kenyon uncovered the clay-paved floors of Natufian huts whose burned posts have given a carbon 14 date of 7800 B.C.E. (± 21 years). The serrated sickle blades and other stone implements show that in the 8th and 7th millennia B.C.E. the inhabitants of the village practiced cereal culture, were skilled in ceramic sculpture, and had a developed religion.

In Palestine the transitional period from the Neolithic period to the Bronze Age is called the Chalcolithic period, whose outline, as well as that of the early, middle, and late Bronze periods, is given in the article ARCHEOLOGY IN ISRAEL. The middle Bronze is the period in which the history of Biblical Palestine begins.   R. PATAI

FROM THE SETTLEMENT OF THE ISRAELITE TRIBES TO THE END OF THE SECOND COMMONWEALTH: 13TH CENTURY B.C.E–C.E. 70

This long period may be divided into Biblical history and the centuries of the Second Commonwealth.

Biblical History. The Biblical history of Hebrew Palestine begins with the appearance of Abraham, who in obedience to God's command migrated from Mesopotamia to the Land of Canaan in the 17th century B.C.E. In the Book of Genesis the divine promise of the land to the seed of Abraham, Isaac, and Jacob is often repeated. Famine forced Jacob to go to Egypt, where his descendants, in spite of slavery and persecution, grew into a sizable nation. Following the Exodus, the miraculous passage through the Red Sea, the Revelation on Mount Sinai, and 40 years of wandering in the Sinai Peninsula under the leadership of Moses, his successor Joshua led the Hebrew tribes across the Jordan into Canaan. The tribes of Reuben and Gad and half of the tribe of Manasseh settled to the east of the Jordan.

The Israelites were not able to subjugate all the inhabitants of the country, and the era of the Judges, who ruled the Israelite tribes after the death of Joshua, was characterized by an almost constant struggle with the Canaanites and other peoples. In the 11th century B.C.E., after having been led for a generation by the prophet Samuel, the Israelites chose Saul as their first King. David, Saul's successor, defeated the coastal Philistines, who had been a constant menace. He also subdued the peoples of Edom, Ammon, and Moab in the east, as well as the Aramaeans in the north, and made them tributaries of his kingdom. After conquering Jerusalem, David transferred the Ark of the Covenant there and made the city the political and religious center of the Jewish people. David's son and successor Solomon built the Temple as well as other magnificent buildings in Jerusalem. Soon after the accession of Solomon's son Rehoboam, the 10 northern tribes, resenting the continued heavy taxation, seceded and established their own kingdom under Jeroboam of the tribe of Ephraim.

Thereafter two Hebrew states existed side by side: the kingdom of Judah in the south, with Jerusalem as its capital, ruled by the descendants of David; and the northern kingdom of Israel, ruled by a succession of dynasties. In the first decades of their separate existence the two sister states warred against each other. Later, conflicts alternated with periods of collaboration. To divert the people of the northern kingdom from making the pilgrimage to Jerusalem, where they might have been induced to transfer their loyalty to the house of David, Jeroboam established places of worship in Dan and Bethel.

The kingdom of Israel had no permanent capital until Omri built Shomron (Samaria) in the early 9th century B.C.E. The dynasty of Omri and its successor, the dynasty of Jehu (842–744 B.C.E.), were the most stable of the northern dynasties. Under the long reign of Jeroboam II (784–744 B.C.E.) the kingdom, which had been plagued by the invasions of the neighboring Aramaeans, attained its greatest power, extending in the east into Transjordan and in the north as far as Damascus and Hamath (Hama). Not long thereafter, however, the Assyrians extended their control over the kingdom. A bid for independence by King Hoshea ended in the liquidation of the kingdom by the Assyrians in 721 B.C.E. The Assyrians deported a large part of the population, replacing the exiles with settlers from other countries.

The kingdom of Judah survived the northern kingdom by more than 130 years. It reached the zenith of its power and prosperity under King Uzziah (784–743 B.C.E.). Eventually, however, Judah became a vassal state of powerful Assyria. After a short period of vassalage to Egypt it became subservient to Babylonia. A revolt by Judah ended in the occupation of Jerusalem and the deportation of King Jehoiachin and dignitaries from the city (597). Following another revolt, the Babylonians destroyed Jerusalem and the Temple and carried off King Zedekiah and the majority of his subjects as captives (586 B.C.E.). The Babylonians appointed as governor of Judah a nobleman, Gedaliah ben Ahikam, who attempted to reorganize life in the conquered country, but was soon assassinated, and the last semblance of Jewish autonomy came to an end.

The 8th to 6th centuries B.C.E. were the age of the great Hebrew prophets, whose teachings made the Hebrew religion a universal ethical monotheism and whose moral standards have remained the unattained ideals of a major part of mankind to this day. The prophets foretold the fall of the Hebrew monarchy, as a punishment for its evil ways, but also comforted the people with the promise that they would eventually return to their land. The hope of return inspired the exiles in faraway Babylonia and found its classic expression in Psalm 137, which contains the outcry "If I forget thee, O Jerusalem, let my right hand forget her cunning."

Second Commonwealth, 538 B.C.E.–C.E. 70. In 539 B.C.E. Cyrus, King of Persia, conquered Babylonia. Shortly thereafter he permitted the Jewish exiles to return and rebuild the Temple in Jerusalem. About 50,000 persons, led by Zerubbabel, a scion of the house of David, returned to the Homeland. They began to rebuild the Temple, but following complaints by the Samaritans, whose offer to participate in the rebuilding of the Sanctuary had been refused, the Persian authorities ordered the cessation of building activities. Shortly after the accession of Darius I to the Persian throne, the Jews, exhorted by the prophets Haggai and Zechariah, resumed the building of the Temple (520 B.C.E.). Darius subsequently confirmed the permission given the Jews by Cyrus to build the Temple, and the structure was completed and dedicated in 516 B.C.E.

The small Jewish community was greatly strengthened by the arrival, about the middle of the 5th century B.C.E., of Ezra the Scribe, accompanied by a large group of exiles. Ezra made it his task to raise the spiritual level of the Jewish community of Palestine and to strengthen religious observance. He instructed the people in the Tora and required all those who had married

heathen wives to dissolve their marriages. Some years later Nehemiah, who was in the service of the King of Persia, arrived in Jerusalem with a small group of exiles. The King subsequently appointed him Governor of Judah (Jewish Palestine). Nehemiah supported Ezra in his spiritual and religious activities, introduced social reforms, and organized the defense of the community against attack by its neighbors. He rebuilt the wall of Jerusalem and took steps to encourage migration to the city.

The conquest of the Persian Empire by Alexander the Great (333 B.C.E.) brought Palestine under Greek rule. After the death of Alexander (323 B.C.E.), the Ptolemies of Egypt and the Seleucids of Syria alternately ruled the country. In the 2d century B.C.E. the attempts of Antiochus Epiphanes to Hellenize the Jews by force and his conversion of the Temple of Jerusalem into a temple of Zeus spurred the Maccabean revolt (167 B.C.E.). Under the leadership of Judah the Maccabee, of the Hasmonean family, the Jews gained religious freedom. After Judah's death, his brothers continued the war against the Syrians. Simon was able to obtain political independence for the Jewish people. In a number of successful wars John Hyrcanus, a son of Simon, and Alexander Janneus, a son of Hyrcanus, enlarged the Jewish-ruled territory until it included all of Biblical Palestine.

Independence came to an end in 63 B.C.E., when the Romans, after conquering Syria, interfered in the affairs of the Jewish state, which was then in the throes of a civil war between Hyrcanus II and Aristobulus II, two brothers of the Hasmonean ruling family. Pompey occupied Jerusalem. From then on the Romans were the real masters of the country, appointing Jewish governors to rule in their name. They detached areas on the coast and in Transjordan (which had been conquered by the Hasmoneans) from the Jewish state, which now included only those parts of the country settled mainly by Jews. Hyrcanus II was made head of the vassal state, which the Romans called Judea. During the invasion of Syria by the Parthians in 40 B.C.E., Antigonus, a son of Aristobulus II, was able with their aid to wrest power from Hyrcanus and his Roman masters, but his reign was short-lived. Herod I the Great, a man of Edomite extraction who was married to the Hasmonean Mariamne, was proclaimed King of Judea by the Romans. With their aid he defeated Antigonus. Herod's long reign (37–4 B.C.E.) was characterized by extreme cruelty. He ruthlessly suppressed all his opponents and had rivals, including members of his family, put to death. To ingratiate himself with his Roman overlords, he embarked on a large-scale program of construction and development, building cities in honor of Rome, erecting pagan temples, introducing pagan games, and contributing funds for the construction of buildings and temples outside Palestine. He expanded the area devoted to agriculture and rebuilt the Temple of Jerusalem on a magnificent scale. The Romans enlarged his kingdom by giving him some of the areas on the coast and in Transjordan, which had been detached from the Jewish state.

After Herod's death the country was divided between his sons Archelaus, Philip, and Antipas. Archelaus ruled over Judea, Idumea, and Samaria with the title Ethnarch. Following complaints by the Jews against his cruel rule, he was exiled by the Romans (C.E. 6). Judea became part of the province of Syria and was ruled by a Roman procurator.

For a short time Judea enjoyed a measure of autonomy under Agrippa, a grandson of Herod. In C.E. 39 he had been installed as King of the areas in Transjordan which after Herod's death had been ruled by his son Philip. Later the Romans enlarged Agrippa's domain by adding to it all the other parts of Palestine. A benevolent ruler, Agrippa loved his people and honored the law. After his death in 44, the whole country became part of the province of Syria and was placed under the rule of Roman procurators, who were responsible to the Roman Prefect in Antioch.

The decades that followed saw the progressive deterioration of Roman-Jewish relations because of the ferocity, greed, and insolence of the Roman procurators and their subordinates. Pillage and excessive taxation, violation of Jewish rights, affronts to Jewish religious sensibilities, and armed attacks by Roman soldiers or by foreigners settled in Judea by Rome and secure under the protective shield of the Romans brought about the rise of revolutionary groups. The country seethed with unrest. Finally, in 66, the explosion occurred. The insurrection began in Jerusalem. The population drove Gessius Florus, the last and most rapacious of the Roman procurators, and his soldiers from the city. A Roman army, hastily dispatched from Syria to subdue Jerusalem, suffered a crushing defeat near Bet Horon. The country was now free from Roman rule, and the Jews prepared to meet the legions they knew would be sent from Rome.

In the spring of 67 a Roman army led by Vespasian and his son Titus set out to reconquer Judea. The same year the Romans conquered Galilee and northern Transjordan. After subjugating the rest of the country, Titus laid siege to Jerusalem in the spring of 70. For about five months the city, whose defense was led by Shimon Bar Giyora and the Zealot Yohanan of Giscala (Gush Halav), respective leaders of two rival rebel groups, withstood Roman onslaughts. In the end, however, Jerusalem fell. The city was razed, the Temple lay in ruins, and the survivors of the siege killed or taken prisoner.

After the fall of Jerusalem, several fortresses, including Massada (M'tzada), near the Dead Sea, still held out. Eventually, they too were taken, and Palestine became a Roman colony.

PALESTINE UNDER THE ROMANS, BYZANTINES, ARABS, CRUSADERS, MAMELUKES, AND TURKS: 70–1882

For centuries Palestine was ruled by a succession of conquerors.

Palestine under the Romans. Following the destruction of Jerusalem, Palestine became a Roman province administered by the commander of the local Roman troops. The war brought great social and demographic changes. Large parts of the country, especially in Judea, which was the center of the fighting, were laid waste. Hundreds of thousands had been killed and tens of thousands sold into slavery by the Romans.

The physical strength of the Jews was ostensibly broken. They bore without protest heavy taxation and provocations by Roman legionaries and expropriation and pillage by Roman settlers. The leadership of the people was in the hands of the Sanhedrin, which was tolerated but not officially recognized by the Romans. Without legal or military force at its command, the Sanhedrin derived its power solely from the moral and religious authority it possessed.

The calm was interrupted by an outbreak of clashes between Jews and Greeks in Alexandria, which was followed by fighting between Jews and their allies on one side, and Greeks and Romans on the other, in Egypt, Cyrenaica, Cyprus, and Mesopotamia and ended in the massacre of the people of many Jewish communities. Naturally these events had their effect on the Jewish community in Palestine. Two decades later, Palestine itself was the scene of a great rebellion.

Led by Simon Bar Kosiba (Bar Kokhba), the rebels defeated the Roman garrison of the country as well as a Roman army that had come to its aid from Syria (132). The Jews enjoyed independence again, but their freedom was short-lived. The Romans mustered large forces for a counterattack. Not daring to meet the Jews in open combat, they planned a gradual reconquest of the country. The revolt came to an end in 135 with the fall, after a long siege, of the fortress of Betar in Judea, where Bar Kokhba and his troops had made a last stand. In this last great rebellion almost 600,000 Jews were slain, large numbers were taken captive and sold as slaves, and Judea was almost completely destroyed.

After the Jewish revolt had been crushed, Emperor Hadrian, rebuilt Jerusalem as a heathen city, Aelia Capitolina, from which all Jews were barred. The Emperor also began to persecute the Jewish religion, and many Jews suffered martyrdom for their unflinching adherence to the precepts of Judaism. Jewish life became somewhat easier under Hadrian's successor, Antoninus Pius, during whose reign (138–61) the Jewish religious leaders of Palestine made strenuous efforts to consolidate Jewish life.

Notwithstanding the great losses the Jews had suffered in the rebellion against Rome and through the settlement of foreign colonists, they still constituted a substantial part of Palestine's population. They formed a majority in Galilee, which had become the hub of Jewish life in Palestine after the suppression of the Bar Kokhba revolt. On the other hand, they were a minority in Judea and in the heathen towns established on the Mediterranean coast.

Another change for the better occurred under the rule of the emperors of the Severus dynasty (193–235). The Jews of Palestine had supported Septimius Severus in his struggle with his rival Pescennius Niger. It may have been in recognition of these services that the Emperor initiated a new policy toward the Jews. The Severi recognized the Nasi (head) of the Sanhedrin as the official spokesman of the Jews, and thus the N'si'ut (patriarchate) and its institutions became the officially recognized autonomous bodies of Palestine Jewry. Judah HaNasi was then Patriarch, and his period was one of peace, economic prosperity, and intense intellectual activity. Judah was the editor of the Mishna, the principal code of Jewish law. His work was the culmination of a process of compiling and arranging the traditions of the Oral Law, which had been begun at a much earlier time, during the days of the Second Jewish Commonwealth.

The era of peace and tranquillity in Palestine came to an end after the death of Alexander Severus (235) owing to the general military anarchy in the Roman Empire and the fighting on its eastern borders. Conditions improved again with the accession of Diocletian in 284.

Following the adoption of Christianity in 312 by the emperor Constantine (306–37), the Christian rulers and Christian officials embarked on efforts to Christianize Palestine. Laws were enacted to limit the influence of Judaism there. Emperor Julian (361–63), who abandoned Christianity and strove to reestablish pagan worship, was very tolerant toward the Jews and even promised to rebuild the Temple in Jerusalem. His rule, however, was cut short by his death in battle against the Persians.

Byzantine Rule, 4th century–640. The successors of Julian were all Christians. The end of the 4th and the beginning of the 5th century witnessed the energetic Christianization of Palestine by the emperors and church leaders. The heathen population of the country adopted the Christian faith. Monasteries and churches sprang up in many localities. All Jews were subject to discriminatory legislation and suffered from the excesses of fanatical monks. In the first half of the 5th century the patriarchate was abolished. However, the Jews continued to regard the Sanhedrin as their sole internal authority.

A respite of several decades, due to schism and polemics within the church, was followed by new anti-Jewish oppression under Justinian (527–65), whose policy was aimed at converting the Jews. He promulgated a series of laws reducing the civic status of the Jews and limiting their religious freedom. During the decades of respite the Jews had begun once more to build synagogues (remnants of these, as at Bet Alfa, are still extant). Justinian prohibited the erection of Jewish houses of worship and converted existing synagogues into churches. He also put an end to the Jewish autonomy that had existed for centuries on the small island of Yotva (Tiran) in the Gulf of Elat ('Aqaba).

The Samaritans, too, were heavily oppressed. Their revolt against the Byzantines in 485 had been ruthlessly crushed. They revolted once more in 529 but again, after an initial success, were brutally suppressed.

Justinian's successors continued his policy of repressing the Jews and Judaism. The harassed Jews found strength and comfort in their religious heritage. During the reign of the early Christian emperors, several Aggadic Midrashim, containing the sermons of the Rabbis to the people, and the Jerusalem Talmud, which incorporated discussions that had taken place in the Palestinian academies, were compiled. The greater part of the Jerusalem Talmud was edited about the turn of the 4th century in Tiberias, which was the seat of Palestine's Jewish religious leadership for several centuries. Under the harsh rule of Justinian, Paytanim (liturgical poets) inspired the people with renewed hope. However, although persecution and repression did not succeed in breaking the Jews spiritually, they considerably weakened the political position of the Jews, who still formed a substantial proportion of the population and maintained compact settlements, especially in Galilee.

In 614 the Persians invaded Palestine. The invaders were aided by the Jews of Galilee, who had formed their own battalions. After conquering Jerusalem, the Persians exiled the Christian population of the city and the Jews were permitted to govern it for several years. Later, however, the Persians, breaking their alliance with the Jews, restored the control of the city to the Christians. In 627 the Persians, under an agreement with the Byzantine emperor Heraclius, withdrew from Palestine. Though he had promised the Jewish leaders security, Heraclius broke his word at the urging of the Christian clergy, persecuted the Jews, and forbade them to enter Jerusalem.

Arab Period, 640–1099. The newly established Byzantine rule did not last long. Palestine was invaded by the Arabs, and by 640 the entire country was under their occupation, Jerusalem having fallen after a prolonged siege about two years earlier. As part of the Arab empire, Palestine was ruled from 661 until 750 by the Umayyad caliphs. They were replaced by the Abbasids. In 969 the secessionist Fatimids of Egypt wrested control of Palestine from the Abbasids, and from then on the country was the scene of frequent encounters between Fatimid forces and their enemies and local Bedouins. In 1071 the Seljuk Turks invaded Palestine, captured Jerusalem, and marched south to Egypt. They were repulsed by the Fatimids, who succeeded in recapturing the Palestinian coast towns and eventually also Jerusalem (1096). On the eve of the Crusaders' arrival in Palestine, the country was divided between the Fatimids, who held the coastal area, and the Seljuks, who occupied the rest of the country to the east and west of the Jordan.

During the first decade of Arab rule in Palestine the country's Jewish population enjoyed prosperity and peace. Jews had aided the Arabs in the conquest of the country, and after its occupation many Jews who had fled Heraclius's persecutions returned, retaking possession of their estates. With the capture of Jerusalem, the Holy City was opened once more to Jewish settlers. However, when the Arabs, not content with political suzerainty, embarked on a policy of Arabization of the country in both the ethnic and the religious senses, the Jewish population was subjected to many pressures. Jewish landowners were displaced by Arab settlers. Jewish *holy places were taken over by the Arabs, who at first shared them with the Jews but then excluded the Jews entirely. Jews and other "nonbelievers" suffered from much discriminatory legislation. The situation improved under the rule of the Fatimids. Being Shi'ites, the Fatimids were not liked by the Sunnite Muslim population of the country. They employed Jews and Christians in their administration. However, the general state of insecurity in the country and a brief period of harsh persecution by the demented caliph al-Hakim caused a further depletion in the Jewish population.

Throughout the Arab period the Jews of Palestine enjoyed internal autonomy. Palestinian Jewry was headed by the Sanhedrin or the Palestinian Talmudical Academy. Originally located in Tiberias, the academy was eventually moved to Jerusalem and Ramle and, after the Seljuk invasion, to Tyre. Aharon Ben Meir, who headed it during the first half of the 10th century, attempted to restore to Palestine Jewry spiritual supremacy over the *Diaspora, especially over Babylonian Jewry, to which hegemony had passed. This attempt failed.

The literary products of Palestine Jewry during this period include Halakhic works; Aggadic Midrashim and liturgical poetry, both of which are permeated with Messianic yearnings; polemics with the *Karaites, many of whom had settled in Palestine; and works on the correct reading and spelling of the Bible text. The present system of *Hebrew vocalization was evolved in Palestine during the Arab period.

Crusaders' Period, 1099–1291. From 1099, when the first Crusaders reached Palestine, until 1291, when the Egyptian Mamelukes finally drove them from the country, Palestine was the scene of bloody fighting between the Christian warriors and the Muslim armies. In the first decades after their arrival the Crusaders succeeded in occupying almost all of the country, including large parts of the territory east of the Jordan River. They took Jerusalem in the first year (1099), after a siege of more than a month. The city was defended by the Muslim inhabitants, aided by the Jews, who defended their own quarters. After the fall of the city, the Crusaders massacred the population.

The power of the Crusaders began to ebb in the last quarter of the 12th century. Saladin, Sultan of Egypt and Syria, dealt them a crushing blow at Hittin, near Tiberias (1187). Later that year he entered Jerusalem. He accorded humane treatment to the Christians of the city, in sharp contrast to the conduct of the conquering Crusaders. Following reconquests by the Christians, a peace treaty negotiated by Saladin and Richard Coeur de Lion (1192) confined the rule of the Crusaders to the Mediterranean coast from Jaffa to Tyre. In subsequent decades the Crusaders were able to enlarge their territory and even retake Jerusalem, but the second half of the 13th century saw the complete elimination of their rule in the country by the Mamelukes.

Throughout the period of the Crusaders, the Jews aided the Muslims in the defense of the cities. They shared the fate of the vanquished Muslims, who were massacred by the conquerors. After hostilities had subsided, however, the Crusaders showed a more tolerant attitude toward the "nonbelievers," who constituted the majority of the population, and the surviving Jews began to rebuild their lives.

The largest Jewish communities at the time were in the coastal cities of Tyre, Acre ('Akko), and Ascalon (Ashk'lon). There was also a rural center of Jewish population in Galilee, but except for a few families who had special permission to live in Jerusalem, Jews were not allowed to settle in that city. The Jerusalem community was reestablished after the conquest of the city by Saladin, who is said to have issued a proclamation urging Jews to return there.

This period saw an influx of Jews from various countries. Many of the immigrants were inspired by a Messianic fervor that had been stirred by persecutions in Europe and by the encounters between Christians and Muslims. Early in the 13th century more than 300 rabbis from France and England came to Palestine. Groups of immigrants continued to come throughout the century, among them Rabbi Yehiel of Paris, who established a Yeshiva in 'Akko. During the short-lived Mongol invasion of Palestine (1260), Jerusalem was destroyed. When Nachmanides, the Spanish Bible commentator, came to Palestine in 1267, he found the city in ruins and only two Jews living there. He proceeded to establish a synagogue and laid the foundations for a new Jewish community in the city.

Mameluke Era, 1291–1516. After the Mamelukes had defeated and expelled the Crusaders, they ruled Palestine and Syria for more than two centuries. Unhampered by attacks from abroad, they reestablished security and order in the country, which for so long had been the scene of Christian-Muslim battles. To prevent new landings and invasion by the Crusaders, they destroyed almost all the harbors of the country. This step greatly damaged Palestine's trade with Europe. On the other hand, the Mamelukes built several Muslim religious institutions and emphasized the sacred character of the Muslim holy places.

In the last half century of Mameluke rule, insecurity and disorder returned to Palestine and Syria, in the wake of revolts prompted by the heavy taxes and tributes imposed by the Mamelukes and by their efforts to press the local Bedouins into armed service against the Ottoman Turks. During this period the country was also plagued by natural disasters and epidemics.

During Mameluke rule there were Jewish communities in Jerusalem, Lod, Ramle, Hebron, Gaza, Safed, and elsewhere, including Transjordan. The largest communities were those of Safed and Jerusalem, numbering 300 and 250 families respectively. Most of the Jews were peddlers or artisans.

Throughout the period, Jews continued to arrive in Palestine from various countries. Among them was Estori Farhi, who arrived early in the 14th century, settled in Bet Sh'an, and wrote the book *Kaftor VaFerah*, the first Hebrew treatise on Palestinography. Toward the end of the 15th century, Rabbi 'Ovadia

Bertinoro, the famous Mishna commentator, arrived in Jerusalem. He found the community, counting only 70 families, in a sad state materially as well as spiritually. Bertinoro became head of the community, founded a Yeshiva, and did much to improve the situation of his flock.

From the Turkish Conquest to the First 'Aliya, 1516–1882. In 1516 Palestine was occupied by the Turks, who were to hold the country with brief interruptions until it was conquered by the British in 1917–18. In the first half century of Turkish rule the country enjoyed stability, the population increased, and agriculture made progress. The Jewish population, too, increased greatly, mainly through the influx of exiles from Spain and Portugal, who had found refuge in communities throughout the Ottoman Empire and from there made their way to Palestine.

The largest Jewish community was in Safed, in which city and its neighboring villages the great majority of the Palestinian Jewish population was concentrated. Some of Jewry's foremost scholars, including Rabbi Jacob Berab, who wanted to reintroduce S'mikha (rabbinic ordination) to pave the way for the Messianic era, Joseph Karo, author of the Shulhan 'Arukh (the most authoritative code of Jewish law), and Isaac Luria, the famous Kabbalist, settled in the city. As a consequence, the spiritual influence of Safed was felt throughout world Jewry.

A sizable Jewish community existed also in Jerusalem. In 1561 Sultan Suleiman the Magnificent leased to Don Joseph Nasi the city of Tiberias, which was then in ruins, along with an adjacent area. Nasi endeavored to develop the city into an autonomous Jewish center. After an initial period of great activity, during which many Jews settled in Tiberias, the project collapsed. There were also Jewish communities in Sh'khem (Nablus), Hebron, and Gaza.

The late 16th and early 17th century saw the attempt of a Lebanese Druze leader, Fakhr ed-Din, to shake off Turkish rule. He was able to establish control over many areas and at one time ruled almost the entire country. Eventually, in 1634, he was defeated by the Turks. In subsequent years there were new but unsuccessful attempts by Druze leaders to gain control of Palestine. During the resulting warfare the Jewish communities of Galilee, especially those of Safed and Tiberias, were almost destroyed.

Jerusalem's Jews, with the other inhabitants of the city, suffered greatly from the despotism of the local ruler in the years 1625–27. Later, the community made a rapid recovery and afforded a haven for refugees from Galilee. The Jerusalem Jewish community was further enlarged by the arrival from Europe of refugees of the Chmielnicki pogroms in the Ukraine (1648–49).

In 1700 Juda HeHasid (Juda the Pious) arrived in Jerusalem with a sizable group of followers. Juda died soon after his arrival, and many of his followers, who were persecuted by the Jews of Jerusalem as suspected adherents of the false Messiah, Shabbetai Tz'vi, eventually returned to Europe.

The middle of the 18th century saw the rise to power of Dhaher el-'Amr. Originally a tax farmer for the greater part of Galilee, Dhaher gradually widened his domain, becoming for all practical purposes the ruler of northern Palestine. His independent activities presented a challenge to the Turks, who sent an army against him. With the aid of his allies, he resisted the Turks for several years and by 1771 controlled almost all of the country. He was killed in 1775.

In the early years of his regime, Dhaher el-'Amr rebuilt the

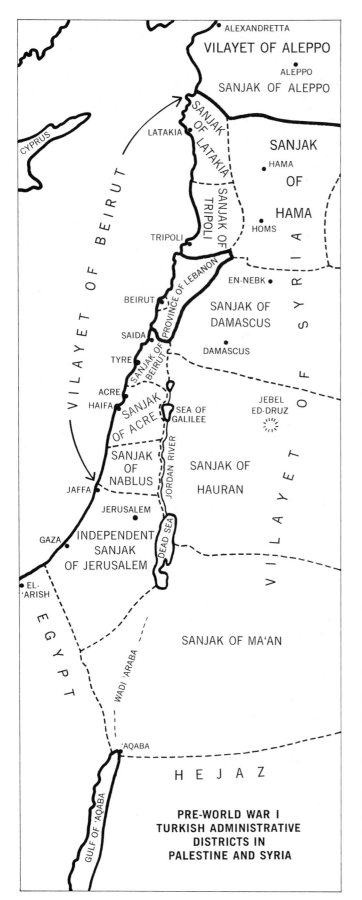

PRE-WORLD WAR I
TURKISH ADMINISTRATIVE
DISTRICTS IN
PALESTINE AND SYRIA

city of Tiberias, making it his first stronghold. At his invitation Rabbi Hayim Abulafia, scion of an old Tiberias Jewish family, came from Smyrna, bringing other Jews with him. Later the young community of Tiberias was augmented by part of the first large group of Hasidic immigrants, who arrived in the country in 1777 (see HASIDIC JEWS IN ISRAEL). Most of the Hasidim settled in Safed; later some of them moved to Tiberias.

In 1798 Napoleon conquered Egypt and soon afterward led an army into Palestine. After occupying El-'Arish, Ramle, Jaffa, and Haifa, he laid siege to 'Akko (March, 1799). The Turks, led by Ahmed el-Jazzar and aided by the British Navy, succeeded in repelling Napoleon's assault on the city, causing heavy losses to the French. Eventually, Napoleon lifted the siege and withdrew with his troops from Palestine.

Ahmed el-Jazzar, Palestine's chief governor from the death of Dhaher el-'Amr (1775) until his own death in 1804, recognized the suzerainty of the Turkish Sultan but was in fact independent. A cruel ruler who maintained his own army and navy, he imposed taxes and tariffs at will. Succeeding governors also displayed a great measure of independent authority.

From 1832 to 1840 Palestine and Syria were occupied by Mohammed 'Ali, the powerful Pasha of Egypt. Defeated by the Pasha's troops, Sultan Mahmud II was forced to reach an agreement with Mohammed 'Ali. The Pasha nominally recognized the Sultan but remained a quasi-independent ruler of an empire that stretched from the southern borders of Anatolia to Khartoum in the Sudan. In 1840–41 intervention by European powers on the side of the Sultan forced Mohammed 'Ali to withdraw from Syria and Palestine. Subsequently the Ottoman Empire strengthened its hold on Palestine by diminishing the power of local rulers and instituting centralized administration by Turkish officials.

During the semi-independent rule of the Turkish governors, the Jews, like the rest of Palestine's population, suffered greatly from internal wars and Bedouin attacks, which the governors were powerless to prevent, and from extortion and arbitrary imposition of taxes. Hayim Farhi, who served as adviser to Ahmed el-Jazzar and succeeding governors, used his influence to have anti-Jewish decrees revoked and to protect the Jews from extortion. Farhi was murdered by Governor 'Abdullah in 1820.

Jews from other countries continued to enter Palestine. Among the newcomers was a group of disciples of the Gaon of Vilna, who settled in Safed in 1808. Later some of them moved to Jerusalem.

Under the rule of Mohammed 'Ali, attempts were made to enforce order, and many tolls and taxes were imposed. Nevertheless, the Jews of Safed, Tiberias, and Hebron suffered greatly during revolts against the Egyptian administration. In 1837 an earthquake claimed hundreds of Jewish victims in Safed and Tiberias.

The great majority of the Jewish population lived on *Halukka, or charity sent from abroad, but a trend toward engaging in productive pursuits gradually emerged. In 1839 Sir Moses *Montefiore visited Palestine for the second time. Encouraged by the desire of the Jews to engage in agriculture, he contemplated renting land from Mohammed 'Ali and establishing agricultural settlements. He hoped that the establishment of such settlements would "induce the return of thousands of our brethren to the Land of Israel." On his way back to England, he was received in Egypt by Mohammed 'Ali, but his negotiations with the Pasha did not make the desired progress.

The intervention of the European powers (1840–41) forced Mohammed 'Ali to withdraw his troops from Palestine and Syria. In subsequent years the European powers sought to widen their influence in the region with a view to establishing themselves there in the event of the division of the Ottoman Empire. More and more foreign consulates came to be established in Palestine. The consuls enjoyed a degree of influence in the country and often would intervene with the Turkish administration on behalf of minorities. More missionary societies opened institutions, many of them financially backed by foreign governments, that perceived of their activities as advancing their particular political interests. The Eastern Question, as the problem of the future of the Turkish provinces in the Levant was called, was not only discussed in the political and diplomatic arenas but was also the subject of articles and tracts published in various European countries.

During this period a variety of schemes for the restoration of the Jews to Palestine was put forward. These were inspired by political, humanitarian, and missionary considerations. The same period saw also the appearance of the forerunners of the *Hoveve Zion movement, who propagated among the Jews the idea of the return to, and rebuilding of, Zion. Although these efforts yielded no immediate practical results and were confined to small circles, they prepared the ground for the actual movement which arose in the 1880s.

Moses Montefiore returned several times to Palestine and took an abiding interest in the welfare of the Jewish population of Palestine. He was instrumental in founding various institutions and housing projects, and helping individual Jews to engage in agriculture and crafts. In 1870 the *Alliance Israélite Universelle established an agricultural school in Mikve Yisrael, which was to play an important role in training Jewish farmers. In 1878 a group of Orthodox Jews from Jerusalem, imbued with the vision of rebuilding a Jewish agriculture in Palestine, established Petah Tikva, the first modern Jewish agricultural settlement in the country.

T. PRESCHEL

NEW YISHUV: 1882–1948

The term "*Yishuv" (more exactly, "new Yishuv," as distinct from the "old Yishuv" that developed in Palestine until 1882) refers to Jews who immigrated to Palestine after 1882 and who, with the aid of the *World Zionist Organization (WZO) and other institutions and of prominent Jews in the Diaspora, developed a network of agricultural and urban settlements, public institutions, and economic enterprises that finally led to the establishment of the State of Israel in May, 1948 (see IMMIGRATION TO PALESTINE AND ISRAEL). From its inception the new Yishuv was fully aware that its achievements would be important stages in the rehabilitation of Palestine, preparatory to making the country the Jewish Homeland.

The development of the Yishuv was influenced by two dominant factors: (1) the vision of the Return to Zion that accompanied the Jewish people through the long years of dispersion and attained practical significance with the liberation of many small nations in the 19th and 20th centuries; and (2) the increase in Europe of anti-Jewish feeling, which at the end of the 19th century assumed a new form—racial hatred, or *anti-Semitism—and expressed itself in an intense political campaign against the Jews, advocating restrictive measures against them, their expulsion from Europe, and in some cases their physical annihilation. Anti-Semitism, and particularly the pogroms of 1881 in Tsarist Russia, launched a mighty stream of migration, with millions of Jews moving from Eastern Europe to lands across the seas. The new Yishuv resulted from a combination of the vision of the Return to Zion with practical efforts to direct part of this migration to the historic National Homeland in order to give the Jewish people equal standing among the peoples of the earth.

The 66-year history of the new Yishuv, from 1882 until the establishment of the Jewish State, may be divided into two main periods, the periods of Ottoman rule (1882–1918) and that of British rule (1918–48). Each of these, in turn, can be subdivided.

First 'Aliya. In 1882 there were about 25,000 Jews in Palestine, almost all of them concentrated in the four holy cities of Jerusalem, Safed, Tiberias, and Hebron. The old Yishuv included *Sephardim and members of various Oriental communities, as well as members of the Ashkenazi (European) communities (see ASHKENAZIM). The Ashkenazim comprised Hasidim and their opponents, the so-called P'rushim. The old Yishuv consisted partly of small merchants and craftsmen but largely of individuals supported partially or entirely by contributions collected throughout the Diaspora. Here and there efforts had been made earlier in the 19th century to promote gainful employment, the establishment of new schools, and even of agricultural settlements (Petah Tikva, Motza, and others).

The first wave of immigration followed the pogroms in Russia and the increase of anti-Jewish persecution in Romania in 1882–83. It resulted in the establishment of the first villages in Judea (Rishon L'Tziyon, 'Ekron, G'dera), Samaria (Zikhron Ya'akov), and Galilee (Rosh Pina, Y'sud HaMa'ala) by organized groups of immigrants who wanted to become farmers. Prominent among these pioneers was the *Bilu group, which considered itself the forerunner of a large pioneering immigration from Russia. This wave of immigration immediately ran into the strong opposition of the Ottoman government, whose political suspicions had been aroused. Because these settlers had no previous experience in agricultural work, particularly under Palestinian conditions, they rapidly exhausted their meager resources and found themselves in difficulties. They were rescued by Baron Edmond de *Rothschild of Paris, who took most of these settlements under his supervision, devoting large sums to their consolidation and expansion and to the purchase of additional tracts of land. To supervise the work of the settlements the baron set up an administration that included experts in various branches of agriculture. The Rothschild-supported settlements were run along paternalistic lines, a practice that at times was resented by the settlers. Despite these shortcomings the Rothschild organization helped protect the settlements from oppressive measures by the Turkish authorities and also developed new branches of agriculture, especially viticulture (see WINE INDUSTRY IN ISRAEL).

In 1890–91 a second wave of immigration arrived from Russia; some of these pioneers set up the villages of Rehovot and Hadera, whose economy depended solely on the private initiative and means of the settlers. In 1896 the villages of B'er Tovya in the south and M'tula in the north were established. These villages were settled by farmhands who had previously worked and acquired agricultural skills in the older settlements. In 1900 Baron de Rothschild transferred the management of his villages to the *Jewish Colonization Association (ICA), which developed new settlements in Lower Galilee (among them Sejera, Mes'ha, Yavn'el, Bet Gan, M'nahemiya, and Mitzpe), based mainly on cereal cultivation.

By the beginning of the 20th century there were in Palestine 20 Jewish villages with a total population of 6,000. The area purchased by Jews (mostly by Baron de Rothschild and the ICA) totaled 400,000 dunams (see DUNAM), including more than 90,000 dunams in Transjordan, which for political reasons were not settled.

This period also saw substantial urban development. An important Jewish community, most of whose inhabitants were closely identified with the way of life evolved in the new villages, arose in Jaffa. By 1904 the number of Jews in Palestine had risen to 50,000 (about one-fifth of these can be considered part of the new Yishuv). The Jewish villages were administered by local committees handling problems arising from relations with government authorities, payment of taxes, defense, and education and even maintaining their own tribunals to adjudicate disputes. In 1903, on the initiative of M'nahem M. *Ussishkin, a meeting of representatives of Jewish communities and villages was held in Zikhron Ya'akov, and an abortive attempt was made to establish a central authority to conduct the affairs of the new Yishuv (see YISHUV, SELF-GOVERNMENT IN THE).

In the 1890s a conflict broke out between Orthodox circles (led by Yehiel Mikhel *Pines and Z'ev *Jawitz) and secular groups (Eliezer *Ben Yehuda and the *B'ne Moshe circle). Resisting pressures from the old Yishuv, the secular-nationalist groups insisted on their right to live in accordance with their own outlook and to educate their children in that spirit. Their influence in the Yishuv grew. Modern Hebrew schools were developed in Jaffa and the villages. In 1903 the Hebrew Teachers Association was founded. It played a major role in developing this type of school and in making the Hebrew language the language of instruction in its schools. See EDUCATION IN ISRAEL.

*Second 'Aliya, 1904–13. The wave of immigration that arrived in Palestine during the decade preceding World War I was known as the Second 'Aliya. It received its impetus from the pogroms that erupted in Russia between 1903 and 1906 and from the ensuing restrictions and persecutions.

The Young Turk Revolution of 1908 did not justify the hope of the Yishuv for relief from Turkish oppression. On the contrary, the revolution was followed by an anti-Zionist press campaign in Turkey and by the beginnings of the Arab nationalist movement (see ARABS AND ZIONISM). In the Turkish Parliament representatives from Palestine and other parts of the

Immigrants brought by 'Aliya Bet arrive in Palestine in defiance of the British White Paper of 1939. [Zionist Archives]

Ottoman Empire warned against the immigration of Jews into the country.

Nevertheless, the Yishuv continued to grow. By the outbreak of World War I the Jewish population in the settlements had doubled, and citrus and almond groves had been developed in addition to vineyards (see CITRUS INDUSTRY IN ISRAEL). Organizations such as Ahuzot (see AHUZA SOCIETIES) and Agudat N'ta'im were founded in Palestine and Diaspora countries to build new Jewish agricultural settlements. In 1908 the WZO began systematic settlement operations in Palestine by opening the first Palestine Office in Jaffa (see PALESTINE OFFICES) under the direction of Arthur *Ruppin.

Important developments took place in the cities of Palestine. In Jerusalem, which maintained its identity as the stronghold of the old Yishuv, the Jerusalem Teachers Seminary (1904) and the *Bezalel School of arts and crafts (1906) were established. In 1909 Tel Aviv, an all-Jewish suburb of Jaffa, was founded. Tel Aviv was the site of the *Herzliya High School, the first Hebrew secondary school in modern Palestine. Prior to World War I, 2,000 of Jaffa's Jews lived in Tel Aviv. In Haifa, where the Jewish population had reached 3,000, construction of the *Technion began. Here and there the beginnings of modern industry appeared (see INDUSTRY IN ISRAEL). By the summer of 1914 the Yishuv numbered 85,000 (about 12 per cent of the population of Palestine).

One of the major problems facing the Yishuv in those days was that of Jewish labor, particularly in the villages. The Jewish settlers employed Arab farmhands from nearby villages and Bedouin camps, with the result that the Jewish farmers became in many instances managers and overseers and one of the basic ideas of the Zionist movement, that of *self-labor, was likely to be undermined. The Zionist leaders in the Diaspora saw the moral, social, and political dangers involved in this development and warned against them. In 1904 there began an *'Aliya of young people from Eastern Europe who considered it their first task to champion and practice self-labor and to form a class of Jewish agricultural workers in the villages (Kibbush 'Avoda; literally, *"Conquest of Labor"). These young people, many of whom had been influenced by the ideas of the Russian revolutionary parties, organized themselves into two parties, *Po'ale Zion and *HaPo'el HaTza'ir, and later formed the agricultural workers' organizations in Judea and Galilee. They began a campaign for the right to be hired as workers in the Jewish settlements.

Soon the problem of Jewish labor became the central issue in the Yishuv. On one side were the Jewish workers, who insisted on a policy of hiring Jews to the exclusion of all others to preserve the national character of the Jewish settlements. On the other side were the Jewish farmers, who argued that Jewish labor was too expensive and not productive enough. Many experiments such as the founding of *auxiliary farms near the larger villages (e.g., 'En Ganim, Nahlat Y'huda) were tried to solve the problem. These efforts increased the immigration of *Yemenite Jews, and their settlement in villages laid the basis of a Jewish agricultural labor force. A more radical solution came with the first experiments conducted by the Palestine Office in cooperation with the workers, in which workers' villages based on self-labor by the individual settlers were set up. In this manner the first villages of the Hityashvut Ha'Ovedet (working settlement), the K'vutzot D'ganya and Kinneret and the cooperative Merhavya, were founded.

Culturally, the Second 'Aliya saw the growth of Hebrew

language and literature (*see* LITERATURE, MODERN HEBREW AND ISRAELI) and Hebrew education. These changes were expressed in the dispute over the language of instruction to be used in the schools, with the Zionist elements pressing for the use of Hebrew. Following the *Language War, a network of Hebrew schools was organized under the direction of the Zionist *Executive and soon accommodated most of the children of the new Yishuv.

Another important problem was the protection of the villages from attack by Arabs and Bedouins. Previously entrusted to local Arab guards, this task was turned over in 1909 to *HaShomer. This group, founded by new immigrants, took over the defense of villages in Galilee and Judea.

World War I, 1914–18. World War I brought hard times to the Yishuv. Hunger and disease struck, the old Yishuv being the hardest hit, for unlike the new Yishuv it had no organized public system of material aid. In the new Yishuv the Va'ad Tziburi (Public Committee), composed of representatives of all groups and settlements, engaged in diligent relief work. Much-needed support, in the form of funds and food, came from the Diaspora, particularly the United States (*see* AMERICAN JEWISH JOINT DISTRIBUTION COMMITTEE).

Complicating the situation and endangering the Yishuv was the attitude of the Turkish Army in Palestine, which viewed the Jews and particularly the Zionists as a foreign and dangerous element. Community leaders and active Zionists were imprisoned or expelled. During the first winter of the war 11,000 Palestinian Jews who were nationals of Russia were exiled to Egypt. The leaders of the Yishuv tried to soften the hard attitude of the Turkish government by demonstrating loyalty to Turkey with such measures as having graduates of the Herzliya High School and the Jerusalem Teachers Seminary volunteer for service in the officers' corps of the Turkish Army. In the spring of 1917, as the battlefront drew nearer southern Palestine, the Jewish residents of Tel Aviv–Jaffa were expelled to northern Palestine. The position of the Yishuv deteriorated after the discovery in October, 1917, of *Nili, a group of youths organized by Aaron *Aaronsohn in order to provide the advancing British with military intelligence. The ensuing wave of persecution and arrests was halted only with the conquest of southern Palestine by the British (November–December, 1917).

Establishment of British Rule, 1918–20. The British conquest of Palestine raised high hopes in the Yishuv, for in the *Balfour Declaration the British government had supported "the establishment in Palestine of a national home for the Jewish people." Operating within the framework of the British Army by that time was the *Jewish Legion, which included battalions recruited from Britain and the United States and, later, also Palestinian Jews. A committee of representatives of the Zionist movement and of different Jewish communities in the Diaspora was formed with the approval of the British government (*see* ZIONIST COMMISSION) and arrived in Palestine to lay the foundations for the large-scale establishment of settlements. Its first task was to rebuild the Yishuv, which had suffered heavily during the war, its numbers having decreased to about 56,000.

Concomitantly with Zionist political achievements there developed an Arab nationalist movement that was linked to similar movements in Syria and other Arab countries. The riots of Syrian Arabs in 1920 endangered the Jewish settlements of eastern Galilee, which organized to defend themselves with the help of HaShomer and Jewish Legion veterans (*see* ARAB RIOTS IN PALESTINE). In one of the clashes with the Arabs in March,

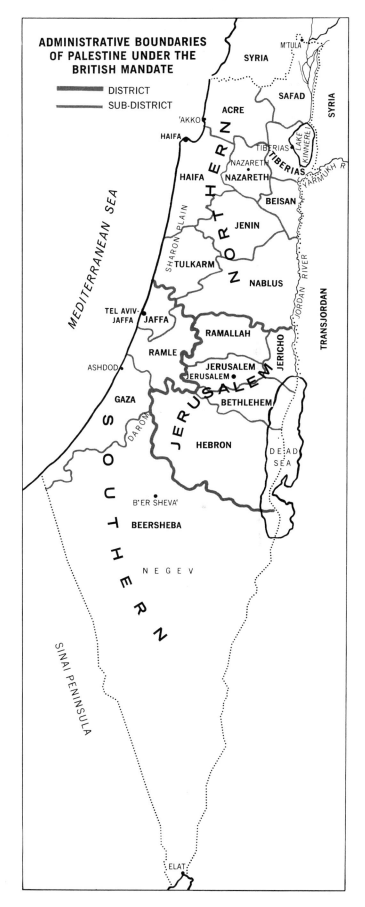

ADMINISTRATIVE BOUNDARIES
OF PALESTINE UNDER THE
BRITISH MANDATE
▬▬▬ DISTRICT
▬▬▬ SUB-DISTRICT

1920, Joseph *Trumpeldor and five of his comrades fell in the defense of Tel Hai, which came to symbolize the heroism of the defenders of the Yishuv. Viewing the promises given the Jews by the British government as an impediment to their Middle Eastern policy, the British military authorities strove to nullify them. The Jewish Legion was disbanded, and restrictions were placed on Jewish immigration and land purchases, while Arab nationalist movements received open support. Anti-Jewish incitement in the press and demonstrations were left unsuppressed; they turned into bloody attacks by Arabs on Jews in Jerusalem at Passover, 1920. Following these riots, 20 of the Jewish defenders of Jerusalem and their leader, Vladimir *Jabotinsky, were arrested and sentenced to long prison terms. As a result, the *Hagana was formed in June, 1920, to undertake the defense of the Yishuv. In the meantime, at the *San Remo Conference of the principal Allied Powers, the *Mandate for Palestine was awarded to Great Britain. The mandate included a commitment by Britain to aid Jewish immigration and settlement. Military rule was replaced by a civil administration, and Sir Herbert *Samuel, a leading Anglo-Jewish statesman and Zionist sympathizer, was sent to Palestine as the first British *High Commissioner.

Third 'Aliya. The immigration wave that followed the war (1919–23) is known as the Third 'Aliya. Among the newcomers were many young pioneers from Russia (*HeHalutz) and Galicia (*HaShomer HaTza'ir), who were fired with revolutionary zeal. The "veteran" workers of the Second 'Aliya welcomed the newcomers and with them founded the *Histadrut (General Federation of Labor), which became one of the most important factors in the development of the Yishuv. However, Palestine was not ready to absorb immigrants without means. For the first year or two, most of the workers eked out a living in government highway construction work in the Jezreel Valley and Lower Galilee. The road gangs gave rise to groups for settlement, the most important being the *G'dud Ha'Avoda V'haHagana 'Al Shem Yosef Trumpeldor, named in memory of Trumpeldor. Large tracts of land were purchased in the Jezreel Valley. There numerous kibbutzim and moshavim (*see* KIBBUTZ; MOSHAV) were established, including Nahalal, 'En Harod, Tel Yosef, K'far Y'hezk'el, Geva', Heftzi-Bah, Bet Alfa, Ginnegar, Mizra', and Balfouriya. However, large-scale plans for new settlements foundered because the Zionist institutions (the *Jewish National Fund and the *Keren HaYesod) were unable to raise the necessary funds for the purchase of additional needed land. A considerable number of workers found employment in Tel Aviv and Haifa in the building trades, which were carried on by private initiative, or as farmhands in the old settlements.

In 1923 the Third 'Aliya ended in the midst of an economic crisis, but the 34,000 persons who had arrived in Palestine in this immigration wave had changed the character of the Yishuv. By then the new Yishuv constituted the majority of the Jewish population of Palestine. The First *Asefat HaNivharim (Elected Assembly; 1920–25) set the new mood when, despite the strong opposition of certain Orthodox circles, it gave women the right to vote and to be elected to any office in the institutions of the Yishuv.

During the early phase of Samuel's administration political tension continued. In May, 1921, Arab rioters attacked Jews in Tel Aviv and Jaffa and in several villages of Judea and Samaria. Jewish self-defense and British intervention put an end to the attacks, but the political results were serious. Plans for the continuation of the Jewish Legion in Palestine were

canceled, and all Jewish immigration was halted temporarily. The *White Paper of June, 1922, gave a limited interpretation to the Balfour Declaration by excluding from the terms of the mandate any relation or reference to all of Transjordan. Nevertheless, the British Mandate for Palestine was approved by the Assembly of the League of Nations on July 22, 1922.

Fourth 'Aliya. The last years of Sir Herbert's administration were a period of quiet and slow development. In 1924 immigration was resumed. Most of the new immigrants were middle-class settlers who brought with them considerable sums of money. They were concentrated especially in the cities, particularly Tel Aviv, and in the citrus-growing villages. In the cities they developed small industries. This 'Aliya gave an impetus to the building trades as well as to the planting of citrus groves. By the end of Samuel's term (1925) there were 108,000 Jews in Palestine. In 1921 Pinhas *Rutenberg had received a franchise to establish the Palestine Electric Corporation (*see* ISRAEL ELECTRIC CORPORATION, LTD.). The Hebrew language was introduced as one of the three official languages of Palestine (the others were English and Arabic). On Apr. 1, 1925, the *Hebrew University of Jerusalem was officially opened in a ceremony attended by Lord Balfour (Arthur James *Balfour).

During the administration of Lord Plumer (Herbert Charles Onslow *Plumer) as High Commissioner (1925–28) peaceful conditions prevailed and the British reduced their security forces. On the other hand, the Fourth 'Aliya entered a period of economic crisis. Many businesses went bankrupt, thousands were unemployed and on relief, and there was a sharp rise in emigration. In 1928 the economy began to show signs of recovery, but for the next three years progress was slow.

This period saw three important developments in Palestine's industries. The Palestine Electric Corporation completed its power plant on the Jordan at Naharayim, construction was begun on a large modern port at Haifa, and a franchise was granted Palestine Potash, Ltd., an enterprise founded by Jewish and British investors to exploit the mineral resources of the Dead Sea (*see* DEAD SEA WORKS COMPANY, LTD.).

During the first 10 years of the British Mandate the Jews had a great opportunity to further the realization of their political objectives through immigration and settlement in Palestine. However, the WZO could not take full advantage of the opportunity because it lacked the necessary organizational and financial resources. Because of the prevailing worldwide economic depression, the efforts of Zionists and non-Zionists in the expanded *Jewish Agency (founded in 1929) failed to secure all the required capital.

During the late 1920s the Arab nationalist movement was revived in Palestine, in large measure owing to the efforts of Hajj Amin *al-Husayni, the mufti of Jerusalem. In 1929, against a background of disputes over Jewish rights at the *Western Wall, a nationwide attack was launched by the Arabs. It began in Jerusalem, from where it quickly spread to all parts of the country. The Jewish communities of Hebron and Safed were destroyed, and dozens of Jews, including women, children, and old persons, were massacred. Several small Jewish villages were abandoned after battles with Arab mobs (Hulda, B'er Tovya). In Jerusalem, Tel Aviv, and Haifa the Hagana with its meager resources repelled the attacks of the Arab mobs and managed to hold its ground until the arrival of British reinforcements. The British officials in Palestine proved unable to cope with the situation, and it took the help of British troops brought from Egypt and Malta to restore order.

The *Shaw Commission, which was sent by the British Colonial Office to investigate the cause of the riots, blamed the outbreaks mainly on the Arabs' fears of loss of their political rights and their economic status as a result of Jewish immigration and settlement. The British government conducted several other investigations, the most important being that undertaken in 1930 by Sir John Hope-Simpson, which in its report stated that Palestine was incapable of absorbing further Jewish immigration until there was further development (see HOPE-SIMPSON REPORT). As a result of these investigations, the British government issued a White Paper in October, 1930 (see PASS-FIELD WHITE PAPER), that sought to restrict further Jewish immigration and land purchases in Palestine. The issuance of this document evoked sharp criticism from leading statesmen and the press, and following negotiations between representatives of the British government and the Jewish Agency, the British Prime Minister, (James) Ramsay *MacDonald, sent a letter to Chaim *Weizmann that in effect canceled the main anti-Zionist recommendations of the White Paper (see ANTI-ZIONISM; MACDONALD LETTER).

The security and political crises of the years 1929–31 accentuated differences within the Zionist movement and the Yishuv. Vladimir Jabotinsky, who since 1922 had led a political struggle against the moderate policy of Chaim Weizmann, demanding that the British be forced to rescind the separation of Transjordan from Palestine, that the Jewish Legion be revived, and that the development of Jewish industry and immigration be pursued more vigorously, intensified his activities. Jabotinsky and his adherents, the Zionists-*Revisionists, directed their main efforts against the Histadrut, which was one of the important public bodies in Palestine supporting Weizmann's policies. Clashes between the two factions reached a peak with the mysterious murder, on June 16, 1933, of Hayim *Arlosoroff, one of the representatives of the labor movement on the Zionist Executive. Even the acquittal (due to lack of evidence) of the two members of the Revisionist movement accused of the murder failed to clear the atmosphere. Attempts by Jabotinsky and David *Ben-Gurion to reach a compromise failed after a referendum of members of the Histadrut (summer, 1935) rejected the proposal of the two leaders for an agreement between the Histadrut and the *Histadrut Ha'Ovdim HaL'umit, the labor organization of the Revisionist movement.

Despite these differences the early 1930s saw progress in the internal organization of the Yishuv. As early as 1927 the British government had recognized the right of the Yishuv to organize as the *K'nesset Yisrael, with explicit permission to certain ultra-Orthodox groups to remain outside this official "community," which represented more than 95 per cent of the Yishuv. The K'nesset Yisrael elected representatives to the Asefat HaNivharim, which in turn elected from among its members the *Va'ad L'umi (National Council). In the early 1930s the Jewish Agency transferred the administration of education and health to these institutions, while reserving the right to make all political and security policy decisions for the Yishuv. Localities in which the population was largely Jewish formed municipalities (e.g., the city of Tel Aviv and local councils in the larger villages) that received the right to operate local services and to tax their residents to support these services.

After the Arab riots of 1929 the Hagana began to play a major role in the life of the Yishuv. It became a national underground organization with thousands of members and a national leadership composed of representatives of the Histadrut and civic groups (e.g., the municipality of Tel Aviv and the *Hitahdut HaIkkarim). It established officers' training courses, storehouses for armaments, and workshops where light arms were manufactured. In the spring of 1931 a group of officers seceded from Hagana to set up a separate organization, the *Irgun Tz'vai L'umi (Etzel), which was supported by various rightist groups, particularly the Revisionist party.

*Fifth 'Aliya. The most important development that took place in this period in the history of the Yishuv was the large immigration wave of 1933–36 (Fifth 'Aliya) and the resulting upsurge in Palestine's economy. During these four years 166,000 newcomers arrived in Palestine as legal immigrants, and thousands more arrived illegally (see ILLEGAL IMMIGRATION). These immigrants, more than 20 per cent of whom came from Nazi Germany, brought large amounts of private capital (about 32,000,000 Palestinian pounds), which were invested in various branches of the economy, particularly construction, industrial enterprises, and citriculture. This mass importation of capital and skill laid the foundation for a stable economic structure.

Beginning in 1934, *Youth 'Aliya brought young people from Germany and settled them in agricultural villages and educational institutions in Palestine. By the end of 1936 Tel Aviv had tripled its population, to 150,000. In Jerusalem, where a water supply system drawing on the sources of the Yarkon River was completed in 1935, population growth was slower. In 1936 the city had 76,000 Jews (60 per cent of the total population). Haifa, whose new port was opened in 1933, had 50,000 Jews (half of the total population). The Palestine Electric Corporation and Palestine Potash, Ltd., expanded their operations and employed thousands of workers. The economic development of the Yishuv was shown by the Levant Fairs, which were held in 1934, 1935, and 1936. At the same time, the pace of agricultural settlement slowed. Among the settlements established during this period, mention should be made particularly of those destroyed in the riots of 1929 which were now rebuilt with funds raised by Jews' throughout the world (e.g., B'er Tovya, Hulda, and Ramat Rahel); the settlements in the Hefer Valley (K'far Witkin, K'far HaHoresh, K'far Hayim, Ma'barot, etc.), which completed the chain of Jewish settlements in the coastal plain; and the settlements of Hityashvut HaElef (Thousand Families Settlement Plan), built by the workers in the larger villages near those villages (K'far Bilu and Gan Sh'lomo near Rehovot, N'ta'im and Bet 'Oved near Nes Tziyona, and Rishpon, K'far Hess, and Ramat HaKovesh in the southern Sharon). There was considerable expansion of middle-class agricultural settlements, many of them initiated by recent arrivals from Germany, who established numerous villages, among them K'far Sh'maryahu, Nahariya, Ramatayim, and Shave Tziyon. As a result of the Fifth 'Aliya, the Yishuv, which by late 1936 numbered 400,000, or about 30 per cent of Palestine's total population, became a key factor in the country, not only because of its economic potential but in sheer numbers.

This development, of course, aroused Arab fears. The Arab nationalist movement, which had received added impetus from the 1929 riots, grew and found increased mass support, particularly among young people. Nationalist parties and youth organizations arose, among them the terrorist group of Sheikh el-Kassem of Haifa, which periodically ambushed and killed individual Jews. When he and his band were wiped out in November, 1935, the sheikh became a symbol of heroism for the Arab nationalists. High Commissioner Sir Arthur *Wauchope (1931–38) was sympathetic to the Zionist cause. When anti-British demonstrations and riots broke out in October, 1933, they were put down vigorously by the British police. In 1935 Wauchope tried to establish a *Legislative Council with limited powers in order to satisfy Arab demands for self-government, but this proposal was strongly opposed by the Jewish Agency and by groups in Britain and therefore was never implemented. The Arab nationalists were given added encouragement by the achievements of the Arabs during this period in Iraq, Egypt, and Syria. The discovery by the British in Jaffa of 537 cases of arms intended for the Hagana increased the tension among the Arabs.

Arab-Jewish Struggle, 1936–39. Following the Arab attacks on Jews in Jaffa on Apr. 19 and 20, 1936, the Arab political parties united and chose an *Arab Higher Committee under the leadership of Amin al-Husayni. The committee proclaimed a general strike against the British and made three demands: (1) the cessation of all Jewish immigration into Palestine, (2) the cessation of all land purchases by Jews, and (3) the formation of a Palestine government. The strike paralyzed a large part of the Arab economy, especially in the cities, but it did not harm the Jewish economy. Jewish enterprises, particularly the transportation network, continued to function. Enterprises with mixed labor forces such as the port of Haifa were able to continue operations because Jewish workers were ready to fill the places of Arab strikers.

Before long violence erupted. Jews were murdered, Jewish property was destroyed, and Jewish-operated transportation was attacked by armed bands. More than 90 Jews were killed during the six months of the Arab strike. The Arab gangs also began to attack British soldiers and police. During the summer of 1936 an attempt was made to organize the armed bands into a military structure under the command of a Syrian officer, Fawzi el-Kawukji, but after a few weeks, during which there were several clashes with the British Army, he was forced to leave the country.

The strike ended in October, 1936, without achieving its political goals. The British government did not accept the strikers' demands. Jewish immigration, although curtailed, continued; Jewish transportation continued under armed guard; and a month after work stopped in Jaffa harbor a new port was opened in Tel Aviv. Large quantities of weapons were distributed by the Palestine government to the Jewish settlements for self-defense purposes within the framework of a special police force (see NOTRIM). The British government appointed a Royal Commission to investigate the Palestine problem (see PEEL COMMISSION). Arriving in Palestine late in 1936, the Commission heard Jewish, Arab, and British witnesses. For about a year (October, 1936–October, 1937) there was a tense quiet in the country, broken by occasional acts of terror.

The report of the Commission, published in June, 1937, declared that, in view of the conflicting views of Jews and Arabs, the mandate was unworkable and that the only way to solve this problem was to partition Palestine into two states, Arab and Jewish. According to this plan (see PARTITION OF PALESTINE), the Jews would have received Galilee, the Jezreel Valley, and the coastal plain from 'Akko to Rehovot. Jerusalem, its surroundings, and a narrow strip connecting the city with the coast were to be under British rule. The rest of the country was to be an Arab State. A committee was appointed by the British government to work out the details of the plan and its implementation.

The partition plan was rejected by the Arab nationalists and aroused considerable differences of opinion among the Jews. Ben-Gurion, Moshe Shertok (Moshe *Sharett), and Weizmann supported the plan; other leaders such as M'nahem M. Ussishkin, Rabbi Meir Berlin (Meir *Bar-Ilan), Berl *Katznelson, and Vladimir Jabotinsky opposed it.

In the summer of 1937 the Arab attacks were resumed and, encouraged by Nazi agents, soon took on the character of an Arab revolt against the British regime. The signal for the uprising was given on Sept. 26, 1937, with the murder in Nazareth of the British acting district officer of Galilee. The mandatory government responded by disbanding the Arab Higher Committee and exiling its members. Only its head, Hajj Amin al-Husayni, succeeded in fleeing to Syria and continuing his activities there.

The Arab attacks were continued until 1939 in the form of raids by armed bands that roamed the country. Officially these bands were linked to the Central Committee in Damascus, but actually each gang operated in its area as it saw fit. The rebels drafted men, imposed taxes, and conducted courts-martial. However, they were unable to form a countrywide organization and received no real support from any foreign power. Nevertheless, they succeeded in gaining control over many rural and hilly regions; at one time, in the summer of 1938, they even held the Old City of Jerusalem. The British then took military action, causing many casualties. About 70 of the Arab rebels were hanged. Late in 1938 the activities of the armed gangs began to subside.

The three years of the Arab Revolt (1936–39) were a difficult period for the Yishuv, which stood the test only thanks to its strong internal organization and the solidarity of its members. Political leadership at the time was in the hands of the Jewish Agency, and defense and security were entrusted to the Hagana. The defense of the Jewish settlements was conducted in cooperation with the British authorities. Notrim, which had been established at the beginning of the disturbances, was expanded and developed; it guarded the borders, the railway lines, the airfields, and so on. The most important unit of this force was the Jewish Settlement Police, which at the end of the disturbances was reorganized into 10 regional units equipped with rifles, machine guns, and armored cars. The Jewish Settlement Police was under the command of British police officers, but its members and even its noncommissioned officers were members of the Hagana and subject to its discipline. In the summer of 1938 the British military authorities formed the *Special Night Squads, in which British soldiers served together with members of the Hagana under the command of Capt. Orde Charles *Wingate. The squads operated at night, using guerrilla tactics to combat the Arab bands in Galilee and the Jezreel Valley. They had a demoralizing effect on the Arab gangs and discouraged Arab villagers from helping them.

The experiences of the Night Squads had a powerful impact on the policies of the Hagana. The change from passive defense, which had been the rule until the disturbances of 1936, to active combat (hot pursuit of the Arab bands) was accompanied by many doubts. From the beginning of the disturbances the Jewish Agency had imposed on the Yishuv a policy of self-restraint (see HAVLAGA) in order to prevent irresponsible reprisals, which chiefly took the form of random attacks on any Arabs who happened to pass by. Many circles in the Yishuv were opposed to Havlaga, afraid that the Arabs would interpret the policy of nonreprisal and self-restraint as a sign of fear or weakness. However, self-restraint helped the Hagana command develop a more effective system of active defense and face-to-face combat with the marauding bands. For this purpose it organized within the Hagana a field force that laid ambushes and pursued the Arab bands in the fields and hills. Thus Hagana assured the safety and indeed the survival of hundreds of settlements. Not even the smallest or most isolated settlement was abandoned during these disturbances. The ever-growing defense needs were supplied by voluntary contributions in which nearly the entire community participated and which were known as *Kofer HaYishuv (Yishuv Redemption).

From both the political and the defense points of view the most important activity during the Arab uprisings was a large-scale accelerated project of establishing Jewish settlements. Groups of settlers, most of them from the kibbutzim, went out to unsettled areas purchased by the Jewish National Fund and founded new settlements, which in view of prevailing conditions had to be erected in the form of fortifications (see "STOCKADE AND TOWER" SETTLEMENTS). More than 50 of these settlements were established in the Bet Sh'an Valley (Nir David, Ma'oz, Tirat Tz'vi, etc.), eastern Upper Galilee (Dan, Dafna, etc.), the Carmel Hills ('En HaShofet, Ramat HaShofet, etc.), the hills of western Galilee on the Lebanese border (Hanita, Elon, etc.), and the Negev (Negba). Arab raiders attempted to attack these settlements but were repelled.

During this period the Hagana became properly organized. Nationwide training courses were unified. Clandestine arms production was increased, and the acquisition of arms abroad was expanded, leading to contacts with governments of countries such as Poland. In the fall of 1939 Hagana established a General Staff that assumed the character of a regular military command. In 1937 Etzel split, and some of its members, including its high command, returned to the fold of Hagana. The rest, comprising mostly Revisionists, continued to exist independently, rejecting control by the Jewish Agency. After one of its members, Sh'lomo *Ben Yosef, had been sentenced to hanging for shooting at an Arab bus, Etzel began a series of reprisals in which random attacks were made on Arab civilians without regard for age or sex. Most of the Yishuv, however, was opposed to these tactics.

During this period of internal strife the Yishuv proved its staying power. More than 500 Jews, including many in Hagana service and on guard duty, were killed by Arab terrorists. Nevertheless, immigration, though it slowed down, did not cease. A result of the Arab strike and boycott was that the Yishuv became more self-sufficient insofar as agricultural production was concerned. It was during these years that the men who were to lead the Israel Army in the *War of Independence (Yigael *Yadin, Yigal *Allon, Moshe *Dayan, and many others) underwent their baptism of fire. The Arab community, rural as well as urban, unable to sell its produce to Jews, suffering from prolonged strikes, and exposed to the extortions of the armed gangs, became well-nigh impoverished. Some well-to-do Arabs left Palestine.

The worldwide war climate following the Munich Agreement led Britain to make a basic change in its policy in Palestine. Although the Arab Revolt had failed, the British government scrapped its partition proposal and published the *White Paper of 1939, in which Britain in effect repudiated its obligations to the Yishuv as set forth in the mandate. Its attitude was based on the assumption that whereas the Jews had no choice but to support the British against Nazi Germany, the Arabs had to be appeased as much as possible in order to keep them from cooperating with the enemy in the event of war. The White Paper met the demands of the Arabs to a great extent: Jewish immigration was restricted (no more than 75,000 Jewish immigrants were to be admitted to Palestine during the ensuing five years), and land purchases by Jews were limited and allowed, on certain conditions, in only a small part of the country. Most important of all, the Arabs were promised that within five years an independent government would be established in Palestine in which they would have a majority and so be in a position to determine the future of the country.

The Yishuv considered the White Paper of 1939 an act of treachery toward the Jewish people. It came at the very moment when the Jewish refugee problem was becoming increasingly acute following the annexation of Austria, the *Kristallnacht* (night of broken glass) in Germany, and the annexation of Czechoslovakia. In response to an appeal by the Jewish Agency, mass demonstrations were held throughout Palestine on the day the White Paper was published (May 17, 1939). Here and there demonstrators clashed with the police.

In 1938–39 the illegal immigration movement, which had been organized in 1937 partly by HeHalutz and the Revisionists, became a mass movement that openly fought the White Paper. Mosad L'Aliya Bet, aided by HeHalutz, by the pioneering youth movements in the Diaspora, and by the Hagana in Palestine, was set up to organize the illegal immigration. In response to the stepped-up efforts by the British to seize the illegal-immigration ships, the Hagana formed special units for the struggle against the British, and clashes broke out between Jews and the British military and police. Jewish settlements were established outside the areas where Jews were permitted to acquire land under the White Paper.

World War II. With the beginning of the war the country was hit by a grave economic crisis, but the isolation of the Middle East from its usual sources of supply stimulated the development of agriculture and industry. Employment rose, and the economic position of the Yishuv improved. On the other hand, the political conflict with Great Britain worsened, for the mandatory government embarked on a policy of vigorous enforcement of the White Paper provisions on Jewish immigration and land purchases. Most of the Yishuv accepted the policy statement of David Ben-Gurion, which called for "war against the Nazis as though there were no White Paper, and a struggle against the White Paper as though there were no war." Only a small minority, the *Lohame Herut Israel (Lehi, or Stern group), called for an increased struggle against the British.

The publication of the *Land Transfer Regulations of February, 1940, set off protest demonstrations that frequently led to clashes with the police. Resentment was fanned by arrests of Hagana men and arms searches and, particularly, by the inhuman treatment the British gave refugees from the Nazi holocaust who attempted to enter Palestine illegally. When the British intercepted a contingent of "illegal" immigrants and transferred the refugees to the *"Patria" for deportation to Mauritius (see MAURITIUS CAMPS), the Hagana sabotaged the ship (Nov. 25, 1940) in Haifa harbor. Unfortunately, more than 250 of the refugees lost their lives when the "Patria" sank. Sixteen hundred other would-be immigrants were deported to Mauritius. The government refused admission to refugees who had reached Turkey aboard the *"Struma" (February, 1942). For some mysterious reason, the ship sank in the Black Sea and 764 refugees perished. The Yishuv put the blame squarely on the mandatory government.

Even while it defied British rule in Palestine, however, the Yishuv wholeheartedly participated in the war effort against the Nazis. British authorities at first were not eager to accept aid from Palestine's Jewish community on an "official" basis, but the exigencies of the war in the Middle East forced them to accept thousands of Palestinian Jewish volunteers (as a mandate, Palestine was not subject to draft laws). Jewish volunteers were accepted particularly for auxiliary services such as the Transport Corps (RASC), the Engineers (RE), and the Women's Auxiliary Corps (ATS) and, later, in combat units, most of which served as territorial guards in Palestine, and in the artillery, which guarded the coasts and important military installations (the port of Haifa, the oil refineries, etc.). The British authorities did everything in their power to play down the "Jewish" character of this recruiting movement and, among other things, forbade the use of national Jewish symbols on badges, banners, and the like. Nevertheless, the various Jewish units, which saw service in the Middle East, Africa, and Italy, attested to the military skills and technical know-how of the Yishuv. Only in the very last months of the war, and after a protracted political struggle, did the British form the *Jewish Brigade, in which Jewish infantry groups and auxiliary units were combined to form a military force that served in the final battles in northern Italy in the spring of 1945. By the end of the war Jewish volunteers in the Palestine military and security forces totaled 30,000.

The war brought acute danger to the Yishuv when the Nazi forces stood at the gates of Palestine (1941–42), and shock and distress when news first came of the full extent of the disaster that had overtaken the Jews of Europe. During those years Hagana set up units for full-time service, called the *Palmah.

Originally intended to defend the Yishuv in the event of a Nazi invasion, Palmah later became active in the political and military struggle against the White Paper. In the period between Italy's entry into the war in 1940 and the decisive victory at El Alamein late in 1942 there was close cooperation between the Jewish Agency and the British Army. Hagana units took part in the invasion of Vichy-controlled Syria, and the first Palmah units were trained by British instructors. It was this mutual cooperation that made possible the landing of 32 Palestinian Jewish *parachutists behind the enemy lines in Europe. When the battle lines moved away from the Middle East and the danger of a Nazi invasion receded, however, the British authorities began to persecute the Hagana. They conducted arms searches in which they encountered opposition from inhabitants of Ramat HaKovesh and Hulda and held show trials in which members of the Hagana were accused of stealing arms from British arsenals.

In 1942 the Zionist movement adopted the *Biltmore Program, which called for a Jewish Commonwealth in Palestine. Most of the Yishuv supported this program and prepared to fight for it once the war ended. Early in 1944 Etzel started a series of sabotage operations against British police installations. These activities, which were contrary to the policy adopted by the official institutions of the Yishuv, led to an internal conflict that sharpened after the slaying of Lord *Moyne, the British Resident Minister in the Middle East, by Lehi in November, 1944. The Hagana then took action to suppress Etzel.

In spite of the inimical attitude of the British Mandatory government, the position of the Yishuv became stronger during the war years. Because the Mediterranean area was cut off from Europe, there was considerable development in the Jewish industry of Palestine, which rendered valuable services to the

American delegation to the World Zionist Conference in London in 1945. From left to right: Louis E. Levinthal, Daniel Frisch, Emanuel Neumann, Juliette Benjamin, Naomi Chertoff, Abba Hillel Silver, Judith G. Epstein, Stephen S. Wise, Rose Halprin, Meyer Weisgal, Israel Goldstein, James G. Heller, Louis Lipsky, and Samuel Margoshes. [Zionist Archives]

Ben Yehuda Street, Jerusalem, after a terrorist explosion on Feb. 22, 1948. [Zionist Archives]

war effort (*see* WAR EFFORT OF THE YISHUV) and provided the Allied forces in the area with vital military and other supplies. The limitations of immigration into the country notwithstanding, some 50,000 Jewish immigrants reached Palestine either legally or illegally. At the end of the war the Yishuv numbered some 580,000 and constituted about one-third of the total population of Palestine.

Final Years of the Mandate, 1945–48. After the defeat of Germany in May, 1945, the Yishuv hoped for a change in British policy in Palestine, particularly in view of the victory in July of the Labor party, which had long supported Zionist views and adopted a pro-Zionist program in the 1945 British elections. However, it soon became apparent that the new government, with Ernest *Bevin as Foreign Secretary, was going to keep the White Paper in force. As a consequence, the Jewish Agency gave the signal for armed resistance to British policy. At the time, the fight was not yet for political independence but merely for the opening of Palestine to the remnants of European Jewry and for the abolition of land purchase restrictions. This struggle was conducted through the T'nu'at HaMeri Ha-'Ivri (Hebrew Resistance movement), in which the Hagana participated with Etzel and the Stern group. After several isolated operations, such as the break from the immigrant detention camp at 'Atlit in October, 1945, Palmah, Etzel, and Lehi joined forces in an all-out resistance campaign, sabotaging

Palestine's rail networks and attacking the central railroad terminal at Lod. These actions were followed by a series of operations designed to cripple coastal patrol stations and radio and radar installations set up to intercept immigrant ships and to paralyze police stations and air and rail traffic. In many instances, large numbers of Jews engaged in demonstrations to interfere with British army and police operations; these activities resulted in numerous casualties.

'Aliya Bet resumed its systematic operations in Europe. Shiploads of Jewish immigrants set sail for Palestine from small ports in Italy, Greece, Romania, and France. The British increased their guard, and most of the ships were intercepted near the shores of Palestine. The passengers were placed in prison camps and released against the limited monthly immigration quota of 1,000 persons, which had been allowed as a temporary measure by the government and was to continue until a final settlement of the Palestine problem was found.

The problem of resettling the survivors of the Nazi holocaust had become a major political factor in the struggle against the White Paper. In August, 1945, Pres. Harry S *Truman proposed that 100,000 refugees be settled in Palestine forthwith. The number of refugees grew steadily through the operations of *B'riha, the organized movement of Eastern European Jews to displaced-persons camps in Central Europe and Italy, from where they hoped to get to Palestine.

Eliezer Kaplan signs Declaration of Independence as David Ben-Gurion and Rabbi Y'huda Leb Maimon, at left, and Moshe Sharett, at right, look on. [Zionist Archives]

Between 1945 and 1948, Mosad L'Aliya Bet brought to Palestine 60 ships carrying a total of about 70,000 immigrants. Most of these refugees were arrested by the British authorities in Palestine. In April, 1946, world opinion was shocked when 1,000 Palestine-bound refugees, held by the Italian authorities in the port of La Spezia, announced a hunger strike. The British government was forced to allow them to enter Palestine. The *Anglo-American Committee of Inquiry, appointed by Great Britain and the United States to investigate the problem of the refugees and Palestine, seconded Truman's proposal to admit 100,000 refugees to Palestine. The refusal of the British government to carry out the recommendations of the Committee set off large-scale operations by the Hebrew Resistance movement in which Palmah units destroyed the bridges linking Palestine with neighboring countries.

On June 29, 1946 (Black Sabbath), the British retaliated with a series of arrests and searches throughout the country. Several members of the Jewish Agency Executive were detained, as were thousands of members of kibbutzim harboring units of the Palmah. In the course of searches conducted for Hagana arms stores, a central arsenal at the kibbutz Yagur was uncovered. The government then decided to intern the refugees seized at sea in Cyprus until such time as the Palestine problem was settled (*see* CYPRUS, DETENTION CAMPS IN).

A few weeks after the Black Sabbath, Etzel blew up British

government offices in the King David Hotel in Jerusalem. Unfortunately, many innocent clerks and civilians, Arabs and Jews, were killed in this operation.

The Jewish Agency called for a cessation of armed resistance and was particularly anxious to avoid direct attacks on British government and army installations. Etzel and Lehi thereupon withdrew from the Hebrew Resistance movement and escalated their attacks on the British. In May, 1947, they broke into *'Akko Prison and freed many of the prisoners.

That year the British hanged seven members of the Irgun. Illegal immigration increased, and transfers of immigrants in the port of Haifa to ships bound for Cyprus were accompanied by demonstrations and, in some cases, by bloody clashes. In July, 1947, the British attempted to return to France a contingent of 4,500 immigrants aboard the *"Exodus 1947." When the refugees refused to leave the ship voluntarily in France, they were brought to the British-occupied zone in Germany and forcibly taken off the ship.

As a result of the resistance activities in all their forms, the British government announced in April, 1947, that the Palestine problem would be turned over to the United Nations. The *United Nations Special Committee on Palestine (UNSCOP), which consisted of the representatives of 11 nations, recommended the partition of Palestine into two independent states, one Arab and one Jewish. This proposal, which was supported by the Soviet Union and the United States, was adopted by the General Assembly of the United Nations on Nov. 29, 1947. The British government thereupon announced that it would do nothing to help implement this decision but would remove its army and administrative establishment from the country by May 15, 1948. The Arabs at once officially declared at the United Nations and in Arab capitals that they would resist the partition scheme by force of arms, and began to attack the Yishuv, setting off the initial phase of the War of Independence. The transition period between December, 1947, and May, 1948, put the Yishuv to a severe test. The British, who deliberately wanted to leave the country in a state of chaos, did nothing to facilitate an orderly transfer of authority.

Ben-Gurion, who had devoted all his energies to the organization of the Yishuv's defense after March, 1947, stood at the helm of Palestine's Jewish community. Hagana and Palmah units repelled Arab attacks on Jewish settlements throughout Palestine. In the meantime, seven new Hagana brigades were organized, and in the spring of 1948 large quantities of arms were acquired from other countries, particularly Czechoslovakia. During the first months of the war Hagana concentrated on the defense of Jewish settlements and the maintenance of lines of communication. The position of Jerusalem was especially difficult; at times the city was entirely cut off from the coastal plain and suffered heavy casualties.

In April, 1948, the Hagana turned from the defensive to the offensive. It launched Operation Nahshon, in which a road was cleared to give temporary access to besieged Jerusalem. The attempt by the Arab Liberation Army, organized by Fawzi el-Kawukji, to break through to Haifa was smashed in a battle near Mishmar Ha'Emek. That spring, too, Tiberias, Haifa, Jaffa, and Safed were taken by the Jewish forces.

Meanwhile, the political struggle continued. The proposal of the United States, on Mar. 19, 1948, to postpone the implementation of the United Nations decision until a new discussion could be held, was rejected by the representative of the Jewish Agency.

Y. SLUTSKY

STATE OF ISRAEL: 1948–

The State of Israel was proclaimed by David Ben-Gurion on May 14, 1948. The *Declaration of Independence was signed by 37 representatives of the WZO and the Jewish Community (K'nesset Yisrael) in Palestine, the two bodies that composed the provisional government and Provisional Council of State. Ben-Gurion headed the new *Government, and Chaim Weizmann was elected President of the Council.

Establishment of the State and War of Independence. The State of Israel replaced the British Mandate, which expired the same day. Although legally the State was based on the United

Proclamation of the State of Israel at the first meeting of the Provisional Council, forerunner of the Knesset, in the Tel Aviv Museum on May 14, 1948. On the platform, left to right: B'khor Shitrit, David Remez, Pinhas Rosen, Peretz Bernstein, Rabbi Y'huda Leb Maimon, David Ben-Gurion (standing), Moshe Shapira, Moshe Sharett, Eliezer Kaplan, Mordecai Bentov, and Aharon Zisling. [Zionist Archives]

Emblem of Israel. [Israel Information Services]

Nations decision of Nov. 29, 1947, in actuality the United Nations took no measures to provide for a peaceful and orderly transfer of authority. The State was accorded de facto recognition by the United States on May 14 and de jure recognition by the Soviet Union on May 18, 1948. Many countries, mainly in Eastern Europe and Latin America, followed suit.

Within a few hours after the establishment of the State, the armies of Egypt, Transjordan, Iraq, Syria, and Lebanon crossed the borders in a strategically coordinated plan to conquer Israel. They were opposed by the Hagana, including units of the Palmah, and the so-called dissident forces Etzel and Lehi. Thus began the War of Independence, the first phase of which ended with the truce that came into effect on June 11, 1948, lasted until July 8, 1948, and gave Israel a chance to consolidate its government and defense forces (*see* ISRAEL DEFENSE FORCES). As the Arab states rejected the United Nations proposal to extend the truce, fighting was renewed, and in 10 days (July 9–18; a second, unlimited truce then began), the Israeli forces considerably increased the territory under their control by capturing Ramle and Lod in the central part of the country and Lower Galilee. One of the problems left unsolved by the renewed truce was the road to Jerusalem, which was blocked by the Transjordanians. During the truce Israel continued to consolidate its position. Jerusalem was proclaimed a "*hold* territory" (August 1), and Dov *Joseph was named military governor.

An Israeli appeal for peace (Aug. 5, 1948) was rejected by the Arabs, although UN Mediator Count Folke *Bernadotte strove untiringly to effect a compromise solution. Also in August, an Israeli currency was introduced, and taxes were levied to pay for war expenditures. Thanks to generous financial support by world Jewry and despite the arbitrary exclusion of the country from the sterling bloc, the main economic problem during Israel's first year was not so much a shortage of foreign currency as the refusal of steamship and air lines to transport goods to a country in a state of war. This refusal, in effect, amounted to a blockade of the new State.

Meanwhile, Count Bernadotte worked out a plan for the settlement of the main issues, which were the cession of the Negev to the Arabs, the cession of western Galilee to the Jews, and the internationalization of Jerusalem. Bernadotte's infringement on Israel's newly acquired sovereignty and the suggested exclusion of the Negev aroused opposition in Israel. On Sept. 17, 1948, he was assassinated in Jerusalem by an extremist group allegedly belonging to Lehi. The Israeli government then took drastic steps to put an end to the activities of splinter groups.

Bernadotte's plan and the discussion in the UN General Assembly in Paris convinced the Israeli leaders that Israel's hold on its territory must be strengthened and its frontiers consolidated. An Israeli attack started in the Negev on Oct. 15, 1948. By October 22, the road to the Negev, which had been isolated, was opened, B'er Sheva' was occupied, and the Egyptian forces in the Faluja area were encircled. Another Israeli attack, in Galilee, ended in the occupation of the whole area (Oct. 29–31, 1948). The last Israeli operation took place in the Negev (Dec. 22, 1948–Jan. 7, 1949) and confirmed Israel's domination of the northern and central Negev. During this operation Israeli forces temporarily invaded Egyptian territory in the Sinai Peninsula. On Jan. 6, 1949, the Egyptians declared their readiness to negotiate an armistice.

A population census, held on Nov. 8, 1948, showed that 782,000 persons were residing in Israel; of these 71,000 were Arabs. On Jan. 25, 1949, elections were held for a Constituent Assembly, which became the first *Knesset of the State. *Mapai emerged as the major party, receiving 33.7 per cent of the votes cast. Next came the left-wing *Mapam, with 14.7 per cent. The religious bloc did well, obtaining 12 per cent of the votes cast. *Herut received only 11.5 per cent, and the lists of the center (*Progressive party) and right wing (General Zionist party; *see* GENERAL ZIONISM) polled no more than 4 and 5 per cent, respectively. Since no one party had a clear majority of seats, a coalition Government had to be formed.

Flag-raising ceremony in Haifa after the departure of the British in 1948. [Histadrut Foto-News]

The elections were watched abroad with much interest. Before they were held, the Export-Import Bank of Washington had granted Israel a loan of $100,000,000. Soon after the elections many Western European countries recognized the State of Israel, and the United States extended de jure recognition.

When he formed a Government, Ben-Gurion insisted on commitment to an agreed program and on acceptance of collective responsibility by the coalition as a whole for the actions of its member parties. Negotiations with Mapam failed, and the religious bloc became the main ally of Mapai. On Mar. 3, 1949, Ben-Gurion introduced the new Government, which won a vote of confidence. The coalition was based on 71 of the 120 members of the Knesset.

During the first half of 1949 armistice negotiations were conducted with the Arab states. On February 24, the general armistice agreement with Egypt was signed on Rhodes (see ARMISTICE AGREEMENTS). Based largely on the existing military situation, it provided for the evacuation of the encircled Egyptian forces in Faluja, which included the then Capt. Gamal Abdel Nasser. In March an armed Israeli column advanced toward the Red Sea to take hold of the southern part of the Negev. It reached Elat on March 12. In the armistice with Lebanon (Mar. 23, 1949), Israel gave up some of the villages that had been occupied by Israeli troops. On April 3, Israel signed an armistice with Jordan in which it agreed to make certain concessions. The armistice with Syria was not signed until July 20, 1949, after difficult negotiations and the establishment of demilitarized zones. No armistice was signed with Iraq, whose forces had also taken an active part in the war. Each of the four armistice agreements contained in its preamble a statement that it was a preliminary toward peace.

Early Years. The consolidation of Israel's position on the international scene culminated in admission to the United Nations in May, 1949. The attempt by the Palestine Conciliation Commission (consisting of representatives of France, the United States, and Turkey) to advance beyond the armistice agreements to a permanent peace settlement failed. At the Lausanne Conference in the summer of 1949, the Arabs demanded that the Arab refugee problem be discussed first as a basis for any negotiations (see ARAB REFUGEES), while the Jews were ready to consider it only as part of a general agreement. Thereafter all conciliation efforts failed. King 'Abdullah of Jordan, the only major figure in the Arab world who was ready to negotiate, was assassinated in July, 1951. The armistice agreements, which remained unchanged, left many vexing problems in Israel's international relations and in its relations with neighboring countries, particularly Syria. See also FOREIGN RELATIONS OF ISRAEL.

Thus, efforts at solving the Palestine problem were confined to securing peace and to dealing with specific issues. In a Tripartite Declaration (May 25, 1950), the United States, Great Britain, and France expressed their desire for a balance of arms and their opposition to any violation of the territorial integrity of Israel and its neighbors.

Israel bent every effort to the task of safeguarding its security and territorial integrity. When the UN General Assembly accepted (Dec. 9, 1949) the plan of the Conciliation Commission to establish an international zone in Jerusalem, Israel reacted by moving the Knesset and the Prime Minister's Office from Tel Aviv to that city. However, between 1950 and 1953 Israel's most important problem in foreign relations was its relations with the great powers. Israel endeavored to follow a

Walter Eytan, Director General of the Israel Ministry of Foreign Affairs, signs the Israel-Egypt armistice at Rhodes on Feb. 24, 1949. Other armistices with Lebanon, Syria, and Transjordan ended the War of Independence. [Zionist Archives]

policy of nonidentification with either East or West, but growing dependence on American aid and the lack of response by the Soviet Union to the vital needs of the State, such as free immigration and economic aid, oriented the country increasingly toward the West. When the Korean War broke out in 1950, Israel condemned the Communist attack and supported United Nations action. On the other hand, it viewed the American-sponsored plan of a Middle East Command with misgiving because of fear that the Arabs, as members of such a command, would be given arms. Relations between Israel and the Soviet Union deteriorated during the second half of 1952 because of the anti-Jewish and anti-Zionist drive in the Communist world, which culminated in the *Slansky trial of November, 1952, and the accusations against the Jewish doctors in Moscow in January, 1953. Israel, including the majority of Mapam, protested the accusations.

Israel's major enterprise between 1949 and 1952 was the absorption of mass immigration. Between 1948 and 1951 a total of 676,749 persons settled in Israel. First came more than 30,000 immigrants from the Cyprus camps and Europe, as well as volunteers for the Israel Army. Then Israel had to accept the Jews from the Eastern European countries, where there was a danger that Jews might soon be forbidden to emigrate. The situation of the Jews in the Arab countries deteriorated so that they, too, had to be rescued. Jewish communities from Bulgaria, Yemen, and Iraq moved to Israel practically in their entirety. Jews also came in great numbers from Poland and Romania. Israel's open-door policy was officially set forth in the Law of *Return, which was enacted in July, 1950. Upon their arrival, the immigrants, sometimes as many as 90,000, were placed in immigrants' camps and supported by the Jewish Agency. Later, all those able to work were moved to Ma'abarot (transit villages; see MA'ABARA), where they were given employment in public works.

The burden of war and security expenditures as well as the need to develop the economy necessitated a policy of austerity. The balance of payments deteriorated owing to the need to absorb masses of immigrants not yet productive and also owing to the partial destruction of the Dead Sea potash works and the closure of the Haifa oil refineries. Food rationing was introduced in the spring of 1949 and clothes rationing in the summer of 1950. The attempt to reduce prices and consumption was intended to effect an equitable distribution of the country's resources, a saving of foreign currency, and an increase in investments. There was an ephemeral success, but the increase in currency in circulation and the inflation that followed gave rise to a black market, caused a reduction in exports, and kept private investment away. Soon there was an acute shortage of foreign currency. *See also* FINANCE IN ISRAEL.

In view of the urgency of settling vacant land and providing food for the country, a major effort was made to strengthen existing agricultural settlements and to promote the establishment of new ones. The government attempted to overcome the economic difficulties by a public campaign against the black market, the lifting of limitations on income, premiums for exports, encouragement of savings, and the sale of State lands (autumn, 1950).

On Mar. 29, 1950, the Law for the Encouragement of Capital Investments was passed by the Knesset, but economic conditions did not then favor large investments from abroad. In the summer of 1950 a conference of Jewish communal leaders, mostly from the United States but also from the United Kingdom, was held in Jerusalem. The Israeli leaders proposed a plan for raising $1,500,000,000 within four years. In May, 1951, Ben-Gurion inaugurated the Israel independence loan, which aimed at raising $500,000,000 within three years (*see* STATE OF ISRAEL BONDS). Meanwhile, in March, 1951, the Israeli government appealed for aid to the government of the United States. That October, Israel was given a grant of $65,000,000, and administrative machinery was set up to handle the aid. The *German-Israel Agreement (Luxembourg Agreement) on reparations, which was signed on Sept. 10, 1952, after prolonged negotiations and a bitter debate in Israel, became a major factor in the Israeli economy. The agreement provided for the payment by West Germany of $715,000,000 within 12 years.

In February, 1952, a new economic policy was inaugurated. Three rates of exchange were fixed for the Israeli pound (IL). A more realistic rate of IL1 to $1 was introduced to encourage investments from abroad, while higher rates of exchange were maintained within the country to keep staple food prices down. A steep rise in prices followed, and additional measures had to be taken in order to curb this inflation. In June, 1952, Levi *Eshkol replaced Eliezer *Kaplan as Minister of Finance.

Some time was to pass before Israel's economy began to be stabilized. The country continued to suffer from a severe shortage of foreign currency. There were bad harvests (as in 1951 and 1952) before the new agricultural settlements were in a position to supplement the food production of the older settlements. Industry was still conducted mainly on a small scale. Kaiser-Frazer was one of the first foreign manufacturers to establish an assembly plant in Israel.

Besides its precarious economic situation, Israel was plagued by political instability. The coalition Government was attacked by the right wing for suppressing private initiative and discouraging private foreign investment by its Socialist image. The left wing, on the other hand, branded the Government's policy as collaboration with imperialism and betrayal of the cause of labor. A decision taken by Mapam in March, 1950, not to join the coalition made the Government dependent on the religious bloc. Municipal elections in November, 1950, brought gains to the General Zionists, who were not part of the coalition. Thus the public expressed its resentment at the Government's economic policy, and the Government seemed to be losing the confidence of the people.

Tension between Mapai and its religious partners in the coalition mounted over the religious education of immigrant children. The government was defeated in the Knesset and resigned. New elections were held in July, 1951. Mapai polled

37.3 per cent of the votes, saving its predominant position in the coalition owing to Ben-Gurion's prestige and to the immigrant vote. General Zionist strength rose from 5.2 to 16.2 per cent of the total vote. Herut's share declined from 11.5 to 6.6 per cent, and Mapam sustained small losses. The coalition resulting from the election was not much different from the one that had preceded it.

The Law on the Status of the World Zionist Organization–Jewish Agency, passed in 1952, officially recognized the Jewish Agency as the agency for immigrant settlement and absorption activities but did not accord it the exclusive right to act as the representative of the Jewish people.

On Nov. 9, 1952, Chaim Weizmann, the first President of Israel, died. On December 8, he was succeeded by Itzhak *Ben Zvi, a veteran member of Mapai and one of the pioneers and founders of the labor movement in Palestine.

Political and Economic Stabilization. The support of the religious bloc became weaker and less reliable. To obtain greater political stability, the General Zionists were brought into the coalition. On Dec. 23, 1952, the new Government won a vote of confidence of 63 to 24. Meanwhile, the Prague Slansky trial had had a severe impact on the left-wing parties. Early in 1953 Mapam debated the question of protesting Soviet anti-Zionist accusations. Moshe *S'ne and a small group of followers left the party and formed a leftist front that later joined the Communist party (*see* COMMUNISTS IN ISRAEL). Two Mapam members of the Knesset switched their allegiance to Mapai. In 1954 Mapam split: the more nationalist and less left-oriented faction of *Ahdut 'Avoda left it and formed an independent party.

In 1953 certain deflationary effects of the new economic policy first made themselves felt. The amount of money in circulation decreased, while prices rose to a point of stabilization. A "gray market" was tolerated alongside the official one, unemployment increased, and a drive for greater efficiency was inaugurated. Thus conditions supposedly favoring economic recovery were created while the main effort of development was still confined chiefly to agriculture and to the initiation of work to exploit the Dead Sea and other mineral resources, which was financed mainly by public investment.

Despite economic grievances, the stabilization of the government was followed by domestic stabilization. The left-wing parties were weakened after the Prague trial. Disagreements with the Orthodox were attenuated after the passage (August, 1953) of a law abolishing all party control of educational institutions and the consequent establishment of State schools. Some Orthodox extremists (*see* N'TURE KARTA), who attempted terrorist measures to force their views on the population, found themselves completely isolated. *See also* RELIGION AND RELIGIOUS ATTITUDES IN ISRAEL.

Events after the death of Joseph Stalin in 1953 removed some of the grounds for Israel's strained relations with the Soviet Union. In July, diplomatic relations between the U.S.S.R. and Israel, which had been broken off by the Soviet Union in February, were restored.

The revolution in Egypt (July, 1952) which deposed King Farouk did not have an immediate effect on Israel. An appeal by Ben-Gurion to the new regime to establish friendly relations with Israel met with no public response. Clashes broke out on the Jordanian border as a result of the incursion of infiltrators into Israel. In the Israeli retaliatory attack on the Jordanian village of Kibya a number of Arabs were killed (Oct. 14, 1953). An Israeli attempt to dig an irrigation canal in the demilitarized zone on the Syrian border caused a dispute with Syria. Under pressure from the United States and following the suspension of American economic aid (October, 1953), Israel altered its original plan, much to the detriment of its agriculture.

On Dec. 7, 1953, Ben-Gurion resigned as Prime Minister and Minister of Defense and retired to the kibbutz S'de Boker. On Jan. 25, 1954, Moshe Sharett presented a coalition Government, which received a vote of confidence of 75 to 23 from the Knesset.

The economic situation continued to improve. The threat of a foreign currency crisis was no longer imminent. Prices were stabilized, and the black market disappeared. There was an increase in foreign currency income, and stabilization was further strengthened by a consolidation loan of $65,000,000. The improvement of the economic situation and an abundance of jobs brought about a decline in idealism and in the willingness of the people, particularly the young, to make sacrifices. From his retreat in S'de Boker Ben-Gurion appealed to the youth of the country to make its choice between self-advancement and personal dedication to the upbuilding of the Homeland.

Suez and the *Sinai Campaign. Apart from border assaults and clashes (11 killed on the Scorpion Ascent, Mar. 17, 1954; an Israeli reprisal attack on Mar. 28, 1954; shooting in Jerusalem on June 30, 1954), the main threat to Israel did not lie in immediate relations with the Arab states but in Anglo-Egyptian negotiations on the evacuation of the Suez area and in the change of attitude of the new administration that had been elected in the United States in November, 1952. Israel was prevented from using the Suez Canal. Its complaint to the UN Security Council was rejected because of a Soviet veto (Mar. 29, 1954). The evacuation of the British from the Suez zone would mean the cession of valuable military bases to Egypt. The Eisenhower-Dulles administration in the United States declared its intention to arm the Arabs and "redress the balance" in American Middle Eastern policy. Assistant Secretary of State Henry Byroade called on Israel to limit immigration and to loosen its ties with world Jewry, concentrating instead on becoming integrated into the Middle East (April–May, 1954). This situation brought about a dispute between those of Israel's political leaders who wished Israel to be a "law-abiding country" as defined by world opinion and those who advocated a firm policy to safeguard Israel's survival and sovereignty. Prime Minister Sharett was the leading advocate of the first trend; Defense Minister Pinhas Lavon, of the second. Against this background, a "security mishap" occurred that later, in 1960, was to cause a considerable stir in Israeli politics.

Israel-Egyptian relations took a turn for the worse when the Israeli freighter "Bat Galim" was seized by the Egyptians while trying to pass through the Suez Canal. Contrary to the wishes of the UN Security Council, the Egyptian government released only the crew, keeping the ship and its cargo (September, 1954–January, 1955). In December, 1954–January, 1955, Egypt held a trial of Jews on charges of espionage and sabotage. Two were sentenced to death and executed; others were given long terms of imprisonment.

Following disagreements between Defense Minister Lavon and army officers as well as dissension within Mapai, Lavon resigned and Ben-Gurion was recalled from retirement, assuming the office of Defense Minister in Sharett's Government on Feb. 21, 1955.

Late in 1954 the border situation deteriorated, with the center of tension shifting from the Jordanian to the Egyptian border; small groups of Egyptian-trained Palestinians infiltrated into Israeli territory, carrying on espionage activities and attacking Israeli villages and settlements. On Feb. 28, 1955, Israel retaliated by attacking an Egyptian military camp in the Gaza Strip and killing 40 Egyptian soldiers.

In January, 1955, the Baghdad Pact was signed. While it did not include Egypt, it alarmed Israel, since under its terms Iraq, another hostile power, was to be armed by the Western powers.

Despite the aggravation of the political situation, the Israeli economy continued to advance. Oil was discovered in marketable quantities in the Negev. German reparations payments were invested in the improvement of communication facilities, and the merchant marine was developed. A new harbor was opened near Haifa, and work started on a pipeline to bring water from the Yarkon River to the Negev (*see* NATIONAL WATER CARRIER). On the other hand, new internal dissension was developing. Professional workers, considering themselves underpaid, voiced demands for salary increases and staged strikes. Demands of this kind as well as increased defense expenditure compelled the government to relax its currency restrictions. Meanwhile, a new phase of settlement policy was inaugurated. The Lakhish area became a model for a new regional type of settlement organization. The region, in which 25 agricultural settlements were set up, was treated as a single unit for purposes of cultivation plans, water usage, and public building. *See also* DEVELOPMENT REGIONS.

Public opinion was greatly excited by the Grünwald-Kasztner trial, in which the conduct of Jewish leadership under Nazi rule was reexamined and Rezső *Kasztner was accused of unjustified contacts with the Nazi authorities. The fact that Kasztner was a member of Mapai was exploited by other parties to discredit the ruling party.

The elections of 1955 brought a setback for Mapai, to 32.2 per cent of the votes cast, and for the General Zionists, who received only 10.2 per cent. The extreme parties did well: Herut's share rose to 12.6 per cent, the reorganized Ahdut 'Avoda polled 8.2 per cent, and Mapam 7 per cent. The election results were interpreted as evidence of dissatisfaction with the Government's "weak" national and economic policy.

The persistence of the problem of religion-State relationships brought unity to the religious camp, differences in social policy being blurred in the face of pressing problems that demanded a concerted effort. In June, 1956, the *Mizrahi and HaPo'el HaMizrahi parties merged to form the National Religious party. *See also* RELIGION AND STATE IN ISRAEL.

On Nov. 2, 1955, Ben-Gurion formed a new Government. The modification in the views of the left-wing parties now enabled him to include these parties in his coalition. His insistence on a firm foreign policy and the predominance of the Ministry of Defense over the Ministry of Foreign Affairs led to the resignation of Foreign Minister Moshe Sharett. On June 18, 1956, Sharett was succeeded by Golda *Meir.

Border clashes between Israel and Egypt were resumed in August, 1955, before the Egyptian-Czechoslovak arms deal was made public. Egyptian commando operations in Israeli areas provoked Israeli retaliation, and an Egyptian attempt to control an area in the demilitarized zone was thwarted by Israeli forces. In November, the focus of tension shifted to the Syrian border. A Syrian attempt to gain a foothold in the Lake

Kinneret area was countered by a large-scale Israeli operation (December, 1955).

The threat to Israel's security increased with the arms deal between Egypt and Czechoslovakia (September, 1955), which was sponsored by the Soviet Union and which weakened Israel's military position in relation to the Arab world. Late in 1955 and during 1956 Israel had reason to consider itself in a state of political as well as military siege. The supply of Czechoslovak arms modernized the Arab war machine. The Baghdad Pact assured the flow of Western arms to Iraq. Sharett's plea for arms for Israel was rejected. U.S. Secretary of State John Foster Dulles stated in August, 1955, that the United States would guarantee the borders between Israel and the Arab countries only if the parties concerned reached an agreement. In a speech delivered at the Guildhall on Nov. 9, 1955, British Prime Minister Anthony Eden called for an arrangement involving a compromise between Israel's actual borders and those assigned to it by the United Nations partition resolution. Egypt's guerrilla campaign against Israel was intensified. The United States refused Israel's request for arms, which would have restored the balance of power in the Middle East. At this critical moment the help of France played a vital role in Israel's security.

The state-of-siege atmosphere in Israel elicited voluntary help in the form of funds, but soon the economy began to feel new strains, currency circulation increased, and prices rose. After the nationalization of the Suez Canal (summer, 1956) the Egyptian border quieted down. In the autumn tension built up along the Israeli-Jordanian border. Acts of terror were met with Israeli retaliation against Jordanian border posts, culminating in the attack on Kalkiliya on Oct. 11, 1956. Great Britain warned Israel that it intended to fulfill its treaty obligations to defend Jordan. The Jordanian government seemed unstable. Iraqi troops moved into Jordan; in elections held on October 22, the pro-Egyptian parties won, and on October 24, Jordan, Syria, and Egypt established a joint military command directed against Israel.

On Oct. 29, 1956, Israel launched the Sinai Campaign. In a single week the Egyptian bases were destroyed, the seaway to Elat was opened, and the Sinai Peninsula, together with the Gaza Strip, was occupied. At the same time, by prearrangement, France and Great Britain tried to take control of the Suez Canal. On November 2, the UN General Assembly called for a cease-fire and a withdrawal of armed forces. Under heavy pressure the Israeli government agreed to withdraw its troops, provided the UN Emergency Force took over. Israel demanded free waterways and the cessation of infiltration, and it insisted that the Egyptian Army stay out of the Gaza Strip. The United States, on the other hand, demanded unconditional withdrawal on Israel's part. Under American pressure Israel complied with the United Nations resolution and withdrew its forces from Sinai in January, 1957, even though its own conditions had been accepted only in part.

In February, 1957, successive resolutions were adopted by the United Nations ordering Israel to withdraw from the Gaza Strip and Sharm el-Sheikh. Although American public opinion was on Israel's side, the United States government threatened Israel with sanctions. Only after some implied promises were received did Israel agree, in March, 1957, to withdraw from the Gaza Strip and Sharm el-Sheikh. United Nations forces took over border posts in both places to prevent infiltration and to assure the free passage of ships through the Gulf of 'Aqaba (Elat).

Years of Tension and Growth. The Sinai Campaign brought quiet to Israel's borders with Egypt. Eden's suggestion of Israeli territorial concessions as the price for a peace settlement with the Arabs was abandoned. Nonetheless, long-range threats resulting from the arms race continued to loom large. Israel's relations with France became closer after the Sinai Campaign; its relations with Germany were broadened to include military cooperation despite reservations and opposition from a substantial segment of Israeli public opinion. On May 7, 1957, after much deliberation and not without misgivings, Israel announced its basic support of the Eisenhower Doctrine for the protection of Middle Eastern states from Communist encroachments on their independence.

The burden placed by the Sinai Campaign on Israel's economy was aggravated by a wave of immigration from Poland, Hungary, and, later, also Romania. On the other hand, the opening of the port of Elat stimulated the development of the Negev. An oil pipeline was laid between Elat and B'er Sheva', and a railway line to B'er Sheva' was finished. At the same time, the biggest drainage enterprise in the Hula area, begun in 1951, was completed. Industry made great strides, and there was a steep rise in income and production.

Internal tensions were now focused mainly on relations with Germany, particularly Israeli military cooperation with Bonn. This dissension provoked two brief Cabinet crises in 1958–59, arising from disagreements between the Prime Minister and the left-wing Ahdut 'Avoda. Conflicts on the issue of religion and state also increased, and on July 1, 1958, the Cabinet ministers representing the religious parties resigned from the Government because of disagreement on the issue of the proper definition of "Who Is a Jew?"

Israel was not directly involved in the major events of the Middle East during 1958. The Iraqi Revolution in July, the instability in Lebanon, and the unrest in Jordan kept Israel alert but passive. Reluctantly, it briefly permitted a British airlift to Jordan, aimed at keeping Jordan independent, to fly over Israeli territory, but pointed out that any alteration in Jordan's status would elicit Israeli action.

The establishment, on Feb. 1, 1958, of the United Arab Republic (UAR) by Egypt and Syria posed a long-range threat to Israel's security. In comparison with this major event, border incidents (Jordan on Mount Scopus; Syria) were of secondary importance. In view of the new weapons such as missiles that had made their appearance in the Middle East, Israel's main concern was the maintenance of a balance of power.

The year 1959 began with ill omens for Mapai in domestic politics. Knesset Speaker Yosef *Sprinzak of Mapai was succeeded by Nahum Nir of Ahdut 'Avoda, who was elected by a wall-to-wall coalition including Mapai. In the elections to the Histadrut held in May, Mapai showed a slight decline in strength, from 37.7 per cent to 35.7 per cent of the total vote, while the vote for the left-wing parties, except the Communists, increased by 3.5 per cent. In the Knesset elections of November, however, a number of factors—popular support of the government's security policy, an economic boom, fear of the exploitation of ethnic tensions by extremists, and the show of a united leadership—combined to secure a victory for Mapai. The party polled 38.2 per cent of the total vote; Herut came next with 13.6 per cent. The left-wing parties lost strength, and the General Zionists received only 6.1 per cent of the total vote. The lists submitted by the immigrant communities failed. The elections reflected a new structure of Israeli society in which

Mapai reduced the traditional influence of the right-wing groups in the middle class. The election results encouraged Ben-Gurion's plan to restructure the country's electoral system by substituting the constituency system of elections for the existing one of proportional representation. This proposal met with opposition outside Mapai, particularly from the smaller parties, which feared that such an electoral reform would end or at least weaken their Knesset representation.

However, foreign affairs demanded first priority. A dispute in the demilitarized zone south of Lake Kinneret elicited retaliatory action by Israeli troops (Feb. 1, 1960). Meanwhile, the new government made an effort to present Israel's case to the planned Big Four Summit Conference; Ben-Gurion went to the United States to meet with Pres. Dwight D. Eisenhower. On that visit, Ben-Gurion also met German Chancellor Konrad Adenauer; the details of their talks were not disclosed, but there was some agreement on German aid to Israel. Later, in March, 1960, Ben-Gurion met British Prime Minister Harold Macmillan. Links with France were strengthened during a meeting with Gen. Charles de Gaulle in June, 1960. Ben-Gurion also paid visits to Brussels and The Hague. During the year Israel's activities in the new African states also made headway. Israeli specialists were sent to African states, and many Africans came to study and be trained in Israel (*see* FOREIGN AID PROGRAM OF ISRAEL).

The unrest within Mapai that had made itself felt since the late 1950s exploded not in a public confrontation but in the so-called Lavon affair. Defense Minister Lavon, who had resigned in 1955, asked Ben-Gurion to clear him of the responsibility for the security mishap that had occurred in 1954. New evidence, not known in 1955, had come to light, tending to exonerate Lavon. He accused persons affiliated with the army and the Defense Ministry of attempting to discredit him in his position as Minister. Ben-Gurion refused to clear Lavon without a judicial investigation, but on Dec. 25, 1960, a seven-member Cabinet committee found that Lavon had not given the controversial order in 1954. On Jan. 31, 1961, Ben-Gurion resigned as Prime Minister. Mapai attempted to appease him by removing Lavon from his post as secretary-general of the Histadrut, accusing him of harming the party by his political campaign methods.

The resolution was carried by a small majority (about 60 per cent) and caused a rift in the party. On Feb. 9, 1961, Lavon resigned from his Histadrut position. When Ben-Gurion was ready to form a new Government, most of his former coalition partners refused to cooperate, and new elections were called for.

The Lavon dispute in Mapai had wider implications. It exacerbated relations between the older leadership and some "young pretenders." The problem of the status of the Histadrut became acute; Ben-Gurion's leadership was challenged. Outside Mapai, the Lavon affair and the premature elections resulted in a union between the General Zionists and the Progressive party; together they established the *Liberal party (Apr. 25, 1961).

The elections to the Fifth Knesset were held after a bitter campaign in which the issue was the moral fitness of Mapai to rule the country and the alleged "threats to democracy." There was no landslide, nor was there a deep split in Mapai. Mapai lost about 4 per cent of its former strength, and the Liberals gained about 3 per cent. After an abortive attempt to present a united front to dictate conditions to Mapai, Levi Eshkol formed a coalition Government headed by

Ben-Gurion and based on Mapai, the National Religious party, and Ahdut 'Avoda. Amid the debate on the Lavon affair and widespread protests against increasingly close ties with Germany, Adolf Eichmann was captured in Argentina and brought to trial in Jerusalem (*see* EICHMANN TRIAL).

The direct threat to Israel's borders was eased when Syria seceded from the UAR on Sept. 29, 1961. At the same time, the UAR Army became entangled in the Yemenite civil war (September, 1962). This, too, eased the threat to Israel, but the arms race, particularly in missiles, remained a source of considerable alarm. Israel's chief concern was to maintain the balance of power in the face of increasing Arab armament. In September, 1962, the United States government approved the sale to Israel of Hawk ground-to-air defensive missiles. This was a change from the previous policy, which had been to refrain from extending direct military aid to Israel.

Israel's relations with Germany were ambiguous. In March, 1963, the Israeli government launched a public campaign to urge the German government to halt the service of German scientists in the UAR. At the same time, relations between Germany and Israel were made closer by economic and military assistance.

In April, 1963, the UAR, Syria, and Iraq signed a manifesto in Cairo calling for an expanded United Arab Republic, including all three countries. The "liberation of Palestine" was proclaimed as the patriotic duty of the Arabs. In response, Ben-Gurion demanded a Soviet-American guarantee of Israel's frontiers or, failing that, a mutual defense pact between Israel and the United States.

In an attempt to stabilize Israel's economy and to direct it toward exports, Finance Minister Eshkol announced a new economic policy on Feb. 9, 1962. The Israeli pound was devalued to 33 cents. The system of multiple rates of exchange was abolished, as were export premiums, subsidies for currency transfer, and most import levies. The devaluation had some beneficial effects on the economy. During 1962 there was an increase in exports. The trend toward devaluation was halted in the second half of 1963 because of monetary expansion and intensive economic activity. During the year there was some anxiety that the European Economic Community (EEC) might strangle Israel's exports (*see* EUROPEAN COMMON MARKET AND ISRAEL). Israel's application for special status within the EEC was not granted. The significance of Israel's relations with the EEC was heightened by the *Arab boycott.

On Apr. 23, 1963, President Ben Zvi died. On May 21, Sh'neur Zalman *Shazar, of Mapai, was elected President. Despite rumors about Ben-Gurion's discontent with the party leadership, his resignation, on June 16, came as a surprise to the public. Eshkol, who was considered his natural successor, introduced a new Cabinet and received a vote of confidence on June 24. In addition to the Premiership, Eshkol assumed the portfolio of Defense. The younger supporters of Ben-Gurion criticized Eshkol's appointments and his national and party policies.

Israel's relations with the great powers were focused on maintaining the balance of power and its defensive strength. Premier Eshkol's official visits to the United States in May and June, 1964, and to France in June and July, were made with this purpose in view. An American plan to cooperate in a huge program of desalination of seawater was suggested by Pres. Lyndon B. Johnson.

The early 1960s were years of considerable economic growth owing to capital inflow and full employment. Wages and salaries rose swiftly, and the inflationary trend hindering exports did not stop after 1962. A project to settle Galilee was initiated; a new town, Karmiel, was inaugurated in October, 1964. The 25th Zionist *Congress, held in Jerusalem from Dec. 30, 1964, to Jan. 11, 1965, urged Israel to take a more active part in the effort to assure Jewish survival in the Diaspora.

An Arab summit conference held in September, 1964, established a joint command against Israel and gave official recognition to the Palestine Liberation Army, whose recruits were to be drafted from among the Arab refugees (see TERRORIST ORGANIZATIONS, ARAB). A showdown with the Arab states was narrowly avoided in the spring of 1965, when the Arabs threatened to attack Israel on the inauguration of the National Water Carrier Project. But the Arab intention to divert the tributaries of the Jordan still posed a threat.

Another crisis developed in Israel's relations with West Germany. After Germany stopped the shipment of arms to Israel (which had continued for some years), German public opinion forced the German government to establish diplomatic relations with Israel, thus endangering its ties with the Arab states (March, 1965).

The year 1965 was a stormy one in Israeli politics. The Mapai conference held in February rejected Ben-Gurion's demand that the inquiry into the Lavon affair be reopened. It decided on an election bloc (Labor Alignment) with Ahdut 'Avoda, temporarily shelving the proposed reform of the proportional system of elections. In May, Ben-Gurion declared Eshkol unfit for the office of Prime Minister and suggested that he himself take the helm again, but the majority in Mapai's Central Committee rejected him. After some hesitation, Ben-Gurion's supporters decided to stand for election on an independent list, *R'shimat Po'ale Yisrael (Rafi), adopting as their main slogan "Constituency System of Elections." On the right, there was an alignment between the Liberals and Herut, the *Gahal bloc, causing a split in the Liberal party, whose minority formed the Independent Liberal party. The Communist party split into two factions. The New Communists, headed by Meir Wilner and Tawfik Toubi, most of whom were Arabs, leaned toward the Chinese Communists. The Israel Communist party (Maki), led by Sh'muel Mikunis and Moshe S'ne, supported the Soviet Union but defended the just national aspirations of the Jewish people.

In September, 1965, elections were held in the Histadrut. The Ma'arakh (Alignment) barely managed to keep its majority (50.8 per cent); Gahal was second, with 15.2 per cent, and Rafi polled only 12.11 per cent. Elections to the Knesset were held in November. The Alignment received 36.7 per cent of the votes cast; Gahal, which offered an alternative, received 21.3 per cent; and Rafi polled only 7.9 per cent. It was clear that the combination of "democracy," "stability," and "soberness" represented by the Alignment appealed to wide strata of the population.

During 1965 Israel lost Martin *Buber, its preeminent philosopher, and Moshe Sharett, its first Foreign Minister and second Prime Minister. The economic situation deteriorated because of an increase in salaries and wages, which the government was unable to resist in an election year. This deterioration was one of the major challenges facing the new government.

Despite the success of the Ma'arakh in the elections, Levi Eshkol's Government was slow to be formed and was completed only in January, 1966. The participation of Mapam was assured, but the National Religious party delayed its entry because of

apprehension over the power of the left bloc. The Government finally formed included the Ma'arakh, Mapam, the National Religious party, the Independent Liberals, and *Po'ale Agudat Israel. The opposition consisted of Gahal, Rafi, and the extreme left. Abba *Eban replaced Golda Meir as Minister of Foreign Affairs.

The new Government hoped to maintain a moderate line in international relations. The split in the Arab camp between the "conservatives" and the "revolutionaries," as reflected in the war in Yemen and in the appearance of such voices as that of the Tunisian President, Habib Bourguiba, gave rise to hopes that an agreement with the Arabs was possible. The "new line" was expressed in relation to the Israeli Arabs; at the end of 1966 military rule in the border areas settled by Arabs was replaced by civilian and police authorities. The Government also attempted to improve relations with the Soviet Union. A small number of immigrants from the U.S.S.R., arriving under the Unification of Families Plan, and an exchange of artists appeared to point to the possibility of rapprochement.

The Government continued to give special attention to relations with the United States. Discussions were held regarding American assistance for the project of seawater desalination in Israel. Military aid supplied by the United States increased in importance, and in February, 1966, the United States government announced the sale of tanks and planes to Israel. However, France was still considered the main supplier of armaments. Relations with West Germany were initiated after an exchange of diplomatic representatives between the two countries. In May, 1966, former Chancellor Konrad Adenauer visited Israel and was received with honors. That month an agreement was reached on a 25-year low-interest loan of 160,000,000 marks. The loan aroused opposition because of its terms and because of the difficult negotiations that had preceded it. President Shazar visited Latin America, and Prime Minister Eshkol visited Africa during the year.

The realities of Arab-Israeli relations did not match expectations. In 1966 there were increasing forays into Israel by Arab terrorist organizations, particularly *el-Fatah, for purposes of sabotage. The Syrian Revolution of February, 1966, resulted in the rise of the extreme Ba'ath faction. This faction aided the Arab terrorists and increased tension in the demilitarized zones. It also had the strong support of the Soviet Union, and thereafter any complaint concerning Syria made by Israel to the UN Security Council could expect a Soviet veto. When, in November, 1966, following several sabotage incidents, Israel undertook a reprisal action against Kafr Samu' in Jordan, it was sharply condemned by the Security Council.

The Government's primary activity was in the economic sphere. A slowing down of economic activity and a policy of deflation were designed to control inflation, regulate the labor force by transferring greater numbers of workers into productive branches of the economy, and reduce the deficit in the trade balance. Deflation succeeded in improving the balance of payments in 1966, but at the cost of a noticeable reduction in the growth of the national product (it rose by only 1.2 per cent, in comparison with 8.2 per cent in 1965). The number of unemployed rose to more than 30,000. Deflation also affected the institutions of higher learning, which had been at the height of their development. Deflation and unemployment, the diminishing number of immigrants, and dissatisfaction with the Government and the administration caused a moral crisis in Israel to the extent that doubts were raised concerning the future of the country. An increasing number of Israelis, many of them in the liberal professions, left the country. Many young people, dissatisfied with what they considered the narrow horizons of Israel, also emigrated.

This situation did not alter the Government. The Ma'arakh, responsible for guiding the State, did not succeed in uniting its component elements (Mapai and Ahdut 'Avoda) and appeared to lack decisiveness. However, no acceptable alternative appeared. Within the Herut party, a group split off, demanding more vigorous opposition to the Government, and formed the Free Center under the leadership of Sh'muel Tamir, a member of the Knesset.

Israel continued to maintain a close relationship with Diaspora Jewry, a relationship manifested in the dedication ceremonies for the new Knesset building in the summer of 1966. The award of the Nobel Prize for literature to Sh'muel Yoseph *Agnon added to the image of Israel's spiritual creativity. At the same time, however, there was increasing doubt about the ability of the Zionist movement to bring immigrants to Israel and to maintain the central position of Israel in the life of Diaspora Jewry.

*Six-day War and Its Aftermath. In May, 1967, Syria's vehement hatred of Israel, abetted by Soviet support, and the activities of the Arab terrorist groups induced the UAR's President Nasser to demand the withdrawal of the UN Emergency Force from the Sinai Peninsula and to concentrate troops there, close the Strait of Tiran, and prepare to go to war against Israel. The resulting crisis created an internal change in Israel. The moral crisis gave way to a spirit of rededication. A Government of National Unity was formed that, for the first time since the creation of the State, included the Herut party within the Gahal framework. Moshe Dayan, representing Rafi, became Minister of Defense. Jews all over the free world, shocked into action by the threat of a second holocaust, gave moral, financial, and volunteer support to the endangered Jewish State. This renewed identification of Diaspora Jewry with the State of Israel also caused the Jews of Israel to feel closer to their coreligionists in other lands.

The Six-day War of 1967 gave the Israeli armies control over the Sinai Peninsula, the entire western bank of the Jordan River, and the Gaulan Heights, thus removing the immediate threat to Israel. In contrast to the situation after the Sinai Campaign, Israel succeeded in resisting international pressures to withdraw from the cease-fire boundaries. This time the United States refused to go along with the Soviet demand for withdrawal, and attempts to force a decision against Israel in the UN General Assembly failed. For a time it even appeared as if the Arabs were ready to start negotiations with Israel. However, at the Khartoum Conference (August, 1967), they announced that they would make no peace with Israel and that they would not recognize it or enter into negotiations with it. Israel persevered in its demand for direct negotiations and for a peace treaty as prerequisites to any concrete discussion of future boundaries.

The General Assembly resolution of Nov. 22, 1967, summed up the United Nations debates in a call for recognition of Israel, secure and recognized boundaries, withdrawal from occupied areas, freedom of navigation, and a solution of the refugee problem—decisions subject to various interpretations. Gunnar Jarring, the Swedish Ambassador to the Soviet Union, was asked to serve as Mediator. Israel continued to uphold the principle of direct negotiations as the only way to peace.

The policy formulated by the Minister of Defense for the occupied areas was aimed at maintaining economic contact with these areas and providing self-government within them. Only Jerusalem was officially annexed by the State of Israel. Israel's victory in the war did not bring about the hoped-for peace with the Arab world. In the succeeding months the Arab states frequently violated the cease-fire agreement. Their rapid rearmament by the Soviet Union enabled them to resume their policy of intransigence. In October, 1967, the UAR attacked and sank the Israel warship "Elat" with rockets.

From time to time there were artillery battles at Suez. Sabotage groups of Palestinian Arabs continued to operate across the borders, but attempts to form fighting units among the Arab inhabitants of the occupied areas failed. After many battles, attempts to penetrate Israel along the Jordan River also failed. Arab sabotage groups were forced to content themselves with shelling settlements from across the borders and with laying mines. They then turned to acts of terrorism in population centers and on the airlines. These activities led to Israeli acts of reprisal, the most significant being the raid early in 1968 on the village of Karameh, Jordan, which had become a center for terrorists, and the raid late in the year against Beirut Airport.

Strict security measures and preparation for a possible resumption of full-scale war necessitated an increase in the size of the Israel Army and in the manufacture of war matériel. The embargo placed by France on the sale of planes to Israel on the eve of the Six-day War was extended in the winter of 1968–69 to cover all armaments. This development necessitated expansion of Israel's own war industry.

Postwar domestic affairs were marked by national and political unification. Despite differences of opinion on acute and basic issues, the Government of National Unity that had been formed in June, 1967, continued in office. In January, 1968, Mapai, Ahdut 'Avoda, and Rafi united to form the *Israel Labor party, which together with Mapam established a coalition in 1969. Simultaneously, debate erupted over the question of the extent of Israeli withdrawal from the areas conquered in the war, in exchange for peace. A second debate concerned policies in occupied areas prior to a permanent peace settlement. One group demanded the establishment of settlements and army bases in, and economic cooperation with, these territories. Others argued for the retention of distinctions between the pre-June, 1967, areas of Israel and the occupied areas.

The war and the contributions and investments that followed, in both the military and the civilian spheres, did away with deflation. There was a labor shortage. The business sector again began to grow, but prices were kept stable to a degree. The defense budget expanded to almost 20 per cent of the national product. Maintaining the occupied areas also involved expenditures, but these were kept down by a policy of "open bridges" to the eastern bank of the Jordan. Simultaneously, development projects were undertaken, the most significant being the laying of a 42-inch pipeline from Elat to Ashk'lon to carry oil from the Red Sea to the Mediterranean.

The war and the response of Diaspora Jewry brought a sizable immigration of Jews from Western countries. Volunteers and students arrived, as did professional people and businessmen. The government took over the task of immigrant absorption from the Jewish Agency. Following a preliminary meeting in August, 1967, a conference of Jewish financiers and economists was convened in April, 1968, to consider additional investment possibilities of $300,000,000 to develop Israel's industry. The devaluation of the pound sterling in November, 1967, forced Israel to devalue its currency accordingly. Meanwhile, Israel's attempts to join the European Common Market were complicated by opposition from France.

Despite the pressing security, political, and economic problems educational reforms were undertaken in 1969, with the goal of transferring the last two grades of the eight-grade elementary schools to an intermediate level, expanding the Free and Compulsory Education Law by degrees, raising teaching standards, and grading classes according to the level of the students. The period following the war also saw the initiation of a television system,

In 1968 Zalman Shazar was reelected President for five years. In 1969 Prime Minister Eshkol died; Golda Meir assumed the Premiership and formed a Government similar to the one headed by her predecessor.

I. KOLATT

ISRAEL, LAND OF. *See* PALESTINE.

ISRAEL ACADEMY OF SCIENCES AND HUMANITIES.

Israeli scholarly and scientific body. At the end of 1958 Prime Minister David *Ben-Gurion, on government authorization, nominated 22 outstanding Israeli scholars and scientists to serve as a preparatory committee for the establishment of an Academy of Sciences and Humanities. A year later these 22 scholars became the founding members of the academy and elected Martin *Buber its first president. In June, 1961, the *Knesset passed the Israel Academy of Sciences and Humanities Law.

The principal aims and functions of the academy are (1) to have a membership of leading scholars in the sciences and humanities who are residents of Israel; (2) to foster and promote work in the sciences and humanities; (3) to advise the government on activities relating to research and scientific planning of national importance; (4) to maintain contact with similar bodies abroad and to represent Israeli sciences and humanities in international bodies and at international conferences; and (5) to publish works contributing to the advancement of the sciences and humanities. Members are elected for life by the annual general membership meeting. The academy is composed of two sections, sciences and humanities. The number of members in each section may not exceed 25, but members above the age of 75 are not counted in that maximum. At the end of 1968 the academy had 48 members, of whom 8 were over the age limit. The academy may admit nonresident members, but it has not yet done so.

The seat of the academy is in Jerusalem. The president of the academy is appointed by the President of the State of Israel (*see* PRESIDENCY OF ISRAEL) on the academy's recommendation for a term of three years, which is renewable. Buber, the first president, resigned in 1962 on the ground of ill health and was succeeded by Prof. Aharon *Katzir-Katchalsky, who was appointed for a second term in 1965, to be succeeded in turn in 1968 by Prof. Gershom *Scholem. Prof. Arye Dvoretsky is vice-president of the academy.

The academy has engaged in and supported, *inter alia*, the following research projects: (1) in the sciences, the flora and fauna of the region and prehistoric excavations and geological survey of the Lower Pleistocene of the central Jordan Valley; and (2) in the humanities, source materials of Jewish history, thought, and religion, and poetry. In the 1960s

it was engaged, in cooperation with the Jewish Theological Seminary of America, in the preparation of a concordance to the Jerusalem Talmud and, in cooperation with the French National Center for Scientific Research, in a survey of Hebrew paleography.

Recent publications of the academy, in addition to the *Proceedings of the Israel Academy of Sciences and Humanities* (in Hebrew and in English), which contains the lectures delivered in the academy, include the first two of the eight volumes of the *Flora Palaestina* (1966), by Michael Zohary; several reports on the excavations at Ubadia, in the central Jordan Valley; Prof. Hayim Jefim Schirmann's *Shirim Hadashim MehaG'niza B'Mitzrayim* (1965, *New Poems from the Genizah in Egypt*); and Solomon Maimon's *Giv'at HaMore*, edited by Samuel Hugo *Bergmann and Nathan *Rotenstreich.

The academy represents Israel in numerous scientific bodies and activities abroad and assists in organizing international scientific activities in Israel. In 1968 the following scholars were members of the academy:

Humanities	*Sciences*
Efrayim E. Urbach, chairman	David Ernst *Bergmann, chairman
Hanokh Albeck	Samuel Agmon
David Ayalon	Joshua Bar-Hillel
Roberto Bachi	Yitzhak Berenblum
Yitzhak Baer	Felix Bergmann
Zeev Ben-Hayim	Abraham Cogan
Samuel Hugo Bergmann	Solly G. Cohen
Joshua Blau	Amos De-Shalit
Ben-Zion *Dinur	Arye Dvoretsky
Sh'muel N. Eisenstadt	Georg Haas
Benjamin *Mazar	Ephraim *Katchalski
Dan Patinkin	Aharon Katzir-Katchalsky
Sh'lomo Pines	Isaac C. Michaelson
Jacob Polotsky	Yuval Ne'eman
Joshua Prawer	Franz Ollendorff
Nathan Rotenstreich	Hayim L. Pekeris
Dov Sadan	Y'huda Leo Picard
Samuel Sambursky	Marcus Reiner
Hayim Jefim Schirmann	Nathan Rosen
Gershom Scholem	Yigal Talmi
Jacob L. Talmon	Hayim Ernst Wertheimer
Gad Tedeschi	Michael Zohary
Naphtali H. *Tur-Sinai	Hermann *Zondek
Hayim Wirszubski	
Yigael *Yadin	

M. AVIDOR

ISRAEL AND THE DIASPORA. The specific character of the Jewish *Diaspora crystallized following the destruction of the Second Jewish Commonwealth in C.E. 70. Prior to that time the Jewish dispersion was not essentially different from that of other peoples, such as the ancient Greeks or, in our own day, the Armenians, Irish, and Chinese, who also had or have a diaspora. A substantial segment of Jewry dwelt outside their Homeland, but the Holy Land was the focus of their lives.

Diaspora and Exile. Although the destruction of Judea by the Romans in C.E. 70 uprooted the greater part of the Jewish population from the soil of Palestine, the Holy Land never remained entirely without Jews, nor did it lose its character as the religious, historic, traditional, and spiritual center of the

Jewish people. Nevertheless, it may be said that from that time on dispersion became *Galut—banishment or exile. The traditional Jewish attitude to Galut is negative: exile is regarded as an abnormal and temporary state. For many centuries Jews, declaring that "for our sins we have been expelled from our Land," prayed several times each day for the return of the people of Israel to their Homeland.

*Assimilation, encouraged by the *emancipation of the Jews in the 18th and 19th centuries, sought to overcome the sense of exile by promoting the unreserved identification of the Jews with the countries in which they resided. It was even asserted that the Diaspora was a blessing rather than a curse, offering as it did a unique opportunity for the dissemination of the concept of monotheism, which the Jews had the privilege and obligation to spread among the nations of the world. In spite of this "mission" theory and similar ideologies, the emotional attachment of the great majority of the Jews to the land of their fathers remained strong. It was this attachment rather than rational arguments that prompted Herzl to prefer Palestine to Argentina or any other place and brought to naught the *East Africa scheme and the various Territorialist plans (see TERRITORIALISM).

Zionist Work for the Diaspora. Zionism, in a sense, normalized the Diaspora inasmuch as it restored to the dispersion a center, if not one actually in existence, then at least one for which to work and strive. The *Basle Program referred to the tasks of the Zionist movement in the Diaspora, listing among the methods for the attainment of the Zionist goal "the strengthening of national Jewish feeling and consciousness" and "organizing the whole of Jewry in suitable local and general bodies." Already in Herzl's time, an increasingly important role was given to what was called *Gegenwartsarbeit*, or work for the improvement of the immediate situation of those Jews in the Diaspora who were not yet ready or able to emigrate to Palestine. *Gegenwartsarbeit* eventually came to include also the struggle for Jewish civil rights. Work in and for the Diaspora had a prominent place in the program adopted by the *Helsingfors Conference of Russian Zionists in 1906. However, some leaders of political Zionism, among them David *Wolffsohn, did not favor this approach; nor was the attitude of organized Zionism to the Diaspora uniform and consistent in later years, when it ranged from Jacob *Klatzkin's *negation of the Diaspora to Itzhak *Grünbaum's bloc of national minorities, which the Zionists formed with other nationalities in the Polish Sejm (Parliament) for the defense of Jewish rights and interests. *Ahad Ha'Am, the proponent and ideologist of spiritual Zionism, who aimed at a spiritual-cultural center in Palestine rather than a political Jewish State, saw in the Diaspora a permanent feature of Jewish life. However, he did not regard it as equal to Eretz Yisrael. His views on the Diaspora were succinctly summed up by his disciple and translator, Sir Leon *Simon: "To Ahad Ha'Am diaspora life, though inescapable, is at best a *pis aller* [makeshift arrangement], national autonomy in the diaspora is a chimera and the only way to preserve a distinctly Jewish type of life outside *Eretz Yisrael* is to build up a strong Jewish national center in *Eretz Yisrael*." Herein lies the fundamental difference between Ahad Ha'Am's views on the Diaspora and those of the Jewish historian Simon *Dubnow, who propounded a philosophy of *Galut nationalism, or autonomism, primarily for the masses of Eastern European Jewry.

The State of Israel and the Diaspora. The *Balfour Declaration in 1917, the confirmation of the British *Mandate for Palestine by the League of Nations in 1922, and the opening of the *Hebrew University of Jerusalem in 1925 were milestones in the crystallization of the Jewish national and cultural center in Palestine.

It is obvious that the restoration of Jewish statehood had a profound effect on the relationship between the center in Israel and the Diaspora. The tasks of the *World Zionist Organization (WZO), which through the establishment of the State had been divested of its central political purpose, were redefined in the so-called Jerusalem Program adopted by the 23d Zionist *Congress in 1951 and incorporated in the new constitution of the WZO in 1960: "The consolidation of the State of Israel, the ingathering of the exiles in *Eretz Israel*, and the fostering of the unity of the Jewish people."

The third part of this three-point program refers to the relationship between Israel and the Diaspora. In stressing the unity of the Jewish people, the program clearly opposes a certain ideological trend that emerged in Israel soon after the establishment of the State, namely, that of numerically insignificant but sometimes vociferous groups, such as the *Canaanites and Semitic Action, which asserted that the Israeli nation was not identical with the Jewish people abroad and should seek close lies with other Middle Eastern countries rather than with Diaspora Jewry. More general than this extreme ideology was an attitudinal development manifested by some of Israel's young *Sabra generation in a lack of understanding for, and interest in, the Jewish people outside Israel. To prevent this type of estrangement between Israeli Jews and those of the Diaspora, a special subject, "Jewish consciousness," was introduced into the curriculum of Israeli schools to acquaint the younger generation with the cultural heritage of Judaism, to stress the bonds between Israel and world Jewry, and to foster feelings of Jewish solidarity (see EDUCATION IN ISRAEL).

On the other hand, it is inconsistent with the classic Zionist ideology to depart from the dualism between Eretz Yisrael and the Diaspora and to assert that American Jewry, instead of being part of the Diaspora (a free, rich, and flourishing Diaspora, to be sure, but a Diaspora nevertheless), is a Jewish center parallel to Israel and analogous to the ancient Jewish center in Babylonia. In Zionist opinion, the graphic symbol of the Jewish position is a circle with Israel as its center rather than an ellipse with two foci, Israel and the United States.

Diaspora Support for Israel. Apart from a small minority—radical assimilationists such as the American Council for Judaism, ultra-Orthodox circles such as the *N'ture Karta, and Jewish Communists—all sections of the Jewish people, whether organized Zionists or non-Zionists, have closely identified themselves with Israel. The emergence of the State of Israel not only put an end to the tragedy of Jewish homelessness but also gave the individual Jew a sense of security which he had not possessed in the past. The Jew was glad to know that there was a country ready and willing to receive him, if for any reason he should be forced to leave his present domicile. The State of Israel has been a source of pride to Diaspora Jewry. It has enhanced the Jews' self-respect and improved their standing in the eyes of gentiles. It now became possible, by pointing to the farmers, workers, and soldiers of Israel, to give the lie to allegations that the Jews were a people of businessmen and intellectuals, averse to physical work and lacking in military prowess.

More often than not, it is a far cry from emotional attachment such as this to real commitment involving actual preparedness for *'Aliya (*immigration) or at least for that of one's children, readiness to make business investments in the Jewish State, regular visits to Israel, and so on. The stimulation and promotion of 'Aliya, one of the main tasks of Zionism, is one of the most important functions of the WZO, but those who think, like David *Ben-Gurion, that every individual Zionist is duty-bound to settle in Israel, are a small minority.

Ben-Gurion's Views. Ben-Gurion's views brought him into conflict with the *American Jewish Committee and its president, Jacob *Blaustein, who was anxious to clarify the relationship between the people of Israel and Diaspora Jewry. In an exchange of views at a luncheon in Jerusalem on Aug. 23, 1950, Ben-Gurion said:

> The Jews of the United States, as a community and as individuals, have only one political attachment and that is to the United States of America. They owe no political allegiance to Israel. In the first statement which the representative of Israel made before the United Nations after her admission to that international organization [he said that] the State of Israel represents and speaks only in behalf of its own citizens and in no way presumes to represent or speak in the name of the Jews who are citizens of any other country. We, the people of Israel, have no desire and no intention to interfere in any way with the internal affairs of Jewish communities abroad....

Although the Prime Minister reiterated Israel's need for immigrants, particularly from the United States, who could contribute a spirit of enterprise and technical know-how, he said that "the decision as to whether they wish to come—permanently or temporarily—rests with the free discretion of each American Jew himself." Ben-Gurion confirmed these views in a letter to Blaustein dated Oct. 2, 1956, and again in a joint statement, signed in Jerusalem by Blaustein and Ben-Gurion on Apr. 23, 1961, in which Ben-Gurion undertook "to do everything within his power to see to it that the agreement [of Aug. 23, 1950] is in future kept in spirit and in letter and to draw the attention of members of the Cabinet and other responsible officers of the Government of Israel to his desire that the spirit and content of the agreement be fully respected."

Zionist Obligations. The resolution of the 26th Zionist Congress in 1965 on "individual Zionist obligations" says on this subject: "The Zionist encourages 'aliya to Israel by the creation of a suitable public climate favorable to 'aliya, by practical aid to the Halutz Youth Movement, and by personal example." It does not expressly stipulate a duty of personal 'Aliya. The material aid given to Israel by the Diaspora and its share in the building of the country have been massive and magnificent. Through the channels of the *United Jewish Appeal in the United States, the United Israel Appeal (*Keren Ha-Yesod), the *Jewish National Fund, and *Youth 'Aliya, Diaspora Jewry, since the establishment of the State of Israel, has contributed over $1,000,000,000, exclusive of the considerable amounts collected and contributed for specific Israeli purposes by *Hadassah, the American Friends of the Hebrew University, *Magen David Adom, and many other groups.

Organizational Links. There are numerous organizational links between Israel and the Diaspora, since the Jewish National Fund, Keren HaYesod, Youth 'Aliya, and other institutions, whose common denominator is their affiliation with the WZO, operate and raise funds not only in the Diaspora but also in Israel. The principal link between these two parts of the Jewish people is the WZO, on whose governing bodies both the Diaspora and Israel are represented, with a relative preponderance of

Israelis despite the fact that Israel today (1968) accounts for no more than 17 per cent of world Jewry and for 35 per cent of the Sh'kalim (see SHEKEL) distributed prior to the 26th Zionist Congress. At the Congress, 180 regular delegates and 18 youth representatives were Israelis, as against 337 regular delegates, 54 youth representatives, and 74 representatives of Jewish communities and organizations in the Diaspora. Among the 103 full-fledged members of the Greater *Actions Committee there were 38 Israelis.

Non-Zionist bodies like *B'nai B'rith, the *World Jewish Congress, and the *World Federation of Sephardi Communities may also be regarded as links between both sections of the Jewish people, because they conduct activities in both Israel and the Diaspora.

The situation in the late 1960s was that the organizational links between Israel and the Diaspora in the field of religion were rather loose and weak, although not only the dominant Orthodox trend but also the beginnings of Conservative and Reform movements in Israel had some connection with their counterparts abroad, especially in the United States.

Law of *Return. The obligation which the State of Israel feels toward the Diaspora is exemplified by the Law of Return, passed by the *Knesset in 1950. It proclaims that every Jew, with few and insignificant exceptions, "has the right to come to Israel as an immigrant," to settle in the country, and to acquire Israeli citizenship by the mere act of immigration.

Israel and Jewish Culture. As far as Jewish culture is concerned, Israel in the 1960s was a center in the making rather than one already in existence. Its influence in most fields of Jewish cultural endeavor was not dominant. Perhaps this could not have been otherwise, in view of the short span of time since the establishment of national independence and of the urgent and grave political, economic, and social problems that beset the State and its citizens.

Question of Dual Loyalty. The accusation of dual loyalty was leveled against Diaspora Zionists from the beginning of the Zionist movement, more by Jewish opponents than by gentiles. It was based on a twofold misconception. First, it disregarded the fact that modern man has multiple loyalties, not only to his country but also to his family, religion, profession, and so on. It is to this argument that the famous dictum made by Louis D. *Brandeis in connection with Zionism, that "multiple loyalties are reprehensible only if they are inconsistent," referred. Normally, these loyalties are not inconsistent but can be reconciled and harmonized. Second, the misconception overlooked the fact that Zionism does not require of its adherents political allegiance to Israel. Only citizens of Israel owe allegiance to the State of Israel.

The ties of Diaspora Zionists and, for that matter, of Jews in general with Israel are spiritual, cultural, religious, and historical, not political. In this respect, the relationship of Diaspora Jewry to Israel is the same as that of Irish Americans to Ireland or of Swede-Finns to Sweden. The emergence of the State has normalized rather than complicated the situation.

While under normal conditions and in a democracy the question of dual loyalty should not arise, it may, and indeed did, arise in countries under totalitarian regimes, which, in many cases, consider interest in, support of, and especially emigration to any non-Communist country an act of disloyalty to the Communist state bordering on treason. This was repeatedly evidenced by the persecution of Zionism and Zionists in Communist countries. Before long anti-Zionism turned into anti-Semitism. The trials of Rudolf Slansky and his followers (*see* SLANSKY TRIAL) or of the Jewish physicians in the Soviet Union had distinct anti-Semitic overtones. Similarly, the anti-Israel campaign launched by Poland following the *Six-day War of 1967 rapidly developed into a full-fledged anti-Semitic drive. Therefore, if the question of Jewish dual loyalty arises in earnest in a totalitarian state that claims the undivided loyalty of its citizens, or perhaps also in special wartime situations, then the underlying cause is not Zionist affiliation, or the existence of the State of Israel, or ties with that State but the status of the Jews as a conspicuous and exposed minority.

Separation of Functions between the State and the WZO. As early as April, 1948, even before the Proclamation of the State, the Greater Actions Committee at its meeting in Tel Aviv attempted to delimit the field of activities of the WZO as against that of the State about to come into existence. The guiding principle was Hafrada (separation of functions). It was resolved that the *Jewish Agency should be active in four areas: immigration to Israel; absorption of immigrants, including Youth 'Aliya; agricultural settlement in Israel; and cultural and organizational activities in the Diaspora. All other functions previously performed by the Jewish Agency were henceforth to devolve on the State. The idea was to give the WZO a well-defined sphere of activity and to avoid over-lapping and the duplication of effort.

The Law on the Status of the World Zionist Organization-the Jewish Agency. In 1952, in order to clarify and enhance the standing of the WZO, the Knesset passed the Law on the Status of the World Zionist Organization–the Jewish Agency. The first articles of this law are quoted here because they are of a declaratory nature and shed light not only on the relationship between the State of Israel and the WZO as such but also on that between the State and the Diaspora as a whole. They also define what may be called the Jewish mission of the State:

  1. The State of Israel regards itself as a creation of the whole Jewish people and, in accordance with its laws, its gates are open to every Jew who desires to immigrate to it.
  2. Since its foundation fifty years ago, the World Zionist Organization has stood at the head of the movement of the Jewish people and its efforts to realize the vision of the generations to return to its Homeland, and, with the assistance of other Jewish circles and bodies, it has borne the chief responsibility for the establishment of the State of Israel.
  3. The World Zionist Organization, which is also the Jewish Agency for Palestine, shall deal, as hitherto, with immigration and direct the projects of immigrant absorption and settlement in the State.
  4. The State of Israel recognizes the World Zionist Organization as the authorized agency which shall continue to work in the State of Israel for the development and the colonization of the country, for the absorption of immigrants from the Diaspora, and for the co-ordination of the activities in Israel of Jewish institutions and associations operating in these fields.

The law recognized the Zionist *Executive as a legal person. It specified that the details of the status of the WZO and the form of its collaboration with the *government of Israel should be determined by a special agreement to be entered into by both parties. This agreement, concluded on July 26, 1954, defines the tasks of the Zionist Executive, elaborating rather than changing the previous terms, as follows:

The organizing of immigration abroad and the transfer of immigrants and their property to Israel; cooperation in the absorption of immigrants in Israel; youth immigration; agricultural settlement in Israel; the acquisition and improvement of land in Israel by the institutions of the Zionist Organization, the Jewish National Fund and the Keren HaYesod; participation in the establishment and the expansion of development enterprises in Israel; the encouragement of private capital investments in Israel; assistance to cultural enterprises and institutions of higher education in Israel; the mobilization of resources for financing these activities; the coordination of the activities in Israel of Jewish institutions and organizations acting within the limits of these functions using public funds.

Coordination Board. The agreement also exempted the Executive from certain taxes and enjoined the government of Israel to consult the Executive in regard to legislation affecting the functions of the Jewish Agency before such legislation was submitted to the Knesset. For the purpose of coordinating activities between the government of Israel and the Zionist Executive in all spheres to which the agreement applies, a special Coordination Board was established, composed of an even number of members, half of whom are ministers of state appointed by the Israeli government and half members of the Zionist Executive.

In practice, however, this arrangement did not work as smoothly as envisaged in the Status Law and in the agreement. The Zionist Executive did not always receive the recognition and consideration which it thought was due the Zionist movement, partly, at least, owing to the view of Prime Minister Ben-Gurion, who, equating Zionism with 'Aliya, did not hold Diaspora Zionism in great esteem. Ben-Gurion even went to such lengths as to compare the WZO to a scaffolding which was essential only as long as the building was under construction.

A distinct change occurred under his successor, Prime Minister Levi *Eshkol, who for many years had combined the office of Minister of Finance of Israel with the post of head of the Land Settlement Department of the Jewish Agency and had always been an outspoken champion of the WZO. This positive attitude found tangible expression in a joint declaration of the government and the Executive of the WZO, published in March, 1964, which stated: "The Government and the Executive consider the strengthening of the Zionist spirit and action amongst the Jewish people in the Diaspora as a matter of joint responsibility, and therefore the Government is vitally interested in the Executive's program of action and will extend full assistance to its implementation."

These developments, occurring in the mid-1960s, augured well for the future and there was reason for hope that the collaboration between the government of the State of Israel and the Zionist movement, as the principal representative of Diaspora Jewry, would henceforth be smooth and fruitful.

A. ZWERGBAUM

ISRAEL ATOMIC ENERGY COMMISSION. *See* ATOMIC RESEARCH IN ISRAEL.

ISRAEL BONDS. *See* STATE OF ISRAEL BONDS.

ISRAEL BROADCASTING SERVICE. The first broadcasting station in Palestine was opened in Jerusalem in April, 1936, as the Palestine Broadcasting Service. Administered by the British Mandatory regime (*see* MANDATE FOR PALESTINE), it had

Educational television is emphasized by the Israel Broadcasting Service. [Israel Information Services]

a British director of programs and subdirectors for a Hebrew Department, an Arabic Department, and a Music Section. The English programs consisted of news, features, and children's programs. The Hebrew and Arabic Departments were organized along similar lines. The Music Section prepared programs mainly for listeners from Western countries, while "Oriental" music was supplied by a special ensemble. In the 12 years of its existence, the Palestine Broadcasting Service instituted regular weekly symphony concerts at the Jerusalem YMCA, formed a Choral Society with members from all communities, organized a Jewish Music Month, and fostered local talent.

When the British Mandate ended and the State of Israel was established in 1948, the service split into the Jordanian station of Ramallah and the Kol Yisrael (Voice of Israel) Broadcasting Service, the latter remaining in its former building in Jerusalem. Kol Yisrael basically continued in organization and structure where the Hebrew and Music Departments had been left in 1948, but in the 1950s it developed an impressive scheme of exchanges with broadcasting stations all over the world. It became a member of the European Union of Broadcasting Services. As of 1968 Israel was a member of the Executive of the Union's Radio Committee.

Administration. Kol Yisrael was a department of the Prime Minister's Office until June, 1965, when the *Knesset set up a Broadcasting Authority to direct the operations of Israel's radio (and later also television) broadcasting services. The Authority has a five-man Board of Directors (in 1970 its Chairman was Hayim *Yahil) which decides on the policies of the broadcasting service, prepares a budget, and supervises performance. The Board is guided in the discharge of its functions by a Council of 31 members, appointed by the President of Israel on *government recommendation after consultation with representative public bodies and educational institutions. By 1969 the Council had set up five program committees: literary, artistic, and drama; musical; educational and scientific; linguistic; and Judaism and the Israeli way of life. The 1966–67 budget for the Authority was IL17,610,000, to be covered by license fees, advertisement and announcement fees, grants, and public performances. In 1968 there was a development budget of IL940,000 to erect a new Broadcasting House in Jerusalem. In addition to its old Jerusalem headquarters, Kol Yisrael also had small studios in Tel Aviv.

Radio Services. Since the *Six-day War of 1967, Israel has been broadcasting daily on four networks for a total of 350 hours

a week in 11 languages. Each day there are special broadcasts (in simple Hebrew, French, English, Romanian, Moroccan Arabic, Yiddish, and Ladino) to acquaint newcomers with Israel and its problems. There are also daily Arabic programs (consisting mainly of information and political commentary but also including entertainment); overseas programs (in 10 languages, including Russian), beamed at Europe and Africa; and a weekly program for North America, prepared with the cooperation of the *Jewish Agency. In addition, Muslim and Christian religious services are broadcast. Kol Yisrael has its own symphony and chamber orchestras, which frequently make their broadcasts from *development towns and kibbutzim (*see* KIBBUTZ).

Television. The introduction of television broadcasting had been discussed in Israel as early as 1960 (early advocates included Theodore *Kollek and Abba *Eban), but it encountered stiff opposition from those who emphasized the high cost of TV, as well as from others who feared that television would ruin Israeli patterns of living, debase culture, and lower tastes. There was considerable opposition also on religious grounds. Still, in 1961 crowds flocked to view closed-circuit broadcasts of the *Eichmann trial. Several years later, the Rothschild Foundation agreed to sponsor an educational television project for schools. By 1965 it had become obvious that the public would welcome television: by then there were some 20,000 TV sets in the country, tuned in to Arab broadcasts from neighboring Syria, Lebanon, and the United Arab Republic. In March, 1967, the Cabinet finally approved plans for general television in which advice was sought from experts in other countries. The execution of these plans received unexpected impetus from the Six-day War, when prompt action had to be taken to counteract the potential influence of Arab hate broadcasts among the population of Israeli-occupied territory. Early broadcasts included a televised concert of the *Israel Philharmonic Orchestra under Leonard Bernstein and the 1968 *Independence Day parade.

The task of heading Israeli television (with headquarters in Jerusalem) was given to Elihu Katz, a professor of mass communications from Chicago who had settled in Israel in 1963. In 1968 Israeli TV was organized under four departments: Arabic and Hebrew News, and Arabic and Hebrew General Programming. Some of the engineering, producing, and directing personnel came to Israel from the United States and Eastern Europe. By the summer of 1968 both Hebrew and Arabic news broadcasts were carried regularly; there were also documentaries and entertainment programs, including a comedy film series whose purpose was to show the face of Israel to the Arabs. In 1968 the Knesset enacted a law that placed television under the control of the Broadcasting Authority.

P. GRADENWITZ

ISRAEL DEFENSE FORCES (IDF). The armed forces of the State of Israel were constituted by an order of the provisional government dated May 31, 1948. They are the successor to the *Hagana, the underground defense organization of the *Yishuv (Jewish population of Palestine) under the *Mandate for Palestine, whose name is incorporated in the original Hebrew name of the Israel Defense Forces, Tz'va Hagana L'Yisrael, or Tzahal.

Character and Responsibilities. The Israel Defense Forces consists of a small nucleus of regular soldiers, who provide the higher echelon of command and staff and the operational,

Israeli paratroopers. [Israel Information Services]

logistical, administrative, technical, and training skeletons of its formations and units. The bulk of its manpower is recruited under the National Security Service Law, whose revised version was approved by the *Knesset in 1959. The law defined as persons of military age all men between the ages of 18 and 49 and women between the ages of 18 and 38 (the provisions of the law applicable to married women are cited below). The basic principle underlying the law was that all persons of military age were obliged to perform military service, usually first as conscripts and then in the reserves. Conscript service was to be 30 months for men and 24 (reduced to 20 in 1963) for women. On termination of conscript service, all persons were assigned to the reserves, where they were liable to draft for a period of 31 days every year to the age of 39 (for women, 34) and for 14 days each year thereafter until retirement age. Commissioned and noncommissioned officers were subject to 7 additional days of service each year.

Exemptions from military service were granted to all girls who could prove objection on religious grounds. Married women were exempted from conscript service and women with children from reserve duty as well. The Minister of Defense has the authority to grant exemptions from military service to certain categories of individuals, such as students at *Yeshivot. Although practically all the Druze citizens of Israel (*see* DRUZE COMMUNITY IN ISRAEL) perform military service, the law still was not enforced in the 1960s in the case of most Arab citizens (*see* ARABS IN ISRAEL).

Figures concerning the numerical strength of the IDF are not published; the ratio between the number of conscripts and that of reserves indicates that the great bulk of the IDF consists of reserves. All able-bodied Israelis, up to the age of 49, on completion of their conscript service serve in the reserves. The preponderance of reserves determines the character of the IDF, which is a citizens' army that considers itself a part of the people and not far removed from the life of the civilian population.

The highest military authority in the land is the chief of the General Staff, the only officer on active service to hold the rank of *rav aluf,* which is roughly equivalent to lieutenant general. He directs and coordinates a unified General Staff, with authority over land, sea, and air forces. The commanders of the latter two forces serve as advisers on the General Staff on matters pertaining to their respective branches. The air force and the navy have their own staffs dealing with their specific

problems. The uniforms of the three branches of service are distinctive, but rank designations, salary scales, general logistical provisions, and service rules are identical in all three.

In the 1960s the country was divided into three territorial commands for operational purposes: Northern, Center, and Southern. A separate nonterritorial command was in charge of all armored forces.

Special Organizations. In addition to the normal constituents of any modern army, such as artillery and the engineer and medical corps, Israel has created two organizations to fulfill the specific needs of the country, Nahal and Gadna', which have aroused particular interest among other young emerging nations.

Nahal (No'ar Halutzi Lohem, or Fighting Pioneer Youth), in addition to military training and operations, is charged with the agricultural training of its soldiers, rendering help to border settlements, and organizing agricultural settlements along the borders. Under the original National Security Service Law, all conscripts, with few exceptions, were supposed to undergo agricultural training in Nahal. Under regulations subject to annual review, however, the Minister of Defense is entitled to authorize exemptions from such service according to the requirements of the forces. In view of the increasingly complex tasks assigned to modern military forces and the length of time required for training in them, such exemptions have become vital in many cases.

Gadna' (G'dude No'ar, or Youth Battalions), successor to the auxiliary Hagana formation of the same name, conducts the premilitary training of youths between the ages of 14 and 18. Under the joint supervision of the Ministries of Education and Culture and Defense, it puts stress on such factors as good citizenship, physical training, and endurance and imparts preliminary technical training to youths planning to enter such highly technical services as the air force, navy, signal corps, and armored troops.

HeN (abbreviation of Hel Nashim, or Women's Army) includes all women serving in the IDF, whose main occupations are clerical and administrative work, nursing, welfare and cultural activities, and signal communications.

Defense and Other Duties. Israel's land frontiers touch four Arab countries, which, with nine other Arab countries constituting the *Arab League, openly declared it their aim to

Israeli troops parade during Independence Day celebrations in 1962. [Israel Information Services]

eliminate "Zionist control of occupied Palestine" and were actively engaged in political and military preparations for an all-out attack. In 1970 the total of their populations was about 100 million, as against 2.5 million for the State of Israel. The maintenance of the IDF in a maximum state of preparedness, therefore, was the first and foremost task of the State as long as such hostility continued. For this purpose, methods were devised to enable the General Staff to mobilize units and to equip and dispatch them to their assigned positions in record time. This emergency mobilization was made by both public and secret channels of communication. Statistics concerning Israel's security budget were not available; it is known, however, that the constant necessity for acquiring the most modern arms, maintaining them, and training soldiers in their use imposes a tremendous burden on the economy of the country.

Since all Israeli citizens, regardless of country of origin or date of arrival in Israel, pass through the IDF, it plays a prominent role in the integration of immigrants. The Department of Education, one of the large administrative units of the IDF, is concerned with supplementing the education of the soldiers, particularly the new immigrants among them who have not had the benefit of formal schooling. The army also provides facilities for training soldiers in various trades and crafts so that they may find gainful employment when they return to civilian life. The Department has its own publishing house and puts out an illustrated weekly, *BaMahane* (In the Camp), as well as a considerable amount of educational material.

The IDF also participates in such tasks as providing teachers for new settlements and organizing large-scale athletic activities, prominent among which is the annual March to Jerusalem, in which thousands of soldiers and civilians of all ages participate. *See also* SINAI CAMPAIGN; SIX-DAY WAR OF 1967.

N. LORCH

ISRAEL ECONOMIC CORPORATION. *See* PEC ISRAEL ECONOMIC CORPORATION.

ISRAEL ELECTRIC CORPORATION, LTD. (formerly Palestine Electric Corporation, Ltd.). Israeli public utility, founded in 1923 by Pinhas *Rutenberg. Rutenberg, who had come to Palestine soon after the Bolshevik Revolution of 1917, devised a plan for supplying cheap electric power and light by harnessing the waters of the Jordan River. His initial approach to authorities in Palestine and London met with little sympathy, but eventually he succeeded in winning over Winston *Churchill, then Colonial Secretary, and in obtaining the active support of Baron Edmond de *Rothschild (who subscribed $450,000 for the project), Sir Alfred Mond (later 1st Baron *Melchett of Landford), and other leading Jews in England and the United States. After debates in both houses of Parliament, the British government approved the Rutenberg project.

The official agreement, which was signed on Sept. 12, 1921, between the *High Commissioner for Palestine, the Crown agents for the colonies, and Rutenberg, provided for the "utilization of the waters of the Rivers Jordan and Yarmukh, and their affluents, for generating and supplying electrical energy." The concession was granted for a term of 70 years. In 1923 Rutenberg, aided by funds from the *Jewish Colonial Trust and the *Jewish Colonization Association (ICA), set up a small diesel plant in Tel Aviv to supply the needs of the city. The network was extended to Jaffa despite opposition from Arab politicians to the introduc-

tion of "Zionist electricity." On Mar. 29, 1923, the Palestine Electric Corporation was officially incorporated in Palestine with an authorized capital of £2,000,000. In 1925 two new power plants, one in Haifa and one in Tiberias, were built.

On Mar. 5, 1926, the preliminary concession of 1921 was officially approved and signed by the High Commissioner for Palestine and Rutenberg as managing director and chairman of the Palestine Electric Corporation. It gave the corporation the exclusive right to utilize the waters of the Jordan and Yarmukh Rivers for the generation of electricity. Work on the Jordan hydroelectric scheme was begun in 1927. As a result of negotiations conducted with Emir 'Abdullah of Transjordan, Rutenberg obtained permission to use land lying within Transjordanian territory. A total of 6,000 dunams of land (*see* DUNAM) was transferred by the Transjordan government to the concession area. The plant constructed on the site, called *Naharayim, was completed in 1932 and functioned until 1948, when it was destroyed by the Arab Legion. In 1935 and 1938 thermal (oil-burning) power stations were erected in Haifa and Tel Aviv. They supplied all the needs of the Arab and Jewish population of Palestine until the independence of Israel.

In 1968 the generating capacity of the company was 1,000 megawatts (1 million kilowatts), and the construction of an additional power station in Tel Aviv with a generating capacity of 428 megawatts was under way. Plans called for completion of this station by 1971.

In the first 20 years of the State of Israel the company prepared in advance the energy that would be required in succeeding years. Thus it laid the foundation for the development of the economy and the raising of the country's *standard of living. The Israel Electric Corporation supplied all the energy requirements of the population and economy of the State.

Beginning early in 1965, in addition to supplying electricity, the company supplied water to the residents of Elat by means of a power station integrated with the local water desalination plant. The generating capacity of the power station was 6,700 kilowatts, and the capacity of the desalination plant 3,800 cubic meters of water per day. In 1968 Elat was linked to the national grid that covers the map of the State and transfers electricity from the three centers of production, Haifa, Tel Aviv, and Ashdod, to all points of consumption of the various types.

As of 1968 the registered share capital of the corporation was IL168,000,000; issued shares amounted to IL126,000,000. The great majority of the shares in the company are held by the *government of Israel. The regular shares are quoted on the London and Tel Aviv stock exchanges.

In 1967–68 the supply system comprised 6,974 kilometers of high-voltage transmission and distribution lines, 5,780 kilometers of low-voltage networks, and distribution transformers with a total capacity of 2,080 megavolt-amperes. The network served 863,000 consumers. Electricity sales in 1967–68 totaled 4,093 million kilowatt-hours, of which 1,325 million were used by industry, 1,007 million for water pumping, and 1,761 million by residential, commercial, and other consumers.

The growth of the Israel Electric Corporation in the first 20 years after the independence of Israel is shown in the table on page 587.

A. SHADMON

ISRAELI. Adjective meaning of Israel or its people. The word is also used as a noun in the sense of a native or inhabitant of Israel.

GROWTH OF THE ISRAEL ELECTRIC CORPORATION, LTD., 1948–68

	1948	1957–58	Average annual growth, 1948 to 1957–58, per cent	1967–68	Average annual growth, 1957–58 to 1967–68, per cent
Population, at year's end (thousands)	873	1,992	+ 9.6	2,724	+ 3.1
Generation:					
Installed generating capacity (megawatts)	70	266	+16.0	1,000	+14.2
System peak load (megawatts)	65	276	+17.4	838	+11.7
Electricity generated (million kilowatt-hours)	314	1,442	+18.4	4,780	+12.7
Load factor (per cent)	57.0	59.7		64.6	
Average fuel oil consumption (grams per kilowatt-hour)	404	309	− 3.0	257	− 1.9
Network:					
Extra-high-voltage and high-voltage lines (route kilometers)	1,662	3,930	+10.0	6,974	+ 5.9
Low-voltage lines (route kilometers)	1,541	3,830	+10.6	5,780	+ 4.2
Distribution transformers (megawatt-amperes)	149	746	+19.6	2,080	+10.8
Manpower:					
Number of employees, at year's end	1,307	4,412	+14.5	5,293	+ 1.8
Electricity sales (million kilowatt-hours):					
Industrial	70	394	+21.2	1,325	+12.9
Water pumping	75	355	+18.9	1,007	+11.0
Residential, commercial, and other	101	452	+18.1	1,761	+14.6
Total	246	1,201	+19.2	4,093	+12.8
Consumers (thousands):					
Residential	99	379	+16.1	744	+ 7.0
Commercial and public	22	54	+10.5	94	+ 5.7
Industrial and other	8	15	+ 7.3	25	+ 5.2
Total	129	448	+14.8	863	+ 6.8
Average annual consumption, per capita (kilowatt-hours)	282	603	+ 9.1	1,503	+ 9.6
Financial data (thousands of *Israeli pounds):					
Total assets, less current liabilities	5,406	233,190		775,069	
Fixed assets, after depreciation	5,233	217,997		703,577	
Capital and reserves	4,116	72,158		166,985	
Gross revenue	2,664	51,341		214,744	
Operating surplus, after depreciation	204	5,910		44,688	
Net profit, after interest, capital, and tax provisions	98	1,463		6,918	

SOURCE: Israel Electric Corporation, Ltd., *Forty-fifth Annual Report*, 1967–68.
*In 1948, IL1=£1; in 1957–58, IL5.04=£1; in 1967–68, IL8.40=£1.

ISRAELI-ARAB WAR OF 1948. *See* WAR OF INDEPENDENCE.

ISRAELI-ARAB WAR OF 1967. *See* SIX-DAY WAR OF 1967.

ISRAELI LITERATURE. *See* LITERATURE, MODERN HEBREW AND ISRAELI.

ISRAEL INSTITUTE OF TECHNOLOGY. *See* TECHNION.

ISRAEL LABOR PARTY. Political party in Israel, formed by mergers between *Mapai, *R'shimat Po'ale Yisrael (Rafi), and *Ahdut 'Avoda on Jan. 21, 1968. The new party (Mifleget Ha'Avoda HaYisr'elit) held its founding convention the same evening in Jerusalem with the President of Israel, the Cabinet, the diplomatic corps, and 22 representatives of 14 Social Democratic parties from other countries in attendance. Golda *Meir was the first secretary-general of the party; she was succeeded by Pinhas *Sapir in the summer of 1968. On Jan. 19, 1969, the Israel Labor party formed an alignment with *Mapam; while retaining their organizational independence, the two formed a united bloc in the *Knesset and the *Histadrut (General Federation of Labor).

ISRAEL LAND DEVELOPMENT COMPANY (ILDC). *See* HEVRAT HAKHSHARAT HAYISHUV.

ISRAEL PHILHARMONIC ORCHESTRA. First all-Jewish symphonic orchestra of high international standing. Originally called the Palestine Orchestra, it opened its first season in December, 1936, at the Levant Fair Grounds in Tel Aviv under the baton of Arturo Toscanini. It was the realization of the vision of Bronislaw *Huberman, who had made it his mission to rescue Jewish musicians from the fascist-dominated countries of Europe and to create a first-rate orchestra with first-desk men from Vienna, Warsaw, Budapest, Berlin, Frankfurt, and other cities. Toscanini volunteered to conduct the first concert, subsequently returning to Palestine for additional series. Many prominent conductors and soloists followed Huberman's call and visited Palestine even during the years of World War II, when the Palestine Orchestra not only performed in the cities and villages of Palestine but also toured the Middle East,

A concert of the Israel Philharmonic Orchestra in the Fredric R. Mann Auditorium, Tel Aviv. [Israel Information Services]

playing in Beirut, Cairo, and Alexandria and in Allied military camps. With the influx of excellent musicians, musical education also improved. The orchestra, organized as a cooperative of musicians and governed by a Board of Directors, all of whom were members of the orchestra, chose the guest conductor system rather than appointing a permanent director, though for short periods internationally known conductors (e.g., Paul Paray and Jean Martinon) agreed to serve as chief conductors. The guest conductor system precluded the creation of a planned artistic policy, but Israeli audiences benefited from the visits of soloists and conductors of international note. The orchestra visited the United States and Canada several times and toured the Far East as well as European countries. It also encouraged Israeli composers, and for its 25th-anniversary season in 1961 it commissioned orchestral works from 10 prominent Israelis. It made recordings for Columbia (England) and Decca Records. Israeli conductors who made regular appearances with the orchestra were Michael Taube, George Singer, Gary *Bertini, Moshe 'Atzmon, Sergiu Commissiona, and Mendi Rodan. The home base of the orchestra was the Fredric R. Mann Auditorium (Hekhal HaTarbut) in Tel Aviv.

See also MUSIC IN ISRAEL.

P. GRADENWITZ

ISRAEL PRIZE. Award offered annually by the Israeli Ministry of Education and Culture on the *Independence Day of Israel for outstanding achievement in various fields, such as Jewish studies, Tora literature, humanities, sciences, and arts. In 1968, on the occasion of the 20th anniversary of Israel's independence, prizes were awarded in the following 15 fields: agriculture, architecture, education, exact sciences, Hebrew literature, humanities, Jewish studies, jurisprudence, medical science, music and dance, natural sciences, painting and sculpture, social sciences, theater, and Tora literature.

ISRAEL PURCHASING SERVICE. *See* AMPAL.

ISRAEL SECURITIES CORPORATION. *See* AMPAL.

ITALIAN JEWS IN ISRAEL. Since Italy never had a large Jewish population, *'Aliya (immigration) from Italy has been small. However, the 2,000 Jews from Italy who lived in Israel in 1966, mostly in Tel Aviv and its environs, were fully integrated into Israeli society.

Before World War II. Because of *assimilation and the economic prosperity of most Italian Jews, 'Aliya from Italy before Mussolini's anti-Jewish legislation of 1938 was extremely small. During the period from 1926 to 1938 it amounted to no more than 150 Jews. Enzo *Sereni, who arrived in Palestine with his family in 1928, was for years almost the sole personification of the "Italkim." Other immigrants from Italy during those years included Giacomo Hirsch, the second *Halutz (pioneer) to arrive; the late Corrado Corinaldi; Giuseppe *Sinigaglia, who had been active in the *Jewish National Fund; and Alfonso *Pacifici, who settled in Jerusalem in 1934 and became involved in a variety of cultural and educational activities.

After the promulgation of the anti-Semitic Fascist laws of 1938, 'Aliya increased. While most of the 'Olim (immigrants) were drawn from the older middle class, the year 1939 also saw the arrival of some 20 young boys and girls who, sponsored by *Youth 'Aliya, took up studies at agricultural schools in Palestine or joined communal settlements there. The 500 Italian

Jews who came to Palestine that year included leaders of Italian Jewry such as E. S. Artom, David U. Cassuto, Gualtiero *Cividalli, Dante *Lattes, Augusto *Levi, Salomone Umberto *Nahon, Mario *Ottolenghi, and David *Prato, who had been active in Italian Jewish and Zionist life.

Some of the immigrants of 1939 joined kibbutzim, predominantly Giv'at Brenner and Rodges (later Yavne). Others enrolled at institutions of higher learning. Five Jews from Italy joined the faculty of the *Hebrew University of Jerusalem; one of them, Julio Racah, a world-renowned physicist, was its rector from 1961 until his untimely death in 1965. A number lectured and held positions of importance also at the Haifa *Technion, the School of Law and Economics, Tel Aviv, and *Tel Aviv University.

Italian Jews also attained prominence in Israel's industry, having set up a knitwear factory, a drug-manufacturing concern, and a tannery. Later, Jewish industrialists and technicians from Italy established a number of important firms manufacturing electrical equipment, paper, and textiles. 'Olim from Italy were represented also in the Israeli *civil service and in the liberal professions. In the field of medicine, at least 15 physicians from the Italian 'Aliya gave of their skill and experience to factories, workshops, and laboratories.

Since World War II. From World War II on about 1,000 additional 'Olim arrived from Italy, but eventually the immigration wave, strong at first, slowed down. The actual number of individuals from Italy who settled in Israel was small but not insignificant proportionally, if one considers the decimation of Italian Jewry in the war. An unusual 'Aliya soon after the war was that of the converts of Sannicandro Garganico, a group of farmers and shepherds who were converted to Judaism *en masse* and who all moved to Israel. The kibbutzim absorbed many of the later 'Aliyot. In 1966 there were Italian Jews in more than 20 of Israel's communal settlements, from Ruhama (where the largest group lived) to S'de Eliyahu, from R'gavim to Gevim, and from Netzer Sereni to Bar 'Am.

Contributions to Israeli Life. As of 1968, Italian Jews were conspicuous in certain basic services of the State. A good many held important posts in the Ministry of Foreign Affairs and in other ministries such as those of Religious Affairs and the Interior, as well as in various State institutions, in the Central Bureau of Statistics, in port management, and in economic organizations. Some were active in aircraft construction and in the growing Israel Air Force, while others held high rank in the military forces.

The Irgun 'Ole Italia (Organization of Immigrants from Italy), which was founded in 1938, occasionally gave loans and other economic assistance to Italian newcomers. A similar organization, Hevrat 'Ole Italia liF'ula Ruhanit (Association of Immigrants from Italy for Cultural Work), limited its activities to cultural areas. Witness to the rapid integration of Italian Jewry in Israel was the number of translations of Hebrew books into Italian and vice versa made by Italian immigrants, an activity which helped foster ties of goodwill and understanding between Israel and Italy.

Still, the participation of Italian Jews in Israeli life, though active and noteworthy, was primarily in terms of individual contributions rather than of group action, as was the case with 'Aliyot from many other countries. One specific contribution by the Italian 'Olim as a group was in the field of religious art, namely, the transfer to Israel of the interiors of entire synagogues and of ceremonial objects from Italian-Jewish communities

A family of Italian Jews in Israel. [Histadrut Foto-News]

that had ceased to exist. Thanks to this project, some 30 synagogues throughout Israel came into possession of authentic pieces of Italian-Jewish religious art. In Jerusalem, next to a synagogue where the ancient Roman ritual had been revived, there was a collection of Jewish ceremonial art from Italy.

G. ROMANO

ITALY: RELATIONS WITH ZIONISM AND ISRAEL. The history of modern Italy's attitude toward Zionism and, later, toward the State of Israel may be divided into three periods: *risorgimento* and liberal monarchy (19th cent.–1922), the Fascist era (1922–45), and the postwar era and the State of Israel (1945–   ).

Risorgimento and Liberal Monarchy, 19th Century–1922. Modern Italy became a united state in the second half of the 19th century, when Victor Emmanuel II assumed the title King of Italy (1861) and Rome was officially occupied by the Italian government (1870). Italian Jews early began to hold important positions in Italian political and economic life as Cabinet ministers, members of Parliament, academicians, and leaders in business and the professions.

Fully occupied with the consolidation of the country's new political independence and unity and with the development of its economy, the Italian government paid little attention to the Palestine problem and the early stirrings of modern Zionism. However, many individual Italians, recalling their own struggle for *risorgimento* (cultural and political rebirth as a nation), sympathized with the national aspirations of the Jewish people. Alessandro Manzoni (1785–1873), the novelist, envisioned the return of the Jews to their ancient Homeland, and Benedetto Mussolino, a fighter for Italian independence under Giuseppe Garibaldi and later a senator, actually urged the British statesman Lord Palmerston to reconstitute the Jewish people as a political nationality in Palestine under British protection.

Victor Emmanuel III, who succeeded to the throne in 1900, had visited Palestine. On Jan. 23, 1904, he received Herzl in audience. It was not the King's first encounter with Zionism; the year before (1903) he had met with Samuel Hirsch *Margulies, chief rabbi of Florence, who had requested an audience to discuss matters of interest to Zionists. Herzl's *Diaries* give a detailed report of his meeting with the King.

Victor Emmanuel demonstrated a lively interest both in Herzl and in his cause, expressing gratification that the Zionists had given up the *East Africa scheme and requesting Herzl to send him a copy of his book *Altneuland* (*Old-New Land). At that meeting Herzl also set forth his plans for the founding of Jewish settlements in Tripolitania, under Italian protection, for Jews who would not find room in Palestine. When the King pointed out that Tripolitania was a Turkish possession, Herzl replied that the Ottoman Empire was bound to collapse before long. In the end the King referred Herzl to Foreign Minister Tommaso Tittoni, who requested (and received) from Herzl a memorandum asking for Italy's intervention with the Sultan on behalf of the Zionist movement. However, Tittoni's reply was noncommittal.

During the Italo-Turkish War (1911–12) the leaders of the Italian Zionist Federation feared that, in view of Zionist contacts with Turkey, Italian Zionists would be accused of sympathizing with the enemy. Accordingly, the federation suspended its activities and the publication of its organ, *L'Idea Sionnista* (The Zionist Idea), for the duration of the conflict.

Having annexed Libya and the Dodecanese Islands in the war with Turkey, Italy developed an interest in the Turkish province of Antalya (Adalia) in Asia Minor, which included the Mediterranean port of Antalya. During World War I Italy's right to the islands, and also to Antalya, was officially recognized in the Treaty of London (Apr. 26, 1915), in which the Allied Powers delineated the share of the Ottoman Empire that Italy would eventually receive if it were to renounce its neutrality and enter the war on the side of the Allies. That treaty made no mention of Palestine.

In the fall of 1916, when Italy first learned of the *Sykes-Picot Agreement between Great Britain and France, it asked for a supplementary accord with the other Allies in order to clarify the vague promises it had received in the Treaty of London. In April, 1917, conversations were held on this issue at Saint-Jean-de-Maurienne between the Prime Ministers of Britain, France, and Italy. In August it was agreed that the form of the international administration to be set up for Palestine under the Sykes-Picot Agreement should be adopted in accord with Italy. Foreign Minister Baron Sidney Constantino Sonnino (1847–1922) was willing to accept an international arrangement in Palestine as the most suitable to foster Italian interests, and the occupation of Haifa and Acre by the British as long as nothing would be done to prejudice Italian commerce in these ports. Believing that the best way to maintain Italian influence in Palestine was to protect Catholic interests there, Sonnino, who was a Protestant (his father had been a Jew), also expressed his concern for the *holy places. To stress its partnership in the projected international regime, Italy sent some 500 soldiers to fight alongside the British in Palestine, but this force was too small to have political importance.

In its attitude toward Zionist aims, Italy now had to exercise caution. If Italy was to be able to compete with the French for the favor of the Catholic Church and to assure the appointment of Italians to important ecclesiastical posts, it could not afford to endanger relations with the Vatican (see VATICAN: RELATIONS WITH ZIONISM AND ISRAEL). Besides, it feared that support for Zionism might provoke the wrath of the Pan-Islamic movement, which could cause disaffection among the Muslim population of Italy's possessions. As early as 1916 Italy showed a deep interest in the Muslim holy places, considering itself a "Muslim" power.

On the other hand, not wanting Great Britain to gain too firm a foothold in Palestine, Italy made vague professions of sympathy to the Zionists. In April, 1917, Nahum *Sokolow came to Rome, where he was received by the Secretary-General of the Foreign Ministry and then by Prime Minister Paolo Boselli, who promised Italian support while still contemplating an international solution for the status of the holy places.

Actually, the Italian government became deeply distrustful of the Zionist movement, which it suspected of being a tool for achieving British predominance in Palestine at Italy's expense. These suspicions seemed confirmed by various statements of Chaim *Weizmann, by reports received from Palestine, and, above all, by the issuance of the *Balfour Declaration (Nov. 2, 1917). Zionism, being actively in favor of a British *Mandate for Palestine, was an obstacle to internationalization, which was considered the best solution for Italy.

In February, 1918, it was felt that Italian Jewry might be utilized to help advance Italy's economic ambitions in Palestine, thus offsetting British influence. The Italian government was therefore eager to have the *World Zionist Organization (WZO) accept two Italian delegates to the *Zionist Commission. Accordingly, when Nahum Sokolow, in a letter (Apr. 22, 1918) to Marchese Guglielmo Imperiali, Italy's Ambassador in London, pressed Italy to give its official endorsement to the Balfour Declaration, Foreign Minister Sonnino, after some hesitation, acceded to Sokolow's request. In a letter to Sokolow (May 9, 1918), Ambassador Imperiali wrote:

> On the instruction of His Excellency Baron Sonnino, His Majesty's Minister of Foreign Affairs, I have the honor to inform you that . . . His Majesty's Government are pleased to confirm the declarations already made through their representatives at Washington, The Hague and Salonica to the effect that they will gladly be prepared to use their best endeavors to facilitate the establishment in Palestine of a Hebrew national center, it being understood that nothing shall be done to prejudice the existing juridical and political status of the existing religious communities or the civil and political rights enjoyed by Israelites in any other country.

On July 30, 1918, two Italian Jews, Comdr. Angelo *Levi-Bianchini and Giacomo Artom, sailed for Palestine as delegates to the Zionist Commission. Acting also as representatives of the Italian government, they studied the economic prospects of Palestine, with emphasis on possibilities for the sale of Italian goods. Their particular task, however, was to prevent Zionism from falling under Britain's exclusive protection.

That same summer, the Italian Foreign Ministry attempted to foment anti-Zionist demonstrations (see ANTI-ZIONISM) and to get in touch with Justice Louis D. *Brandeis in the belief that the influential American Zionist leader would prefer an international regime to British rule in Palestine. In the fall of 1918 Meli Lupi di Soragna, the representative of the Italian government in Jerusalem, attempted secretly to spark a movement of Christians, Muslims, and anti-Zionist Orthodox Jews to work for the internationalization of Palestine and against the British and the Zionists. (It was only the final decision on the Palestine Mandate at the *San Remo Conference in 1920 that put an end to this activity.)

Foreign Minister Sonnino was a member of the Council of Ten at the Paris Peace Conference, which heard the presentation of the Zionist case in February, 1919. In May, after Levi-Bianchini's return to Italy, plans were made to enlist the services of Sephardi Jews (see SEPHARDIM) in order to counteract the influence of Jewish groups favoring French or British rule in Palestine. Levi-Bianchini, who had used his influence a month before to thwart Arab plans for a Nebi Musa holiday pogrom in Jerusalem, was entrusted with the mission of establishing contact with Sephardim in the Mediterranean region, many of whom were of Italian descent. For this purpose he was given command of an Italian naval vessel, the "Coatit," which plied the Mediterranean from July to November, 1919, calling at the principal eastern Mediterranean ports. The plan was to induce the Sephardim to spearhead a great movement in support of Italy's ambitions in Palestine. To this end the study of *Hebrew was to be introduced in certain Italian-language schools abroad, young Sephardim were to be invited to enroll at the Collegio Rabbinico Italiano in Florence, and a special secretariat for Sephardi Jews was to be established in Rome.

All through those years, a trend of public opinion in Italy slowly evolved in favor of Zionism. An influential non-Jewish committee called Pro Israele was active in Rome under the leadership of Sen. Francesco Ruffini. A number of other men of importance in public life were members of the committee, but its influence on government policy is difficult to assess.

When the San Remo Conference (April, 1920) decided to assign the Mandate for Palestine to Great Britain, Italy raised no objections, directing its efforts solely toward weakening French influence in Palestine and the role of France as the protector of Catholic interests there.

During the years immediately following World War I the Vatican's concern for the holy places, the widespread idea that Zionism was a cover for British imperialist ambitions (others in Italy equated Zionism with Russian Bolshevism), and a desire not to endanger its position in the Arab world kept Italy from giving official support to Zionism. In April, 1922, Chaim Weizmann, in the course of his travels to various European countries on behalf of the World Zionist movement, visited Rome, where he met a number of Italian statesmen, including former Prime Minister Luigi Luzzatti (himself a Jew), Foreign Minister Carlo Schanzer, and Colonial Minister Giovanni Amendola. Weizmann was received also by King Victor Emmanuel III, who according to Weizmann's account in his autobiography, *Trial and Error*, had a photograph of Herzl on his desk but failed to give Weizmann a clear answer to his question concerning the reasons for Italian and Vatican opposition to Zionism. The Italian officials who met with Weizmann told him that they would support Zionist aspirations if an Italian Jew were to be placed on the Zionist *Executive, Italian industry were to be given a share in the economic development of Palestine, and Jewish capital were invested in Italy.

In the summer of 1922 Vladimir *Jabotinsky, then a member of the Zionist Executive, visited Rome to hold conversations with the Italian government concerning Italy's stand on the Palestine Mandate, which was about to be placed before the Council of the League of Nations for final ratification. During his visit he attempted to explain to officials the advantages that could accrue to Italy in the Middle East from a Jewish National Home in Palestine.

Fascist Era, 1922–45. In October, 1922, Benito Mussolini and his Fascist party assumed control of Italy. The policies of Mussolini and his government with regard to Zionism underwent numerous changes, determined at first by a desire to counteract British influence in the Middle East and, later, by relations with Nazi Germany.

Although the first Fascist government included a former chairman of Pro Israele (Giovanni Colonna di Cesarò, Minister of Posts), the initial attitude of the Mussolini regime toward Zionism was distinctly cool. At a meeting with Weizmann in Rome in January, 1923, Mussolini indicated his belief that the Zionists were merely pawns in Great Britain's power game. He voiced this view also to a visiting delegation of Italian Jews, adding that to support Zionism not only would pose a risk of Arab hostility but would also endanger the civil status of Jews all over Europe.

Stiff and consistent opposition to Zionist aims came from Marchese Alberto Theodoli, the Italian who served as chairman of the League of Nations Permanent Mandates Commission from the mid-1920s until the late 1930s. For almost his entire tenure of office, Theodoli, who had married into an Arab family, posed as the defender of Arab and Catholic rights in Palestine and opposed every constructive suggestion for the Jewish Homeland.

When, in 1926, Italy once again became concerned with the eastern Mediterranean area, Palestine, as in the days of Sonnino, took a secondary place after Smyrna (İzmir) and Antalya in Italy's calculations. Since pro-Arab policies seemed to have yielded few positive results, Fascist Italy adopted a more favorable attitude toward Zionism. In September of that year, Mussolini again received Weizmann. This time he extended his good wishes for the success of the Zionist movement and asked Weizmann to arrange for the participation of Italian companies in the construction of the port of Haifa. Mussolini continued to show a lively interest in the Zionist program, expressing his sympathy for Zionism also to Nahum Sokolow when the latter met with him in November, 1926. In an interview with Victor *Jacobson on June 8, 1927, Mussolini showed understanding for Zionism and assured him of his support of the return of the Jewish people to its Homeland.

Cherishing visions of a new Roman Empire in the Mediterranean region, Mussolini sought to exploit the growing Zionist discontent with the British Mandate in the hope that the mandate might eventually be transferred to Italy.

The 1929 Concordat with the Holy See, which redefined the relationship between the Vatican and Fascist Italy, coupled with Mussolini's initial distrust of Adolf Hitler, who came to power in 1933, encouraged Italy to explore the possibility of forming closer ties with the Zionist movement at the expense of the British. In April, 1933, Weizmann called on Mussolini to ask his aid in the emigration of 50,000 German Jews to Palestine. At another meeting between Weizmann and Mussolini in Rome (February, 1934), the latter agreed to allow a certain number of German-Jewish refugees to pass through Italy on their way to Palestine.

The Fascists began to favor the Revisionist movement (*see* REVISIONISTS) because it was considered anti-British. In 1934 the *B'rit Trumpeldor (Betar) movement established the Betar Maritime School in Civitavecchia. This school, which began instruction with some 30 young Revisionists recruited from 15 countries, was in operation for $3\frac{1}{2}$ years under the leadership of Yirmiyahu *Halpern. It provided Sabbath services and kosher food for its students.

Nonetheless, although the Italian government appeared disposed to support the rebirth of a Jewish Homeland in Palestine, it did not particularly favor the dissemination of Zionist propaganda among Italian Jews. Certain Fascist newspapers launched a violently anti-Zionist campaign. The result was a heated dispute with Jewish news media and a split within Italian Jewry, which led to the appearance in Turin in 1934 of an anti-Zionist periodical, *La Nostra Bandiera* (Our Flag), edited by Ettore Ovazza.

The League of Nations condemnation of the invasion of Ethiopia in 1935 helped bring Italy closer to Hitler and his Nazi regime. The appointment of Count Galeazzo Ciano as Foreign Minister in the summer of 1936 and the formation of the Rome-Berlin Axis that October marked the end of Mussolini's flirtation with Zionism. Count Ciano and Marchese Theodoli received Nahum *Goldmann as late as May 4, 1937, but Mussolini that same month welcomed 100 Palestinian Arab youth leaders. It was clear that Italy was adopting an increasingly pro-Arab line. As early as May 13, 1936, the British press had openly charged Italy with fomenting Arab unrest in Palestine through Italian agents in order to embarrass the British government. When Mussolini visited Libya in March, 1937, he proclaimed himself the "protector of Islam."

This period saw the appearance of a virulent anti-Semitic and anti-Zionist book, *Gli Ebrei in Italia* (The Jews in Italy). Written by Paolo Orano, a close friend of Mussolini, the book attacked the Italian Jews for their "Zionist propaganda, tendencies and language" and stated that there was a profound conflict between the duties of the Jews as Italian patriots and their attitude toward the Zionist movement. The publication of Orano's book set off a new anti-Zionist campaign in the press, replete with accusations that Zionism was a tool of British imperialism and an insult to the Arabs, with whom Italy maintained friendly relations. Despite Ciano's assurance on June 6, 1937, to David *Prato, chief rabbi of Rome, that the Italian government had not changed its favorable attitude toward the Jews, it became known that the anti-Zionist campaign had been started by Mussolini himself. The anti-Semitic "racial" laws of October, 1938, marked the final break in relations between Fascist Italy and the Zionist movement. *See also* ANTI-SEMITISM.

In contrast, the sympathies of a great many people of Italy were with the Jews. During World War II many Italians, frequently with the tacit approval of the authorities, sheltered Jewish refugees and saved thousands of Italian Jews from arrest by the Gestapo after Hitler's occupation of Italy.

Postwar Era and the State of Israel, 1945– . After World War II there was much sympathy in Italy for the Jewish people, particularly among the Italians who had participated in the anti-Nazi resistance movement. It was no coincidence that during the years immediately preceding the establishment of the State of Israel Italy became one of the most important bases for *illegal immigration and *Hagana arms purchases.

At the same time, the new postwar democratic government felt it unwise to antagonize the Arab world by lending official support to Zionism. Having lost its colonies in Africa, Italy hoped to find a large market for its products among the Arab nations. Besides, it still had important political, economic, and religious interests in the Middle East. Hence when the State of Israel was established in 1948 (Italy was not a member of the United Nations at the time), it was the Italian Communist party that urged the Italian government to recognize the new State "without ado." Nonetheless, Italy did not extend even de facto recognition to Israel until Oct. 1, 1948, when the two countries exchanged consular representatives. De jure recogni-

tion did not come until Feb. 7, 1949. Israel's first Consul in Rome was Arie Oron; the first Minister Plenipotentiary was Sh'lomo Ginossar. (In 1956 ambassadorial rank was given to the diplomatic representatives of the two countries.)

During the years that followed, Israeli Cabinet ministers frequently visited Italy. In March, 1952, Foreign Minister Moshe *Sharett came to Rome to sign a trade agreement and met with Pres. Luigi Einaudi. Golda *Meir paid a number of official visits to Italy. When she was Minister of Labor, she spent several days in Rome (February, 1954). As Foreign Minister, she was received by Pres. Giovanni Gronchi (October, 1957), by Premier Amintore Fanfani (August, 1958), and, to discuss the possibility of Israel's entrance into the European Common Market, by Foreign Minister Giuseppe Saragat (February, 1964).

Several Italian state enterprises resisted *Arab boycott pressures aimed at Israel. In reply to a Saudi Arabian request that all goods shipped from Italy to Saudi Arabia carry a statement that only gentile firms were involved in their manufacture, Minister of Industry and Trade Pietro Campilli declared that such a statement would violate the Italian Constitution, which forbids racial discrimination. Israel participated in the fairs of Bari and Milan (the latter featuring an Israeli pavilion) and in the Venice Biennale. In May, 1955, the *Israel Philharmonic Orchestra toured Italy; it performed at the Maggio Fiorentino and La Scala and, privately, for Pope Pius XII.

Italy consistently attempted to maintain neutrality toward the Israel-Arab conflict. Pro-Arab pressures were exerted by the Ente Nazionale Idrocarburi (ENI), the government-owned oil agency which, along with the national oil company of Egypt (from 1958, United Arab Republic), was engaged in exploiting the petroleum resources of the Sinai Peninsula and Saudi Arabia and also had projects concerning Iraq. In October, 1958, Premier Fanfani sent Republican party leader Randolfo Pacciardi to various Arab states and Israel on a fact-finding mission. Pacciardi brought back reports of Soviet infiltration in several Arab countries and expressed admiration for the achievements of the State of Israel. Fanfani also lent his support to a series of unofficial conferences on Mediterranean cooperation that met in Florence. A meeting that ended on Oct. 6, 1958, was attended by influential private individuals from Great Britain, the United States, the Soviet Union, the United Arab Republic, Israel, North Africa, Italy, Greece, Turkey, Spain, and Yugoslavia, who discussed Middle Eastern tensions on a nonofficial basis. In January, 1959, Fanfani paid an official visit to Cairo, where, at a press conference held at the Italian Embassy, he declared, "I have always stated that Israel is a historical and geographical reality. It is the task of political leaders to acknowledge realities."

The years 1961 and 1962 saw reciprocal official visits of economic, agricultural, and parliamentary missions. However, Italy's concern for Arab sensibilities resulted in a failure to invite Israel to participate in the Mediterranean Olympics held in Naples in September, 1963. In March, 1965, Premier Aldo Moro declared his intention to maintain "the best of relations" with Israel but to preserve ties of "friendship and understanding" with the Arab world.

In the *Six-day War of 1967, Italian public opinion was enthusiastically in favor of Israel. Although the Communist party and the Italian Socialist party of Proletarian Unity supported the Soviet position, the Unified Socialist party, along with the Republican party, defended Israel's right to exist. It was probably the influence of the latter two parties that finally induced the Italian government to abandon neutrality for a more favorable attitude toward Israel, as shown by Italy's vote at the emergency session of the UN General Assembly held in June. Premier Moro reaffirmed the right of every member state of the United Nations to territorial integrity and protection from the threat and use of force. "The withdrawal of [Israeli] troops [from Arab lands] is necessary but not enough. If the United Nations limited themselves to [insisting on] this, they would become accomplices to a return to the situation which has caused two wars within twenty years," he said.

All this was in contrast to the supposedly neutral but actually pro-Arab line apparently followed by Fanfani, a Christian Democrat, and dictated by a desire to safeguard Italy's economic interests and role in the Arab world. Support for Israel came from Christian Democratic leaders and the rightist Liberal party. At the same time, Italy maintained cordial relations with all the countries of the Arab world.

After the war some sectors of the population and even the non-Communist press began to show a somewhat cooler attitude toward Israel. Certain newspapers controlled by the ENI went so far as to carry articles that recalled the Fascist press of the 1930s, particularly in their allusions to Jewish "dual loyalties."

In July, 1968, Italy assisted in diplomatic negotiations for the return of the *El 'Al jetliner that had been hijacked and forced to land in Algeria.   S. MINERBI

ITALY, ZIONISM IN. Italian Jewry acquired civic and political rights late in the 19th century. Within a few years, Italian Jews, long assimilated to the language and culture of Italy, attained important positions at universities, in the army, in finance, and in politics. Some entered Parliament. Early in the 20th century, two Jews, Leone Wollemborg (1859–1932) and Giuseppe Ottolenghi (1838–1904), became Cabinet ministers, and Luigi Luzzatti (1841–1927) was Prime Minister in 1910–11.

Early Years. It is against this background that one must view the slow headway made by Zionism in Italy. Typical of the initial reaction was the prophecy of *Il Vessillo Israelitico*, the Jewish periodical with the widest circulation in Italy at the time, to the effect that the Zionist movement launched by Herzl in Basle with the 1st Zionist *Congress would prove "a colossal failure." Even in those early days, however, there were in Italy some rabbis and young Jewish intellectuals, including Dante *Lattes, who reacted differently and launched a debate on Zionism in *Il Corriere Israelitico*, which was published in Trieste (then part of Austria).

No delegates from Italy attended the 1st Zionist Congress in 1897, but Felice *Ravenna, a young lawyer who was to become the recognized leader of Italian Zionism, attended the 2d Congress in 1898, as an observer. The 2d Congress was pleased to note the sympathy expressed for Zionism by the Italian-Jewish anthropologist Cesare Lombroso.

In September, 1899, the first Italian Zionist conference was held in Ancona, and on Oct. 20, 1901, the Italian Zionist Federation was founded in Modena.

Although the interest in Palestine of the early Italian Zionists was mostly cultural and humanitarian, political Zionism gained strength, owing mostly to the initiative of a number of rabbis and young men, including Carlo A. Conigliani, Amedeo and

Benvenuto Donati, Carlo Levi, Bernardo *Dessau, Gino Arias, and Angelo *Sullam, all of whom enthusiastically spread the idea of Zionism.

The Italian-Jewish press developed an increasing interest in the problems of Zionism. Two Zionist periodicals made their appearance. One, *L'Idea Sionnista*, a monthly which published the records of the Zionist Federation, lasted from 1901 until 1911; the other, *L'Eco Sionnistica d'Italia*, which was more Socialist in viewpoint, was published during the year 1908. The older *Corriere Israelitico*, though not exclusively Zionist, also played an important role in the interpretation and dissemination of Zionist ideas.

The Italian delegates to the 6th Zionist Congress (Basle, 1903) all were in favor of the *East Africa scheme, and Bernardo Dessau was appointed to the commission set up for the study of possibilities for Jewish colonization in Africa.

Herzl relied on the assistance of an Italian go-between and on the advice of Italian Zionists when he visited Italy for his audiences with King Victor Emmanuel III and Pope Pius X. Herzl was given a cordial reception in Italy. On Jan. 26, 1904, he had an interview with Foreign Minister Tommaso Tittoni. On February 4 of that year, Herzl sent a memorandum to Tittoni (through Ravenna, who was then president of the Italian Zionist Federation), summarizing the views and aspirations of Zionism.

In subsequent years the geographic center of Italian Zionist activity shifted to Florence, where students and faculty members (such as Rabbis Samuel Hirsch *Margulies and Zvi Peretz *Chajes) of the Collegio Rabbinico Italiano spread the message of Zionism. In Florence, too, at the time was Alfonso *Pacifici, a Zionist leader who exerted considerable influence on Jewish opinion.

World War I and the Postwar Years. In 1915, because of wartime difficulties, the *Corriere Israelitico* was forced to suspend publication after 53 years. Several months later, in January, 1916, a new Zionist weekly, *Israel*, made its first appearance in Florence under the direction of Lattes and Pacifici.

Italy's entry into the war in 1915 on the side of the Allied Powers, and the *Balfour Declaration, gave new impetus to Zionism there. Capt. Angelo *Levi-Bianchini of the Italian Navy, a Jew, represented his government in a diplomatic mission in the Middle East. At the instance of the Italian government, Levi-Bianchini and Dr. Giacomo Artom were included as representatives of Italian Jewry in the *Zionist Commission which went to Palestine in 1918. In April, 1920, Levi-Bianchini went to the *San Remo Conference to persuade the Italian delegation to support Zionist aspirations.

In 1918 Felice Ravenna called a small meeting of Zionist leaders in Bologna to plan means of bringing about a revival of Zionist activities in Italy. That October, a Zionist conference was held in Trieste, marking the rebirth of the Italian Zionist Federation.

February, 1921, saw the founding of a Jewish publishing house, the Casa Editrice Israel. On May 2 of that year, Carlo Alberto *Viterbo assumed the leadership of the Zionist Federation after the resignation of Felice Ravenna and of first vice-president Angelo Sullam.

During that decade, Ciro *Glass made his influence felt in Florence in the ranks of Zionist leaders. Thanks in large measure to the organizational work of Rabbi David *Prato, fund raising made considerable headway. In 1920 a single donor turned over 1,000,000 lire to the *Jewish National Fund. Delegates were regularly sent to Zionist Congresses, and the participation of Zionists in the Jewish community councils was accepted.

A Juniors' Congress held in Leghorn in 1924 drew an enthusiastic audience. In 1926 Enzo *Sereni was the first Italian *Halutz (pioneer) to settle in Palestine. The entry of Umberto *Nahon into Zionist activity in 1927 marked the intensification of Italian Zionist organizational life and of closer contact with the *World Zionist Organization.

Late in 1927, the Italian Zionist Federation helped bring into being the Comitato Italia-Palestina (Italy-Palestine Committee), whose aim was to promote good relations between Italy and Palestine and to create goodwill for Zionism in Italian government circles. This committee, presided over by Prince Pietro Lanza di Scalea, included many well-known members of Italy's political, cultural, and literary circles.

Zionism under Fascism. The first phase in the relationship between Italian Zionism and Mussolini's government lasted up to the Italo-Ethiopian War (1935–36), until which time the Zionist Federation was allowed to function unhindered. The climate was favorable, and in 1931 the Foreign Ministry and the Ministry of the Interior gave permission for the holding of the 18th Zionist Congress at the Adriatic resort of Abbazia. (In the end, however, it was decided to hold the Congress in Basle.)

In 1933–34, Chaim *Weizmann and Nahum *Goldmann met with Mussolini. Also, the *Revisionists, headed by Vladimir *Jabotinsky, attempted to seek a rapprochement with the Mussolini government. It was the Revisionist movement which revived *L'Idea Sionnista* and continued to publish this Zionist periodical until 1938. When the Revisionists seceded from the World Zionist Organization, a branch of the *New Zionist Organization (NZO) was formed in Italy with Leone *Carpi, a lawyer, at its head. In 1934 the Revisionists promoted the establishment of a Jewish naval academy at Civitavecchia, Latium. The school's program of study was directed by an Italian officer, but the administration of the institution was in the hands of the youth organization *B'rit Trumpeldor (Betar). A total of 200 students went through the training course of the academy, which was in operation from 1935 until 1938.

In October, 1935, at the outbreak of the Italo-Ethiopian War, the Italian government, hoping that the Jews of Italy might induce their coreligionists in England to use their influence to prevent the application of economic sanctions against Italy, entrusted Dante Lattes and Angiolo Orvieto with an ad hoc mission. Lattes and Orvieto went to London to meet with Weizmann and other Jewish leaders and then proceeded on similar errands to Geneva and Paris. The mission, however, did not accomplish its intended purpose.

As it became increasingly clear that Italy had no chance of initiating political action with regard to Palestine, and as Berlin and Rome moved closer to one another, political contacts between the Italian government and representatives of the Zionist movement gradually came to an end.

Despite the difficulty of carrying on its work without giving offense to the Mussolini regime, the Zionist movement in Italy continued to be active. Until its publication was stopped by the government in 1938, the weekly *Israel* followed an editorial policy of dignity and self-respect. The Zionist Federation, then headed by Augusto *Levi, managed even to maintain the Hakhsharot (agricultural training centers; *see* HAKHSHARA). It sponsored training centers at Orciano and San Marco, where young Jews from Germany and Western Europe were prepared for settlement in Palestine. Drives for the Jewish National Fund and *Keren HaYesod (Palestine Foundation Fund) continued, the contributions being sent abroad at the official rate of exchange. In addition, the Italian Zionist Federation held regular elections and sent delegates to the Zionist Congresses of Prague (1933), Lucerne (1935), and Zurich (1937).

The years following the Italo-Ethiopian War saw a steady deterioration in the situation of Italian Jewry. There were anti-Semitic press campaigns and overt anti-Jewish attacks. These manifestations of hostility set off conflicts within the Jewish community itself, with the so-called Italians of Jewish faith hoping to improve matters by officially dissociating themselves from the Zionist movement through openly anti-Zionist declarations.

The anti-Jewish laws of 1938 put an end to all forms of free Jewish organizational activity. But even though Jewish refugees were expelled and Jews forbidden to attend public schools, Italian *anti-Semitism never took the appalling forms of the Hitler brand, not even after Italy's entry into World War II in June, 1940.

A wave of emigration began. With nearly all of Jewish communal life except for religious and philanthropic activity going underground, most of Italy's Zionist leaders made ready to leave for Palestine. Max Varadi, after organizing several *Youth 'Aliya groups and superintending the distribution of the last available *immigration certificates through the Palestine Office at Trieste (*see* PALESTINE OFFICES), left for Palestine in May, 1940. During the period from 1938 until Italy's entry into the war in 1940, 504 Jews left for Palestine, as contrasted with a total of 150 during the decade from 1928 to 1938. The Italian 'Olim (immigrants) readily found their place on the cultural, industrial, economic, and political scene of Palestine.

World War II and the Postwar Years. During the war years, Italian Jewry suffered deportation and other great hardships. At the same time, Italy was the scene of various Jewish underground activities, including those of the *Jewish Brigade and *B'riha. Liberation and the end of the war brought a revival of Zionist activity. In December, 1944, *Israel* resumed publication under the direction of Carlo Alberto Viterbo. In April, 1948, *La Rassegna Mensile di Israel* was revived, with Dante Lattes as editor. At a meeting of remnants of Zionist groups in Rome on Jan. 12 and 13, 1945, chaired by Viterbo, the Italian Zionist Federation was reorganized. That August, the federation held its first postwar conference.

The presence of Palestinian soldiers on Italian soil, the historic struggle for an independent Jewish State, and the establishment of Israel brought about an upsurge of interest in Zionism and Palestine. During the period from 1945 to 1948, 422 Jews left Italy for Palestine; during the first seven years of Israel's existence (1948–55) *'Aliya from Italy totaled 621. Those remaining in Italy participated with unprecedented enthusiasm in fund-raising campaigns and other pro-Israel endeavors.

In the early postwar period the presidency of the Italian Zionist Federation was held almost uninterruptedly by Viterbo, except for the years 1949–51, when the office was occupied by Astorre *Mayer and Renzo Levi. In 1961 the headquarters of the organization was transferred from Rome to Milan. Thereafter the presidency was occupied by Mrs. Giovanna Luzzatto Ajo, Renzo *Bonfiglioli, Miss Maria Luisa Mayer, and David Schaumann.

Activities of the Zionist Federation in the 1960s included study meetings, Hebrew courses, Ulpanim (*see* ULPAN), camping, trips to Israel, participation in international seminars, and fund-raising campaigns. Sh'lihim (emissaries; *see* SHALIAH) sent by the *Jewish Agency, the Jewish National Fund, Keren HaYesod, and the various political parties of Israel helped Italian Zionists acquire a greater knowledge of Israel and the forces that were shaping it.

The reaction to the *Six-day War of 1967 by Italian Zionists as well as by Italian Jews in general was one of great enthusiasm. Many volunteered to go to Israel to help in the war effort; at the same time the collection of funds for the emergency campaign reached an unprecedented peak. All this was facilitated by the favorable attitude of the Italian government and the Italian people.   G. ROMANO

IZFA (Intercollegiate Zionist Federation of America). *See* STUDENT ZIONIST ORGANIZATION.

IZSÁK, EDE. Hungarian Zionist leader (b. Szatmár-Németi, Hungary, 1887). Izsák studied at the Gymnasium of Szatmár-Németi (now Satu-Mare, Romania), where he founded the Kadimah Zionist youth movement. While studying medicine in Budapest, he was elected general secretary and vice-president of Makkabea (Maccabiah), the Hungarian Zionist student organization (*see* HUNGARY, ZIONISM IN). He played a leading role in the work of the *Jewish National Fund in Hungary (1920–24) and in the Hungarian Zionist Organization, first as a member of its Executive (1920–30) and then as its president (1930–34). Izsák also served the *Keren HaYesod (Palestine Foundation Fund) as its cochairman (1934–38) and president (1943–44). In 1940 he founded the Yavne Library, a Zionist publishing house which produced 15 volumes, and he wrote a number of medical texts. After the German occupation of Hungary in March, 1944, he left the country with the Kasztner group (*see* KASZTNER, REZSŐ RUDOLF) and settled in Tel Aviv.

                                      R. L. BRAHAM

J

JABOTINSKY, VLADIMIR YEVGENIEVICH (Z'ev Yona Jabotinsky). Writer, orator, poet, and Zionist leader (b. Odessa, Russia, 1880; d. Hunter, N.Y., 1940). Reared in a traditional middle-class Jewish family, Jabotinsky occasionally took *Hebrew lessons from Y'hoshu'a *Rawnitzky as a boy but, as he admitted in his autobiography, had "no inner contact with Judaism in his youth." In 1898 he went to Bern and Rome to study law and also served as foreign correspondent of the *Odesskiya Novosti* under the pen name Altalena.

In the spring of 1903, when a pogrom in Odessa seemed imminent, Jabotinsky was one of the initiators of the first Zionist self-defense group. After the *Kishinev pogrom, he threw himself into Zionist work. At the 6th Zionist *Congress (Basle, 1903) he voted against the *East Africa scheme and left the Congress hall with the other objectors to the plan. Between 1903 and 1914 he was the foremost Zionist speaker and journalist in Russia and was one of the chief architects of the Helsingfors Program (*see* HELSINGFORS CONFERENCE) and of *Synthetic Zionism.

After the Young Turk Revolution of 1908, Jabotinsky was put in charge of several Zionist periodicals (in French, Hebrew, and Ladino) in Constantinople and of Zionist political work among both Jews and non-Jews. Following his return to Russia in 1910, he launched a crusade to make Hebrew the language of instruction in all Jewish schools, visiting 50 Jewish communities in Russia to lecture on "The Language of Our Culture." This concept met with strong opposition not only in assimilationist and Yiddishist circles but also among leading Zionists, who considered it extremist and utopian.

After the outbreak of World War I, Jabotinsky advanced, and almost singlehandedly promoted, the idea of a *Jewish Legion as part of the British Army. Among Zionist leaders only Chaim *Weizmann and Montague David *Eder supported his plan. In 1917, when the British government consented to the formation of the 38th Battalion of Royal Fusiliers, Jabotinsky enlisted in it as a private. He was soon promoted to the rank of lieutenant, headed the company that was the first to cross the Jordan River, and was decorated and mentioned in dispatches.

After the war, Jabotinsky joined the *Zionist Commission and for a time headed its Political Department. Anticipating anti-Jewish outbreaks by Arab extremists, abetted by the British Army, Jabotinsky undertook the formation of the first *Hagana units, which he led during the bloody Jerusalem riots in April, 1920 (*see* ARAB RIOTS IN PALESTINE). For this he was sentenced by a British military court to 15 years at hard labor. Following a storm of indignant protest from Jews as well as gentiles in Palestine, England, and the United States, Jabotinsky was amnestied by Sir Herbert *Samuel on July 8, 1920, and the verdict was quashed in 1921.

In March, 1921, Jabotinsky joined the Zionist *Executive. At the 12th Zionist Congress (Karlovy Vary, September, 1921), he was reelected to the Executive and shared with Chaim Weizmann the political responsibility for acquiescing in Winston *Churchill's *White Paper of June, 1922. During the Congress, Jabotinsky signed an agreement with Prof. Maxim Slavinsky, representative of Simon Petlyura's Ukrainian government-in-exile, which was then preparing a march into the Bolshevik-held Ukraine: a noncombatant Jewish gendarmerie force was to follow in the rear of Petlyura's army to ensure the safety of the Jewish population in areas occupied by the Ukrainian units. In many Zionist circles this agreement with a "pogrom regime" was strongly criticized.

Dissatisfied with the policies of the Palestine administration under Sir Herbert Samuel and with what he considered lack of resistance to the British anti-Zionist policy, Jabotinsky resigned from the Executive in January, 1923. In the same year he founded *B'rit Trumpeldor (Betar). In 1925 the World Union of Zionists-*Revisionists (B'rit Herut-HaTzohar) was formed in Paris with Jabotinsky as president. He made Paris his headquarters until 1936, except for a brief period in 1928–29 when he lived in Jerusalem as director of the Judea Insurance Company and edited the daily *Do'ar HaYom*. In 1930, while he was on a lecture tour in South Africa, the British adminstration canceled his return visa, thus preventing him from ever returning to Palestine.

In 1933 Jabotinsky vigorously espoused the case of two young Revisionists, Abraham Stavsky and Zvi Rosenblatt (see STAVSKY TRIAL), who had been accused of assassinating the Jewish labor leader Hayim Victor *Arlosoroff. Both youths were acquitted the following year. In 1934 Jabotinsky concluded with David *Ben-Gurion agreements that were intended to ease internal Zionist conflicts and to regularize the relationship between the *Histadrut (General Federation of Labor) and the Revisionist *Histadrut Ha'Ovdim HaL'umit (National Workers Federation); these agreements were rejected, however, by a Histadrut plebiscite.

Vladimir Jabotinsky.
[Keren HaYesod]

After the establishment, in 1929, of the enlarged *Jewish Agency, with 50 per cent of the seats allocated to non-Zionists, and after the refusal of the 17th Zionist Congress (1931) to define the aim of Zionism as the founding of a Jewish State, Jabotinsky seceded from the *World Zionist Organization and, at a congress held in Vienna in 1935, representing 713,000 voters, founded an independent *New Zionist Organization with himself as president and with headquarters in London. Jabotinsky conducted a vigorous campaign against the plan for the *partition of Palestine, and his testimony before the *Peel Commission (London, February, 1937) was much discussed. Simultaneously, he inaugurated the "policy of alliances" with governments interested in solving the problem of their Jewish minorities through an internationally sponsored 10-year plan under which 1.5 million Eastern European Jews would be evacuated to Palestine. On the eve of World War II, he revived the Max *Nordau plan providing for the transfer of the first million Jews within one year. Since 1932 Jabotinsky, intent on breaking the prohibitive British *immigration regulations, had been advocating *illegal immigration, which, beginning in 1936, became a major activity of his movement. He sided with those groups in the Hagana which, as opposed to the official Zionist line of *Havlaga (self-restraint) toward Arab terror, insisted on a policy of active retaliation. In all matters of major policy, he was the supreme commander of the *Irgun Tz'vai L'umi.

With the outbreak of World War II, Jabotinsky advocated the creation of a Jewish army to fight Nazi Germany. In February, 1940, he went to the United States, where he died of a heart ailment on Aug. 3, 1940, in the B'rit Trumpeldor summer camp at Hunter, N.Y. In his last will he wrote: "Should I be buried outside of Palestine, my remains may not be transferred to Palestine except by order of a future Jewish government in that country." An order to this effect was issued by Prime Minister Levi *Eshkol, and, in July, 1964, the remains of Jabotinsky and his wife were reburied on Mount Herzl in Jerusalem.

J. SCHECHTMAN

JABOTINSKY INSTITUTE (Makhon Jabotinsky). Institute founded in 1935 in Tel Aviv to collect and preserve manuscripts, documents, and historical material connected with the activities of Revisionism (see REVISIONISTS), Zionism in general, and affiliated institutions and organizations. It consists of two sections, the institute proper and the museum. The archives, which have been classified under the supervision of specialists from the *Hebrew University of Jerusalem, are available to students of institutions of higher learning in Israel and to institutes of Zionist and historical research.

Jabotinsky Institute building, Tel Aviv. [Jabotinsky Institute]

In the 1960s the institute cooperated with the Institute for Zionist Research of Tel Aviv University and with the Institute of Contemporary Jewry of the Hebrew University and was represented on the Supreme Council of the National Archives attached to the Prime Minister's Office. The museum exhibited documents, photographs, models, arms, flags, and other objects connected with the activities of the Zionist movement and its affiliated organizations. The museum of the *Irgun Tz'vai L'umi and the museum of the Revisionist and *B'rit Trumpeldor (Betar) partisans and ghetto fighters in Nazi-occupied Europe were affiliated with the institute. The library of the institute contained about 10,000 volumes in more than 10 languages.

In the 1960s the Jabotinsky Institute was governed by a Board of Directors representing the *Herut movement, Betar, *Histadrut Ha'Ovdim HaL'umit, Misdar Jabotinsky, the Association of Former Members of the Irgun, the Association of Former Partisans and Ghetto Fighters, and representatives of the family of Vladimir *Jabotinsky. Its budget was covered by voluntary contributions from Israel and the *Diaspora and by allocations from the Ministry of Education and Culture, municipalities, and institutions represented on the Board of Directors. It published historical studies on *illegal immigration, on the Warsaw ghetto revolt, and on the first Jewish self-defense unit in Odessa in 1903, and *Pirsumim*, a quarterly publication of documents and material from the archives of the institute.

I. BENARI

JACOBS, ROSE GELL. Zionist leader in the United States (b. New York, 1888). A graduate of the New York Training School for Teachers, Rose Gell taught school on New York's lower East Side. She was one of the charter members of *Hadassah, founded by Henrietta *Szold in New York in 1912. From 1920 to 1925 Mrs. Jacobs was editor of the *Hadassah Newsletter*. She also served as acting national president (1920–23), national vice-president (1924–28), and national president (1930–32, 1935–37) of Hadassah. In 1937 she was elected honorary national vice-president for life.

Rose Gell Jacobs.
[Hadassah]

Mrs. Jacobs made the first of many visits to Palestine at the time of her marriage in 1914. In 1929 she was a delegate to the Constituent Assembly of the *Jewish Agency, and in 1937 she became a member of the Agency's Executive. She represented Hadassah at the Zionist Conference held in Karlovy Vary in 1922 and at numerous Zionist Congresses (see CONGRESS, ZIONIST). During her second term as Hadassah president, she initiated *Youth 'Aliya activities in the United States, attending the first conference of Youth 'Aliya in the Netherlands in 1935. She was the only woman delegate at the *St. James Conference held in London in 1939.

An initiator of the building program of the Hadassah-University Hospital on Mount Scopus, Mrs. Jacobs represented Hadassah at the dedication of the hospital and the *Hebrew University–Hadassah Medical School in 1939. In 1940 she organized in Palestine the Emergency Committee for Hadassah Projects in Palestine (other members were Judah L. *Magnes, Julius *Simon, and Henrietta Szold, chairman). As president of the Esco Foundation for Palestine in 1946, she was instrumental in publishing its two-volume work, *Palestine: A Study of Jewish, Arab and British Policies* (1947).

G. HIRSCHLER

JACOBSON, CHARLOTTE STONE. Zionist leader in the United States (b. New York, 1914). Mrs. Jacobson joined *Hadassah in the 1940s, serving as president of the Bronx chapter from 1948 to 1951, when she was elected to the National Board of Directors of the organization. In 1952 she was elected to the National Executive of Hadassah and became national secretary, holding the latter office until 1955, when she was named national chairman for Zionist affairs. She was national vice-president (1957–60), national treasurer (1960–64), and national president (1964–68) of Hadassah. In 1968 she was appointed national chairman of the Hadassah medical organization and was elected a member of the Executive of the *Jewish Agency.

As head of Hadassah, Mrs. Jacobson was responsible for the collection and airlifting of $3,000,000 worth of drugs and medical supplies to Israel before and during the *Six-day War of 1967. A few days after the war she arrived in Israel, where, acting on behalf of Hadassah, she took official possession again of the Hadassah hospital facilities on Mount Scopus, which had stood empty and isolated as an Arab-surrounded enclave for over 19 years. A member of the Hadassah delegation to the *Zionist General Council and of the Committee on Administration of the American Zionist Council (see EMERGENCY COMMITTEE FOR ZIONIST AFFAIRS; she was chairman of the council's Executive in 1960–61), Mrs. Jacobson attended every Zionist *Congress from the 23d (Jerusalem, 1951) on.

JACOBSON, VICTOR. Zionist leader (b. Simferopol, Crimea, Russia, 1869; d. Bern, Switzerland, 1934). Active in the Zionist movement from his student days on, he played a prominent role in Zionism in Russia and was, beginning with the 3d Zionist *Congress (1899), a member of the Zionist *Actions Committee. In 1906 he was appointed manager of the Beirut branch office of the Anglo-Palestine Company (see BANK L'UMI L'YISRAEL), and two years later he became political representative of the *World Zionist Organization (WZO) in Constantinople and director of the Anglo-Levantine Banking Company.

A member of the Zionist *Executive from 1913 to 1921, Jacobson was in charge of Zionist political activity in Turkey and other countries and early in 1914 conducted negotiations with Arab politicians and journalists in an attempt to persuade them that if they would cease opposing Jewish endeavors in Palestine, the Jews would help them realize their own national ambitions. In 1915–16 he was in Berlin, and late in 1916 he became head of the *Copenhagen Bureau of the WZO. There he assiduously cultivated contacts with the German Embassy to help avert the threat to the Jewish community of Palestine due to Turkey's entry into World War I. In 1918 he released the Copenhagen Manifesto. In 1919, when the headquarters of the WZO was moved to London, he too moved to the British capital.

Jacobson resigned from the Zionist Executive in 1921. In 1925 he was appointed representative of the WZO at the League of Nations and head of the Zionist political office in Paris. In a secret memorandum in 1932 he suggested the *partition of Palestine. At the 18th Zionist Congress (1933), when Nahum *Sokolow was president of the WZO, he was again elected a member of the Zionist Executive, while retaining his posts in Geneva and Paris.

JAFFA (Heb., Yafo). Ancient town adjoining Tel Aviv, with which it forms the twin city of Tel Aviv–Yafo.

Biblical and Roman Times. Jaffa is first mentioned on a pylon of Thutmose III at Karnak (16th cent. B.C.E.). Excavations of its ancient tell (mound) yielded remains chiefly from the middle and late Bronze Ages, including a brick wall and monumental gate and inscriptions of Rameses II (1290–1223 B.C.E.). Antiquities found in the Tel Aviv and Jaffa area are exhibited in the Tel Aviv–Jaffa Museum of Antiquities.

In the conquest of Canaan by the Children of Israel, the area near Jaffa was occupied by the tribe of Dan. The Bible narrates that the cedars of Lebanon used for the construction of the First and Second Temples were shipped to Jerusalem via the "Sea of Jaffa." The prophet Jonah, fleeing from God, embarked at Jaffa. In 701 B.C.E., Sennacherib, King of Assyria, conquered the city, which was subsequently held by the Persians and Phoenicians. Alexander the Great, who conquered Pal-

Port of Jaffa. [Israel Government Tourist Office]

estine in 332 B.C.E., made Jaffa a Greek city. During the Hasmonean revolt, the pagan population of the city, enraged by the successes of Judah the Maccabee, enticed many of their Jewish fellow citizens into boats and drowned them. Judah thereupon raided the city, which was eventually occupied by his brother Jonathan and later by Simon, another brother, who converted it into a Jewish city.

In the beginning of the wars between Rome and Judea, Jaffa was a center of Jewish insurrection. Roman troops slaughtered the population and pillaged and burned the city. After the retreat of the Romans, Jews returned to Jaffa and with their boats harassed Roman sea trade and communications. The city was subsequently taken by the Romans in a surprise attack. Thousands of Jews attempted to flee by boat but were overtaken by a storm and drowned.

Byzantine and Arab Rule. In the period following the destruction of the Second Temple and especially after the suppression of the Bar Kokhba revolt, a large Jewish community again developed in the city. During the period of Byzantine rule, Jews were persecuted by their Christian fellow citizens and left Jaffa. Under Arab rule, a Jewish community was again established, and existed until the arrival of the Crusaders in 1099. In the wars between the Crusaders and the Muslims, Jaffa was a much-embattled city and changed hands several times. In 1268 it was finally retaken by the Muslims, who razed it to the ground.

Turkish Period. In subsequent centuries, Jaffa was only a small town and at times was deserted altogether. It was not until the 18th century that it began to regain some of its former importance. However, its renewed growth as a seaport and

trade center was interrupted by new wars, which followed one another in quick succession.

In 1770 the city was taken by the Bedouin sheikh Dhaher el-'Amr and in the following years was the scene of fighting between this sheikh and the Turks and their respective allies. In 1799 Napoleon conquered Jaffa. Not long after the withdrawal of the French, the city was again a battlefield, this time between rival Turkish troops. The period from 1810 to 1820 saw important reconstruction work carried out by Abu Nabbut, the governor of the city. From 1831 to 1840 Jaffa was held by Mohammed 'Ali, the Turkish governor of Egypt, who had proclaimed himself independent of the Sultan.

Jewish *immigration into the country and the establishment of Jewish settlements during the late 19th century contributed to Jaffa's expansion, and a large Jewish community began to develop in the city. Between 1886 and 1892 the Jewish quarters of N've Tzedek and N've Shalom were built. In 1891 the *Hoveve Zion movement opened an executive office in Jaffa, and in 1908 the *World Zionist Organization established an office there to direct settlement efforts. In 1909 the building of a suburb called Tel Aviv was begun, and Jaffa itself became the center of Jewish reconstruction activities.

World War I and Interwar Years. The outbreak of World War I brought development to a standstill. In 1917 the Turks ordered the evacuation of Jews from the city, which was taken by the British during their offensive in November of that year.

The expansion of neighboring Tel Aviv in the period following World War I stimulated the growth of Jaffa. In March, 1921, Jaffa Arabs attacked and killed dozens of Jews in the city. There were additional Jewish victims in Jaffa during the *Arab riots of August, 1929, when Jaffa Arabs attempted to attack Tel Aviv but were repelled. Similar attempts were foiled during the Arab riots of 1936–39.

The development of the harbor at Haifa had an adverse effect on the port of Jaffa. The establishment in 1936 of the seaport of Tel Aviv, as a result of the refusal of the Arabs

Clock tower in the center of Jaffa. [Israel Government Tourist Office]

of Jaffa to handle the goods of Jews, brought about a further decline in the importance of Jaffa's harbor.

*War of Independence and Union with Tel Aviv. During the Arab attacks on Jews following the United Nations *partition resolution of Nov. 29, 1947 (*see* UNITED NATIONS AND PALESTINE-ISRAEL), the Arabs of Jaffa shelled Tel Aviv. In April, 1948, the *Irgun Tz'vai L'umi launched a counterattack and, after two days of fighting, succeeded in penetrating Jaffa's defenses and cutting off the Manshiye quarter from the rest of the city. However, further progress of the Jewish forces was barred by British military intervention. On May 13, 1948, with the evacuation of the British from the city, Jaffa surrendered to the Jews.

During the fighting, the city was abandoned by the great majority of its 70,000 inhabitants and only 3,000 remained. Jaffa was subsequently resettled with new Jewish immigrants and in 1949 officially joined Tel Aviv to become the twin city of Tel Aviv–Yafo. In 1965 the port of Jaffa was closed down as a result of the construction of the Ashdod port.

T. PRESCHEL

JAFFE (YAFFE), BEZALEL. Zionist leader (b. Grodno, Russia, 1868; d. Tel Aviv, 1925). Jaffe founded a *Hoveve Zion society in Grodno and with the advent of political Zionism became one of its early adherents. He attended early Zionist Congresses (*see* CONGRESS, ZIONIST) and at the 7th Congress (Basle, 1905) was elected to the Greater *Actions Committee. He was also a member of the Central Committee of Russian Zionists and participated in the *Helsingfors Conference (1906). In 1909 he settled in Palestine, where for many years he directed the *G'ula land purchase society. He was the head of the Jewish Community Board of Tel Aviv–Jaffa and a member of the *Va'ad L'umi (National Council). In addition to his widespread communal activities, Jaffe was active in educational work.

JAFFE (YOFFE), LEIB. Head of *Keren HaYesod, poet, and Zionist publicist (b. Grodno, Russia, 1875; d. Jerusalem, 1948). Jaffe joined the Hibbat Zion movement (*see* HOVEVE

Leib Jaffe.
[Zionist Archives]

ZION) at an early age and began composing Zionist poems in Russian in the early 1890s and in Hebrew in 1897. He studied at the University of Heidelberg, where he became a close friend of Hermann *Schapira, attended the 1st Zionist *Congress (1897) and practically all succeeding Congresses during his lifetime, participated in the formation of the *Democratic

Faction at the 5th Congress (1901), and was one of the organizers of the opposition to the *East Africa scheme. A leading Zionist in Russia, Jaffe was a member of the Central Committee of Russian Zionists (1906–18) and of the Zionist *Actions Committee (1907–11). He edited the Zionist official organs *Dos Yidishe Folk* (1907), **Ha'Olam* (1909), and *Yevreiskaya Zhizn* (1915–17).

In 1917 Jaffe was president of the Zionist Organization of Moscow. The next year he settled in Vilna, where he edited a number of Zionist publications in Yiddish and became president of the Zionist Organization of Lithuania. In 1920 he settled in Palestine, where he edited **Ha'Aretz* for several years and was a member of the *Zionist Commission (Va'ad HaTzirim). He joined the staff of the Keren HaYesod (Palestine Foundation Fund) in 1923, became its joint managing director (1926–48), and traveled throughout the world on its behalf. He also served as a political emissary for Zionism in South America and Eastern Europe. He was killed in the bombing of the Keren HaYesod building in Jerusalem in March, 1948.

Jaffe wrote a book of reminiscences about Hermann Schapira and edited a memorial volume dedicated to the 1st Zionist Congress. His memoirs, essays, diaries, and letters were published in three volumes (1948, 1964, 1968).

B. JAFFE

JAFFE, MORDECAI GIMPEL. Rabbi and pioneer in Palestine (b. Lithuania, 1820; d. Y'hud, near Petah Tikva, 1891). After studying at the Yeshiva of Volozhin, he served first as rabbi of Derechin and then for 40 years in Ruzhany, both in Grodno District. When Sir Moses *Montefiore visited Russia in 1846, Jaffe presented him with a memorandum on the situation of the Jews in his area. Jaffe supported Rabbi Zvi Hirsch *Kalischer's activities for the establishment of settlements in Palestine. In the debate which arose following the Russian pogroms of 1881 as to whether Jews should emigrate to the United States or to Palestine, he publicly came out in favor of the latter. After Rabbi Sh'muel *Mohilever had obtained the consent of Baron Edmond de *Rothschild to establish an experimental settlement in Palestine, Jaffe helped him select settlers from the village of Pavlovka, near Ruzhany, who established 'Ekron. Jaffe participated in the conference convened by Mohilever in Białystok in 1883 for the purpose of setting up a central office for the *Hoveve Zion movement. In 1888 he emigrated to Palestine and settled in Y'hud, where he headed a Yeshiva. The next year, he urged the Jewish colonists to observe the Sh'mita (Biblical sabbatical year) laws and proposed that financial assistance be given to those who did so. Bezalel and Leib *Jaffe were his grandsons.

I. KLAUSNER

JAHRESKONFERENZ (Annual Conference). Biennial conference held within the *World Zionist Organization (WZO) between 1902 and 1922, in the years during this period when no Zionist *Congress was held. Provisions for this conference were made by the 5th Zionist Congress (Basle, 1901), when it was decided to hold the Congress biennially rather than annually. The Jahreskonferenz, sometimes referred to as the Little Congress, was actually an extended meeting of the Greater *Actions Committee, attended not only by the members of that committee but also by the president and vice-presidents of the previous Congress, the presidents of all permanent commissions, the presidents of the Zionist federations and amalgamated Zionist organizations of the various countries, the directors of Zionist banking institutions, the members of the *Congress Tribunal, the legal adviser of the Congress, and the auditors of the WZO.

The conference had only a limited measure of authority and could not exercise the full powers of a Zionist Congress. It was authorized only to examine the accounts of the WZO, accept resolutions, and draw up a program of activity for the ensuing year. It had no right to conduct elections of committees or officials or to make any changes in the Zionist program adopted by the Congresses.

Annual conferences were held in 1902 (Vienna, Oct. 28–30), 1904 (Vienna, Aug. 17–19), 1906 (Cologne, Aug. 28–31), 1908 (Cologne, Aug. 11–13), 1910 (Berlin, June 27–29), 1912 (Berlin, Sept. 1–3), 1920 (London, July 7–22; *see* LONDON ZIONIST CONFERENCE OF 1920), and 1922 (Karlovy Vary, Aug. 25–Sept. 1). After the 12th Zionist Congress (Karlovy Vary, 1921) the Jahreskonferenz was renamed Zentralrat (Central Council). A conference had been scheduled for the summer of 1924 but was canceled by the Actions Committee. The 14th Congress (Vienna, 1925) decided to abolish the annual conference and turned over its powers to the Actions Committee.

JALJULIYA. Arab village northeast of Petah Tikva. Population (1968): 1,900.

JAMAL (DJEMAL) PASHA, AHMED. Turkish statesman and soldier (b. Mytilene, Lesbos, 1872; d. Tiflis, Russia, 1922). A leader of the Young Turk Revolution, he became military governor of Adana in 1908 and governor-general of Baghdad in 1911. During the Balkan Wars he commanded a division. In 1913 he was made Minister of Public Works and the following year Minister of the Navy. Subsequently, he was one of the triumvirate that ruled the Ottoman Empire.

During World War I, Jamal Pasha commanded the Fourth Army in Palestine and Syria. In 1915 he conducted an abortive campaign to conquer the Suez Canal. During his wartime stay in Palestine, he persecuted the Jewish population in general and the Zionists in particular. Early in the war, he ordered all enemy aliens in Palestine, most of whom were Jews, either to adopt Turkish citizenship or to leave the country. Many leaders of Palestine's Jewish community were exiled. In the spring of 1917 the population of Jaffa and Tel Aviv was expelled into the interior of the country. Following the exposure of the *Nili spy organization in the same year, Jamal Pasha and his aides intensified their harassment of the Jewish settlers.

After the collapse of the Ottoman Empire, Jamal Pasha went to Russia and thence to Afghanistan, where he wielded great influence. He was assassinated in Tiflis while visiting there on behalf of the Afghans.

T. PRESCHEL

JAMMER, MOSHE (Max). Israeli physicist, president and rector of *Bar-Ilan University (b. Berlin, 1915). After obtaining a teacher's diploma in physics at the University of Vienna, he settled in Israel in 1935 and attended the *Hebrew University of Jerusalem.

Jammer served in the British Army (1942–45) and in the *War of Independence, after which he taught physics and the history and philosophy of science at the Hebrew University until 1952, when he was appointed visiting lecturer at Harvard University. In 1956 he was an associate professor at the University of Oklahoma and subsequently was appointed professor and head of the physics department at Bar-Ilan University. In 1958–59 he was research professor at Boston University and in 1962 was elected rector of Bar-Ilan University.

In the 1960s Jammer was a visiting professor at various universities in Europe and the United States. He was a member of several scientific organizations, and in 1961 he received the Physics Prize of the American Academy of Arts and Sciences. From 1966 on he was both rector and president of Bar-Ilan University. He is the author of numerous studies in modern physics.

JANABIB. Bedouin tribe in the B'er Sheva' area. Population (1968): 246.

JANCO, MARCEL. Israeli painter (b. Bucharest, 1895). Janco studied architecture at the Federal Polytechnic School in Zurich and during World War I helped establish the revolutionary art movement known as Dada. After a stay in Paris, he returned to Romania, where he founded Contimporanul, the country's first modernist movement, and was active also as an architect.

Political developments forced Janco to flee to Palestine in 1940. There he established himself as a leader of progressive art. In 1953 he founded the artists' colony 'En Hod on the ruins of an ancient village on Mount Carmel. Four years later he was commissioner of the Israel Pavilion in São Paulo, Brazil. His paintings, often inspired by the people and landscape of Israel, are representational yet highly stylized. They have been exhibited widely in Israel, as well as all over Europe and in the United States.

A. WERNER

JANNER, SIR BARNETT. Public figure and Zionist leader in England (b. Cardiff, Wales, 1892). Janner joined the Cardiff Zionist Society at an early age and became active in the Welsh University Students' Union. Moving to London in 1929, he was a member of Parliament for the Liberal party from 1931 to 1935 and, beginning in 1945, for the Labor party. He served as president of the *Board of Deputies of British Jews from 1955 to 1964 and was one of the two honorary secretaries (the other was the Marquess of Hartington) of the Parliamentary Palestine Committee, formed in 1929. On July 8, 1946, Janner led a Zionist deputation that presented a memorandum ("Let My People Go!") to Prime Minister Clement Attlee. He was president of the Zionist Federation of Great Britain and Ireland (*see* GREAT BRITAIN, ZIONISM IN) and of the European Council of the *World Confederation of General Zionists, vice-president of the Anglo-Israel Parliamentary Group, and a member of the *Actions Committee and of the Conference on Jewish Material Claims against Germany (*see* GERMAN-ISRAEL AGREEMENT).

In January, 1961, Janner was knighted in recognition of his services as president of the Board of Deputies. In 1970 he was elevated to the peerage as Baron Janner of the City of Leicester. Janner's wife, Elsie Sybil Janner (Lady Janner), J.P., is active in Jewish communal life.

J. FRAENKEL

JAPAN, ZIONISM IN, AND RELATIONS WITH ISRAEL. The Jewish population of the four main islands of Japan never exceeded 1,000. The first Jews to settle in the country came from Europe, Turkey, and the Middle East after Japan had been opened to the West in 1854. The first synagogue in the country was founded by Russian Jews in Nagasaki in the 1890s. *Sephardim from Iraq and Iran came to Kobe. Later, particularly following the Russian Revolution of 1917, Jews settled also in Yokohama and Tokyo. During World War II many Jewish refugees from Nazism stayed in Kobe and Yokohama for varying periods. After the war some Jews left the country, but others arrived from Communist China, and Jewish business and professional people came from the United States, Israel, and Europe (many of them representing business concerns in those countries) and settled in Tokyo. In 1968 there were in Japan 1,000 Jews, in a total population of 99,920,000; of these, about 500 to 600 lived in Tokyo.

Before the Establishment of the State of Israel, 1904–48. A report to the 7th Zionist *Congress (Basle, 1905) mentioned Nagasaki as one of the cities in the Far East having a Zionist organization. At that time the future Palestine pioneer Joseph *Trumpeldor, then a soldier in the Russian Army, was in a Japanese prison camp, having been taken captive in the Russo-Japanese War (1904–05). It was during his year in captivity that he conceived a plan to go to Palestine with a few friends and to set up a communal settlement there.

When the *Balfour Declaration was issued in November, 1917, Japan endorsed it promptly in the form of a statement by the Japanese Ambassador in London.

In 1920 Israel *Cohen visited Japan on behalf of the *World Zionist Organization. In Kobe, where he found some 200 Jews (about half were from England, the United States, and Iraq; the other half were Russian refugees), he established a Zionist society with a membership of 70 and S. Yabroff as president. At a meeting in Yokohama, where there were many Russian Jews, Cohen raised several hundred pounds sterling. In his autobiography, *A Jewish Pilgrimage* (1956), Cohen reports that, in order to obtain permission to hold the Yokohama meeting, he had to convince the police that Zionism was not identified with communism even though many Zionists were of Russian origin.

The position of the Japanese government in the 1920s was not unfriendly toward Zionism. In the fall of 1926, Mr. Kuroki, the Japanese Consul at Port Said, visited the offices of the Zionist *Executive in Jerusalem to obtain literature on Zionist activity in Palestine and elsewhere. In December, 1929, Foreign Minister Baron Kijuro Shidehara sent a congratulatory message to *Israel's Messenger*, the Jewish newspaper published in Shanghai (*see* CHINA, ZIONISMS IN), on the occasion of the 12th anniversary of the Balfour Declaration. The death that September of a former Foreign Minister, Baron Gi-ichi Tanaka, was noted in Zionist circles as the loss of a friend.

In the 1930s Tabun Sakai founded an organization in Tokyo (for native Japanese only) whose main function was to support the rebuilding of a Jewish Homeland in Palestine. Bishop Juji Nakada (d. 1939) of the Holiness Church preached his belief that the return of the Jewish people to Palestine was a prerequisite for the coming of the Messiah and began to raise funds "for the kingdom of the Jewish people."

As the Japanese government established closer ties with Nazi Germany, however, there was a rise in *anti-Semitism in Japan. In 1937 the Japanese authorities banned Zionist fund-raising campaigns. After Japan entered World War II on the side of the Axis Powers in 1941, the Japanese policy was to treat the Jews well insofar as they could be of use to the country but to watch them carefully and to give no support to "Jewish national" movements.

Japan and the State of Israel, 1948–   . When the State of Israel was established, Japan was still under Allied occupation. Diplomatic relations between Israel and Japan were established as of May 15, 1952, a little more than two weeks after Japan had officially regained its sovereignty. Joseph I. *Linton became Israel's first envoy to Japan. The Japanese Legation in Israel and Israel's Legation in Japan were raised to embassy level in 1963.

From 1948 on a variety of cultural and commercial exchanges took place between Japan and Israel. The new Jewish State excited the intellectual curiosity of many Japanese students, who went to Israel to study *kibbutz life or to take advanced training at the Haifa *Technion and the *Hebrew University on Israeli scholarships. In return, Israelis received grants from Japan for study in that country. Israel was the first country to send medical aid to Nagoya when that city was struck by a typhoon in October, 1959. In the spring and summer of 1961, Japanese anthropologists and geographers undertook excavations in Israel to study prehistoric man. The *Israel Philharmonic Orchestra was accorded a warm reception in Japan. In the early 1960s a textile plant was set up in the Negev with the help of Japanese experts, and Israel had ships built in Japanese shipyards.

Among the high Israeli government officials who visited Japan were Mordecai *Bentov, as Minister of Development (1959), Pinhas *Sapir, as Minister of Commerce and Industry (1959), and Golda *Meir, as Foreign Minister (1962). In Japan, Prince Mikasa, the youngest brother of Emperor Hirohito, was in the early 1960s the patron of a society for Japan-Israel friendship (founded in 1958), one of whose aims was to foster closer relations between Israel and Japan.

Following the *Six-day War of 1967 relations between Japan and Israel continued friendly.

G. HIRSCHLER

JARBLUM, MARC (Mord'khai). Writer, journalist, and Zionist leader in France and Israel (b. Warsaw, 1887). One of the founders of Poland's *Po'ale Zion party, Jarblum was arrested in Warsaw in 1905 because of his political activities. In 1906 he was in Cracow, editing *Dos Yidishe Arbeter Vort*, the first Po'ale Zion newspaper in Poland. The next year he moved to Paris, where he became active in the French Socialist party. While visiting Warsaw in 1911, he was arrested and deported to Russia but escaped a year later and returned to Paris, where he helped disseminate the ideals of *Labor Zionism among Jewish immigrants. During World War I he met the French Socialist leader Léon *Blum and gained his sympathy for Zionism. Shortly after the 1917 Russian Revolution, Jarblum went to Russia and then to Warsaw, where he edited a Yiddish-language Po'ale Zion periodical, *Der Yunge Yidishe Kemfer*. A few years later he returned to Paris. From 1933 on he was editor of *Unzer Vort*, the organ of the Po'ale Zion–*Hitahdut in France, and in 1936, editor of *Di Naye Tzeit*, a right-wing Po'ale Zion weekly. In 1937 he was elected to the Central Bureau of Po'ale Zion–Hitahdut and, at the 20th Zionist *Congress held in Zurich that year, to the Zionist *Actions Committee.

After the Nazi occupation of Paris in 1940, Jarblum moved to the unoccupied zone of France and became active in the French and French-Jewish resistance movements. After the

Nazi occupation of all of France in November, 1942, he went into hiding from the Gestapo. In the summer of 1943 he escaped to Switzerland, where he worked with the *American Jewish Joint Distribution Committee and the *World Jewish Congress. Returning to Paris after the liberation in 1944, he played an important role in gaining the sympathy of French leaders for the United Nations Palestine *partition resolution. In subsequent years he served successively as president and honorary president of the Zionist Federation of France and of the Federation of Jewish Associations of France. As correspondent in France for *Davar and for Yiddish newspapers in the United States, South America, and Poland, he was in a position to help many Jewish refugee writers in France.

In 1953 Jarblum settled in Israel, where he served on the Executive Committee of *Histadrut (General Federation of Labor) until 1964. He published numerous books and pamphlets on the Palestine problem, Soviet Jewry, and the struggle against Nazism. He was named a knight of the French Legion of Honor in 1948 and an officer 10 years later.

JASINOVSKY, ISRAEL (Isidor). Lawyer (b. Grodno District, Russia, 1842; d. Warsaw, 1917). Jasinovsky received a religious education. In 1876 he settled in Warsaw, where he opened a law practice. He was among the first Warsaw Jews to rally to the *Hoveve Zion movement. Jasinovsky attended the *Kattowitz Conference in 1883 and the Hoveve Zion conference held in that city in 1884. Elected to the Central Committee of the movement, he later headed its Warsaw office. Jasinovsky was a spokesman for the nonobservant elements of the movement, opposing the religious demands made by Sh'muel *Mohilever and other rabbis. He helped draw up the statutes of the *Odessa Committee and attended its first general meeting in 1890.

Joining political Zionism at its inception, he attended the first seven Zionist Congresses (see CONGRESS, ZIONIST) and was a member of the *Actions Committee. After the 7th Congress he joined the Territorialist movement. In 1906 he represented the *Jewish Territorial Organization at a Brussels conference convened by David *Wolffsohn to discuss means of aiding Jewish émigrés.

I. KLAUSNER

JAT. Arab village east-southeast of Hadera. Population (1968): 3,000.

JAT. Druze village east-northeast of ʿAkko. Population (1968): 510.

JAVITS, JACOB KOPPEL. Attorney and legislator in the United States (b. New York, 1904). Raised on New York's lower East Side as the son of immigrant parents, Javits obtained a law degree from New York University (1926) and opened a law practice in New York City. During World War II he served first in a civilian capacity in the Army Chemical Warfare Board, then was commissioned in the army, serving in the European and Pacific theaters. He was a member of the U.S. House of Representatives (1946–54) and attorney general of the state of New York (1954–56). In 1956 he was elected to the U.S. Senate; in 1970 he was still serving as Senator from New York and as a member of various Senate committees. A spokesman for the liberal wing of the Republican party, he initiated legislation on civil rights, civil liberties, health, education, and labor.

Actively involved in numerous Jewish communal and pro-Israel organizations, Javits was an articulate supporter of Zionism and the State of Israel. As a member of the House of Representatives Committee on Foreign Affairs, he went to Israel on a study mission in November, 1951, submitting a report (Feb. 29, 1952) on his findings to the House. He frequently took the Senate floor on behalf of Israel, and after the *Six-day War of 1967 he proposed a conference of all Middle Eastern nations and other countries with an interest in the area in order to promote understanding between Israel and the Arab states and plan for the economic development of the entire region.

JAWITZ, Z'EV. Historian, author, educator, and religious Zionist philosopher (b. Kolno, Russian Poland, 1847; d. London, 1924). Son of a wealthy manufacturer and banker, he studied the Bible, the Talmud, *Hebrew, modern languages, geography, and history with private tutors. After an unsuccessful venture in business, he turned to a literary career. His first article, published under a pseudonym in 1881, outlined his religious Zionist views and incorporated practical suggestions for the settlement of Palestine: draining Lake Hula, seeking sources of water, development of the hot springs of Tiberias, paving roads, utilization of quarries and Dead Sea minerals, afforestation, and development of agricultural industries.

Jawitz lived for some time in Y'hud, near Petah Tikva, continuing his literary activity and serving as spiritual guide and teacher in Zikhron Yaʿakov. In 1890 he moved to Jerusalem, where he devoted all his time to writing. He wrote several Hebrew textbooks and published a periodical to which he contributed studies in Hebrew linguistics and other fields as well as short stories describing the life of the new settlements. He also began his magnum opus, the 14-volume *Toldot Yisrael* (History of the Jews), in which he stressed the uniqueness of Jewish religion and culture and devoted much space to a description of the internal spiritual life of the Jews. However, his books did not sell, and since he was unable to support himself in Jerusalem, he went in 1897 to Vilna, where he lectured and gave private lessons.

Jawitz became active in Zionist organizations in Vilna and in 1902 was instrumental in founding the *Mizrahi movement there, editing its publication for two years. In 1906 he began a period of migration to Homburg, Antwerp, Leeds, and London. In addition to his major work on Jewish history, he published textbooks, ideological articles on religion and politics, works on religious Zionist education, and research on the Hebrew language and prayers. He also wrote stories about the life of the *Yishuv (Jewish population of Palestine), collected legends of the rabbis, and translated poems and stories.

Y. RAPHAEL

JEBEL ET-TUR. *See* OLIVES, MOUNT OF.

JERUSALEM. Capital of Israel. Population (1968): 278,000.

No other city has played such a predominant role in the history, culture, religion, and consciousness of a people as has Jerusalem in the life of Jewry and Judaism. Throughout centuries of exile Jerusalem remained alive in the hearts of Jews everywhere as the Holy City and spiritual center of their lives. They never ceased to mourn its destruction and to pray and hope for its restoration as their national and religious

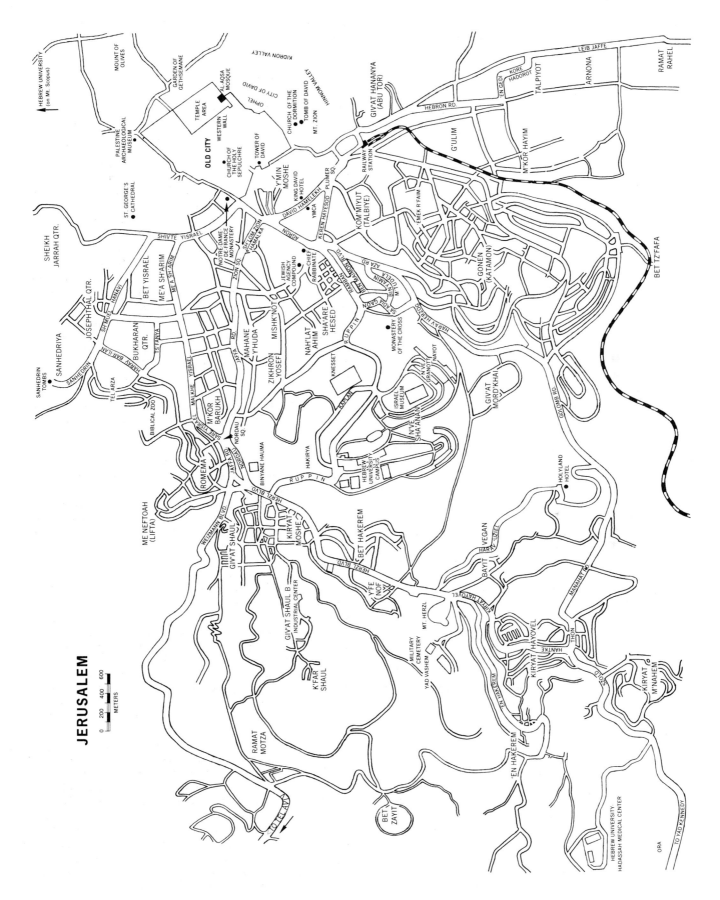

JERUSALEM

0   200   400   600
METERS

HEBREW UNIVERSITY
(on Mt. Scopus)

MOUNT OF OLIVES

GARDEN OF GETHSEMANE

KIDRON VALLEY

AL AQSA MOSQUE

TEMPLE AREA

CITY OF DAVID

OPHEL

CHURCH OF THE DORMITION

TOMB OF DAVID

MT. ZION

HINNOM VALLEY

WESTERN WALL

PALESTINE ARCHAEOLOGICAL MUSEUM

OLD CITY

CHURCH OF THE HOLY SEPULCHRE

TOWER OF DAVID

Y'MIN MOSHE

KING DAVID HOTEL

RAILWAY STATION

GIV'AT HANANYA (ABU TOR)

HEBRON RD.

LEIB JAFFE

RAMAT RAHEL

ARNONA

TALPIYOT

KORE HADOROT

EN GEDI

G'ULIM

M'KOR HAYIM

ST. GEORGE'S CATHEDRAL

SHEIKH JARRAH QTR.

SHIVTE YISRAEL

NOTRE DAME / DE FRANCE MONASTERY

 SHA'UL HAMELEKH

ZION SQ.

SHLOM ZION HAMALKA

BET YISRAEL

ME'A SHARIM

ME'A SH'ARIM

DAVID HAMELEKH

PLUMER SQ.

KEREN HAYESOD

YMCA

AGRON

KOM'MIYUT (TALBIYE)

EMEK R'FAIM

JOSÉPHTHAL QTR.

SHMUEL HANAVI

TSFANYA

SANHEDRIYA

SANHEDRIN

HARAV BAR ILAN

SANHEDRIN TOMBS

TEL ARZA

BIBLICAL ZOO

BUKHARAN QTR.

JAFFA RD.

MAHANE Y'HUDA

M'KOR BARUKH

ZIKHRON YOSEF

MISHK'NOT

NAH'LAT AHIM

JEWISH AGENCY COMPOUND

CHIEF RABBINATE

RAMBAN BLVD

BEN MAIMON BLVD

AZA RD.

RUPPIN

SHA'ARE HESED

MONASTERY OF THE CROSS

GONEN (KATAMON)

HARAV HERZOG

BET TZ'FAFA

SABA ISRAEL

NORDAU SQ.

KNESSET

KAPLAN

ISRAEL MUSEUM

NVE GRANOT

GIV'AT MORD'KHAI

NAYOT

GOLOMB RD.

HOLYLAND HOTEL

ME NEFTOAH (LIFTA)

ROMEMA

JAFFA RD.

BINYANE HAUMA

RUPPIN

HAKIRYA

HEBREW UNIVERSITY CAMPUS

NVE SHA'ANAN

WEIZMANN BLVD

GIV'AT SHAUL

KIRYAT MOSHE

BET HAKEREM

HERZL BLVD

HERZL BLVD

VEGAN

HARA UZIEL

BAYIT VEGAN

KIRYAT HAYOVEL

MANAHAT RD.

GIV'AT SHAUL B INDUSTRIAL CENTER

Y'FE NOF

MILITARY CEMETERY

MT. HERZL

YAD VASHEM

KIRYAT HAYOVEL

HANTKE

THON

KIRYAT M'NAHEM

K'FAR SHAUL

RAMAT MOTZA

TO TEL AVIV

EN HAKEREM

BET ZAYIT

HEBREW UNIVERSITY HADASSAH MEDICAL CENTER

ORA

TO YAD KENNEDY

capital. These sentiments found their succinct expression in the words first uttered by the early exiles in Babylonia: "If I forget thee, O Jerusalem, let my right hand wither."

Prehistoric and archeological evidence indicates that Jerusalem was settled in the Paleolithic era and that it remained populated through the subsequent prehistoric periods. Written documentation of its history begins with Akkadian cuneiform and Egyptian hieroglyphic inscriptions and shows that it was an important city long before the Israelite conquest of the Land of Canaan.

Biblical and Roman Times. The city of Jerusalem (Canaanite, Urusalim; Heb., Y'rushalayim) was first taken by the Israelites under King David, who made it his capital and transferred the Ark of the Covenant there. David's son Solomon enlarged Jerusalem and built the Temple, establishing the city as the nation's permanent religious center. Under Solomon's son Rehoboam, the northern tribes seceded. Jerusalem remained the capital of the southern kingdom of Judah until the conquest of Judah by the Babylonian ruler Nebuchadnezzar in 586 B.C.E. Nebuchadnezzar destroyed the Temple and the city and deported most of Judah's population.

After the return of the exiles from Babylonia, Jerusalem was resettled and the Temple rebuilt. The new Jewish settlement continued to develop under Alexander the Great and the Egyptian Ptolemies, who replaced Persian rule in the country. Under the subsequent regime of the Syrian Seleucids, the Jews suffered from religious persecution. Antiochus Epiphanes looted the Temple treasures and desecrated the Sanctuary by erecting an altar to Zeus there. After hard fighting, the Maccabees captured the city and rededicated the Temple. The Hasmonean rulers, who eventually were to gain complete independence, fortified Jerusalem and carried out various building projects.

In 63 B.C.E., the city was occupied by Pompey, and Roman rule began. Herod, who reigned with Roman support, built new fortifications in the city, rebuilt the Temple on a magnificent scale, and erected other prominent edifices. Jerusalem was then the focus of Jewish life, not only for the Jews of the country but also for those of the ever-widening *Diaspora who made pilgrimages to the Temple on the major festivals.

Following a Jewish rebellion crowned with temporary success, Jerusalem and the Temple were destroyed by the Romans in the year C.E. 70. This event marked the end of the Second Jewish Commonwealth.

More than 60 years after the destruction of Jerusalem a new Jewish rebellion, led by Bar Kokhba, briefly liberated the city. After the suppression of this revolt, the Romans built a new city over the ruins of Jerusalem and called it Aelia Capitolina. Jews were not permitted to live in the city or even to approach it, under pain of death.

Byzantine and Arab Rule. The emperor Constantine (r. 325–37) replaced the pagan temples in Jerusalem with Christian churches and encouraged Christians to settle there. Jerusalem thus became a Christian city, remaining so with a brief interruption until its conquest by the Arabs in 637.

During the short reign of Julian (361–63), Jews were allowed to settle in the city. This Roman Emperor, who earned the epithet Apostate from the Christians, also planned to rebuild the Jewish Temple, but his untimely death prevented the realization of his plan. In 614 the city was occupied by the Persians, who were helped by the Jews. For three years the Jews governed Jerusalem, which was abandoned by the Chris-

tians who had survived the fighting and the massacre that followed. In 628 the Byzantines returned to the city and massacred the Jews.

The caliph Omar, who took Jerusalem from the Byzantines, built a Muslim mosque in the Temple area. This mosque was later rebuilt as the Dome of the Rock by the Umayyad caliph 'Abd al-Malik, who proclaimed Jerusalem a city holy to the Muslims. The Arabs permitted Jews to settle in the city, and both Jews and Christians could freely practice their religions. The Jewish community grew and prospered, and the Palestine Gaonate moved from Tiberias to Jerusalem. In 969 Jerusalem passed into the hands of the Fatimid rulers of Egypt. Early in the 11th century the city's Jewish community suffered greatly from persecution, but the situation later improved. At that time many Jews from the Byzantine provinces made the pilgrimage to Jerusalem.

The Crusaders took the city in 1099 and slaughtered the Jews. In 1187 Jerusalem was recaptured by Saladin, in the 13th century it was held for short periods by the Crusaders, and in 1260 it was destroyed by the Mongols. When Nachmanides came there in 1267, he found only two Jews. He urged the Jews, who had fled from the Mongol invaders, to return to the city and organized a Jewish community. In 1400 the city was again destroyed by the Mongols. In 1488 'Ovadia Bertinoro, a famous commentator of the Mishna, found 70 Jewish families in Jerusalem and did much to consolidate the community.

Turkish Period. As a consequence of the Turkish conquest of Palestine (1516–17), closer contact was established between the local Jewish communities founded in the Ottoman Empire by the exiles from Spain and Portugal. Many of the latter migrated to Palestine, and by 1522 there was a sizable Jewish community in Jerusalem, which continued to grow throughout the 16th century.

Even during the 17th and 18th centuries, when the country was beset by tribal wars and the population was oppressed by despotic local governors, Jewish *immigration to the country and to Jerusalem itself did not cease. In 1700 Rabbi Juda He-Hasid and a sizable group of his followers arrived in Jerusalem from Poland. The newcomers suffered from extreme poverty and persecution by the Arabs as well as by their fellow Jews, who suspected them of being followers of the false Messiah Shabbetai Tz'vi.

In 1806 there were about 2,000 Jews in Jerusalem; by 1819 their number had grown to 3,000. In subsequent decades the Jewish population was further augmented by the arrival of Jews from Safed who fled because of plunderings and the epidemics and earthquake of 1834–37. Jewish immigrants from Europe, too, began to settle in Jerusalem under the protection of their countries of origin, which then opened consulates in the city.

In 1856 Jerusalem had a total population of about 18,000, including nearly 6,000 Jews, 2,000 Christians, and 10,000 Muslims. Each of the three communities had its own quarter in the city, which was still confined to the small area within the walls built by the Turks in the 16th century. The increase in the city's population, however, necessitated the establishment of new residental quarters outside the walls. The first, Mishk'not Sha'ananim, was built in 1860. It was followed by other new Jewish residential quarters. *Me'a Sh'arim was built in 1874. The Christians began to build outside the walls in 1878 and the Muslims toward the end of the century.

Aerial view of the Old City of Jerusalem. [Trans World Airlines]

The *First 'Aliya (1882–1904) brought many newcomers to Jerusalem. By 1890 the city had about 40,000 inhabitants, more than half of whom were Jews.

The greater part of the Jews of Jerusalem had lived on charity (*see* HALUKKA). In the 1880s, however, the character of Jewish Jerusalem began to change. Modern educational and medical institutions and enterprises were established. The turn of the century saw a further increase in the city's population and in the modernization of its life. In 1912 Jerusalem had 75,000 inhabitants, of whom more than 48,000 were Jews, 10,000 Muslims, and nearly 17,000 Christians.

World War I and the British Mandate. During World War I the city's population, as well as that of the country as a whole, suffered greatly from the despotism of the Turkish military authorities. Enemy aliens were expelled, and Ottoman citizens were recruited into the army or pressed into forced labor. Hunger and epidemics were rampant. The population shrank to 50,000.

When the British occupied the city in December, 1917, they were enthusiastically greeted by its inhabitants. British rule in the country ushered in a new period in the life of Jerusalem, which became the seat of the British military authorities and later of the mandatory administration (*see* MANDATE FOR PALESTINE). The city began to develop rapidly, largely because of the influx of Jews.

The *Arab riots of 1920, 1929, and 1936–39, during which many Jews in the city were killed, did not stop Jewish building activity. For reasons of comfort and security, however, many Jews left the Old City and moved to the newer Jewish quarters.

During the 30 years of the British regime in Palestine, many important Jewish institutions were established in Jerusalem. In 1925 the *Hebrew University of Jerusalem, which also housed the *Jewish National and University Library, was dedicated on Mount *Scopus. In 1939 the *Hadassah-University Hospital and Hebrew University–Hadassah Medical School, also on Mount Scopus, were opened. The *Va'ad L'umi (National Council) and the Chief *Rabbinate had their seats in Jerusalem. The Executive offices of the *World Zionist Organization (WZO) and of the *Jewish Agency were located there.

In 1931 Jerusalem had 93,000 inhabitants, of whom about

The new city of Jerusalem seen from the YMCA. [Trans World Airlines]

54,000 were Jews. In 1947 there were 100,000 Jews in a total population of 165,000.

During the Jewish underground struggle against the British between 1944 and 1948, Jerusalem was the scene of numerous attacks. In July, 1946, the *Irgun Tz'vai L'umi blew up the headquarters of the British administration in the King David Hotel. Early in 1947 the British established in Jerusalem and other main cities heavily fortified security zones, surrounded by barbed wire, for their personnel and offices. However, these could not prevent the Jewish underground from reaching its targets. During that year the Irgun struck in Jerusalem at various British establishments within the security zones, including the officers' club at Goldschmidt House and the military barracks in the Schneller Compound.

Soon after the United Nations *partition resolution of Nov. 29, 1947 (*see* UNITED NATIONS AND PALESTINE-ISRAEL), Arab riots broke out in the country. In Jerusalem, which according to the United Nations decision was to be internationalized, Arabs attacked Jews in various sections, pillaged a Jewish shopping district, and laid siege to the Jewish quarter of the Old City, cutting it off from the Jewish population in the modern town.

While Arab attacks increased in the city, a group of British police and soldiers carried out attacks against the Jewish population. In February, 1948, they blew up the printing plant of the *Palestine Post* (later *Jerusalem Post*) and part

of Ben Yehuda Street, one of the main thoroughfares. In March, a wing of the Jewish Agency headquarters was blown up by terrorists.

In April, Arabs ambushed in the Sheikh Jarrah quarter a convoy carrying Jewish scientists, physicians, and nurses to the university and hospital on Mount Scopus and killed many of them. Sheikh Jarrah was subsequently occupied by the *Palmah (commandos), but British military action forced them to withdraw.

*War of Independence. At an early stage of their attacks during the War of Independence, the Arabs tried to cut off Jewish Jerusalem from the Jewish settlements in the coastal plain by attacking Jewish traffic on the Tel Aviv–Jerusalem highway To supply Jewish Jerusalem with food and other necessities, escorted convoys were organized. The system of convoys, which suffered heavily from Arab attacks based on the Arab villages on both sides of the road, failed, and by the end of March the situation of Jewish Jerusalem had become critical. Food supplies were running out. There were also shortages of water and electricity. Early in April, *Hagana, in a large-scale action that involved the capture of Arab villages and strongholds along the road, succeeded temporarily in opening the highway to Jerusalem, and large convoys, bringing food and ammunition, could reach the city. The road was soon closed again to Jewish traffic, and only in June, after the *Israel Defense Forces had built the *K'vish HaG'vura (Road of

Valor), which circumvented Arab positions, did large supplies pour into Jewish Jerusalem again.

The beginning of May, 1948, saw the Jewish forces in the city on the offensive. Arab quarters that threatened Jewish neighborhoods were captured. Later the positions evacuated by the British were occupied. With the British evacuation on May 15, the Arab Legion officially joined in the battle. The legion shelled the Jewish quarters heavily but, with the exception of the reconquest of Sheikh Jarrah, which had been taken by the Jews after the departure of the British, did not succeed in penetrating the Jewish defense of the modern town.

While modern Jerusalem, cut off again from the supply base in the plain, successfully resisted the onslaught of the Arab forces, which now included Egyptians, who advanced from the south, in addition to the Arab Legion and Arab irregulars, the fewer than 2,000 Jews in the Jewish quarter of the Old City, most of them aged or infirm, surrendered on May 28 after months of siege and weeks of heroic fighting. Fierce fighting lasted in Jerusalem until June 11, when the first truce came into force. It was renewed after the expiration of the truce on July 8, and though a second truce came into effect on July 18, skirmishes and exchanges of fire continued until a cease-fire was arranged by local Jewish and Arab commanders in November, 1948.

Capital of Israel. Jerusalem emerged from the fighting a divided city. Most of the modern city and the Jewish institu-

Tower of David. [Zelda Haber]

Street scene in Jerusalem. [Zelda Haber]

tions on Mount Scopus were held by the Jews. The Old City and the Sheikh Jarrah quarter, which separated the modern city from Mount Scopus, were in Arab hands.

On May 14, 1948, when the Jewish State was proclaimed, Jerusalem was not officially included in the territory of the new State. The United Nations resolution had envisaged an international city, open to Jews, Muslims, and Christians, because of the *holy places of the three world religions located there. Since 19 of these 22 sites were in the Old City, its conquest by Jordan invalidated the entire purpose of the resolution. Israel therefore no longer felt bound to certain of its provisions. On August 1, the Israeli government declared new Jerusalem an area of military occupation to be ruled under Israeli law. In February, 1949, the new city was declared an integral part of the State of Israel, and in December was proclaimed its capital. Subsequently the *Knesset (Parliament), the ministries, and all the major government offices were moved there from Tel Aviv. Jerusalem also remained the headquarters of the Jewish Agency, the WZO, and numerous national institutions.

Since the establishment of the State, Jerusalem has grown rapidly both in size and in population. Quarters abandoned by the Arabs have been resettled with Jewish immigrants, and new neighborhoods have been built. Besides *tourism, new light industries such as diamond cutting and polishing (*see* DIAMOND INDUSTRY IN ISRAEL), plastics, and the manufacture

Kennedy Memorial, near Jerusalem. [Israel Government Tourist Office]

of shoes have been developed. Additional hotels and pensions have been opened. An entirely new center was developed, stretching westward from the city. It contains the new campus of the Hebrew University and the Jewish National and University Library; a complex of *museums including the Israel Museum, the Shrine of the Book (housing the Dead Sea Scrolls and finds of the Bar Kokhba period), the Samuel Bronfman Biblical and Archeological Museum, the Bezalel National Art Museum, and the Billy Rose Art Garden; and the Knesset building, various ministries, and the huge convention center (Binyane HaUma). The entire complex is interlinked by gardens and groves of trees. Farther west is the new Hebrew University–Hadassah Medical School and School of Dental Medicine, the largest and most modern institution of its kind in the Middle East. From the suburb of Bet HaKerem to 'En HaKerem ('En Karem) a series of new housing estates for immigrants and veteran settlers has mushroomed.

Educational and cultural institutions and facilities in the city also include many *Yeshivot and Talmudic research institutes (such as the Yad HaRav Maimon, *Yad HaRav Herzog, and the Hebron, Mir, and Rabbi Kook Yeshivot), the *Israel Academy of Sciences and Humanities, the *Hebrew Language Academy, the Hebrew Union College Biblical and Archeological School, the *Schocken Institute for Jewish Research, the American Student Center of the Jewish Theo-

logical Seminary, the New Bezalel School of Arts and Crafts (*see* BEZALEL SCHOOL), the Rubin Academy of Music (*see* MUSIC IN ISRAEL), *Hekhal Sh'lomo (seat of the Chief Rabbinate), the Yeshurun Synagogue, and the Bet Ha'Am. Mount Herzl is the last resting place of the founder of political Zionism, of other prominent Zionist leaders, and of soldiers who fell in the defense of the State. Nearby is Har HaZikaron (Memorial Mount), so called for *Yad VaShem, the memorial to Europe's 6 million Jewish martyrs, erected on it.

Mount *Zion, in the town proper adjoining the wall of the Old City, is the reputed site of the tomb of King David and one of the most revered Jewish holy places in the State. The *Western Wall (Wailing Wall), the most important of Jewish holy places in the country, is in the Old City. From 1948 until the *Six-day War of 1967 it was inaccessible to Jews from Israel.

Between 1949 and 1967 the security position of the city was improved. In the Judean Mountains, overlooking several new roads that linked the capital to the coastal plain and the Negev, a chain of villages was established. These villages not only protected Jerusalem's lifelines but also provided the capital with fresh vegetables, milk, fruit, and other food supplies.

The Six-day War resulted in the establishment of Jewish control over the Arab-held sectors of the city. On the first day of the war (June 5), after the Jordanians had initiated hostilities, Israeli forces counterattacked. By that evening Israeli troops had occupied Arab localities to the south of the city, and the following night, after fierce fighting, they gained control of the modern Arab quarters to the north of the Old City (Sheikh Jarrah, the American colony). On the morning of June 7, Israeli forces occupied the Mount of *Olives, thus sealing off the Old City, which was stormed soon thereafter.

Immediately after their entry into the Old City, the Israeli soldiers made their way to the Western Wall and held a religious service there. The heads of the State and of the Israel Army were among the first to pay homage to the liberated Wall. The general public was permitted access to the Wall a few days later. On the first day, which happened to be the festival of Shavu'ot (Pentecost), 200,000 Jews from all parts of the country made the pilgrimage to the Wall, from which they had been barred for 19 years.

On June 28, Hayim Moshe *Shapira, the Minister of the Interior, acting in accordance with a new law passed by the Knesset authorizing him to extend the jurisdiction of Israeli municipalities to parts of the newly won areas, issued an order enlarging the limits of Jerusalem to include the Old City and the modern Arab quarters and thereby effecting the unification of the formerly divided city. A day later the barriers between Jewish and Arab Jerusalem (thereafter referred to as West and East Jerusalem, respectively) were removed, and the population of both sectors began to intermingle freely.

Soon after the unification of the city, the Israeli authorities made plans for the rebuilding of the Jewish quarter of the Old City, for the restoration of its historic synagogues, which had been razed by the Arabs, and for the reopening of the Hebrew University and Hadassah buildings on Mount Scopus. The Chief Rabbinate, which established its court in the Old City in a building near the Western Wall, declared the 28th of Iyar, the day of the liberation of the Old City, a day of thanksgiving.

The Old City of Jerusalem and its immediate vicinity are the site of some of the most important holy places of Christianity and Islam, including the Church of the Holy Sepulchre, the Garden and churches of Gethsemane on the slopes of the Mount of Olives, the Church of the Dormition on Mount Zion, and the Haram ash-Sharif area with the Mosque of al-Aqsa and the Dome of the Rock, as well as numerous Christian and Muslim religious institutions. Because of these holy places and their historical associations, Jerusalem is considered the Holy City also by Christianity and Islam and is called in Arabic el-Quds, meaning "the Holy."

From 1965 on the mayor of the city was Theodore *Kollek. In 1968 the city had an area of 25,000 acres and a population of 278,000 (Jewish, 210,000). The school population (including Hebrew University, religious seminaries, and adult education courses) was 89,500 (West Jerusalem, 71,500; East Jerusalem, 18,000). The municipal budget was IL74,837,000, and there were approximately 4,000 municipal employees.

T. PRESCHEL

JERUSALEM ACADEMY OF MEDICINE. Institution devoted to the furtherance of medical research and the promotion of public health in the State of Israel. It was formed in 1957 by the Israel Medical Association. Special committees of the academy are concerned with urban sanitation and hygiene, cancer research, infant mortality, and the combating of poi-

soning and rheumatic fever. The academy also has formed a Diabetes Society and conducted a campaign against smoking. Other activities have included a breast cancer detection clinic and a marriage-counseling bureau. Lectures, courses, and other educational programs have been arranged to instruct the public in healthy living.

In 1966 the academy maintained a medical reference library and an exhibit on Jewish physicians and Jewish contributions to medicine. Directed by Prof. Sussman Muntner, it published Hebrew medical textbooks and early medical literature written by Jews.

The academy's headquarters, a four-story building in Jerusalem, contains the 500-seat Meier Segals Auditorium, which serves as a convention hall for local and international scientific gatherings. Membership is open to all qualified physicians, resident and nonresident, regardless of origin and creed.

A. BRAND-AURABAN, M.D.

JERUSALEM POST. Israeli English-language daily founded in Jerusalem in 1932 as the *Palestine Post.* Its editors have been Gershon *Agron (1932–55) and Ted R. Lurie (1955–). Feeling the need for a Palestine English-language daily with a high standard of journalism that would gain the respect of the mandatory authorities (*see* MANDATE FOR PALESTINE) and attract readers capable of speaking effectively in high places on behalf of the Jewish National Home in Palestine, Agron published the first issue of the *Post* (1,200 copies) on Dec. 1, 1932. The statement of policy carried on the front page of that issue said:

> . . . the studied purpose will be the present and future welfare of the country and of its people, and the Management will make no attempt to conceal its conviction that such welfare is best assured by a full realization of the British policy in Palestine as defined in the Mandate.

Even in the face of growing Arab unrest in the middle and late 1930s (*see* ARAB RIOTS IN PALESTINE), the *Post* insisted that, given the goodwill of all concerned, the British Mandate was workable. At the same time, it consistently endeavored to keep the mandatory authorities aware of their moral obli-

The Jerusalem Post *is circulated in all parts of Israel.* [Keren Ha-Yesod]

gation to the Jewish Homeland. It also lost no opportunity to point out that Arab unrest had not been caused by the Jewish National Home in Palestine but by the anti-British and anti-foreign attitudes of Arab nationalists throughout the Middle East. The columns of the paper were always open to Arab writers, and Yussef Hanna, an Egyptian-born Arab and editor of the Jaffa daily *Falastin*, supplied the *Post* with Arab news for more than a decade until Arab terrorist elements forced him to stop doing so.

The proclamation of the *White Paper of 1939, in which Britain in effect repudiated the obligations it had undertaken in the *Balfour Declaration, produced a change in the *Post*'s tone. The *Post* began to place increased stress on Jewish achievements in the rebuilding of the Homeland and to voice open criticism of Britain's Palestine policies. However, it adhered to the official posture of the leaders of the *Yishuv (Jewish population of Palestine): nonviolent resistance to British-imposed anti-Jewish restrictions and opposition to counterterrorist activities by the *Irgun Tz'vai L'umi.

With the outbreak of World War II, the *Post* gave priority to the Allied war effort, aiding in the recruitment of Palestine Jews for the British armed forces. For a time it published a special edition for the Allied occupation forces in. Syria. Agron was a member of the Jewish delegation to the founding conference of the United Nations (San Francisco, April–June, 1945). During the debate that took place in the Yishuv on the future of the country, the *Post* espoused the cause of a Jewish State. On Feb. 1, 1948, its headquarters was blown up by a bomb planted by British soldiers, but the paper appeared the next morning as usual. Indeed, in all the years of its existence the *Post* has appeared without interruption except on Oct. 7, 1936, when it was suspended for one day by the mandatory authorities. It continued to publish even during the siege of Jerusalem in the *War of Independence, receiving news of the war by a circuitous route from Tel Aviv via London and issuing stenciled editions when there was not enough electric power to operate the presses.

With the establishment of the State of Israel, it was decided to continue the *Post* as a "foreign-language" paper with no explicit political party affiliation, addressing itself not only to Israelis but also to the English-reading public abroad. On Apr. 23, 1950, the paper was renamed the *Jerusalem Post*. When Agron was elected mayor of Jerusalem in 1955, the editorship of the *Post* was taken over by Ted R. Lurie, who had been Agron's assistant from the inception of the paper. In the 1960s the *Post*, in addition to its daily issues, published a weekend magazine supplement and an airmail weekly overseas edition. In the nearly four decades of the *Post*'s existence, its roster of writers has included Michael *Comay, David Courtney (Roy Elston), Blanche *Dugdale, Abba *Eban, Eliyahu *Elath, Leo Kohn, Eliezer *Livneh, and Reuben (Zaslany) Shiloah.   G. HIRSCHLER

JERUSALEM PROGRAM. *See* CONGRESS, ZIONIST (23d, 27th).

JEWISH AGENCY FOR ISRAEL. Article 4 of the *Mandate for Palestine, confirmed by the League of Nations in 1922, provided for the recognition of an appropriate "Jewish Agency" as a "public body for the purpose of advising and cooperating with the Administration of Palestine in such economic, social and other matters as may affect the establishment of the Jewish National Home and the interests of the Jewish population in Palestine, and, subject always to the control of the Administration, to assist and take part in the development of the country." Article 6 of the mandate stipulated that the British administration of Palestine should, "in cooperation with the Jewish Agency," encourage close settlement by Jews on the land. Article 11 provided that the administration might arrange with the Jewish Agency "to construct or operate, upon fair and equitable terms, any public works, services and utilities, and to develop any of the natural resources of the country, insofar as these matters are not directly undertaken by the Administration." The mandate itself recognized the *World Zionist Organization (WZO) as such Jewish Agency (art. 4) and directed the WZO to "take steps in consultation with His Britannic Majesty's Government to secure the cooperation of all Jews who are willing to assist in the establishment of the Jewish National Home." The WZO, on its part, undertook to take steps to secure such cooperation.

Pre-State History. Soon thereafter negotiations were initiated by the WZO and, in particular, by Chaim *Weizmann, its president, with prominent Jews not affiliated with the WZO. Among these were Louis *Marshall and Felix M. *Warburg in the United States, Lord *Melchett in Great Britain, Léon *Blum in France, and Oskar *Wassermann in Germany. The plan for the establishment of an expanded Jewish Agency (JA) by the inclusion of non-Zionist Jewish leaders was opposed by several leading Zionists, among them Itzhak *Grünbaum, Nahum *Goldmann, and Vladimir *Jabotinsky. These opponents of the plan feared that a mixed Zionist and non-Zionist body would retard rather than advance the implementation of the Zionist program and endanger its political character. They remained in the minority, however, and after six years of negotiations the 16th Zionist *Congress (Zurich, 1929) approved the establishment of the expanded JA by a vote of 230 to 30, with 45 abstentions. Immediately after the Congress, the Constituent Assembly of the JA convened in Zurich and, after adopting a constitution, elected the governing bodies.

The purpose of the expanded JA was, to quote the preamble of its constitution, "to give adequate representation to non-Zionists to enable them, jointly with the Zionist Organization, to participate in the privileges and responsibilities of the Jewish Agency." The expanded JA was to be based on the principle of parity between Zionists and non-Zionists, that is, prominent Jews and organizations supporting the building of the National Home without identifying themselves with the political aspirations of Zionism. Therefore, the governing bodies of the JA were composed of 50 per cent Zionists, elected by the Zionist Congress, and 50 per cent non-Zionists from 26 countries; most strongly represented were the United States (44 members in the Council of the JA), Poland (14 members), the British Commonwealth (11 members), and Germany (7 members). The constitution provided that the president of the WZO should be the president of the JA.

The object of the JA, as stated in article 3 of its constitution in general terms, was "to discharge the functions of the JA as set forth in the Mandate" and, more specifically, to encourage and further Jewish *immigration to Palestine, to make provision for meeting Jewish religious needs, to foster the *Hebrew language and Jewish culture, to acquire land as Jewish property, in particular for the *Jewish National Fund, and to promote agricultural settlement.

After the establishment of the expanded JA, the JA and the WZO were two distinct and separate bodies, though headed by the same president. However, for a variety of reasons, among them the death of Louis Marshall, in whom Weizmann had placed great hopes and who died shortly after the Zurich session, the 50 per cent participation of non-Zionists in the JA and its organs did not work in practice and the Zionist element became preponderant. This development was accelerated owing to World War II and the Nazi holocaust, in which many of the communities to be represented in the JA were completely destroyed. The supreme organs of the JA, the Council and the Administrative Committee, did not meet after 1939. The last non-Zionist member of the JA Executive resigned in 1947. Thus, the Executives of the JA and the WZO became in fact identical, and so did the two organizations themselves.

One of the main tasks of the JA during the period of the British administration of Palestine was to represent the Zionist movement and world Jewry at large before the mandatory government, the League of Nations, and the British government in London. Insofar as the British Mandatory government of Palestine was concerned, its position was that the JA was not entitled to take part in the government of the country but merely to cooperate with the mandatory authorities in matters affecting the development of the Jewish National Home. For the *Yishuv (Jewish population of Palestine), however, the JA became the dominant force by virtue of its activities in agricultural and urban settlement, its specialized institutions, and its considerable economic resources. It was to the JA that the Yishuv looked for political guidance. Its role was summed up by the *Peel Commission in 1937 as follows: "It may be said that the Jewish Agency has used to the fullest extent the position conferred on it by the Mandate. In the course of time it has created a complete administrative apparatus. This powerful and efficient organization amounts, in fact, to a Government existing side by side with the Mandatory Government."

Development in the State of Israel. The legal and structural identity of the JA and the WZO has been maintained in the first 20 years of the State of Israel and was confirmed and emphasized by the Law on the Status of the World Zionist Organization–Jewish Agency. The difference between the JA and the WZO has become one of terminology rather than of substance; in practice, the name WZO indicates activities and functions in respect to the *Diaspora, while the designation JA is used mostly in connection with work in and for Israel. Insofar as ideological aspects are concerned, the name WZO is preferred, while JA is used when the institutional side, offices, and staff are referred to.

In the second decade of the State of Israel schemes were repeatedly put forward for reconstituting the JA as a separate entity. According to one plan, the WZO was to include only Zionists personally committed to *'Aliya (immigration to Israel) while all the other "friends of Israel" were to be organized in a wider framework analogous to the former expanded JA. This proposal and similar ones were not realized; instead, the 27th Zionist Congress (Jerusalem, 1968) resolved that a special 'Aliya movement be set up within the WZO and its territorial branches.

Although the JA was not established as a special institution, the joint body of the WZO-JA was broadened by the affiliation of elements typical of the former expanded JA. The new constitution of the WZO of 1960 stipulated that national and international Jewish organizations might be admitted as mem-

Jewish Agency compound in Jerusalem. [Zionist Archives]

bers provided they accepted the Zionist program. Whereas the organizations as such must subscribe to the program, it is not required that each of their members be a Zionist. The admission of such bodies, advocated and promoted by Nahum Goldmann, then president of the WZO-JA, meant a broadening of its base that was to some degree similar to the inclusion of non-Zionists in the expanded JA in 1929. Indeed, quite a number of Jewish organizations availed themselves of the opportunity to join the WZO-JA; thus, at the 25th Zionist Congress (Jerusalem, 1960–61), 14 representatives of "associate members" from seven countries participated, among them the *World Federation of Sephardi Communities, the *World Jewish Congress, and community organizations from several countries, particularly in South America. On the eve of the 27th Zionist Congress in 1968, the World Union of Jewish Students was admitted as a full member; it was represented at the Congress by 20 delegates with voting rights.

Division of Functions. It was realized long before May 15, 1948, that the future independent and sovereign Jewish State would shortly be fully responsible for the conduct of its domestic and foreign affairs and that some functions hitherto exercised by the JA would have to be transferred to the State. On the other hand, it was obvious that the State would not and could not deal with all matters that had been in the purview of the JA (in particular, immigration, absorption of immigrants, and settlement), not only for financial reasons but also because they were a global Jewish responsibility and not an internal affair of Israel. It was felt that the JA would be needed to express the partnership of the Jewish people all over the world with Israel in the historic enterprise of building the State and to channel and utilize properly the aid that was expected and forthcoming from Diaspora Jewry.

A month before the *Declaration of Independence, the *Zionist General Council resolved that after the formation of the provisional government of Israel "the jurisdiction of the Zionist *Executive should comprise settlement, immigration and all related matters including *Youth 'Aliya, Zionist information, organization, propaganda and culture, education in the diaspora, youth and *HeHalutz [pioneering movements], the development of Jerusalem and the National Funds." This principle of Hafrada (separation of functions, especially in that the same persons—with the exception of Eliezer *Kaplan—should not serve in both the JA and the government) was confirmed in a somewhat modified form by the resolutions of the subsequent sessions of the Zionist General Council in August–September, 1948, and of the 23d Zionist Congress in 1951.

Consequently, whereas some functions previously exercised by the JA (such as political activities) devolved on the government of Israel, other, exactly defined tasks were to remain the sole responsibility of the WZO-JA. The idea underlying the principle of Hafrada was, on the one hand, to leave the JA with a well-defined sphere of activities and, on the other, to avoid overlapping and duplication.

Status Law. The mutual relations of the State and the JA were put on a firm legal basis by the Law on the Status of the World Zionist Organization–Jewish Agency of 5713 (1952), article 4 of which declares: "The State of Israel recognized the WZO as the authorized agency that will continue to operate in the State of Israel for the development and settlement of the country, the absorption of immigrants from the diaspora and the coordination of the activities in Israel of Jewish institutions and organizations active in those fields." The law reaffirmed the identity of the WZO and the JA, article 3 beginning with the words "The World Zionist Organization, which is also the Jewish Agency. . . . " This identity is also expressed in the very name of the law. The Executive of the WZO-JA was recognized as a legal person with special tax privileges.

The details of the status of the WZO-JA and the forms of collaboration between its Executive and the government of Israel were, as provided in article 7 of the law, to be determined by a covenant, which was entered into in 1954. The covenant laid down, *inter alia*, that the government was to "consult the Executive in regard of legislation especially impinging on the functions of the Executive before such legislation is submitted to the *Knesset." The covenant also redefined the tasks and responsibilities of the Executive, elaborating rather than changing the definitions in the Status Law. For the coordination of joint or related activities of both partners a Coordination Board, consisting of an equal number of ministers and Executive members, was set up.

In practice, the mutual relations of the government and the Executive were not always free from friction, caused both by objective circumstances and by the views of Prime Minister David *Ben-Gurion, who, equating 'Aliya with Zionism, suggested that the WZO-JA had outlived its usefulness. Relations improved considerably under his successor, Levi *Eshkol, who for years had served as treasurer of the JA and Minister of Finance in the government of Israel.

After the *Six-day War of 1967 various proposals were put forward to delimit anew the respective functions of the government and the JA Executive. In particular, it was suggested that while the WZO-JA should remain in charge of immigration, the absorption and integration of immigrants should become largely a responsibility of the government because only the government had the power and means to take care of education, provision of work, medical care, and other services. Therefore a new Ministry for the Absorption of Immigrants was set up, it being stipulated that in future the JA should also be in charge of the initial reception of newcomers and should continue to take care of refugees and destitute immigrants. On the other hand, after the Six-day War the JA made large contributions to the budget of various social services in Israel which otherwise could not have been maintained on the previous level because of the considerably increased burden of defense expenditure that the government had to shoulder.

Organization. After the WZO and the Jewish Agency had become one and the same body (from 1947 on), the organs of the JA (Congress, General Council, Executive, judicial bodies, comptroller) were identical with those of the WZO. In the 1929–47 period, when the JA was constituted on a 50 per cent Zionist and 50 per cent non-Zionist basis, the Zionist representatives were designated by the Zionist Congress, while those of the non-Zionists were appointed in the various countries "in such manner as may appear in each case to be best suited to local conditions; provided it be recognized as a guiding principle that the method of appointment be so far as practicable of a democratic character." The gradual transformation of the JA, and in particular of its Executive, into a body of preponderantly Zionist composition and character had a legal basis in article 7 of the constitution of the expanded JA, which stipulated that the WZO was entitled to fill seats remaining vacant if nominations up to the requisite numbers had not been made by the non-Zionist members of the Council.

The Council of the JA was its "supreme governing body," the "final authority in all matters within its jurisdiction . . . " entrusted with the task of "laying down the guiding principles of policy." According to the "schedule of allotment of seats" attached to the constitution, the Council was to be composed of 112 Zionist and 112 non-Zionist members, but in practice smaller numbers were appointed in subsequent years. Ordinary meetings of the Council were to take place once in two years, as a rule at the time and venue of the Zionist Congress.

The Administrative Committee, meeting in the intervals between sessions of the Council for the purpose of receiving and considering reports from the Executive and exercising general authority and supervision over the activities of the Agency, was composed of 20 Zionist and 20 non-Zionist members.

The Executive of the JA was charged with the conduct of its current business. Though it was stated that its seat should be in Jerusalem, in view of the necessity of being in regular and close contact with the mandatory power, an office of the Executive, under the direction of its president, was maintained in London.

Departments and Activities. The Executive of the JA operates through departments, whose number and organization changed in the course of time. As a rule, each department is headed by one member of the Executive, but it happened that more than one member was in charge of one department (e.g., the Department of Immigration and Absorption of Immigrants in 1967) and, even more frequently, that there were Executive members without portfolio.

Some departments maintained during the mandatory period were abolished after the establishment of the State since their responsibilities were taken over by the government of Israel, among them the Labor Department, the Department of Trade and Industry, the Department of Artisans and Small Trade, and the Maritime Department. The functions of the Political Department were entrusted to the Ministry of Foreign Affairs. Some departments were of a temporary character; among these were the Department for the Settlement of German Jews, created after Hitler's seizure of power; the Department for the Settlement of Ex-servicemen, after World War II; and the Department for Immigrants from Middle East Countries, in the early 1950s. In 1967, in connection with the 27th Zionist Congress (1968), a general and thorough re-organization of the JA departments was carried out, resulting in the merger of some departments and in a reduction of the total number. Since that Congress, the JA has had the following departments.

Department for Immigration and Absorption of Immigrants. This department was formed by the amalgamation of the former separate units for immigration, absorption, and economy. Its task is to encourage, organize, and carry out immigration to Israel, to take care of the reception of immigrants on their arrival, and to assist them in their economic, social, and cultural absorption and integration.

Although the Israeli Law of *Return (1950) grants every Jew (with very few and insignificant exceptions for reasons of health and security) the right to come to Israel and settle in the country, not every prospective immigrant has been in a position to effect his immigration without assistance. The majority of the immigrants, especially those from Communist and Muslim countries, had neither the means nor the possibility of organizing their immigration on their own, and it was the JA that stepped in and took care of their 'Aliya. Moreover, many immigrants from the affluent countries of the Western world depend on the monetary and organizational aid of the JA.

The tasks connected with immigration are performed with the help of special emissaries and 'Aliya offices all over the free world. The most important of these offices are in New York, London, Paris, Marseille, Geneva, Vienna, Frankfurt on the Main, Naples, and Buenos Aires.

Methods for absorption of immigrants changed in the course of time according to the available resources and the specific composition and requirements of the 'Aliya in question. The general pattern, particularly in periods of mass 'Aliya, was as follows: the JA received the immigrant on his arrival, gave him temporary or permanent shelter, and during the first stages even fed him, provided him with equipment and transportation, gave him a cash loan or a grant to cover his initial expenditure, and afforded him medical and social services.

A significant contribution to the integration and absorption of new immigrants is made by the Ulpanim (*see* ULPAN) of the JA. At an Ulpan the immigrant is given intensive Hebrew courses and, in some cases, full board and accommodation. The Ulpanim located in settlements combine the study of Hebrew with agricultural work. In the mid-1960s, when it appeared that immigration from "countries of stress" was drawing to an end and that the free countries of the West would be the main source of future 'Aliya, new media for absorption and integration were devised. A network of hostels, and later, on a larger scale, of absorption centers, was established. There newcomers, especially professional persons and university graduates, could live for several months until they acquired a working knowledge of the language and found employment and permanent housing. At the time of the mass immigration during the first years of the State ways had to be found for coping with the great influx of mostly destitute immigrants. These included the Ma'abarot (transit camps; *see* MA'ABARA), which the JA supplied with all vital services; and the direct transfer of immigrants to new settlements under the "From Ship to Village" scheme. In the late 1960s, the immigrants, especially those from the West, were given individual treatment, the tendency being to establish each newcomer, insofar as possible, in an occupation in which he could utilize both his training and his skills.

Youth 'Aliya Department. This department was established in 1934 to rescue Jewish children from Nazi Germany and make them productive citizens of Eretz Yisrael. After World War II Youth 'Aliya cared mainly for war orphans. During the mass immigration of 1948–52 it provided special training and education for immigrant children who had come to Israel with their families. In the 1960s Youth 'Aliya also took charge of underprivileged children born or brought up in Israel. It provided its wards not only with education but also with clothing, social and medical services, vocational training, and recreation. In the late 1960s about 12,000 youngsters were being educated in the framework of Youth 'Aliya.

Until the late 1960s collective and cooperative villages, children's villages, and agricultural boarding schools were the main instruments of absorption utilized by Youth 'Aliya. Recent years saw the addition of day centers, which functioned mainly in the new development areas.

Agricultural Settlement Department. The task of this department is not only to set up agricultural settlements of various types but to provide the settlers with housing, livestock, and equipment, establish economic and social institutions in the villages, train the settlers for agriculture, and organize marketing and supplies. The time of mass immigration was also one of mass settlement: in the single year 1949 no fewer than 120 new villages were set up. In later years, a new method of regional settlement was introduced. Entire districts such as Ta'anakh, Lakhish, and 'Adulam were opened up. Rural and urban centers were established in addition to villages, so that each region formed an organic unit. In the 1960s the activities of the department centered in the consolidation and expansion of existing settlements rather than the foundation of new ones. Nevertheless, new settlement work was not discontinued; thus in 1967, 10 new villages were added. By 1968 some 150 villages, which had reached economic independence, could be released from the care of the department, while more than 300 villages remained in its charge.

Youth and HeHalutz Department. The departments considered thus far work mostly in and for Israel. The activities of this department and those that follow pertain mainly to the Diaspora. The Youth and HeHalutz Department is charged with the guidance and support of pioneering *youth movements and Zionist youth organizations as well as with the care of various organizations of Jewish youth in general. In 1968 it assisted some 200 organizations in 36 countries. The department set up in Jerusalem a Central Educational Institute for Jewish Youth from the Diaspora, through which some 3,600 youth instructors passed during a 20-year period. Of these, 1,500 settled in Israel after completing their terms of duty as instructors.

The department holds annual Summer Institutes of 6 to 8 weeks' duration, in which students and adolescents from the Diaspora participate. The participants are offered short seminars, study tours, and periods of work in kibbutzim. The department also has charge of projects of more extensive work in Israel, such as *Sh'nat Sherut (Year of Service) and Sherut La'Am (Service to the People). After the Six-day War it dealt with thousands of young Jewish volunteers who had come to help Israel.

Department of Education and Culture in the Diaspora; Department of Religious Education and Culture in the Diaspora. These departments were set up in 1949 and 1951 respectively.

In the holocaust most European centers of Jewish learning were destroyed, and the Zionist movement recognized that one of its main responsibilities was to help meet the need for Jewish education outside Israel. Teacher emissaries are sent to the Diaspora, particularly to the smaller communities. The *Hayim Greenberg Institute and the Rav Gold Institute for the training of teachers in the Diaspora operate in Jerusalem. The departments are also engaged in training teachers in other countries. Among their main tasks are the dissemination of the Hebrew language and the dispatch abroad of large quantities of textbooks and other educational material.

Department for Organization and Information. This department is responsible for the convention and operation of the governing bodies of the WZO-JA (the Zionist Congress, General Council, etc.) and for the implementation of their resolutions. It maintains contact with the members of the WZO, particularly the *Zionist territorial organizations, and aids their activities. The department also arranges seminars for key Zionist workers, both in Israel and in other countries. Among the important projects of the department are the Zionist Library, which publishes Zionist classics and basic works on Zionism, and the Division for Research on the Diaspora.

It is the responsibility of this department to inform the Jewish public, particularly Zionist bodies in other countries, of the activities of the JA and, in cooperation with the government, of various aspects of life in Israel by means of article services, series of booklets, production and distribution of films, exhibitions, and so on. The department is also a partner in Kol Zion laGola, the broadcasting station which for a number of countries has become the only channel of direct information from Israel. Attached to the department are the Central Zionist Archives, founded as early as 1919 and including the largest collection of material relating to the Zionist movement and the history of Eretz Yisrael in modern times (*see* LIBRARIES AND ARCHIVES, ZIONIST), as well as the Bureau for Jewish Communities and Organizations, set up to strengthen ties between these bodies and the WZO-JA.

Other Units. Apart from the main operational departments, the JA comprises several independent or semi-independent units, such as the *Bialik Foundation and the Publishing Section, for the publication of literary and scientific works in Hebrew (both original and in translation), and the Search Bureau for Missing Relatives, established after the holocaust. The Personnel Department is in charge of the staff of the JA, which in September, 1967, numbered 3,228.

Treasury. In concluding the list of the JA departments with the Treasury, a few words on the budget and finances of the Agency are in order. The main sources of income (in millions of Israeli pounds) in 1966–67 were the United Israel Appeal in the United States (103.2), the *Keren HaYesod in other countries (36.7), special Youth 'Aliya campaigns (9.9), heirless property (12.8), collection of debts, realization of property, and so on (13.4), government participation in agricultural settlement (38.9), and loans (94.6); the total income was IL 309,500,000. The main items of expenditure (in millions of Israeli pounds) were immigration (20.7), absorption (40.9), Youth 'Aliya (23.4), agricultural settlement (75.5), and educational and organizational operations (55.0). The remainder of the income was allocated to debt service, general administration, and so on. By virtue of its greatly increased income from emergency campaigns conducted after the Six-day War, the JA could substantially augment its allocations and so relieve the government of Israel of responsibility for many social services. The expenditure budget of the JA for 1967–68 was composed as follows (in millions of Israeli pounds): immigration, absorption, and Youth 'Aliya, 417.9; housing of immigrants, 278.5; agricultural settlement, 178.6; educational and cultural operations in Israel, 158.5; such operations in other countries, 24.4; general administration, 11.0; debt service, 83.0; and reserve, 4.5; or a total of 1,156.

American Section. Following World War II, the leadership of the WZO in the Diaspora passed from London to New York, and an American Section of the Agency Executive evolved. A beginning was made at the World Zionist Conference that met in London in August, 1945, when Louis *Lipsky, Abba Hillel *Silver, and Stephen S. *Wise were made members of the World Executive, but this group functioned only intermittently in the United States.

Following the 22d Zionist Congress (Basle, 1946), an American Section of the Executive was formally established under the chairmanship of Silver. It included Rabbi Z'ev (Wolf) *Gold, Hayim *Greenberg, Rose *Halprin, and Emanuel *Neumann, as well as Moshe Shertok (Moshe *Sharett), who came from Jerusalem, and Nahum Goldmann, who had come from Europe. The American Section was to look after the interests of the WZO and the JA in the United States, with particular reference to political affairs. The latter became its immediate and almost exclusive interest when the British government, early in 1947, decided to refer the Palestine problem to the United Nations, placing a great and unexpected responsibility on the American Section. One of its earliest steps was to assemble a staff of experts from Palestine, Europe, Latin America, and the United States to help establish and maintain contact with numerous delegations to the United Nations. It was also most desirable to maintain contact with important sections of the American Jewish community. Regular meetings were held with the community's representatives, and it was with their knowledge and consent that the JA was recognized by the United Nations as the official Jewish representative body for consultation with the United Nations. On May 8, 1947, the delegation of the American Section, headed by Silver, was seated, and Silver, as spokesman, made the first official presentation of the Jewish case before the United Nations. *See also* UNITED NATIONS AND PALESTINE-ISRAEL.

Throughout 1947 and in 1948, the American Section worked intensively to secure favorable action by the United Nations. Staff efforts to reach and influence the delegates of various nations were directed by Shertok, as head of the Political Department of the Agency, while questions of general policy were under the supervision of Silver, as chairman. The work was carried on consistently during the special session of the General Assembly in the spring of 1947, in connection with the *United Nations Special Committee on Palestine (UNSCOP), in the regular sessions of the General Assembly in the fall of 1947, and finally in the organs of the United Nations in 1948. In addition, many capitals and centers of government in various parts of the world were approached by emissaries or directly from New York. Special attention was devoted to the United States government, largely through the American Zionist Emergency Council and the American Section itself (*see* EMERGENCY COMMITTEE FOR ZIONIST AFFAIRS).

It was through the concentration of effort and intensive activity of the American Section that the *partition resolution was adopted by the General Assembly on Nov. 29, 1947. The struggle was continued into the spring of 1948, when proposals for substituting an international trusteeship over Palestine failed of adoption. Discussions on trusteeship were finally terminated on May 14, 1948, when Silver announced Israel's Declaration of Independence to the United Nations and Pres. Harry S *Truman immediately announced United States recognition of the new State, following a request presented by Eliyahu Epstein (Eliyahu *Elath), the JA representative in Washington.

Although the attention of the American Section was thus concentrated on the major political objectives, it dealt with many other problems. In its early years it operated as a purchasing mission for the JA in Jerusalem and subsequently for the State of Israel and as an instrumentality to promote American investment in Israel, a function that was later taken over by missions of the Israel government. After the establishment of the State, with an embassy in Washington and a consulate in New York, the functions and activities of the American Section were readjusted. Its activities became concentrated largely in fields of education and culture, youth work, and 'Aliya.

Working with Zionist youth organizations and with youth groups in synagogues, community centers, and college campuses, the Youth Department of the Jewish Agency, subsequently cooperating with the *American Zionist Youth Foundation, fostered intensive educational programs and helped develop a Zionist youth movement in the United States. Each summer its study and work groups brought thousands of American youths to Israel for summer programs.

The Education and Tora Education Departments of the American Section have made significant contributions to the promotion of Jewish and Hebrew studies in the United States, helped bring hundreds of Israeli educators to the United States to teach for one or two years in American Jewish educational institutions, conducted seminars for Jewish educators, and arranged visits to Israel by large groups of Jewish educators, university students, and Bar Mitzva youths. The Herzl Foundation, another department of the Agency, has also been active in the field of education and culture through the adult education program of the *Theodor Herzl Institute, the monthly magazine *Midstream*, and the *Herzl Press, which has published more than 100 titles since its founding in 1956, including the *Encyclopedia of Zionism and Israel*.

Since 1947 the American Section, through its 'Aliya Department and the Israel 'Aliya Center, has devoted its major efforts to the development of an American 'Aliya. The section also operates in the area of information and public relations and has published books and brochures interpreting Zionism to the Western world. In addition, it maintains close relations with the United Israel Appeal, in which it is represented, the Jewish National Fund, and other Israel fund-raising organizations in the United States, seeking to develop the best possible climate for American fund-raising efforts on behalf of Israel. Since 1960 the American Section has operated from its own headquarters at 515 Park Avenue, New York.

Achievements and Perspectives. The achievements of the JA during the first two decades of the State are strikingly illustrated by the following statistics. Of the 1.3 million Jewish immigrants to Israel, the overwhelming majority were brought to the country with the help and by means of the JA. About 110,000 children and adolescents were educated and trained by Youth 'Aliya, and more than 90,000 new immigrants learned Hebrew in the Ulpanim of the JA. Together with the govern-

ment of Israel, the JA was instrumental in supplying 200,000 permanent dwelling units to new immigrants. The JA established 490 new settlements, or twice the number of villages founded in the preceding two generations, and about 140,000 persons were absorbed in them. About 30,000 teachers and young persons from the Diaspora participated in educational projects in Israel, 1,500 Israeli teachers undertook educational missions abroad, and 600,000 young persons, affiliated with 200 youth organizations, received educational guidance. From the rise of the State to the end of March, 1967, the JA spent $2,163,000,000 on its varied activities.

It may be said that the existence and operations of a body such as the JA are unique, but so is the position of the Jewish people, because its majority lives outside its national State. As long as this position obtains, the JA is likely to retain its *raison d'être* as the framework through which the Diaspora discharges its responsibilities toward new immigrants and helps develop and consolidate the State of Israel.

A. ZWERGBAUM

JEWISH AND ARAB LABOR. The early history of relations between Jewish and Arab labor in Palestine, during the *Second 'Aliya (1904–14) and *Third 'Aliya (1920–24) periods, is dealt with in the article "CONQUEST OF LABOR." In the beginning of the mandatory period (*see* MANDATE FOR PALESTINE) the British Mandatory government and the British Army created a labor market in which both Jewish and Arab workers found employment. From the point of view of these employers, the Arab workers had the advantage of receiving low wages. The Jews demanded their share in government employment according to their percentage in the population and among taxpayers. As early as 1919 a binational (Jewish and Arab) labor federation, the Federation of Railroad, Postal, and Telegraph Workers, was established. In 1925, with the growth of Arab nationalist sentiment, the Arab workers seceded from this federation. Later they founded their own Palestine Arab Workers Society.

The *Histadrut (General Federation of Labor) found it both necessary and desirable to raise the standard of living of the Arab workers of Palestine and so prevent the competition represented by the low wages they received. This endeavor led the Histadrut to attempt to organize the Arab workers. In 1927 it decided to form a federated body based on the Histadrut itself as the organization of Jewish workers and on a parallel organization of Arab workers. The name chosen for the new federation was B'rit Po'ale Eretz Yisrael (Federation of the Workers of Palestine). The B'rit was active in encouraging organizational and trade union activities among the Arab workers employed by the British Mandatory government of Palestine, by international enterprises, and in Arab-owned factories.

In view of the fact that Jewish workers were excluded from the Arab economy, the Histadrut insisted on reserving the Jewish economic sector as the domain of Jewish workers only. The absorption of Jewish workers in this sector was a prerequisite for the creation of a Jewish laboring class, which in turn could make a contribution to the development of the Jewish National Home. Moreover, the Histadrut opposed all suggestions to limit Jewish workers to the skilled branches of the economy.

These were the antecedents of the struggles for Jewish labor in the early 1930s, when the Histadrut demanded that Jewish orange grove owners employ only Jewish workers in their expanding plantations. In particular, the Histadrut was opposed to the importation from the Hauran of cheap Arab labor that was attracted to the widening labor market in Palestine. Left-wing elements in the Histadrut demanded closer cooperation with Arab workers and hoped that a joint class struggle of the workers of the two peoples would bring the Arab proletariat closer to Zionism.

The *Arab riots of 1936 severed connections between the Jewish and Arab economies of Palestine. By that time the number of Arab workers had reached about 30,000, of whom approximately 20 per cent were employed by Jews, whereas in the Arab economic sector no Jews were employed because Arab employers invariably preferred cheap Arab labor. The prevailing economic crisis and the severance of relations with the Jewish economy gave rise to a difficult situation for the Arab workers.

During World War II both a critical shortage of workers and a rise in the cost of living prevented conflicts over Jewish labor within the Jewish economy. In the Arab economy, the same developments led to the unionization of Arab workers, in which the Jewish-Arab B'rit Po'ale Eretz Yisrael took an active part and which received help from the social services of the Histadrut. In addition, a left-oriented Arab workers' organization was founded.

Following the establishment of the State of Israel in 1948, the problem of the relationship between Jewish and Arab labor underwent a basic change. The competition of cheap labor was a thing of the past, and the Israeli labor market was gradually opened to Arab workers. The Arab economy did not develop markedly, with the exception of the agricultural sector, while the demand for workers in the Jewish economy increased. This situation brought an influx of Arab workers into the Jewish economy, even in places at some distance from Arab settlements.

Late in 1953 the Histadrut opened its trade unions to Arab workers. In 1959 complete equality of wages and fringe benefits was given to Arab workers and workers from other minorities in all Histadrut organizations. The activities of the Histadrut in the Arab sector were expanded in the fields of organization, cooperation, health, and education.

In the mid-1960s about 20,000 Arab workers were employed in the Jewish economy of Israel, and their numbers continued to increase. After the *Six-day War of 1967 more than 15,000 Arabs from the West Bank and the Gaza Strip found employment in Israel.

I. KOLATT

JEWISH BRIGADE. Established formally by a decision of the British War Cabinet in September, 1944, the Jewish Brigade Group (HaHayil) was the final organization created by the British government in its reluctant partial compliance with Jewish demands for an all-Jewish military corps under Jewish insignia on the side of the Allied Powers against the Axis in World War II. Although it was formally established five years after the outbreak of the war, its origins go back to the autumn of 1939, when 130,000 Palestinian Jews registered as volunteers for military service against the Axis. After the first several hundred Palestine Jews had volunteered for service in pioneer units, a decision of the British War Cabinet brought into being 16 companies of infantry, which were given the name Palestinian Buffs, from an East Kent regiment known as the Buffs. Even in this concession in establishing what were termed the first fighting units of Palestinians, the British government, seeking to preserve the principles of the

Brig. Ernest Frank Benjamin inspects the 2d Battalion of the Jewish Brigade in November, 1944. [Zionist Archives]

*White Paper of 1939, set a limit to recruitment for the Jewish units, explaining that parity had to be maintained between Jewish and Arab companies. The continuing pressure of the *Jewish Agency and other groups and "Committees for a Jewish Army," as well as the deteriorating military situation on the North African front, resulted in an announcement from the British government in August, 1942, to the effect that Jewish battalions would be recruited in Palestine, for "general service in the Middle East." These battalions were confined to guard duties and were not placed in frontline service.

Pressure for a Jewish army therefore continued, much of it in the United States. The rabbinical organization adopted resolutions favoring the establishment of a Jewish army, and the National Conference of the *United Palestine Appeal called upon Pres. Franklin D. *Roosevelt to urge Britain to act favorably on the request for a Jewish armed force. When the British government pleaded the shortage of military equipment as an excuse for not arming the Jewish units, the American Zionist Emergency Council (*see* EMERGENCY COMMITTEE FOR ZIONIST AFFAIRS) suggested that the Jewish units be armed through a direct lend-lease action by the United States. A clear indication of the weight of American pressure on the British government is to be found in the memoirs of Sir Winston *Churchill, in which he reveals that on his journey to Quebec in August, 1943, for a meeting with President Roosevelt, he took along Maj. Gen. Orde *Wingate, who was being considered "as Commander in Chief of a Jewish Army when formed."

In this struggle, led by Moshe Shertok (Moshe *Sharett), for the formation of a Jewish army, a significant role was played by the soldiers of the already existing Jewish units. To begin with, the units wanted to be accorded the right to a Jewish insignia and Jewish colors. A mass refusal to wear the Palestinian emblem (a replica of a Palestinian mandatory coin) by members of the 3d Jewish Battalion had resulted in a court-martial and a mass trial with leading Jews giving testimony on the character of Jewish symbols and national emblems. The 2d Jewish Battalion raised the Jewish colors when, after months of agitation (led by Jacob Rubin, Ben-Zion

Appelbaum, Jacob Ariel, Amos Ben-Gurion, and others), the entire battalion was disarmed and put under house arrest. Although the total numerical strength of the Jewish Brigade Group could not be determined with accuracy, its component units—the Jewish Palestinian Regiment (composed of the three Jewish infantry battalions), communications, artillery, engineers, transport, supply and ammunition, medical corps, and military police—amounted to a military corps of 5,000, completely self-sustaining in terms of military functions and combat readiness.

The brigade was assembled in October, 1944, at Burg el-'Arab, near Alexandria, and early in November it was shipped out to Italy, where it was incorporated into the British Eighth Army. Brig. Ernest Frank Benjamin, of the Royal Engineers, a Canadian-born Jew, was appointed commander of the Jewish Brigade Group.

In the months between November, 1944, and the end of February, 1945, the brigade was concentrated around Fiuggi, in central Italy, and underwent a period of intensive combat training. Early in March, 1945, the brigade moved north to the frontline, taking up positions at Alfonsine, north of Ravenna. The brigade did outstanding service in two major assaults on German positions, on Mar. 19 and 20, 1945. After two weeks it was moved to Faenza for a brief rest prior to taking up positions on the Senio River vis-à-vis a German paratroop division. While on this front, the brigade became part of the American Fifth Army commanded by Gen. Mark Clark. During the final push to the north, when the spring offensive began on Apr. 9, 1945, the Jewish Brigade units led the crossing of the Senio in the direction of Imola, on the way to Bologna. The collapse of Nazi resistance on this front freed the bulk of the brigade from combat, while some of its specialized units participated in the pursuit of the retreating enemy farther north. In the brief period of direct combat on the Alfonsine-Senio fronts the brigade lost 30 dead and 70 wounded; 21 were awarded medals, and 78 were mentioned in dispatches. In May, 1945, the brigade moved to the northern frontier of Italy for a rest. It was then that it began a most significant chapter in its history.

Shaken by its first contacts with the remnants of European Jewry, the entire brigade, officers and enlisted men, turned into an army of rescuers, giving away their rations, their clothing, and their bedding to their broken and destitute fellow Jews. Groups of the brigade spread out over Austria and Germany, making contact with and organizing concentration camp survivors and paving the way for their mass migration to Palestine. This important work continued unabated even after the brigade had been transferred to Belgium and the Netherlands in July, 1945 (see B'RIHA). The growing tensions in Palestine and the anti-Zionist policies of the British government naturally affected the brigade units in Europe as well. A hunger strike, the clandestine publication of a pamphlet for Allied troops in Europe, and other forms of resistance to British policies in Palestine hastened the enforcement of Britain's decision to disband the Jewish Brigade Group. In the summer of 1946 the brigade was finally dissolved.

Throughout the existence of the Jewish battalions, the Jewish Regiment, and the Jewish Brigade Group, committees of volunteers on the company, battalion, regiment, and brigade levels played an active role in Jewish national endeavors. After the end of military operations, the brigade briefly published a mimeographed biweekly, *BaMa'avak* (In the Struggle;

edited by Jacob Rubin), and later it launched a Hebrew daily, *HaHayil* (under the editorship of Rubin, Hayim Ben Asher, and M. Silberthal). These publications were part of an intensive cultural program developed by the Jewish Brigade Group and the Jewish Palestinian units before it. With the establishment of the State of Israel, volunteers of the Jewish units provided the young Israeli Army with a nucleus of experienced officer personnel and veteran fighters.

J. RUBIN

JEWISH CHRONICLE. British Jewry's central weekly, founded in 1841. Its establishment coincided with the beginning of the historic growth of British sympathy for a Jewish Palestine. After Abraham Benisch, who had arrived in London in 1841 to propagate Jewish settlement in Palestine, became editor of the *Chronicle* in 1855, news items concerning Palestine were given a prominent place and every event was faithfully recorded. The readers were kept well informed of all that took place in the four holy cities (Jerusalem, Tiberias, Safed, and Hebron) and of Christian and Jewish proposals for colonization.

All the precursors of Zionism, from Mordecai Manuel *Noah to Moses *Hess, appeared in the pages of the *Jewish Chronicle*. In 1867 letters from Henri Dunant (who wrote that the Jewish "rights to Palestine are superior to all others") and from Father *Ignatius of the Order of St. Benedict, as well as from Rabbi Judah Solomon Hai *Alkalai and others, were published in it. Laurence *Oliphant contributed articles from Palestine for many years. The *Chronicle* acquainted its public with the historic achievements of Baron Edmond de *Rothschild, the activities of the Palestine Exploration Fund in London and of the *Hoveve Zion movement, and the efforts of Col. Albert Edward Williamson *Goldsmid, Elim Henry *d'Avigdor, and others.

Asher I. Myers, who became editor of the *Jewish Chronicle* after the death of Benisch in 1878, was present when Herzl delivered his first Zionist talk to the *Order of Ancient Maccabeans in 1895. He asked Herzl for an article, which was published under the title "A Solution of the Jewish Problem" on Jan. 17, 1896, nearly one month prior to the publication of The *Jewish State. Myers was, and remained, an opponent of Herzl's Zionism. In the same issue of the *Chronicle* he explained his opposition in an editorial, "A Dream of a Jewish State"; still, he opened his columns to discussions of Herzl's plans. He sent Morris Duparc to the 1st Zionist *Congress (1897), and the reports of Zionist Congresses were always printed in the *Chronicle* in detail. Almost every issue contained reports, commentaries, or letters on Zionism. Herzl's "Autobiography" was published in the *Jewish Chronicle* on Jan. 14, 1898.

When Herzl died, the paper published many pages of tributes but retained its negative attitude toward political Zionism. The great change came when the Zionists acquired the *Jewish Chronicle*. The *Chronicle* was first offered to Leopold J. *Greenberg, who wanted to acquire it for the *World Zionist Organization. He got in touch with David *Wolffsohn, Herzl's successor, who agreed, and early in 1907 Wolffsohn, Joseph *Cowen, Jacobus H. *Kann, Leopold *Kessler, and Greenberg, as editor, decided to purchase the shares of the paper for themselves.

During World War I, the *Jewish Chronicle* strongly supported the Zionist policy. The British government postponed the publication of the *Balfour Declaration until Nov. 9, 1917, in order to give the *Chronicle* the chance to print it at the same time as the general press.

Greenberg sponsored the formation of Vladimir *Jabotinsky's *Jewish Legion but was firm in his opposition to the policy of Chaim *Weizmann and attacked the Palestine administration. After his death in November, 1931, Jacob Morris Rich became editor, and in 1934 the *Jewish Chronicle* merged with the *Jewish World* (founded in 1873). From 1936 to 1946, Ivan M. *Greenberg, the son of Leopold Greenberg, was editor. An admirer of Jabotinsky, Greenberg called for the establishment of a Jewish State and criticized the policy of the British government and also the official Zionist policy. In 1946 John Maurice Shaftesley became editor, to be succeeded in 1958 by William Frankel. For years David F. Kessler, the son of Leopold Kessler, was chairman and managing director.

J. FRAENKEL

JEWISH COLONIAL TRUST LTD. (Jüdische Colonialbank).

First financial instrument of the *World Zionist Organization, established in accordance with the decisions of the 1st (1897) and 2d (1898) Zionist Congresses (*see* CONGRESS, ZIONIST) and registered in London in 1899. The Jewish Colonial Trust was the form in which the Jewish Company, envisioned by Herzl in his *Jewish State* (1896) as the commercial arm of the *Society of Jews, was realized. The objectives of the Colonial Trust were to promote Jewish settlement in Palestine, grant credit to prospective settlers there, and acquire from "any state or other authority" any "concession, decrease, rights, powers and privileges" deemed likely to advance the Zionist cause. More specifically, Herzl at the time regarded the Trust as the organ that would acquire the hoped-for *Charter from the Turkish government. Accordingly, Herzl exhausted himself in strenuous efforts to have the bank established at the earliest possible moment. He hoped that the Zionist movement might then be in a position to obligate the Ottoman Empire by means of a large loan.

Originally, Herzl hoped to win the support of Jewish millionaires in England, France, and elsewhere for the project. Failing to enlist the aid of these individuals, he decided to build the Jewish Colonial Trust with small subscriptions from the Jewish masses. This approach had a tremendous psychological impact: for the first time in modern history, Jews were being asked not

Herzl with members of the Council of the Jewish Colonial Trust. [Zionist Archives]

to contribute to a philanthropic undertaking but to share in a productive enterprise that would aid the rebirth of the people. Herzl himself put much of his personal fortune into subscriptions for the bank.

The Jewish Colonial Trust began operating in 1902. The authorized capital was £2,000,000, of which only £395,000 was subscribed. It was raised by the sale of £1 shares. Control of the Trust was assured by its charter, which provided that 100 founders' shares were to be vested in a supervisory Council, consisting exclusively of members of the Zionist *Actions Committee. The first president of the Trust was Herzl's devoted lieutenant David *Wolffsohn, who was aided by Jacobus *Kann. These men, who had had extensive business experience, frequently had differences with Herzl, who had no business background but insisted on interfering in the management of the bank.

In 1902 the Trust established a subsidiary, the Anglo-Palestine Company Ltd. (later the Anglo-Palestine Bank Ltd.; *see* BANK L'UMI L'YISRAEL), which opened an office in Jaffa in 1903. In addition to its central offices in London, the Trust maintained a branch office in the city's East End.

The Trust invested its funds in a variety of industrial and financial ventures in both Palestine and other countries, including the Palestine Electric Corporation (*see* ISRAEL ELECTRIC CORPORATION, LTD.) and the Bank HaPo'alim (Workers' Bank). In 1934, after the Trust had suffered great losses, its affairs were taken over by its subsidiary, the Anglo-Palestine Bank. The Trust ceased its banking activities and became a holding company for the stock of the bank. In 1955 it became an Israeli company.

JEWISH COLONIZATION ASSOCIATION (ICA).

Jewish philanthropic organization established in 1891 by Baron Maurice de *Hirsch with the aim of settling Jews in agricultural settlements in North and South America. Having failed to obtain the approval of the Tsarist Russian government for a proposal for the economic and political rehabilitation of the Jewish masses within Russia, Baron de Hirsch felt that the only solution for the Jews in countries of oppression would be mass emigration to the Western Hemisphere. For the implementation of this program he endowed and incorporated in London in 1891 the Jewish Colonization Association (ICA) as a joint stock company with a capital of £2,000,000 ($10,000,000), a sum he subsequently quadrupled. Of the 20,000 shares of

Certificate issued by the Jewish Colonial Trust Ltd. in 1901. [Zionist Archives]

£200 each, Hirsch held 19,993, the rest being held by Jewish leaders in London and Paris. In 1893 Hirsch distributed his shares among the *Anglo-Jewish Association and the Jewish communities of Brussels, Berlin, and Frankfurt on the Main, retaining for his lifetime the voting rights of the shares given the London organization so as to direct ICA's activities as its chairman. The purpose of the association, as defined in article 3 of its statutes, was

> . . . to assist and promote the emigration of poor and needy Jews from any part of Europe or Asia where they are oppressed by special restriction laws and where they are deprived of political rights, to any other part of the world where they can enjoy these and other rights pertaining to man. To this effect the Association proposes agricultural colonies in diverse regions of North and South America, as also in other territories.

ICA's first and main object was the colonization of Russian and Romanian Jews in Argentina. Here ICA had acquired about 750,000 hectares of land, of which a little less than 500,000 hectares were cultivated by about 3,500 families. The entire Jewish population in the colonies and the surrounding countryside never exceeded 35,000 to 40,000 persons. Moreover, there was a steady migration from rural to urban areas, and although many colonists prospered, their children preferred to become doctors, lawyers, scholars, or businessmen in the cities. Hirsch's great hope of eventually bringing 3.5 million Jews from Russia and settling them largely as farmers never materialized.

ICA bought land also in Brazil and supported farmers there as well as in Canada and the United States (through the Industrial Removal Office). It helped Jewish farmers in Russia before World War I and in the succession states (Poland, Estonia, Latvia, Lithuania, and Bessarabia in Romania) after the war. Contrary to assumptions in some circles, however, ICA did not participate in settling Jews in Birobidzhan, Cyprus, the Balkans, and Asia Minor (Turkey). Among other ICA activities was assistance to vocational schools and credit and producer cooperative societies.

In Palestine, in which ICA had taken an interest as early as 1896, it took over (1899) from Baron Edmond de *Rothschild the task of consolidating the colonies supported by him, for which purpose the baron provided a fund of 15,000,000 francs ($3,000,000). This task was handed over in 1924 to the newly formed *Palestine Jewish Colonization Association (PICA). After the *Arab riots of 1929, ICA resumed activities in Palestine through a subsidiary, EMICA. Since the establishment of the State of Israel, ICA has concentrated its work there, participating with the Israel *government, the *Jewish Agency, or both, in the consolidation and establishment of 41 settlements (1968) and supporting agricultural research (at the *Hebrew University of Jerusalem and the *Weizmann Institute of Science) and agricultural training (Mikve Yisrael Agricultural School and scholarships at other schools). To meet political and economic emergency situations facing Jewish communities in Europe, ICA has cooperated in the relief work of the Hebrew Immigrant Aid Society (HIAS) and the *American Jewish Joint Distribution Committee (JDC).

K. GRUNWALD

JEWISH COMMUNITY OF PALESTINE. *See* YISHUV.

JEWISH COMPANY. *See* OLD-NEW LAND.

JEWISH DAY SCHOOLS, ZIONIST (in England). *See* GREAT BRITAIN, ZIONISM IN.

JEWISH EDUCATION IN THE DIASPORA. Of the estimated 11,350,000 Jews living outside the State of Israel in 1968, 2,824,000 resided in the Soviet Union and its satellites. Jewish educational activity was prohibited in the Soviet Union and severely curtailed in Soviet-dominated countries. As a result, Jewish education in the 1960s was geographically coextensive, with only minor deviations, with the free world.

Early Years. In the period preceding the *Haskala (Enlightenment), Jews lived in restricted, self-contained geographic areas, and their religious, educational, communal, social, and intellectual activities revolved around traditional (Orthodox) beliefs and practice. Opportunities for secular studies were mostly unavailable. Jewish studies of a secular character were practically unknown. Jews who had a modicum of knowledge and education in secular matters were usually self-educated.

JEWISH SCHOOL POPULATION AND SCHOOL ENROLLMENT IN THE DIASPORA, 1966

Country	Jewish population	Jewish school-age population*	Children enrolled in Jewish schools	Percentage of children attending Jewish schools
Western Europe	985,404	163,235	63,088	39
United States	5,531,500	1,106,300	540,323	50
Canada	250,000	50,000	23,903	48
South and Central America	673,850	127,386	35,381	28
Arab countries†	119,900	23,990	23,761	99
Iran	80,000	16,000	10,685	67
Republic of South Africa	113,000	23,000	13,313	58
Australia	67,000	13,460	6,915	57
Total	7,820,654	1,523,361	717,369	47
U.S.S.R. and its satellites‡	2,695,300			

*Aged 5–17, except in the United States, where the figure includes children aged 3–17 years.

†Includes an estimated Jewish population of 70,000 in Morocco and 23,000 in Tunisia.

‡Reports from Romania, Hungary, and Yugoslavia indicated some measure of Jewish education programming. Owing to lack of communication with the Jews in these countries, however, no reliable statistics could be obtained.

The Jewish school curriculum consisted of the classic Jewish sacred texts: the prayer book, the Bible (Pentateuch with Rashi's commentary), and Talmud. In the self-contained and inner-directed Jewish community, Jewish education was not limited to formal classroom study. Life all around was deeply Jewish, and the Jewish way of life was the only one known to, and followed by, the Jews.

The traditional Jewish education and way of life were not directly conducive to the growth and development of modern Jewish *nationalism. However, the age-old hopes and aspirations for the Return to Zion, as expressed in daily prayer and observances on the holidays and festivals and in the classic texts, were the latent forces in the advent of the Zionist movement in the late 19th and early 20th century. Naturally, the practical realization of Jewish nationalism required, in addition, secular knowledge and an awareness of the national aspirations prevailing among other nationality groups.

The Haskala movement was the springboard for such a development in Western Europe and ultimately in Eastern Europe as well. Influenced by the European intellectual revolution and the rising tide of nationalism, the Haskala spearheaded the scientific study of Judaism, stimulated the revival of the *Hebrew language, and accelerated the rise of Jewish nationalism.

One of the earliest results of the Haskala in the field of Jewish education was the establishment by the *Alliance Israélite Universelle of a large network of Jewish schools in the Balkans and in Muslim countries from Persia (Iran) in the east to Morocco in the west. While the educational orientation of the Alliance schools was largely French, they also gave their students a good Jewish education, with Hebrew studies receiving increasing emphasis as the years passed. Until 1920 the Alliance schools were the largest single educational system in the Jewish world.

Modern Jewish education, calling as it did for the revival of the Hebrew language as the key to national renascence, played a major role in the Zionist movement at the end of the 19th and in the first decade of the 20th century. At World Zionist Congresses (see CONGRESS, ZIONIST) and special conferences devoted to the Hebrew language and Hebrew culture, the Zionists, beginning with the 1st Congress (Basle, 1897), called on Jews everywhere " . . . to establish organizations for maintaining institutions for instruction in the Hebrew language." By encouraging and later successfully conducting full-time Jewish elementary and secondary schools in Palestine, where Hebrew was the language of instruction as well as of everyday conversation, the Zionists exerted a great influence on the development of Hebrew education in Eastern Europe.

The influence of the modern Hebrew literati, the zealous teachers under the influence of Eliezer *Ben Yehuda and the leaders who advocated the use of the Hebrew language as a living tongue, was considerable and lasting. In 1902, at the *Minsk Conference, *Ahad Ha'Am proclaimed the famous slogan "Capture the schools." In the spirit of this slogan, the Zionist Hebrew-speaking organization *Hoveve S'fat 'Ever established Hebrew schools in a number of communities.

In Tsarist Russia, including Poland, Estonia, Latvia, Lithuania, and Bessarabia, where the major part of world Jewry was living in the early 20th century, both Zionism and Hebrew education had to function under severe political and other restrictive conditions. As a consequence, modern Jewish education made little headway. The typical Jewish educational institutions in Poland and Russia proper until after World War I were the private Heder (elementary-level one-room school; plural, Hadorim), the Talmud Tora (community-sponsored Orthodox Jewish school), and the Yeshiva (or Talmudic academy). Statistical information for this period is scanty. Thus, for example, in 1915 there were 2,112 private Hadorim and only 70 Talmud Toras in five districts (Podolsk, Volyn, Chernigov, Poltava, and Lublin).

In Western European countries, Jewish education took a different direction. There, the gradual *emancipation and enfranchisement of the Jews, the resulting greater educational, economic, and social opportunities, and increasing tolerance on the part of the state to religions other than the established creed brought about far-reaching changes in Jewish communal life. Jewish education in Western Europe was not accorded the position of primacy it enjoyed in the East. In contrast to Jewish education in Eastern Europe, which centered on Jewish tradition and nationhood, Jewish schools in the West tended to stress the religious rather than the historic and national differences between Jews and their neighbors. In general, Jewish education in Western Europe received less time and emphasis than Jewish studies in the East. Adjustment to the culture of the non-Jewish community became an important goal. Zionism, nationalism, and Hebraism did not play the role they were given in the East, and the threat of cultural *assimilation became very real.

Between the Two World Wars. With the fall of the Tsarist government in Russia in March, 1917, a period of intensive nationalist educational activity began among the small nations achieving independence in Eastern Europe. This was also a period of intensive educational activity among the Jews. The development of Jewish education in Eastern Europe between the two world wars was aided by the granting of cultural autonomy to the minorities living in the provinces that had seceded from Russia. In Estonia and Latvia, under the terms of the cultural autonomy, all the Jewish schools were supervised and financed by the government. Hebrew and Yiddish were recognized equally as languages of instruction. In Lithuania the Jewish schools were under the jurisdiction of a Ministry for Jewish Affairs. See also AUTONOMY, JEWISH.

In Poland the cultural autonomy accorded to minority groups did not extend to Yiddish schools. Hebrew schools, however, were given such recognition, and the first Hebrew all-day elementary school was opened in Goniądz, Białystok Province, in 1916, one year after the founding of the first Hebrew high school in Vilna. Under the stimulus of cultural autonomy in Eastern Europe and the short-lived liberal Russian regime before the coming of Bolshevism, the number of both Hebrew and Yiddish educational institutions greatly increased.

In 1921 the Polish Zionist Organization (see POLAND, ZIONISM IN) initiated the *Tarbut organization to coordinate, establish standards for, and supervise the Hebrew school movement in Poland. In the schools affiliated with Tarbut, instruction was conducted entirely in Hebrew and the students were thoroughly Palestine-motivated. The Tarbut form of organization later spread to the other Eastern European countries.

In 1935 the Polish Tarbut school system comprised 72 Hebrew kindergartens, 133 all-day elementary schools, 9 all-day secondary schools, and 4 evening schools with a combined enrollment of more than 40,000. There were also two Orthodox religious central organizations conducting the Horev and Yavne schools.

Yiddish education, too, developed during this period. It began as a folk movement late in the 19th century, when "jargon circles," prohibited by the government, were organized clandestinely for the teaching of Yiddish and arithmetic. The rise of Yiddishist education was an expression of the need felt for democratization of Jewish communal life, an indication of the strength and depth of Jewish folk spirit among the Jewish masses and a demonstration of the changing economic, political, and spiritual conditions in the Jewish community. The Yiddish educational institutions were later transplanted to the Americas. In 1935 the Yiddish educational institutions of Poland numbered more than 100, with a combined enrollment of more than 15,000. The Yiddish schools were affiliated with the Zentrale Yidishe Shul Organizacie (ZISHO).

Jewish education in this period of change and transition was threefold in motivation and character: (1) the continuing classic traditional education on different levels, still strong and vibrant; (2) the modern Hebraist educational institutions with a strong Zionist orientation; and (3) the Yiddish-oriented educational institutions with strong secular leanings. World War II, Nazism, and the spread of communism put an end to all Jewish education in Eastern Europe and destroyed almost all the Jewish educational institutions in Western Europe as well.

Development since World War II. Following World War II attempts were made to reestablish and expand Jewish education in the Western European countries. This effort was spearheaded by the Department of Education of the *American Jewish Joint Distribution Committee and the Department of Education and Culture of the *Jewish Agency for Israel. The latter, for example, sent educational Sh'lihim (emissaries; see SHALIAH) and, in cooperation with local communal and educational organizations, established seminars for Jewish teachers from the Diaspora. In one year (1959–60) the Jewish Agency sent some 135 educational Sh'lihim to 24 countries.

In 1966 only 39 per cent of all Jewish children of elementary and secondary school age in Western Europe (including Great Britain) were receiving some measure of formal Jewish education. On the Continent, of every 100 children of school age, 4 attended all-day Jewish schools, 16 attended supplementary schools, and 80 received no Jewish education at all. In Great Britain more than half of the children aged 5 through 17 received some measure of Jewish education. Of these, about 30 per cent attended day schools, and 70 per cent supplementary schools.

In Arabic-speaking countries, where Jewish life was restricted and precarious, Jewish education consisted of the classic religious texts. In India, Iran, and the North African countries, the Alliance Israélite Universelle, Otzar HaTora, *ORT, the Lubavich Hasidic movement, and the Department of Education and Culture of the Jewish Agency were active and effective in the establishment and maintenance of schools and the training of teachers. The climate of insecurity in which these Jewries lived, particularly after the *Six-day War of 1967, caused the disintegration of the Jewish communities and their Jewish educational systems.

Development in the Americas. Although Jewish settlement in the Americas is more than 300 years old, it was not until the early 20th century that Jewish communities in the United States and other American countries showed large-scale growth. The American Jewish community is composed of heterogeneous immigrant elements that came from many different parts of the world. All of them made provision for the instruction of their young in the Jewish tradition. Because Jewish experience was so varied, however, each immigrant group gave its own interpretation to the Jewish educational goal. The early Jewish educational institutions established by the Spanish-Portuguese and German immigrants attempted to duplicate their European counterparts, as did the schools established by the Eastern European newcomers at a later date.

The large number of Eastern European Jews who went to the United States between 1881 and 1914 had been influenced by the Haskala, the Hibbat Zion movement (see HOVEVE ZION), the Hebraic and the Yiddish renaissance, and, particularly, the Heder M'tukan (the "improved" traditional elementary school). Their attitudes, molded by these influences, expressed themselves in the Jewish educational institutions they established in the United States.

The arrival of trained teachers, dedicated to the revival of Hebrew as a living language, also left its mark on Jewish education in the United States. Some of the teachers became pioneers in the effort to modernize Jewish education through the establishment of schools in which Hebrew was taught as a living language. Efforts of this type had been anticipated by earlier educational pioneers, the first among whom was Sundel Hirsch Neumann, who in 1893 established a private school where Hebrew was taught as a modern language and modern methods of teaching were introduced.

Noteworthy in this field of endeavor was the modern Hebrew school established in Baltimore by Dr. Samson Benderly, who came to the United States from Safed, Palestine, and under whose leadership the first Bureau of Jewish Education was established in New York in 1910. The bureau pioneered in the development of new curricula, texts, and methods for Jewish schools and laid the foundation for communal responsibility for Jewish education. The work of the Bureau of Jewish Education profoundly influenced the subsequent development of American Jewish education.

In the first two decades of the 20th century it appeared as if the communal Talmud Tora, which tended to be Hebraist and Zionist as well as religious in orientation, would be the typical supplementary Jewish school in the United States. However, the synagogues belonging to the major groupings of American Judaism (Orthodox, Conservative, and Reform) began to set up their own Sunday and Hebrew schools. By the 1930s these congregational schools seemed to have become the Jewish educational institutions most acceptable to American Jews.

Following World War II the center of Jewish education shifted from Eastern Europe to the Americas. American Jews, not directly affected by the war, founded a vast network of elementary, secondary, all-day, and supplementary schools and educational camps, as well as schools for the training of teachers and central community and national agencies for Jewish education. In the United States alone, almost 4,000 Jewish educational institutions were founded, in which (in the mid-1960s) about 540,000 children of school age (3 through 17) were enrolled. Some children were still attending Talmud Toras and a very small number were enrolled in Yiddishist schools, but the preponderant number was found in the congregational Sunday schools, receiving a minimal Jewish education. About 10 per cent attended all-day elementary and secondary schools. The growth of these day schools with their intensive Jewish curriculum is a significant phenomenon in American Jewish education. In Canada, about the same proportion of children received a Jewish education, with one-third attending day schools.

However, Jewish education for the majority of the children is supplementary, taking place in the afternoon after attendance at the public schools. The school curriculum consists of prayers, customs, holidays, Bible study, Bar Mitzva preparation and confirmation, and Hebrew-language instruction. In most schools Israel is not studied as a separate subject but is incorporated in the study of the holidays, Tu BiSh'vat and Yom Ha'Atzmaut celebrations, *Jewish National Fund projects, and Israeli songs and dances.

In Latin America, about 28 per cent of the Jewish children attended Jewish schools in the mid-1960s. Of the total enrollment, 31 per cent attended all-day schools.

Jewish education in the Diaspora faced many problems, the gravest of them being a serious shortage of qualified teachers.
See also EDUCATION IN ISRAEL.

U. Z. ENGELMAN AND A. P. GANNES

JEWISH FELLOWSHIP. *See* LEAGUE OF BRITISH JEWS.

JEWISH FRONTIER. American Labor Zionist journal (*see* LABOR ZIONISM) published in New York since 1934 as the monthly organ of the Labor Zionist Organization of America–*Po'ale Zion and the League for Labor Israel. It has consistently followed the policy enunciated in an editorial in its first issue:

We feel that there must be a publication which will interpret contemporary events in Palestine and take its stand on the frontiers of Jewish life throughout the world. We represent that synthesis in Jewish thought which is nationalist without being chauvinist, and which stands for fundamental economic reconstruction without being communist.

In addition to articles and editorials on current events, the *Jewish Frontier* has devoted much space to poetry, short stories, scholarly essays, and book reviews. It has had permanent correspondents in Israel and, beginning in 1958, has printed a special 32-page quarterly supplement entitled *Israel from Within*, to which leading Israeli journalists and public figures have been regular contributors. Attention has been given also to Jewish life in other countries and to social problems at home and abroad. The editors and managing editors have included Hayim *Greenberg, Hayim *Fineman, Ben Halpern, Shlomo Katz, and Marie *Syrkin.

C. B. SHERMAN

JEWISH LEGION. Jewish military units formed by volunteers in World War I to fight alongside British troops for the liberation of Palestine from Turkish rule.

Formation and War Service. The idea of the Jewish Legion was advanced by Vladimir *Jabotinsky after Turkey entered the war on the side of the Central Powers on Oct. 30, 1914. In Alexandria, Egypt, he found several thousand Palestinian Jews who had been expelled by the Turkish authorities and, with Joseph *Trumpeldor, organized a 500-man volunteer corps for service in Palestine. When the British authorities agreed to assign to them only auxiliary and not fighting duties

Recruits for the Jewish Legion in Jerusalem in 1917. [Zionist Archives]

American recruits for the Jewish Legion in New York in 1918. [Zionist Archives]

at a non-Palestinian front, Trumpeldor accepted the offer and led the *Zion Mule Corps, the first Jewish military formation, on the Gallipoli front. Jabotinsky, however, refused to join him and in 1915–16 unsuccessfully sought to win understanding and support for the Jewish Legion in Rome, Paris, and London. In the British capital he was cold-shouldered by the War Office and met with the disapproval of the entire Zionist leadership, which feared Turkish reprisals against the *Yishuv (Jewish population of Palestine); the only exception was Chaim *Weizmann, who volunteered assistance. The small group of supporters included Meir *Grossman, Jacob *Landau, Pinhas *Rutenberg, Joseph *Cowen, and Dr. Montague David *Eder. Appeals to the Jewish youth in London's East End to volunteer for the legion were frustrated by apathy, abuse, and obstruction.

Late in 1916, 120 former Zion Mule Corps soldiers, who volunteered again for the British Army, arrived in London and were assigned as a unit to the 20th London Battalion, thus forming the nucleus of the legion. Having enlisted as a private, Jabotinsky, with Trumpeldor, submitted a petition to the British Cabinet for the formation of a Jewish Legion for Palestine. On Aug. 23, 1917, the establishment of a Jewish

regiment was announced in the London *Gazette.* The official name was the 38th Battalion, Royal Fusiliers, commanded by Lieut. Col. John Henry *Patterson, with Jabotinsky holding the rank of lieutenant. After training in England and Egypt, the battalion arrived in Palestine in June, 1918, and was assigned to active frontline duty. It was later joined by the 39th Battalion under Lieut. Col. Eleazar *Margolin. On September 23, Jabotinsky's company captured the strategically important Jordan ford Umm esh-Shert. This unit and the two companies of Colonel Margolin's battalion were among the first to enter Transjordan.

Early in 1918 a strong movement for the formation of a Palestinian Legion developed among the Jews in southern Palestine, which by that time had been liberated by the British Army. Authorization for recruitment arrived in May, and within the first few weeks more than 1,000 men volunteered. They were organized into the 40th Battalion, Royal Fusiliers, under the command of Col. M. F. Scott, and sent for training to Egypt, where they were kept until December, 1918, so that they missed the decisive September offensive.

During the first three years of the war, some American Zionists, with the notable exceptions of Louis D. *Brandeis

A battalion of the Jewish Legion parades in London, in July, 1919.
[Zionist Archives]

and Nachman *Syrkin, were strongly opposed to Jabotinsky's project and occasionally even ridiculed such a venture. As late as the middle of 1917, the labor party *Po'ale Zion was opposed to Jewish participation and American involvement in the war, as were David *Ben-Gurion and Itzhak *Ben Zvi, who, after their expulsion from Palestine, met Trumpeldor in Alexandria but remained unconvinced that the formation of Jewish units to fight for the Allied cause was in the interest of the Yishuv. It was not until the issuance of the *Balfour Declaration on Nov. 2, 1917, that they started a campaign for the enlistment of volunteers in the British Army (the United States had not declared war on Turkey). The first group of 150 volunteers left for military training in Canada in February, 1918; Ben-Gurion and Ben Zvi enlisted late in April, and a total of 2,700 men were ultimately recruited. In August, several contingents left for further training in England and then in Egypt, where they joined the 39th Battalion. The training was so lengthy that most of the American volunteers reached Palestine only when the war was already over.

Postwar Activities. Early in 1919 the three Jewish battalions (the 38th, 39th, and 40th) in liberated Palestine numbered more than 5,000 men, or about one-sixth of the entire British Army of Occupation. The major component (34 per cent) of this total consisted of volunteers from the United States, followed by the Palestinians (30 per cent), volunteers from England (28 per cent), Canada (6 pet cent), and Argentina (1 per cent), and Turkish prisoners of war (1 per cent). After the victorious conclusion of the Palestine Campaign, the name Royal Fusiliers was changed to Judean Regiment. Its insignia was a *Menora with the Hebrew word "Kadima" (Forward). In addition to the 5,000 men in active service, about 5,600 (mostly Americans, with a sprinkling of Canadians) enlisted before Armistice Day and went through basic training in England; they were subsequently demobilized.

As long as the legion retained its full strength, occupying strategically crucial positions, peace and order prevailed in Palestine. The situation began to deteriorate with the progressive whittling down of the "Judeans." The anti-Zionist British military administration was eager to effect their demobilization as early as possible. Largely because of this official attitude, the volunteers from the United States were eagerly awaiting discharge and repatriation. Appeals by leaders of the

Jewish community that they remain in Palestine to safeguard the security of the Yishuv were of little avail; very few believed that there was any real danger of Arab violence. A marked tendency toward speedy repatiation also developed among the legionnaires from England, who, however, remained in Palestine longer than any other group of Jewish soldiers from overseas. The desire for demobilization among the Palestinian volunteers was motivated mostly by their eagerness to resume work on the country's upbuilding. All this contributed to the shrinking of the legion's strength. In the second part of 1919 only two of the three battalions were still in existence, and by the spring of 1920 only 300 to 400 men remained. This was the time of the first bloody anti-Jewish assaults by the Arabs at Tel Hai (February, 1920) and Jerusalem (April, 1920; *see* ARAB RIOTS IN PALESTINE).

Late in the summer of 1919, 80 men of the 40th Battalion, mostly Palestinian volunteers, were ordered to proceed to Egypt, where violent anti-British riots had broken out. Risking a court-martial, the battalion unanimously refused to go lest the Arabs interpret such a move as cooperation by Palestinian Jews in suppressing the Egyptian nationalist movement. Strongly backed by its non-Jewish commander, Colonel Scott, the legionnaires finally made their cause prevail. When, in May, 1921, anti-Jewish riots broke out in Jaffa, Colonel Margolin, without asking official permission, brought his soldiers, fully armed, from Sarafand to Tel Aviv and stopped the pogrom. Because of this he was forced to resign, and the liquidation of the legion was stepped up.

In 1921 the Executive of the World Zionist Organization (*see* EXECUTIVE, ZIONIST) requested of the British government that the 38th to 40th Royal Fusiliers (Judeans), as established in 1917–18, "continue to form part of the British Forces in Palestine." The request, subsequently endorsed by the 12th Zionist *Congress, remained unheeded. The Palestine government promised to facilitate the settlement of demobilized legionnaires on government land but did not keep that promise. In 1932, 60 former Judeans from the United States, Canada, and Argentina founded Avihayil, a Moshav 'Ovdim (small-holders' settlement; *see* MOSHAV) north of N'tanya on land made available for this purpose by the *Jewish National Fund.

The legion provided, in fact, the first cadres of post-World War I *'Aliya (immigration). It also was the breeding ground for the Yishuv's political leadership. It was in the 40th (Palestinian) Battalion that the *Ahdut 'Avoda movement (an amalgam of Po'ale Zion and nonparty Laborites, among them Privates Levi *Eshkol and Berl *Katznelson) was born, and several members of the *Hagana High Command up to 1939 were former legionnaires; Ya'akov *Dori, the first chief of staff of the Israel Defense Army, was also a legion man.

J. SCHECHTMAN

JEWISH NATIONAL AND UNIVERSITY LIBRARY, JERUSALEM. National library of the State of Israel and central library of the *Hebrew University of Jerusalem.

Development and Functions. The library was developed from a small collection started in 1884 by a group of Jerusalem intellectuals and incorporated in 1892 into a library founded by the *B'nai B'rith lodge in Jerusalem. The idea of a national library was conceived by Dr. Joseph *Chasanovich, a Biały-stok physician, who, in 1895, sent a collection of Hebrew books to Jerusalem which formed the nucleus of the library. In 1920 the library with its 30,000 books was taken over by the *World

Zionist Organization and named the Jewish National Library. Since the opening of the Hebrew University in 1925, it has been known as the Jewish National and University Library. In 1929 the library was transferred to Mount Scopus into a building named for David *Wolffsohn.

In 1948 the university campus was cut off from Jewish Jerusalem, and the library had to start again from scratch in the city. Strenuous efforts were made to build up new collections, partly by salvaging hundreds of thousands of books from the public and private libraries of destroyed Jewish communities in Europe. In 1960 the library moved to its new home on the new university campus in Giv'at Ram.

The library fulfills a threefold function: (1) As the national library of the Jewish people, it collects books, manuscripts, periodicals, and other material reflecting the life and culture of the Jewish people. Its collections of Judaica and Hebraica are the largest in the world. (2) As the central library of the Hebrew University, it collects publications with particular reference to education and research and includes several departmental libraries, among them the Julius Jarcho Medical Library. (3) As the central library of the State of Israel, it makes its services available to the population as a whole.

Collections and Activities. In 1970 the library, along with the departmental libraries, had 2 million volumes, more than 7,000 manuscripts, and a comprehensive collection of Hebrew incunabula (rare books printed before 1500). The library regularly received more than 15,000 periodicals. Among its outstanding special collections were the Schwadron Collection of Jewish Autographs and Portraits, including manuscripts of Albert *Einstein; the Friedenwald Collection on Medicine, in particular on Jews in medicine; and the archives of *Ahad Ha'Am, Joseph *Klausner, and others.

Since 1924 the library has published a bibliographical quarterly, *Kiryat Sepher*, the first part of which contains the current national bibliography while the other sections are devoted to bibliographies and studies in book lore. The Institute of Microfilms of Hebrew Manuscripts, the Institute for Hebrew Bibliography, and the Jewish Music Research Center are housed in the library.

The Graduate Library School of the Hebrew University is an associated library project of the UN Educational, Scientific

Jewish National and University Library building on the Hebrew University campus in Jerusalem. [Israel Information Services]

and Cultural Organization (UNESCO) and has a special wing in the library donated by the *Pioneer Women of the United States.

The library assists other libraries by supplying duplicates and professional advice and is the center for bibliographic activities in Israel. It is also the center for international library loans and exchanges, the depository library of the United Nations and its agencies, and the representative of the Smithsonian Institution in Washington.

C. D. WORMANN

JEWISH NATIONAL FUND (JNF; Keren Kayemet L'Yisrael). Fund for the afforestation and reclamation of the land of Israel, originally set up to purchase land in Palestine.

Formation and Early Development. The Jewish National Fund was the brainchild of Prof. Hermann *Schapira, who proposed the idea at the 1st Zionist *Congress (Basle, 1897). The land to be bought by the Fund could be neither sold nor mortgaged, thus remaining in perpetuity the property of the Jewish people; it was to be leased to settlers for 49-year periods. Action was not taken on the proposal until the 5th Zionist Congress (1901), to which it was submitted in a reformulated version by Johann *Kremenetzky with strong encouragement from Herzl. Contributions began to pour in at once, and that same year saw the creation of two fund-raising devices: the blue collection boxes, many thousands of which were placed in Jewish homes all over the world; and the JNF stamp, which also served as an educational device. In the very early days of the State of Israel, JNF stamps were even used for postage.

In the Fund's early years, the struggle between the adherents of the political approach, who opposed settlement efforts and land acquisition until political rights were secured for the Jews in Palestine, and those who insisted on starting practical settlement work at once left its mark on the newly founded Fund. The decision of the 6th Zionist Congress (1903) to begin acquiring land was virtually the first step of the *World Zionist Organization (WZO) in settlement work, followed two years later by the acquisition of the first tract of land in Palestine. Although appreciable sums of money had accumulated, the first land purchases, for K'far Hittim, Hulda, and Ben Shemen, were not made until 1905.

On Apr. 8, 1907, the JNF was registered under the British Companies Act as an association limited by guarantee and not having a capital divided into shares. Its first subscribers were Max *Bodenheimer, Leopold J. *Greenberg, Alexander *Marmorek, Jacob *Moser, M'nahem M. *Ussishkin, Otto *Warburg, and David *Wolffsohn. With the transfer of World Zionist headquarters to Cologne, the JNF moved there also (1907), with Bodenheimer as director. This transition marked the beginning of practical work in Palestine by the WZO in accordance with decisions taken by the 8th Zionist Congress (1907).

The expenses of the Palestine Office (set up in 1908; *see* PALESTINE OFFICES) were covered, in the main, by JNF allocations. As the only public fund available to the WZO at the time, the JNF carried a good part of the financial burden of settlement in areas like D'ganya and Kinneret, and provided loans for Ahuzat Bayit, the nucleus of what later became Tel Aviv. The Fund was severely criticized for these departures from its original purpose (the purchase of land), but Bodenheimer argued that these activities were in keeping with the JNF Charter, which provided for investment in any project that

Conference of Jewish National Fund leaders before the 16th Zionist Congress (Zurich, 1929). Seated from left to right are Emanuel Neumann, Berl Katznelson, Yitzhak Elazari-Volcani, M'nahem M. Ussishkin, Sh'lomo Salman Schocken, Rabbi Meir Berlin, and Abraham Granott. [Jewish National Fund]

would further the rebuilding and resettlement of Palestine. It was in this spirit that the JNF aided the immigration of *Yemenite Jews and projects such as the Bezalel National Art Museum, and that it supplied land for the building of the *Herzliya High School in Tel Aviv and the *Technion in Haifa. By the outbreak of World War I, there were on JNF land seven agricultural settlements, constituting 16 per cent of all agricultural settlements in the country.

World War I and the Interwar Years. With the coming of World War I, JNF headquarters was moved to The Hague, where Nehemia *de Lieme was elected its chairman in 1919, serving until his resignation in 1921. During the war the JNF ran appeals to finance special work projects for the unemployed in Palestine and increased its landholdings to 21,000 dunams (*see* DUNAM). Theoretical aspects of the Palestine land problem were explored by the Fund in journals and pamphlets issued in several languages. An important part in this work was played by Abraham *Granott, then secretary of the Fund's central office and for many years the Fund's outstanding theorist.

The *London Zionist Conference of 1920, which dealt with the upbuilding of Palestine, also formulated a policy whereby the activities of the JNF would be confined to the acquisition of land for agricultural settlement and the *Keren HaYesod (Palestine Foundation Fund), established at that conference, would engage in the establishment of settlements on land so acquired. The JNF thereafter acquired large tracts of land in the Jezreel Valley. This purchase, the largest single

land acquisition by the JNF, was initiated by Ussishkin, who from 1923 until his death in 1941 was the chairman of the Board of Directors of the JNF. Ussishkin, who was the driving spirit of the JNF, lent it prestige and made it a major financial as well as an educational factor in Zionist activity.

In September, 1922, JNF headquarters was moved to Jerusalem. Land was purchased in urban sections and in the vicinity of smaller settlements for the construction of workers' housing. However, the main emphasis still continued to be placed on the acquistion of farmland. By April, 1923, the JNF had purchased 100,000 dunams of land in Palestine, following a policy of acquiring large and continuous areas so as to develop a considerable Jewish-owned territorial concentration. In the late 1920s the JNF purchased the Hefer Valley and Haifa Bay, where kibbutzim (*see* KIBBUTZ), cooperative settlements, workers' housing developments, Yemenite settlements, work projects for women, and agricultural schools were soon set up. By 1932 the JNF had collected nearly £P3,000,000 and had acquired more than 300,000 dunams, representing about 60 per cent of Jewish-owned land in Palestine.

The start of large-scale Jewish *immigration from Germany following Hitler's rise to power marked the beginning of a new era for the JNF. After the *Arab riots of 1936 pointed up the importance of areas remote from main centers of settlement, the Fund purchased the Bet Sh'an Valley. It also bought land near the borders, particularly in Galilee. With the announcement of the plan for the *partition of Palestine, it became JNF policy to acquire land in areas excluded from the proposed Jewish State and to form settlements there (see "STOCKADE AND TOWER" SETTLEMENTS). By 1939 JNF landholdings were close to 500,000 dunams, and the 21st Zionist Congress (Geneva, 1939) commended the JNF for having bought more than 100,000 dunams of land in the late 1930s, making possible the creation of many new settlements during a period of Arab riots and highway murders.

World War II and Development under the State of Israel. The *White Paper of 1939 severely limited the possibilities for Jewish land purchase in Palestine. Under the *Land Transfer Regulations of 1940, the country was divided into three zones; in two of these, 17 million dunams were barred to Jewish purchase. Nevertheless, during the first year after the issuance of the White Paper, the JNF succeeded in buying 30,000 dunams within the forbidden zones.

After the death of Ussishkin in 1941, the directorship of the JNF was assumed by Granott. Granott served until 1960 and was succeeded by Jacob *Tsur. The directorate of the Fund was composed of Zionist leaders representing all sectors and factions in the *Yishuv as well as in the *Diaspora.

Following the Nazi destruction of Eastern European Jewry during World War II, American Jewry effectively came to the aid of the JNF. In the four years 1940–43, JNF income amounted to 40 per cent of the total amount it had been able to raise during the entire previous period of its existence. Of this sum, 56 per cent was contributed by American Jewry.

During the struggle with the British Mandatory government after World War II (see MANDATE FOR PALESTINE), the JNF participated increasingly in settlement projects, particularly in the Negev, where work began in the 1940s. When the State of Israel was established, its *boundaries as approved by the United Nations partition resolution of Nov. 29, 1947, were to a considerable degree determined by the extent of Jewish-owned land and actual Jewish settlement in Palestine. The JNF had received a measure of encouragement in 1946, when the report of the *Anglo-American Committee of Inquiry recommended the abolition of the 1940 Land Transfer Regulations and their replacement by legislation permitting the sale, rental, and use of land in Palestine without considerations of race, community, or religion.

As of Nov. 29, 1947, the day the UN General Assembly voted for the Jewish State, the JNF had acquired 928,000 dunams of land. With the rise of the State, which became the effective owner of all State lands and abandoned properties, the JNF shifted its activities from the acquisition of additional land to the reclamation of uncultivable land (see LAND RECLAMATION IN ISRAEL), the building of roads to assure accessibility, and amelioration so as to render the land fit for settlement. Seeking to disperse the population of the country and to prevent excessive concentration in the central areas, the Fund turned its attention to the reclamation of barren soil in border areas and other unsettled territories.

In the beginning, these plans and policies created a certain overlapping in the work of the JNF and of the State of Israel. Negotiations begun on the initiative of Granott led to an agreement between the Fund and the State. The agreement, signed in 1960, provided for two separate bodies: (1) a Government Land Authority headed by the Minister of Agriculture, which was to manage all State and JNF lands in accordance with a unified policy assuring ownership of the land by the State and the JNF, respectively; and (2) a Land Development Authority, set up within the JNF, which was to be in charge of land reclamation, afforestation, and certain other forms of land development. This agreement was based on the Basic Law: Lands in Israel, enacted by the *Knesset in 1960. Under this arrangement, the JNF remained under the control and authority of the WZO.

In the 1960s the JNF became increasingly concerned with land improvement operations and border road construction. It continued to be active in the establishment of frontier settlements that posed special agricultural and security problems. Thus border outposts were set up in places like Mount Gilboa, Modi'in, and Almagor, as well as along the Lebanese frontier. Particular attention was given to Galilee, where Jewish settlement was most sparse. Development work, including drilling for water and dam construction, was carried on also in the south, as was large-scale afforestation throughout the country. In the first 20 years of Israel's statehood the JNF reclaimed 388,000 dunams of land, planted 80 million trees, and constructed 1,900 kilometers of border highways.

In the United States the JNF conducts its own fund-raising efforts for the afforestation and land development of Israel. It also serves as a broad-based educational force in bringing the message of Israel into the school and home and to the general public.

G. KRESSEL

JEWISH STATE, THE (Der Judenstaat). Treatise by Herzl, written in German and published in Vienna on Feb. 14, 1896. The German title, *Der Judenstaat*, defies exact rendition into English. Most often translated as *The Jewish State*, the caption literally means "The Jews' State"—a fine semantic difference that exerted considerable influence on the direction and course of the World Zionist movement (see ZIONISM, HISTORY OF). Subtitled "An Attempt at a Modern Solution of the Jewish Question," the tract contains a dispassionate examination of the status of the Jewish people among the nations and a detailed plan for creating a state in which the Jews would reconstitute their national life in a territory of their own.

Considered a basic tract of Zionism, *The Jewish State*, containing some 23,000 words, is tersely written and simply structured. It includes a brief preface, an introductory section followed by four short aphoristic chapters, and a conclusion.

Background. Herzl's goal in *The Jewish State* was nothing less than the regeneration of the Jewish nation as a political entity. The task seemed impossible. The Jews had settled throughout the world; they were a minority everywhere, possessed no common territory, spoke many languages, and followed different traditions; and their religious ideology had become splintered as a result of *emancipation and reform. There was no Jewish nation in the political sense; there were only Jewish communities scattered throughout the world.

Keenly aware of the magnitude of the Jewish problem, Herzl stressed the power inherent in the idea of a national territory. He noted that no human being was "wealthy or powerful enough to transplant a people from one place of residence to another." Only an idea could create the necessary momentum. The idea of a Jewish State, he strongly believed, had the power to motivate Jewry, for Jews had "dreamed this princely dream through the long night of their history. 'Next year in Jerusalem' is our ancient watchword." It was simply a matter of showing that the vague dream could be transformed into reality.

The starting point of Herzl's ideology, as presented in *The*

DER

JUDENSTAAT.

VERSUCH

EINER

MODERNEN LÖSUNG DER JUDENFRAGE

VON

THEODOR HERZL

DOCTOR DER RECHTE.

LEIPZIG und WIEN 1896.

M. BREITENSTEIN'S VERLAGS-BUCHHANDLUNG

WIEN, IX., WÄHRINGERSTRASSE 5.

Title page of the original German edition of Herzl's The Jewish
State. [Zionist Archives]

Jewish State, was his analysis of the Jewish question. For
Herzl, the root of the problem was the Jew's feeling of homelessness—the sensation of being unwanted, an alien even in
the country of his birth. The sense of homelessness, Herzl
declared, existed even though Jews had sincerely tried everywhere to merge with the national communities in which they
lived, seeking only to preserve the faith of their fathers. It was
not permitted, though the Jews were loyal patriots, sometimes
even superloyal. In vain did they make the same sacrifices of
life and property as their fellow citizens, strive to enhance the
fame of their native land, or augment its wealth by trade and
commerce. In their native lands where they had lived for centuries, they were still described as aliens, "often by men whose
ancestors had not yet come at a time when Jewish sighs had
long been heard in the country. The majority decided who
the alien is. . . ."

Keeping pace with this feeling of homelessness, and often
resulting directly from it, was the phenomenon of *anti-Semitism. The forms of its occurrence varied from country to country,
but one thing was clear to Herzl: anti-Semitism existed wherever
Jews lived in large numbers. Moreover, the longer anti-
Semitism was dormant, the more violently did it finally erupt.
"The infiltration of immigrating Jews attracted to a land by
apparent security, and the rising class status of native Jews,
combine powerfully to bring about a revolution."

What were the causes of anti-Semitism? Its earliest cause,
Herzl believed, was the factor of religious differences, which

originated in the Middle Ages. Modern anti-Semitism was
due largely to economic factors and had developed out of the
emancipation of the Jews following the French Revolution.
When civilized nations awoke to the inhumanity of discriminatory legislation and enfranchised the Jews, however, it was too
late. In the ghetto, Herzl noted, the Jews had developed into
a bourgeois people, and they had emerged from it as a full-
fledged rival to the middle class. "Thus, we found ourselves
thrust upon emancipation into this bourgeois circle, where we
have a double pressure to sustain from within and from without."

In keeping with a common 19th-century Western and Central
European belief, Herzl thought that the equal rights of the Jews
before the law could not be rescinded where they had once
been granted. Hence, he reasoned, anti-Semitism would grow
because "the very impossibility of getting at the Jews nourishes
and deepens hatred of them."

No matter what the cause of anti-Semitism, economic,
political, or religious, the results were always the same. It
inevitably led to bloodshed, poverty, destruction of property,
and demoralization. It was a vicious circle, Herzl believed,
because "oppression naturally creates hostility against oppres-
sors, and our hostility in turn increases the pressure."

In *The Jewish State* Herzl emphasized that the constant oppression of the Jews would produce one positive effect: it would
weld the Jews into one united people. The feeling of fellowship among the Jews, which had begun to crumble after the
era of emancipation, was strengthened anew by anti-Semitism.
"Therefore," he concluded, "we are now and shall remain,
whether we would or not, a group of unmistakable cohesive-
ness. We are a people [*Wir sind ein Volk*]—our enemies have
made us one whether we will it or not, as has repeatedly happened in history. Affliction binds us together, and thus united,
we suddenly discover our strength."

Herzl's statement that the Jews were a *Volk* stirred the Jewish
intellectuals of both Eastern and Western Europe. The Yiddish
word *Folk* denotes an important Jewish concept. The Jews of
Eastern Europe were thrilled when Dr. Herzl, of the famous
Neue Freie Presse, spoke their language, as it were, and declared
his adherence to *dos Yidishe Folk*. Nor was that all. Not only
did Herzl declare the Jews to be a people; he declared them
to be *one* people. And so the assimilationists of Western
Europe and the tradition-bound Jews of Eastern Europe,
regarded by the former as unimproved and backward, were
to be members of one body, suffused with one spirit, and
sharing one common destiny.

Herzl's nationalistic appeal to the Jewish people was heightened by its Messianic overtones. Among the Eastern European
Jews, in particular, Herzl stimulated the old dream of a return
to the Promised Land, even though he had not ruled out
other territories as possible sites for a Jewish State. "Shall
we choose Palestine or Argentina? We shall take what is given
us, and what is selected by Jewish public opinion." The Messianic appeal was not anticipated by Herzl but was inherent
in the concepts of nationalism. For modern European nationalism had drawn from the old monotheistic religions not only
their exclusiveness but also their profound belief in a forthcoming "end of days," an era of ultimate fulfillment.

Throughout his exposition in *The Jewish State* Herzl shows
an awareness of the power of nationalism, its attractions and
its dangers. ". . . it might be said," he writes, "that we ought
not to create new distinctions between people; we ought not

to raise fresh barriers but make instead the old ones disappear. But men who think in this manner are amiable visionaries, and the idea of a native land will still flourish when the dust of their bones will have vanished tracelessly in the winds. . . ."

Herzl also knew that there was considerable danger in bringing Jewish *nationalism into the glaring light of international politics. His was an age of political unrest, in which strong currents of national revolt and international rivalry could be discerned under the smooth surface of apparent peace. Had Herzl's theory contained the faintest suggestion of the use of force, his efforts to gain the support of both the international community of nations and the Jews themselves would have miscarried. It was as a peaceful emancipator, therefore, that Herzl appeared before the Jews of Europe. His plan contemplated no force of arms. It depended largely upon international discussion, diplomacy, and positive political action.

The very nature of Herzl's approach to the Jewish question produced in his treatise a rejection of those solutions that advocated the use of violence and those that ignored the question of nationalism. In the latter category Herzl placed two concepts that enjoyed some popularity among Jews in the last quarter of the 19th century: the doctrine of *assimilation and the ultrareligious, or "ghetto," doctrine.

The idea of assimilation was based on the belief that the Jews were not a people at all but only an aggregation with vestigial religious doctrines and tenets that separated them from their neighbors. Its adherents were convinced that the Jews would eventually become an organic part of the peoples among whom they lived. Assimilation, they reasoned, would eliminate the causes of anti-Semitism.

Reared in a family that believed in assimilation, Herzl had great difficulty trying to shed its effects. His struggle with the concept of assimilation is strongly evident in *The Jewish State*. Prior to writing this treatise he even believed that anti-Semitism, if exerted steadily, could act as a stimulant to hasten the assimilation process.

Nevertheless, it can be seen in *Der Judenstaat* that Herzl's attitude had undergone a basic change and that he had taken a new position on assimilation. He now felt that assimilation was unacceptable and even impossible for the Jewish people as a whole. He saw that assimilation was dependent on factors beyond the control of the Jews: a desire for widespread intermarriage on the part of the majority population and sufficient time (at least one or two generations) to permit nearly complete assimilation to take place. Neither of these conditions seemed likely to obtain. The rapid rise of anti-Semitism made this clear. Furthermore, from a nationalistic point of view assimilation was undesirable, since the "distinctive nationality of the Jews neither can, will, nor must perish. . . . Whole branches of Jewry may wither and fall away. The tree lives on."

The adherents of the ultrareligious, or ghetto, solution of the Jewish question argued that it was incumbent on the Jews to remain separate from other peoples, to follow strictly their sacred religious laws, and particularly to await the coming advent of the Messiah. Herzl considered this point of view sterile.

The Jewish question, he believed, was neither a social nor a religious problem, even though it sometimes took these forms. Boldly he noted, " . . . it is a national question, and to solve it we must first of all establish it as an international political problem to be discussed and settled by the civilized nations of the world in council." Since the Jewish question was a national

one with international ramifications, it could only be resolved, Herzl concluded, by the creation of a special instrument to encompass both these factors: a Jewish State, recognized and secured by international agreement, to which Jews could migrate and in which they could freely settle on a large scale.

The rise of the Jewish State, Herzl was convinced, would put an end to anti-Semitism. He reasoned that, with the large-scale migration of the bulk of European Jewry to the new state, the economic foundations of anti-Semitism (the modern cause of this evil) would crumble and collapse. Those Jews who chose to remain behind in the lands of their birth after the creation of the Jewish State could then easily be absorbed, as all bars to assimilation would be let down in the absence of economic competition from the Jewish middle classes.

Creating the State. How was this national state to be achieved? The first step, Herzl believed, was to convince the Jewish people of the need for a Jewish State. He recognized that if one man were to attempt to create a state it would be folly, but he believed it practicable if the will of a whole people were behind it. National consciousness would lead to the awakening of the national will. "Those Jews who want a state will have it."

The skills and knowledge the Jews had acquired since their emancipation would now serve them in laying the foundation of a modern state. Herzl felt ". . . we are strong enough to form a state, and indeed a model state, for we possess all the requisite human and material resources." Besides, in recent history other peoples, such as the Greeks, the Romanians, the Serbs, and the Bulgarians, had successfully attained statehood.

It seemed to Herzl that anti-Semitism would provide the motive for creating the Jewish State. The sheer force of Jewish suffering and misery (*Judennot*) would act as a propelling force to set in motion a migration to the projected state.

Herzl's plan for creating a state called for the formation of two organizations, the *Society of Jews and the Jewish Company (see OLD-NEW LAND). The Society of Jews would make the necessary preparations for the establishment of a state, while the Jewish Company would deal with the economic interests of the Jews in the countries from which they were migrating. The Society was to provide the Jews with an authoritative political organ, explore and educate public opinion, determine the political preconditions for mass migration, search out suitable territory for a state, and negotiate with the Great Powers for its acquisition and for the granting of a political *Charter that would guarantee Jewish sovereignty. Thereafter, the Society of Jews would give instructions to the Jewish Company concerning immigration, land purchase, and colonization. In addition, the Society would prepare the legal and administrative groundwork for the future state. In brief, the Society would be the forerunner of the state; for it "will be recognized, to put it in the terminology of international law, as a state-creating power, and this recognition will in effect mean the creation of the state."

Of course, the task of establishing a state could not be carried out without adequate financial support. The Jewish Company would have the task of supplying such aid. It would help those who chose to leave their old homes and would organize commerce, trade, and industry in the new country. Thus the Jewish Company would provide an orderly and equitable method of liquidating the business interests of Jewish emigrants and compensate the various countries for the loss of Jewish income and taxes. In the new country the Jewish

Title page of a Yiddish edition of The Jewish State *published in Russia in 1899.* [Zionist Archives]

Company would purchase land and equipment for settlement, erect temporary housing for workmen, and provide financial help for incoming settlers. The Company, as Herzl conceived it, was transitional, and he assumed that its functions in the new land would eventually be assumed by the state.

How and where would the Company be organized? Herzl felt that the Jewish Company should be set up as a joint-stock company, incorporated in England under British laws and protection. Its principal center would be in London, and the Company's capital would be about 1,000,000,000 marks ($200,000,000). Herzl offered three approaches to the task of creating the capital stock of the Jewish Company, leaving the selection of the best method to the Society of Jews, which would use its prestige to establish the credit of the Company among the Jewish people. It was Herzl's hope that wealthy Jewish financiers would subscribe the necessary funds. He favored this method because it seemed the simplest and swiftest means of obtaining the requisite financial resources while providing investment opportunities with the possibility of a fair return. His second approach, to be used in the event that financiers were reluctant to help, was an appeal to small banks. If this, too, were unsuccessful, Herzl proposed to capitalize the Jewish Company through the direct subscription of funds by the Jewish masses.

How would the Society of Jews, the forerunner of the state, come into being? Could it legally act on behalf of the Jewish communities of the world? To answer these questions Herzl drew upon his knowledge of Roman law, particularly the ancient juridic institution of the *negotiorum gestio*. Under this concept, any person or group could protect the property of an incapacitated or absent party without receiving a warrant from the owner to do so. A person acting in this manner derived his mandate from what the law deemed to be a "higher necessity" and was designated a *gestor*, the manager or caretaker of affairs not strictly his own.

A state, Herzl stressed, is created by a nation's struggle for existence. In the process of such a struggle it is often impossible to obtain proper authority in due form beforehand. In fact, any preliminary attempt to obtain a regular decision from the majority would probably ruin the undertaking at the outset, for partisan divisions would render the people defenseless against external dangers. "We cannot," he stated, "all be of one mind; the *gestor* therefore simply takes the leadership into his hands and marches in the van." Action by the *gestor* of a state is sufficiently authorized if the *dominus* (the principal) is prevented either by want of will or by some other reason from helping himself. "However, the *gestor* by his intervention becomes similar to the *dominus* and is bound by the agreement *quasi ex contractu*. This is the legal relationship existing before, or, more correctly, created simultaneously with, the state."

Since the Jews were dispersed throughout the world, they were not in a position to conduct their own political affairs nor could they protect themselves against common dangers. They were, Herzl believed, unable to create a state without the help of a *gestor*. The Jewish *gestor*, however, would not be a single individual because such a person would appear ridiculous. Furthermore, since he might appear to be working for his own gain, he might seem contemptible. The *gestor* of the Jews was to be a corporate person, such as the Society of Jews. After 1897 the *gestor* became, in fact, the World Zionist *Congress.

Inherent in this theory were the answers to the important political questions: who shall rule, and what group or class should enjoy a privileged position in the Jewish State? The Society of Jews, or *gestor*, would "arise out of the circle of energetic English Jews whom I apprised of my scheme in London." Herzl had in mind the *Order of Ancient Maccabeans, an organization of prominent English Jews. The order, he felt, would either become the Society of Jews or serve as the model for the Society. In terms of class structure, the Society, if it closely paralleled its model, would be composed of an elite of Jewish community leaders, religious, economic, and intellectual, drawn from the upper and middle classes.

It would be the middle class of Jewry, however, that would benefit most from a Jewish State. It would be this class that would do the most to spread the idea of a state and provide the necessary technical and professional manpower for the national movement.

Once the state was established, Herzl foresaw very little change in the power structure, no matter what form the government took. Both power and privilege would remain in the upper and middle classes, with the latter acting as the backbone of the state's bureaucracy. From the ranks of the middle class, Herzl predicted, would come a "surplus intelligentsia" that would provide the state with an aristocracy of talent.

Herzl was convinced that his plans for the intelligentsia would meet with the latter's full approval. A unity of interest existed between the needs of the intelligentsia and the needs of the Jewish State. The differentiation that had marked the rise of this middle class had created a strong class solidarity. Economic pressures brought about by older and more firmly established social groups were threatening to destroy this feeling of union.

The "surplus intelligentsia" of the Jewish middle class, Herzl believed, would gradually sink and become a helpless revolutionary-minded proletariat unless its energies were diverted toward the goal of creating a Jewish State. These factors would be quickly grasped by the intelligentsia and compel it to support a state that strengthened its claims as a class. The intelligentsia would secure its own ends and at the same time give to the state the power and authority it required.

Character. Apart from this description of the forces and instruments that would make possible a national Jewish State, Herzl included in the pages of *The Jewish State* many practical suggestions on statecraft. These ideas, which were in large measure derived from his personal observations and experiences, made the book more readable and gave additional substance to his theory of the state.

Herzl buttressed his theoretical concepts with concrete suggestions on such diverse subjects as agriculture, civil service, treaties, education, communications, shipping and transport, trade, and taxation. In addition, he attempted to anticipate and forestall the attacks that he knew would be made on his book and its blueprint for a Jewish State. Illustrative of Herzl's thinking and approach to these problems were his comments on capitalism and its institutions, labor, law, the military, and the press and his defense against the possible charge that he had written a utopian work.

Like those of other Central European thinkers in the second half of the 19th century, Herzl's thoughts on capitalism were strongly influenced by the ideological struggle between the proponents of "scientific socialism" and their rivals, the "state Socialists." Herzl was favorably disposed to state socialism and adopted most of the arguments of this school in his book. Society had grown so complex, he believed, that the classical concepts of capitalism were in dire need of revision. What was needed most were positive, state-sponsored programs of political and economic reform and the use of state power to weed out speculation and exploitation. The abuses of laissez faire had to be curbed if capitalism was to survive. Nevertheless, Herzl did not wish to see the demise of all capitalistic institutions. Thus, for instance, he placed great value on the need for free enterprise. In his introduction he noticed that the technical progress achieved in his era had enabled even the "dullest minds with the dimmest of visions" to note the appearance of new commodities all about them. The spirit of free enterprise had created them. Without such enterprise, labor remained static: "All our material welfare has been brought about by men of enterprise . . . the spirit of private enterprise must, indeed, be encouraged in every possible way." Risk, with its reward of profits, was to remain the privilege of private capital. To assure the healthy growth of private enterprise in his proposed state, Herzl recommended protective tariffs, state-controlled labor agencies, and national bureaus of statistical research to aid employers in their daily labor and marketing problems.

Herzl's views of private property reflected the influence of Hegelian philosophy, state Socialist tenets, Roman law, and the writings of the French 18th-century philosopher Montesquieu. Private property, he strongly felt, was the mainstay of capitalism and also of individual liberty and therefore had to be freely developed in the Jewish State. Although Herzl was adamant about the rights of individuals to enjoy private property, he felt no compunction about the superior right of the state to interfere with private property rights whenever such action was deemed necessary. Nonetheless, he stressed that the state act in an equitable manner and not in an arbitrary fashion.

Herzl's exposure to the acceptance of Hegelian and state Socialist doctrines also shaped his attitude toward labor. Keenly aware of the seamy side of laissez faire politics, he vigorously avoided, like his philosophical mentors, the empty abstractions of the Manchester school of economics. He was convinced that the Manchester theorists had no appreciation of the higher duties of the state in the protection of the working class. This basically paternalistic outlook appears throughout *The Jewish State* and reflects ideas that had slowly evolved in Herzl's mind and writings during the period 1882–96. Typical of this formative period were his thoughts about labor outlined in his 1892–93 correspondence with Baron Johann von Chlumecky, a prominent member of the Austrian Parliament. In these letters Herzl first stressed the concept which he was later to incorporate and feature prominently in *The Jewish State*, that the condition of unskilled, destitute workers could be ameliorated by a state-sponsored system of work relief (*assistance par le travail*).

From the ranks of Jewish unskilled labor drawn chiefly from the great reservoirs of Russia and Romania, Herzl theorized in *The Jewish State*, it would be possible to fashion an army of workers. This labor force, directed by the Jewish Company and organized along military lines, would carry out the gigantic physical task of building a viable state. In accordance with a preconceived plan, its members would construct "roads, bridges, railways and telegraph installations, regulate rivers and build their own dwellings." This army, composed solely of volunteers, would operate under a strict disciplinary code. To stimulate the growth of this labor force, Herzl recommended promotions for merit, bonuses, pensions, insurance, educational benefits, and the opportunity to work one's way up to private proprietorship. In addition, the Jewish Company would build attractive schools for the children of the labor force and provide numerous social services as well as amusement centers and religious facilities for their parents.

Furthermore, in the initial state-building phase the army of unskilled workers, who would not receive pay for their labor, would be fully protected by the Jewish Company. Herzl felt that a "truck system," that is, the practice of paying workmen's wages in goods instead of in money, would have to be applied in the first few years of settlement. This system would prevent the labor force from being victimized by unscrupulous merchants. However, Herzl visualized that payment of wages would be made for overtime work during this period.

The state not only would protect the labor force from being exploited but would also establish a new legal standard workday, the seven-hour day. Following the path indicated by such work experiments in Belgium and England, Herzl suggested that there be "fourteen hours of labor, in shifts of three and a half hours. . . . A healthy man can do a great deal of concentrated work in three and a half hours. After a recess of the same length of time—devoted to rest, to his family and to his education under guidance—he is quite fresh for work again. Such labor can do wonders. The seven-hour day thus implies fourteen hours of joint labor—more than that cannot be put into a day."

So deeply ingrained in his thinking was the seven-hour day that Herzl considered creating a national flag for the future Jewish state that would symbolize this work standard for the benefit of the rest of the world. He suggested "a white flag with seven golden stars. The white field symbolizes our pure new life; the stars are the seven golden hours of our working day. For we shall march into the Promised Land carrying the badge of honor" (*see* FLAG, ZIONIST AND ISRAELI).

Women and children were to be excluded from the labor force. The Jewish Company was to bear the burden of caring for the needs of these dependents. The homes of the laborers would be built by the labor army and resemble "neither those melancholy workmen's barracks of European towns, nor those miserable rows of shanties which surround factories." Even though economics would compel a certain uniformity in construction, all efforts would be made to create spacious garden towns consisting of clusters of detached houses. Each labor community would take advantage of the natural conformation of the land in order to prevent the growth of hypertropic cities. The unskilled workers, Herzl stressed, would have the opportunity "to earn their houses as permanent possessions by means of their work—not immediately, but after three years of good conduct."

Within the sphere of the state, Herzl believed, there were two distinct kinds of law, the law that governs the state (constitutional) and the law by which the state governs (ordinary). Although Herzl recognized the importance of the former, he devoted little attention to it and stressed instead the development of ordinary law in his proposed state. He emphasized that when the state began to approach realization, the Society of Jews would appoint a council of jurists to lay the groundwork for its laws. During the transition period this council would act on the principle that every immigrant Jew was to be judged according to the laws of the country he had left behind. Thereafter legal uniformity was to be sought. The laws would be modern, making use of the best precedents available, and indeed might become a model code, embodying all just social demands.

Herzl's identification of the state with justice indicated that he had taken a definite stand on the question as to whether the law was to be above the state or the state above the law. His legal training compelled him to side against those who placed the state above the law and exalted the state as a power agency. Yet Herzl was not completely willing to reject the value of state power if it was used judiciously and for the common welfare of a nation's citizens.

This balanced approach to the question of state power was also evident in Herzl's thoughts on the role of the military in the Jewish State. He stressed that an army would be necessary, if only to preserve order internally and defend the state against an external enemy. Under no circumstances, however, would it be used for the aggrandizement of the state, nor would it ever be allowed to dominate the state.

Herzl felt that public opinion had to have an outlet in a modern state. The great organs of opinion, particularly the newspapers, provided such an outlet and were necessary for good government. As the chief purveyors of news and opinion, the newspapers therefore had a grave responsibility to their public and their nation. Although freedom of the press was essential, there were reasonable limitations to such liberty. Libel and slander, for example, could not be justified under freedom of the press. Herzl therefore felt that in the Jewish State there should be some limitations to freedom of the press in order to safeguard innocent people from slander or libel. As long as a newpaper in the Jewish State did not violate ethical principles and common decency, however, it could print what it wished. It would even oppose the government and governmental policy without fear of recriminations or retaliation.

Herzl greatly feared that many people would consider *The Jewish State* utopian. His attitude was understandable in view of the times. The last two decades of the 19th century had been marked by an unusual number of publications dealing with the same theme, the need to rebuild or reform society along modern lines. Some of these works were completely visionary. Others, notably the books of the French Socialists (Cabet, Fourier, Blanc, Saint-Simon, Proudhon), were dubbed utopian by the "scientific Socialists," Friedrich Engels and Karl Marx, to discredit their authors and their themes. The term "utopian" was applied by the Marxists to all reformers who did not accept the division of society into classes, the inevitability of class struggle, and the certainty of social revolution. Apprehensive of such criticism, Herzl met the issue of utopianism head on. In the preface of his treatise he addressed his would-be critics by noting that "it would be no disgrace to have written an idealist Utopia. And very likely I could also assure myself easier literary success while avoiding all responsibility, if I were to offer this [state] plan in the form of romantic fiction to a public that seeks to be entertained. But this is no amiable Utopia such as have been projected in abundance before and since Sir Thomas More. And it seems to me that the situation of the Jews in various lands is grave enough to make quite superfluous any attention-getting tricks."

In many ways *The Jewish State* represented a complete break with utopian tradition. It contained nothing suggestive of a perfect society, nor did it reveal any tendency to mold individuals into uniform creatures with identical wants and reactions, devoid of all emotions and passions. Individuality and individual expression were not to be crushed on either esthetic or moral grounds. Private property and the family were to remain intact rather than be sacrificed to the unity of the state, as demanded by most utopias.

Similarly, Herzl's work lacked the symmetry so beloved by all utopians. The settings of most utopias are invariably artifical and tend to neglect natural regions in favor of perfectly round islands and perfectly straight rivers. Herzl dealt with concrete territories: Palestine and Argentina.

Reaction to Publication. The publication of *Der Judenstaat* aroused a storm of controversy almost without parallel in modern Jewish history. Immediately after the appearance of the first edition (3,000 copies) a vehement campaign was launched against Herzl and his publisher, Dr. Max Breitenstein. Doubts were expressed about the personal integrity of the author. The leaders of the Union of Austrian Jews and of the Vienna Jewish Community flung bitter reproaches at the publisher and forced him to issue the first counterbrochure against Herzl's work (*National Judaism*, by Chief Rabbi Moritz *Güdemann). The press, both Jewish and non-Jewish, was generally unfavorable to Herzl's plan. A number of journalists alluded to the adventurer who would like to become king of the Jews. The *Neue Freie Presse*, of which Herzl was literary editor, kept silent about *Der Judenstaat* and maintained this policy until the author's death. The *Allgemeine Zeitung* of Vienna said that Zionism was a madness born of despair. The *Allgemeine Zeitung* of Munich described the treatise as a fantastic dream of a feuilletonist whose mind had been unhinged by Jewish enthusiasm. Even among the *Hoveve Zion (Lovers of Zion) there were many who feared that so clear an exposition of nationalism would cause the Turkish government to take steps to destroy the Jewish settlements in Palestine. Assimilationist elements of Western Jewry were disturbed by the declaration that a Jewish people as such existed and that it constituted a single entity throughout the world. Similarly, many lay leaders of Western Jewry and, with few exceptions, the rabbis, both Orthodox and Reform, utterly condemned Herzl's ideas as contrary to the fundamental principles of Judaism. The Orthodox opponents were antagonistic because they believed his plans violated the ancient Messianic idea of Jewish redemption: human realization of the restoration of Israel was considered futile and impious. They were also alarmed by Herzl's emphasis on a political and economic solution to the Jewish question. Many of the Reform rabbis opposed Herzl's theories on the ground that they negated the doctrine of the "mission of Israel," that is, the concept that God desired the Jews to be dispersed among the nations of the world to teach their neighbors the ideals of ethical monotheism.

On the other hand, *The Jewish State* was greeted with enthusiastic support by Jewish youth groups throughout Europe. Disciples, especially Jewish university students, began to rally around Herzl, and he soon found himself the leader of a viable nationalistic movement. Prominent men such as the critic Max *Nordau and the poet Richard *Beer-Hofmann were swept off their feet by his message and sang its praises. Others soon followed suit.

However, it was on the Jewish masses of Eastern Europe that Herzl's ideas made their greatest impression. Little was known there of the contents of *The Jewish State*, for it had been kept out of these areas by Russian censorship. Only its title captured the attention of the Jews, as did the stories told of the author—the Western Jew who had returned to his people to lead them to the Promised Land. Thus, overnight *Der Judenstaat* catapulted Herzl into the forefront of Jewish political affairs, a position he was to retain until his untimely death in 1904.   J. ADLER

JEWISH STATE PARTY.
Zionist party formed by Meir *Grossman, Robert *Stricker, Richard *Lichtheim, Selig Eugen *Soskin, Ya'akov *Cahan, Barukh Weinstein, and Herzl Rosenblum, after a split in the Revisionist movement, in 1933.

The new Zionist party adhered to the basic principles of Revisionism but, unlike the latter, remained within the WZO and abided by Zionist discipline. It participated in elections to the 18th Zionist *Congress (Prague, 1933) with a list of seven delegates. During that Congress the party held its first preliminary convention, which was attended by dissident Revisionists from Austria, England, France, Latvia, Lithuania, Palestine, Poland, Romania, and South Africa. It constituted itself as the Jewish State party, was recognized by the WZO as a *Sonderverband* (separate union), and was granted representation on the *Zionist General Council and the boards of directors of the national funds. In Palestine Barukh Weinstein, who had been elected to the *Asefat HaNivharim (Elected Assembly) on the

Revisionist slate in 1930, left the Revisionist party and was recognized by the Assembly as the representative of the Jewish State party.

The first world conference of the party met in Paris in 1937, prior to the convocation of the 20th Zionist Congress in Zurich. The rejection by the conference of the British proposal for the *partition of Palestine and the establishment of a Jewish State in only a small part of Palestinian territory prompted Richard Lichtheim and Selig Eugen Soskin to resign from the Jewish State party. Elected chairman of the party's Executive, Meir Grossman led the party's opposition to the partition plan at the 20th Zionist Congress. During that Congress the party published a daily newspaper, *Congress Tribune*. That same year the headquarters of the Jewish State party, under Weinstein's direction, was set up in Palestine.

In the wake of the secession of Grossman and his associates, a group of *B'rit Trumpeldor (Betar) members left that movement and formed the youth movement B'rit HaKana'im. It adopted the same program as Betar as well as Betar's paramilitary character. The movement, which had branches in Austria, Czechoslovakia, Poland, Romania, Germany, and Palestine, at its first conference (Lucerne, 1935) elected a Provisional High Command composed of Reuben Feldschuh (Ben-Shem), Natalie Rotman, and Fritz Richter and headed by Ya'akov Cahan.

On the eve of World War II the Jewish State party had a registered membership of 8,000. With the outbreak of the war the party ceased its activities, and in 1946 it merged with the World Union of Zionists-Revisionists under the name United Zionists-Revisionists. Grossman, Weinstein, and several of their associates subsequently joined the General Zionist party (*see* GENERAL ZIONISM).   I. BENARI

JEWISH STATE PROJECTS.
See JEWISH TERRITORIAL ORGANIZATION; RESTORATION MOVEMENT; TERRITORIALISM.

JEWISH TELEGRAPHIC AGENCY.
Worldwide agency for the dissemination of Jewish news, providing daily reports of news of Jewish interest to the Jewish and secular press and to subscribing organizations. The Jewish Telegraphic Agency (JTA) was founded in London in 1919 by Jacob *Landau, an Austrian-born Zionist journalist, and Meir *Grossman, later a founder of the World Union of Zionists-Revisionists (*see* REVISIONISTS), as a continuation of the Jewish Correspondence Bureau, which Landau had set up in The Hague in 1917 to present the case of the Jewish people and of the Zionist movement to the world. With Landau as president and managing director (1919–51), the JTA established branch offices in Paris, Warsaw, Berlin, and Jerusalem (where it was known as the Palestine Telegraphic Agency, now the Israel News Agency).

In the early 1920s JTA headquarters was moved from London to New York, from where the agency was further extended to Latin America and South Africa. The JTA was one of the major sources of information on the *Arab riots of 1929 and on the Nazi persecution of Jews in Germany from 1933 on. Its correspondents gave detailed coverage to Nazi excesses against Jews, and during World War II were among the first to reveal the Nazi extermination of European Jewry. By 1970 the JTA had offices and correspondents on every continent and provided a daily feature service. In the United States it is (1970) a nonprofit communal organization administered by a group of directors.

JEWISH TERRITORIAL ORGANIZATION. Organization founded in 1905 to find a territory anywhere in the world suitable for Jewish settlement on an autonomous basis (*see also* TERRITORIALISM). The Jewish Territorial Organization (ITO, from its Yiddish initials) was founded in August, 1905, in Basle, by 40 dissident delegates to the 7th Zionist *Congress, after the Congress had finally rejected the *East Africa scheme for Jewish settlement. The leading spirit behind it was the writer Israel *Zangwill, who was to be its president until its official disbandment in 1925. A friend of Herzl (who had died the year before), Zangwill felt that political Zionism, committed as it was to Palestine, which seemed impossible of attainment, was a captive of the past, while his movement looked to the future and to more practical possibilities for Jewish settlement. In its charter the ITO announced as its purpose "to procure a territory upon an autonomous basis for those Jews who cannot or will not remain in the lands in which they at present live." To this end, the ITO proposed to unite all those in agreement with its objectives, to get in touch with governments and public and private institutions, and to create financial institutions and labor bureaus to carry out its aims. Zangwill obtained the support of a group of influential Jewish leaders, among them British Jews such as Sir Francis *Montefiore, Leopold de Rothschild. Meyer Spielman, Carl Stettauer, and Lucien Wolf. At one time Nathan *Birnbaum, who had coined the term "Zionism," was a member of Zangwill's movement. Zangwill received encouragement also from American Jewish leaders including Jacob H. *Schiff, Oscar S. *Straus, Cyrus L. *Sulzberger, and Mayer Sulzberger. He obtained many adherents also in Russia, Poland, and Romania, where Jews were ready to emigrate to whatever country would offer itself.

Within weeks of the founding of his movement, Zangwill initiated political action. In a letter to Alfred Lyttelton, who had succeeded Joseph *Chamberlain as British Colonial Secretary, Zangwill asked that the site in the British East Africa Colony originally offered for Jewish settlement be kept in reserve until the Territorialists had had an opportunity to discuss the matter with the British government. In his reply (Sept. 16, 1905), Lyttelton stated that in view of the official Zionist rejection of the East Africa scheme, he had already instructed the Commissioner for the East Africa Protectorate not to reserve the area any longer. To this news, Zangwill replied (Sept. 20, 1905) that his organization would soon submit another Jewish settlement proposal to the government. However, this discussion soon became purely academic, for a year later Lyttelton went out of office with the Conservative party's fall from power. Zangwill himself gradually abandoned the East Africa project, partly "from the fear that our neo-Jewish civilization would be based on black labor." His plan for an autonomous Jewish settlement had included not only full autonomy at least with regard to control of Jewish immigration but also complete *self-labor on the part of the settlers. Later, however, he was to say that had there been such a Jewish settlement in East Africa at the time of World War I, it could have been of great help to the British in the war and therefore in a position to claim and take over the *Mandate for Palestine.

Meanwhile, Zangwill's supporters all over the world organized themselves. In January, 1906, the Socialist-Territorialists formed an organization in New York that set up branches in many other cities in the United States. Their parent group was the Socialist Zionist Workers' party of Russia, which had early eliminated Palestine as a possible Jewish Homeland because of its lack of natural resources and the political instability of the area. Led by Nachman *Syrkin, that party had walked out of the 7th Zionist Congress, with Syrkin attacking the Zionist "fixation on Palestine" as the "moribund traditionalism of aimless and backward sectors among the Jewish masses as well as of the reactionary nationalist sectors of the Jewish intelligentsia." Ten years later, Syrkin was to change his mind and return to the Zionist fold.

In April, 1906, the American Federation of the Jewish Territorial Organization was founded in New York at the call of Cyrus L. Sulzberger, who served as its chairman. Other officers of the federation, which started branches also in Philadelphia and Baltimore, included Rev. Goodman Lipkind of New York (secretary), Daniel Guggenheim, Oscar S. Straus, and Mayer Sulzberger. In Russia, ITO had offices in Kiev (directed by Dr. David Jochelman), Warsaw, Yekaterinoslav, Białystok, Kaunas, Grodno, and Vilna. ITO's first international convention was held in London in August, 1907. In that city, Oscar S. Straus arranged a meeting between the Territorialists and the Zionists in an effort to see whether a common platform could not be developed, but the Territorialists maintained they had nothing in common with Zionism since the latter insisted on Palestine (and no other country) as a Jewish Homeland.

During the years that followed, ITO made an intensive, scientifically conducted search for a region to acquire and settle as "ITO-land." A Geographical Committee organized expeditions to the areas in question. Briefly, in 1905, Surinam (Netherlands Guiana) was considered (it was to be considered again in 1938). In 1908 Cyrenaica (Libya) was studied by an expedition that was headed by the distinguished explorer John W. Gregory. Montague David *Eder, who later became prominent in the World Zionist movement, also participated in this expedition. The following year an expedition was sent to Mesopotamia (now Iraq). In 1912 Gregory headed an expedition to the Portuguese territory of Angola. Zangwill, accompanied by David Jochelman, went to Portugal to call on the Portuguese President, who seemed to favor the project. Gregory was to submit his report on his findings to an international ITO conference scheduled for the fall of 1914 in Zurich, but owing to the outbreak of World War I the conference was never held and the Angola project was abandoned. Zangwill also considered possibilities in Canada, but was informed by Prime Minister Sir Wilfred Laurier that he had come 10 years too late. The international conference held in Vienna in June, 1912, discussed the suitability of Honduras. ITO also explored the suitability of Australia and even of Mexico and Siberia. In each case, the plans came to naught; either the territory was found unsuitable owing to climatic conditions, particularly a lack of water, or the ITO encountered political obstacles such as opposition from the government concerned or anticipated opposition from the indigenous population.

Zangwill, while not prepared at any time to abandon the primary objective of his organization (an autonomous Jewish settlement), faced the realities of the situation and sought to keep ITO active through practical work on a useful secondary objective. In 1907 he founded the ITO Emigration Regulation Department, which took over the Galveston emigration scheme that had been started in Germany the year before under the leadership of a group of Berlin Jewish philanthropists and of Arthur Meyerowitz, assistant director of the North German Lloyd Steamship Company. The object of the plan was to shunt Jewish emigration away from the large seaports and cities of the east coast of the United States and to divert the stream of mass Jewish immigration to the less crowded Southern and Western parts of the country or even to South America. To this end, North German Lloyd established a special passenger line to take immigrants to Galveston, Tex., rather than to one of the Eastern seaports. A Jewish Immigrant Information Bureau, headed by Morris D. Waldman, was organized in Galveston with the cooperation of the United States government. The project, which received most of its financial support from Jacob H. Schiff, got much help from David Jochelman in Kiev. Between 1906 and 1914 some 10,000 Jews landed in Galveston and settled in the Southern part of the United States. The project was abandoned several weeks before the outbreak of World War I because of lack of transportation facilities and the increasingly unsympathetic attitude of the newly organized U.S. Department of Labor, which had assumed authority in matters of immigration. World War I then halted all ITO activity.

The issuance of the *Balfour Declaration in November, 1917, brought about a change of heart in Zangwill and many of his followers. Many former Territorialists returned to the *World Zionist Organization. British patriot that he was, Zangwill himself, though skeptical of the vague wording of the declaration, hailed what he called the "historic achievement" of Zionism in the "region of diplomacy." Addressing a mass meeting in London early in December, 1917, he said it was the duty of all Jews and particularly of the ITO "to see that this is followed by a similar achievement in the more difficult region of practice." However, he soon became convinced that the British government had not given the declaration the interpretation originally intended by David *Lloyd George and Arthur James *Balfour. Speaking at a rally of the *American Jewish Congress in Carnegie Hall, New York, in October, 1923, Zangwill deplored the acceptance by Zionist leadership of the progressive whittling down of the declaration by the British government. He called political Zionism a failure for having been unable to realize its aims.

Nevertheless, Zangwill felt that, given the Balfour Declaration, the Palestine effort should be accorded a chance. Besides, many of his followers had defected and ITO was suffering from lack of funds. He hoped at least to resume the Galveston scheme, but that hope was dashed by the death of Jacob H. Schiff, its main supporter, in 1920. In 1925 Zangwill officially dissolved the Jewish Territorial Organization. However, with increasing British restrictions on Jewish *immigration to Palestine, on the one hand, and the growing need for places of refuge owing to Hitler's rise to power, on the other, Zangwill's movement was revived in the form of organizations such as the Freeland Movement for Jewish Territorial Colonization.

G. HIRSCHLER

JEWISH TOYNBEE HALLS. Social centers maintained by Zionist groups in Central and Eastern Europe. The establishment of Jewish Toynbee Halls was initiated by Leon *Kellner and modeled on the London Toynbee Hall, a non-Jewish social settlement which he had come to know during his visit to London in 1900 on the occasion of the 4th Zionist *Congress. On his return to Vienna, Kellner published an article in Die *Welt (Oct. 19, 1900), calling on his fellow Jews to follow the lead of the British and to establish centers where the poor would be able to spend their evenings in hospitable surroundings, listening to lectures, readings, and concerts or participating in discussions. The call found a warm response, and soon Jewish Toynbee Halls were established by Zionists in Vienna and other cities of Europe, especially in Galicia. The Jewish Toynbee Halls were an important instrument of Jewish adult education, particularly in the period preceding World War I.

JEWISH WORLD. Illustrated weekly newspaper and review, published in London from 1873 to 1934. Founded by George Lewis Lyon (1838–1904), a financial journalist, it was first edited by Myer David Davis (1830–1912). Among its editors were Samuel Levy Bensusan, Jacob *de Haas, John Raphael, Lucien Wolf, Stanley Fay, Myer Jack Landa, and David Spiro. For a time it published a Yiddish supplement, edited by Jacob *Hodess. In 1913 the *Jewish Chronicle became the proprietor of the Jewish World, and in 1934 the two were amalgamated.

The Jewish World published articles by various Zionist leaders, as well as by the non-Jewish precursors of Zionism Henry Wentworth Monk and the painter Holman Hunt, and, especially under Jacob de Haas, gave its support to Herzl and modern Zionism.

J. FRAENKEL

JEZREEL (YEZRE'EL) VALLEY ('Emek Yezre'el, commonly known as the 'Emek). Only transverse valley in Israel linking the Mediterranean coast with the Jordan Valley. It is a tectonic trough, filled with deep alluvium and bounded by the steep slopes of Mount Carmel in the south and Lower Galilee in the north. With a length of 17 miles and a maximum width of 12 miles, it forms the largest interior valley of Israel.

The Jezreel Valley has the shape of a triangle, of which each apex forms a gateway to an adjoining valley. In the west the Kishon River, the only drainage of the valley, forms the narrow gap known as Sha'ar Ha'Amakim, which connects the Jezreel Valley with the Z'vulun Valley. In the southeast the narrow Harod Valley continues the trend of the valley toward the Bet Sh'an Valley, and in the northeast the 'Emek K'salon (at the foot of Mount Tabor) leads toward Lake Kinneret. Throughout history the Jezreel Valley served as the main crossroads for the northern part of the country and as the strategic center of all decisive battles for the domination of Palestine.

The Kishon River, which is subject to heavy flooding, turned most of the valley into a malarial swamp, occupied only by Bedouins. After the acquisition of large tracts by the *Jewish National Fund, drainage and settlement operations were begun in 1921, and for many years the name of the valley was synonymous with the labor movement and communal settlement. The valley eventually became, in fact, the most densely settled rural area in Israel. Its central parts were utilized mainly for unirrigated grain crops, while large irrigated areas along its fringes yielded deciduous fruits and vegetables and dairy products. In modern times, too, the valley served as a main traffic artery, and the highways converged at 'Afula, which thus became the central town of the valley, with a population of 16,400 in 1968.

Y. KARMON

JISH. Arab village northwest of Safed. Inhabited mostly by Maronite Christians. Population (1968): 1,650.

The old Hebrew name, Gush Halav, is preserved in the name of the village. Gush Halav was an important town and fortress in the Second Temple period. Its archeological remains in Jish include tombs and a synagogue from the 2d century. The Maronite church of the village is built on top of another ancient synagogue. These remains, in addition to numerous Talmudic references, show that the town was a Jewish center even after its conquest by the Romans just prior to their destruction of Jerusalem (C.E. 70). Jews again lived in Gush Halav from the Middle Ages to the 19th century; they were engaged mainly in oil production.

JISR AZ-ZARQA. Arab village in the Hadera area. Population (1968): 2,210.

JNF. *See* JEWISH NATIONAL FUND.

JOFFE, ELIEZER LIPA. Agricultural pioneer and author (b. Khotin District, Bessarabia, Russia, 1882; d. Nahalal, 1942). In 1904 Joffe went to the United States to study new methods in agriculture. While there he helped found the first American *HeHalutz organization, and he also organized a pioneer group, HaIkkar HaTza'ir (The Young Farmer). In 1910 he settled in Palestine and founded on the Kinneret Farm another HaIkkar HaTza'ir group, which engaged in cooperative farming. Joffe was among the founders of *HaPo'el HaTza'ir and a volunteer for the *Jewish Legion in World War I. After the war he settled in Nahalal and became one of the founders and directors of T'nuva, the *Histadrut's marketing cooperative for agricultural products.

Beginning in 1902, Joffe published several books and articles on vegetable growing and animal husbandry as well as on historical and linguistic subjects. He was the first editor of *HaSade* (The Field) and an editor of *Gan HaYerek* (The Vegetable Garden), both agricultural journals. His collected writings were published posthumously in two volumes in 1957.

JOFFE, HILLEL. Physician and Palestine pioneer (b. Bristovka, Ukraine, Russia, 1864; d. Haifa, 1936). Joffe studied medicine in Geneva and subsequently worked at ophthalmological clinics in Paris and at a hospital in Simferopol, in the Crimea. An early adherent of the *Hoveve Zion movement, he settled in Palestine in 1891 and practiced medicine in various localities. He rendered invaluable aid to the Jewish settlers, who were beset by epidemics, and initiated and organized measures against malaria and cholera. Some years before World War I he moved to Zikhron Ya'akov, where he established a hospital and trained medical personnel.

From 1895 to 1905 Joffe was the representative of Hoveve Zion in Palestine. He participated as medical expert in the El-'Arish Expedition organized by Herzl in 1903 (*see* EL-'ARISH SCHEME). In the same year he took part in the conference of Palestine Jewish representatives held in Zikhron Ya'akov to establish a countrywide Jewish organization and was elected to its leadership. He was also a Palestine delegate to the 4th and 7th Zionist Congresses, held in 1900 and 1905, respectively (*see* CONGRESS, ZIONIST).

Joffe was the author of a number of medical papers, including several dealing with malaria and its cure. *Dor Ma'palim*, a book containing his memoirs and letters, was published in 1939.

JOINT DISTRIBUTION COMMITTEE. *See* AMERICAN JEWISH JOINT DISTRIBUTION COMMITTEE.

JORDAN, KINGDOM OF. *See* TRANSJORDAN.

JORDAN-NEGEV PROJECT. *See* NATIONAL WATER CARRIER.

JORDAN RIVER. Largest river in historical Palestine, flowing in a deep depression forming the historical boundary between western Palestine and Transjordan. Its total length (including its many bends) is 205 miles, while the length of its valley in a straight line is only 87 miles, of which 29 miles lie within the State of Israel. Another 17 miles form the boundary between Israel and the kingdom of Jordan, while the remainder lies within Jordanian territory, forming the 1967 cease-fire line between Israel and Jordan.

Most of the waters of the Jordan originate from the snows and rains that descend on Mount Hermon. The northernmost source, which is in Lebanon, is the Hasbani River (Heb., Snir). The Banias (Hermon) River originates in Syria, while the largest source, the Dan River, lies within Israel territory though very close to the Syrian border. After a short distance in the Hula Valley, the sources combine to form the Jordan River. After crossing the area formerly comprising the lake and swamps of Hula, the river drops in a deep gorge from an elevation of 230 feet above sea level to 686 feet below sea level and enters Lake Kinneret. It leaves the lake at its southern end, near D'ganya, and after a few miles receives its main tributary, the Yarmukh River. Lined by a dense gallery forest, it meanders through the floor of the Jordan depression, which becomes more arid toward the south until it turns into a whitish desert a short distance south of the Israeli border. Finally, the Jordan enters the Dead Sea in a small delta at 1,296 feet below sea level.

The average flow of the Jordan near its mouth is about 900 million cubic meters, of which about half is supplied by the Yarmukh and half by the outflow from Lake Kinneret. The contribution of the other tributaries is balanced by evaporation.

By 1970 only the part of the valley within Israel had been irrigated. In no part of the kingdom of Jordan was the river used for irrigation. About one-third of the total water carried by the Jordan is being pumped out of Lake Kinneret and transported by the *National Water Carrier over the watershed toward the coastal plain and the Negev.

Y. KARMON

JORDAN VALLEY. Deepest depression on the surface of the earth, forming part of the great Syro-African Rift Valley. Its average width ranges from 4 to 8 miles. Its bottom lies 2,500 to 3,700 feet below its rims. The climate of the valley is mostly arid and much warmer than that of the surrounding parts.

The valley runs in a straight line from north to south but is divided into various stretches by steplike slopes. The northernmost part is the Hula Valley (average altitude, 300 feet above sea level), where the Jordan River is formed; its lake and swamps were drained. The next step is Lake Kinneret (695 feet below sea level). The name Jordan Valley in a narrow sense is applied to the area lying between Lake Kinneret and the Yarmukh River, one of the most fertile regions of Israel. Here the eastern part of the valley (the whole of it farther

The Jordan flows into Lake Kinneret. [El Al Israel Airlines]

south) lies within Jordanian territory. It is covered with a whitish, saline marl, which makes for barren soil, and has an arid climate. The Jordanian Ghor project was a plan to irrigate part of the valley with water from the Yarmukh River. The southern end of the Jordan Valley is formed by the Dead Sea.   Y. KARMON

JORDAN VALLEY AUTHORITY. Plan for the utilization of the waters of the Jordan River developed by Walter C. *Lowdermilk in his book *Palestine: Land of Promise* (1944). Lowdermilk suggested the damming of all headwaters of the Jordan near the northern border of Israel, partly on Syrian and Lebanese territory, and their flow by gravity to the Bet N'tofa Valley, which was suggested as the main reservoir, and from there, along a line similar to the way of the *National Water Carrier, to the Negev. He also recommended the digging of a canal from Haifa to the Dead Sea, which would carry seawater and utilize the drop of 1,200 feet for the production of electricity.

These proposals evoked the interest of Emanuel *Neumann, who organized the Commission on Palestine Surveys, including a group of prominent laymen and an Engineering Consulting Board. The engineering group was headed by Abel Wolman, who was chairman of the U.S. Water Resources Board. Neumann also secured the cooperation of the Tennessee Valley Authority, headed by David Lilienthal, whose staff made available expert advice and guidance. Under the auspices of the commission, engineering studies were carried on for several years. They resulted in a detailed report, published in 1948 under the title *TVA on the Jordan*, by James B. Hays. It was presented to Moshe *Sharett, Foreign Minister of Israel, and served in part as the basis for Israel's Jordan River diversion and the building of its large-scale irrigation project.

Y. KARMON

JOSEPH, DOV (Bernard). Israeli lawyer and Cabinet minister (b. Montreal, 1899). A founder and early president of the *Young Judaea movement in Canada, Joseph interrupted his law studies (McGill and Laval Universities, 1915–21) to enlist in the *Jewish Legion. In 1921 he settled in Jerusalem, where he engaged in private law practice until 1948, obtaining a Ph.D. degree from London University in 1929. He early became associated with the *Jewish Agency, serving as the legal adviser of its Political Department from 1936 to 1945, as a member of its Executive from 1945 to 1948, and its treasurer from 1956 to 1961.

Joseph worked closely with Moshe *Sharett, head of the Political Department, representing Palestinian Jewry before the British Mandatory authorities (*see* MANDATE FOR PALESTINE). During World War II he was chairman of the Jerusalem board that recruited Jews for the British Army. On June 29, 1946, he was one of the four members of the Jewish Agency Executive to be arrested by the British authorities and detained in Latrun. As a member of the Political Committee of the *World Zionist Organization (WZO), he was sent to the United States in September, 1947, to take part in last-minute efforts to obtain a favorable vote in the United Nations on the *partition resolution. On his return to Jerusalem that December, he was appointed cochairman of the Jerusalem Emergency Committee, a body formed by the Jewish Agency and the *Va'ad L'umi (National Council). As military governor of Jerusalem during the period of siege (1948–49), he was responsible for the administration of the city's food supplies and emergency services.

Dov Joseph.
[Israel Information Services]

A member of the First, Second, and Third Knessets (1949–59; *see* KNESSET), Joseph held a variety of Cabinet posts. As Minister of Supply and Rationing (1949–50), he was in charge of the austerity program. He subsequently was Minister of Communications (1950–51), Minister of Trade (1951–52; and briefly during that period also Minister of Justice), Minister of State (1952–53), Minister of Development (1953–55; and briefly during that period also Minister of Health), and Minister of Justice (1961–65). He wrote two books: *British Rule in Palestine* (1948), a study of the legal and moral validity of the British Mandate, the *Balfour Declaration, and the case of the Jews and the Arabs; and *The Faithful City: The Siege of Jerusalem, 1948* (1960), an account of the beleaguerment of Jerusalem by the Arab Legion.

JOSEPHTHAL, GIORA (GEORG). Zionist leader and member of the Israeli Cabinet (b. Nürnberg, Germany, 1912; d. Lucerne, Switzerland, 1962). During his student days in Berlin and Munich, Josephthal, who had joined the Zionist movement at 17, became active in Jewish social work. When Hitler rose to power (1933), he was appointed head of the Youth Department of the Jewish Communities of Bavaria. In 1934 he moved to Berlin as head of the bureau that organized *Youth 'Aliya. Early in 1936 he became secretary-general of the pioneering organization *HeHalutz in Germany.

Settling in Palestine in 1938, Josephthal worked with the *Jewish Agency (1939–43), first in London to help rescue German HeHalutz leaders and then at the 'Atlit detention camp. After serving in the British Army (1943–45), he became head of the Jewish Agency's Absorption Department (1945–56). From 1952 on he served simultaneously as treasurer of the Agency. In 1952 he was cochairman of the Israeli delegation that negotiated the German reparations agreement (*see* GERMAN-ISRAEL AGREEMENT), and subsequently served as chairman of the board of the Reparations Corporation. In 1955 he negotiated the agreement whereby the Bonn government was to compensate Israel for heirless property left by Jews in Germany.

In 1956 Josephthal was elected secretary-general of the *Mapai party. Elected to the *Knesset in 1959, he served as Minister of Labor from 1960 to 1961, when he was given the portfolio of Development and Housing, a position he held until his death. Josephthal promoted the idea of *development towns and was a founder (1945) of Gal'ed, a kibbutz set up near Zikhron Ya'akov by Halutzim (pioneers; *see* HALUTZIYUT) from Germany. A collection of his writings and speeches, *The Responsible Attitude: The Life and Opinions of Giora Josephthal* (ed. by Ben Halpern and Shalom Wurm), was published in 1966.

JU'AMIS. Bedouin tribe in the Nazareth area. Population (1968): 233.

JUDE, DER. Jewish nationalist German-language monthly, founded in 1916 by Martin *Buber as "an independent organ for the knowledge and furtherance of living Judaism." In the first issue Buber stressed the need to restore the modern Jew to the living Jewish national community, the creation of which he regarded as the major aim of Zionism. The periodical attracted some of the best spiritual forces within the Jewish national movement, writers and scholars of both Western and Eastern Europe. Its contents included essays and studies on Jewish history and literature, on Jewish religious, national, and ethical values, on current Jewish problems, and on the problems and tasks of Zionism. The periodical appeared regularly until 1924. Thereafter issues appeared only irregularly; these were devoted to special themes such as *anti-Semitism and Jewish peoplehood (1925), education (1926), Judaism and Germanism (1926), and Judaism and Christianity (1927). There was a special issue (1928) to honor Martin Buber on the occasion of his 50th birthday.

JUDEA. Historically, Judea (Heb., Y'huda) is the name of the area most of which was occupied by the tribe of Judah (Y'huda) in premonarchic days and which, following the death of King Solomon, became the southern kingdom of Judah, ruled by the Davidic dynasty until its destruction by the Babylonians in 586 B.C.E. (*see* ISRAEL, HISTORY OF). In Jewish consciousness Judah has ranked next to its capital, Jerusalem, and its sacred mountain, Zion, as the symbol of the Holy Land and of Biblical history and as the focus of Jewish longing for a return to the ancestral soil.

Judea is the southern section of the central mountains of historic Palestine, 56 miles long and 34 miles wide. Its area is approximately 1,750 square miles. Until the *Six-day War of 1967 only the foothills in the south (the Sh'fela) and a small section of the western mountain slopes (Jerusalem corridor) lay within Israel, as did the southeastern extremity of the Judean Desert.

A view of the Judean Mountains. [Israel Information Services]

Geologically, Judea is a wide, asymmetric anticline, whose layers slope steeply toward the west; its eastern flank has been markedly disturbed by the Jordan Rift Valley and consecutive faulting.

Three longitudinal divisions can be discerned. In the west lie the foothills of the Sh'fela, which gradually ascend from the coastal plain toward the steep slope of the mountains. They reach an altitude of 1,300 feet.

The central and widest division consists of the Judean Mountains, which are composed mainly of dolomites and hard limestones. Their long western flanks, which descend steeply toward the Sh'fela, are dissected by numerous wadis (*see* WADI) into almost isolated spurs, but along the watershed a level crest appears which in places reaches a width of 2 or 3 miles. This crest carries the only lengthwise road (in ancient as well as in modern times). Along it are situated the historic towns of Hebron, Bethlehem, Jerusalem, and Bet El (Ramallah), as is the only airfield at Kalandia, which served Arab Jerusalem from 1948 to 1967.

The Judean Mountains can be divided into three parts. The northernmost, the Mountains of Bet El, contains the highest elevation (Ba'al Hatzor, 3,340 feet), receives the most abundant rainfall, and is densely settled by Arab villages. The central part, the Jerusalem Mountains, forms a low saddle with an average elevation of 2,450 feet. Throughout history this saddle offered the easiest route for crossing the range and was a factor in the rise of Jerusalem as the center of Judea. The southern part, the Hebron Hills, is the largest part of the Judean Mountains, again reaching altitudes of over 3,250 feet. Its climate is more arid, and its villages are very large but widely scattered.

The easternmost division of Judea is the Judean Desert.

Y. KARMON

JUDEAN DESERT. Eastern slope of the Judean Mountains, descending toward the lower Jordan Valley and the Dead Sea. Its climate is arid because of the rain shadow of the mountains. Alternating hard and soft limestones have created steep steps, sometimes showing cliffs 1,000 to 1,500 feet high. Numerous dry riverbeds dissect the area steeply and form canyons in the hard rocks. Owing to its steepness and dissection, most of the desert is almost impassable; the only historic route leads from Jerusalem to Jericho, the sole oasis in the lower Jordan Valley. A few springs, fed by underground

Dry riverbeds (wadis) cut through the Judean Desert. [Israel Information Services]

water from the Judean Mountains, enabled refugees, hermits, or monasteries to exist nearby. In ancient times, the Judean Desert served as a place of refuge for the Essenes; in it, too, were found the famous Dead Sea Scrolls. Its southeastern sector lies within Israel and contains its only oasis, 'En Gedi, as well as the ruins of M'tzada (Massada). The new town of 'Arad marks the point of contact between the Judean Desert and the Negev.

Y. KARMON

JUDELEVITZ (YUDELEVITZ), DAVID. Palestine pioneer (b. Iaşi, Romania, 1863; d. Rishon L'Tziyon, 1943). Judelevitz went to Palestine in 1882 with the settlers who established Zamarin (*see* ZIKHRON YA'AKOV) and joined the *Bilu group that worked at a variety of jobs in Jerusalem. He learned the craft of knife sharpening and went to Paris to perfect his skill. After returning to Palestine in 1888, he became a teacher in Rishon L'Tziyon, the first to teach general subjects in the *Hebrew language. He wrote Hebrew textbooks, initiated the establishment of the first Hebrew kindergarten in the country, and in 1892 helped organize the Asefat HaMorim, the precursor of the Histadrut HaMorim, or Teachers Association. He contributed to the Hebrew press and was one of the editors of the Hebrew children's paper *'Olam Katan.*

In 1903 he went to the Far East to sell Palestine wines. From 1906 to 1924 he resided in Alexandria as the representative of the Carmel Mizrahi Company. During World War I he helped the Palestine Jewish refugees in Egypt and aided in the formation of the *Zion Mule Corps. After his return to Palestine, he continued to work for Carmel Mizrahi. Judelevitz was the editor of *LeDivre Y'me Ha'Itonut B'Eretz Yisrael* (On the History of the Press in the Land of Israel, 2 vols., 1935–36) and of *Sefer Rishon L'Tziyon* (The Book of Rishon L'Tziyon, 1941).

I. KLAUSNER

JUDENSTAAT, DER. *See* JEWISH STATE, THE.

JUDEYDA. Arab village east of 'Akko. Population (1968): 1,970.

JUDICIARY IN ISRAEL. The law courts of the State of Israel are divided into civil courts and religious courts. The principal civil courts are the magistrates' courts, the district courts, and the Supreme Court, all of which exercise jurisdiction in civil and criminal matters.

Civil Courts. Magistrates' courts are established in each district and subdistrict. They may try civil actions pertaining

The caves of the Judean Desert have yielded ancient manuscripts to archeologists. [Israel Government Tourist Office]

to the possession or use of immovable property, or the partition of immovable property or the use thereof, irrespective of the value of the subject matter of the action, and other civil actions where the amount of the claim or the value of the subject matter does not exceed IL3,000. They may also try offenses punishable by not more than three years' imprisonment. Usually, a single judge tries a case. Judgments of a magistrates' court may be appealed to the district court of the district in which the magistrates' court exercises jurisdiction.

District courts have unlimited jurisdiction as courts of first instance in all civil and criminal matters not within the jurisdiction of a magistrates' court, all matters not within the exclusive jurisdiction of any other court or tribunal, and matters within the concurrent jurisdiction of any other court or tribunal as long as such court or tribunal does not deal with them. Cases are tried mostly before a single judge. District courts also hear appeals, before a bench of three, from judgments and decisions of magistrates' courts. Judgments of district courts sitting in first instance are appealable to the Supreme Court, as are other court decisions in civil matters and the judgments of a district court sitting as an appellate court, if leave to appeal has been granted in the decision or judgment or by the President or other justice of the Supreme

Court chosen by the President, or by the Supreme Court. There are five district courts (Jerusalem, Tel Aviv–Yafo, Haifa, Nazareth, and B'er Sheva'), having jurisdiction in the Jerusalem District, the Tel Aviv and Central Districts, the Haifa District and 'Akko Subdistrict, the Northern District excluding the 'Akko Subdistrict, and the Southern District, respectively.

The Supreme Court, the highest court in Israel, has jurisdiction as an appellate court from the district courts in all matters, both civil and criminal (sitting as a court of civil appeal or as a court of criminal appeal), and as a court of first instance (sitting as a high court of justice) in matters in which it considers it necessary to grant relief in the interests of justice and which are not within the jurisdiction of any other court or tribunal. In particular, it has the authority (1) to issue orders for the release of persons unlawfully detained or imprisoned; (2) to issue orders to State or local authorities and their officials and to other bodies and persons performing public functions under the law, requiring them to take or to refrain from taking any action in the performance of their functions according to law and, if they were unlawfully elected or appointed, to refrain from taking action; (3) to issue orders to courts, tribunals, and bodies of persons other than magistrates' courts, district courts, and religious courts, having judicial or quasijudicial powers under the law, to adjudicate in any particular matter, and to set aside any unlawful proceeding or decision; and (4) to issue orders to religious courts to deal with any specific matter not within their jurisdiction. The Supreme Court sits in Jerusalem and is composed of such number of members as the *Knesset, by resolution, determines. Starting with 5 members in 1948, it grew to a total of 10 members in the 1960s, including a President and a permanent Deputy President. The bench is composed mainly of 3 justices, and in exceptional cases of 5 or 7 or 9 justices; certain procedural and interim decisions can be made by single members.

In addition to the civil courts described above, there are traffic magistrates, municipal courts, tribal courts, and military courts. Traffic magistrates are appointed as are judges of a magistrates' court, but for a limited period. They have jurisdiction to try offenses against the Road Transport Ordinance or any rules or bylaws made thereunder.

Municipal courts, established under the Municipal Courts Ordinance of 1928 in certain municipal areas, have jurisdiction to try offenses against municipal regulations and bylaws and certain other offenses, such as town planning offenses, committed within the municipal area. The maximum sentence which such courts may impose is a fine of IL750 or 15 days' imprisonment, or both such penalties, for any one offense. The members are laymen appointed by the Minister of Justice, save for stipendiary magistrates in Tel Aviv, Jerusalem, Petah Tikva, Ramat Gan, and Haifa, who are also appointed by the Minister.

Tribal courts for the subdistrict of B'er Sheva', composed of sheikhs appointed by the Minister of Justice, may apply tribal custom insofar as it is not repugnant to natural justice or morality.

The military courts are the various courts-martial and a Military Court of Appeal established under the Military Justice Law of 5715 (1955) to deal with offenses by soldiers and army employees; military courts established under the Defense (Emergency) Regulations of 1945 to try offenses against those regulations committed in Israel; and military courts established under the Prevention of Infiltration (Offenses and Jurisdiction) Law of 5714 (1954) to try offenses against that law.

There are also numerous tribunals, boards, and committees established under various laws, as need arises, to deal with special classes of cases, in many of which a judge presides, such as the General Claims Tribunal, the Shipping Tribunal, the Water Affairs Tribunal, rent tribunals, the National Insurance Appeal Tribunal, the Restrictive Trade Practices Board, the Employment Service Supreme Objection Committee, the Land Betterment Tax Objection Committee, and the Customs Agents Objection Committee. Under the Commissions of Inquiry Law of 5729 (1968), when the government appoints a commission of inquiry under the law to inquire into and report upon a matter of vital public importance, the President of the Supreme Court must appoint the chairman and other members of the commission and the chairman must be a Supreme Court justice or a district court judge.

Under the Courts Law of 1957, every Court is guided by a rule laid down by a higher court, and a rule laid down by the Supreme Court binds every court except itself. The procedure in the civil courts in civil and criminal matters is modeled on that of the English courts except that there is no trial by jury.

As of 1968 there was no provision for judicial review of statutes. Consequently no court had the authority to declare any law of the Knesset invalid, but every court was competent to invalidate subsidiary legislation, such as regulations, orders, and bylaws, on the ground of illegality or unreasonableness, as well as legal provisions antedating the State, if these were contrary to any law of the Knesset.

Religious Courts. The religious courts are rabbinical courts, Muslim religious courts, Christian religious courts, and Druze religious courts.

The rabbinical courts have exclusive jurisdiction in matters of marriage and divorce of Jews in Israel who are citizens or residents of the State and in every matter connected with a claim for divorce filed therein in Israel by a Jew or Jewess. In all other matters of personal status such as inheritance, legitimation of minors, or guardianship, they have jurisdiction with the consent of all the parties concerned.

The Muslim religious courts have exclusive jurisdiction in all matters of personal status over Muslims who are not foreigners and also over Muslims who are foreigners if, under the law of their country, they are subject to the jurisdiction of Muslim religious courts in such matters.

Such *Christian communities and churches as had judicial systems of their own under Ottoman and British administrations (the so-called recognized Christian communities) have retained these systems. The Christian religious courts have exclusive jurisdiction in matters of marriage, divorce, and alimony of members of their community other than foreigners and concurrent jurisdiction with the civil courts in such matters for members of their community who are foreigners but agree to abide by their jurisdiction. The Christian religious courts have jurisdiction also in all other matters of personal status of all members of their community, whether foreigners or not, with the consent of all parties to the action, except that such courts may not grant a decree of dissolution of marriage to a citizen of a foreign country.

The Druze religious courts have exclusive jurisdiction in matters of divorce of members of the *Druze community in Israel who are citizens or residents of the State. In matters of personal status in which they do not have exclusive jurisdiction such as inheritance, legitimation of minors, or guardianship, they may assume jurisdiction with the consent of all the parties concerned.

In cases where any action of personal status involves members of different religious communities, the President of the Supreme Court decides which court shall have jurisdiction, and whenever a question arises as to whether or not a case is one of personal status within the exclusive jurisdiction of a religious court, the matter must be referred to a special tribunal composed of two justices of the Supreme Court and the President of the highest court of the religious community concerned.

The judgments of the religious courts are enforced as are the judgments of the civil courts. The chief execution officer may refuse to enforce a judgment of a religious court given in excess of its jurisdiction or contrary to natural justice, but the validity of his refusal can be reviewed by the Supreme Court sitting as a high court of justice. The Supreme Court may also issue an order prohibiting a religious court from dealing with a matter not within its jurisdiction.

Judges. Under the Judges Law of 1953, the judges of all the civil courts are appointed by the President of the State of Israel on nomination by a Nominations Committee of nine persons, submitted to the President by the Minister of Justice. The Nominations Committee, which must be listed in *R'shumot* (the official Israeli gazette), consists of the Minister of Justice, who acts as chairman, another Cabinet Minister chosen by the government, the President of the Supreme Court and two other justices of the Supreme Court chosen by the Court as a whole for a period of three years, two members of the Knesset elected by the Knesset by secret ballot, and two practicing advocates elected by the Chamber of Advocates.

Whenever the Minister of Justice determines that a new judge should be appointed, he must give notice to that effect in *R'shumot* and convene the Nominations Committee. Names of candidates may be proposed by the Minister of Justice, the President of the Supreme Court, or jointly by any three members of the Committee. Candidates may submit their own names to the Committee, but the Committee does not limit its list of candidates to persons who have submitted their own names. The promotion of judges is regulated in the same manner as their initial appointment.

The Minister of Justice submits the name of the candidate selected by the Nominations Committee to the President of the State, who then makes the appointment without further consideration. The President signs the instrument of appointment in the presence of the candidate, who then and there makes an affirmation of loyalty to the State and its laws and undertakes to fulfill the Biblical injunctions to judge the people justly, not to distort justice, and to favor none.

A judge is normally required to retire on pension at the age of 70. In cases of physical disability and on the strength of a medical opinion given in accordance with general rules laid down by the Nominations Committee, the Committee may decide at an earlier date that the judge is unable to perform his duties for reasons of health. A judge may retire on a pension at the age of 60 if he has held office for 20 years, or at the age of 65 if he has held office for 15 years, or at any age if he so requests and his request is approved by the Nominations Committee.

If a judge submits a letter of resignation to the Minister of Justice, his resignation takes effect three months later unless the Minister agrees to accept it at shorter notice. No person may be appointed a judge in any court whatsoever if he is not a citizen of the State of Israel, nor may a candidate for appointment having any other citizenship in addition to Israeli citizenship be appointed until he has done all that is required of him for his release from that other allegiance if the laws of the country of which he is a citizen enable him to be released from his citizenship.

The following persons are qualified for appointment to the Supreme Court: (1) any person who has held office as a judge of a district court for at least 5 years; (2) a member of the legal profession (i.e., a person who is listed, or is entitled to be listed, on the Roster of Advocates in Israel and who, continuously or intermittently for not less than 10 years, including at least 5 years in Israel, has been engaged in one or more of the following: the legal profession, a judicial or other legal function in the service of the State of Israel or any other service approved by the Minister of Justice, or the teaching of law at a university or school of law approved by the Minister of Justice); and (3) any person who is considered an eminent jurist. The following are qualified to be appointed to the district court: (1) any person who has held office as a judge of a magistrates' court for a period of at least 4 years; and (2) a member of the legal profession who has engaged in that profession for at least 6 years, including at least 3 years in Israel. Appointment as judge of a magistrates' court is open to any member of the legal profession who has engaged in that profession for not less than 3 years, including at least 1 year in Israel.

The salary of a judge and other payments to be made to him, either during or after his term of office, as well as the payments to be made to his dependents after his death, and judges' pensions are fixed by the Finance Committee of the Knesset independently of the rules pertaining to the fixing of salary and other payments to other State employees. The salary of the President of the Supreme Court is on a par with that of the Prime Minister; that of the other Supreme Court justices is on a par with that of Cabinet members, while the salaries of the other members of the judiciary are fixed on a corresponding graduated scale. In order to ensure, among other things, the independence of the judiciary, the salaries of the judges are the highest in the State service.

Every judge is subject to the jurisdiction of a court of discipline, the members of which are chosen in each case by the justices of the Supreme Court. A complaint against a judge may be submitted to the court of discipline by the Minister of Justice, and only by him, on one of the following grounds: improper conduct in the carrying out of judicial functions, behavior unbecoming a judge in Israel, conviction for an offense involving moral turpitude, and determination by the Nominations Committee that the judge obtained his appointment in an unlawful manner. The court of discipline submits its findings to the Minister of Justice. If it is found that a judge is not qualified to continue to exercise his functions, the Minister brings that finding before the President of the State, who then removes the judge from office. Only the Attorney General may file a criminal charge against a judge, and such a charge will be tried only by a district court composed of three judges.

The provisions of the law regarding the qualifications (including Israeli citizenship), manner of appointment, term of office, salaries, and other emoluments of the judges of the rabbinical courts (Dayanim), the judges of the Muslim religious courts (kadis), and the judges of the Druze religious courts closely follow those of the Judges Law regarding the civil judiciary with appropriate modifications. Those provisions are contained in the Dayanim Law of 1955, the Kadis Law of 1961, and the Druze Religious Courts Law of 1962, respectively.

All the judges of the religious courts are appointed by the President of the State, on nomination by a Nominations Committee, the composition of which is similar to that for the civil judiciary. The nominations are submitted by the Minister of Religious Affairs, who acts as chairman of the Committee.

Arbitration. Until the Arbitration Law of 5728 (1968) came into force on Jan. 1, 1969, arbitration was governed by the Palestine Arbitration Ordinance of 1926, the provisions of which were based upon those of the United Kingdom Arbitration Act of 1889. The law retains substantially the English system of arbitration but contains a number of new provisions designed to improve and accelerate arbitration proceedings with a view to encouraging persons to resort to arbitration and so reduce to some extent the ever-increasing volume of work of the courts. As under the ordinance, an arbitration award must be confirmed by a competent court before it can be enforced as if it were a judgment of the court. It may be set aside by the competent court upon one of 10 grounds specified in the law, upon the application of one of the parties to the arbitration made within the prescribed period, unless the court is satisfied that no injustice has been caused. Unless the parties to the arbitration otherwise agree, the arbitrator must act in the manner appearing to him to be the most effective for arriving at a just and speedy decision and decide according to the best of his judgment in the light of the material submitted to him, and he is not bound by the substantive law, the rules of evidence, or the rules of procedure obtaining in the courts.

The law follows the ordinance in empowering the arbitrator to fix his fee, but it also empowers the competent court, upon the application of a party to the arbitration, to reduce the fee fixed by the arbitrator without the consent of the parties if it considers that the fee is excessive. Under the ordinance, the competent court was empowered to remove an arbitrator if he misconducted himself or willfully neglected to act upon the submission after having been requested to do so by written notice served upon him by a party to the submission. Under the law, the competent court may remove an arbitrator when it becomes evident that he is not worthy of the confidence of the parties, when his conduct during the course of the arbitration causes delay in the making of the award, or when he is unable to perform his functions.

H. E. BAKER

JÜDISCHE COLONIALBANK. *See* JEWISH COLONIAL TRUST LTD.

JÜDISCHE RUNDSCHAU. Central forum of German Zionism. Originally a nonpartisan Berlin German-Jewish weekly, founded in 1895 and entitled *Israelitische Rundschau*, the paper was taken over in 1902 by Heinrich *Loewe, who changed its name to *Jüdische Rundschau* (Jewish Review) and made it the recognized organ of Zionism in Germany. The *Rundschau* also maintained a publications department. Editors after Loewe (who served until 1910) were Julius Becker, Hugo *Herrmann, Leo *Herrmann, Max Mayer, Fritz Loewenstein, and Robert *Weltsch, who edited the paper from 1919 until its suspension by the Nazis in 1938.

The *Rundschau*, which consistently maintained a high intellectual level, was a factor of considerable influence in World Zionist circles. For the sake of the unity of the Zionist movement, it opposed the *Kharkov Conference (October, 1903), at which the Russian Zionists rebelled against Herzl's advocacy of the *East Africa scheme. After the 7th Zionist *Congress (Basle, 1905) had rejected the plan, however, the *Rundschau* strongly opposed Israel *Zangwill's *Jewish Territorial Organization and supported "practical" work in the settlement of Palestine (*see* PRACTICAL ZIONISM).

For nearly two decades the *Rundschau*, while striving for an objective presentation of all views within the Zionist movement, reflected the philosophy of Robert Weltsch, a pacifist and an intellectual adherent of socialism, who put great stress on education and cultural activity. Weltsch called for a policy of understanding with the Arabs and accommodation with the British Mandatory authorities (*see* MANDATE FOR PALESTINE), which he considered prerequisites for the realization of the cultural ideals of *Ahad Ha'Am and the social ethics of Aharon David *Gordon. Weltsch and the *Rundschau* tended to favor a binational arrangement in Palestine— a Jewish National Home based on cooperation between Jews and Arabs rather than an independent Jewish State.

When Hitler came to power in January, 1933, the *Rundschau*, in terms that were articulate but sufficiently camouflaged to avoid action by the Nazi authorities, offered encouragement to the Jews in facing Nazi attacks. It also endeavored to sustain the spirit of its readers. The issue of Apr. 4, 1933, carried Weltsch's editorial "Wear the Yellow Badge with Pride," which called on the Jews of Germany to find new strength and hope in their heritage and to further the upbuilding of the Jewish National Home in Palestine. This article had a powerful impact on Zionists and non-Zionists alike. To aid prospective emigrants to Palestine, the *Rundschau* published supplements of news from the *Yishuv (Jewish population of Palestine) and lessons in the Hebrew language. During the early years of the Nazi regime the *Rundschau* was closed down time and again, but in each instance Weltsch was able to persuade the Nazi authorities to permit the paper to reappear. It was not until November, 1938, that the *Rundschau* was finally closed down by the Nazis. The paper reappeared briefly (1939–40) in Palestine under Weltsch's editorship as the *Jüdische Weltrundschau*.

G. HIRSCHLER

JULIS. Druze village east-northeast of 'Akko. Population (1968): 1,850.

JUNG ISRAEL (Young Israel). Pre-Herzlian Zionist organization founded in 1892 in Berlin to promote a sense of national unity among the Jewish people through the furtherance of Jewish life and knowledge. One of its founders was Heinrich *Loewe. Jung Israel was deeply influenced also by the ideas of Nathan *Birnbaum, with whom it collaborated. Though it never had a large membership, it played a prominent part in the dissemination of the idea of Jewish nationhood among Jewish university students in Germany. In 1893 Jung Israel was the initiator of a planned international conference of all (pre-Herzlian) Zionist associations, and it participated in practical work in Palestine through its cooperation with *Esra and other Palestine settlement societies. In 1896 it was instrumental in arranging the first exhibit of Palestinian Jewish produce at the Berlin Exhibition of Trade and Industry.

The association existed for about five years. It was later replaced by the Berliner Zionistische Vereinigung (Zionist Association of Berlin).

JUNIOR HADASSAH. Youth department of *Hadassah. Its membership consisted of girls from high school senior age (17) to 25 years. Its program stressed Jewish education, leadership training, and special projects in Israel, for which it raised funds.

The movement developed in 1916 with groups forming simultaneously in Baltimore, Boston, and Rochester. In 1920 it was established as a national organization offering a Hebrew cultural program to its membership and adopting 186 war orphans in Palestine. In 1921 Junior Hadassah undertook the project of developing a model children's village at Meir Sh'feya, which it maintained for more than 30 years. In 1966 its Israel program included contributions to special projects for the Meir Sh'feya youth village, the Henrietta *Szold-Hadassah School of Nursing, the *Jewish National Fund, and the kibbutzim HaSol'lim in Lower Galilee and 'En HaSh'losha in the western Negev.

The continuing emphasis on educational and cultural activities was reflected both in the domestic program of Junior Hadassah and in its activities relating to Israel. Groups received program and education kits which highlighted the relevance of Judaism to American Jewish girls and which helped to foster close ties with Israel.

Junior Hadassah inaugurated a summer seminar leadership training program at Camp Cejwin, N.Y. In addition, members were offered opportunities to study, work, and travel in Israel through the Summer Institute in Israel and the Junior Hadassah section of the American Students' Program of the American Friends of the *Hebrew University of Jerusalem. The former,

a two-month course, included work periods at Meir Sh'feya and at a kibbutz. The latter, a full-year program open to girls with at least two years of college, included an *Ulpan for the study of Hebrew and a regular college curriculum.

In November, 1967, Junior Hadassah and *Young Judaea merged under the name HaShahar (Dawn). A. KAPLAN

JURDIYA. Arab village in the 'Akko area. Population (1968): 379.

JUVENILE DELINQUENCY IN ISRAEL. *See* CRIME IN ISRAEL.